Analyzing Moral Issues

Fifth Edition

JUDITH A. BOSS

Connect
Learn
Succeed™

Published by McGraw-Hill, an imprint of The McGraw-Hill Companies, Inc., 1221 Avenue of the Americas, New York, NY 10020. Copyright © 2010, 2008, 2005, 2002, 1999. All rights reserved. No part of this publication may be reproduced or distributed in any form or by any means, or stored in a database or retrieval system, without the prior written consent of The McGraw-Hill Companies, Inc., including, but not limited to, in any network or other electronic storage or transmission, or broadcast for distance learning.

This book is printed on acid-free paper.

1 2 3 4 5 6 7 8 9 0 DOC/DOC 0 9

ISBN: 978-0-07-353574-6
MHID: 0-07-353574-5

Editor in Chief: *Michael Ryan*
Editorial Director: *Beth Mejia*
Publisher: *Frank Mortimer*
Sponsoring Editor: *Mark Georgiev*
Developmental Editor: *Craig Leonard*
Managing Editor: *Nicole Bridge*
Marketing Manager: *Pam Cooper*
Media Project Manager: *Jennifer Barrick*
Production Editor: *Alison Meier*
Design Coordinator: *Margarite Reynolds*
Cover Design: *Kay Lieberherr*
Photo Credit: *Royalty-Free/CORBIS*
Production Supervisor: *Laura Fuller*
Production Service: *Anne Draus, Scratchgravel Publishing Services*
Composition: *New Baskerville 9.5/12 by Laserwords*
Printing: *45# New Era Matte Plus, R. R. Donnelley & Sons*

Credits: A credits section for this book begins on page C-1 and is considered an extension of the copyright page.

Library of Congress Cataloging-in-Publication Data
Boss, Judith A.
  Analyzing moral issues / Judith A. Boss.—5th ed.
      p. cm.
  Includes bibliographical references and index.
  ISBN-13: 978-0-07-353574-6 (alk. paper)
  ISBN-10: 0-07-353574-5 (alk. paper)
  1. Ethical problems.   2. Applied ethics.   I. Title.
  BJ1031.B68 2010
  170—dc22

                                                    2009028593

The Internet addresses listed in the text were accurate at the time of publication. The inclusion of a Web site does not indicate an endorsement by the author or McGraw-Hill, and McGraw-Hill does not guarantee the accuracy of the information presented at these sites.

www.mhhe.com

Contents

Preface   xi

CHAPTER 1   **Moral Theory**   1

Moral Philosophy   2

What Is the Purpose of Moral Theories?   2

The Types of Moral Theories   3

Relativism in Ethics   4

Moving Beyond Ethical Relativism   11

Morality and Religion   15

Universal Moral Theories   18

Ethical Egoism   19

Utilitarianism   22

Deontology: The Ethics of Duty   26

Rights-Based Ethics   32

Virtue Ethics   37

Conclusion   41

ARISTOTLE, from *Nicomachean Ethics*   42

AYN RAND, from *The Fountainhead*   47

JEREMY BENTHAM, from *An Introduction to the Principles of Morals and Legislation*   50

JOHN STUART MILL, from *Utilitarianism*   52

IMMANUEL KANT, from *Fundamental Principles of the Metaphysic of Ethics*   54

JOHN RAWLS, from *A Theory of Justice*   59

JOHN LOCKE, from *Two Treatises of Civil Government*   62

NEL NODDINGS, from *Caring: A Feminine Approach to Ethics and Moral Education*   65

CONFUCIUS, from *The Analects*   68

THICH NHAT HANH, "The Five Mindfulness Trainings"   71

CHAPTER 2   ## Abortion   73

Background   73
The History of Abortion in the United States   74
The U.S. Supreme Court *Roe v. Wade* Decision   75
Abortion and Religion   78
Methods of Abortion   79
The Moral Issues   80
Conclusion   85

JUDITH JARVIS THOMSON, "A Defense of Abortion"   86
JOHN T. NOONAN JR., "An Almost Absolute Value
   in History"   97
MARY ANNE WARREN, "The Moral Significance
   of Birth"   102
DON MARQUIS, "Why Abortion Is Immoral"   108
SERRIN M. FOSTER, "Refuse to Choose: Women Deserve Better
   Than Abortion"   113
STEPHEN D. HALES, "Abortion and Fathers' Rights"   117

Case Studies   125

CHAPTER 3   ## Genetic Engineering, Cloning, and Stem Cell Research   131

The History of Genetic Engineering   131
The Human Genome Project   132
Genetic Engineering   132
Cloning   133
Stem Cell Research   136
The Moral Issues   137
Conclusion   143

JULIAN SALVULESCU, "Genetic Interventions and the Ethics of Enhancement
   of Human Beings"   144
JUDITH A. JOHNSON AND ERIN D. WILLIAMS, "Human Cloning: Ethical
   and Social Issues"   150
LEON KASS, "The Wisdom of Repugnance: Why We Should Ban the Cloning
   of Humans"   158
JAMES R. LANGEVIN, "Statement in Support of H.R. 810, the Stem Cell Research
   Enhancement Act"   166
GEORGE W. BUSH, "Stem Cell Research Policy"   167

Case Studies   169

CHAPTER 4   ## Euthanasia   177

What Is Euthanasia?   177
The Philosophers on Euthanasia   178
The Contemporary Debate over Euthanasia   180
Euthanasia Legislation   181
Physician-Assisted Suicide   182
The Hospice Movement   184
The Moral Issues   185
Conclusion   189

JAMES RACHELS, "Active and Passive Euthanasia"   190
MARGARET PABST BATTIN, "The Case for Euthanasia"   195
J. GAY-WILLIAMS, "The Wrongfulness of Euthanasia"   203
JOHN HARDWIG, "Is There a Duty to Die?"   207
SUSAN M. WOLF, "A Feminist Critique of Physician-Assisted Suicide"   214

Case Studies   222

CHAPTER 5   ## The Death Penalty   228

History of the Death Penalty   228
The Death Penalty Today   228
The Death Penalty: Juvenile and Mentally Retarded Offenders   232
The Medicalization of Executions   232
DNA Testing   233
The Philosophers on the Death Penalty   233
The Moral Issues   235
Conclusion   239

ERNEST VAN DEN HAAG, "The Ultimate Punishment: A Defense
   of Capital Punishment"   240
CHRISTOPHER W. MORRIS, "Punishment and Loss of Moral Standing"   245
HUGO ADAM BEDAU, "Capital Punishment"   251
JEFFREY REIMAN, "Why the Death Penalty Should be Abolished in
   the United States"   261
HELEN PREJEAN, "Would Jesus Pull the Switch?"   267

Case Studies   272

CHAPTER 6   ## Drug and Alcohol Use   278

What Is a Drug?   278
The History of Drug and Alcohol Use   279

Legal and Illegal Drugs   280
Drug and Alcohol Use Today   281
Drug and Alcohol Use Among College Students   283
Drugs in Sports   284
The Disease Model of Addiction   285
The Moral Model of Addiction   286
The Philosophers on Drug and Alcohol Abuse   286
The Moral Issues   287
Conclusion   290

Thomas Szasz, "The Ethics of Addiction"   291
James Q. Wilson, "Against the Legalization of Drugs"   299
Douglas N. Husak, "A Moral Right to Use Drugs"   307
Laura Dean-Mooney and John McCardell, "Two Takes on
   the 21 Drinking Age"   314
Thomas H. Murray, "Drugs, Sports, and Ethics"   317

Case Studies   324

CHAPTER 7 Sexual Intimacy and Marriage   330

Religious and Cultural Attitudes Toward Sexuality and Marriage   330
Sexual Intimacy and Love   331
Marriage   332
Homosexuality and Same-Sex Marriages   333
Cohabitation and Premarital Sex   334
The Philosophers on Sexuality and Marriage   335
Adultery and Infidelity   336
Sex and Violence   336
Prostitution and the Sex Trade   338
The Moral Issues   338
Conclusion   341

The Vatican, "Declaration on Sexual Ethics"   341
Sara Ruddick, "Better Sex"   346
Michael Ruse, "Is Homosexuality Bad Sexuality?"   353
Margaret H. Marshall and Robert J. Cordy, *Goodridge v. Department
   of Public Health* (2003)   361
Richard Wasserstrom, "Is Adultery Immoral?"   370
Lois Pineau, "Date Rape: A Feminist Analysis"   377

Case Studies   383

CHAPTER 8   ## Feminism, Motherhood, and the Workplace   390

Feminism   390

The Philosophers on Women   394

Motherhood   395

Women in the Workplace   397

Sexual Harassment   399

The Moral Issues   400

Conclusion   401

SIMONE DE BEAUVOIR, "The Second Sex"   402

RUTH GROENHOUT, "Essentialist Challenges to Liberal Feminism"   406

LINDA HIRSHMAN, "Homeward Bound"   415

CATHY YOUNG, "The Return of the Mommy Wars"   421

GLORIA STEINEM, "Women Are Never Front-Runners"   424

STEVEN GOLDBERG, "The Logic of Patriarchy"   426

KATIE ROIPHE, "Reckless Eyeballing: Sexual Harassment
  on Campus"   432

Case Studies   439

CHAPTER 9   ## Freedom of Speech   445

What Is "Freedom of Speech"?   445

Limitations on Freedom of Speech   446

The First Amendment to the U.S. Constitution   447

Freedom of Speech in Cyberspace   448

Pornography   449

Hate Speech as Protected Speech   450

Speech Codes and Free Speech Zones on College Campuses   452

The Philosophers on Freedom of Speech   454

The Moral Issues   455

Conclusion   459

JOHN STUART MILL, from *On Liberty*   459

CATHARINE A. MACKINNON, "Pornography, Civil Rights, and Speech"   467

CHARLES R. LAWRENCE III, "If He Hollers Let Him Go: Regulating
  Racist Speech on Campus"   475

NADINE STROSSEN, "Hate Speech and Pornography: Do We Have
  to Choose Between Freedom of Speech and Equality?"   484

STANLEY FISH, "There's No Such Thing as Free Speech,
  and It's a Good Thing, Too"   493

ALAN M. DERSHOWITZ, "Political Correctness, Speech Codes, and Diversity"   499

CASS R. SUNSTEIN, "The First Amendment in Cyberspace"   502

Case Studies   507

CHAPTER 10   **Racial Discrimination and Global Justice**   514

Defining the Key Terms   514

The Philosophers on Racism   516

The Roots of American Racism   517

Racism Today   521

Globalization, Immigration, and Racism   524

The Moral Issues   525

Conclusion   527

LYNDON B. JOHNSON, "To Fulfill These Rights"   528

JORGE GARCIA, "The Heart of Racism"   530

BERNARD R. BOXILL, "The Color-Blind Principle"   540

MICHAEL LEVIN, "Race, Biology, and Justice"   546

WILLIAM I. ROBINSON, "'Aqui Estamos y No Nos Vamos!' Global Capital and Immigrant Rights"   554

THOMAS POGGE, "World Poverty and Human Rights"   559

Case Studies   565

CHAPTER 11   **War and Terrorism**   571

Background   571

The Philosophers on War and Terrorism   572

The Just-War Tradition   575

Weapons of Mass Destruction   578

Pacifism and Conscription   579

The Moral Issues   580

Conclusion   584

ELIZABETH ANSCOMBE, "War and Murder"   585

C. A. J. COADY, "War and Terrorism"   591

SOHAIL H. HASHMI, "Interpreting the Islamic Ethics of War and Peace"   599

JONATHAN GRANOFF, "Nuclear Weapons, Ethics, Morals and Law"   608

DAVID LUBAN, "The War on Terrorism and the End of Human Rights"   613

STEPHEN JOEL TRACHTENBERG, "Sharing the Burden"   620

Ron Paul, "Conscription: The Terrible Price of War"   624

Jonathan Granoff, "Peace and Security"   627

Case Studies   630

CHAPTER 12   **Animal Rights and Environmental Ethics**   637

The Legal and Moral Status of Nonhuman Animals   637

The Legal and Moral Status of the Environment   639

The Philosophers on the Moral Value of Nonhuman Animals and the Environment   639

Animal Farming, Environmental Degradation, and Vegetarianism   641

Global Warming and Climate Change   643

Animal Experimentation   644

The Moral Issues   645

Conclusion   648

Tom Regan, "The Moral Basis of Vegetarianism"   649

Jan Narveson, "Animal Rights Revisited"   655

Peter Singer, from *Animal Liberation*   660

Carl Cohen, "Do Animals Have Rights?"   669

Aldo Leopold, "The Land Ethic"   676

Bill Devall and George Sessions, "Deep Ecology"   680

Al Gore, "Perspective on Global Warming"   685

Karen J. Warren, "The Power and the Promise of Ecological Feminism, Revisited"   687

Case Studies   694

Glossary   G-1

Endnotes   N-1

Credits   C-1

Index   I-1

Preface

Although there are several approaches to teaching college ethics, the use of moral issues is probably the most popular as well as the most appealing to students. The moral issues approach, on its own, however, has some drawbacks. It often fails to provide students with the analytical tools necessary for making real-life moral decisions. Students may also come to confuse "ideology," or the holding of certain views on issues, with morality itself. This, in turn, may contribute to "moral passivity" in which

> great numbers of people, the young and educated especially, feel they have an adequate moral identity merely because they hold the "right" views on such matters as ecology, feminism, socialism, and nuclear energy. They may lead narrow, self-indulgent lives . . . yet still feel a moral advantage over those who actively work to help the needy but who are, in their eyes, ideologically unsound.*

Analyzing Moral Issues provides a corrective to these drawbacks by combining the appeal and strengths of the moral issues approach with a solid foundation in moral theory and moral reasoning. In addition to giving an overview of some of the major moral issues in our society, it introduces students to both Western and non-Western moral theories.

THE ORGANIZATION OF THE BOOK

The Moral Theory Chapter

Chapter 1 covers the major moral theories. It also includes a section on moral development. When grounded in moral theory, the moral issues approach can engage the students' interest and connect abstract theory to what is going on in the world around them. Connecting theory to real-life moral decisions encourages students to accept personal responsibility for their moral choices rather than substituting ideology for character development. This chapter is followed by ten short readings from world philosophers and scholars.

---

*Christina Sommers, "Where Have All the Good Deeds Gone?" *Hastings Center Report*, August 1982, pp. 13–14.

THE READING SELECTIONS

The reading selections following Chapters 2 through 12 begin with a bridge between moral theory and moral issues by showing students how to apply moral reasoning to an actual philosophical reading on a moral issue—Judith Jarvis Thomson's "A Defense of Abortion." Each chapter includes readings from traditional Western moral philosophers as well as readings that represent non-Western, multicultural, feminist, religious, and legal perspectives. The readings have been selected to introduce students to diverse and opposing viewpoints regarding the particular issue under discussion.

The Eleven Issues Chapters

Chapters 2–12 each cover a different contemporary moral issue. Each issue is related, when possible, to the students' everyday experience, thus connecting their lives as college students to wider societal issues. While students' lives may not be directly affected by broader issues such as capital punishment, as citizens in a democratic society they will be directly responsible for formulating policy regarding these issues. Bringing in broader social issues also requires students to extend their range of moral concern beyond their immediate community, which is one of the goals of a college education.

The introduction to each chapter includes a historical background of the issue and an overview of the traditional philosophical perspectives on the issue presented. Following is a summary of each of the eleven chapters.

Chapter 2, Abortion: Despite its legalization, abortion remains one of the most divisive moral issues. This chapter looks at the history of the abortion debate and some of the key moral issues underlying this debate, such as women's rights and the moral status of the fetus. It also raises the issues of selective abortion and discrimination.

Chapter 3, Genetic Engineering, Cloning, and Stem Cell Research: Cloning entered the ethics spotlight in 1997 with the announcement of the birth of Dolly, the first mammal to be cloned from an adult cell. This chapter explores some of the moral issues raised by new reproductive technologies, stem cell research, cloning, and other forms of genetic engineering. In doing so, it also addresses the issue of personhood as well as the morality of trying to control what it means to be a human.

Chapter 4, Euthanasia: Euthanasia has become an important moral issue mainly because of advances in medical technology that permit physicians to extend life. The demand for legalized euthanasia is also a reflection of the emphasis on personal autonomy and freedom in modern society. This chapter focuses primarily on the question of voluntary, active euthanasia and the debate over physician-assisted suicide.

Chapter 5, The Death Penalty: The issue of capital punishment touches on the most basic questions of justice and what is meant by the moral value of human life. This chapter looks at both the legal and moral issues involved in the debate over the death penalty. In addition to questions regarding the morality of the death penalty, it also challenges students to think about the more basic question of the morality of punishing wrongdoers.

Chapter 6, Drug and Alcohol Use: Drug and alcohol use among college students has increased dramatically since 1990. This chapter looks at some of the moral issues involved in the use of both legal and illegal drugs. It also includes an examination of the disease model and the moral model of addiction.

Chapter 7, Sexual Intimacy and Marriage: Most Americans regard sexual intimacy, especially outside of marriage, as an ethical hotbed. This chapter provides students with the background information as well as the moral issues raised in the debates over cohabitation, same-sex marriages, divorce, prostitution, and rape.

Chapter 8, Feminism, Motherhood, and the Workplace: Feminism takes different forms. This chapter gives an overview of the types of feminism and how each addresses issues such as the nature of men and women, motherhood, the division of labor in the home, and special rights for parents in the workplace.

Chapter 9, Freedom of Speech: Freedom of speech needs to be considered in context and in light of other values that may conflict with it. In this chapter, freedom of speech is analyzed primarily in the context of hate speech—especially on college campuses—pornography, and restrictions on speech in cyberspace. Also examined are the moral implications of the First Amendment for regulating these types of speech.

Chapter 10, Racial Discrimination and Global Justice: Racism is perpetuated and reinforced at both the institutional and the individual level. This chapter examines the roots of racism in Western philosophy, American culture, and globalization, as well as policies—such as affirmative action, reparation for slavery, and redistribution of global wealth—that are designed to overcome the effects of racism.

Chapter 11, War and Terrorism: War and terrorism have become a prominent moral issue in the United States following September 11, 2001. This chapter discusses the differences between war and terrorism and examines the question of whether either is morally justified and, if so, under what conditions.

Chapter 12, Animal Rights and Environmental Ethics: This chapter explores questions regarding the moral status of nonhuman animals and the environment, as well as our obligations toward other animals and nonhuman nature. In particular, it challenges students to rethink anthropocentrism and to question whether human practices such as meat-eating, animal experimentation, hunting, and deforestation are morally acceptable.

The Critical Reading and Discussion Questions

Analyzing Moral Issues encourages students to apply critical thinking skills to each reading through the use of critical reading and discussion questions. Each reading is preceded by a short introduction and a set of critical reading questions related to the main points raised in the reading. The discussion questions at the end of each reading require students to think more deeply about the arguments and concepts raised in that particular reading. The discussion questions also encourage students to relate these concepts and arguments to the different moral theories and other readings in the book as well as to real-life moral issues in their own lives.

Case Studies

Each moral issues chapter includes, at the end, several case studies related to the particular moral issue. The majority of these case studies are based on real-life events.

The case studies have been updated for the fifth edition to reflect changes in policies and issues as well as national and international events, including the appointment of a new administration under President Obama. Placing the issue within a real-world context encourages students to apply theory and moral reasoning to actual situations that they might encounter in their own lives.

Some of the case studies involve moral dilemmas that force students to defend a particular position on a controversial issue. Discussion of real-life moral dilemmas has been shown to enhance a student's ability to engage in effective moral reasoning. However, exclusive focus on dilemmas runs the danger of leaving students with the impression that there are no right and wrong answers and that morality is all relative. Therefore, other cases focus on issues that are fairly straightforward but that require introspection and reflection.

ACKNOWLEDGMENTS

I thank the reviewers for their helpful suggestions: Robert Schimoler, University of Saint Mary; Larry Waggle, St. Norbert College; Cassandra Evans, San Diego City College; Alban Urbanas, University of Delaware; Vickey Milligan, North Central State College; Matthew Pamental, Northern Illinois University; Csaba Nyiri, University of Toledo; Joy Raser, University of Saint Mary; Mike Steinman, Mira Costa College; Kitty Henderson, Austin Community College; Octavio Roca, Miami Dade College; Jo Ann Hedleston, Colorado State University; Chris Frakes, University of Colorado, Colorado Springs; Todd Shumpert, Bloomfield College; and A. David Kline, University of North Florida.

Thanks to my editor, Mark Georgiev, development editor, Craig Leonard, and managing editor, Nicole Bridge, for their enthusiastic support and suggestions. Heart-felt thanks go to Peggy Tropp for her excellent job of editing the fifth edition. I would also like to express my appreciation to Wesley Hall, permissions editor, for his assistance in obtaining permissions for the reading selections in this edition, and to Alison Meier, production editor, and Anne Draus, production service, for keeping the book on schedule. In addition, I am grateful to the many authors who gave me permission to use their writings in this edition. My deepest gratitude also goes out to the many people, including Michael Jackson, reference librarian at Brown University, and my daughter Alyssa Boss, Esq., who assisted me with my research and provided feedback on the manuscript. Thanks also to Emily Petit, my intern, for her assistance in preparing the fifth edition. Last, but not least, I would like to thank my former assistant, James Nuzum, for his continuing enthusiasm, his dedication to this project, and his invaluable input and assistance in putting this text together.

Moral Theory

Adolf Hitler once said, "What good fortune for those in power that people do not think." In the early 1960s, Yale psychologist Stanley Milgram conducted an experiment on obedience to determine if Americans would be as ready to blindly follow the orders of an authority figure as were the Nazis.

In Milgram's experiment, subjects were led to believe that they were delivering a series of increasingly painful electric shocks as part of an experiment on the effect of punishment on learning. In fact, the person who was playing the role of the learner was an accomplice of the experimenter and was not actually receiving the shocks. When the subjects balked upon hearing the screams of pain from the learner, they were urged to continue by an experimenter wearing a white lab coat. Despite the feigned protests of the learner, about two-thirds of the subjects obeyed the experimenter and continued delivering what they believed were potentially fatal electric shocks.

The findings of this experiment suggest that people can be persuaded to torture, and perhaps even kill, another person simply at the urging of an authority figure. A film made of the experiment revealed that those who were most likely to give in to the urging of the authority figure knew that what they were doing was wrong but were unable to articulate *why* it was wrong.[1] Those who were able to resist the authority figure, on the other hand, were able to provide justifications, in the form of moral principles and moral theory, for their refusal; they were able to say *why* continuing to deliver the shocks was wrong. Milgram wrote of his findings:

> Ordinary people, simply doing their jobs, and without any particular hostility on
> their part, can become agents in a terribly destructive process. Moreover, even
> when the destructive effects of their work become patently clear, and they are
> asked to carry out actions incompatible with fundamental standards of morality,
> relatively few people have the resources needed to resist.[2]

Like the subjects in the Milgram experiment, many of us also lack the resources necessary to critically analyze moral issues. For example, in a study of how college students judge social issues, such as abortion, pornography, and homosexuality, researchers found that many students had inconsistent "informational assumptions"; they were unable to offer a well-reasoned justification for their position on an issue, shifting positions depending on the questions asked.[3] This inability hinders many of us from engaging in thoughtful discussions of issues such as euthanasia, abortion, capital

1

punishment, animal rights, and environmental ethics. Like the Milgram subjects, simply deferring to those in authority or refusing to take a stand can contribute to a life-and-death decision for those affected.

MORAL PHILOSOPHY

Moral philosophy is the study of the values and guidelines by which we live, as well as the justification of these values and guidelines. There are two traditional subdivisions in moral philosophy: (1) normative ethics and (2) theoretical ethics.

Normative ethics is concerned with the study of the values and guidelines by which we live. Normative ethics also includes the study of moral issues—the primary focus of this text. **Applied ethics** is the application of normative ethics to actual cases. The emerging field of global ethics, for example, is concerned with the application of normative ethics to global issues such as the disparities of wealth between nations, international trade and immigration policy, war and peace, and global warming.

Theoretical ethics, also known as **metaethics,** is concerned with the justification of these values and guidelines. These justifications involve skill in moral reasoning and critical thinking. The study of moral issues and applied or normative ethics is built on an understanding of moral reasoning and theoretical ethics.

If we simply begin debating moral issues without first establishing this foundation, our arguments may be weak and can easily collapse like the proverbial house built on sand. Without the ability to critically analyze or offer theoretical underpinning for our position on an issue, we are unable to effectively defend it or respond to others' arguments. This inability contributes to the feeling that our position is simply a matter of personal opinion. "Well," we may say with a shrug of the shoulders, "we all have a right to our opinions." Having a right to our own opinion, however, is not the same as saying that all opinions are equally reasonable.

Or, in our frustration, we may resort to using logical fallacies, glaring at our opponents in an attempt to intimidate them, or attacking their character; we may make wild generalizations that we are unable to back up, or we may simply change the topic. We see this especially in highly polarized issues such as the current abortion debate where emotions run high.

The moral rightness or wrongness of a position or action, such as delivering potentially lethal shocks to a subject in an experiment, is not a matter of personal feeling or opinion but of reason. The study of moral theory and reasoning helps us recognize and organize these general principles and moral concerns. It is up to us as critical thinkers to decide which arguments are the strongest and to come up with a well-reasoned position that takes into account the strengths of all sides of the argument.

WHAT IS THE PURPOSE OF MORAL THEORIES?

Most people, if given a choice, would prefer to skip moral theory and get on with discussions of real-life moral issues. Theory is often contrasted with action. This is a false dichotomy, since it is theory that informs our actions. Knowing how to ground discussions of moral issues in moral theory and good moral reasoning will make us less vulnerable to persuasive, but logically incorrect, thinking.

A **theory** is a conceptual framework for explaining a set of facts or concepts. In moral philosophy, theory *explains* why a certain action—such as torturing babies—is wrong and why we *ought* to act in certain ways and be a certain type of person. Moral theory also helps us *clarify, critically analyze,* and *rank* the moral concerns raised by particular moral issues.

A good theory should also be able to explain the whole range or scope of morality, not just particular types of actions. For example, the theory that morality is a private choice is inadequate for dealing with choices such as rape, torture, and genocide, since these actions affect other people. In addition, a theory should take into account what we, upon reflection, believe to be right. Aristotle (384–322 B.C.E.), for example, takes as the starting point in developing his moral theory the moral intuitions of ordinary people. Moral theory, however, goes beyond our everyday notions about morality. It requires consistency in our thinking and the weeding out of those commonly held beliefs about morality that are inconsistent or superfluous.

Moral theories can be compared to road maps. A good theory offers *guidance* or signposts for thinking about and resolving moral issues. Although we may just happen to come upon a good solution, a moral theory, like a road map, makes it more likely that we will reach our destination with the least amount of wrong turns and aggravation. Like maps, not all theories are equally good. Some may be good as far as they go, but they leave out too much. In this case we may want to combine them with other theories or "maps." Other moral theories, such as ethical subjectivism, lead us down dead ends. Knowing about the strengths and weaknesses of the different moral theories can save us from heading down these dead ends!

Theories also shape our worldviews. We all approach the world with certain assumptions that, loosely, form our theories about what to expect in the world. In any culture there are certain theories that are so embedded in the cultural worldview that they are uncritically assumed to be true. For example, in Western culture the theory that humans are superior to and separate from other animals (**anthropocentrism**) is rarely questioned. This is reflected in our language, where the common use of the term *animal* does not include humans. Rather than uncritically adopting the prevailing theories of our culture, we need to ask first if their assumptions can be justified or if they embody false views.

THE TYPES OF MORAL THEORIES

There are two main types of moral theories: (1) ethical relativism and (2) universalist or objectivist. An **ethical relativist** claims that morality is invented or created by people; therefore morality, like fashion, can vary from time to time and from person to person. **Universalist** or **objectivist moral theories,** in contrast, state that there are fundamental, objective moral principles and values that are universally true for all people, independent of their personal beliefs or culture.

In his study of moral development, psychologist Lawrence Kohlberg found that while 90 percent of adult Americans acknowledge universal moral principles such as equality, they believe, for the most part, that morality is relative to or created by society.[4] For the majority of Americans, being morally good means following the norms and values of their society or culture—whether this be their peer culture, their church,[5] their country, or a combination of these. The theory that morality is relative to societal norms is known in moral philosophy as **cultural relativism.** Rather than promote tolerance as a universal moral value, ethical relativism breeds suspicion of those who are different and allows exploitation of the weak by the powerful as long as it is culturally sanctioned.

Because of this, it is important that we learn how to analyze different moral theories. As critical thinkers and students of moral philosophy, we cannot be content with simply accepting the norms of our culture or dismissing morality as a matter of personal opinion. Rather than depend on the opinions of others and risk getting off course, we can use theory as a guide as we make our way through the often bewildering morass of moral issues that confront us in modern life.

EXERCISES

1. What do you mean when you say that something is morally right or morally wrong? Use specific examples from your life experience to illustrate your answer.
2. Make a list of guidelines and values that you use in making moral decisions. Are your values and guidelines consistent? Where did you get these guidelines and values? Do they give you sufficient guidance in resolving difficult moral issues? Explain.
3. Choose a moral issue. Discuss how the guidelines and values you listed in the previous answer help shape your position on that issue.

RELATIVISM IN ETHICS

There is one thing a professor can be absolutely certain of: almost every student entering the university believes, or says he believes, that truth is relative.

—Allan Bloom, *The Closing of the American Mind*

The fact of moral disagreement raises the question of whether there are objective or universal moral principles. Cultural and individual disagreements, fueled by popular clichés such as "morality is all relative," "do what you feel is right," "don't force your values on me," and "who am I to judge?" create serious doubts in people's minds about whether moral issues can ever be resolved, or whether meaningful dialogue between those holding opposing positions is even possible.

According to ethical relativists, there are no independent or objective moral standards. Instead, morality is *created* by people. In other words, humans, either individually or collectively, are the ultimate measure of what is right and wrong.

Ethical Subjectivism

What I feel is right is right. What I feel is wrong is wrong.

—Jean-Jacques Rousseau

Ethical relativism can be subdivided into ethical subjectivism and cultural relativism. **Ethical subjectivists** claim that individual people create their own morality. There are no objective moral truths—only individuals' **opinions** or preferences. What is right for you may be wrong for me, depending on our respective feelings. You may feel that racism is wrong; I may feel that white supremacy is morally right. You may feel that it is wrong to eat meat; I may feel it is right for me. The rightness or wrongness of our actions depends solely on how each of us *feels* about racism or meat-eating.

Do not confuse ethical subjectivism with the obviously true, descriptive statement that "whatever a person believes is right for him or her is what that person believes is right for him or her." Ethical subjectivism goes beyond this by claiming that sincerely believing or feeling that something is right *makes* it right for the individual. Because morality is merely a matter of personal opinion, we can never be mistaken about what is right and wrong. In other words, my actions in terrorizing black students on campus are morally commendable and perhaps even morally obligatory, so long as I personally feel that what I am doing is right.

When asked if he thought what he did was wrong, convicted serial killer Craig Price calmly replied, "Morality is a private choice." If morality is simply a matter of personal opinion, there is no point in trying to use rational arguments to convince the racist or the serial killer that what he did was wrong, any more than it would make sense to try to convince me that I really don't like cashew nuts. Furthermore, there would not be any point in proceeding further in a moral-issues course.

When people's views come into conflict, those who are strongest will be able to impose their agenda on others, as Craig Price did. Under ethical subjectivism we do not have to tolerate other people's views or even their lives unless, of course, we feel that tolerance is right for us. Ethical subjectivism, in other words, provides no guidance for reaching moral decisions when there is a question of what to do. Returning to the metaphor of moral theories as a road map, ethics subjectivism is rather like a map that always says "You're wherever you think you are." Clearly, such a map would not be of much use, especially if we are lost and trying to get to a particular destination.

What Would the World Be Like If We Took Ethical Subjectivism Seriously?   Ethical subjectivism is one of the weakest moral theories. If taken seriously, it permits people to exploit and hurt others without having to justify their actions. As a theory, it does not provide a satisfactory explanation for why certain actions are wrong. In real life we generally make moral judgments independently of anyone's feelings toward the action. Indeed, the fact that a serial killer enjoys torturing and killing his victims or that a child molester sincerely believes that his young victims enjoy being raped only makes their actions more horrific. If ethical subjectivism were true, the opposite would be the case: Our moral heroes would be **sociopaths**—people who act solely on their feelings, without concern for any universal moral principles.

Cultural Relativism

> *We recognize that morality differs in every society, and is a convenient term for socially approved habits.*

> —Ruth Benedict (1933)

The modern theory of cultural relativism developed primarily out of late nineteenth- and early twentieth-century studies of "simple" cultures by prominent anthropologists such as Ruth Benedict, Emile Durkheim, William Graham Sumner, and Franz Boas. Like ethical subjectivists, **cultural relativists** maintain that standards of right and wrong are created by people. It is societal norms, however, rather than the opinions of isolated individuals, that form the basis of morality. Public opinion, not private opinion, determines what is right and wrong. There are no objective universal moral standards that hold for all people in all cultures, only different cultural customs.

Cultural relativists are not merely arguing that *some* moral values are relative to culture. They claim that *all* moral values are nothing more than cultural customs and laws. Because there are no universal moral standards, the moral values of one culture cannot be judged to be any better or worse than those of any other culture. Headhunting, for example, is right or wrong only within a particular cultural context. In some New Guinea cultures, it was at one time considered morally commendable for a young man to give his sweetheart a shrunken head as a trophy. In our country such an action would be regarded as highly immoral and evidence of serious mental illness. Similarly, if a culture believes that women should be kept in subjection, women have a moral obligation to be submissive to their fathers or husbands, and men have a moral right, and perhaps a moral duty, to use brute force should their women deviate from the cultural norm. While it is wrong in our culture for men to beat their wives, according to a cultural relativist it is wrong *only* because it goes against cultural norms.

Cultural Relativism Is Not the Same as Sociological Relativism   Cultural relativism is a moral theory about what *ought to be*. **Sociological relativism** is a descriptive rather than normative theory. It is simply the observation that there is disagreement among cultures regarding moral values. Unlike cultural relativism, sociological relativism draws no conclusions about the rightness or wrongness of these values. Sociological relativists leave open the possibility that a culture may be mistaken about its moral values (such as Nazi Germany or the headhunting cultures) and that there *may* be universal moral principles that all cultures ought to respect. Cultural relativism, on the other hand, claims that if a culture believes something is morally right, that in itself makes it morally right. Because morality is nothing more than custom, there are no legitimate grounds for criticizing the moral practices of other cultures.

Morality may also change within a culture over time, much like fashions. Slavery is now considered immoral in the United States. Two hundred years ago, however, slavery was not only *believed to be* morally acceptable by the majority, it *was,* according to cultural relativists, morally acceptable. If morality is synonymous with conformity to cultural norms, it was the abolitionists, not the slaveholders, who were immoral. Similarly, Martin Luther King Jr. was immoral for protesting the segregation laws of the South.

For cultural relativists, if something is legal or at least culturally acceptable, whether it be slavery, abortion, capital punishment, prostitution, or pornography, it is, by definition, morally acceptable. Things that are illegal—such as recreational drug use, human cloning, assisted suicide, and same-sex marriage—are immoral according to the cultural relativist.

Cultural Relativism Is Based on Faulty Reasoning   Cultural relativism argues from the fact that a culture believes something, such as slavery, *is* moral, to the conclusion that that is the way things *ought to be*. In logic this type of faulty reasoning is known as the naturalist fallacy. The **naturalist fallacy** draws a conclusion about what ought to be, based on what is. As noted earlier, the fact that people believe something to be true, whether it be the flatness of the earth, creationism, or the morality of slavery, does not make it true or moral in itself.

What If Cultural Relativism Is True?   Further analysis of cultural relativism reveals that, like ethical subjectivism, it is fraught with problems and contradictions.

Cultural relativism offers no criteria for distinguishing between reformers, such as Martin Luther King Jr. and Susan B. Anthony, who may break the law as an act of conscience, and common criminals. Both the social reformer and the criminal break cultural norms; both, therefore, are immoral. Identifying what is moral with what is legal is problematic, since some laws—such as laws supporting slavery or prohibiting women from voting—are clearly unjust and reasonable people believe they should be changed.

Because it identifies morality with maintaining the status quo, cultural relativism cannot explain moral progress. Yet most people believe that the abolition of slavery in the United States, the civil rights movement, and granting women full rights of citizenship all represented moral progress. Similarly, cultural relativism cannot account for the fact that most people believe that there are ways in which their own society can be improved. Not only does cultural relativism prevent criticism of other cultures, it also rules out the possibility of engaging in a rational critique of one's own cultural customs.

Cultural relativism encourages blind conformity to cultural norms rather than rational analysis of moral issues. Rather than using dialogue, we resolve a moral issue simply by taking a poll or calling a lawyer. But surely this is not an accurate description of how we make moral decisions or resolve moral issues. Legalizing abortion and capital punishment did not stop moral debate over those two issues. Futhermore, the fact that most Americans eat meat is irrelevant to someone who is struggling with the morality of meat-eating.

Cultural relativism does not work in pluralistic cultures. Although it may have been possible a century ago for anthropologists to identify the cultural norms of relatively isolated and static cultures, in the rapidly changing modern world it is becoming more and more difficult to draw sharp distinctions between cultures or even to figure out what our own cultural norms are. Most of us are members of several cultures or subcultures. We may be members of a Catholic, Cambodian, Native American, African American, or homosexual subculture whose values may conflict with those of the wider culture. Indeed, the so-called dominant cultural values are sometimes simply the values held by a small group of people who happen to hold the power in that culture.

We also cannot assume that simply because the majority holds a certain value that it is desirable. In his essay *On Liberty,* at the end of Chapter 9, John Stuart Mill (1806–1873) argues that basing public policy on the will of the people can result in the "tyranny of the majority." Suppression of freedom of speech and religion, censorship of the press, and discrimination against minorities have all, at some time, had the blessing of the majority.

The belief that there are no shared universal moral values can lead to suspicion and mistrust of people from other cultures or subcultures, rather than tolerance and a sense of community. We may feel that "they" do not share our respect for life; that people from other cultures may even have dangerous values. Because cultural relativism rules out the possibility of rational discussion when cross-cultural values come into conflict and persuasion fails, groups may resort to either apathy and isolationism when the values of other cultures are not a threat, or to violence when another culture's values or actions create a threat to one's own way of life. We can see this in the current conflict involving the United States and Iraq and other Middle Eastern countries.

This being said, even though relativist moral theories may not stand up under the scrutiny of critical analysis, they contain at least a grain of truth. Cultural relativism reminds us that culture and history are important in the moral life. Our traditions, our religious values, and our political and social institutions all shape the way in which we apply moral values. Although culture may not be the source of fundamental moral principles and values, it influences how they are interpreted and prioritized. In their concern to disavow ethical relativism, too many philosophers have divorced morality from the actual historical and cultural settings in which we make our moral decisions, but cultural relativism takes this observation too far. Although the *application* of specific moral principles is relative to cultures (as noted in the Eskimo example later in this chapter), this does not imply that these moral principles are the *creation* of cultures.

Global ethicists reject the reduction of morality to cultural customs and the uncritical defense of traditional knowledge and local customs—particularly oppressive customs. Cultural relativism is a reminder of how easily we can confuse custom and tradition with morality. Because of this, we need to be able to critically analyze not just issues that are controversial but also customs that society accepts as perfectly moral.

Ethical Relativism and Doublethink   The simplicity and popularity of the two types of ethical relativism make them particularly seductive. Ethical subjectivism absolves people of ever having to deliberate before making a moral judgment, whereas cultural relativism absolves people from moral responsibility so long as they follow the crowd. At the same time, almost everyone wants others to treat them with respect and be held morally culpable for their hurtful actions.

In his book *1984*, George Orwell coined the term **doublethink** to describe when people simultaneously hold two contradictory views and believe both to be true. Some people jump back and forth between the different theories, depending on what is more expedient in a particular situation. For example, some students may argue that morality is a private choice when it comes to something they are doing, such as binge drinking or cheating on a test or using hate speech. At the same time, they may be morally critical of teachers who break cultural norms by using sexist or racist language in class or playing favorites in grading tests. Ethical subjectivism and cultural relativism, however, are mutually exclusive theories. A person cannot consistently believe both that morality is created by individuals and that morality is a cultural creation.

Some people who claim that they are relativists may also bring universal moral principles concerning justice and respect in through the back door. They may argue that sexist and racist language is disrespectful or that playing favorites in grading is unfair. They may even cite the Golden Rule or some form of it. Because the two types of theories are based on contradictory claims regarding the source of morality, however, both forms of ethical relativism are incompatible with universalist theories.

What About Moral Disagreement?

But if ethical relativism is incorrect, how can we explain the lack of agreement among individuals and cultures? The fact that people disagree does not necessarily mean that there are no objective moral principles. People can disagree for a number of reasons.

They may be mistaken about their facts. At one time most people believed that the earth was flat, but it turns out they were mistaken. Physicians used to routinely lie to dying cancer patients, believing that the truth would be so upsetting that it might kill them. It wasn't until the 1970s that studies were carried out that showed physicians to be wrong. There may also be objective moral standards, even though there may be disagreement regarding their application to particular situations and issues.

Disagreement can also occur because natural conditions and religious beliefs influence the expression of a particular moral value. In 1941 Gontran de Poncins wrote the following about the Kabloona, an Eskimo culture living in the Canadian arctic.

> One observer was told of an Eskimo who was getting ready to move camp and was concerned about what to do with his blind and aged father, who was a burden to the family. One day the old man expressed a desire to go seal hunting again, something he had not done for many years. His son readily assented to this suggestion, and the old man was dressed warmly and given his weapons. He was then led out to the seal grounds and was walked into a hole in the ice into which he disappeared.[6]

Is cultural relativism the only way to explain the difference between the Kabloona and modern Americans? Modern Americans can hire caregivers or put their ailing parents or grandparents in nursing homes. The Kabloona, on the other hand, were a nomadic people; there were no nursing homes or hospitals or spare bedrooms in the house. As nomadic people their lives depended on following the seal herds. To take a blind and ailing parent on one of these treks could have resulted in starvation, not just of the elderly parent, but of the whole family. In addition, the son, as was the tradition, respected his father's autonomy, waiting until he requested the "hunting" trip.

What was different here, in other words, were not the fundamental moral values of respect for life, family loyalty, and personal autonomy, but different conditions that placed limitations on how these values could best be *applied*. In other words, the Kabloona practice can be explained as an example of *sociological relativism*. Saving the lives of many took precedence over prolonging the father's life. The question of when, if ever, it is morally permissible to assist a terminally ill person in taking his or her life is not one limited to the Kabloona culture. The introduction of medical technology that can prolong the lives of the elderly and the dying has brought the issues of death with dignity and assisted suicide to the forefront in our own culture.

People may also disagree about moral issues not because they hold fundamentally different moral values, but because they *rank* or prioritize them differently. Both Aristotle and the Confucians give a high ranking to community and social values. Libertarians, on the other hand, place a higher value on individual autonomy and freedom. Moral theory helps us recognize and rank these values and in so doing helps us come to a resolution that honors as many moral values as possible.

Relativism, Personhood, and Moral Community

Variations in cultural norms can also occur because of differences in how cultures define their moral communities. According to anthropologist Clyde Kluckholn, there are universal moral values that are recognized by all cultures. No culture, for example, approves of indiscriminate lying, cheating, or stealing. Random violence is also prohibited universally. Every culture also makes arrangements for the care of its children. These moral values, however, apply only to members of a particular culture's **moral community**— that is, to those who are seen as having moral value. Headhunters, for example, always select their victims from outside their immediate community.

Beings who have moral worth are known in moral philosophy as **persons.** Persons are beings who are worthy of respect as valuable in themselves, rather than simply because of their usefulness or value to someone else. The widespread identification of *person* with *human being* in our culture betrays our anthropocentric bias; the use of the term *man* for all humans also shows our patriarchal bias. In coming up with a rational and consistent definition of the moral community, it is important to look beyond culturally biased terms.

Cultural Relativism and Ethnocentrism   Cultural relativism defines moral community in terms of **ethnocentrism:** Someone, or something, has moral value only because society grants this status. Those who are granted moral status by their culture receive the protection and support of the community. Moreover, those who are closer to the center of the moral community receive more privileges and protection. Those who are **marginalized**—such as women, homosexuals, blacks, and Hispanics—have less access to economic and social benefits. When members of a marginalized group transgress cultural norms, they are not given the same protection as those in power. For example, in the United States, blacks are more likely to receive the death penalty.[7] Beings who are outside the moral community—such as nonhuman animals, fetuses, and the environment in our culture—can be treated as a "means only" and disposed of, eaten, or exploited solely for the benefit of those within the moral community.

In Buddhist cultures and some Native American cultures, the moral community is defined very broadly to include all living beings—human and nonhuman. Other cultures define their moral community more narrowly. For a group of beings to be excluded from the moral community, they first have to be "depersonalized." Before embarking on their "final solution," the German Supreme Court in 1936 ruled that "the Jew is only a rough copy of a human being, with human like facial traits but nonetheless . . . lower than any animal . . . otherwise nothing." In the 1857 *Dred Scott v. Sanford* decision, the United States Supreme Court reaffirmed that the slave was "property in the strictest sense of the word" and an "inferior being that had no rights which the white man was bound to respect." In the 1973 *Roe v. Wade* decision, which legalized abortion, the Court declared that "the word 'person,' as used in the Fourteenth Amendment, does not include the unborn" (see pages 76–77).

The cultural definition of the moral community is, to a large extent, politically and economically motivated and serves to maintain the status quo. By protecting the interests of those in power and morally sanctioning the marginalization and exploitation of other groups, cultural relativism promotes ethnocentrism and legitimates hatred and discrimination. Problems such as racism and sexism exist in our culture, in part, because the majority of American adults are cultural relativists.

The power of our cultural worldview is more pervasive than most of us realize. Many people, while giving lip service to the universal principle of equality, tacitly adopt the prevailing cultural view of the moral community. In the study mentioned earlier of how college students judge social issues, slightly more than half of the students interviewed evaluated homosexuality in a positive light, stating that it was a personal preference just like heterosexuality.[8] When the same students were presented with a hypothetical example of their own child being homosexual, however, 92 percent shifted their position, stating that this would not be morally acceptable or desirable. In other words, they shifted from a definition based on the principle of equality to the cultural definition of the moral community that marginalizes homosexuals (see Chapter 7). To avoid getting mired in doublethink, it is important to be aware of how the cultural definition of the moral community shapes viewpoints on moral issues.

Unlike cultural relativism, universalist theories of morality require rational criteria for personhood and that the exclusion of a particular group from the moral community be justified. Much of the dissension over abortion and animal rights stems from disagreement over the definition of moral community and personhood. Thus, any debate on these issues must be based on a rational and consistent definition of these key terms. Mary Anne Warren in her article on abortion (see Chapter 2), for example, devotes considerable space to defining personhood. As with slavery, justifying practices such as meat-eating or abortion on the grounds of tradition or legality just won't do.

EXERCISES

1. Philosopher Stephen Satris argues that the ethical relativism of most college students is intended not as a well-thought-out philosophical theory but as an "invincible suit of armor" to "prevent or close off dialogue and thought."[9] Do you agree? Discuss an instance when you, or someone else, used ethical subjectivism as a means of ending the discussion on a moral issue.
2. Do your views on issues coincide, for the most part, with those of your culture or subculture? To what extent do you use widespread agreement as support for the "rightness" of your position on issues such as abortion or capital punishment?
3. George Orwell predicted that doublethink would become more and more prevalent as people lost the ability to think critically. Do you agree with Orwell? What are some instances of doublethink in debates on moral issues?
4. What criteria do you use to decide who or what is included in and excluded from the moral community? Are you satisfied with your criteria? Discuss how your definition of personhood affects your views on the moral issues included in this text.

MOVING BEYOND ETHICAL RELATIVISM

Moral thought, then, seems to behave like all other kinds of thought. Progress through the moral levels and stages is characterized by increasing differentiation and increasing integration, and hence is the same kind of progress that scientific theory represents.

—Lawrence Kohlberg, *The Philosophy of Moral Development*
(1971)

Just as children must one day leave their parents and strike out on their own if they are to continue maturing, so too must we put behind us the dictates of our peer group or culture as the ultimate moral authority and seek a more solid and reliable foundation for everyday moral decisions. Both types of ethical relativism—ethical subjectivism and cultural relativism—are inadequate as explanations of how we make real-life moral decisions and as guides for what we ought to do. Universalist moral theories offer an alternative to ethical relativism. These theories claim that morality is universal and objective and, as such, exists independently of personal or cultural opinions.

The Stage Theory of Moral Development

According to developmental psychologists, there are innate cognitive structures that are fundamental to all humans. These structures include—among others—causality, time and space, and moral excellence. In his study of moral reasoning, psychologist Lawrence Kohlberg found that humans move through distinct **stages of moral development** (see chart on page 14). These stages are universal and cross-cultural and represent "transformations in the organization of thought, rather than increasing knowledge of cultural values." The earlier stages are not so much replaced by higher stages as incorporated into them—much as elementary school arithmetic becomes part of understanding complex statistical analysis. People move on to the next or "higher" stage only when they find their current type of moral reasoning inadequate. This generally occurs when they encounter a crisis that their current mode of thinking cannot satisfactorily resolve.

Young children use primarily egoistic or preconventional moral reasoning. Morality is simply a matter of satisfying their own needs. While they recognize basic moral principles such as justice, they apply this principle egocentrically only to themselves, demanding fair treatment from others but not caring whether others are treated justly.

In the second or conventional stage of moral reasoning, people look to others, whether it be their peers or societal norms, for their moral values. In other words, they adopt cultural relativism. The transition to the conventional stage generally takes place during early adolescence. While egoistic reasoning may be effective in helping the young child get what he or she wants, in high school and college, egoism is more likely to alienate the egoist from his or her peers.

Conventional moral reasoners are concerned with pleasing others and respecting social rules. Their position on a moral issue is generally determined by what their peers believe, or, at the higher level of conventional reasoning, what is legal. As a developmental stage, conventional moral reasoning helps to socialize young people and move them beyond egoism to a concern for community values and the needs of others.

The final stage, according to Kohlberg, is that of principled reasoning. In justifying this as a more desirable or higher stage than the previous stages, he points out that people at this stage prefer it to their earlier stages. In addition, most world philosophers have long held that autonomous moral reasoning, universality and impartiality, and a concern for justice for all are the hallmarks of sound moral reasoning.

Kohlberg used only males in formulating his theory on moral development. Not surprisingly, his stage theory has been criticized for not taking into account the way women think about moral issues. Through her interviews with women and a study of women in literature, Harvard psychologist Carol Gilligan concluded that women's moral development tends to follow a different path than men's: Men tend to be duty- and principle-oriented; women are more context-oriented and tend to view the world in a more emotional and personal way.[10] Women's moral judgment, Gilligan found, is characterized by concern for themselves and others, accepting and maintaining responsibility within relationships, attachment, and self-sacrifice.

Although Gilligan's and Kohlberg's theories emphasize different aspects of moral development, their stages are roughly parallel. The preconventional stage in both theories includes the egoists and ethical subjectivists who put their needs before those of others. Conventional moral reasoners, in both theories, are cultural relativists. The different descriptions of the conventional stage are not surprising given the different ways in which men and women are socialized in our culture. Men, for the most part, are socialized to be the upholders of law and order—whether it be the law of the land or the rules laid down by their peer culture. Women, on the other hand, are taught that being a good woman involves self-sacrifice and placing the welfare of others before her own. As Susan Wolf points out in her article on feminism and euthanasia (see Chapter 4), this can make women more vulnerable to pressure to choose euthanasia.

In both theories the postconventional stage is represented by autonomous moral reasoning, in which a person looks to transcultural universal values—whether in the form of abstract principles of justice and respect or moral sentiments such as compassion and empathy. Developing an awareness that respect applies to all persons involves being able to empathize with others. Sociopaths, who lack the ability to empathize, also lack any sense of moral duty. In addition, Gilligan's postconventional stage entails that women realize that principles of justice and respect apply to themselves as well as to others. Recent research has shown that most people—men and women alike— use both the care and the justice perspective in their moral reasoning. Both Gilligan and Kohlberg came to acknowledge that moral maturity involves the development and integration of both perspectives.[11] Indeed, scores on Kohlberg's Moral Judgment Interview are significantly related to those of the Ethic of Care Interview.[12]

The preference for one of the two perspectives can show up in how students debate moral issues. Women, as well as some men, at the conventional stage of moral reasoning may fail to speak up or challenge someone for fear of offending them. Males at Kohlberg's conventional stage may conform to the rules of their peer culture or confuse what is moral with what is legal. Studies of drinking on campuses, for example, show that freshmen men are more likely than women to succumb to peer pressure to engage in heavy drinking and drug use. Female freshmen, in contrast, are more likely to refrain from drinking and drug use, because of concern for how it will affect their families.[13] (For more on the issue of drinking on campuses, see Chapter 6, pages 283–284.)

Being wary of peer pressure and being concerned about the impact of our actions on our relationships are both important in moral decision making. Being aware of your own moral-decision-making style can help you cultivate your strengths and overcome your weaknesses, as well as appreciate the strengths and contributions of other perspectives in moral decision making and discussions of moral issues.

College and Moral Development

Moral maturity entails making our own well-reasoned moral decisions rather than simply following the dictates of the crowd or going with our selfish desires.

🍃 STAGES OF MORAL REASONING

Stage	Kohlberg[14]	Gilligan[15]
Preconventional	Punishment (avoid punishment) Egoist (satisfy one's own needs; consider the needs of others only if it benefits you)	Self-centered (view one's own needs as all that matters)
Conventional	Good boy/nice girl (please others; concern for others' approval; conformity to peer norms) Society-maintaining (respect authority and social rules; maintain the existing social order)	Self-sacrificing (view others' needs as more important)
Postconventional	Social contract (obey useful social rules; appeal to social consensus as long as minimal basic rights are safeguarded) Conscience and universal principles (autonomously recognize universal rules, such as justice and equality; respect for equal dignity of each individual)	Mature care ethics (balance one's own needs and the needs of others)

When young people begin college, they may discover that what they thought were clear-cut cultural norms and values are not so uncontroversial after all. Their cherished worldviews may come into conflict with those of others, especially people from different cultural backgrounds. This, in turn, leads them to question some of their own cultural norms. During this transition period, students are torn between the rejection of moral values that are culturally relative and the reluctance to commit to universal moral principles (postconventional moral reasoning). This conflict can manifest itself in hedonistic disregard for any moral values—either relative or universal.[16]

Unfortunately, like the majority of Americans, most college students do not complete the transition to postconventional moral reasoning, but instead move into a higher level of conventional moral reasoning. Although they may become less dependent on the opinions of their peers, the trade-off is that they become more conforming to wider societal norms. The good news is that college experiences such as community service learning, contact with people from diverse backgrounds, and classes in which moral worldviews are challenged can significantly enhance a student's moral development.

The Importance of Moral Development and Ethics Education

Could culturally approved holocausts like the one that happened in Nazi Germany happen today in the United States? Most of us think that we would draw the line at participating in such atrocities. If laws were enacted ordering, let's say, the euthanasia of all people over 65, or mandatory destruction of all genetically "imperfect" fetuses, would we go along with these laws? Although these practices may make us feel uncomfortable, if we identify morality with cultural norms, on what grounds are we going to oppose them?

One purpose of ethics education is to help students make the transition to post-conventional moral reasoning by providing them with the resources to make effective moral decisions that they will not come to regret later. Unlike moral indoctrination, ethics education is not about telling people what is right and wrong. Most people "know" right from wrong.[17] In the Milgram experiment, for example, many of the subjects were openly distressed and "knew" that what they were doing was wrong, but they were unable to say why. Ethics education helps us articulate moral values and apply moral theory and moral reasoning to a particular issue or real-life moral decision.[18]

The study of moral theory and the reasoning underlying moral issues also help motivate people. Research has found that people who are morally mature and better at moral reasoning are more motivated to act on their beliefs.[19] People at the higher stages of moral development not only sympathize with those who are suffering, but take active steps to help alleviate that suffering. They are willing to speak out on behalf of themselves and others when they witness an injustice and will take effective and well-thought-out action to correct the injustice.

Moral action also involves striving to be the best person we can be. Virtuous people, those who regard morality as important to their self-identity, are more likely to do the right thing and to get involved in social action.[20] Taking a class in ethics helps us on our journey to becoming the best people we can be.

EXERCISES

1. Which perspective—Kohlberg's justice or Gilligan's care perspective—best describes the way you approach discussions of moral issues? To what extent do you draw from both perspectives? Illustrate your answer with specific examples.
2. Has the college experience enhanced your moral development and, if so, how? Discuss what motivated you to change. Are you more satisfied with your current strategy? Explain, using specific examples.
3. Have your views on any of the issues covered in this chapter changed or been called into doubt as a result of your college experience? Explain.
4. Discuss a time when you went along with others even though you "knew" that what they were doing was morally questionable. Discuss strategies you might have used that would have made it easier for you to resist peer pressure and to do the right thing.
5. Discuss ways in which you are engaged in moral action. What motivates you to take action? Illustrate your answer with an example.

MORALITY AND RELIGION

> *A list of virtues or duties drawn up by a Buddhist would not differ very greatly from one drawn up by a Christian, a Confucianist, a Muhammadan or a Jew. Formally all of the ethico-religious systems are universalist in scope.*
>
> —Morris Ginsberg, *Reason and Unreason in Society* (1947)

Many people look to religion for moral guidance. The concept of God in the major world religions is intimately connected with that of moral goodness.[21] People worship God, in part, because God represents perfect goodness. Worshipping reaffirms these moral values. This raises the question of the connection between religion and morality. Is morality dependent on religion, or does it exist independently of religion?

The Divine Command Theory

The first position, that something is moral merely because God approves of it, is known as the divine command theory. Just as morality for the cultural relativist is relative to cultural norms, for the divine command theorist morality is relative to what God commands or wills. There are no independent, universal moral standards by which to judge God's commands. No other justification is necessary for an action to be right other than God's commanding it. The story of Abraham and Isaac in the Bible, in which God commanded Abraham to sacrifice his son, is often used as an example of divine command theory. Abraham was not the last parent to claim that God commanded them to kill their child. In 2001, Texas housewife Andrea Yates drowned her five children, ranging in age from six months to seven years, to save them from Satan. Her justification: God commanded her to do so.

Even more disturbing is the use of divine command theory to justify war and terrorism. Radical Islamic terrorist groups such as al-Qaeda believe that God has commanded them to destroy infidels (see Chapter 11). The terrorists who flew the airplanes into the World Trade Center and the Pentagon on September 11, 2001, justified their actions using the divine command theory. Divine command has also been invoked by former President George W. Bush, who believed that he was given a divine mandate to carry out God's will in declaring war on these radical Islamic groups.[22] If we respond that God would not have commanded anyone to do something horrible, we are implying that there are independent moral standards by which we can judge God's commands.

If we accept the divine command theory, the only way to resolve a moral issue would be to wait for God to speak to us. There are no other criteria for deciding right from wrong. If someone claims that God spoke to her and commanded her to blow up a bus, we have no independent criteria for judging whether she, in fact, heard God or not. Under the divine command theory, God's commands are arbitrary; they are based only on divine whim. Most religious people reject divine command theory. They believe that actions such as genocide are not arbitrary but a matter of reason.

Natural Law Theory

Natural law theorists maintain that God commands something *because* it is moral, not the other way around. Whereas religious teachings may affirm universal moral principles, morality exists independently of religion and God's commands. According to the natural law theory, morality is grounded in rational human nature rather than in God's commands or personal feelings or cultural norms. Morality is universally binding on everyone, no matter what their religion or lack thereof.

According to Thomas Aquinas (c. 1225–1274), it is through the "light of natural reason," given to us by God, that humans discern moral or natural law (see page 573). These moral laws are very general and exist in the form of guidelines, such as the

Golden Rule and the Ten Commandments (Decalogue). The Muslim Qur'an also contains a universal moral code similar to the Decalogue that is a universal "message to all the worlds" (81:27). Moral law is also teleological; it directs us toward a particular purpose or goal of the natural order. It is incumbent upon us as rational beings to discern how these moral laws apply at a particular time in history and in a particular case. In her article on the death penalty (see pages 267–272), Helen Prejean adopts this approach by asking if God would return pain for pain and torture for torture. She concludes that God would not.

Although natural law theory is often identified with the Catholic Church, one need not be Catholic—or even believe in God—to subscribe to this theory. Martin Luther King Jr. subscribed to some form of natural law theory and rejected divine command theory. Aristotle believed that, rather than being created by God, the moral law has always been part of the natural order. Variations of natural law theory are also found in non-Western cultures, such as the Akan tribe of Ghana.[23]

Natural law ethicists reject cultural relativism. According to them a human or civil law (legislation) or tradition is moral only to the extent that it is in accord with natural or moral law. If a law is unjust, we may have a moral obligation to disobey it. A human law is unjust if it is degrading to humans, such as laws that permit torture or slavery. Laws that are discriminatory, such as segregation laws and, perhaps, affirmative action, may also be unjust.

Civil disobedience, on the grounds of obedience to a higher moral law, has a long history in this country. In engaging in civil disobedience, the dissident can use only moral means and must be nonviolent and open about his or her actions. Members of animal liberation groups break into laboratories and set animals free; anti-abortionists block women from entering abortion clinics; anti-nuclear activists block roads leading to nuclear power plants and military establishments; and in the back of his Volkswagen van, Dr. Jack Kevorkian—despite repeated warnings from the courts—continued to assist terminally ill people in ending their lives, until he was put in jail. In each of these cases, the people engaged in civil disobedience justified their actions on the grounds of a higher moral law. (For a more in-depth discussion of civil disobedience, see page 579.)

Universality and Religious Ethics

In discussing moral issues, it may be tempting to dismiss a particular position as a religious issue, especially if we are unsure of how to defend our own position. Antislavery arguments were dismissed for many years as the rantings of fanatic Quakers who were trying to force their religious views on the southerners. Today certain moral positions on abortion, stem cell research, and homosexuality are dismissed as religious views. The fact that a specific religion takes an official stand on a certain moral issue, however, does not imply that the issue is religious rather than moral. In discussing these and similar issues, we must be careful to separate the moral issues involved from specific religious doctrines.

Most theologians and philosophers maintain that morality exists independently of religion—that religious ethics are not fundamentally different from philosophical ethics. Although a moral code is incorporated into the doctrine of most religions, moral issues can be discussed without appealing to religion. When people who are religious use the terms *right* and *wrong*, they generally mean the same thing as someone who is not religious. Religious differences tend to fall away in most serious discussions of moral issues because moral disputes can be discussed and even resolved without bringing religion into the equation.[24]

EXERCISES

1. How, if at all, have your religious beliefs shaped your morality? Is there a difference between religious and secular morality in your life? What happens when your religion and your culture take different positions on a particular moral issue? How do you resolve the conflict? Use specific examples.
2. Fyodor Dostoyevsky in *The Brothers Karamazov* (1880) writes, "If God doesn't exist, everything is permissible." Discuss his claim that morality is dependent on the existence of God. What, if anything, would be different about your moral beliefs and behavior if God did not exist? Explain, using specific examples.
3. Discuss a case in which someone justified a position that most people would consider immoral, such as an act of aggression against a particular group of people, on the grounds that God commanded him or her to take this position. How would you respond to such a person?
4. Choose a controversial topic, such as abortion, euthanasia, or homosexuality, that is sometimes regarded as a religious issue. Can the morality of these practices be discussed without bringing in religious doctrine? Support your answer.

UNIVERSAL MORAL THEORIES

Two things fill the mind with ever new and increasing admiration and awe, the oftener and more steadily we reflect on them: the starry heavens above and the moral law within.

—Immanuel Kant, *Critique of Practical Reason* (1788)

Like natural law theorists, most moral philosophers believe that there are moral principles that are universal and objective. There are several different *universalist theories*, including natural law theory, ethical egoism, utilitarianism, deontology, rights ethics, and virtue ethics. They all agree, however, that there are universal moral principles that are binding on all people regardless of their personal opinions, culture, or religion and that these moral principles are *discovered* rather than created by people. Although individual interests or cultural customs, as noted in the example about the Kabloona, can influence how a particular moral principle is applied, fundamental moral principles are universal and transcultural.

Just as scientists disagree about the origin of the universe or the nature of gravity, people may disagree about the source and nature of these principles and sentiments. Some philosophers believe that we intuitively know what is morally right and wrong; others argue that reason is the primary source of moral knowledge. The fact of disagreement, however, does not mean that objective universal moral principles do not exist, anymore than it follows that disagreement about the source of the universe or the nature of gravity means that the universe and gravity do not exist.

There is a lot of overlap between the different universalist theories. Instead of being mutually exclusive, like ethical subjectivism and cultural relativism, universalist theories, for the most part, emphasize particular aspects of morality.

ETHICAL EGOISM

The achievement of his own happiness is man's highest moral purpose.
—Ayn Rand, *The Virtue of Selfishness* (1964)

Ethical egoists argue that morality involves the pursuit of our rational self-interests. It differs from ethical subjectivism in that it is concerned with a person's best interests, not simply what each person feels is right for him or her. We may feel something is the right action for us only to later discover the error of our ways. Ethical egoists also maintain that egoism should be universalized and that the world would be a better place if we all pursued our rational self-interests.

Gyges's Ring

The story of Gyges's ring in Plato's *Republic* is often used to illustrate ethical egoism. In this dialogue, Glaucon tries to convince Socrates that it is better for people to do only that which benefits themselves. "Those who practice justice," Glaucon argues, "do it unwillingly because they lack the power to do injustice."

To make his point he tells the story of Gyges, a shepherd who finds a gold ring. Before long, Gyges notices that when he turns the setting of the ring so it faces the inside of his hand, he becomes invisible to those around him. When he realizes his power, he arranges to become a messenger to the king. When he arrives at the king's residence, he seduces the queen, kills the king, and takes over the empire. (For the full text of Gyges's ring, go to http://classics.mit.edu/Plato/republic.3.ii.html.)

Psychological Egoism and Ethical Egoism

There are two main types of egoism: ethical egoism and psychological egoism. **Ethical egoism** is a normative or moral theory about how things *ought* to be. We ought to act in our own best self-interests. **Psychological egoism,** in contrast, is a descriptive theory about how things *are.* Humans by nature are selfish[25] and out for themselves.

Thomas Hobbes (1588–1679) was a psychological egoist. He believed that people are basically selfish, aggressive, and quarrelsome. Without society, he argued, we would all live in a "**state of nature**" in which life would be "solitary, poor, nasty, brutish, and short." Like Glaucon, Hobbes believed that we agree to live within a society and obey certain rules only because it benefits us. To those opponents of psychological egoism who point out people who do noble deeds, Hobbes replies that we perform great acts of charity and altruism only because we delight in demonstrating our powers and superiority by showing the world that we are more capable than those we serve. (To read chapters 13–15 in Hobbes's *Leviathan,* in which he discusses ethical egoism, go to http://oregonstate.edu/instruct/phl302/texts/hobbes/leviathan-contents.html.)

🔥 ETHICAL EGOISM: CONSIDERATIONS FOR THINKING ABOUT MORAL ISSUES

- **Determine what is in your rational self-interests:** What will bring me the greatest happiness? Am I being reasonable in considering what is in my best self-interests?
- **Act in ways that promote your rational self-interests:** Which action or plan will best promote my goal of happiness?
- **Interact with others based on the principle of trade:** Will this exchange give me back something of equal value? Or are other people asking for something that they neither have earned nor deserve?

Sociobiologists, such as E. O. Wilson, also believe that humans, like other animals, are genetically programmed to act in ways that further their own self-interests. Even altruism is fundamentally selfish, because it increases our chances of passing on our genes to future generations.

One of the problems with psychological egoism is that it is not falsifiable. No matter what happens, psychological egoism argues that it must have been motivated by self-interest. People smoke because it gives them pleasure; they sabotage relationships because it gets them off the hook; they commit suicide to escape a painful existence or, in the case of suicide bombers, to enter the bliss of heaven. Thus, as a theory, psychological egoism is based on circular reasoning and, as such, is useless in explaining human behavior or offering guidelines for what we should do.

Ayn Rand and Rational Ethical Egoism

According to rational ethical egoist Ayn Rand (1905–1982), humans are rational and fundamentally solitary individuals, each pursuing his or her own personal self-interests. Unlike psychological egoists, ethical egoists do not believe that we always act in our best self-interests. We need to use our reason to determine what is best for us. Also, we should do things for others only when we can expect to get something of similar value in exchange. This type of voluntary cooperation Rand referred to as the principle of trade or justice. When we each pursue our rational self-interests, we actually promote the common good. In line with this, Rand concluded that laissez-faire capitalism is the only economic system compatible with respect for the integrity of the individual human.

While E. O. Wilson believes that altruism is compatible with egoism, Rand maintained that it is a vice. Altruists, according to her, give things to people who have neither earned them nor deserve them. This turns the recipients of altruism or charity into parasites or second-handers. The only good people can do for each other, Rand writes, is "hands off." Because of this she was opposed to the welfare state or any sort of handouts as degrading to both the giver and the receiver. Taxing people to redistribute resources to second-handers is, in her view, a form of theft. The sole purpose of government is to protect our individual rights to pursue our rational self-interests. If everyone were allowed to pursue their rational self-interests and engage in voluntary trade, the result would be the most efficient use of resources and human talent.

To learn more about Rand's ethical egoism, see the reading in this chapter from her novel *The Fountainhead*.

The Strengths and Limitations of Ethical Egoism

One of the strengths of ethical egoism is that it contains two important truths: (1) We all want to be happy, and (2) pursuing our interests is important to our happiness. Ethical egoism encourages us to stand up for ourselves, to take responsibility for our lives, and not to let other people take advantage of us.

But are there only two alternatives, self-sacrifice or the pursuit of our self-interests? Indeed, is the pursuit of our self-interests even the best path to happiness? By having individual happiness as its only goal, ethical egoism becomes self-defeating—a phenomenon known as the hedonist paradox. If we are focused only on our own happiness, we often end up feeling frustrated and alienated. A review of studies worldwide on what makes people happy found that "self-actualization values" such as inner-directedness, independence, individualism, and productive work were not associated with greater happiness. Instead, values and activities that were not motivated by self-interest—such as helping others, sympathy, friendship, tolerance, and forgiveness—were most highly correlated with happiness.[26]

Another limitation is that ethical egoism does not provide guidelines for resolving conflicts of interest between people. Protecting people's liberty rights is insufficient to guarantee that everyone will have the freedom to pursue their rational self-interests. In a world of limited resources and opportunities, people's self-interests sometimes come into conflict. When this happens, the rich and powerful will generally be able to assert their self-interests at the expense of those with less power. Ethical egoism may work well in a community of equals. However, the world falls far short of this ideal. The devastating effects of this ideology on people and nations that are not in positions of economic power are becoming more evident with the increasing accumulation of wealth in the hands of fewer and fewer people and the destruction of the environment in the name of economic progress.

In "The Land Ethic" (Chapter 12), Aldo Leopold rejects individualism and ethical egoism as destructive to the environment and proposes instead a more communitarian approach. Thomas Pogge, in "World Poverty and Human Rights" (Chapter 10), likewise argues that the wealthier nations have a moral obligation to help alleviate the suffering of poor nations. Buddhist ethicists also reject ethical egoism in favor of a more holistic approach.

EXERCISES

1. Imagine that you found a ring that could make you invisible. Discuss how you might use such a ring. For example, would you use it to cheat on tests or to rob banks in order to distribute the money to the needy? Would the world be a better place if everyone had such a ring? Support your answers.
2. Discuss the claim by psychological egoists that people, by nature, are selfish. Discuss how you might go about proving or disproving the theory.

3. Discuss how your life would be affected if all your interactions with other people were based on "trade." Do you agree with Rand that the principle of trade is the same as justice? Support your answer.
4. Are students who receive government-funded college scholarships parasites or second-handers under Rand's definition? If so, do we have a moral obligation to get rid of any scholarship assistance? Why or why not? Support your answers.
5. Discuss the possible ramifications of ethical egoism and Rand's principle of trade for globalization and economic trade between wealthy and developing countries.

UTILITARIANISM

The happiness of the individuals, of whom a community is composed, that is their pleasures and their security, is the end and the sole end which the legislator ought to have in view.

—Jeremy Bentham, *Principles of Morals and Legislation* (1789)

Modern utilitarian theory was developed by English philosopher and social reformer Jeremy Bentham (1748–1832) in response to the flagrant injustices and the desperate needs of workers during the Industrial Revolution. Bentham's goal was to develop a practical ethical theory that could provide a secure, scientific foundation for developing social policy and legislation.

Jeremy Bentham: Father of Modern Utilitarian Theory

Bentham's utilitarian theory was inspired primarily by the theories of Epicurus (341–270 B.C.E.) and David Hume (1711–1776). Hume and Epicurus both argued that certain traits are virtues because of their utility, or usefulness. Those traits that promote happiness have the greatest utility. Bentham took this one step further by arguing that utility provides the *only* source of political obligation for the state; it is utility alone that proves the test of what a law ought to be and which laws ought to be obeyed.

Utilitarianism states that the morality of an action or policy is determined solely by its consequences. Utilitarians maintain that the desire for happiness is universal and that we intuitively recognize it as the greatest good. Happiness is synonymous with pleasure, unhappiness with pain. Actions are right to the extent that they tend to promote overall happiness, and wrong to the extent that they tend to promote overall unhappiness. Furthermore, what counts is not just individual or even human happiness, but the sum of the happiness of the whole community of **sentient beings**—that is, those beings who are capable of feeling pleasure and pain.

The Principle of Utility: Promoting Happiness and Minimizing Pain

In determining which action or policy has the greatest utility (produces the greatest amount of happiness) we cannot rely on a majority vote, since people's choices are not always well-informed. The majority, either because of ignorance about an issue or because of irrational traditions and prejudice, may be mistaken about what is the best course of action. Nor can we rely on feelings alone, such as sympathy, because feelings can also mislead us. Instead, we need a rational principle by which to guide our actions.

> **THE UTILITARIAN CALCULUS: SEVEN FACTORS TO TAKE INTO CONSIDERATION IN DETERMINING THE MOST MORAL ACTION OR DECISION**
>
> 1. *Intensity:* Strength of the pleasure and pain. The greater the pleasure the higher the value; the greater the pain the lower the value.
> 2. *Duration:* Length of time the pain and pleasure will last.
> 3. *Certainty:* Level of probability that the pleasure or pain will occur.
> 4. *Propinquity:* How near in time the pleasure or happiness will occur.
> 5. *Fecundity:* Extent to which the pleasure will produce more pleasure.
> 6. *Purity:* The pleasure does not cause pain at the same time.
> 7. *Extent:* The number of sentient beings affected by the action.

This principle is the *principle of utility,* or the *greatest happiness principle:*

> Actions are right in proportion as they tend to promote happiness, wrong as they tend to produce the reverse of happiness.[27]

In deciding which action or policy is the most morally compelling, we need only measure the total amount of pleasure and the total amount of pain involved in the alternatives, and choose the alternative with the greatest net pleasure. Because the interests of all sentient beings count, the pain caused by human practices to other animals—such as animal agriculture and research using nonhuman animals—also has to be taken into consideration.

John Stuart Mill's Reformulation of Utilitarianism

Jeremy Bentham advocated equality and impartiality. He argued that all pleasures, whether those of a pig or a human, are equal. **Equality,** according to him, is not a description of actual equality of ability; rather, it is a moral ideal or prescription of how we ought to treat all sentient beings. The happiness of any one individual is no more or less important than that of any other.

Utilitarian John Stuart Mill disagreed with Bentham, arguing that intellectual pleasures, such as listening to a symphony or reading a great book, are *qualitatively* better than those of the body, such as eating or basking in the sun. In other words, the intellectual pleasures experienced by humans, though they may be less intense at times, are morally preferable to the simple pleasures of a pig. This is not to say that the pleasures of the pig should not count at all. In fact, utilitarians, such as Peter Singer, continue to be in the forefront of the animal-welfare movement (see Chapter 12, pages 660–669).

Utilitarianism and Social Reform

Utilitarian theory has had a profound influence on social reform and the shaping of public policy. Jeremy Bentham was an advocate of animal welfare and prison reform. John Stuart Mill spoke out eloquently on behalf of equal opportunities for women, freedom of the press, and the legalization of homosexual acts between consenting adults. Contemporary discussions of capital punishment, euthanasia, animal welfare, genetic engineering, stem cell research, pornography, legalization of drugs, and environmental ethics all have utilitarian components.

Unlike most moral theories, utilitarian theory adopts a practical bottom-up approach. It begins with the actual happiness of the people and other sentient beings rather than imposing morality and social ideals on them from above. The principle of utility requires that we do not take refuge in ideological slogans, cultural traditions, or personal opinion, but that we instead examine our position on moral issues in light of the actual consequences. This entails overcoming our ignorance regarding the extent to which our lifestyle is built upon the suffering of other people or animals.

Utilitarianism requires that we first do our research. For example, is capital punishment, in fact, an effective deterrent? Does viewing pornography and violence, in fact, cause people to behave more violently? Does permitting people who are openly homosexual to teach in schools, in fact, make children more likely to become homosexuals?

We also need to look at possible consequences of our decisions. Would censorship of hate speech and pornography cause more harm than allowing hate speech and pornography? Are terrorism or a preemptive attack on another country ever justified if other avenues have failed to remove a leader who inflicts massive suffering on his people? Would legalizing recreational drugs result in more or in less drug abuse and drug-related crime? Would condoning voluntary euthanasia put us on the slippery slope toward involuntary euthanasia? Would legalizing same-sex marriage lead to the breakdown of traditional marriage? In their report on "Human Cloning" (Chapter 3, pages 150–157), Judith Johnson and Erin Williams examine the question of whether seemingly valid uses of cloning might open the door to undesirable uses of the technology.

Finally, we need to balance harm and benefit. Is the harm that human activities cause to the environment and to other animals justified by the benefit the products bring to humans? Would permitting parents to genetically engineer their children result in more overall happiness for society, or less?

The Strengths and Limitations of Utilitarianism

Utilitarian theory is a powerful tool for formulating social policies. It is also a reminder that tradition alone cannot serve as a foundation for morality.

One of the strengths of utilitarian theory is that it challenges us to rethink our traditional notions about moral community. If we are going to exclude or marginalize people or other animals, we have to offer a rational justification for our decision. We cannot exclude other animals based on irrational religious doctrines that claim that only humans are created in the image of God. Nor can we justify expending expensive limited resources on humans who are no longer sentient simply on the grounds that they are human (see Chapter 4, pages 195–203).

The utilitarian insistence on equality and impartiality is both one of its greatest strengths and one of its weaknesses. Justice as impartiality assumes that people living in a community share a common conception of the good. In reality, however, people have different needs and goals. The capitalist's idea of happiness, for example, is not the same as that of the religious contemplative. John Rawls (1921–2002) pointed out that justice demands not only impartiality, but that we treat people fairly and in proportion to their needs and merits. A person who works hard deserves a raise or a good grade because he

---

■ UTILITARIAN CONSIDERATIONS FOR THINKING ABOUT MORAL ISSUES

- **Determine who or what will be affected:** Who will be caused pain or pleasure?
- **Look at the possible consequences:** What are both the long-term and short-term consequences of the different alternatives?
- **Maximize happiness:** Which solution will bring about the greatest net happiness?
- **Minimize pain:** Which solution will cause the least pain and suffering to those affected by the decision?

---

or she has done a good job. Utilitarians, in contrast, are not concerned with what a person deserves, but whether giving rewards based on merit produces the most utility.

There are other desirable goals in life besides pleasure. Most people agree that goals such as friendship, spiritual growth, and appreciation of the aesthetic are also desirable. On the other hand, utilitarian theory reminds us that one of the primary purposes of morality is not to make our lives more tedious or to make us feel more guilt-ridden, but to improve the quality of our lives by promoting ideals and behavior that provide optimal conditions for us to flourish, both as individuals and as a community.

By claiming that only consequences count, utilitarianism underplays the importance of individual integrity and personal responsibility. In considering only consequences when determining the rightness and wrongness of an action, utilitarian theory may require us to act in ways that violate our integrity and our conscience. For example, say that a particularly heinous murder, which the community believes to have been racially motivated, has created racial tension, looting, and killing in that community. The police have been unable to find the murderer. It also seems fairly certain that the community rampage will continue until someone is brought to "justice." In desperation the police arrest a man—an unsavory character who has a history of petty crime— who they know is not guilty of the murder. As a judge, you can bring about more pleasure and restore social harmony by convicting the man and giving him the death penalty. What should you do? The utilitarian would probably say we should send the man to death row. But our actions do not happen just as part of a wider context of the general good; each of us is also responsible for what we do as individuals.

Because only pleasure has intrinsic value, utilitarian theory allows us to use people as a means toward that end, rather than requiring us to respect people as ends in themselves. In the previous example, the accused man was used as a means to social harmony. In addition, to pressure the judge into bringing about the death of an innocent person to prevent the death of others is to treat the judge as a means only.

Utilitarian theory is not so much wrong as incomplete. Despite its limitations, utilitarian theory provides valuable guidelines for discussions of issues in social ethics. Although other moral philosophers may regard other moral considerations as more fundamental than the principle of utility, as deontologist John Rawls writes, "all ethical doctrines worth our attention take consequences into account in judging rightness. One which did not would simply be irrational, crazy."[28]

EXERCISES

1. Utilitarian theory is frequently used to formulate social policies regarding issues like AIDS testing and distribution of social benefits such as scholarships and medical care. Find some examples of utilitarian thinking in current public or college policies. Explain why these policies represent utilitarian thinking.
2. Does social ethics require a different strategy than personal moral decision making? If so, how do the two strategies differ? On what grounds can you justify these differences?
3. Do you agree with Mill that human intellectual pleasures have greater moral value than the pleasures of other animals? Discuss how adopting either Bentham's or Mill's position would influence public policy on the use of nonhuman animals to benefit humans.
4. Both Confucianism and feminist care ethics teach that our concern should be strongest for our family and friends. Utilitarian theory, in contrast, teaches that our concern for others' happiness should be impartial. Discuss these two competing concepts of moral obligation. Support your answer using examples from your own life as a college student.

DEONTOLOGY: THE ETHICS OF DUTY

> *Look to your own duty; do not tremble before it.*
>
> —Bhagavad Gita

Deontological theories regard duty as the basis of morality. *Duty,* or doing what is right for its own sake, is the foundation of morality. There are strong strands of deontology in Confucianism and Hindu ethics as well as in many Western philosophies.

Immanuel Kant and the Categorical Imperative

Deontologist Immanuel Kant (1724–1804) believed that we should do our duty purely out of **good will,** not because of rewards or punishment or other consequences. A person of good will can be depended on to do what is right, even when other motives are absent. An action that is done out of sympathy or because one enjoys helping others, rather than out of a sense of duty, may be praiseworthy, but it has no moral value.

Kant also argued that if there is a universal moral law and if it is to be morally binding, it must be based on reason. According to Kant, the most fundamental moral principle is the **categorical imperative.** He came up with two formulations of the categorical imperative. The first formulation states:

> Act only on that maxim by which you can at the same time will that it should become a universal law.

Kant believed that all rational beings would recognize the categorical imperative as universally binding. Because reason provides the foundation of morality, this makes humans and other rational beings very special in Kant's mind. Whereas rational beings have free will, everything else in nature operates according to physical laws. Because autonomy is essential for dignity, only rational beings have intrinsic worth. Rational beings can therefore never be treated as expendable, but must be treated with dignity as ends in themselves. This ideal is summed up in the second formulation of the categorical imperative:

> So act as to treat humanity, whether in thine own person or in that of any other, in every case as an end in itself, never as a means only.

The categorical imperative is a formal principle that provides a framework for deriving moral maxims or duties, such as "Do not lie" and "Help others in distress," that can be applied in specific situations. When deciding if a particular maxim creates a moral duty, we need only ask, keeping in mind that rational beings must be treated with dignity, whether we would will that it be a universal law.

The *Golden Rule* in Judeo-Christian ethics, and the law of **reciprocity** in Confucian ethics are both similar to the categorical imperative. The Golden Rule states, "Do unto others as you would have them do unto you." Similarly, when Confucius (551–479 B.C.E.) was asked if there is a single principle that can be used as a guide to conduct in our lives, he replied, "Do not impose on others what you yourself do not desire."[29]

Universalization

Universalization is one of the trademarks of morality: Moral maxims or duties, by their very nature, apply to everyone and under all circumstances. It is inconsistent, for example, to argue that it is wrong for others to lie but that it is okay for us. If it is wrong to lie, it is wrong for everyone. If we could make an exception of ourselves whenever it is to our advantage, the moral rule "Do not lie" would be meaningless. If we are unwilling to universalize a particular moral maxim—that is, apply it consistently in all similar cases—we should either modify the maxim or toss it out.

A good moral maxim must be consistent with the demands of the categorical imperative. But, unlike the categorical imperative itself, moral maxims are open for debate. For example, many people question whether we would want to universalize, as did Kant, a maxim that states, "Do not commit suicide." Kant, of course, was writing in the days before medical technology could artificially extend the dying process. Some people believe that refusing to help someone die who is suffering terribly is disrespectful and, hence, violates the second formulation of the categorical imperative. What moral maxims, then, can we come up with for shaping a policy on euthanasia and assisted suicide? Would we want to universalize a maxim that states, "Physicians have a duty to carry out the requests of their patients"? This may sound good in some situations, but what about one in which a student is temporarily depressed because she got a poor grade on an exam and requests medical assistance in committing suicide? Further consideration of this maxim reveals so many exceptions that it proves to be of little use in making moral decisions.

W. D. Ross: Duties Are Prima Facie

Kant argued that universalizing moral maxims requires that they be absolutely binding in all circumstances. If it is wrong to lie, then, according to him, it is *always* wrong to lie, no matter what the circumstance. He also believed that because morality is based on reason, there could never be a conflict between moral duties.

Most moral philosophers, while agreeing with Kant that moral duties or maxims are universal, disagree that they are also absolute. Moral duties are prima facie rather than absolute. **Prima facie duties** are universal moral duties that may on occasion be overridden by stronger moral claims.

According to W. D. Ross (1877–1971), moral duties cannot be absolute, because there are particular situations in which they come into conflict. The moral duty of nonmaleficence, for example, could conflict with the moral duty to keep a promise when keeping that promise could result in death or injury. Because duties are context-bound, the particular circumstances and possible consequences will affect which moral duties are most important in any given situation.

Unlike Kant, Ross also believed that consequences matter when applying moral principles. Moral duties, however, cannot be overridden by nonmoral duties or considerations such as obeying the law or financial success. When there is a conflict between moral and nonmoral duties, we ought to do what is morally right.

Seven Prima Facie Duties

Ross came up with a list of seven prima facie duties that he claimed we intuitively know. These include duties concerning the consequences of our actions, such as the duty of **nonmaleficence** (do no harm) and the duty of **beneficence** (increase happiness)—two duties also recognized by utilitarians. **Ahimsa,** or the principle of nonviolence, in Buddhist ethics, is a version of the principle of nonmaleficence and is the most fundamental moral principle in Buddhist ethics. Buddhists such as Thich Nhat Hanh oppose meat-eating because it violates this principle.

Although almost all ethicists agree that we have a positive duty to refrain from harming others, they disagree about whether we have a positive duty of beneficence—that is, to perform altruistic actions. Both Judith Jarvis Thomson in her essay "A Defense of Abortion" (Chapter 2) and Margaret Pabst Battin in "The Case for Euthanasia" (Chapter 4) discuss the question of whether we have a positive duty of beneficence to the unborn and those who are dying, and, if so, what the limits of this duty are.

We also have duties that stem from past obligations. The duty of **fidelity** arises from past commitments and promises. We have a commitment to our fellow students, to our parents, and to our children. The duty of fidelity or filial piety is particularly important in Confucian ethics and generally takes precedence over individual liberty rights. Some philosophers argue that part of the physician's commitment to his or her patients is to assist dying patients who request assistance in committing suicide. Others argue that the duty of nonmaleficence is more compelling in this case and that physicians should refuse to carry out actions that cause lethal harm to their patients.

The duty of **gratitude** is evoked when we receive gifts or unearned favors and services from others. Some environmental ethicists argue that we have a duty of gratitude toward the earth because it nourishes and sustains us.

The duty of **reparation** is also based on past actions. It requires making up for past harms we have caused others. Affirmative action is an attempt to make up for past harms to women and minorities (see Chapter 10, page 523). Some philosophers argue that affirmative action is unjust and that justice in this case is a more compelling duty than reparation.

W. D. ROSS'S SEVEN PRIMA FACIE DUTIES

Future-Looking Duties
  Beneficence   the duty to do good acts to promote happiness
  Nonmaleficence   the duty to do no harm and to prevent harm

Duties Based on Past Obligations
  Fidelity   duties arising from past commitments and promises
  Reparation   duties that stem from past harms to others
  Gratitude   duties based on past favors and unearned services

Ongoing Duties
  Self-Improvement   the duty to improve our knowledge and virtue
  Justice   the duty to give each person equal consideration

Finally, there are two ongoing duties: self-improvement and justice. **Self-improvement** entails striving to improve our moral knowledge and our virtue. Self-improvement requires that we work to overcome our ignorance by becoming well-informed about moral issues and that we be open to new ideas. In addition, being a virtuous person requires that we use our moral knowledge to make this world a better place.

Justice

Justice is the seventh prima facie duty. Many philosophers consider justice to be our most important social duty. The ongoing duty of **justice** requires that we give each person equal consideration. Because laws and social institutions are generally the agencies for balancing conflicting interests, the issue of justice is closely tied with that of "the good society." As noted earlier, however, not all laws are just, nor are all demands for justice addressed by law.

There are two types of justice: retributive justice and distributive justice. **Retributive justice** requires punishment for wrongdoing in proportion to the magnitude of the crime. Both Immanuel Kant and Ernest van den Haag argue that the only suitable punishment for murder is the death penalty. Hugo Adam Bedeau and Helen Prejean, on the other hand, claim that the death penalty is immoral because it violates the underlying moral principle of respect for persons. Buddhist philosophers also oppose the death penalty as being in conflict with the principle of nonviolence (*ahimsa*).

Distributive justice refers to the fair distribution of benefits and burdens in a society. Benefits include education, emergency medical care, police protection, legal representation, and economic opportunities. Taxes, jury duty, and military conscription are examples of shared burdens. Distributive justice becomes a concern when (1) there are conflicts of interest and (2) people have competing claims for certain limited or scarce societal goods. Because there are not enough good jobs and college scholarships for everyone, the distribution of these goods is an issue of justice. John Hardwig (Chapter 4) supports euthanasia on the grounds that it is unjust that those who are dying long, lingering deaths get such a disproportionate share of medical and other resources. He claims that in cases such as these, we have a duty to die.

Distributive justice also requires impartiality. We should treat equals equally and unequals in proportion to their differences. In his reading "Sharing the Burden" (Chapter 11), Stephen Joel Trachtenberg argues in favor of military conscription on the grounds that it fairly distributes the responsibility of defending the country. In addition, in a just society, we all deserve a fair opportunity to pursue our goals. Charles R. Lawrence III argues that hate speech creates an atmosphere on campuses in which certain groups of people are denied this opportunity (see Chapter 9, pages 475–483). Aristotle, on the other hand, focused more on merit as the key criterion in distributive justice. He was opposed to democracy, preferring instead an oligarchy, or an elitist political system based on merit. Those who are most talented and most virtuous, and who have contributed most to society, ought to get a greater share of the privileges and opportunities.

John Rawls and Justice as Fairness

In his book *A Theory of Justice,* John Rawls maintains that justice requires not only impartiality but also treating people fairly and in proportion to their needs as well as their merits. There are inequalities of birth and natural endowment (what Rawls calls the "natural lottery") and historic circumstances, such as slavery, that create undeserved disadvantages for certain people. Simply redistributing opportunities or wealth does not solve the root problem as long as the underlying conditions that disadvantage certain people still exist. What is needed, Rawls argues, is a change in the social system so that it does not permit these injustices to occur in the first place.

Rawls's solution is to base justice upon a social contract that is unbiased and impartial. To do this, he proposes that we use a conceptual device that he calls the **"veil of ignorance,"** where everyone is ignorant of the advantages or disadvantages he or she will receive in this life. Under these conditions, Rawls argues, all rational people would agree upon the following two principles of justice:

1. Each person is to have an equal right to the most extensive basic liberty compatible with a similar liberty for others.

2. Social and economic inequalities are to be arranged so that both are (a) reasonably expected to be to everyone's advantage and (b) attached to positions and offices open to all.

While it is impossible to truly forget our advantages and disadvantages in this life, the "veil of ignorance" provides a conceptual tool for thinking impartially about moral issues. Rawls's theory of justice has been used to reform social institutions and to develop policy in areas such as health care reform and education.

Moral Dilemmas and Resolving Moral Issues

Any of the above duties can come into conflict with one another. When moral duties and other moral concerns conflict, we have a **moral dilemma.** Because moral duties are prima facie, when an issue involves a moral conflict, we must carefully weigh each duty, decide which are the most compelling, and try to arrive at a resolution that honors as many duties as possible.

According to Ross, there is no formula for determining what we should do in a moral dilemma. Whereas the general duties may be self-evident, judgment about our

---

DEONTOLOGY: CONSIDERATIONS FOR THINKING ABOUT MORAL ISSUES

- **Universality:** Are we willing to universalize our rules and assumptions?
- **Reciprocity:** How would we want to be treated in a similar situation?
- **Respect:** Is our position on an issue respectful of all persons affected, or does it entail treating some as a means only?
- **Impartiality:** Are we treating equals equally?
- **Identify relevant duties:** What are the relevant duties in this particular situation?
- **Prioritize duties:** If there is a conflict of duties, which duties are the most important?

---

duties in a particular case is not. Because of this we need to use reason and creativity in making judgments. Ross believed that this lack of clarity is due to the nature of moral decision making, which, he claims, is more like creating a work of art than solving a mathematical problem. When there is a moral dilemma, no solution is going to be completely satisfactory. Different people may come to different solutions because they prioritize duties differently. The purpose of moral deliberation is to arrive at the *best* solution, given the circumstances.

Strengths and Limitations of Deontology

Kant's deontology, because of its abstractness and lack of specificity, suffered a decline in popularity during the past century. It is making a comeback, however, in part because of disillusionment with ethical relativism. Many contemporary philosophers, such as John Rawls, while adopting the basics of deontology, have revised it or combined it with the strengths of other theories, such as social contract theory and utilitarianism, so it is more useful in everyday moral decision making.

Kantian deontology, with its claim that duties are absolute and that there are no conflicts between moral rules, cannot provide guidance in situations where there is a moral dilemma. Although prima facie deontology has overcome this limitation to some extent, it has been criticized for failing to provide a strategy for ranking conflicting duties.

Deontology sacrifices community in the name of individual autonomy. In Kantian deontology in particular, the private life replaces the public life as the sphere of moral actions. According to philosophers such as Confucius and Aristotle, humans are first and foremost social or political beings. Kant's assumption that people are basically autonomous, private units who are free to carry out the moral law fails to take into consideration that we are all part of a wider social network of relationships that places restraints on the actions of some people and bestows privilege on others.

The deontologist's overriding concern with duty and justice fails to take into account the important role of sentiment and care in morality. Feminist care ethicists, such as Carol Gilligan and Nel Noddings (see pages 65–68) claim that deontology, or what they call the "justice perspective," ignores caring in relationships. Practical morality, they argue, is constructed dialectically through interaction with others, not merely by an autonomous examination of the dictates of reason. Indeed, as studies with sociopaths have shown, reason without the ability to empathize with others seems unable to produce the categorical imperative or to inspire us to respect others.

Deontology ignores consequences. Kant's denial that consequences are morally relevant has been criticized by utilitarians as well as by modern deontologists. Even if we agree that consequences are not as important as duty, most philosophers still believe that they must be taken into consideration. Indeed, John Stuart Mill points out that the categorical imperative by its very nature requires that we take consequences into account when adopting moral rules. According to Mill, rational people would not universalize a moral rule that would harm, rather than benefit, the moral community.

Few philosophers accept Kant's deontology in its entirety; nevertheless, Kantian deontology is one of the most influential moral philosophies in modern history. Despite its shortcomings, the strengths and richness of deontology far outshine its weaknesses.

It would be a mistake to consider any philosophical or scientific theory a complete statement about a phenomenon. One of the characteristics of a good theory is that it is open-ended and generates further thought. In this respect, deontology has made important contributions to the study of ethics. In particular, with its emphasis on the dignity of the individual, deontology has had a major influence on the development of rights ethics in Western and non-Western philosophies.

EXERCISES

1. List the fundamental moral assumptions or maxims that you use in discussing moral issues such as capital punishment, affirmative action, same-sex marriage, or war. Examine each of these maxims in light of universality.
2. Select a moral issue that involves a moral dilemma. List the duties that support the "pro" side of the issue, then list the moral duties that support the "con" side of the issue. Which duties are the most compelling? Discuss possible solutions that take the most duties into account.
3. Is it morally acceptable to euthanize people who have terminal illnesses and who request physician-assisted suicide? Discuss the contributions both utilitarians and deontologists would make to a debate on this issue.
4. Discuss whether the use of torture on terrorist suspects, who in all likelihood have information that endangers the American public, violates Kant's categorical imperative. Discuss also how a utilitarian would answer this question and how Kant might respond to their argument.

RIGHTS-BASED ETHICS

> *We hold these truths to be self-evident, that all men are created equal, that they are endowed by their Creator with certain inalienable Rights, that among these are Life, Liberty and the Pursuit of Happiness.*
>
> —United States Declaration of Independence (July 4, 1776)

Before the eighteenth century, the focus of moral theory was primarily on duty. The language of rights in Western philosophy emerged primarily in the context of the growing confrontation with the principle of absolute sovereignty. In 1948 the United Nations issued the Universal Declaration of Human Rights as "a common standard of achievement for all peoples and all nations." Its preamble states that human rights are not simply a Western creation but belong to people everywhere.

Moral rights are not the same as legal rights, although in a just society the two would overlap. Moral rights instead are generally seen as either (1) natural and existing independently or (2) derived from duties.

John Locke's Natural Rights Ethics

The philosophical doctrine of **natural rights** first appeared in Western philosophy in the seventeenth century as a demand for equality for all people. According to natural rights ethicists such as John Locke (1632–1704), these rights stem from our human nature and are self-evident and God-given. Humans alone have moral rights because of our creation in the image of God. These natural rights include a right to own property, a right to marry and have children, and a right to punish someone who has wronged us. The right of private punishment, which exists in a state of nature, is turned over to the state when we agree to form a civil society.

The doctrine of natural rights had a profound influence on the thinking of Thomas Jefferson, who drafted the Declaration of Independence. The impact of natural rights in the United States is evident in the way that moral rights are generally equated with human rights and are discussed without any reference to correlative duties. For example, freedom of speech, in the cases of pornography and hate speech, is sometimes depicted as a natural right that exists independently of any duty of nonmaleficence or concerns for the harm caused to others by the speech.

Whether hate speech constitutes a legitimate interest that should be protected is up for debate. In Chapter 9, Charles R. Lawrence III argues that we do not have a right to use hate speech because it causes harm to those targeted by it.

Ayn Rand and Laissez-Faire Capitalism

Ayn Rand (1905–1982) was one of the foremost contemporary defenders of natural rights ethics. According to her, the United States is the first society created upon natural rights ethics. Only through free enterprise and laissez-faire capitalism, she argued, can individual rights and a free society be sustained.

Like Locke, Rand believed that rights exist prior to and independently of duties. Moral rights define and protect our freedoms without imposing obligations on anyone else. For example, the right to own property does not entail an obligation to provide people with property. The ideal society is one that protects people's individual liberty rights so they can freely pursue their interests.

Although she agreed with John Locke that rights exist prior to and independent of duties, she disagreed with him about the source of these rights. The source of our rights, she argued, is not God, but man's rational nature.

Rights and Duties

Most philosophers maintain that moral rights do not stand on their own but are linked to or derived from duties. Utilitarians and deontologists both see rights as entailing duties. For example, the duty of nonmaleficence requires that people refrain from interfering

---

🌿 TWO TYPES OF MORAL RIGHTS

- **Liberty rights:** The right to be left alone to pursue our legitimate interests. *Legitimate interests* are those that do not violate other people's similar and equal interests. Examples include freedom of speech and freedom of religion.
- **Welfare rights:** The right to receive certain social goods necessary for us to pursue our legitimate interests. Examples include public schools and police protection.

---

with other people's rights to pursue their interests. Rights, as noted earlier, are also limited by the duty of nonmaleficence. The duty of fidelity entails a right to expect others to keep their promises and the right of children to receive proper care from their parents. According to duty-based rights ethics, rights protect us as persons who ought to be treated with respect. Because we are entitled to certain rights, others have a duty to honor these rights. Al Gore, for example, maintains that our children have a right to a good future, a right that creates a duty on our part to clean up environmental pollution that is contributing to global warming.

Natural rights ethicists like Locke and Rand, in contrast, maintain that our possession of a right does not imply that someone else has a duty to honor that right. Under natural rights ethics, being able to actually claim our rights boils down to having the power— generally political or economic power—to assert ourselves. Because the environment and nonhuman animals lack the power of assertion, they lack rights.

Unlike John Locke, Tom Regan argues that rights stem from interests (see Chapter 12, pages 649–654). Because nonhuman animals have interests, such as not being confined or eaten, they also have rights that we have a duty to respect. Similarly, Catharine MacKinnon argues that women have a right not to be raped, molested, or used solely for pleasure and profit; therefore, publishers have a corresponding duty not to produce hard-core pornography. In his article on "Abortion and Fathers' Rights," Steven Hales argues that if a woman has a liberty right to escape future duties to her progeny through abortion, then the principle of equality entails that fathers also have a right of refusal to avoid future burdens such as child support (see Chapter 2, pages 117–124).

Liberty and Welfare Rights

Moral rights are generally divided into liberty rights and welfare rights. **Welfare rights** entail the right to receive certain social goods such as education, medical care, and police protection. Welfare rights are important because without a minimal standard of living or education, we cannot pursue our legitimate interests. Socialist and Marxist countries place more emphasis on welfare rights.

Liberty rights, in contrast, entail the right to be left alone to pursue our legitimate interests without interference from the government or other people. Liberty rights include autonomy, privacy, freedom of speech, freedom to own property, and freedom from harassment and confinement. Our **legitimate interests** are those that do not violate other people's similar and equal interests. For example, a misogynist may have an interest in keeping women out of the workplace, but this does not give him the right to discriminate in hiring, because doing so would violate women's rights to equal opportunity.

In the United States, we tend to place more emphasis on liberty rights. People, such as Ayn Rand, who emphasize liberty rights are known as **libertarians.** Libertarians believe that personal **autonomy**—the freedom to make our own decisions—is the highest moral value. According to libertarians, respect for others means allowing them freedom to develop and exercise the capacities that are necessary for them to pursue their concept of the good. This includes freedom of speech and privacy as well as freedom from coercive interference from the government.

According to deontologists, our liberty rights are limited by our duty to respect others as well as ourselves; we do not have a right to harm ourselves or neglect our own welfare. Kant regarded suicide as "an abomination because it involves the misuse of freedom to destroy oneself and one's freedom."[30] In contrast, Dr. Jack Kevorkian, a libertarian, considers suicide to be one of our most fundamental rights.

The emphasis on liberty rights at the expense of welfare rights tends to handicap those who are unable to assert their liberty rights either because of natural disadvantages or because of traditional roles that limit their options. Supporters of affirmative action, such as Bernard Boxill, point out that merely being granted access to societal goods, such as jobs and education, will not ensure that people will actually be able to purchase these goods without facing discrimination or harassment (see Chapter 10, pages 540–545).

Like duties, most rights are prima facie and may come into conflict with one another or with duties. A white man's right to a college education may conflict with a duty of reparation toward African Americans who have been harmed by our public education system. The welfare rights of nonhuman animals, if they have rights, may come into conflict with our search for a cure for cancer using animals as subjects.

The Strengths and Limitations of Rights Ethics

Rights ethics is an important component of a comprehensive moral theory. Nevertheless, there are some shortcomings, especially with natural rights ethics.

The theological basis of natural rights ethics, which privileges humans as a special creation, is difficult, if not impossible, to justify on either rational philosophical or empirical grounds. Natural rights ethics has given a moral blessing to the exploitation of other animals and the environment. The reduction of nonhuman animals and the environment to the status of resources for humans has had a devastating effect on the environment.

The separation of rights from duties fails to take into account the limitations placed on marginalized groups by societal traditions. Natural rights ethicists such as Rand and Locke assume that in a free society everyone is equally able to pursue their concept of the good life. Not all people are equally capable of asserting their rights, however. Traditional roles, for example, give men and people born into wealthy families greater access to resources, thus disadvantaging women and poorer people in a free marketplace. If the right to accumulate property is not constrained by the duty of distributive justice, the gap between the haves and have-nots will become greater and greater.

> ### ✍ RIGHTS ETHICS: CONSIDERATIONS FOR THINKING ABOUT MORAL ISSUES
>
> - **Identify the relevant rights:** What are the liberty rights in the moral issue? What welfare rights are at stake in the issue?
> - **Identify the legitimate interests:** Does exercising any of these rights infringe on the equal and similar rights of others?
> - **Prioritize rights and duties:** If there is a conflict of rights and/or duties, which ones are most important?

The claim that pursuing liberty rights does not impose obligations on others is false. The libertarian model of rights actually depends on the backing of an extensive and expensive legal and police system. Liberty rights to own property and businesses, for example, are protected by tax monies, some of which are forcibly taken from people who are too poor to own property.

The assertion by natural rights ethicists that rights are self-evident leaves us with no criteria for determining which claims are legitimate rights. The belief that rights need no justification has led to a proliferation of demands for certain rights. Former U.S. ambassador to the United Nations Jeane Kirkpatrick compares the current proliferation of rights declarations with "writing letters to Santa Claus"; they are based on wishful thinking rather than any reasonable expectations.[31] Without any criteria for justifying rights, there is no way to decide which rights are frivolous and which should be taken seriously. For this reason, most philosophers argue that rights must be grounded in duties and, in particular, the fundamental duty of respect for the dignity of others.

Although rights ethics is problematic if it is used as a complete explanation of morality, rights are important because they protect our dignity as persons. If we do not have rights, all our claims to be treated with respect simply amount to requests for favors and privileges.

Although few philosophers deny that rights are morally meaningful, the origin and nature of rights have been the focus of considerable debate. The claim that rights are based on the principle of equality has prompted animal rights advocates such as Tom Regan to question why this principle should not also be extended to other animals (see Chapter 12). Buddhist ethicists go even further and extend the concept of rights to all of nature. The extension of the concept of rights to all humans—and even to nonhumans—has been a difficult endeavor, but one that has been very fruitful in calling our attention to the dignity of those who are different from us.

EXERCISES

1. Are rights self-evident, as natural rights ethicists argue? List some rights that you consider to be important in making moral decisions. On what grounds do you justify these rights? Which are welfare rights? Which are liberty rights?
2. Do you agree with Ayn Rand that capitalism is the only system that can protect our individual freedoms? Or does it merely further empower those who are already privileged? Support your answers.

3. Do we have a moral right to property and inheritance acquired through someone else's forced labor, such as slave labor and the exploitation of people living under conditions of poverty? If not, do we have a duty of reparation to those who were forced to work to provide us with our property? Explain.

4. Select a moral issue that involves a conflict between rights or between rights and duties. List the rights and duties that support the "pro" side of the issue, then list the rights and duties that support the "con" side of the issue. Which rights and/or duties are the most compelling? Discuss possible solutions that take the greatest number of rights into account.

VIRTUE ETHICS

The rule of virtue can be compared to the Pole Star which commands the homage of the multitude of Stars without leaving its place.

—Confucius, *The Analects*, book 4:4

Virtue ethics emphasizes right being over right action. The sort of people we are constitutes the heart of our moral life. More important than the rules or principles we follow is our character. Virtue ethics, however, is not an alternative to ethical theories that stress right conduct, such as utilitarianism and deontological theories. Rather, virtue ethics and theories of right action complement each other.

A virtue is an admirable character trait or disposition to habitually act in a manner that benefits ourselves and others. The actions of virtuous people stem from a respect and concern for the well-being of themselves and others. Compassion, courage, generosity, loyalty, and honesty are all examples of virtues.

Virtues are often spoken of as though they were discrete, individual traits; but virtue is more correctly defined as an overarching quality of goodness that gives unity and integrity to a person's character. "If the will be set on virtue," Confucius taught, "there will be no practice of wickedness."[32] Because virtuous people are motivated to act in ways that benefit society, the cultivation of a virtuous character is an important aspect of social ethics. For example, generous people are more likely to act in ways that benefit those who are least well-off in society. Honesty is an important social virtue because without honest communication, society would soon collapse.

Buddhism, care ethics, and the moral philosophies of David Hume, Aristotle, and Jesus of Nazareth are often classified as virtue ethics. Confucian ethics has strong strands of both virtue ethics and deontology.

Aristotle: Reason and Virtue

Aristotle divided virtues into two categories: intellectual virtues and moral virtues. The intellectual virtues are cultivated through growth and experience, the moral virtues through habit. Wisdom is the most important virtue because it makes all other virtues (intellectual and moral) possible. The role of **habituation,** including repeated exposure to particular types of stimuli and behavior, in the development of virtuous and vicious behavior is one of the questions involved in censorship of pornography and campus restrictions on drinking and drug use.

> ### 🍃 ARISTOTLE'S DOCTRINE OF THE MEAN[33]
>
> | Deficit (Vice) | Mean (Virtue) | Excess (Vice) |
> | --- | --- | --- |
> | cowardice | courage | foolhardiness |
> | inhibition | temperance | overindulgence/intemperance |
> | miserliness | liberality | prodigality/extravagance |
> | shabbiness | magnificence | bad taste/vulgarity |
> | poor spiritedness | gentleness | irascibility |
> | peevishness/surlyness | friendliness | obsequiousness/flattery |
> | malice | righteous indignation | envy |
> | boorishness | wittiness | buffoonery |
> | shamelessness | modesty | shame |

Aristotle believed that all life has a function that is peculiar to its particular life-form. The function peculiar to human life, he claimed, is the exercise of reason. The function of the excellent man, therefore, "is to exert such activities well." Virtue, which is essential to the good life, involves living according to reason. Only by living in accord with reason can we achieve happiness and inner harmony.

Aristotle also believed that people by nature are political animals. The purpose of the state is to promote the virtuous or good life. Justice is the primary virtue of the state; unless a state is just and encourages the development of virtue in its citizens, it has no power to make its citizens good.

According to Aristotle's **doctrine of the mean,** most virtues entail finding the mean between excess and deficiency. For example, courage is the mean between cowardice (a deficit) and foolhardiness (an excess); liberality lies between miserliness and extravagance. Aristotle writes, "virtue discovers the means and deliberately chooses it."

This should not be misinterpreted as advising us to be wishy-washy or to compromise our moral standards. The doctrine of the mean is meant to apply to virtues, not to our positions on social issues. By suggesting that we seek the mean, Aristotle was not referring to being lukewarm or a fence-straddler but to seeking what is *reasonable*. Indeed, the most effective moral reformers have taken positions that differed sharply from the status quo. The abolitionists and early feminists were considered extremists and fanatics.

The doctrine of the mean is found in moral philosophies throughout the world. Confucians as well as Buddhist ethicists teach that the mean is that which is consistent with harmony and equilibrium, or the Way (Tao).

Confucian Virtue Ethics

Confucius was one of the most important Chinese philosophers. Although he died one century before the birth of Aristotle, there are remarkable similarities between the two men. Both taught that virtue, in general, involves hitting the mean between excess and deficit; both emphasized the role of habituation in the cultivation of virtue; and both believed that virtue is essential for individual and social harmony. Confucius also taught that a virtuous person is a person of good will who puts duty first.

Like Aristotle, Confucius believed that a virtuous society and individual virtue are inseparable. People are happiest and most virtuous when they are living in a just and well-ordered society. It is the rulers, therefore, who have the greatest power to promote virtue in society and individuals. If the actions and policies of the government are consistent with the Way, the common people will also be good, and there will be no need for the government to use punishment to maintain order.

Buddhist Virtue Ethics

Buddhist ethics affirms the absolute worth of all living beings. Buddhism rejects individualism as an illusion; we exist only as members of a community. Because we are all part of the same web of being, to be true to ourselves is to extend concern for everything that lies in our path of experience. The virtuous person is motivated not by self-interest, but by a concern to benefit all living beings.

Like Aristotle and Confucius, Buddhists believe that good and evil—virtue and vice—are expressed in our actions. Engaging in destructive actions makes it more likely that we'll repeat that behavior in the future; engaging in virtuous actions makes it more likely that we'll repeat that behavior in the future. A good society encourages the development of moral wisdom and virtue. We cannot resolve the problems that plague modern society by encouraging an individualism, such as that advocated by natural rights ethics, that allows people to pursue their concept of good at the expense of other human and nonhuman beings.

Nietzsche and the *Übermensch*

Friedrich Nietzsche was an outspoken critic of cultural relativism, what he called herd morality. He was particularly critical of traditional bourgeois Christian morality that, he claimed, forms the basis of modern Western morality. This morality, which extols meekness, unconditional forgiveness, self-sacrifice, and equality as virtues, he argued, is destructive to individual integrity and growth.

Nietzsche's *Übermensch*, or superman, is a person of integrity and self-mastery who is able to rise above the morality of the crowd and exercise the "will to power," which entails the will to grow, courage, generosity toward the vanquished, and human nobility. In contrast, weak people extol humility and self-sacrifice as virtues. Thus, traditional Christian or Western bourgeois morality drags the best and strongest people down to the lowest common denominator.

Nietzsche's ethics have often been misinterpreted as the will to dominate and subjugate others. However, truly strong or virtuous people are not cruel, nor do they desire to subjugate others. While Nietzsche apparently admired Jesus as an example of an *Übermensch,* he condemned modern Christianity, arguing that it bears little resemblance to that which was promoted by Jesus.

Care Ethics

Care ethics emphasizes caring over considerations of justice and impartiality. Care ethics, as a moral theory, developed primarily out of Carol Gilligan's study of women's moral reasoning. In her interviews with women and through her study of women in literature, Gilligan concluded that women's moral development tends to follow a different path than

---

🌿 VIRTUE ETHICS: CONSIDERATIONS FOR THINKING ABOUT MORAL ISSUES

- **Seeking the mean:** Does the trait we are encouraging represent a balance between excess and deficiency?
- **Social policies:** Does this social policy or resolution to a social issue encourage the development of virtue in the people affected by it?
- **Relationships:** What relationships are involved in this moral issue?
- **Caring and caring for:** How can we best nurture these relationships both as the "ones-caring" and the "ones-cared-for"?

---

men's. Men, she found, tend to base their moral decisions on duty- and principle-oriented moral theories; women are more context-oriented and concerned with relationships.

Care ethics has also been influenced by David Hume's ethics, which emphasizes moral sentiment over moral reasoning. According to him, it is primarily sympathy rather than reason that motivates us to act morally. Sympathy opens us up to others by breaking down the "we/them" barriers that impede the development of caring relationships.

According to feminist care ethicist Nel Noddings, we are at our moral best when we are "caring and being cared for." Ecofeminist Karen Warren expands care ethics to include all living creatures and all of nature. Unlike abstract moral principles, sympathy joins us to others in a caring relationship (see Chapter 12, pages 687–694). It is care, not rational calculations or an abstract sense of duty, that creates moral obligations. Caring is also ranked highly in Confucian ethics, where traditional family ties and loyalty are extremely important.

Care, however, is not enough. When our personal inclination to care is lacking, our commitment to an ideal or principle of caring motivates us to do what is right. On this point care ethicists and deontologists find common ground. A person of good will—a person who is truly virtuous and caring—can be counted on to act out of a sense of duty even when the immediate emotional inclination to do so is lacking.

Care ethicists maintain that moral sentiments such as compassion and sympathy are forms of knowledge that should be taken seriously in discussing social issues and formulating social policy. Philosopher Virginia Held, for example, disagrees with the traditional division wherein justice belongs to the public sphere and care to the private domain of family, friends, and charity.[34] Just as justice is needed in the family, so is the care perspective needed in the public domain. Care ethics plays a central role in the hospice movement's opposition to euthanasia and its belief that we should work on providing a more caring and supportive environment for those who are dying. In her article opposing capital punishment, Helen Prejean enjoins her readers to see prisoners who are condemned to death row from a care perspective as well as a justice perspective (see Chapter 5, pages 267–272).

Like Prejean, care ethicists do not want to dispense with justice; rather, they want to see the two approaches used together in formulating social policy. Care ethics serves as a corrective to our traditional views by demanding that we recognize welfare rights as basic rights. It also requires that we respect others in relationships as individuals with their own needs, rather than adopting a paternalistic attitude. Although care ethics is often associated with feminism, some feminists reject it on the grounds that it reinforces traditional stereotypes of women's roles in the family and in society.

The Strengths and Limitations of Virtue Ethics

The primary criticism of virtue ethics is that it is incomplete. It has also been criticized for its lack of coherence as a bag-of-virtues approach. This criticism is based on a misunderstanding of the nature of virtue, however. Virtue ethicists do not mean virtue to imply a list of unrelated character traits, but rather a unity of character.

Virtue ethics does not offer sufficient guidance for making real-life moral decisions. While a virtuous character may be enough to motivate the saint and those at the higher stages of moral development, most of us also need formal guidelines.

On the other hand, virtue ethics gives abstract principles regarding duties and rights a personal face. Virtue ethicists are not suggesting that we ignore moral principles; they are saying that virtue is more fundamental than duty. Nor does virtue ethics entail discarding reason and relying solely on our "good" feelings. In the virtuous person, reason and feeling complement and confirm one another.

Virtue ethics goes beyond pure duty- and rights-based ethics. It directly challenges the individual to rise above ordinary moral demands and to work toward creating a society in which it is easier for everyone to be virtuous and enjoy the good life.

EXERCISES

1. Which motivates you more to take action, a sense of justice or a feeling of sympathy for other persons? Illustrate your answer with specific examples.
2. Discuss possible social policies for dealing with an issue such as hate speech, pornography, or alcohol and drug use on campus. Which policies are most likely to promote virtue in citizens? Support your answer.
3. Select a specific moral issue that is covered in this text. Discuss ways in which the care perspective might help in coming up with a resolution.
4. Examine the contemporary notion of nation-building in light of the Confucian concept of the virtuous society. Should virtue be imposed on the leadership of other nations, as is happening in Iraq and, if so, do other nations have a moral obligation to impose virtue in government, or at least their concept of a virtuous government, in wayward nations? Support your answer.

CONCLUSION

Moral issues are complex. No one theory offers the complete truth or perfect solution to a moral issue. On the other hand, theories can work together to provide us with more comprehensive tools for effectively analyzing moral issues. Theories help us recognize and prioritize moral principles and concerns. We should not simply discard a theory because it has limitations, but adopt a multidimensional approach that draws from the strengths of each of the theories. Whether the theory is deontological and oriented toward autonomy and the careful delineation of rules and rights; or utilitarian and concerned with consequences and maximizing benefits; or virtue-based and focused on making us better, more caring people—all of the universalist theories have the same ultimate goal: to provide a rational basis for making better moral decisions.

🖋 SUMMARY OF READINGS ON MORAL PHILOSOPHY

Aristotle, "Nicomachean Ethics." Living the good life—the life of virtue—is our most important human activity.

Rand, "The Fountainhead." Rational ethical egoism is the moral ideal.

Bentham, "An Introduction to the Principles of Morals and Legislation." A moral action or policy is one that maximizes pleasure and minimizes pain.

Mill, "Utilitarianism." Some pleasures should count more than other pleasures.

Kant, "Fundamental Principles of the Metaphysic of Ethics." Moral laws should be logically consistent and universally binding.

Rawls, "A Theory of Justice." Justice as fairness is the most basic requirement of a social contract.

Locke, "Two Treatises of Civil Government." People unite into political societies to protect and enjoy their natural rights.

Noddings, "Caring: A Feminine Approach to Ethics and Moral Education." Care and sympathy offer better guidance than principled moral reasoning.

Confucius, "The Analects." People are happier and more virtuous when they are living in a just, well-ordered society.

Nhat Hanh, "The Five Mindfulness Trainings." Mindfulness is fundamental to living a moral life.

Although moral theory offers guidance, theory alone does not offer specific solutions. An understanding of the relevant facts, cultural traditions and conditions, practical wisdom, and sound moral reasoning are all necessary adjuncts to theory.

🖋 ARISTOTLE

Nicomachean Ethics

Aristotle was born in Stagira, a Greek colony north of Athens. He spent most of his childhood in Macedonia, where his father, Nicomachus, was a court physician. Aristotle was a scientist, philosopher, logician, poet, and psychologist who wrote hundreds of works, including poems, treatises, and books. *Nicomachean Ethics* is one of Aristotle's best-known works. In it, Aristotle argues that living the good life—the life of virtue—is our most important human activity. Because the peculiar function of humans is the

---

Nicomachean Ethics, from *The Basic Works of Aristotle,* ed. by Richard McKeon (New York: Random House, 1941). Copy of an earlier translation by Benjamin Jowett (1817–1893). Notes have been omitted. (To read the complete text of *Nicomachean Ethics* online, go to http://classics.mit.edu/Aristotle/nicomachean.)

exercise of reason, virtue involves living according to reason. Only by doing so can we achieve happiness, inner harmony, and a well-ordered society.

After the death of his teacher Plato, Aristotle took on the education of Alexander the Great, future king of Macedonia, who set out to conquer the world. After Alexander the Great's untimely death in 323 B.C.E., Aristotle was charged with impiety. He fled to Euboea, where he died in Babylon a year later.

Aristotle is sometimes dismissed as being too much of an elitist to be relevant for today's democracies. His critique of democracy, however, is a timely warning against the dangers of relying on majority rule as the criterion for deciding what is just.

Critical Reading Questions

1. How does Aristotle go about analyzing the term *good*?
2. According to Aristotle, what is the most important human activity? What is the final end of human activity?
3. What is the relationship between morality and happiness?
4. What is virtue? What are the two types of virtue?
5. What does Aristotle mean by habituation? What does habituation have to do with becoming virtuous? What is the role of the state in helping citizens become virtuous?
6. What does Aristotle mean when he says that goodness is the quality that hits the mean? Is virtue always a matter of hitting the mean?
7. What are some examples of excesses and deficits? How do we avoid them?

Book I

CHAPTER 1

Every art and every inquiry, and similarly every action and pursuit, is thought to aim at some good; and for this reason the good has rightly been declared to be that at which all things aim. But a certain difference is found among ends; some are activities, others are products apart from the activities that produce them. Where there are ends apart from the actions, it is the nature of the products to be better than the activities. . . .

CHAPTER 7

Let us again return to the good we are seeking, and ask what it can be. It seems different in different actions and arts; it is different in medicine, in strategy, and in the other arts likewise. What then is the good of each? Surely that for whose sake everything else is done. In medicine this is health, in strategy victory, in architecture a house, in any other sphere something else, and in every action and pursuit the end; for it is for the sake of this that all men do whatever else they do. Therefore, if there is an end for all that we do, this will be the good achievable by action, and if there are more than one, these will be the goods achievable by action.

So the argument has by a different course reached the same point; but we must try to state this even more clearly. Since there is evidently more than one end, and we choose some of these (e.g., wealth, flutes, and in general instruments) for the sake of something else, clearly not all ends are final ends; but the chief good is evidently something final. Therefore, if there is only one final end, this will be what we are seeking, and if there are more than one, the most final of these will be what we are seeking. Now we call that which is in itself worthy of pursuit more final than that which is worthy of pursuit for the sake of something else, and that which is never desirable for the sake of something else more final than the things that are desirable both in themselves and for the sake of that other thing, and therefore we call final without qualification that which is always desirable in itself and never for the sake of something else.

Now such a thing happiness, above all else, is held to be; for this we choose always for itself and never for the sake of something else, but honour, pleasure, reason, and every virtue we choose indeed for themselves (for if nothing resulted from them we should still choose each of them), but we choose them also for the sake of happiness, judging that by means of them we shall be happy. Happiness, on the other hand, no one chooses for the sake of these, nor, in general, for anything other than itself. . . .

Presumably, however, to say that happiness is the chief good seems a platitude, and a clearer account of what it is is still desired. This might perhaps be given, if we could first ascertain the function of man. For just as for a flute-player, a sculptor, or any artist, and, in general, for all things that have a function or activity, the good and the "well" is thought to reside in the function, so would it seem to be for man, if he has a function. Have the carpenter, then, and the tanner certain functions or activities, and has man none? Is he born without a function? Or as eye, hand, foot, and in general each of the parts evidently has a function, may one lay it down that man similarly has a function apart from all these? What then can this be? Life seems to be common even to plants, but we are seeking what is peculiar to man. Let us exclude, therefore, the life of nutrition and growth. Next there would be a life of perception, but *it* also seems to be common even to the horse, the ox, and every animal. There remains, then, an active life of the element that has a rational principle; of this, one part has such a principle in the sense of being obedient to one, the other in the sense of possessing one and exercising thought. And, as "life of the rational

element" also has two meanings, we must state that life in the sense of activity is what we mean; for this seems to be the more proper sense of the term. Now if the function of man is an activity of soul which follows or implies a rational principle, . . . : if this is the case, [and we state the function of man to be a certain kind of life, and this to be an activity or actions of the soul implying a rational principle, and the function of a good man to be the good and noble performance of these, and if any action is well performed when it is performed in accordance with the appropriate excellence: if this is the case,] human good turns out to be activity of soul in accordance with virtue, and if there are more than one virtue, in accordance with the best and most complete.

But we must add "in a complete life." For one swallow does not make a summer, nor does one day; and so too one day, or a short time, does not make a man blessed and happy. . . .

Book II

CHAPTER 1

Virtue, then, being of two kinds, intellectual and moral, intellectual virtue in the main owes both its birth and its growth to teaching (for which reason it requires experience and time), while moral virtue comes about as a result of habit, whence also its name *ethike* is one that is formed by a slight variation from the word *ethos* (habit). From this it is also plain that none of the moral virtues arises in us by nature, for nothing that exists by nature can form a habit contrary to its nature. For instance the stone which by nature moves downwards cannot be habituated to move upwards, not even if one tries to train it by throwing it up ten thousand times; nor can fire be habituated to move downwards, nor can anything else that by nature behaves in one way be trained to behave in another. Neither by nature, then, nor contrary to nature do the virtues arise in us; rather we are adapted by nature to receive them, and are made perfect by habit.

Again, of all the things that come to us by nature we first acquire the potentiality and later exhibit the activity (this is plain in the case of the senses; for it was not by often seeing or often hearing that we got these senses, but on the contrary we had them before we used them, and did not come to have them by using them); but the virtues we get by first exercising them, as also happens in the case of the arts as well. For the things we have to learn before we can do them, we learn by doing them, e.g. men become builders by building and lyre-players by playing the lyre; so too we become just by doing just acts, temperate by doing temperate acts, brave by doing brave acts.

This is confirmed by what happens in states; for legislators make the citizens good by forming habits in them, and this is the wish of every legislator, and those who do not effect it miss their mark, and it is in this that a good constitution differs from a bad one.

Again, it is from the same causes and by the same means that every virtue is both produced and destroyed, and similarly every art; for it is from playing the lyre that both good and bad lyre-players are produced. And the corresponding statement is true of builders and of all the rest; men will be good or bad builders as a result of building well or badly. For if this were not so, there would have been no need of a teacher, but all men would have been born good or bad at their craft. This, then, is the case with the virtues also; by doing the acts that we do in our transactions with other men we become just or unjust, and by doing the acts that we do in the presence of danger, and being habituated to feel fear or confidence, we become brave or cowardly. The same is true of appetites and feelings of anger; some men become temperate and good-tempered, others self-indulgent and irascible, by behaving in one way or the other in the appropriate circumstances. Thus, in one word, states of character arise out of like activities. This is why the activities we exhibit must be of a certain kind; it is because the states of character correspond to the differences between these. It makes no small difference, then, whether we form habits of one kind or of another from our very youth;

it makes a very great difference, or rather *all* the difference.

CHAPTER 2

Since, then, the present inquiry does not aim at theoretical knowledge like the others (for we are inquiring not in order to know what virtue is, but in order to become good, since otherwise our inquiry would have been of no use), we must examine the nature of actions, namely how we ought to do them; for these determine also the nature of the states of character that are produced, as we have said. Now, that we must act according to the right rule is a common principle and must be assumed—it will be discussed later, i.e. both what the right rule is, and how it is related to the other virtues. . . .

First, then, let us consider this, that it is the nature of such things to be destroyed by defect and excess, as we see in the case of strength and health (for to gain light on things imperceptible we must use the evidence of sensible things); both excessive and defective exercise destroys the strength, and similarly drink or food which is above or below a certain amount destroys the health, while that which is proportionate both produces and increases and preserves it. So too is it, then, in the case of temperance and courage and the other virtues. For the man who flies from and fears everything and does not stand his ground against anything becomes a coward, and the man who fears nothing at all but goes to meet every danger becomes rash; and similarly the man who indulges in every pleasure and abstains from none becomes self-indulgent, while the man who shuns every pleasure, as boors do, becomes in a way insensible; temperance and courage, then, are destroyed by excess and defect, and preserved by the mean.

But not only are the sources and causes of their origination and growth the same as those of their destruction, but also the sphere of their actualization will be the same; for this is also true of the things which are more evident to sense, e.g. of strength; it is produced by taking much food and undergoing much exertion, and it is the strong man that will be most able to do these things. So too is it with the virtues; by abstaining from pleasures we become temperate, and it is when we have become so that we are most able to abstain from them; and similarly too in the case of courage; for by being habituated to despise things that are terrible and to stand our ground against them we become brave, and it is when we have become so that we shall be most able to stand our ground against them. . . .

CHAPTER 5

Next we must consider what virtue is. Since things that are found in the soul are of three kinds—passions, faculties, states of character—virtue must be one of these. By passions I mean appetite, anger, fear, confidence, envy, joy, friendly feeling, hatred, longing, emulation, pity, and in general the feelings that are accompanied by pleasure or pain; by faculties the things in virtue of which we are said to be capable of feeling these, e.g. of becoming angry or being pained or feeling pity; by states of character the things in virtue of which we stand well or badly with reference to the passions, e.g. with reference to anger we stand badly if we feel it violently or too weakly, and well if we feel it moderately; and similarly with reference to the other passions.

Now neither the virtues nor the vices are *passions,* because we are not called good or bad on the ground of our passions, but are so called on the ground of our virtues and our vices, and because we are neither praised nor blamed for our passions (for the man who feels fear or anger is not praised, nor is the man who simply feels anger blamed, but the man who feels it in a certain way), but for our virtues and our vices we *are* praised or blamed.

Again, we feel anger and fear without choice, but the virtues are modes of choice or involve choice. . . . Further, in respect of the passions we are said to be moved, but in respect of the virtues and the vices we are said not to be moved but to be disposed in a particular way.

For these reasons also they are not *faculties;* for we are neither called good nor bad, nor praised nor blamed, for the simple capacity of feeling the passions; again, we have the faculties by nature, but we are not made good or bad by nature; we have spoken of this before.

If, then, the virtues are neither passions nor faculties, all that remains is that they should be *states of character.*

Thus we have stated what virtue is in respect of its genus.

CHAPTER 6

We must, however, not only describe virtue as a state of character, but also say what sort of state it is. We may remark, then, that every virtue or excellence both brings into good condition the thing of which it is the excellence and makes the work of that thing be done well; e.g. the excellence of the eye makes both the eye and its work good; for it is by the excellence of the eye that we see well. Similarly the excellence of the horse makes a horse both good in itself and good at running and at carrying its rider and at awaiting the attack of the enemy. Therefore, if this is true in every case, the virtue of man also will be the state of character which makes a man good and which makes him do his own work well. . . .

Virtue, then, is a state of character concerned with choice, lying in a mean, i.e. the mean relative to us, this being determined by a rational principle, and by that principle by which the man of practical wisdom would determine it. Now it is a mean between two vices, that which depends on excess and that which depends on defect; and again it is a mean because the vices respectively fall short of or exceed what is right in both passions and actions, while virtue both finds and chooses that which is intermediate. Hence in respect of its substance and the definition which states its essence virtue is a mean, with regard to what is best and right an extreme.

But not every action nor every passion admits of a mean; for some have names that already imply badness, e.g. spite, shamelessness, envy, and in the case of actions adultery, theft, murder; for all of these and suchlike things imply by their names that they are themselves bad, and not the excesses or deficiencies of them. It is not possible, then, ever to be right with regard to them; one must always be wrong. Nor does goodness or badness with regard to such things depend on committing adultery with the right woman, at the right time, and in the right way, but simply to do any of them is to go wrong. It would be equally absurd, then, to expect that in unjust, cowardly, and voluptuous action there should be a mean, an excess, and a deficiency; for at that rate there would be a mean of excess and of deficiency, an excess of excess, and a deficiency of deficiency. But as there is no excess and deficiency of temperance and courage because what is intermediate is in a sense an extreme, so too of the actions we have mentioned there is no mean nor any excess and deficiency, but however they are done they are wrong; for in general there is neither a mean of excess and deficiency, nor excess and deficiency of a mean.

Discussion Questions

1. Discuss Aristotle's claim that every act and inquiry aims at some good (goal). Is there a single end toward which all human behavior is directed? If so, does this justify the regulation of people's behavior, including media censorship, by the government so they are more likely to achieve this end? Use specific examples to support your answer.

2. Do colleges have a duty to help students become virtuous people by creating an atmosphere in which good behavior becomes habitual for them? Support your answer. Should campus administrations prohibit certain excessive behaviors in order to make it easier for students to become good people? Discuss your answer in light of regulations on hate speech, cheating, and drug and alcohol abuse.

3. Aristotle warned against the rule of the many, arguing that "the many are more corruptible than the few." Is the fact that the United States is a democracy an impediment to getting the United States to comply with international policies? Discuss whether important public policies, especially those that affect the international community, should be left up to the experts or to majority rule.

AYN RAND

The Fountainhead

Philosopher, novelist, and playwright Ayn Rand (1905–1982) was one of the foremost contemporary defenders of ethical egoism and natural rights ethics. Born in St. Petersburg, Russia, she immigrated to the United States in 1926. Strongly opposed

---

The Fountainhead (Philadelphia: The Blakiston Company, 1943), pp. 736–742. Reprinted with permission of The Estate of Ayn Rand.

to collectivism and Soviet communism, she championed rational ethical egoism and the capitalist system it supported.

In the selection from her novel *The Fountainhead,* Howard Roark is presented as her ideal of the moral person and rational ethical egoist. Roark, a successful architect, lives his life entirely for himself and his values.

Critical Reading Questions

1. What does Roark mean when he says, "Man cannot survive except through his mind"?
2. What is the relationship between "the mind" and individualism?
3. What is a "second-hander" and why does Roark view second-handers as immoral?
4. What is the nature of "proper relationships"?
5. Why does egotism offer a better alternative in living the good life than altruism?

Roark stood before them as each man stands in the innocence of his own mind. But Roark stood like that before a hostile crowd—and they knew suddenly that no hatred was possible to him. For the flash of an instant, they grasped the manner of his consciousness. Each asked himself: do I need anyone's approval?—does it matter?—am I tied? And for that instant, each man was free—free enough to feel benevolence for every other man in the room.

It was only a moment; the moment of silence when Roark was about to speak. . . .

"Man cannot survive except through his mind. He comes on earth unarmed. His brain is his only weapon. Animals obtain food by force. Man has no claws, no fangs, no horns, no great strength of muscle. He must plant his food or hunt it. To plant, he needs a process of thought. To hunt, he needs weapons, and to make weapons—a process of thought. From this simplest necessity to the highest religious abstraction, from the wheel to the skyscraper, everything we are and everything we have comes from a single attribute of man—the function of his reasoning mind.

"But the mind is an attribute of the individual. There is no such thing as a collective brain. There is no such thing as a collective thought. An agreement reached by a group of men is only a compromise or an average drawn upon many individual thoughts. It is a secondary consequence.

The primary act—the process of reason—must be performed by each man alone. . . .

"Nothing is given to man on earth. Everything he needs has to be produced. And here man faces his basic alternative: he can survive in only one of two ways—by the independent work of his own mind or as a parasite fed by the minds of others. The creator originates. The parasite borrows. The creator faces nature alone. The parasite faces nature through an intermediary. . . .

"The basic need of the second-hander is to secure his ties with men in order to be fed. He places relations first. He declares that man exists in order to serve others. He preaches altruism.

"Altruism is the doctrine which demands that man live for others and place others above self.

"No man can live for another. He cannot share his spirit just as he cannot share his body. But the second-hander has used altruism as a weapon of exploitation and reversed the base of mankind's moral principles. Men have been taught every precept that destroys the creator. Men have been taught dependence as a virtue.

"The man who attempts to live for others is a dependent. He is a parasite in motive and makes parasites of those he serves. The relationship produces nothing but mutual corruption. It is impossible in concept. The nearest approach to it in reality—the man who lives to serve others—is the slave. If physical slavery is repulsive, how much more repulsive is the concept of servility of the spirit? The conquered slave has a vestige of honor. He has the merit of having resisted and of considering his condition evil. But the man who enslaves himself voluntarily in the name of love is the basest of creatures. He degrades the dignity of man and he degrades the conception of love. But this is the essence of altruism. . . .

"Here the basic reversal is most deadly. The issue has been perverted and man has been left no alternative—and no freedom. As poles of good and evil, he was offered two conceptions: egotism* and altruism. Egotism was held to mean the sacrifice of others to self. Altruism—the sacrifice of self to others. This tied man irrevocably to other men and left him nothing but a choice of pain: his own pain borne for the sake of others or pain inflicted upon others for the sake of self. When it was added that man must find joy in self-immolation, the trap was closed. Man was forced to accept masochism as his ideal—under threat that sadism was his only alternative. This was the greatest fraud ever perpetrated on mankind.

"This was the device by which dependence and suffering were perpetuated as fundamentals of life.

"The choice is not self-sacrifice or domination. The choice is independence or dependence. The code of the creator or the code of the second-hander. This is the basic issue. It rests upon the alternative of life or death. The code of the creator is built on the needs of the reasoning mind which allows man to survive. The code of the second-hander is built on the needs of a mind incapable of survival. All that which proceeds from man's independent ego is good. All that which proceeds from man's dependence upon men is evil.

"The egotist in the absolute sense is not the man who sacrifices others. He is the man who stands above the need of using others in any manner. He does not function through them. He is not concerned with them in any primary matter. Not in his aim, not in his motive, not in his thinking, not in his desires, not in the source of his energy. He does not exist for any other man—and he asks no other man to exist for him. This is the only form of brotherhood and mutual respect possible between men. . . .

"In all proper relationships there is no sacrifice of anyone to anyone. An architect needs clients, but he does not subordinate his work to their wishes. They need him, but they do not order a house just to give him a commission. Men exchange their work by free, mutual consent to mutual advantage when their personal interests agree and they both desire the exchange. If they do not desire it, they are not forced to deal with each other. They seek further. This is the only possible form of relationship between equals. Anything else is a relation of slave to master, or victim to executioner. . . ."

---

*Rand is using the term *egotism* in the sense that the text is using *egoism*.

Discussion Questions

1. Analyze Rand's argument that if we lived in a perfectly laissez-faire society, always following our own rational self-interest and not hindering others from following theirs, then conflicts between one person's self-interest and another's would not arise. Support your conclusion with specific examples.

2. Discuss Rand's claim in the reading that the only good we can do for each other is hands-off. What effect would this approach have on people who now depend on others, a view which, she says, allows voluntary charity under certain circumstances, such as social service and government agencies, for certain services?

3. Is Rand's depiction of the proper relationship between people in which there is "no sacrifice of anyone to anyone" an appropriate model for personal and family relationships? If not, discuss why not.

4. Discuss how Rand might have responded to Barack Obama's election promise to increase taxes on the rich and redistribute the money to poor and middle-income families.

JEREMY BENTHAM

An Introduction to the Principles of Morals and Legislation

English jurist, philosopher, and social reformer Jeremy Bentham (1748–1832) was born in London and lived during a period of remarkable political and economic changes, including the American and French Revolutions and the Industrial Revolution. He developed his utilitarianism theory primarily as a tool of social reform in response to the injustices of his time and the desperate needs of the poor and exploited workers.

In the following excerpt, Bentham explains what he means by the principle of utility and how to determine if an action or policy conforms to the principle.

Critical Reading Questions

1. What does Bentham mean when he says that "nature has placed mankind under the governance of two sovereign masters"?
2. What is utility and what is the principle of utility?
3. What is meant by the interest of the community, and who or what is included in this community?
4. How are the community and the individuals who comprise it related?
5. What ends should legislatures keep in mind when formulating laws and public policies?

I. Nature has placed mankind under the governance of two sovereign masters, *pain* and *pleasure.* It is for them alone to point out what we ought to do, as well as to determine what we shall do. On

An Introduction to the Principles of Morals and Legislation (London: Clarendon Press, 1907). Some notes have been omitted. The complete book is available online at www.econlib .org/library/Bentham/bnth.PML.html.

the one hand the standard of right and wrong, on the other the chain of causes and effects, are fastened to their throne. They govern us in all we do, in all we say, in all we think: every effort we can make to throw off our subjection, will serve but to demonstrate and confirm it. In words a man may pretend to abjure their empire: but in reality he will remain subject to it all the while. The *principle of utility* recognises this subjection, and assumes it for the foundation of that system, the object of which is to rear the fabric of felicity by the hands of reason and of law. Systems which attempt to question it, deal in sounds instead of sense, in caprice instead of reason, in darkness instead of light.

. . .

II. . . . By the principle* of utility is meant that principle which approves or disapproves of every action whatsoever, according to the tendency which it appears to have to augment or diminish the happiness of the party whose interest is in question: or, what is the same thing in other words, to promote or to oppose that happiness. I say of every action whatsoever; and therefore not only of every action of a private individual, but of every measure of government.

III. By utility is meant that property in any object, whereby it tends to produce benefit, advantage, pleasure, good, or happiness, (all this in the present case comes to the same thing) or (what comes again to the same thing) to prevent the happening of mischief, pain, evil, or unhappiness to the party whose interest is considered: if that party be the community in general, then the happiness of the community: if a particular individual, then the happiness of that individual.

---

*The principle here in question may be taken for an act of the mind; a sentiment; a sentiment of approbation; a sentiment which, when applied to an action, approves of its utility, as that quality of it by which the measure of approbation or disapprobation bestowed upon it ought to be governed.

IV. The interest of the community is one of the most general expressions that can occur in the phraseology of morals: no wonder that the meaning of it is often lost. When it has a meaning, it is this. The community is a fictitious *body*, composed of the individual persons who are considered as constituting as it were its *members*. The interest of the community then is, what?—the sum of the interests of the several members who compose it.

V. It is in vain to talk of the interest of the community, without understanding what is the interest of the individual. A thing is said to promote the interest, or to be *for* the interest, of an individual, when it tends to add to the sum total of his pleasures: or, what comes to the same thing, to diminish the sum total of his pains.

VI. An action then may be said to be conformable to the principle of utility, or, for shortness sake, to utility, (meaning with respect to the community at large) when the tendency it has to augment the happiness of the community is greater than any it has to diminish it.

. . .

. . . Pleasures then, and the avoidance of pains, are the *ends* which the legislator has in view: it behoves him therefore to understand their *value*. Pleasures and pains are the *instruments* he has to work with: it behoves him therefore to understand their force, which is again, in other words, their value.

Discussion Questions

1. Bentham argued that punishment is an evil because it increases pain. Discuss what policy a utilitarian would propose for dealing with hardened and dangerous criminals or with people who are suspected terrorists.
2. Does social or public ethics require a different strategy than personal ethics? If so, how do the two strategies differ? On what grounds can you justify the difference?
3. Using the principle of utility, develop a public policy regarding human cloning.
4. Discuss whether the practice of meat-eating can be morally justified in light of Bentham's principle of utility.

🍃 JOHN STUART MILL

Utilitarianism

John Stuart Mill (1806–1873) was educated by his father James Mill, with the help of Jeremy Bentham, to carry on the utilitarian tradition. When Mill was about twenty, he experienced a nervous breakdown and sank into a deep depression that lasted for two years. During this time, he began to question some of the tenets of utilitarian theory, particularly Bentham's insistence on the equality of pleasures.

Like Bentham, Mill was interested in legislation and social reform. However, unlike Bentham, Mill believed that certain pleasures should count more than others.

Critical Reading Questions

1. What is the principle of utility, and what are the only things that the principle of utility regards as desirable moral ends?
2. Which pleasures does Mill regard as superior?
3. What method does Mill use for determining which pleasures are of a higher quality?
4. Whose interests should be taken into account when determining the utility of an action?
5. What is the relationship between the principle of utility and the Golden Rule?

The creed which accepts as the foundation of morals, Utility, or the Greatest Happiness Principle, holds that actions are right in proportion as they tend to promote happiness, wrong as they tend to produce the reverse of happiness. By happiness is intended pleasure, and the absence of pain; by unhappiness, pain, and the privation of pleasure. To give a clear view of the moral standard set up by the theory, much more requires to be said; in particular, what things it includes in the ideas of pain and pleasure; and to what extent this is left an open question. But these supplementary explanations do not affect the theory of life on which this theory of morality is grounded—namely, that pleasure, and freedom from pain,

are the only things desirable as ends; and that all desirable things (which are as numerous in the utilitarian as in any other scheme) are desirable either for the pleasure inherent in themselves, or as means to the promotion of pleasure and the prevention of pain. . . .

It is quite compatible with the principle of utility to recognise the fact, that some *kinds* of pleasure are more desirable and more valuable than others. It would be absurd that while, in estimating all other things, quality is considered as well as quantity, the estimation of pleasures should be supposed to depend on quantity alone.

If I am asked, what I mean by difference of quality in pleasures, or what makes one pleasure more valuable than another, merely as a pleasure, except its being greater in amount, there is but one possible answer. Of two pleasures, if there be one to which all or almost all who have experience of both give a decided preference, irrespective of

Originally published in three installments in *Fraser's Magazine*, 1861. (Mill's complete book is available online at http://etext.library.adelaide.edu.au/m/mill/john_stuart/ m645u.)

any feeling of moral obligation to prefer it, that is the more desirable pleasure. If one of the two is, by those who are competently acquainted with both, placed so far above the other that they prefer it, even though knowing it to be attended with a greater amount of discontent, and would not resign it for any quantity of the other pleasure which their nature is capable of, we are justified in ascribing to the preferred enjoyment a superiority in quality, so far outweighing quantity as to render it, in comparison, of small account.

Now it is an unquestionable fact that those who are equally acquainted with, and equally capable of appreciating and enjoying, both, do give a most marked preference to the manner of existence which employs their higher faculties. Few human creatures would consent to be changed into any of the lower animals, for a promise of the fullest allowance of a beast's pleasures; no intelligent human being would consent to be a fool, no instructed person would be an ignoramus, no person of feeling and conscience would be selfish and base, even though they should be persuaded that the fool, the dunce, or the rascal is better satisfied with his lot than they are with theirs. . . . It is better to be a human being dissatisfied than a pig satisfied; better to be Socrates dissatisfied than a fool satisfied. And if the fool, or the pig, are of a different opinion, it is because they only know their own side of the question. The other party to the comparison knows both sides.

. . .

According to the Greatest Happiness Principle, as above explained, the ultimate end, with reference to and for the sake of which all other things are desirable (whether we are considering our own good or that of other people), is an existence exempt as far as possible from pain, and as rich as possible in enjoyments, both in point of quantity and quality; the test of quality, and the rule for measuring it against quantity, being the preference felt by those who in their opportunities of experience, to which must be added their habits of self-consciousness and self-observation, are best furnished with the means of comparison. This, being, according to the utilitarian opinion,

the end of human action, is necessarily also the standard of morality; which may accordingly be defined, the rules and precepts for human conduct, by the observance of which an existence such as has been described might be, to the greatest extent possible, secured to all mankind; and not to them only, but, so far as the nature of things admits, to the whole sentient creation.

. . .

I must again repeat, what the assailants of utilitarianism seldom have the justice to acknowledge, that the happiness which forms the utilitarian standard of what is right in conduct, is not the agent's own happiness, but that of all concerned. As between his own happiness and that of others, utilitarianism requires him to be as strictly impartial as a disinterested and benevolent spectator. In the golden rule of Jesus of Nazareth, we read the complete spirit of the ethics of utility. To do as you would be done by, and to love your neighbour as yourself, constitute the ideal perfection of utilitarian morality. As the means of making the nearest approach to this ideal, utility would enjoin, first, that laws and social arrangements should place the happiness, or (as speaking practically it may be called) the interest, of every individual, as nearly as possible in harmony with the interest of the whole; and secondly, that education and opinion, which have so vast a power over human character, should so use that power as to establish in the mind of every individual an indissoluble association between his own happiness and the good of the whole; especially between his own happiness and the practice of such modes of conduct, negative and positive, as regard for the universal happiness prescribes; so that not only he may be unable to conceive the possibility of happiness to himself, consistently with conduct opposed to the general good, but also that a direct impulse to promote the general good may be in every individual one of habitual motives of action, and the sentiments connected therewith may fill a large and prominent place in every human being's sentient existence. If the impugners of the utilitarian morality represented it to their own minds in this its true character, I know not what recommendation possessed by any other morality they could possibly affirm to be wanting to it; what more beautiful or more exalted developments of human nature any other ethical system can be supposed to foster, or what springs of action, not accessible to the utilitarian, such systems rely on for giving effect to their mandates. . . .

———

A selection from Mill's *On Liberty* is included after Chapter 9, "Freedom of Speech."

Discussion Questions

1. Analyze Mill's argument that the life of a dissatisfied human is preferable to that of a satisfied pig. Is his distinction between the different pleasures justified? If so, on what basis?
2. How does Mill's concept of pleasure differ from that of Bentham's? Which definition is more useful? Apply Mill's concept of the quality of pleasures to moral issues involving nonhuman animals—for example, meat-eating, keeping animals in zoos, and the use of animals in experimentation.
3. Discuss Mill's use of sentience as a criterion for determining whose interests should be taken into account. Using this criterion, what would Mill's position most likely be regarding euthanasia and "partial-birth" abortion?
4. Discuss the legalization of drugs and pornography in light of Mill's theory.

IMMANUEL KANT

Fundamental Principles of the Metaphysic of Ethics

An intellectual giant, Immanuel Kant (1724–1804) was born in Germany. In 1755 he got a job as privatdocent at the University of Konigsberg, making Kant the first of the major philosophers to be a professional university teacher. One of his students wrote that they "never left a single lecture in his ethics without having become better men." He remained at the university as a professor until poor health forced him to retire in 1796. People came from all over to consult Kant on all sorts of issues. He died in 1804, having spent his entire life in Konigsberg.

Unlike the utilitarians, Kant was more concerned with establishing a metaphysical foundation for morality than in coming up with an ethical system that could be used for formulating social policy. He believed that only reason could provide this

———

Fundamental Principles of the Metaphysic of Ethics, trans. by Thomas Kingsmill Abbott (London: Longmans, Green and Co., Ltd., 1926). Some notes have been omitted. (To read Kant's work online, go to www.bartleby.com/32/601.html.)

foundation. If moral law is to be morally compelling, he argued, it must be logically consistent as well as absolutely binding.

Critical Reading Questions

1. What is the Good Will? What is the relevance of the Good Will in making decisions regarding social policy?
2. What gives an action moral worth?
3. Why does Kant reject utilitarianism as the foundation of morality?
4. Why does Kant argue that moral maxims must be universal rather than relative?
5. What is the categorical imperative? How does it differ from a hypothetical imperative? Give examples of both types of imperatives.
6. What does it mean for a being to be an "end in itself"? What gives a being value as an end in itself?
7. What is the difference between treating a being as an end in itself and treating a being as a means only? Why is it wrong to treat persons as means only?

Nothing can possibly be conceived in the world, or even out of it, which can be called good without qualification, except a Good Will. Intelligence, wit, judgment, and the other *talents* of the mind, however they may be named, or courage, resolution, perseverance, as qualities of temperament, are undoubtedly good and desirable in many respects; but these gifts of nature may also become extremely bad and mischievous if the will which is to make use of them, and which, therefore, constitutes what is called *character,* is not good. It is the same with the *gifts of fortune.* Power, riches, honour, even health, and the general well-being and contentment with one's condition which is called *happiness,* inspire pride, and often presumption, if there is not a Good Will to correct the influence of these on the mind, and with this also to rectify the whole principle of acting, and adapt it to its end. . . .

A Good Will is good not because of what it performs or effects, not by its aptness for the attainment of some proposed end, but simply by virtue of the volition, that is, it is good in itself, and considered by itself is to be esteemed much higher than all that can be brought about by it in favour of any inclination, nay, even of the sum total of all inclinations. Even if it should happen that, owing to special disfavour of fortune, or the niggardly provision of a step-motherly nature, this will should

wholly lack power to accomplish its purpose, if with its greatest efforts it should yet achieve nothing, and there should remain only the Good Will (not, to be sure, a mere wish, but the summoning of all means in our power), then, like a jewel, it would still shine by its own light, as a thing which has its whole value in itself. Its usefulness or fruitlessness can neither add to nor take away anything from this value. . . .

To be beneficent when we can is a duty; and besides this, there are many minds so sympathetically constituted that, without any other motive of vanity or self-interest, they find a pleasure in spreading joy around them, and can take delight in the satisfaction of others so far as it is their own work. But I maintain that in such a case an action of this kind, however proper, however amiable it may be, has nevertheless no true moral worth, but is on a level with other inclinations, *e.g.* the inclination to honour, which, if it is happily directed to that which is in fact of public utility and accordant with duty, and consequently honourable, deserves praise and encouragement, but not esteem. For the maxim lacks the moral import, namely, that such actions be done *from duty,* not from inclination. Put the case that the mind of that philanthropist was clouded by sorrow of his own extinguishing all sympathy with the lot of others, and that while he still has the power to benefit others in distress, he is not touched by their trouble because he is absorbed with his own; and now suppose that he tears himself out of his dead insensibility, and performs the action without any inclination to it, but simply from duty, then first has his action its genuine moral worth. . . .

Thus the moral worth of an action does not lie in the effect expended from it, not in any principle of action which requires to borrow its motive from this expected effect. For all these effects—agreeableness of one's condition, and even the promotion of the happiness of others—could have been also brought about by other causes, so that for this there would have been no need of the will of a rational being; whereas it is in this alone that the supreme and unconditional good can be found. The preeminent good which we call moral can therefore consist in nothing else than *the conception of law* in itself, *which certainly is only possible in a rational being*, in so far as this conception, and not the expected effect, determines the will. . . .

But what sort of law can that be, the conception of which must determine the will, even without paying any regard to the effect expected from it, in order that this will may be called good absolutely and without qualification? As I have deprived the will of every impulse which could arise to it from obedience to any law, there remains nothing but the universal conformity of its actions to law in general, which alone is to serve the will as a principle, *i.e.* I am never to act otherwise than *so that I could also will that my maxim should become a universal law.* Here now, it is the simple conformity to law in general, without assuming any particular law applicable to certain actions, that serves the will as its principle, and must so serve it, if duty is not to be a vain delusion and a chimerical notion. The common reason of men in its practical judgments perfectly coincides with this, and always has in view the principle here suggested. Let the question be, for example: May I when in distress make a promise with the intention not to keep it? I readily distinguish here between the two significations which the question may have: Whether it is prudent, or whether it is right, to make a false promise. The

former may undoubtedly often be the case. . . . The shortest way, however, and an unerring one, to discover the answer to this question whether a lying promise is consistent with duty, is to ask myself, Should I be content that my maxim (to extricate myself from difficulty by a false promise) should hold good as a universal law, for myself as well as for others? and should I be able to say to myself, "Every one may make a deceitful promise when he finds himself in a difficulty from which he cannot otherwise extricate himself"? Then I presently become aware that while I can will the lie, I can by no means will that lying should be a universal law. For with such a law there would be no promises at all, since it would be in vain to allege my intention in regard to my future actions to those who would not believe this allegation, or if they overhastily did so would pay me back in my own coin. Hence my maxim, as soon as it should be made a universal law, would necessarily destroy itself. . . .

I do not indeed as yet *discern* on what this respect is based (this the philosopher may inquire), but at least I understand this, that it is an estimation of the worth which far outweighs all worth of what is recommended by inclination, and that the necessity of acting from *pure* respect for the practical law is what constitutes duty, to which every other motive must give place, because it is the condition of a will being good *in itself,* and the worth of such a will is above everything. . . .

Everything in nature works according to laws. Rational beings alone have the faculty of acting according *to the conception* of laws, that is according to principles, *i.e.* have a *will.* Since the deduction of actions from principles requires *reason,* the will is nothing but practical reason. . . .

The conception of an objective principle, in so far as it is obligatory for a will, is called a command (of reason), and the formula of the command is called an Imperative.

All imperatives are expressed by the word *ought* [or *shall*], and thereby indicate the relation of an objective law of reason to a will, which from its subjective constitution is not necessarily determined by it (an obligation). They say that something would be good to do or to forbear, but they say it to a will which does not always do a thing because it is conceived to be good to do it. . . .

Now all *imperatives* command either *hypothetically* or *categorically*. The former represent the practical necessity of a possible action as means to something else that is willed (or at least which one might possibly will). The categorical imperative would be that which represented an action as necessary of itself without reference to another end, *i.e.* as objectively necessary.

Since every practical law represents a possible action as good, and on this account, for a subject who is practically determinable by reason, necessary, all imperatives are formulæ determining an action which is necessary according to the principle of a will good in some respects. If now the action is good only as a means *to something else,* then the Imperative is *hypothetical;* if it is conceived as good *in itself* and consequently as being necessarily the principle of a will which of itself conforms to reason, then it is *Categorical.* . . .

An imperative which commands a certain conduct immediately, without having as its condition any other purpose to be attained by it . . . is Categorical. It concerns not the matter of the action, or its intended result, but its form and the principle of which it is itself a result; and what is essentially good in it consists in the mental disposition, let the consequence be what it may. This Imperative may be called that of Morality. . . .

When I conceive a hypothetical imperative in general I do not know beforehand what it will contain until I am given the condition. But when I conceive a Categorical Imperative I know at once what it contains. For as the imperative contains besides the law only the necessity that the maxims* shall conform to this law, while the law contains

no conditions restricting it, there remains nothing but the general statement that the maxim of the action should conform to a universal law, and it is this conformity alone that the imperative properly represents as necessary.

There is therefore but one Categorical Imperative, namely this: *Act only on that maxim whereby thou canst at the same time will that it should become a universal law.*

Now if all imperatives of duty can be deduced from this one imperative as from their principle, then, although it should remain undecided whether what is called duty is not merely a vain notion, yet at least we shall be able to show what we understand by it and what this notion means.

Since the universality of the law according to which effects are produced constitutes what is properly called *nature* in the most general sense (as to form), that is, the existence of things so far as it is determined by general laws, the Imperative of duty may be expressed thus: *Act as if the maxim of thy action were to become by thy will a Universal Law of Nature.* . . .

A man reduced to despair by a series of misfortunes feels wearied of life, but is still so far in possession of his reason that he can ask himself whether it would not be contrary to his duty to himself to take his own life. Now he inquires whether the maxim of his action could become a universal law of nature. His maxim is: From self-love I adopt it as a principle to shorten my life when its longer duration is likely to bring more evil than satisfaction. It is asked then simply whether this principle founded on self-love can become a universal law of nature. Now we see at once that a system of nature of which it should be a law to destroy life by means of the very feeling whose special nature it is to impel to the improvement of life would contradict itself, and therefore could not exist as a system of nature; hence that maxim cannot possibly exist as a universal law of nature, and consequently would be wholly inconsistent with the supreme principle of all duty. . . .

We have thus established at least this much, that if duty is a conception which is to have any import and real legislative authority for our actions, it can

---

*A *maxim* is a subjective principle of action, and must be distinguished from the *objective principle,* namely, practical law. The former contains the practical rule set by reason according to the conditions of the subject (often its ignorance or its inclinations), so that it is the principle on which the subject *acts;* but the law is the objective principle valid for every rational being, and is the principle on which it *ought to act,* that is, an imperative.

only be expressed in Categorical, and not at all in hypothetical imperatives. We have also, which is of great importance, exhibited clearly and definitely for every practical application the content of the Categorical Imperative, which must contain the principle of all duty if there is such a thing at all. . . .

If then there is a supreme practical principle or, in respect of the human will, a Categorical Imperative, it must be one which, being drawn from the conception of that which is necessarily an end for every one because it is *an end in itself*, constitutes an *objective* principle of will, and can therefore serve as a universal practical law. The foundation of this principle is: *rational nature exists as an end in itself.* Man necessarily conceives his own existence as being so: so far then this is a *subjective* principle of human actions. But every other rational being regards its existence similarly, just on the same rational principle that holds for me: so that it is at the same time an objective principle, from which as a supreme practical law all laws of the will must be capable of being deduced. Accordingly the practical imperative will be as follows: *So act as to treat humanity, whether in thine own person or in that of any other, in every case as an end withal, never as means only.* We will now inquire whether this can be practically carried out.

To abide by the previous examples:

Firstly, under the head of necessary duty to oneself: He who contemplates suicide should ask himself whether his action can be consistent with the idea of humanity *as an end in itself.* If he destroys himself in order to escape from painful circumstances, he uses a person merely as a *mean* to maintain a tolerable condition up to the end of life. But a man is not a thing, that is to say, something which can be used merely as means, but must in all his actions be always considered as an end in himself. I cannot, therefore, dispose in any way of a man in my own person so as to mutilate him, to damage or kill him. (It belongs to ethics proper to define this principle more precisely so as to avoid all misunderstanding, *e.g.* as to the amputation of the limbs in order to preserve myself; as to exposing my life to danger with a view to preserve it, &c. This question is therefore omitted here.)

Secondly, as regards necessary duties, or those of strict obligation, toward others; he who is thinking of making a lying promise to others will see at once that he would be using another man *merely as a mean,* without the latter containing at the same time the end in himself. For he whom I propose by such a promise to use for my own purposes cannot possibly assent to my mode of acting towards him, and therefore cannot himself contain the end of this action. This violation of the principle of humanity in other men is more obvious if we take in examples of attacks on the freedom and property of others. For then it is clear that he who transgresses the rights of men, intends to use the person of the others merely as means, without considering that as rational beings they ought always to be esteemed also as ends, that is, as beings who must be capable of containing in themselves the end of the very same action.

Discussion Questions

1. Kant formulated his views on suicide long before medical technology was developed that could be used to extend the dying process. What would Kant's position most likely be on physician-assisted suicide? Is physician-assisted suicide always incompatible with the categorical imperative? Support your answers.

2. The categorical imperative requires that we treat persons as ends in themselves and never as means only. Develop a policy on affirmative action for college admissions that is based on the categorical imperative.

3. Can hate speech ever be compatible with the categorical imperative? Why or why not? If not, what is your moral duty, as a person of good will, if you witness or are the victim of hate speech? Support your answers.

4. Although Kant excluded nonhuman animals from the moral community, he was opposed to cruelty to other animals on the grounds that it makes us more likely to be cruel to people. Is enjoying the products of animal agriculture morally acceptable so long as we are not directly involved or do not witness the pain or extinction of other species? Discuss how Kant's definition of personhood and the moral community would influence his position on vegetarianism or environmental issues.

JOHN RAWLS

A Theory of Justice

Harvard philosopher and political theorist John Rawls (1921–2002) was primarily concerned with providing a theoretical framework for formulating social policy. Rawls argued that utilitarian theory is too obscure and simplistic to deal with many of the issues facing modern society. In his book *A Theory of Justice*, he offers an alternative by combining deontology with a social contract approach to social ethics.

According to Rawls, justice as fairness is the most basic requirement of the social contract. This element of justice, he argues, is absent in strict utilitarian theory. Rawls believed that under a "veil of ignorance," people will come up with two principles of justice outlined in the reading. By applying these two principles, we can resolve disputes in social ethics and formulate social policies that are just.

Rawls's theory of justice has been tremendously influential in discussions of public policy in areas such as health care and welfare reform.

Critical Reading Questions

1. What is "the first virtue of social institutions"?
2. What does Rawls mean by a "social contract" and what is its relevance to resolving moral issues?
3. What is the "original position of equality"? Does this position actually exist or has it ever existed in the past?
4. What is the "veil of ignorance" and what is its purpose?
5. What does Rawls mean by "justice as fairness"?
6. What are the two principles of justice that would be chosen in the original position? How are these principles to be applied in resolving social issues?
7. Why does Rawls reject the principle of utility as one that would be chosen in the original position?
8. What are the basic rights, according to Rawls? Does he place more emphasis on liberty rights or on welfare rights?

A Theory of Justice (Cambridge, Mass.: Harvard University Press, 1971). Notes have been omitted.

Justice as Fairness

THE ROLE OF JUSTICE

Justice is the first virtue of social institutions, as truth is of systems of thought. A theory however elegant and economical must be rejected or revised if it is untrue; likewise laws and institutions no matter how efficient and well-arranged must be reformed or abolished if they are unjust. Each person possesses an inviolability founded on justice that even the welfare of society as a whole cannot override. . . .

A society is a more or less self-sufficient association of persons who in their relations to one another recognize certain rules of conduct as binding and who for the most part act in accordance with them. Suppose further that these rules specify a system of cooperation designed to advance the good of those taking part in it. Then, although a society is a cooperative venture for mutual advantage, it is typically marked by a conflict as well as by an identity of interests. There is an identity of interests since social cooperation makes possible a better life for all than any would have if each were to live solely by his own efforts. There is a conflict of interests since persons are not indifferent as to how the greater benefits produced by their collaboration are distributed, for in order to pursue their ends they each prefer a larger to a lesser share. A set of principles is required for choosing among the various social arrangements which determine this division of advantages and for underwriting an agreement on the proper distributive shares. These principles are the principles of social justice: they provide a way of assigning rights and duties in the basic institutions of society and they define the appropriate distribution of the benefits and burdens of social cooperation. . . .

THE MAIN IDEA OF THE THEORY OF JUSTICE

My aim is to present a conception of justice which generalizes and carries to a higher level of abstraction the familiar theory of the social contract as found, say, in Locke, Rousseau, and Kant. In order to do this we are not to think of the original contract as one to enter a particular society or to set up a particular form of government. Rather, the guiding idea is that the principles of justice for the basic structure of society are the object of the original agreement. They are the principles that free and rational persons concerned to further their own interests would accept in an initial position of equality as defining the fundamental terms of their association. These principles are to regulate all further agreements; they specify the kinds of social cooperation that can be entered into and the forms of government that can be established. This way of regarding the principles of justice I shall call justice as fairness.

Thus we are to imagine that those who engage in social cooperation choose together, in one joint act, the principles which are to assign basic rights and duties and to determine the division of social benefits. Men are to decide in advance how they are to regulate their claims against one another and what is to be the foundation charter of their society. . . .

In justice as fairness the original position of equality corresponds to the state of nature in the traditional theory of the social contract. This original position is not, of course, thought of as an actual historical state of affairs, much less as a primitive condition of culture. It is understood as a purely hypothetical situation characterized so as to lead to a certain conception of justice. Among the essential features of this situation is that no one knows his place in society, his class position or social status, nor does any one know his fortune in the distribution of natural assets and abilities, his intelligence, strength, and the like. . . . The principles of justice are chosen behind a veil of ignorance. This ensures that no one is advantaged or disadvantaged in the choice of principles by the outcome of natural chance or the contingency of social circumstances. Since all are similarly situated and no one is able to design principles to favor his particular condition, the principles of justice are the result of a fair agreement or bargain. . . . The original position is, one might say, the appropriate initial status quo, and thus the fundamental agreements reached in it are fair. This explains the propriety of the name "justice as fairness": it conveys the idea that the principles of justice are agreed to in an initial situation that is fair. . . .

In working out the conception of justice as fairness one main task clearly is to determine which principles of justice would be chosen in the original position. To do this we must describe this situation in some detail and formulate with care the problem of choice which it presents. . . . It may be observed, however, that once the principles of justice are thought of as arising from an original agreement in a situation of equality, it is an open question whether the principle of utility would be acknowledged. Offhand it hardly seems likely that persons who view themselves as equals, entitled to press their claims upon one another, would agree to a principle which may require lesser life prospects for some simply for the sake of a greater sum of advantages enjoyed by others. . . .

I shall maintain instead that the persons in the initial situation would choose two rather different principles: the first requires equality in the assignment of basic rights and duties, while the second holds that social and economic inequalities, for example inequalities of wealth and authority, are just only if they result in compensating benefits for everyone, and in particular for the least advantaged members of society. These principles rule out justifying institutions on the grounds that the hardships of some are offset by a greater good in the aggregate. . . .

TWO PRINCIPLES OF JUSTICE

I shall now state in a provisional form the two principles of justice that I believe would be chosen in the original position. . . .

The first statement of the two principles reads as follows.

First: each person is to have an equal right to the most extensive basic liberty compatible with a similar liberty for others.

Second: social and economic inequalities are to be arranged so that they are both (a) reasonably expected to be to everyone's advantage, and (b) attached to positions and offices open to all. . . .

By way of general comment, these principles primarily apply, as I have said, to the basic structure of society. They are to govern the assignment of rights and duties and to regulate the distribution of social and economic advantages. As their formulation suggests, these principles presuppose that the social structure can be divided into two more or less distinct parts, the first principle applying to the one, the second to the other. They distinguish between those aspects of the social system that define and secure the equal liberties of citizenship and those that specify and establish social and economic inequalities. The basic liberties of citizens are, roughly speaking, political liberty (the right to vote and to be eligible for public office) together with freedom of speech and assembly; liberty of conscience and freedom of thought; freedom of the person along with the right to hold (personal) property; and freedom from arbitrary arrest and seizure as defined by the concept of the rule of law. These liberties are all required to be equal by the first principle, since citizens of a just society are to have the same basic rights.

The second principle applies, in the first approximation, to the distribution of income and wealth and to the design of organizations that make use of differences in authority and responsibility, or chains of command. While the distribution of wealth and income need not be equal, it must be to everyone's advantage, and at the same time, positions of authority and offices of command must be accessible to all. One applies the second principle by holding positions open, and then, subject to this constraint, arranges social and economic inequalities so that everyone benefits.

These principles are to be arranged in a serial order with the first principle prior to the second. This ordering means that a departure from the institutions of equal liberty required by the first principle cannot be justified by, or compensated for, by greater social and economic advantages. The distribution of wealth and income, and the hierarchies of authority, must be consistent with both the liberties of equal citizenship and equality of opportunity. . . .

Discussion Questions

1. Is the "veil of ignorance" a useful conceptual device for formulating public policy on issues of social justice? Do you agree with Rawls that people under the veil of ignorance would come up with his two principles of justice? Explain why or why not.
2. How should social benefits, such as a college education, be distributed? Apply Rawls's two principles of justice in developing a public policy on affirmative action in college admissions.
3. Does pornography violate Rawls's first principle of justice? Support your answer.
4. Given that genetic engineering and cloning will probably be an option only for well-off parents, discuss whether it is fair to use public tax money to fund research on cloning and genetic engineering. Support your answer.

 JOHN LOCKE

Two Treatises of Civil Government

British philosopher John Locke (1632–1704) was born into a liberal Puritan family that was heavily involved in political activism. Locke's theory of natural rights emerged primarily as a protest against the idea that the king possessed divine rights. Locke believed that God created the earth as a resource for humans. These natural rights ethics had a profound effect on the founders of the United States, especially Thomas Jefferson.

In the following selection, from *Two Treatises of Civil Government,* Locke defends our right to own property and explains why people in a state of nature come together to form a political society.

Critical Reading Questions

1. How does Locke define political power?
2. What is the state of nature? What rights do humans have in a state of nature?
3. What is the law of nature?
4. Why does Locke argue that civil society is preferable to a state of nature?
5. According to Locke, why do humans have a right to the resources of the earth?
6. How do humans, as individuals, make these resources their property?
7. What are the limits on what we can claim as our property?
8. According to Locke, why do people come together to form a political society?
9. What are the advantages and disadvantages of living in a political society?

OF THE STATE OF NATURE

4. To understand political power aright, and derive it from its original, we must consider what estate all men are naturally in, and that is, a state of perfect freedom to order their actions, and dispose of their possessions and persons as they think fit, within the bounds of the law of Nature, without asking leave or depending upon the will of any other man.

A state also of equality, wherein all the power and jurisdiction is reciprocal, no one having more than another, there being nothing more evident than that creatures of the same species and rank, promiscuously born to all the same advantages of Nature, and the use of the same faculties, should also be equal one amongst another, without subordination or subjection, unless the lord and master of them all should, by any manifest declaration of his will, set one above another, and confer on him by an evident and clear appointment an undoubted right to dominion and sovereignty.

. . .

6. But though this be a state of liberty, yet it is not a state of license; though man in that state have an uncontrollable liberty to dispose of his person or possessions, yet he has not liberty to destroy himself, or so much as any creature in his possession, but where some nobler use than its bare preservation calls for it. The state of nature has a law of nature to govern it, which obliges everyone; and reason, which is that law, teaches all mankind who will but consult it, that, being all equal and independent, no one ought to harm another in his life, health, liberty, or possessions. For men being all the workmanship of one omnipotent and infinitely wise Maker, they are his property, . . .

. . .

15. . . . "for as much as we are not by ourselves sufficient to furnish ourselves with competent store

"Natural Rights," from *Two Treatises of Civil Government* (London: A & J Churchill, 1698). Notes have been omitted. (For the complete text, go to www.constitution.org/jl/2ndtreat.htm.)

of things needful for such a life as our Nature doth desire, a life fit for the dignity of man, therefore to supply those defects and imperfections which are in us, as living single and solely by ourselves, we are naturally induced to seek communion and fellowship with others; this was the cause of men uniting themselves as first in politic societies." But I, moreover, affirm that all men are naturally in that state, and remain so till, by their own consents, they make themselves members of some politic society, . . .

OF PROPERTY

. . .

25. God, who hath given the world to men in common, hath also given them reason to make use of it to the best advantage of life and convenience. The earth and all that is therein is given to men for the support and comfort of their being. And though all the fruits it naturally produces, and beasts it feeds, belong to mankind in common, as they are produced by the spontaneous hand of Nature, and nobody has originally a private dominion exclusive of the rest of mankind in any of them, as they are thus in their natural state, yet being given for the use of men, there must of necessity be a means to appropriate them some way or other before they can be of any use, or at all beneficial, to any particular men. . . .

26. Though the earth and all inferior creatures be common to all men, yet every man has a "property" in his own "person." This nobody has any right to but himself. The "labour" of his body and the "work" of his hands, we may say, are properly his. Whatsoever, then, he removes out of the state that Nature hath provided and left it in, he hath mixed his labour with it, and joined to it something that is his own, and thereby makes it his property. It being by him removed from the common state Nature placed it in, it hath by this labour something annexed to it that excludes the common right of other men. For this "labour" being the unquestionable property of the labourer, no man

but he can have a right to what that is once joined to, at least where there is enough, and as good left in common for others.

OF THE BEGINNING OF POLITICAL SOCIETIES

95. Men being, as has been said, by nature all free, equal, and independent, no one can be put out of this estate and subjected to the political power of another without his own consent, which is done by agreeing with other men, to join and unite into a community for their comfortable, safe, and peaceable living, one amongst another, in a secure enjoyment of their properties, and a greater security against any that are not of it. This any number of men may do, because it injures not the freedom of the rest; they are left, as they were, in the liberty of the state of Nature. When any number of men have so consented to make one community or government, they are thereby presently incorporated, and make one body politic, wherein the majority have a right to act and conclude the rest.

96. For, when any number of men have, by the consent of every individual, made a community, they have thereby made that community one body, with a power to act as one body, which is only by the will and determination of the majority.

. . .

99. Whosoever, therefore, out of a state of Nature unite into a community, must be understood to give up all the power necessary to the ends for which they unite into society to the majority of the community, unless they expressly agreed in any number greater than the majority. And this is done by barely agreeing to unite into one political society, which is all the compact that is, or needs be, between the individuals that enter into or make up a commonwealth. And thus, that which begins and actually constitutes any political society is nothing but the consent of any number of free-men capable of majority, to unite and incorporate into such a society. And this is that, and that only, which did or could give beginning to any lawful government in the world. . . .

Discussion Questions

1. Do you agree with Locke that people can exist outside of civil society in a "state of nature"? Support your answer.
2. Discuss Locke's claim that there is a law of nature that gives individuals living in a state of nature the right to punish transgressors. Does the lack of an international government mean that nations are living in a state of nature? Discuss whether this justifies the use of war against nations that violate our property rights.
3. Natural rights ethicists claim that human equality is self-evident. What does this mean? What are the implications of this belief for public policy on gay rights?
4. Ralph Waldo Emerson once said that "people say law but they mean wealth." In the United States 90 percent of the resources are owned by 10 percent of the people. Compare and contrast the capitalist system of property ownership, as supported by Ayn Rand, with Locke's philosophy. Use specific examples to illustrate your answer.

NEL NODDINGS

Caring: A Feminine Approach to Ethics and Moral Education

American philosopher Nel Noddings is a professor at Stanford University. Care ethics, which expands on Carol Gilligan's studies of women's moral reasoning, is currently one of the most influential feminist theories in moral philosophy. Unlike the analytical approach of most earlier philosophers, care ethics stresses the contextual aspect of morality. We are at our moral best, according to Noddings, when we are caring and being cared for in relationships.

In the selection from her book *Caring: A Feminine Approach to Ethics and Moral Education,* Noddings illustrates the role of feelings or sentiment in morality. It is care, not an abstract sense of duty, that creates moral obligations.

Although Noddings does not altogether reject the use of principled moral reasoning, she believes that as an ideal, care offers us guidance in actual situations and relationships that an abstract ethics of duty cannot provide.

Critical Reading Questions

1. What does Noddings mean by the term *care*?
2. How do we demonstrate caring for others?
3. What are the limitations on caring? Do we, for example, have a moral obligation to care for people we do not know or people we do not like?
4. What is the difference between natural caring and ethical caring?
5. What, according to Noddings, is the "ethical ideal" or "vision of the best self"?
6. Why does Noddings consider the ethical ideal of caring preferable to moral principles as a guide to moral actions?
7. Why does Noddings reject the principle of universality and the principle of universal love?
8. On what grounds does Noddings claim that we do not have moral obligations to other animals?
9. What does Noddings mean when she says that an ethic of care is a "feminine," as opposed to a "masculine," ethic?

Caring: A Feminine Approach to Ethics and Moral Education (Berkeley: University of California Press, 1984).

From Natural to Ethical Caring

David Hume long ago contended that morality is founded upon and rooted in feeling—that the "final sentence" on matters of morality, "that which renders morality an active virtue"—"... this final sentence depends on some internal sense or feeling, which nature has made universal in the whole species. For what else can have an influence of this nature?"

What is the nature of this feeling that is "universal in the whole species"? I want to suggest that morality as an "active virtue" requires two feelings and not just one. The first is the sentiment of natural caring. There can be no ethical sentiment without the initial, enabling sentiment. In situations where we act on behalf of the other because we want to do so, we are acting in accord with natural caring. A mother's caretaking efforts in behalf of her child are not usually considered ethical but natural. Even maternal animals take care of their offspring, and we do not credit them with ethical behavior. . . .

Recognizing that ethical caring requires an effort that is not needed in natural caring does not commit us to a position that elevates ethical caring over natural caring. Kant has identified the ethical with that which is done out of duty and not out of love, and that distinction in itself seems right. But an ethic built on caring strives to maintain the caring attitude and is thus dependent upon, and not superior to, natural caring. The source of ethical behavior is, then, in twin sentiments—one that feels directly for the other and one that feels for and with that best self, who may accept and sustain the initial feeling rather than reject it.

We shall discuss the ethical ideal, that vision of best self, in some depth. When we commit ourselves to obey the "I must" even at its weakest and most fleeting, we are under the guidance of this ideal. It is not just any picture. Rather, it is our best picture of ourselves caring and being cared for. . . .

I feel the moral "I must" when I recognize that my response will either enhance or diminish my ethical ideal. It will serve either to increase or decrease the likelihood of genuine caring. My response affects me as one-caring. In a given situation with someone I am not fond of, I may be able to find all sorts of reasons why I should not respond to his need. I may be too busy. He may be undiscerning. The matter may be, on objective analysis, unimportant. But, before I decide, I must turn away from this analytic chain of thought and back to the concrete situation. Here is this person with this perceived need to which is attached this importance. I must put justification aside temporarily. Shall I respond? How do I feel as a duality about the "I" who will not respond?

I am obliged, then, to accept the initial "I must" when it occurs and even to fetch it out of recalcitrant slumber when it fails to awake spontaneously. The source of my obligation is the value I place on the relatedness of caring. This value itself arises as a product of actual caring and being cared-for and my reflection on the goodness of these concrete caring situations. . . .

Let me say here, however, why it seems preferable to place an ethical ideal above principle as a guide to moral action. It has been traditional in moral philosophy to insist that moral principles must be, by their very nature as moral principles, universifiable. If I am obligated to do X under certain conditions, then under sufficiently similar conditions you also are obligated to do X. But the principle of universifiability seems to depend, as Nietzsche pointed out, on a concept of "sameness." In order to accept the principle, we should have to establish that human predicaments exhibit sufficient sameness, and this we cannot do without abstracting away from concrete situations those qualities that seem to reveal the sameness. In doing this, we often lose the very qualities or factors that gave rise to the moral question in the situation. That condition which makes the situation different and thereby induces genuine moral puzzlement cannot be satisfied by the application of principles developed in situations of sameness.

This does not mean that we cannot receive any guidance from an attempt to discover principles that seem to be universifiable. We can, under this sort of plan, arrive at the doctrine of "prima facie duty" described by W. D. Ross. Ross himself, however, admits that this doctrine yields no real guidance for moral conduct in concrete situations. It guides us in abstract moral thinking; it tells us, theoretically, what to do, "all other things being equal." But other things are rarely if ever equal. . . .

Our obligation is limited and delimited by relation. We are never free, in the human domain, to abandon our preparedness to care; but, practically, if we are meeting those in our inner circles adequately as ones caring and receiving those linked to our inner circles by formal chains of relation, we shall limit the calls upon our obligation quite naturally. We are not obliged to summon the "I must" if there is no possibility of completion in the other. I am not obliged to care for starving children in Africa, because there is no way for this caring to be completed in the other unless I abandon the caring to which I am obligated. I may still choose to do something in the direction of caring, but I am not obliged to do so. When we discuss our obligation to animals, we shall see that this is even more sharply limited by relation. We cannot refuse obligation in human affairs by merely refusing to enter relation; we are, by virtue of our mutual humanity, already and perpetually in potential relation. Instead, we limit our obligation by examining the possibility of completion. In connection with animals, however, we may find it possible to refuse relation itself on the grounds of a species-specific impossibility of any form of reciprocity in caring. . . .

One under the guidance of an ethic of caring is tempted to retreat to a manageable world. Her public life is limited by her insistence upon meeting the other as one-caring. So long as this is possible, she may reach outward and enlarge her circles of caring. When this reaching out destroys or drastically reduces her actual caring, she retreats and renews her contact with those who address her. If the retreat becomes a flight, an avoidance of the call to care, her ethical ideal is diminished. Similarly, if the retreat is away from human beings and toward other objects of caring—ideas, animals, humanity-at-large, God—her ethical ideal is virtually shattered. This is not a judgment, for we can understand and sympathize with one who makes such a choice. It is more in the nature of a perception: we see clearly what has been lost in the choice.

Our ethic of caring—which we might have called a "feminine ethic"—begins to look a bit mean in contrast to the masculine ethics of universal love or universal justice. But universal love is illusion. Under the illusion, some young people retreat to the church to worship that which they cannot actualize; some write lovely poetry extolling universal love; and some, in terrible disillusion, kill to establish the very principles which should have entreated them not to kill. Thus are lost both principles and persons.

Discussion Questions

1. Compare and contrast the moral philosophies of Nel Noddings and Immanuel Kant. What is the source and role of duty or moral obligation in care ethics?
2. Does care require reciprocity in a relationship as Noddings claims? Discuss the implications of her ethics for issues such as abortion and euthanasia. Does a pregnant woman have a moral obligation to her fetus? Is euthanasia morally permissible for members of a family who are unable to reciprocate caring?
3. Discuss how a care ethicist might approach issues in environmental ethics such as global warming and preservation of wildlife. Is care ethics adequate for dealing with these issues? Support your answer.
4. Pornography takes women out of relationships and objectifies them. While a care ethicist might be morally opposed to pornography because of this, discuss how this would translate into a public policy regarding pornography in the media.

5. Some judges hear victims' statements before sentencing. To what extent should a sentence depend on the willingness of the family and friends of the victim to express care for the guilty party? Is capital punishment permissible if no one wants to be in a caring relationship with the guilty party? Is it fair that one's moral worth as a person is judged by others' willingness to care? Support your answers.

 CONFUCIUS

The Analects

Confucius (551–479 B.C.E.) lived during the period of the "hundred philosophers" (the late sixth to the early third centuries B.C.E.), which paralleled the golden age in Greek philosophy. Confucius traveled for many years with his pupils. Much of the writing in *The Analects* is directed toward the rulers, since it is the rulers who have the most power to advance virtue in society and individuals.

As a teacher, Confucius radically changed Chinese philosophy by focusing on our duties to humanity rather than on spiritual concerns. Like Aristotle, Confucius believed that humans were happiest and found it easiest to be virtuous when they were living in a just and well-ordered society.

Critical Reading Questions

1. What does Confucius mean by "benevolence"?
2. Does Confucius think that virtue or benevolence is relative or the same for all people?
3. Which does Confucius value more—personal freedom or social harmony?
4. What duties do children have toward their parents?
5. What does Confucius mean when he says that the "gentleman is not invariably for or against anything. He is on the side of what is moral"?
6. Why is trust the most important social virtue?
7. What is the root of injustice?
8. What does Confucius say about punishment?
9. Why do we have crime? What is the role of government and social policy in promoting virtuous behavior?

The Analects, trans. by D. C. Lau (London: Penguin Classics, 1979). Notes have been omitted.

Book I

. . .

3. The Master said, "It is rare, indeed, for a man with cunning words and an ingratiating face to be benevolent."

4. Tseng Tzu said, "Every day I examine myself on three counts. In what I have undertaken on another's behalf, have I failed to do my best? In my dealings with my friends have I failed to be trustworthy in what I say? Have I passed on to others anything that I have not tried out myself?" . . .

6. The Master said, "A young man should be a good son at home and an obedient young man abroad, sparing of speech but trustworthy in what he says, and should love the multitude at large but cultivate the friendship of his fellow men. If he has any energy to spare from such action, let him devote it to making himself cultivated." . . .

8. The Master said, "A gentleman who lacks gravity does not inspire awe. A gentleman who studies is unlikely to be inflexible.

"Make it your guiding principle to do your best for others and to be trustworthy in what you say. Do not accept as a friend anyone who is not as good as you.

"When you make a mistake, do not be afraid of mending your ways." . . .

Book IV

1. The Master said, "Of neighbourhoods benevolence is the most beautiful. How can the man be considered wise who, when he has the choice, does not settle in benevolence?" . . .

4. The Master said, "If a man sets his heart on benevolence, he will be free from evil."

5. The Master said, . . . "If the gentleman forsakes benevolence, in what way can he make a name for himself? The gentleman never deserts benevolence, not even for as long as it takes to eat a meal. If he hurries and stumbles one may be sure that it is in benevolence that he does so."

6. The Master said, "I have never met a man who finds benevolence attractive or a man who finds unbenevolence repulsive. A man who finds benevolence attractive cannot be surpassed. A man who finds unbenevolence repulsive can, perhaps, be counted as benevolent, for he would not allow what is not benevolent to contaminate his person. . . .

7. The Master said, "In his errors a man is true to type. Observe the errors and you will know the man." . . .

10. The Master said, "In his dealings with the world the gentleman is not invariably for or against anything. He is on the side of what is moral." . . .

12. The Master said, "If one is guided by profit in one's actions, one will incur much ill will." . . .

13. The Master said, "The gentleman understands what is moral. The small man understands what is profitable." . . .

15. The Master said, "In serving your father and mother you ought to dissuade them from doing wrong in the gentlest way. If you see your advice being ignored, you should not become disobedient but remain reverent. You should not complain even if in so doing you wear yourself out." . . .

Book XII

. . .

2. Chung-kung asked about benevolence. The Master said, "When abroad behave as though you were receiving an important guest. When employing the services of the common people behave as though you were officiating at an important sacrifice. Do not impose on others what you yourself do not desire. In this way you will be free from ill will whether in a state or in a noble family." . . .

10. Tzu-chang asked about the exaltation of virtue and the recognition of misguided judgement. The Master said, "Make it your guiding principle to do your best for others and to be trustworthy in what you say, and move yourself to where rightness is, then you will be exalting virtue. When you love a man you want him to live and when you hate him you want him to die. . . .

16. The Master said, "The gentleman helps others to realize what is good in them; he does not help them to realize what is bad in them. The small man does the opposite."

17. Chi K'ang Tzu asked Confucius about government. Confucius answered, "To govern (*cheng*) is to correct (*cheng*). If you set an example by being correct, who would dare to remain incorrect?" . . .

19. Chi K'ang Tzu asked Confucius about government, saying, "What would you think if, in order to move closer to those who possess the Way, I were to kill those who do not follow the Way?"

Confucius answered, "In administering your government, what need is there for you to kill? Just desire the good yourself and the common people will be good. The virtue of the gentleman is like wind; the virtue of the small man is like grass. Let the wind blow over the grass and it is sure to bend." . . .

21. Fan Ch'ih was in attendance during an outing to the Rain Altar. He said, "May I ask about the exaltation of virtue, the reformation of the depraved and the recognition of misguided judgement?" The Master said, "What a splendid question! To put service before the reward you get for it, is that not exaltation of virtue? To attack evil as evil and not as evil of a particular man, is that not the way to reform the depraved? To let a sudden fit of anger make you forget the safety of your own person or even that of your parents, is that not misguided judgement?"

22. Fan Ch'ih asked about benevolence. The Master said, "Love your fellow men."

He asked about wisdom. The Master said, "Know your fellow men." Fan Ch'ih failed to grasp his meaning. The Master said, "Raise the straight and set them over the crooked. This can make the crooked straight." . . .

23. Tzu-kung asked about how friends should be treated. The Master said, "Advise them to the best of your ability and guide them properly, but stop when there is no hope of success. Do not ask to be snubbed." . . .

Book XIII

11. The Master said, "How true is the saying that after a state has been ruled for a hundred years by good men it is possible to get the better of cruelty and to do away with killing." . . .

13. The Master said, "If a man manages to make himself correct, what difficulty will there be for him to take part in government? If he cannot make himself correct, what business has he with making others correct?" . . .

Discussion Questions

1. In light of what Confucius says about the relative importance of personal freedom and social harmony, discuss concerns he would have regarding the regulation of hate speech and pornography. Compare and contrast his approach with that of John Stuart Mill.
2. Discuss whether filial duty requires us to carry out a parent's or grandparent's wish for assistance in committing suicide. If so, is the duty to carry out these types of requests absolute or prima facie? Support your answer.

3. Compare the Confucian principle of reciprocity to Kant's categorical imperative.
4. Why is Confucius opposed to capital punishment? Discuss alternatives to capital punishment that Confucius might propose.

THICH NHAT HANH

The Five Mindfulness Trainings

Thich Nhat Hanh is a Vietnamese Buddhist monk, poet, and peace worker. In the following excerpt from his book *The Path of Emancipation,* Thich Nhat Hanh presents a summary of each of the five mindfulness trainings, which are fundamental aspirations for those seeking to live the mindful and moral life.

Critical Reading Questions

1. What do the five mindfulness trainings remind us to be aware of in living our lives?
2. What particular behaviors and attitudes does each of the five mindfulness trainings address?

FIRST MINDFULNESS TRAINING

Aware of the suffering caused by the destruction of life, I am committed to cultivating compassion and learning ways to protect the lives of people, animals, plants, and minerals. I am determined not to kill, not to let others kill, and not to condone any act of killing in the world, in my thinking, and in my way of life.

SECOND MINDFULNESS TRAINING

Aware of the suffering caused by exploitation, social injustice, stealing, and oppression, I am committed to cultivating loving kindness and

"The Five Mindfulness Trainings." Reprinted from *The Path of Emancipation: Talks from a 21 Day Mindfulness Retreat* (2000, pp. 277–279) by Thich Nhat Hanh with permission of Parallax Press, Berkeley, California. www.parallax.org

learning ways to work for the well-being of people, animals, plants, and minerals. I will practice generosity by sharing my time, energy, and material resources with those who are in real need. I am determined not to steal and not to possess anything that should belong to others. I will respect the property of others, but I will prevent others from profiting from human suffering or the suffering of other species on Earth.

THIRD MINDFULNESS TRAINING

Aware of the suffering caused by sexual misconduct, I am committed to cultivating responsibility and learning ways to protect the safety and integrity of individuals, couples, families, and society. I am determined not to engage in sexual relations without love and a long-term commitment. To preserve the happiness of myself and others, I am determined to respect my commitments and the commitments of others. I will do everything in my power to protect children from sexual abuse and to prevent couples and families from being broken by sexual misconduct.

FOURTH MINDFULNESS TRAINING

Aware of the suffering caused by unmindful speech and the inability to listen to others, I am committed to cultivating loving speech and deep listening in order to bring joy and happiness to others and relieve others of their suffering. Knowing that words can create happiness or suffering, I am determined to speak truthfully, with words that inspire self-confidence, joy, and hope. I will not spread news that I do not know to be certain and will not criticize or condemn things of which I am not sure. I will refrain from uttering words that can cause division or discord, or that can cause the family or the community to break. I am determined to make all efforts to reconcile and resolve all conflicts, however small.

FIFTH MINDFULNESS TRAINING

Aware of the suffering caused by unmindful consumption, I am committed to cultivating good health, both physical and mental, for myself, my family, and my society by practicing mindful eating, drinking, and consuming. I will ingest only items that preserve peace, well-being, and joy in my body, in my consciousness, and in the collective body and consciousness of my family and society. I am determined not to use alcohol or any other intoxicant or to ingest foods or other items that contain toxins, such as certain TV programs, magazines, books, films, and conversations. I am aware that to damage my body or my consciousness with these poisons is to betray my ancestors, my parents, my society, and future generations. I will work to transform violence, fear, anger, and confusion in myself and in society by practicing a diet for myself and for society. I understand that a proper diet is crucial for self-transformation and for the transformation of society.

Discussion Questions

1. What does Thich Nhat Hanh mean by "mindfulness"? Relate the concept of mindfulness to that of living the virtuous life. Choose one of the five trainings and discuss it in light of your own moral values, conduct, and aspirations.
2. To what extent is your life based on mindfulness? How might the five mindfulness trainings be applied to your relationships with your family, friends, faculty, and other students? Be specific.
3. Are you ingesting "toxins" in your life? If so, what are some of these toxins? Discuss how these toxins affect your outlook on life, your feelings about yourself, and your relations with others.
4. Are the five mindfulness trainings relevant to the issues facing us today, such as abortion, global warming, and war? Using the relevant mindfulness trainings, come up with a plan or guidelines for addressing one of these issues on either a personal or a national level.
5. Discuss the five mindfulness trainings in light of Kant's categorical imperative, Bentham's utilitarian principle, and Noddings's care ethics.

Abortion

There is probably no more controversial issue in bioethics today, or one that touches so many lives, as abortion. Prior to the early 1960s, however, there was little public debate over the morality of abortion or support for reform of the restrictive abortion laws that had been on the books in the United States since the turn of the century.

In 1962 Sherri Finkbine, the star of a popular Arizona children's show and mother of four, discovered that the drug thalidomide, which she had taken early in her pregnancy to help her sleep, could cause birth defects such as missing limbs or seal-like flippers, paralysis, and malformed internal organs. After much tortured soul-searching, the Finkbines decided that the best course of action for them was abortion.

Shortly before the scheduled day for her abortion, Sherri Finkbine decided to go public in order to warn other women about the dangers of thalidomide. As a result of the publicity, the hospital, fearful of legal prosecution, withdrew its consent to perform the abortion. Sherri Finkbine eventually obtained an abortion in Sweden. The fetus was severely deformed. Sherri Finkbine's tragic ordeal helped galvanize public support for relaxing laws regulating therapeutic abortions.

BACKGROUND

Abortion involves the intentional termination of a pregnancy resulting in the death of the fetus. Abortion was legalized in the United States in January 1973 by the U.S. Supreme Court *Roe v. Wade* ruling. Between 1973, when 760,000 abortions were performed, and 1980, the national abortion rate increased rapidly every year. It continued to increase at a slower rate between 1980 and 1990. The abortion rate has been steadily decreasing since 1990, when 1.6 million abortions were reported, to 1.2 million abortions in 2005, the lowest level since 1976.[1] The decline is attributed in part to better contraception use among teenagers and to decreasing public support of abortion, as well as to advances in prenatal technology, such as real-time ultrasound, that allow us to visualize the fetus. Nevertheless, the abortion rate in the United States is still higher than that in most other industrialized nations.

In the United States today, about 20 percent of pregnancies are ended by abortion. Of these, 61 percent are performed at less than eight weeks of gestation and 88 percent at less than thirteen weeks.[2] Rates are highest among black women. The primary reasons women seek abortions are that having a child would interfere with their education, work, or ability to care for dependents and that they could not afford to have a baby now.[3] Three percent of abortions are performed because of the mother's health problems, 1 percent because of rape and incest, and another 1 percent because of fetal abnormalities.[4]

According to the World Health Organization, approximately 42 million abortions were performed worldwide in 2003. China, the United States, Japan, and Russia have the highest number of abortions.[5] Abortion rates have been dropping globally, with the largest declines being in Eastern Europe and central Asia. The abortion rate in China, which accounted for one-third of the world's abortions in 1996, has declined more than 20 percent since then.[6] Poverty seems to be one of the factors most closely associated with abortion, in the United States as well as worldwide.

THE HISTORY OF ABORTION IN THE UNITED STATES

Abortion was not uncommon in America during the colonial period up until the late 1800s. It was not the abortion itself that was usually condemned but the violation of other social taboos, such as sexual relations outside of marriage, that led to the abortion.[7] Many middle- and upper-class women also used abortion as a means of birth control.

During the early 1820s, physicians began to take an interest in the legal regulation of abortion.[8] In 1821, Connecticut passed the country's first antiabortion law. Early nineteenth-century antiabortion laws, for the most part, applied only to women "quick with child." It was generally believed at this time that the unborn child did not come to life until "quickening"—the moment, generally between sixteen and eighteen weeks, when the pregnant woman first feels the movement of her fetus. Despite laws against abortion, folk remedies and patented medicines continued to be widely available to women.

In the mid-nineteenth century, the newly founded American Medical Association (AMA) spearheaded a movement to outlaw abortion. In an 1859 resolution, the AMA condemned abortion as an "unwarranted destruction of human life," calling upon state legislators to pass or toughen their existing antiabortion laws.[9]

Although many people blamed the prevalence of abortion on feminist ideas, the early feminists disapproved of abortion, which they considered to be "a revolting outrage against . . . our common humanity" and a form of infanticide.[10] Unlike the physicians, however, the feminists did not think that outlawing abortion without getting to the root cause of abortion—the oppression of women—would have the desired effect. Instead they wanted the *need* for abortion to be eliminated. "We want prevention, not merely punishment," Susan B. Anthony wrote in 1869. "We must reach the root of the evil, and destroy it."[11] Elizabeth Cady Stanton also regarded abortion as just one more result of degradation of women.[12] Serrin Foster, in "Refuse to Choose: Women Deserve Better Than Abortion," presents the pro-life feminists' argument that abortion is immoral except to save the life of the mother.

By 1900 every state had laws prohibiting or restricting abortion; all but six included a "therapeutic exception" in their abortion laws. These laws remained virtually unchanged until the 1960s.

Several events during the 1960s led to an increasing dissatisfaction with the restrictive abortion laws. These included an increase in the number of women in the workforce, a desire for smaller families, increased publicity about the dangers of illegal abortion, improvements in the safety of surgical abortion, and a series of front-page stories chronicling the desperate circumstances of women such as Sherri Finkbine who were denied legal therapeutic abortions. The thalidomide tragedy was closely followed by a German measles epidemic in the United States. Many pregnant women who came down with German measles were unable to obtain legal abortions in the United States. As a result of this outbreak, 15,000 babies were born with birth defects—including blindness, mental retardation, and heart problems—between 1963 and 1966.

Fueled by the publicity generated by these tragedies, the push for legal reform came primarily from the medical and legal professions. Although most people supported more liberal laws regarding the regulation of therapeutic abortions, there was little public support in the late 1960s for nontherapeutic abortions or "abortion on demand"—what later became known as the **pro-choice** position.[13]

In 1969 Planned Parenthood, which had historically been opposed to abortion, reversed its position and came out in support of repealing all antiabortion laws. The following year the AMA voted to support a physician's right to perform abortions if the woman's social and economic circumstances would make it difficult for her to have a baby. These changes, together with the first legal acknowledgment of a constitutional "right to privacy" in the 1965 Supreme Court *Griswold v. Connecticut* case, provided lawyers with the grist they needed to challenge the constitutionality of existing antiabortion laws. Between 1967 and 1970, twelve states, including California, Hawaii, New York, Alaska, and Washington, repealed their restrictive abortion laws.

THE U.S. SUPREME COURT *ROE V. WADE* DECISION

In January 1973 the Supreme Court in *Roe v. Wade* ruled that the Texas antiabortion law violated a woman's fundamental constitutional right to privacy as implied in the Fourteenth Amendment. It also ruled that the fetus was not a person according to the Fourteenth Amendment. The effect of this ruling was to legalize abortion, at least prior to viability, throughout the United States. **Viability** is defined as "the capacity to survive disconnection from the placenta."[14] After viability, set at twenty-eight weeks, the state has a legitimate interest in "potential life" and can pass laws to regulate abortion. Selections from the *Roe v. Wade* majority ruling can be found on pages 76–77.

Rather than settling the abortion question, *Roe v. Wade* has left Americans deeply divided. The challenge to *Roe v. Wade* comes not only from the **pro-life** movement but also from pro-choice groups who would like to see all restrictions on abortion removed.

ROE V. WADE: EXCERPTS FROM THE MAJORITY OPINION

[Justice Blackmun delivered the opinion of the Court]

It is . . . apparent that at common law, at the time of the adoption of our Constitution, and throughout the major portion of the nineteenth century, abortion was viewed with less disfavor than under most American statutes currently in effect. Phrasing it another way, a woman enjoyed a substantially broader right to terminate a pregnancy than she does in most states today. . . .

Three reasons have been advanced to explain historically the enactment of criminal abortion laws in the nineteenth century and to justify their continued existence.

[First] It has been argued occasionally that these laws were the product of a Victorian special concern to discourage illicit sexual conduct. . . .

A second reason is concerned with abortion as a medical procedure. When most criminal abortion laws were first enacted, the procedure was a hazardous one for the woman. . . . Modern medical techniques have altered this situation. . . .

The third reason is the state's interest—some phrase it in terms of duty—in protecting prenatal life. Some of the argument for this justification rests on the theory that a new human life is present from the moment of conception. . . . Only when the life of the pregnant mother herself is at stake, balanced against the life she carries within her, should the interest of the embryo or fetus not prevail. Logically, of course, a legitimate state interest in this area need not stand or fall on acceptance of the belief that life begins at conception or at some other point prior to live birth. In assessing the state's interest, recognition may be given to the less rigid claim that as long as at least *potential* life is involved, the state may assert interests beyond the protection of the pregnant woman alone. . . .

The Constitution does not explicitly mention any right of privacy. . . . [Earlier Supreme Court] decisions make it clear that only personal rights that can be deemed "fundamental" or "implicit in the concept of ordered liberty" . . . are included in this guarantee of personal privacy. They also make it clear that the right has some extension to activities relating to marriage . . . [and] procreation. . . .

We therefore conclude that the right of personal privacy includes the abortion decision, but that this right is not unqualified and must be considered against important state interests in regulation.

. . . [N]o case could be cited that holds that a fetus is a person within the meaning of the Fourteenth Amendment. . . . All this, together with our observation, *supra,* that throughout the majority portion of the nineteenth century prevailing legal abortion practices were far freer than they are today, persuades us that the word "person," as used in the Fourteenth Amendment, does not include the unborn. . . .

There has always been strong support for the view that life does not begin until live birth. . . . Physicians and their scientific colleagues have . . . tended to focus either upon conception or upon live birth or upon the interim point at which the fetus becomes "viable," that is, potentially able to live outside the mother's womb, albeit with artificial aid. Viability is usually placed at about seven months (28 weeks) but may occur earlier, even at 24 weeks. . . .

With respect to the state's important and legitimate interest in the health of the mother, the compelling point, in the light of present medical knowledge, is at approximately the end of the first trimester. This is so because of the now established medical fact . . . that until the end of the first trimester mortality in abortion is less than mortality in normal childbirth. It follows that, from and after this point, a state may regulate the abortion procedure to the extent that the regulation reasonably relates to the preservation and protection of maternal health. Examples of permissible state regulation in this area are requirements as to the qualifications of the person who is to perform the abortion. . . .

With respect to the state's important and legitimate interest in potential life, the "compelling" point is at viability. This is so because the fetus then presumably has the capability of meaningful life outside the mother's womb. State regulation protective of fetal life after viability thus has both logical and biological justifications. If the state is interested in protecting fetal life after viability, it may go so far as to proscribe abortion during that period except when it is necessary to preserve the life or health of the mother. . . .

Fifty-four percent of Americans in a 2007 Gallup poll took a moderate view on abortion, saying it "should be legal only under certain circumstances," while 28 percent maintained that it "should be legal under all circumstances."[15] Support for abortion is strongest when the woman's life or physical health is endangered.

There is less acceptance of abortion among young people today. According to the 2007 Freshman Survey, support among college students for legalized abortion has declined since 1990. In 2007, 57 percent of freshmen supported legalized abortion under some or all circumstances, compared to 64.9 percent of freshmen in 1990. In line with trends found in the general population, female college students and African American students are less supportive of legalized abortion.[16]

The rise in violence against abortion clinics and abortion providers and the reluctance of younger doctors to perform abortions have contributed to a decline in the number of facilities providing abortions. The number of providers in 2000 was 37 percent lower than in 1982, the all-time high. The number of hospitals that perform abortions has also declined.[17]

Since 1973 most states have passed legislation that places restrictions on abortion. These restrictions include parental and spousal notification requirements, mandatory waiting periods, mandatory counseling, and bans on federal funding for abortions. Several bills for a constitutional amendment that would overturn *Roe v. Wade* have been introduced, including the Human Life Amendment, which would extend "personhood" or legal protection to "all human beings."

In the 1992 *Planned Parenthood v. Casey* case, the U.S. Supreme Court replaced the trimester framework used in *Roe v. Wade* with a floating viability line. Since modern technology keeps pushing back the date of viability, this ruling has the potential of placing further restrictions on a woman's opportunity to obtain an abortion. Indeed, since the passing of *Roe v. Wade,* the age of viability has been pushed back a month to 23–24 weeks and may occur as early as 20–21 weeks.

In the 2000 *Stenberg v. Carhart* case, the U.S. Supreme Court struck down a Nebraska law that banned **"partial-birth" abortion.** This decision was reversed by the federal Partial-Birth Abortion Ban Act of 2003. The act was immediately challenged. In 2007, the Supreme Court upheld the ban, stating that it did not violate the Constitution.

In *Hill v. Colorado,* the U.S. Supreme Court ruled in favor of a Colorado statute that restricted protesters from coming within eight feet of women who were within one hundred feet of an entrance to an abortion clinic. Three years previously the Court had upheld a New York law that established buffer zones around abortion clinics in which antiabortion demonstrations are prohibited. These restrictions have been challenged as a violation of the protesters' rights. In 2006 a federal court ruled that a Florida law restricting abortion protesters violates their freedom of speech.

The appointments to the U.S. Supreme Court of John Roberts, who once stated that *Roe v. Wade* was wrongly decided and should be overturned, and of Samuel Alito, who has expressed similar views, may tip the scales against *Roe v. Wade.*

The fact that abortion is currently legal—at least under most circumstances—does not mean that it is moral; nor does believing that abortion is immoral necessarily imply that it ought to be outlawed. The resolution of most moral issues that confront us as a society involves not just discerning right from wrong, but determining how best to embody this moral wisdom in a just public policy. This involves balancing concerns about abortion with other concerns such as equal rights for women. As both Confucius and Aristotle maintain, good laws and public policy are important because they make it easier for people to be virtuous.

ABORTION AND RELIGION

Although the pro-life stand is often labeled as the "religious" position, religious views on abortion vary widely. Muslims believe that human life is sacred and that the fetus is a person with rights under the law from the moment of "ensoulment." This is tempered by practical concerns, however, and Islamic law generally permits early abortions on medical and health grounds.[18]

In Hinduism the killing of a conscious fetus carries the same penalty as the murder of a learned Brahman. However, the current emphasis on having sons in many Asian countries, including India and China, has led to a high rate of selective abortion despite laws in some countries specifically prohibiting abortion for sex selection.

There is little mention of abortion in the Bible, and what there is is ambiguous. Orthodox Jews emphasize passages in Genesis that teach that, because we are created in the image of God, all human life is inviolable and sacred. Thus abortion is prohibited except to save the life of the mother. Liberal and reform Jews, on the other hand, point out that Adam did not become a living being or fully human until God breathed life into him. Likewise, the infant does not become a *nephesh,* or a person with a soul, until he or she takes the first breath of air. Abortion, therefore, is morally permissible at any time during the pregnancy.

The position of the early Christian Church was similar to that of the Orthodox Jews. The *Didache,* written no later than A.D. 100, contains a prohibition against abortion, calling those who procure abortions "destroyers of God's image." The only exception to the prohibition was abortion to save the life of the mother.

Unlike the early Church, Thomas Aquinas set the time of ensoulment at forty days for males and eighty days for females. Based on this distinction, for centuries the Church regarded late-term abortions as more sinful than early abortions. The belief that early abortions are less morally problematic is still common today. In the nineteenth century, the Roman Catholic Church changed its position, returning to the early Christian prohibition against abortion at any time of the pregnancy.

The reaction of modern Protestants to abortion is varied. Most fundamentalist, evangelical, and African American Protestant churches take a position similar to that of the Roman Catholics, whereas most mainstream Protestant churches take a moderate stand, supporting abortion prior to viability.

The moral controversy over abortion cannot be resolved simply by uncritically accepting religious dogma. At the same time, the arguments used by the different religions should not be dismissed offhand, because they are generally based on philosophical rather than purely theological arguments. Good ethical analysis, while eschewing arguments based solely on faith, entails being open to, listening to, and subjecting to critical analysis the moral arguments put forth by the various religions.

METHODS OF ABORTION

There are three primary types of abortions: medical abortions, surgical abortions, and medical induction of uterine contractions. The method used depends primarily on the time of gestation.

Medical Abortions

Medical abortions include the morning-after pill and mifepristone, popularly known as RU 486. Medical abortions can be done only early in pregnancy.

The morning-after pill. The **morning-after pill** is actually a high dose of birth control pills taken over the three days following intercourse. The doses may prevent ovulation, prevent fertilization, or, prevent the blastocyst from implanting in the uterine wall. This method is 75 percent successful at preventing an implanted pregnancy.

Mifepristone (RU 486). Mifepristone was approved by the U.S. Food and Drug Administration (FDA) in 2000 for sale to the public, thus decreasing the need for surgical abortions in early pregnancies. Mifepristone induces menstruation, thus expelling the implanted embryo. It is more than 90 percent effective in terminating pregnancies of less than seven weeks' gestation.

Surgical Abortions

Most abortions are still performed surgically. The 98- to 99-percent success rate of surgical abortion is much higher than that of medical abortion.

Dilation and curettage (D & C). Dilation and curettage involves expanding the cervix of the uterus so a curette can be inserted to scrape the surface of the uterine wall. This method has fallen out of favor because of the risk of puncturing the uterus, which, in turn, can cause maternal hemorrhaging and even death.

Vacuum aspiration (D & E). The development in China in the early 1960s of the safer vacuum aspiration method was accompanied by a sharp decline in the death rate in women from abortions. Also known as dilation and evacuation (D & E), vacuum aspiration was first used in the United States in the late 1960s. This method is similar to D & C, but the fetus is suctioned rather than scraped out of the uterus. Today most abortions in the United States are vacuum aspirations.

Intact dilation and extraction (IDX or "partial-birth" abortion). This method is used only in late-term abortions. After partially delivering an intact fetus feet-first, the doctor punctures the fetus's skull, suctions out the brain, and then crushes the skull so the fetus can fit easily through the birth canal. Prior to a 2003 federal law banning "partial-birth" abortion, an estimated 2,200 such abortions were performed annually.[19] (See Case Study 5.)

Hysterectomy and hysterontomy. Surgical removal of the fetus is generally reserved for late-term abortions. A hysterectomy entails the surgical removal of the whole uterus; a hysterontomy, the removal of the fetus through an incision in the uterus. Because of the number of fetuses that survive these procedures and the high incidence of maternal complications, these methods are rarely used except in emergencies.

Medical Induction of Uterine Contractions

Abortions between sixteen and twenty weeks can be carried out using either surgical removal of the fetus or medical induction of uterine contractions.

Saline solution. With a saline abortion, about 200 milliliters of amniotic fluid is withdrawn from the amniotic sac and replaced with saline solution. Although the saline solution is meant to kill the fetus, this method occasionally results in a live birth.

Prostaglandins. This method involves an intramuscular or intravaginal injection of prostaglandins to induce labor. The use of prostaglandins is associated with fewer live births than using just saline solution.

THE MORAL ISSUES

The Moral Status of the Fetus

By eight weeks all organs and structural features are in place and the fetus resembles a very small newborn child. The question of fetal personhood is important because persons have rights that we ought to respect. Is there a distinct point when embryos or fetuses achieve personhood, or do they gradually achieve this status based on developmental criteria?

John Noonan maintains that there is no distinction between biological humanhood and personhood. We have moral value simply because we have a human genotype. Therefore, even the zygote is a person with moral standing. Mary Anne Warren, in contrast, argues that a fetus does not become a person until sometime after birth, when the infant becomes a "socially responsive member of a human community."

Most definitions of personhood fall between these extremes. According to utilitarians, only sentient beings need to be given moral consideration. Abortion, therefore, becomes a moral issue only after the fetus is able to experience pain. While there is controversy over whether, and when, the fetus is able to feel pain or whether it simply responds reflexively to external stimuli, most physicians agree that by thirteen weeks the fetus can experience pain.[20] A related developmental milestone that has been suggested as marking the beginning of personhood is the presence of brainwaves, which occurs at about six weeks.[21] This criterion has the advantage of being symmetrical with definitions of the end of personhood. On the other hand, an adult whose brainwaves have ceased is no longer alive, whereas an embryo, despite lack of a brain, is.

Viability replaced quickening after the 1973 *Roe v. Wade* ruling as the most widely accepted point for granting the fetus moral rights. Viability is problematic as a criterion, however, because personhood becomes dependent on medical technology rather than on any characteristic of the fetus. In 1950, viability occurred at about thirty weeks' gestation. When the *Roe v. Wade* decision was handed down in 1973, medical technology had advanced to the point where viability occurred at twenty-four weeks. Now fetuses as young as twenty weeks are surviving. If an artificial womb, or another means for the young fetus to breathe and survive outside the womb, is created, viability could occur much earlier, making *Roe v. Wade* a pro-life ruling.

A final criterion is that of potentiality, according to which the potential to develop into a full-fledged adult confers personhood on a fertilized egg. Noonan's definition of personhood embraces this criterion. Thomson, on the other hand, rejects it in her analogy between human development and the development of an acorn into an oak tree.

The moral status of the fetus is currently being challenged at both ends of the continuum in debates on the morality of embryonic stem cell research, which involves the destruction of embryos, and debates on "partial-birth" abortion, which was outlawed in 2003. For more on the moral issues surrounding cloning human stem cells, see Chapter 3, "Genetic Engineering, Cloning, and Stem Cell Research."

Some people, frustrated with the lack of consensus on a definition of personhood, argue that it is better left to personal or religious opinion. To say that one's definition of personhood is a matter of opinion, however, is to mire the debate in ethical subjectivism. Not only is abortion morally permissible, if in one's opinion a fetus is not a person, but so would be infanticide, slavery, and genocide, so long as the perpetrators believe that their victims are not persons. Because of this implication, it is important that we give careful consideration to the criteria for personhood and the implications of these criteria, and not uncritically accept cultural definitions or those that are politically and economically expedient, as happened with declaring slaves nonpersons.

Some abortion rights advocates oppose granting the fetus rights or personhood at any stage, arguing it will weaken a woman's legal right to an abortion. On the other hand, denying the fetus any moral status, pro-life feminists point out, denies the pregnant woman's special status and relationship with her unborn child and limits her options. The moral status and rights of the fetus are also an issue in maternal alcohol and drug use (see Case Study 2).

Even if we grant the fetus some moral status, as Judith Jarvis Thomsom does, it is still possible to argue that abortion is morally permissible under some circumstances. If a fetus is a person who can feel pain, however, the method used for abortion becomes a moral concern, since it is wrong to cause unnecessary pain.

Don Marquis, in his article "Why Abortion Is Immoral," argues that the killing of human beings who are able to enjoy their future experiences is wrong because it deprives them of the value of their future. Because the fetus, like an adult human, has a future that he or she can value, abortion, according to Marquis, is immoral.

The Rights and Autonomy of the Mother

Some people think that the emphasis on the personhood of the fetus has been at the expense of concerns about the rights of the woman. Thomson argues that even though the fetus may have moral standing, the rights of the mother, in most though not all cases, outweigh those of the fetus.

Mary Anne Warren likewise maintains that a woman's liberty rights or autonomy is paramount; women should have the right to make decisions about their own bodies. To deny women this basic right, according to Warren, is to treat them as a means only. Steven Hales argues that women have a right to abortion as a mechanism to avoid future burdens. Opponents of abortion, in response, argue that autonomy is not an absolute right. While women have a moral right to control their bodies, this right does not extend to abortion, because abortion involves destroying the body of an unborn child.

The extent to which women have a right to control their own bodies also arises in the debate over whether women have a responsibility to refrain from prenatal behaviors, such as drug and alcohol use, that may harm fetuses. Fetal alcohol syndrome, according to the Centers for Disease Control, is the leading cause of mental retardation in the United States. More infants are born with fetal alcohol syndrome than the combined total of Down's syndrome, spina bifida, muscular dystrophy, and HIV. Women who smoke during pregnancy are also at higher risk for having babies with low birth weight, respiratory problems, and sudden infant death syndrome (SIDS).

Advocates of abortion rights argue that as long as we have a patriarchal society in which pregnant women and mothers are socially and economically disadvantaged, abortion must remain a legitimate alternative. To have it otherwise is to deny women full and equal participation in society. Autonomy is especially an issue when the pregnancy is the result of rape or when the woman is a teenager (see Case Study 4). Justice is also an issue in access to abortion services. Restrictive abortion laws, lack of money, unavailability of a clinic in one's area, and harassment outside of abortion clinics—all contribute to a situation in which some women, especially poor women, do not have adequate access to abortion. Many providers have stopped performing abortions because of death threats and violence against clinics (see Case Study 3). Pro-life feminists such as Serrin Foster, in contrast, maintain that abortion degrades women, by pitting women's rights against babies' rights, and harms women because it removes the incentive for government, schools, and workplaces to provide resources for pregnant women to continue their education and careers.

It should be noted that a right to have an abortion to avoid future unjust burdens applies only to burdens caused by the pregnancy and giving birth, since adoption provides a mechanism for avoiding the burdens of raising the child after birth. Because adoption is an option, the decision to carry a pregnancy to term and the decision to raise the child should be seen as two separate decisions. This being said, the burdens of pregnancy in terms of discrimination faced in the workplace, and the stigma and pain of giving up a child for adoption, are still very real. Whether or not permissive abortion policies are exacerbating this injustice needs further study.

Abortion and Fathers' Rights and Duties

Service providers of contraception and abortion have focused almost exclusively on women. The exclusion of fathers when it comes to abortion decisions is reflected in the U.S. Supreme Court ruling in *Planned Parenthood of Central Missouri v. Danford* (1976), which stated that fathers have no rights over a child in the womb. This raises the question of whether fathers should have rights. Most Americans say they should have at least limited rights. A 2003 Gallup poll found that 67 percent of women and 78 percent of men favored laws requiring married women to notify their husbands before seeking an abortion.

In his article "Abortion and Fathers' Rights," Steven Hales argues that because women have a right to avoid future burdens through abortion, the principle of equality requires that men should also have the right of refusal when it comes to contributing to the support of his child after birth. Women have a similar right through the mechanism of adoption, in which the natural parents can turn over their rights and obligations toward their child to the adoptive parents (see Case Study 6).

Others maintain that it is fair to force fathers to pay child support should a woman decide to keep her child, even though she does not have a duty to consult the father about whether to terminate the pregnancy. This is because men bear some responsibility for the child's conception and birth, and because of the social consequences of the father's refusing to support his child. Indeed, studies show that unmarried fathers are far more interested in their children than we generally give them credit for.

Selective Abortion and the Principle of Discrimination

Unlike elective abortion, in which the pregnancy itself is unwanted, in **selective abortion** it is the particular fetus, rather than the pregnancy, that is unwanted. Discrimination is a key issue in selective abortion. About 7 percent of infants are born with a physical and/or mental disorder. Prenatal diagnosis provides parents with information about most of these disorders as well as the gender of the fetus. The overwhelming majority of pregnancies in which the fetus is diagnosed as having a genetic disorder are terminated by selective abortion.

In countries such as China and India, where sons are preferred, selective abortion may be used more for sex selection than for genetic disorders. As a result, there is a great discrepancy in some parts of India and China between the number of males and the number of females.[22] India banned the use of abortion intended for sex selection in 1994 and China followed suit in 2003. However, these laws have been hard to enforce given the strong preference for boys in parts of these countries and the easy availability of ultrasound for determining the gender of the fetus (see Case Study 1).

Abortion for sex selection is legal in the United States, where there is a preference for sons as firstborn and only children. American physicians are most supportive worldwide of the practice, citing the woman's autonomy as their reason for performing the procedure.[23] With increasing knowledge of the human genome, geneticists may soon be able to prenatally diagnose tendencies toward obesity, cancer, and homosexuality—to name only a few traits that most Americans consider undesirable in their children.[24]

It is now possible for women to purchase over-the-counter prenatal genetic testing kits at their local pharmacy. This enables women to make a decision about whether or not to terminate a pregnancy without first seeking genetic counseling. Whether this development will enhance women's autonomy or put additional pressure on parents to have the perfect baby (one of the "right" gender) remains to be seen.

The principle of nondiscrimination requires that humans not be denied benefits or equal treatment for morally irrelevant reasons, such as sex or skin color or physical abilities. Does selective abortion involve discrimination against females, people with handicaps, and other socially unacceptable people? Even if it does involve discrimination, this has to be weighed against women's autonomy as well as against the social consequences of having "undesirable" children who will be a burden on their parents and on society.

Consequentialist Arguments: Abortion as a Benefit to Born Children

Those who favor a permissive abortion policy point to the harmful consequences of restrictive abortion policies. These include complications and deaths from self-induced and illegal abortions, overpopulation, the burden on women of mandatory motherhood, at least during the nine months of pregnancy, and the burden on society when unwanted children are neglected or abandoned.

The use of consequentialist or utilitarian arguments requires that we base our arguments in fact, rather than conjecture. One of the arguments for abortion rights, summarized in the slogan Pro-Child/Pro-Choice, is that they not only benefit women but also benefit children by ensuring that all born children are wanted children. However, studies have not shown that abortion leads to a decrease in child abuse nor that it improves the quality of life of born children.

Indeed, some pro-life feminists maintain that abortion, rather than benefiting children, has led to a devaluation of children and an increase in child abuse. While the general well-being of the nation remained relatively stable in the 1970s, declining slightly in the first part of the 1980s, the "social health" of children and youth began a steady course of decline beginning in 1974, the year after abortion was legalized.[25] In addition, the rates of child abuse began rising after 1973, increasing 566 percent between 1977 and 1980.[26] The rate of child abuse leveled off after 1993 along with a drop in the rate of abortion. However, as of 2003 it still remained almost four times what it was in the 1970s.[27] These figures cannot be attributed solely to better reporting of child abuse cases because most of the improvement in reporting techniques took place in the early 1980s in response to the alarming increase in child abuse. A study conducted at Johns Hopkins Hospital by the Baltimore, Maryland, Department of Social Services of 532 abused children found that previous abortions and stillbirths place a family at significantly higher risk for child abuse, independently of other factors such as socioeconomic and marital status.[28] While a positive correlation between child abuse and previous abortions may sound counterintuitive, psychiatrist Phillip Nye suggests that by legitimating the death of the fetus in utero we have weakened the normal instinctual restraint and social taboo against the use of violence against young children dependent on our care.[29]

On the other hand, the harms to born children may be corrected by creating better support systems for parents and young children. These harms also have to be weighed against the harm to women of depriving them of control over their bodies during pregnancy. In any case, we cannot argue in favor of abortion on the grounds that it benefits born children. Instead, we must be willing to examine the morality of abortion, using factually correct premises and consistent arguments.

CONCLUSION

As members of a pluralistic society, can we ever reach a resolution to the current abortion debate? Should we even bother to try? Why can't we just be tolerant of other people's views: "If you don't believe in abortion, don't have one." Unfortunately, the

---

✍ SUMMARY OF READINGS ON ABORTION

Thomson, "A Defense of Abortion." Abortion may be morally permissible, even if the fetus is a person.

Noonan, "An Almost Absolute Value in History." Abortion is rarely, if ever, morally justifiable since any being conceived by human parents is a person.

Warren, "The Moral Significance of Birth." Abortion is morally justified because personhood does not begin until after birth.

Marquis, "Why Abortion Is Immoral." Abortion is immoral because it deprives the fetus of his or her future.

Foster, "Refuse to Choose: Women Deserve Better Than Abortion." Abortion is immoral because it harms women and pits women's rights against babies' rights.

Hales, "Abortion and Fathers' Rights." If a mother can escape parenthood through abortion, then fathers should also be able to refuse to take on the future burdens of parenthood.

hands-off approach doesn't work, because those who are opposed to abortion are not merely expressing a personal opinion about abortion; they are saying that abortion is wrong because it violates universal moral principles. Furthermore, to claim that we should be tolerant of other people's moral opinions is to advocate tolerance not only of abortion but also of other practices. Few of us would be willing to carry a bumper sticker sporting the slogan "If you don't believe in slavery, don't own slaves."

Ethical analysis should not be a matter of personal opinion or majority consensus. It should be logical and consistent in its application. Until we can approach the issue of abortion rationally, it is unlikely to be resolved. The following readings are an invitation to rethink the abortion issue with an open and analytical mind.

JUDITH JARVIS THOMSON

A Defense of Abortion

Judith Jarvis Thomson is a professor of philosophy at the Massachusetts Institute of Technology. Her article "A Defense of Abortion," published two years before *Roe v. Wade*, has become a classic in the abortion debate. Rather than attempt to refute the premises that the fetus is a person and that every person has a right to life, Thomson argues that abortion may be morally permissible even if these premises are true. Even if the fetus has a right to life, this right does not entail the right to have whatever one needs—including use of a woman's body—to stay alive.

Critical Reading Questions

1. What is Thomson's position regarding the personhood of the fetus?
2. How does Thomson use the violinist analogy to illustrate the relationship between the fetus and the woman?
3. What conclusion regarding the rights of the fetus and the mother and the moral permissibility of abortion does Thomson draw based on the violinist analogy?
4. Why does Thomson reject the "extreme" pro-life view of abortion?
5. Which position on abortion is Thomson addressing when she uses the analogy of a person being trapped in a tiny house with a rapidly growing child?
6. How does Thomson respond to the pro-life argument that if the fetus has a right to life, abortion is unjust killing?
7. What analogy does Thomson use to justify abortion in cases of contraceptive failure?

"A Defense of Abortion," *Philosophy and Public Affairs* 1, no. 1 (1971): 47–66. Notes have been omitted. This article has been annotated using the guidelines set forth in the "Critical Reading" portion of the *Online Learning Center* for this book.

8. Are there any circumstances, according to Thomson, in which abortion is not morally permissible?
9. What is the difference between a Minimally Decent Samaritan and a Good Samaritan? What is the relevance of this distinction in the abortion debate?
10. On what grounds does Thomson draw a moral distinction between the right to have an abortion and the right to secure the death of an unborn child?

Most opposition to abortion relies on the premise that the fetus is a human being, a person, from the moment of conception. The premise is argued for, but, as I think, not well. Take, for example, the most common argument. We are asked to notice that the development of a human being from conception through birth into childhood is continuous; then it is said that to draw a line, to choose a point in this development and say "before this point the thing is not a person, after this point it is a person" is to make an arbitrary choice, a choice for which in the nature of things no good reason can be given. It is concluded that the fetus is, or anyway that we had better say it is, a person from the moment of conception. But this conclusion does not follow. [Similar things might be said about the development of an acorn into an oak tree, and it does not follow that acorns are oak trees, or that we had better say they are.] Arguments of this form are sometimes called "slippery slope arguments"—the phrase is perhaps self-explanatory—and it is dismaying that opponents of abortion rely on them so heavily and uncritically.

[margin: CA 1: Fetus is a person]

[margin: J.T.'s response to CA 1]

[margin: Oak tree analogy]

I am inclined to agree, however, that the prospects for "drawing a line" in the development of the fetus look dim. I am inclined to think also that [we shall have to agree that the fetus has already become a human person well before birth.] Indeed, it comes as a surprise when one first learns how early in its life it begins to acquire human characteristics. By the tenth week, for example, it already has a face, arms and legs, fingers and toes; it has internal organs, and brain activity is detectable. On the other hand, I think that the premise is false, that the fetus is not a person from the moment of conception. A newly fertilized ovum, a newly implanted clump of cells, is no more a person than an acorn is an oak tree. But I shall not discuss any of this. For it seems to me to be of great interest to ask what happens if, for the sake of argument, we allow the premise. . . .

[margin: Definition of key term "person"]

[margin: Premise #1: Fetus is a person]

[margin: Explanation of premise #1]

I propose, then, that [we grant that the fetus is a person from the moment of conception.] How does the argument go from here? Something like this, I take it. [Every person has a right to life.] So the fetus has a right to life. No doubt the [mother has a right to decide what shall happen in and to her body;] everyone would grant that. But surely a person's right to life is stronger and more stringent than the mother's right to decide what happens in and to her body, and so outweighs it. [So the fetus may not be killed; an abortion may not be performed.]

[margin: CA 2: The fetus may not be killed]

[margin: Premise #1 and premise #2: Fetus has a right to life / Premise #3: The mother has a right to life]

It sounds plausible. But let me ask you to imagine this. You wake up in the morning and find yourself back to back in bed with an unconscious violinist. A famous unconscious violinist. He has been found to have a fatal kidney ailment, and the Society of Music Lovers has canvassed all available medical records and found that you alone have the right blood type to help. They have therefore kidnapped you, and last night the violinist's circulatory system was plugged into yours, so that your kidneys can be used to extract poisons from his blood as well as your own. The director of the hospital now tells you, "Look, we're sorry the Society of Music Lovers did this to you—we would have never permitted it if we had known. But still, they did it, and the violinist is now plugged into you. To unplug you would be to kill him. But never mind, it's only for nine months. By then he will have recovered from his ailment, and can be safely unplugged from you." Is it morally incumbent on you to accede to this situation? No doubt it would be very nice of you if you did, a great kindness. But do you *have* to accede to it? What if it were not nine months, but nine years? Or longer still? What if the director of the hospital says, "Tough luck, I agree, but you've now got to stay in bed, with the violinist plugged into you, for the rest of your life. Because remember this. All persons have a right to life, and violinists are persons. Granted you have a right to decide what happens in and to your body, but a person's right to life outweighs your right to decide what happens in and to your body. So you cannot ever be unplugged from him." [I imagine you would regard this as outrageous, which suggests that something really is wrong with that plausible-sounding argument I mentioned a moment ago.]

J.T.'s response to CA 2: violinist analogy

Rejection of CA 2

In this case, of course, you were kidnapped; you didn't volunteer for the operation that plugged the violinist into your kidneys. Can those who oppose abortion on the ground I mentioned make an exception for a pregnancy due to rape? Certainly. They can say that persons have a right to life only if they didn't come into existence because of rape; or they can say that all persons have a right to life, but that some have less of a right to life than others, in particular, that those who came into existence because of rape have less. But these statements have a rather unpleasant sound. Surely the question of whether you have a right to life at all, or how much of it you have, shouldn't turn on the question of whether or not you are the product of a rape. And in fact the people who oppose abortion on the ground I mentioned do not make this distinction, and hence do not make an exception in case of rape. . . .

Explanation

Some won't even make an exception for a case in which continuation of the pregnancy is likely to shorten the mother's life; they regard abortion as impermissible even to save the mother's life. Such cases are nowadays very rare, and many opponents of abortion do not accept this extreme view. All the same, it is a good place to begin: a number of points of interest come out in respect to it.

1. Let us call the view that abortion is impermissible even to save the mother's life "the extreme view." I want to suggest first that it does not issue from the argument I mentioned earlier without the addition of some fairly powerful premises. Suppose a woman has become pregnant, and now learns that she has a cardiac condition such that she will die if she carries the baby to term. What may be done for her? The fetus, being a person, has a right to life, but as the mother is a person too, so has she a right to life. Presumably they have an equal right to life. How is it supposed to come out that an abortion may not

CA 3: Extreme pro-life view

J.T.'s response to extreme view

be performed? If mother and child have an equal right to life, shouldn't we perhaps flip a coin? Or should we add to the mother's right to life her right to decide what happens in and to her body, which everybody seems to be ready to grant—the sum of her rights now outweighing the fetus' right to life?

The most familiar argument here is the following. We are told that performing the abortion would be directly killing the child, whereas doing nothing would not be killing the mother, but only letting her die. Moreover, in killing the child, one would be killing an innocent person, for the child has committed no crime, and is not aiming at his mother's death. . . .

Premise #4: It is not murder to perform an abortion to save your life

If directly killing an innocent person is murder, and thus is impermissible, then the mother's directly killing the innocent person inside her is murder, and thus is impermissible. But [it cannot seriously be thought to be murder if the mother performs an abortion on herself to save her life. It cannot seriously be said that she *must* refrain, that she *must* sit passively by and wait for her death.] Let us look again at the case of you and the violinist. There you are, in bed with the violinist, and the director of the hospital says to you, "It's all most distressing, and I deeply sympathize, but you see this is putting an additional strain on your kidneys, and you'll be dead within the month. But you *have* to stay where you are all the same. Because unplugging you would be directly killing an innocent violinist, and that's murder, and that's impermissible." If anything in the world is true, it is that you do not commit murder, you do not do what is impermissible, if you reach around to your back and unplug yourself from that violinist to save your life.

violinist analogy explanation of premise #4

Rejection of CA 3: Extreme pro-life position

The main focus of attention in writings on abortion has been on what a third party may or may not do in answer to a request from a woman for an abortion. This is in a way understandable. Things being as they are, there isn't much a woman can safely do to abort herself. So the question asked is what a third party may do, and what the mother may do, if it is mentioned at all, is deduced, almost as an afterthought, from what is concluded that third parties may do. But it seems to me that to treat the matter in this way is to refuse to grant to the mother that very status of person which is so firmly insisted on for the fetus. For we cannot simply read off what a person may do from what a third party may do. Suppose you find yourself trapped in a tiny house with a growing child. I mean a very tiny house, and a rapidly growing child—you are already up against the wall of the house and in a few minutes you will be crushed to death. The child on the other hand won't be crushed to death; if nothing is done to stop him from growing he'll be hurt, but in the end he'll simply burst open the house and walk out a free man. Now I could well understand it if a bystander were to say, "There's nothing we can do for you. We cannot choose between your life and his, we cannot be the ones to decide who is to live, we cannot intervene." But it cannot be concluded that you too can do nothing, that you cannot attack it to save your life. However innocent the child may be, you do not have to wait passively while it crushes you to death. Perhaps a pregnant woman is vaguely felt to have the same status of house, to which we don't allow the right of self-defense. But if the woman houses the child, it should be remembered that she is a person who houses it. . . .

Sub conclusion and Premise #6: A woman can defend herself against threats from the unborn child even if it results in child's death

Explanation of rejection of CA 3 Analogy of house with growing child

Premise #5: A pregnant woman's body is her own

In sum, [a woman surely can defend her life against the threat to it posed by the unborn child, even if doing so involves its death.] And this shows also that the extreme view of abortion is false, and so we need not canvass any other possible ways of arriving at it from the argument I mentioned at the outset.

CA 4: Self defense allows only mother to perform abortion

2. The extreme view should of course be weakened to say that while abortion is permissible to save a mother's life, it may not be performed by a third party, but only by the mother herself. But this cannot be right either. For what we have to keep in mind is that the mother and the unborn child are not like two tenants in a small house which has, by an unfortunate mistake, been rented to both: the mother *owns* the house. The fact that she does adds to the offensiveness of deducing that the mother can do nothing from the supposition that third parties can do nothing. But it does nothing more than this: it casts a bright light on the supposition that third parties can do nothing. Certainly it lets us see that a third party who says "I cannot choose between you" is fooling himself if he thinks this is impartiality. If Jones has found and fastened on a certain coat, which he needs to keep from freezing, but which Smith also needs to keep him from freezing, then it is not impartiality that says "I cannot choose between you" when Smith owns the coat. Women have said again and again "This body is *my* body!" and they have reason to feel angry, reason to feel that it has been like shouting in the wind. . . .

J. T.'s rejection of CA 4: Smith owns the coat

We should really ask what it is that says "no one may choose" in the face of the fact that the body that houses the child is the mother's body. It may be simply a failure to appreciate this fact. But it may be something more interesting, namely the sense that one has a right to refuse to lay hands on people, even where it would be just and fair to do so, even where justice seems to require that somebody do so. This justice might call for somebody to get Smith's coat back from Jones, and yet you have a right to refuse to be the one to lay hands on Jones, a right to refuse to do physical violence to him. This, I think, must be granted. But then what should be said is not "no one may choose," but only "*I* cannot choose," and indeed not even this, but "*I* will not *act*," leaving it open that somebody else can or should, and in particular that anyone in a position of authority, with the job of securing people's rights, both can and should. So this is no difficulty. I have not been arguing that any given third party must accede to the mother's request that he perform an abortion to save her life, but only that he may. . . .

J. T.'s rejection of CA 4: Smith owns the coat

CA 5: The child's right to life is stronger than the mother's rights

3. Where the mother's life is not at stake, the argument I mentioned at the outset seems to have a much stronger pull. "Everyone has a right to life, so the unborn person has a right to life." And isn't the child's right to life weightier than anything other than the mother's own right to life, which she might put forward as ground for an abortion?

This argument treats the right to life as if it were unproblematic. It is not, and this seems to me to be precisely the source of the mistake.

For we should now, at long last, ask what it comes to, to have a right to life. In some views having a right to life includes having a right to be given at least the bare minimum one needs for continued life. But suppose that what in fact *is* the bare minimum a man needs for continued life is something he has no right at all to be given? If I am sick unto death, and the only thing that will save my life is the touch of Henry Fonda's cool hand on my fevered brow, then all the same, I have no right to be given the touch of Henry Fonda's cool hand on my fevered brow. It would be frightfully nice of him to fly in from the West Coast to provide it. It would be less nice, though no doubt meant well, if my friends flew out to the West Coast and carried Henry Fonda back with them. But I have no right at all against anybody that he should do this for me. Or again, to return to the story told earlier, the fact that for continued life that violinist needs the continued use of your kidneys does not establish that he has a right to be given the continued use of your kidneys. He certainly has no right against you that *you* should give him continued use of your kidneys. For nobody has any right to use your kidneys unless you give him such a right; and nobody has the right against you that you shall give him this right—if you do allow him to go on using your kidneys, this is a kindness on your part, and not something he can claim from you as his due. . . .

J.T.'s reply to CA 5: Henry Fonda analogy

But I would stress that I am not arguing that people do not have the right to life—quite to the contrary, it seems to me that the primary control we must place on the acceptability of an account of rights is that it should turn out in that account to be a truth that all persons have a right to life. [I am arguing only that having a right to life does not guarantee having either a right to be given the use of or a right to be allowed continued use of another person's body—even if one needs it for life itself.] So the right to life will not serve the opponents of abortion in the very simple and clear way in which they seem to have thought it would.

Premise #7: It is a kindness rather than an obligation to let someone else use our body

4. There is another way to bring out the difficulty. In the most ordinary sort of case, [to deprive someone of what he has a right to is to treat him unjustly.] Suppose a boy and his small brother are jointly given a box of chocolates for Christmas. If the older boy takes the box and refuses to give his brother any of the chocolates, he is unjust to him, for the brother has been given a right to half of them. But suppose that, having learned that otherwise it means nine years in bed with that violinist, you unplug yourself from him. You surely are not being unjust to him, for you gave him no right to use your kidneys, and no one else can have given him any such right. But we have to notice that in unplugging yourself, you are killing him; and violinists, like everybody else, have a right to life, and thus in the view we were considering just now, the right not to be killed. So here you do what he supposedly has a right you shall not do, but you do not act unjustly to him in doing it.

Premise #8: It is unjust to deprive someone of something to which they have a right

Explanation of premise #8

The emendation which may be made at this point is this: [the right to life consists not in the right not to be killed, but rather in the right not to be killed unjustly.] This runs a risk of circularity, but never mind: it would enable us to square the fact that the violinist has a right to life with the fact that you do not act unjustly toward him in unplugging yourself, thereby killing him. For if you do not kill him unjustly, you do not violate his right to life, and it is no wonder you do him no injustice.

Premise #9: The right to life consists only of the right not to be killed unjustly

But if this emendation is accepted, the gap in the argument against abortion stares us plainly in the face: it is no means enough to show that the fetus is a person, and to remind us that all persons have a right to life—we need to be shown also that killing the fetus violates its right to life, i.e., that abortion is unjust killing. And is it?

I suppose we may take it as a datum that in a case of pregnancy due to rape the mother has not given the unborn person a right to the use of her body for food and shelter. Indeed, in what pregnancy could it be supposed that the mother has given the unborn person such a right? It is not as if there were unborn persons drifting about the world, to whom a woman who wants a child says "I invite you in."

But it might be argued that there are other ways one can have acquired a right to the use of another person's body than by having been invited to use it by that person. Suppose a woman voluntarily indulges in intercourse, knowing of the chance it will issue in pregnancy, and then she does become pregnant; is she not in part responsible for the presence, in fact the very existence, of the unborn person inside her? No doubt she did not invite it in. But doesn't her partial responsibility for its being there itself give it a right to the use of her body? If so, then her aborting it would be more like the boy's taking away the chocolates, and less like your unplugging yourself from the violinist—doing so would be depriving it of what it does have a right to, and thus would be doing it an injustice. . . .

> *CA 6: If mother "invites" fetus to use her body, it is unjust to then kill the fetus*

The first thing to be said about this is that it is something new. Opponents of abortion have been so concerned to make out the independence of the fetus, in order to establish that it has a right to life, just as its mother does, that they have tended to overlook the possible support they might gain from making out [that the fetus is *dependent* on the mother, in order to establish that she has a special kind of responsibility for it,] a responsibility that gives it rights against her which are not possessed by any independent person—such as an ailing violinist who is a stranger to her.

> *Premise #10: The fetus is dependent on the mother*

On the other hand, this argument would give the unborn person a right to its mother's body only if her pregnancy resulted from a voluntary act, undertaken in full knowledge of the chance a pregnancy might result from it. It would leave out entirely the unborn person whose existence is due to rape. Pending the availability of some further argument, then, we would be left with the conclusion that unborn persons whose existence is due to rape have no right to the use of their mothers' bodies, and thus that aborting them is not depriving them of anything they have a right to and hence is not unjust killing.

> *J. T.'s response to CA 6: J. T.'s people seeds analogy*

And we should also notice that it is not at all plain that this argument really does not go even as far as it purports to. For there are cases and cases, and the details make a difference. If the room is stuffy, and I therefore open a window to air it, and a burglar climbs in, it would be absurd to say, "Ah, now he can stay, she's given him a right to the use of her house—for she is partially responsible for his presence there, having voluntarily done what enabled him to get in, in full knowledge that there are such things as burglars, and that burglars burgle." It would be still more absurd to say this if I had had bars installed outside my windows, precisely to prevent burglars from getting in, and a burglar got in only because of a defect in the bars. It remains equally absurd if we imagine it is not a burglar who climbs in, but an innocent person who blunders or falls in. Again, suppose it were like this: people-seeds drift about in the air like pollen, and if you open your windows, one may drift in and take root in your carpets or upholstery. You don't want children, so you fix up your windows with fine mesh screens, the very best you can buy. As can happen, however, and on very, very rare occasions does happen, one of the screens is defective; and a seed drifts in and takes root. Does the person–plant who now develops have a right to the use of your house? Surely not—despite the fact that you voluntarily opened your windows, you knowingly kept carpets and upholstered furniture, and you knew that screens were sometimes defective. Someone may argue that you are responsible for its rooting, that it does have a right to your house, because after all you *could* have lived out your life with bare floors and furniture, or with sealed windows and doors. But this won't do—for by the same token anyone can avoid a pregnancy due to rape by having a hysterectomy, or anyway by never leaving home without a (reliable!) army.

It seems to me that the argument we are looking at can establish at most that [there are *some* cases in which the unborn person has a right to the use of its mother's body,] and therefore [*some* cases in which abortion is unjust killing.] There is room for much discussion and argument as to precisely which, if any. But I think we should sidestep this issue and leave it open, for at any rate the argument certainly does not establish that all abortion is unjust killing.

5. There is room for yet another argument here, however. [We surely must all grant that there may be cases in which it would be morally indecent to detach a person from your body at the cost of his life.] Suppose you learn that what the violinist needs is not nine years of your life, but only one hour: all you need to do to save his life is to spend one hour in that bed with him. Suppose also that letting him use your kidneys for that one hour would not affect your health in the slightest. Admittedly you were kidnapped. Admittedly you did not give anyone permission to plug him into you. Nevertheless it seems to me plain you *ought* to allow him to use your kidneys for that one hour—it would be indecent to refuse.

Again, suppose pregnancy lasted only an hour, and constituted no threat to your life or health. And suppose that a woman becomes pregnant as a result of rape. Admittedly she did not voluntarily do anything to bring about the existence of a child. Admittedly she did nothing at all which would give the unborn person a right to the use of her body. All the same it might well be said, as in the newly emended violinist story, that she *ought* to allow it to remain for that hour—that it would be indecent in her to refuse.

Now some people are inclined to use the term "right" in such a way that it follows from the fact that you ought to allow a person to use your body for the hour he needs, that he has the right to use your body for the hour he needs, even though he has not been given that right by any person or act. They may say that it follows also that if you refuse, you act unjustly toward him. This use of the term is perhaps so common that it cannot be called wrong; nevertheless it seems to me to be an unfortunate loosening of what we would do better ↓

[handwritten left margin:] Premise #11: There are some cases where the fetus has a right to the mother's body

[handwritten right margin:] Sub conclusion and premise #12: There are some cases where abortion is unjust killing

[handwritten right margin:] Explanation of premise #10: The violinist analogy revisited

to keep a tight rein on. Suppose the box of chocolates I mentioned earlier had not been given to both boys jointly, but was given only to the older boy. There he sits, stolidly eating his way through the box, his small brother watching enviously. Here we are likely to say "You ought not to be so mean. You ought to give your brother some of those chocolates." My own view is that it just does not follow from the truth of this that the brother has any right to any of the chocolates. If the boy refuses to give his brother any, he is greedy, stingy, callous—but not unjust. . . .

So my own view is that even though you ought to let the violinist use your kidneys for the one hour he needs, we should not conclude that he has a right to do so—we should say that if you refuse, you are, like the boy who owns all the chocolates and will give none away, self-centered and callous, indecent in fact, but not unjust. And similarly, that even supposing a case in which a woman pregnant due to rape ought to allow the unborn person to use her body for the hour he needs, we should not conclude that he has a right to do so; we should conclude that she is self-centered, callous, indecent, but not unjust, if she refuses. The complaints are no less grave; they are just different. . . .

6. We have in fact to distinguish between two kinds of Samaritan: the Good Samaritan and what we might call the Minimally Decent Samaritan. . . . The Good Samaritan went out of his way, at some cost to himself, to help one in need of it. . . . [in Luke 10:30–35]

Premise #13: Even if there are cases in which the mother ought to allow the unborn child to use her body, this does not mean the child has a right to her body

Explanation of two types of Samaritans

Key terms: Good Samaritan and Minimally Decent Samaritan

These things are a matter of degree, of course, but there is a difference, and it comes out perhaps most clearly in the story of Kitty Genovese, who, as you will remember, was murdered while thirty-eight people watched or listened, and did nothing at all to help her. A Good Samaritan would have rushed out to give direct assistance against the murderer. Or perhaps we had better allow that it would have been a Splendid Samaritan who did this, on the ground that it would have involved a risk of death for himself. But the thirty-eight not only did not do this, they did not even trouble to pick up a phone to call the police. Minimally Decent Samaritanism would call for doing at least that, and their not having done it was monstrous.

After telling the story of the Good Samaritan, Jesus said "Go, and do thou likewise." Perhaps he meant that we are morally required to act as the Good Samaritan did. Perhaps he was urging people to do more than is morally required of them. At all events it seems plain that [it was not morally required of any of the thirty-eight that he rush out to give direct assistance at the risk of his own life,] and that [it is not morally required of anyone that he give long stretches of his life—nine years or nine months—to sustaining that life of a person who has no special right (we were leaving open the possibility of this) to demand it.]

Premise #14: We are only morally required to be Minimally Decent Samaritans

Premise #15: Being a Minimally Decent Samaritan does not require us to give long stretches to sustain the life of someone who has no special rights

Indeed, with one rather striking class of exceptions, no one in any country in the world is *legally* required to do anywhere near as much as this for anyone else. The class of exceptions is obvious. My main concern here is not the state of the law in respect to abortion, but it is worth drawing attention to the fact that in no state in this country is any man compelled by law to be even a Minimally Decent Samaritan to any person; there is no law under which charges could be brought against the thirty-eight who stood by while Kitty Genovese died. . . .

I should think, myself, that Minimally Decent Samaritan laws would be one thing, Good Samaritan laws quite another, and in fact highly improper. But we are not here concerned with the law. What we should ask is not whether anybody should be compelled by law to be a Good Samaritan, but whether we must accede to a situation in which somebody is being compelled—by nature, perhaps—to be a Good Samaritan. We have, in other words, to look now at third-party interventions. I have been arguing that no person is morally required to make large sacrifices to sustain the life of another who has no right to demand them, and this even where the sacrifices do not include life itself; we are not morally required to be Good Samaritans or anyway Very Good Samaritans to one another. But what if a man cannot extricate himself from such a situation? What if he appeals to us to extricate him? It seems to me plain that there are cases in which we can, cases in which a Good Samaritan would extricate him. There you are, you were kidnapped, and nine years in bed with that violinist lie ahead of you. You have your own life to lead. You are sorry, but you simply cannot see giving up so much of your life to the sustaining of his. You cannot extricate yourself, and ask us to do so. I should have thought that—in light of his having no right to the use of your body—it was obvious that we do not have to accede to your being forced to give up so much. We can do what you ask. There is no injustice to the violinist in our doing so.

Explanation of premises #14 and #15

7. Following the lead of opponents of abortion, I have throughout been speaking of the fetus merely as a person, and what I have been asking is whether or not the argument we began with, which proceeds only from the fetus' being a person, really does not establish its conclusion. I have argued that it does not.

But of course there are arguments and arguments, and it may be said that I have simply fastened on the wrong one. It may be said that what is important is not merely the fact that the fetus is a person, but that it is a person for whom the woman has a special kind of responsibility issuing from the fact that she is the mother. And it might be argued that all my analogies are therefore irrelevant—for you do not have that special responsibility for that violinist, Henry Fonda does not have that special kind of responsibility for me. And our attention might be drawn to the fact that men and women both *are* compelled by law to provide support for their children.

CA 1: The woman has a special kind of obligation toward her fetus because she is the mother

I have in effect dealt (briefly) with this argument in section 4 above; but a (still briefer) recapitulation now may be in order. [Surely we do not have any such "special responsibility" for a person unless we have assumed it, explicitly or implicitly.] If a set of parents do not try to prevent a pregnancy, do not obtain an abortion, and then at the time of birth of the child do not put it out for adoption, but rather take it home with them, then they have assumed responsibility for it, they have given it rights, and they cannot *now* withdraw support from it at the cost of its life because they now find it difficult to go on providing for it. But if they have taken all reasonable precautions against having a child, they do not simply by virtue of their biological relationship to the

J. T.'s response to CA 1

Premise #16: We do not have a responsibility for another person unless we have assumed it

child who comes into existence have a special responsibility for it. They may wish to assume responsibility for it, or they may not wish to. And I am suggesting that if assuming responsibility for it would require large sacrifices, then they may refuse. . . .

8. My argument will be found unsatisfactory on two counts by many of those who want to regard abortion as morally permissible. First, while I do argue that abortion is not impermissible, I do not argue that it is always permissible. There may well be cases in which carrying the child to term requires only Minimally Decent Samaritanism of the mother, and this is a standard we must not fall below. I am inclined to think it a merit of my account precisely that it does *not* give a general yes or a general no. It allows for and supports our sense that, for example, a sick and desperately frightened fourteen-year-old schoolgirl, pregnant due to rape, may *of course* choose abortion, and that any law which rules this out is an insane law. And it also allows for and supports our sense that in other cases resort to abortion is even positively indecent. It would be indecent in the woman to request an abortion, and indecent in a doctor to perform it, if she is in her seventh month, and wants the abortion to avoid the nuisance of postponing a trip abroad. The very fact that the arguments I have been drawing attention to treat all cases of abortion, or even all cases of abortion in which the mother's life is not at stake, as morally on a par ought to have made them suspect at the outset.

Secondly, while I am arguing for the permissibility of abortion in some cases, I am not arguing for the right to secure the death of the unborn child. It is easy to confuse these two things in that up to a certain point in the life of the fetus it is not able to survive outside the mother's body; hence removing it from her body guarantees its death. But they are importantly different. I have argued that you are not morally required to spend nine months in bed, sustaining the life of that violinist; but to say this is by no means to say that if, when you unplug yourself, there is a miracle and he survives, you then have to turn around and slit his throat. You may detach yourself even if this costs him his life; you have no right to be guaranteed his death, by some other means, if unplugging yourself does not kill him. There are some people who will feel dissatisfied by this feature of my argument. A woman may be utterly devastated by the thought of a child, a bit of herself, put out for adoption and never seen or heard of again. She may therefore want not merely that the child be detached from her, but more, that it die. Some opponents of abortion are inclined to regard this as beneath contempt—thereby showing insensitivity to what is surely a powerful source of despair. All the same, I agree that the desire for the child's death is not one which anybody may gratify, should it turn out to be possible to detach the child alive.

At this place, however, it should be remembered that we have only been pretending throughout that the fetus is a human being from the moment of conception. A very early abortion is surely not the killing of a person, and so is not dealt with by anything I have said here.

[margin note, left: Part 1 of conclusion: Abortion is permissible except in cases where it falls beneath the standard of Minimally Decent Samaritan]

[margin note, left: Part 2 of conclusion: The woman does not have a right to secure the death of her child, but only to remove it from her body]

Discussion Questions

1. In her analogies does Thomson take her presumption of the personhood of the fetus as seriously as she does the personhood of the mother? Support your answer.

2. Imagine that you find a baby or toddler in your winter cabin. There is no one else around to help care for the child and, because of heavy snows, no way to get to town for the next eight months. Assuming that you have enough food in the cabin for both of you, do you have a moral obligation, as a Minimally Decent Samaritan, to let the child share your cabin for the next eight months? Would it be morally permissible for you to put the child outside even though you knew she would certainly die of exposure if you did? Discuss the analogy between this case and that of abortion.

3. Does Thomson's argument that the fetus has no right to the mother's womb justify killing the fetus? Does Thomson do an adequate job of distinguishing between the right of a mother to have an abortion and the moral injunction against taking the life of the fetus? Support your answers.

4. Thomson argues that we have no responsibility for another person unless we have voluntarily assumed it. Discuss the implications of Thomson's argument for cases in which the woman chose to continue her pregnancy when the father did not want to have the child. Does the father have any moral obligation toward the child in terms of child support and sharing in the care of the child?

5. Discuss how Thomson would most likely stand in the debate over late-term "partial-birth" abortions.

JOHN T. NOONAN JR.

An Almost Absolute Value in History

John Noonan is a professor of law at the University of California at Berkeley. Like Thomson's "A Defense of Abortion," Noonan's 1970 article on abortion remains one of the classics in abortion debates. Both Noonan and Thomson begin with the presumption that the fetus is a person with moral standing. Unlike Thomson, however, Noonan draws the conclusion that abortion is rarely, if ever, morally justified.

"An Almost Absolute Value in History," *The Morality of Abortion: Legal and Historical Perspectives* (Cambridge, Mass.: Harvard University Press, 1970), 51–59. Notes have been omitted.

Critical Reading Questions

1. What, according to Noonan, is the most fundamental question in the abortion debate?
2. What does Noonan mean by "ensoulment"? Why does he claim that the notion of ensoulment does not require a theological basis?
3. On what grounds does Noonan reject viability as the point that distinguishes persons from nonpersons?
4. On what grounds does Noonan reject experience and the possession of memories as an argument in support of abortion?
5. On what grounds docs Noonan reject both parental feelings toward the fetus and social visibility as morally irrelevant to the moral status of the fetus?
6. What criterion does Noonan use to define personhood? What support does he offer for his definition?
7. What analogy does Noonan offer to support his argument that even if we are not sure that the fetus is a person, we should give the fetus the benefit of the doubt?
8. How does Noonan use "biological probabilities" to support his argument that the fetus is a person?
9. How does Noonan suggest that we resolve conflicts between the rights of the fetus and the rights of the mother?
10. What philosophical principle is, according to Noonan, equivalent to the scriptural command to "love your neighbor as yourself" and how does it apply to the fetus?

The most fundamental question involved in the long history of thought on abortion is: how do you determine the humanity of a being? To phrase the question that way is to put in comprehensive humanistic terms what the theologians either dealt with as an explicitly theological question under the heading of "ensoulment" or dealt with implicitly in their treatment of abortion. The Christian position as it originated did not depend on a narrow theological or philosophical concept. . . . The theological notion of ensoulment could easily be translated into humanistic language by substituting "human" for "rational soul"; the problem of knowing when a man is a man is common to theology and humanism.

If one steps outside the specific categories used by the theologians, the answer they gave can be analyzed as a refusal to discriminate among human beings on the basis of their varying potentialities. Once conceived, the being was recognized as man because he had man's potential. The criterion for humanity, thus, was simple and all-embracing: if you are conceived by human parents, you are human.

The strength of this position may be tested by a review of some of the other distinctions offered in the contemporary controversy over legalizing abortion. Perhaps the most popular distinction is in terms of viability. Before an age of so many months, the fetus is not viable, that is, it cannot be removed from the mother's womb and live apart from her. To that extent, the life of the fetus is absolutely dependent on the life of the mother. This dependence is made the basis of denying recognition to its humanity.

There are difficulties with this distinction. One is that the perfection of artificial incubation may make the fetus viable at any time: it may be removed and artificially sustained. Experiments with animals already show that such a procedure is possible. This hypothetical extreme case relates to an actual difficulty: there is considerable elasticity to the idea of viability. Mere length of life is not an exact measure. The viability of the fetus depends on the extent of its anatomical and functional development. . . .

The most important objection to this approach is that dependence is not ended by viability. The fetus is still absolutely dependent on someone's care in order to continue existence; indeed a child of one or three or even five years of age is absolutely dependent on another's care for existence; uncared for, the older fetus or the younger child will die as surely as the early fetus detached from the mother. The unsubstantial lessening in dependence at viability does not seem to signify any special acquisition of humanity.

A second distinction has been attempted in terms of experience. A being who has had experience, has lived and suffered, who possesses memories, is more human than one who has not. Humanity depends on formation by experience. The fetus is thus "unformed" in the most basic human sense. . . .

This distinction is not serviceable for the embryo which is already experiencing and reacting. The embryo is responsive to touch after eight weeks and at least at that point is experiencing. At an earlier stage the zygote is certainly alive and responding to its environment. The distinction may also be challenged by the rare case where aphasia has erased adult memory: has it erased humanity? More fundamentally, this distinction leaves even the older fetus or the younger child to be treated as an unformed inhuman thing. Finally, it is not clear why experience as such confers humanity. It could be argued that certain central experiences such as loving or learning are necessary to make a man human. But then human beings who have failed to love or to learn might be excluded from the class called man.

A third distinction is made by appeal to the sentiments of adults. If a fetus dies, the grief of the parents is not the grief they would have for a living child. The fetus is an unnamed "it" till birth, and is not perceived as personality until at least the fourth month of existence when movements in the womb manifest a vigorous presence demanding joyful recognition by the parents.

Yet feeling is notoriously an unsure guide to the humanity of others. Many groups of humans have had difficulty in feeling that persons of another tongue, color, religion, sex are as human as they. Apart from reactions to alien groups, we mourn the loss of a ten-year-old boy more than the loss of his one-day-old brother or his 90-year-old grandfather. The difference felt and the grief expressed vary with the potentialities extinguished, or the experience wiped out; they do not seem to point to any substantial difference in the humanity of baby, boy, or grandfather.

Distinctions are also made in terms of sensation by the parents. The embryo is felt within the womb only after about the fourth month. The embryo is seen only at birth. What can be neither seen nor felt is different from what is tangible. If the fetus cannot be seen or touched at all, it cannot be perceived as man.

Yet experience shows that sight is even more untrustworthy than feeling in determining humanity. By sight, color became an appropriate index for saying who was a man, and the evil of racial discrimination was given foundation. Nor can touch provide the test; a being confined by sickness, "out of touch" with others, does not thereby seem to lose his humanity. To the extent that touch still has appeal as a criterion, it appears to be a survival of the old English idea of "quickening"—a possible mistranslation of the Latin *animatus* used in the canon law. To that extent touch as a criterion seems to be dependent on the Aristotelian notion of ensoulment, and to fall when this notion is discarded.

Finally, a distinction is sought in social visibility. The fetus is not socially perceived as human. It cannot communicate with others. Thus, both subjectively and objectively, it is not a member of society. As moral rules are rules for the behavior of members of society to each other, they cannot be made for behavior toward what is not yet a member. Excluded from the society of men, the fetus is excluded from the humanity of men.

By force of the argument from the consequences, this distinction is to be rejected. It is more subtle than that founded on an appeal to physical sensation, but it is equally dangerous in its implications. If humanity depends on social recognition, individuals or whole groups may be dehumanized by being denied any status in their society. Such a fate is fictionally portrayed in *1984* and has actually been the lot of many men in many societies. In the Roman empire, for example, condemnation to slavery meant the practical denial of most human rights; in the Chinese Communist world, landlords have been classified as enemies of the people and so treated as nonpersons by the state. Humanity does not depend on social recognition, though often the failure of society to recognize the prisoner, the alien, the heterodox as human has led to the destruction of human beings. Anyone conceived by a man and a woman is human. Recognition of this condition by society follows a real event in the objective order, however imperfect and halting the recognition. Any attempt to limit humanity to exclude some group runs the risk of furnishing authority and precedent for excluding other groups in the name of the consciousness or perception of the controlling group in the society.

A philosopher may reject the appeal to the humanity of the fetus because he views "humanity" as a secular view of the soul and because he doubts the existence of anything real and objective which can be identified as humanity. One answer to such a philosopher is to ask how he reasons about moral questions without supposing that there is a sense in which he and the others of whom he speaks are human. Whatever group is taken as the society which determines who may be killed is thereby taken as human. A second answer is to ask if he does not believe that there is a right and wrong way of deciding moral questions. If there is such a difference, experience may be appealed to: to decide who is human on the basis of the sentiment of a given society has led to consequences which rational men would characterize as monstrous. . . .

There is a kind of continuity in all life, but the earlier stages of the elements of human life possess tiny probabilities of development. Consider for example, the spermatozoa in any normal ejaculate: there are about 200,000,000 in any single ejaculate, of which one has a chance of developing into a zygote. Consider the oocytes which may become ova: there are 100,000 to 1,000,000 oocytes in a female infant, of which a maximum of 390 are ovulated. But once spermatozoon and ovum meet and the conceptus is formed, such studies as have been made show that roughly in only 20 percent of the cases will spontaneous abortion occur. In other words, the chances are about 4 out of 5 that this new being will develop. At this stage in the life of the being there is a sharp shift in probabilities, an immense jump in potentialities. . . .

It may be asked, What does a change in biological probabilities have to do with establishing humanity? The argument from probabilities is not aimed at establishing humanity but at establishing an objective discontinuity which may be taken into account in moral discourse. As life itself is a matter of probabilities, as most moral reasoning is an estimate of probabilities, so it seems in accord with the structure of reality and the nature of moral thought to found a moral judgment on the change in probabilities at conception. The appeal to probabilities is the most commonsensical of arguments, to a greater or smaller degree all of us base our actions on probabilities, and in morals, as in law, prudence and negligence are often measured by the account one has taken of the probabilities. If the chance is 200,000,000 to 1 that the movement in the bushes into which you shoot is a man's, I doubt if many persons would hold you careless in shooting; but if the chances are 4 out of 5 that the movement is a human being's, few would acquit you of blame. Would the argument be different if only one out of ten children conceived came to term? Of course this argument would be different. This argument is an appeal to probabilities that actually exist, not to any and all states of affairs which may be imagined.

The probabilities as they do exist do not show the humanity of the embryo in the sense of a demonstration in logic any more than the probabilities of the movement in the bush being a man demonstrate beyond all doubt that the being is a man. The appeal is a "buttressing" consideration, showing the plausibility of the standard adopted. The argument focuses on the decisional factor in any moral judgment and assumes that part of the business of a moralist is drawing lines. One evidence of the nonarbitrary character of the line drawn is the difference of probabilities on either side of it. If a spermatozoon is destroyed, one destroys a being which had a chance of far less than 1 in 200 million of developing into a reasoning being, possessed of the genetic code, a heart and other organs, and capable of pain. If a fetus is destroyed, one destroys a being already possessed of the genetic code, organs, and sensitivity to pain, and one which had an 80 percent chance of developing further into a baby outside the womb who, in time, would reason.

The positive argument for conception as the decisive moment of humanization is that at conception the new being receives the genetic code. It is this genetic information which determines his characteristics, which is the biological carrier of the possibility of human wisdom, which makes him a self-evolving being. A being with a human genetic code is man. . . .

Even with the fetus weighed as human, one interest could be weighed as equal or superior: that of the mother in her own life. The casuists between 1450 and 1895 were willing to weigh this interest as superior. Since 1895, that interest was given decisive weight only in the two special cases of the cancerous uterus and the ectopic pregnancy. In both of these cases the fetus itself had little chance of survival even if the abortion were not performed. As the balance was once struck in favor of the mother whenever her life was endangered, it could be so struck again. The balance reached between 1895 and 1930 attempted prudentially and pastorally to forestall a multitude of exceptions for interests less than life.

The perception of the humanity of the fetus and the weighing of fetal rights against other human rights constituted the work of the moral analysts. But what spirit animated their abstract judgments? For the Christian community it was the injunction of Scripture to love your neighbor as yourself. The fetus as human was a neighbor; his life had parity with one's own. The commandment gave life to what otherwise would have been only rational calculation.

The commandment could be put in humanistic as well as theological terms: do not injure your fellow man without reason. In these terms, once the humanity of the fetus is perceived, abortion is never right except in self-defense. When life must be taken to save life, reason alone cannot say that a mother must prefer a child's life to her own. With this exception, now of great rarity, abortion violates the rational humanist tenet of the equality of human lives.

Discussion Questions

1. Noonan argues that parents' feelings toward their fetus are morally irrelevant. Discuss how a care ethicist, such as Nel Noddings, might respond to Noonan's argument.

2. According to Noonan, "anyone conceived by a man and a woman is human [a person]." Evaluate the premises he offers in support of this definition of personhood.

3. Imagine a conversation between Noonan and Thomson. How might Thomson respond to Noonan's claim that abortion is never right except in cases of self-defense?

4. While Noonan supports the Catholic position on abortion, he points out that this position can be supported on rational philosophical or humanistic premises. Discuss whether Noonan does an adequate job of supporting his position on abortion using only philosophical premises.

MARY ANNE WARREN

The Moral Significance of Birth

Mary Anne Warren is a professor of philosophy at San Francisco State University. Warren defends a pro-choice position on abortion: Women have a fundamental right to make their own decisions about their bodies. After rejecting the traditional criteria of personhood, Warren argues that personhood does not begin until after birth. Because the fetus is not a person, abortion can be justified under any circumstances.

Critical Reading Questions

1. According to Warren, what is the relationship between moral and legal rights?
2. What are Warren's arguments against the use of the "intrinsic-properties assumption" and the "single-criterion assumption" as the foundation of moral rights?
3. Why does Warren reject both sentience and viability as sufficient conditions for personhood?
4. What arguments does Warren use in support of self-awareness as a condition for personhood?
5. Why does Warren consider early infanticide morally preferable to infanticide after a few weeks, even though the two-week-old infant is not yet a person?
6. What arguments does Warren use to support her claim that, in our society, we should extend protection to human infants even though they are not yet persons?
7. What is the relationship, according to Warren, between personhood and being a member of a community?
8. What does Warren mean when she says that granting legal personhood to the fetus is "necessarily incompatible" with respect for the personhood of women?

Does birth make a difference to the moral rights of the fetus/infant? Should it make a difference to its legal rights? Most contemporary philosophers believe that birth cannot make a difference to moral rights. If this is true, then it becomes difficult to justify either a moral or a legal distinction between late abortion and infanticide. I argue that the view that birth is irrelevant to moral rights rests upon two highly questionable assumptions about the theoretical foundations of moral rights. If we reject these assumptions, then we are free to take account of the contrasting biological and social relationships that make even relatively late abortion morally different from infanticide.

"The Moral Significance of Birth," *Hypatia* 4, no. 3 (Fall 1989): 46–65. Notes have been omitted.

English common law treats the moment of live birth as the point at which a legal person comes into existence. Although abortion has often been prohibited, it has almost never been classified as homicide. In contrast, infanticide generally is classified as a form of homicide, even where (as in England) there are statutes designed to mitigate the severity of the crime in certain cases. But many people—including some feminists—now favor the extension of equal legal rights to some or all fetuses (S. Callahan 1984, 1986). The extension of legal personhood to fetuses would not only threaten women's right to choose abortion, but also undermine other fundamental rights. I will argue that because of these dangers, birth remains the most appropriate place to mark the existence of a new legal person. . . .

THE DENIAL OF THE MORAL SIGNIFICANCE OF BIRTH

The view that birth is irrelevant to moral rights is shared by philosophers on all points of the spectrum of moral views about abortion. For the most conservative, birth adds nothing to the infant's moral rights, since all of those rights have been present since conception. Moderates hold that the fetus acquires an equal right to life at some point after conception but before birth. The most popular candidates for this point of moral demarcation are (1) the stage at which the fetus becomes viable (i.e., capable of surviving outside the womb, with or without medical assistance), and (2) the stage at which it becomes sentient (i.e., capable of having experiences, including that of pain). For those who hold a view of this sort, both infanticide and abortion at any time past the critical stage are forms of homicide, and there is little reason to distinguish between them either morally or legally.

Finally, liberals hold that even relatively late abortion is sometimes morally acceptable, and that at no time is abortion the moral equivalent of homicide. However, few liberals wish to hold that infanticide is not—at least sometimes—morally comparable to homicide. Consequently, the presumption that being born makes no difference to one's moral rights creates problems for the liberal view of abortion. Unless the liberal can establish some grounds for a general moral distinction between late abortion and early infanticide, she must either retreat to a moderate position on abortion, or else conclude that infanticide is not so bad after all.

To those who accept the intrinsic-properties assumption, birth can make little difference to the moral standing of the fetus/infant. For birth does not seem to alter any intrinsic property that could reasonably be linked to the possession of a strong right to life. Newborn infants have very nearly the same intrinsic properties as do fetuses shortly before birth. . . .

Prenatal neurophysiology and behavior suggest that human fetuses begin to have rudimentary sensory experiences at some time during the second trimester of pregnancy. . . .

These two theories are worth examining, not only because they illustrate the difficulties generated by the intrinsic-properties and single-criterion assumptions, but also because each includes valid insights that need to be integrated into a more comprehensive account. Both Sumner and Tooley are partially right. Unlike "genetic humanity"—a property possessed by fertilized human ova—sentience and self-awareness are properties that have some general relevance to what we may owe another being in the way of respect and protection. However, neither the sentience criterion nor the self-awareness criterion can explain the moral significance of birth.

THE SENTIENCE CRITERION

Both newborn infants and late-term fetuses show clear signs of sentience. For instance, they are apparently capable of having visual experiences. Infants will often turn away from bright lights, and those who have done intrauterine photography have sometimes observed a similar reaction in the late-term fetus when bright lights are introduced in its vicinity. Both may respond to loud noises, voices, or other sounds, so both can probably have auditory experiences. They are evidently also responsive to touch, taste, motion, and other kinds of sensory stimulation.

The sentience of infants and late-term fetuses makes a difference to how they should be treated, by contrast with fertilized ova or first-trimester fetuses. Sentient beings are usually capable of experiencing painful as well as pleasurable or effectively neutral sensations. . . . Thus, sentient beings may plausibly be said to have a moral right not to be deliberately subjected to pain in the absence of any compelling reason. For those who prefer not to speak of rights, it is still plausible that a capacity for sentience gives an entity some moral standing. . . .

But it is not clear that sentience is a sufficient condition for moral equality, since there are many clearly-sentient creatures (e.g., mice) to which most of us would not be prepared to ascribe equal moral standing. . . .

The 1973 *Roe v. Wade* decision treats the presumed viability of third-trimester fetuses as a basis for permitting states to restrict abortion rights in order to protect fetal life in the third trimester, but not earlier. Yet viability is relative, among other things, to the medical care available to the pregnant woman and her infant. Increasingly sophisticated neonatal intensive care has made it possible to save many more premature infants than before, thus altering the average age of viability. Someday it may be possible to keep even first-trimester fetuses alive and developing normally outside the womb. The viability criterion seems to imply that the advent of total ectogenesis (artificial gestation from conception to birth) would automatically eliminate women's right to abortion, even in the earliest stages of pregnancy. At the very least, it must imply that as many aborted fetuses as possible should be kept alive through artificial gestation. But the mere technological possibility of providing artificial wombs for huge numbers of human fetuses could not establish such a moral obligation. A massive commitment to ectogenesis would probably be ruinously expensive, and might prove contrary to the interests of parents of children. The viability criterion forces us to make a hazardous leap from the technologically possible to the morally mandatory.

The sentience criterion at first appears more promising as a means of defending a moderate view of abortion. It provides an intuitively plausible distinction between early and late abortion. Unlike the viability criterion, it is unlikely to be undermined by new biomedical technologies. . . .

The strong version of the sentience criterion treats sentience as a sufficient condition for having full and equal moral standing. The weak version treats sentience as sufficient for having some moral standing, but not necessarily full and equal moral standing. . . .

[According to the strong version] any being which has even minimal capacities for sensory experience is the moral equal of any person. If we accept this theory, then we must conclude that not only is late abortion the moral equivalent of homicide, but so is the killing of such sentient nonhuman beings as mice. . . . [According to the weak version] all sentient beings have some moral standing, but beings that are more highly sentient have greater moral standing than do less highly sentient beings. This weaker version of the sentience criterion leaves room for a distinction between the moral standing of mice and that of sentient humans—provided, that is, that mice can be shown to be less highly sentient. However, it will not support the moral equality of late-term fetuses, since the relatively undeveloped condition of fetal brains almost certainly means that fetuses are less highly sentient than older human beings. . . .

THE SELF-AWARENESS CRITERION

Although newborn infants are regarded as persons in both law and common moral conviction, they lack certain mental capacities that are typical of persons. They have sensory experiences, but, as Tooley points out, they probably do not yet think, or have a sense of who they are, or a desire to continue to exist. It is not unreasonable to suppose that these facts make some difference to their moral standing. Other things being equal, it is surely worse to kill a self-aware being that wants to go on living than one that has never been self-aware and that has no such preference. If this is true, then it is hard to avoid the conclusion that neither abortion nor infanticide is quite as bad as the killing of older human beings. And indeed many human societies seem to have accepted that conclusion. . . .

But if infanticide is to be considered, it is better that it be done immediately after birth, before the bonds of love and care between the infant and the mother (and other persons) have grown any stronger than they may already be. Postponing the question of the infant's acceptance for weeks or months would be cruel to all concerned. Although an infant may be little more sentient or self-aware at two weeks of age than at birth, its death is apt to be a greater tragedy—not for it, but for those who have come to love it. I suspect that this is why, where infanticide is tolerated, the decision to kill or abandon an infant must usually be made rather quickly. If this consideration is morally relevant—and I think it is—then the self-awareness criterion fails to illuminate some of the morally salient aspects of infanticide. . . .

WHY PROTECT INFANTS?

I have already mentioned some of the reasons for protecting human infants more carefully than we protect most comparably-sentient nonhuman beings. Most people care deeply about infants, particularly—but not exclusively—their own. Normal human adults (and children) are probably "programmed" by their biological nature to respond to human infants with care and concern. For the mother, in particular, that response is apt to begin well before the infant is born. But even for her it is likely to become more intense after the infant's birth. The infant at birth enters the human social world, where, if it lives, it becomes involved in social relationships with others, of kinds that can only be dimly foreshadowed before birth. It begins to be known and cared for, not just as a potential member of the family or community, but as a socially present and responsive individual. . . . The newborn is not yet self-aware, but it is already (rapidly becoming) a social being.

Thus, although the human newborn may have no intrinsic properties that can ground a moral right to life stronger than that of a fetus just before birth, its emergence into the social world makes it appropriate to treat it as if it had such a stronger right. This, in effect, is what the law has done, through the doctrine that a person begins to exist at birth. . . .

Another reason for condemning infanticide is that, at least in relatively privileged nations like our own, infants whose parents cannot raise them can usually be placed with people who will love them and take good care of them. This means that infanticide is rarely in the infant's own best interests, and would often deprive some potential adoptive individual or family of a great benefit. . . .

But have I not left the door open to the claim that infanticide may still be justified in some places, e.g., where there is severe poverty and a lack of accessible adoption agencies or where women face exceptionally harsh penalties for "illegitimate" births? I have, and deliberately. The moral case against the toleration of infanticide is contingent upon the existence of morally preferable options. Where economic hardship, the lack of contraception and abortion, and other forms of sexual and political oppression have eliminated all such options, there will be instances in which infanticide is the least tragic of a tragic set of choices. In such circumstances, the enforcement of extreme sanctions against infanticide can constitute an additional injustice.

WHY BIRTH MATTERS

I have defended what most regard as needing no defense, i.e., the ascription of an equal right to life to human infants. Under reasonably favorable conditions that policy can protect the rights and interests of all concerned, including infants, biological parents, and potential adoptive parents.

But if protecting infants is such a good idea, then why is it not a good idea to extend the same strong protections to sentient fetuses? The question is not whether sentient fetuses ought to be protected: of course they should. Most women readily accept the responsibility of doing whatever they can to ensure that their (voluntarily continued) pregnancies are successful, and that no avoidable harm comes to the fetus. Negligent or malevolent actions by third parties which result in death or injury to pregnant women or their potential children should be subject to moral censure and legal prosecution. A just and caring society would do much more than ours does to protect the health of all its members, including pregnant women.

The question is whether the law should accord to late-term fetuses *exactly the same* protections as are accorded to infants and older human beings.

The case for doing so might seem quite strong. . . .

But there is one crucial consideration which this argument leaves out. It is impossible to treat fetuses *in utero* as if they were persons without treating women as if they were something less than persons. The extension of equal rights to sentient fetuses would inevitably license severe violations of women's basic rights to personal autonomy and physical security. In the first place, it would rule out most second-trimester abortions performed to protect the women's life or health. Such abortions might sometimes be construed as a form of self-defense. But the right to self-defense is not usually taken to mean that one may kill innocent persons just because their continued existence poses some threat to one's own life or health. If abortion must be justified as self-defense, then it will rarely be performed until the woman is already in some extreme danger, and perhaps not even then. Such a policy would cost some women their lives, while others would be subjected to needless suffering and permanent physical harm.

Other alarming consequences of the drive to extend more equal rights to fetuses are already apparent in the United States. In the past decade it has become increasingly common for hospitals or physicians to obtain court orders requiring women in labor to undergo Caesarean sections, against their will, for what is thought to be the good of the fetus. . . . Forced Caesareans threaten to reduce women to the status of inanimate objects—containers which may be opened at the will of others in order to get at their contents. . . .

Another danger in extending equal legal protections to sentient fetuses is that women will increasingly be blamed, and sometimes legally prosecuted, when they miscarry or give birth to premature, sick, or abnormal infants. It is reasonable to hold the caretakers of infants legally responsible if their charges are harmed because of their avoidable negligence. But when a woman miscarries or gives birth to an abnormal infant, the cause of harm might be traced to any of an enormous number of actions or circumstances which would not normally constitute any legal offense. She might have gotten too much exercise or too little, eaten the wrong foods or the wrong quantity of the right ones, or taken or failed to take certain drugs. She might have smoked, consumed alcohol, or gotten too little sleep. She might have "permitted" her health to be damaged by hard work, by unsafe employment conditions, by the lack of affordable medical care, by living near a source of industrial pollution, by a physically or mentally abusive partner, or in any number of other ways.

Are such supposed failures on the part of pregnant women potentially to be construed as child abuse or negligent homicide? If sentient fetuses are entitled to the same legal protections as infants, then it would seem so. . . .

Such an approach to the protection of fetuses authorizes the legal regulation of virtually every aspect of women's public and private lives, and thus is incompatible with even the most minimal right to autonomy. Moreover, such laws are apt to prove counterproductive, since the fear of prosecution may deter poor or otherwise vulnerable women from seeking medical care during pregnancy. I am not suggesting that women whose apparent negligence causes prenatal harm to their infants should always be immune from criticism. However, if we want to improve the health of infants we would do better to provide the services women need to protect their health, rather than seeking to use the law to punish those whose prenatal care has been less than ideal. . . .

Such arguments will not persuade those who deeply believe that fetuses are already persons, with equal moral rights. How, they will ask, is denying legal equality to sentient fetuses different from denying it to any other powerless group of human beings? If some human beings are more equal than others, then how can any of us feel safe? The answer is twofold.

First, pregnancy is a relationship different from any other, including that between parents and already-born children. It is not just one of innumerable situations in which the rights of one individual may come into conflict with those of another; it is probably the *only* case in which the legal personhood of one human being is necessarily incompatible with that of another. Only in pregnancy is the organic functioning of one human individual biologically inseparable from that of another. This organic unity makes it impossible for others to provide the fetus with medical care or any other presumed benefit, except by doing something to or for the woman. To try to "protect" the fetus other than through her cooperation and consent is effectively to nullify her right to autonomy, and potentially to expose her to violent physical assaults such as would not be legally condoned in any other type of case. The uniqueness of pregnancy helps to explain why the toleration of abortion does not lead to the disenfranchisement of other groups of human beings, as opponents of abortion often claim. . . .

But, granting the uniqueness of pregnancy, why is it *women's* rights that should be privileged? If women and fetuses cannot both be legal persons then why not favor the fetus, e.g., on the grounds that they are more helpless, or more innocent, or have a longer life expectancy? It is difficult to justify this apparent bias towards women without appealing to the empirical fact that women are already persons in the usual, nonlegal sense—already thinking, self-aware, fully social beings—and fetuses are not. Regardless of whether we stress the intrinsic properties of persons, or the social and relational dimensions of personhood, this distinction remains. Even sentient fetuses do not yet have either the cognitive capacities or the richly interactive social involvements typical of persons.

This "not yet" is morally decisive. It is wrong to treat persons as if they do not have equal basic rights. Other things being equal, it is worse to deprive persons of their most basic moral and legal rights than to refrain from extending such rights to beings that are not persons. This is one important element of truth in the self-awareness criterion. If fetuses were already thinking, self-aware, socially responsive members of communities, then nothing could justify refusing them the equal protection of the law. In that case, we would sometimes be forced to balance the rights of the fetus against those of the woman, and sometimes the scales might be almost equally weighted. However, if women are persons and fetuses are not, then the balance must swing toward women's rights.

CONCLUSION

Birth is morally significant because it marks the end of one relationship and the beginning of others. It marks the end of pregnancy, a relationship so intimate that it is impossible to extend the equal protection of the law to fetuses without severely infringing women's most basic rights. Birth also marks the beginning of the infant's existence as a socially responsive member of a human community. Although the infant is not instantly transformed into a person at the moment of birth, it does become a biologically separate human being. As such, it can be known and cared for as a particular individual. It can also be vigorously protected without negating the basic rights of women. There are circumstances in which infanticide may be the best of a bad set of options. But our own society has both the ability and the desire to protect infants, and there is no reason why we should not do so.

We should not, however, seek to extend the same degree of protection to fetuses. Both late-term fetuses and newborn infants are probably capable of sentience. Both are precious to those who want children; and both need to be protected from a variety of possible harms. All of these factors contribute to the moral standing of the late-term fetus, which is substantial. However, to extend equal legal rights to fetuses is necessarily to deprive pregnant women of the rights to personal autonomy, physical integrity, and sometimes life itself. *There is room for only one person with full and equal rights inside a single human skin.* That is why it is birth, rather than sentience, viability, or some other prenatal milestone that must mark the beginning of legal personhood.

REFERENCES

Callahan, Sidney. 1984. Value choices in abortion. In *Abortion: Understanding differences.* Sidney Callahan and Daniel Callahan, eds. New York and London: Plenum Press.

Callahan, Sidney. 1986. Abortion and the sexual agenda. *Commonweal,* April 25, 232–238.

Tooley, Michael. 1983. *Abortion and infanticide.* Oxford: Oxford University Press.

Discussion Questions

1. Does Warren confuse cultural norms and legal rights with moral rights? Can she defend her position without reference to cultural norms and legal rights? Use specific examples to support your answers.
2. Discuss Warren's claim that deontology, rights ethics, and care ethics all support abortion and early infanticide. Would a utilitarian also agree with her position? Discuss how a Buddhist might respond to Warren's argument.
3. Critically evaluate Warren's claim that self-concept is necessary for personhood. Discuss the implications of accepting this criterion for the moral standing of infants and brain-damaged, senile, and comatose humans. Would Warren permit euthanasia for these groups of humans?
4. Massachusetts Institute of Technology psychology professor Steven Pinker claims that the killing of newborn babies is perfectly natural and has been practiced and accepted in most cultures. "To a biologist," he points out, "birth is as arbitrary a milestone as any other . . . so how do you provide grounds for outlawing neonaticide? The facts don't make it easy."[30] Discuss how Warren might respond to Pinker.
5. The United Nations Population Fund advocates abortion as a means of population control, especially in areas of the world that are already plagued by overpopulation, such as China and India.[31] Discuss what Warren would most likely think of this policy.

DON MARQUIS

Why Abortion Is Immoral

Don Marquis is a professor of philosophy at the University of Kansas. Marquis disagrees with philosophers such as Warren who believe that birth is morally significant in terms of the value of a human's life. He argues instead that while abortion may sometimes be morally permissible, the moral presumption against killing a fetus is as

---

"Why Abortion Is Immoral," *Journal of Philosophy* 86 (April 1989). Some notes have been omitted.

strong as the moral presumption against killing an adult human or newborn because abortion deprives the victims of the value of the activities, experiences, and enjoyments of their future.

Critical Reading Questions

1. What is the major presumption of Marquis's argument that abortion is immoral?
2. Why, according to Marquis, is it wrong to kill adult humans?
3. What does Marquis mean by the phrase a "future like ours"?
4. What are the implications of Marquis's argument for the killing of nonhuman animals? What are the implications of Marquis's argument for euthanasia?
5. On what grounds does Marquis dismiss arguments against abortion that depend on the category of personhood?
6. Why is a "future like ours" of value to the fetus? Why is it wrong to deprive a fetus of this future?
7. What are the implications of Marquis's argument for the use of contraception?

The view that abortion is, with rare exceptions, seriously immoral has received little support in the recent philosophical literature. No doubt most philosophers affiliated with secular institutions of higher education believe that the anti-abortion position is either a symptom of irrational religious dogma or a conclusion generated by seriously confused philosophical argument. The purpose of this essay is to undermine this general belief. This essay sets out an argument that purports to show, as well as any argument in ethics can show, that abortion is, except possibly in rare cases, seriously immoral, that it is in the same moral category as killing an innocent adult human being. . . .

A necessary condition of resolving the abortion controversy is a more theoretical account of the wrongness of killing. After all, if we merely believe, but do not understand, why killing adult human beings such as ourselves is wrong, how could we conceivably show that abortion is either immoral or permissible?

In order to develop such an account, we can start from the following unproblematic assumption concerning our own case: it is wrong to kill *us*. Why is it wrong? Some answers can be easily eliminated. It might be said that what makes killing us wrong is that a killing brutalizes the one who kills. But the brutalization consists of being inured to the performance of an act that is hideously immoral; hence, the brutalization does not explain the immorality. It might be said that what makes killing us wrong is the great loss others would experience due to our absence. Although such hubris is understandable, such an explanation does not account for the wrongness of killing hermits, or those whose lives are relatively independent and whose friends find it easy to make new friends.

A more obvious answer is better. What primarily makes killing wrong is neither its effect on the murderer nor its effect on the victim's friends and relatives, but its effect on the victim. The loss of one's life is one of the greatest losses one can suffer. The loss of one's life deprives one of all the experiences, activities, projects, and enjoyments that would otherwise have constituted one's future. Therefore, killing someone is wrong, primarily because the killing inflicts (one of) the greatest possible losses on the victim. To describe this as the loss of life can be misleading, however. The change in my biological state does not by itself make killing me wrong. The effect of the loss of my biological life is the loss to me of all those activities, projects, experiences, and enjoyments which would otherwise have constituted my future personal life. These activities, projects, experiences, and enjoyments are either valuable for their own sakes or are means to something else that is valuable for its own sake. Some parts of my future are not valued by me now, but will come to be valued by me as I grow older and as my values and capacities change. When I am killed, I am deprived both of what I now value which would have been part of my future personal life, but also what I would come to value. Therefore, when I die, I am deprived of all of the value of my future. Inflicting this loss on me is ultimately what makes killing me wrong. This being the case, it would seem that what makes killing *any* adult human being prima facie seriously wrong is the loss of his or her future. . . .

The view that what makes killing wrong is the loss to the victim of the value of the victim's future gains additional support when some of its implications are examined. In the first place, it is incompatible with the view that it is wrong to kill only beings who are biologically human. It is possible that there exists a different species from another planet whose members have a future like ours. Since having a future like that is what makes killing someone wrong, this theory entails that it would be wrong to kill members of such a species. Hence, this theory is opposed to the claim that only life that is biologically human has great moral worth, a claim which many anti-abortionists have seemed to adopt. This opposition, which this theory has in common with personhood theories, seems to be a merit of the theory.

In the second place, the claim that the loss of one's future is the wrong-making feature of one's being killed entails the possibility that the futures of some actual nonhuman mammals on our own planet are sufficiently like ours that it is seriously wrong to kill them also. Whether some animals do have the same right to life as human beings depends on adding to the account of the wrongness of killing some additional account of just what it is about my future or the futures of other adult human beings which makes it wrong to kill us. No such additional account will be offered in this essay. Undoubtedly, the provision

of such an account would be a very difficult matter. Undoubtedly, any such account would be quite controversial. Hence, it surely should not reflect badly on this sketch of an elementary theory of the wrongness of killing that it is indeterminate with respect to some very difficult issues regarding animal rights.

In the third place, the claim that the loss of one's future is the wrong-making feature of one's being killed does not entail, as sanctity of human life theories do, that active euthanasia is wrong. Persons who are severely and incurably ill, who face a future of pain and despair, and who wish to die will not have suffered a loss if they are killed. It is, strictly speaking, the value of a human's future which makes killing wrong in this theory. This being so, killing does not necessarily wrong some persons who are sick and dying. Of course, there may be other reasons for a prohibition of active euthanasia, but that is another matter. Sanctity-of-human-life theories seem to hold that active euthanasia is seriously wrong even in an individual case where there seems to be good reason for it independently of public policy considerations. This consequence is most implausible, and it is a plus for the claim that the loss of a future of value is what makes killing wrong that it does not share this consequence.

In the fourth place, the account of the wrongness of killing defended in this essay does straightforwardly entail that it is prima facie seriously wrong to kill children and infants, for we do presume that they have futures of value. Since we do believe that it is wrong to kill defenseless little babies, it is important that a theory of the wrongness of killing easily account for this. Personhood theories of the wrongness of killing, on the other hand, cannot straightforwardly account for the wrongness of killing infants and young children.* Hence, such theories must add special ad hoc accounts of the wrongness of killing the young. The plausibility of such ad hoc theories seems to

---

*Feinberg, Tooley, Warren, and Engelhardt have all dealt with this problem.

be a function of how desperately one wants such theories to work. The claim that the primary wrong-making feature of a killing is the loss to the victim of the value of its future accounts for the wrongness of killing young children and infants directly; it makes the wrongness of such acts as obvious as we actually think it is. . . .

The claim that the primary wrong-making feature of a killing is the loss to the victim of the value of its future has obvious consequences for the ethics of abortion. The future of a standard fetus includes a set of experiences, projects, activities, and such which are identical with the futures of adult human beings and are identical with the futures of young children. Since the reason that is sufficient to explain why it is wrong to kill human beings after the time of birth is a reason that also applies to fetuses, it follows that abortion is prima facie seriously morally wrong.

This argument does not rely on the invalid inference that, since it is wrong to kill persons, it is wrong to kill potential persons also. The category that is morally central to this analysis is the category of having a valuable future like ours; it is not the category of personhood. The argument to the conclusion that abortion is prima facie seriously morally wrong proceeded independently of the notion of person or potential person or any equivalent. . . .

Of course, this value of a future-like-ours argument, if sound, shows only that abortion is prima facie wrong, not that it is wrong in any and all circumstances. Since the loss of the future to a standard fetus, if killed, is, however, at least as great a loss as the loss of the future to a standard adult human being who is killed, abortion, like ordinary killing, could be justified only by the most compelling reasons. The loss of one's life is almost the greatest misfortune that can happen to one. Presumably abortion could be justified in some circumstances, only if the loss consequent on failing to abort would be at least as great. Accordingly, morally permissible abortions will be rare indeed unless, perhaps, they occur so early in pregnancy that a fetus is not yet definitely an individual. Hence, this argument should be taken as showing

that abortion is presumptively very seriously wrong, where the presumption is very strong—as strong as the presumption that killing another adult human being is wrong.

How complete an account of the wrongness of killing does the value of a future-like-ours account have to be in order that the wrongness of abortion is a consequence? This account does not have to be an account of the necessary conditions for the wrongness of killing. Some persons in nursing homes may lack valuable human futures, yet it may be wrong to kill them for other reasons. Furthermore, this account does not obviously have to be the sole reason killing is wrong where the victim did have a valuable future. This analysis claims only that, for any killing where the victim did have a valuable future like ours, having that future by itself is sufficient to create the strong presumption that the killing is seriously wrong. . . .

In this essay, it has been argued that the correct ethic of the wrongness of killing can be extended to fetal life and used to show that there is a strong presumption that any abortion is morally impermissible. If the ethic of killing adopted here entails, however, that contraception is also seriously immoral, then there would appear to be a difficulty with the analysis of this essay.

But this analysis does not entail that contraception is wrong. Of course, contraception prevents the actualization of a possible future of value. Hence, it follows from the claim that futures of value should be maximized that contraception is prima facie immoral. This obligation to maximize does not exist, however; furthermore, nothing in the ethics of killing in this paper entails that it does. The ethics of killing in this essay would entail that contraception is wrong only if something were denied a human future of value by contraception. Nothing at all is denied such a future by contraception, however. . . .

At the time of contraception, there are hundreds of millions of sperm, one (released) ovum and millions of possible combinations of all of these. There is no actual combination at all. Is the subject of the loss to be a merely possible combination? Which one? This alternative does not yield an actual subject of harm either. Accordingly, the immorality of contraception is not entailed by the loss of a future-like-ours argument simply because there is no nonarbitrarily identifiable subject of the loss in the case of contraception.

The purpose of this essay has been to set out an argument for the serious presumptive wrongness of abortion subject to the assumption that the moral permissibility of abortion stands or falls on the moral status of the fetus. Since a fetus possesses a property, the possession of which in adult human beings is sufficient to make killing an adult human being wrong, abortion is wrong. This way of dealing with the problem of abortion seems superior to other approaches to the ethics of abortion, because it rests on an ethics of killing which is close to self-evident, because the crucial morally relevant property clearly applies to fetuses, and because the argument avoids the usual equivocations on "human life," "human being," or "person."

The argument rests neither on religious claims nor on Papal dogma. It is not subject to the objection of "speciesism." Its soundness is compatible with the moral permissibility of euthanasia and contraception. It deals with our intuitions concerning young children.

Finally, this analysis can be viewed as resolving a standard problem—indeed, *the* standard problem—concerning the ethics of abortion. Clearly, it is wrong to kill adult human beings. Clearly, it is not wrong to end the life of some arbitrarily chosen single human cell. Fetuses seem to be like arbitrarily chosen human cells in some respects and like adult humans in other respects. The problem of the ethics of abortion is the problem of determining the fetal property that settles this moral controversy. The thesis of this essay is that the problem of the ethics of abortion, so understood, is solvable.

Discussion Questions

1. Without bringing in the concept of "personhood," discuss why it is wrong to kill newborns and adult humans. Apply your criteria to the killing of fetuses.
2. Break down Marquis's argument into its premises and conclusion. Analyze the argument. Are the premises acceptable? Are the premises complete? Does the conclusion follow from the premises? If not, come up with a counterargument that addresses Marquis's concerns.
3. Apply Marquis's argument to the use of RU 486. Discuss whether his argument against abortion would or would not preclude the use of the early abortion pill.
4. If we accept Marquis's claim that abortion is a prima facie wrong because it destroys the future of the fetus, are there circumstances where continuing the pregnancy might damage the woman's future to such an extent that it overrides the value of her fetus's future? How about situations in which the fetus has a severe genetic anomaly associated with a life of suffering and/or death shortly after birth?
5. Discuss how both Thomson and Warren might respond to Marquis's argument.

SERRIN M. FOSTER

Refuse to Choose: Women Deserve Better Than Abortion

Serrin Foster is president of Feminists for Life of America, an organization that is dedicated to eliminating and finding practical solutions to the root causes that drive women to seek abortions. In her article Foster points out that feminists have traditionally been opposed to abortion. She argues that, rather than benefiting women, abortion harms women.

Critical Reading Questions

1. What was the position of feminists over the last two centuries on abortion?
2. What does Foster mean when she says that making abortion a woman's choice also makes abortion her problem?
3. How do colleges generally react when a student becomes pregnant?
4. According to Foster, how does abortion harm women?
5. What options does Foster propose instead of abortion?

For more than two centuries feminists have opposed abortion.

British feminist author Mary Wollstonecraft decried, in scathing 18th century terms, the sexual exploitation of women in *A Vindication of the Rights of Women*. She went on to condemn those who would "either destroy the embryo in the womb or casting it off when born" saying: "Nature in everything deserves respect, and those who violate her laws seldom violate them with impunity."

Elizabeth Cady Stanton, who in 1848 organized the first women's convention in Seneca Falls, New York, and suffragist organizer Susan B. Anthony were active in the abolitionist movement. Their basic belief in the rights of all human beings extended to women, slaves, and children—born and unborn. While history books are filled with their efforts to win rights for women, it is less

"Refuse to Choose: Women Deserve Better Than Abortion," Feminists for Life, 2005.

well known that the early American feminists also opposed abortion.

Without known exception, the early feminists condemned abortion in the strongest terms. Susan B. Anthony and Elizabeth Cady Stanton's radical feminist newspaper, *The Revolution,* called abortion "child murder." Stanton classified abortion as a form of "infanticide" and said, "When we consider that women have been treated as property, it is degrading to women that we should treat our children as property to be disposed of as we see fit." . . .

Sarah Norton, the first woman to successfully argue admission to Cornell University, wrote in an 1870 edition of the *Sisters' Weekly*, "Child murderers practice their profession without let or hindrance, and open infant butcheries unquestioned. . . . Is there no remedy for this antenatal murder? . . . Perhaps there will come a day when . . . an unmarried mother will not be despised because of her motherhood . . . and when the right of the unborn to be born will not be denied or interfered with."

Feminists who fought for the rights of women—to vote, sit on a jury, testify on their own behalf, control their own money, and defend themselves from marital rape—also fought for our right to life.

Yet like today's pro-life feminists, they recognized that women do not have to bear children to share in this celebration of womanhood. Susan B. Anthony, once complimented by a friend who thought that she would have made a wonderful mother, responded, "Sweeter even than to have had the joy of caring for children of my own has it been to me to help bring about a better state of things for mothers generally, so their unborn little ones could not be willed away from them."

Alice Paul, Anthony's successor and author of the original Equal Rights Amendment, once told a friend, "Abortion is the ultimate exploitation to women."

Properly defined, feminism is a philosophy that embraces basic rights for all human beings without exception—without regard to one's race, religion, sex, size, age, location, disability or parentage. Feminism rejects the use of force to dominate, control, or destroy one another. Abortion violates the core principles of feminism: nondiscrimination, nonviolence and justice for all.

In our own day Feminists for Life's Honorary Chair Patricia Heaton, winner of two Emmy awards and a bestselling author, says, "Women experiencing an unplanned pregnancy also deserve unplanned joy." The sad reality is that the "unplanned joy" Patricia Heaton envisions for women is all too rare. Instead, women experiencing an unplanned pregnancy often end up experiencing the tragic violence of abortion.

OUR BODY. OUR CHOICE.
OUR *PROBLEM.*

Statistics gathered by abortion supporters reveal that the overarching reasons women with unintended pregnancies turn to abortion are lack of financial resources and lack of emotional support. Many women also say they felt abandoned, or even coerced into having an abortion. Despite child support laws, some fathers threaten to withhold support. Domestic violence against pregnant women at the hands of a partner is being reported with greater frequency. . . .

The women at highest risk of resorting to abortion are those of college age. One out of five abortions is performed on a college student. For many years, Feminists for Life's College Outreach Program has been listening to women on campuses across the country. Women who tested positive for pregnancy at a campus health center tell us—almost universally—that the next words they heard from clinic staff were "I'm so sorry."

Then they were handed a business card for a local abortion clinic. University counselors and professors echo this message, telling students that they can't possibly continue their education and have a child—as if pregnancy makes women incapable of reading, writing or thinking.

Resources are similarly lopsided. Some colleges offer $300 loans for an abortion, but no financial aid if the young woman gives birth. Pregnant and parenting students report that housing, maternity coverage, childcare and telecommuting options are nonexistent on many campuses, and expensive on others. Women who are visibly pregnant are stared at like exotic animals when they cross the campus.

Forcing a woman to choose between sacrificing her education or career plans and sacrificing her child is not much of a "free choice."

Beyond the campus, support is also lacking for any choice other than abortion. Pregnant and parenting women in the workplace still cannot count on basic benefits such as maternity coverage, job sharing, flex time, telecommuting, or the ability to make a living wage.

Even well meaning family and friends often fail to give women what they really need and want—congratulations and unconditional support. Instead of saying "How can I help?" they say, "A baby will ruin your life."

In other words, most women "choose" abortion precisely because they believe they have no other choice.

More than 30 years since the U.S. Supreme Court handed down the *Roe v. Wade* decision legalizing abortion, the pro-choice mantra "Our body, Our choice" still means the same thing: Our problem. Abortion is not a measure of society's success in meeting the needs of women; it's a measure of its failure.

ABORTION HARMS WOMEN

The damage that abortion causes to women's bodies can result in infertility, future miscarriages, and even death. Second-term abortions performed on teens with a family history of breast cancer elevate their risk of breast cancer. Many women carry emotional scars from the experience. Studies from Finland, Great Britain, Canada and the United States reveal higher rates of suicide, attempted suicide and psychiatric admissions among women who have had an abortion compared to women who have given birth.

Feminists for Life board member Marion Syversen had two abortions as a teenager while living in an extremely abusive home. She supports studies of abortion's impact on women—especially since abortion is the most common surgery in America. Reminded that former Surgeon General C. Everett Koop said it was problematic to study the impact of abortion because half the women who had them may deny it, Syversen responded, "Well, doesn't that tell you something? If it was such a great thing we'd all be talking about it!"

At a July 2002 briefing on Capitol Hill, actor and Feminists for Life Honorary Co-Chair Margaret Colin challenged members of Congress to "remember the woman" and ask themselves, "Is this the best we can do for her?" Abortion is a symptom of—never a solution to—the problems faced by women. Americans like to say. "Failure is not an option." Yet abortion has completely failed as a social policy designed to aid women. Women have had to settle for far less than they need and deserve.

REFUSE TO CHOOSE

Abstract rhetoric that pits "women's rights" against "the baby" does nothing to solve the unmet needs of women. As a result, more than a million times a year in America, women lay their bodies down or swallow a bitter pill. Every day that goes by with the needs of pregnant women unmet is another day marked by thousands of abortions. Although Americans are deeply divided on abortion, there is no disagreement that the number of abortions needs to be reduced. No compassionate person wants a woman to suffer through the personal tragedy of abortion.

Abortion is a reflection that we have not met the needs of women. Susan B. Anthony urged activists to address the root causes that drive women to abortion. It's time for feminism to return to its roots with a women-centered plan to significantly eliminate abortion.

Women's advocates on both sides need to work together for better outcomes for women and children. We should seek a comprehensive review of the reasons that drive women to abortion. We must listen to women from all walks of life—women who have had abortions, single and married mothers, birthmothers. Men should be welcomed as partners in problem solving. We need to listen, to hear women and create a step-by-step plan to systematically eliminate the root causes that drive so many women to abortion—primarily the lack of financial resources and lack of emotional support.

We need to engage those in higher education, healthcare, technology, corporations, small businesses, the entertainment industry, government and the media to help redirect the debate toward positive outcomes for all concerned.

We must begin by finding solutions for those at highest risk of abortion—college women, young working women and low-income women.

College campuses should reexamine their policies, attitudes and support for pregnant and parenting students and staff. Through programs like Feminists for Life's Pregnancy Resource

Forums, people on all sides of the debate within the campus community can put aside their differences to address the needs of pregnant and parenting students, including housing, childcare and maternity benefits in student healthcare plans.

Family-friendly workplaces that offer childcare, flex time and telecommuting solutions can help lessen the pressure on women to choose between their careers and their children. Farsighted employers like Steelcase Corporation of Michigan set up offices in the homes of employees who are new parents to help them telecommute.

Pregnancy care centers need funding to assist women to follow through on nonviolent, life-affirming choices—whether that involves married parenthood, single parenthood, extended family or co-parenting options, or adoption.

We need to replicate the success achieved in Pennsylvania, where abortions have been greatly reduced through state funding of resource centers that promote life-affirming alternatives. Pennsylvania law also mandates that a woman seeking an abortion be accurately and adequately informed about the procedure, fetal development, and the father's rights and responsibilities so she can make an informed choice. The late Governor Robert Casey knew that women deserve—and can handle—this information. We can work with states to implement the State Children's Health Insurance Program (SCHIP), whose services include prenatal care for low-income women and their unborn children.

It is also important that we reverse the negative attitudes toward children and parenting that have become so prevalent in our culture. Our society needs once again to cherish motherhood, champion fatherhood, and celebrate the benefits and rewards of parenthood.

RETURN TO FEMINISM'S ROOTS

In 1869, Mattie Brinkerhoff wrote in *The Revolution:* "When a man steals to satisfy hunger, we may safely conclude that there is something wrong in society. So when a woman destroys the life of her unborn child, it is evidence that either by education or circumstances she has been greatly wronged." Every woman deserves better, and every child deserves a chance at life.

It is time to reaffirm the strength and dignity of women, the importance of fathers, and the value of every human life. It's time women refuse to choose between sacrificing education and career plans or sacrificing their children. We must raise expectations and focus our efforts on what is best for women, children and families—so that one day soon we will look back at this barbaric practice and wonder why any woman ever felt coerced into suffering through an abortion.

Women deserve better.

Discussion Questions

1. Identify the premises in Foster's argument. Discuss whether they support her conclusion. Are her responses to the counterarguments effective?
2. Discuss how Foster would most likely respond to Thomson's conclusion that abortion may be morally defensible even if the fetus is a person. Which person makes the better argument and why?
3. Discuss how both a utilitarian and a rights ethicist would most likely respond to Foster's argument.
4. Foster argues that by making abortion a woman's choice, it makes abortion her problem. What does she mean by this? Do you agree with her that abortion is rarely a "free choice"? Support your answer.

5. Foster points out that women who are college students are at the highest risk for resorting to abortion. Why do you think this is the case? Discuss policies that might be instituted at your college to reduce the need for abortion and the moral justification of these policies.

STEVEN D. HALES

Abortion and Fathers' Rights

Steven Hales is a professor of philosophy at Bloomsburg University in Pennsylvania. In "Abortion and Fathers' Rights," Hales argues that if a mother can escape the burdens of future duties to her progeny through abortion, then men should also be able to escape future duties to their progeny through the mechanism of refusal.

Critical Reading Questions

1. What are the three widely accepted principles, according to Hales, regarding abortion and parental rights?
2. What is the basis for a woman's right to an abortion?
3. Why does Hales maintain that these three principles are prima facie inconsistent?
4. How does Hales resolve the apparent conflict between the principle of equality, the father's moral duty to his future children, and the woman's right to avoid future child-rearing duties through abortion?
5. What is the fourth "commonly accepted principle" and why does Hales reject it in some cases?
6. What is a right of refusal? How and under what conditions would a father carry it out?
7. How does Hales use Judith Jarvis Thomson's violinist analogy to support his conclusion regarding a father's right of refusal?
8. How does Hales respond to the argument that the father's obligation is to the mother, not the future child?
9. How does Hales respond to the argument that by bearing the burden of pregnancy, a woman receives the "benefit of guaranteed paternal support"?
10. How does Hales respond to the appeal to social welfare arguments that state that it is in the interests of society that a father be compelled to support his children?

"Abortion and Fathers' Rights," in *Reproduction, Technology, and Rights,* ed. by James M. Humber and Robert F. Almeder (Totowa, N.J.: 1996), 5–26. Notes have been omitted.

THE PROBLEM

In this chapter I argue that three widely accepted principles regarding abortion and parental rights are *prima facie* jointly inconsistent. These principles are probably accepted by most who consider themselves feminists, so the conundrum posed is particularly acute for them. There is one obvious way of resolving the inconsistency. However, as will be made clear, this solution is prevented by a fourth principle—that fathers have an absolute obligation to provide material support for their children. I argue that this principle is false, that fathers have no such absolute obligation, and thereby provide a way of making the first three principles consistent.

These three principles are apparently inconsistent.

1. Women have the moral right to get abortions on demand, at their discretion. They can make unilateral decisions whether or not to abort, and are not morally obligated to consult with the father, or any other person, before reaching a decision to abort. Moreover, neither the father nor any other person can veto or override a mother's decision about the disposition of the unborn fetus. She has first and last say about what happens in, and to, her body.

The principle formulated here is an extreme one. More moderate versions might replace it. . . . Such modifications will not substantially affect what will be said about fathers' rights, given suitable changes, *mutatis mutandis,* in the description of those rights.

2. Men and women have equal moral rights and duties, and should have equal legal rights and duties. . . .

3. Parents have a moral duty to provide support for their children once they are born. Any legal duties of support (e.g., child welfare laws or court-enforced child support) should supervene on this moral duty.

Given both (2) and (3), we can conclude that the mother and father have equal moral obligations toward their child once it is born. Although it is an interesting question as to *why* (3) is true (even granting that it is), the issue before us here is the distribution of rights and duties *before* the child is born, particularly during the pregnancy of the mother. Principle (1) tells us that the mother has the right to an abortion during her pregnancy. Since (2) tells us that men and women have equal moral rights, it seems that we can therefore conclude that men also have a right to an abortion. On the face of it, this seems either absurd or trivial: absurd because men clearly cannot get pregnant, and so it is silly to talk about them having a right to an abortion; and trivial because it may be true that this conditional right is trivially true of men: If one is pregnant, then one may get an abortion. So for a man to insist on his right to an abortion appears pointless. However, it is pointless only if we understand the right to an abortion in a certain way, viz, the right to an abortion is the right to end one's *own* pregnancy.

Why would anyone care about having a right to an abortion? There are a variety of reasons some women no longer want to be pregnant: They cannot afford another child, they are not psychologically prepared to be a parent, a child would hinder the lifestyle they wish to pursue, they do not want to endure the hardship of pregnancy, and so on. All of these reasons have to do with burdens or hardships that the mother faces in the future. For whatever reason, the mother is not (currently) willing to suffer these hardships, and so has an abortion in order to avoid them. Fortunately, the duties and burdens that the mother wants to escape are ones that she can in fact morally escape. She has no obligation to endure the hardship of pregnancy (according to [1]), nor any absolute, inevitable duty to shoulder the burden of an infant. True, these are burdens and duties that she faces if she continues with the pregnancy, but they are ones that she can avoid by having an abortion. Thus, it seems that the motivation for wanting a right to an abortion is because a mechanism is wanted to avoid future duties and burdens. Abortion constitutes just such a mechanism.

If it were immoral to avoid these future duties of childrearing (i.e., if they were absolute and morally inexorable), then clearly there could be no *right* to an abortion. Her right to an abortion is a liberty right; that is, having the right tells us that it is morally permissible for her to have an abortion. . . .

Now consider the case of the father. He, too, is facing future duties; in fact (aside from pregnancy itself), the same ones as the mother, as (2) and (3) specify. However, the father, having participated in conception, cannot escape the future duties he will have toward the child. The father can decide that he cannot afford another child, that he is not psychologically prepared to be a parent, that a child would hinder the lifestyle he wishes to pursue, and so on, to no avail. He is completely subject to the decisions of the mother. If she decides to have the child, she thereby ensures that the father has certain duties; duties that it is impossible for him to avoid. Even more, the mother is solely in charge: If she wants to have an abortion and the father does not want her to, she may anyway. If she does *not* want to have an abortion and the father does want her to, it is permissible for her to refuse to have one. If there is any conflict between the mother and the father here, the mother's wishes win out. . . .

It might be argued that, although true, this is an unavoidable (and hence acceptable) consequence of biology. The mother has some kind of absolute right over the disposition of her body, and in a battle of rights, these rights over one's body trump all other rights in the fray. So the fact that the fetus is in her body ensures that she has final say over it. Not only is this "right over one's body" supposed to guarantee that the mother can abort over the father's objections, but also that she can carry the child to term even if the father insists on an abortion. . . .

The difficulty is that it seems that we might agree to all of this and still argue that the father is ill treated. Even if biology prevents men and women from having *absolutely identical* means to exercise their rights, it remains that what we should do is try to achieve equal opportunity to exercise rights as much as possible. Perhaps we will never attain complete equality (biology may prevent us), but we should try our best.

Another objection is that since the father does *eo ipso* have a right to avoid future duties (he just has no opportunity or mechanism to exercise this right), (2) is satisfied, and (1)—(3) are consistent. However, I think it is plausible that genuine equality insists that not only do persons have various liberty rights, but also that they should have equality of opportunity to exercise these rights. So long as some, but not all, persons are equipped with the means to exercise their rights, we cannot say that people have *really* been provided with equal rights. So, even if fathers do have a right to avoid future duties, without any way of acting on this right, the equality principle (2) has *not* been satisfied. . . .

So, in order for us to satisfy our goal of achieving equality as best we can, we should not only admit that fathers have a right to avoid future duties, but there needs to be some mechanism by which they can, by personal fiat, exercise that right. Mothers have the right and a mechanism—the mechanism of abortion. The mechanism employed by fathers, of course, need not be abortion. The important thing to note is that even if we grant that the father cannot avail himself of *abortion* as a way out, it is a giant step from here to conclude that he cannot avail himself of *any* way out. Perhaps it will do to say that, sometime during the span of time that a mother may permissibly abort, a father may simply declare that he refuses to assume any future obligations. If we are prepared to speak loosely of mothers having the right to an abortion, we might also loosely talk of fathers having the right of refusal. By admitting that fathers have this right, we more closely approximate the ideal of moral parity. The right of refusal is to be designed as a parallel (as demanded by [2]) of the mother's right to an abortion (as specified in [1]). Let us put it this way: A man has the moral right to decide not to become a father (in the social, non-biological sense) during the time that the woman he has impregnated may permissibly abort. He can make a unilateral decision whether to refuse fatherhood, and is not morally obliged to consult with the mother or any other person before reaching a decision. Moreover, neither the mother nor any other person can veto or override a man's decision about becoming a father. He has first and last say about what he does with his life in this regard.

Suppose that the mother is pregnant and the father tells her during the time that she may permissibly abort, "I think this was a big mistake, we should not have done this, I regret that you are pregnant, and wish you would have an abortion." The mother, according to principle (1), may fairly respond, "Sorry, I want the child, and will carry it to term even though you want me to abort." If the father has the right of refusal, he can justly respond, "OK, if that is your decision, have the child, but it will be solely your responsibility. I want out of the deal, and I do not want to have anything to do with the child or any responsibilities toward it." More than this will be needed, of course. The mother's declared intention to have an abortion does not constitute having one, nor is her declaration as expensive, difficult, and unappealing as the actual abortion. An adequate legal implementation of a father's right of refusal will involve written contracts and sufficient penalties to the father to make the exercise of his right of refusal as costly to him (in the broadest sense) as the mother's exercise of her right to an abortion is to her. Fathers should not find exercising a right of refusal to be more appealing than mothers generally find getting an abortion, but they should not find it less appealing either.

The right of refusal solved the problem of inconsistency among our three moral principles. However, this solution is blocked by a fourth commonly accepted principle:

4. Fathers are under an absolute moral obligation to provide for the welfare of their children, despite the intentions or desires of the father before the birth of the child. Something close to this is reflected in the law, and serves to underwrite paternity suits and at least some of the complaints about "deadbeat dads." . . .

Those willing to defend something like (4) often have in mind a case of a longish relationship in which the woman gets pregnant and the father, unwilling to be burdened with a child, ends the relationship, or leaves town. Surely the father should not be allowed to just saddle the mother with the child and get off scot-free. He willingly and voluntarily engaged in sex and knowingly took the risks in full awareness of the possibility of pregnancy. For him just to leave the mother and have no future duties toward the child is to dump 100 percent of the burden on the mother when she only assumed 50 percent of the risk. This, advocates of (4) claim, is manifestly unfair—it means that (ignoring disease and such) sex has no consequences for men, and massive consequences for women. This is why we need a principle like (4) that ensures that there are consequences for men too, and one of the reasons that we must protect a woman's right to an abortion, à la principle (1).

It is important to note that in the discussion of (4) that will follow, I will not be discussing the obligations of fathers to continue to support children that they have already been voluntarily supporting. . . . Principle (4) has solely to do with the connection between paternal obligations and prenatal paternal desires.

Admitting that fathers have the right of refusal provided a way of making principles (1), (2), and (3) consistent. The introduction of (4) rejects this solution, and once again generates inconsistency. The mother has the right to do something that the father does not have the right to do: get out of any future commitment to the (yet unborn) child by personal fiat. The mother can get out of it by terminating the life of the fetus, and the father cannot get out of it in any way, not even by refusal. Again principle (2) is violated.

There seem to be only four options. The first is that we can abandon principle (1). There are two ways of giving up (1). The first is to say that the conservative is right after all, and abortions really are impermissible. The second is to maintain that abortions continue to be permissible, but there must be some sort of mechanism for paternal consent. Mothers will have to consult with fathers before they are allowed to have abortions, and (perhaps) fathers will be allowed to insist that mothers have abortions if the father so decides. Women will no longer have complete control over their bodies, and will be subject (at least in part) to the decisions of men.

We can abandon principle (2). Men and women do not have equal rights and duties, or striving for a balance of powers with respect to the exercising of rights is not a valuable goal. Somehow the biological asymmetry of childbirth gives rise to an insuperable moral asymmetry. I suspect that most who accept all three principles will opt for rejection of (2), the equality principle. However, even though one might (with some plausibility) argue that biology prevents fathers from having a right to procure an abortion or insist that the mother have one, it is *much* harder to argue that biology forbids fathers from having a right of refusal. At the very least, such a right has no obvious connection to biology.

We can reject principle (3). Parents do not have an obligation to provide support for their children. Among other problems with this approach, it will entail the rejection of principle (4), whereas rejecting principle (4) will not require us to jettison (3). Thus, other things being equal, if getting rid of the comparably weaker (4) alone will restore consistency, we are better off doing that than getting rid of both (3) and (4).

The last alternative is that we can abandon principle (4) and grant that fathers have a right of refusal. If a father-to-be declares his refusal to accept fatherhood (with attendant legal details) and skips town, abandoning his pregnant girlfriend, he is perhaps callous and unfeeling, but he has not done anything morally wrong. He is no more unfeeling than if the mother intentionally aborted over his strong objections. Just as she can abort the fetus at her discretion, so too can he exercise the right of refusal at his. She can get out of the deal when she wants, and so can he. To reject (4) and accept a father's right of refusal is a radical change in most people's ordinary beliefs. If taken to heart in a broader social context, I believe it would ultimately result in considerable legal change with respect to paternity suits and court-ordered child support. This is the position for which I will argue.

THE SOLUTION

Since all four of the principles seem plausible, and rejecting any one is distasteful, an argument in favor of rejecting any particular one over the others is needed. I will first marshall the arguments in favor of rejecting (4), and then consider other solutions to the dilemma. I will argue that rejecting (4), counterintuitive as it is, is the most cogent solution available. This is why I claimed above that no line-drawing project is needed to adjudicate the cases seemingly relevant to evaluating (4). Principle (4) is false in every case. There are three arguments that I will develop to support the rejection of (4). Two arguments are suggested by positions taken by Judith Thomson in her well-known "A Defense of Abortion," and the last is an analogy that imports our moral intuitions from a logically parallel case.

Thomson's arguments are meant to support (1), and they do. But they also pave the way for abandoning (4). Thomson writes, "[Unless they implicitly or explicitly accept special responsibility] nobody is morally *required* to make large sacrifices, of health, of all other interests and concerns, of all other duties and commitments, for nine years, or even for nine months, in order to keep another person alive."

It is this dilemma that provides much of the support for principle (1). Without accepting some kind of special responsibility for the gestating fetus, the mother is under no obligation to keep it alive, even if it is a person. It is a direct consequence of (1) that the act of conception alone is insufficient to require of the mother that she make major personal sacrifices—most immediately the sacrifice of pregnancy and childbirth. Yet the father has done no more than participate in conception, and as a result he is required to make major personal sacrifices once the child is born. If conceiving alone does not count as accepting any special responsibility for a person for the mother, then it does not count as accepting any sort of special responsibility for a person for the father either. But (4) seems to deny this.

Another Thomsonian argument also supports this position. Her famous violinist case shows that someone who is the victim of a selfish, unilateral act (such as being kidnapped by the Society of Music Lovers, or being raped) is not obligated to make major personal sacrifices. By "unilateral" here, I mean that the victim had no say in what would happen, or, put another way, was kept out of the decision-making loop. Yet if the mother were to carry on with a pregnancy over the father's strong objections, it seems that her act is a selfish, unilateral one. Continuing with the pregnancy was her personal decision, and executed with regard only for her motives and desires. The father was kept out of the loop entirely. That the mother can do all of this is ensured by (1). So it seems on Thomsonian grounds that the father should then be exempt from having to make major personal sacrifices (such as 18 years of child support). But (4) tells us that he is not exempt. . . .

COMPETITORS AND THEIR PROBLEMS

There are, of course, other ways out. One is to find a way to resolve the inconsistency among the four principles without giving any up. Another is to give up either (1) or (2) while retaining (4). A third approach is to agree that fathers have a right of refusal, and find some way of ensuring that fathers pay child support anyway, in spite of this right. The arguments for rejecting (1) are legion, well-known, and will not be rehashed here. I suspect that (2) will be a likely target of those wishing to keep (4), but I have no idea how an argument against retaining (2) (at least as an ideal) might proceed, and so I cannot evaluate such an argument here. But I have been able to identify two arguments that purport to resolve the inconsistency among the four principles, and one that tries to accommodate my results while keeping the feminist preanalytic data, and will consider these in turn.

The first argument that attempts to resolve the inconsistency is this: It is not that the father especially has a commitment to the future child, but rather he has an obligation toward the mother. This commitment consists in something like a responsibility to help support their progeny. So there are not any future duties toward a child that he could escape by having a right of refusal. His duties are toward the mother.

However, this does not seem right, because the mother has no analogous commitment toward the father. She has no responsibility to help the father support their progeny, since such a responsibility would entail a duty to the fetus that it be carried to term. One cannot support something by killing it. Yet the mother clearly has no such duty toward the fetus, as (1) tells us. . . . The mother can avoid future duties through abortion, and the father cannot. And principle (4) rules out the analogous paternal right of refusal. The problem remains.

A second argument that purports to resolve the inconsistency is this: The mother undergoes the burden of pregnancy, and receives the benefit of guaranteed paternal support. The father, by contrast, has the benefit of not having to suffer the burden of pregnancy and childbirth, and instead shoulders the burden of necessarily having to help support the child once it is born. Each party has their respective burdens and benefits, and these benefits and burdens are distributed more or less evenly. Thus, the equality principle (2) is satisfied, and (1), (3), and (4) are retained.

I think that there are several difficulties with this approach. The first is that although pregnancy is undoubtedly a burden of some sort, it is relatively short compared to the legal burden under which the father labors. The mother is pregnant for nine months, and in most cases is not suffering for much of that time. The father, by contrast, is obliged to pay considerable sums of income over a period of 18 years. The father's burden lasts 27 times as long. The distribution of burdens hardly seems equitable. It will not help to say that the mother has the same 18-year burden of support, since she *volunteered* to support the child by having it. The father, we are supposing, would have preferred the mother to have an abortion. Since the mother volunteered to support the child and the father did not, it does not seem right to say that she has the same *burden* as the father. We can appeal to the maxim of *volenti non fit injuria* here.

Another problem is this: If anyone should have more duties toward the child, it ought to be the mother, not the father. After all, she is the one who allowed (or is allowing) the fetus to gestate and mature in her body. Thus, it seems that she is establishing some kind of agreement with the fetus that when it is born she will provide for its well-being. The father, on the other hand, has not allowed the fetus to gestate and continue, and, let us suppose, strongly opposes its existence. Moreover, he explicitly rejects the idea that he has duties or future obligations toward the fetus or the child it will become. It is strange, then, to insist that the duties the father acquires after the child is born are just as strong as the mother's. If anything, it would seem that the mother should have *more* and *stronger* duties than the father.

But these are really just side concerns. The central problem with the argument is that it, too, only sidesteps the real issue. We can grant the burden/benefit argument and still generate inconsistency. The mother can escape her burden of pregnancy by personal decision—having an abortion as guaranteed by (1). The father cannot escape his burden of support, either by abortion or by refusal (as insisted on by [4]). So the mother still has something he lacks—a morally permissible escape from future duties.

The final objection I will consider grants that (4) is false—fathers have a right to avoid future duties, and ought to be legally granted the mechanism of refusal in order to have a means of exercising this right. Nevertheless, the objection goes, society can override the individual rights of fathers if it is in the best interest of society as a whole. Just as society can declare the right of eminent domain, and occasionally override the individual rights of property owners by building a highway through their front lawns, so too can society decide that the general public welfare is benefited by placing strong duties on fathers, and the individual rights of fathers are justifiably outweighed by these policy concerns. Moreover, we are generally prepared to grant that it is morally permissible for social concerns to outweigh the concerns of individuals. Thus, recognizing the falsity of (4) need not give rise to major social change. The intuitions behind (4) can be preserved even if (4) is jettisoned.

There are two main paths this objection can take: The interest of the state in benefiting children, and the interest of the state in benefiting mothers. . . .

Consider, then, the first path of this objection. The state decides that it is in the interest of society at large that children be assured of a certain level of financial security or material comfort. To promote this interest, the state does not distribute the burden evenly across all citizens, but instead levies a special tax on a subset. More specifically, the biological parents of these children are obliged to pay for their upbringing (of course, special provisions will have to be built into the law to excuse biological parents when the child is adopted). In the case where the mother voluntarily submits to this (by not exercising her right to an abortion), and the father does not (by actively exercising his right to refusal), the father's rights are overridden, and he is still legally bound to pay child support.

One difficulty specific to this strategy is that we are on thin ice if we are prepared to engage in a wholesale suppression of individual rights for the pecuniary benefit of children. There are many children who would be better off living with adoptive parents than with their natural parents. Children born into poverty will, *ceteris paribus,* have worse life prospects than those children born to well-off parents. It would benefit these children, *ceteris paribus,* to take them from their natural parents and place them with wealthy adoptive parents. But surely this is wrong, and it is wrong because it unjustly usurps the rights of natural parents to keep their children. There are cases (e.g., child abuse) in which we might allow society to take children from their parents, but poverty is not one of them. Yet this case and the case of the father seem parallel: Society overrides the right of a biological parent(s) for the financial benefit of children. If we refuse to allow society to take children away from poor parents, so too should we refuse to allow society to override a father's right of refusal.

Let us consider the second path the social welfare objection might take. The state decides that as a contingent matter of fact, women have unequal standing in our society. They make statistically significantly less amounts of money than men doing equal jobs, and they are not proportionately represented in positions of power in the government and in business. One practical result of this is that single mothers raising children have a much more difficult time, and a greater burden, than single fathers raising children. Thus, in order to alleviate this burden, the state decides to override systematically the father's right to refusal. This amounts roughly to an affirmative action program for women: Equal treatment in one domain is temporarily suspended with the intention of addressing inequalities in another domain. Once other social inequities between men and women have been adequately resolved, fathers will be allowed to resume their exercise of a right of refusal.

Again, one should note that this path accepts the main conclusion of this chapter—that fathers have a right of refusal. What the argument rejects is the inference from this right to immediate social and legal change. There are several difficulties with the second path of the social welfare argument, and it is hard to tell *a priori* which of these is the most serious. One is that much more argument is needed to show that overriding the father's right of refusal is the best way to address the issue of unequal burdens in single parenting. Since it is presumably in the *state's* interest, or the interest of society in general, to sponsor such an affirmative action program, it may be that society in general ought to pay for it. Another problem is that even if overriding the father's right of refusal is shown to be the best solution, considerable argument is then needed to demonstrate that it is also fair or just to suppress this right. For example, suppose that the national economy (and hence society as a whole) is best served if slavery were still allowed. This in no way means that we are therefore justified in reinstating slavery. Moreover, the reason that we are not thereby justified in reinstating slavery is because slavery impermissibly violates individual rights.

In addition, there are two wholly general problems with the strategy of appealing to the general social welfare in order to maintain the *status quo*. One is this: Suppose that on the ground of

eminent domain, the state decided to build a highway across the front lawns of all and only Jewish citizens, all the while maintaining that Jews have a right to own property unmolested. Clearly this "right" would then amount to nothing but a ruse. So too, by telling fathers that they have a right to get out of future obligations through refusal but then invariably forcing these obligations on them anyway, it is clear that their "right" is an empty one. Granting such a right is mere trickery with words. One might object here that fathers do indeed have the right of refusal, it is just that their right is overridden—and there is nothing unusual or odd about overriding a right. This is true. But if a right is uniformly and consistently overridden, to the point that no one can exercise it except at some vague point in the distant future, one becomes suspicious as to whether there is a real right here. If a woman's right to an abortion is consistently overridden by society throughout her life, with a promise of allowing her to exercise it in the nebulous future, there is legitimate question of whether she really has this right.

The second problem is a danger looming for the partisans of principle (1). If a father's right of refusal can easily be trumped by society, then it might well be that a mother's right to an abortion can also easily be trumped. Society might decide, for example, that mothers do indeed have a right to elective abortion, but that social unrest over the abortion issue would be best alleviated by universally suppressing this right. . . .

So appeal to the general social welfare is a dangerous move at best, and a mere trick at worst. I conclude that it does not provide a plausible alternative to the conclusion for which I have argued—that the intentions and desires of the father before the birth of his child are in fact relevant to his duty to provide for the welfare of his children. If the mother can escape future duties to her progeny via the mechanism of abortion, the father also can escape future duties to his progeny via the mechanism of refusal.

Discussion Questions

1. Hales uses Thomson's argument in her "A Defense of Abortion" to support his position that fathers have a right of refusal. Would Thomson agree with Hales's reasoning? Discuss how both Thomson and Marquis might respond to Hales's argument.

2. According to Gallup polls, most women are morally opposed to abortion on demand. Do fathers still have a moral right of refusal in cases where a woman, because of moral objections to abortion, cannot in good conscience avoid future obligations to her progeny through an abortion? Support your answer.

3. In a response to Hales's article,[32] James Humber argues that it is not unjust to require reluctant fathers to contribute financially to child support for women who choose to keep their children after birth since both parents contributed to the conception of the child and the mother is already unequally burdened or harmed by parenthood even if the father does contribute child support. Hales responds that the woman freely chose to continue the pregnancy and raise the child so there is no harm and, consequently, she deserves no redress.[33] Discuss the merits of both arguments.

4. Discuss how a care ethicist, a utilitarian, or a Confucian would most likely respond to Hales's argument.

CASE STUDIES

1. THE UNWANTED DAUGHTERS

Chandra and Ramdas Malik were poor farmers who lived in a small village outside of Bombay. They had one son and one daughter. Although they would have welcomed the birth of another son, they did not want another daughter, because the required dowry to her future husband's family would have been financially crippling for them. Sons also provided the best social security for elderly parents, because daughters were absorbed into their husbands' families. In India minivans carrying ultrasound equipment cruise the countryside, providing prenatal diagnosis of the sex of fetuses. Although the price of an ultrasound was high, it was worth it to the Maliks. "Better 800 rupees now for an abortion," Ramdas Malik said before the procedure, "than tens of thousands of rupees later for a dowry."[34] The ultrasound operator informed them that the child was a boy. Malik let out a sigh of relief.

Chandra Malik's cousin, Indira, emigrated to Canada in 1979. Two years later she married a successful engineer, John Sarava. With her son and daughter now in high school, Indira Sarava had decided to return to college when she found out she was pregnant. Because she was forty, Indira had amniocentesis at sixteen weeks to see if the fetus had any genetic disorders. The following week Dr. Lee called her and said, "Congratulations. You're going to have a healthy baby girl!" Two weeks later Indira asked him to perform an abortion. She explained that although she would have continued the pregnancy had it been a boy, she is not interested in having another daughter. Her husband John is opposed to the abortion. He points out that having another daughter would not be a burden for the family since they are financially secure. Also, because he is semiretired, he is willing to do most of the child care.

Discussion Questions

1. Discuss how a cultural relativist would respond to each of the above scenarios. Are you satisfied with the answers? Would it have made a difference if either the Maliks or Indira Sarava had requested the abortion because the fetus had Down syndrome? Explain.

2. Although the Maliks did not have an abortion, they intended to if the fetus had been a girl. What is the role of intention in moral responsibility? Discuss what Thomson would think regarding the morality of the Maliks' actions in seeking prenatal diagnosis for sex selection. If sex selection is morally impermissible, does this create a moral obligation on the part of physicians administering prenatal diagnosis to withhold information about the gender of the fetus? Support your answers.

3. Does the father have any rights when it comes to deciding whether a pregnancy should be terminated? How would Hales most likely respond to the Sarava case?

4. Sometimes, because of the position of the fetus or material floating in the amniotic fluid, ultrasound misdiagnoses the sex of the fetus. Much to the Maliks' dismay, their son turns out to be a girl. They wrap the newborn in a rag and abandon her in a ditch beside a road. Is their action morally acceptable? Would your answer be different if the Canadian couple had done the same? Support your answers.

5. Although most Americans disapprove of abortion for sex selection, they regard abortion for genetic disorders as morally permissible. Is this distinction morally justified? Discuss whether the principle of equality should apply to people born with physical or mental handicaps as well as to females.

---

2. JENNIFER JOHNSON: MATERNAL DRUG USE AND FETAL RIGHTS

When twenty-three-year-old Jennifer Johnson arrived to give birth to her fourth child, hospital drug tests found traces of cocaine in her blood. It was later revealed that her other children had all been cocaine-affected babies. Johnson was arrested in a crack house. A Florida judge found her guilty of delivery (through the umbilical cord) of a controlled substance to a child. Johnson was sentenced to fifteen years' probation, drug treatment, random drug testing, and educational and vocational training. She was also ordered to participate in an intensive prenatal care program if she should ever become pregnant again.[35]

According to the Physicians Committee for Responsible Medicine, an estimated one in five pregnant women uses illegal drugs.[36] The cost of caring for a cocaine-exposed infant can run into the millions of dollars. In response, several states have passed civil child abuse and neglect laws, which state that taking illicit drugs or alcohol during pregnancy constitutes child abuse. As a result of these laws, thousands of women have lost custody of their children and some have even been jailed or placed in mandatory drug treatment programs.

A South Carolina law allows public hospitals to test pregnant women for drug use and to give the results to the police without the woman's consent. More than thirty women have been arrested under the South Carolina law. As in the case of Jennifer Johnson, addicted women can avoid prison by agreeing to undergo drug treatment.[37]

Discussion Questions

1. Discuss whether hospitals that routinely perform drug tests on any pregnant woman "suspected of being a drug user" are violating the privacy rights of the woman. Discuss how Ayn Rand and Mary Anne Warren might respond to this question.

2. Discuss whether pregnant women who plan to carry their fetus to term have a moral obligation to refrain from using substances that are harmful to the fetus. If so, does such an obligation necessarily depend on the personhood or moral status of the fetus? Can we have a duty to refrain from behavior that might harm persons who do not yet exist? If so, what is the moral basis of this duty? Support your answers.

3. Joyce Arthur of the Pro-Choice Action Network, argues that "fetal alcohol syndrome is serious," but to legislate any kind of coercion on pregnant women is the wrong way to go. Studies have shown that . . . if women fear some sort of coercive intervention, they will completely forego any prenatal care whatsoever."[38] Instead, she suggests that we need better "social resources and supports" in terms of money, counseling, and so on for expectant mothers. Others disagree, arguing that this view is degrading to women, and that women who abuse alcohol and drugs while pregnant should be held responsible. Discuss the two proposed approaches.

4. Should a pregnant woman's behavior that is potentially harmful to the fetus be regulated by law? Discuss how Warren and Foster would each stand on the morality of passing laws to protect the fetus from the mother's use of toxic substances.

5. Come up with a public policy for resolving the conflict between maternal and fetal rights. Consider the views of Confucius, Aristotle, rights ethicists, utilitarians, and care ethicists in arriving at your solution.

---

3. THE LIMITS OF PROTEST: BOMBING OF ABORTION CLINICS

Since 1977, antiabortion activists have committed more than 2,400 acts in at least twenty-eight states and the District of Columbia including bombings, assaults, death threats, and even murders.[39] In 1982, a physician who performed abortions and his wife were kidnapped in Illinois. Three clinics were also bombed in Florida and Virginia. Following this there were a rash of bombings, assaults, and arsons, including more than twenty-five incidents in 1984. Since then several health care providers and staff have been murdered and many others seriously injured.

In 1994, in response to increasing violence and threats against abortion providers, Congress passed the Freedom of Access to Clinic Entrances Act ("FACES") which "prohibits use of force, obstruction and property damage intended to interfere with reproductive health care services" and allowed the establishment of buffer zones around clinics.[40] Following this, abortion-related crime at clinics declined somewhat, only to rise again in 1997. During 1997 alone there were six bombings, sixty-five acts of vandalism, and sixty-two cases of stalking.[41] A 2006 study found that almost half of all abortion clinics continue to experience some harassment, and 7 percent of the clinics, or their staff, were the targets of major violence.[42] Because of the violence and emotional toll from the harassment, many providers have stopped performing abortions.

Discussion Questions

1. The people who are protesting at the clinics believe that *Roe v. Wade* is unjust and that abortion is murder. They compare the abortion clinics with the death camps in Nazi Germany. Is this analogy accurate? Support your answer.
2. Paul Hill was executed in 2003 for killing two people at a Pensacola, Florida, abortion clinic. Hill maintained to the end that what he did was moral because he saved more lives, the lives of the unborn, than he took. He also believed that God condoned his action and would reward him in the afterlife. Do you agree with Hill's argument? Discuss how a divine command ethicist and a natural law ethicist might each respond to Hill's claim regarding the morality of his actions.
3. What are the limits of protest against what is seen as an unjust law? Discuss the morality of vandalism, harassment, stalking, bombing clinics, and causing injury to abortion providers as forms of protest.
4. Should abortion clinics have a legal right, despite freedom of speech, to create buffer zones around their clinics to prohibit antiabortion protesters from approaching clients and abortion providers and talking to them or passing out pamphlets? Support your answer. Discuss how a rights ethicist would balance the rights of the protesters against those of the people who want to use the services of the clinic.

---

4. DATE RAPE AND ABORTION

Lisa, an eighteen-year-old college freshman, attends a fraternity party with her twenty-year-old boyfriend, Derek. Although alcohol is forbidden on campus, there is plenty of liquor at the party. Derek and his roommate have already started drinking when Lisa arrives. Lisa reluctantly agrees to join them in a drink. After a few drinks, she becomes so tipsy that she can't stand up, so she lies down on Derek's bed. Derek's roommate winks and tells him to "go for it." Then he leaves the room. Derek then has sex with Lisa, who neither consents nor protests.

The next morning Lisa deeply regrets what has happened. She tells Derek that she is worried she might be pregnant. He gives her the name of an out-of-town doctor and reassures her that the doctor will take care of everything. Lisa goes to the doctor that morning. The doctor gives her the morning-after pill.

Lisa doesn't tell anyone else what has happened, nor does she keep her follow-up appointment with the doctor. When her periods don't return and she begins putting on weight, she dismisses the changes as stress. Six months after the incident, Lisa goes to the doctor for what she thinks are stomach problems or possibly a tumor. After examining her, the doctor tells her that she is six months pregnant.

Discussion Questions

1. Although the abortion rate among teenagers is declining, a disproportionate number of late-term abortions are performed on teenagers, because many teens do not recognize the early signs of pregnancy.[43] Would a late-term "partial-birth" abortion be morally justified in Lisa's case? State why or why not.

2. Is using the morning-after pill contraception or abortion? If the morning-after pill is an abortifacient, is there any difference morally between using the morning-after pill and having a late-term abortion?

3. Is this a case of rape? Is this relevant in regard to whether the abortion is morally permissible? Support your answers.

4. Discuss the responsibility, if any, of the other people involved. Should the boyfriend be punished for having sex with Lisa when she was drunk? Is the fact that he was also drunk morally relevant? Should he have to pay for or share Lisa's medical expenses or be compelled to provide support for the child if she decides not to have a late-term abortion? To what extent is the college or fraternity responsible for what happened? Do they owe Lisa a duty of reparation?

5. The United States has one of the highest teen pregnancy, birth, and abortion rates in the world. Discuss the moral issues involved in policies, such as promoting sexual abstinence or a "safe-sex or no-sex" approach, aimed at discouraging teen pregnancies. Discuss how a utilitarian, a rights ethicist, and a virtue ethicist might respond to these policies.

5. "PARTIAL-BIRTH" ABORTION

When a family immigrated from India to Michigan in 1997, they moved into a two-bedroom apartment, where the sixteen-year-old son and eleven-year-old daughter shared a bedroom. The following spring the girl, now twelve, began complaining of abdominal pains. At first her physician passed them off as digestion problems. However, it turned out that she was twenty-seven weeks pregnant. Furthermore, the father of the baby was the brother. The family requested an abortion.

An ultrasound in Vikki Stella's thirty-second week of pregnancy revealed that something was very wrong with her baby. More tests revealed that the fetus had several abnormalities, including a fluid-filled cranium with no brain tissue at all. Stella did not wish to continue a pregnancy with a fetus that had no chance of survival after birth. She had a "partial-birth" abortion.

Discussion Questions

1. What are the moral issues involved in these two cases? Discuss what you might say to each of the two women if you were on the hospital ethics board and they came to you for advice.

2. Should "partial-birth" abortion be illegal except to save the life of the mother? What about cases like the one above in which a girl does not know she is pregnant until late in her pregnancy? Support your answers.

3. Some ethicists consider "partial-birth" abortion infanticide. They maintain that the right to an abortion provides only for the termination of a pregnancy, not a dead child. The most a woman can claim is a severance right to be freed from the excessive burdens of pregnancy, not a right to have someone else kill her child. Discuss the strengths and weaknesses of this position.

6. THE RELUCTANT DAD

Rose and Joe have been living together in a monogamous relationship for more than a year—since the beginning of their junior year at college. They both agreed at the time they moved in together that either could leave the relationship at any time. Although they were using birth control, Rose has unexpectedly become pregnant.

Joe suggests that she get an abortion and offers to pay for it. However, because Rose is morally opposed to abortion, she resigns herself to having the baby. Joe does not bring up the subject again. When Rose is six months pregnant, Joe decides to leave. He leaves a short note saying, "It was fun while it lasted, but it's time for me to move on."

Rose is distraught. Even though it had never been discussed, she had thought that she and Joe would raise the baby together.

Discussion Questions

1. Make a list of the relevant facts, moral principles, rights, and other moral issues (such as the moral status of the fetus) involved in this case. Which moral considerations are most compelling? Based on your analysis, come to a conclusion regarding Joe's moral responsibility, if any, to Rose and/or the baby.
2. Discuss what you would do if you were in Rose's position. Critically evaluate your course of action in light of the moral concerns you have listed.
3. Would it have made a difference regarding Joe's moral responsibilities in this case if he had left the relationship at the time Rose found out she was pregnant rather than staying for another five months? What if they had not been living together and the pregnancy had been the result of casual, consensual sex? Support your answers.
4. Discuss how both Noonan and Hales would most likely respond regarding Joe's responsibility in this case.

C H A P T E R   3

Genetic Engineering, Cloning, and Stem Cell Research

It was one of the most controversial birth announcements in history: On February 23, 1997, Ian Wilmut and a team of scientists at the Roslin Institute in Edinburgh, Scotland, announced to the world that they had created the first genetic clone of an adult mammal. The new arrival was a lamb called Dolly. Unlike any other mammal ever born, Dolly was created asexually from a single cell from her mother's udder. Dolly's genetic makeup was identical to her mother's. The announcement of Dolly's birth set off a flurry of debate over the morality of human cloning. Giving greater urgency to the debate is the completion of the Human Genome Project, which is expected to revolutionize both medicine and society.

THE HISTORY OF GENETIC ENGINEERING

The desire to improve humans through genetic engineering goes back at least to the time of Plato (c. 427–347 B.C.E.). In his *Republic,* Plato proposed the use of selective breeding as a means of improving society.[1] The term **eugenics** was first used by English scientist Francis Galton, a cousin of Charles Darwin, to describe the study of human improvement by genetic means.

Eugenics fell out of favor in the mid-twentieth century as a result of the eugenic programs that used sterilization to prevent the reproduction of people who were deemed unfit. The United States was one of the first nations to engage in compulsory sterilization. State laws regarding eugenic sterilization were upheld by the U.S. Supreme Court in 1927 in *Buck v. Bell.* Between 1907 and 1963, more than 64,000 people were forcibly sterilized in the United States. Although the eugenics programs in the United States never reached the magnitude and level of coerciveness of those in Nazi Germany, memories of the state-run programs of involuntary sterilization have left Americans feeling uneasy with talk of genetic engineering.

In 1962 James Watson and Francis Crick won a Nobel Prize for their discovery of the molecular structure of DNA. During the latter part of the twentieth century, reproductive technology focused primarily on the problem of infertility and prenatal diagnosis of birth defects. The development of amniocentesis in 1966 provided a method for diagnosing chromosomal disorders in the fetus. The ability to genetically engineer and even clone humans has awakened fears of a resurgence of large-scale human eugenics programs.

THE HUMAN GENOME PROJECT

The **Human Genome Project** (HGP), a worldwide cooperative effort to map the entire human genetic makeup or **genome,** began in 1990. In 2003, the complete human genome sequence was released to the public.[2] The HGP has led to a dramatic increase in the number of genetic tests, with more the 1,500 now available for diagnosing genetic diseases and conditions.

This knowledge leads to a staggering array of reproductive options. Parents may soon be able to have their fetuses tested for genes that incline the child to obesity, shortness, nearsightedness, depression, alcoholism, Alzheimer's disease, sexual orientation, and even "risk-taking behavior." Parents theoretically could seek genetic therapy or enhancement to alter the genetic makeup of their fetus or preimplant embryo by overriding or replacing "undesirable" genes with more "desirable" ones. Parents may even be able to choose the genetic traits they want in their children or have children who are clones of themselves or some famous person.

The ability to manipulate a person's genome, or **genotype,** raises myriad ethical questions. Is it moral to tamper with our genetic makeup? If so, are there limits that should be placed on the use of genetic engineering and cloning? Do people at risk for carrying certain debilitating genetic diseases have a right not to know their genetic status? Indeed, do they have a right not to be born? Can information about human DNA be owned? Indeed, what does it mean to be human?

The findings of the HGP also raise the issue of our relationship to nonhuman nature and our anthropocentric belief that we are somehow qualitatively different and superior to other living beings. Humans have only about 23,000 genes—far fewer than the 100,000 previously assumed. Other animals, such as dogs, as well as many plants are more genetically complex than humans. The Human Genome Project has also opened the door to creating new genomes from scratch. In 2008 geneticist Craig Venter assembled 582,970 base pairs of genes to create the genome of a completely new organism—a synthetic bacterium.

GENETIC ENGINEERING

Genetic engineering includes both **gene therapy,** in which a new gene is introduced to override a defective gene, and **genetic enhancement,** which involves the manipulation of the **germ cell**—in this case the egg—to improve the genetic code of a being, (see Case Study 2).

By the late 1980s, scientists were genetically altering food by taking genetic material from fish, bacteria, viruses, and insects and adding it to fruits, grains, and vegetables to improve durability and quality. **Transgenic** animals and plants are those with introduced genes from another species. In 1992 the FDA declared that genetically modified (GM) crops are safe and do not need FDA approval before marketing. Although the majority of crops now grown in the United States are genetically modified, the FDA has not yet approved the commercial sale of GM animals for agriculture, with the exception of milk from genetically engineered cows. Scientists are also working on genetically engineering algae that can be used to produce biofuel for automobiles. For more on the moral issues surrounding the use of genetically modified plants and animals, see Chapter 12.

Scientists began experimenting in the 1990s with mass-producing drugs by inserting human genes into bacteria. Scientists are also experimenting with **chimeras**—embryos created from the genetic material of two different species. In late 1997 the same institute that had produced Dolly announced that by blending the two technologies—cloning and genetic engineering—it had created five almost-identical transgenic lambs with human genes that produce factor IX, a blood-clotting substance used in treating hemophilia. The possibility of using genetic engineering in conjunction with cloning to produce "perfect" humans raises the ante in the debate.

There are two types of gene therapy: somatic cell therapy and germ line therapy. In **somatic cell therapy,** normal genes are introduced to produce something, such as an enzyme or protein, that is lacking because of a genetic defect. Somatic cell therapy is a treatment; it does not get rid of the defective gene, nor does it change a person's genotype. Therefore, the defective gene can still be passed on to future generations.

Germ line therapy, in contrast, actually alters the genetic structure of germ line cells—the sperm and the ova—so that the genotype of future generations is also altered. It is even possible to synthesize completely new genes and chromosomes, thus overriding the human genetic code itself. It may be possible to protect offspring against AIDS or certain types of cancer through the use of germ line therapy. As of the beginning of 2009, the FDA has not approved any form of gene therapy and all gene therapy remains experimental.

Both types of genetic engineering can also be used for genetic enhancement and the creation of "designer babies." Geneticists are now able to create artificial genes and even whole chromosomes that can be passed on to offspring.[3] Some computer scientists are even talking of "upgrading" humans by combining genetic engineering with robotics. Dr. Gregory Stock writes, "In the not-too-distant future, it will be looked at as kind of foolhardy to have a child by normal conception."[4]

CLONING

Cloning is the process of producing genetically identical individuals through asexual reproduction. There are currently two types of cloning: (1) blastocyst (embryo) splitting and (2) somatic cell nuclei transfer (SCNT). Nuclei transfer can be further subdivided into nuclei transfer using embryonic or fetal cells and nuclei transfer using adult cells.

PROPOSED USES OF GENETIC ENGINEERING AND CLONING TECHNOLOGY

- **A solution to infertility:** Couples who are infertile could clone one of themselves in order to have a child that is genetically related to at least one parent.
- **Replacement children:** Parents could clone a child to replace one that has died or is dying.
- **Replicating desirable genomes:** Nuclei transfer from adult cells could be used to create clones of people of great genius, talent, and beauty.
- **Genetic testing and gene therapy:** Genetic tests could predict genetic diseases and gene therapy could be used to override or replace the defective gene(s).
- **Prolonging human life:** The identification of the genes responsible for aging may help us to extend the average human life span to ninety or even one hundred years or more.
- **Stem cell (regenerative) medicine:** Stem cells could be used to repair or replace damaged tissues for diseases such as Alzheimer's and spinal cord injuries.
- **Directing our evolution:** We may be able to direct human evolution, as well as that of other species, by replacing selected genes or adding new genes.
- **Agriculture:** Scientists could genetically engineer and clone animals and plants that produce high-quality food.
- **Medicinal animals:** Transgenic animals with human genetic material could be cloned to be used as drug factories or as models for human diseases.
- **Genetically guided drugs:** The development of genome scanning would allow pharmaceutical manufacturers to custom-tailor drugs to a person's genome.[5]
- **Research tools:** Cloned animals could be infected with human diseases such as AIDS or cancer, and different therapies could be tried on them.
- **Organ donors:** Animals could be genetically altered so their organs are compatible with human organs. Human clones could also be used for organ transplants (see Case Study 4).
- **Endangered and extinct species:** Endangered species could be cloned to ensure their survival. Extinct animals could be cloned if viable cells are obtainable.

Blastocyst (embryo) splitting involves separating cells at the **blastocyst** or preimplantation stage of development. At this stage, the two to eight cells are not yet specialized into different organ systems, and each cell is still capable of reproducing an entire organism, as occurs naturally in the case of identical twins. In 1993 researchers at George Washington University announced that they had created the first clones of human embryos. This event touched off the first round of debates on the morality of human cloning.

In *nuclei transfer using embryonic or fetal cells,* the nucleus from an early embryo is transferred to an unfertilized egg from which the original nucleus has been removed. Nuclei transfer using embryonic cells has been used in cloning mice, rabbits, sheep, and cattle. The first successful cloning in vertebrate animals (animals with backbones), using nuclei transfer from tadpoles, was accomplished in 1952. In 1997 Don

Wolf at the Oregon Regional Primate Research Center created two monkey clones from embryonic cells.

Nuclei transfer using adult cells involves taking the nucleus from the cell of an adult and transferring it into a mature egg from which the nucleus has been removed. Prior to the cloning of Dolly, this type of cloning had never succeeded. Since the birth of Dolly in 1997, mice, cows, pigs, and even human embryos have been cloned using this method. Because the new nucleus has the full complement of forty-six chromosomes, the renucleated egg and the person who contributed the new nucleus will be virtually genetically identical, with the exception of a very small contribution of DNA material from the mitochondria[6] of the host egg. Unlike blastocyst splitting, which is limited by the number of cells in a blastocyst, nuclei transfer from adult cells makes it possible for anyone—man, woman, or child—to be cloned in any quantity. With the ability to store cells that outlive their donors, it may someday even be possible to clone the dead, including members of extinct species. Indeed, 80 percent of the woolly mammoth's genome has been sequenced (see Case Study 6, "Jurassic Park Revisited"). Scientists are also working on the genome of Neanderthal man.

Shortly after the birth of Dolly, an advertisement appeared on the Internet from a Bahamas-based group called Clonaid, which offered to clone people for $200,000 or to save a person's cells after death for future cloning. Clonaid announced the birth of the first human clone on December 26, 2002 (see Case Study 1). They also claim that four other cloned babies have since been born. However, they refuse to release the identities of the mothers and infants. Many scientists remain skeptical about these claims to have cloned humans. Since then, other scientists have claimed to have cloned human embryos from adult DNA, including South Korean Hwang Woo-suk, whose widely acclaimed work on human cloning and stem cell research turned out to be a fraud. To date, no claims to have cloned humans from adult DNA have been substantiated.

Putting the Brakes on Research on Human Cloning

Following the announcement of Dolly's birth, many countries established temporary bans on human-cloning research. The European Commission on the Ethical Implications of Biotechnology also came out in 1997 with a statement of "condemnation of human reproductive cloning."[7] In 2005 the United Nations voted to approve a nonbinding global ban on human cloning; however, it lacks the legal power to enforce the ban.

The 1997 Cloning Prohibition Act in the United States banned for a period of five years the use of cloning for the creation of humans. In 2003 the act was updated and placed a further five-year ban on human cloning. This law affects only research using federal money, however. The private sector is still free to engage in human-cloning research. Some legislators are calling for a permanent ban on cloning. This is in line with public opinion. Polls show that the great majority of Americans oppose human cloning.[8] The selection at the end of this chapter from the 2006 Congressional Research Service Report for Congress on Human Cloning addresses the ethical, religious, and legal issues involved in cloning for therapeutic and reproductive purposes.

STEM CELL RESEARCH

Many medical researchers believe that embryonic stem cell research holds great promise for curing disease and the development of a new specialty known as "regenerative medicine." Human embryonic **stem cells** are pluripotent—that is, they have the potential to become any one of the more than 220 cell types that make up the human body. Embryonic stem cells are extracted from embryos that are a few days old and are a tiny round ball of cells. Researchers are hopeful that they can use these cells to repair damaged spinal cords; reverse the damage of Parkinson's disease, Alzheimer's disease, stroke, and osteoporosis; fight cancer; and cure diabetes, cystic fibrosis, blindness, and deafness, to name only some of the possible uses of this technology.

Embryonic stem cell research is prohibited or legally restricted in most countries. Most existing embryonic stem cell lines come from discarded embryos from fertility clinics and from donated eggs.

Sixty-four percent of Americans support "medical research using stem cells obtained from human embryos."[9] Support is based primarily on utilitarian moral theory. Advocates, including notables such as Nancy Reagan, Michael J. Fox, and Christopher Reeve (1952–2004), point to the potential of stem cell research to help thousands, perhaps even millions of people who are suffering from devastating diseases and disabilities. They also note that the embryos that would be used would have been discarded anyway. U.S. Congressman James Langevin defends this view in his speech at the end of the chapter in favor of the Stem Cell Research Enhancement Act of 2005.

Opponents of embryonic stem cell research argue that human personhood starts at conception and stem cell research, by killing the embryo, is a violation of the sanctity of human life. In 2006 President Bush vetoed the Stem Cell Research Enhancement Act of 2005, which had passed both the Senate and the House by solid majorities. The bill would have permitted the use of federal funding for work with certain stem cell lines created from excess frozen IVF (in vitro fertilization) embryos.

Unlike his predecessor, President Obama supports embryonic stem cell research. In 2009 President Obama rescinded the ban on federal funding for use of new embryonic stem cells in research. In any case, it is possible that the debate may soon become passé if researchers develop a method for using adult stem cells or those from the umbilical cord blood of fetuses or newborns.

Researchers are also looking into cloning a patient's own DNA, adding it to a donor's unfertilized egg, and then extracting cells from the growing embryo. However, this brings up the same moral and legal problems as were raised by therapeutic cloning. To date, no cures have been verified using stem cell technology.

In 2007 scientists from Wake Forest University and Harvard University announced that they had found stem cells in amniotic fluid donated by pregnant women that may show the same promise as embryonic stem cells. Since amniotic fluid can be withdrawn from the mother without harm to the mother or fetus, it may offer an alternative that overcomes the moral objections to using embryonic stem cells.

THE MORAL ISSUES

Human Dignity

According to Kant, human dignity requires that humans be treated as ends in themselves. Cloning, Leon Kass argues, is immoral because it treats humans as commodities rather than as ends in themselves, since clones are valued only for their desirable genome (see Case Study 7). However, the fact that we value our children—whether they are clones or "natural" children—for their desirable genomes does not mean that we do not also respect them for who they are. Also, the argument that it is undignified for one person to have the same genome as another is questionable, given that we do not consider it an affront to dignity to be one of a set of identical twins—and clones are merely "delayed" twins. On the other hand, it is argued, cloning may violate human dignity in a way that natural twinning does not, because cloning reduces people to their genetic codes.

In 1672 British philosopher and scientist Robert Boyle (1627–1691) expressed the following view of the human body: "I think the physician is to look upon the patient's body as an engine that is out of order." The idea that the human body can be reduced to an elaborate machine continues to dominate medicine and medical research. In defense of the Vatican's 1987 statement condemning artificial fertilization and the generation of human life outside the body, Cardinal Joseph Ratzinger (now Pope Benedict XVI) told a news conference, "We encourage scientific research, but science is not [an] absolute, to which everything must be subordinated and eventually sacrificed, including the dignity of man."[10] **Reductionism** removes the human body from its social and personal context and reduces it to an object to be studied and manipulated. To have someone else define who we are removes our sense of self-control over our bodies, which is essential to our self-identity and well-being.

Because cloning and stem cell research both involve the destruction of surplus embryos, they raise the same issues of personhood found in the abortion debate. Some bioethicists maintain that embryos are not persons and therefore do not deserve our moral concern. Former President George W. Bush opposed embryonic stem cell research on the grounds that it is a violation of the inherent worth and dignity of the human embryo.

Genetic enhancement has been condemned as tampering with a child's self-identity and right to choose his or her own future. However, other bioethicists point out that parents make environmental interventions—including making their children eat a healthy diet, sending them to school and dance classes, and getting them vaccinated against certain diseases—that benefit the children by modifying their phenotype. If it is laudable on the part of parents to control their child's environment in order to produce the "best" offspring possible, why not also use genetic interventions to attain the same goals? Why are genetic interventions regarded as a violation of the child's dignity or self-identity while environmental ones are not? Thus, the critics of reductionism and genetic engineering are using as a premise the very assumption they reject ("we are essentially our genes") to support their conclusion. There is also concern that clones, because they are human inventions, may be denied the rights of full personhood. Clones could be mass produced to act as drones for the "real" humans. On the other hand, clones, because of their more desirable genomes, might become a new master race, while "natural" humans are relegated to an inferior role.

🖋 KEY DEFINITIONS

- **Genetic engineering:** The introduction of new genes or the manipulation of the genetic code to correct a defective gene or to enhance the genetic code. There are two types of genetic engineering:
  1. *Gene line therapy:* Changing the genetic code of germ line cells (the ova and sperm). These changes will be inherited by future generations.
  2. *Somatic cell therapy:* Introducing normal genes to correct an existing genetic problem. These changes will not be inherited.

- **Cloning:** The process of producing genetically identical individuals through asexual reproduction. There are two types of cloning:
  1. *Blastocyst (embryo) splitting:* Splitting up the cells of the early embryo so that each cell produces an identical individual, as occurs in natural twinning.
  2. *Somatic cell nuclei transfer (SCNT):* Taking the nucleus from an adult cell and transferring it into a mature egg from which the nucleus has been removed in order to produce an identical copy of the adult donor.

- **Stem cell research:** Stem cells are cells that give rise to specific types of tissue. These cells may be used to repair or replace damaged tissue. There are two types of stem cells:
  1. *Embyonic stem cells:* Stem cells from embryos a few days old. These cells have the potential of becoming any tissue in the human body.
  2. *Adult stem cells:* Stem cells from adults or children. These cells are less flexible in their ability to form different tissues.

Gene Patents and Owning Life

The patenting of genetic material has been accelerated by the Human Genome Project (HGP). Although the HGP was adamant that data on the human genome remain in the public domain,[11] in the United States and many other countries, human cells that have been genetically modified can be owned and patented. About 20 percent of the human genome is currently patented or owned by governments, universities, and private corporations, with the United States, China, and Japan being the countries with the most patents. Several companies have obtained patents on individual human genes as well as on genetically engineered animals such as Harvard's oncomouse, which has a gene for cancer (see Case Study 5). Can we, or should we, draw the line at patenting genetically engineered humans? How great a deviation from the human genome is required before we can consider a genetically engineered being a nonhuman that can, legally at least, be used as a means only? Questions have already been raised by lawyers about whether genetically enhanced "designer" children will need permission from the company that owns the patent on their designer genes before they can legally pass the genes on to children of their own.

Scientists and biotech companies have also scouted the globe in search of rare genetic traits that may have future market potential. The Human Genome Diversity Project (HGDP), a separate project from the Human Genome Project, was established to expand the scope of genome research by collecting blood samples from groups of isolated indigenous people. Less than 1 percent of the human genome is responsible for the differences between groups of people. Samples of blood for genetic analysis have been gathered from indigenous groups such as the Bantu and the Mbuti pygmy people in Africa, the Papuans of New Guinea, the Mayan and Pima people of Central and North America, and the Cambodians and Han of Asia, to name only a few.

The project, dubbed the "Vampire Project" and "bio-colonialism" by its critics, has been heavily criticized, especially by indigenous groups, as an extension of white colonialism that treats the bodies of indigenous people as commodities to be exploited. There is also concern that the information will be used to promote racism and deny rights to certain groups based on their "genetic model." The project has now been officially halted because of criticism and withdrawal of funding.

Defining "Perfection" and "Disease"

What does it means to be a "perfect," or even a "healthy," human? Who determines this? Should we define *perfect* in terms of the consequences for the wider community and the species? Or should it be a private decision left up to parents? By being allowed to impose their concept of perfection on their offspring, the parent generation will control the destiny of subsequent generations. The world, however, does not sit still. Talents that may be appropriate today may be passé in years to come. The reject of today may be the genius of tomorrow's world.

Like "perfection" and "health," the concept of "disease" is difficult to define. What distinguishes a disease from discomfort or the suffering caused by variations in cultural norms? Is shortness or homosexuality a disease? Also, are cloning and genetic enhancement the best uses of our limited medical resources? Genetically engineering animals that can produce valuable drugs and organs for humans may drastically reduce that cost of manufacturing these drugs. On the other hand, a utilitarian would balance this against the pain and suffering caused to these animals (see Case Study 3).

The Right to Be Unique

President Clinton, in announcing the federal ban on funding for research on human cloning, affirmed that "human life is unique, born of a miracle, a 'profound gift.'"[12] Cloning is regarded by many of its opponents as a violation of a purported "right to be unique." Cloning, it is argued, robs the clone of his or her sense of uniqueness. Leon Kass expresses concern that clones will be burdened with genetic identities—those of their parents—that have already lived, thus creating a serious self-identity problem.

Natural twins, however, as Judith Johnson and Erin Williams point out, have a sense of self-identity. Although genes provide the building blocks for individuals, they do not determine who we are. Who we are is the result of the interaction between our genetic inheritance and our social and cultural environment. Thus, the idea that we could clone an army of identical Hitlers, or any group of people, who lack a unique identity has no scientific basis.

Interfering with Nature

There are two strands to the argument that genetic engineering and cloning are wrong because they interfere with nature. The first states that nature and the right to create new life belong to God and that we should not encroach on God's domain. This objection is somewhat vague: What exactly do we mean by "creating" as opposed to "reproducing" life? What exactly is included in God's domain? This argument is also irrelevant to those who do not believe in God.

The second strand implicit in this argument is the assumption that "natural" and "good" are invariably linked. However, we are constantly interfering with nature in the name of morality. Indeed, the primary purpose of medicine is to prevent diseases by interfering with their natural courses. This argument, which is based on the naturalistic fallacy, is one of the weakest arguments against cloning.

A related argument is that species have integrity as biological units and we should not disrupt the natural boundaries between species. Again this argument assumes that *natural* and *good* are synonymous. The species-integrity argument is also reminiscent of the racial-purity argument. Just what is the moral value in keeping groups biologically separate? In addition, the distinction between species is not as distinct as biologists once thought. Genetic exchange between species occurs in nature without human interference as well as in cloning combined with genetic engineering.

Redefining Parenthood and Family

Kass argues that cloning would wreak havoc with our ideas of parenting and family. In particular, he questions the wisdom of separating reproduction from sexuality and the family, which is the fundamental unit of all societies. Without grounding parenting in the family, the care of children loses its natural grounding. The act of conjugal love, therefore, is the only method of human procreation consistent with the dignity of man.

Clones break this connection between family and children, because a clone comes from a single parent and may also be that parent's identical twin. What's more, cloning will make men reproductively superfluous. A woman who wants to clone herself would not need a man. On the other hand, a man who wanted to clone himself would need a woman to provide both the egg and a womb.

Kass's critics maintain that the right to have two parents is an artificial right, not a genuine one. As for making men superfluous, cloning would not make social fatherhood obsolete. Clones could still have two social parents. Also, cloning may be the only chance for some couples to have a child who is genetically related to them. The father could provide the nucleus and the mother the egg. That way the mother would at least contribute some material—the DNA from her mitochondria—to their child.

Autonomy and Reproductive Rights

Autonomy is one of the most fundamental human rights. The desire of parents to have a child who is "their own genetic child" is already widely accepted. In cases of infertility or serious genetic disorders, cloning may provide a way for parents to realize this dream. Like Kass, we may find repugnant or arrogant the idea of people cloning themselves, or of parents using genetic engineering to produce the "perfect" child, but these feelings do not, in themselves, make these practices morally wrong so long as the children's interests are protected after birth.

On the other hand, given the high cost of genetic engineering and cloning, making it available could severely curtail reproductive freedom for parents who cannot afford it. Parents who had a less-than-perfect child in a society full of perfect children would put their child at risk for failure and discrimination. In the 1980 case *Curlander v. Bio-Science*

Laboratories, a California court ruled that a child with a genetic defect could bring a "wrongful life" suit against her parents for not undergoing prenatal screening and aborting her. This case could set a precedent for children who do not meet certain social and physical standards to sue their parents because their parents did not have their genome genetically engineered to remove "flaws." Thus, what began as a reproductive right could turn into a duty to have "perfect" children.

Justice as Fairness

Genetic engineering might give children who are products of this technology an unfair advantage. Studies show that there is an association between good-looking executives and business success. Overweight women earn less, on the average, and buyers prefer more attractive salespeople. In another study, subjects gave good-looking criminals sentences that were 20 percent lighter than others. As for the argument that beauty is a cultural construct, even little babies prefer to look at what most people would consider beautiful faces.[13] If people should be given equal treatment, then do parents or society have an obligation to provide genetic enhancement for certain children who may suffer a disadvantage because they may not be as good-looking as their peers?

Being denied the opportunity for genetic engineering or enhancement because of cost constraints could draw even tighter boundaries around membership in privileged classes and further increase the gap between the rich, who can afford such technology, and the poor. Technology that nullifies the need to have "inferior" children may render policy makers less sympathetic to those who are disadvantaged. John Rawls acknowledges that eugenics could create a caste system that divides society into separate biological populations. He also points out, however, that justice as fairness entails that the talents of those with greater abilities would have to be used for the common advantage. Whether this would happen in actual practice is another question.

Another related issue is the use of genetic tests to identify harmful genes, such as those that increase the risk of breast cancer, alcoholism, bipolar (manic-depressive) disorder, or Huntington's disease. The Genetic Information Nondiscrimination Act of 2008 prohibits employers and health insurance companies from requiring genetic tests and from discriminating based on genetic information.

Consequentialist Arguments

These arguments weigh the harms of genetic engineering, cloning, and stem cell research against the benefits. Because we have little experience with these technologies, we have to rely for the most part on speculation in determining whether the harms outweigh the benefits.

Even research to improve our knowledge has its dangers. In 1999, eighteen-year-old Jesse Glesinger died following a gene therapy experiment at the University of Pennsylvania that was thought by the researchers to be relatively safe. Another blow to genetic therapy research came in 2003 when it was learned that two children being treated in a French gene therapy trial had developed a leukemia-like condition.

Some bioethicists maintain that because the possibility for misuse of cloning is so great, all human cloning ought to be banned. Kass fears that cloning and genetic engineering may lead to the mass production of children and the breakdown of parent–child relationships. Johnson and Williams also express concern about the safety of human cloning. Others point to the benefits of cloning to infertile couples, noting that cloning does not harm the offspring, because the clone owes his or her very existence to the cloning process.

Some biologists are concerned that cloning will undermine human diversity. Almost all of us carry several recessive genes that are potentially debilitating. Will cleaning up the gene pool by getting rid of these harmful genes amount to throwing the baby out with the bathwater? By culling genes that may be harmful today, we become less flexible genetically. This in turn may make us less capable, as a species, of adapting to sudden climate changes or of resisting new diseases. A case in point is the gene for sickle-cell anemia. In this genetic disorder, found primarily in people of African descent, the red blood cells have a tendency to become distorted into a sickle shape. These distortions can precipitate a "sickle-cell crisis," which is characterized by severe pain. On the other hand, sickle-cell anemia also provides a measure of immunity against malaria—a potentially deadly disease that is rampant in some parts of Africa. The deletion of this gene and others from the human gene pool could also make us less resistant to future diseases. On the other hand, we now have the potential of creating unlimited biodiversity.

There is also concern about the breeding of cloned herds of agricultural animals and plants—a practice that results in a genetically homogeneous population. Because of this, the whole herd or crop could be wiped out by a single disease. In 1970 half of the maize crop in the United States was lost to one disease—the southern corn leaf blight. The loss was attributed to lack of genetic diversity in the plant.

We also do not yet know the full effect of using adult cells to create clones. Although the incidence of death among the fetuses and offspring of clones is higher than normal, this problem may be resolved with better cloning technology. Initially, there were also fears that cells cloned from an adult animal would age prematurely. However, a later study found that cells from clones actually have longer life spans than the original cells.[14] Obviously much more research is needed on the effects of cloning.

Consequential or utilitarian arguments are key in the embryonic stem cell research debate, with advocates emphasizing the potentially great benefits of this technology for relieving human suffering. Langevin uses consequentialist arguments in his defense of stem cell research. The use of genetically guided drugs, tailored to a person's particular genome, could also greatly decrease drug-related side effects associated with the "one size fits all" approach to drugs and increase the effectiveness of the treatment. Currently medicines have only a 30 to 40 percent chance of working on a particular patient.[15] Genetically engineering crops also has the potential to greatly increase yield and thereby reduce world hunger. On the other hand, it is unrealistic to think that we can genetically engineer some organisms without affecting the rest of the biosphere.

The Rights of Nonhuman Animals

In our belief that humans exist outside and above the natural world, we often forget that we are not just *like* animals—we *are* animals. One of the surprising findings of the Human Genome Project is how much humans are genetically like other animals

---

SUMMARY OF READINGS ON GENETIC ENGINEERING, CLONING, AND STEM CELL RESEARCH

Salvulescu, "Genetic Interventions and the Ethics of Enhancement of Human Beings." Parents have a moral obligation to use genetic intervention to improve the quality of their child's life.

Johnson and Williams, "Human Cloning: Ethical and Social Issues." Both reproductive and therapeutic human cloning raise several ethical issues.

Kass, "The Wisdom of Repugnance." Human cloning violates important human values and should be prohibited.

Langevin, "Statement in Support of H.R. 810, the Stem Cell Research Enhancement Act." Embryonic stem cell research should be permitted because of the many people it will benefit.

Bush, "Stem Cell Research Policy." Stem cell research is prohibited because human embryos are unique human lives that have inherent dignity.

---

and even plants. For example, humans and chimpanzees share more than 98 percent of their genomes in common. There are also more parallels between human development and the development of "lower" animals than was previously assumed.[16] What are we to make of this? Can we continue to justify the moral wedge between humans and nonhuman animals? Does our animal status lessen the moral value of humans, or does the close relationship of humans to other animals mean that we should extend moral respect to all animals, as Buddhists and animal-rights advocates do? If other animals have moral status, can we justify the cloning and genetic engineering of animals as a means to benefit humans?

Another issue is the inclusion of human genetic material in other animals. Do other animals with human genetic material deserve the moral respect now reserved only for humans? What are the moral implications of the breeding of transgenic animals for species integrity? Will the concept of species someday become morally irrelevant? Cloning and genetic engineering may bring an end to the traditional line now drawn between humans and other species of animals; indeed, it may even obliterate the concept of species. Whether this is morally desirable remains to be seen.

CONCLUSION

The ability to genetically engineer and clone humans is a milestone in history. How are we, as morally responsible citizens, going to respond to this new technology? We must resist the temptation to use the temporary ban on cloning as an opportunity to sweep the moral issues under the rug or to dismiss cloning offhand as too bizarre to be morally acceptable. Such a head-in-the-sand approach may simply encourage the development of unregulated back-alley cloning clinics.

There are compelling arguments on both sides of the cloning and genetic engineering debates. These concerns also address issues related to abortion and the use of nonhuman animals in medical experiments. How should we balance the different moral concerns? During the temporary ban, college students and others will have an opportunity to actively engage in policy making.

JULIAN SALVULESCU

Genetic Interventions and the Ethics of Enhancement of Human Beings

Julian Salvulescu is the Uehiro Chair in Practical Ethics and the Director of the Oxford Uehiro Centre for Practical Ethics at the University of Oxford in England. In this reading Salvulescu argues that parents have a moral obligation to use genetic enhancement to improve the quality and well-being of their children's lives.

Critical Reading Questions

1. What are some of the ways in which we already practice enhancement?
2. How does Salvulescu use the analogies of the Neglectful and the Lazy Parents to support his argument that choosing not to enhance is wrong?
3. On what grounds does Salvulescu conclude that there is no relevant moral difference between environmental and genetic interventions?
4. On what grounds does Salvulescu argue that if we have an obligation to treat and prevent disease, then we should also have an obligation to use genetic enhancement to prevent those diseases?
5. How does Salvulescu respond to the objection that genetic enhancement is playing God or goes against nature?
6. How does Salvulescu respond to the genetic discrimination objection?
7. How does Salvulescu respond to the "perfect child" objection?
8. How does Salvulescu respond to the objection that enhancement goes against human nature and is an affront to human dignity?
9. How does Salvulescu respond to the objection that enhancements are self-defeating?

Julian Salvulescu, "Genetic Interventions and the Ethics of Enhancement of Human Beings," in Bonnie Steinbock, ed., *The Oxford Handbook of Bioethics,* excerpts from pp. 516–535 (Oxford: Oxford University Press, 2007). By permission of Oxford University Press. Some notes have been omitted.

Should we use science and medical technology not just to prevent or treat disease, but to intervene at the most basic biological levels to improve biology and enhance people's lives? By enhance, I mean help them to live a longer and/or better life than normal. There are various ways in which we can enhance people but I want to focus on biological enhancement, especially genetic enhancement.

There has been considerable recent debate on the ethics of human enhancement. A number of prominent authors have been concerned about or critical of the use of technology to alter or enhance human beings, citing threats to human nature and dignity as one basis for these concerns. The President's Council Report entitled *Beyond Therapy* was strongly critical of human enhancement. Michael Sandel, in a widely discussed article, has suggested that the problem with genetic enhancement "is in the hubris of the designing parents, in their drive to master the mystery of birth . . . it would disfigure the relation between parent and child, and deprive the parent of the humility and enlarged human sympathies that an openness to the unbidden can cultivate. . . . [T]he promise of mastery is flawed. It threatens to banish our appreciation of life as a gift, and to leaves us with nothing to affirm or behold outside our own will.[1] . . .

In this chapter, I will take a more provocative position. I want to argue that far from being merely permissible, we have a moral obligation or moral reason to enhance ourselves and our children. Indeed, we have the same kind of obligation as we have to treat and prevent disease. Not only *can* we enhance, we *should* enhance. . . .

CURRENT INTEREST IN ENHANCEMENT

There is great public interest in enhancement of people. Women employ cosmetic surgery to make their nose smaller, their breasts larger, their teeth

---

[1]Sandel, M. (2004) The case against perfection. *Atlantic Monthly*, April 2004, 51–62.

straighter and whiter, to make their cheekbones higher, their lips bigger and to remove wrinkles and fat. Men, too, employ many of these measures, as well as pumping their bodies with steroids to increase muscle bulk. The beauty industry is testimony to the attraction of enhancement. Body art, such as painting and tattooing, and body modification, such as piercing, have, since time began, represented ways in which humans have attempted to express their creativity, values and symbolic attachments through changing their bodies. . . .

Many people attempt to improve their cognitive powers through the use of nicotine, caffeine and drugs like Ritalin and Modavigil.

Mood enhancement typifies modern society. People use psychological "self-help," prozac, recreational drugs and alcohol to feel more relaxed, socialize better and feel happier. . . .

More radical forms of biological enhancement appear possible . . . by replacing aging tissue with healthy tissue. We could live longer than the current maximum of 120 years.

But instead of the radical prolongation of length of life, I want to focus on the radical improvement in quality of life through biological manipulation. Some sceptics believe this is not possible. The skeptic claims that it is our environment, or culture, that defines us, not genetics. But a quiet walk in the park demonstrates the power of a great genetic experiment: dog breeding. It is obvious that different breeds of dog differ in temperament, intelligence, physical ability and appearance. . . . Dog breeds are all genetic—for over ten thousand years we have bred some 300–400 breeds of dog from early canids and wolves. The St. Bernard is known for its size, the greyhound for its speed, the bloodhound for its sense of smell. . . . These characteristics have been developed by a crude form of genetic selection—selective mating or breeding.

Today we have powerful scientific tools in animal husbandry—genetic testing, artificial reproduction and cloning are all routinely used in the farming industry to create the best stock. Scientists are now starting to look at a wider range of complex behaviours. Changing the brain's reward centre genetically may be the key to changing behaviour.

Gene therapy has been used to turn lazy monkeys into workaholics by altering the reward centre in the brain.[2] In another experiment, researchers used gene therapy to introduce a gene from the monogamous male prairie vole, a rodent which forms life-long bonds with one mate, into the brain of the closely related but polygamous meadow vole.[3] . . .

But could biological enhancement of human beings really be possible? Selective mating has been occurring in humans ever since time began. . . . As products of evolution, we select our mates, both rationally and instinctively, on the basis of their genetic fitness—their ability to survive and reproduce. Our (subconscious) goal is the success of our offspring.

With the tools of genetics, we can select offspring in a more reliable way. The power of genetics is growing. Embryos can now be tested not only for the presence of genetic disorder (including some forms of bowel and breast cancer), but also for less serious genetic abnormalities, such as dental abnormalities. . . . Research is going on in the field of behavioural genetics to understand the genetic basis of aggression and criminal behaviour, alcoholism, anxiety, antisocial personality disorder, maternal behaviour, homosexuality and neuroticism. . . .

This raises a new question: should we try to engineer better, happier people? While at present genetic technology is most efficient at selecting among different embryos, in the future it will be possible to genetically alter existing embryos, with considerable progress already being made to the use of this technology for permanent gene therapy of disease. There is no reason that such technology could not be used to alter non-disease genes in the future.

[2]Liu, Z. et al. *PNAS Online* doi:10.1073/pnas.0403639101
[3]Lim, M. (2004) *Nature* **429** 754–757.

THE ETHICS OF ENHANCEMENT

. . .

First Argument for Enhancement: Choosing Not to Enhance Is Wrong

Consider the case of the Neglectful Parents. The Neglectful Parents give birth to a child with a special condition. The child has a stunning intellect but requires a simple, readily available, cheap dietary supplement to sustain his intellect. But they neglect the diet of this child and this results in a child with a stunning intellect becoming normal. This is clearly wrong.

But now consider the case of the Lazy Parents. They have a child who has a normal intellect but if they introduced the same dietary supplement, the child's intellect would rise to the same level as the child of the Neglectful Parent. They can't be bothered with improving the child's diet so the child remains with a normal intellect. Failure to institute dietary supplementation means a normal child fails to achieve a stunning intellect. The inaction of the Lazy Parents is as wrong as the inaction of the Neglectful Parents. It has exactly the same consequence: a child exists who could have had a stunning intellect but is instead normal.

Some argue that it is not wrong to fail to bring about the best state of affairs. This may or may not be the case. But in these kinds of cases, when there are no other relevant moral considerations, the failure to introduce a diet which sustains a more desirable state is as wrong as the failure to introduce a diet which brings about a more desirable state. The costs of inaction are the same, as are the parental obligations.

If we substitute "biological intervention" for "diet," we see that in order not to wrong our children, we should enhance them. Unless there is something special and optimal about our children's physical, psychological or cognitive abilities, or something different about other biological interventions, it would be wrong not to enhance them.

Second Argument: Consistency

. . .

In general, we accept environmental interventions to improve our children. Education, diet and training are all used to make our children better people and increase their opportunities in life. We train children to be well behaved, co-operative and intelligent. Indeed, researchers are looking at ways to make the environment more stimulating for young children to maximise their intellectual development. . . .

Some argue that genetic manipulations are different because they are irreversible. But environmental interventions can equally be irreversible. Child neglect or abuse can scar a person for life. It may be impossible to unlearn the skill of playing the piano or riding a bike, once learnt. One may be wobbly, but one is a novice only once. . . .

If the outcome is the same, why treat biological manipulation differently to environmental manipulation? Not only may a favourable environment improve a child's biology and increase a child's opportunities, so too may direct biological interventions. Couples should maximise the genetic opportunity of their children to lead a good life and a productive, cooperative social existence.

There is no relevant moral difference between environmental and genetic intervention.

Third Argument: No Difference to Treating Disease

If we accept the treatment and prevention of disease, we should accept enhancement. The goodness of health is what drives a moral obligation to treat or prevent disease. But health is not what ultimately matters—health enables us to live well: disease prevents us from doing what we want and what is good. Health is instrumentally valuable— valuable as a resource that allows us to do what really matters, that is, lead a good life.

What constitutes a good life is a deep philosophical question. . . . Disease is important because it causes pain, is not what we want and stops us engaging in those activities that giving meaning to life. . . . Life is about managing risk to health and life to promote well-being.

Beneficence—the moral obligation to benefit people—provides a strong reason to enhance people in so far as the biological enhancement increases their chance of having a better life. . . .

Many of our biological and psychological characteristics profoundly affect how well our lives go. In the 1960s Walter Mischel conducted impulse control experiments where 4-year-old children were left in a room with one marshmallow, after being told that if they did not eat the marshmallow, they could later have two. Some children would eat it as soon as the researcher left, others would use a variety of strategies to help control their behaviour and ignore the temptation of the single marshmallow.

A decade later, they reinterviewed the children and found that those who were better at delaying gratification had more friends, better academic performance and more motivation to succeed. Whether the child had grabbed for the marshmallow had a much stronger bearing on their SAT scores than did their IQ.[4]

Impulse control has also been linked to socio-economic control and avoiding conflict with the law. The problems of a hot and uncontrollable temper can be profound. . . .

"[A]ll purpose goods" . . . are traits which are valuable regardless of which kind of life a person choose to live. They give us greater all round capacities to live a vast array of lives. Examples include intelligence, memory, self-discipline, patience, empathy, a sense of humour, optimism and just having a sunny temperament. All of these characteristics . . . may have some biological and psychological basis capable of manipulation with technology.

Technology might even be used to improve our *moral character*. We certainly seek through good instruction and example, discipline and other methods to make better children. It may be

[4]Mischel, W., Shoda, Y., Peake, P. K. (1988) The nature of adolescent competencies predicted by preschool delay of gratification. *Journal of Personality & Social Psychology* **54** (4) 687–696.

possible to alter biology to make people predisposed to be more moral by promoting empathy, imagination, sympathy, fairness, honesty, etc.

In so far as these characteristics have some genetic basis, genetic manipulation could benefit us. There is reason to believe that complex virtues like fairmindedness may have a biological basis. . . .

Summary: The Case in Favour of Enhancement

What matters is human well-being, not only treatment and prevention of disease. Our biology affects our opportunities to live well. The biological route to improvement is no different to the environmental. Biological manipulation to increase opportunity is ethical.

If we have an obligation to treat and prevent disease, we have an obligation to try to manipulate these characteristics to give an individual the best opportunity of the best life. . . .

OBJECTIONS

1. Playing God or Against Nature

This objection has various forms. Some people in society believe that children are a gift, of God or of Nature, and that we should not interfere in human nature. Most people implicitly reject this view—we screen embryos and fetuses for diseases, even mild correctible diseases. We interfere in Nature or God's will when we vaccinate, provide pain relief to women in labour . . . and treat cancer. No one would object to the treatment of disability in a child, if it were possible. Why then, not treat the embryo with genetic therapy if that intervention is safe? This is no more thwarting God's will than giving antibiotics.

Another variant of this objection is that we are arrogant to assume we can have sufficient knowledge to meddle with human nature. Some people object that we cannot know the complexity of the human system, which is like an unknowable magnificent symphony. To attempt to enhance one characteristic may have other unknown, unforeseen effects elsewhere in the system. We should not play God—we should be humble and recognise the limitations of our knowledge. Unlike God, we are not omnipotent or omniscient.

A related objection is that genes are pleiotropic—which means they have different effects in different environments. The gene or genes which predispose to manic depression may also be responsible for heightened creativity and productivity.

One response to both these objections is to limit our interventions, until our knowledge grows, to selections between different embryos and not intervene to enhance particular embryos or people. Since we would be choosing between complete systems on the basis of their type, we would not be interfering with the internal machinery. In this way, selection is less risky than enhancement. . . .

We must do adequate research before intervening. And because the benefits may be less than when we treat or prevent disease, we may require the standards of safety to be higher than for medical interventions. But we must weigh the risks against the benefit. If confidence is justifiably high, and benefits outweigh harms, we should enhance.

Once technology affords us the power to enhance our and our children's lives, to fail to do so will be to be responsible for the consequences. To fail to treat our children's disease is to wrong them. To fail to prevent them getting depression is to wrong them. To fail to improve their physical, musical, psychological and other capacities is to wrong them, just as it would be to harm them if we gave them a toxic substance that stunted or reduced these capacities. . . .

There is no moral reason to preserve some traits—such as uncontrollable aggressiveness, a sociopathic personality or extreme deviousness. Tell the victim of rape and murder that we must preserve the natural balance and diversity.

2. Genetic Discrimination

Some people fear the creation of a two class society of the enhanced and the unenhanced, where the inferior unenhanced are discriminated against and disadvantaged all through life.

We must remember that nature allots advantage and disadvantage with no gesture to fairness. Some are born horribly disadvantaged, destined to die after short and miserable lives. Some suffer great genetic disadvantage while others are born gifted, physically, musically or intellectually. There is no secret that there are "gifted" children naturally. Allowing choice to change our biology will, if anything, be more egalitarian—allowing the ungifted to approach the gifted. There is nothing fair about the natural lottery—allowing enhancement may be more fair. . . .

3. The Perfect Child, Sterility and Loss of the Mystery of Life

If we engineered perfect children, this objection goes, the world would be a sterile, monotonous place where everyone is the same and the mystery and surprise of life is gone.

It is impossible to create perfect children. We can only attempt to create children with better opportunities of a better life. There will necessarily be difference. Even in the case of screening for disability, like Down syndrome, 10% of people choose not to abort a pregnancy known to have Down syndrome. People value different things. There will never be complete convergence. Moreover, there will remain massive challenges for individuals to meet in their personal relationships and in the hurdles our unpredictable environment presents. There will remain much mystery and challenge—we will just be better able to deal with these. We will still have to work to achieve, but our achievements may have greater value.

4. Against Human Nature

One of the major objections to enhancement is that it is against human nature. Common alternative phrasings are that enhancement is tampering with our nature or an affront to human dignity. I believe that what separates us from other animals is our rationality, our capacity to make normative judgements and act on the basis of reasons. When we make decisions to improve our lives by biological and other manipulations, we express our rationality and express what is fundamentally important about our nature. And if those manipulations improve our capacity to make rational and normative judgements, they further improve what is fundamentally human. Far from being against the human spirit, such improvements express the human spirit. To be human is to be better.

5. Enhancements Are Self-Defeating

Another familiar objection to enhancement is that enhancements will have self-defeating or other adverse social effects. A typical example is increase in height. If height is socially desired, then everyone will try to enhance the height of their children at great cost to themselves and the environment (as taller people consume more resources), with no advantage in the end since there will be no relative gain.

If a purported manipulation does not improve well-being or opportunity, there is no argument in favour of it. In this case, the manipulation is not an enhancement. In other cases, such as enhancement of intelligence, the enhancement of one individual may increase that individual's opportunities only at the expense of another. So-called positional goods are goods only in relative sense.

But many enhancements will have both positional and non-positional qualities. Intelligence is good not just because it allows an individual to be more competitive for complex jobs, but because it allows an individual to more rapidly process information in her own life, and to develop greater understanding of herself and others. These non-positional effects should not be ignored. . . .

Nonetheless, if there are significant social consequences of enhancement, this is of course a valid objection. But it is not particular to enhancement—there is an old question about how far individuals in society can pursue their own self-interest at cost to others. It applies to education, health care, and virtually all areas of life. . . .

CONCLUSION

Enhancement is already occuring. In sport, human erythropoietin boosts red blood cells. Steroids and growth hormone improve muscle strength. Many people seek cognitive enhancement—nicotine, ritalin, modavigil, caffeine. Prozac, recreational drugs and alcohol all enhance mood. Viagra is used to improve sexual performance.

And of course mobile phones and aeroplanes are examples of external enhancing technologies.

In the future, genetic technology, nanotechnology, and artificial intelligence may profoundly affect our capacities.

Will the future be better or just disease-free? We need to shift our frame of reference from health to life enhancement. What matters is how we live. . . .

I believe to be human is to be better. Or, at least, to strive to be better. We should be here for a *good* time, not just a *long* time. Enhancement, far from being merely permissible, is something we should aspire to achieve.

Discussion Questions

1. Discuss Salvulescu's claim that there is no difference morally between environmental and genetic enhancement. If there is no relevant difference between the two, does this create a moral obligation for parents to use genetic enhancement to prevent disease and improve the quality of their child's life? Support your answer.
2. Make a list of the harms and benefits of prenatal genetic enhancement. Reviewing the list, discuss how a utilitarian might respond to the use of genetic enhancement by parents. Where, if at all, might a utilitarian draw the line between acceptable and unacceptable uses of genetic enhancement and why?
3. Imagine that you can roll back the clock and your parents have been given the option to genetically enhance you shortly after your conception. Would you have wanted them to genetically enhance you? Explain your reasoning.

JUDITH A. JOHNSON AND ERIN D. WILLIAMS

Human Cloning: Ethical and Social Issues

The following is an excerpt from a Report for Congress prepared by Judith Johnson, a specialist in life sciences, and Erin Williams, a specialist in bioethical policy with the Congressional Research Service. In the report, they explore the various moral issues raised by both therapeutic and reproductive human cloning as well as different types of governmental restrictions proposed for human cloning.

"Human Cloning," Congressional Research Service Report for Congress, Library of Congress, July 20, 2006, pp. 14–42. Some notes have been omitted.

Critical Reading Questions

1. What positions do the President's Council on Bioethics, Clonaid, and the Catholic Church each take regarding the morality of reproductive cloning?
2. Why do Johnson and Williams reject the argument that reproductive cloning is immoral because it does not involve a conjugal union?
3. Why is safety one of the primary moral concerns in reproductive cloning?
4. On what grounds do Johnson and Williams reject the "identity," "commodification," "familiar relationships," and "societal view of children" arguments against reproductive cloning?
5. Why does therapeutic cloning have more support in the scientific community than reproductive cloning?
6. What are some of the benefits and harms of therapeutic cloning to society?
7. What are some of the concerns regarding the moral status of the cloned embryo and its use and destruction?
8. What are the arguments for and against paying women for donating eggs for cloning?
9. What are the five types of restrictions government might place on human cloning, and what are the arguments for and against each type of restriction?

ETHICAL AND SOCIAL ISSUES

The possibility of using cloning technology not just for therapeutic purposes but also for reproducing human beings raises profound moral and ethical questions. . . . In July 2002, the President's Council on Bioethics issued its report, *Human Cloning and Human Dignity,* which contained two opinions and sets of recommendations: one of the 10–7 majority, and one of the minority. The majority and minority both opposed reproductive cloning. It was on the topic of therapeutic cloning, which the majority opposed and the minority favored, that the Council was split.

A predecessor to the President's Council, the National Bioethics Advisory Commission (NBAC), recommended, in *Cloning Human Beings,*[1] the continuation of a moratorium on federal funding for reproductive purposes with a call for voluntary compliance from the private sector. It further

recommended the enactment of legislation with a three- to five-year sunset clause banning cloning for reproductive purposes. However, it made clear that all measures taken should "be carefully written so as not to interfere with other important areas of scientific research."[2]

Various other organizations, individuals, and councils have issued opinions and reports on cloning as well. Some, such as the United States Conference of Catholic Bishops (USCCB), oppose human cloning for any purpose. . . . Others, such as a group of forty Nobel Laureates, former First Lady Nancy Reagan, and former President Gerald Ford, would allow regulated cloning for therapeutic purposes, but disallow it for reproductive ones. Still others, such as Dr. Severino Antinori, and Clonaid, favor cloning for reproductive purposes, and even claim to have created human clones via SCNT.

The human cloning debate centers around a number of different ethical and pragmatic issues. Exploration of these issues reveals variation in ethical and moral as well as factual beliefs. The following

---

[1] National Bioethics Advisory Commision, *Cloning Human Beings,* June 1997.

[2] Ibid., p. iv.

discussion breaks down the arguments surrounding human cloning according to these issues, demonstrating both the complexity of the issues and the points of resonance among the groups.

ISSUES INVOLVED IN CLONING FOR REPRODUCTIVE PURPOSES

As Clonaid advertised and the President's Council acknowledged, supporters of reproductive cloning favor it because it might "allow infertile couples to have genetically-related children,"[3] enable families to avoid genetic disease in their genetically-related children, facilitate the replication of specific persons (such as lost loved ones), or to create ideal transplant donors. Likewise, the NBAC recognized that some of the principles that underlie these purposes are a "presumption in favor of individual liberty," that "human reproduction [is] particularly personal and should remain free of constraint, . . . [and] as a society, we ought not limit the freedom of scientific inquiry.[4] However, for a number of other reasons, the idea of cloning for reproductive purposes is presently rejected by most groups and organizations, including the President's Council and NBAC. Of the groups and individuals listed in the Ethical and Social Issues section, only Clonaid and Dr. Antinori favor reproductive cloning at this time. . . .

Procreation Without Conjugal Union

According to the USCCB, *Donum Vitae*[5] instructs that "attempts or hypotheses for obtaining a human being without any connection with sexuality

through 'twin fission,' cloning or parthenogenesis are to be considered contrary to the moral law, since they are in opposition to the dignity both of human procreation and of the conjugal union.[6] This objection to reproductive cloning, that procreation should be limited to conjugal unions, is not supported by most groups. If accepted, it would lead to a rejection of other forms of assisted reproduction, such as in vitro fertilization (IVF). . . .

Safety

The most agreed upon objection to human reproductive cloning is one of safety. The President's Council on Bioethics concluded that, "[g]iven the high rates of morbidity and mortality in the cloning of other mammals, we believe that cloning-to-produce-children would be extremely unsafe, and that attempts to produce a cloned child would be highly unethical."[7] The National Bioethics Advisory Commission reached a consensus in its objection to reproductive cloning "because current scientific information indicate[d] that this technique [was] not safe in humans. . . ."[8] The National Academies agrees with this line of reasoning, given that animal experimentation has demonstrated that "only a small percentage of attempts are successful," "many of the clones die during gestation," and "newborn clones are often abnormal, or die."[9] While these objections about safety are widely held, they may be temporary in nature. As research advances, it may become less risky, and thus some may find it less objectionable to attempt reproductive human cloning.

[3]President's Council on Bioethics, *Human Cloning and Human Dignity,* July 2002, p. xxvii. (Hereafter cited as President's Council, *Human Cloning.*)

[4]National Bioethics Advisory Commission, *Cloning Human Beings,* June 1997, p. 72.

[5]*Donum Vitae* ("The Gift of Life"), which addresses the Catholic view of morality of many modern fertility procedures, was issued in 1987 by the Sacred Congregation for the Doctrine of the Faith at [http://www.nccbuscc.org/prolife/tdocs/donumvitae.htm], accessed July 9, 2004.

[6]John Haas, "Begotten Not Made: A Catholic View of Reproductive Technology," *United States Conference of Catholic Bishops, Pro Life Activities,* June 2003, at [http://www.usccb.org/prolife/programs/rlp/98rlphaa.htm], accessed July 9, 2004.

[7]President's Council, *Human Cloning,* p. xxiii.

[8]National Bioethics Advisory Commission, *Cloning Human Beings,* June 1997, p. iii.

[9]*Scientific and Medical Aspects of Human Reproductive Cloning* (Washington: National Academies Press, 2002), p. 93. The report on human cloning is available at [http://www.nap.edu/catalog/10285.html?onpi_topnews_011802].

Unlike concerns about safety, other types of objections, while not so widely held, may be more lasting because they are not likely to be alleviated by scientific progress. These tend to be philosophical in nature. . . .

Identity

Some objections to reproductive cloning are based upon fears that cloned children will have difficulty with their identities "because each will be genetically virtually identical to a human being who has already lived and because the expectations for their lives may be shadowed by constant comparisons to the life of the 'original.'"[10] These concerns are dismissed by others, who point out that this argument rests largely on "the crudest genetic determinism."[11] They cite both the effect that environment plays on individual development, and the lack of difficulty with identity experienced by naturally occurring identical twins.[12]

Commodification

Other philosophical objections have to do with a fear that cloned children "might come to be considered more like products of a designed manufacturing process than 'gifts' whom their parents are prepared to accept as they are. Such an attitude toward children could also contribute to increased commercialization and industrialization of human procreation."[13] This, in turn, may fuel a new eugenics in which parents select not only whether to have a child, but which child to have. Others point out that these types of concerns were raised about most forms of assisted reproduction (such as in vitro fertilization and preimplantation genetic diagnosis), which have not led to objectification. In addition, if being born is considered to

be a benefit to the one born, "to the extent that the technology is used to benefit the child . . . no objectification of the child takes place."[14]

Familial Relationships

A complicated lineage has also been introduced as an objection to reproductive cloning: "By confounding and transgressing the natural boundaries between generations, cloning could strain the social ties between them. Fathers could become "twin brothers" to their "sons"; mothers could give birth to their genetic twins; and grandparents would also be the "genetic parents" of their grandchildren. Genetic relation to only one parent might produce special difficulties for family life."[15] Others point out that children "born through assisted reproductive technologies may also have complicated relationships to genetic, gestational, and rearing parents . . . [yet] there is no evidence that confusion over family roles has harmed children born through assisted reproductive technologies, although the subject has not been carefully studied."[16]

Societal View of Children

Concerns have been voiced about the effects of cloning on society: "Cloning-to-produce-children would affect not only the direct participants but also the entire society that allows or supports this activity. Even if practiced on a small scale, it could affect the way society looks at children and set a precedent for future nontherapeutic interventions into the human genetic endowment or novel forms of control by one generation over the next."[17] This objection is rejected by others, who argue that "people can, and do, adapt in socially redeeming ways to new technologies. . . . [A] child

[10]President's Council, *Human Cloning,* July 2002, p. xxviii.
[11]National Bioethics Advisory Commission, *Cloning Human Beings,* June 1997, p. 65. Note: *genetic determinism* is the idea that a person's identity and development are primarily or entirely the result of his or her genetic makeup.
[12]President's Council, *Human Cloning,* July 2002, p. 103.
[13]Ibid., pp. xxviii–xxix.

[14]National Bioethics Advisory Commission, *Cloning Human Beings,* June 1997, p. 70.
[15]President's Council, *Human Cloning,* July 2002, p. xxix.
[16]National Bioethics Advisory Commission, *Cloning Human Beings,* June 1997, p. 66.
[17]President's Council, *Human Cloning,* July 2002, p. xxix.

born through somatic cell nuclear transfer could be loved and accepted like any other child . . ."[18]

ISSUES INVOLVED IN CLONING FOR THERAPEUTIC PURPOSES[19]

Cloning for therapeutic purposes is more broadly supported than reproductive cloning, and the issues involved are somewhat different. The safety concerns of reproductive cloning do not apply in therapeutic cloning, placing much of the scientific community, such as the National Academies, in favor of it. . . .

Relief of Human Suffering and Moral Status of Cloned Embryos

The central debate over therapeutic cloning rests on the relative weight ascribed to potential research benefits, and that ascribed to cloned embryos themselves. All sides generally agree that research involving cloning may generate biomedical advancements that relieve human suffering. As described by the President's Council, the research "may offer uniquely useful ways of investigating and possibly treating many chronic debilitating diseases and disabilities, providing relief to millions."[20] Yet a majority of Council members were dissuaded from the research, arguing that "[i]f we permit this research to proceed, we will effectively be endorsing the complete transformation of nascent human life into nothing more than a resource tool."[21] . . .

The Council's minority offered an opposing viewpoint: "We believe there are sound moral reasons for not regarding the embryo, in its earliest

stages as the moral equivalent of a human person" but rather as having a "developing and intermediate moral worth that commands our special respect."[22] The minority based its opinion on the fact that, at the blastocyst stage (the one useful for stem cell research, for example), the cells are still undifferentiated and could still be split and develop into two separate twinned embryos, "suggesting that the earliest stage embryo is *not yet* an individual."[23] Furthermore, they note that the possibility for the development of a human child from a cloned embryo would require its transference to a uterus, as is currently the case with IVF.[24] IVF often results in the creation of embryos that remain unimplanted, and is permitted in the United States. For all of the above reasons, the Council minority, NBAC, Nancy Reagan, Gerald Ford, and the Nobel Laureates support therapeutic cloning.

. . . At the December 2004 Council meeting, Dr. William Hurlbut, . . . who objects to the destruction of human embryos and voted for the moratorium, made a proposal to explore the possibility of using SCNT in combination with techniques to ensure that the group of cells created cannot give rise to human life but can generate embryonic stem cells . . . "morally akin to a complex tissue culture and thereby bypass moral concerns about the creation and disruption of human embryos."[25] Some have criticized Dr. Hurlbut's proposal to create something that is not an embryo, yet generates embryonic stem cells, as one focused on a "semantic issue, not a scientific one."[26] Others have lauded Dr. Hurlbut's proposals as a potential scientific solution to a moral problem. Included among them is Dr. Leon Kass, the Chair of the Council

[18]National Bioethics Advisory Commission, *Cloning Human Beings,* June 1997, p. 67.

[19]For purposes of this section, the term "therapeutic purposes" is meant to include the use of cloning technology for both the research underlying treatments and the treatments themselves.

[20]President's Council, *Human Cloning,* July 2002, pp. xxxi, xxxiii.

[21]Ibid., p. xxxiii.

[22]Ibid., p. xxxi.

[23]Ibid., p. 136.

[24]Ibid.

[25]President's Council on Bioethics, Presentation of Dr. William Hurlbut in "Transcript of the President's Council on Bioethics," Dec. 3, 2004, Washington, D.C., at [http://www.bioethics.gov/transcripts/dec04/session6.html].

[26]Kirsty Horsey, "When Is an Embryo Not an Embryo?" *BioNews,* no. 287, Dec. 6, 2004, at [http://www.bionews.org.uk/commentary.lasso?storyid=2372].

and a well-known opponent of embryo destruction, who said the proposal raises the possibility that, "the partisans of scientific progress and the defenders of nascent human life can go forward in partnership without anyone having to violate things they hold dear."[27]

Deliberate Creation for Use/Destruction

A second set of considerations underlying the debate have to do with a moral aversion to the prospect of creating life in order to destroy it. As a majority of the President's Council pointed out, cloning for therapeutic purposes requires "the creation of human life expressly and exclusively for the purpose of its use in research, research that necessarily involves its destruction, . . . transform [ing] nascent human life into nothing more than a resource tool."[28] . . .

The Council minority countered that the "embryos would not be 'created for destruction,' but for use in the service of life and medicine."[29] Further, the "practice of sacrificing the life of the unborn in order to save the life of the pregnant woman—while not a moral parallel to the case of using cloned embryos for biomedical research—shows that there is some moral precedent for subordinating nascent human life to more developed human life."[30]

Moral Harm or Benefit to Society

The effect of therapeutic cloning upon society has been debated by opponents and proponents alike. The President's Council majority fear negative effects, such as the subjugation of weak members of society, or genetic manipulation of developing life: "As much as we wish to alleviate suffering now and to leave our children in a world where suffering can be more effectively relieved, we also want

to leave them in a world . . . that honors moral limits, that respects all life whether strong or weak, and that refuses to secure the good of some human beings by sacrificing the lives of others."[31] Approving therapeutic cloning would harm society by "crossing the boundary from sexual to asexual reproduction, thus approving in principle the genetic manipulation and control of nascent human life."[32] . . .

Counter arguments have been made by those who note that "[h]istorically, scientific inquiry has been protected and even encouraged because of the great societal benefit the public recognizes in maintaining the sanctity of knowledge and the value of intellectual freedom."[33] In addition, they note that cloning is replication, rather than transformation: "In an important sense, cloning is not the most radical thing on the horizon. Much more significant . . . would be the ability to actually alter or manipulate the genome of offspring, . . . which could then lead to a child being born with characteristics other than it would have had. . . ."[34]

Going Too Far or Drawing Appropriate Limitations

Some, such as the majority of the President's Council and USCCB, believe that policies allowing therapeutic cloning would create a slippery slope, "opening the door to other moral hazards, such as cloning-to-produce-children or research on later-stage embryos and fetuses."[35] Others . . . believe that it is possible to circumscribe acceptable practices with good policy. "Both the federal government and the states already regulate the researchers' methods in order to protect the rights

---

[27]David Brown, "Two Stem Cell Options Presented; Human Embryos Wouldn't Be Killed," *Washington Post,* Dec. 4, 2004, A1.
[28]President's Council, *Human Cloning,* July 2002, p. xxxiii.
[29]Ibid., p. xxxi.
[30]Ibid., pp. 137–138.

[31]Ibid., p. xxxiv.
[32]Ibid., p. xxxiv.
[33]National Bioethics Advisory Commission, *Cloning Human Beings,* June 1997, p. 75.
[34]J. A. Robertson, "A Ban on Human Cloning Research Is Unjustified," *Testimony before the National Bioethics Advisory Commission* (Mar. 14, 1997), in National Bioethics Advisory Commission, *Cloning Human Beings,* June 1997, p. 68.
[35]President's Council, *Human Cloning,* p. xxxiv.

of research subjects and community safety."[36] Government might regulate "the secure handling of embryos, licensing and prior review of research projects, the protection of egg donors, and the provision of equal access to benefits."[37]

Egg Procurement

. . . The prospect of paying women for their eggs, which has been debated in the context of seeking donor eggs both for reproductive purposes (for example, to enable women who do not produce their own eggs to become pregnant), and for research purposes, is not unheard of in the United States. According to a 2000 study by the American Society of Reproductive Medicine (ASRM), some IVF programs reportedly offered as much as $5,000 for one egg retrieval cycle, though $2,500 appeared to be a more common amount. . . . The questions are, is payment for egg donation ever acceptable, and if so, what amount is appropriate?

Several arguments have been put forth in favor of payment for egg donation, many focused on donation for reproductive purposes. First, some have argued that payment creates incentives to increase the number of egg donors, thus facilitating research and benefitting infertile couples. Second, some reason that payment for eggs gives women parity with sperm donors, who may be compensated for donating gametes at a lower rate, given that they require a much less involved procedure. Third, some allege that fairness dictates that women who donate eggs ought to be able to benefit from their action. Fourth, some claim that pressures created by financial incentives may be no greater than those experienced by women asked to make altruistic egg donations for relatives or friends, and may thus not rise to the level of coercion. These are the types of arguments that led ASRM to recommend in 2000 that sums of up to $5,000 may be appropriate for typical egg donation, while sums of up to $10,000 may possibly

be justified if there are particular difficulties a woman must endure to make her donation.

Several arguments have also been put forth against payment for egg donation. First, some voiced fears that payment might lead to the exploitation of women, particularly poor women, and the commodification of reproductive tissues. Second, some have argued that payment for eggs for research purposes might undermine public confidence in endeavors such as human ESR. Arguments such as these have prompted both the NAS and the PCBE to recommend that women not be paid for donating their eggs for research purposes. It also led the PCBE to note that in theory, there is the possibility that eggs could be procured from ovaries harvested from cadavers, which might at least alleviate concerns related to coercion.

It is worth noting that a woman may choose to undergo egg retrieval for her own reproductive purposes, which would effectively take the process of egg procurement out of the research arena and avoid the question of payment entirely. (For example, this could be an option for a woman seeking IVF because her fallopian tubes are blocked.)

Types of Restrictions

One final set of arguments center around the types of actions that the government may take with respect to therapeutic and/or reproductive cloning. These include permitting, regulating, funding, discouraging, and temporarily or permanently banning the practices. As a starting point, NBAC offers: "In the United States, governmental policies that prohibit or regulate human actions require justification because of a general presumption against governmental interference in individual activities."[38] . . .

The most permissive approach available, permitting cloning with no restrictions, is not supported by any of the individuals or organizations referenced herein. By contrast, the next most permissive approach, regulating cloning, is supported

---

[36]National Bioethics Advisory Commission, *Cloning Human Beings,* June 1997, p. 75.
[37]President's Council, *Human Cloning,* p. xxxviii.

[38]National Bioethics Advisory Commission, *Cloning Human Beings,* June 1997, p. 78.

by the Council minority, NBAC, Nancy Reagan, Gerald Ford, and the Nobel Laureates as appropriate for therapeutic cloning, so as to enable it to continue in accordance with socially accepted scientific research practices. As summarized by the Council minority, "We believe that this research could provide relief to millions of Americans, and that the government should therefore support it, within sensible limits imposed by regulation."[39]

A voluntary prohibition, the third most permissive approach, was recommended by NBAC as the appropriate immediate response to reproductive cloning by the private sector. NBAC called for "an immediate request to all firms, clinicians, investigators, and professional societies in the private and non-federally funded sectors to comply voluntarily with the intent of the federal moratorium."[40]

As a longer term approach, NBAC recommended the fourth most permissive approach, a temporary ban on reproductive cloning. "Federal legislation [should] be enacted to prohibit anyone from attempting, whether in a research or clinical setting, to create a child through somatic cell nuclear transfer. It is critical, however, that such legislation include a sunset clause to ensure that Congress will review the issue after a specified time period (three to five years) in order to decide whether the prohibition continues to be needed."[41] . . . The National Academies also recommended a ban on reproductive cloning, and did not call it temporary but did add that it should be reconsidered every five years. On the topic of therapeutic rather than reproductive cloning, a majority of the Council recommended a temporary moratorium as the proper approach, because it would "reaffirm the principle that science can progress while upholding the community's moral norms, and would therefore reaffirm the community's moral support for science and biomedical technology."[42]

The most restrictive approach to cloning, a permanent ban, was proposed by the Council minority and majority, and Nancy Reagan as appropriate for reproductive cloning. "By permanently banning cloning-to-produce-children, this policy gives force to the strong ethical verdict against [it], unanimous in the Council . . . and widely supported by the American people."[43] This approach is also favored by the USCCB not only for reproductive cloning, but also for therapeutic cloning.

One related issue, that of the use of federal funding for therapeutic cloning, has also been discussed. No proposals have been made by any of the groups or individuals listed above for the use of federal funding for reproductive cloning. Opponents of funding therapeutic cloning, such as the Council majority, have expressed concern that use of federal funding for therapeutic cloning would put "the federal government in the novel and unsavory position of mandating the destruction of nascent human life."[44] Proponents of federal funding for therapeutic cloning . . . cite as support the advancements that might be powered by the infusion of federal dollars into the research, as well as the ethical protections that would attach with the money.

---

[39]President's Council, *Human Cloning*, p. xxxviii.
[40]National Bioethics Advisory Commission, *Cloning Human Beings*, June 1997, p. 105.
[41]Ibid.

[42]President's Council, *Human Cloning*, p. xxxvii.
[43]President's Council, *Human Cloning*, p. xxxiv.
[44]President's Council, *Human Cloning*, p. xxxvi.

Discussion Questions

1. Johnson and Williams regard safety, including possible abnormalities in clones, as the strongest argument against legalizing reproductive cloning. However, parents who are carriers of genetic disorders, such as Tay-Sachs disease and cystic fibrosis, are allowed to have children even though there is a good chance they will pass these

often devastating disorders on to their children. Discuss whether laws should be passed restricting parents who are carriers of serious genetic disorders from having children.

2. Discuss the claim that reproductive cloning is similar to other types of assisted reproduction, such as in vitro fertilization, and as such should be permitted.

3. The arguments for therapeutic cloning are based primarily on its benefits to society. Discuss how a utilitarian and a deontologist might respond.

4. The issue of paying women for eggs to be used in cloning raises the question of exploitation of poor women who might be tempted to sell their eggs, especially since harvesting eggs may lead to future health problems. Indeed, there already is an international trade in human eggs for fertility clinics, with women in some impoverished nations receiving up to $250 for their eggs. Should there be legal restrictions on the donation and sale of eggs? Or should women have a liberty right to decide how to use their bodies in this case? Support your answers. Discuss how both a rights ethicist and a care ethicist might answer this question.

5. Discuss the types of governmental restrictions for and against reproductive and therapeutic cloning. Working in small groups, develop a policy for each type of cloning that takes into account the various moral concerns.

 LEON KASS

The Wisdom of Repugnance: Why We Should Ban the Cloning of Humans

Leon Kass, who has an MD in internal medicine and a PhD in biochemistry, is on the Committee on Social Thought at the University of Chicago. From 2001 to 2005, he was chair of the President's Council on Bioethics. Kass was one of the first scholars to openly express concern about the morality of human cloning. In this reading he gives reasons why people should trust their initial feeling of repugnance toward cloning.

Critical Reading Questions

1. What does Kass mean when he says that cloning is "the perfect embodiment of the ruling opinions of our new age"?

2. Why does Kass claim that cloning is dehumanizing?

3. What, according to Kass, is the most common reaction of people regarding the prospect of cloning humans? What is the source of this reaction?

"The Wisdom of Repugnance: Why We Should Ban the Cloning of Humans," *The New Republic* 216, no. 22 (1997): 17–26.

4. According to Kass, what are some of the moral values violated by cloning? What are some of the inherent dangers?

5. Why, in Kass's view, is sexual reproduction morally preferable to cloning? What effects would cloning have on parent–child and husband–wife relationships?

6. On what grounds does Kass claim that the independence of clones would be subverted by their maker?

7. What is the moral significance of the differences between "making" and "begetting"?

8. Why does Kass reject Robertson's "right to reproduction" as a justification of cloning?

9. Why is Kass concerned about cloning taking us down a "slippery slope"?

TAKING CLONING SERIOUSLY, THEN AND NOW

Cloning first came to public attention roughly thirty years ago, following the successful asexual production, in England, of a clutch of tadpole clones by the technique of nuclear transplantation. . . .

Much has happened in the intervening years. . . . We have become accustomed to new practices in human reproduction: not just in vitro fertilization, but also embryo manipulation, embryo donation and surrogate pregnancy. Animal biotechnology has yielded transgenic animals and a burgeoning science of genetic engineering, easily and soon to be transferable to humans.

Even more important, changes in the broader culture make it now vastly more difficult to express a common and respectful understanding of sexuality, procreation, nascent life, family, and the meaning of motherhood, fatherhood and the links between the generations. . . .

Cloning turns out to be the perfect embodiment of the ruling opinions of our new age. Thanks to the sexual revolution, we are able to deny in practice, and increasingly in thought, the inherent procreative teleology of sexuality itself. But, if sex has no intrinsic connection to generating babies, babies need have no necessary connection to sex. Thanks to feminism and the gay rights movement, we are increasingly encouraged to treat natural heterosexual difference and its preeminence as a matter of "cultural construction."

But if male and female are not normatively complementary and generatively significant, babies need not come from male and female complementarity. Thanks to the prominence and the acceptability of divorce and out-of-wedlock births, stable, monogamous marriage as the ideal home for procreation is no longer the agreed-upon cultural norm. For this new dispensation, the clone is the ideal emblem: the ultimate "single-parent child."

Thanks to our belief that all children should be *wanted* children (the more high-minded principle we use to justify contraception and abortion), sooner or later only those children who fulfill our wants will be fully acceptable. Through cloning, we can work our wants and wills on the very identity of our children, exercising control as never before. Thanks to modern notions of individualism and the rate of cultural change, we see ourselves not as linked to ancestors and defined by traditions, but as projects for our own self-creation, not only as self-made men but also man-made selves; and self-cloning is simply an extension of such rootless and narcissistic self-re-creation. . . .

Human cloning, though it is in some respects continuous with previous reproductive technologies, also represents something radically new, in itself and in its easily foreseeable consequences. The stakes are very high indeed. I exaggerate, but in the direction of the truth, when I insist that we are faced with having to decide nothing less than whether human procreation is going to remain human, whether children are going to be made rather than begotten, whether it is a good thing, humanly speaking, to say yes in principle to the road which leads (at best) to the dehumanized rationality of *Brave New World*. This is not business as usual, to be fretted about for a while but finally to be given our seal of approval. We must rise to the occasion and make our judgments as if the future of our humanity hangs in the balance. For so it does. . . .

THE WISDOM OF REPUGNANCE

"Offensive." "Grotesque." "Revolting." "Repugnant." "Repulsive." These are the words most commonly heard regarding the prospect of human cloning. Such reactions come both from the man or woman in the street and from the intellectuals, from believers and atheists, from humanists and scientists. Even Dolly's creator has said he "would find it offensive" to clone a human being.

People are repelled by many aspects of human cloning. They recoil from the prospect of mass production of human beings, with large armies of look-alikes, compromised in their individuality; the idea of father-son or mother-daughter twins; the bizarre prospects of a woman giving birth to and rearing a genetic copy of herself, her spouse or even her deceased father or mother; the grotesqueness of conceiving a child as an exact replacement for another who has died; the utilitarian creation of embryonic genetic duplicates of oneself, to be frozen away or created when necessary, in case of need for homologous tissues or organs for transplantation; the narcissism of those who would clone themselves and the arrogance of others who think they know who deserves to be cloned or which genotype any child-to-be should be thrilled to receive; the Frankensteinian hubris to create human life and increasingly to control its destiny; man playing God. Almost no one finds any of the suggested reasons for human cloning compelling; almost everyone anticipates its possible misuses and abuses. Moreover, many people feel oppressed by the sense that there is probably nothing we can do to prevent it from happening. This makes the prospect all the more revolting.

Revulsion is not an argument; and some of yesterday's repugnancies are today calmly accepted—though, one must add, not always for the better. In crucial cases, however, repugnance is the emotional expression of deep wisdom, beyond reason's power fully to articulate it. Can anyone really give an argument fully adequate to the horror which is father-daughter incest (even with consent), or having sex with animals, or mutilating a corpse, or eating human flesh, or even just (just!) raping or murdering another human being? Would anybody's failure to give full rational justification for his or her revulsion at these practices make that revulsion ethically suspect? Not at all. On the contrary, we are suspicious of those who think that they can rationalize away our horror, say, by trying to explain the enormity of incest with arguments only about the genetic risks of inbreeding.

The repugnance of human cloning belongs in this category. We are repelled by the prospect of cloning human beings not because of the strangeness or novelty of the undertaking, but because we intuit and feel, immediately and without argument, the violation of things that we rightfully hold dear. Repugnance, here as elsewhere, revolts against the excesses of human willfulness, warning us not to transgress what is unspeakably profound. Indeed, in this age in which everything is held to be permissible so long as it is freely done, in which our given human nature no longer commands respect, in which our bodies are regarded as mere instruments of our autonomous rational wills, repugnance may be the only voice left that speaks up to defend the central core of our humanity. Shallow are the souls that have forgotten how to shudder. . . .

THE PROFUNDITY OF SEX

To see cloning in its proper context, we must begin not, as I did before, with laboratory technique, but with the anthropology—natural and social—of sexual reproduction.

Sexual reproduction—by which I mean the generation of new life from (exactly) two complementary elements, one female, one male, (usually) through coitus—is established (if that is the right term) not by human decision, culture or tradition, but by nature; it is the natural way of all mammalian reproduction. By nature, each child has two complementary biological progenitors. Each child thus stems from and unites exactly two lineages. In natural generation, moreover, the precise genetic constitution of the resulting offspring is determined by a combination of nature and chance, not by human design: each human child shares the common natural human species genotype, each child is genetically (equally) kin to each (both) parent(s), yet each child is genetically unique.

These biological truths about our origins foretell deep truths about our identity and about our human condition altogether. Every one of us is at once equally human, equally enmeshed in a particular familial nexus of origin, and equally individuated in our trajectory from birth to death. . . . Though less momentous than our common humanity, our genetic individuality is not humanly trivial. It shows itself forth in our distinctive appearance through which we are everywhere recognized; it is revealed in our "signature" marks of fingerprints and our self-recognizing immune system; it symbolizes and foreshadows exactly the unique, never-to-be-repeated character of each human life.

Human societies virtually everywhere have structured child-rearing responsibilities and systems of identity and relationship on the bases of these deep natural facts of begetting. The mysterious yet ubiquitous "love of one's own" is everywhere culturally exploited, to make sure that children are not just produced but well cared for and to create for everyone clear ties of meaning, belonging and obligation. But it is wrong to treat such naturally rooted social practices as mere cultural constructs (like left- or right-driving, or like burying or cremating the dead) that we can alter with little human cost. What would kinship be without its clear natural grounding? And what would identity be without kinship? We must resist those who have begun to refer to sexual reproduction as the "traditional method of reproduction," who would have us regard as merely traditional, and by implication arbitrary, what is in truth not only natural but most certainly profound.

Asexual reproduction, which produces "single-parent" offspring, is a radical departure from the natural human way, confounding all normal understandings of father, mother, sibling, grandparent, etc., and all moral relations tied thereto. It becomes even more of a radical departure when the resulting offspring is a clone derived not from an embryo, but from a mature adult to whom the clone would be an identical twin; and when the process occurs not by natural accident (as in natural twinning), but by deliberate human design and manipulation; and when the child's (or children's) genetic constitution is preselected by the parent(s) (or scientists). Accordingly, as we will see, cloning is vulnerable to three kinds of concerns and objections, related to these three points: cloning threatens confusion of identity and individuality, even in small-scale cloning; cloning represents a giant step (though not the first one) toward transforming procreation into manufacture, that is, toward the increasing depersonalization of the process of generation and, increasingly, toward the "production" of human children as artifacts, products of human will and design (what others have called the problems of "commodification" of new life); and cloning—like other forms of eugenic engineering of the next generation—represents a form of despotism of the cloners over the cloned, and thus (even in benevolent cases) represents a blatant violation of the inner meaning of parent-child relations, of what it means to have a child, of what it means to say "yes" to our own demise and "replacement."

Human procreation, in sum, is not simply an activity of our rational wills. It is a more complete activity precisely because it engages us bodily, erotically and spiritually, as well as rationally. There is wisdom in the mystery of nature that has joined the pleasure of sex, the inarticulate longing for union, the communication of the loving embrace and the deep-seated and only partly articulate desire for children in the very activity by which we continue the chain of human existence and participate in the renewal of human possibility. Whether or not we know it, the severing of procreation from sex, love and intimacy is inherently dehumanizing, no matter how good the product.

We are now ready for the more specific objections to cloning.

THE PERVERSITIES OF CLONING

First, an important if formal objection: any attempt to clone a human being would constitute an unethical experiment upon the resulting child-to-be. As the animal experiments (frog and sheep) indicate, there are grave risks of mishaps and deformities. Moreover, because of what cloning means, one cannot presume a future cloned child's consent to be a clone, even a healthy one. Thus, ethically speaking, we cannot even get to know whether or not human cloning is feasible.

I understand, of course, the philosophical difficulty of trying to compare a life with defects against nonexistence. Several bioethicists, proud of their philosophical cleverness, use this conundrum to embarrass claims that one can injure a child in its conception, precisely because it is only thanks to that complained-of conception that the child is alive to complain. But common sense tells us that we have no reason to fear such philosophisms. For we surely know that people can harm and even maim children in the very act of conceiving them, say, by paternal transmission of the AIDS virus, maternal transmission of heroin dependence or, arguably, even by bringing them into being as bastards or with no capacity or willingness to look after them properly. And we believe that to do this intentionally, or even negligently, is inexcusable and clearly unethical.

The objection about the impossibility of presuming consent may even go beyond the obvious and sufficient point that a clonant, were he subsequently to be asked, could rightly resent having been made a clone. At issue are not just benefits and harms, but doubts about the very independence needed to give proper (even retroactive) consent, that is, not just the capacity to choose but the disposition and ability to choose freely and well. It is not at all clear to what extent a clone will truly be a moral agent. For, as we shall see, in the very fact of cloning, and of rearing him as a clone, his makers subvert the cloned child's independence, beginning with that aspect that comes from knowing that one was an unbidden surprise, a gift, to the world, rather than the designed result of someone's artful project.

Cloning creates serious issues of identity and individuality. The cloned person may experience concerns about his distinctive identity not only because he will be in genotype and appearance identical to another human being, but, in this case, because he may also be twin to the person who is his "father" or "mother"—if one can still call them that. What would be the psychic burdens of being the "child" or "parent" of your twin? The cloned individual, moreover, will be saddled with a genotype that has already lived. He will not be fully a surprise to the world. People are likely always to compare his performances in life with that of his alter ego. True, his nurture and his circumstances in life will be different; genotype is not exactly destiny. Still, one must also expect parental and other efforts to shape the new life after the original—or at least to view the child with the original version always firmly in mind. Why else did they clone from the star basketball player, mathematician and beauty queen—or even dear old dad—in the first place?

Since the birth of Dolly, there has been a fair amount of doublespeak on this matter of genetic identity. Experts have rushed in to reassure the public that the clone would in no way be the same person, or have any confusions about his or her identity. . . .

Curiously, this conclusion is supported, inadvertently, by the one ethical sticking point insisted on by friends of cloning: no cloning without the donor's consent. Though an orthodox liberal objection, it is in fact quite puzzling when it comes from people who also insist that genotype is not identity or individuality, and who deny that a child could reasonably complain about being made a genetic copy. If the clone of Mel Gibson would not be Mel Gibson, why should Mel Gibson have grounds to object that someone had been made his clone? We already allow researchers to use blood and tissue samples for research purposes of no benefit to their sources: my falling hair, my expectorations, my urine and even my biopsied tissues are "not me" and not mine. Courts have held that the profit gained from uses to which scientists put my discarded tissues do not legally belong to me. Why, then, no cloning without consent—including, I assume, no cloning from the body of someone who just died? What harm is done the donor, if genotype is "not me"? Truth to tell, the only powerful justification for objecting is that genotype really does have something to do with identity, and everybody knows it. . . . The insistence on donor consent unwittingly reveals the problem of identity in all cloning.

Genetic distinctiveness not only symbolizes the uniqueness of each human life and the independence of its parents that each human child rightfully attains. It can also be an important support for living a worthy and dignified life. Such arguments apply with great force to any large-scale replication of human individuals. But they are sufficient, in my view, to rebut even the first attempts to clone a human being. . . .

Human cloning would also represent a giant step toward turning begetting into making, procreation into manufacture (literally, something "handmade"), a process already begun with in vitro fertilization and genetic testing of embryos. With cloning, not only is the process in hand, but the total genetic blueprint of the cloned individual is selected and determined by the human artisans. To be sure, subsequent development will take place according to natural processes; and the resulting children will still be recognizably human. But we here would be taking a major step into making man himself simply another one of the manmade things. Human nature becomes merely the last part of nature to succumb to the technological project, which turns all of nature into raw material at human disposal, to be homogenized by our rationalized technique according to the subjective prejudices of the day.

How does begetting differ from making? In natural procreation, human beings come together, complementarily male and female, to give existence to another being who is formed, exactly as we were, *by what we are:* living, hence perishable, hence aspiringly erotic, human beings. In clonal reproduction, by contrast, and in the more advanced forms of manufacture to which it leads, we give existence to a being not by what we are but by what we intend and design. As with any product of our making, no matter how excellent, the artificer stands above it, not as an equal but as a superior, transcending it by his will and creative prowess. Scientists who clone animals make it perfectly clear that they are engaged in instrumental making; the animals are, from the start, designed as means to serve rational human purposes. In human cloning, scientists and prospective "parents" would be adopting the same technocratic mentality to human children: human children would be their artifacts.

Such an arrangement is profoundly dehumanizing, no matter how good the product. Mass-scale cloning of the same individual makes the point vividly; but the violation of human equality, freedom and dignity are present even in a single planned clone. And procreation dehumanized into manufacture is further degraded by commodification, a virtually inescapable result of allowing baby-making to proceed under the banner of commerce. . . .

Finally, and perhaps most important, the practice of human cloning by nuclear transfer—like other anticipated forms of genetic engineering of the next generation—would enshrine and aggravate a profound and mischievous misunderstanding of the meaning of having children and of the parent-child relationship. When a couple now chooses to procreate, the partners are saying yes to the emergence of new life in its novelty, saying yes not only to having a child but also, tacitly, to having whatever child this child turns out to be. In accepting our finitude and opening ourselves to our replacement, we are tacitly confessing the limits of our control. In this ubiquitous way of nature, embracing the future by procreating means precisely that we are relinquishing our grip, in the very activity of taking up our own share in what we hope will be the immortality of human life and the human species. This means that our children are not *our* children: they are not our property, not our possessions. Neither are they supposed to live our lives for us, or anyone else's life but their own. To be sure, we seek to guide them on their way, imparting to them not just life but nurturing, love, and a way of life; to be sure, they bear our hopes that they will live fine and flourishing lives, enabling us in small measure to transcend our own limitations. Still, their genetic distinctiveness and independence are the natural foreshadowing of the deep truth that they have their own and never-before-enacted life to live. They are sprung from a past, but they take an uncharted course into the future.

Much harm is already done by parents who try to live vicariously through their children. Children are sometimes compelled to fulfill the broken dreams of unhappy parents: John Doe Jr. or the III is under the burden of having to live up to his forebear's name. Still, if most parents have hopes for their children, cloning parents will have expectations. In cloning, such overbearing parents take at the start a decisive step which contradicts the entire meaning of the open and forward-looking nature of parent-child relations. The child is given a genotype that has already lived, with full expectation that this blueprint of a past life ought to be controlling of the life that is to come. Cloning is inherently despotic, for it seeks to make one's children (or someone else's children) after one's own image (or an image of one's choosing) and their future according to one's will. In some cases, the despotism may be mild and benevolent. In other cases, it will be mischievous and downright tyrannical. But despotism—the control of another through one's will—it inevitably will be.

MEETING SOME OBJECTIONS

The defenders of cloning, of course, are not wittingly friends of despotism. Indeed, they regard themselves mainly as friends of freedom: the freedom of individuals to reproduce, the freedom of scientists and inventors to discover and devise and to foster "progress" in genetic knowledge and technique. They want large-scale cloning only for animals, but they wish to preserve cloning as a human option for exercising our "right to reproduce." . . .

We have here a perfect example of the logic of the slippery slope, and the slippery way in which it already works in this area. Only a few years ago, slippery slope arguments were used to oppose artificial insemination and in vitro fertilization using unrelated sperm donors. Principles used to justify these practices, it was said, will be used to justify more artificial and more eugenic practices, including cloning. . . .

The principle of reproductive freedom as currently enunciated by the proponents of cloning logically embraces the ethical acceptability of sliding down the entire rest of the slope—to producing children ectogenetically from sperm to term (should it become feasible) and to producing children whose entire genetic makeup will be the product of parental eugenic planning and choice. If reproductive freedom means the right to have a child of one's own choosing, by whatever means, it knows and accepts no limits.

But, far from being legitimated by a "right to reproduce," the emergence of techniques of assisted reproduction and genetic engineering should compel us to reconsider the meaning and limits of such a putative right. In truth, a "right to reproduce" has always been a peculiar and problematic notion. Rights generally belong to individuals, but this is a right which (before cloning) no one can exercise alone. Does the right then inhere only in couples? Only in married couples? Is it a (woman's) right to carry or deliver or a right (of one or more parents) to nurture and rear? Is it a right to have your own biological child? Is it a right only to attempt reproduction, or a right also to succeed? Is it a right to acquire the baby of one's choice?

The assertion of a negative "right to reproduce" certainly makes sense when it claims protection against state interference with procreative liberty, say, through a program of compulsory sterilization.

But surely it cannot be the basis of a tort claim against nature, to be made good by technology, should free efforts at natural procreation fail. Some insist that the right to reproduce embraces also the right against state interference with the free use of all technological means to obtain a child. . . . When the exercise of a previously innocuous freedom now involves or impinges on troublesome practices that the original freedom never was intended to reach, the general presumption of liberty needs to be reconsidered. . . .

Though I recognize certain continuities between cloning and, say, in vitro fertilization, I believe that cloning differs in essential and important ways. . . . Can the defenders of cloning show us today how, on their principles, we will be able to see producing babies ("perfect babies") entirely in the laboratory or exercising full control over their genotypes (including so-called enhancement) as ethically different, in any essential way, from present forms of assisted reproduction? Or are they willing to admit, despite their attachment to the principle of continuity, that the complete obliteration of "mother" or "father," the complete depersonalization of procreation, the complete manufacture of human beings and the complete genetic control of one generation over the next would be ethically problematic and essentially different from current forms of assisted reproduction? If so, where and how will they draw the line, and why? I draw it at cloning, for all the reasons given.

BAN THE CLONING OF HUMANS

What, then, should we do? We should declare that human cloning is unethical in itself and dangerous in its likely consequences. In so doing, we shall have the backing of the overwhelming majority of our fellow Americans, and of the human race, and (I believe) of most practicing scientists. Next, we should do all that we can to prevent the cloning of human beings. We should do this by means of an international legal ban if possible, and by a unilateral national ban, at a minimum. . . .

Discussion Questions

1. Feeling repugnance does not, in itself, signal that the object of our repugnance is immoral; repugnance can arise from cultural conditioning as well. For example, people once felt repugnance at the thought of interracial marriage. Discuss whether Kass provides a convincing argument for his claim that our repugnance toward human cloning is based on "deep wisdom" rather than cultural constructs.

2. One of Kass's objections to cloning is that there are too many risks of mishaps and deformities. Would cloning be morally acceptable if it were perfected to the point where the chances of mishaps and deformities were significantly less than relying on sexual reproduction? How would Kass answer this question?

3. Discuss Kass's concerns regarding the autonomy and identity of a clone.

4. Kass argues that whereas using preimplantation to create a healthy child may be morally acceptable, the use of cloning to produce a healthy child never is. Is this distinction justified? Support your answer.

5. Discuss how Johnson and Williams would most likely respond to Kass's arguments against reproductive human cloning. Which person makes the better arguments? Support your answer.

JAMES R. LANGEVIN

Statement in Support of H.R. 810, the Stem Cell Research Enhancement Act

James R. Langevin is a member of the U.S. House of Representatives from Rhode Island. In his statement Langevin argues that embryonic stem cell research is consistent with the pro-life position because of the number of people's lives it would benefit.

Critical Reading Questions

1. How have Langevin's life experiences shaped his views on stem cell research?
2. What does Langevin mean by "pro-life"?
3. What are some of the promises held out by stem cell research?
4. What does Langevin mean when he refers to stem cell research as one of the great moments in medical history?

Mr. Speaker, I rise in strong support of H.R. 810. I want to acknowledge the bipartisan effort that has gone into this legislation and the incredible grassroots movement that has built support for this groundbreaking medical research. It has been inspirational to see so many people putting aside politics and partisanship to address this issue, which affects the lives of millions of Americans.

I am one of those millions. At 16, I was an Explorer Scout in my hometown police station. One afternoon, in the police locker room, a gun accidentally discharged. The bullet severed my spinal cord, and I have been paralyzed ever since.

This experience shapes my perspective in many ways. Above all, it has given me tremendous appreciation and respect for life. My life as a quadriplegic is filled with challenges and obstacles, yet I am grateful for every minute. This gratitude has become a passion—and it has motivated me to help create a culture that values and protects life from its beginning to its end.

To me, being pro-life also means fighting for policies that will eliminate pain and suffering and help people enjoy longer, healthier lives. And to me, support for embryonic stem cell research is entirely consistent with that position. What could be more life-affirming than using what otherwise would be discarded to save, extend and improve countless lives?

This research offers the opportunity to discover cures and treatments for diseases like Parkinson's, Alzheimer's, ALS, diabetes, spinal cord injury, and many others. But it will take not only the talent of our scientists, but also the support of our government to realize its potential. We have a responsibility to ensure that this research proceeds, and that it does so with ethical safeguards and strict guidelines. By permitting research only on excess embryos created in the in-vitro fertilization process, and by establishing a clear, voluntary consent process for donors, H.R. 810 meets this responsibility.

Stem cell research gives us hope, and a reason to believe. I believe one day, a child with diabetes will no longer face a lifetime of painful shots and tests. I believe one day, families will no longer watch in agony as a loved one with Parkinson's or

"Statement in Support of H.R. 810, the Stem Cell Research Enhancement Act," U.S. House of Representatives, May 24, 2005.

Alzheimer's gradually declines. I believe one day, I will walk again.

There are a few moments in medical history when we can clearly identify a giant step forward in improving countless lives. We saw it with the discovery of antibiotics, and with the advent of organ transplants.

Mr. Speaker, I believe that adult and embryonic stem cell research is another of these great moments. Today we have a historic opportunity to make a difference for millions of Americans, and I urge my colleagues to vote in favor of H.R. 810.

Discussion Questions

1. Discuss Langevin's claim that his position is consistent with a pro-life position. Is his argument that the embryos from IVF would have been destroyed anyway morally relevant from a pro-life point of view? Support your answer.
2. Which moral theory does Langevin primarily use to justify his support of stem cell research? Discuss how a utilitarian and a deontologist would each most likely respond to his argument.
3. Some opponents of embryonic stem cell research are concerned that it will lead to women seeking IVF in order to donate the embryos to research. Discuss how Langevin and advocates of embryonic stem cell research might respond to this concern.

GEORGE W. BUSH

Stem Cell Research Policy

In the following press release, former President George W. Bush explains his reasons for vetoing H.R. 810, the Stem Cell Research Enhancement Act of 2005. He argues that human embryos are unique human lives that have inherent dignity and, as such, should not be destroyed.

Critical Reading Questions

1. What is Bush's position on the use and potential of science, including stem cell research, to cure diseases?
2. What is Bush's position on the moral status of embryos and the use of leftover embryos from fertility treatments?

"President Discusses Stem Cell Research Policy," Office of the Press Secretary, The White House, July 19, 2006.

3. On what grounds does Bush argue that his approach to stem cell research is a "balanced approach"?
4. Why does Bush believe that the Stem Cell Research Enhancement Act of 2005 crossed the "moral line"?

Congress has just passed and sent to my desk two bills concerning the use of stem cells in biomedical research. These bills illustrate both the promise and perils we face in the age of biotechnology. In this new era, our challenge is to harness the power of science to ease human suffering without sanctioning the practices that violate the dignity of human life. . . .

Like all Americans, I believe our nation must vigorously pursue the tremendous possibility that science offers to cure disease and improve the lives of millions. We have opportunities to discover cures and treatments that were unthinkable generations ago. Some scientists believe that one source of these cures might be embryonic stem cell research. Embryonic stem cells have the ability to grow into specialized adult tissues, and this may give them the potential to replace damaged or defective cells or body parts and treat a variety of diseases.

Yet we must also remember that embryonic stem cells come from human embryos that are destroyed for their cells. Each of these human embryos is a unique human life with inherent dignity and matchless value. We see that value in the children who are with us today. Each of these children began his or her life as a frozen embryo that was created for in vitro fertilization, but remained unused after the fertility treatments were complete. Each of these children was adopted while still an embryo, and has been blessed with the chance to grow up in a loving family.

These boys and girls are not spare parts. They remind us of what is lost when embryos are destroyed in the name of research. They remind us that we all begin our lives as a small collection of cells. And they remind us that in our zeal for new treatments and cures, America must never abandon our fundamental morals.

Some people argue that finding new cures for disease requires the destruction of human embryos like the ones that these families adopted. I disagree. I believe that with the right techniques and the right policies, we can achieve scientific progress while living up to our ethical responsibilities. That's what I sought in 2001, when I set forth my administration's policy allowing federal funding for research on embryonic stem cell lines where the life and death decision had already been made. . . .

Since I announced my policy in 2001, advances in scientific research have also shown the great potential of stem cells that are derived without harming human embryos. My administration has expanded the funding of research into stem cells that can be drawn from children, adults, and the blood in umbilical cords, with no harm to the donor. And these stem cells are already being used in medical treatments.

With us today are patients who have benefited from treatments with adult and umbilical-cord-blood stem cells. And I want to thank you all for coming. They are living proof that effective medical science can also be ethical. Researchers are now also investigating new techniques that could allow doctors and scientists to produce stem cells just as versatile as those derived from human embryos. . . .

We must pursue this research. And so I direct the Secretary of Health and Human Services, Secretary Leavitt, and the Director of the National Institutes of Health to use all the tools at their disposal to aid the search for stem cell techniques that advance promising medical science in an ethical and morally responsible way.

Unfortunately, Congress has sent me a bill that fails to meet this ethical test. This legislation would overturn the balanced policy on embryonic stem cell research that my administration has followed for the past five years. This bill would also undermine the principle that Congress, itself, has followed for more than a decade, when it has prohibited federal funding for research that destroys human embryos.

If this bill would have become law, American taxpayers would, for the first time in our history, be compelled to fund the deliberate destruction of human embryos. And I'm not going to allow it.

I made it clear to the Congress that I will not allow our nation to cross this moral line. I felt like crossing this line would be a mistake, and once crossed, we would find it almost impossible to turn back. Crossing the line would needlessly encourage a conflict between science and ethics that can only do damage to both, and to our nation as a whole. If we're to find the right ways to advance ethical medical research, we must also be willing, when necessary, to reject the wrong ways. So today, I'm keeping the promise I made to the American people by returning this bill to Congress with my veto.

As science brings us ever closer to unlocking the secrets of human biology, it also offers temptations to manipulate human life and violate human dignity. Our conscience and history as a nation demand that we resist this temptation. America was founded on the principle that we are all created equal, and endowed by our Creator with the right to life. We can advance the cause of science while upholding this founding promise. We can harness the promise of technology without becoming slaves to technology. And we can ensure that science serves the cause of humanity instead of the other way around. . . .

Discussion Questions

1. Discuss how Langevin would most likely respond to Bush's argument that embryos left over from fertility treatment should be treated with moral respect since they can be adopted by families.
2. Is Bush being consistent in allowing stem cell lines developed before 2001 to be used for research while forbidding federal funding for the use of stem cells acquired after 2001? Support your answer.
3. Would it be morally acceptable to use stem cells if they could be extracted from embryos without killing them? Support your answer. Discuss how Bush and opponents of embryonic stem cell research might answer this question.
4. Even if embryos are persons with rights, does the great potential benefit to society justify the killing of embryos for therapeutic purposes? After all, we have sacrificed the lives of thousands of American military men and women in wars (some of whom were conscripted) in order to benefit society and save lives. Discuss how Bush might respond to this argument.

CASE STUDIES

1. EVE: THE WORLD'S FIRST CLONED HUMAN?

On December 26, 2002, Clonaid, a Bahamas-based company, announced the birth of Eve—the world's first cloned human. According to Clonaid, they fused over two hundred human eggs with adult cells in order to get ten that appeared normal. The other four cloned children, they claim, were born in 2003.

After initially agreeing to DNA testing on Eve, Clonaid CEO Brigitte Boisselier told the press that Clonaid would not reveal the identity of the mother and child, or cooperate in performing genetic tests to confirm that the mother and child were clones. Clonaid said they were concerned that lawsuits filed in the United States and the Netherlands were making testing impossible because the tests would be used to try and identify the parent and child and take them into custody.

Some people fear that the real reason for Clonaid's refusal is that Eve may have developed serious medical problems. Others dismiss Clonaid's claim that they cloned a human child as a hoax, calling Clonaid a "rogue organization" founded by members of a sect who believe that humans were created by extraterrestrials.[17] Despite claims by Clonaid, as well as geneticists in China who claim to have successfully grown eighty cloned human embryos, there is no verifiable evidence to date of any human clones' having been born.

Discussion Questions

1. If Clonaid was indeed successful in cloning the first human babies, were they acting immorally? Discuss how Johnson and Williams, and Kass might each respond to these questions.

2. An American couple offered Clonaid $500,000 to clone their dead infant. The couple have other children and are not infertile. According to a spokesperson at Clonaid, "They just want to give this particular genome another chance."[18] Is cloning a liberty right? Would we be interfering with the couple's reproductive rights if we denied them the opportunity of cloning their lost child? Discuss your answer in light of some of the arguments for and against cloning put forth in this chapter.

3. Discuss the moral issues involved in the destruction of large numbers of embryos in order to produce a clone. Relate your answers to the debates about personhood.

4. Given the additional health risks associated with cloning, should the courts try to force Clonaid to reveal the identity of Eve (if, in fact, she exists) and her mother? What if the child is found to have serious medical problems—is this sufficient reason for the state to take custody of her? Do parents have a duty to forgo having children who are genetically related to them (through cloning or by normal means) if doing so puts the future children at risk? Support your answers. Discuss also how Johnson and Williams might answer these questions.

2. GENETIC ENGINEERING AND THE FOUNTAIN OF YOUTH

Genetic engineering is increasingly being used for purposes that go beyond therapy. Scientists have genetically engineered nematodes and mice that live well beyond their natural life span and are hoping to discover the genetic fountain of youth for humans as well. If successful, the field of age-extending medicine promises to be very lucrative.

One strategy being explored is to clone our own cells, tissues, and organs and to make them younger by correcting any genetic errors as well as by stopping the shrinkage of the telomeres. As our cells age, the telomeres (ends of the chromosomes) get shorter until they eventually die. The cloned, genetically modified cells or tissues could be introduced into our bodies to replace aging and damaged tissues.

Another technique that shows promise is to use gene therapy to boost the natural antioxidants that fight free radicals, which cause aging. These techniques could potentially boost the human life span by decades. If they work, scientists are considering germ line therapy so the life-boosting changes in our genomes will be inherited by future generations.

Discussion Questions

1. Imagine that you have been offered a chance to be genetically engineered so that your life would be extended by fifty years. Would you accept the offer? Support your answers.
2. One of the criticisms of life-extending genetic engineering is that it is unnatural and interferes with nature. Is the fact that it is unnatural for humans to live beyond 120 years morally relevant? Support your answer.
3. Discuss the moral implications of age-extending genetic engineering on issues of justice and fairness, including global justice.

---

3. DOLLY AND HER SISTERS: GENETICALLY ENGINEERING ANIMALS WITH HUMAN GENES

In December 1997 the same scientists who brought Dolly into the limelight achieved another breakthrough with the birth of five almost-identical transgenic Dorset lambs—that is, animals with genetic material from another species, in this case humans. The lambs carry a gene to produce factor IX, a blood-clotting substance used in treating a rare form of hemophilia known as hemophilia B or Christmas disease.

The Edinburgh-based firm PPL Therapeutics announced that it wants to eventually establish herds of sheep carrying human genes to produce proteins and blood products for treating diseases such as hemophilia and osteoporosis. In 1998 George and Charlie, two Holsteins, were born. They were cloned from genetically engineered fetal cells that included human genes so their milk would contain valuable human proteins such as factor IX.[19] Two years later five piglets were cloned from an adult female by PPL Therapeutics.[20] PPL plans to use them to develop and clone genetically modified pigs whose organs can be used for transplantation into humans. It is hoped that organs from transgenic pigs will go a long way toward solving the current organ shortage.

Trans Ova Genetics in Iowa is currently genetically engineering cows with human genes, then cloning them and inoculating them against biological agents such as anthrax, smallpox, and botulism in the hope that the transgenic cows will eventually produce human antibodies that can be used as an antidote in case of biological warfare.[21] Mice, however, are by far the most commonly used transgenic animals in medical research. Transgenic mice are used to test new medicines and vaccines, and to study and develop treatments for human diseases such as arthritis.

Discussion Questions

1. Research with transgenic animals involves treating them as a means only. Also, transgenic animals, because of the introduction of foreign genetic material, tend to have more health problems. Discuss the moral issues involved in genetically modifying and cloning other animals to benefit humans.
2. What does it mean to be human? How many human genes must beings have before they merit the respect accorded to persons? Are the genetically engineered animals mentioned in this case study part human because they carry human genes? If so, how does that affect the moral respect we should show them?
3. Discuss how a utilitarian might think about the practice of genetically engineering and cloning lambs to produce factor IX to benefit humans with hemophilia B and genetically engineering pigs so their organs can be used by humans.

---

4. USING CLONES AS ORGAN DONORS

One of the proposed uses of genetic engineering is the creation of human organs for transplantation. One method of doing this would be to clone a person's own cells and then use the embryonic stem cells to grow the needed tissue or organ.

Jeremy has been waiting for a kidney transplant for two years and despairs of ever getting one.[22] He knows that his chances of getting the kidney he so badly needs from a compatible human donor are probably only about 5 percent.

His physician tells him of an experiment using embryonic stem cells to grow organs. The process entails creating a clone of Jeremy and then destroying the embryo so that the stem cells can be harvested. The process, the physician tells him, can be carried out in vitro. However, the success rate in getting the stem cells to differentiate into a functional kidney is very low, and it may take many attempts before the procedure is successful, if at all. Jeremy is faced with a moral dilemma. He is opposed to abortion but also realizes that this may be his only chance for survival.

Discussion Questions

1. Role-play a situation in which Jeremy comes to you for assistance in resolving his moral dilemma. Have one student play the role of Jeremy and the other the role of an ethics student. When you are finished, share your insights with the class.
2. The cloning of embryos for transplantation tissue raises the issue of abortion. Is the destruction of embryos to obtain tissue for transplantation morally different from an abortion when the woman doesn't want the pregnancy? What about harvesting organs from terminally ill newborns? Support your answers.
3. Discuss whether the use of cloned human embryos for organ transplants and medical research is morally preferable to the current practice of using sentient nonhuman animals for organ transplants and medical experimentation.
4. Many people consider a brain a prerequisite for personhood. Biologists have succeeded in creating mouse embryos that fail to develop a head. According to biologist Jonathan Slack, we could do the same with human embryos.[23] These headless, and hence nonsentient, humans, he says, could serve as "organ sacs"

for organ transplants as well as subjects for medical research. Discuss the moral issues involved in genetically engineering and cloning headless humans for organ transplants and medical research.

5. PATENTING GENETICALLY ENGINEERED LIFE-FORMS

In 1873 Louis Pasteur received a U.S. patent for the manufacture of a yeast that was free of disease. The first patent in the United States for a genetically engineered life-form was granted in 1980 when the U.S. Supreme Court, in *Diamond v. Chakrabarty*, held that a man-made microorganism was a new and useful "manufacture," and hence patentable. Since then, more than 3 million genome-related patents have been filed with the U.S. Patent and Trademark Office (USPTO), some of which cover methods of genetically engineering humans. The United States does not permit patents on humans because this would violate Amendment 13 of the U.S. Constitution, which forbids slavery. The year 2007 marked the first application for a patent for an artificial, man-made life-form—a microbe.

Despite the legal status of biopatents, there is still considerable controversy about the morality of the practice. Canada does not permit patents for "higher life-forms," such as the oncomouse. China, India, and Thailand prohibit the patenting of any animal. The European Union, only permits such patents "provided the potential benefits of the 'invention' outweigh the ethical and moral considerations, in particular the suffering of animals."[24]

People who favor biopatents argue that researchers should be rewarded for their discoveries. People would not put the money and years into genetic research unless they had some mechanism of protecting their inventions and investment through patents. Those who are opposed question the assumption that science will advance faster if researchers can have exclusive rights to their inventions. They also point out that the monopoly on certain products and the high royalty costs owed to patent holders may discourage product development since the high costs would be passed on to the consumer, as is currently happening in the pharmaceutical industry. Finally, there is the question of whether it is moral to patent a part of nature or to own life-forms.

Discussion Questions

1. Humans have long set themselves apart from other animals as morally superior, a special creation. However, as philosopher Mary Midgley once put it, "We are not just *like* other animals; we *are* animals." Analyze the following argument: Humans are not a special creation but simply another species of mammal. It is morally acceptable to patent genetically engineered mammals such as mice. Therefore, it is also morally acceptable to genetically engineer and patent human life-forms.
2. Discuss the arguments for and against patenting life-forms. Working in a group, put together a policy for issuing patents for animals. Which moral theories were most useful in providing guidelines for the policy?
3. One of the current issues under debate is the morality of patenting human/nonhuman animal chimeras. (A chimera, named after the mythological fire-breathing creature that had a lion's head, a goat's body, and a serpent's tail, is an artificially

produced being with genes from two or more species.) If it is morally acceptable to patent other mammals, such as mice, should human/nonhuman chimeras also be patentable? Support your answer.

4. Religious leaders denounced the *Diamond v. Chakrabarty* Supreme Court decision, calling for a moratorium on the patenting of life-forms. They argue that genetic engineers should not play God or create new organisms. To grant patents on animal or plant genomes is to usurp the "ownership rights of God." Evaluate their argument. Discuss also how John Locke might respond to this argument.

6. *JURASSIC PARK* REVISITED

In his book *Jurassic Park,* Michael Crichton envisions a world in which extinct dinosaur species are resurrected by cloning DNA from fossils. His fantasy may soon become a reality. One of the proposed uses for cloning is to save endangered species by creating clones of the few remained members of the species or by saving samples of their DNA before they become extinct. Researchers are also working on sequencing the genome of the woolly mammoth, the Tasmanian tiger, and the quagga (a relative of the zebra).

In 2005 genomist Stephen Schuster from Penn State University purchased a mammoth hair on Ebay from a Russian dealer. As of January 2009, he and his colleagues have finished sequencing 80 percent of the genome of the woolly mammoth. Scientists hope to produce a mammoth clone, using an elephant as the surrogate mother, in the not too distant future.

While the prospect of bringing back the woolly mammoth is exciting for some, others are concerned that reintroducing extinct species will upset the balance of nature. Some people also fear that cloning programs for preserving endangered species may divert resources from efforts to save the natural habitats of these species.

Scientists are also working on sequencing the genome of our prehistoric relative, Neanderthal man (*homo neanderthalensis*). Reviving Neanderthal man through cloning could provide valuable information about human evolution and about other earlier species of humanoids. It could also open a Pandora's box of moral quandaries, including what it means to be human and the moral standing of our human relatives.

Discussion Questions

1. Is it morally acceptable, and perhaps even desirable, to clone species that have already passed into extinction? Discuss the moral issues raised by cloning extinct animals such as mammoths and dinosaurs. Does the knowledge we might acquire from cloning already-extinct species justify it?

2. Is it morally acceptable to use cloning to preserve endangered species? Is there a morally relevant difference between preserving species that are on their way to extinction and resurrecting extinct species?

3. It is now believed that Neanderthal man, rather than being a subspecies of *homo sapiens* (modern humans) was a distinct species. Should bans against human cloning apply to Neanderthal man? How about prehistoric members of our own

species, such as Cro-Magnon man? Discuss the moral issues involved in cloning in these cases.

7. MY FATHER, MY SON[25]

Dianne's father was on his deathbed. Her father was an only child, and she had no children, so Dianne decided she wanted to have her "father" as a baby. She wrote to a British geneticist, asking for information on cloning her father. "My father," she explained, "is a remarkable man and I intend to see that he goes on in the world. . . . I am writing in the hope that you can help me find information on where human cloning may be performed now. There must be organizations that are actively pursuing cloning, and I want to contact them and see if there is a possibility of cloning my father. I have little time left to pursue this venture, and I would greatly appreciate your assistance." Dianne offered to be the host mother for the clone of her father.

Derek, who read Dianne's correspondence on the Internet, was horrified at her request. "The desire to clone a passed-on loved one," he says, "seems to me to be grotesque. It brings to mind the Stephen King book *Pet Sematary*. The clone would be a disappointment to the donor's relatives, in that the original personality could never be completely duplicated. Additionally, the clone would not be able to live its own life; it would be forced to live in a predefined, unattainable role."

Discussion Questions

1. Discuss how you might respond to Dianne if she came to you with her request.
2. Discuss Derek's reaction to Dianne's request. How might Kass explain Derek's repugnance toward Dianne's request? Discuss whether the repugance in this case is morally relevant.
3. Does the fact that the relative's donors might be disappointed, as Derek argues, or the concern that the clone may be deprived of an open future, override Dianne's reproductive autonomy? Support your answer.
4. Discuss whether the clone of Dianne's father would be harmed by being a clone. Would it make a difference morally if Dianne's father had concurred with her request? Support your answer.

8. DO WE OWN OUR BODY TISSUE?

Gus Stokes has been HIV positive for more than twenty years, yet he has developed no symptoms of AIDS. His physician, Dr. Sharma, thinks that Stokes might have a genetic antibody to AIDS. If this gene could be identified, it is possible that it could be reproduced and used in somatic gene therapy, thus possibly saving the lives of millions of people who are HIV positive. When Dr. Sharma asks Stokes for permission to use a sample of his blood for research, Stokes refuses. "This body is my own," he says, "and I don't want anyone messing with my genes and giving them to other people."

Dr. Sharma already has several samples of Stokes's blood left over from routine medical tests. What should Dr. Sharma do?

Discussion Questions

1. Should Dr. Sharma use the blood sample and not tell Stokes? Indeed, does she have a moral obligation to do so? Or does Stokes have a moral right to refuse to let scientists use his tissue for a possible cure for AIDS? Support your answers.
2. Discuss how a utilitarian and a rights ethicist might each respond to this scenario.
3. Dr. Sharma decides to go ahead and use the blood sample. After two years of research, she comes up with a cure for AIDS based on a synthesized version of the antibody in Stokes's blood. Who, if anyone, should own the patent to the synthetic antibody? Does she have a moral obligation to inform Stokes that the cure was based on his blood sample? What if she suspects that Stokes would charge an exorbitant amount for the treatment if he owned the patent, whereas she is willing to market it at cost? Support your answers.

CHAPTER 4

Euthanasia

In 1975 twenty-one-year-old Karen Ann Quinlan went into a coma after having a few drinks at a party. Apparently, she had eaten very little in the days before the party and had also taken some drugs—perhaps tranquilizers. She was rushed to the hospital, where doctors connected her to a respirator. Unfortunately, by this time the lack of oxygen had caused permanent brain damage. Her parents, convinced that Karen would not have wanted to be kept alive by artificial means, asked the hospital to disconnect her from the respirator machine. The hospital refused.

The resulting controversy and court battles brought the issue of euthanasia to the public's attention. In 1976 the New Jersey Supreme Court ruled that Karen Quinlan's right to privacy had been violated by the hospital. As a result, she was removed from the machine and moved to a nursing home to die in peace. More recently, the Terri Schiavo case has renewed interest in the development of legal guidelines for euthanasia.

WHAT IS EUTHANASIA?

The term **euthanasia** comes from the Greek *eu* and *thanatos* meaning "good death." Euthanasia has come to mean painlessly bringing about the death of a person who is suffering from a terminal or incurable disease or condition.

Euthanasia can be classified as active or passive, voluntary or involuntary. Combining these two dimensions, a particular act of euthanasia can fall into one of four categories: active voluntary, passive voluntary, active involuntary, and passive involuntary (see box, next page).

Although physicians in the United States are permitted to withhold treatment for a dying patient, the law prohibits active euthanasia. This position is consistent with both that of the American Medical Association (AMA) and the British Medical Society.

> For humane reasons, with informed consent, a physician may do what is
> medically necessary to alleviate severe pain, or cease or omit treatment to permit
> a terminally ill patient to die when death is imminent. . . . Even if death is not
> imminent but a patient is beyond doubt permanently unconscious . . . it is not
> unethical to discontinue all means of life-prolonging medical treatment . . .

<table>
<tr><td colspan="3" align="center">**Active**</td></tr>
</table>

Active involuntary: Giving an incompetent person, such as an infant or person in a coma, a lethal injection.

Active voluntary: Physician-assisted suicide; administering a lethal injection at a patient's request.

Involuntary ⟵   ⟶ **Voluntary**

Passive involuntary: Withholding life support or medical treatment from an incompetent person as in the Baby Doe and Karen Quinlan cases.

Passive voluntary: Withholding life support or medical treatment at the patient's direct request or indirectly through a living will.

Passive

[which] includes medication and artificially or technologically supplied respiration, nutrition or hydration.

— AMA COUNCIL ON SCIENTIFIC AFFAIRS AND COUNCIL
ON ETHICAL AND JUDICIAL AFFAIRS (1990)

It should be noted that the distinction between active and passive euthanasia is sometimes unclear and often depends on the intention of the person carrying out the action. In the Netherlands, where active, voluntary euthanasia is legal, there is no sharp line drawn between active and passive euthanasia. **Voluntary euthanasia** requires that the patient be **competent**—that is, rational and able to make his or her own health care decisions.

In his article at the end of this chapter, James Rachels asks whether the distinction between active and passive euthanasia is morally justified. J. Gay-Williams in "The Wrongfulness of Euthanasia" argues that passive euthanasia is not strictly euthanasia since it does not involve intentional killing; rather, it is an effort to spare a person "additional and unjustified suffering" by withholding further treatment. In this chapter we will primarily consider the morality of active euthanasia.

THE PHILOSOPHERS ON EUTHANASIA

The contemporary philosophical debate on euthanasia has been influenced primarily by ancient Greek and Judeo-Christian views on death. Greek physicians regarded health as a human ideal par excellence. Because human worth and social usefulness depended on one's state of health, chronically sick people were expendable. Plato favored euthanasia of deformed and sickly infants because they would be a burden on the polis. The early Stoics taught that humans ought to quit life nobly when they are no longer socially useful. The Stoic attitude toward dying is reflected in John Hardwig's article "Is There a Duty to Die?"

Not all Greek philosophers agreed with the Stoics. Aristotle believed that willful euthanasia was wrong. Virtue, he argued, requires that we face death bravely rather than take the cowardly way out by quitting life in the face of pain and suffering. The Pythagoreans, who wrote the Hippocratic oath, also opposed euthanasia on the grounds that we are the possessions of the gods. To kill ourselves is to sin against the gods:

> Never will I give a deadly drug, not even if I am asked for one, nor will I give any advice tending in that direction.

> —Hippocratic Oath

The theme that humans are owned by God is also found in Hebrew scriptures (Gen. 2:2–27). As creations of God, no human has the right to destroy his or her life or wantonly take the life of another. This understanding of human life as inherently precious and belonging to God has been immensely influential on the Jewish, Christian, and Islamic views on euthanasia. In the Jewish tradition, death should never be hastened; physicians who kill patients, even if their intention is to relieve pain and suffering, are considered murderers. According to the Islamic religion, illness and suffering are part of God's will. Taking a life interferes with God's will.

In Buddhist philosophy self-willed death, even in cases of suffering and pain, violates the principle of the sanctity of life. It is also wrong because (1) suffering is a means to work out bad karma and (2) a person who assists in suicide or euthanasia will be negatively affected by that participation. Hinduism also teaches that suffering should be endured. Those who deliberately shorten their lives will carry their negative karma into a later life. The Dalai Lama teaches:

> Your suffering is due to your own karma, and you have to bear the fruit of that karma anyway in this life or another, unless you can find some way of purifying it. In that case, it is considered to be better to experience the karma in this life of a human where you have more abilities to bear it in a better way, than, for example, an animal who is helpless and can suffer even more because of that.[1]

Thomas Aquinas incorporated the Aristotelian and biblical prohibition against euthanasia and suicide into his natural law theory, arguing that suicide is unnatural and immoral for three reasons:

> First, everything naturally loves itself, the result being that everything naturally keeps itself in being. . . . Secondly, because every part, as such, belongs to the whole . . . and so, as such, he belongs to the community. Hence by killing himself he injures the community as the Philosopher [Aristotle] declares. Thirdly, because life is God's gift to man, and is subject to His power, Who kills and makes to live. Hence whoever takes his own life sins against God. . . . For it belongs to God alone to pronounce sentence of death and life.

Using the model of Jesus on the cross, Christians emphasize the redemptive aspect of suffering. John Locke regarded self-killing as cowardly, contrary to nature, and opposed to the commandments of God. His view is echoed in the modern Protestant prohibition of active euthanasia, although most Protestants agree that it is morally acceptable to withhold or discontinue treatment that is merely prolonging the dying process.

Immanuel Kant regarded suicide and voluntary euthanasia as immoral. Suicide does not fulfill the requirements of the categorical imperative because it involves a contradiction—that of exercising our autonomy to destroy our autonomy by destroying ourselves. People who want to end their lives also show a lack of respect for themselves by viewing their lives as a means only rather than an end. The prohibition of euthanasia remained pretty much unchallenged right up to the end of the nineteenth century.[2]

THE CONTEMPORARY DEBATE OVER EUTHANASIA

It was not until the end of the nineteenth century that the public began questioning the prohibition of euthanasia. Public debate over euthanasia turned to horror when it was learned that in Nazi Germany up to a hundred thousand mentally ill and disabled children and adults "considered incurable according to the best available human judgment" were, to use official language, "granted a mercy death."[3] The memory of this terrible event still haunts Germany, which now prohibits euthanasia.

The public debate over euthanasia resumed with the development of new life-sustaining technologies such as the mechanical respirator. In 1957, troubled by the ethical problems involved in resuscitating unconscious individuals, the International Congress of Anesthesiology sought moral guidance from Pope Pius XII. The pope responded that physicians should not act without the consent of the family. Physicians also have a moral duty to use ordinary, but not "extraordinary," measures to prolong life. The pope's position was supported by the Catholic Church's "principle of double effect."

The **principle of double effect** states that if an act has two effects, one intended (in this case to end pain and suffering) and the other unintended (the death of the patient), terminating treatment may be morally permissible if it is the only way to bring about the intended effect. This distinction between passive euthanasia, where death is an unintended effect, and active euthanasia, where the intention is to directly bring about the death of the patient, has remained unchallenged for years.

Public opinion began shifting in favor of legalized euthanasia in the early 1970s. In 1973, 53 percent of Americans supported legalized euthanasia. By 2005 this figure had risen to 75 percent. The debate gained momentum with the 2005 Terri Schiavo case. Terri Schiavo had suffered irreversible brain damage and had been in a persistent vegetative state since 1990. Her husband requested that the feeding tube be removed. Her parents disagreed with the decision. The courts repeatedly rejected the parents' request to make the hospital reinsert the feeding tube that kept their daughter alive.

Support for physician-assisted suicide, on the other hand, is somewhat lower, having declined since reaching a high of 65 percent in 2001 to 49 percent in 2007. Men are significantly more likely than women to support legalized euthanasia and physician-assisted suicide.[4] Support for legalizing euthanasia and physician-assisted suicide tends to be higher in other Western countries. Support for euthanasia is especially high in France and in the Netherlands, where active voluntary euthanasia has been legal for several years.

Support for euthanasia of incurably ill people is also high in China, where there is a tradition in some parts of euthanizing unwanted infant girls. There is currently a movement afoot to legalize and regulate euthanasia.[5] Although Japanese views on euthanasia have been influenced by the Buddhist repugnance of killing, the influence of the Shinto religion's glorification of self-willed death for the benefit of the country has led to a more permissive attitude toward euthanasia than in other Buddhist countries.

Muslims are opposed to euthanasia on the grounds that human life is sacred and belongs to Allah. The Qur'an states, "Do not take life, which Allah made sacred, other than in the course of justice" (*Qur'an* 17:33) and "And no person can ever die except by Allah's leave and at an appointed term" (*Qur'an* 3:145).[6]

Judaism likewise forbids active euthanasia as murder. Israel recently passed a law that will allow euthanasia by a timer machine, which shuts down a patient's respiratory system, and hence does not violate Jewish law. The Roman Catholic Church, as well as some other Christian denominations, also prohibits euthanasia. However, some Catholics support euthanasia in cases of unremitting and severe pain or irreversible brain damage.

EUTHANASIA LEGISLATION

The 1976 California Natural Death Act became the first law in the United States to address the issue of decision making on the part of incompetent individuals. The act allowed individuals, under certain circumstances, to make decisions in advance about the kind of treatment they would receive at the end of their lives.

Most people, however, do not have a living will. A 2005 Pew Research study found that only 29 percent of Americans had either prepared written advanced directives regarding their medical care or appointed a durable power of attorney for health care. Thus, it is not surprising that many terminally ill patients end up in a "highly undesirable state"—that is, being kept alive despite their apparent wishes or despite family requests to terminate treatment.[7]

In the 1990 landmark case *Cruzan v. Director, Missouri Department of Health,* the U.S. Supreme Court ruled that every competent individual has a constitutional liberty right to be free of unwanted medical treatment if there is "clear and convincing evidence" of the patient's desire to have the medical treatment withdrawn. The Court left it up to the states to decide for incompetent individuals. (See Case Study 1.)

In 1994 the citizens of Oregon approved Ballot Measure 16 (the "Oregon Death with Dignity Act"), which would legalize euthanasia under certain conditions. The Oregon Death with Dignity Act took effect in 1997 following a lengthy court appeal process. Since then, more than 250 people—mostly cancer patients—have chosen to end their lives under the conditions of the law, which requires that

- patients must be in their final six months of terminal illness;
- patients must make two oral requests and one written request to die, separated by a two-week period;
- patients must be mentally competent to make a decision; and
- two doctors must confirm the diagnosis.

Oregon's Death with Dignity Act was challenged in 2002 by U.S. Attorney General John Ashcroft, who charged that prescribing barbiturates to induce death is illegal under the Controlled Substances Act. The U.S. District Court ruled in favor of *Ashcroft v. Oregon*. The case was appealed to the U.S. Supreme Court, and in 2006 the Court in *Gonzales v. Oregon* ruled in favor of Oregon, stating that the Controlled Substances Act does not give the attorney general the power to prevent physicians from prescribing controlled substances to patients for the purpose of euthanasia, if it is permitted by the law of the state.

Oregon, Washington, and Montana are the only states where physician-assisted suicide is legal. Physician-assisted suicide is also legal in the Netherlands, Switzerland, Luxembourg, Thailand, and Belgium, although it is tolerated in several other countries. The debate over euthanasia is perhaps nowhere so intense as in the Netherlands. Although active euthanasia was only legalized in 2001, it has been tolerated for many years. The law in the Netherlands permits euthanasia only for "medically classified physical or mental diseases and afflictions." Many people are critical of this law on the grounds that it has too much potential for abuse. Indeed, active euthanasia is involved in an estimated 3 to 5 percent of deaths in the Netherlands.[8] In 2008, medical authorities in the Netherlands reported the fourth consecutive annual increase in the number of euthanasia cases, up from 1,815 in 2003 to 2,120 in 2006.[9] Unlike the Oregon law, physicians in the Netherlands are not required to determine whether the patient is of "sound mind" or competent to make such a decision. A Dutch study found that at least 50 percent of these patients were suffering from serious depression when they requested euthanasia.[10] Children who are "hopelessly ill" or handicapped are also the target of euthanasia in the Netherlands, leading to the charge that the Dutch have already started down the slippery slope to involuntary euthanasia.

PHYSICIAN-ASSISTED SUICIDE

Americans are split over whether **physician-assisted suicide**—a type of active euthanasia in which a physician assists the patient in bringing about his or her death—should be legal. Because of laws against euthanasia, most physicians who help patients die do not go public. One notable exception is Dr. Jack Kevorkian, a retired pathologist and trained physician. In 1990 Kevorkian helped Janet Adkins, an Oregon woman who was suffering from the early stages of Alzheimer's disease, to end her life. The vision of Adkins lying dead on the crisp white sheets in the back of Kevorkian's rusting '68 Volkswagen van has become permanently etched onto the American psyche. Since 1990, Kevorkian has presided over the deaths of more than one hundred other people. In April 1999 a Michigan judge sentenced Kevorkian to ten to twenty-five years in prison for second-degree murder. Kevorkian was released on parole in 2007.

The publicity surrounding Kevorkian has sparked intense debate over the morality of physician-assisted suicide. Kevorkian's detractors dubbed him "Dr. Death." Surgeon General C. Everett Koop denounced him as "a serial killer who should be put away."[11] Kevorkian's opponents also point out that he is a pathologist, not a psychiatrist. Unlike health care workers, who know their patients for a long time, Kevorkian hardly knew

CRUZAN V. MISSOURI DEPARTMENT OF HEALTH (1990): EXCERPTS FROM THE MAJORITY OPINION

Chief Justice Rehnquist delivering the opinion of the Court:

Petitioner Nancy Beth Cruzan was rendered incompetent as a result of severe injuries sustained during an automobile accident. Copetitioners Lester and Joyce Cruzan, Nancy's parents and coguardians, sought a court order directing the withdrawal of their daughter's artificial feeding and hydration equipment after it became apparent that she had virtually no chance of recovering her cognitive faculties. The Supreme Court of Missouri held that because there was no clear and convincing evidence of Nancy's desire to have life sustaining treatment withdrawn under such circumstances, her parents lacked authority to effectuate such a request. . . .

At common law, even the touching of one person by another without consent and without legal justification was a battery. . . . This notion of bodily integrity has been embodied in the requirement that informed consent is generally required for medical treatment. . . . The logical corollary of the doctrine of informed consent is that the patient generally possesses the right not to consent, that is, to refuse treatment. . . .

As a general matter, the State—indeed, all civilized nations—demonstrate their commitment to life by treating homicide as a serious crime. Moreover, the majority of States in this country have laws imposing criminal penalties on one who assists another to commit suicide. We do not think a State is required to remain neutral in the fact of an informed and voluntary decision by a physically able adult to starve to death. . . . We believe Missouri may legitimately seek to safeguard the personal element of this choice through the imposition of heightened evidentiary requirements. . . .

In sum, we conclude that a State may apply a clear and convincing evidence standard in proceedings where a guardian seeks to discontinue nutrition and hydration of a person diagnosed to be in a persistent vegetative state. We note that many courts which have adopted some sort of substituted judgement procedure in situations like this, whether they limit consideration of evidence to the prior expressed wishes of the incompetent individual, or whether they allow more general proof of what the individual decision would have been, required a clear and convincing standard of proof for such evidence. The Supreme Court of Missouri held that in this case the testimony adduced at trial did not amount to clear and convincing proof of the patient's desire to have hydration and nutrition withdrawn.

The judgment of the Supreme Court of Missouri is Affirmed.

Justice O'Connor concurring . . . The liberty interest in refusing medical treatment flows from decisions involving the States' invasion into the body. Because our notions of liberty are inextricably entwined with our idea of physical freedom and self-determination, the Court has often deemed state incursions into the body repugnant. . . .

(continued)

(continued from page 183)

The State's artificial provision of nutrition and hydration implicates identical concerns. Artificial feeding cannot readily be distinguished from other forms of medical treatment. . . . Feeding a patient by means of a nasogastric tube requires a physician to pass a long flexible tube through the patient's nose, throat, and esophagus and into the stomach. Because of the discomfort such a tube causes, many patients need to be restrained forcibly and their hands put into large mittens to prevent them from removing the tube. . . . Requiring a competent adult to endure such procedures against her will burdens the patient's liberty, dignity, and freedom to determine the course of her own treatment.

[I] emphasize that the Court does not today decide the issue whether a State must also give effect to the decision of a surrogate decisionmaker. In my view, such a duty may well be constitutionally required to protect the patient's liberty interest in refusing medical treatment. Few individuals [however] provide explicit oral and written instructions regarding their interest to refuse medical treatment should they become incompetent. States which decline to consider any evidence other than such instructions may frequently fail to honor a patient's intent. Such failures might be avoided if the State considered an equally probative source of evidence: the patient's appointment of a proxy to make health care decisions on her behalf. [Cruzan neither left instructions nor appointed a proxy.]

Today's decision does not preclude a future determination that the Constitution requires the State to implement the decisions of a patient's duly appointed surrogate. Nor does it prevent States from developing other approaches for protecting an incompetent individual's liberty interest in refusing medical treatment. . . .

his; he knew Janet Adkins only two days before participating in her death. Kevorkian, on the other hand, sees himself as a defender of liberty.

THE HOSPICE MOVEMENT

The modern **hospice** movement was founded in 1967 by British physician Cicely Saunders to help people die with dignity rather than with fear. The first hospice program in the United States opened in 1974. The philosophy behind hospice is to provide **palliative care**—pain relief, comfort, and compassion—to the dying. As such, hospice has been active in the development of pain control. Hospice also emphasizes attention to the emotional needs of the patient and the patient's family.

There are currently more than 4,700 hospice programs in the United States. According to the National Hospice and Palliative Care Organization, 1.4 million terminally ill patients received services from hospice in 2008, up more than eightfold from 1990.

Hospice is opposed to the legalization of euthanasia. "If one of our patients requests euthanasia," Saunders once wrote, "it means we are not doing our job." Saunders continued:

> We are not so poor a society that we cannot afford time and trouble and money to help people live until they die. We owe it to all those for whom we can kill the pain which traps them in fear and bitterness. To do this we do not have to kill them. . . . To make voluntary [active] euthanasia lawful would be an irresponsible act, hindering help, pressuring the vulnerable, abrogating our true respect and responsibility to the frail and the old, the disabled and dying.[12]

Hospice believes that providing terminally ill people with better palliative care allows them to live their last days in relative comfort and dignity. Advocates of euthanasia maintain that while the hospice program is wonderful for many people, there are still cases in which pain cannot be controlled, and euthanasia should be an option.

THE MORAL ISSUES

The Sanctity of Life

Most Western philosophers believe that human life has intrinsic worth. Legalizing euthanasia will weaken this respect for human life. If life has intrinsic worth, our right not to be killed cannot be overridden, even at our own request.

A variation of this theme is the religious argument, cited by Islam, Judaism, and Roman Catholicism, that our lives are a gift from God and, therefore, we are not free to end them on our own terms. However, physicians are continuously working to prevent death and suffering. Does this interfere with God's will? Furthermore, those who do not believe in God argue that people are not owned by God. As beings with intrinsic moral worth, we have inalienable rights that cannot be waived by anyone else—including God. One of the most fundamental of these rights is the right of autonomy.

Autonomy and Self-Determination

Autonomy requires two conditions: freedom from outside control and moral agency. According to Margaret Pabst Battin, autonomy is one of the two key principles in the euthanasia debate. Autonomy requires that, in general, physicians respect a competent person's choices in determining his or her medical treatment, including euthanasia. If euthanasia is a positive right, as Battin claims, physicians may even have a duty to assist their patients in dying.

Some ethicists argue that autonomy and self-determination have been given too much weight in the euthanasia debate and that people do not have a right to do anything they want. In addition, the leap between claiming that people have a right to end their lives and the claim that it is morally acceptable for physicians to assist in this process is not as self-evident as most advocates of active euthanasia would have us believe.

There is also the danger that making euthanasia available will compromise our autonomy. Some people may feel pressured by circumstances, such as lack of medical insurance or family support, into requesting euthanasia. Susan Wolf argues that, given the traditional view of women as self-sacrificing, women are especially vulnerable to these sorts of pressures.

Nonmaleficence and the Principle of *Ahimsa*

The principle of nonmaleficence or "do no harm" is one of the strongest moral principles. In the Buddhist prohibition against euthanasia, *ahimsa* is the deciding principle. Battin, on the other hand, argues that the principle of nonmaleficence and the duty to relieve pain and suffering may, at times, require euthanasia.

Compassion and the Principle of Mercy

The **principle of mercy** is based on the duty of nonmaleficence. It states that we have a duty both (1) not to cause further pain and suffering and (2) to relieve pain and suffering. Most philosophers agree that the first part of this duty justifies refusal of futile and painful treatment, even though withdrawing or withholding such treatment may result in an earlier death for the patient. Both Rachels and Battin agree that pain relief is a universal duty of physicians and that this duty may entail a positive obligation to use active euthanasia when it is the only way to end pain and suffering.

Hospice, on the other hand, maintains that the appropriate response to suffering is compassionate care, not conceding to a patient's request to be put to death. The Vatican likewise opposes euthanasia. In the Terri Schiavo case, Pope John Paul II stated that feeding tubes are "morally obligatory" for most patients in persistent vegetative states as long as the feeding tube "provides nourishment" and "alleviates suffering."

Death with Dignity

The expressions "death with dignity" and the "good death" are often heard in euthanasia debates. The number one fear of most people is not fear of dying or of pain, but of loss of control and dignity.[13] Advocates of euthanasia argue that respect for the dignity of life entails allowing a person to die with dignity as well, rather than spend the last days of life hooked up to machines and wasting away. Some opponents of euthanasia, in contrast, believe that the good death involves courageously accepting the suffering entailed in dying.

Gay-Williams maintains that survival or the inclination to continue living is a natural human goal. Since human dignity comes from seeking our ends, euthanasia is a violation of human dignity and, therefore, diminishes our humanness.

Quality of Life: Pain and Suffering

Human life is more than mere biological existence. Battin points out that the ability to be in relationships with family and friends, to have hopes for the future, and to live without constant pain are all basic goods. When isolation, pain, and suffering outweigh any expectation of enjoying the goods of life, the quality of that life becomes a negative value and death may be preferable.

Pain, however, such as that associated with most cancers, can be relieved in up to 90 percent of cases. Despite this, many terminally ill people are not offered palliative care. A 2002 national survey found that 59 percent of people gave the quality of end-of-life care a fair or poor rating when it comes to making sure patients were as comfortable and pain-free as possible at the end of life.[14] This is blamed, in part, not on the lack of effective pain relievers, but on Western society's opiophobia—fear of drug addiction and abuse.[15]

On the other hand, why should only physical pain count? There are other types of suffering, such as lifelong disability, loneliness, and depression. Should there be a moral distinction between wanting to die because one is depressed or facing chronic illness and the pain associated with a terminal illness? (See Case Study 2.)

Another issue is determining the quality of life of incompetent patients, such as people in comas and children with disabilities. Who, if anyone, should decide if their lives are worth living? If we answer that euthanasia should be voluntary only, we have to ask ourselves if it is fair that incompetent people be doomed to lives of suffering and hopelessness. Hardwig also asks if it is fair that society and families be forced to bear the burden of maintaining the lives of hopelessly ill people.

Ordinary Versus Extraordinary Treatment

The AMA, while opposing euthanasia, allows the withdrawal of extraordinary treatment. Ordinary medical treatment includes measures that have a reasonable hope of benefiting the patient, whereas **extraordinary treatments** provide no reasonable hope of benefiting the patient. This brings up the question of just when treatment becomes extraordinary. How should we draw the line between prolonging life and prolonging the dying process? Is using chemotherapy on an ailing eighty-five-year-old with cancer ordinary or extraordinary treatment? Also, what counts as a reasonable hope? Is continuing to keep a patient in a coma on artificial life support, even though there is only slight hope of recovery, ordinary or extraordinary treatment?

The Principle of Double Effect: Letting Die Versus Actively Killing

The traditional distinction between active and passive euthanasia rests on intention. In **active euthanasia,** the intention is to cause the death of another person. In **passive euthanasia,** there is a "double effect": the death of the person is an unintended consequence of the intended effect—the elimination of pain and suffering.

Some philosophers claim that this distinction is hypocritical and that physicians are morally responsible for both intended and foreseen consequences. Rachels argues that knowing that high doses of painkillers may hasten a person's death is an action as much as is administering a lethal injection on request. Both involve decision and action on the part of the physician. Indeed, he claims there may be cases in which active euthanasia is the more humane alternative.

The Physician's Role as Healer

Some opponents of physician-assisted suicide and euthanasia, such as Gay-Williams, argue that expecting physicians to be agents of death runs contrary to their training as healers and comforters and may damage trust in the patient–physician relationship. This argument, however, does not rule out euthanasia. The act of euthanasia could instead be left to others, perhaps people like Dr. Kevorkian or "death technicians," who specialize in it.

Patient Competence

Two of the problems in deciding who should be a candidate for euthanasia are (1) determining if a patient is rational and competent to make such a decision and (2) determing whether it is a sincere request for death or simply a cry for help. What, in other words, are the patient's real intentions? Furthermore, if the patient is incompetent, how do we determine what is in the patient's best interests? Some people argue that physicians or close family members can usually be counted on to respect a patient's self-determination, whereas others, such as Wolf, question the insidious effect of cultural biases on these decisions.

Some claim that the request, especially in cases in which the patient is able to carry out the suicide without assistance, is often a cloaked request for help. Suicide prevention workers point out that people who are suicidal often feel a sense of depression, hopelessness, and despair. Rather than seeking to end their lives, the request to die is really an expression of that despair and, as such, is a cry for help.

Justice and the Principle of Equality

Some opponents of euthanasia maintain that it is always unjust because it involves the death of an innocent person. Battin, on the other hand, maintains that the duty of justice may require euthanasia, especially in cases in which keeping a person alive is tremendously expensive.

Wolf expresses concern that euthanasia may be unjust because it unfairly targets certain groups. In a society that holds up self-sacrifice as a virtue for women, women are especially vulnerable to pressures to put the needs and desires of others before their own. The physician-assisted death of Judith Curren, who was later alleged to have been abused by her husband, is just one case in point.

Another concern is our society's negative view of people who are disabled and the tendency to devalue their lives. While it may be countered that disabled people fall outside the scope of euthanasia because they are not terminally ill, the facts show that infants and children with disabilities, such as Baby Doe, are also vulnerable to euthanasia. A study of infant deaths at the special-care unit of the Yale–New Haven Hospital between 1970 and 1972 revealed that of 299 deaths, 14 percent were associated with the withholding or withdrawal of treatment in cases of severe congenital disorders.[16]

Burdens to Society and a Duty to Die

The majority of Dutch and American doctors favor physician-assisted suicide for a patient in excruciating pain.[17] However, they differ in their justifications of euthanasia. Dutch doctors are more likely to support physician-assisted suicide in cases in which a patient finds life meaningless; American physicians are more likely to consider a patient's fear of being a burden as a justification for euthanasia.

Both Hardwig and Battin argue that when costly medical resources are needed to sustain a human life, the principle of justice may warrant involuntary active euthanasia. End-of-life costs account for 10 percent of total health care spending in the United States and 27 percent of Medicare expense.[18] In contrast, it costs only a few dollars to deliver a lethal injection.

The baby boomers, those 78 million Americans born between 1945 and 1961, are the largest generation in American history. The aging baby boomer population can be expected to drive up health care costs in the next few decades. Are these health care dollars well spent, or do the elderly have what Hardwig calls "a duty to die"? Hardwig argues that burden to family and society creates a duty to die. According to him, there comes a time in life when we have a duty to let go. In a nonegalitarian society, however, where the lives of certain groups are valued less than others, a duty to die might come into conflict with the principle of justice by unfairly targeting certain people, such as women, the poor, and the disabled.

The Finality of Death Versus the Hope of Recovery

Although rare, there are cases in which a patient comes out of a coma or makes a miraculous recovery despite a prognosis of imminent death or irreversible brain damage. Jackie Cole suffered a stroke and massive bleeding in her brain. The doctors predicted that without artificial life support she would be dead within a few days. Before slipping into a coma, she had made it clear that she did not want to be kept alive by artificial means. The court, however, refused her husband's petition to have life support withdrawn. Six days later Cole awoke from the coma and slowly began to recover.[19]

What is a reasonable cost of sustaining hope? Do cases like Jackie Cole's justify spending millions of dollars keeping comatose people alive in hopes that a few of them will come out of it? Gay-Williams, an opponent of euthanasia, says yes. If euthanasia is legal, we are more likely to give up hope as well as not put as much effort into research for new cures.

Slippery Slope Argument

Even if euthanasia can be morally justified in principle, there may still be problems when it comes to legalizing it because of the difficulty of drawing the line between who should and who should not be eligible. If there is no definite line to stop abuses, it will be easy to slip down the slope toward greater and greater acceptance of euthanasia. A report from the Netherlands found that Dutch physicians "sometimes act without patient requests in performing euthanasia and that there was a sense among some patients that they had a duty to die."[20] The right to euthanasia, in other words, can slip into a duty to die. If euthanasia is an option, it will also be easy to redefine chronic medical conditions as terminal illnesses to justify the euthanasia of people who have Alzheimer's or of children with genetic disorders, a practice that has already begun to some extent.[21]

CONCLUSION

The moral issues surrounding euthanasia are complex. Many of the relevant principles come into conflict with one another and need to be carefully weighed. A further complication is the uncertainty of medical prognoses and the presence of subjective factors in assessing patients' requests for euthanasia. In addition, public policies on euthanasia need to be drafted within the wider social context. As with abortion, the judgment that euthanasia, or at least certain types of it, is morally acceptable does not imply that the law should permit it.

🍃 JAMES RACHELS

Active and Passive Euthanasia

Utilitarian POV

James Rachels (1941–2003) was a professor of philosophy at the University of Alabama. In his celebrated article "Active and Passive Euthanasia," which first appeared in the *New England Journal of Medicine* in 1975, Rachels argues that the traditional distinction between active and passive euthanasia cannot be morally justified. He also points out that there are cases in which active euthanasia may be morally preferable to passive euthanasia.

Critical Reading Questions

1. What is the AMA's position on euthanasia?
2. What is the distinction between active and passive euthanasia?
3. Why is passive euthanasia worse in some cases, according to Rachels, than active euthanasia?
4. What does Rachels think of the practice of allowing newborns with Down syndrome to die?
5. What point is Rachels illustrating with the analogy of Smith and Jones and the death of their six-year-old cousin?
6. How important, in Rachels's view, is the role of intention in justifying euthanasia?
7. According to Rachels, what is the crucial issue in euthanasia?
8. Why does Rachels claim that the AMA position as well as the current laws on euthanasia are inconsistent?

James Rachels, "Active and Passive Euthanasia," *New England Journal of Medicine*, Vol. 292 (January 9, 1975), pp. 78–81. Copyright © 1975 Massachusetts Medical Society. All rights reserved. Reprinted with permission.

The distinction between active and passive euthanasia is thought to be crucial for medical ethics. The idea is that it is permissible, at least in some cases, to withhold treatment and allow a patient to die, but it is never permissible to take any direct action designed to kill the patient. This doctrine seems to be accepted by most doctors, and it is endorsed in a statement adopted by the House of Delegates of the American Medical Association on December 4, 1973:

> The intentional termination of the life of one human being by another—mercy killing—is contrary to that for which the medical profession stands and is contrary to the policy of the American Medical Association.

> The cessation of the employment of extraordinary means to prolong the life of the body when there is irrefutable evidence that biological death is imminent is the decision of the patient and/or his immediate family. The advice and judgement of the physician should be freely available to the patient and/or his immediate family.

However, a strong case can be made against this doctrine. In what follows I will set out some of the relevant arguments, and urge doctors to reconsider their views on this matter.

To begin with a familiar type of situation, a patient who is dying of incurable cancer of the throat is in terrible pain, which can no longer be satisfactorily alleviated. He is certain to die within a few days, even if present treatment is continued, but he does not want to go on living for those days since the pain is unbearable. So he asks the doctor for an end to it, and his family joins in the request.

Suppose the doctor agrees to withhold treatment, as the conventional doctrine says he may. The justification for his doing so is that the patient is in terrible agony, and since he is going to die anyway, it would be wrong to prolong his suffering needlessly. But now notice this. If one simply withholds treatment, it may take the patient longer to die, and so he may suffer more than he would if more direct action were taken and a lethal injection given. This fact provides strong reason for

thinking that, once the initial decision not to prolong his agony has been made, active euthanasia is actually preferable to passive euthanasia, rather than the reverse. To say otherwise is to endorse the option that leads to more suffering rather than less, and is contrary to the humanitarian impulse that prompts the decision not to prolong his life in the first place.

Part of my point is that the process of being "allowed to die" can be relatively slow and painful, whereas being given a lethal injection is relatively quick and painless. Let me give a different sort of example. In the United States about one in 600 babies is born with Down's syndrome. Most of these babies are otherwise healthy—that is, with only the usual pediatric care, they will proceed to an otherwise normal infancy. Some, however, are born with congenital defects such as intestinal obstructions that require operations if they are to live. Sometimes, the parents and the doctor will decide not to operate, and let the infant die. Anthony Shaw describes what happens then:

> When surgery is denied [the doctor] must try to keep the infant from suffering while natural forces sap the baby's life away. As a surgeon whose natural inclination is to use the scalpel to fight off death, standing by and watching a salvageable baby die is the most emotionally exhausting experience I know. It is easy at a conference, in a theoretical discussion, to decide that such infants should be allowed to die. It is altogether different to stand by in the nursery and watch as the dehydration and infection wither a tiny being over hours and days. This is a terrible ordeal for me and the hospital staff—much more so than for the parents who never set foot in the nursery.[*]

I can understand why some people are opposed to all euthanasia, and insist that such infants must be allowed to live. I think I can also understand why other people favor destroying these babies quickly and painlessly. But why should anyone favor letting "dehydration and infection wither a tiny being over hours and days"? The doctrine that says that a

---

[*]Shaw A: "Doctor, Do We Have a Choice?" *The New York Times Magazine,* January 30, 1972, p. 54.

baby may be allowed to dehydrate and wither, but may not be given an injection that would end its life without suffering, seems so patently cruel as to require no further refutation. The strong language is not intended to offend, but only to put the point in the clearest possible way.

My second argument is that the conventional doctrine leads to decisions concerning life and death made on irrelevant grounds.

Consider again the case of the infants with Down's syndrome who need operations for congenital defects unrelated to the syndrome to live. Sometimes, there is no operation, and the baby dies, but when there is no such defect, the baby lives on. Now, an operation such as that to remove an intestinal obstruction is not prohibitively difficult. The reason why such operations are not performed in these cases is, clearly, that the child has Down's syndrome and the parents and doctor judge that because of that fact it is better for the child to die.

But notice that this situation is absurd, no matter what view one takes of the lives and potentials of such babies. If the life of such an infant is worth preserving, what does it matter if it needs a simple operation? Or, if one thinks it better that such a baby should not live on, what difference does it make that it happens to have an unobstructed intestinal tract? In either case, the matter of life and death is being decided on irrelevant grounds. It is the Down's syndrome, and not the intestines, that is the issue. The matter should be decided, if at all, on that basis, and not be allowed to depend on the essentially irrelevant question of whether the intestinal tract is blocked.

What makes this situation possible, of course, is the idea that when there is an intestinal blockage, one can "let the baby die," but when there is no such defect there is nothing that can be done, for one must not "kill" it. The fact that this idea leads to such results as deciding life or death on irrelevant grounds is another good reason why the doctrine should be rejected.

One reason why so many people think that there is an important moral difference between active and passive euthanasia is that they think killing someone is morally worse than letting someone

die. But is it? Is killing, in itself, worse than letting die? To investigate this issue, two cases may be considered that are exactly alike except that one involves killing whereas the other involves letting someone die. Then, it can be asked whether this difference makes any difference to the moral assessments. It is important that the cases be exactly alike, except for this one difference, since otherwise one cannot be confident that it is this difference and not some other that accounts for any variation in the assessment of the two cases. So, let us consider this pair of cases:

In the first, Smith stands to gain a large inheritance if anything should happen to his six-year-old cousin. One evening while the child is taking his bath, Smith sneaks into the bathroom and drowns the child, and then arranges things so that it will look like an accident.

In the second, Jones also stands to gain if anything should happen to his six-year-old cousin. Like Smith, Jones sneaks in planning to drown the child in his bath. However, just as he enters the bathroom Jones sees the child slip and hit his head, and fall face down in the water. Jones is delighted; he stands by, ready to push the child's head back under if it is necessary, but it is not necessary. With only a little thrashing about, the child drowns all by himself, "accidentally," as Jones watches and does nothing.

Now Smith killed the child, whereas Jones "merely" let the child die. That is the only difference between them. Did either man behave better, from a moral point of view? If the difference between killing and letting die were in itself a morally important matter, one should say that Jones's behavior was less reprehensible than Smith's. But does one really want to say that? I think not. In the first place, both men acted from the same motive, personal gain, and both had exactly the same end in view when they acted. It may be inferred from Smith's conduct that he is a bad man, although that judgment may be withdrawn or modified if certain further facts are learned about him—for example, that he is mentally deranged. But would not the very same thing be inferred about Jones from his conduct? And would not the same further considerations also be relevant to any modification of this judgment? Moreover, suppose Jones pleaded, in his own defense, "After all, I didn't do anything except just stand there and watch the child drown. I didn't kill him; I only let him die." Again, if letting die were in itself less bad than killing, this defense should have at least some weight. But it does not. Such a "defense" can only be regarded as a grotesque perversion of moral reasoning. Morally speaking, it is no defense at all.

Now, it may be pointed out, quite properly, that the cases of euthanasia with which doctors are concerned are not like this at all. They do not involve personal gain or the destruction of normal healthy children. Doctors are concerned only with cases in which the patient's life is of no further use to him, or in which the patient's life has become or will soon become a terrible burden. However, the point is the same in these cases: the bare difference between killing and letting die does not, in itself, make a moral difference. If a doctor lets a patient die, for humane reasons, he is in the same moral position as if he had given the patient a lethal injection for humane reasons. If his decision was wrong—if, for example, the patient's illness was in fact curable—the decision would be equally regrettable no matter which method was used to carry it out. And if the doctor's decision was the right one, the method used is not itself important.

The AMA policy statement isolates the crucial issue very well; the crucial issue is "the intentional termination of the life of one human being by another." But after identifying this issue, and forbidding "mercy killing," the statement goes on to deny that the cessation of treatment is the intentional termination of a life. This is where the mistake comes in, for what is the cessation of treatment, in these circumstances, if it is not "the intentional termination of the life of one human being by another"? Of course it is exactly that, and if it were not, there would be no point to it.

Many people will find this judgment hard to accept. One reason, I think, is that it is very easy to conflate the question of whether killing is, in itself, worse than letting die, with the very different question of whether most actual cases of killing are more reprehensible than most actual cases of letting die. Most actual cases of killing are clearly terrible (think, for example, of all the murders reported in the newspapers), and one hears of such cases every day. On the other hand, one hardly ever hears of a case of letting die, except for the actions of doctors who are motivated by humanitarian reasons. So one learns to think of killing in a much worse light than of letting die. But this does not mean that there is something about killing that makes it in itself worse than letting die, for it is not the bare difference between killing and letting die that makes the difference in these cases. Rather, the other factors—the murderer's motive of personal gain, for example, contrasted with the doctor's humanitarian motivation—account for different reactions to the different cases.

I have argued that killing is not in itself any worse than letting die; if my contention is right, it follows that active euthanasia is not any worse than passive euthanasia. What arguments can be given on the other side? The most common, I believe, is the following:

> The important difference between active and passive euthanasia is that, in passive euthanasia, the doctor does not do anything to bring about the patient's death. The doctor does nothing, and the patient dies of whatever ills already afflict him. In active euthanasia, however, the doctor does something to bring about the patient's death: he kills him. The doctor who gives the patient with cancer a lethal injection has himself caused the patient's death; whereas if he merely ceases treatment, the cancer is the cause of death.

A number of points need to be made here. The first is that it is not exactly correct to say that in passive euthanasia the doctor does nothing, for he does do one thing that is very important: he lets the patient die. "Letting someone die" is certainly different, in some respects, from other types of action—mainly in that it is a kind of action that one may perform by way of not performing certain other actions. For example, one may let a patient die by way of not giving medication, just as one may insult someone by way of not shaking his hand. But for any purpose of moral assessment, it is a type of action nonetheless. The decision to let a patient die is subject to moral appraisal in the same way that a decision to kill him would be subject to moral appraisal: it may be assessed as wise or unwise, compassionate or sadistic, right or wrong. If a doctor deliberately let a patient die who was suffering from a routinely curable illness, the doctor would certainly be to blame for what he had done, just as he would be to blame if he had needlessly killed the patient. Charges against him would then be appropriate. If so, it would be no defense at all for him to insist that he didn't "do anything." He would have done something very serious indeed, for he let his patient die.

Fixing the cause of death may be very important from a legal point of view, for it may determine whether criminal charges are brought against the doctor. But I do not think that this notion can be used to show a moral difference between active and passive euthanasia. The reason why it is considered bad to be the cause of someone's death is that death is regarded as a great evil—and so it is. However, if it has been decided that euthanasia— even passive euthanasia—is desirable in a given case, it has also been decided that in this instance death is no greater an evil than the patient's continued existence. And if this is true, the usual reason for not wanting to be the cause of someone's death simply does not apply.

Finally, doctors may think that all of this is only of academic interest—the sort of thing that philosophers may worry about but that has no practical bearing on their own work. After all, doctors must be concerned about the legal consequences of what they do, and active euthanasia is clearly forbidden by the law. But even so, doctors should also be concerned with the fact that the law is forcing upon them a moral doctrine that may well be indefensible, and has a considerable effect on their practices. Of course, most doctors are not now in the position of being coerced in this matter, for they do not regard themselves as merely going along with what the law requires. Rather, in statements such as the AMA policy statement that I have quoted, they are endorsing this doctrine as a central point of medical ethics. In that statement, active euthanasia is condemned not merely as illegal but as "contrary to that for which the medical profession stands," whereas passive euthanasia is approved. However, the preceding considerations suggest that there is really no moral difference between the two, considered in themselves (there may be important moral differences in some cases in their *consequences,* but, as I pointed out, these differences may make active euthanasia, and not passive euthanasia, the morally preferable option). So, whereas doctors may have to discriminate between active and passive euthanasia to satisfy the law, they should not do any more than that. In particular, they should not give the distinction any added authority and weight by writing it into official statements of medical ethics.

Discussion Questions

1. Discuss Rachels's claim that withholding treatment or assistance, as in the case of an infant with Down syndrome, is the moral equivalent of intentional termination of life.
2. Discuss how Rachels would most likely view the legalization of physician-assisted suicide. Would it matter to him if the person was not terminally ill but requested it?
3. What would Rachels think of the hospice practice of using large doses of morphine to alleviate pain, knowing that it might shorten a patient's life? Is this practice an example of euthanasia? Support your answers.
4. Discuss what Rachels would most likely recommend in the cases of Nancy Cruzan and Terri Schiavo.

MARGARET PABST BATTIN

The Case for Euthanasia

Margaret Pabst Battin is a professor of philosophy and adjunct professor of internal medicine, Division of Medical Ethics, at the University of Utah. She is also author of the book *The Least Worst Death* (1994). Battin argues that the moral values of mercy, justice, and autonomy support the legalization of euthanasia.

Critical Reading Questions

1. What is the principle of mercy? What two duties does this principle establish for physicians and caregivers? What common medical practices, in Battin's view, go against this principle?
2. According to Battin, does the principle of mercy justify both passive and active euthanasia? What examples does Battin use to illustrate this?
3. What is Battin's response to the argument that euthanasia is no longer necessary because of advances in pain control and palliative care?
4. What is Battin's response to the argument that life itself is a benefit and ought to be preserved?
5. What is the principle of autonomy, and why is it fundamental to the euthanasia debate? How, according to Battin, is the principle of autonomy conceptually tied to the principle of mercy in the euthanasia debate?
6. What are "limited paternalism" and "extended paternalism"? When is it responsible for physicians to deny patient requests for euthanasia? When is it irresponsible?
7. According to Battin, does patient autonomy create a moral obligation for physicians to perform euthanasia?
8. How does the principle of justice, according to Battin, support euthanasia?
9. What is Battin's response to those who argue that legalizing euthanasia will take us down the slippery slope to a Nazi-type scenario?
10. What is Battin's position on physician-assisted suicide?

Because it arouses questions about the morality of killing, the effectiveness of consent, the duties of physicians, and equity in the distribution of resources, the problem of euthanasia is one of the most acute and uncomfortable contemporary problems in medical ethics. It is not a new problem; euthanasia has been discussed—and practiced—in both Eastern and Western cultures from the earliest historical times to the present. But because of medicine's new technological capacities to extend life, the problem is much more pressing than it has been in the past, and both the discussion and practice of euthanasia are more widespread. Despite this, much of

"The Case for Euthanasia." from *Health Care Ethics,* ed. by D. VanDeVeer and Tom Regan (Philadelphia, Penn.: Temple University Press, 1987), 58–95. Some notes have been omitted.

contemporary Western culture remains strongly opposed to euthanasia: doctors ought not kill people, its public voices maintain, and ought not let them die if it is possible to save life.

I believe that this opposition to euthanasia is in serious moral error—on grounds of mercy, autonomy, and justice. I shall argue for the rightness of granting a person a humane, merciful death, if he or she wants it, even when this can be achieved only by a direct and deliberate killing. . . .

THE CASE FOR EUTHANASIA, PART I: MERCY

The case for euthanasia rests on three fundamental moral principles: mercy, autonomy, and justice.

The principle of mercy asserts that *where possible, one ought to relieve the pain or suffering of another person, when it does not contravene that person's wishes, where one can do so without undue costs to oneself, where one will not violate other moral obligations, where the pain or suffering itself is not necessary for the sufferer's attainment of some overriding good, and where the pain or suffering can be relieved without precluding the sufferer's attainment of some overriding good.* This principle might best be called the principle of medical mercy, to distinguish it from principles concerning mercy in judicial contexts. . . . Contexts that require mercy sometimes require euthanasia as a way of granting mercy—both by direct killing and by letting die. . . .

"Relief of pain is the least disputed and most universal of the moral obligations of the physician," writes one doctor. "Few things a doctor does are more important than relieving pain," says another.[1] These are not simply assertions that the physician ought "do no harm," as the Hippocratic oath is traditionally interpreted, but assertions of positive obligation. . . .

This principle of mercy establishes two component duties:

1. the duty not to cause further pain or suffering; and

2. the duty to act to end pain or suffering already occurring.

Under the first of these, for a physician or other caregiver to extend mercy to a suffering patient may mean to refrain from procedures that cause further suffering—provided, of course, that the treatment offers the patient no overriding benefits. So, for instance, the physician must refrain from ordering painful tests, therapies, or surgical procedures when they cannot alleviate suffering or contribute to a patient's improvement or cure. . . .

Of course, whether a painful test or therapy will actually contribute to some overriding good for the patient is not always clear. Nevertheless, the principle of mercy directs that where such procedures can reasonably be expected to impose suffering on the patient without overriding benefits for him or her, they ought not be done. . . .

In such cases, the principle of mercy demands that the "treatments" no longer be imposed, and that the patient be allowed to die.

But the principle of mercy may also demand "letting die" in a still stronger sense. Under its second component, the principle asserts a duty to act to end suffering that is already occurring. Medicine already honors this duty through its various techniques of pain management. . . . But there are some difficult cases in which pain or suffering is severe but cannot be effectively controlled, at least as long as the patient remains sentient at all. Classical examples include tumors of the throat (where agonizing discomfort is not just a matter of pain but of inability to swallow, "air hunger," or acute shortness of breath), tumors of the brain or bone, and so on. Severe nausea, vomiting, and exhaustion may increase the patient's misery. In these cases, continuing life—or at least continuing consciousness—may mean continuing pain. Consequently, mercy's demand for euthanasia takes hold here: mercy demands that the pain, even if with it the life, be brought to an end.

Ending the pain, though with it the life, may be accomplished through what is usually called "passive euthanasia," withholding or withdrawing treatment that could prolong life. In the most indirect of these cases, the patient is simply not given treatment that might extend his or her life—say, radiation therapy in advanced cancer. . . .

But the second component of the principle of mercy may also demand the easing of pain by means more direct than mere allowing to die; it may require *killing*. This is usually called "active euthanasia," and despite borderline cases (for instance, the ancient Greek practice of infanticide by exposure), it can in general be conceptually distinguished from passive euthanasia. In passive euthanasia, treatment is withheld that could support failing bodily functions, either in warding off external threats or in performing its own processes; active euthanasia, in contrast, involves the direct interruption of ongoing bodily processes that otherwise would have been adequate to sustain life. However, although it may be possible to draw a conceptual distinction between passive and active euthanasia, this provides no warrant for the ubiquitous view that killing is morally worse than letting die. Nor does it support the view that withdrawing treatment is worse than withholding it. If the patient's condition is so tragic that continuing life brings only pain, and there is no other way to relieve the pain than by death, then the more merciful act is not one that merely removes support for bodily processes and waits for eventual death to ensue; rather, it is one that brings the pain—and the patient's life—to an end *now*. . . .

But, it may be objected, the cases we have mentioned to illustrate intolerable pain are classical ones; such cases are controllable now. Pain is a thing of the medical past, and euthanasia is no longer necessary, though it once may have been, to relieve pain. . . . Particularly impressive are the huge advances under the hospice program in the amelioration of both the physical and emotional pain of terminal illness, and our culturewide fears of pain in terminal cancer are no longer justified: cancer pain, when it occurs, can now be controlled in virtually all cases. We can now end the pain without also ending the life.

This is a powerful objection, and one very frequently heard in medical circles. Nevertheless, it does not succeed. It is flatly incorrect to say that all pain, including pain in terminal illness, is or can be controlled. Some people still die in unspeakable agony. With superlative care, many kinds of pain can indeed be reduced in many patients, and adequate control of pain in terminal illness is often quite easy to achieve. Nevertheless, complete, universal, fully reliable pain control is a myth. Pain is not yet a "thing of the past," nor are many associated kinds of physical distress. . . . Finally, there are cases in which pain control is theoretically possible but for various extraneous reasons does not occur. Some deaths take place in remote locations where there are no pain-relieving resources. Some patients are unable to communicate the nature or extent of their pain. And some institutions and institutional personnel who have the capacity to control pain do not do so, whether from inattention, malevolence, fears of addiction, or divergent priorities in resources.

In all these cases, of course, the patient can be sedated into unconsciousness; this does indeed end the pain. But in respect of the patient's experience, this is tantamount to causing death: the patient has no further conscious experience and thus can achieve no goods, experience no significant communication, satisfy no goals. Furthermore, adequate sedation, by depressing respiratory function, may hasten death. . . .

The principle of mercy holds that suffering ought to be relieved—unless, among other provisos, the suffering itself will give rise to some overriding benefit or unless the attainment of some benefit would be precluded by relieving the pain. But it might be argued that life itself is a benefit, always an overriding one. Certainly life is usually a benefit, one that we prize. But unless we accept certain metaphysical assumptions, such as "life is a gift from God," we must recognize that life is a benefit because of the experiences and interests associated with it. . . . Philippa Foot treats this as a conceptual point: "Ordinary human lives, even very hard lives, contain a minimum of basic goods, but when these are absent the idea of life is no longer linked to that of good."[2]

Such basic goods, she explains, include not being forced to work far beyond one's capacity; having the support of a family or community; being able to more or less satisfy one's hunger; having hopes for the future; and being able to lie down to rest at night. When these goods are missing, she asserts, the connection between *life* and *good* is broken, and we cannot count it as a benefit to the person whose life it is that his life is preserved.

These basic goods may all be severely compromised or entirely absent in the severely ill or dying patient. . . . Yet even for someone lacking all of what Foot considers to be basic goods, the experiences associated with life may not be unrelievedly negative. We must be very cautious in asserting of someone, even someone in the most abysmal-seeming conditions of the severely ill or dying, that life is no longer a benefit, since the way in which particular experiences, interests, and "basic goods" are valued may vary widely from one person to the next. . . .

It is true that contemporary pain management techniques do make possible the control of pain to a considerable degree. But unless pain and discomforting symptoms are eliminated altogether without loss of function, the underlying problem for the principle of mercy remains: how does *this* patient value life, how does he or she weigh death against pain? We are accustomed to assume that only patients suffering extreme, irremediable pain could be candidates for euthanasia at all and do not consider whether some patients might choose death in preference to comparatively moderate chronic pain, even when the condition is not a terminal one. Of course, a patient's perceptions of pain are extremely subject to stress, anxiety, fear, exhaustion, and other factors, but even though these perceptions may vary, the underlying weighing still demands respect. This is not just a matter of differing sensitivities to pain, but of differing values as well: for some patients, severe pain may be accepted with resignation or even pious joy, whereas for others mild or moderate discomfort is simply not worth enduring. . . .

If the sufferer is the best judge of the relative values of that suffering and other benefits to himself, then his own choices in the matter of mercy ought to be respected. To impose "mercy" on someone who insists that despite his suffering life is still valuable to him would hardly be mercy; to

withhold mercy from someone who pleads for it, on the basis that his life could still be worthwhile for him, is insensitive and cruel. Thus, the principle of mercy is conceptually tied to that of autonomy, at least insofar as what guarantees the best application of the principle—and hence, what guarantees the proper response to the ostensive premise in the argument from mercy—is respect for the patient's own wishes concerning the relief of his suffering or pain.

To this issue we now turn.

THE CASE FOR EUTHANASIA, PART II: AUTONOMY

The second principle supporting euthanasia is that of (patient) autonomy: *one ought to respect a competent person's choices, where one can do so without undue costs to oneself, where doing so will not violate other moral obligations, and where these choices do not threaten harm to other persons or parties.* This principle of autonomy, though limited by these provisos, grounds a person's right to have his or her own choices respected in determining the course of medical treatment, including those relevant to euthanasia: whether the patient wishes treatment that will extend life, though perhaps also suffering, or whether he or she wants the suffering relieved, either by being killed or by being allowed to die. It would of course also require respect for the choices of the person whose condition is chronic but not terminal, the person who is disabled though not dying, and the person not yet suffering at all, but facing senility or old age. Indeed, the principle of autonomy would require respect for self-determination in the matter of life and death in any condition at all, provided that the choice is freely and rationally made and does not harm others or violate other moral rules. Thus, the principle of autonomy would protect a much wider range of life-and-death acts than those we call euthanasia, as well as those performed for reasons of mercy. . . .

It is often objected that autonomy in euthanasia choices should not be recognized in practice, whether or not it is accepted in principle, because such choices are often erroneously made. One version of this argument points to physician error. . . . People diagnosed as dying rapidly of inexorable cancers have survived, cancer-free, for dozens of years; people in cardiac failure or long-term irreversible coma have revived and regained full health. . . .

A second argument pointing to the possibility of erroneous choice on the part of the patient asserts the very great likelihood of impairment of the patient's mental processes when seriously ill. Impairing factors include depression, anxiety, pain, fear, intimidation by authoritarian physicians or institutions, and drugs used in medical treatment that affect mental status. Perhaps a person in good health would be capable of calm, objective judgment even in such serious matters as euthanasia, so this view holds, but the person as patient is not. Depression, extremely common in terminal illness, is a particular culprit: it tends to narrow one's view of the possibilities still open; . . . A choice of euthanasia in terminal illness, this view holds, probably reflects largely the gloominess of the depression, not the gravity of the underlying disease or any genuine intention to die.

If this is so, ought not the euthanasia request of a patient be ignored for his or her own sake? According to a limited paternalistic view (sometimes called "soft" or "weak" paternalism), intervention in a person's choices for his or her own sake is justified if the person's thinking is impaired. Under this principle, not every euthanasia request should be honored; such requests should be construed, rather, as pleas for more sensitive physical and emotional care.

It is no doubt true that many requests to die are pleas for better care or improved conditions of life. But this still does not establish that all euthanasia requests should be ignored, because the principle of paternalism licenses intervention in a person's choices just *for his or her own good*. Sometimes the choice of euthanasia, though made in an impaired, irrational way, may seem to serve the person's own good better than remaining alive. Thus, since the paternalist, in intervening, must act for the sake of the person in whose liberty he or she interferes, the paternalist must take into account not only the costs for the person of failing to interfere with a euthanasia decision when euthanasia was not warranted (the cost is death, when death was not in this person's interests) but also the costs for that person of interfering in a decision that was warranted (the cost is continuing life—and continuing suffering—when death would have been the better choice). The likelihood of these two undesirable outcomes must then be weighed. To claim that "there's always hope" or to insist that "the diagnosis could be wrong" in a morally responsible way, one must weigh not only the cost of unnecessary death to the patient but also the costs to the patient of dying in agony if the diagnosis is right and the cure does not materialize. . . .

As with limited paternalism, extended "strong" or "hard" paternalism—permitting intervention not merely to counteract impairment but also to avoid great harm—provides a special case when applied to euthanasia situations. The hard paternalist may be tempted to argue that because death is the greatest of harms, euthanasia choices must always be thwarted. But the initial premise of this argument is precisely what is at issue in the euthanasia dispute itself, as we've seen: is death the worst of harms that can befall a person, or is unrelieved, hopeless suffering a still worse harm? The principle of mercy obliges us to relieve suffering when it does not serve some overriding good; but the principle itself cannot tell us whether sheer existence—life—is an overriding good. In the absence of an objectively valid answer, we must appeal to the individual's own preferences and values. . . .

To claim that an incessantly pain-racked but conscious person cannot make a rational choice in matters of life and death is to misconstrue the point: he or she, better than anyone else, can make such a choice, based on intimate acquaintance with pain and his or her own beliefs and fears about death. If the patient wishes to live, despite such suffering, he or she must be allowed to do so; or the patient must be granted help if he or she wishes to die.

But this introduces a further problem. The principle of autonomy, when there are no countervailing considerations on paternalistic grounds or on grounds of harm to others, supports the practice of voluntary euthanasia and, in fact, any form of rational, voluntary suicide. We already recognize a patient's right to refuse any or all medical treatment and hence correlative duties of noninterference on the part of the physician to refrain from treating the patient against his or her will. But does the patient's right of self-determination also give rise to any positive obligation on the part of the physician or other bystander to actively produce death? . . . Although we usually recognize only that the principle of autonomy generates rights to noninterference, in some circumstances a right of self-determination does generate claims to assistance or to the provision of goods. . . .

Some singularly sympathetic cases—like that of the completely paralyzed cerebral palsy victim Elizabeth Bouvier—have brought this issue to public attention. But notice that in euthanasia situations, most persons are handicapped with respect to producing for themselves an easy, "good," merciful death. The handicaps are occasionally physical, but most often involve lack of knowledge of how to bring this about and lack of access to means for so doing. . . . Full autonomy is not achieved until one can both choose and act upon one's choices. It is here, in these cases of "handicap" that afflict many or most patients, that rights to self-determination may generate obligations on the part of physicians (provided, perhaps, that they do not have principled objections to participation in such activities themselves). The physician's obligation is not only to respect the patient's choices but also to make it possible for the patient to act upon his or her choices. This means supplying the knowledge and equipment to enable the person to stay alive, if he or she so chooses; this is an obligation physicians now recognize. But it may also mean providing the knowledge, equipment, and help to enable the patient to die, if that is his or her choice; this is the other part of the physician's obligation, not yet recognized by the medical profession or the law in the United States.

This is not to say that any doctor should be forced to kill any person who asks that: other contravening considerations—particularly that of ascertaining that the request is autonomous and not the product of coerced or irrational choice, and that of controlling abuses by unscrupulous physicians, relatives, or patients—would quickly override. Nor would the physician have an obligation to assist in "euthanasia" for someone not severely ill. But when the physician is sufficiently familiar with the patient to know the seriousness of the condition and the earnestness of the patient's request, when the patient is sufficiently helpless, and when there are no adequate objections on grounds of personal scruples or social welfare, then the principle of autonomy—like the principle of mercy— imposes on the physician the obligation to help the patient in achieving an easy, painless death.

THE CASE FOR EUTHANASIA, PART III: JUSTICE

Although the term "euthanasia" traditionally was employed in cases in which "good death" meant the avoidance of suffering, in recent years use of the term has been extended to cover cases in which the patient is neither suffering nor capable of choosing to die. . . .

This argument from justice is usually employed only to justify the denial of treatment, that is, to justify passive euthanasia; but similar considerations also favor active euthanasia. Passive euthanasia is often practiced upon unsalvageable patients by withholding treatment if a medical crisis occurs: for instance, no-code orders are issued, or pneumonias are not treated, or electrolyte imbalances not corrected if they occur. If justice demands that, despite the prima facie claims of these patients, the resources allocated to their care are better assigned somewhere else, then we must notice that *passive* euthanasia does not provide the most just redistribution of these resources. To "allow" the patient to die may still involve enormous expenditures of money, scarce supplies, or caregiver time.

This is most evident in cases of "irretrievably inaccessible" patients, for whom no considerations of mercy or autonomy override the demands of justice in weighing claims. . . . The total cost of maintaining a permanently comatose woman, who was injured in a riding accident in 1956 at age twenty-seven and died eighteen years later, has been estimated at just over $6,000,000; this care provided her with not a single moment of conscious life.[3] The record survival for a coma patient is thirty-seven years and 111 days.[4] The argument from justice demands that these patients, since their claims for care are so weak as to have virtually no force at all, be killed, not simply allowed to die.

OBJECTION TO THE ARGUMENT FROM JUSTICE: THE SLIPPERY SLOPE

But if justice, under the distributive principle employed here, licenses the killing of permanently comatose patients, will it not also license the killing of still-conscious, still-competent dying patients, perhaps still salvageable, close or not so close to death? What extensions of the scope of this principle might be made, should resources become still more scarce? These concerns introduce the "wedge" or "slippery slope" argument, which holds that although some acts of euthanasia may be morally permissible (say, on grounds of mercy or autonomy), to allow them to occur will set a logical precedent for, or will causally result in, consequences that are morally repugnant. Just as Hitler's 1938 "euthanasia" program for mentally defective, senile, and terminally ill Aryans paved the way for the establishment of the extermination camps several years later, it is argued, so permissive euthanasia policies invite irreversible descent down that slippery slope that leads to mass murder. . . .

As it is usually posed, the form of the argument that points to the Nazi experience does not succeed: the forces that brought the mass extermination camps into being were not *caused* by the earlier euthanasia program, and, other things being equal, the extermination camps for Jews would

no doubt have been established had there been no euthanasia program at all. To argue that permitting euthanasia now will lead to death camps like Hitler's is to overlook the many other political, social, and psychological factors of the Nazi period. Yet the wedge argument cannot be simply discarded; the factors operating to favor the slide from morally warranted euthanasia to murder are probably much stronger than we realize. They are best seen, I think, as misunderstandings or corruptions of the very principles that favor euthanasia: mercy, autonomy, and perhaps most prominently, justice.

A contemporary version of the wedge argument holds that to permit euthanasia at all—including cases justified on grounds of mercy, autonomy, or justice—will in the presence of strong financial incentives lead to circumstances in which people are killed who are not suffering or who do not wish to die. Furthermore, to permit some doctors to allow their patients to die or to kill them would invite cavalier attitudes concerning the lives of the patients and, in addition to financial incentives, ordinary greed, insensitivity, hastiness, and self-interest, would cause some doctors to let their patients die—or kill them—when there was no moral warrant for doing so. Doctors treating difficult or unresponding patients would find an easy way out. Medical blunders could be more easily covered up, and doctors might use euthanasia as a way of avoiding criticism in cases that were medically difficult to treat. Particularly important, perhaps, are societal and political pressures, most evident in cost-containment policies, to which doctors might respond. After all, to permit earlier, less expensive death would ease the enormous pressures on third-party insurers, public welfare, and the Social Security system: euthanasia is less expensive than continuing medical care. . . .

Is there any reason to think such practices would actually occur? The reasons are closer to hand than one might imagine. Rather than predicting the future, we need simply look to our present practices for evidence that violations of the moral limits to euthanasia can occur. . . .

The wedge argument assumes, without adequate justification, that the rights of those who may become the victims of abuses of a practice outweigh the rights of those who become victims if a practice is prohibited to whose benefits they are morally entitled and urgently need.

To protect those who might wrongly be killed or allowed to die might seem a stronger obligation than to satisfy the wishes of those who desire release from pain, analogous perhaps to the principle in law that "better ten guilty men go free than one be unjustly convicted." . . . But to require the person who chooses to die to stay alive in order to protect those who might unwillingly be killed sometime in the future is to impose an extreme harm—intolerable suffering—on that person, which he or she must bear for the sake of others. Furthermore, since, as we've seen, the question of which is worse, suffering or death, is person-relative, we have no independent, objective basis for protecting the class of persons who might be killed at the expense of those who would suffer intolerable pain; perhaps our protecting ought to be done the other way around. . . .

CONCLUSION: EUTHANASIA AND SUICIDE

It may be objected that requiring the patient to choose between death and life, insofar as the patient must antecedently consider treatment decisions that affect the circumstances and timing of his or her own demise, is equivalent to requiring the patient's consideration of suicide. In a sense, it is; but this is also the more general solution to the euthanasia problem. Although euthanasia is indeed warranted on grounds of mercy, autonomy, and justice, these principles can be more effectively and safely honored by permitting suicide, perhaps assisted by the physician who has care of the patient or a family member under the advice of the physicians, and supplemented by nonvoluntary euthanasia *only* when the patient is permanently comatose or otherwise irretrievably inaccessible. Not only do practical reasons like avoiding greed and manipulation on the part of the physicians or the institutions controlling them speak for preferring physician-assisted suicide to physician-initiated euthanasia, but there are conceptual reasons as well. The conditions that distinguish morally permissible euthanasia from impermissable murder all involve matters that the patient, not the physician, is in a privileged position to know. To extend mercy, the physician must know how the patient weights suffering against death, and at what point *for the patient* death becomes the lesser of two evils. To respect the patient's autonomy, the physician must know what his or her preferences are, given the alternatives available, in the matter of dying. And to exercise justice, the physician must know what treatment the patient realistically desires. . . . Consequently, since the risk of misinterpretation is great and the possibility of manipulation or coercion high, the physician should not be the one to *initiate* the choice. Rather, he or she must be prepared to assist the patient who chooses death, just as he or she is prepared to assist the patient who chooses continuing life. . . .

NOTES

1. Edmund D. Pellegrino, M.D., "The Clinical Ethics of Pain Management in the Terminally Ill," *Hospital Formulary* 17 (November 1982): 1495–1496; and Marcia Angell, "The Quality of Mercy," *New England Journal of Medicine* 306 (January 1982): 98–99.
2. Philippa Foot, "Euthanasia," *Philosophy & Public Affairs* 6 (Winter 1977): 95.
3. This case, originally presented in the *Illinois Medical Journal* and reprinted in *Connecticut Medicine* with commentary from medical, ethical, and legal experts, is summarized in *Concern for Dying* 8 (Summer 1982): 3.
4. President's Commission for the Study of Ethical Problems in Medicine and Biomedical and Behavioral Research, *Defining Death: Medical, Legal, and Ethical Issues in the Determination of Death* (Washington, D.C.: Government Printing Office, 1981), 18, citing the *Guiness Book of World Records* regarding the case of Elaine Esposito.

Discussion Questions

1. Dr. Jack Kevorkian claimed that his mission was one of mercy. He also maintained that by allowing patients to administer the lethal injections themselves, he was respecting their autonomy. Discuss whether Battin would approve of Kevorkian's "mercy killings."

2. In a note in her article, Battin asks us to try the following thought experiment. Discuss the questions at the end of the experiment.

   Imagine that you have been captured by a gang of ruthless and superlatively clever criminals, whom you know with certainty will never be caught or change their minds. They plan either to execute you now or to torture you unremittingly for the next twenty years and then put you to death. Which would be worse? Does your view change if the length of the torture period is reduced to twenty days or twenty minutes, and, if so, why? How severe must the torture be?

3. Is Battin's claim that life has worth only if it is a benefit and contains "a minimum of basic goods" consistent with the deontological principle that rational beings have intrinsic worth? Discuss which interpretation of the value of rational human life, Battin's or Kant's, you find more compelling.

4. David Lewis, an AIDS counselor in Vancouver, British Columbia, helped eight friends with AIDS take lethal doses of drugs that had been prescribed earlier by a doctor. The men had begged to die; none of them wanted to suffer anymore, he told a reporter. "To refuse to help them would be criminal."[22] Did Lewis make the morally right decision? Support your answer using the principles of mercy and autonomy as well as Battin's concept of limited paternalism.

5. Discuss Battin's claim that distributive justice supports involuntary active euthanasia in cases in which costly medical resources are needed to sustain life. Relate your answer to the Terri Schiavo case.

J. GAY-WILLIAMS

The Wrongfulness of Euthanasia

J. Gay-Williams opposes euthanasia. Euthanasia, Gay-Williams argues, violates our natural inclination to continue living and precludes the possibility of a "miraculous" recovery or that a new cure may be found. In addition, euthanasia violates the medical professional's commitment to save lives.

"The Wrongfulness of Euthanasia," from Ronald Munson, *Intervention and Reflection: Basic Issues in Medical Ethics*, 6th ed. (Belmont, CA: Wadsworth, 1996), pp. 156–159. Note: J. Gay-Williams is a pseudonym. The author wishes that no personal information be released.

Critical Reading Questions

1. On what grounds does Gay-Williams reject the argument that compassion for people who are dying supports euthanasia?
2. Why does Gay-Williams claim that "passive euthanasia" is not euthanasia at all?
3. What is the argument from nature, and why does it rule out euthanasia as a moral option?
4. Why, according to Gay-Williams, is euthanasia a violation of human dignity?
5. What is the argument from self-interest and why, according to Gay-Williams, does euthanasia work against our self-interest?
6. In what ways would allowing euthanasia contribute to a decline in the quality of medical care?
7. What does Gay-Williams mean by "euthanasia as a policy is a slippery slope"?

My impression is that euthanasia—the idea, if not the practice—is slowly gaining acceptance within our society. Cynics might attribute this to an increasing tendency to devalue human life, but I do not believe this is the major factor. The acceptance is much more likely to be the result of unthinking sympathy and benevolence. Well-publicized, tragic stories like that of Karen Quinlan elicit from us deep feelings of compassion. We think to ourselves, "She and her family would be better off if she were dead." It is an easy step from this very human response to the view that if someone (and others) would be better off dead, then it might be all right to kill that person. Although I respect the compassion that leads to this conclusion, I believe the conclusion is wrong. I want to show that euthanasia is wrong. It is inherently wrong, but it is also wrong judged from the standpoints of self-interest and of practical effects.

Before presenting my arguments to support this claim, it would be well to define "euthanasia." An essential aspect of euthanasia is that it involves taking a human life, either one's own or that of another. Also, the person whose life is taken must be someone who is believed to be suffering from some disease or injury from which recovery cannot reasonably be expected. Finally, the action must be deliberate and intentional. Thus, euthanasia is intentionally taking the life of a presumably hopeless person. Whether the life is one's own or that of another, the taking of it is still euthanasia.

It is important to be clear about the deliberate and intentional aspect of the killing. If a hopeless person is given an injection of the wrong drug by mistake and this causes his death, this is wrongful killing but not euthanasia. The killing cannot be the result of accident. Furthermore, if the person is given an injection of a drug that is believed to be necessary to treat his disease or better his condition and the person dies as a result, then this is neither wrongful killing nor euthanasia. The intention was to make the patient well, not kill him. Similarly, when a patient's condition is such that it is not reasonable to hope that any medical procedures or treatments will save his life, a failure to implement the procedures or treatments is not euthanasia. If the person dies, this will be as a result of his injuries or disease and not because of his failure to receive treatment.

The failure to continue treatment after it has been realized that the patient has little chance of benefiting from it has been characterized by some as "passive euthanasia." This phrase is misleading and mistaken. In such cases, the person involved is not killed (the first essential aspect of euthanasia), nor is the death of the person intended by the withholding of additional treatment (the third essential aspect of euthanasia). The aim may be to spare the person additional and unjustifiable pain, to save him from the indignities of hopeless manipulations, and to avoid increasing the financial and emotional burden on his family.

When I buy a pencil it is so that I can use it to write, not to contribute to an increase in the gross national product. This may be the unintended consequence of my action, but it is not the aim of my action. So it is with failing to continue the treatment of a dying person. I intend his death no more than I intend to reduce the GNP by not using medical supplies. His is an unintended dying, and so-called "passive euthanasia" is not euthanasia at all.

1. THE ARGUMENT FROM NATURE

Every human being has a natural inclination to continue living. Our reflexes and responses fit us to fight attackers, flee wild animals, and dodge out of the way of trucks. In our daily lives we exercise the caution and care necessary to protect ourselves. Our bodies are similarly structured for survival right down to the molecular level. When we are cut, our capillaries seal shut, our blood clots, and fibrogen is produced to start the process of healing the wound. When we are invaded by bacteria, antibodies are produced to fight against the alien organisms, and their remains are swept out of the body by special cells designed for clean-up work.

Euthanasia does violence to this natural goal of survival. It is literally acting against nature because all the processes of nature are bent towards the end of bodily survival. Euthanasia defeats these subtle mechanisms in a way that, in a particular case, disease and injury might not.

It is possible, but not necessary, to make an appeal to revealed religion in this connection. Man as trustee of his body acts against God, its rightful possessor, when he takes his own life. He also violates the commandment to hold life sacred and never to take it without just and compelling cause. But since this appeal will persuade only those who are prepared to accept that religion has access to revealed truths, I shall not employ this line of argument.

It is enough, I believe, to recognize that the organization of the human body and our patterns of behavioral responses make the continuation of life a natural goal. By reason alone, then, we can recognize that euthanasia sets us against our own nature. Furthermore, in doing so, euthanasia does violence to our dignity. Our dignity comes from seeking our ends. When one of our goals is survival, and actions are taken that eliminate that goal, then our natural dignity suffers. Unlike animals, we are conscious through reason of our nature and our ends. Euthanasia involves acting as if this dual nature—inclination towards survival and awareness of this as an end—did not exist. Thus, euthanasia denies our basic human character and requires that we regard ourselves or others as something less than fully human.

2. THE ARGUMENT FROM SELF-INTEREST

The above arguments are, I believe, sufficient to show that euthanasia is inherently wrong. But there are reasons for considering it wrong when judged by standards other than reason. Because death is final and irreversible, euthanasia contains within it the possibility that we will work against our own interest if we practice it or allow it to be practiced on us. Contemporary medicine has high standards of excellence and a proven record of accomplishment, but it does not possess perfect and complete knowledge. A mistaken diagnosis is possible, and so is a mistaken prognosis. Consequently, we may believe that we are dying of a disease when, as a matter of fact, we may not be. We may think that we have no hope of recovery when, as a matter of fact, our chances are quite good. In such circumstances, if euthanasia were permitted, we would die needlessly. Death is final and the chance of error too great to approve the practice of euthanasia.

Also, there is always the possibility that an experimental procedure or a hitherto untried technique will pull us through. We should at least keep this option open, but euthanasia closes it off. Furthermore, spontaneous remission does occur in many cases. For no apparent reason, a patient simply recovers when those all around him, including his physicians, expected him to die. Euthanasia would just guarantee their expectations and leave no room for the "miraculous" recoveries that frequently occur.

Finally, knowing that we can take our life at any time (or ask another to take it) might well incline us to give up too easily. The will to live is strong in all of us, but it can be weakened by pain and suffering and feelings of hopelessness. If during a bad time we allow ourselves to be killed, we never have a chance to reconsider. Recovery from a serious illness requires that we fight for it, and anything that weakens our determination by suggesting that there is an easy way out is ultimately against our own interest. Also, we may be inclined towards euthanasia because of our concern for others. If we see our sickness and suffering as an emotional and financial burden on our family, we may feel that to leave our life is to make their lives easier. The very presence of the possibility of euthanasia may keep us from surviving when we might.

3. THE ARGUMENT FROM PRACTICAL EFFECTS

Doctors and nurses are, for the most part, totally committed to saving lives. A life lost is, for them, almost a personal failure, an insult to their skills and knowledge. Euthanasia as a practice might well alter this. It could have a corrupting influence so that in any case that is severe doctors and nurses might not try hard enough to save the patient. They might decide that the patient would simply be "better off dead" and take the steps necessary to make that come about. This attitude could then carry over to their dealings with patients less seriously ill. The result would be an overall decline in the quality of medical care.

Finally, euthanasia as a policy is a slippery slope. A person apparently hopelessly ill may be allowed to take his own life. Then he may be permitted to deputize others to do it for him should he no longer be able to act. The judgment of others then becomes the ruling factor. Already at this point euthanasia is not personal and voluntary, for others are acting "on behalf of" the patient as they see fit. This may well incline them to act on behalf of other patients who have not authorized them to exercise their judgment. It is only a short step, then, from voluntary euthanasia (self-inflicted or authorized), to directed euthanasia administered to a patient who has given no authorization, to involuntary euthanasia conducted as part of a social policy. Recently many psychiatrists and sociologists have argued that we define as "mental illness" those forms of behavior that we disapprove of. This gives us license then to lock up those who display the behavior. The category of the "hopelessly ill" provides the possibility of even worse abuse. Embedded in a social policy, it would give society or its representatives the authority to eliminate all those who might be considered too "ill" to function normally any longer. The dangers of euthanasia are too great to all to run the risk of approving it in any form. The first slippery step may well lead to a serious and harmful fall.

I hope that I have succeeded in showing why the benevolence that inclines us to give approval of euthanasia is misplaced. Euthanasia is inherently wrong because it violates the nature and dignity of human beings. But even those who are not convinced by this must be persuaded that the potential personal and social dangers inherent in euthanasia are sufficient to forbid our approving it either as a personal practice or as a public policy.

Suffering is surely a terrible thing, and we have a clear duty to comfort those in need and to ease their suffering when we can. But suffering is also a natural part of life with values for the individual and for others that we should not overlook. We may legitimately seek for others and for ourselves an easeful death, as Arthur Dyck has pointed out. Euthanasia, however, is not just an easeful death. It is a wrongful death. Euthanasia is not just dying. It is killing.

Discussion Questions

1. Evaluate Gay-Williams's argument that humans' natural goal is survival. What about cases in which the patient is in a persistent vegetative state and, presumably, no longer has conscious goals? Support your answers.
2. Battin argues that the duty of beneficence (mercy) supports euthanasia. Discuss how Gay-Williams might respond to Battin. Who makes the stronger argument?
3. One of the arguments Gay-Williams uses against legalizing voluntary euthanasia is that it will lead us down the slippery slope to involuntary euthanasia. Discuss how Gay-Williams might respond to Battin's argument that the slippery slope argument does not provide sufficient justification to warrant making euthanasia illegal. Working in small groups, write a bill that might overcome the slippery slope problem. Share and critically analyze your proposed legislation with others in the class.
4. Would the use of machines, such as Kevorkian's Mercitron—a device that allowed patients to self-administer a lethal injection—overcome Gay-Williams's objection to euthanasia? Support your answer.

JOHN HARDWIG

Is There a Duty to Die?

John Hardwig is a professor of philosophy and medical ethics at East Tennessee State University. Hardwig rejects the current emphasis on patient autonomy as the critical issue in euthanasia. Because of modern technology, more and more elderly people are saved from acute illness only to eventually die lingering and costly deaths from chronic illnesses. Hardwig argues that when this happens and we become a burden on our family and loved ones, we may have a duty to die.

Critical Reading Questions

1. Why does Hardwig claim that most of us probably do believe in the existence of a duty to die? What examples does he use to support his claim?
2. What are some of the developments in modern medicine that have made the duty to die an important issue?
3. According to Hardwig, what "American fantasy" has led bioethics to see euthanasia as a private decision?
4. How does Hardwig answer the question, Whose life is it, anyway?

"Is There a Duty to Die?" *Hastings Center Report* 27, no. 2 (1997): 34–42. Notes have been omitted.

5. What are some of the burdens imposed on loved ones who have to care for an old, ailing family member? What obligations, if any, do these families have toward their old and ailing members?
6. What, according to Hardwig, are some of the most serious objections to the idea that there is a duty to die? How does he respond to these objections?
7. What are some of the guidelines Hardwig gives for deciding if someone has a duty to die? Who should make the decision about when a person has a duty to die?
8. According to Hardwig, how does a duty to die affirm rather than compromise our moral agency and human dignity?
9. Why does our fear of death, according to Hardwig, prevent us from finding meaning in death?

When Richard Lamm made the statement that old people have a duty to die, it was generally shouted down or ridiculed. The whole idea is just too preposterous to entertain. Or too threatening. In fact, a fairly common argument against legalizing physician-assisted suicide is that if it were legal, some people might somehow get the idea that they have a duty to die. These people could only be the victims of twisted moral reasoning or vicious social pressure. It goes without saying that there is no duty to die.

But for me the question is real and very important. I feel strongly that I may very well some day have a duty to die. I do not believe that I am idiosyncratic, morbid, mentally ill, or morally perverse in thinking this. I think many of us will eventually face precisely this duty. But I am first of all concerned with my own duty. . . .

CIRCUMSTANCES AND A DUTY TO DIE

Do many of us really believe that no one ever has a duty to die? I suspect not. I think most of us probably believe that there is such a duty, but it is very uncommon. Consider Captain Oates, a member of Admiral Scott's expedition to the South Pole. Oates became too ill to continue. If the rest of the team stayed with him, they would all perish. After this had become clear, Oates left his tent one night, walked out into a raging blizzard, and was never seen again. That may have been a heroic thing to do, but we might be able to agree that it was also no more than his duty. It would have been wrong for him to urge—or even to allow—the rest to stay and care for him.

This is a very unusual circumstance—a "lifeboat case"—and lifeboat cases make for bad ethics. But I expect that most of us would also agree that there have been cultures in which what we would call a duty to die has been fairly common. These are relatively poor, technologically simple, and especially nomadic cultures. In such societies, everyone knows that if you manage to live long enough, you will eventually become old and debilitated. Then you will need to take steps to end your life. The old people in these societies regularly did precisely that. Their cultures prepared and supported them in doing so.

Those cultures could be dismissed as irrelevant to contemporary bioethics; their circumstances are so different from ours. But if that is our response, it is instructive. It suggests that we assume a duty to die is irrelevant to us because our wealth and technological sophistication have purchased exemption for us . . . except under very unusual circumstances like Captain Oates's.

But have wealth and technology really exempted us? Or are they, on the contrary, about to make a duty to die common again? We like to think of modern medicine as all triumph with no dark side. Our medicine saves many lives and enables us to live longer. That is wonderful, indeed. We are all glad to have access to this medicine. But our medicine also delivers most of us over to chronic illnesses and it enables many of us to survive longer than we can take care of ourselves, longer than we know what to do with ourselves, longer than we even are ourselves.

The costs—and these are not merely monetary—of prolonging our lives when we are no longer able to care for ourselves are often staggering. If further medical advances wipe out many of today's "killer diseases"—cancer, heart attacks, strokes, ALS, AIDS, and the rest—then one day most of us will survive long enough to become demented or debilitated. These developments could generate a fairly widespread duty to die. . . .

Let me be clear. I certainly believe that there is a duty to refuse life-prolonging medical treatment and also a duty to complete advance directives refusing life-prolonging treatment. But a duty to die can go well beyond that. There can be a duty to die before one's illnesses would cause death, even if treated only with palliative measures. In fact, there may be a fairly common responsibility to end one's life in the absence of any terminal illness at all. Finally, there can be a duty to die when one would prefer to live. . . .

THE INDIVIDUALISTIC FANTASY

Because a duty to die seems such a real possibility to me, I wonder why contemporary bioethics has dismissed it without serious consideration. I believe that most bioethics still shares in one of our deeply embedded American dreams: the individualistic fantasy. This fantasy leads us to imagine that lives are separate and unconnected, or that they could be so if we chose. . . .

Within a health care context, the individualistic fantasy leads us to assume that the patient is the only one affected by decisions about her medical treatment. If only the patient were affected, the relevant questions when making treatment decisions would be precisely those we ask: What will benefit the patient? Who can best decide that? The pivotal issue would always be simply whether the patient wants to live like this and whether she would consider herself better off dead. "Whose life is it, anyway?" we ask rhetorically.

But this is morally obtuse. We are not a race of hermits. Illness and death do not come only to those who are all alone. Nor is it much better to think in terms of the bald dichotomy between "the interests of the patient" and "the interests of society" (or a third-party payer), as if we were isolated individuals connected only to "society" in the abstract or to the other, faceless members of our health maintenance organization.

Most of us are affiliated with particular others and most deeply, with family and loved ones. Families and loved ones are bound together by ties of care and affection, by legal relations and obligations, by inhabiting shared spaces and living units, by interlocking finances and economic prospects, by common projects and also commitments to support the different life projects of other family members, by shared histories, by ties of loyalty. This life together of family and loved ones is what defines and sustains us; it is what gives meaning to most of our lives. We would not have it any other way. We would not want to be all alone, especially when we are seriously ill, as we age, and when we are dying.

But the fact of deeply interwoven lives debars us from making exclusively self-regarding decisions, as the decisions of one member of a family may dramatically affect the lives of all the rest. The impact of my decisions upon my family and loved ones is the source of many of my strongest obligations and also the most plausible and likeliest basis of a duty to die. "Society," after all, is only very marginally affected by how I live, or by whether I live or die.

A BURDEN TO MY LOVED ONES

Many older people report that their one remaining goal in life is not to be a burden to their loved ones. Young people feel this, too: when I ask my undergraduate students to think about whether their death could come too late, one of their very first responses always is, "Yes, when I become a burden to my family or loved ones." Tragically, there are situations in which my loved ones would be much better off—all things considered, the loss of a loved one notwithstanding—if I were dead.

The lives of our loved ones can be seriously compromised by caring for us. The burdens of providing care or even just supervision twenty-four hours a day, seven days a week are often overwhelming. When this kind of caregiving goes on for years, it leaves the caregiver exhausted, with no time for herself or life of her own. . . .

I am not advocating a crass, quasi-economic conception of burdens and benefits, nor a shallow, hedonistic view of life. Given a suitably rich understanding of benefits, family members sometimes do benefit from suffering through the long illness of a loved one. Caring for the sick or aged can foster growth, even as it makes daily life immeasurably harder and the prospects for the future much bleaker. Chronic illness or drawn-out death can also pull a family together, making the care for each other stronger and more evident. If my loved ones are truly benefiting from coping with my illness or debility, I have no duty to die based on burdens to them.

But it would be irresponsible to blithely assume that this always happens, that it will happen in my family, or that it will be the fault of my family if they cannot manage to turn my illness into a positive experience. Perhaps the opposite is more common: . . .

Our families and loved ones also have obligations, of course—they have the responsibility to stand by us and to support us through debilitating illness and death. They must be prepared to make significant sacrifices to respond to an illness in the family. I am far from denying that. Most of us are aware of this responsibility and most families meet it rather well. . . .

OBJECTIONS TO A DUTY TO DIE

To my mind, the most serious objections to the idea of a duty to die lie in the effects on my loved ones of ending my life. But to most others, the important objections have little or nothing to do with family and loved ones. Perhaps the most common objections are: (1) there is a higher duty that always takes precedence over a duty to die; (2) a duty to end one's own life would be incompatible with a recognition of human dignity or the intrinsic value of a person; and (3) seriously ill, debilitated, or dying people are already bearing the harshest burdens and so it would be wrong to ask them to bear the additional burden of ending their own lives. . . .

An example of the first line of argument would be the claim that a duty to God, the giver of life, forbids that anyone take her own life. It could be argued that this duty always supersedes whatever obligations we might have to our families. But what convinces us that we always have such a religious duty in the first place? And what guarantees that it always supersedes our obligations to try to protect our loved ones? . . .

Secondly, religious considerations aside, the claim could be made that an obligation to end one's own life would be incompatible with human dignity or would embody a failure to recognize the intrinsic value of a person. But I do not see that in thinking I had a duty to die I would necessarily be failing to respect myself or to appreciate my dignity or worth. Nor would I necessarily be failing to respect you in thinking that you had a similar duty. There is surely also a sense in which we fail to respect ourselves if in the face of illness or death, we stoop to choosing just what is best for ourselves. Indeed, Kant held that the very core of human dignity is the ability to act on a self-imposed moral law, regardless of whether it is in our interest to do so. We shall return to the notion of human dignity.

A third objection appeals to the relative weight of burdens and thus, ultimately, to considerations of fairness or justice. The burdens that an illness creates for the family could not possibly be great enough to justify an obligation to end one's life— the sacrifice of life itself would be a far greater burden than any involved in caring for a chronically ill family member.

But is this true? Consider the following case:

An 87-year-old woman was dying of congestive heart failure. Her APACHE score predicted that she had less than a 50 percent chance to live for another six months. She was lucid, assertive, and terrified of death. She very much wanted to live and kept opting for rehospitalization and the most aggressive life-prolonging treatment possible. That treatment successfully prolonged her life (though with increasing debility) for nearly two years. Her 55-year-old daughter was her only remaining family, her caregiver, and the main source of her financial support. The daughter duly cared for her mother. But before her mother died, her illness had cost the daughter all of her savings, her home, her job, and her career.

This is by no means an uncommon sort of case. Thousands of similar cases occur each year. Now, ask yourself which is the greater burden:

a) To lose a 50 percent chance of six more months of life at age 87?

b) To lose all your savings, your home, and your career at age 55?

Which burden would you prefer to bear? Do we really believe the former is the greater burden? . . .

I think most of us would quickly agree that (b) is a greater burden. That is the evil we would more hope to avoid in our lives. . . .

This point does not depend on a utilitarian calculus. Even if death were the greatest burden (thus disposing of any simple utilitarian argument), serious questions would remain about the moral justifiability of choosing to impose crushing burdens on loved ones in order to avoid having to bear this burden oneself. . . .

WHO HAS A DUTY TO DIE?

Suppose, then, that there can be a duty to die. Who has a duty to die? And when? To my mind, these are the right questions, the questions we should be asking. Many of us may one day badly need answers to just these questions. . . .

Some may object that it would be wrong to put a loved one in a position of having to say, in effect,

"You should end your life because caring for you is too hard on me and the rest of the family." Not only will it be almost impossible to say something like that to someone you love, it will carry with it a heavy load of guilt. On this view, you should decide by yourself whether you have a duty to die and approach your loved ones only after you have made up your mind to say good-bye to them. Your family could then try to change your mind, but the tremendous weight of moral decision would be lifted from their shoulders.

Perhaps so. But I believe in family decisions. Important decisions for those whose lives are interwoven should be made together, in a family discussion. Granted, a conversation about whether I have a duty to die would be a tremendously difficult conversation. The temptations to be dishonest could be enormous. Nevertheless, if I am contemplating a duty to die, my family and I should, if possible, have just such an agonizing discussion. It will act as a check on the information, perceptions, and reasoning of all of us. But even more importantly, it affirms our connectedness at a critical juncture in our lives and our life together. Honest talk about difficult matters almost always strengthens relationships. . . .

I cannot say when someone has a duty to die. Still, I can suggest a few features of one's illness, history, and circumstances that make it more likely that one has a duty to die. I present them here without much elaboration or explanation.

1. A duty to die is more likely when continuing to live will impose significant burdens—emotional burdens, extensive caregiving, destruction of life plans, and, yes, financial hardship—on your family and loved ones. . . .

2. A duty to die becomes greater as you grow older. As we age, we will be giving up less by giving up our lives, if only because we will sacrifice fewer remaining years of life and a smaller portion of our life plans. . . .

3. A duty to die is more likely when you have already lived a full and rich life. You have already had a full share of the good things life offers.

4. There is greater duty to die if your loved ones' lives have already been difficult or impoverished, if they have had only a small share of the good things that life has to offer (especially if through no fault of their own).

5. A duty to die is more likely when your loved ones have already made great contributions—perhaps even sacrifices—to make your life a good one. Especially if you have not made similar sacrifices for their well-being or for the well-being of other members of your family.

6. To the extent that you can make a good adjustment to your illness or handicapping condition, there is less likely to be a duty to die. A good adjustment means that smaller sacrifices will be required of loved ones and there is more compensating interaction for them. . . .

7. There is less likely to be a duty to die if you can still make significant contributions to the lives of others, especially your family. . . .

8. A duty to die is more likely when the part of you that is loved will soon be gone or seriously compromised. Or when you soon will no longer be capable of giving love. Part of the horror of dementing disease is that it destroys the capacity to nurture and sustain relationships, taking away a person's agency and the emotions that bind her to others.

9. There is a greater duty to die to the extent that you have lived a relatively lavish lifestyle instead of saving for illness or old age. . . . It is a greater wrong to come to your family for assistance if your need is the result of having chosen leisure or a spendthrift lifestyle. . . .

CAN THE INCOMPETENT HAVE A DUTY TO DIE?

. . . I am tempted to simply bypass the entire question by saying that I am talking only about competent persons. But the idea of a duty to die clearly raises the specter of one person claiming that another—who cannot speak for herself—has such a duty. So I need to say that I can make no sense of the claim that someone has a duty to die if the person has never been able to understand moral obligation at all. To my mind, only those who were formerly capable of making moral decisions could have such a duty.

But the case of formerly competent persons is almost as troubling. Perhaps we should simply stipulate that no incompetent person can have a duty to die, not even if she affirmed belief in such a duty in an advance directive. . . .

But for me personally, very urgent practical matters turn on their resolution. If a formerly competent person can no longer have a duty to die (or if other people are not likely to help her carry out this duty), I believe that my obligation may be to die while I am still competent, before I become unable to make and carry out that decision for myself. Surely it would be irresponsible to evade my moral duties by temporizing until I escape into incompetence. And so I must die sooner than I otherwise would have to. On the other hand, if I could count on others to end my life after I become incompetent, I might be able to fulfill my responsibilities while also living out all my competent or semi-competent days. Given our society's reluctance to permit physicians, let alone family members, to perform aid-in-dying, I believe I may well have a duty to end my life when I can see mental incapacity on the horizon.

There is also the very real problem of sudden incompetence—due to a serious stroke or automobile accident, for example. For me, that is the real nightmare. If I suddenly become incompetent, I will fall into the hands of a medical-legal system that will conscientiously disregard my moral beliefs and do what is best for me, regardless of the consequences for my loved ones. And that is not at all what I would have wanted!

SOCIAL POLICIES AND A DUTY TO DIE

The claim that there is a duty to die will seem to some a misplaced response to social negligence. If our society were providing for the debilitated, the chronically ill, and the elderly as it should be, there would be only very rare cases of a duty to die. . . .

I cannot claim to know whether in some abstract sense a society like ours should provide care for all who are chronically ill or debilitated. But the fact is that we Americans seem to be unwilling to pay for this kind of long-term care, except for ourselves and our own. In fact, we are moving in precisely the opposite direction—we are trying to shift the burdens of caring for the seriously and chronically ill onto families in order to save costs for our health care system. As we shift the burdens of care onto families, we also dramatically increase the number of Americans who will have a duty to die.

I must not, then, live my life and make my plans on the assumption that social institutions will protect my family from my infirmity and debility. To do so would be irresponsible. More likely, it will be up to me to protect my loved ones.

A DUTY TO DIE AND THE MEANING OF LIFE

A duty to die seems very harsh, and often it would be. It is one of the tragedies of our lives that someone who wants very much to live can nevertheless have a duty to die. It is both tragic and ironic that it is precisely the very real good of family and loved ones that gives rise to this duty. Indeed, the genuine love, closeness and supportiveness of family members is a major source of this duty: we could not be such a burden if they did not care for us. Finally, there is deep irony in the fact that the very successes of our life-prolonging medicine help to create a widespread duty to die. . . .

We do not even ask about meaning in death, so busy are we with trying to postpone it. But we will not conquer death by one day developing a technology so magnificent that no one will have to die. Nor can we conquer death by postponing it ever longer. We can conquer death only by finding meaning in it.

Although the existence of a duty to die does not hinge on this, recognizing such a duty would go some way toward recovering meaning in death. . . .

First, recognizing a duty to die affirms my agency and also my moral agency. I can still do things that make an important difference in the lives of my loved ones. Moreover, the fact that I still have responsibilities keeps me within the community of moral agents. My illness or debility has not reduced me to a mere moral patient (to use the language of the philosophers). . . .

To treat me as if I had no moral responsibilities when I am ill or debilitated implies that my condition has rendered me morally incompetent. Only small children, the demented or insane, and those totally lacking in the capacity to act are free from moral duties. There is dignity, then, and a kind of meaning in moral agency, even as it forces extremely difficult decisions upon us.

Second, recovering meaning in death requires an affirmation of connections. If I end my life to spare the futures of my loved ones, I testify in my death that I am connected to them. It is because I love and care for precisely these people (and I know they care for me) that I wish not to be such a burden to them. By contrast, a life in which I am free to choose whatever I want for myself is a life unconnected to others. . . .

This need not be connections with other people. Some people are deeply tied to land (for example, the family farm), to nature, or to a transcendent reality. But for most of us, the connections that sustain us are to other people. . . .

I don't know about others, but these reflections have helped me. I am now more at peace about facing a duty to die. Ending my life if my duty required might still be difficult. But for me, a far greater horror would be dying all alone or stealing the futures of my loved ones in order to buy a little more time for myself. I hope that if the time comes when I have a duty to die, I will recognize it, encourage my loved ones to recognize it too, and carry it out bravely.

Discussion Questions

1. Discuss how Aristotle would reply to Hardwig's argument that there is a duty to die once we have become burdensome. Compare and contrast Aristotle's likely public policy on euthanasia with the one proposed by Hardwig.
2. Hardwig protests that he is "not advocating a crass, quasi-economic conception of burdens and benefits." Discuss ways, if any, in which Hardwig's argument differs from that of pure utilitarianism. Does the expected dramatic increase in the elderly population in the next few decades add weight to Hardwig's duty to die? If so, discuss whether this duty should be enforced through legislation.
3. Hardwig draws a comparison between modern society and primitive societies. Looking back at the example of the Kabloona Eskimo in Chapter 1, would Hardwig approve of the practice of walking elderly people into holes in the ice? Compare and contrast this situation with that of an elderly person with a chronic illness in a modern hospital.
4. Hardwig claims that the duty to die is consistent with Immanuel Kant's claim that "human dignity rests on the capacity for moral agency within a community of those who respect the demands of morality." Kant, however, was opposed to suicide and euthanasia. Discuss how Hardwig might reconcile his claim with Kant's position.
5. Discuss whether feminist care ethicist Nel Noddings would agree with Hardwig that the duty to die is consistent with an ethics of care.
6. Would Battin agree with Hardwig that there are times when we have a duty to die? Discuss your answer using her three principles of autonomy, mercy, and justice.

SUSAN M. WOLF

A Feminist Critique of Physician-Assisted Suicide

Susan Wolf is an associate professor of law and medicine at the University of Minnesota Law School and an associate at the University of Minnesota's Center for Biomedical Ethics. In her essay Wolf argues that euthanasia practices are gender-biased. The traditional view of women as self-sacrificing puts subtle pressures on women to request euthanasia, as well as on doctors to comply with their requests.

"A Feminist Critique of Physician-Assisted Suicide," from Susan M. Wolf, "Gender, Feminism, and Death: Physician-Assisted Suicide and Euthanasia," in *Feminism and Bioethics,* ed. by Susan M. Wolf (New York: Oxford University Press, 1996), 282–317. Copyright 1996 the Hastings Center. Some notes have been omitted.

Critical Reading Questions

1. How does Wolf support her claim that there are gender differences that might contribute to women being more affected by the legalization of euthanasia?
2. What are some of the implications of the research findings of Lawrence Kohlberg and Carol Gilligan on the euthanasia debate?
3. How does Wolf use the "Debbie" case as well as the Kevorkian cases to support her argument that euthanasia is gender-biased?
4. According to Wolf, why did Kevorkian's female patients request his assistance in their suicides?
5. What are some of the traditional female virtues? How, according to Wolf, do traditional views contribute to the greater likelihood that women will request euthanasia?
6. What are the three objections Wolf raises to the rights-based argument for euthanasia?
7. Why does Wolf reject the argument that euthanasia can be based on a physician's duty of beneficence?
8. According to Wolf, why does linking an ethics of justice to an ethics of care require that euthanasia remain illegal?
9. Why does Wolf, despite her opposition to euthanasia, claim that "physicians must honor patients' requests to be free of unwanted life-sustaining treatment"? How does she use care ethics to justify her position?

The debate in the United States over whether to legitimate physician-assisted suicide and active euthanasia has reached new levels of intensity. . . .

Yet the debate over whether to legitimate physician-assisted suicide and euthanasia (by which I mean active euthanasia, as opposed to the termination of life-sustaining treatment) is most often about a patient who does not exist—a patient with no gender, race, or insurance status. This is the same generic patient featured in most bioethics debates. Little discussion has focused on how differences between patients might alter the equation.

Even though the debate has largely ignored this question, there is ample reason to suspect that gender, among other factors, deserves analysis. The cases prominent in the American debate mostly feature women patients. This occurs against a backdrop of a long history of cultural images revering women's sacrifice and self-sacrifice. . . .

What sort of gender effects might we expect? There are four different possibilities. First, we

might anticipate a higher incidence of women than men dying by physician-assisted suicide and euthanasia in this country. This is an empirical claim that we cannot yet test; we currently lack good data in the face of the illegality of the practices in most states and the condemnation of the organized medical profession. . . .

There may, however, be a second gender effect. Gender differences may translate into women seeking physician-assisted suicide and euthanasia for somewhat different reasons than men. Problems we know to be correlated with gender—difficulty getting good medical care generally, poor pain relief, a higher incidence of depression, and a higher rate of poverty—may figure more prominently in women's motivation. Society's persisting sexism may figure as well. And the long history of valorizing women's self-sacrifice may be expressed in women's requesting assisted suicide or euthanasia.

The well-recognized gender differences in suicide statistics also suggest that women's requests for physician-assisted suicide and euthanasia may more often than men's requests be an effort to change an oppressive situation rather than a literal request for death. . . .

Third, gender differences may also come to the fore in physicians' decisions about whether to grant or refuse requests for assisted suicide or euthanasia. The same historical valorization of women's self-sacrifice and the same background sexism that may affect women's readiness to request may also affect physicians' responses. Physicians may be susceptible to affirming women's negative self-judgments. This might or might not result in physicians agreeing to assist; other gender-related judgments (such as that women are too emotionally labile, or that their choices would not be taken seriously) may intervene. But the point is that gender may affect not just patient but physician.

Finally, gender may affect the broad public debate. The prominent U.S. cases so far and related historical imagery suggest that in debating physician-assisted suicide and euthanasia, many in our culture may envision a woman patient. . . .

The debate over physician-assisted suicide and euthanasia so starkly raises questions of rights, caring, and context that at this point it would take determination *not* to bring to bear a literature that has been devoted to understanding those notions. Indeed, the work of Lawrence Kohlberg bears witness to what an obvious candidate this debate is for such analysis. It was Kohlberg's work on moral development, of course, that provoked Carol Gilligan's *In a Different Voice,* criticizing Kohlberg's vision of progressive stages of moral maturation as one that was partial and gendered. Gilligan proposed that there were really two different approaches to moral problems, one that emphasized generalized rights and universal principles, and the other that instead emphasized contextualized caring and the maintenance of particular human relationships. She suggested that although women and men could use both approaches, women tended to use the latter and men the former. . . .

The euthanasia debate thus demands analysis along the care, rights, and context axes that the Kolhberg–Gilligan debate has identified. Kolhberg himself used this problem to reveal how well respondents were doing in elevating general principles over the idiosyncrasies of relationship and context. It is no stretch, then, to apply the fruits of more than a decade of feminist critique. . . .

GENDER IN CASES, IMAGES, AND PRACTICE

The tremendous upsurge in American debate over whether to legitimate physician-assisted suicide and euthanasia in recent years has been fueled by a series of cases featuring women. The case that seems to have begun this series is that of Debbie, published in 1988 by the *Journal of the American Medical Association (JAMA).*[1] *JAMA* published this now infamous, first-person, and anonymous account by a resident in obstetrics and gynecology of performing euthanasia. Some subsequently queried whether the account was fiction. Yet it successfully catalyzed an enormous response.

The narrator of the piece tells us that Debbie is a young woman suffering from ovarian cancer. The resident has no prior relationship with her, but is called to her bedside late one night while on call and exhausted. Entering Debbie's room, the resident finds an older woman with her, but never pauses to find out who that second woman is and what relational context Debbie acts within. Instead, the resident responds to the patient's clear discomfort and to her words. Debbie says only one sentence, "Let's get this over with." It is unclear whether she thinks the resident is there to draw blood and wants that over with, or means something else. But on the strength of that one sentence, the resident retreats to the nursing station, prepares a lethal injection, returns to the room, and administers it. The story relates this as an act of mercy under the title, "It's Over, Debbie," as if in caring response to the patient's words.

The lack of relationship to the patient; the failure to attend to her own history, relationships, and resources; the failure to explore beyond the patient's presented words and engage her in conversation;

the sense that the cancer diagnosis plus the patient's words demand death; and the construal of that response as an act of mercy are all themes that recur in later cases. The equally infamous Dr. Jack Kevorkian has provided a slew of them.

They begin with Janet Adkins, a 54-year-old Oregon woman diagnosed with Alzheimer's disease. Again, on the basis of almost no relationship with Ms. Adkins, on the basis of a diagnosis by exclusion that Kevorkian could not verify, prompted by a professed desire to die that is a predictable stage in response to a number of dire diagnoses, Kevorkian rigs her up to his "Mercitron" machine in a parking lot outside Detroit in what he presents as an act of mercy.

Then there is Marjorie Wantz, a 58-year-old woman without even a diagnosis. Instead, she has pelvic pain whose source remains undetermined. By the time Kevorkian reaches Ms. Wantz, he is making little pretense of focusing on her needs in the context of a therapeutic relationship. Instead, he tells the press that he is determined to create a new medical specialty of "obiatry." Ms. Wantz is among the first six potential patients with whom he is conferring. When Kevorkian presides over her death there is another woman who dies as well, Sherry Miller. Miller, 43, has multiple sclerosis. Thus neither woman is terminal.

The subsequent cases reiterate the basic themes. And it is not until the ninth "patient" that Kevorkian finally presides over the death of a man. By this time, published criticism of the predominance of women had begun to appear.

Kevorkian's actions might be dismissed as the bizarre behavior of one man. But the public and press response has been enormous, attesting to the power of these accounts. Many people have treated these cases as important to the debate over physician-assisted suicide and euthanasia. Nor are Kevorkian's cases so aberrant—they pick up all the themes that emerge in "Debbie." . . .

Prevailing values have imbued women's deaths with a specific meaning. Indeed, Carol Gilligan builds on images of women's suicides and sacrifice in novels and drama, as well as on her own data, in finding a psychology and even an ethic of self-sacrifice among women. Gilligan finds one of the "conventions of femininity" to be "the moral equation of goodness with self-sacrifice." "[V]irtue for women lies in self-sacrifice. . . ."[2]

Given this history of images and the valorization of women's self-sacrifice, it should come as no surprise that the early cases dominating the debate about self-sacrifice through physician-assisted suicide and euthanasia have been cases of women. In Greek tragedy only women were ever candidates for sacrifice and self-sacrifice, and to this day self-sacrifice is usually regarded as a feminine not masculine virtue. . . .

Analyzing the early cases against the background of this history also suggests hidden gender dynamics to be discovered by attending to the facts found in the accounts of these cases, or more properly the facts not found. What is most important in these accounts is what is left out, how truncated they are. We see a failure to attend to the patient's context, a readiness on the part of these physicians to facilitate death, a seeming lack of concern over why these women turn to these doctors for deliverance. A clue about why we should be concerned about each of these omissions is telegraphed by data from exit polls on the day Californians defeated a referendum measure to legalize active euthanasia. Those polls showed support for the measure lowest among women, older people, Asians, and African Americans, and highest among younger men with postgraduate education and incomes over $75,000 per year. The *New York Times* analysis was that people from more vulnerable groups were more worried about allowing physicians actively to take life. This may suggest concern not only that physicians may be too ready to take their lives, but also that these patients may be markedly vulnerable to seeking such relief. Why would women, in particular, feel this?

Women are at greater risk for inadequate pain relief. Indeed, fear of pain is one of the reasons most frequently cited by Americans for supporting legislation to legalize euthanasia. Women are also at greater risk for depression. And depression appears to underlie numerous requests for physician-assisted suicide and euthanasia. These factors suggest that women may be differentially driven to consider requesting both practices.

That possibility is further supported by data showing systematic problems for women in relationship to physicians. As an American Medical Association report on gender disparities recounts, women receive more care even for the same illness, but the care is generally worse. Women are less likely to receive dialysis, kidney transplants, cardiac catheterization, and diagnostic testing for lung cancer. The report urges physicians to uproot "social or cultural biases that could affect medical care" and "presumptions about the relative worth of certain social roles."[3]

This all occurs against the background of a deeply flawed health care system that ties health insurance to employment. . . . In the U.S. two-tier health care system, men dominate in the higher-quality tier, women in the lower. . . .

Women may also be driven to consider physician-assisted suicide and euthanasia out of fear of otherwise burdening their families. . . . The history and persistence of family patterns in this country in which women are expected to adopt self-sacrificing behavior for the sake of the family may pave the way too for the patient's request for death. Women requesting death may also be sometimes seeking something other than death. The dominance of women among those attempting but not completing suicide in this country suggests that women may differentially engage in death-seeking behavior with a goal other than death. Instead, they may be seeking to change their relationships or circumstances.

In analyzing why women may request physician-assisted suicide and euthanasia, and why indeed the California polls indicate that women may feel more vulnerable to and wary of making that request, we have insights to bring to bear from other realms. Those insights render suspect an analysis that merely asserts women are choosing physician-assisted suicide and active euthanasia, without asking why they make that choice. The analogy to other forms of violence against women behind closed doors demands that we ask why the woman is there, what features of her context brought her there, and why she may feel

there is no better place to be. Finally, an analogy [to domestic violence] counsels us that the patient's consent does not resolve the question of whether the physician acts properly in deliberately taking her life through physician-assisted suicide or active euthanasia. The two people are separate moral and legal agents.

This leads us from consideration of why women patients may feel vulnerable to these practices, to the question of whether physicians may be vulnerable to regarding women's requests for physician-assisted suicide and euthanasia somewhat differently from men's. There may indeed be gender-linked reasons for physicians in this country to say "yes" to women seeking assistance in suicide or active euthanasia. In assessing whether the patient's life has become "meaningless," or a "burden," or otherwise what some might regard as suitable for extinguishing at her request, it would be remarkable if the physician's background views did not come into play on what makes a woman's life meaningful or how much of a burden on her family is too much.

Second, there is a dynamic many have written about operating between the powerful expert physician and the woman surrendering to his care. It is no accident that bioethics has focused on the problem of physician paternalism. Instead of an egalitarianism or what Susan Sherwin calls "amicalism,"[4] we see a vertically hierarchical arrangement built on domination and subordination. When the patient is female and the doctor male, as is true in most medical encounters, the problem is likely to be exacerbated by the background realities and history of male dominance and female subjugation in the broader society. Then a set of psychological dynamics are likely to make the male physician vulnerable to acceding to the woman patient's request for active assistance in dying. . . .

FEMINISM AND THE ARGUMENTS

. . . Advocacy of physician-assisted suicide and euthanasia has hinged to a great extent on rights claims. The argument is that the patient has a right to self-determination or autonomy that entitles her to assistance in suicide or euthanasia. The strategy is to extend the argument that self-determination entitles the patient to refuse unwanted life-sustaining treatment by maintaining that the same rationale supports patient entitlement to more active physician assistance in death. Indeed, it is sometimes argued that there is no principled difference between the termination of life-sustaining treatment and the more active practices.

The narrowness and mechanical quality of this rights thinking, however, is shown by its application to the stories recounted above. That application suggests that the physicians in these stories are dealing with a simple equation: given an eligible rights bearer and her assertion of the right, the correct result is death. What makes a person an eligible rights bearer? Kevorkian seems to require neither a terminal disease nor thorough evaluation of whether the patient has non-fatal alternatives. Indeed, the Wantz case shows he does not even require a diagnosis. Nor does the Oregon physician-assisted suicide statute require evaluation or exhaustion of non-fatal alternatives; a patient could be driven by untreated pain, and still receive physician-assisted suicide. And what counts as an assertion of the right? For Debbie's doctor, merely "Let's get this over with." Disease plus demand requires death. . . .

Feminist critiques suggest three different sorts of problems with the rights equation offered to justify physician-assisted suicide and euthanasia. First, it ignores context, both the patient's present context and her history. The prior and surrounding failures in her intimate relationships, in her resources to cope with illness and pain, and even in the adequacy of care being offered by the very same physician fade into invisibility next to the bright light of a rights bearer and her demand. In fact, her choices may be severely constrained. . . .

Second, in ignoring context and relationship, the rights equation extols the vision of a rights bearer as an isolated monad and denigrates actual dependencies. Thus it may be seen as improper to ask what family, social, economic, and medical supports she is or is not getting; this insults her

individual self-governance. Nor may it be seen as proper to investigate alternatives to acceding to her request for death; this too dilutes self-rule. Yet feminists have reminded us of the actual embeddedness of persons and the descriptive falseness of a vision of each as an isolated individual. . . . Indeed, the very meaning of the patient's request for death is socially constructed; that is the point of the prior section's review of the images animating the debate. If we construe the patient's request as a rights bearer's assertion of a right and deem that sufficient grounds on which the physician may proceed, it is because we choose to regard background failures as irrelevant even if they are differentially motivating the requests of the most vulnerable. We thereby avoid real scrutiny of the social arrangements, governmental failures, and health coverage exclusions that may underlie these requests. We also ignore the fact that these patients may be seeking improved circumstances more than death. We elect a myopia that makes the patient's request and death seem proper. We construct a story that clothes the patient's terrible despair in the glorious mantle of "rights." . . .

In fact, there are substantial problems with grounding advocacy for the specific practices of physician-assisted suicide and euthanasia in a rights analysis, even if one accepts the general importance of rights and self-determination. I have elsewhere argued repeatedly for an absolute or near-absolute moral and legal right to be free of unwanted life-sustaining treatment. Yet the negative right to be free of unwanted bodily invasion does not imply an affirmative right to obtain bodily invasion (or assistance with bodily invasion) for the purpose of ending your own life.

Moreover, the former right is clearly grounded in fundamental entitlements to liberty, bodily privacy, and freedom from unconsented touching; in contrast there is no clear "right" to kill yourself or be killed. Suicide has been widely decriminalized, but decriminalizing an act does not mean that you have a positive right to do it and to command the help of others. . . .

There are even less grounds for concluding that there is a right to be killed deliberately on request, that is, for euthanasia. There are reasons why a victim's consent has traditionally been no defense to an accusation of homicide. . . . Similarly, acceding to a patient's request to be killed wipes out the possibility of her future exercise of her liberty. The capacity to command or permit another to take your life deliberately, then, would seem beyond the bounds of those things which you have a right grounded in notions of liberty. . . .

Finally, the rights argument in favor of physician-assisted suicide and euthanasia confuses two separate questions: what the patient may do, and what the physician may do. After all, the real question in these debates is not what patients may request or even do. It is not at all infrequent for patients to talk about suicide and request assurance that the physician will help or actively bring on death when the patient wants; that is an expected part of reaction to serious disease and discomfort. The real question is what the doctor may do in response to this predictable occurrence. That question is not answered by talk of what patients may ask; patients may and should be encouraged to reveal everything on their minds. Nor is it answered by the fact that decriminalization of suicide permits the patient to take her own life. The physician and patient are separate moral agents. Those who assert that what a patient may say or do determines the same for the physician, ignore the physician's separate moral and legal agency. They also ignore the fact that she is a professional, bound to act in keeping with a professional role and obligations. They thereby avoid a necessary argument over whether the historic obligations of the physician to "do no harm" and "give no deadly drug even if asked" should be abandoned. Assertion of what the patient may do does not resolve that argument.

The inadequacy of rights arguments to legitimate physician-assisted suicide and euthanasia has led to a different approach, grounded on physicians' duties of beneficence. This might seem to be quite in keeping with feminists' development of an ethics of care. Yet the beneficence argument in the euthanasia context is a strange one, because it asserts that the physician's obligation to relieve suffering permits or even commands her to annihilate the person who is experiencing the suffering. Indeed, at the end of this act of beneficence, no patient is left to experience its supposed benefits. . . .

What does feminism have to offer these debates? Feminists too have struggled extensively with the question of method, with how to integrate detailed attention to individual cases with rights, justice, and principles. Thus in criticizing Kohlberg and going beyond his vision of moral development, Carol Gilligan argued that human beings should be able to utilize both an ethics of justice and an ethics of care. "To understand how the tension between responsibilities and rights sustains the dialectic of human development is to see the integrity of two disparate modes of experience that are in the end connected. . . . In the representation of maturity, both perspectives converge. . . ."[5] What was less clear was precisely how the two should fit together. And unfortunately for our purposes, Gilligan never took up Kolhberg's mercy killing case to illuminate a care perspective or even more importantly, how the two perspectives might properly be interwoven in that case. . . .

Here we find the beginning of an answer to our dilemma. It appears that we must attend to both context and abstraction, peering through the lens of both care and justice. Yet our approach to each will be affected by its mate. Our apprehension and understanding of context or cases inevitably involves categories, while our categories and principles should be refined over time to apply to some contexts and not others. Similarly, our understanding of what caring requires in a particular case will grow in part from our understanding of what sort of case this is and what limits principles set to our expressions of caring; while our principles should be scrutinized and amended according to their impact on real lives, especially the lives of those historically excluded from the process of generating principles. . . .

Against this background, arguments for physician-assisted suicide and euthanasia—whether grounded on rights or beneficence—are automatically suspect when they fail to attend to the vulnerability of women and other groups. . . .

To institute physician-assisted suicide and euthanasia at this point in this country—in which many millions are denied the resources to cope with serious illness, in which pain relief and palliative care are by all accounts woefully mishandled, and in which we have a long way to go to make proclaimed rights to refuse life-sustaining treatment and to use advanced directives working realities in clinical settings—seems, at the very least, to be premature. Were we actually to fix those other problems, we have no idea what demand would remain for these more drastic practices and in what category of patients. . . .

The required interweaving of principles and caring, combined with attention to the heightened vulnerability of women and others, suggests that the right answer to the debate over legitimating these practices is at least "not yet" in this grossly imperfect society and perhaps a flat "no." Beneficence and caring indeed impose positive duties upon physicians, especially with patients who are suffering, despairing, or in pain. Physicians must work with these patients intensively; provide first-rate pain relief, palliative care, and symptomatic relief; and honor patients' exercise of their rights to refuse life-sustaining treatment and use advance directives. Never should the patient's illness, deterioration, or despair occasion physician abandonment. Whatever concerns the patient has should be heard and explored, including thoughts of suicide, or requests for aid or euthanasia.

Such requests should redouble the physician's efforts, prompt consultation with those more expert in pain relief or support care, suggest exploration of the details of the patient's circumstances, and a host of other efforts. What such requests should not do is prompt our collective legitimation of the physician's saying "yes" and actively taking the patient's life. The mandates of caring fail to bless killing the person for whom one cares. Any such practice in the United States will inevitably reflect enormous background inequities and persisting societal biases. And there are special reasons to expect gender bias to play a role. . . .

CONCLUSION

Some will find it puzzling that elsewhere we seek to have women's voices heard and moral agency respected, yet here I am urging that physicians not accede to the request for assisted suicide and euthanasia. Indeed, as noted above, I have elsewhere maintained that physicians must honor patients' requests to be free of unwanted life-sustaining treatment. In fact, attention to gender and feminist argument would urge some caution in both realms. . . . Finally there is a difference between the two domains. As I have argued above, there is a strong right to be free of unwanted bodily invasion. Indeed, for women, a long history of being harmed specifically through unwanted bodily invasion such as rape presents particularly compelling reasons for honoring a woman's refusal of invasion and effort to maintain bodily intactness. When it comes to the question of whether women's suicides should be aided, however, or whether women should be actively killed, there is no right to command physician assistance, the dangers of permitting assistance are immense, and the history of women's subordination cuts the other way. Women have historically been seen as fit objects for bodily invasion, self-sacrifice, and death at the hands of others. The task before us is to challenge all three. . . .

NOTES

1. See "It's Over, Debbie," *Journal of the American Medical Association* 259 (1988): 272.
2. Carol Gilligan, *In a Different Voice* (Cambridge, MA: Harvard University Press, 1982), 70.
3. Council on Ethical and Judicial Affairs, American Medical Association, "Gender Disparities in Clinical Decision Making," *Journal of the American Medical Association* 266 (1991): 559–62.
4. Susan Sherwin, *No Longer Patient: Feminist Ethics and Health Care* (Philadelphia: Temple University Press, 1992), 157.
5. See Gilligan, *In a Different Voice*, 174.

Discussion Questions

1. Do you agree with Wolf that women are more likely than men to request as well as receive euthanasia? If so, does this necessarily imply that euthanasia is gender-biased?

2. Are the women in your class more likely than the men to say that they would choose euthanasia should they become a burden to their families? If so, how do they justify their decisions? Which of Gilligan's levels of moral reasoning does the reasoning represent? Does conventional moral reasoning contribute to injustice? Discuss.

3. Polls show that women are significantly more likely than men to oppose the legalization of euthanasia. Why do you think this is the case? Support your answer.

4. Discuss how Wolf might reply to Battin's argument that, for the most part, we can trust the physician to serve as a check in preventing "ill-considered" physician-assisted suicide and involuntary euthanasia.

5. Should euthanasia be prohibited because some women run into sexist attitudes? Would Wolf support physician-assisted suicide in an egalitarian society? If not, what other conditions would she require? Discuss the specific steps we would have to take in the United States before legalizing euthanasia.

CASE STUDIES

1. NANCY CRUZAN: SEVEN YEARS IN A PERSISTENT VEGETATIVE STATE

In 1983 twenty-five-year-old Nancy Cruzan's car crashed after skidding out of control on a patch of ice. She was thrown from the car and landed facedown in a ditch, where she nearly suffocated. Although paramedics restored her breathing, her brain had gone without oxygen for thirteen minutes. When doctors told Nancy's parents that she was in a vegetative state, they requested that the hospital disconnect all life supports, including the feeding tubes in her stomach. They told the doctors that they knew she would not want to be kept alive with machines. Although the hospital complied with the request that Nancy be taken off the respirator, it decided not to remove the feeding tube, arguing that food and water were not medical treatment or artificial life support but merely part of basic care.

The Cruzans turned to the courts for help. In 1990 the case reached the U.S. Supreme Court *(Cruzan v. Missouri Department of Health),* which ruled that a person has a constitutional right to refuse life-support treatment, including food and water. The Court also ruled, however, that the state could limit that right for incompetent people by requiring that the surrogate decision makers provide "clear and convincing" proof of the "patient's desire to have hydration and nutrition withdrawn." The Cruzans recruited several of Nancy's coworkers to testify that she had clearly stated that she did not want to be kept alive by artificial means. On December 14, 1990, a Missouri court finally gave the Cruzans permission to remove the feeding tube. Nancy died twelve days later.

Discussion Questions

1. Read the excerpts on pages 183–184 from the United States Supreme Court opinion on *Cruzan v. Missouri Department of Health*. If you had been one of the Supreme Court justices, would you have concurred with the ruling or dissented? Explain your position in a paragraph giving your opinion, as a Supreme Court justice, of the case.
2. Discuss the hospital's claim that a feeding tube is not medical treatment or artifial life support.
3. Are the principles of autonomy and mercy relevant in this case? Is it morally relevant that Nancy did not seem to be in any pain? Does the physician have a moral obligation to Nancy? If so, do these principles apply to the physician's relationship with the parents?
4. Discuss how Battin's principle of limited paternalism applies to the physician, the parents, and the judge in this case.
5. Compare and contrast the recommendations Battin, Hardwig, and Gay-Williams would each have made in this case. What would you have done had you been Nancy's physician? Support your position.
6. Discuss who should make the decision in cases in which incompetent people have not made their wishes explicitly known in a document such as a living will.

---

2. DR. KEVORKIAN AND THE ASSISTED SUICIDE OF JUDITH CURREN[23]

On August 15, 1996, Judith Curren, a forty-two-year-old mother of two young daughters, committed suicide with the assistance of Dr. Jack Kevorkian. Unlike most of Kevorkian's clients, Curren was not terminally ill; she was suffering from depression, chronic fatigue syndrome, and fibromyalgia—a benign but painful inflammation of fibromuscular tissue.

Curren's husband, psychiatrist Franklin Curren, who was present at his wife's death, was a strong supporter of physician-assisted suicide and his wife's choice to end her life.[24] Kevorkian was surprised when he read a press release a few days later stating that Dr. Curren had been charged with assaulting his wife just three weeks earlier. This was not the first domestic assault charge that had been brought against Curren by his wife.[25]

When questioned about the role that domestic violence may have played in Judith Curren's decision to end her life, Kevorkian replied he had asked the Currens if there had been any trouble in the family and that they had said no. "You can't know what goes on domestically," Kevorkian added in defense of his action.

Discussion Questions

1. Kevorkian justifies his actions on the grounds that it would be immoral, similar to torture, not to help people in excruciating pain who request his help. Discuss how Battin would most likely respond to this argument.
2. Kevorkian claims that he has never caused a death, but merely helped people exercise their last civil right. His supporters claim that he was a "prisoner of

conscience," a "martyr to the cause of the right to choose to die." Derek Humphry, founder of the Hemlock Society, wrote following Kevorkian's conviction: "The severity of the sentence on Kevorkian will drive the practice of voluntary euthanasia and assisted suicide even further underground. It will not stop it . . . Kevorkian's martyrdom—self-imposed as it is—will speed up the day when voluntary euthanasia for the dying is removed from the legal classification of 'murder' and recognized as a justifiable act of compassion."[26] Do you agree?

3. Judith Curren was not terminally ill at the time of her death. Should physician-assisted suicide be extended to anyone who desires it? Discuss how you would respond if someone you knew who was depressed and/or suffering from a chronic illness asked you to assist in his or her suicide.

4. Wolf argues that many people consider euthanasia because they lack adequate pain control medication or medical insurance to seek proper treatment, or because they feel they have become a burden to their friends and family. Discuss these objections to euthanasia in light of the Judith Curren case.

5. According to research, women who adopt traditional views of women as self-sacrificing are more likely to be victims of domestic violence. Discuss this in light of the Judith Curren case. Is physician-assisted suicide in these cases simply an extension of violence against women? Discuss how both Wolf and Nel Noddings (Chapter 1) might answer this question.

6. John Stuart Mill argues that security and a safe environment are "the most indispensable of all necessaries after physical nutriment."[27] Would allowing physicians to assist in the suicide of their terminally ill patients damage this sense of security and safety in a physician–patient relationship? Or would it expand the freedom of the dying patient to choose his or her own destiny? Support your answer.

---

3. "FINAL EXIT": HOW TO COMMIT SUICIDE

In February 2000, "Final Exit," a show on how to commit suicide, was aired on late-night cable television in two Oregon cities. The program, which was produced by Hemlock Society founder Derek Humphry, laid out in detail the tools and drugs needed to end one's life quickly and painlessly and offered practical advice on "keeping clear of the law." The show was also intended to arouse public opposition to federal legislation that would impose sanctions on physicians who prescribe lethal drugs to their terminally ill patients.

Barbara Coombs Lee, who led the initiative to get the legislation passed, criticized the video as "irresponsible and potentially dangerous for some people. . . . There is information about how a person could die using very readily available tools and drugs, and for some people who may be mentally unbalanced or acting impulsively, that could be dangerous information."[28]

In response, the cable station and the producers of the show pointed out that this information is already widely available. The program was based on Humphry's book, *Final Exit,* which has sold more than a million copies and is available in twelve languages. "I feel strongly," says Cindy Noblitt, co-producer of the video, "that if we are truly free, that an individual should have the right to decide when and how to end their lives . . . I think it's a central role of the media to provide complete and accurate information to the public that they may need to make those hard decisions in their lives."[29]

Discussion Questions

1. Analyze the arguments put forth by both Lee and Noblitt. What premises do they use, or could they use, to support their conclusions? Which person presents the stronger argument and why?
2. Should there be limits on freedom of speech when it comes to publicizing methods for killing oneself or others? Should suicide machines such as Kevorkian's Mercitron or Australian Dr. Nitschke's "COGen" (a machine, which the Hemlock Society hopes to market, that pumps carbon dioxide through a nasal tube and is used with a sedative to assist a person to die) be made available to the general public? Present your conclusion in the form of a policy statement for the media.
3. In her article Battin argues that a patient's autonomy may be compromised because of lack of knowledge about humane methods for ending his or her life. Discuss whether the principle of autonomy creates a moral obligation for physicians to provide patients who request it with information on how to die.

---

4. DONALD COWART: "PLEASE, LET ME DIE"

In 1973 twenty-six-year-old jet pilot and sometime rodeo performer Donald Cowart was standing in a field with his father when there was a violent explosion caused by leaking gas. The explosion killed his father and sent Donald, whose body was engulfed in flames, running for half a mile. When a farmer found him, Cowart, who was in excruciating pain from burns covering more than 65 percent of his body, asked for a gun so he could kill himself. The farmer refused his request and called an ambulance. Cowart asked the paramedics not to drive him to the hospital but to leave him in the field to die. They instead administered lifesaving measures and took him to the hospital.

Cowart lost both his eyes and all his fingers and underwent several operations for skin grafts and amputations. After he was released from the hospital, Cowart attempted suicide several times. Eventually, he completed a law degree. Cowart frequently speaks at medical conferences on issues relating to euthanasia. He still insists that the hospital staff who treated him for his burns violated his right to self-determination in keeping him alive.

Discussion Questions

1. Discuss whether the paramedics did the morally right thing in treating Cowart, even though he asked them not to. What moral principles and concerns are relevant to this decision?
2. Imagine that you are Cowart's best friend and that you found him. Discuss whether the fact that you are his friend, rather than a stranger or a medical professional, is relevant in making your decision to end his suffering or call an ambulance.

3. Some people argue that suicide attempts are really a cry for help. Does the fact that Cowart never successfully committed suicide, despite repeated attempts, suggest that he was mistaken about his own wishes to end his life? How can a physician determine if a request for euthanasia is genuine? How might Battin, Gay-Williams, and Wolf each respond to this question?

4. Many people think that euthanasia is morally acceptable only when a person is dying. Is the fact that Cowart did not have a terminal condition relevant? Support your answer.

5. THE DEATH OF "BABY DOE"

When Baby Doe was born in an Indiana hospital in 1982, his parents were at first over-joyed. Their joy turned to dismay, however, when they learned that their son had Down syndrome. It was later found that the baby also had a malformed esophagus, which pre-vented food from entering his stomach. Whereas a blockage in the esophagus can be easily corrected by surgery, there is no cure for Down syndrome. The parents, believ-ing that their son might be severely retarded, refused to give approval for the surgery. Without the surgery or a feeding tube, the baby would starve to death. The hospital administration took the case to court. The judge who heard the case concluded that Baby Doe's parents had the right to make an informed decision regarding the course of treatment for their child. Baby Doe died, five days after his birth, of starvation and dehydration.

Discussion Questions

1. Do parents have a right to make euthanasia decisions for children who are not terminally ill? Is the assumption that parents will act in the best interests of their children justified? Support your answers.

2. Rachels uses the Baby Doe case to illustrate how passive euthanasia can sometimes cause more suffering than active euthanasia. If it is morally permissible for parents to allow their infants to die, should active euthanasia be used instead?

3. The death of Baby Doe created an uproar from people concerned about the rights of the disabled. Columnist George Will, himself the father of a child with Down syndrome, accused the parents of being cruel and treating their child and those like him as less than human. Do you agree with Will? Support your answer.

4. Anencephaly is a congenital disorder in which the brain, with the exception of some rudimentary function in the brain stem, fails to develop. It is virtually always fatal within a few weeks after birth. As the brain stem function begins to fail, other organs may become damaged prior to heart failure. Because of this, the organs of these infants are rarely useful for donation following their death. Should the law be changed to allow the euthanasia of infants who are going to die anyway so their organs can be harvested for organ transplant? Discuss how a utilitarian and a rights ethicist might each respond to this question.

6. ROBERT LATIMER: MURDERER OR ANGEL OF MERCY?

In a courtroom in the quiet farming community of Battleford, Saskatchewan, twelve jurors declared Robert Latimer guilty of second-degree murder. Fours years earlier, on October 24, 1993, Latimer, a canola and wheat farmer, had trudged through the snow with his severely disabled twelve-year-old daughter, Tracy, cradled in his arms and placed her gently in the cab of the family pickup truck. He watched through the window as the cab filled with deadly carbon monoxide fumes. Seven minutes later Tracy was dead.

Twelve days earlier Laura Latimer, Tracy's mother, had taken Tracy to the doctor, who recommended the removal of her right thigh bone to ease her pain. Both she and Robert cried as they thought about their daughter's prospects for the future. They had already tried placing her in a group home, but she was so unhappy she lost a sixth of her weight. "It would be better for Tracy if she died," Laura told her husband. She was relieved when, twelve days later, she came home and found Tracy dead.

Was this an act of mercy or a cold-blooded murder? As a result of his actions, Latimer received a life sentence with no access to parole for at least ten years. He was denied day parole in December 2007 on the grounds that he had failed to develop any insight into his crime during his time in prison.

Latimer's supporters argue that he is "a loving man and a decent father" who acted out of compassion; he deserves leniency, not a prison sentence. If the proper legal and social supports for mercy killing had been in place, Latimer would not have taken the law into his own hands. Many disabled-rights activists see things differently, however. "What that [granting leniency] says is that it's all right to kill your child with a disability because she may encounter some discomfort," says a spokesperson for the Council of Canadians with Disabilities.[30]

Discussion Questions

1. Mercy killing is usually seen as justified only when there is no other way to relieve pain and suffering. According to witnesses at the trial, however, Tracy Latimer experienced no more pain than many other people with disabilities. The prosecutor told the jury, "Pain is a condition of life, not a reason for death. Must a person like Tracy die because another person cannot bear to watch her fight?" Should other kinds of suffering besides unremitting pain, such as the suffering of the caregivers, be taken into account in justifying mercy killing?
2. Compare and contrast this case with that of Baby Doe. Is it morally relevant that Baby Doe was allowed to die, whereas Tracy was actively killed? How would Rachels respond to these two case studies?
3. Seventy-one percent of Americans in a 2007 Gallup poll supported physician-assisted suicide and euthanasia for terminally ill people, but less than half of respondents feel that relatives or friends should be allowed to commit the deed. Is this distinction morally relevant? Discuss in light of the Robert Latimer case study.

C H A P T E R   5

The Death Penalty

Fred Simmons and Bob Moore were on their way from Florida to Georgia when they stopped to pick up two hitchhikers, Tony Gregg and Floyd Allen. At a rest stop outside of Atlanta, Gregg told Allen that he was going to rob Simmons and Moore. As Simmons and Moore were returning to the car, Gregg pulled a gun and fired three shots at them. The two men fell into a ditch. Gregg then got out of the car and shot them both point-blank in the head.

Gregg was found guilty of armed robbery and two counts of murder and given the death penalty. Gregg appealed his sentence. The death penalty had been ruled unconstitutional in 1972 by the U.S. Supreme Court in *Furman v. Georgia* on the grounds that it had been arbitrarily administered. In response, the state of Georgia had overhauled its death penalty laws to make them less arbitrary. In 1976 the U.S. Supreme Court in *Gregg v. Georgia* ruled that Georgia's revised statutes were constitutional, thus overturning the 1972 ruling that had banned the death penalty.

HISTORY OF THE DEATH PENALTY

The **death penalty,** also known as **capital punishment,** is the infliction of death by the state as punishment for a crime. In the Middle Ages, the purpose of punishment was as much to save the criminal's soul as to protect society from harm. Torture instruments, isolation, hard labor, horrendous living conditions, the gallows, and burning at the stake were used to terrorize criminals to the point that they would repent their evil ways and cry out for God's mercy.

During the nineteenth century, public executions were abolished in most of Europe and North America. Rather than abolish the death penalty, however, societies moved executions behind the walls of an impersonal penal system. It wasn't until the mid-twentieth century that there was a worldwide movement to abolish the death penalty.

THE DEATH PENALTY TODAY

During the 1980s and 1990s, many countries abolished the death penalty. As of 2009, more than two-thirds of all countries had abolished the death penalty in law or in practice, including all of western Europe, Canada, Australia, and most Central American,

South American, and African countries. The United States is the only Western democracy that still uses the death penalty. Both the United Nations and the European Union support abolition of the death penalty. The use of the death penalty has been declining worldwide, with 1,252 executions officially recorded in 2007. Eighty-eight percent of these executions took place in five countries—China, Iran, Pakistan, Saudi Arabia, and the United States.[1]

Although the death penalty is permitted in most Islamic countries, the Koran's law of retributive justice or *lex talionis*—"an eye for an eye and a tooth for a tooth"—has been softened to permit the payment of "blood money." The imposition of the Islamic penal code and the death penalty on both Muslims and non-Muslims has become a controversial issue in Malaysia and other Asian countries that have both Islamic and non-Islamic populations, including Buddhists, Hindus, and Christians. (See Case Study 5.)

Unlike Islamic law, Jewish law interprets the Old Testament law of retributive justice to prohibit capital punishment. According to the Jewish Mishnah, it is murder for the courts to execute a person.

Many Christian churches likewise regard capital punishment as being inconsistent with the sanctity of human life. Capital punishment is illegal in almost all Protestant and Catholic countries, with the exception of the United States. The Roman Catholic papal encyclical *Evangelium Vitae* expressly forbids capital punishment. Although the U.S. bishops have issued statements opposing the death penalty, the majority of U.S. Catholics support capital punishment.[2]

Prior to the 1970s, there was not much public support for the death penalty in the United States. In a 1971 Roper poll, Americans overwhelmingly responded that society has a duty to reform criminals and give them a second chance.[3] The death penalty was ruled unconstitutional by the U.S. Supreme Court in the 1972 *Furman v. Georgia* case. The Court ruled that the unlimited discretion given to judges and juries to impose the death penalty led to its capricious and arbitrary use.

Between 1967 and 1977, there were no executions in the United States. The escalating violent crime rate in the 1970s led to increasing public support for the death penalty for murder. The media's extensive coverage of the most brutal and horrific cases, and the onslaught of violent crime on television and in movies, intensified people's fear of and anger over violent crime and their demand for harsher punishment.

In 1976 the U.S. Supreme Court in *Gregg v. Georgia* reversed the earlier ruling, saying that Georgia's new "guided discretion" laws had removed the arbitrariness of sentencing from the death penalty. All but fifteen states reinstated the death penalty. A decline in violent crime beginning in the late 1990s convinced many Americans that strict punishment, including capital punishment, was the solution to the nation's crime rate.

The number of executions more than tripled between 1994 and 1999, when ninety-eight people were executed.[4] The year 2002, when there were seventy-one executions, saw the first decrease since 1976 in the number of executions and the number of prisoners under sentence of death.[5] Thirty-seven executions were carried out in 2008, down from forty-two in 2007. The number of prisoners on death row is also decreasing.[6] These rates can be expected to continue declining, with numerous reprieves because of DNA evidence and legislation restricting imposition of the death penalty.

🖊 U.S. SUPREME COURT *GREGG V. GEORGIA* (1976): EXCERPTS FROM THE MAJORITY OPINION*

[Justice Potter Stewart delivered the opinion of the Court.]

The issue in this case is whether the imposition of the sentence of death for the crime of murder under the law of Georgia violates the Eighth and Fourteenth Amendments. . . .

The Court on a number of occasions has both assumed and asserted the constitutionality of capital punishment. In several cases that assumption provided a necessary foundation for the decision, as the Court was asked to decide whether a particular method of carrying out a capital sentence would be allowed to stand under the Eighth Amendment. But until *Furman v. Georgia,* 408 U.S. 238 (1972), the Court never confronted squarely the fundamental claim that the punishment of death always, regardless of the enormity of the offense or the procedure followed in imposing the sentence, is cruel and unusual punishment in violation of the Constitution. Although this issue was presented and addressed in *Furman,* it was not resolved by the Court. . . . We now hold that the punishment of death does not invariably violate the Constitution.

The phrase ["cruel and unusual" punishment] first appeared in the English Bill of Rights of 1689. . . . The American draftsmen, who adopted the English phrasing in drafting the Eighth Amendment, were primarily concerned with proscribing "tortures" and other "barbarous" methods of punishment. . . .

In the earliest cases raising Eighth Amendment claims, the Court focused on particular methods of execution to determine whether they were too cruel to pass constitution muster. The constitutionality of the sentence of death itself was not at issue, and the criterion used to evaluate the mode of the sentence of death itself was not at issue. . . .

But the Court has not confined the prohibition embodied in the Eighth Amendment to "barbarous" methods that were generally outlawed in the 18th century. Instead, the Amendment has been interpreted in a flexible and dynamic manner. The Court early recognized that "a principle to be vital must be capable of wider application than the mischief which gave it birth" *Weems v. United States* (1910). Thus the Clause forbidding "cruel and unusual" punishments "is not fastened to the obsolete but may acquire meaning as public opinion becomes enlightened by a humane justice.". . .

But our cases also make clear that public perceptions of standards of decency with respect to criminal sanctions are not conclusive. A penalty also must accord with "the dignity of man," which is the "basic concept underlying the Eighth Amendment." This means, at least, that the punishment not be "excessive.". . . First, the punishment must not involve the unnecessary and wanton infliction of pain *Furman v. Georgia* (1972). . . .

In the discussion to this point we have sought to identify the principles and considerations that guide a court in addressing an Eighth Amendment claim. We

---

* Footnotes omitted.

now consider specifically whether the sentence of death for the crime of murder is a per se violation of the Eighth and Fourteenth Amendments to the Constitution. We note first that history and precedent strongly support a negative answer to this question.

The imposition of the death penalty for the crime of murder has a long history of acceptance in the United States and in England.

It is apparent from the text of the Constitution itself that the existence of capital punishment was accepted by the framers. At the time the Eighth Amendment was ratified, capital punishment was a common sanction in every state. Indeed, the first Congress of the United States enacted legislation providing death as the penalty for specified crimes. . . .

The death penalty is said to serve two principal social purposes: retribution and deterrence of capital crimes by prospective offenders.

In part, capital punishment is an expression of society's moral outrage at particularly offensive conduct. This function may be unappealing to many, but it is essential in an ordered society that asks its citizens to rely on legal processes rather than self-help to vindicate their wrongs. . . .

Capital punishment may be the appropriate sanction in extreme cases as an expression of the communities' belief that certain crimes are themselves so grievous an affront to humanity that the only adequate response may be the death penalty.

In November 2001, President George W. Bush created military commissions that have the power to impose the death penalty on people convicted of "international terrorism." (See Case Study 2). In 2003 Attorney General John Ashcroft asked lawmakers on Capitol Hill to expand the death penalty to cover people who are accused of perpetrating terrorist activities, even though they may not be directly involved in the actual killings. Over 3,000 "foot-soldiers of terror" have been captured since the passage of the USA Patriot Act following September 11, 2001.[7] So far no international terrorists have been executed under the new laws.

The United States has the highest incarceration rate in the world, with 1 out of every 133 people in this country in prison.[8] This is five times the rate of any other Western nation. Of the 2.3 million people in prison in the United States in 2008, about 3,000 are on death row.[9] Blacks are disproportionately represented both on death row and in the prison population. A black male in the United States has a 1 in 3 chance of being in prison sometime in his life, compared to 1 in 6 for a Hispanic male, and 1 in 17 for a white male.[10]

Support for the death penalty for a person convicted of murder began rising in the 1980s and peaked in 1994 at 80 percent. A 2008 Gallup poll reported that support had dropped to 64 percent, the lowest level since 1978. And, if given the option of life imprisonment without parole, support for the death penalty drops to 47 percent. Support for the death penalty among college freshmen is about the same as that found in the general public.[11] Men are more likely than women to favor the death penalty. The most striking difference is based on race, however, with white people being more than twice as likely as black people to support the death penalty.[12] White people are also more likely to believe that the death penalty is being applied fairly.[13]

Despite continuing support for capital punishment, the vast majority of murderers do not receive the death penalty. Of the 20,000 homicides that occur in an average year in the United States, fewer than 300 convicted murderers are sentenced to death.[14] Of those sentenced to death, 99 percent are poor and have to rely on public defenders.[15] While blacks make up only 12 percent of the U.S. population, they represent more than 40 percent of death row inmates. According to Amnesty International, however, the greatest predictive factor in giving the death penalty is not the race of the criminal, but the race of the victim. Although blacks and whites are victims of murder in almost equal numbers, 80 percent of death penalties involved white victims.

THE DEATH PENALTY: JUVENILE AND MENTALLY RETARDED OFFENDERS

In 1999, in one of the worst school shootings in history, Eric Harris and Dylan Klebold opened fire on their classmates at Columbine High School in Littleton, Colorado. Thirteen people were killed and twenty-one others wounded before the two boys finally turned the guns on themselves, ending both the rampage and their own lives.

In addition to the racial and socioeconomic disparities in the application of the death penalty, violent crime among **juveniles** has raised the moral issue of whether people under eighteen should be put to death. Should children who kill be subjected to the same penalties as adults? A total of 226 death sentences for juveniles have been imposed since 1973. Twenty-two juvenile offenders were executed in the United States between 1976 and April 2005, when the U.S. Supreme Court in *Roper v. Simmons* ruled that the execution of juvenile offenders violates the Eighth Amendment to the Constitution. Iran, Saudi Arabia, Yemen, and Pakistan are the only countries that have executed juvenile offenders since 2005, and Iran is the only one to have done so in 2008.

In June 2003 in *Atkins v. Virginia,* the Supreme Court ruled that executing people who are mentally retarded (an IQ of 70 or lower) violates the Eighth Amendment of the U.S. Constitution, which prohibits "cruel and unusual punishments." This decision affects an estimated 5 to 10 percent of people on death row.[16] Reaction to this decision was mixed. Justice Scalia wrote the dissenting opinion in *Atkins v. Virginia,* arguing "if we accept the concept of blanket incapacity, we relegate people with retardation to second-class citizenship, potentially permitting the state to abrogate the exercise of such fundamental interests as the right to marry, to have and rear one's children, to vote or such everyday entitlements as entering into contracts or making a will."

THE MEDICALIZATION OF EXECUTIONS

The gas chamber, firing squads, and hanging have all been used in the United States and continue to be used in some other countries. Lethal injection, however, is the most common method of execution in the United States.[17]

The adoption of lethal injection in 2000 as the standard method of execution has led to what some call "medicalized execution." Although it is claimed that lethal injection is more humane than earlier methods of execution, the use of medical knowledge to kill people has created a conflict between medical professionals and penal officials. (See Case Study 4.) In 1980 the American Medical Association (AMA) adopted a resolution that states, "A physician, as a member of a profession dedicated to the preservation of life. . . should not be a participant in a legally authorized execution."

Despite consensus on the part of every national and international physicians' organization that physician participation in an execution violates medical ethics and the Hippocractic oath, which enjoins physicians to do everything in their power to relieve suffering and prevent death, most states require the presence of a physician in the death chamber.[18] To protect physicians from censure by their colleagues, some prisons keep the identity of participating physicians secret, even paying them in cash in order to thwart attempts to identify them. In California, one of the states that requires a physician's presence at executions, a group of physicians is suing the state prison system, charging that requiring physicians to participate in executions forces them to violate their professional code of ethics—"First of all, do no harm."

DNA TESTING

Although support among the medical community for physician participation in executions is low, it is likely with the increased use of DNA testing in capital cases that more and more physicians will be called upon to testify in court. This role for physicians is more in line with the Hippocratic oath. Since 1973, more than 130 death row prisoners, some of whom had spent ten to twenty years in prison, have been released because of new evidence showing that they were innocent of the crime. Many of these prisoners were exonerated on the basis of DNA testing.

Although DNA samples from the crime scene are not available in most cases, nor is DNA testing infallible in determining guilt and innocence, a study using random sampling of prisoners where DNA evidence was available concluded that between 7 and 10 percent of convicted death row prisoners are innocent.[19] This error rate, many people believe, is morally unacceptable.

The U.S. Supreme Court is currently (in spring 2009) hearing arguments concerning a defendant's constitutional right to DNA testing in murder trials.[20]

THE PHILOSOPHERS ON THE DEATH PENALTY

Capital punishment became an issue during the Enlightenment period, with its increasing emphasis on individual rights and the inherent dignity of the individual. According to natural rights ethicist John Locke, the right to life is the primary human right. This right, however, can be forfeited if we violate another person's right to life. Locke writes in his *Second Treatise of Government:*

> Every Man hath a right to punish the Offender, and be Executioner of the Law of Nature. . . . Thus it is, that every Man in the State of Nature, has a Power to kill a Murderer, both to deter others from doing the like injury, which no Reparation

can compensate . . . and also to secure Men from the attempts of a Criminal, who having renounced Reason. . . . hath by the unjust Violence and Slaughter he hath committed upon one, declared War against all Mankind, and therefore may be destroyed as a *Lyon* or a *Tyger,* one of those wild Savage Beasts, with whom Men can have no Society nor Security: And upon this is grounded the great Law of Nature, *Who so sheddeth Man's Blood, by Man shall his Blood be shed.*[21]

The right to punish, including the right to administer the death penalty, is transferred to the state when people enter a social contract. Governments assume the prerogative to punish wrongdoers in order to prevent society from degrading into a state of disorder and anarchy, or what Locke refers to as a "state of nature." For more on the social contract, see the reading from John Locke at the end of Chapter 1.

The main objection to capital punishment came from social reformers such as Karl Marx and utilitarian Jeremy Bentham. Bentham opposed punishment in general because it subtracts from the total happiness of the community. He wrote. "All punishment is evil." The deliberate infliction of suffering on a person who has committed an evil, such as murder, he argued, merely adds more evil and suffering to the world. Punishment, therefore, can be justified only if it is the *only* way to remove an even greater evil.[22]

Not all utilitarians oppose the death penalty. John Stuart Mill believed that the benefits of capital punishment outweighed the harms. In an 1868 speech delivered in the British House of Commons, Mill called the death penalty appropriate for brutal crimes, arguing that it has a deterrent effect.[23] Both Ernest van den Haag and Hugo Adam Bedau examine the deterrent argument in their readings at the end of this chapter.

Immanuel Kant rejected consequentialist arguments for capital punishment. A murderer must die, he argued, not because of any social benefits but because this is the only way to satisfy the requirement of retributive justice. Kant writes:

> The penal law is a categorical imperative; and woe to him who creeps through the serpent-windings of utilitarianism to discover some advantage that may discharge him from the justice of punishment, or even from the due measure of it. . . . For if justice and righteousness perish, human life would no longer have any value in the world. . .
>
> But what is the mode and measure of punishment which public justice takes as its principle and standard? It is just the principle of equality, by which the pointer of the scale of justice is made to incline no more to the one side than the other. It may be rendered by saying that the undeserved evil which any one commits on another, is to be regarded as perpetrated on himself. ". . . If you strike another, you strike yourself; if you kill another, you kill yourself." This is the right of retaliation (jus talionis) . . . whoever has committed murder must die.[24]

Kant maintained that not only does the state have a right to punish; wrongdoers also have a right to *be* punished. Punishment, including the death penalty, affirms the criminals' dignity by acknowledging that they are responsible for their actions. Denying people the right to punishment is to deny that they are rational beings capable of responsibility for their own decisions. Jeffrey Reiman, in his article at the end of this chapter, rejects Kant's argument with regard to the death penalty. He argues that there are other types of punishment that can meet these moral requirements.

Marx rejected the Kantian justification of capital punishment based on retributive justice. He argued that an abstract theory, like the theory of retributive justice, is unable to take into account the unfair relations among different groups of people, especially in a capitalist society. Helen Prejean addresses this issue in the reading "Would Jesus Pull the Switch?" at the end of this chapter.

Both Buddhist and Confucian philosophers reject the death penalty. Buddhists oppose capital punishment because it violates the principle of *ahimsa,* or "no harm." Confucius believed that crime is a symptom of a disordered state. It is the rulers, rather than individual citizens, who have the most power to advance virtue in society and individuals. Because it is easiest for people to be virtuous when they are living in a just and well-ordered society, a state where there is a problem with crime needs to work on developing social policy that is more conducive to individual virtue and social harmony.

Contemporary philosophers are divided over capital punishment. Van den Haag and Christopher Morris support it. Bedau, Reiman, and Prejean, on the other hand, call for abolition of the death penalty.

THE MORAL ISSUES

Deterrence

Van den Haag argues that the threat of death is the ultimate deterrent. **Deterrence** is based on the assumption that the more severe the punishment for an action, the less likely people are to engage in it. If fear of punishment is removed, ordinarily law-abiding citizens may become violent and lawless.

Abolitionists of the death penalty point out that studies have not found any connection between the use of capital punishment and the rate of violent crime. Indeed, in Canada, the homicide rate peaked in 1975, the year *before* the abolition of the death penalty, and continued to decline for the next ten years.[25] In the United States, by contrast, two of the states with the most executions since 1979 have had an increase in murder rates following the reinstitution of the death penalty.[26] Because capital punishment has not been shown to have a deterrent effect, abolitionists argue, we are not saving innocent lives, but rather adding to the loss of human life.

Incapacitation

Whereas deterrence has the goal of keeping others from committing similar crimes, **incapacitation** is aimed at the specific person who was convicted of the crime and is based on an analogy between capital punishment and self-defense. The death penalty, it is argued, is the only way to ensure that a murderer will never kill again. Just as people have the right to use lethal force to protect themselves, so too does the government have the right to use the death penalty to protect society from dangerous criminals.

Opponents of capital punishment, such as Prejean and Bedau, maintain that life imprisonment, including the use of restraints and the isolation of those who pose a threat to guards and fellow inmates, is sufficient to incapacitate a would-be repeat murderer. Self-defense justifies the killing of a wrongdoer only during the commission of a violent crime. Several states now have life imprisonment without the possibility of parole as an alternative to the death penalty.

Retributive Justice

Many supporters of the death penalty, including Kant, Locke, and van den Haag, state that it doesn't matter whether capital punishment is a deterrent. Retributive justice alone justifies the death penalty. Retribution is not the same as revenge. Revenge is based on a personal desire for retaliation; retribution, on the other hand, is the impersonal carrying out of punishment to "cancel out" an evil act. A person who commits a crime creates a debt that must be paid to society.

One of the underlying principles of retributive justice is **proportionality.** Retributive justice requires that the severity of the punishment be proportionate to the crime, what Kant called the "equality of crime and punishment." The only appropriate payment for murder is death. As long as the debt remains unpaid, there is a sort of imbalance in the community or universe—a state of injustice exists until the debt is paid. Kant also argues that rather than denying the criminal's worth and dignity, retributive justice assumes moral worth and dignity by acknowledging that the criminal is a rational person who can be held morally responsible for his or her actions.

Some philosophers, including Bentham, question whether there is a moral duty of retribution. How can one act of violence cancel out another? Both Bedau and Reiman argue that the principle of retributive justice does not require an exact fit between the crime and the punishment. We do not rape rapists or burn the homes of arsonists; the deliberate killing of a murderer is also an inappropriate punishment. Instead, the appropriate moral response to wrongdoing is to demand that wrongdoers provide restitution to their victims. The goals of restitution are incompatible with capital punishment, because death removes all possibility of victim compensation.

Many opponents of capital punishment question Kant's assumption that retributive justice is required on the grounds that murder is based on a rational decision. Evidence indicates that, rather than being a rational decision, the great majority of murders are carried out impulsively, in the heat of passion, with little deliberation over the possible consequences. If murder is not based on a rational decision, murderers cannot be held morally responsible for their actions. Hence, the requirement of retributive justice that the murderer have a particular state of mind, when applied in practice, rules out capital punishment in most if not all cases. (See Case Study 3.)

Human Dignity and the Sanctity of Human Life

Some opponents of capital punishment, including Prejean and the Buddhists, claim that all deliberate taking of human life is wrong. The use of the death penalty diminishes the value of human life and lowers us to the level of the criminal. Prejean rejects the retributivist argument, arguing instead that it is degrading and inconsistent with respect for the dignity of persons. Because humans have intrinsic moral value, it is wrong to deprive them of their lives.

Human Rights and Moral Standing

Both the United Nations and Amnesty International oppose the death penalty on the grounds that it violates human rights. The human-rights argument has also been used to *support* capital punishment. Like Locke, Morris maintains that humans have certain fundamental rights, such as the right to life; but he also argues that those who violate other people's right to life by murdering them in turn forfeit their own right to life. Because they have forfeited this right, capital punishment cannot be said to violate it.

Prejean questions the logic of this argument, which is known as *reciprocity retributivism,* concluding that it does not take into account unfairness in society. Rather than setting wrongs right, capital punishment can further perpetuate an unfair status quo that denies certain groups of people full rights.

Distributive Justice and the Principle of Equality

There is concern that capital punishment is unfairly distributed. Tibetans are disproportionately represented on death row in China. In the United States, blacks are six times more likely than whites to end up on death row. Poorer defendants are also more likely to get the death penalty, because they cannot afford good defense lawyers.[27]

Some opponents of capital punishment argue that it is an extension of the slavery mentality, whereby the death penalty was frequently used on slaves who committed crimes against whites. They point out that all of the states that executed eight or more prisoners in the years since the Supreme Court declared capital punishment to be constitutional were Confederacy states.

In a study of why white Americans support the death penalty more than black Americans, researchers found that in some areas of the United States racial prejudice against blacks is the strongest predictor of support for the death penalty.[28] Furthermore, although all sixteen states that formed the Confederacy have the death penalty, outside of the former slave-owning states most have either abolished it or do not use it even though it is still on the books.

Van den Haag maintains the distribution-of-justice argument is irrelevant to capital punishment. The principle of equality requires not the abolition of the death penalty, but that all those guilty of murder—whether white or black—receive it. Even if the death penalty is applied in a discriminatory manner, this does not mean that capital punishment itself is wrong; it means that too many murderers who deserve the death penalty are getting off.

Utilitarian (Consequentialist) Arguments

Because pain is essential to punishment, utilitarians maintain that punishment is permissible only if it leads to an overall decrease in pain and an increase in pleasure for society. Studies have not shown this to be the case, however.

First of all, capital punishment has not been proven to have a deterrent effect. In addition, the death penalty can be expensive. Because of the lengthy appeal process and the time prisoners spend on death row, the average cost associated with a death penalty case can amount to several million dollars—up to three times higher than for life imprisonment.[29] Most of these costs are incurred prior to and during trials, as trials for capital offenses are costly and time-consuming. In California, which has the death penalty but has not carried out an execution since 2006, the death penalty system is estimated to have cost taxpayers about $138 million in 2008 alone.[30]

Capital punishment has also been denounced as cruel and inhumane. Amnesty International writes: "International law states that torture or cruel, inhuman, or degrading punishments can never be justified. The cruelty of the death penalty is self-evident." In some cases, such as in the execution of Stanley "Tookie" Williams in California in 2005 and that of Angel Nieves Diaz in Florida in December 2006, lethal injection can take more than half an hour to kill a person, due to difficulty in administering the needle or to insufficient doses of lethal chemicals, causing the prisoner pain and suffering. Witnesses in the Diaz execution said that "the whole process appeared to be torture."[31]

In her article, Prejean vividly describes the cruelty of the death penalty, both during the execution and during the long wait before it. In a 1983 electrocution in Alabama, it took three attempts and fourteen minutes to kill the prisoner.

The suffering of the criminal awaiting execution also has to be considered in a utilitarian calculus. The average time spent on death row before execution in the United States is ten years. French writer Albert Camus (1913–1960) once wrote that the moral contradiction inherent in a punishment that imitates the violence that it claims to abhor is only made worse by the premeditated nature of capital punishment.

According to **social contract** theory, governments are formed to protect themselves against danger. One of the primary purposes of capital punishment is to protect society against dangerous people. Some opponents of the death penalty, however, argue that it actually reduces public safety by draining public resources that could be used for crime prevention and drug treatment.

The death penalty has repercussions that reach far beyond the death chamber. The ripple effect reaches out to the family and friends of both the murder victim and the condemned person, as well as to society in general. Does capital punishment ease the grief of the murder victim's family? What is the effect of participating in an execution on medical professionals, who are sworn to save lives? Does violent punishment reinforce or legitimate violence in society in general?

Finality and the Risk of Errors

In 2003 New York City Mayor Michael Bloomberg expressed his opposition to the death penalty because of the number of innocent people who are executed. The death penalty also removes the possibility of restitution and repentance, as happened in the case of Karla Faye Tucker. (See Case Study 1.)

In addition to incorrect verdicts revealed by DNA testing, errors can occur because of flaws in the legal procedure. A Columbia University Law School study found that between 1973 and 1995 more than two-thirds of death sentences had been overturned in the appeal process because of "procedural flaws or unsound evidence."[32] The report concluded that the American capital punishment system is "fraught with error" mainly due to three factors: incompetent defense lawyers, flawed instructions to jurors, and procedural misconduct such as suppressed evidence.

Van den Haag dismisses these mistakes as part of the cost of doing justice. He points out that nearly all activities, such as construction work or even driving a car, carry risks and can cost the lives of innocent bystanders. However, we don't give up these activities. Bedau and Prejean, on the other hand, believe that the risk of executing innocent people is morally unacceptable, especially when there is an alternative such as life imprisonment without the possibility of parole.

Care Ethics

Prejean claims that one reason people favor the death penalty is that we don't identify with the condemned persons; we don't see them as humans like us. Before we can discuss the morality of capital punishment, we first have to see those who are condemned from a care perspective rather than a pure justice perspective.

Adopting Jesus Christ as her role model, Prejean maintains that we ought to love and care for people despite what they may have done. We should return compassion and good for evil, rather than evil for evil as the retributivists claim.

Why Punish?

Most people assume that punishment is the appropriate moral response to wrongdoing. However, does justice require punishment as the retributive justice theorists claim? Or is the punishment paradigm actually counterproductive and harmful to society?

One of the greatest frustrations of our criminal justice system is that criminals often come out in worse shape than when they went in. One study found that prisoners and guards interacted primarily at the lowest level of moral development—avoiding coercion and punishment. Within each group, however, they interacted primarily at Kohlberg's stage two of moral development—mutual benefit. The researchers concluded that prison life tends to mold prisoners into a morality lower than their "private best" outside the prison environment. In other words, the punishment paradigm, rather than making society safer, may actually be harming society by turning out more-hardened criminals.[33]

CONCLUSION

Capital punishment raises the issue of the moral value and dignity of humans who, apparently, are at the most despicable end of the spectrum, and who have little or no respect for the dignity of those whom they brutally massacre. The debate over the death penalty also leads to a reexamination of the punishment paradigm that underlies capital punishment. Even if the death penalty can be morally justified in theory, it does not necessarily follow that it should be used in practice. Creating a just public policy regarding capital punishment requires balancing moral theory with the realities of human nature and society.

🍃 SUMMARY OF READINGS ON THE DEATH PENALTY

Van den Haag, "The Ultimate Punishment: A Defense of Capital Punishment." The primary purpose of capital punishment is not deterrence but retributive justice.

Morris, "Punishment and Loss of Moral Standing." Those who violate the social contract lose some moral standing, including the right to life in the case of a murderer.

Bedau, "Capital Punishment." Capital punishment is inconsistent with the principle of respect for human dignity.

Reiman, "Why the Death Penalty Should Be Abolished in the United States." There are better ways morally to satisfy the requirement of retributive justice for murder than the death penalty.

Prejean, "Would Jesus Pull the Switch?" Capital punishment is brutal and a violation of human intrinsic value.

🍃 ERNEST VAN DEN HAAG
—————————

The Ultimate Punishment:
A Defense of Capital Punishment

Ernest van den Haag (1914–2002) was a professor of jurisprudence and public policy at Fordham University. A well-known advocate of the death penalty, van den Haag argues that the primary purpose of capital punishment is to satisfy the demands of retributive justice.

Critical Reading Questions

1. How does van den Haag respond to the argument that capital punishment is morally wrong because it is applied in a discriminatory manner?
2. According to van den Haag, which is the more important value, equality or justice, and why?
3. On what grounds does van den Haag argue that justice requires the death penalty?
4. How does van den Haag respond to the objection that sometimes innocent people are executed?
5. Does van den Haag think that capital punishment is an effective deterrent? Does his argument depend on its being an effective deterrent?

———————

"The Ultimate Punishment: A Defense of Capital Punishment," *The Harvard Law Review* 99 (1986): 1662–1669. Notes have been omitted.

6. What is the "rule of retaliation"? What, according to van den Haag, is the relevance of retaliation to the capital punishment debate?
7. How does van den Haag respond to the argument that capital punishment legitimates killing?
8. According to van den Haag, why does the principle of retribution require capital punishment for some crimes?
9. How does van den Haag respond to the argument that capital punishment is degrading to human dignity?

In an average year about 20,000 homicides occur in the United States. Fewer than 300 convicted murderers are sentenced to death. But because no more than thirty murderers have been executed in any recent year, most convicts sentenced to death are likely to die of old age. Nonetheless, the death penalty looms large in discussions: it raises important moral questions independent of the number of executions.

The death penalty is our harshest punishment. It is irrevocable: it ends the existence of those punished, instead of temporarily imprisoning them. Further, although not intended to cause physical pain, execution is the only corporal punishment still applied to adults. These singular characteristics contribute to the perennial, impassioned controversy about capital punishment.

I. DISTRIBUTION

Consideration of the justice, morality, or usefulness of capital punishment is often conflated with objections to its alleged discriminatory or capricious distribution among the guilty. Wrongly so. If capital punishment is immoral *in se,* no distribution among the guilty could make it moral. If capital punishment is moral, no distribution would make it immoral. Improper distribution cannot affect the quality of what is distributed, be it punishments or rewards. Discriminatory or capricious distribution thus could not justify abolition of the death penalty. Further, maldistribution inheres no more in capital punishment than in any other punishment.

Maldistribution between the guilty and the innocent is, by definition, unjust. But the injustice does not lie in the nature of the punishment. Because of the finality of the death penalty, the most grievous maldistribution occurs when it is imposed upon the innocent. However, the frequent allegations of discrimination and capriciousness refer to maldistribution among the guilty and not to the punishment of the innocent.

Maldistribution of any punishment among those who deserve it is irrelevant to its justice or morality. Even if poor or black convicts guilty of capital offenses suffer capital punishment, and other convicts equally guilty of the same crimes do not, a more equal distribution, however desirable, would merely be more equal. It would not be more just to the convicts under sentence of death.

Punishments are imposed on persons, not on racial or economic groups. Guilt is personal. The only relevant question is: does the person to be executed deserve the punishment? Whether or not others who deserve the same punishment, whatever their economic or racial group, have avoided execution is irrelevant. If they have, the guilt of the executed convicts would not be diminished, nor would their punishment be less deserved. To put the issue starkly, if the death penalty were imposed on guilty blacks, but not on guilty whites, or, if it were imposed by a lottery among the guilty, this irrationally discriminatory or capricious distribution would neither make the penalty unjust, nor cause anyone to be unjustly punished, despite the undue impunity bestowed on others.

Equality, in short, seems morally less important than justice. And justice is independent of distributional inequalities. The ideal of equal justice demands that justice be equally distributed, not that it be replaced by equality. Justice requires that as many of the guilty as possible be punished, regardless of whether others have avoided punishment. To let these others escape the deserved punishment does not do justice to them, or to society. But it is not unjust to those who could not escape. . . .

Recent data reveal little direct racial discrimination in the sentencing of those arrested and convicted of murder. The abrogation of the death penalty for rape has eliminated a major source of racial discrimination. Concededly, some discrimination based on the race of murder victims may exist; yet, this discrimination affects criminal victimizers in an unexpected way. Murderers of whites are thought more likely to be executed than murderers of blacks. Black victims, then, are less fully vindicated than white ones. However, because most black murderers kill blacks, black murderers are spared the death penalty more often than are white murderers. They fare better than most white murderers. The motivation behind unequal distribution of the death penalty may well have been to discriminate against blacks, but the result has favored them. Maldistribution is thus a straw man for empirical as well as analytical reasons.

II. MISCARRIAGES OF JUSTICE

In a recent survey Professors Hugo Adam Bedau and Michael Radelet found that 7000 persons were executed in the United States between 1900 and 1985 and that 25 were innocent of capital crimes. Among the innocents they list Sacco and Vanzetti as well as Ethel and Julius Rosenberg. Although their data may be questionable, I do not doubt that, over a long enough period, miscarriages of justice will occur even in capital cases.

Despite precautions, nearly all human activities, such as trucking, lighting, or construction, cost the lives of some innocent bystanders. We do not give up these activities, because the advantages, moral or material, outweigh the unintended

losses. Analogously, for those who think the death penalty just, miscarriages of justice are offset by the moral benefits and the usefulness of doing justice. For those who think the death penalty unjust even when it does not miscarry, miscarriages can hardly be decisive.

III. DETERRENCE

Despite much recent work, there has been no conclusive statistical demonstration that the death penalty is a better deterrent than are alternative punishments. However, deterrence is less than decisive for either side. Most abolitionists acknowledge that they would continue to favor abolition even if the death penalty were shown to deter more murders than alternatives could deter. Abolitionists appear to value the life of a convicted murderer or, at least, his non-execution, more highly than they value the lives of innocent victims who might be spared by deterring prospective murderers.

Deterrence is not altogether decisive for me either. I would favor retention of the death penalty as retribution even if it were shown that the threat of execution could not deter prospective murderers not already deterred by the threat of imprisonment. Still, I believe the death penalty, because of its finality, is more feared than imprisonment, and deters some prospective murderers not deterred by the threat of imprisonment. Sparing the lives of even a few prospective victims by deterring their murderers is more important than preserving the lives of convicted murderers because of the possibility, or even the probability, that executing them would not deter others. Whereas the lives of the victims who might be saved are valuable, that of the murderer has only negative value, because of his crime. Surely the criminal law is meant to protect the lives of potential victims in preference to those of actual murderers.

Murder rates are determined by many factors; neither the severity nor the probability of the threatened sanction is always decisive. However, for the long run, I share the view of Sir James

Fitzjames Stephen: "Some men, probably, abstain from murder because they fear that if they committed murder they would be hanged. Hundreds of thousands abstain from it because they regard it with horror. One great reason they regard it with horror is that murderers are hanged." Penal sanctions are useful in the long run for the formation of the internal restraints so necessary to control crime. The severity and finality of the death penalty is appropriate to the seriousness and finality of murder.

IV. INCIDENTAL ISSUES: COST, RELATIVE SUFFERING, BRUTALIZATION

Many nondecisive issues are associated with capital punishment. Some believe that the monetary cost of appealing a capital sentence is excessive. Yet most comparisons of the cost of life imprisonment with the cost of execution, apart from their dubious relevance, are flawed at least by the implied assumption that life prisoners will generate no judicial costs during their imprisonment. At any rate, the actual monetary costs are trumped by the importance of doing justice.

Others insist that a person sentenced to death suffers more than his victim suffered, and that this (excess) suffering is undue according to the *lex talionis* (rule of retaliation). We cannot know whether the murderer on death row suffers more than his victim suffered; however, unlike the murderer, the victim deserved none of the suffering inflicted. Further, the limitations of the *lex talionis* were meant to restrain private vengeance, not the social retribution that has taken its place. Punishment—regardless of the motivation—is not intended to revenge, offset, or compensate for the victim's suffering, or to be measured by it. Punishment is to vindicate the law and the social order undermined by the crime. This is why a kidnapper's penal confinement is not limited to the period for which he imprisoned his victim; nor is a burglar's confinement meant merely to offset the suffering or the harm he caused his victim; nor is it meant only to offset the advantage he gained.

Another argument heard at least since Beccaria is that, by killing a murderer, we encourage, endorse, or legitimize unlawful killing. Yet, although all punishments are meant to be unpleasant, it is seldom argued that they legitimize the unlawful imposition of identical unpleasantness. Imprisonment is not thought to legitimize kidnapping; neither are fines thought to legitimize robbery. The difference between murder and execution, or between kidnapping and imprisonment, is that the first is unlawful and undeserved, the second a lawful and deserved punishment for an unlawful act. The physical similarities of the punishment to the crime are irrelevant. The relevant difference is not physical, but social.

V. JUSTICE, EXCESS, DEGRADATION

We threaten punishments in order to deter crime. We impose them not only to make the threats credible but also as retribution (justice) for the crimes that were not deterred. Threats and punishments are necessary to deter and deterrence is a sufficient practical justification for them. Retribution is an independent moral justification. Although penalties can be unwise, repulsive, or inappropriate, and those punished can be pitiable, in a sense the infliction of legal punishment on a guilty person cannot be unjust. By committing the crime, the criminal volunteered to assume the risk of receiving a legal punishment that he could have avoided by not committing the crime. The punishment he suffers is the punishment he voluntarily risked suffering and, therefore, it is no more unjust to him than any other event for which one knowingly volunteers to assume the risk. Thus, the death penalty cannot be unjust to the guilty criminal.

There remain, however, two moral objections. The penalty may be regarded as always excessive as retribution and always morally degrading. To regard the death penalty as always excessive, one must believe that no crime—no matter how heinous—could possibly justify capital punishment. Such a belief can neither be corroborated nor refuted; it is an article of faith.

Alternatively, or concurrently, one may believe that everybody, the murderer no less than the victim, has an imprescriptible (natural?) right to life. The law therefore should not deprive anyone of life. I share Jeremy Bentham's view that any such "natural and imprescriptible rights" are "nonsense upon stilts."

Justice Brennan has insisted that the death penalty is "uncivilized," "inhuman," inconsistent with "human dignity" and with "the sanctity of life," that it "treats members of the human race as nonhumans, as objects to be toyed with and discarded," that it is "uniquely degrading to human dignity" and "by its very nature, [involves] a denial of the executed person's humanity." Justice Brennan does not say why he thinks execution "uncivilized." Hitherto most civilizations have had the death penalty, although it has been discarded in Western Europe, where it is currently unfashionable probably because of its abuse by totalitarian regimes.

By "degrading," Justice Brennan seems to mean that execution degrades the executed convicts. Yet philosophers, such as Immanuel Kant and G. F. W. Hegel, have insisted that, when deserved, execution, far from degrading the executed convict, affirms his humanity by affirming his rationality and his responsibility for his actions. They thought that execution, when deserved, is required for the sake of the convict's dignity. (Does not life imprisonment violate human dignity more than execution, by keeping alive a prisoner deprived of all autonomy?)

Common sense indicates that it cannot be death—our common fate—that is inhuman. Therefore, Justice Brennan must mean that death degrades when it comes not as a natural or accidental event, but as a deliberate social imposition. The murderer learns through his punishment that his fellow men have found him unworthy of living; that because he has murdered, he is being expelled from the community of the living. This degradation is self-inflicted. By murdering, the murderer has so dehumanized himself that he cannot remain among the living. The social recognition of his self-degradation is the punitive essence of execution. To believe, as Justice Brennan appears to, that the degradation is inflicted by the execution reverses the direction of causality.

Execution of those who have committed heinous murders may deter only one murder per year. If it does, it seems quite warranted. It is also the only fitting retribution for murder I can think of.

Discussion Questions

1. Do you agree with van den Haag that retributive justice is more important than equality? Support your answer.
2. Are you satisfied with van den Haag's argument that miscarriages of justice, in which innocent people are executed, are offset by the moral benefits of retributive justice? Discuss whether his response is consistent with human dignity and the categorical imperative, which states that we should never treat a person as a means only.
3. U.S. criminal defense attorney Clarence Darrow (1857–1938) was an outspoken opponent of the death penalty. Darrow believed that human behavior is determined by circumstances out of our control and, therefore, does not deserve to be punished. In his "Address to the Prisoners in the Chicago County Jail," Darrow told the inmates:

   In one sense, everybody is equally good and equally bad. We all do the best we can under the circumstances . . . there were circumstances that drove you to do exactly the thing which you did. You could not help it any more than we outside can help taking the positions we take. . . .

> I will guarantee to take from this jail, or any jail in the world, five hundred men who have been the worst criminals and law-breakers who ever got into jail, and I will go down to our lowest streets and take five hundred of the most abandoned prostitutes, and go out somewhere where there is plenty of good land, and will give them a chance to make a living, and they will be as good people as the average in the community.[34]

Do you agree with Darrow? Discuss how van den Haag might respond to Darrow's claim that criminals are simply products of their environments.

4. Discuss how a care ethicist, such as Carol Gilligan or Nel Noddings, might respond to van den Haag's justice-based argument. Is van den Haag's justification of capital punishment consistent with a care ethics approach? Support your answer.

CHRISTOPHER W. MORRIS

Punishment and Loss of Moral Standing

Christopher Morris is a professor of philosophy at Bowling Green University in Ohio. In his article Morris presents a social contract theory of punishment. He argues that people who intentionally violate the social contract by engaging in wrongdoing lose some moral standing and, hence, forfeit some of their moral rights. Those who murder forfeit their right to life.

Critical Reading Questions

1. According to Morris, what is the moral status of a wrongdoer?
2. How does Morris define punishment? What is the purpose of punishment?
3. What distinction does Morris make between justice and benevolence? Which of these moral duties is more relevant to the question of punishment?
4. How does Morris define justice? Why, according to him, should we act justly?
5. What is the "doctrine of the circumstances of justice"?
6. According to Morris, what does it mean for someone to have "moral standing"?
7. What is the "forfeiture justification of punishment"?
8. According to Morris, why would a rational person choose to be just?
9. What are some of the objections to the forfeiture justification of punishment? How does Morris respond to these objections?

"Punishment and Loss of Moral Standing," *Canadian Journal of Philosophy* 21, no. 1 (March 1991): 53–80. Some notes have been omitted.

I. THE MORAL JUSTIFICATION OF PUNISHMENT

. . . I shall argue that wrongdoers do not possess moral rights that stand in the way of their being punished. Thus punishment of wrongdoers will not be unjust.

What is punishment? The matter of the definition of punishment is complicated, as well as controversial. It will suffice for my purposes to have a general characterization of the notion. As such, punishment is the intentional imposition of some pain, unpleasantness, or deprivation for an offense committed by the culprit. It may be imposed so as to teach the offender a lesson, to deter others from similar acts, or to exact retribution. . . .

Criminal penalties are often recommended or defended as effective deterrents, or as appropriate means of retribution for certain offenses or at least of expressing the seriousness with which we view them. It is usually, and quite naturally, assumed that such penalties must consequentially be justified— that is, *morally* justified—if they are to be inflicted. In particular, it is usually thought that a particular kind of moral justification is required in the standard cases of punishment—namely, justification with reference to *justice*.

It is common to think of morality as having different parts or virtues. It is controversial how to understand these parts or even how to distinguish them. But it is widely thought that justice is different from the virtues of friendship, courage, moderation, and the like. More importantly, justice is usually distinguished from charity or benevolence, although there is less agreement here. The standard distinction is to understand justice to pertain to what individuals are *owed*, to what they may *claim*, to what they have a *right*. Benevolence, by contrast, is a virtue that attaches itself directly to the well-being of others. It is exemplified by taking an interest in others' welfare independently of that to which they have a claim. . . .

Typically, infringements of liberty or intentional infliction of pain violate moral rights to be free and not to be harmed. Thus, it would normally be thought that punishment requires a rationale in terms of justice. The state's involvement, it is usually thought, will only strengthen this requirement.

Now the moral rights of criminals do not stand in the way of punishment if we may justifiably *infringe* or *override* them. I do not, however, wish to defend either of these two possibilities. Instead I shall argue that punishment will not be unjust when wrongdoers lose the moral rights that would otherwise protect them against harm or loss. I turn now to the conception of justice that will be the basis of my approach to punishment.

II. JUSTICE BY CONVENTION

Justice is the moral virtue that is concerned with what is *owed* or *due* to individuals. It is that to which individuals appeal when they claim that to which they have a moral *right* (though this is not to say that the domain of rights exhausts that of justice). Recent discussions of justice have focused largely on principles of distributive justice, but this narrow focus should not let us lose sight of the larger virtue.

There is a long western tradition, dating back to Antiphon, Glaucon, and Epicurus, developed by Hobbes, Hume, and Rousseau, and continued in various ways by Rawls, Harsanyi, Mackie, Harman, Scanlon, Gauthier, and Kavka that understands justice to be a type of mutually agreeable convention. According to this tradition, justice consists of principles, rules, and norms that ideally serve to advance the interests and aims of all in certain situations. This tradition is dubbed "contractarian" as it often understands the terms of justice to be the outcome of a hypothetical bargain or "social contract." It might be less misleading to think of contemporary representatives of this tradition as offering a "rational choice" conception of morality after John Rawls's famous remark, "The theory of justice is a part, perhaps the most significant part, of the theory of rational choice."[1]

The account of justice offered by this tradition is designed to answer two traditional questions: what does justice require? and why be just? . . .

The indirect advantages of justice may normally be such that few individuals can wish to forego them. The advantages of injustice may, however, be sufficiently great that individuals are tempted to act unjustly. When then is it rational to be just? The principles of conduct that would emerge from the hypothetical bargain that rational choice ethicists use to determine the requirements of justice are those to which it is rational to agree. For such principles, if complied with, secure everyone's advantage. Without them, life would be nasty, brutish, and short, depending on the efficacy of alternative means of social control (e.g., law, superstition, kinship relations). However, granting that we have a reason to agree to such principles—even to grant that they define what justice is—what reason do we have to comply with their requirements? . . .

One of the conditions—one of the "circumstances of justice," to use Rawls's phrase—giving rise to the need for justice is the possibility of mutual benefit. Others are the capacity and willingness of rational beings to impose constraints on their behavior. In the absence of such conditions, one has no reason to abide by the constraints of justice in one's conduct toward others. This is important, for it effectively means that in the absence of (1) mutual benefit or of (2) the capacity or (3) willingness to be just, individuals are not constrained by justice in their behavior toward one another. The answer that contractarian theorists give to the question "why be just?" commits them to the view just expressed, that in the absence of certain conditions there is no reason to act justly; we may call this view "the *doctrine* of the circumstances of justice." This doctrine is crucial to my understanding of the justification of punishment. I turn now to a brief account of *moral standing.*

Let us say that a *moral object* is something that is an object of moral consideration. A *direct* moral object is something *to* which (or to whom) that consideration is paid or owed; an *indirect* moral object is something *about* or *concerning* which moral consideration is paid. The latter is a *beneficiary* of the moral consideration. . . .

To have *moral standing* is to be owed (some) moral consideration, that is, to be a direct moral object. To be a mere indirect moral object is *not* to possess moral standing. In terms of these notions and distinctions, people typically are direct moral objects and have moral standing. . . .

We may contrast the notion of a moral object with that of a *moral subject.* The latter is something that has moral duties or may be expected to give moral consideration to direct moral objects. We usually understand adult humans to be moral subjects, while non-human animals and young infants are not so regarded; presumably *agency* would be necessary to being a moral subject.

Supposing that the "circumstances of justice" be satisfied, rational choice or contractarian moral theory understands rational humans, capable and willing to impose moral constraints on their conduct toward others, as moral subjects and direct moral objects. Thus, for this theory, as for most others, in normal circumstances adult humans have moral obligations and are owed certain moral considerations. . . .

Now contractarian moral theory will imply that in the circumstances of justice all humans capable and willing to impose constraints on their behavior toward others have full moral standing. . . .

III. WRONGDOING AND LOSS OF MORAL STANDING

To have moral standing is to be owed (some) moral consideration. Justice consists in part of a set of moral rights, the most important of which, we may assume, are those to life, liberty, and property. To lose some such rights is to lose some of one's moral standing. I wish to argue that wrongdoers lose some of their rights and some of their moral standing, and that some wrongdoers lose all of their rights (or never possessed the full set) and retain at most what I have called partial moral standing. In other words, I shall defend a type of forfeiture theory, one according to which part (but only part) of the justification for punishment rests in the fact that wrongdoers lack certain rights, the presence of which would normally suffice to block the appropriate punishment. . . .

The first way in which wrongdoers can lose rights is less controversial or novel than the second; so I shall spend less time developing it. We may suppose that the conventions that determine justice, according to the contractarian tradition, have built into them provisions for penalties in the event of violation. Consider a club or organization established for the benefit of its members. It will have rules, respect of which will further the ends of the members. Without supposing duplicity on the part of the latter, it would be reasonable for them to include sanctions, however mild, for the violation of these rules; sanctions may provide assurance that others will not take advantage of one's cooperative behavior. Similarly, we may suppose that the rules of morality have built into them penalties, which may be applied whenever individuals act wrongly, that is, in violation of the rules.

The conception of justice characteristic of the contractarian tradition is that of an "artificial" system—to use the predicate favored by Hobbes and Hume—which ideally serves the interests of members of society. Given the imperfections of human rationality, it would be unwise to desire a system without sanctions for violations of its norms. That is, since we may expect that ordinary humans, without manifesting unwillingness to abide by the constraints of justice, will violate these constraints on occasion, when the temptation proves to be difficult to resist, we build into these constraints penalties for violations. . . .

The normal rights of individuals, then, are suspended whenever they violate the constraints of justice. The *act* of wrongdoing may cause the wrongdoer to lose, if only temporarily, certain rights. . . .

Criminal acts, then, insofar as they manifest the agent's unwillingness to comply with the requirements of justice, lead to (some) loss of moral standing. This is a simple consequence of the conditional nature of contractarian justice. What rights are thus lost? Alan H. Goldman makes the following suggestion:

> if we ask which rights are forfeited in violating rights of others, it is plausible to answer just those rights that one violates (or an equivalent set).

One continues to enjoy rights only as long as one respects those rights in others: violation constitutes forfeiture. But one retains those rights which one has continued to respect in others.[2]

Wrongdoers, then, may lose (some of) their rights by their acts. The act alone may cause this loss insofar as the conventions of justice have penalties and the requisite suspension of duties built in. Further, the act, insofar as it manifests an unwillingness to abide by the constraints of justice, will bring about this loss; in some cases, the unwillingness revealed by the act may show that we mistakenly cooperated with the wrongdoer. Inflicting pain or deprivation of property or liberty on wrongdoers as a response to their acts is not unjust for they have lost, through their acts, the moral rights that would otherwise stand in the way of such treatment. Their status is analogous to exile; they are banished, not from a physical space but from a moral space. They have lost, at least in part, their membership in the moral community.

The forfeiture account may be independently appealing for retributive and other reasons. It may be thought that loss of the rights that wrongdoers violate is actually a most appropriate punishment for individuals unwilling to respect the requirements of justice. The intuitive appeal here may be similar to that of *lex talionis* in retributive theories. Further, it might be argued that punishing wrongdoers in ways that emphasize the relation between the rights they have violated and those they have thereby lost best *expresses* the community's outrage or anger at the wrongful act. Insofar as punishment has an expressive function, the criminal's forfeiture of moral rights would be both a consequence of his or her wrongdoing and an expression of the moral community's consequent outrage. . . .

IV. THE DEATH PENALTY

The forfeiture account may be illustrated by an application to the death penalty. A discussion of capital punishment in light of the forfeiture thesis may provide a different understanding of the issues than is usually found in the contemporary literature. Consider the cases of contract killers, war criminals, tyrants, and certain terrorists who are unwilling to abide by the constraints of justice in their conduct toward others. . . .

Such people clearly lack full moral standing on a contractarian account of justice. They show by their conduct that they are unwilling to abide by the constraints of justice with most others. With respect to the latter, they themselves lack the protection that justice normally affords people. Suppose that they are apprehended, tried, and convicted of their crimes. Would it be *unjust* to execute them? No, for they lack full moral standing and thus the protection of justice. By their unwillingness to impose the constraints of justice on their conduct toward others, they lose the protection of justice. . . .

[W]e have no moral obligations of justice to contract killers, war criminals, tyrants, and genuine terrorists, or other individuals who place themselves outside the constraints of justice. Were it to be wrong to execute them, we would not be wronging *them* were we to do so; *they* would have no grounds of justice to complain.

We normally possess moral rights to life and to liberty. It is a controversial matter among ethicists exactly how these rights are to be understood, thus the contemporary debates over abortion, euthanasia, nuclear deterrence, and other issues. But at least part of the content of such moral rights is the obligation of others to refrain from intentionally taking one's life or from interfering with one's liberty when such is not necessary in order to protect the equal liberty of others or to serve some other important good. Such characterizations are imprecise, but they will serve my purpose.

Justice gives us our basic moral rights to life and liberty. Most theories of justice, contractarian or other, should have little trouble accounting for these rights, at least as I have characterized them. Thus, normally when we intentionally take another's life or interfere with their liberty, we must justify our actions with reference to justice, given their rights to life and liberty. Since taking or thus restricting another's life or liberty appear to be

violations of their moral rights to life or liberty, a moral justification, one which makes reference to justice, seems required. Usually we will seek to show that the rights in question were *overridden* by some moral consideration. . . .

In the cases of the contract killers, war criminals, tyrants, and terrorists, I am suggesting that their moral rights to life or liberty are not overridden. (Indeed, I believe that this is not possible with respect to the moral right to life since I believe that this right is not *defeasible,* though I do not propose to argue this here.) Instead I am arguing that we do not have to give standard *moral* justifications for executing contract killers, war criminals, tyrants, or terrorists because so killing them would neither be a violation nor an overriding of their moral rights to life or liberty. Rather, they no longer have, or never had, such moral rights. Thus we merely need sufficient reason to execute them. To use Hobbes' language, such individuals have only the "right" of nature, that is, mere Hohfeldian liberties that entail no correlative obligations on the part of others. . . .

V. OBJECTIONS

Many will find my account counter-intuitive and will reject the idea that some humans, no matter how amoral, lose their rights and moral standing. And there are many objections that will be, and have been, made. I shall discuss some of these.

Much crime is committed by the destitute in the urban underclass. It may be argued that the account I have offered "does not apply" to them, as "they are *outside* of the circumstances of justice to begin with and have nothing to forfeit." It is unclear what exactly the objection is, for if individuals who commit crimes lack certain rights to begin with, then no rights stand in the way of their being punished for their acts, and the first part of a justification for punishment is complete. This criticism might be the same as that which finds the very idea of someone without full moral standing objectionable. Now there *is* a serious question about the implications of our moral theories for the plight of those in our cities who have no or lit-tle stake in the social order. My view is that there are compelling contractarian arguments for some redistribution to the poor and destitute to give them a stake in the social order and bring them into the circumstances of justice. But that would seem to be another matter entirely than the sub-ject of this essay.

It might be argued that the forfeiture account would permit various forms of cruel punishment—for instance, the death penalty—and that this constitutes an objection. If cruelty involves indif-ference to another's pain or suffering, then pun-ishment as I have characterized it may well be cruel. However, if cruelty involves taking pleasure in another's suffering, then cruelty is not part of the account that I am offering. For on the view that I am defending, the reasons for punishment are independent of the grounds for the permissibility of punishment.

It is a criticism, however, of many of our institu-tions to point out that our motivations are mixed and include elements of cruelty or malice. Were we to dispose of certain amoral criminals by impris-oning or executing them, accepting the account I have offered, but do so largely from malice and revenge, then our practices would be vulnerable to criticism. Supposing that the criminal in question lacks the moral rights that justice accords, then cruelty will be an objection only insofar as (1) it is contrary to benevolence or some other virtue, (2) it is bad public policy, or (3) we have obliga-tions to others that prohibit us from treating any human cruelly. It is likely that, e.g., torture will virtually always be ruled out for these reasons, though I do not propose to argue this here. . . .

VI. CONCLUSION

Punishment, I have argued, is justified in part because wrongdoers lose the moral rights that would otherwise stand in the way of their being harmed in the manner that we do when we pun-ish. Moral standing is to some degree lost, and moral rights are to some degree forfeited, by wrongdoers.

It might be argued that the position I have put forward does not take justice seriously. I disagree. The forfeiture account I have developed links in a certain way being a direct moral object with being a moral subject. Rational humans who are not will-ing to impose the constraints of justice on their conduct toward others are not themselves pro-tected by these constraints. In my view, *that* is to take justice seriously.

NOTES

1. *A Theory of Justice* (Cambridge, MA: Harvard Uni-versity Press, 1971), 16; see also 172. It is clear from his most recent writings, if not from some of the ele-ments of *A Theory of Justice,* that Rawls does not really endorse the view of moral theory expressed by his remark.
2. Alan H. Goldman, "The Paradox of Punishment," *Philosophy & Public Affairs* 9 (1979): 44.

Discussion Questions

1. Consider the story of Gyges's ring in Plato's *Republic* in which Glaucon argues that people are naturally selfish and will behave unjustly whenever they have the oppor-tunity (see Chapter 1). Do people behave justly only to avoid punishment or public censure, as Glaucon claims? Or do people behave justly because it mutually benefits them, as Morris claims? Support your answer.
2. In a footnote to his article, Morris draws an analogy between forfeiture of rights and exile or banishment of criminals. Someone "violates certain fundamental norms of society (or displeases the rulers) and is stripped of citizenship and banished from

the land." Socrates, he notes, was offered the choice of exile or the death penalty; he chose the latter. Most people believe, however, that the execution of Socrates by the state was not morally justified. Does the death of Socrates and others who question societal norms and laws demonstrate a flaw in the contractual concept of justice? Discuss how Morris might respond to this question.

3. Following World War II, the tribunal at the United Nations Nuremberg Trials compiled a charter with a list of universal standards of justice. Between 1945 and 1949, almost 200 Nazis were tried under this new charter. Of these, 161 were found guilty and 36 sentenced to death. Discuss how a social contractarian such as Morris would respond to the use of the death penalty for the Nazi war criminals. Because the Nazis did not violate their own community's social contract, and the Nuremberg charter was not written until after the war, did the United Nations act unjustly by punishing the Nazis for being "good" citizens?

4. Should foreign terrorist suspects or enemy combatants who are acting according to their cultural or group norms be subjected to the death penalty by the United States? Discuss how Morris might answer this question.

HUGO ADAM BEDAU

Capital Punishment

Hugo Adam Bedau is a professor of philosophy at Tufts University and a well-known opponent of capital punishment. In the following selection, Bedau examines the death penalty in light of important relevant moral values, such as the sanctity of life and the right to life. Bedau also questions the morality of punishment.

Critical Reading Questions

1. What, according to Bedau, is one of the most important moral values?
2. What is the relationship between the sanctity of human life and the right to life? Why, according to Bedau, is the death penalty inconsistent with these two values?
3. Why does Bedau reject Locke's argument that the right to life is forfeited by murderers?
4. On what grounds does Bedau reject Kant's claim that retributive justice requires capital punishment for murder?

"Capital Punishment," in *Matters of Life and Death,* ed. by Tom Regan (New York: McGraw-Hill, 1993), 160–192. Some notes have been omitted.

5. According to Kant, in what state of mind must a murderer be to be held morally responsible for his or her actions? Why does Bedau reject Kant's reasoning on this point?

6. On what grounds does Bedau reject utilitarian arguments for capital punishment?

7. What are the nature and purpose of punishment, according to Bedau?

8. Why does Bedau conclude that the death penalty violates the dignity of persons?

9. On what grounds does Bedau reject the social defense argument for the death penalty?

10. On what grounds does Bedau reject consequentialist arguments, such as deterrence, incapacitation, and crime prevention, for the death penalty?

11. On what grounds does Bedau argue that retributive justice does not require the death penalty for murder?

12. According to Bedau, why does capital punishment demean society as well as the criminal being executed?

INTRODUCTION

When we confront the task of evaluating punishments from the moral point of view, a host of questions immediately arises: Who should be punished? What offenses and harms should be made liable to punishment? What is involved in making the punishment fit the crime? Are some punishments too cruel or barbaric to be tolerated no matter how effective they may be in preventing crime? Are some criminals so depraved or dangerous that no punishment is too severe for them? What moral principles should govern our thinking about crime and punishment?

To give reasonable answers to such questions, we need to appeal to a wide variety of empirical facts. We will want to know, for example, what would happen to the crime rate if no one were punished at all, or if all offenders were punished more leniently or more severely than is now usual. We would want to know whether the system of criminal justice operates with adequate efficiency and fairness when it metes out punishment, or whether the severest punishments tend to fall mainly on some social, racial, or economic classes. But we will want to settle other things besides these matters of fact. Social values, moral ideals, ethical principles are also involved, and we will want to know which values and which ideals they are and how to evaluate them as well.

Central among these ethical considerations are the value, worth, and dignity of persons—the victims of crime, the offenders, and the rest of society. How, exactly, does our belief in the value of human life, the worth of each person, our common humanity and our common dignity, bear on the nature and methods of punishment as seen from the moral point of view?

. . . From an historical perspective, one of the most important relevant ethical values is the idea of *the sanctity of human life.* . . .

So far as the death penalty is concerned, it might seem that once it is granted that human life is sacred or that everyone has an equal right to life, the death penalty is morally indefensible. Such a punishment seems obviously inconsistent with such ideals as human worth and value. The opposite, however, is true if we let history be our guide. Chief among the traditional defenders of capital punishment have been religious and secular thinkers who sincerely believed in these ideals. In fact, these thinkers usually invoked the sanctity of human life and the right to life as part of their defense and justification of death for murderers and other criminals. To see how such a seemingly paradoxical doctrine can be maintained, as well as to begin our examination of the major issues involved in the moral evaluation of the death penalty, we must scrutinize the traditional doctrine of the right to life.

I. THE RIGHT TO LIFE AND CAPITAL PUNISHMENT

The Doctrine of Natural Rights

The general idea shared by many philosophers, beginning in the seventeenth century, was that each person by nature—that is, apart from the laws of the state and simply by virtue of being born a human being—had the right to live. It followed from this that it was a violation of this right to murder another person, and that it was the responsibility of government to protect human rights, prohibit murder, and try to arrest, convict, and punish anyone guilty of this crime. Thus, the right to life can be thought of, first, as underlying the prohibition against murder common to the criminal law of all countries. . . .

The right to life seems to pose a problem for a policy of capital punishment. Even if a person has committed murder (so the argument runs) and has therewith intentionally violated another's right to life, the criminal still has his or her own right to life. Would it not be a violation of the murderer's right for him or her to be put to death as punishment? If so, must not capital punishment be morally wrong? . . .

Forfeiting the Right to Life

Locke argued that although a person's right to life is natural and inalienable, it can be "forfeited" and is forfeited whenever one person violates that right in another. [W. D. Ross] has put the point clearly: "The offender, by violating the life, liberty, or property of another, has lost his own right to have his life, liberty, or property respected. . . ."[1] The idea is a familiar one, although there are troubling and unanswered questions: To whom is it forfeited? Can this right, once forfeited, ever be restored? . . .

Difficulties with Locke's Theory

There are various objections to the classic theory of the right to life, two of which deserve to be mentioned here. First, underlying Locke's doctrine of natural rights and wholly independent of it are two important assumptions. One is that punishment under law is necessary for social defense. (By "social defense" is meant the prevention of crime, by means of deterrence and incapacitation, as well as by the reduction of incentives and opportunities for the commission of crimes. Thus, prisons, police forces, controlling the sale of firearms, locks on doors, and threats of punishment can all be regarded as methods of social defense.) The other is that justice requires retribution—criminals deserve to be punished, and the punishment must fit the crime. Such beliefs lead to the conclusion that the punishment for murder and other crimes should be death, and they force Locke to make some accommodation in his theory of natural rights. The device he hit upon, as we have just seen, and one that generations of later thinkers have also adopted, is to declare that the right to life could be forfeited under certain conditions.

Against Locke's doctrine several objections deserve to be considered. First of all, there are other alternatives. . . . [S]uppose it is argued that although punishments typically constitute harms or deprivations to the person who undergoes them, the quality and extent of the deprivations [are] an open question. What is necessary is that the deprivation be imposed on the offender regardless of his or her preferences and choice. On this view, while it would be necessary for the offender to forfeit some rights in order to be punished, it would not be necessary to forfeit the right to life. Yet another possibility is to regard the right to life as an absolute right, one that it is always wrong to violate. Whether any of these alternatives can be better supported than the doctrine of forfeiture need not be resolved here. They do show that forfeiture of rights as Locke presents it is not the only way to permit punishment under a theory of natural rights.

Another difficulty with Locke's doctrine is that it seems to collapse two distinct issues into one. It is one thing to appeal to forfeiting rights in order to permit society to punish the guilty offender in the first place. It is quite another to appeal to forfeiture of rights in order to decide which among the available punishments is the appropriate one. . . . There is no intrinsic feature of any natural right, including the right to life, that makes it subject to loss through forfeiture. The only basis for supposing that any right is forfeited rather than grossly violated by society when it punishes an offender by death is that just retribution and social defense together require the death penalty for offenders guilty of a crime of this sort. If this requirement turns out to be false, unsubstantiated, or doubtful, then the claim that a criminal's right to life has been forfeited turns out to be equally false, unsubstantiated, or doubtful. . . .

Even if it is concluded that a murderer or violent criminal does forfeit the natural right to life, it does not follow that a murderer *must* be put to death. . . . This is often overlooked by those who insist that the death penalty is justified because murderers forfeit their lives. Forfeiting one's *right* to life is not identical with forfeiting one's life. . . .

Finally, we should note that Locke's doctrine of forfeiture makes his theory of natural rights vulnerable to utilitarian reasoning, and with devastating effect. The chief attraction of the idea of natural rights is that it provides each of us with moral armor (our rights) to protect us against burdens and deprivations that might be imposed on the ground that they are in the interests of the many or good for society in the long run. . . .

The Dignity of Persons

Although Kant by no means repudiated the doctrine of natural rights, he elevated to primary importance a different idea, the supreme worth or dignity of each person. The most famous single passage in which this doctrine and Kant's views on the punishment of murder are brought together runs as follows:

> If . . . he has committed a murder, he must die. In this case, there is no substitute that will satisfy the requirements of legal justice. There is no sameness of kind between death and remaining alive even under the most miserable conditions, and consequently there is no equality between the crime and the retribution unless the criminal

is judicially condemned and put to death. But the death of the criminal must be kept entirely free of any maltreatment that would make an abomination of the humanity residing in the person suffering it.[2] . . .

For Kant, that idea of the dignity of man enters explicitly only to rule out any aggravations and brutality accompanying the sentence of death and its execution. For Kant, the dignity of man underlies the whole idea of society of free and rational persons choosing to submit themselves to a common rule of law that includes the punishment of crimes. Accordingly, in punishment, "a human being can never be manipulated merely as a means to the purposes of someone else. . . . His innate personality protects him against such treatment. . . ."[3] Kant's appeal to the dignity of man requires him to rule out any role for social defense in the justification of capital punishment.

As the above passage also shows, underlying Kant's belief in the appropriateness of punishing murder with death is a principle of just retribution. This is reminiscent of Locke's view. . . . The chief difference between Kant and Locke is that Locke thinks it is proper to take into account not only just retribution but also social defense to determine proper punishments, whereas Kant unequivocally rules out the latter. What Kant has done is to present us with two moral ideas—the dignity or worth of each person as a rational creature, and the principle of retribution—that he regards as inextricably tied together. The latter principle he explained in the following way:

> What kind and what degree of punishment does public legal justice adopt as its principle and standard? None other than the principle of equality . . . , that is, the principle of not treating one side more favorably than the other. Accordingly, any undeserved evil that you inflict on someone else among the people is one that you do to yourself. Only the Law of retribution . . . can determine exactly the kind and degree of punishment.[4] . . .

Kant, as is obvious from his remarks, thought that retribution *required* the death penalty for murder.

He is not alone in holding this view; it has widespread appeal even today. . . .

Difficulties with Kant's Theory

In the course of presenting Kant's views, we have already identified three respects in which his theory is vulnerable. One is that, like Locke's, it assumes that just retribution *requires* capital punishment for murder, an assumption that may be unnecessary and in any case is not proved. Another difficulty is that, unlike Locke's theory, Kant's seems to make no room whatever for the role of social defense in the justification of punishment. . . .

Finally, the third objection follows from the fact that Kant's theory is so obviously abstract and unempirical from beginning to end. If we really take seriously the idea of the dignity of the human person, then it may be that we will be led in case after case of actual crime to reject Kant's reasoning on the ground that it is inapplicable in light of the actual facts of the case. Kant's theory tells us what to do only with ideally rational killers; what we need is a theory that tells us how to cope with the actual persons who kill, and how to do that in a way that acknowledges our common humanity with both the victim and the offender, as well as the injustices to which all social systems are prone and the wisdom of self-restraint in the exercise of violence, especially when undertaken deliberately and in the name of justice.

Utilitarianism and the Death Penalty

. . . Just as Kant disregarded considerations of consequences in evaluating the morality of capital punishment, so utilitarians disregard any appeals to natural rights or the dignity of the human person. . . . The utilitarian, therefore, regards the death penalty as justified by the degree to which it advances the general welfare. Accordingly, its justification proceeds in the following manner: (1) Consider the practice of the death penalty and all its present and future consequences—for the executed offenders, for the victims of crime, their friends and families, and the rest of society. (2) Consider each of the alternative modes of punishment that might be imposed and the consequences of each were it to be employed. (3) Decide in favor of the death penalty rather than any alternative only if, in light of all of the facts, its practice would have the greatest net balance of benefit over burden for everyone affected by it.

Two things are noteworthy about such a pattern of reasoning. First, everything depends on the facts, and diverse issues of fact are always in question. Moreover, these facts are not likely to remain constant in a given society decade after decade, much less from one society to another. The result is that it may be very difficult to reach agreement on all of them, as the unending debate over the deterrent efficacy of executions attests. When that happens, reasonable utilitarians will have to agree to disagree with each other over whether the death penalty should be retained, modified, or abolished for this or that crime. We have, in fact, a perfect illustration of precisely such a disagreement between the two most influential classic utilitarian philosophers. Jeremy Bentham (1748–1832) strongly opposed the death penalty throughout his life and in one of his last essays argued forcefully for its complete abolition in England and France. His student, John Stuart Mill (1806–1873), however, when he was a member of Parliament in the 1860s, argued with comparable firmness against abolition of the death penalty for murder. . . .

A second point of interest is that the general welfare is an extremely abstract, remote, and elusive end-state to serve as the good to be aimed at in choosing among alternative penal policies. Utilitarians have devoted much energy to trying to give shape and content to this idea. . . .

II. THE MORALITY OF PUNISHMENT

As a first step toward providing a fresh setting for the rest of our discussion, it is useful to have a general sketch before us of why it is rational for society to have a system of punishment at all, quite apart from whether the death penalty is used as one of the modes of punishment. We are not likely to assess the morality of capital punishment correctly unless we understand the morality of punishment in general. . . .

The Right to Punish

Society is organized by reference to common norms that forbid anyone and everyone to engage in certain sorts of harmful conduct. When someone deliberately, willfully, and knowingly violates such rules, and therewith harms the innocent, the offender has violated the rights of others and immediately becomes liable to a punitive response. Since the norms were originally designed to provide protection to every person, and since (so we also assume) the culprit knew in advance that his or her conduct was prohibited because it would be injurious to others, and since he or she freely and knowingly chose nevertheless to violate the norm, society cannot simply ignore the violation and continue to treat the offender as if no wrong had been done. It must attempt to bring the offender to judgment. . . .

Punishment, therefore, serves the complex function of reinforcing individual compliance with a set of social norms deemed necessary to protect the rights of all the members of society. Once it has been determined that one of these norms has been deliberately violated, then there is no alternative but to set in motion the system of criminal justice that culminates in the punishment of the guilty offender.

Such a system is essentially retributive in at least two respects. Crime must be punished, and the punishment must fit the crime. The theory relied upon here certainly acknowledges the first of these contentions. Punishment by its nature pays back an offender who has inflicted suffering and indignity on an innocent victim by inflicting suffering and indignity on the offender. Justice, more than any other consideration (social defense, reform of the offender), dictates that all crimes be liable to punishment, and that a reasonable portion of social resources (public expenditures) be allocated to the arrest, conviction, and punishment of offenders. . . .

Modes of Punishment

What sorts of punishments are available to society to inflict on offenders? What are the sorts of things any person could be deprived of that would count as punishment? Obviously, one could have one's money or property confiscated, or be deprived of the right to future earnings or an inheritance. But because so much crime against property and against the person is committed by the poor and untalented, by persons with no property and no prospects of any, and because the stolen property is so often disposed of prior to the offender's arrest, it is often pointless to levy punishments in the form of fines or confiscations. . . .

For reasons such as these society has long preferred to take other things of intrinsic value from persons in the name of punishment—notably their freedom and their bodily integrity. Everybody, rich and poor, young and old, male and female, has life and limb and some degree of liberty to lose. . . .

III. THE SEVERITY AND INDIGNITY OF THE DEATH PENALTY

Is Capital Punishment an Untimely and Undignified Death?

Some defenders of capital punishment have complained that opposition to the death penalty entails an overestimation of the value of human life; it tends to ignore that we will all die eventually. All that capital punishment does, according to this objection, is to schedule a person's death at a definite time and place, by a definite mode, and for a definite reason. This raises a new question for us, namely, how the idea of the value, worth, dignity, or sanctity of human life can be made consistent with human mortality.

Even though death is a fact of life, emphasizing the worth of human life is a way of giving sense to the familiar notions of "untimely" death and of an "undignified" death. These terms are admittedly vague and have application in a wide variety of settings, but they also have a place where crime and punishment are concerned. Other things being equal, if a death is brought about by one person killing another, as in murder, then it is an untimely death. If a death is brought about in a way that causes terror during the dying or disfigurement of the body, then it is an undignified death. This, of course, is exactly what murder and capital punishment both typically do. . . .

Why Death Is More Severe than Imprisonment

. . . Roughly, of two punishments, one is more severe than the other depending on its duration and on its interference with things a person so punished might otherwise do. Death is interminable, whereas it is always possible to revoke or interrupt a life sentence. Death also makes compensation impossible, whereas it is possible to compensate a prisoner in some way for wrongful confinement even if it is not possible to give back any of the liberty that was taken away. Of most importance, death permits of no concurrent experiences or activities, whereas even a life-term prisoner can read a book, watch television, perhaps even write a book or repair a television set, and experience various social relations with other people. Death eliminates the presupposition of all experience and activity: life itself. For these reasons, the death penalty is unquestionably the more severe punishment, no matter how painless and dignified the mode of execution might be. . . .

The Indignity of Corporal Punishments

In addition to the severity of the death penalty, the killing of persons as punishment shares certain important features with other modes of corporal punishment—maiming, flogging, branding—once widely practiced in our society but now abandoned. All these other methods of corporal punishment have been adandoned in part because they are now seen to violate the dignity of the person being punished. . . .

Why has death as a punishment escaped the nearly universal condemnation visited on all these other punishments with which it is historically and naturally associated? In part, it may be owing to

a failure of imagination. Whereas we all know or can easily and vividly imagine the pain and humiliation involved in other corporal punishments, executions today are carried out away from public view, they are quickly over, and the person punished by death is no longer in our midst as a constant reminder. Other factors come into play, too. One is the belief that in some cases there is truly no alternative, because if the criminal were not killed there would be too much risk that he or she would repeat the crime. If so, then neither retribution nor deterrence, but rather incapacitation turns out to be the last line of defense. . . .

IV. CAPITAL PUNISHMENT AND SOCIAL DEFENSE

The Analogy with Self-Defense

Capital punishment, it is sometimes said, is to the body politic what self-defense is to the individual. If the latter is not morally wrong, how can the former be? To assess the strength of this analogy, we need first to inspect the morality of self-defense.

Except for absolute pacifists, who believe it is morally wrong to use violence even to defend themselves or others from undeserved aggression, most of us believe that it is not morally wrong and may even be our moral duty to use violence to prevent aggression directed against either ourselves or innocent third parties. The law has long granted persons the right to defend themselves against the unjust aggressions of others, even to the extent of using lethal force to kill an assailant. . . .

The foregoing account assumes that the person acting in self-defense is innocent of any provocation of the assailant. It also assumes that there is no alternative to victimization except resistance. In actual life, there may be a third alternative: escape, or removing oneself from the scene of the imminent aggression. Hence, the law imposes on us the "duty to retreat." . . . The rule is this: Use of deadly force is justified only to prevent loss of life in immediate jeopardy where a lesser use of force cannot reasonably be expected to save the life that is threatened. . . .

The rationale for self-defense as set out above illustrates two moral principles of great importance to our discussion. One is that if a life is to be risked, then it is better that it be the life of someone who is guilty (in this context, the initial assailant) rather than the life of someone who is not (the innocent potential victim). . . . [F]airness dictates that the guilty aggressor ought to be the one to run the risk.

The other principle is that taking life deliberately is not justified so long as there is any feasible alternative. One does not expect miracles, of course, but in theory, if shooting a burglar through the foot will stop the burglar and enable one to call the police for help, there is no reason to shoot to kill. Likewise, if the burglar is unarmed, there is no reason to shoot at all. . . . In these ways the law shows a tacit regard for the life even of a felon and discourages the use of unnecessary violence even by the innocent. . . .

Deterrence, Incapacitation, and Crime Prevention

The analogy with self-defense leads naturally to the empirical and the conceptual questions surrounding the death penalty as a method of crime prevention. Notice first that crimes can be prevented without recourse to punishment; we do that when we take weapons from offenders, protect targets by bolts and alarms, and educate the public to be less vulnerable to victimization. As for punishment, it prevents crimes by *incapacitation* and by *deterrence*. . . . Executing a murderer prevents crimes by means of *incapacitation* to the extent that the murderer would have committed further crimes if not executed. Incapacitating a murderer will not have any preventative benefits, however, unless the murderer would otherwise have committed some further crimes. (In fact relatively few murderers turn out to be homicidal recidivists.) Nor is killing persons the only way to incapacitate them; isolation and restraints will suffice. Executing a murderer prevents crimes by means of *deterrence* to the extent that others are frightened into not committing any capital crimes by the knowledge that

convicted offenders are executed. Thus, successful deterrence is prevention by a psychologically effective threat; incapacitation, if it prevents crimes at all, does so by physically disabling the offender.

The Death Penalty and Incapacitation

Capital punishment is unusual among penalties because its incapacitative effects limit its deterrent effects. The death penalty can never deter an executed person from further crimes. At most, it incapacitates the executed person from committing them. . . . But incapacitation is not identical with prevention. Prevention by means of incapacitation occurs only if the executed criminal would have committed other crimes if he or she had not been executed and had been punished only in some less incapacitative way (e.g., by imprisonment). . . .

This is the nub of the problem. There is no way to know in advance which if any of the incarcerated or released murderers will kill again. It is useful in this connection to remember that the only way to guarantee that no horrible crimes ever occur is to execute *everyone* who might conceivably commit such a crime. Similarly, the only way to guarantee that no convicted murderer ever commits another murder is to execute them all. No modern society has ever done this, and for two hundred years Western societies have been moving steadily in the opposite direction. . . .

The Death Penalty and Deterrence

. . . For half a century, social scientists have studied the questions whether the death penalty is a deterrent and whether it is a better deterrent than the alternative of imprisonment. Their verdict, while not unanimous, is nearly so. Whatever may be true about the deterrence of lesser crimes by other penalties, the deterrence achieved by the death penalty for murder is not measurably any greater than the deterrence achieved by long-term imprisonment. . . .

If the death penalty and long-term imprisonment are equally effective (or ineffective) as deterrents to murder, then the argument for the death penalty on grounds of deterrence is seriously weakened. One of the moral principles identified earlier now comes into play: Unless there is a good reason for choosing a more rather than a less severe punishment for a crime, the less severe penalty is to be preferred. This principle obviously commends itself to anyone who values human life and who concedes that, all other things being equal, less pain and suffering is always better than more. . . .

V. CAPITAL PUNISHMENT AND RETRIBUTIVE JUSTICE

No discussion of the morality of punishment would be complete without taking into account the two leading principles of retributive justice relevant to the capital punishment controversy. One is the principle that crimes ought to be punished. The other is the principle that the severity of a punishment ought to be proportional to the gravity of the offense. These are moral principles of recognized weight. Leaving aside all questions of social defense, how strong a case for capital punishment can be made on their basis? How reliable and persuasive are these principles themselves?

Crime Must Be Punished

. . . Fortunately, this principle need not be in dispute between proponents and opponents of the death penalty. Even defenders of the death penalty must admit that putting a convicted murderer in prison for years is a punishment of that criminal. The principle that crime must be punished is neutral to our controversy, because both sides acknowledge it.

The other principle of retributive justice is the one that seems to be decisive. Under *lex talionis,* it must always have seemed that murderers ought to be put to death. . . . The strategy for opponents of the death penalty is to argue either that (1) this principle is not really a principle of justice after all, or that (2) to the extent it is, it does not require death for murderers, or that (3) in any case it is not the only principle of punitive justice. As we shall see, all these objections have merit. . . .

Is Death Sufficiently Retributive?

Those who advocate capital punishment for murder on retributive grounds must face the objection that, on their own principles, the death penalty in some cases is morally inadequate. How could death in the electric chair or the gas chamber or before a firing squad or by lethal injection suffice as just retribution, given the savage, brutal, wanton character of so many murders? How can retributive justice be served by anything less than equally savage methods of execution? . . .

. . . Where the quality of the crime sets the limits of just methods of punishment, as it will if we attempt to give exact and literal implementation to *lex talionis,* society will find itself descending to the cruelties and savagery that criminals employ. What is worse, society would be deliberately authorizing such acts, in the cool light of reason, and not (as is usually true of vicious criminals) impulsively or in hatred and anger or with an insane or unbalanced mind. Moral constraints, in short, prohibit us from trying to make executions perfectly retributive. Once we grant that such constraints are proper, it is unreasonable to insist that the principle of "a life for a life" nevertheless by itself justifies the execution of murderers. . . .

As the French writer Albert Camus once remarked:

> For there to be an equivalence, the death penalty would have to punish a criminal who had warned his victim of the date at which he would inflict a horrible death on him and who, from that moment onward, had confined him at his mercy for months. Such a monster is not encountered in private life.[5]

Differential Severity Does Not Require Executions

What, then, emerges from our examination of retributive justice and the death penalty? If retributive justice is thought to consist in *lex talionis,* all one can say is that this principle has never exercised more than a crude and indirect effect on the actual punishments meted out by society. . . .

But retributive justice need not be identified with *lex talionis*. One may reject that principle as too crude and still embrace the retributive principle that the severity of punishments should be graded according to the gravity of the offense. Even though one need not claim that life imprisonment (or any kind of punishment other than death) "fits" the crime of murder, one can claim that this punishment is the proper one for murder. To do this, the schedule of punishments accepted by society must be arranged so that this mode of imprisonment is the most severe penalty used. Opponents of the death penalty can embrace this principle of retributive justice, even though they must reject a literal *lex talionis*.

Equal Justice and Capital Punishment

During the past generation, the strongest practical objection to the death penalty has been the inequity with which it has been applied. . . . All the sociological evidence points to the conclusion that the death penalty is the poor man's justice; hence the slogan, "Those without the capital get punishment." The death penalty is also racially sensitive. . . .

Let us suppose that the factual basis for such a criticism is sound. What follows for the morality of capital punishment? Many defenders of the death penalty have been quick to point out that since there is nothing intrinsic about the crime of murder or rape dictating that only the poor or only racial-minority males will commit it, and since there is nothing overtly racist about the statutes that authorize the death penalty for murder or rape, capital punishment itself is hardly at fault if in practice it falls with unfair impact on the poor and the black. . . . At worst such results stem from defects in the system of administering criminal justice. . . .

We can look at these statistics in another way to illustrate the same point. . . . Persons are sentenced to death and executed not because they have been found to be uncontrollably violent or hopelessly poor risks for safe confinement and release. Instead, they are executed because at trial they had a poor defense (inexperienced or overworked

counsel); they had no funds to bring sympathetic witnesses to court; they are transients or strangers in the community where they are tried; the prosecuting attorney wanted the publicity that goes with "sending a killer to the chair"; there were no funds for an appeal or for a transcript of the trial record; they are members of a despised racial or political minority. In short, the actual study of why particular persons have been sentenced to death and executed does not show any careful winnowing of the worst from the bad. It shows that those executed were usually the unlucky victims of prejudice and discrimination, the losers in an arbitrary lottery that could just as well have spared them, the victims of the disadvantages that almost always go with poverty. A system like this does not enhance human life; it cheapens and degrades it. . . .

VI. CONCLUSION

Our discussion of the death penalty from the moral point of view shows that there is no one moral principle that has paramount validity and that decisively favors one side of the controversy. Rather, we have seen how it is possible to argue either for or against the death penalty, and in each case to be appealing to moral principles that derive from the worth, value, or dignity of human life. . . .

My own view of the controversy is that, given the moral principles identified in the course of our discussion (including the overriding value of human life), and given all the facts about capital punishment, the balance of reasons favors abolition of the death penalty. The alternative to capital punishment that I favor, as things currently stand, is long-term imprisonment. Such a punishment is retributive and can be made more or less severe to reflect the gravity of the crime. It gives adequate (though hardly perfect) protection to the public. It is free of the worst defect to which the death penalty is liable: execution of the innocent. It tacitly acknowledges that there is no way for a criminal, alive or dead, to make complete amends for murder or other grave crimes against the person. Last but not least, long-term imprisonment has symbolic significance. The death penalty, more than any other kind of killing, is done by officials in the name of society and on its behalf. Each of us, therefore, has a hand in such killings. Unless they are absolutely necessary they cannot be justified. Thus, abolishing the death penalty represents extending the hand of life even to those who by their crimes have "forfeited" any right to live. A penal policy limiting the severity of punishment to long-term incarceration acknowledges that we must abandon the folly and pretense of attempting to secure perfect justice in an imperfect world. . . .

NOTES

1. W. D. Ross, *The Right and the Good.* Oxford: Clarendon Press, 1930, pp. 60–61.
2. Immanuel Kant, *The Metaphysical Elements of Justice* (1797), Indianapolis, Ind.: Bobbs-Merrill (1965), translated by John Ladd, p. 102.
3. Ibid., p. 100.
4. Ibid., p. 101.
5. Albert Camus, *Resistance, Rebellion, and Death.* New York: Knopf, 1961, p. 199.

Discussion Questions

1. Bedau maintains that the forfeiture-of-rights argument is problematic because it can be used to justify the death penalty for almost any crime. Do you agree with Bedau? Use the execution of Socrates to illustrate your answer.
2. Bedau claims that Kant's criteria for determining a murderer's "state of mind" at the time of the crime are too ambiguous to be useful. Make up a list of criteria that might be used in determining if a murderer should be held morally blameworthy. Make a list of criteria that might be used in determining if a murderer should get the death penalty. Are the two lists the same? Discuss why or why not.
3. Compare and contrast the arguments of Bedau and van den Haag regarding the morality of capital punishment. Which person presents the more compelling argument? Support your answer.
4. What if a society were dissolved, not by common agreement, but because of a natural disaster or a civil war that led to the collapse of the government and, with it, the penal system? Discuss whether Bedau would permit the death penalty in situations in which there is no other effective means of incapacitating dangerous criminals.

𝄞 JEFFREY REIMAN

Why the Death Penalty Should Be Abolished in the United States

Jeffrey Reiman is a professor of philosophy at American University. In this selection Reiman concludes that one can accept retributivism, as well as the claim that the murderers deserve to die for their offense, without accepting the claim that murderers ought to receive the death penalty.

"Why the Death Penalty Should Be Abolished," from Louis P. Pojman and Jeffrey Reiman, *The Death Penalty: For and Against* (Lanham, Md.: Rowman & Littlefield, 1998), 67, 87–100. Some notes have been omitted.

Critical Reading Questions

1. What are the two arguments used by advocates of the death penalty?
2. What does Reiman mean when he says the "desert creates a *right to punish,* not a duty to do so"?
3. What is the standard problem confronting those who justify retributivism?
4. What is the "retributivist principle," and how is it related to the justice of *lex talionis*?
5. What is the relationship between *lex talionis* and the Golden Rule?
6. What conclusion does Reiman draw about retributive justice from the Hegelian and Kantian approaches?
7. Why is it important to figure out what penalties are equivalent to the crimes?
8. According to Reiman, when is the desire for revenge rational?
9. According to Reiman, what types of punishment are monstrous and unacceptable?
10. Who has the right to punish in a civil state?
11. How does Reiman determine the top and the bottom of the range of acceptable punishment? What is the role of deterrence in setting these limits?
12. How does "proportional retributivism" modify the requirements of *lex talionis*?

Death penalty advocates commonly press two claims in favor of executing murderers. The first is that the death penalty is a just punishment for murder, a murderer's just deserts. On this line of thought, we do injustice to the victims of murder if we do not execute their murderers. The second claim is that the death penalty is necessary to deter potential murderers. Here, the suggestion is that we do injustice to potential victims of murder if we do not execute actual ones. I accept that the death penalty is a just punishment for some murders—some murderers' just deserts—and that, if the death penalty were needed to deter future murders, it would be unjust to future victims not to impose it. Notice, then, that I accept two of the strongest points urged in favor of the death penalty. If, granting these strong points, I can show that it would still be wrong to impose the death penalty, that should be a strong argument indeed. . . .

DEATH AND DESERT

In this section, I aim to show that execution is justly deserved punishment for some murders, *as a step toward arguing that it is not unjust to punish murder less harshly.* Note, then, that the fact that a punishment is justly deserved does not, in my view, entail that someone has a duty to impose that punishment. Rather, I shall argue in this section that desert creates *a right to punish,* not a duty to do so. To prepare the ground for this argument, I present here three commonplace observations that support the view that desert does not entail a duty to give what is deserved: First, the victim of an offense has the moral right to forgive the offending party rather than punish him though he deserves to be punished; second, we have no duty (not even a prima facie duty) to torture torturers even if they deserve to be tortured; and third, though great benefactors of humanity deserve to be rewarded, no one necessarily has a duty to provide that reward. At most, there is a very weak and easily overridden duty to provide the reward. On the other hand, I will claim that, when the state punishes a criminal, the state has a duty to punish in a way that does not trivialize the harm suffered by the criminal's victim. However, we shall see that this duty is compatible with administering punishment that is less than the full amount deserved. . . .

1. Retributivism, *Lex Talionis,* and Just Desert

There is nothing self-evident about the justice of the *lex talionis* or, for that matter, of retributivism. The standard problem confronting those who would justify retributivism is that of overcoming the suspicion that it does no more than sanctify the victim's desire to hurt the offender back. Since serving that desire amounts to hurting the offender simply for the satisfaction that the victim derives from seeing the offender suffer, and since deriving satisfaction from the suffering of others seems primitive, the policy of imposing suffering on the offender for no other purpose than giving satisfaction to his victim seems primitive as well. Consequently, defending retributivism requires showing that the suffering imposed on the wrongdoer has some worthy point beyond the satisfaction of victims. In what follows, I shall try to identify a proposition—which I call the *retributivist principle*—that I take to be the nerve of retributivism. I think this principle accounts for the justice of the *lex talionis* and indicates the point of the suffering demanded by retributivism. . . .

I think that we can see the justice of the *lex talionis* by focusing on the striking affinity between it and the Golden Rule. The Golden Rule mandates, "Do unto others as you would have others do unto you," while the *lex talionis* counsels, "Do unto others as they have done unto you." It would not be too far-fetched to say that the *lex talionis* is the law enforcement arm of the Golden Rule, at least in the sense that if people were actually treated as they treated others, then everyone would necessarily follow the Golden Rule, because then people could only willingly act toward others as they were willing to have others act toward them. This is not to suggest that the *lex talionis* follows from the Golden Rule, but rather that the two share a common moral inspiration: the equality of persons. Treating others as you *would* have them treat you means treating others as equal to you, because it implies that you count their suffering to be as great a calamity as your own suffering, that you count your right to impose suffering on them as

no greater than their right to impose suffering on you, and so on. The notion of the equality of persons leads to the *lex talionis* by two approaches that start from different points and converge.

I call the first approach "Hegelian" because Hegel held (roughly) that crime upsets the equality among persons and that retributive punishment restores that equality by "annulling" the crime. We have seen, acting according to the Golden Rule implies treating others as your equals. Conversely, violating the Golden Rule implies the reverse: Doing to another what you would *not* have that other do to you violates the equality of persons by asserting a right toward the other that the other does not possess toward you. Doing back to you what you did "annuls" your violation by reasserting that the other has the same right toward you that you assert toward him. Punishment according to the *lex talionis* cannot heal the injury that the other has suffered at your hands; rather, it rectifies the indignity he has suffered, by restoring him to equality with you.

This Hegelian account of retributivism provides us with a nonutilitarian conception of crime and punishment. This is so because "equality of persons" here does not mean equality of concern for their happiness, as it might for a utilitarian. On a utilitarian understanding of equality, imposing suffering on a wrongdoer equivalent to the suffering she has imposed would have little point (unless such suffering were exactly what was needed to deter future would-be offenders). Rather, equality of concern for people's happiness would lead us to impose as little suffering on the wrongdoer as is compatible with promoting the happiness of others. Instead of seeing morality as administering doses of happiness to individual recipients, the Hegelian retributivist envisions morality as maintaining the relations appropriate to equally sovereign individuals. . . . The victim (or his representative, the state) . . . has the right to rectify this loss of standing relative to the criminal by meting out a punishment that reduces the criminal's sovereignty to the degree to which she vaunted it above her victim's. It might be thought that this is a duty, not just a right, but that is surely too much. The victim has the right to forgive the violator without imposing punishment. This suggests that it is by virtue of having the right to punish the violator—having authority over the violator's fate equivalent to the authority over the victim's fate that the violator wrongly took—rather than having the duty to punish the violator, that the victim's equality with the violator is restored.

I call the second approach "Kantian" because Kant held (roughly) that, since reason (like justice) is no respecter of the sheer difference among individuals, when a rational being decides to act in a certain way toward his fellows, he implicitly authorizes similar action by his fellows toward him. A version of the Golden Rule, then, is a requirement of reason: Acting rationally, one always acts as he would have others act toward him. Consequently, to act toward a person as he has acted toward others is to treat him as a rational being, that is, as if his act were the product of a rational decision. From this, it may be concluded that we have a duty to do to offenders what they have done, since this amounts to according them the respect due rational beings. And Kant asserts as much. Here, too, however, the assertion of a duty to punish seems excessive, since, if this duty arose because doing to people what they have done to others is necessary to accord them the respect due rational beings, then we would have a duty to do to all rational persons *everything*—good, bad, or indifferent—that they do to others. The point, rather, is that, by his acts, a rational being *authorizes* others to do the same to him; he doesn't *compel* them to. Here, again, the argument leads to a right, rather than a duty, to exact the *lex talionis*. It should be clear that the Kantian argument, like the Hegelian one, rests on the equality of persons. A rational agent implicitly authorizes having done to him action similar to what he has done to another only if he and the other are similar in the relevant ways.

The Hegelian and Kantian approaches arrive at the same destination from opposite sides. . . . Taken together, these approaches support the following proposition: *The equality and rationality of persons imply that an offender deserves, and his victim has the right to impose on him, suffering equal to that which he imposed on the victim*. This is the proposition I call the *retributivist principle*. This principle provides that the *lex talionis* is the criminal's just desert and the victim's—or, as her representative, the state's—right. . . .

I do not contend that it is easy or even always possible to figure out what penalties are equivalent to the harms imposed by offenders. Hugo Bedau, for example, has observed that, apart from murder and possibly some other crimes against the person, "we have no clear intuitions at all about what such equivalences consist in."[1] Even if this is so, however, it is still worth knowing what the criterion of deserved punishment is. . . . [K]nowing what criminals deserve according to *lex talionis* gives us something at which to aim, a target in light of which we might eventually sharpen our intuitions.

When I say that, with respect to the criminal, the point of retributive punishment is to impress upon him his equality with his victim, I mean to be understood quite literally. If the sentence is just and the criminal rational, then the punishment should normally *force* upon him recognition of his equality with his victim, recognition of their shared vulnerability to suffering and their shared desire to avoid it, as well as recognition of the fact that he counts for no more than his victim in the eyes of their fellows. For this reason, the retributivist requires that the offender be sane not only at the moment of his crime, but also at the moment of his punishment—while this latter requirement would be largely pointless (if not downright malevolent) to a utilitarian. Incidentally, it is, I believe, the desire that the offender be forced by suffering punishment to recognize his equality with his victim, rather than the desire for that suffering itself, that constitutes what is rational in the desire for revenge. . . .

It seems, then, reasonable to take the equality and rationality of persons as implying moral desert in the way asserted in the retributivist principle. I shall assume henceforth that the retributivist principle is true.

2. The Top and the Bottom End of the Range of Just Punishments

The truth of the retributivist principle establishes that *lex talionis* is the offender's just desert; but, since it establishes this as a right of the victim rather than the victim's duty, it does not settle the question of whether or to what extent the victim or the state ought to exercise this right and exact the *lex talionis*. This is a separate moral question because strict adherence to the *lex talionis* amounts to allowing criminals, even the most barbaric of them, to dictate our punishing behavior. . . . It seems certain that there are at least some crimes, such as rape or torture, that we ought not to try to match. And this is not merely a matter of imposing an alternative punishment that produces an equivalent amount of suffering, as, say, some number of years in prison that might "add up" to the harm caused by a rapist or a torturer. Even if no amount of time in prison would add up to the harm caused by a torturer, it still seems that we ought not to torture him even if this were the only way of making him suffer as much as he has made his victim suffer. Or consider someone who has committed several murders in cold blood. On the *lex talionis*, it would seem that such a criminal might justly be brought to within an inch of death and then revived (or to within a moment of execution and then reprieved) as many times as he has killed (minus one), and then finally executed. But surely this is a degree of cruelty that would be monstrous.

Since the retributivist principle establishes the *lex talionis* as the victim's right, it might seem that the question of how far this right should be exercised is "up to the victim." Indeed, this would be the case in the state of nature. But once, for all the good reasons familiar to readers of Locke, the state comes into existence, public punishment replaces private, and the victim's right to punish reposes in the state. With this, the decision as to how far to exercise this right goes to the state as well. . . .

I suspect that it will be widely agreed that the state ought not to administer punishments of the sort described above even if required by the letter of the *lex talionis* and that, thus, even granting the justice of *lex talionis*, there are occasions on which it is morally appropriate to diverge from its requirements. . . .

The implication of the notion that justice permits us to avoid extremely cruel punishments is that there is a range of just punishments that includes some that are just though they exact less than the full measure of the *lex talionis*. What are the top and bottom ends of this range? . . .[A]ll punishments within the range of just punishments must be sufficient to deter rational people generally from the crime in question. Assume, then, for purposes of simplicity, that we are trying to identify the range of just punishments from within a series of punishments of increasing harshness all of which suffice to provide adequate deterrence.

Within this series of punishments, the top end of the range of just punishments is given by *lex talionis,* and the bottom end is, in a way, as well. Based on the argument of the previous section, the top end, the point after which more or harsher punishment is undeserved and thus unjust, is reached when we impose a punishment that is equivalent to the harm caused by the criminal (including both the harm done to his immediate victim and the harm done to the law-abiding by his unfair taking of advantage). As for the bottom end, recall that, if the retributivist principle is true, then denying that the offender deserves suffering equal to that which she imposed amounts to denying the equality and rationality of persons. From this, it follows that we fall below the bottom end of the range of just punishments when we act in ways that are incompatible with the *lex talionis* at the top end. We do injustice to the victim when we treat the offender in a way that is no longer compatible with sincerely believing that she deserves to have done to her what she has done to her victim. In this way, the range of just punishments remains faithful to the victim's right.

This way of understanding just punishment enables us to formulate proportional retributivism so that it is compatible with acknowledging the justice of the *lex talionis*. If we take the *lex talionis* to spell out the offender's just desert, and if other moral considerations require us to refrain from matching the injury caused by the offender while still allowing us to punish justly, then surely we impose just punishment if we impose the closest morally acceptable approximation to the *lex talionis*. Proportional retributivism, then, in requiring that the worst crime be punished by the society's worst punishment and so on, could be understood as translating the offender's just desert into its nearest equivalent in the society's table of morally acceptable punishments. Then, the two versions of retributivism (*lex talionis* and proportional) are related in that the first states what just punishment would be if nothing but the offender's just desert mattered and the second locates just punishment at the meeting point of the offender's just desert and the society's moral scruples.

Inasmuch as proportional retributivism modifies the requirements of the *lex talionis* only in light of other moral considerations, it is compatible with believing that the *lex talionis* spells out the offender's just desert, much in the way that modifying the obligations of promisers in light of other moral considerations is compatible with believing in the binding nature of promises. That a person is justified in failing to keep a promised appointment because she acted to save a life is compatible with still believing that promises are binding. So, too, justifiably doing less than *lex talionis* requires in order to avoid cruelty is compatible with believing that offenders still deserve what *lex talionis* would impose.

Proportional retributivism so formulated preserves the point of retributivism and remains faithful to the victim's right that is its source. Since it punishes with the closest morally acceptable approximation to the *lex talionis*, it effectively says to the offender: You deserved the equivalent of what you did to your victim, and you are getting less only to the degree that our moral scruples limit us from duplicating what you have done. Such punishment, then, affirms the equality of persons by respecting, *as far as seems morally permissible*, the victim's right to impose suffering on the offender equal to what she received, and it affirms the rationality of the offender by treating him as

authorizing others to do to him what he has done, though they take him up on it only *as far as it seems to them morally permissible*. Needless to say, the alternative punishments must in some convincing way be comparable in gravity to the crimes that they punish, or else they will trivialize the harms those crimes caused and be no longer compatible with sincerely believing that the offender deserves to have done to him what he has done to his victim and no longer capable of impressing upon the criminal his equality with the victim. . . .

To sum up: When, because we are simply unable to duplicate the criminal's offense, we modify the *lex talionis* to call for imposing on the offender as nearly as possible what he has done, we are still at the top end of punishment justified via *lex talionis*, modifying the *lex talionis* only for reasons of practical possibility. When, because of our own moral scruples, we do less than this, we still act justly as long as we punish in a way that is compatible with sincerely believing that the offender deserves the full measure of the *lex talionis*. If this is true, then it is not unjust to spare murderers as long as they can be punished in some other suitably grave way. For example, a natural life sentence with no chance of parole might be a civilized equivalent of the death penalty—after all, people sentenced to life imprisonment have traditionally been regarded as "civilly dead."

It might be objected that no punishment short of death will serve the point of retributivism with respect to murderers because no punishment short of death is commensurate with the crime of murder. For, while some number of years of imprisonment may add up to the amount of harm done by rapists or assaulters or torturers, no number of years will add up to the harm done to the victim of murder. But justified divergence from the *lex talionis* is not limited only to changing the form of punishment while maintaining equivalent severity. . . . If justice allows us to refrain from these penalties, then justice allows punishments that are not equal in suffering to their crimes. It seems to me that if the objector grants this much, then she must show that a punishment less than death is not merely incommensurate to the harm caused by murder, but so far out of proportion to that harm that it trivializes the harm and thus effectively denies the equality and rationality of persons. . . .

I take it, then, that the justice of the *lex talionis* implies that it is just to execute murderers, but not that it is unjust to spare them as long as they are systematically punished in some other suitably

grave way—and as long as the deterrence requirement can be satisfied. . . .

NOTES

1. Hugo Bedau, personal correspondence to author.

Discussion Questions

1. Discuss how Morris would most likely respond to Reiman's claim that the principle of retributivism does not require the death penalty for murder. Which person presents the stronger argument? Support your answer.
2. Should an exception in the use of the death penalty be made for terrorists who kill hundreds of people? Discuss how Reiman would most likely handle cases of international terrorism.
3. One of Reiman's premises is that all people are moral equals. However, in practice, certain groups of people are denied full and equal rights and have been morally degraded by social practices and attitudes. Discuss whether prejudice and lack of social and economic equality should be taken into consideration in determining punishment.
4. Reread the quote from lawyer Clarence Darrow in question 3 on pages 244–245. Role-play a conversation between Reiman and Darrow regarding Darrow's claim that criminals are simply products of their environment.
5. Examine how the principle of retributivism, as explicated by Reiman, would apply to children and teenagers who kill. For example, should the boys responsible for the Columbine High School killings, had they lived, have received the same punishment as an adult would receive? Support your answer.

HELEN PREJEAN

Would Jesus Pull the Switch?

Helen Prejean is a member of the Sisters of St. Joseph of Medaille in Louisiana. Through her work with inner-city residents in New Orleans, she became involved in ministry to death row inmates at the Louisiana State Prison in Angola. Prejean takes a natural ethics approach to the question "Would Jesus Pull the Switch?" She concludes that Jesus would not, nor would God condone such an action.

"Would Jesus Pull the Switch?" *Salt of the Earth,* March/April 1997, http://salt.claretianpubs.org/issues/deathp/prejean.html.

Critical Reading Questions

1. Why did Prejean get involved with death row inmates?
2. What do the Bible and Jesus say about the death penalty?
3. On what grounds does Prejean reject the concept of a God who metes out hurt for hurt and torture for torture?
4. According to Prejean, what is the connection between capital punishment and racism?
5. According to Prejean, why is the death penalty essentially torture?
6. What do the *UN Universal Declaration on Human Rights* and Pope John Paul II in "The Gospel of Life" each say about torture and the death penalty?
7. On what grounds does Prejean reject the argument that the government has a right to kill?
8. Why does the United States still have the death penalty, and how does Prejean view the future of the death penalty in this county?

I was scared out of my mind. I went into the women's room because it was the only private place in the death house, and I put my head against the tile wall and grabbed the crucifix around my neck. I said, "Oh, Jesus God, help me. Don't let him fall apart. If he falls apart, I fall apart."

I had never watched anybody be killed in front of my eyes. I was supposed to be Patrick Sonnier's spiritual advisor.

I was in over my head.

All I had agreed to in the beginning was to be a pen pal to this man on Louisiana's death row. Sure, I said, I could write letters. But the man was all alone, he had no one to visit him.

It was like a current in a river, and I got sucked in. The next thing I knew I was saying, "OK, sure, I'll come visit you.". . .

But I had no idea that at the end, on the evening of the execution, everybody has to leave the death house at 5:45 p.m., everybody but the spiritual advisor. The spiritual advisor stays to the end and witnesses the execution. . . .

People ask me all the time, "What are you, a nun, doing getting involved with these murderers?" You know how people have these stereotypical ideas about nuns: nuns teach; nuns nurse the sick.

I tell people to go back to the gospel. Look at who Jesus hung out with: lepers, prostitutes, thieves—the throwaways of his day. If we call ourselves Jesus' disciples, we too have to keep ministering to the marginated, the throwaways, the lepers of today. And there are no more marginated, thrown-away, and leprous people in our society than death-row inmates.

There's a lot of what I call "biblical quarterbacking" going on in death-penalty debates: people toss in quotes from the Bible to back up what they've already decided anyway. People want to not only practice vengeance but also have God agree with them. The same thing happened in this country in the slavery debates and in the debates over women's suffrage.

Religion is tricky business. Quote that Bible. God said torture. God said kill. God said get even.

Even the Pauline injunction "Vengeance is mine, says the Lord, I will repay" (Rom. 12:19) can be interpreted as a command and a promise—the command to restrain individual impulses toward revenge in exchange for the assurance that God will be only too pleased to handle the grievance in spades.

That God wants to "get even" like the rest of us does not seem to be in question.

One intractable problem, however, is that divine vengeance (barring natural disasters, so-called acts of God) can only be interpreted and exacted by human beings, very human beings.

I can't accept that.

Jesus Christ, whose way of life I try to follow, refused to meet hate with hate and violence with violence. I pray for the strength to be like him.

I cannot believe in the God who metes out hurt for hurt, pain for pain, torture for torture. Nor do I believe that God invests human representatives with such power to torture and kill. The paths of history are stained with the blood of those who have fallen victim to "God's Avengers." Kings, popes, military generals, and heads of state have killed, claiming God's authority and God's blessing. I do not believe in such a God. . . .

But here's the real reason why I got involved with death-row inmates: I got involved with poor people. It took me a while to wake up to the call of the social gospel of Jesus. For years and years when I came to the passages where Jesus identified with poor and marginated people I did some fast-footed mental editing of the scriptures: poor meant "spiritually poor."

When I read in Matthew 25, "I was hungry and you gave me to eat," I would say, "Oh there's a lot of ways of being hungry." "I was in prison, and you came to visit me,"—"Oh, there's a lot of ways we live in prison, you know." . . .

But later that year I finally got it. I began to realize that my spiritual life had been too ethereal, too disconnected. To follow Jesus and to be close to Jesus meant that I needed to seek out the company of poor and struggling people.

So in June 1981 I drove a little brown truck into St. Thomas, a black, inner-city housing project in New Orleans, and began to live there with four other sisters.

Growing up a Southern white girl right on the cusp of the upper class, I had only known black people as my servants. Now it was my turn to serve them.

It didn't take long to see that for poor people, especially poor black people, there was a greased track to prison and death row. As one Mama in St. Thomas put it: "Our boys leave here in a police car or a hearse."

It didn't take long to see how racism worked. When people were killed in St. Thomas and you looked for an account of their deaths in the newspaper, you'd find it buried on some back page as a three-line item. When other people were killed, it was front-page news. . . .

I began to understand that some life is valued and some life is not.

One day a friend of mine from the Prison Coalition Office casually asked me if I'd be a pen pal to someone on death row in Louisiana.

I said, "Sure." But I had no idea that this answer would be my passport to a strange and bizarre country. . . .

I wrote Patrick about life at Hope House in St. Thomas, and he told me about life in a 6-by-8-foot cell, where he and 44 other men were confined 23 hours a day. . . .

Patrick was on death row four years before they killed him.

I made a bad mistake. When I found out about Patrick Sonnier's crime—that he had killed two teenage kids—I didn't go to see the victims' families. I stayed away because I wasn't sure how to deal with such raw, unadulterated pain. I was a coward. I only met them at Patrick's pardon-board hearing. They were there to demand Patrick's execution. I was there to ask the board to show him mercy. It was not a good time to meet.

Here were two sets of parents whose children had been ripped from them. I felt terrible. I was powerless to assuage their grief. It would take me a long time to learn how to help victims' families, a long time before I would sit at their support-group meetings and hear their unspeakable stories of loss and grief and rage and guilt. . . .

I don't see capital punishment as a peripheral issue about some criminals at the edge of society that people want to execute. I see the death penalty connected to the three deepest wounds of our society: racism, poverty, and violence.

In this country, first the hangman's noose, then the electric chair, and now the lethal-injection gurney have been almost exclusively reserved for those who kill white people.

The rhetoric says that the death penalty will be reserved only for the most heinous crimes, but when you look at how it is applied, you see that in fact there is a great selectivity in the process. When the victim of a violent crime has some kind of status, there is a public outrage, and especially when the victim has been murdered, death—the ultimate punishment—is sought.

But when people of color are killed in the inner city, when homeless people are killed, when the "nobodies" are killed, district attorneys do not seek to avenge their deaths. Black, Hispanic, or poor families who have a loved one murdered not only don't expect the district attorney's office to pursue the death penalty—which, of course, is both costly and time-consuming—but are surprised when the case is prosecuted at all. . . .

In regard to this first and deepest of America's wounds, racism, we'd have to change the whole soil of this country for the criminal-justice system not to be administered in a racially biased manner.

The second wound is poverty. Who pays the ultimate penalty for crimes? The poor. Who gets the death penalty? The poor. After all the rhetoric that goes on in legislative assemblies, in the end, when the net is cast out, it is the poor who are selected to die in this country.

And why do poor people get the death penalty? It has everything to do with the kind of defense they get.

When I agreed to write to Patrick Sonnier, I didn't know much about him except that if he was on death row in Louisiana he had to be poor. And that holds true for virtually all of the more than 3,000 people who now inhabit death-row cells in our country.

Money gets you good defense. That's why you'll never see an O.J. Simpson on death row. As the saying goes: "Capital punishment means them without the capital get the punishment."

I had to learn all this myself. My father was a lawyer. I used to think, "Well, they may not get perfect defense, but at least they get adequate defense."

I tell you it is so shocking to find out what kind of defense people on death row actually have had.

The man I have been going to see on death row now for over six years is a young black man who was convicted for the killing of a white woman in a small community in Many, Louisiana. He had

an all-white jury, and he was tried, convicted, and sentenced to death in just one week. Dobie Williams has now been on death row for 10 years, and I believe he's innocent. But it is almost impossible for us to get a new trial for him. Why? Because if his attorney did not raise any objections at his trial, we cannot bring them up in appeals.

Finally, the third wound is our penchant for trying to solve our problems with violence. When you witness an execution and watch the toll this process also takes on some of those who are charged with the actual execution—the 12 guards on the strap-down team and the warden—you recognize that part of the moral dilemma of the death penalty is also: who deserves to kill this man?

On my journey with murder victims' families, I have seen some of them go for vengeance. I have seen families watch executions in the electric chair and still be for vengeance. I have also witnessed the disintegration of families because some parents got so fixated on vengeance that they couldn't love their other children any more or move on with life. . . .

Patrick had tried to protect me from watching him die. He told me he'd be OK. I didn't have to come with him into the execution chamber. "The electric chair is not a pretty sight, it could scare you," he told me, trying to be brave.

But I said, "No, no, Pat, if they kill you, I'll be there." . . .

Being in that death house was one of the most bizarre, confusing experiences I have ever had. It wasn't like visiting somebody dying in a hospital, where you can see the person getting weaker and fading. Patrick was so fully alive, talking and responding to me and writing letters to people and eating.

I'd look around at the polished tile floors—everything so neat—all the officials following a protocol, the secretary typing up forms for the witnesses to sign afterwards, the coffee pot percolating, and I kept feeling that I was in a hospital and the final act would be to save this man's life.

It felt strange and confusing because everyone was so polite. They kept asking Patrick if he needed anything. The chef came by to ask him if he liked his last meal—the steak (medium rare), the potato salad, the apple pie for dessert.

When the warden with the strap-down team came for him, I walked with him. God heard his prayer, "Please, God, hold up my legs." It was the last piece of dignity he could muster. He wanted to walk.

I saw this dignity in him, and I have seen it in the three men I have accompanied to their deaths. I wonder how I would hold up if I were walking across a floor to a room where people were waiting to kill me.

The essential torture of the death penalty is not finally the physical method of death: bullet or rope or gas or electrical current or injected drugs. The torture happens when conscious human beings are condemned to death and begin to anticipate that death and die a thousand times before they die. They are brought close to death, maybe four hours away, and the phone rings in the death house, and they hear they have received a stay of execution. Then they return to their cells and begin the waiting all over again. . . .

The U.N. Universal Declaration on Human Rights states that there are two essential human rights that every human being has: the right not to be tortured and the right not to be killed.

I wish Pope John Paul II in his encyclical "The Gospel of Life" had been as firm and unconditional as the U.N.

The pope still upholds the right of governments to kill criminals, even though he restricts it to cases of "absolute necessity" and says that because of improvements in modern penal systems such cases are "very rare, if not practically nonexistent."

Likewise, the U.S. Catholic bishops in their 1980 "Statement on Capital Punishment," while strongly condemning the death penalty for the unfair and discriminatory manner in which it is imposed, its continuance of the "cycle of violence," and its fundamental disregard for human dignity, also affirm in principle the right of the state to kill.

But I believe that if we are to have a firm moral bedrock for our society, we must establish that no

one may be permitted to kill—no one—and that includes government. . . .

In this last decade of the 20th century, U.S. government officials kill citizens with dispatch with scarcely a murmur of resistance from the Christian citizenry. In fact, surveys of public opinion show that those who profess Christianity tend to favor capital punishment slightly more than the overall population—Catholics more than Protestants.

True, in recent years leadership bodies of most Christian denominations have issued formal statements denouncing the death penalty, but generally that opposition has yet to be translated into aggressive pastoral initiatives to educate clergy and membership on capital punishment. I do not want to pass judgment on church leaders, but I invite them to work harder to do the right thing.

I also believe that we cannot wait for the church leadership to act. We have to put our trust in the church as the people of God; things have to come up from the grassroots.

The religious community has a crucial role in educating the public about the fact that government killings are too costly for us, not only financially, but—more important—morally. Allowing our government to kill citizens compromises the deepest moral values upon which this country was conceived: the inviolable dignity of human persons. . . .

I have no doubt that we will one day abolish the death penalty in America. One day all the death instruments in this country—electric chairs, gas chambers, and lethal-injection needles—will be housed behind velvet ropes in museums.

Today, however, executions are still the order of the day, and people are being executed at an ever-increasing rate in this country.

People are scared of crime, and they've been manipulated by politicians who push this button for all it's worth. For politicians, the death penalty is a convenient symbol and an easy way to prove how tough they are on criminals and crime. It allows them to avoid tackling the complex issue of how to get to the roots of crime in our communities.

But we may be close to bottoming out, which has to happen before momentum can build in the other direction. Right now we may be at just the beginning of the dawning of consciousness.

The death penalty is firmly in place, but people are beginning to ask, "If this is supposed to be the solution, how come we're not feeling any better? How come none of us feels safer?" People are beginning to realize that they have been duped and that the death penalty has not so much to do with crime as it has to do with politics. . . .

When people support executions, it is not out of malice or ill will or hardness of heart or meanness of spirit. It is, quite simply, that they don't know the truth of what is going on.

And that is not by accident. The secrecy surrounding executions makes it possible for executions to continue. I am convinced that if executions were made public, the torture and violence would be unmasked and we would be shamed into abolishing executions. . . .

When you accompany someone to the execution, as I have done three times as a spiritual advisor, everything becomes very crystallized, distilled, and stripped to the essentials. You are in this building in the middle of the night, and all these people are organized to kill this man. And the gospel comes to you as it never has before: Are you for compassion, or are you for violence? Are you for mercy, or are you for vengeance? Are you for love, or are you for hate? Are you for life, or are you for death? . . .

In his last words [Patrick Sonnier] expressed his sorrow to the victims' family. But then he said to the warden and to the unseen executioner behind the plywood panel, "but killing me is wrong, too." . . .

Discussion Questions

1. Prejean maintains that all humans have intrinsic moral value—"Nobody is disposable human waste." Do you agree with Prejean? Does moral respect require that people be treated with dignity even when they treat others as "disposable human waste"? Support your answers.
2. Both Immanuel Kant and John Locke disagree with Prejean's interpretation of the Bible, arguing instead that the Bible demands retributive justice: "Who so sheddeth Man's Blood, by Man shall his Blood be shed." Discuss how Prejean might respond to Locke's and Kant's interpretations of biblical imperatives regarding retributive justice.
3. Prejean argues that the death penalty in this country is linked to racism and poverty. Does the fact that people who are nonwhite and poor are more likely to get the death penalty make it unjust and, hence, immoral? Discuss how van den Haag might respond to Prejean as well as how Prejean might respond to van den Haag.
4. According to psychologist Carol Gilligan, moral maturity entails integrating the justice and the care perspectives. Develop a policy on capital punishment that draws from both perspectives.

CASE STUDIES

1. KARLA FAYE TUCKER: THE REPENTANT MURDERER

There's no question that thirty-eight-year-old Karla Faye Tucker of Texas was guilty of murder. In 1983, while strung out on drugs, Tucker hacked her two helpless victims to death with a pickax. She even boasted afterward that the killing gave her a sexual thrill.

Tucker later came to regret her deeds. She found God, she said, and was a changed person. "God reached down inside of me and literally uprooted all of that stuff and took it out and poured himself in." Tucker became involved in a prison-run program counseling young people to stay away from crime. "The world per se may not believe I deserve forgiveness," she told the world in an ABC interview, "but God says He's forgiven me."

More than one hundred people gathered outside the Texas prison on February 3, 1998, the day of her scheduled execution, some protesting the death penalty and hoping for a stay of execution, others rallying in support of her execution. Despite pleas for her pardon, Tucker was executed that evening by lethal injection.

Discussion Questions

1. Women make up only 1.4 percent of the death row population. Is the fact that the vast majority of violent crime is committed by young men relevant to the practical application of capital punishment? Because women, in general, do not need deterring, can capital punishment be justified in Tucker's case?

2. A survey of seven hundred death row inmates found that most share certain characteristics. Seven out of ten began their criminal careers as children, going on to commit more and more serious crimes, crimes that often included killing, before the murder that landed them on death row.[35] Like most inmates on death row, Tucker had a rough childhood. A former prostitute, she was using marijuana by age eight and heroin at age eleven. She was on drugs when she committed the murders. Is any of this relevant to her moral responsibility for her action?

3. One of the arguments against the death penalty is that people change. Capital punishment denies people the opportunity for growth, whereas other types of punishment do not. It is generally years before a death sentence is finally carried out. Meanwhile some people, like Tucker, go through major changes and moral growth. Should this be taken into consideration? Is it fair to punish people for a crime they committed during a different "stage" in their lives? Support your answers.

2. TERRORISM AND THE DEATH PENALTY

Shortly after 9:00 A.M. on April 19, 1995, a fireball ripped through the plate-glass doors of the Alfred P. Murrah Federal Building in Oklahoma City, collapsing all nine floors on the north side, killing 168 people and injuring 850. In June 1997, Timothy McVeigh was found guilty of murder and conspiracy and sentenced to death for his role in the bombing. McVeigh was executed by lethal injection on June 11, 2001, just three months before the deadly September 11 terrorist attacks on the Twin Towers in New York City that killed 2,975 people.

In December 2008, Khalid Sheik Mohammed and four other men imprisoned at Guantanamo Bay, Cuba, who were charged with coordinating the 9/11 attacks, announced that they wanted to abandon their defenses and enter a guilty plea before President Obama took office, thus daring Washington to give them the death penalty. Before his election, Obama had pledged to close Guantanamo and get rid of military war crime trials in which a prisoner could be sentenced to death without a jury trial.

If the five men got their wish and received the death penalty, they would be hailed as martyrs by their supporters and members of the terrorist organization al-Qaeda. None of the five showed any repentance for what they had done if, in fact, they were guilty. In a statement, one of the men reaffirmed his allegiance to Osama bin Laden and expressed his hope that the heart of the United States would be struck with weapons of mass destruction.[36]

Discussion Questions

1. Prejean argues that capital punishment is inconsistent with the intrinsic value of human life. Nobody, she writes, is disposable human waste. Despite their terrible crimes, murderers are human beings and deserve to be treated with dignity. Do you agree? Does morality require that terrorists like McVeigh and the 9/11 terrorists, who allegedly treat others as "disposable human waste," be treated with dignity?

2. The terrorists who were directly responsible for the destruction of the World Trade Center and the attack on the Pentagon died in the attacks. Does retributive justice require that people who order murders, but do not carry them out themselves, receive the death penalty? What about cases such as the alleged 9/11 masterminds who are seeking the death penalty in order to achieve martyrdom? Support your answers. Discuss how Kant and van den Haag would most likely respond to these questions.

3. French existentialist Albert Camus claimed that there is a moral contradiction in a policy, such as capital punishment, that imitates the violence it claims to hate.[37] Do you agree with Camus? Are we as a community made a little less virtuous by executing McVeigh and other convicted terrorists? Support your answers.

4. Can social contract theory and the concept of forfeiture of rights be used to justify the execution of people from other countries, such as the 9/11 terrorists, who violate our social contract—especially for actions that might be considered a capital crime in one culture but a heroic act in their own? Relate your answer to how Morris might respond to use of the death penalty for foreign terrorists.

---

3. "BORN KILLERS": CAPITAL PUNISHMENT AND THE GENETIC LOTTERY

Sociopaths make up 20 percent of prison inmates in the United States, and 50 percent of prison inmates responsible for the most serious and violent crimes, such as murder, armed robbery, and kidnapping.[38] Violent or destructive behavior in sociopaths may begin to manifest itself during childhood or adolescence.

In 1989, fifteen-year-old Craig Price murdered three of his neighbors. When the police arrived at the Heaton home in Warwick, Rhode Island, they found three mutilated bodies. Joan Heaton, thirty-nine, had been stabbed with a knife eleven times, strangled, and bitten in the face. Her daughter Jennifer, ten, had been stabbed sixty-two times. Melissa, eight, had been stabbed eight times and her skull crushed.

Price was arrested shortly after the bodies were found. Police later discovered that two years earlier Price had murdered another neighbor. He also had a record of assaults, burglaries, and other crimes.

Does Price think what he did was immoral? When asked about the murders, Price shrugged his shoulders and responded: "Morality is a private choice." According to Police Captain Kevin Collins, who witnessed Price's confessions to the four murders, "He just loves to kill. There's no doubt . . . that he's going to kill again."[39]

There is nothing unusual about Price's background: He came from what seemed to be a good family and lived in a middle-class neighborhood. Price is in all likelihood a sociopath, a person whose cerebral cortex, because of the genetic lottery, is incapable of processing emotional stimuli like a normal brain. Because sociopaths have no sense of guilt, remorse, or concern for the well-being of others, they are impervious to rehabilitation efforts.

Males with an extra Y chromosome also have a genetic predisposition to violent crime. Although the majority of XYY males do not engage in violent behavior, studies have found that maximum-security prison hospitals have a much higher than normal incidence of XYY males.

Discussion Questions

1. Sociopathy can be fairly accurately identified using brain imaging along with psychological testing. Likewise, the presence of the XYY chromosome can be detected through genetic testing. Should violent criminals be compelled to take these tests, or would this be a violation of their rights? If a violent criminal is a sociopath, he or she is very likely to continue a life of violence both in jail and after release. Should this be taken into consideration in sentencing sociopaths?

2. Because Price was a minor at the time of his sentencing, he could not be tried as an adult. Under Rhode Island law, the maximum sentence for juveniles, regardless of their crimes, is detention in the training school until they turn twenty-one. Should children who kill be treated and punished as adults? Discuss how Reiman would most likely respond to this question.

3. Plato maintained that a human without a conscience is not a person and, as such, lacks moral standing. Because sociopaths are not persons, he makes a provision in his *Republic* for the execution of those "whose souls are incurably evil." Do you agree with Plato? Should sociopaths who murder automatically receive the death penalty? Or does the inability of sociopaths to distinguish right from wrong mean that the concept of retributive justice and punishment is inapplicable to them? Is it fair that people who are disadvantaged by the "genetic lottery" be punished? Support your answers. Discuss also how Bentham and Kant might answer these questions.

4. The science fiction thriller *Alien* 3 opens with Lieutenant Ripley (Sigourney Weaver) crash-landing on the planet Fiorina "Fury" 161, a maximum-security correctional facility for "double-Y-chromosome" offenders. These violent offenders are not part of the "mainstream human race" but, in the words of the prison doctor, "alternative people" set apart from others by their genome and the bar codes indelibly tattooed on their heads. Discuss whether life imprisonment or exile on an isolated planet is preferable to the death penalty for violent offenders.

5. Discuss whether it would be appropriate for courts to use genetic screening to determine whether a person has a genetic tendency toward violence. Should these

genetic test results be available to parents as well as to schools and employers? Would it be morally justifiable to "tattoo" people who have a genetic predisposition toward violence along with a history of violence? Support your answers.

---

4. INSIDE A TEXAS DEATH CHAMBER

Texas has been dubbed "the execution capital of the free world." Journalist Michael Graczyk of the Houston bureau of the Associated Press has witnessed about seventy executions. "It's my job," he says. "It's like going to cover a baseball game or a basketball game." In the past, executions were scheduled for midnight; now they are held at 6 P.M. for the convenience of those involved. As the prisoner is ushered into the death chamber, guards stand around talking about their kids, Little League, and what they're going to do on their day off. There is no blood, no sense of horror, no scream of anguish as the needle is inserted into the inmate's arm. When the execution is over, it just looks like the inmate went to sleep. Graczyk wrote, after the execution of brutal murderer Billy Joe Woods, "It was bizarre to look around and see all these people just doing their job. It was just another day at the office."[40]

Outside a handful of anti–death penalty advocates are crying, "Murderer!"—not at the man about to be executed, but at the gray-shirted guards. Later they chanted into a megaphone, "God bless Billy Woods. God bless Billy Woods."

Discussion Questions

1. Does the death penalty brutalize and numb all those who participate in it, as abolitionists claim? Discuss how van den Haag might respond to this objection to capital punishment.
2. Prejean argues that capital punishment creates sympathy for the murderer, as in the case of Billy Woods. Does it weaken respect for the authority of the law if the state is seen as the murderer and the death row inmate as the victim? Support your answer. Discuss how a social contractarian would answer this question.
3. Executions involving lethal injection generally require the presence of a physician. Should physicians participate in executions, or does this require them to go against their professional code of ethics—specifically, the principle of nonmaleficence or "Do no harm"—as the AMA claims? If not physicians, who should carry out executions? Or does the principle of nonmaleficence forbid anyone from executing another person? Support your answers.
4. Prejean suggests making executions public. It is the secrecy surrounding executions, she maintains, that keeps the public from realizing just how brutal capital punishment really is. Discuss whether executions should be open to the public.

---

5. ADULTERY AND EXECUTION BY STONING

In October 2001, Safiya Yakubu Hussaini, a divorced mother of five children in Nigeria, was sentenced to death by stoning for adultery. The male partner in the alleged adultery was allowed to go free. The gender-discriminatory nature of the sentence created an international furor. Members of the World Women Parliamentarians, which represents 130 countries, adopted a motion calling for amnesty for Hussaini. The Secretary General of the Council of Europe also called on the Nigerian president to grant her a reprieve.

Safiya Yakubu Hussaini was finally acquitted by the *Sharia* State Court of Appeals in Sokoto state in March 2003 and allowed to go free. However, in the same month another divorced woman, Amina Lawal Kurami, was sentenced to death by stoning by the *Sharia* court in the Nigerian Katsina state for adultery and having a baby out of wedlock. As in the previous case, charges were dropped against the father.

Discussion Questions

1. According to cultural relativists, if sentencing women who commit adultery to death by stoning is considered morally acceptable in a culture, then the practice is, by definition, morally acceptable. Do you agree? If so, is it morally wrong for people from other countries and cultures to condemn and "impose their moral values" on Nigeria in trying to get the sentences overturned? If not, why not?
2. Discuss the moral issues involved in this case. Is the fact that the women knew that adultery was a crime punishable by death morally relevant in holding them responsible for their actions? What about the gender differences in the way the case was handled?
3. The *Sharia* courts in northern Nigeria were set up only for Muslims and are different from courts in the rest of Nigeria. The Nigerian Minister of Justice, Kanu Agabi, sent a letter to the governors of the Muslim Nigerian states saying that they should not impose punishments more severe than those imposed on other Nigerians, because doing so is "deliberately flouting the Constitution" of Nigeria. Is Kanu Agabi violating Muslims' religious freedom by holding them to a non-Muslim standard of punishment? To what extent should we respect the values of different subcultures within a nation when it comes to punishment?
4. Relate your answer to the previous question to the use of corporal punishment (spanking, beating, and other physical punishment) for children by religious sects, such as the House of Prayer and the Church of God (Restoration) in the United States. Is the use of corporal punishment on children morally acceptable if the parents believe it is acceptable and/or their religion calls for it? Should the government interfere or punish the parents? Support your answers.

C H A P T E R   6

Drug and Alcohol Use

Scott Krueger was looking forward to balancing the challenging demands of an engineering major at MIT, early-morning crew practice, and an active social life at Phi Gamma Delta, one of the thirty fraternities at MIT. In the fall of 1997, however, the fraternity pledge passed out during a Greek Week celebration after downing sixteen drinks in an hour. When Krueger's fraternity brothers noticed he was having trouble breathing, they called an ambulance.

By the time rescue workers arrived, Krueger was already comatose. His blood alcohol level was later found to be more than five times the legal driving limit. A few days later, Krueger's distraught parents had him removed from life support. Krueger is only one of hundreds of college students whose lives are cut short or devastated every year as a result of drug and alcohol abuse.

In September 2000 Krueger's parents were awarded a $6 million settlement by the university. This unprecedented financial settlement and MIT's declared commitment to change the college conditions that contributed to Krueger's death have spurred other colleges to make similar commitments to create a safer and more secure campus environment for students.

WHAT IS A DRUG?

Drugs, for the purpose of this chapter, are defined as chemicals that enter the bloodstream and are easily transported to the brain, where they alter the way we feel, with predictable results. Alcohol, by this definition, is a type of drug. Drugs can be smoked, injected, snorted, or swallowed.

Drug abuse is defined as "taking a drug or drugs for purposes other than those for which the drug or drugs were intended, and/or the illicit use of a drug or drugs which can cause harm (not necessarily physical) to oneself and/or others."[1] One of the risks of alcohol and drug use is addiction. **Addiction** is "a behavioral pattern of drug use, characterized by overwhelming involvement with the use of a drug [compulsive use], the securing of its supply, and a high tendency to relapse after withdrawal."[2]

DRUG CLASSIFICATIONS

Classification	Drugs	Effects[3]
Stimulants	Amphetamines, cocaine, prescription diet pills, nicotine, caffeine	Alertness; a sense of power; enhanced performance
Depressants	Alcohol, anti-anxiety drugs and sleeping pills containing benzodiazepine and barbiturates	Drowsiness and sedation
Opiates	Prescription painkillers, codeine, heroin, Demerol, methadone, morphine	Diminished or no pain; sense of euphoria
Hallucinogens	LSD, "magic mushrooms," peyote, MDMA ("ecstasy"), mescaline	Intensified perception and sense experience; hallucinations
Cannabinols	All forms of marijuana	Mellowness
Inhalants/ Solvents	Acetone, aerosol gases, glue, paint thinner, correction fluid	Giddiness and confusion
Performance enhancement	Anabolic and androgenic steroids	Increased muscle mass

THE HISTORY OF DRUG AND ALCOHOL USE

Alcohol is the most widely used drug in North America. Wine and beer have been used since ancient times for their pleasurable effects, in medicine, with meals, and in religious ceremonies. Even the *Mayflower* carried a good supply of "bere."

Distilled spirits were first produced in Europe about 1300 and were often referred to as "aqua vitae" because of their purported powers to prolong life. In 1606, alarmed by the increase in drunkenness, the British government made intoxication a statutory offense with the Act of Repression of the Odious and Loathsome Sin of Drunkedness.

Laws in the colonies were relatively lenient and geared primarily toward controlling drunkenness and disorderly conduct. A Connecticut law prohibited drinking for more than one-half hour at a time. A 1760 Virginia law prohibited ministers from "drinking to excess and inciting riots."

The temperance movement of the late nineteenth and early twentieth centuries was spearheaded by groups such as the Women's Christian Temperance Union (WCTU) and the Anti-Saloon League. The WCTU opposed drinking primarily because of its destructive effect on the family. The problem was also blamed on the influx of immigrants from Europe and Ireland, with their decadent drinking habits.

In 1919 the Eighteenth Amendment to the Constitution outlawed the sale and consumption of alcohol. Despite lack of unanimous support for the amendment, most prohibitionists thought that Americans would not violate their Constitution.

They were mistaken. Although alcohol consumption declined during the first few years of prohibition, it began to climb again during the 1920s. Ratification of the Eighteenth Amendment ushered in an era of organized crime and a vast illegal liquor trade, known as "bootlegging," under the control of such notorious gangsters as Al Capone. The cost of trying to stamp out illegal drinking soared into the millions of dollars. It soon became apparent that prohibition was too unpopular and too expensive to enforce. The Eighteenth Amendment was repealed in 1933 by the Twenty-first Amendment, although some states continued to have local prohibition laws as late as 1966.

Alcohol consumption hit another peak about 1980. Once again the tide of public opinion turned against alcohol. This time it was the medical profession that led the crusade. Rather than denounce alcohol as a moral failing, as had the early prohibitionists, the medical establishment declared alcoholism to be a disease. The disease model continues to dominate attitudes toward alcohol use in the United States today.

Attitudes toward drug use have followed a similar course. Hallucinogenic drugs have been used since antiquity both for pleasure and for religious purposes. Apparently, the techniques of ecstatic trances used by some Hindu yogis involved the use of drugs. The peyote cult of Mexico also used drug-induced ecstasy in mystical and religious rituals. LSD, which was popular in the 1960s, has been similarly credited with helping users get in touch with a deeper mystical wisdom. Marijuana also became popular in the late 1960s and 1970s. Much of the marijuana was imported from Jamaica, where the Rastafarians considered marijuana (ganja) to be the "wisdom weed" and used it in religious rites and for spiritual wisdom. Western philosophers and psychologists, with their emphasis on reason as the source of knowledge, tend to dismiss these experiences as merely drug induced and, hence, unreal.

Drugs have also been widely used for medicinal purposes. Opium was available in a crude form prior to 1800 and was valued by physicians for its calming effect and as a cure for gastrointestinal illnesses. Morphine, a derivative of opium, became a popular painkiller after 1870. When heroin, a derivative of morphine, was introduced into medical practice in the late 1800s, it was actively promoted by the American Medical Association (AMA) and pharmaceutical companies as a cure for many ailments. The easy availability of these drugs in the late nineteenth century was accompanied by a substantial increase in the number of drug addicts.[4]

Cocaine was first isolated from the coca leaf in the mid-nineteenth century. It became popular as a general tonic and for sinusitis and hay fever. The exhilarating effects of cocaine made it a popular additive in medicine, soda, and wine. In the United States, blacks were blamed by prohibitionists for the "cocaine problem." Even though studies failed to confirm the widespread use of cocaine by blacks, the fear of an uprising of "euphoric" blacks was used, in part, to justify an era of lynchings and segregation.

LEGAL AND ILLEGAL DRUGS

State laws regulating the use of morphine and cocaine were first enacted in the United States in the 1890s. Federal prohibition of drugs was not attempted initially because it was thought to be unconstitutional. Libertarians, physicians, and the major

---

✍ SECTION 1 OF THE EIGHTEENTH AMENDMENT TO THE UNITED STATES CONSTITUTION

[Adopted January 29, 1919]

Section 1. After one year from the ratification of this article the manufacture, sale, or transportation thereof into, or the exportation thereof from the United States and all territories subject to the jurisdiction thereof for beverage purposes is hereby prohibited.

---

pharmaceutical societies protested the outlawing of opiates, cocaine, and cannabis, substances they relied heavily on for symptom relief. Despite support for the medicinal use of drugs, by the mid-1920s the federal government moved to eliminate all heroin use.

The Pure Food and Drug Act of 1906 was the first federal legislation to regulate the use of opium. Because opium was imported from China, opposition to opium was used to reinforce anti-Chinese sentiment and the persecution of Chinese immigrants.

It is sometimes assumed that the division between legal and illegal drugs is based on rational criteria, but this isn't the case. Alcohol, nicotine (tobacco), and marijuana are currently the three most frequently used drugs in the United States. Yet marijuana, which rarely causes physiological addiction or serious illness, is illegal whereas alcohol and tobacco are not. According to an AMA study, tobacco is the number one "actual cause of death" in the United States; alcohol is number three. Tobacco kills one out of every three users, ending their lives prematurely by an average of fifteen years. Globally it is responsible for 5 million deaths a year, making it the leading cause of death in the world.[5] More than 80 percent of these deaths occur in the developing world in countries such as China, India, and Indonesia, where tobacco companies are aggressively marketing cigarettes in order to make up for lost revenue due to declining smoking in most industrialized nations.[6]

The abuse of legal over-the-counter or prescription drugs, inhalants, or solvents can also lead to addiction, serious health problems, and even death. Heroin, morphine, and cocaine, in contrast, are responsible for fewer than 8,500 deaths a year, while marijuana has yet to be implicated as responsible in anyone's death.[7]

The most recent wave of antidrug laws comes at a time when the public is divided over the wisdom of drug prohibition. Does the state have a right to prohibit or protect adults from using drugs? Is drug abuse a moral, legal, medical, or religious issue? Which drugs should be prohibited and which allowed?

DRUG AND ALCOHOL USE TODAY

More than 13 million Americans currently use illicit drugs. Another 60 million are addicted to cigarettes and 33 million binge on alcohol.[8] Seventy-three percent of Americans believe that the drug problem in the United States today is "very" or "extremely" serious, with women and people from lower-income families more likely to be concerned about the problem of illicit drugs.[9]

The use of illicit drugs by youth peaked in 1981, when 66 percent of American youth under the age of eighteen admitted to having tried illegal drugs.[10] When the George H. W. Bush administration declared an official "war on drugs," it had strong public support. Illicit drug use began declining during the 1980s. However, despite tougher laws and some initial victories, the success of the "war" was short-lived. During the mid-1990s, drug use began rising again, especially among young people. And marijuana has become ten to fifteen times more potent with the use of genetic engineering to alter the plant to make it resistant to attempts by drug agencies to destroy the crop through the use of pesticides.

By 1994 polls showed that approximately 19 percent of eighth graders, 36 percent of high school seniors, and 75 percent of people in their twenties had tried illicit drugs.[11] The rate gradually fell to 41 percent, then rose again to 54 percent in 2001.[12]

Marijuana is the most widely used illicit drug in the United States. Nearly 69 million Americans over the age of twenty-one have used marijuana at least once.[13] By tenth grade, 21 percent of teenagers report that they are current users of marijuana. By their senior year, 24 percent are users.[14] Although marijuana was made illegal in 1937, medical marijuana under a doctor's prescription is currently legal in Canada, Belgium, Austria, Great Britain, the Netherlands, and in fifteen states in the United States. In 2005 the U.S. Supreme Court ruled that the federal government can block the backyard cultivation of marijuana, thus greatly limiting its availability for medical use.

Support for legalization of marijuana varies widely by age, gender, and religious affiliation, with younger men and people who are liberal and unaffiliated with a religious group being most supportive of legalization. According to a 2005 Gallup poll, 44 percent of men between the ages of eighteen and forty-nine support the legalization of marijuana compared to 34 percent of women in the same age group. Only 17 percent of people who attend church regularly support legalization.

In 2001 Canada legalized the use of marijuana for medical purposes, and in 2003 decriminalized marijuana possession, so small-time users do not face the threat of jail and a criminal record. People caught with 15 grams or less receive a citation and fine, similar to a traffic ticket. This move has created tension between Canada and the United States, where possession of even a small amount of marijuana is punishable by up to a year in jail. (See Case Study 6.) There is currently a bill (HR 5843) in Congress that, if passed, would permit the possession of small amounts of medical marijuana for personal use. Singapore, where the penalty for trafficking marijuana is death, has some of the toughest marijuana laws.

Possession of small amounts of marijuana has also been decriminalized in England and most parts of Australia. Although marijuana is technically illegal in the Netherlands, possession of less than 5 grams or five plants is not prosecutable. In countries such as Jamaica and India, where marijuana is used in traditional religious rites, its use is generally tolerated, though not legal.

Although the use of the drug peyote by Native Americans in religious rituals was legalized in the United States in 1994, the Rastafarians, a religious sect originating in Jamaica that uses marijuana in religious rites, have been unsuccessful so far in getting marijuana legalized in this country for religious purposes.

Cocaine is the second most popular illicit drug in the United States. White males, at 12 percent, are twice as likely to use cocaine as black, Hispanic, and Native American males. African Americans, on the other hand, are more likely to use heroin. Because heroin-related offenses in the United States receive much more severe legal penalties than cocaine use or alcohol-related crimes such as drunk driving, blacks bear a disproportionate burden with respect to enforcement of drug laws. Blacks are also more likely than whites to receive convictions for similar drug-related offenses.[15] A study in the state of Washington found that African Americans, who made up only 3 percent of the state's population, received nearly 20 percent of the drug sentences.[16] This disparity was attributed in part to racial profiling.

Tobacco, although legal, is one of the most deadly and addictive drugs. It is responsible for one in five deaths in the United States and one in every three worldwide. Tobacco use has declined 40 percent since 1965, with the largest drop being among college graduates.[17] People who smoke are also smoking fewer cigarettes, probably because of the greater restrictions on smoking in public places and the workplace as well as increased concerns about the health risks of smoking.

In 2007, 20.8 percent of Americans were smokers. Half of all adults who smoke were regular smokers before their eighteenth birthday.[18] The prevalence of smoking is highest among young adults (23.8 percent) and lowest among people over the age of sixty-five (8.8 percent). Rates are also higher among men as well as Native Americans, whites, and Hispanics.[19]

Alcohol is a drug that in moderation may have health benefits. Slightly under two-thirds of Americans drink alcohol—a figure that has remained relatively steady since 1940. Most Americans drink responsibly. Excessive alcohol use, however, has health risks. Alcohol is responsible for more than six times as many deaths—75,000 a year in the United States alone—as all illicit drugs combined. These include deaths due to accidents, violence, alcohol poisoning, liver disease, neurological disorders, cancer, and suicide.[20]

DRUG AND ALCOHOL USE AMONG COLLEGE STUDENTS

In 1984 the drinking age was raised from eighteen to twenty-one throughout the United States in an attempt to curb drunk-driving accidents. However, the drinking-age laws have had little effect on the actual drinking habits of college students. After dropping off from a high in the mid-1980s, drug and alcohol use among college students began to rise again in the 1990s. A 1997 *Time* magazine article described American colleges as "among the nation's most alcohol-drenched institutions."[21] American undergraduates in 1999 drank 4 billion cans of beer and spent an average of $446 on alcoholic beverages—more than they spent on soft drinks and textbooks combined.[22] Male college students are more likely to drink and to binge drink than are female students.[23]

Binge drinking, defined as five or more drinks in a row for men and four or more for women, is a serious problem on many campuses in both the United States and Canada.[24] According to the National Institute on Alcohol Abuse, 1,700 college students die each year from alcohol-related injuries, including automobile accidents.

Members of fraternities and sororities are at the highest risk of excessive drinking, because intoxication is viewed as an acceptable aspect of Greek life.[25] Excessive alcohol use in fraternity hazing is once again on the upswing. (See Case Study 1.)

In addition to such problems as poor concentration, lower grade-point average (GPA), and health risks, binge drinking among college students is linked to intentional violence, including assault, homicide, rape, brawls, vandalism, and burglary, as well as being the victim of aggression, in part because being intoxicated makes the person an easier target for a predator.[26]

Of students who do not engage in binge drinking, 87 percent reported problems caused by students who do. These problems ranged from unwanted sexual advances and property damage to having sleep or studying interrupted.[27] Some 696,000 college students have been assaulted by a student who had been drinking. About half of all date rapes on campuses are associated with alcohol consumption.[28] Alcohol use is also a causal factor in suicide.

Illicit drug use in particular is up among college students. In 2004, 33.7 percent of college students reported using marijuana and 5.4 percent cocaine. The figure is roughly equivalent to that for high school seniors.[29] Despite the prevalence of marijuana use among high school and college students, only 38 percent of U.S. college freshmen polled in 2007 thought marijuana should be legal.[30] The increase in marijuana use among teens and young adults in the past ten years has been of particular concern because it is regarded by some as a "gateway drug" that may lead to the use of so-called hard drugs.

College drug use and binge drinking take a huge toll in terms of damage to health and cognitive functioning, violence, property damage, and liability costs to the fraternities and colleges associated with drunken parties. Would lowering the legal drinking age to eighteen make the problem of drinking on campus better or worse? Laura Dean-Mooney and John McCardell debate the wisdom of lowering the drinking age and the effect it might have on college campuses in their readings at the end of this chapter.

DRUGS IN SPORTS

Two weeks after the close of the summer 2000 Olympics in Sydney, Australia, the International Olympic Committee medical commission recommended that German wrestler Alexander Leipold be stripped of his gold medal. Leipold had tested positive for the steroid nandrolone after defeating American Brandon Slay in freestyle wrestling. Leipold denied taking the steroid and said he had no idea of how he could have tested positive. He is only one of forty-seven athletes who were suspended from the Sydney games for doping offenses, the highest number ever in the history of the Olympics. Apparently, mandatory drug testing has been ineffective. Both the 2004 and 2008 Olympics were also dogged by drug scandals and allegations of wrongdoing.

Anabolic steroids, such as nandrolone, are testosterone-based drugs that stimulate muscle growth and help athletes recover faster from injuries. However, use of these steroids also increases by fivefold the risk of heart attacks and strokes and may contribute to the development of liver disease.

Despite the harms associated with performance-enhancement drugs, their use in sports appears to be on the increase. Football is the toughest on drug use by professional athletes and hockey the most lenient, with basketball and baseball being somewhere in between the two.[31] According to one estimate, between 20 and 40 percent of major league baseball players were using testosterone-based drugs in 2000.[32]

In addition to steroids, growth hormones, and testosterone, blood doping is used by some athletes in sports that demand great endurance, such as cycling. Blood doping entails injecting a synthetic version of EPO, a hormone that stimulates the bone marrow to produce more red blood cells, which carry oxygen to the muscles. Because EPO is a naturally occurring substance in the body, it is difficult to detect through blood tests. In 2005, French authorities accused American cyclist Lance Armstrong, six-time winner of the Tour de France, of doping practices, an accusation that he denied. The incident raised the hackles of many Americans who were already miffed at France because of their opposition to U.S. military involvement in Iraq.

College sports are also plagued by drug use. (See Case Study 3.) Peer pressure is a factor in the increased use of steroids by college athletes and young people who want to improve their appearance.[33] The American College of Sports Medicine reports that more than 6 percent of high school and college athletes have taken steroids without a doctor's permission.[34] A policy at Duke University calls for unannounced drug testing, including tests for performance-enhancing as well as recreational drugs, for all college athletes. The first violation is handled by treatment and counseling, the third violation by permanent suspension from the team.

The use of performance-enhancing drugs raises several moral issues. Does the duty of self-improvement require that athletes refrain from using drugs that will harm their bodies over the long run? Is it fair that athletes who use these drugs have a competitive advantage? Should drug testing be mandatory, or does mandatory drug testing violate the autonomy of the athlete? Is the use of performance-enhancing drugs in sports inherently coercive since it puts pressure on athletes to use drugs if they want to win? In his reading at the end of this chapter, Thomas Murray opposes drug use in sports on the grounds that it is inherently coercive.

In addition to enhancing athletic performance, drugs can also be used to enhance personality. People may drink a glass of alcohol at a party to overcome social awkwardness and shyness, or use antidepressants to become a happier, less self-occupied person. (See Case Study 4.)

THE DISEASE MODEL OF ADDICTION

The therapeutic revolution in the mid-twentieth century involved relabeling certain behaviors, previously attributed to moral weakness, as diseases. The **disease model of addiction** views addiction primarily as an individual medical problem rather than a social or moral problem. According to this model, it is not lack of willpower or moral character that separates addicts from nonaddicts. Addiction is a pathological state. Addicts abuse drugs because they are ill; they are biologically different from nonaddicts. People who harm others or break the law while under the influence of alcohol or drugs should receive treatment, not punishment, because they were no more in control of what they did when "under the influence" than an epileptic having a seizure.

The disease model of addiction was first articulated in the 1940s by Elvine M. Jellinek of the Yale Center of Alcoholic Studies.[35] It has since become the official view of both the AMA and the World Health Organization (WHO). In 1956 the AMA recognized drug addiction as a "chemical dependency" and, therefore, a disease like diabetes or cancer. In 1977 the AMA added alcoholism to its list of illnesses, defining it as "an illness characterized by significant impairment that is directly associated with persistent and excessive use of alcohol. Impairment may involve physiological, psychological, or social dysfunction." Although abstinence may arrest the disease of addiction, the disease itself can never be cured because it is biologically based. Recent advances in genetics lend weight to the disease model of addiction and the idea of the "addictive personality."[36] (See Case Study 2.)

Alcoholics Anonymous (AA) is based primarily on the disease model. A fundamental assumption of the AA Twelve Steps program is that healing can occur only when alcoholics admit their powerlessness over addiction and turn the healing process over to a "higher power." The "one disease [addiction], one treatment [abstinence]" approach of AA currently dominates the medical field. (See Case Study 5.)

THE MORAL MODEL OF ADDICTION

Addiction, according to the **moral model of addiction,** is a freely chosen vice. Many people, including psychiatrist Thomas Szasz, question the validity of the medical model and call for a return to the moral model. Resisting or overcoming addiction is simply a matter of willpower. The religious view that alcoholism is a sin, the prohibition legislation of the early twentieth century, and the "Just Say No" campaign are all based on the moral model of addiction.

Most positions on addiction lie somewhere between the two extremes. Although AA is based primarily on the disease model, accepting moral responsibility for one's actions is also a key part of the recovery process. Similarly, most supporters of the moral model acknowledge that there are social, personal, and genetic factors that make it more likely that certain people will become addicts. However, unlike predispositions to other diseases, such as breast cancer and diabetes, a person who is genetically predisposed to addiction can avoid it altogether by avoiding the substances that may lead to addiction. Therefore, people who harm others while under the influence of alcohol or drugs should be held morally responsible for their choices and actions. Under the moral model, punishment is an appropriate response to drug-related crime.

THE PHILOSOPHERS ON DRUG AND ALCOHOL ABUSE

Aristotle rejects the disease model of addiction. According to him, virtue entails acting according to reason. People who are drunk are "acting in ignorance." Thus, addicts give up their essential humanity by giving up control of their actions. We need have no sympathy for a person whose health is destroyed by excessive drinking or drug abuse.

Unlike a person whose illness is involuntary, a drunkard is responsible for his ignorance "since it was open to him to refrain from getting drunk."[37]

Although Aristotle would probably not object to the use of drugs and alcohol in moderation, Buddhists are morally opposed to any use of drugs or alcohol because a "clear and composed mind" is necessary to achieve moral perfection and enlightenment. According to Buddha, all human suffering is caused by people whose minds are confused and their reason dulled.

Muslims are also opposed to the use of alcohol and drugs. Alcohol use is a moral failing similar to slander. According to Muslim philosophy, "When a person drinks he becomes intoxicated; when he is intoxicated he raves; and when he raves he falsely accuses."[38]

Libertarians favor a permissive policy on drug and alcohol use. John Stuart Mill opposed the U.S. prohibition laws of the 1850s as an unjustified interference with people's liberty. He wrote, "Over himself, over his own body and mind, the individual is sovereign."[39] Although Mill acknowledged that drug or alcohol users can harm others by rendering themselves incapable of working, this does not justify prohibiting drugs, because society can afford to absorb these losses for the sake of liberty.

THE MORAL ISSUES

Virtue Ethics and the Good Life

Virtue ethicists encourage us to improve our character through self-examination and the practice of virtuous behavior. Addiction interferes with our ability to engage in philosophical self-examination and to seek the higher good.

Virtue, in most cases, requires us to seek the mean between excess and deficit. The doctrine of the mean requires that we use our reason to discern where the mean is for us. According to the disease model, the use of any amount of a drug is excessive for addicts. However, for other people, moderation may be appropriate and consistent with the good and virtuous life. Recent studies at Harvard University have found that light and moderate drinkers are healthier and live longer than total abstainers. Morphine is another drug where excess for one person may be a deficiency for another. Although it can be addictive, to refuse a dying cancer patient morphine because of fear of addiction is to err on the side of deficiency.

Confucius believed that government bears the primary responsibility for promoting virtue in citizens. The purpose of laws is to make it easier for people to be virtuous. James Q. Wilson argues that if drugs are legal, many people will prefer the pleasure of drug excess over treatment and virtuous behavior. Douglas Husak counters that it is not the place of government to impose on citizens an ideal of human excellence. It is up to each of us to responsibly determine our own concept of the good life.

Human Dignity and the Categorical Imperative

Kant's categorical imperative states that we should never use ourselves as a means only. Addicts debase themselves by using themselves as a means only—to get a fix through drugs or alcohol. Addiction is tempting because it "fixes" our disquiet and malaise.

Addiction distracts us from our lives and relieves us of the burden, the frustration, the boredom, and the search for meaning in our lives. Addiction *becomes* the meaning of life. Because drug abuse and addiction prevent us from being fully human, they are incompatible with human dignity.

As rational moral agents, we are responsible for our choices and actions. The disease model is problematic in that it places the burden of "curing" addiction on physicians rather than on the individual, thus allowing addicts to abdicate personal responsibility for their behavior. Passing off responsibility for our destructive and disrespectful behavior is inconsistent with human dignity and freedom.

Autonomy, Liberty Rights, and the Principle of Noninterference

Autonomy involves our ability to make free choices. Both Szasz and Husak argue that prohibiting recreational drug use violates our autonomy. The "right of self-medication," Szasz writes, is a fundamental right. Enforcement procedures are not only futile, but an infringement on people's liberty rights. They reject the disease model of addiction. Drug addicts are autonomous, because any person of "reasonable firmness" can stop using drugs.

Not everyone agrees that adult drug users are acting autonomously. Murray maintains that the use of performance-enhancing drugs in sports is "inherently coercive." In sports, in which one's professional success may ride on using performance-enhancing drugs, the pressure to use these drugs may seriously compromise the athlete's autonomy. Like Major League Baseball, the National Football League and the National Basketball Association have banned many performance-enhancing drugs, but they balk at mandatory blood testing, saying that making players give blood violates their privacy.

The principle of noninterference states that interference with adults' free choice must be justified. However, most drug and alcohol addicts begin as children. In the United States, the average age is twelve for the first use of alcohol and thirteen for the first use of illicit drugs.[40] Judges in both Massachusetts and Iowa have upheld a school's right to search students for drugs, ruling in *Iowa v. Marzel Jones* (2003) that the school's interest in maintaining "a controlled and disciplined environment" overrules a student's right to privacy.

Pleasure

Pleasure is the most common reason college students give for using alcohol and drugs.[41] According to some utilitarians, the use of drugs for pleasure is not necessarily at odds with the good life and may even contribute to it. However, they draw the line at drug use that interferes with living the good life.

Paternalism and Harm to Self

Paternalism permits interfering with people's choices for their own good. Drugs and alcohol can be harmful to self. The life of an average alcoholic, for example, is fifteen years shorter than that of a nonalcoholic.[42]

The belief that drug and alcohol abuse is a disease promotes a paternalistic approach to drug and alcohol regulation. Laws prohibiting alcohol and tobacco use by children are generally based on the principle of paternalism. Given that so many untimely adult deaths involve tobacco and alcohol abuse, however, shouldn't paternalism extend to adults as well? If adults use these and other drugs in a manner that is harmful to themselves, isn't their "decision" to do so by definition irrational and, hence, not a free and autonomous choice?

Prohibition based on paternalism can come into conflict with the principle of autonomy. The use of coercion—even "well-meaning" coercion—in an attempt to regulate a person's character is an affront to human dignity and freedom. Should we prohibit drugs for all because drugs seriously impair the autonomy of some? The belief that people use drugs "against their will," that they have "lost control of their lives," or that drug users are "morally deficient" is demeaning. It may be better to let addicts continue harming themselves rather than deny them at least some control over their lives.

Furthermore, because people do not like to be told what to do, paternalism can backfire. There was a dramatic increase in drug use, especially among young people, following President Bush's declaration of war on drugs. Studies also suggest that raising the drinking age from eighteen to twenty-one throughout the United States may actually have exacerbated the bingeing problem on campuses. In addition to the lure of forbidden fruit, students are now more likely to drink in private places like their dorms and fraternities or in bars that are lax in checking for proper ID.[43]

Nonmaleficence and Preventing Harm to Others

One of the most common arguments for drug prohibition is protection of public health and safety. Although restrictions based on paternalism are often considered an affront to personal dignity, most people acknowledge that coercion is justified to prevent people from harming one another.

Wilson argues that the harms of legalizing drugs outweigh those of prohibition. Drug abuse, he points out, is hardly a victimless crime. It is associated with health problems, reduced job productivity, family violence, crime, fetal alcohol syndrome, drug-addicted newborns, and suicide. Many of these costs are passed on to society. Twenty percent of Medicare funds go to the treatment of problems stemming from alcohol and drug abuse. Indeed, elderly patients are more likely to be hospitalized for conditions related to alcohol abuse than for heart attacks.[44] The cost of treating infants born to cocaine/crack mothers was estimated in the mid-1990s to be $500 million a year.[45]

Prosecuting and punishing drug-related crimes cost taxpayers more than $30 billion a year. In 2005, 53 percent of inmates in federal prisons and 20 percent of those in state prisons were drug offenders.[46] The majority of drug-related criminal charges in the United States involve marijuana. Of these, two-thirds are for simple possession.[47] Indeed, there is a marijuana-related arrest in the United States every 38 seconds, with marijuana-related arrests outnumbering those for all violent crimes.[48]

Husak supports legalizing recreational drugs. Harm to others is a powerful argument for working toward decreasing drug and alcohol abuse, but it is not obvious that legal prohibition is the best solution; drug education may be more effective. Making drugs illegal forces up their price, thus encouraging users to resort to crime to pay for their habit. Much of the street violence in our cities is attributable to the illicit sale of drugs rather than to the actual effects of the drugs themselves. In addition, because street dealers are already criminals, drug prohibition brings young people seeking drugs into contact with the criminal element.

There are also hidden costs of illegal drug use and alcoholism in terms of domestic violence and the breakup of families. In addition, the cost of health care for alcoholics is more than double that for nonalcoholics; much of this cost is borne by taxpayers and employers. Smokers also use more medical resources and have longer hospital stays than nonsmokers. Indeed, lung cancer has now become the leading cause of cancer deaths in women.

CONCLUSION

Drug and alcohol use raises two concerns. The first relates to virtue ethics: We have a personal responsibility to abstain from harmful drugs or drugs that are addictive. If addiction is a disease, virtue dictates that addicts or potential addicts are morally responsible for avoiding drugs and/or alcohol and for seeking a cure, or at least avoiding situations in which they could harm others. On the other hand, the moderate use of certain drugs may actually enhance the good life. Knowing the difference between excess and moderation involves the development of wisdom and character.

The second issue relates to social policy. Some philosophers maintain that drugs should be prohibited. Most people agree that harm to others is a strong justification for restricting drug use; however, they disagree over the best means to achieve the objective of minimizing harm.

⬖ SUMMARY OF READINGS ON DRUG AND ALCOHOL USE

Szasz, "The Ethics of Addiction." People who abuse drugs and alcohol are not sick and should be held morally accountable.

Wilson, "Against the Legalization of Drugs." Drugs should be illegal because the harms of legalizing drugs outweigh the harms of prohibition.

Husak, "A Moral Right to Use Drugs." There is nothing inherently wrong about using recreational drugs; therefore, they should be legal for adults.

Dean-Mooney and McCardell, "Two Takes on the 21 Drinking Age." A forum on whether or not the drinking age should be lowered to eighteen.

Murray, "Drugs, Sports, and Ethics." Drug use in sports is immoral because it restricts the free choice of competing athletes.

THOMAS SZASZ

The Ethics of Addiction

Thomas Szasz is a professor emeritus of psychiatry at the State University of New York Upstate Medical Center and author of several books on psychiatry, including *The Myth of Mental Illness.* In this article Szasz rejects the disease model of addiction. Citing John Stuart Mill's principle of no harm, Szasz argues that drug laws do not respect the right of citizens to exercise control over their own lives. Therefore, all prohibition laws should be repealed, at least for adults.

Critical Reading Questions

1. What is the World Health Organization definition of drug abuse? Why does Szasz maintain that this definition is a moral rather than a medical judgment?
2. According to Szasz, what "propaganda" is used by proponents of the disease model of addiction to justify the prohibition of drug use?
3. Why does Szasz reject the prohibition argument that some drugs are dangerous?
4. According to Szasz, why do people become addicted? Why does Szasz reject the prohibition argument that drug addiction is different from addiction to other substances?
5. According to Szasz, what are the primary reasons people take drugs? Which of these reasons is identified with "drug abuse"?
6. What arguments does Szasz use to support his position for the legalization of drugs?
7. On what grounds does Szasz argue that the "right of self-medication" is a fundamental right? Should there be any limitations on this right?
8. Why does Szasz support the prohibition of drug and alcohol sales to minors?
9. What are the two principal methods of legitimizing policy in the United States? How have these two methods been used to legitimize the prohibition of drugs?
10. On what grounds does Szasz reject the current medical concept of drug abuse and drug treatment programs?
11. According to Szasz, why are we in need of a "medical reformation"?
12. On what grounds does Szasz argue that we have a constitutional right to use drugs and alcohol?
13. How does Szasz use John Stuart Mill's philosophy to support his position?

"The Ethics of Addiction," *Harper's Magazine* 244 (April 1972): 74–79.

AN ARGUMENT IN FAVOR OF LETTING AMERICANS TAKE ANY DRUG THEY WANT TO TAKE

To avoid cliches about "drug abuse," let us analyze its official definition. According to the World Health Organization, "Drug addiction is a state of periodic or chronic intoxication detrimental to the individual and to society, produced by the repeated consumption of a drug (natural or synthetic). Its characteristics include: 1) an overpowering desire or need (compulsion) to continue taking the drug and to obtain it by any means, 2) a tendency to increase the dosage, and 3) a psychic (psychological) and sometimes physical dependence on the effects of the drug."

Since this definition hinges on the harm done to both the individual and society, it is clearly an ethical one. Moreover, by not specifying what is "detrimental," it consigns the problem of addiction to psychiatrists who define the patient's "dangerousness to himself and others."

Next, we come to the effort to obtain the addictive substance "by any means." This suggests that the substance must be prohibited, or is very expensive, and is hence difficult for the ordinary person to obtain (rather than that the person who wants it has an inordinate craving for it). If there were an abundant and inexpensive supply of what the "addict" wants, there would be no reason for him to go to "any means" to obtain it. Thus by the WHO's definition, one can be addicted only to a substance that is illegal or otherwise difficult to obtain. This surely removes the problem of addiction from the realm of medicine and psychiatry, and puts it squarely into that of morals and law.

In short, drug addiction or drug abuse cannot be defined without specifying the proper and improper uses of certain pharmacologically active agents. The regular administration of morphine by a physician to a patient dying of cancer is the paradigm of the proper use of a narcotic; whereas even its occasional self-administration by a physically healthy person for the purpose of "pharmacological pleasure" is the paradigm of drug abuse.

I submit that these judgments have nothing whatever to do with medicine, pharmacology, or psychiatry. They are moral judgments. Indeed, our present views on addiction are astonishingly similar to some of our former views on sex. Until recently, masturbation—or self-abuse, as it was called—was professionally declared, and popularly accepted, as both the cause and the symptom of a variety of illnesses. Even today, homosexuality—called a "sexual perversion"—is regarded as a disease by medical and psychiatric experts as well as by "well-informed" laymen.

To be sure, it is now virtually impossible to cite a contemporary medical authority to support the concept of self-abuse. Medical opinion holds that whether a person masturbates or not is medically irrelevant; and that engaging in the practice or refraining from it is a matter of personal morals or life-style. On the other hand, it is virtually impossible to cite a contemporary medical authority to oppose the concept of drug abuse. Medical opinion holds that drug abuse is a major medical, psychiatric, and public health problem; that drug addiction is a disease similar to diabetes, requiring prolonged (or lifelong) and careful, medically supervised treatment; and that taking or not taking drugs is primarily, if not solely, a matter of medical responsibility.

Thus the man on the street can only believe what he hears from all sides—that drug addiction is a disease, "like any other," which has now reached "epidemic proportions," and whose "medical" containment justifies the limitless expenditure of tax monies and the corresponding aggrandizement and enrichment of noble medical warriors against this "plague."

PROPAGANDA TO JUSTIFY PROHIBITION

Like any social policy, our drug laws may be examined from two entirely different points of view: technical and moral. Our present inclination is either to ignore the moral perspective or to mistake the technical for the moral.

Since most of the propagandists against drug use seek to justify certain repressive policies because of the alleged dangerousness of various drugs, they often falsify the facts about the pharmacological properties of the drugs they seek to prohibit. They do so for two reasons: first, because many substances in daily use are just as harmful as the substances they want to prohibit; second, because they realize that dangerousness alone is never a sufficiently persuasive argument to justify the prohibition of any drug, substance, or artifact. Accordingly, the more they ignore the moral dimensions of the problem, the more they must escalate their fraudulent claims about the dangers of drugs.

To be sure, some drugs are more dangerous than others. It is easier to kill oneself with heroin than with aspirin. But is also easier to kill oneself by jumping off a high building than a low one. In the case of drugs, we regard their potentiality for self-injury as justification for their prohibition; in the case of buildings, we do not.

Furthermore, we systematically blur and confuse the two quite different ways in which narcotics may cause death: by a deliberate act of suicide or by accidental overdosage.

Every individual is capable of injuring or killing himself. This potentiality is a fundamental expression of human freedom. Self-destructive behavior may be regarded as sinful and penalized by means of informal sanctions. But it should not be regarded as a crime or (mental) disease, justifying or warranting the use of the police powers of the state for its control.

Therefore, it is absurd to deprive an adult of a drug (or of anything else) because he might use it to kill himself. To do so is to treat everyone the way institutional psychiatrists treat the so-called suicidal mental patient: they not only imprison such a person but take everything away from him—shoelaces, belts, razor blades, eating utensils, and so forth—until the "patient" lies naked on a mattress in a padded cell—lest he kill himself. The result is degrading tyrannization.

Death by accidental overdose is an altogether different matter. But can anyone doubt that this danger now looms so large precisely because the sale of narcotics and many other drugs is illegal? Those who buy illicit drugs cannot be sure what drug they are getting or how much of it. Free trade in drugs, with governmental action limited to safeguarding the purity of the product and the veracity of the labeling, would reduce the risk of accidental overdose with "dangerous drugs" to the same levels that prevail, and that we find acceptable, with respect to other chemical agents and physical artifacts that abound in our complex technological society.

This essay is not intended as an exposition on the pharmacological properties of narcotics and other mind-affecting drugs. However, I want to make it clear that in my view, *regardless* of their danger, all drugs should be "legalized" (a misleading term I employ reluctantly as a concession to common usage). Although I recognize that some drugs—notably heroin, the amphetamines, and LSD, among those now in vogue—may have undesirable or dangerous consequences, I favor free trade in drugs for the same reason the Founding Fathers favored free trade in ideas. In an open society, it is none of the government's business what idea a man puts into his mind; likewise, it should be none of the government's business what drug he puts into his body.

WITHDRAWAL PAINS FROM TRADITION

It is a fundamental characteristic of human beings that they get used to things: one becomes habituated, or "addicted," not only to narcotics, but to cigarettes, cocktails before dinner, orange juice for breakfast, comic strips, and so forth. It is similarly a fundamental characteristic of living organisms that they acquire increasing tolerance to various chemical agents and physical stimuli: the first cigarette may cause nothing but nausea and headache; a year later, smoking three packs a day may be pure joy. Both alcohol and opiates are "addictive" in the sense that the more regularly they are used, the more the user craves them and the greater his tolerance for them becomes. Yet none of this involves any mysterious process of "getting hooked." It is simply an aspect of the universal biological propensity for *learning,* which is especially well developed in man. The opiate habit, like the cigarette habit or food habit, can be broken—and without any medical assistance—provided the person wants to break it. Often he doesn't. And why, indeed, should he, if he has nothing better to do with his life? Or, as happens to be the case with morphine, if he can live an essentially normal life while under its influence?

Actually, opium is much less toxic than alcohol. Just as it is possible to be an "alcoholic" and work and be productive, so it is (or, rather, it used to be) possible to be an opium addict and work and be productive. . . .

I am not citing this evidence to recommend the opium habit. The point is that we must, in plain honesty, distinguish between pharmacological effects and personal inclinations. Some people take drugs to help them function and conform to social expectations; others take them for the very opposite reason, to ritualize their refusal to function and conform to social expectations. Much of the "drug abuse" we now witness—perhaps nearly all of it—is of the second type. But instead of acknowledging that "addicts" are unfit or unwilling to work and be "normal," we prefer to believe that they act as they do because certain drugs—especially heroin, LSD, and the amphetamines—make them "sick." If only we could get them "well," so runs this comforting view, they would become "productive" and "useful" citizens. To believe this is like believing that if an illiterate cigarette smoker would only stop smoking, he would become an Einstein. With a falsehood like this, one can go far. No wonder that politicians and psychiatrists love it.

The concept of free trade in drugs runs counter to our cherished notion that everyone must work and idleness is acceptable only under special conditions. In general, the obligation to work is greatest for healthy, adult, white men. We tolerate idleness on the part of children, women, Negroes, the aged, and the sick, and even accept the responsibility to support them. But the new wave of drug abuse affects mainly young adults, often white males, who are, in principle at least, capable of working and supporting themselves. But they refuse: they "drop out"; and in doing so, they challenge the most basic values of our society.

The fear that free trade in narcotics would result in vast masses of our population spending their days and nights smoking opium or mainlining heroin, rather than working and taking care of their responsibilities, is a bugaboo that does not deserve to be taken seriously. Habits of work and idleness are deep-seated cultural patterns. Free trade in abortions has not made an industrious people like the Japanese give up work for fornication. Nor would free trade in drugs convert such a people from hustlers to hippies. Indeed, I think the opposite might be the case: it is questionable whether, or for how long, a responsible people can tolerate being treated as totally irresponsible with respect to drugs and drug-taking. In other words, how long can we live with the inconsistency of being expected to be responsible for operating cars and computers, but not for operating our own bodies?

Although my argument about drug-taking is moral and political, and does not depend upon showing that free trade in drugs would also have fiscal advantages over our present policies, let me indicate briefly some of its economic implications.

The war on addiction is not only astronomically expensive; it is also counterproductive. On April 1, 1967, New York State's narcotics addiction control program, hailed as "the most massive ever tried in the nation," went into effect. "The program, which may cost up to $400 million in three years," reported the *New York Times,* "was hailed by Governor Rockefeller as 'the start of an unending war.'" . . . In short, the detection and rehabilitation of addicts is good business. We now know that the spread of witchcraft in the late Middle Ages was due more to the work of witchmongers than to the lure of witchcraft. Is it not possible that the spread of addiction in our day is due more to the work of addictmongers than to the lure of narcotics?

Let us see how far some of the monies spent on the war on addiction could go in supporting people who prefer to drop out of society and drug themselves. Their "habit" itself would cost next to nothing; free trade would bring the price of narcotics down to a negligible amount. . . .

. . . free trade in narcotics would be more economical for those of us who work, even if we had to support legions of addicts, than is our present program of trying to "cure" them. Moreover, I have not even made use, in my economic estimates, of the incalculable sums we would save by reducing crimes now engendered by the illegal traffic in drugs.

THE RIGHT OF SELF-MEDICATION

Clearly, the argument that marijuana—or heroin, methadone, or morphine—is prohibited because it is addictive or dangerous cannot be supported by facts. For one thing, there are many drugs, from insulin to penicillin, that are neither addictive nor dangerous but are nevertheless also prohibited; they can be obtained only through a physician's prescription. For another, there are many things, from dynamite to guns, that are much more dangerous than narcotics (especially to others) but are not prohibited. As everyone knows, it is still possible in the United States to walk into a store and walk out with a shotgun. We enjoy this right not because we believe that guns are safe but because we believe even more strongly that civil liberties are precious. At the same time, it is not possible in the United States to walk into a store and walk out with a bottle of barbiturates, codeine, or other drugs.

I believe that just as we regard freedom of speech and religion as fundamental rights, so we should also regard freedom of self-medication as a fundamental right. Like most rights, the right of self-medication should apply only to adults; and it should not be an unqualified right. Since these are important qualifications, it is necessary to specify their precise range.

John Stuart Mill said (approximately) that a person's right to swing his arm ends where his neighbor's nose begins. And Oliver Wendell Holmes said that no one has a right to shout "Fire!" in a crowded theater. Similarly, the limiting condition with respect to self-medication should be the inflicting of actual (as against symbolic) harm on others.

Our present practices with respect to alcohol embody and reflect this individualistic ethic. We have the right to buy, possess, and consume alcoholic beverages. Regardless of how offensive drunkenness might be to a person, he cannot interfere with another person's "right" to become inebriated so long as that person drinks in the privacy of his own home or at some other appropriate location, and so long as he conducts himself in an otherwise law-abiding manner. In short, we have a right to be intoxicated—in private. Public intoxication is considered an offense to others and is therefore a violation of the criminal law. It makes sense that what is a "right" in one place may become, by virtue of its disruptive or disturbing effect on others, an offense somewhere else.

The right to self-medication should be hedged in by similar limits. Public intoxication, not only with alcohol but with any drug, should be an offense punishable by the criminal law. Furthermore, acts that may injure others—such as driving a car—should, when carried out in a drug-intoxicated state, be punished especially strictly and severely. The right to self-medication must thus entail unqualified responsibility for the effects of one's drug-intoxicated behavior on others. For unless we are willing to hold ourselves responsible for our own behavior, and hold others responsible for theirs, the liberty to use drugs (or to engage in other acts) degenerates into a license to hurt others.

Such, then, would be the situation of adults, if we regarded the freedom to take drugs as a fundamental right similar to the freedom to read and worship. What would be the situation of children? Since many people who are now said to be drug addicts or drug abusers are minors, it is especially important that we think clearly about this aspect of the problem.

I do not believe, and I do not advocate, that children should have a right to ingest, inject, or otewise use any drug or substance they want. Children do not have the right to drive, drink, vote, marry, or make binding contracts. They acquire these rights at various ages, coming into their full possession at maturity, usually between the ages of eighteen and twenty-one. The right to self-medication should similarly be withheld until maturity.

In short, I suggest that "dangerous" drugs be treated, more or less, as alcohol is treated now. Neither the use of narcotics, nor their possession, should be prohibited, but only their sale to minors. Of course, this would result in the ready availability of all kinds of drugs among minors—though perhaps their availability would be no greater than it is now, but would only be more visible and hence more easily subject to proper controls. This arrangement would place responsibility for the use of all drugs by children where it belongs: on parents and their children. This is where the major responsibility rests for the use of alcohol. It is a tragic symptom of our refusal to take personal liberty and responsibility seriously that there appears to be no public desire to assume a similar stance toward other "dangerous" drugs.

Consider what would happen should a child bring a bottle of gin to school and get drunk there. Would the school authorities blame the local liquor stores as pushers? Or would they blame the parents and the child himself? There is liquor in practically every home in America and yet children rarely bring liquor to school. Whereas marijuana, Dexedrine, and heroin—substances children usually do not find at home and whose very possession is a criminal offense—frequently find their way into the school.

Our attitude toward sexual activity provides another model for our attitude toward drugs. Although we generally discourage children below a certain age from engaging in sexual activities with others, we do not prohibit such activities by law. What we do prohibit by law is the sexual seduction of children by adults. The "pharmacological seduction" of children by adults should be similarly punishable. In other words, adults who give or sell drugs to children should be regarded as offenders. Such a specific and limited prohibition—as against the kinds of generalized prohibitions that we had under the Volstead Act or have now with respect to countless drugs—would be relatively easy to enforce. Moreover, it

would probably be rarely violated, for there would be little psychological interest and no economic profit in doing so.

THE TRUE FAITH: SCIENTIFIC MEDICINE

What I am suggesting is that while addiction is ostensibly a medical and pharmacological problem, actually it is a moral and political problem. We ought to know that there is no necessary connection between facts and values, between what is and what ought to be. Thus, objectively quite harmful acts, objects, or persons may be accepted and tolerated—by minimizing their dangerousness. Conversely, objectively quite harmless acts, objects, or persons may be prohibited and persecuted—by exaggerating their dangerousness. It is always necessary to distinguish—and especially so when dealing with social policy—between description and prescription, fact and rhetoric, truth and falsehood.

In our society, there are two principal methods of legitimizing policy: social tradition and scientific judgment. More than anything else, time is the supreme ethical arbiter. Whatever a social practice might be, if people engage in it, generation after generation, that practice becomes acceptable.

Many opponents of illegal drugs admit that nicotine may be more harmful to health than marijuana; nevertheless, they urge that smoking cigarettes should be legal but smoking marijuana should not be, because the former habit is socially accepted while the latter is not. This is a perfectly reasonable argument. But let us understand it for what it is—a plea for legitimizing old and accepted practices, and for illegitimizing novel and unaccepted ones. It is a justification that rests on precedent, not evidence.

The other method of legitimizing policy, ever more important in the modern world, is through the authority of science. In matters of health, a vast and increasingly elastic category, physicians play important roles as legitimizers and illegitimizers. This, in short, is why we regard being medicated by a doctor as drug use, and self-medication (especially with certain classes of drugs) as drug abuse.

This, too, is a perfectly reasonable arrangement. But we must understand that it is a plea for legitimizing what doctors do, because they do it with "good therapeutic" intent; and for illegitimatizing what laymen do, because they do it with bad self-abusive ("masturbatory" or mind-altering) intent. This justification rests on the principles of professionalism, not of pharmacology. Hence we applaud the systematic medical use of methadone and call it "treatment for heroin addiction," but decry the occasional nonmedical use of marijuana and call it "dangerous drug abuse."

Our present concept of drug abuse articulates and symbolizes a fundamental policy of scientific medicine—namely, that a layman should not medicate his own body but should place its medical care under the supervision of a duly accredited physician. Before the Reformation, the practice of True Christianity rested on a similar policy—namely, that a layman should not himself commune with God but should place his spiritual care under the supervision of a duly accredited priest. The self-interests of the church and of medicine in such policies are obvious enough. What might be less obvious is the interest of the laity: by delegating responsibility for the spiritual and medical welfare of the people to a class of authoritatively accredited specialists, these policies—and the practices they ensure—relieve individuals from assuming the burdens of responsibility for themselves. As I see it, our present problems with drug use and drug abuse are just one of the consequences of our pervasive ambivalence about personal autonomy and responsibility.

I propose a medical reformation analogous to the Protestant Reformation: specifically, a "protest" against the systematic mystification of man's relationship to his body and his professionalized separation from it. The immediate aim of this reform would be to remove the physician as intermediary between man and his body and to give the layman direct access to the language and contents of the pharmacopoeia. If man had unencumbered access to his own body and the means of chemically altering it, it would spell the end of medicine, at least as we now know it. This is why, with faith in scientific medicine so strong, there is little interest in this kind of medical reform. Physicians fear the loss of their privileges; laymen, the loss of their protections. . . .

LIFE, LIBERTY, AND THE PURSUIT OF HIGHS

Sooner or later we shall have to confront the basic moral dilemma underlying this problem: does a person have the right to take a drug, any drug—not because he needs it to cure an illness, but because he wants to take it?

The Declaration of Independence speaks of our inalienable right to "life, liberty, and the pursuit of happiness." How are we to interpret this? By asserting that we ought to be free to pursue happiness by playing golf or watching television, but not by drinking alcohol, or smoking marijuana, or ingesting pep pills?

The Constitution and the Bill of Rights are silent on the subject of drugs. This would seem to imply that the adult citizen has, or ought to have, the right to medicate his own body as he sees fit. Were this not the case, why should there have been a need for a Constitutional Amendment to outlaw drinking? But if ingesting alcohol was, and is now again, a Constitutional right, is ingesting opium, or heroin, or barbiturates, or anything else, not also such a right? If it is, then the Harrison Narcotic Act is not only a bad law but is unconstitutional as well, because it prescribes in a legislative act what ought to be promulgated in a Constitutional Amendment.

The questions remain: as American citizens, should we have the right to take narcotics or other drugs? If we take drugs and conduct ourselves as responsible and law-abiding citizens, should we have a right to remain unmolested by the government? Lastly, if we take drugs and break the law, should we have a right to be treated as persons accused of crime, rather than as patients accused of mental illness?

These are fundamental questions that are conspicuous by their absence from all contemporary discussions of problems of drug addiction and drug abuse. The result is that instead of debating the use of drugs in moral and political terms, we define our task as the ostensibly narrow technical problem of protecting people from poisoning themselves with substances for whose use they cannot possibly assume responsibility. This, I think, best explains the frightening national consensus against personal responsibility for taking drugs and for one's conduct while under their influence. . . .

To me, unanimity on an issue as basic and complex as this means a complete evasion of the actual problem and an attempt to master it by attacking and overpowering a scapegoat—"dangerous drugs" and "drug abusers." There is an ominous resemblance between the unanimity with which all "reasonable" men—and especially politicians, physicians, and priests—formerly supported the protective measures of society against witches and Jews, and that with which they now support them against drug addicts and drug abusers.

After all is said and done, the issue comes down to whether we accept or reject the ethical principle John Stuart Mill so clearly enunciated: "The only purpose [he wrote in *On Liberty*] for which power can be rightfully exercised over any member of a civilized community, against his will, is to prevent harm to others. His own good, either physical or moral, is not a sufficient warrant. He cannot rightfully be compelled to do or forbear because it will make him happier, because in the opinions of others, to do so would be wise, or even right. . . . In the part [of his conduct] which merely concerns himself, his independence is, of right, absolute. Over himself, over his own body and mind, the individual is sovereign."

By recognizing the problem of drug abuse for what it is—a moral and political question rather than a medical or therapeutic one—we can choose to maximize the sphere of action of the state at the expense of the individual, or of the individual at the expense of the state. In other words, we could commit ourselves to the view that the state, the representative of many, is more important than the individual; that it therefore has the right, indeed the duty, to regulate the life of the individual in the best interests of the group. Or we could commit ourselves to the view that individual dignity and liberty are the supreme values of life, and that the foremost duty of the state is to protect and promote these values.

In short, we must choose between the ethic of collectivism and individualism, and pay the price of either—or of both.

Discussion Questions

1. What, according to Szasz, are some of the myths surrounding the notion of drug addiction? Discuss how Elvine Jellinek (see page 286) might respond to Szasz. Which person presents the stronger argument? Support your answers.

2. Is Szasz being logically consistent in his rejection of legal access to drugs and alcohol for teenagers? If it is wrong for children to use certain "dangerous" drugs, why isn't it also wrong for adults to use the same drugs? Should "immature" adults who abuse drugs and alcohol also be legally prohibited from using these substances? Support your answers.

3. Is Szasz committing the fallacy of appeal to tradition when he argues that we have a constitutional right to use drugs? Or can his argument for a "right of self-medication" stand without appeal to the Constitution? Support your answers.

4. Moonshining—the illegal production and sale of distilled spirits—is an underground art in some rural parts of the Atlantic provinces in Canada. The Royal Canadian Mounted Police have been receiving a growing number of tips about the whereabouts of illegal stills, as well as complaints from public-spirited neighbors.

Discuss whether laws that prohibit moonshining violate the right of citizens to exercise control over their own lives. Discuss also how Szasz would respond to this question.

JAMES Q. WILSON

Against the Legalization of Drugs

James Q. Wilson is a professor of public policy at Pepperdine University and former chair of the National Advisory Council for Drug Abuse Prevention. He is also the author of *The Moral Sense* and *Crime and Human Nature*. In this article Wilson rejects the libertarian view that citizens have the right to use drugs and to drink anything they want. Instead, Wilson argues that the harms of legalizing drugs outweigh the harms of prohibition.

Critical Reading Questions

1. What arguments does Wilson use to show that drug prohibition is morally justified?
2. What is Wilson's view on the disease model of addiction?
3. What evidence does Wilson use to support his position that legalizing drugs would increase their use?
4. Which drugs does Wilson think should be prohibited and why?
5. Why does Wilson reject the concept of drug abuse as a "victimless crime"?
6. Why is Wilson appalled by the argument that drug abusers should be allowed to kill themselves?
7. How does Wilson respond to the antiprohibition argument that the illegality of drugs increases crime?
8. According to Wilson, what are some of the benefits of making drugs illegal?
9. According to Wilson, why would drug treatment be less successful if drugs were legal?
10. What is Wilson's view on the morality of tobacco use? What are the similarities and differences, according to Wilson, of tobacco use and cocaine use?
11. What is Wilson's view on the morality of alcohol use?
12. Why does Wilson dislike the "war on drugs" metaphor? What metaphor does he prefer?
13. According to Wilson, what is the role of science in helping us understand and cope with addiction?

"Against the Legalization of Drugs," *Commentary* 89, no. 2 (February 1990): 21–28.

In 1972, the President appointed me chairman of the National Advisory Council for Drug Abuse Prevention. Created by Congress, the Council was charged with providing guidance on how best to coordinate the national war on drugs. (Yes, we called it a war then, too.) In those days, the drug we were chiefly concerned with was heroin. When I took office, heroin use had been increasing dramatically. Everybody was worried that this increase would continue. Such phrases as "heroin epidemic" were commonplace.

That same year, the eminent economist Milton Friedman published an essay in *Newsweek* in which he called for legalizing heroin. His argument was on two grounds: as a matter of ethics, the government has no right to tell people not to use heroin (or to drink or to commit suicide); as a matter of economics, the prohibition of drug use imposes costs on society that far exceed the benefits. Others, such as the psychoanalyst Thomas Szasz, made the same argument. . . .

That was 1972. Today, we have the same number of heroin addicts that we had then—half a million, give or take a few thousand. Having that many heroin addicts is no trivial matter; these people deserve our attention. But not having had an increase in that number for over fifteen years is also something that deserves our attention. What happened to the "heroin epidemic" that many people once thought would overwhelm us?

The facts are clear: a more or less stable pool of heroin addicts has been getting older, with relatively few new recruits. In 1976 the average age of heroin users who appeared in hospital emergency rooms was about twenty-seven; ten years later it was thirty-two. More than two-thirds of all heroin users appearing in emergency rooms are now over the age of thirty. Back in the early 1970s, when heroin got onto the national political agenda, the typical heroin addict was much younger, often a teenager. . . .

Why did heroin lose its appeal for young people? When the young blacks in Harlem were asked why they stopped, more than half mentioned "trouble with the law" or "high cost" (and high cost is, of course, directly the result of law enforcement).

Two-thirds said heroin hurt their health; nearly all said they had had a bad experience with it. We need not rely, however, simply on what they said. In New York City in 1973–75, the street price of heroin rose dramatically and its purity sharply declined, probably as a result of the heroin shortage caused by the success of the Turkish government in reducing the supply of opium base and of the French government in closing down heroin-processing laboratories located in and around Marseilles. These were short-lived gains for, just as Friedman predicted, alternative sources of supply—mostly in Mexico—quickly emerged. But the three-year heroin shortage interrupted the easy recruitment of new users. . . .

RELIVING THE PAST

Suppose we had taken Friedman's advice in 1972. What would have happened? We cannot be entirely certain, but at a minimum we would have placed the young heroin addicts (and, above all, the prospective addicts) in a very different position from the one in which they actually found themselves. Heroin would have been legal. Its price would have been reduced by 95 percent (minus whatever we chose to recover in taxes). Now that it could be sold by the same people who make aspirin, its quality would have been assured—no poisons, no adulterants. Sterile hypodermic needles would have been readily available at the neighborhood drugstore, probably at the same counter where the heroin was sold. No need to travel to big cities or unfamiliar neighborhoods—heroin could have been purchased anywhere, perhaps by mail order.

There would no longer have been any financial or medical reason to avoid heroin use. Anybody could have afforded it. We might have tried to prevent children from buying it, but as we have learned from our efforts to prevent minors from buying alcohol and tobacco, young people have a way of penetrating markets theoretically reserved for adults. Returning Vietnam veterans would have discovered that Omaha and Raleigh had been converted into the pharmaceutical equivalent of Saigon.

Under these circumstances, can we doubt for a moment that heroin use would have grown exponentially? Or that a vastly larger supply of new users would have been recruited? . . .

But we need not rely on speculation, however plausible, that lowered prices and more abundant supplies would have increased heroin usage. Great Britain once followed such a policy and with almost exactly those results. Until the mid-1960s, British physicians were allowed to prescribe heroin to certain classes of addicts. (Possessing these drugs without a doctor's prescription remained a criminal offense.) For many years this policy worked well enough because the addict patients were typically middle-class people who had become dependent on opiate painkillers while undergoing hospital treatment. There was no drug culture. The British system worked for many years, not because it prevented drug abuse, but because there was no problem of drug abuse that would test the system.

All that changed in the 1960s. A few unscrupulous doctors began passing out heroin in wholesale amounts. One doctor prescribed almost 600,000 heroin tablets—that is, over thirteen pounds—in just one year. A youthful drug culture emerged with a demand for drugs far different from that of the older addicts. As a result, the British government required doctors to refer users to government-run clinics to receive their heroin.

But the shift to clinics did not curtail the growth in heroin use. Throughout the 1960s the number of addicts increased—the late John Kaplan of Stanford estimated by fivefold—in part as a result of the diversion of heroin from clinic patients to new users on the streets. An addict would bargain with the clinic doctor over how big a dose he would receive. The patient wanted as much as he could get, the doctor wanted to give as little as was needed. The patient had an advantage in this conflict because the doctor could not be certain how much was really needed. Many patients would use some of their "maintenance" dose and sell the remaining part to friends, thereby recruiting new

addicts. As the clinics learned of this, they began to shift their treatment away from heroin and toward methadone, an addictive drug that, when taken orally, does not produce a "high" but will block the withdrawal pains associated with heroin abstinence.

Whether what happened in England in the 1960s was a mini-epidemic or an epidemic depends on whether one looks at numbers or at rates of change. Compared to the United States, the numbers were small. In 1960 there were 68 heroin addicts known to the British government; by 1968 there were 2,000 in treatment and many more who refused treatment. (They would refuse in part because they did not want to get methadone at a clinic if they could get heroin on the street.) Richard Hartnoll estimates that the actual number of addicts in England is five times the number officially registered. At a minimum, the number of British addicts increased by thirtyfold in ten years; the actual increase may have been much larger. . . .

The United States began the 1960s with a much larger number of heroin addicts and probably a bigger at-risk population than was the case in Great Britain. Even though it would be foolhardy to suppose that the British system, if installed here, would have worked the same way or with the same results, it would be equally foolhardy to suppose that a combination of heroin available from leaky clinics and from street dealers who faced only minimal law-enforcement risks would not have produced a much greater increase in heroin use than we actually experienced. My guess is that if we had allowed either doctors or clinics to prescribe heroin, we would have had far worse results than were produced in Britain, if for no other reason than the vastly larger number of addicts with which we began. We would have had to find some way to police thousands (not scores) of physicians and hundreds (not dozens) of clinics. If the British civil service found it difficult to keep heroin in the hands of addicts and out of the hands of recruits when it was dealing with a few hundred people, how well would the American civil service have accomplished the same tasks when dealing with tens of thousands of people?

BACK TO THE FUTURE

Now cocaine, especially in its potent form, crack, is the focus of attention. Now as in 1972 the government is trying to reduce its use. Now as then some people are advocating legalization. Is there any more reason to yield to those arguments today than there was almost two decades ago?*

I think not. If we had yielded in 1972 we almost certainly would have had today a permanent population of several million, not several hundred thousand, heroin addicts. If we yield now we will have a far more serious problem with cocaine.

Crack is worse than heroin by almost any measure. Heroin produces a pleasant drowsiness and, if hygienically administered, has only the physical side effects of constipation and sexual impotence. Regular heroin use incapacitates many users, especially poor ones, for any productive work or social responsibility. They will sit nodding on a street corner, helpless but at least harmless. By contrast, regular cocaine use leaves the user neither helpless nor harmless. When smoked (as with crack) or injected, cocaine produces instant, intense, and short-lived euphoria. The experience generates a powerful desire to repeat it. If the drug is readily available, repeat use will occur. Those people who progress to "bingeing" on cocaine become devoted to the drug and its effects to the exclusion of almost all other considerations—job, family, children, sleep, food, even sex. Dr. Frank Gawin at Yale and Dr. Everett Ellinwood at Duke report that a substantial percentage of all high-dose, binge users become uninhibited, impulsive, hypersexual, compulsive, irritable, and hyperactive. Their moods vacillate dramatically, leading at times to violence and homicide.

---

*I do not take up the question of marijuana. For a variety of reasons—its widespread use and its lesser tendency to addict—it presents a different problem from cocaine or heroin.

Women are much more likely to use crack than heroin, and if they are pregnant, the effects on their babies are tragic. . . . Cocaine harms the fetus and can lead to physical deformities or neurological damage. Some crack babies have for all practical purposes suffered a disabling stroke while still in the womb. The long-term consequences of this brain damage are lowered cognitive ability and the onset of mood disorders. Besharov estimates that about 30,000 to 50,000 such babies are born every year, about 7,000 in New York City alone. There may be ways to treat such infants, but from everything we now know treatment will be long, difficult, and expensive. Worse, the mothers who are most likely to produce crack babies are precisely the ones who, because of poverty or temperament, are least able and willing to obtain such treatment. In fact, anecdotal evidence suggests that crack mothers are likely to abuse their infants.

The notion that abusing drugs such as cocaine is a "victimless crime" is not only absurd but dangerous. Even ignoring the fetal drug syndrome, crack-dependent people are, like heroin addicts, individuals who regularly victimize their children by neglect, their spouses by improvidence, their employers by lethargy, and their coworkers by carelessness. Society is not and could never be a collection of autonomous individuals. We all have a stake in ensuring that each of us displays a minimal level of dignity, responsibility, and empathy. We cannot, of course, coerce people into goodness, but we can and should insist that some standards must be met if society itself—on which the very existence of the human personality depends—is to persist. Drawing the line that defines those standards is difficult and contentious, but if crack and heroin use do not fall below it, what does? . . .

HAVE WE LOST?

Many people who agree that there are risks in legalizing cocaine or heroin still favor it because, they think, we have lost the war on drugs. "Nothing we have done has worked" and the current federal policy is just "more of the same." Whatever the costs of greater drug use, surely they would be less than the costs of our present, failed efforts.

That is exactly what I was told in 1972—and heroin is not quite as bad a drug as cocaine. We did not surrender and we did not lose. We did not win, either. What the nation accomplished then was what most efforts to save people from themselves accomplish: the problem was contained and the number of victims minimized, all at a considerable cost in law enforcement and increased crime. Was the cost worth it? I think so, but others may disagree. What are the lives of would-be addicts worth? I recall some people saying to me then, "Let them kill themselves." I was appalled. Happily, such views did not prevail.

Have we lost today? Not at all. High-rate cocaine use is not commonplace. The National Institute of Drug Abuse (NIDA) reports that less than 5 percent of high-school seniors used cocaine within the last thirty days. . . . Medical examiners reported in 1987 that about 1,500 died from cocaine use; hospital emergency rooms reported about 30,000 admissions related to cocaine abuse. . . .

In some neighborhoods, of course, matters have reached crisis proportions. Gangs control the streets, shootings terrorize residents, and drug-dealing occurs in plain view. The police seem barely able to contain matters. But in these neighborhoods—unlike at Palo Alto cocktail parties—the people are not calling for legalization, they are calling for help. And often not much help has come. Many cities are willing to do almost anything about the drug problem except spend more money on it. The federal government cannot change that; only local voters and politicians can. It is not clear that they will.

It took about ten years to contain heroin. We have had experience with crack for only about three or four years. Each year we spend perhaps $11 billion on law enforcement (and some of that goes to deal with marijuana) and perhaps $2 billion on treatment. Large sums, but not sums that should lead anyone to say, "We just can't afford this any more."

The illegality of drugs increases crime, partly because some users turn to crime to pay for their habits, partly because some users are stimulated by certain drugs (such as crack or PCP) to act more violently or ruthlessly than they otherwise would, and partly because criminal organizations seeking to control drug supplies use force to manage their markets. These also are serious costs, but no one knows how much they would be reduced if drugs were legalized. Addicts would no longer steal to pay black-market prices for drugs, a real gain. But some, perhaps a great deal, of that gain would be offset by the great increase in the number of addicts. These people, nodding on heroin or living in the delusion-ridden high of cocaine, would hardly be ideal employees. Many would steal simply to support themselves, since snatch-and-grab, opportunistic crime can be managed even by people unable to hold a regular job or plan an elaborate crime. Those British addicts who get their supplies from government clinics are not models of law-abiding decency. Most are in crime, and though their per-capita rate of criminality may be lower thanks to the cheapness of their drugs, the total volume of crime they produce may be quite large. Of course, society could decide to support all unemployable addicts on welfare, but that would mean that gains from lowered rates of crime would have to be offset by large increases in welfare budgets.

Proponents of legalization claim that the costs of having more addicts around would be largely if not entirely offset by having more money available with which to treat and care for them. The money would come from the taxes levied on the sale of heroin and cocaine.

To obtain this fiscal dividend, however, legalization's supporters must first solve an economic dilemma. If they want to raise a lot of money to pay for welfare and treatment, the tax rate on the drugs will have to be quite high. Even if they themselves do not want a high tax rate, the politicians' love of "sin taxes" would probably guarantee that it would be high anyway. But the higher the tax, the higher the price of the drug, and the higher the price the greater the likelihood that addicts will turn to crime to find the money for it and that criminal organizations will be formed to sell tax-free drugs at below-market rates. If we managed to keep taxes (and thus prices) low, we would get that much less money to pay for welfare and treatment and more people could afford to become addicts. There may be an optimal tax rate for drugs that maximizes revenue while minimizing crime, bootlegging, and the recruitment of new addicts, but our experience with alcohol does not suggest that we know how to find it.

THE BENEFITS OF ILLEGALITY

The advocates of legalization find nothing to be said in favor of the current system except, possibly, that it keeps the number of addicts smaller than it would otherwise be. In fact, the benefits are more substantial than that.

First, treatment. All the talk about providing "treatment on demand" implies that there is a demand for treatment. That is not quite right. There are some drug-dependent people who genuinely want treatment and will remain in it if offered; they should receive it. But there are far more who want only short-term help after a bad crash; once stabilized and bathed, they are back on the street again, hustling. And even many of the addicts who enroll in a program honestly wanting help drop out after a short while when they discover that help takes time and commitment. Drug-dependent people have very short time horizons and a weak capacity for commitment. These two groups—those looking for a quick fix and those unable to stick with a long-term fix—are not easily helped. Even if we increase the number of treatment slots—as we should—we would have to do something to make treatment more effective.

One thing that can often make it more effective is compulsion. Douglas Anglin of UCLA, in common with many other researchers, has found that the longer one stays in a treatment program, the better the chances of a reduction in drug dependency. But he, again like most other researchers, has found that drop-out rates are high. He has also found, however, that patients who enter treatment under legal compulsion stay in the program longer

than those not subject to such pressure. . . . If for many addicts compulsion is a useful component of treatment, it is not clear how compulsion could be achieved in a society in which purchasing, possessing, and using the drug were legal. It could be managed, I suppose, but I would not want to have to answer the challenge from the American Civil Liberties Union that it is wrong to compel a person to undergo treatment for consuming a legal commodity.

Next, education. We are now investing substantially in drug-education programs in the schools. Though we do not yet know for certain what will work, there are some promising leads. But I wonder how credible such programs would be if they were aimed at dissuading children from doing something perfectly legal. We could, of course, treat drug education like smoking education: inhaling crack and inhaling tobacco are both legal, but you should not do it because it is bad for you. . . .

Again, it might be possible under a legalized regime to have effective drug-prevention programs, but their effectiveness would depend heavily, I think, on first having decided that cocaine use, like tobacco use, is purely a matter of practical consequences; no fundamental moral significance attaches to either. But if we believe—as I do—that dependency on certain mind-altering drugs is a moral issue and that their illegality rests in part on their immorality, then legalizing them undercuts, if it does not eliminate altogether, the moral message.

That message is at the root of the distinction we now make between nicotine and cocaine. Both are highly addictive; both have harmful physical effects. But we treat the two drugs differently, not simply because nicotine is so widely used as to be beyond the reach of effective prohibition, but because its use does not destroy the user's essential humanity. Tobacco shortens one's life, cocaine debases it. Nicotine alters one's habits, cocaine alters one's soul. The heavy use of crack, unlike the heavy use of tobacco, corrodes those natural sentiments of sympathy and duty that constitute our human nature and make possible our social life. To say, as does [Ethan] Nadelmann

[Executive Director of Drug Policy Alliance], that distinguishing morally between tobacco and cocaine is "little more than a transient prejudice" is close to saying that morality itself is but a prejudice.

THE ALCOHOL PROBLEM

... Alcohol, like heroin, cocaine, PCP, and marijuana, is a drug—that is, a mood-altering substance—and consumed to excess it certainly has harmful consequences: auto accidents, bar-room fights, bedroom shootings. It is also, for some people, addictive. We cannot confidently compare the addictive powers of these drugs, but the best evidence suggests that crack and heroin are much more addictive than alcohol.

Many people, Nadelmann included, argue that since the health and financial costs of alcohol abuse are so much higher than those of cocaine or heroin abuse, it is hypocritical folly to devote our efforts to preventing cocaine or drug use. But as Mark Kleiman of Harvard has pointed out, this comparison is quite misleading. What Nadelmann is doing is showing that a *legalized* drug (alcohol) produces greater social harm than *illegal* ones (cocaine and heroin). But of course. Suppose that in the 1920s we had made heroin and cocaine legal and alcohol illegal. Can anyone doubt that Nadelmann would now be writing that it is folly to continue our ban on alcohol because cocaine and heroin are so much more harmful?

And let there be no doubt about it—widespread heroin and cocaine use are associated with all manner of ills. Thomas Bewley found that the mortality rate of British heroin addicts in 1968 was 28 times as high as the death rate of the same age group of non-addicts, even though in England at the time an addict could obtain free or low-cost heroin and clean needles from British clinics. Perform the following mental experiment: suppose we legalize heroin and cocaine in this country. In what proportion of auto fatalities would the state police report that the driver was nodding off on heroin or recklessly driving on a coke high? In what proportion of spouse-assault and child-abuse cases would

the local police report that crack was involved? In what proportion of industrial accidents would safety investigators report that the forklift or drill-press operator was in a drug-induced stupor or frenzy? We do not know exactly what the proportion would be, but anyone who asserts that it would not be much higher than it is now would have to believe that these drugs have little appeal except when they are illegal. And that is nonsense.

An advocate of legalization might concede that social harm—perhaps harm equivalent to that already produced by alcohol—would follow from making cocaine and heroin generally available. But at least, he might add, we would have the problem "out in the open" where it could be treated as a matter of "public health." That is well and good, *if* we knew how to treat—that is, cure—heroin and cocaine abuse. But we do not know how to do it for all the people who would need such help. We are having only limited success in coping with chronic alcoholics. Addictive behavior is immensely difficult to change, and the best methods for changing it—living in drug-free therapeutic communities, becoming faithful members of Alcoholics Anonymous or Narcotics Anonymous—require great personal commitment, a quality that is, alas, in short supply among the very persons—young people, disadvantaged people—who are often most at risk for addiction.

Suppose that today we had, not 15 million alcohol abusers, but half a million. Suppose that we already knew what we have learned from our long experience with the widespread use of alcohol. Would we make whiskey legal? I do not know, but I suspect there would be a lively debate. The Surgeon General would remind us of the risks alcohol poses to pregnant women. The National Highway Traffic Safety Administration would point to the likelihood of more highway fatalities caused by drunk drivers. The Food and Drug Administration might find that there is a nontrivial increase in cancer associated with alcohol consumption. At the same time the police would report great difficulty in keeping illegal whiskey out of our cities, officers being corrupted by bootleggers, and alcohol addicts often resorting to crime to feed their habit.

Libertarians, for their part, would argue that every citizen has a right to drink anything he wishes and that drinking is, in any event, a "victimless crime."

However the debate might turn out, the central fact would be that the problem was still, at that point, a small one. The government cannot legislate away the addictive tendencies in all of us, nor can it remove completely even the most dangerous addictive substances. But it can cope with harms when the harms are still manageable.

SCIENCE AND ADDICTION

One advantage of containing a problem while it is still containable is that it buys time for science to learn more about it and perhaps to discover a cure. Almost unnoticed in the current debate over legalizing drugs is that basic science has made rapid strides in identifying the underlying neurological processes involved in some forms of addiction. Stimulants such as cocaine and amphetamines alter the way certain brain cells communicate with one another. . . .

When dopamine crosses the synapse between two cells, it is in effect carrying a message from the first cell to activate the second one. In certain parts of the brain that message is experienced as pleasure. After the message is delivered, the dopamine returns to the first cell. Cocaine apparently blocks this return, or "reuptake," so that the excited cell and others nearby continue to send pleasure messages. When the exaggerated high produced by cocaine-influenced dopamine finally ends, the brain cells may (in ways that are still a matter of dispute) suffer from an extreme lack of dopamine, thereby making the individual unable to experience any pleasure at all. This would explain why cocaine users often feel so depressed after enjoying the drug. Stimulants may also affect the way in which other neurotransmitters, such as serotonin and noradrenaline, operate. . . .

Tragically, we spend very little on such research, and the agencies funding it have not in the past occupied very influential or visible posts in the federal bureaucracy. If there is one aspect of the "war on drugs" metaphor that I dislike, it is its tendency to focus attention almost exclusively on the troops in the trenches, whether engaged in enforcement or treatment, and away from the research-and-development efforts back on the home front where the war may ultimately be decided.

I believe that the prospects of scientists in controlling addiction will be strongly influenced by the size and character of the problem they face. If the problem is a few hundred thousand chronic, high-dose users of an illegal product, the chances of making a difference at a reasonable cost will be much greater than if the problem is a few million chronic users of legal substances. Once a drug is legal, not only will its use increase but many of those who then use it will prefer the drug to the treatment: they will want the pleasure, whatever the cost to themselves or their families, and they will resist—probably successfully—any efforts to wean them away from experiencing the high that comes from inhaling a legal substance.

Discussion Questions

1. Wilson claims that tobacco, unlike cocaine, corrodes our natural sentiments of sympathy and duty. Do you agree? Should tobacco be made illegal across the board for people of all ages? Or is there a relevant moral distinction between cocaine and tobacco as Szasz claims? Support your answers.

2. Compare and contrast Wilson's position on the legalization of drugs, for minors and for adults, with that of Thomas Szasz.

3. Discuss how Wilson would most likely react to the Canadian Marijuana Medical Access Regulations (2001) legalizing the use of marijuana for medical purposes.[49]

4. Preemployment drug screening and employee drug testing have become common-place since the 1980s. The majority of Fortune 500 companies, for example, now have drug-testing programs.[50] Some colleges are also considering mandatory drug-screening programs for undergraduates. Discuss how Wilson and Szasz would each respond to mandatory drug testing in the workplace and on college campuses.

5. Studies show that people under twenty-five are more likely to binge on drugs and alcohol than people over twenty-five. Are people who engage in excessive drug and alcohol use simply morally immature? Support your answer in light of Lawrence Kohlberg's and Carol Gilligan's stages of moral development. If moral immaturity is a factor in drug and alcohol abuse, discuss how this knowledge might be incorporated into a policy on your campus regarding drug use and drug education.

DOUGLAS N. HUSAK

A Moral Right to Use Drugs

Douglas Husak is a professor of philosophy at Rutgers University. In this article he crit-ically analyzes the various arguments against drug use, including those based on harm and the virtue-based argument of James Q. Wilson. Husak concludes that there is noth-ing inherently immoral about drug use, apart from any harm it may cause. Instead of outlawing drugs, we should use drug education programs to combat harmful use.

Critical Reading Questions

1. According to Husak, what is the current status of the "war on drugs"?
2. According to Husak, why has a war been declared on illegal drugs?
3. What is a "drug" and why is this term, as it is commonly used, confusing?
4. What is a "recreational drug"? How does it differ from a "nonrecreational drug"?
5. What have been some of the consequences of the "get-tough" policy on drugs?
6. What are some of the arguments for the criminalization of drugs?
7. Why does Husak reject Wilson's argument against the legalization of drugs?
8. What is the difference between maintaining that adults have a right to use drugs and advocating drug use?
9. What are the similarities, according to Husak, between his position on drugs and the pro-choice position on abortion?
10. What policy does Husak suggest regarding drug abuse?

"A Moral Right to Use Drugs," in *Drugs and Rights* (New York: Cambridge University Press, 1992), 10–12, 14–18, 20–21, 44–45, 50–51, 56–60, 63–68, 251–256. Some notes have been omitted.

Accurate or not, the perception that drug use is out of control has triggered an enormous state response. Illegal drugs have become the single most important concern of our criminal justice system. Although estimates are imprecise, tens of billions of dollars are probably spent to enforce LAD [laws against drugs] every year, and the less direct costs of the war on drugs are several times greater. . . .

About 750,000 of the 28 million illegal drug users are arrested every year. Between one-quarter and one-third of all felony charges involve drug offenses. . . . As a result, courts have become clogged, and prison overcrowding is legendary. The U.S. Sentencing Commission has estimated that within fifteen years the Anti-Drug Abuse Act passed by Congress in 1986 will cause the proportion of inmates incarcerated for drug violations to rise from one-third to one-half of all defendants sentenced to federal prison. The costs of punishment threaten to drain the treasury, as each prisoner requires expenditures of between $10,000 and $40,000 per year. Since the average punishment for a drug conviction has risen to seventy-seven months in prison, each new inmate will cost taxpayers approximately $109,000 for the duration of the sentence.

Law enforcement officials continue to exercise broad discretion in arresting and prosecuting drug offenders. More than three-quarters of those arrested are eventually charged with possession, typically of marijuana. Many crimes of possession involve amounts that include a presumption of intent to distribute. Sometimes the quantity of drugs that creates this presumption is small. . . .

The true extent of the war on drugs cannot be measured in quantities of dollars spent or numbers of defendants punished. The enforcement of drug laws has diminished precious civil liberties, eroding gains for which Americans have made major sacrifices for over two centuries. Increasingly common are evictions, raids, random searches, confiscations of driver's licenses, withdrawals of federal benefits such as education subsidies, and summary forfeitures of property. . . .

First, why do so many Americans use recreational drugs? Or, more specifically, why do so many Americans use the kinds of recreational drugs of which the majority disapproves? The power of drugs per se can only be part of the explanation. Illegal drug use is less prevalent in many countries where drugs are plentiful, inexpensive, and higher in quality than those available in America. A more viable strategy to combat drugs might attempt to identify and change the conditions peculiar to America that have led to widespread use. . . . It is hard to see how a long-term solution to the drug problem can be found without knowing why so many Americans are motivated to break the law in the first place. . . .

A second issue is typically neglected in understanding and evaluating the war on drugs: Why has war been declared on illegal drugs? The simplistic answer is that drugs pose a threat to American society comparable to that of an invading enemy. Self-protection requires the mobilization of resources equivalent to those employed in time of war. For reasons that will become clear, I do not believe that this answer can begin to explain the extraordinary efforts of the state in combating drugs. Few wars—and certainly not the war on drugs—can be understood as a purely rational response to a grave social crisis. . . .

The public fears that America is a nation in decline. Crime, poverty, poor education, corporate mismanagement, and an unproductive and unmotivated work force are cited as evidence of this deterioration. Who, or what, should be blamed? The political climate limits the range of acceptable answers. Conservatives will not allow liberals to blame institutional structures for our problems. The difficulty cannot be that government has failed to create the right social programs to help people. Nor will liberals allow conservatives to blame individuals for our problems. The difficulty cannot be that people are lazy, stupid, or egocentric. What alternative explanations remain?

Illegal drugs provide the ideal scapegoat. Drugs are alleged to be so powerful that persons cannot be blamed very much for succumbing to them, as they could be blamed for not studying or working. And drugs are so plentiful and easy to conceal that government cannot be blamed very much for failing to eliminate them. Even better, most drugs are smuggled from abroad, so Americans can attribute our decline to the influence of foreigners. In blaming drugs, politicians need not fear that they will antagonize a powerful lobby that will challenge their allegations and mobilize voters against them. Almost no organized bodies defend the interests of drug users. Illegal drugs represent a "no-lose" issue, the safest of all political crusades.

A scapegoat would be imperfect unless there were at least some plausibility in the accusations of drug prohibitionists. Perhaps illegal drug use *has* increased crime, contributed to poverty, exacerbated the decline of education, and decreased the productivity of workers. Sometimes it may have done so in dramatic ways. The stories of the most decrepit victims of drug abuse lend themselves to biographies and television docudramas that make a deep and lasting impression on viewers. Everyone has seen vivid images of persons who were driven by drugs to commit brutal crimes, abandon their children, steal from their friends, drop out of school, stop going to work, and perhaps even die. In light of these consequences, who can condone illegal drug use? . . .

A third and final issue about the war on drugs raises a matter that I will explore in greater depth: If there is to be a war on drugs, against which drugs should it be waged? . . .

How is "drug" defined by those who make the effort to define it at all? The answer depends on the discipline where an answer is sought. Perhaps the most frequently cited medical definition is "any substance other than food which by its chemical nature affects the structure or function of the living organism." Undoubtedly this definition is too broad. Nonetheless, I tentatively propose to adopt it until a better alternative becomes available.

Notice that this definition refers only to the pharmacological effect of a substance and not to its legal status. For two reasons, "drugs" must not be defined as synonymous with "illegal drugs." First, it would be absurd to suppose that a non-drug could become a drug, or that a drug could become a non-drug, simply by a stroke of the pen. A legislature can change the legal classification of a substance, but not the nature of that substance; it has no more power to decide that a substance is a drug than to decide that a substance is a food. Second, a philosophical study designed to evaluate the moral rights of drug users can hardly afford to rely uncritically on the existing legal status of substances, since the legitimacy of these determinations is part of what is under investigation. To suppose that "drugs" means "illegal drugs" begs important questions and concedes much of what I will challenge. In what follows, I will use the word "drug" to refer to both legal and illegal substances that satisfy the medical definition I cited.

No doubt this usage will create confusion. Despite the desirability of distinguishing "drugs" from "illegal drugs," there is ample evidence that the public tends to equate them. Surveys indicate, for example, that whereas 95 percent of adults recognize heroin as a drug, only 39 percent categorize alcohol as a drug, and a mere 27 percent identify tobacco as a drug. This tendency is pernicious. The widespread premise that only illegal substances are drugs lulls persons into accepting unsound arguments such as the following: Drugs are illegal; whatever is illegal is bad; we drink alcohol; what we do isn't bad; therefore, alcohol is not a drug. Clear thinking about this issue is impossible unless one realizes that whether a substance is a drug is a different question from whether that substance is or should be illegal. . . .

RECREATIONAL DRUG USE

As the examination of the Controlled Substances Act demonstrates, war has not really been declared on *drugs*. War has been declared on persons who make a certain *use* of drugs. I will describe this use as *recreational*.

By "recreational use," I mean consumption that is intended to promote the pleasure, happiness, or euphoria of the user. . . . Interviews with users indicate that they are most likely to consume drugs on two general occasions. First, they use drugs to attempt to improve what they anticipate will be a good time. Hence drug use is frequent during parties, concerts, and sex. Second, they use drugs to attempt to make mindless and routine chores less boring. Hence drug use is frequent during house cleaning and cooking. I regard these as paradigm examples of recreational use. . . .

The concept of recreational use can be clarified by contrasting it with other purposes for using drugs. The most familiar nonrecreational reason to use drugs is medical. Although most drug use is either recreational or medical, these categories do not begin to exhaust the purposes for which drugs are consumed. Some persons take drugs for the explicit purpose of committing suicide. Others take drugs ceremonially, in the course of religious rituals. Still others take drugs in order to enhance their performance in competitive sports. . . .

Undoubtedly my focus on recreational drug use will give rise to the criticism that my approach is academic, middle-class, and unresponsive to the realities of drug use in impoverished neighborhoods. Drug use in ghettos, it will be said, is not recreational. The less fortunate members of our society do not use drugs to facilitate their enjoyment at concerts but to escape from the harsh realities of their daily lives. Here, at least, gloom and despair play a central role in explaining the high incidence of drug use. . . .

The empirical facts are ambiguous in proving that illegal drug use is a special problem for the black community. Only 20 percent of all illegal drug users are black. Whites are more likely than blacks to have tried illegal drugs, and cocaine in particular, at some time in their lives. The more drug prohibitionists succeed in portraying drug use as a ghetto phenomenon, born of frustration and despair, the easier it is to lose sight of the repudiation of liberal values that LAD entails. As I will emphasize time and time again, too much of our policy about illegal drug use is based on generalizations from worst-case scenarios that do not conform to the reality of typical drug use. I hope to undermine the inaccurate stereotypes of drug use and drug users reinforced by this objection. LAD prohibits drug use by members of all races and classes; a legal policy applicable to all should not be based on the perceived problems of a few.

THE DECRIMINALIZATION MOVEMENT

. . . Courts and jails have become clogged as a result of "get-tough" policies toward drug offenders. . . . In many jurisdictions, delays in criminal cases not involving drugs or in the adjudication of civil disputes have become intolerable. The number of Americans behind bars has recently exceeded the one million mark and sets new records every day. . . . As a result of overcrowding by nonviolent drug offenders, violent criminals are less likely to serve long prison terms. . . .

Among the more serious effects of prohibition is discrimination against the poor, who increasingly consume a higher and higher percentage of illegal drugs. Although two-thirds of weekly drug users in New York State in 1987 were white, 91 percent of the persons convicted and sentenced to state prison for drug-related offenses were either black or Hispanic. Therapeutic treatment is frequently provided for middle- and upper-class users; prison is the preferred mode of "treatment" for the underprivileged. . . .

Finally and most significantly, the war on drugs is counterproductive in making criminals of tens of millions of Americans whose behavior is otherwise lawful. Most drug users are lucky to escape detection. Others are less fortunate. . . . Even those who are eventually acquitted spend tremendous sums of time and money defending themselves in court. . . .

ARGUMENTS FOR CRIMINALIZATION

Defenses of and attacks against arguments for decriminalization have become so familiar that it is easy to forget that the burden of proof should be placed on those who favor the use of criminal penalties. When arguing about criminalization, most philosophers begin with a "presumption of freedom," or liberty, which places the onus of justification on those who would interfere with what a person wants to do. . . .

A second and equally familiar presumption cuts in the opposite direction. A "presumption in favor of the status quo" allocates the burden of proof on those who oppose any change in current laws against the use of recreational drugs. No one has any clear idea about what weight to assign to these "clashing presumptions." For this reason, it is probably unproductive to worry too much about who should bear the burden of proof on this issue. . . .

I assume without much argument that a respectable defense of criminal legislation must demonstrate that it is needed to prevent *harm*. Everyone agrees that persons lack a moral right to cause harm, so criminal laws that prohibit harmful conduct do not violate the basic principles I have described. . . . But in the absence of harm, criminal sanctions are undeserved and unjustified.

The least controversial rationale in favor of criminalization is that the conduct to be prohibited is harmful *to others*. Many legal philosophers, following the lead of [John Stuart] Mill, believe that harm to others is a necessary condition that any criminal law must satisfy in order to be justified. . . . A more controversial rationale in favor of criminalization is that drug use should be prohibited because it is harmful *to users* themselves. . . .

Many philosophers are quick to point out that "no man is an island" and that whatever harms oneself also harms others or at least is capable of doing so. Perhaps there are no examples of "pure" or "unmixed" paternalism, that is, of an interference with liberty that is justifiable solely on the ground that the conduct to be prohibited harms the doer. I do not maintain otherwise. I do not suppose that a given activity can harm the doer but not others. The distinction between harm to oneself and harm to others is *not* a distinction between kinds of laws, but rather it is a distinction between *rationales* for laws. Any law might be defended by more than one rationale. . . .

My premise that the use of the criminal sanction should require harm can be questioned. Perhaps arguments can be marshaled in support of LAD that do not depend on harm, either to oneself or to others. According to *legal moralism*, the wrongfulness of conduct per se, apart from its harmful effects, is a sufficient reason to impose criminal punishment.

Many drug prohibitionists resort to legal moralism in support of LAD. [William] Bennett [drug czar under President George H. W. Bush] replies to the cost-benefit analyses of decriminalization theorists as follows: "I find no merit in the legalizers' case. The simple fact is that drug use is wrong. And the moral argument, in the end, is the most compelling argument." There can be no doubt that popular objections to illegal recreational drug use are often couched in the strongest possible moral terms. Drug use is frequently portrayed as sinful and wicked. . . .

For two reasons, however, I will have little to say about legal moralism here. First, this principle is extremely problematic. No one has presented a compelling case in favor of legal moralism; responses from philosophers have been almost entirely negative. One recurrent theme of their attack is that legal moralism might be used to enforce community prejudice. The requirement that criminal liability presupposes a *victim* who has been *harmed* helps to assure that persons will not be punished simply for doing what those with political power do not want them to do.

Second, the application of legal moralism to LAD is utterly baffling. Why would anyone believe the drug use per se is immoral, apart from any harm it might cause? . . .

What, exactly, do drug prohibitionists believe to be immoral about recreational drug use? Two alternatives are possible. Does the alleged wrong consist in the act of drug use per se, or in the alteration of consciousness that drug use produces? The former alternative seems unlikely. Suppose that the physiology of persons were altered so that a given drug no longer produced any psychological effect. Could anyone continue to believe that the use of that drug would still be immoral? In any event, contemporary Americans widely reject the view that the act of drug use is inherently wrong. Few condemn the moderate use of alcohol. . . .

The latter alternative seems no more attractive. Why should the alteration of consciousness produced by drug use be immoral, apart from any harm that might result? Some theorists have proposed that practices such as long-distance running and meditation can trigger natural neurological reactions that alter consciousness in respects that are phenomenologically indistinguishable from the effects of drug use. No one has suggested that such practices are immoral, and for good reason. . . .

Perhaps many Americans share a vague conviction that some but not all ways of altering consciousness, by the use of some but not all drugs, is immoral. If this conviction could be defended, the particular experience of alcohol intoxication might be upheld as morally permissible, whereas the experiences of intoxication produced by various illegal drugs could be condemned. As it stands, however, this conviction is a conclusion in search of an argument. Typically, persons appeal to harm, either to oneself or to others, in attempts to differentiate between intoxication from alcohol and intoxication from illegal drugs. In this guise, the argument should be taken seriously. . . .

Moral objections to drug use might also be derived from an ideal of human excellence. Drug use might not be conducive to the attainment of a particular conception of virtue. These arguments are frequently endorsed by drug prohibitionists. According to Bennett, "Drug use degrades human character, and a purposeful, self governing society ignores its people's character at great peril." James Q. Wilson confines his virtue-based arguments to illegal drugs: "Tobacco shortens one's life, cocaine debases it. Nicotine alters one's habits, cocaine alters one's soul." What conception of virtue is employed here? . . . According to this tradition, drug use, like any other recreational activity, is suspect. Recreational activities are nonaltruistic and self-indulgent. . . .

The answer is that virtue-based arguments fail to support criminal punishment for recreational drug use. Bennett is correct that a society should not "ignore its people's character." But it does not follow that the protection of character is an appropriate objective of the criminal law. The prohibitions of the criminal law describe the minimum of acceptable behavior beneath which persons are not permitted to sink. Virtue-based considerations cannot be used to show that moderate self-indulgence, as well as any temporary impairment

of rationality and autonomy brought about by most incidents of drug use, fall below this permissible level. The criminal law should not enforce a particular conception of human excellence, however attractive it may be. . . .

MISINTERPRETATIONS

I have concluded that the arguments in favor of believing that adults have a moral right to use drugs recreationally are more persuasive than the arguments on the other side. . . .

First, the conclusion that adults have a moral right to use drugs recreationally does not amount to advocating drug use. . . . This basic distinction is widely appreciated in most other contexts. Adults have the moral right to preach communism or to practice Buddhism. Yet no one who defends this right would be misunderstood to recommend a conversion to communism or Buddhism.

Nonetheless, one of the most widely voiced objections to the proposal to repeal LAD is that it would express the wrong symbolism about drug use, especially among adolescents. . . .

In order to dispel the impression that support for a right to use drugs is tantamount to encouraging drug use, those who reject LAD should be described as endorsing a *pro-choice* position on recreational drug use. This label has been carefully crafted by persons who uphold the right of women to terminate their pregnancies. These persons are not "pro-death," or "anti-life," as their critics would like the public to believe. Perhaps many of them would not elect abortion as their own solution to an unwanted pregnancy. Still, they believe that women have the right to make this choice for themselves. Misunderstanding would be avoided if the debate about the decriminalization of recreational drug use borrowed this terminology. The conclusion that adults have a moral right to use drugs recreationally should be described as the pro-choice position on recreational drug use. . . .

Should the rights of adults be infringed in order to ensure that the wrong message is not received by the public (to whom this argument extends very little credit)? The main problem is that this rationale for LAD would not allow the decriminalization of *any* activity that is less than exemplary. At bottom, this argument is simply another utilitarian defense of the status quo. The rights of some adults should not be sacrificed so that others do not misinterpret a message. . . .

A second related but distinct misunderstanding of my position is as follows. The conclusion that adult use of recreational drugs is protected by a moral right does not entail that drug use is beyond moral reproach. The exercise of a moral right may be subject to criticism. Perhaps all recreational drug use, legal and illegal, is morally tainted. . . . In any event, some instances of recreational drug use are morally objectionable, beyond those in the special circumstances in which users create an impermissible risk of harm to others. These objectionable instances might be described by the pejorative term *drug abuse.* . . .

If the moral right to use drugs recreationally is to be respected, the need to minimize disutility leaves society with little choice but to discourage drug abuse. The process by which this goal is reached might loosely be described as "drug education." But this process differs from drug education as it is usually conceived. Most educational programs are prevention programs. As so designed, education has generally been deemed a failure, largely because it has not been shown to achieve its objective of decreasing drug use. Yet there may be more reason for optimism if the goal of education is to decrease drug abuse.

As so construed, drug education may never have been tried. No existing educational program has attempted either to separate use from abuse or to indicate how abuse might be avoided by means other than abstinence. The introduction of scientifically respectable materials in drug education programs has been politically unacceptable. . . .

Since I make no attempt to solve America's drug problem as a matter of social policy, I will hazard only one final observation about the prospects for success that drug education as so conceived will minimize drug abuse. To demand that recreational drug users show restraint over the time, place, and quantity of their consumption is not to require the impossible. In fact, virtually every drug user exhibits some degree of control over her consumption. The means by which users manage to avoid abuse deserves careful study and extensive publicity. Perhaps a successful educational program should seek out responsible drug users. . . . To respect the moral right of adults to use recreational drugs may be painful, at least in the short run. But the protection of moral rights has a value to Americans that is not easily expressed in the utilitarian calculus of costs and benefits in which the decriminalization debate is usually cast.

Discussion Questions

1. Former Virginia Governor L. Douglas Wilder proposed mandatory drug testing of all college students. Discuss some of the moral arguments for and against Wilder's proposal. Develop a policy on drug testing for your campus. What might some of the objections be? Discuss how you would defend your policy against objectors.
2. Does Husak present a convincing rebuttal of James Q. Wilson's argument against the legalization of drugs? Discuss how Wilson might respond to Husak's criticism.
3. Do you accept Husak's comparison of the right to use drugs and the pro-choice position in the abortion debate? Support your answer.
4. Do you agree with Husak that drug education, rather than LAD, is the best policy for dealing with drug abuse? Support your answer. Discuss what sort of drug education program would be most effective on your campus.
5. Florida State University in Tallahassee is one of many colleges working with local police and businesses to reduce alcohol abuse by its students. Recently, a bar near

the university put on a "Valentine's Day 'No date, get drunk! Free beer all night.'" The event was advertised at the college. How should universities respond to this type of aggressive advertising aimed at college students? What stance would Wilson and Husak each most likely take? Support your answers.

LAURA DEAN-MOONEY AND JOHN MCCARDELL

Two Takes on the 21 Drinking Age

Laura Dean-Mooney, national president of Mothers Against Drunk Driving, and John McCardell, president emeritus of Middlebury College in Vermont, debate the wisdom of keeping the drinking age at twenty-one or lowering it to age eighteen. In particular, they debate the question in the context of the Choose Responsibility initiative signed by nearly 130 college and university presidents stating that the current legal drinking age of twenty-one contributes to a culture of binge drinking on campuses.

Critical Reading Questions

1. What evidence does Laura Dean-Mooney present to support her conclusion that the drinking age should remain at age twenty-one?
2. According to Dean-Mooney, why is drinking harmful to young adults?
3. On what grounds does McCardell oppose legislation setting the drinking age at twenty-one?
4. What evidence does McCardell use to support his conclusion that raising the drinking age from eighteen to twenty-one has not been effective in curbing problem drinking on college campuses?
5. What solution does McCardell put forth to curb problem drinking on college campuses?

A Lower Age Would Be Unsafe

LAURA DEAN-MOONEY

As the fall semester begins at colleges across the country, campuses once again face the challenge of combating underage and binge drinking. This is a serious and difficult issue for colleges, for

communities, and for parents like me who are preparing to send a son or daughter to college.

Unfortunately, more than 100 college presidents have chosen to address the issue by signing on to a misguided initiative that ostensibly favors a debate but is supported by a group, Choose Responsibility, whose sole aim is lowering the drinking age from 21 to 18 years old. Mothers Against Drunk Driving is open to a discussion about solving the problems of underage and binge drinking. But the discussion must be based on facts, and, in this case, the facts are clear: 21 saves lives.

Since states began setting the legal drinking age at 21, the law has been one of the most studied in our history. The evidence is overwhelming: More than 50 high-quality scientific studies all found the 21 law saves lives, both on and off the road. And the public agrees: 72 percent of adults think that lowering the drinking age would make alcohol more accessible to kids, and nearly half think that it would increase binge drinking among teens, according to a new Nationwide Insurance poll.

This is why stakeholders from scientific, medical, and public health organizations have joined MADD to form the Support 21 Coalition: We believe in basing public health policy on sound medical research and are committed to highlighting the lifesaving impact of the 21 drinking age.

Twenty-one isn't just an arbitrary number set by Congress—more than 20 states already had laws setting the drinking age there in 1984. And since the 21 law was widely enacted, the number of young people killed annually in crashes involving drunk drivers under 21 has been cut in half, from more than 5,000 individuals in the early 1980s to around 2,000 in 2005. By the end of 2005, the 21 drinking age had saved nearly 25,000 American lives—approximately 1,000 lives a year.

The Support 21 Coalition stands behind the indisputable scientific research that demonstrates lowering the drinking age would make the difficult problems of underage and binge drinking far worse. Research indicates that when the minimum legal drinking age is 21, people under age 21 drink less overall and continue to do so through their early 20s. When the drinking age has been lowered, injury and death rates significantly increased.

Lowering the age of those who have easy access to alcohol would shift responsibility for underage drinking to high school parents and educators.

A neurotoxin. Research has shown that the harmful effects of alcohol abuse are magnified on a teenager's still-developing brain. The adolescent brain is a work in progress, marked by significant development in areas of the brain responsible for learning, memory, complex thinking, planning, inhibition, and emotional regulation. The neu-

rotoxic effect of excessive alcohol use is a danger to these key regions of the maturing adolescent brain.

A person's brain does not stop developing until their early to mid-20s. During this period, alcohol negatively affects all parts of the brain, including cognitive and decision-making abilities as well as coordination and memory. Adolescent drinkers not only do worse academically but are also at greater risk for social problems like depression, violence, and suicidal thoughts.

Lowering the drinking age would have dangerous long-term consequences: Early teen drinkers are not only more susceptible to alcoholism but to developing the disease earlier and more quickly than others.

The problem of binge drinking on college campuses needs to be addressed, but lowering the drinking age would be not only short-sighted but deadly. The simple fact is that the 21 law saves lives and is, therefore, nonnegotiable.

The Status Quo Has Bombed

JOHN MCCARDELL

It is time to rethink the drinking age. That's the message of nearly 130 college and university presidents who have signed on to the Amethyst Initiative, which declares that the 21 drinking age does not work and has created a culture of binge drinking on campus. While the initiative intentionally does not prescribe a specific new policy, it seeks a debate that acknowledges the current law's failure. (As a former college president, I am not a signatory, but I have helped spearhead the effort.)

The National Minimum Legal Drinking Age Act could not, constitutionally, mandate a national drinking age. Instead, it allowed the states to set the age as they chose. If, however, the age was lower than 21, the state would forfeit 10 percent of its federal highway appropriation.

End of debate. Until now.

As the discussion renews in earnest throughout the media and society, "science" will be used to support the status quo. Yet any survey of the evidence at hand shows that the data are peskily inconsistent. The National Institute on Alcohol Abuse and Alcoholism, a respected authority, believes that the 21-year-old drinking age works. Yet its website reveals that of 5,000 Americans under the age of 21 who die of alcohol-related causes each year, only 1,900 are traffic fatalities, meaning the remaining 3,100 occur *off* the highways. Drunk teens behind the wheel are less of a problem than those drinking in private.

And drinking continues to be widespread among adolescents: The institute says that 75 percent of 12th graders, two thirds of 10th graders, and two fifths of eighth graders have consumed alcohol. Not surprisingly, the institute concludes that we have an "enormous public health issue." The Institute of Medicine notes that "more youth drink than smoke tobacco or use illegal drugs." The estimated annual social cost of underage drinking is $53 billion. These statistics will most likely not be offered in support of the current law.

Moreover, the evidence that raising the drinking age has been primarily responsible for the decline in alcohol-related traffic fatalities (a trend that effectively stopped in the mid-1990s and has been inching upward) is underwhelming. One survey of research on this subject revealed that about half of the studies looked at found a cause-and-effect relationship between the 21 drinking age and diminishing alcohol-related traffic fatalities—and half showed no relationship whatsoever.

Hidden drinking. Yet college presidents are pilloried for daring to question our current laws. Even though many students who enter their institutions have already consumed alcohol, the presidents are labeled "shirkers" and "lawbreakers" for not enforcing an unenforceable law. The more they crack down on campus drinking, the more they simply force that behavior into clandestine locations, often off campus, beyond their sight and their authority.

Where, after all, does "binge drinking" take place? Not in public places, from which the law has effectively banned alcohol consumption, but in locked dorm rooms, off-campus apartments, farmers' fields, and other risky environments.

The "abstinence" message—the only one legally permissible—is failing, as prohibition has always failed. Presidents looking for a solution find such remarkable documents as the 2002 "Call to Action," written by a National Institutes of Health task force, which advises presidents to, in effect, break the law. It describes programs to "reduce," not eliminate, alcohol consumption. It recommends teaching "students basic principles of moderate drinking." In short, it advises what others have condemned.

Effective laws reflect not abstract, unattainable ideals but rather social and cultural reality. The reality in this case is that one is a legal adult at age 18; that alcohol is present in the lives of young adults ages 18 to 20; that most of the rest of the world has come out in a very different place on this issue; and that the 21-year-old drinking age is routinely evaded. Either we are a nation of lawbreakers, or this is a bad law.

Discussion Questions

1. Critically analyze the arguments presented by Dean-Mooney and by McCardell. Which person presents the stronger argument and why?
2. The United States has the highest legal drinking age in the world. In most of the world, the legal drinking age is sixteen or eighteen; some countries, such as Portugal and China, have no minimum age. Is this information relevant to the debate over the legal drinking age in the United States? Use research to support your answer.
3. One of the most common arguments for lowering the drinking age is that eighteen-year-olds in the United States are able to legally marry, drive a car, hunt,

and serve combat duty in the military. Does it logically follow from this that they should also be permitted to drink alcohol? Support your argument.

4. Does a prohibition of drinking on campus make it more likely or less likely that you and others you know will drink? Does it affect where you drink? Discuss what effect lowering the drinking age would have on your drinking behavior and that of other students.

5. What policy does your campus have regarding drinking on campus? Working in small groups come up with a policy that you think would be most effective in curbing binge drinking on your campus.

THOMAS H. MURRAY

Drugs, Sports, and Ethics

Thomas H. Murray is president of The Hastings Center and former director of the Center of Biomedical Ethics at Case Western Reserve University in Cleveland, Ohio. In this paper, Murray argues against the use of performance-enhancing drugs, such as steroids, in sports. Murray concludes that drug use in sports is immoral because it restricts the free choice of competing athletes.

Critical Reading Questions

1. What is the difference between pleasure-enhancing and performance-enhancing drugs? What are some examples of the latter?

2. What are anabolic and androgenic steroids? What are some of the desired effects of these drugs?

3. What are some of the other performance-enhancing drugs used in sports? What are some of the advantages and drawbacks of using high doses of these drugs?

4. Why do athletes take anabolic steroids? What are some of the risks?

5. According to Murray, what is the "inherent coerciveness" involved in the use of drugs in competitive sports?

6. According to Murray, why are the current policies prohibiting drugs in sports problematic and insufficient?

7. What are the three reasons cited by ethicists that justify restriction of liberties?

8. According to Murray, under what circumstances can restrictions on certain liberties actually work to preserve liberty? Do these circumstances apply to the restriction of performance-enhancing drugs?

"Drugs, Sports, and Ethics," in *Feeling Good and Doing Better: Ethics and Nontherapeutic Drug Use,* ed. by Thomas H. Murray, Willard Gaylin, and Ruth Macklin (Clifton, N.J.: Humana Press, 1984), 107–126. Some notes have been omitted.

9. Why can't restrictions on performance-enhancing drugs be justified on the basis of harm to oneself? What is the relevance of Aristotle's concept of *eudaimonia,* or the good life, to the self-harm argument?
10. What does Murray mean by "free choice under pressure"? How does the use of performance-enhancing drugs violate this free choice?
11. According to Murray, who bears the primary responsibility for drug use among athletes?

Our images of the nonmedical drug user normally include the heroin addict nodding in the doorway, the spaced-out marijuana smoker, and maybe, if we know that alcohol is a drug, the wino sprawled on the curb. We probably do not think of the Olympic gold medalist, the professional baseball player who is a shoo-in for the Hall of Fame, or the National Football League lineman. Yet these athletes and hundreds, perhaps thousands, of others regularly use drugs in the course of their training, performance, or both. I am talking not about recreational drug use—athletes who use drugs for pleasure or relaxation probably no more or less than their contemporaries with comparable incomes—but about a much less discussed type of drug use: taking drugs to enhance performance.

It is a strange idea. . . . Performance-enhancing drug use is so common and so tolerated in some forms that we often fail to think of it as "drug" use. The clearest example is the (caffeinated) coffee pot, which is as much a part of the American workplace as typewriters and timeclocks. We drink coffee (and tea or Coke) for the "lift" it gives us. The source of "that Pepsi feeling" and the "life" added by Coke is no mystery—it is caffeine or some of its close chemical relatives, potent stimulants to the human central nervous system. Anyone who has drunk too much coffee and felt caffeine "jitters," or drunk it too late at night and been unable to sleep can testify to its pharmacological potency. Caffeine and its family, the xanthines, can stave off mental fatigue and help maintain alertness, very important properties when we are working around potentially dangerous machines, fighting through a boring report, or driving a long stretch. In other words, caffeine can enhance our ability to perform tasks that would otherwise be so fatiguing that we might do them badly, or even harm ourselves or others in trying.

But is caffeine a drug? The fact that it is not under the control of doctors is irrelevant. . . .

About the only definition of "drugs" that would exclude things like caffeine and alcohol would be one that arbitrarily excludes them because of their wide availability and long and extensive history of use. Any reasonable definition of "drug" based on its effects on the human organism would have to include these two as well as nicotine and a number of other common substances.

Caffeine, then, is a performance-enhancing drug. . . . What the drug is used for and the intention behind the use—not the substance itself—determines whether we describe it as medical or non-medical; as pleasure- or performance- or health-enhancing.

DRUGS ON THE PLAYING FIELD

The area of human endeavor that has seen the most explosive growth in performance-enhancing drug use is almost certainly sport. At the highest levels of competitive sports, where athletes strain to improve performances already at the limits of human ability, the temptation to use a drug that might provide an edge can be powerful. Is this kind of drug use unethical? Should we think of it as an expression of liberty? Or do the special circumstances of sport affect our moral analysis? In particular, should liberty give way when other important values are threatened, and when no one's good is advanced? These questions frame the discussion that follows. . . .

Drugs did not enter sport in a major way until the 1960s. The 1964 Olympics were probably the first in which steroids were used. A group of steroids related to the masculinizing hormone testosterone was synthesized. These steroids are valued for two principal effects, which they have in varying proportions: androgenic, or masculinizing, and anabolic, or tissue-building. . . .

Those who lift or throw weights appear to have been the first to use steroids, and even today use them most. An informal, confidential survey of weight lifters revealed that between 90 and 100 percent used steroids. A recent study of power-lifters and body builders outside the Olympics, where athletes are a bit less reluctant to talk about their use of performance-enhancing drugs, found almost universal use of steroids as part of training. . . .

At about the same time that steroids were introduced into amateur sports, amphetamines and related stimulants were finding their way into professional sports. We know the most about professional baseball and football. But ignorance about other sports is just that—ignorance—and should not be taken to mean that performance-enhancing drugs are not used in those sports. . . .

WHY ATHLETES TAKE ANABOLIC STEROIDS

Many athletes persist in using performance-enhancing drugs despite official disapproval, possible disqualification, and even risk to their own health. They do so in the face of expert opinion that casts doubt on the effectiveness of the drugs they take. What leads them to jeopardize their futures as athletes, and possibly their very health, for what some medical people claim is an illusory advantage? The best case to illuminate these questions is steroid use among Olympic athletes. Nowhere else are the penalties greater, the efficacy more contended, or the possible health effects more serious. . . .

A recent report in *The Lancet* acknowledged, "Unquestionably, anabolics improve live weight gain, carcass weight, feed efficiency, and percentage meat in some species."[1] Although the report was referring to the practice of mixing steroids with livestock feed, it might have referred equally to humans. Aside from the genitals, the major active site for anabolic–androgenic steroids is skeletal muscles. The action of steroids on muscle tissue is probably related to their effect on nitrogen metabolism—dietary nitrogen is utilized more efficiently in androgenized tissue. There is even suggestive evidence that androgens may act directly on heart tissue; androgen receptors are found in atrial and ventrical myocardial cells.

Athletes also believe that anabolic–androgenic steroids make them more aggressive, and thus enable them to train harder. The case for this, as with most behavioral rather than physiological effects, is more elusive. . . .

AN UNSIGHTLY ARRAY OF RISKS

Along with the effects athletes desire to obtain from steroids come others not so welcome. Again, the lack of careful scientific information on chronic, high-dose usage forces us to rely on anecdotal reports and reasonable inferences. The anecdotes can be frightening. It is important to bear in mind that, despite being billed as "anabolic" steroids, all these drugs are related to testosterone and have a mix of anabolic and androgenic effects. . . . Therefore, any potent anabolic is also going to have a mix of androgenic effects. In male athletes this leads to a well-known decrease in fertility, since the synthetic androgen interferes with the normal feedback loop linking endogenous testosterone with sperm production. Other effects include acne (a real giveaway for steroid use, according to one athlete), and less visibly, cholesterol buildup and altered liver function. Athletes today are likely to have located a doctor who is willing to help them monitor some of the more subtle effects.

The impact on female athletes, like the East German swimmers, is more visible, and potentially catastrophic. Patricia Connelly, former Olympian and now coach, has lamented the use of steroids by women saying it robs them of their womanliness. The obvious changes—lowered voice, increased body hair, masculinized build—are probably reversible. Other changes are less well understood and potentially more dangerous. I have heard reports of two women, world champions in the 1970s, who appeared to age with stunning rapidity. One—in her early thirties—began to grow bald, developed age spots and wrinkles on her skin. . . .

Facing such an unpleasant, poorly understood, and unsightly array of risks, why do athletes persist in using steroids? The answer lies in the nature of international, or for that matter professional, athletic competition. In his Senate testimony, Harold Connelly said ". . . the overwhelming majority of the international track and field athletes I have known would take anything and do anything short of killing themselves to improve their athletic performance." The pressures are almost as intense in professional football. As one former player describes it: "It's hard to get violent every Sunday at 1 P.M." Amphetamines permitted athletes to play with the necessary aggressive intensity. . . . The intense competition at the highest levels of sport calls for every effort the athletes can make, and pushes them to seek every possible advantage over their competitors. . . .

In a competitive endeavor, participants will be pressed to use any means available to achieve a competitive advantage. The higher the stakes, the more intense the competition, the more total the commitment, the more likely people are to use exceptional means. For the international amateur or professional athlete this has often come to include drugs. The pressure to use exists when people *believe* that something confers a competitive advantage, whether or not this is objectively true. There is, then, an *inherent coerciveness* present in these situations: when some choose to do what gives them a competitive edge, others will be pressed to do likewise, or resign themselves to either accepting a competitive disadvantage, or leaving the endeavor entirely. . . .

AN ETHICAL ACCOUNT

Now we can confront the fundamental ethical question: May athletes use drugs to enhance their athletic performance? The International Olympic Committee has given an answer of sorts by flatly prohibiting "doping" of any kind. This stance creates at least as many problems as it solves. It requires an expensive and cumbersome detection and enforcement apparatus, turning athletes and officials into mutually suspicious adversaries. It leads Olympic sports medicine authorities to proclaim that drugs like steroids are ineffective, a charge widely discounted by athletes, and thereby decreases the credibility of Olympic officials. Drug use is driven underground, making it difficult to obtain sound medical data on drug side-effects. . . .

Any argument for prohibiting or restricting drug use by Olympic athletes must contend with a very powerful defense of such use based on our concept of individual liberty. We have a strong legal and moral tradition of individual liberty that proclaims the right to pursue our life plans in our own way, to take risks if we so desire and, within very broad limits, to do with our own bodies what we wish. This right in law has been extended unambiguously to competent persons who wish to refuse even life-saving medical care. More recently, it has been extended to marginally competent persons who refuse psychiatric treatment. Surely, competent and well-informed athletes have a right to use whatever means they desire to enhance their performance.

Those who see performance-enhancing drug use as the exercise of individual liberty are unmoved by the prospect of some harm. They believe it should be up to the individual, who is assumed to be a rational, autonomous, and uncoerced agent, to weigh probable harms against benefits, and choose accordingly to his or her own value preferences. It would be a much greater wrong, they would say, to deny people the right to make their own choices. Why should we worry so much about some probabilistic future harm for athletes when many other endeavors pose even greater dangers? High-steel construction work and coal-mining, mountain-climbing, hang-gliding, and auto-racing are almost certainly more dangerous than using steroids or other common performance-enhancing drugs.

Reasons commonly given to limit liberty fall into three classes: those that claim that the practice interferes with capacities for rational choice; those that emphasize harms to self; and those that emphasize harms to others. The case of performance-enhancing drugs and sport illustrates a fourth reason that may justify some interference with liberty, that given the social nature of the enterprise, performance-enhancing drug use in sport is inherently coercive. But first the other three reasons.

There is something paradoxical about our autonomy: we might freely choose to do something that would compromise our future capacity to choose freely. Selling yourself to slavery would be one way to limit liberty, making one's body the property of another person. If surrendering autonomous control over one's body is an evil and something we must refuse to permit, how much worse is it to destroy one's capacity to *think* clearly and independently? Yet that is one thing that might happen to people who abuse certain drugs. We may interfere with someone's desire to do a particular autonomous act if that act is likely to cause a general loss of the capacity to act autonomously. In this sense, forbidding selling yourself into slavery and forbidding the abuse of drugs likely to damage your ability to reason are similar *restrictions* on liberty designed to *preserve* liberty.

This argument applies only to things that do in fact damage our capacity to reason and make autonomous decisions. Although some of the more powerful pleasure-enhancing drugs might qualify, no one claims that performance-enhancing drugs like the steroids have any deleterious impact on reason. This argument, then, is irrelevant to the case of performance-enhancing drugs.

Destroying one's reasoning ability is a special kind of harm to oneself, but there are many other kinds of harm, and they constitute a potential argument in favor of curtailing liberty. Aristotle, in the Nicomachean Ethics, described a conception of *eudaimonia,* or the good life, in which the perfection of natural excellences was a central component. Our physical abilities, character traits, and above all our intellect were all to be perfected. We can infer from this that persons have a duty to do whatever is in their power to perfect their talents, and forsake whatever would interfere with that development. Aristotle might have no hesitation in condemning most or all pleasure-enhancing drug use, but his principle, which paraphrased is "People should develop their natural excellences," stumbles over the case of athletes and performance-enhancing drugs. Athletes use the drugs precisely to perfect their natural excellences. Our objection would have to be that drug use is an improper means to that end, since the end itself is especially commendable in the Aristotelian worldview. We could argue that drug use is wrong because, on balance, it hurts the pursuit of excellence more than it helps it. But then we are reduced to arguing about the facts—improved performances versus side effects. And if it turns out that the drugs work with minimal, reversible side effects, we would say that they are morally justified under the perfection-of-excellence principle.

Another way to put the Aristotelian objection is that we should not use unnatural means—drugs—to perfect natural excellences—athletic abilities. It is difficult to make this stick as a *moral,* and not merely an esthetic, objection. Although we recognize that certain means of perfecting our natural excellences are generally regarded as illegitimate and may be dismissed as "unnatural," the judgments are always with respect to specific ends. A prosthetic hand might be "unnatural" and unfair for the purpose of pitching baseball, but not objectionable if it allowed an injured novelist to operate a typewriter. Even in so narrow a case as drugs in sport, all depends on context. If we would not object to a diabetic athlete using insulin, could we object to a depressed one using an antidepressant, to an exhausted one using a stimulant? We can draw lines, but based on complex practical understandings, rather than solid, simple principles delineating the "natural" from the "unnatural." . . .

A second class of reasons to limit liberty says that we may interfere with some actions when they result in wrong to others. The wrong done may be direct. Lying, cheating, or other forms of deception are unavoidable when steroid use is banned, yet one persists in the practice. Of course, we could lift the ban, and then the steroid use need no longer be deceptive; it could be completely open to the same extent as other training aids. . . .

The wrong we do to others may be indirect. We could make ourselves incapable of fulfilling some duty we have to another person. For example, a male athlete who marries and promises his wife that they will have children makes himself sterile with synthetic anabolic steroids (a probable side effect). He has violated his moral duty to keep a promise. This objection could work, but only where the duty is clearly identifiable and not overly general, and the harm is reasonably foreseeable. . . . Except for cases like the sterile athlete reneging on his promise, instances where athletes make themselves incapable of fulfilling some specific duty to others would probably be rare. In any case, we cannot get a general moral prohibition on drug use in sports from this principle, only judgments in particular cases.

We may also do a moral wrong to others by taking unnecessary risks and becoming a great burden to family, society, or both. The helmetless motorcyclist who suffers severe brain damage in an accident is a prototypical case. Increasingly, people are describing professional boxing in very similar terms. Although this might be a good reason to require motorcyclists to wear helmets or to prohibit professional boxing matches, it is not a sound reason to prohibit steroid use. No one claims that the athletes using steroids are going to harm themselves so grievously that they will end up seriously brain-damaged or otherwise unable to care for themselves. Though the harms they do to themselves may be substantial, they are not disabling.

"FREE CHOICE UNDER PRESSURE"

So far we have not found any wrong done to others that is serious and likely to occur when athletes, at the top of the competitive ladder, commonly use performance-enhancing drugs. Let us look at the problem more closely. Olympic and professional sport, as a social institution, is an intensely competitive endeavor, and there is tremendous pressure to seek a competitive advantage. If some athletes are believed to have found something that gives them an edge, other athletes will feel pressed to do the same, or leave the competition. Unquestionably, coerciveness operates in the case of performance-enhancing drugs and sport. Where improved performance can be measured in fractions of inches, pounds, or seconds, and that fraction is the difference between winning and losing, it is very difficult for athletes to forego using something that they believe improves their competitor's performance. Many athletes do refuse; but many others succumb; and still others undoubtedly leave rather than take drugs or accept a competitive handicap.

Under pressure, decisions to take performance-enhancing drugs are anything but purely "individual" choices. My alleged liberty to take performance-enhancing drugs, which is very hard to oppose from an individualistic conception of morality, is counterbalanced by the pressure I place on my fellow competitors. My "free" choice contains an element of coercion. If enough people like me choose to use performance-enhancing drugs, then the freedom of others not to use them is greatly diminished.

But can we say that "freedom" has actually been diminished because others are using performance-enhancing drugs? I still have a choice whether to participate in the sport at all. In what sense is my freedom impaired by what the other athletes may be doing? If we take freedom or liberty in the very narrow sense of noninterference with my actions, then my freedom has not been violated, because no one is prohibiting me from doing what I want, whether that be throwing the discus, taking steroids, or selling real estate. But if we take freedom to be one of a number of values, whose purpose is to support the efforts of persons to pursue reasonable life plans without being forced into unconscionable choices by the actions of others, then the coerciveness inherent when many athletes use performance-enhancing drugs and compel others to use the same drugs, accept a competitive handicap or leave the competition can be seen as a genuine threat to one's life plan. When a young person has devoted years to reach the highest levels in an event, only to find that to compete successfully he or she must take potentially grave risks to health, we have, I think, as serious a threat to human flourishing as many restrictions on liberty. . . .

My conclusions are complex. First, the athletes who are taking performance-enhancing drugs that have significant health risks are engaging in a morally questionable practice. They have turned a sport into a sophisticated game of "chicken." Most likely, each athlete feels pressed by others to take drugs, and does not feel he or she is making a free choice. The "drug race" is analogous to the arms race.

Second, since the problem is systemic, the solution must be too. The IOC has concentrated on individual athletes, and even then it has been inconsistent. This is the wrong place to look. Athletes do not use drugs because they like them, but because they feel compelled to. Rather than merely punishing those caught in the social trap, why not focus on the system? A good enforcement mechanism should be both ethical and efficient. To be ethical, punishment should come in proportion to culpability and should fall on *all* the guilty parties—not merely the athletes. Coaches, national federations, and political bodies that encourage, or fail to strenuously discourage, drug use, are all guilty. Current policy punishes only the athlete.

To be efficient, sanctions should be applied against those parties who can most effectively control drug use. Ultimately, it is the athlete who takes the pill or injection, so he or she ought to be one target of sanctions. But coaches are in an extraordinary influential position to persuade athletes to take or not to take drugs. Sanctions on coaches whose athletes are caught using drugs could be very effective. Coaches, not wanting to be eliminated from future competitions, might refuse to take on athletes who use performance-enhancing drugs.

Finally, although I am not in a position to elaborate a detailed plan to curtail performance-enhancing drug use in sports, I have tried to establish several points. Despite the claims of individual autonomy, the use of performance-enhancing drugs is ethically undesirable because it is coercive, has significant potential for harm, and advances no social value. Furthermore, any plan for eliminating its use should be just and efficient, in contrast to current policies.

Can we apply this analysis of drug use in sports to other areas of life? One key variable seems to be the social value that the drug use promotes, weighed against the risks it imposes. If we had a drug that steadied a surgeon's hand and improved his or her concentration so that surgical errors were reduced at little or no personal risk, I would not fault its use. If, on the other hand, the drug merely allowed the surgeon to operate more quickly and spend more time on the golf course with no change in surgical risk, its use would be at best a matter of moral indifference. Health, in the first case, is an important social value, one worth spending money and effort to obtain. A marginal addition to leisure time does not carry anywhere near the same moral value.

A careful, case-by-case, practice-by-practice weighing of social value gained against immediate and long-term risks appears to be the ethically responsible way to proceed in deciding the merits of performance-enhancing drugs.

NOTES

1. Editorial: "Anabolics in Meat Production," *Lancet*, March 27, 1982, pp. 721–722.

Discussion Questions

1. Compare and contrast Murray's position on drugs with that of a libertarian such as Thomas Szasz. Does the use of performance-enhancing drugs fall under Szasz's "right of self-medication"? Support your answer.

2. If we reject Aristotle's distinction between natural and unnatural means to perfection, could his virtue ethics and concept of *eudaimonia* be used to support the use of performance-enhancing drugs? If so, under what circumstances? For example, is it morally acceptable to use performance-enhancing drugs—such as caffeine, amphetamines, or other stimulants—before taking an exam, performing on stage, going to a job interview, or driving long distances at night? Support your answers.

3. What type of policy might Murray suggest regarding the use of performance-enhancing drugs in sports? How would it differ from current policies? Who would be penalized most severely by this policy? Who would benefit the most? Explain.

CASE STUDIES

1. FRATERNITIES AND ALCOHOL: THE DEATH OF BENJAMIN WYNNE[51]

Much of the criticism of binge drinking on college campuses is focused on the Greek system. A Harvard study found that 86 percent of fraternity-house residents are binge drinkers. Binge drinking can be deadly.

In August 1997 twenty-year-old Benjamin Wynne of Louisiana State University was accepted as a pledge with the Sigma Alpha Epsilon fraternity. To celebrate, Wynne and the other pledges got rip-roaring drunk. The festivities started with an off-campus keg party in which beer was funneled through a rubber hose into the drinker's mouth. Following this, the Sigma Alpha Epsilon brothers headed to Murphy's Bar, which was near the campus, and drank "Three Wise Men," a 151-proof drink made from rum, whiskey, and a liqueur. The festivities ended with the brothers wheeling the pledges back to campus in shopping carts because they were too drunk to walk.

Police were called to the fraternity house several hours later. They found almost two dozen men passed out on the living-room floor, including Wynne who was dying of alcohol poisoning. Three other brothers were hospitalized. The autopsy showed that Wynne had consumed the equivalent of twenty-four drinks the night before. When rescue workers arrived, he was already comatose. A few days later, his distraught parents had him removed from life support. This was not an isolated event. According to the National Institutes of Health, alcohol drinking by college students is a contributing factor in an estimated 1,700 student deaths, 599,000 injuries, and 97,000 cases of sexual assault and date rape each year.[52]

Discussion Questions

1. Who bears responsibility for the death of Benjamin Wynne? Did the brothers have a moral responsibility to keep the pledges from drinking to excess? Does the bartender who served Wynne bear part of the responsibility for his death? Discuss what you would have done had you been at Murphy's Bar that evening.

2. Studies show that a permissive attitude on campus toward alcohol encourages students to drink more heavily than they otherwise would.[53] Outright prohibition, however, isn't necessarily the answer. Louisiana State University had a no-alcohol policy in effect the day Wynne died. Create a policy for your campus regarding

alcohol use. What moral concerns are most important in the creation of your policy? Given the fact that alcohol abuse is associated primarily with the Greek system, should fraternities and sororities be banned? Support your answers.

3. Some bars rely on college students for most of their business. These bars sometimes distribute handbills to students walking across campus and put fliers under doors in freshman dormitories. Should bars and alcohol companies be prohibited from advertising on college campuses?

4. Rutgers University has a dormitory especially for students who are recovering alcoholics and drug addicts. The cost of maintaining the dorm, which includes four people to run a substance-abuse program, is about $300,000 a year. Does the university have a duty to provide rehabilitative services to students who are alcoholics and drug abusers? If so, should these programs be voluntary or mandatory? Support your answers.

5. The primary justification of mandatory drug testing is the utilitarian argument that drug and alcohol use have a negative effect on productivity. Does this justify mandatory drug testing of college students? Support your answer. Discuss how Wilson and Husak might answer this question.

---

2. BASEBALL STAR MICKEY MANTLE: SHOULD ALCOHOLICS RECEIVE LIVER TRANSPLANTS?

In 1995 sixty-three-year-old Yankee baseball star and Hall-of-Famer Mickey Mantle lay critically ill in a Dallas Hospital, his liver destroyed by forty years of alcohol abuse.

Alcoholism is associated with a liver disease known as alcohol-related end-stage liver disease (ARESLD). In the United States, more than half of all deaths from liver disease are related to chronic alcoholism.[54] Mantle was given two to five weeks to live. The only hope for people with end-stage liver disease is a liver transplant. Livers are very scarce, however, and the waiting list is long. Only a fraction of those who need liver transplants ever get one.

The night after Mantle was hospitalized, a suitable donor was found. Mantle was moved to the top of the recipient list and soon received a new liver, even though the American Medical Association in 1991 had proposed as a general guideline that patients with alcohol-related liver disease should not compete equally with other people who need liver transplants.[55] Mantle died shortly after of a failed liver transplant.

Discussion Questions

1. How should scarce resources, such as organs, be allocated? Is it fair to move to the top of an organ transplant list people who are famous, or who still might make great contributions to society? Should the fact that a person's disease is related to lifestyle be taken into consideration in allocating scarce resources? Given the fact that there are livers available for only one-third of the people who need transplants,[56] should active alcoholics such as Mickey Mantle even be considered for liver transplants? Discuss how a supporter of the disease model of addiction and a supporter of the moral model of addiction might each answer these questions.

2. Studies show that the medical costs of alcohol and tobacco users are much higher than those of nonusers. Who should be responsible for the costs incurred in Mantle's liver transplant? Should private and public medical insurance plans cover these costs? Or, should alcohol and tobacco users have to cover the medical costs related to their use of these substances? Should tobacco companies have to foot the bill for diseases caused by tobacco use? Support your answers.

3. Libertarian John Taylor argues that people such as Mickey Mantle and rock star Jerry Garcia, who died of a heart attack at age fifty-three after decades of drug abuse and related health problems, have a right to choose their own ideal of the good life.[57] Taylor writes that both Mantle and Garcia "chose lives that valued recklessness, intensity, sensation, and, in a word, fun over mere longevity. As a result they died at the onset of old age rather than at its outer limits." Do you agree with Taylor? Should the fact that Mantle chose the life he lived mean that he also forfeited his right to a liver transplant? Support your answers.

3. WINNING AT ALL COSTS: DRUGS IN SPORTS

You are the captain and star player on your college basketball team, which has made the finals. A wealthy entrepreneur, who is an avid basketball fan and alumnus of your college, has promised to make a $60 million donation to your school *if* your team wins the finals. Your college desperately needs the money. It is currently in serious financial trouble and has been forced to lay off faculty and cut back on academic programs.

A few weeks before the game, the wealthy entrepreneur offers you a banned performance-enhancing substance. He assures you that you will not get caught, because the substance has been slightly altered so that it cannot be detected. He also tells you that he will make a $60 million donation even if your team loses, but only on the condition that you take the drug for the next two weeks. The team you are playing in the finals is better than yours and has won the finals the past two years in a row. According to a noted sports analyst, the odds against your winning are eight to one.[58]

Discussion Questions

1. What should you do? Would your answer be any different if the wealthy entrepreneur had also offered to give *you* $1 million if you agreed to use the drug? Would your answer be any different if you found out that the opposing team was going to be using performance-enhancing drugs? Explain your answers.

2. In a 1995 poll, 198 athletes, most of them U.S. Olympians or aspiring Olympians, were asked if they would take a banned performance-enhancing drug if the following two guarantees were made: (1) You will not be caught and (2) you will win. Of the 198 athletes, 195 said yes; 3 said no. Does the fact that almost 99 percent of the athletes polled were willing to use drugs under certain circumstances undermine the argument that performance-enhancing drugs should be banned because they violate free choice? Discuss how Murray would most likely answer these questions.

3. Both the alcohol and the tobacco industries use professional sports to advertise their products. For every hour of professional sports programming, there are

2.4 alcohol commercials, many of which are very appealing to children and young adults.[59] Tobacco companies, such as Virginia Slims, also sponsor women's sporting events, thus encouraging girls to think that there is a connection between smoking and being slim, athletic, and liberated. The large number of teenage girls who have taken up smoking following its ad campaigns is a testimony to the success of Virginia Slims ads. Discuss whether alcohol and tobacco advertisements should be more strictly regulated or banned altogether. Support your answers.

4. PROZAC: ENHANCING MORALITY THROUGH DRUGS[60]

Although the role of drugs in lowering inhibitions against immoral behavior is widely acknowledged, there is considerable resistance to the similar idea that certain drugs may actually enhance moral behavior. People who suffer from depression can become self-preoccupied to the point of seeming indifferent to the consequences of their actions for others. According to Peter Kramer, author of *Listening to Prozac*, treatment with a drug such as Prozac can in some cases "turn a morally unattractive person into an admirable one."[61] Prozac can also numb feelings, however.

Kramer cites the case of Phillip, an undergraduate who was undergoing psychotherapy because of humiliation he had received from his parents. Initially, Phillip resisted the use of medication. As his depression became more severe, however, Phillip agreed to try Prozac. Although he felt better on the Prozac, he also hated it. He felt phony. Why? Because he had been robbed of his disdain, resentment, and rage without having to first work through it.[62]

Prozac is used not only by people who feel depressed or overwhelmed by the challenges of life; many use it as a means of self-transformation. According to Kramer, using Prozac can increase autonomy and life choices by "lend[ing] people courage and allow[ing] them to choose life's ordinary risky undertakings."[63]

Discussion Questions

1. Is it morally admirable to use drugs in our quest for self-realization and moral maturity? Support your answer. Discuss how both Aristotle and a Buddhist might respond to this question.
2. The use of mood-altering drugs such as Prozac has been criticized for masking our true personalities or essences, as well as for freeing us from having to "struggle with reality." Do you agree? What is meant by "essence" and "reality"?
3. Prozac use is more prevalent among women than among men. Unlike Valium, which made women more compliant, Prozac is described as the "feminist drug" because it seems to transform some people into assertive, self-confident high achievers who are socially adept. Given this, would it be morally desirable for women who put others' needs before their own to take Prozac? Support your answer. Discuss how care ethicists Carol Gilligan and Nel Noddings might each answer this question.
4. Is unhappiness or depression necessarily an indication of a moral failing? Discuss your answer in light of Phillip's experience.

5. Discuss the following statement by Peter Kramer, author of *Listening to Prozac:*

> Working with Prozac has heightened my awareness of the extent to which compulsion is a basis for moral actions. Is it a sound basis? Surely one could make the case that what is compelled is inherently amoral; what characterizes moral action is choice. Still, in addressing this effect of Prozac [tempering compulsive behavior], we face the least irrational, most cogent aspect of pharmacological Calvinism: perhaps diminishing pain can dull the soul.[64]

5. THE ALCOHOLICS ANONYMOUS CONFESSION OF A DOUBLE MURDERER[65]

On New Year's Eve 1989, Donald Cox broke into a couple's bedroom and slashed their throats. The murder remained unsolved until Cox confessed his brutal crime at an AA meeting. Following the confession, one of the AA members called the police. Should this confession be admitted as evidence in a court of law?

According to Cox and his lawyers, the rules of AA obligate members to confess their transgressions. Because confession is part of the recovery process in AA, it should remain confidential, like confessions made to a priest or a psychiatrist. "It doesn't seem right," his lawyer Adele Walker argued. "It's like he's being punished for recovering." Furthermore, if confessions made during AA meetings did not remain confidential, AA would not be nearly as effective in helping alcoholics.

On the other hand, it is also an AA principle that alcoholics must accept responsibility for their actions, even when they are drunk. Although Cox claimed that he was drunk at the time of the murders and tried the "drunken stupor–temporary insanity" defense at his trial, he had no trouble recalling what had happened on that tragic New Year's Eve.

Discussion Questions

1. Should the fact that Cox made his confession as part of his recovery absolve him of responsibility for his actions? Support your answer. Discuss how supporters of the disease model and the moral model of addiction might each respond to this question.
2. Discuss what moral principles are in conflict when confidential confessions of murder or other horrific crimes—or plans to commit crimes—are made at AA meetings or to priests or psychiatrists. Which principles and moral concerns are most compelling?
3. Discuss what you would have done had you been at the AA meeting the night Cox confessed. Support your position.
4. Should people who commit crimes under the influence of drugs or alcohol be given stiffer penalties, as in drunk-driving violations? Or should they be treated with greater leniency? Support your answers. Discuss how a utilitarian as well as supporters of the disease model and the moral model might respond to these questions.

6. DECRIMINALIZING MARIJUANA

In March 2003 Jorge Lopez crossed the Canadian border to buy marijuana for his wife, Juanita, who was suffering from unrelenting pain in her joints from a severe form of arthritis. None of the prescription drugs had worked for her. She was bedridden and even contemplating suicide. He did not tell her he was going, fearing that she would try to stop him because of the risks to him. Medical marijuana had been legalized in Canada in 2001 for use by patients with AIDS wasting syndrome, multiple sclerosis, severe pain associated with cancer and chemotherapy, spinal cord injuries, epilepsy, and severe forms of arthritis. In addition, in December 2002 the Canadian Parliament had recommended that marijuana possession be decriminalized, which allowed Mr. Lopez to get some from a friend in Vancouver who grew small amounts for his own personal use.

When Mr. Lopez crossed back over the border into the state of Washington carrying 16 ounces of marijuana for his wife, he was arrested for possession and sentenced to one year in jail. Juanita Lopez pleaded, unsuccessfully, for his release. She died before he was released.[66]

Discussion Questions

1. Should Mr. Lopez have gone to Canada to buy marijuana for his wife? Support your answer. Discuss how a care ethicist might respond to this question.
2. Should marijuana be legalized and, if so, under what conditions? What moral principles and rights are at stake in this debate? Discuss how Wilson and Husak would most likely respond to the laws regarding marijuana use.
3. John Walters, director of the United States Office of Drug Control Policy, opposes the Canadian law, arguing that it will exacerbate the illegal marijuana trade from Canada to the United States and that it will allow growers in Canada to produce high-potency marijuana that, like crack, may be more addictive and dangerous. Discuss Walters's concerns. Do countries have a moral obligation to consider the needs and laws of neighboring countries when changing their own laws?
4. Discuss the morality of American college students' crossing the border to buy marijuana in Canada for recreational use. Do we have a moral obligation to abide by the laws of our society?
5. The Rastafarians, who use marijuana in religious ceremonies, have sought exemption from the marijuana laws in both Canada and the United States. Should they be granted an exemption? Do the current marijuana laws violate the Rastafarians' right to freedom of religion? Support your answers.

Sexual Intimacy and Marriage

Adam and Brooke, both seniors at Boston University, had been living together in off-campus housing for seven months. The arrangement was initially just a way of saving money since it was cheaper to live off campus and share expenses than to live in a dormitory. Although they did not talk about it, Brooke had come to regard the relationship as a testing ground for marriage. Adam, on the other hand, continued to regard the living arrangement mainly in terms of convenience and believed Brooke thought likewise. One day Brooke discovered that Adam was seeing another woman, Jennifer. When Brooke confronted him, he shrugged it off and told her that he and Jennifer were thinking of renting an apartment together after graduation. Brooke was devastated and accused him of betrayal. "What's the big deal?" he said, surprised at her reaction. "I haven't done anything wrong. After all, we're not married and haven't made any promises of sexual fidelity or a commitment to a long-term relationship."

RELIGIOUS AND CULTURAL ATTITUDES TOWARD SEXUALITY AND MARRIAGE

The sexual revolution that began in the late 1960s discarded the traditional notion of sexual morality and instead urged people to free themselves from sexual guilt and shame and to freely enjoy the pleasure of sexuality. Was this a desirable move from a moral point of view, or a sign of declining morals in our society?

Jewish, Christian, and Islamic attitudes toward sexuality have been shaped by teachings in the Bible and the Qu'ran, which regard heterosexual marriage as the only proper setting for sexual intimacy. Sex outside of heterosexual marriage is considered wrong because it is in conflict with God's natural law. According to Catholic natural law ethics, contraception is also wrong because it interferes with procreation, the natural end of sexuality. The Catholic position on sexual morality is explained in the Vatican's 1973 "Declaration on Sexual Ethics." Michael Ruse challenges the belief that procreation is the only moral end to sexuality and that homosexuality is "bad sexuality."

The prohibition against homosexuality, adultery, and fornication has been incorporated into the legal system of most of the Western and Islamic world. State laws punishing homosexual acts have only recently been repealed in the United States. In Iran more than three hundred people were executed between 1990 and 1996 for violation of laws prohibiting homosexuality.[1] In some sub-Saharan Islamic cultures, adulterers, especially women, are still stoned to death.[2]

The sale of contraception has also been regulated by laws. The prohibition against contraception was based primarily on the scriptural imperative to go forth and multiply, and the belief that the only legitimate end for sexual activity was procreation.[3] In 1969, the U.S. Supreme Court in *Griswold v. Connecticut* ruled that married people should be able to obtain contraception. In "Better Sex," Sara Ruddick argues that mutual pleasure is also a natural end of sexual intercourse. Therefore, contraception is morally permissible.

SEXUAL INTIMACY AND LOVE

The romantic view of sex links sex to love. The notion of romantic love became popular in the nineteenth and twentieth centuries, particularly in the years following World War II, when it became linked to courtship and marriage. The connection between love, sexual intimacy, and marriage remains an enduring theme. Nearly half of all paperback fiction books sold in the United States are romance novels, the majority of popular songs are about romantic love, and most movies and television shows have romance at least as a subplot.[4]

Sexual intimacy entails, at a minimum, consent between two adults. In Islamic countries that permit polygamy, there could be up to five adults involved. While polygamy is relatively rare in Islamic nations, it is still practiced in Africa. (See Case Study 4.) Lois Pineau, in her reading, emphasizes the importance of consent and good communication to sexual intimacy in dating relationships. But does sexual intimacy require love? Is mutual enjoyment and respect sufficient? Can one-night encounters count as sexual intimacy? Even if we concede that sexual intimacy requires mutual love, what do we mean by love and what does it add to a sexual relationship?

Sara Ruddick maintains that sex is morally preferable if it involves attempting to secure benefits not just for oneself but for the person cared for, a situation that is more likely to occur in a loving relationship. However, consensual sex outside of a loving relationship may still be morally permissible. Richard Wasserstrom, in his reading on adultery, explores the connection between sexual intimacy, love, and exclusivity.

Clearly, sexual desire can exist independently from love. Traditional views of sexual desire regard it as debasing and, hence, morally suspect. Sex outside of marriage, according to this view, involves the use of the other as a means only, which is a violation of Kant's categorical imperative. A person who sexually desires another person objectifies that person. Because of this, pornography, prostitution, adultery, and premarital sex are wrong.

However, while sex that exploits another person as a means only may be morally questionable, why must sex affirm one's moral worth or involve an exclusive commitment in order to be morally permissible? What about prostitution between consenting

---

🖋 THE DEFENSE OF MARRIAGE ACT

United States Congress
September 21, 1996

No State, territory, or possession of the United States, or Indian tribe, shall be required to give effect to any public act, record, or judicial proceeding of any other State, territory, possession, or tribe respecting a relationship between persons of the same sex that is treated as a marriage under the laws of such other State, territory, possession, or tribe, or a right or claim arising from such a relationship.

In determining the meaning of any Act of Congress, or of any ruling, regulation, or interpretation of the various administrative bureaus and agencies of the United States, the word "marriage" means only a legal union between one man and one woman as husband and wife, and the word "spouse" refers only to a person of the opposite sex who is a husband or wife.

---

adults? We engage in other bodily activities with others (e.g., contact sports and massage) because these activities bring us pleasure or profit without feeling we have to be in an intimate relationship with the other or affirm their moral worth.

MARRIAGE

The tradition of romantic love is firmly entrenched in our views on marriage. In a survey of Americans between the ages of twenty and twenty-eight, 94 percent said that the most important thing to look for in a marital partner is that the person is your "soul mate."[5] The majority of Americans also regard romantic love, rather than procreation, as the major purpose of marriage.

While marriage customs may differ from culture to culture, marriage between a man and woman is the ideal in almost all cultures. In Islam, as well as Orthodox Judaism, marriage is a holy duty.[6] Most people, however, regard marriage as morally permissible and even desirable, but not a duty. In the Catholic Church, because sexuality is associated with sin, a chaste, unmarried life is also held up as an ideal; indeed, it is required for priests and nuns.

Most people believe that marriage should be between two people of the opposite sex. According to the book of Genesis, God gave man and woman complementary natures. When united in marriage, men and women constitute a unit that is more balanced and greater than the sum of its parts. Because male and female natures complement each other, sex roles are exaggerated in a marriage and bind the couple together.

The core expectations of marriage, at least in modern Western society, are that "it typically involves sexual intimacy, economic domestic cooperation, and a voluntary commitment to sustaining this relationship."[7] In addition, marriage entails a moral commitment—"the feeling that one ought to continue a relationship, that one has a moral obligation to continue," and structural commitments involving joint property and shared friends.[8] In this sense, marriage is different from casual sex.

Marriage is sometimes compared with a contract agreement. Some couples insist on premarital agreements, legally binding contracts that detail in advance the allocation of all financial and property assets if the marriage should come to an end. Opponents of premarital agreements argue that marriage is a lifelong commitment, not a business contract. Premarital agreements indicate a lack of trust and commitment on the part of each partner. A marriage, they argue, is indissoluble or permanent because the two are of one flesh: "What God hath joined together, let no man put asunder."[9] Some radical feminists maintain that if free consent is a condition for a valid marriage, then most marriages can be annulled since women do not freely choose marriage but are pressured into it because of lack of social and economic equality.

The marriage rate began dropping in the late 1970s. However, since 1980, college women have been marrying at a higher rate than less educated, poorer women, a reverse of the previous trend. There is also an increasing racial, as well as economic, divide between those who are married and those who are not. In 1960, the marriage rate for blacks was only slightly lower than that for whites. Now fewer than half of black adults are married.

The divorce rate has also been declining since 1980, with marriages being most stable among couples with college educations. Although two-thirds of Americans, according to a 2007 Gallup poll, regard divorce as morally acceptable, they tend to be ambivalent about it. The indissolubility of marriage is important in the Catholic Church. Divorce not only violates natural law, but can harm children. Divorce is also discouraged under Islamic law. Furthermore, only men can initiate a divorce. There was no place for divorce under ancient Hindu law. However, the current Hindu Marriage Act permits divorce under limited circumstances, such as cruelty, adultery, or desertion.

Is divorce morally unacceptable? Do the ease and social acceptability of divorce weaken the institution of marriage as well as harm children? What about cases of loveless marriages, domestic violence, or marriages without sexual intimacy?

HOMOSEXUALITY AND SAME-SEX MARRIAGES

Homosexuality is a modern term, coined in 1869 as a category of scientific investigation. The belief that homosexuality is a deviation from the norm was reinforced by Sigmund Freud (1856–1939), who wrote that homosexuality resulted from a boy's inability to resolve his Oedipal conflict and sexual attraction to his mother. For many decades, the mental health community accepted Freud's definition of homosexuality as a perversion and mental disorder. The high prevalence of HIV/AIDS, which was first diagnosed in 1977 among homosexuals, fueled the public's belief that homosexuality was inherently unhealthy and immoral. It wasn't until 1994 that the American Medical Association revoked the disease model and its position that medical professionals should seek to change the sexual orientation of homosexuals.

Despite this reversal, the belief that homosexuality is immoral and deviant is still pervasive in American society. Although support for same-sex marriage has increased since the late 1990s, the majority of Americans (58 percent) polled by Gallup in 2008 still oppose it. Indeed, attitudes against homosexuals on this side of the Atlantic, with the exception of Canada, tend to be more severe than in Europe and non-Islamic Asia. Until 2003, when the U.S. Supreme Court ruled antisodomy laws unconstitutional in *Lawrence v. Texas,* several states had laws that punished homosexuality by up to twenty-five years in prison.

Same-sex marriage is legal in the Netherlands, Belgium, Canada, Spain, and South Africa. In addition, homosexual couples have full legal rights in several European countries.[10] In the United States, as of this writing, same-sex marriage is illegal in all states except Connecticut, Iowa, Maine, Massachusetts, New Hampshire, and Vermont.

The Defense of Marriage Act, signed by President Bill Clinton in 1996, defines marriage as a union between a man and a woman. Some people are pushing to make the act a constitutional amendment. They argue that same-sex marriage degrades the institution of traditional marriage. (See Case Study 5.)

COHABITATION AND PREMARITAL SEX

Acceptance of sex outside of marriage was highest in the late 1960s through the 1980s. However, it declined during the late 1990s among the general public as well as on college campuses. According to a 2007 Gallup poll, only 59 percent of Americans believe that sex between an unmarried man and woman is morally acceptable. Casual sex is especially frowned on. Many people disapprove of premarital sex because they believe it interferes with the deepening of a couple's relationship in other areas. They maintain that premarital chastity is the best way to guarantee marital commitment and faithfulness.

Even though almost half of Americans state that sex outside of marriage is immoral, 95 percent of American adults, including the majority of older teens, have had sex before marriage, a figure that has remained relatively stable since the 1950s.[11] This raises the question of the effectiveness of sex education in schools that encourages teenagers to wait until adulthood or marriage to have sex. (See Case Study 1.)

While two-thirds of the women in one study stated that they hoped to meet their future husbands in college, another study found that courtship is no longer part of the college scene. Instead, dating and courtship have been supplanted by "hanging out" and sexual encounters that are usually either casual "hookups" with no emotional commitment or "joined at the hip" cohabitation.[12] The number of unmarried couples living together has increased tenfold since 1960. Cohabitation is prevalent among college students, with 30 to 40 percent of college students cohabiting at any given time.[13] (See Case Study 2.) **Cohabitation,** formerly called "living together," is defined as people of the opposite sex living together, having sex together on a regular basis, and sharing living expenses.

Two of the primary reasons for cohabitation are readily available sex and convenience. Students also cohabitate as a symbol of their emancipation and freedom to make their own decisions. Another reason, especially among women, is cohabitation as a testing ground for marriage. However, the great majority of people who cohabitate do not eventually get married. Indeed, couples who cohabitate before marriage have a significantly higher divorce rate[14] and rate their marriages less positively than couples who did not cohabitate before marriage.[15] Cohabitation is also associated with a higher risk of domestic violence than is marriage.[16] The longer two people cohabitate, the greater the chance they will marry, with 58 percent who have cohabited for at least three years eventually marrying. Does this mean that consensual sex outside of marriage is wrong? Ruddick explores this question in her reading.

THE PHILOSOPHERS ON SEXUALITY AND MARRIAGE

Aristotle maintained that there are inherent gender differences and that inequality is an inevitable aspect of marriage. Marriage and the home are the domain of women, the state the primary focus of men. While family is necessary to meet our physical needs, the state is the proper moral sphere. The family contributes to the human good, which is participation in the state.

For Augustine and Thomas Aquinas, only sexuality within marriage between a man and a woman was morally permissible. Augustine regarded sexual intercourse for the purpose of begetting children as good, and desire for intercourse without this purpose as a depravity or a "sin against nature." Homosexual unions cannot be marital since they can never form a "biological unit" and produce children. This philosophy still informs the position of the Catholic Church on sexuality and marriage.

Immanuel Kant wrote that because the sexual impulse treats the other as an object of one's enjoyment rather than as a person, it is a debasement of our humanity and shameful. Sexuality is compatible with morality only in a marriage between a man and a woman because in marriage a person dedicates not only his or her sexuality but his or her whole person to the other and, in so doing, "constitutes a unity of will."[17] Homosexuality, however, is a travesty because it involves the use of the other person as an object and, like masturbation, the misuse of the sexual facilities and "runs counter to the ends of humanity to preserve the species without forfeiture of the person."[18]

Georg Hegel believed that "woman has her substantial destiny in the family." In a marriage the wife cedes rule to the husband on the basis of her natural inferiority. Sex roles, including maternity, are a product of marriage and, according to Hegel, necessary for marital unity.[19] Jean-Jacques Rousseau likewise believed that men's and women's duties in a marriage are based on the sexual division of labor as dictated by nature. It is by fulfilling their feminine and maternal duties that women achieve freedom.

It was not until the end of the eighteenth century, in Mary Wollstonecraft's *A Vindication of the Rights of Woman*, that the idea emerged of marriage as a union of equals. She envisioned marriage as a union of moral equals united by reason. The traditional marriage contract, Wollstonecraft argued, is a "fraudulent sexual contract" based on force and domination and resting on women's slavery that denies them access to reason. She believed that if women were better educated and given greater freedom, marriage could become like a friendship of equals.

Wollstonecraft's arguments were expanded by utilitarian John Stuart Mill and Harriet Taylor in the nineteenth century. Like Wollstonecraft, Mill and Taylor regarded marriage as a higher form of friendship based on equality and mutual esteem. This type of marriage, they argued, would bring greater social benefits than one based on inequality.

ADULTERY AND INFIDELITY

In Homer's *Odyssey*, Odysseus was warned of the sirens whose mesmerizing song bewitched men. Blinded by lust, sailors would wreck their ships on the jagged rocks or drown trying to reach the sirens. Odysseus, a happily married man, wisely asked that his men tie him to the mast of the ship and not let him loose no matter how much he begged.

Ninety-one percent of Americans think that **adultery,** or extramarital affairs, is morally wrong.[20] Despite widespread disapproval, however, adultery is on the increase, especially among women. Dr. Shirley Glass, a Baltimore psychologist and infidelity researcher, estimates that 25 percent of wives and 44 percent of husbands have extramarital affairs, often with coworkers.[21] (See Case Study 6.)

Some married people are also turning to strangers in chat rooms and to Internet pornography sites for companionship. Online forums or "sex-cussion" groups are playing an increasing role in the breakup of marriages. In some cases, online relationships can lead to real-life meetings and adultery. But even if they don't, is Internet "virtual sex" still immoral or adulterous?

In the reading "Is Adultery Immoral?" Wasserstrom argues that it is not the extramarital sexual act per se that is immoral, but the deception, the breaking of an implicit promise of sexual loyalty to one's spouse. However, he continues, a commitment to sexual exclusivity is not a necessary condition of marriage. In "open marriages," spouses have agreed to allow extramarital sexual relations. Other philosophers disagree, maintaining that the promise to be sexually loyal to one's spouse is implicit in the marriage vow no matter what the two partners may say to the contrary.

SEX AND VIOLENCE

A disproportionate number of assaults and murders occur within the context of intimate sexual relationships. **Domestic violence** (sometimes called intimate violence) is defined as violence within a home or an intimate sexual relationship. According to the Centers for Disease Control, domestic violence is the leading cause of death for women ages 15–44. More than a thousand women are killed each year by intimate partners, and another 2 million injured. The number of deaths has declined from about 1,500 since the passage in 1994 of the Violence against Women Act which raises awareness of the problem and funds programs addressing domestic violence. Of these funds, $140 million is earmarked for programs to stop violence against women on college campuses.[22] At Kansas State University, 90 percent of all calls to the Crisis Center involve victims of intimate violence.[23] This raises the question of the moral responsibility of emergency room medical professionals and college personnel to recognize and report suspected domestic violence. Are these statistics an artifact of gender inequality? Or does sexual intimacy, with its high emotions and emphasis on exclusivity, promote violence?

Rape seems to be a uniquely human phenomenon.[24] In her book *Against Our Will: Men, Women and Rape,* Susan Brownmiller argues that rape is a crime of violence—a conscious process of intimidation by men to keep women in a state of fear—rather than an act of sexual passion. Rape is also used in war and in prison among inmates as a form of intimidation and means of maintaining the power structure. Rape, as Lois Pineau points out in her reading on date rape, is viewed more ambiguously than most crimes. Women who say they have been raped are often met with suspicion and insinuations that they somehow provoked the attack. Furthermore, many women are reluctant to report rape. Rape shield laws have been passed in some states that protect women from being cross-examined about their sexual pasts.

Most rapists are known by their victims. Fraternities in particular have been called "rape-prone contexts" (see Case Study 7). Fraternity men are involved in more than 90 percent of all gang rapes on campus.[25] Some fraternities use women as bait to attract new members by having "Little Sisters," attractive undergraduates who attend and serve as hostesses at fraternity parties. Little Sisters are "sexual assets," and fraternities often promise prospective recruits sexual access to these women. The use of women as sexual objects and pawns in a game, some argue, encourages fraternities to see women as objects and rape as a sport.[26] Men are the predators, women their prey. Some universities' guidelines, such as those at Antioch College, require students to give explicit verbal consent throughout each step of a sexual activity to ensure that there is no misunderstanding.

A survey in *Ms.* magazine reported that one-fourth of all college women are victims of rape or attempted rape. However, 75 percent of the women described as rape victims did not define their experience as rape. Pineau suggests that this is because women have been socialized to see their oppression and violation as normal. Others, such as Katie Roiphe, argue that the problem lies in the definition of date rape used by what she calls "rape crisis" feminists. Instead of helping women overcome oppression, Roiphe argues that the "rape crisis" approach buys into the myth that women are naïve, passive, innocent, and helpless. (See Chapter 8, pages 432–439.) Another controversial issue is whether rape can occur in the context of marriage. Does the marriage vow or contract ensure sexual access even when one of the partners is not interested?

Pedophilia is often considered a form of rape. Pedophiles seek sexual intimacy with children. Most, though not all, people believe that sex with children, even if it is limited to fondling, is wrong because children cannot consent. Pedophilia also often involves a violation of trust and the duty of fidelity, since most victims of pedophiles know their abuser, who is often a trusted authority figure such as a parent or priest.

Another form of violence associated with sexual intimacy is stalking, an obsessive behavior that causes the victim to fear for her or his safety. Eighty-five percent of stalkers are current or former husbands, cohabiting partners, or boyfriends.[27] Stalking, however, is not limited to women. In the 1987 film *Fatal Attraction,* Glenn Close portrays an obsessive woman stalking her former lover, played by Michael Douglas.

What are we to make of these findings? Are sexual intimacy and sexual desire inherently fraught with sin and danger? Should they be avoided except in marriage and for procreation? Or is the problem social? In a perfect and just world, would intimate violence be nonexistent?

PROSTITUTION AND THE SEX TRADE

The United States, with the exception of Nevada and Rhode Island (although as of July 2009 there is a bill in the Rhode Island legislature to recriminalize prostitution), is one of the few Western nations where prostitution is illegal. Although prostitution is not, using Ruddick's definition, "complete" or "better sex," should it be illegal? Is it immoral?

One of the feminist critiques of prostitution is that it legitimates the subordination of women as a class by degrading women and reinforcing the patriarchal hierarchy. Prostitution also reinforces economic disparities, since woman who are poor and who have been sexually abused as children are more likely to become prostitutes. Networks exist that lure impoverished foreign women and children into prostitution rings under the guise of dating and employment agencies or marriage bureaus. Prostitution, whether the prostitutes are minors or adults, is also thought to be harmful to the social good and to public health because prostitutes are disproportionately afflicted with HIV/AIDS and other sexually transmitted diseases, and for this reason it should remain illegal.

Those who favor legalizing prostitution for adult sex workers, including several organizations of sex workers in this country,[28] respond that women gain some benefits from voluntary prostitution because it may be the best employment available to them. Many prostitutes work in terrible conditions, marginalized from the rest of society. Placing prostitutes—sex workers—outside of legal protection puts further burdens on them, making them more vulnerable to predators and pimps who exploit them. Legalizing prostitution and removing the stigma would help overcome many of the degrading aspects of prostitution as it currently exists in the United States. In addition, without regulation, there is no requirement that prostitutes get tested and treated for sexually transmitted diseases (STDs) or that clients use safe-sex practices.

In Canada, where prostitution is legal, full-service, safe-sex work is the accepted norm. Prices are lower because the cost to the sex worker is lower, since there is no need to pay pimps or "protection fees" to organized crime. The right of sex workers to advertise their services in public print is also protected in Canada.

Proponents of legalizing prostitution in the United States maintain that we should not place any significance on the sexual use of the body but leave it up to each individual, as a liberty right. People "sell" their bodily services in many professions— masseurs, athletes, surgeons, dentists, ballroom dancers. However, we do not consider these uses of the body immoral. Shouldn't it also be a sex worker's right to choose how to use her or his own body?

THE MORAL ISSUES

Dignity and Respect for Persons

What is morally good sex? The concept of moral goodness is linked to the well-being and dignity of our fellow human beings. Some philosophers argue that sex outside of heterosexual marriage violates respect for human dignity since it entails using the other merely as an object or tool for one's pleasure. Sex within a marriage, on the other hand, affirms the other's worth and dignity. But if providing sexual pleasure to one's spouse is simply a means of attaining your own sexual pleasure, isn't this still treating the other merely as a means rather than as a person? Also, sex within a marriage may not be based on respect, while sex outside of marriage may.

Autonomy and Consent

Consensual sex is noncoercive and involves mutual consent. Imposing our sexual desires on others without their consent is an affront to the other's dignity. It is for this reason that adults having sex with children is considered immoral. Rape is also immoral because it is imposed upon a person by intimidation or force. However, what about a man "wining and dining" a woman to get her to agree to have sex with him, or a woman engaging in seductive behavior to entice a man to have sex with her—do these behaviors count as coercion, or are they just part of the "courting" process?

Arguments against prostitution also focus mainly on the socially coercive nature of the institution, especially where the prostitutes' autonomy is severely compromised because they have few other viable options for earning a livelihood.

Radical feminists argue that because of unequal economic and social power, even when women consent to a sexual relationship the problem of coercion remains. Marriage is viewed as an exchange of sex for money and power, both of which men, in general, have more of. All sexual relationships, even within marriage, unless initiated by the woman, involve lack of consent on the part of women because consent is not possible in an unequal relationship.[29] One questionable assumption underlying this view is that women do not enjoy sex for its own sake and would not agree to it unless there was some element of coercion or external benefit attached to the sexual encounter. While this may be true in some cases, it is certainly not true in all cases.

Fidelity and Trust

Although consent may be a necessary condition for sex to be morally acceptable, it is not sufficient. Two people may freely consent to sexual intercourse, but the relationship may still be immoral because it is adulterous and violates the principle of fidelity. Wasserstrom explores these issues in the reading "Is Adultery Immoral?" Some people maintain that couples who are dating steadily or cohabiting, such as Adam and Brooke in the opening scenario, have a tacit agreement to remain faithful. Deception can also occur if we pretend we are someone we are not, exaggerate our good qualities, omit relevant information about our past, or use insincere words of love to win the other person's affection.

Divorce is a violation of the prima facie duty of fidelity and the marriage commitment. However, is it necessarily immoral? Are there situations in which divorce might be morally preferable because of the harms involved in staying together, such as a loveless marriage or one shattered by domestic violence and infidelity?

Justice and Equality

Some feminists regard the institution of marriage as inherently unjust. The traditional view of marriage, which is tied to sex roles, has been seen as a hindrance to the realization of justice in marriage as well as the recognition of same-sex marriages.

Polygamous marriages, some argue, are even more unequal because they exploit women and reduce them to commodities.

Homosexuals also face discrimination. Discrimination is not inherently wrong; however, unequal treatment must be based on morally relevant differences between two groups. For example, children are not allowed to drive automobiles because of their lack of maturity. Are there similar rational grounds to deny same-sex couples the right to marry? Massachusetts Chief Justice Margaret Marshall, in *Goodridge v. Department of Health* (2003), argues that denying same-sex couples the right to marry is a violation of the principle of equality.

Unnatural

One of the arguments against homosexuality and same-sex marriage, as well as contraception, is that they are unnatural. The underlying assumption is that the sole purpose of sex is procreation of the species. One weakness of this argument is the ambiguity of the term *unnatural*. Does unnatural mean contrary to the "laws of human nature"? Ruse points out that homosexual behavior is found throughout human societies as well as in other species of animals. Or does "unnatural" mean "uncommon"? This definition is also problematic. There are many uncommon traits and behavior, such as great genius, beauty, or moral fortitude, that we regard as desirable rather than immoral.

Natural can also be defined in terms of function based on the assumption that certain parts of our body were designed, by God or evolution, for specific functions. But why do we have to restrict ourselves to using something only for the function for which it was supposedly designed? Isn't part of human creativity the ability to see new possibilities in things? We use our other bodily parts—feet, hands, arms—in many ways.

Consequentialist Considerations

Many of the arguments against sex outside of marriage are based on beliefs about its harmful consequences. Couples who cohabitate have a higher rate of intimate violence. If they marry, they have a higher divorce rate. However, does this mean that cohabiting is immoral, or simply that people should be more discerning, and perhaps even more committed, before getting into such an arrangement?

Adultery and infidelity can be harmful to the third party. However, if adultery is condemned on the grounds of harm to the third party, then is adultery morally acceptable if the adulterous parties take care that their secret will not be discovered?

Homosexual behavior, it is argued, is wrong because it is offensive to those who are forced to witness public displays of affection. However, a feeling of offense or disgust is not a harm, according to utilitarians, and is not on its own sufficient grounds for declaring certain behaviors to be immoral.

The Common Good

Heterosexual marriage, most philosophers maintain, contributes to the common good of society. Laws that prohibit same-sex marriage are justified on the grounds that they preserve the stability of the family. Other institutions and practices that threaten the stability of marriage, such as prostitution, cohabitation, polygamy, and adultery, are

---

 SUMMARY OF READINGS ON SEXUAL INTIMACY AND MARRIAGE

The Vatican, "Declaration on Sexual Ethics." Sexual acts should occur only within marriage.

Ruddick, "Better Sex." Better sex brings benefit to those engaging in it and is also complete and natural.

Ruse, "Is Homosexuality Bad Sexuality?" Although some people may regard homosexuality as a perversion, it is not immoral.

Marshall and Cordy, "*Goodridge v. Department of Public Health* (2003)." Arguments are presented for and against the legalization of same-sex marriage.

Wasserstrom, "Is Adultery Immoral?" Adultery in general is immoral because it involves deception.

Pineau, "Date Rape: A Feminist Analysis." Good sex requires communication and consent. To engage in sex without consent is rape.

---

also regarded as immoral for these same reasons. Whether legalizing or accommodating these practices will weaken the institution of marriage remains to be seen. The institution of marriage does not seem to have been weakened nor the common good damaged in countries where these practices are legal.

CONCLUSION

For sex to be moral it must, at a minimum, be based on mutual and informed consent, and not be coercive or deceptive. Whether marriage or love and sexual intimacy are required for sex to be morally permissible remains open to debate.

 THE VATICAN

Declaration on Sexual Ethics

The Declaration on Sexual Ethics was issued by the Vatican on December 29, 1975. In it the writers defend the doctrine, based on natural law ethics and scriptural text, that sexual acts must occur only in the context of marriage. Premarital sex, homosexuality, and masturbation are all condemned.

Vatican Statement, "Persona Humana: Declaration on Certain Questions Concerning Sexual Ethics." Given at Rome, at the Sacred Congregation for the Doctrine of the Faith, on December 29, 1975.

Critical Reading Questions

1. Why did the Vatican feel the need to issue the "Declaration on Sexual Ethics"?
2. What is the connection between sexuality and human dignity?
3. What is the source of morality?
4. Why is marriage between a man and a woman the only framework in which sexual intimacy is moral?
5. What is the moral relationship between sexuality and procreation?
6. Why is premarital sex immoral?
7. Why is homosexuality immoral? How should the Church respond to people who are homosexual?
8. What is the Vatican's position on the morality of masturbation?

1. According to contemporary scientific research, the human person is so profoundly affected by sexuality that it must be considered as one of the factors which give to each individual's life the principal traits that distinguish it. In fact it is from sex that the human person receives the characteristics which, on the biological, psychological and spiritual levels, make that person a man or a woman, and thereby largely condition his or her progress towards maturity and insertion into society. Hence sexual matters, as is obvious to everyone, today constitute a theme frequently and openly dealt with in books, reviews, magazines, and other means of social communication.

In the present period, the corruption of morals has increased, and one of the most serious indications of this corruption is the unbridled exaltation of sex. . . .

2. The Church cannot remain indifferent to this confusion of minds and relaxation of morals. It is a question, in fact, of a matter which is of the utmost importance both for the personal lives of Christians and for the social life of our time . . . since the erroneous opinions and resulting deviations are continuing to spread everywhere, the Sacred Congregation for the Doctrine of the Faith, by virtue of its function in the universal Church and by a mandate of the Supreme Pontiff, has judged it necessary to publish the present Declaration.

3. The people of our time are more and more convinced that the human person's dignity and vocation demand that they should discover, by the light of their own intelligence, the values innate in their nature, that they should ceaselessly develop these values and realize them in their lives, in order to achieve an ever greater development.

In moral matters man cannot make value judgments according to his personal whim: "In the depths of his conscience, man detects a law which he does not impose on himself, but which holds him to obedience. . . . For man has in his heart a law written by God. To obey it is the very dignity of man; according to it he will be judged."[1] . . . .

Therefore there can be no true promotion of man's dignity unless the essential order of his nature is respected. Of course, in the history of civilization many of the concrete conditions and needs of human life have changed and will continue to change. But all evolution of morals and every type of life must be kept within the limits imposed by the immutable principles based upon every human person's constitutive elements and essential relations—elements and relations which transcend historical contingency.

These fundamental principles, which can be grasped by reason, are contained in "the divine law—eternal, objective, and universal—whereby God orders, directs, and governs the entire universe and all the ways of the human community, by a plan conceived in wisdom and love. . . .

4. Hence, those many people are in error who today assert that one can find neither in human nature nor in the revealed law any absolute and immutable norm to serve for particular actions other than the one which expresses itself in the general law of charity and respect for human dignity. . . .

But in fact, divine Revelation and, in its own proper order, philosophical wisdom, emphasize the authentic exigencies of human nature. They thereby necessarily manifest the existence of immutable laws inscribed in the constitutive elements of human nature and which are revealed to be identical in all beings endowed with reason.

Furthermore, Christ instituted his Church as "the pillar and bulwark of truth."[2] With the Holy Spirit's assistance, she ceaselessly preserves and transmits without error the truths of the moral order, and she authentically interprets not only the revealed positive law but "also . . . those principles of the moral order which have their origin in human nature itself"[3] and which concern man's full development and sanctification. . . .

5. Since sexual ethics concern certain fundamental values of human and Christian life, this general teaching equally applies to sexual ethics. In this domain there exist principles and norms which the Church has always unhesitatingly transmitted as part of her teaching, however much the opinions and morals of the world may have been opposed to them. These principles and norms in no way owe their origin to a certain type of culture, but rather to knowledge of the divine law and of human nature. . . .

It is these principles which inspired the exhortations and directives given by the Second Vatican Council for an education and an organization of social life taking account of the equal dignity of man and woman while respecting their difference. . . .

In this regard the Council declares that the moral goodness of the acts proper to conjugal life, acts which are ordered according to true human dignity, "does not depend solely on sincere intentions or on an evaluation of motives. It must be determined by objective standards. These, based on the nature of the human person and his acts, preserve the full sense of mutual self-giving and human procreation in the context of true love."[4]

These final words briefly sum up the Council's teaching—more fully expounded in an earlier part of the same Constitution—on the finality of the sexual act and on the principal criterion of its morality: it is respect for its finality that ensures the moral goodness of this act.

This same principle, which the Church holds from divine Revelation and from her authentic interpretation of the natural law, is also the basis of her traditional doctrine, which states that the use of the sexual function has its true meaning and moral rectitude only in true marriage.

6. It is not the purpose of the present declaration to deal with all the abuses of the sexual faculty, nor with all the elements involved in the practice of chastity. Its object is rather to repeat the Church's doctrine on certain particular points, in view of the urgent need to oppose serious errors and widespread aberrant modes of behavior.

7. Today there are many who vindicate the right to sexual union before marriage, at least in those cases where a firm intention to marry and an affection which is already in some way conjugal in the psychology of the subjects require this completion, which they judge to be connatural. This is especially the case when the celebration of the marriage is impeded by circumstances or when this intimate relationship seems necessary in order for love to be preserved.

This opinion is contrary to Christian doctrine, which states that every genital act must be within the framework of marriage. However firm the intention of those who practice such premature sexual relations may be, the fact remains that these relations cannot ensure, in sincerity and fidelity, the interpersonal relationship between a man and a woman, nor especially can they protect this relationship from whims and caprices. Now it is a stable union that Jesus willed, and he restored its original requirement, beginning with the sexual difference. "Have you not read that the creator from the beginning made them male and female and that he said: This is why a man must leave father and mother, and cling to his wife, and the two become one body? They are no longer two, therefore, but one body. So then, what God has united, man must not divide."[5]. . . . Through marriage, in fact, the love of married people is taken up into that love which Christ irrevocably has for the Church,[6] while dissolute sexual union[7] defiles the temple of the Holy Spirit which the Christian has become. Sexual union therefore is only legitimate if a definitive community of life has been established between the man and the woman. . . .

Experience teaches us that love must find its safeguard in the stability of marriage, if sexual intercourse is truly to respond to the requirements of its own finality and to those of human dignity. These requirements call for a conjugal contract sanctioned and guaranteed by society—a contract which establishes a state of life of capital importance both for the exclusive union of the man and the woman and for the good of their family and of the human community. Most often, in fact, premarital relations exclude the possibility of children. What is represented to be conjugal love is not able, as it absolutely should be, to develop into paternal and maternal love. Or, if it does happen to do so, this will be to the detriment of the children, who will be deprived of the stable environment in which they ought to develop in order to find in it the way and the means of their insertion into society as a whole.

The consent given by people who wish to be united in marriage must therefore be manifested externally and in a manner which makes it valid in the eyes of society. . . .

8. At the present time there are those who, basing themselves on observations in the psychological order, have begun to judge indulgently, and even to excuse completely, homosexual relations between certain people. This they do in opposition to the constant teaching of the Magisterium and to the moral sense of the Christian people.

A distinction is drawn, and it seems with some reason, between homosexuals whose tendency comes from a false education, from a lack of normal sexual development, from habit, from bad example, or from other similar causes, and is transitory or at least not incurable; and homosexuals who are definitively such because of some kind of innate instinct or a pathological constitution judged to be incurable.

In regard to this second category of subjects, some people conclude that their tendency is so natural that it justifies in their case homosexual relations within a sincere communion of life and love analogous to marriage insofar as such homosexuals feel incapable of enduring a solitary life.

In the pastoral field, these homosexuals must certainly be treated with understanding and sustained in the hope of overcoming their personal difficulties and their inability to fit into society. Their culpability will be judged with prudence. But no pastoral method can be employed which would give moral justification to these acts on the grounds that they would be consonant with the condition of such people. For according to the objective moral order, homosexual relations are acts which lack an essential and indispensable finality. In Sacred Scripture they are condemned as a serious depravity and even presented as the sad consequence of rejecting God.[8] This judgment of Scripture does not of course permit us to conclude that all those who suffer from this anomaly are personally responsible for it, but it does attest to the fact that homosexual acts are intrinsically disordered and can in no case be approved.

9. The traditional Catholic doctrine that masturbation constitutes a grave moral disorder is often called into doubt or expressly denied today. It is said that psychology and sociology show that it is a normal phenomenon of sexual development, especially among the young. . . .

This opinion is contradictory to the teaching and pastoral practice of the Catholic Church. Whatever the force of certain arguments of a biological and philosophical nature, which have sometimes been used by theologians, in fact both the Magisterium of the Church—in the course of a constant tradition—and the moral sense of the faithful have declared without hesitation that masturbation is an intrinsically and seriously disordered act. The main reason is that, whatever the motive for acting in this way, the deliberate use of the sexual faculty outside normal conjugal relations essentially contradicts the finality of the faculty. For it lacks the sexual relationship called for by the moral order, namely the relationship which realizes "the full sense of mutual self-giving and human procreation in the context of true love."[9] All deliberate exercise of sexuality must be reserved to this regular relationship. . . . The frequency of the phenomenon in question is certainly to be linked with man's innate weakness following original sin; but it is also to be linked with the loss of a sense of God, with the corruption of morals engendered by the commercialization of vice, with the unrestrained licentiousness of so many public entertainments and publications, as well as with the neglect of modesty, which is the guardian of chastity. . . .

In the pastoral ministry, in order to form an adequate judgment in concrete cases, the habitual behavior of people will be considered in its totality, not only with regard to the individual's practice of charity and of justice but also with regard to the individual's care in observing the particular precepts of chastity. In particular, one will have to examine whether the individual is using the necessary means, both natural and supernatural, which Christian asceticism from its long experience recommends for overcoming the passions and progressing in virtue. . . . .

NOTES

1. *Pastoral Constitution on the Church in the World of Today,* no. 16: *AAS* 58 (1966) 1037 [*TPS* XI, 268].
2. 1 *Tm* 3, 15.
3. *Declaration on Religious Freedom,* no. 14: *AAS* 58 (1966) 940 [*TPS* XI, 93].
4. *Loc. cit.;* see also no. 49: *AAS* 58 (1966) 1069–1070 [*TPS* XI, 291–292].
5. *Mt* 19, 4–6.
6. See *Eph* 5, 25–32.
7. Extramarital intercourse is expressly condemned in 1 *Cor* 5, 1; 6, 9; 7, 2; 10, 8; *Eph* 5, 5–7; 1 *Tm* 1, 10; *Heb* 13, 4; there are explicit arguments given in 1 *Cor* 6, 12–20.
8. *Rom* 1:24–27: . . . . See also what St. Paul says of sodomy in 1 *Cor* 6, 9; 1 *Tm* 1, 10.
9. *Pastoral Constitution on the Church in the World of Today,* no. 51: *AAS* 58 (1966) 1072 [*TPS* XI, 293].

Discussion Questions

1. The Vatican argues that procreation is the only proper end of the sexual act. Does this claim logically follow from the fact that procreation occurs as a result of the sexual act? Support your answer.
2. Does the claim that the primary purpose of marriage is the procreation and raising of children reduce marriage to a means to an end? How might the authors of the "Declaration of Sexual Ethics" respond to this question? Support your answers.
3. Discuss the Vatican's condemnation of homosexuality. Does calling homosexuality a pathological state merely beg the question and avoid the issue? Support your answers.
4. Seventy-five percent of Americans believe that Catholic priests should be allowed to marry and continue to function as priests.[30] How would the authors of the Vatican's "Declaration of Sexual Ethics" most likely respond to these views? Is requiring celibacy contrary to natural law or harmful to the social good? Support your answers.

SARA RUDDICK

Better Sex

Sara Ruddick is professor emeritus at Eugene Lang College at the New School for Social Research. She is also the author of *Maternal Thinking: Towards a Politics of Peace.* In this reading, Ruddick distinguishes between incomplete and complete or better sex. Better sex, she argues, is sex that increases the benefit of the act for the person engaging in it. Better sex is also complete and natural.

Critical Reading Questions

1. What analogy does Ruddick discuss between driving and sexual experiences, and why does she reject this analogy?
2. What are the three characteristics that Ruddick maintains have been used to "distinguish some sex acts as better than others"?
3. Upon what does the "completeness of a sexual act" depend?
4. In what ways might a sexual act be incomplete?
5. How, according to Ruddick, do "perverted" sexual acts differ from "natural" sexual acts?
6. According to Ruddick, what is the moral significance of perversions such as homosexuality?
7. What type(s) of perversion are immoral and on what grounds?
8. What is the moral significance of complete sex?
9. What are the dangers of passivity and distancing ourselves from our sexual desires?
10. In what three ways are complete sex acts morally superior to incomplete sex acts?
11. What is the connection between sex and other emotions?

It might be argued that there is no specifically sexual morality. . . . Sexual experiences, like experiences in driving automobiles, render us liable to specific moral situations. As drivers we must guard against infantile desires for revenge and excitement. As lovers we must guard against cruelty and betrayal, for we know sexual experiences provide special opportunities for each. We drive soberly because, before we get into a car, we

believe that it is wrong to be careless of life. We resist temptations to adultery because we believe it wrong to betray trust, whether it be a parent, a sexual partner, or a political colleague who is betrayed. As lovers and drivers we act on principles that are particular applications of general moral principles. . . . There is no specifically sexual morality, and none should be invented. Or so it might be argued.

When we examine our moral "intuitions," however, the analogy with driving fails us. Unburdened of *sexual* morality, we do not find it easy to apply general moral principles to our sexual lives.

"Better Sex," in *Philosophy and Sex*, revised edition, ed. by Robert Baker and Frederick Elliston (Amherst, N.Y.: Prometheus Books, 1994), 280–299.

The "morally average" lover can be cruel, violate trust, and neglect social duties with less opprobrium precisely *because* he is a lover. . . .

Our intuitions vary but at least they suggest we can use "good" sex as a positive weight on some moral balance. What is that weight? Why do we put it there? How do we, in the first place, evaluate sexual experiences? On reflection, should we endorse these evaluations? These are the questions whose answers should constitute a specifically sexual morality.

In answering them, I will first consider three characteristics that have been used to distinguish some sex acts as better than others—greater pleasure, completeness, and naturalness. Other characteristics may be relevant to evaluating sex acts, but these three are central. If they have *moral* significance, then the sex acts characterized by them will be better than others not so characterized. . . .

A characteristic renders a sex act morally preferable to one without that characteristic if it gives, increases, or is instrumental in increasing the "benefit" of the act for the person engaging in it. . . . A benefit may then be described as an experience, relation or object that anyone who properly cares for another is obliged to attempt to secure for him. Criteria for the virtue of care and for benefit are reciprocally determined, the virtue consisting in part in recognizing and attempting to secure benefits for the person cared for. . . .

A characteristic renders a sex act morally preferable to one without that characteristic if either the act is thereby more just or the act is thereby likely to make the person engaging in it more just. Justice includes giving others what is due them, taking no more than what is one's own, and giving and taking according to prevailing principles of fairness.

A characteristic renders a sex act morally preferable to one without that characteristic if because of the characteristic the act is more virtuous or more likely to lead to virtue. A virtue is a disposition to attempt, and an ability to succeed in, good acts—acts of justice, acts that express or produce excellence, and acts that yield benefits to oneself or others.

SEXUAL PLEASURE

Sensual experiences give rise to sensations and experiences that are paradigms of what is pleasant. . . .

Sexual pleasure is a species of sensual pleasure with its own conditions of arousal and satisfaction. Sexual acts vary considerably in pleasure, the limiting case being a sexual act where no one experiences pleasure even though someone may experience affection or "relief of tension" through orgasm. Sexual pleasure can be considered either in a context of deprivation and its relief or in a context of satisfaction. . . . Sexual pleasure is "a primary distinctively poignant pleasure experience that manifests itself from early infancy on. . . . Once experienced it continues to be savored. . . ."[1]

Sexual pleasure, like addictive pleasure generally, does not, except very temporarily, result in satiety. Rather, it increases the demand for more of the same while sharply limiting the possibility of substitutes. The experience of sensual pleasures, and particularly of sexual pleasures, has a pervasive effect on our perceptions of the world. We find bodies inviting, social encounters alluring, and smells, tastes, and sights resonant because our perception of them includes their sexual significance. . . .

COMPLETE SEX ACTS

The completeness of a sexual act depends upon the *relation* of the participants to their own and each other's *desire*. A sex act is complete if each partner allows himself to be "taken over" by an active desire, which is desire not merely for the other's body but also for his active desire. Completeness is hard to characterize, though complete sex acts are at least as natural as any others—especially, it seems, among those people who take them casually and for granted. . . . "What we try to possess, then, is not just a body, but a body brought to life by consciousness."[2] "It is important that the partner be aroused, and not merely aroused, but aroused by the awareness of one's desire."[3]

The precondition of complete sex acts is the "embodiment" of the participants. Each participant submits to sexual desires that take over consciousness and direct action. . . . Desire is pervasive and "overwhelming," but it does not make its subject its involuntary victim (as it did the Boston Strangler, we are told), nor does it, except at its climax, alter capacities for ordinary perceptions, memories, and inferences. . . .

We may often experience ourselves as relatively disembodied, observing or "using" our bodies to fulfill our intentions. On some occasions, however, such as in physical combat, sport, physical suffering, or danger, we "become" our bodies; our consciousness becomes bodily experience of bodily activity. Sexual acts are occasions for such embodiment; they may, however, fail for a variety of reasons, for example, because of pretense or an excessive need for self-control. If someone is embodied by sexual desire, he submits to its direction. Spontaneous impulses of desire become his movements—some involuntary, like gestures of "courting behavior" or physical expressions of intense pleasure, and some deliberate. His consciousness, or "mind," is taken over by desire and the pursuit of its object, in the way that at other times it may be taken over by an intellectual problem or by obsessive fantasies. But unlike the latter takeovers, this one is bodily. A desiring consciousness is flooded with specifically sexual feelings that eroticize all perception and movement. Consciousness "becomes flesh."

Granted the precondition of embodiment, complete sex acts occur when each partner's embodying desire is active and actively responsive to the other's. This second aspect of complete sex constitutes a "reflexive mutual recognition" of desire by desire.[4]

The partner *actively* desires another person's desire. Active desiring includes more than embodiment, which might be achieved in objectless masturbation. It is more, also, than merely

being aroused by and then taken over by desire, though it may come about as a result of deliberate arousal. It commits the actively desiring person to her desire and requires her to identify with it—that is, to recognize herself as a sexual agent as well as respondent. (Active desiring is less encouraged in women, and probably more women than men feel threatened by it.)

The other recognizes and responds to the partner's desire. . . . Imperviousness to desire is the deepest defense against it. We have learned from research on families whose members tend to become schizophrenic that such imperviousness, the refusal to recognize a feeling for what it is, can force a vulnerable person to deny or to obscure the real nature of his feelings. Imperviousness tends to deprive even a relatively in-vulnerable person of his efficacy. The demand that our feelings elicit a response appropriate to them is part of a general demand that *we* be recognized, that our feelings be allowed to make a difference.

There are many ways in which sexual desire may be recognized, countless forms of submission and resistance. In complete sex, desire is recognized by a responding and active desire that commits the other, as it committed the partner. Given responding desire, both people identify themselves as sexually desiring the other. They are neither seducer nor seduced, neither suppliant nor benefactress, neither sadist nor victim, but sexual agents acting sexually out of their recognized desire. . . . Returned and endorsed desire becomes one of the features of an erotically structured perception. Desiring becomes desirable. (Men are less encouraged to desire the other's active and demanding desire, and such desiring is probably threatening to more men than women.)

In sum, in complete sex two persons embodied by sexual desire actively desire and respond to each other's active desire. Although it is difficult to write of complete sex without suggesting that one of the partners is the initiator, while the other responds, complete sex is reciprocal sex. The partners, whatever the circumstances of their coming together, are equal in activity and responsiveness of desire.

Sexual acts can be partly incomplete. A necrophiliac may be taken over by desire, and a frigid woman may respond to her lover's desire without being embodied by her own. Partners whose sexual activities are accompanied by private fantasies engage in an incomplete sex act. . . .

There are many possible sex acts that are pleasurable but not complete. The desire for a sleeping woman, for example, is possible only "in so far as this sleep appears on the ground of consciousness."[5] This seems much too strong. Some lovers desire that their partners resist, others like them coolly controlled, others prefer them asleep. We would not say that there was anything abnormal or less fully sexual about desire. Whether or not complete sex is preferable to incomplete sex (the question to which I shall turn shortly), incompleteness does not disqualify a sex act from being fully sexual.

SEXUAL PERVERSION

The final characteristic of allegedly better sex acts is that they are "natural" rather than "perverted." The ground for classifying sexual acts as either natural or unnatural is that the former type serve or could serve the evolutionary and biological function of sexuality—namely, reproduction. "Natural" sexual desire has as its "object" living persons of the opposite sex, and in particular their postpubertal genitals. The "aim" of natural sexual desire—that is, the act that "naturally" completes it—is genital intercourse. Perverse sex acts are deviations from the natural object (for example, homosexuality, fetishism) or from the standard aim (for example, voyeurism, sadism). Among the variety of objects and aims of sexual desire, I can see no other ground for selecting some as natural, except that they are of the type that can lead to reproduction. . . .

The connection of sexual desire with reproduction is not sufficient to yield the concept of perversion, but it is surely necessary. [Thomas] Nagel, however, thinks otherwise. There are, he points out, many sexual acts that do not lead to reproduction but that we are not even inclined to call perverse—for example, sexual acts between partners who are sterile. Perversion, according to him, is a psychological concept while reproduction is (only?) a physiological one. . . .

Nagel is right about our judgments of particular acts, but he draws the wrong conclusions from those judgments. The perversity of sex acts does not depend upon whether they are intended to achieve reproduction. "Natural" sexual desire is for heterosexual genital activity, not for reproduction. The ground for classifying that desire as natural is that it is so organized that it *could* lead to reproduction in normal physiological circumstances. The reproductive organization of sexual desires gives us a *criterion* of naturalness, but the *virtue* of which it is a criterion is the "naturalness" itself, not reproduction. . . .

. . . To say a sex act is perverted is to pass a conventional judgment about characteristics of the act, which could be evident to any observer. As one can pretend to be angry but not to shout, one can pretend to a complete, but not to a natural, sex act (though one may, of course, conceal desires for perverse sex acts or shout in order to mask one's feelings). As Nagel himself sees, judgments about particular sex acts clearly differentiate between perversion and completeness. Unadorned heterosexual intercourse where each partner has private fantasies is clearly "natural" and clearly "incomplete," but there is nothing prima facie incomplete about exclusive oral-genital intercourse or homosexual acts. . . .

IS BETTER SEX REALLY BETTER?

Some sex acts are, allegedly, better than others insofar as they are more pleasurable, complete, and natural. What is the moral significance of this evaluation? In answering this question, official sexual morality sometimes appeals to the social consequences of particular types of better sex acts. For example, since dominantly perverse organizations of sexual impulses limit reproduction, the merits of perversion depend upon the need to limit or increase population. Experience of sexual pleasure may be desirable if it promotes relaxation and communication in an acquisitive society, undesirable if it limits the desire to work or, in armies, to kill. The social consequences of complete sex have not received particular attention, because the quality of sexual experience has been of little interest to moralists. It might be found that those who had complete sexual relations were more cooperative, less amenable to political revolt. If so, complete sexual acts would be desirable in just and peaceable societies, undesirable in unjust societies requiring revolution.

The social desirability of types of sexual acts depends on particular social conditions and independent criteria of social desirability. . . . .

THE BENEFIT OF SEXUAL PLEASURE

. . . The most eloquent detractors of sexual experience have admitted that it provides sensual pleasures so poignant that once experienced they are repeatedly, almost addictively, sought. Yet, unlike other appetites, such as hunger, sexual desire can be permanently resisted, and resistance has been advocated. How can the prima facie benefits of sexual pleasure appear deceptive?

There are several grounds for complaint. Sexual pleasure is ineradicably mixed, frustration being part of every sexual life. The capacity for sexual pleasure is unevenly distributed, cannot be voluntarily acquired, and diminishes through no fault of its subject. If such a pleasure were an intrinsic benefit, benefit would in this case be independent of moral effort. Then again, sexual pleasures are not serious. Enjoyment of them is one of life's greatest recreations, but none of its business. And finally, sexual desire has the defects of its strengths. Before satisfaction, it is, at the least, distracting . . . . Like psychosis, sexual desire turns us from "reality"—whether the real be God, social justice, children, or intellectual endeavor. This turning away is more than a social consequence of desire, though it is that. Lovers themselves feel that their sexual desires are separate

from their "real" political, domestic, ambitious, social selves. . . .

. . . More than other well-known desires (for example, desire for knowledge, success, or power), sexual desire is simply and completely satisfied upon attaining its object. Partly for this reason, even if we are overtaken by desire during sexual experience, our sexual experiences do not overtake us. Lovers turn away from the world while loving, but return—sometimes all too easily—when loving is done. The moralist rightly perceives sexual pleasure as a recreation, and those who upon realizing its benefits make a business of its pursuit appear ludicrous. The capacity for recreation, however, is surely a benefit that any human being rightly hopes for who hopes for anything. . . . Thus, though priest, revolutionary, and parent are alike in fearing sexual pleasure, this fear should inspire us to psychological and sociological investigation of the fearing rather than to moral doubt about the benefit of sexual pleasure.

THE MORAL SIGNIFICANCE OF PERVERSION

What is the moral significance of the perversity of a sexual act? Next to none, so far as I can see. Though perverted sex may be "unnatural" both from an evolutionary and developmental perspective, there is no connection, inverse or correlative, between what is natural and what is good. Perverted sex is sometimes said to be less pleasurable than natural sex. We have little reason to believe that this claim is true and no clear idea of the kind of evidence on which it would be based. In any case, to condemn perverse acts for lack of pleasure is to recognize the worth of pleasure, not of naturalness.

There are many other claims about the nature and consequences of perversion. Some merely restate "scientific" facts in morally tinged terminology. Perverse acts are, by definition and according to psychiatric theory, "immature" and "abnormal," since natural sex acts are selected by criteria of "normal" sexual function and "normal" and "mature" psychological development. But there is no greater connection of virtue with maturity and normality than there is of virtue with nature. . . .

If perverted sex acts did rule out normal sex acts, if one were *either* perverted *or* natural, then certain kinds of sexual relations would be denied some perverts—relations that are benefits to those who enjoy them. It seems that sexual relations with the living and the human would be of greater benefit than those with the dead or with animals. But there is no reason to think that heterosexual relations are of greater benefit than homosexual ones. It might be that children can only be raised by heterosexual couples who perform an abundance of natural sex acts. If so (though it seems unlikely), perverts will be denied the happiness of parenthood. . . .

Some perversions are immoral on independent grounds. Sadism is the obvious example, though sadism practiced with a consenting masochist is far less evil than other, more familiar forms of aggression. Voyeurism may seem immoral because, since it must be secret to be satisfying, it violates others' rights to privacy. Various kinds of rape can constitute perversion if rape, rather than genital intercourse, is the aim of desire. Rape is seriously immoral, a vivid violation of respect for persons. . . .

THE MORAL SIGNIFICANCE OF COMPLETENESS

Complete sex consists in mutually embodied, mutually active, responsive desire. Embodiment, activity, and mutual responsiveness are instrumentally beneficial because they are conducive to our psychological well-being, which is an intrinsic benefit. . . .

The mutual responsiveness of complete sex is also instrumentally beneficial. It satisfies a general desire to be recognized as a particular "real" person and to make a difference to other particular "real" people. The satisfaction of this desire in sexual experience is especially rewarding, its thwarting especially cruel. Vulnerability is increased in complete sex by the active desiring of the partners. . . . Passivity in respect to one's own sexual desire not only limits sexual pleasure but, more seriously, limits the

extent to which the experience of sexual pleasure can be included as an experience of a coherent person. With passivity comes a kind of irresponsibility in which one can hide from one's desire, even from one's pleasure, "playing" seducer or victim, tease or savior. Active sexual desiring in complete sex acts affords an especially threatening but also especially happy occasion to relinquish these and similar roles. To the extent that the roles confuse and confound our intimate relations, the benefit from relinquishing them in our sexual acts, or the loss from adhering to them then, is especially poignant.

In addition to being beneficial, complete sex acts are morally superior for three reasons. They tend to resolve tensions fundamental to moral life; they are conducive to emotions that, if they become stable and dominant, are in turn conducive to the virtue of loving; and they involve a preeminently moral virtue—respect for persons. . . .

The connection between sex and certain emotions—particularly love, jealousy, fear, and anger—is as evident as it is obscure. Complete sex acts seem more likely than incomplete pleasurable ones to lead toward affection and away from fear and anger, since any guilt and shame will be extrinsic to the act and meliorated by it. It is clear that we need not feel for someone any affection beyond that required (if any is) simply to participate with him in a complete sex act. However, it is equally clear that sexual pleasure, especially as experienced in complete sex acts, is conducive to many feelings—gratitude, tenderness, pride, appreciation, dependency, and others. These feelings magnify their object who occasioned them, making him unique among men. When these magnifying feelings become stable and habitual they are conducive to love—not universal love, of course, but love of a particular sexual partner. However, even "selfish" love is a virtue, a disposition to care for someone as her interests and demands would dictate. Neither the best sex nor the best love require each other, but they go together more often than reason would expect— often enough to count the virtue of loving as one of the rewards of the capacity for sexual pleasure exercised in complete sex acts. . . .

Finally, as Sartre has suggested, complete sex acts preserve a respect for persons. Each person remains conscious and responsible, a "subject" rather than a depersonalized, will-less, or manipulated "object." Each actively desires that the other likewise remain a "subject." Respect for persons is a central virtue when matters of justice and obligation are at issue. Insofar as we can speak of respect for persons in complete sex acts, there are different, often contrary requirements of respect. . . . Respect for persons, typically and in sex acts, requires that *actual present* partners participate, partners whose desires are recognized and endorsed. Respect for persons typically requires taking a distance from both one's own demands and those of others. But in sex acts the demands of desire take over, and equal distance is replaced by mutual responsiveness. . . . In sex acts, another person is so clearly a means to satisfaction that she is always on the verge of becoming merely a means. . . . In complete sex acts, instrumentality vanishes only because it is mutual and mutually desired. Respect requires encouraging, or at least protecting, the autonomy of another. In complete sex, autonomy of will is recruited by desire, and freedom from others is replaced by frank dependence on another person's desire. Again the respect consists in the reciprocity of desiring dependence, which bypasses rather than violates autonomy. . . .

While complete sex is morally superior because it involves respect for persons, incomplete sex acts do not necessarily involve immoral disrespect for persons. . . . Masturbation, for example, allows only the limited completeness of embodiment and often fails of that. But masturbation only rarely involves disrespect to anyone. . . . Sex acts provide one context in which respect for persons can be expressed. That context is important both because our sexual lives are of such importance to us and because they are so liable to injury because of the experience and the fear of the experience of disrespect. . . .

To say that complete sex acts are preferable to incomplete ones is not to court a new puritanism. There are many kinds and degrees of incompleteness. Incomplete sex acts may not involve a disrespect for persons. Complete sex acts only *tend* to be good for us, and the realization of these tendencies depends upon individual lives and circumstances of sexual activity. The proper object of sexual desire is sexual pleasure. It would be a foolish ambition indeed to limit one's sexual acts to those in which completeness was likely. Any sexual act that is pleasurable is prima facie good, though the more incomplete it is—the more private, essentially autoerotic, unresponsive, unembodied, passive, or imposed—the more likely it is to be harmful to someone.

ON SEXUAL MORALITY: CONCLUDING REMARKS

There are many questions we have neglected to consider because we have not been sufficiently attentive to the quality of sexual lives. For example, we know little about the ways of achieving better sex. When we must choose between inferior sex and abstinence, how and when will our choice of inferior sex damage our capacity for better sex? . . .

Some of the traditional sexual vices might be condemned on the ground that they are inimical to better sex. Obscenity, or repeated public exposure to sexual acts, might impair our capacity for pleasure or for response to desire. Promiscuity might undercut the tendency of complete sex acts to promote emotions that magnify their object. Other of the traditional sexual vices are neither inimical nor conducive to better sex, but are condemned because of conflicting nonsexual benefits and obligations. For example, infidelity qua infidelity neither secures nor prevents better sex. The obligations of fidelity have many sources, one of which may be a past history of shared complete sex acts, a history that included promises of exclusive intimacy. Such past promises are as apt to conflict with as to accord with a current demand for better sex. I have said nothing about how such a conflict would be settled. I hope I have

shown that where the possibility of better sex conflicts with obligations and other benefits, we have
a *moral dilemma,* not just an occasion for moral
self-discipline.

The pursuit of more pleasurable and more
complete sex acts is, among many moral activities, distinguished not for its exigencies but for its
rewards. Since our sexual lives are so important to
us, and since, whatever our history and our hopes,
we are sexual beings, this pursuit rightly engages
our moral reflection. It should not be relegated to
the immoral, nor to the "merely" prudent.

NOTES

1. George Klein, "Freud's Two Theories of Sexuality," in
   L. Berger, ed., *Clinical-Cognitive Psychology: Models and
   Integrations* (Englewood Cliffs, N.J.: Prentice-Hall,
   1969), pp. 131–81.
2. Maurice Merleau-Ponty, *Phenomenology of Perception,*
   p. 167.
3. Thomas Nagel, "Sexual Perversion," *The Journal of
   Philosophy* 66, no. 1 (January 16, 1969).
4. Nagel, "Sexual Perversion," p. 254.
5. Sartre, *Being and Nothingness,* p. 386.

Discussion Questions

1. Do you agree with Ruddick's three criteria of better sex? If so, why? If not, develop a
   list of alternative criteria and explain why they are morally preferable.
2. Discuss how the Vatican might respond to Ruddick's definition of complete or better sex acts. Which view do you find more morally acceptable and why?
3. Using Ruddick's criteria, are minors (people under eighteen years of age) capable of
   engaging in complete sex acts? Discuss the type of policy Ruddick would most likely
   recommend for a residential high school regarding sexual relationships among the
   students.
4. Using Ruddick's criteria, can prostitution and/or adultery involve better or complete
   sex? If so, does this mean that prostitution and adultery are morally acceptable in
   these cases?
5. Is Ruddick promoting a "new Puritanism" by claiming that complete sex acts tend
   to be morally preferable to incomplete ones? Support your answer.

MICHAEL RUSE

Is Homosexuality Bad Sexuality?

Michael Ruse is a professor of philosophy at Florida State University. Ruse examines
the argument that homosexuality is "bad sexuality" because it is unnatural and abnormal. He concludes that, although some people may see homosexuality as a perversion,
it is not immoral.

"Is Homosexuality Bad Sexuality?" in *Homosexuality: A Philosophical Inquiry* (Oxford, England: Basil
Blackwell, 1988), 179–192. Some notes have been omitted.

Critical Reading Questions

1. What were the conventions regarding homosexuality in ancient Greece?
2. Why, according to Ruse, were both Socrates and Plato opposed to the physical consummation of homosexual relationships?
3. What does the Bible say regarding the morality of homosexuality?
4. Why, according to Thomas Aquinas, is homosexuality a violation of natural law?
5. What are the kinds of *crimina carnis*? How does Kant use the concept of *crimina carnis* in his analysis of the morality of homosexuality?
6. What was Jeremy Bentham's position on the morality of homosexuality? On what grounds does Bentham oppose outlawing it?
7. What is the source, according to Ruse, of the argument in Western philosophy that homosexuality is unnatural? How does Ruse respond to this argument?
8. According to Ruse, why do so many people regard homosexuality as a perversion? What does Ruse mean when he says that this kind of thinking involves a paradox?
9. On what grounds does Sara Ruddick argue that homosexuality is a perversion? How does Ruse respond to her argument?
10. What is the relationship among naturalness, perversion, and morality?
11. Why do people find perversion so disgusting?
12. What does Ruse mean when he says that the question of the perversity of homosexuality is more of an empirical than a prescriptive matter?
13. What does Ruse mean when he says that perversion, when applied to homosexuality, is a relative concept?
14. What is the difference between moral indignation and disgust?

Is homosexuality, inclination and behavior, an acceptable way for a human being to feel and act, or is it pernicious? Undoubtedly, although there will be less unanimity on this matter today than there would have been (say) a hundred years ago, for a good many people the answer will seem obvious—that homosexuality is aesthetically revolting and morally gross; that in all its aspects it is wrong, and that this is a conclusion not merely confirmed by modern thought but underlined by the whole western religious/philosophical tradition. . . .

The Greeks, so the story would go, accepted and even promoted homosexual relations. Furthermore, this attitude is to be found in the greatest of their philosophers, most especially Plato. The Jews, however, both those of the Old and New Testaments, uniformly and unambiguously condemned all forms of homosexuality. It merited the punishment of man and of God. And it is this latter position which has prevailed ever since, thanks to the rise of Christianity, a religion which has such deep roots in Judaism.

But is this story true? Let us turn to the sources, beginning first with the Greeks. As is so often the case, popular opinion has a very inadequate grasp of the whole. It is indeed true that by the time of "classical Greece". . .—a time which firmly includes the life span of the philosopher Plato (428–347 BC)—overt homosexuality was a well-established tradition and acceptable part of the Greek life style. But the sexuality of classical Greece was apparently not simply an unrestrained free-for-all, with any two or more people doing whatsoever they liked, to whomsoever they liked. Specifically, the homosexuality one hears about was very much an upper-class phenomenon, strongly associated with the enforced segregation of the sexes, and highly stylized, with emotions rather than actions playing a major role. The central focus was a bond which would be formed between a somewhat older and a somewhat younger man (ideally, a 25-year-old paired with a 15-year-old). It seems to have been rare indeed (and certainly not proper) for two men of exactly the same age to have fallen in love and to have had any kind of physical relationship. Moreover, after marriage the need for (and acceptability of) homosexual relations fell away rapidly. (It is assumed that an analogous story can be told about women, although we know far less about lesbianism. It seems, for some unknown reason, to have been a taboo subject for the male writers.)

The constraint about ages was accompanied also by a constraint about emotions. The older man (the *erastes* or lover) was expected to feel strong sexual emotion for the younger man or boy (the *eromenos* or loved one), admiring his beauty, wanting to get physically close to him, and being prepared to court him with gifts and favors. The boy, however, was not expected to feel the same kind of sexual attraction in response, but rather to admire his older lover, looking upon him as an ideal or model, and wanting to make him happy. This convention about love and ages helped dictate the nature of the physical sexual relations. Officially at least, sodomy was definitely taboo, not to mention things like fellatio. Being sodomized was considered far too degrading. . . . Hence, the usual method of intercourse between upper-class lovers was somewhat limited, in a stylized manner. The erastes, the older, would push his penis between the thighs of the eromenos, the younger, and bring himself to ejaculation this way, "intercrurally." The boy was not supposed to ejaculate in return—indeed, he was supposed to find the whole business rather asexual, and to remain unaroused throughout. No doubt there was frequently a gap between the ideal and the actual.

Against this background we can understand Plato's position on homosexuality. . . . Plato, tradition has it, was unmarried and fairly exclusively homosexual in orientation. Be this as it may, [his teacher] Socrates and his (exclusively male) companions lived, thought, and behaved very much in the homosexual milieu described above as being the norm for upper-class Athenians. In Plato's early writings (which report, fairly authentically, on actual Socratic discussions or dialogues), we get repeated, unself-conscious references to the sexual pangs that an older man would feel for a boy or younger man, and the liaisons that would spring up between them. . . .

Although there is much talk of sexual desire, which seems even to be cherished, both Socrates and Plato unambiguously reject and condemn all taking of homosexual attraction to the point of intercourse and orgasm. . . .

Why were Socrates and Plato so strongly against physical homosexual relations? There is an obvious reason, which had nothing to do with homosexuality per se. Both Socrates and Plato were reflecting an important attitude of their society and class, namely a great respect for self-constraint and control. Emotions were seen as things which took control of one, and the man who could withstand them gained stature in his and his colleagues' eyes. . . .

For the mature Plato, therefore, control is essential. To read Plato's early and middle writings as providing a license for homosexual inclination and behavior is not to read them properly. Homosexual attraction is accepted and even venerated, but consummation is condemned. The man who lets his passions thus govern his reason is an object of pity. This, however, is not quite all that there is to Plato's treatment of homosexuality. Towards the end of his life he developed his ideas yet further, and indeed he arrived at a position by a line of argument that was profoundly to influence subsequent thinking on the matter of homosexuality. Simply and categorically Plato condemned homosexual behavior because it is "unnatural." It is not done by the animals. No more should it be done by us.

> Anyone who, in conformity with nature, proposes to re-establish the law as it was before Laios, declaring that it was right not to join with men and boys in sexual intercourse as with females, adducing as evidence the nature of animals and pointing out that [among them] male does not

touch male for sexual purposes, since that is not natural, he could, I think, make a very strong case. (Plato, *Laws*, 836c–e, trans. Dover 1978: 166)

The opposition to homosexual acts becomes absolute. . . .

THE JUDAEO/CHRISTIAN TRADITION

Let us turn now to Judaism and its breakaway offspring, Christianity. Here, on the surface at least, popular opinion does seem closer to the truth. The primary source of information about the positions of the Jews and the early Christians is obviously the Bible, Old and New Testaments. In the Old Testament, there are two main sources of information about the positions taken by God and his chosen people on the subject of homosexuality: the story of Sodom and Gomorrah, and various scattered dictates about homosexual practices. Both sources apparently tell the same tale: homosexual behavior is abhorrent in the eyes of the Lord and therefore morally barred to humankind. As it happens, the Sodom and Gomorrah story about the citizens of Sodom, who wanted to have homosexual intercourse with two of God's angels, has been the subject of much Biblical reinterpretation. Most pertinently, it has been argued that the homosexual theme of the Sodom and Gomorrah story is a later interpolation. But the "holiness Code" of Leviticus is unambiguous.

> Thou shalt not lie with mankind, as with womankind: it is abomination. (Leviticus xviii.22)

> If a man also lie with mankind, as he lieth with a woman, both of them have committed an abomination: they shall surely be put to death; their blood shall be upon them. (Leviticus xx.13)

In the New Testament, one likewise finds passages which categorically prohibit homosexual behavior. As is usual on matters of sex, it was not the founder himself who pronounced on these matters, but his chief proselytizer, Paul.

> the men, leaving the natural use of the woman, burned in their lust one toward another, men

> with men working unseemliness, and receiving in themselves that recompense of their error which was due. (Romans i.27)

> Be not deceived: neither fornicators, nor idolators, nor adulterers, nor effeminate, nor abusers of themselves with men, nor thieves, nor covetous, nor drunkards, nor revilers, nor extortioners, shall inherit the kingdom of God. (I Corinthians vi.9–10)

> law is not made for a righteous man, but for the lawless and unruly . . . for abusers of themselves with men . . . (I Timothy i.9–10)

Nor is lesbian behavior neglected.

> God gave them up unto vile passions: for their women changed the natural use into that which is against nature . . . (Romans i.26)

. . . The most detailed philosophical discussion of homosexuality by a Christian thinker is to be found in the writings of the thirteenth-century theologian St. Thomas Aquinas. Aquinas's treatment of homosexuality, as of most moral issues, depends crucially on the notion of "natural law." . . . Coming to sexuality, Aquinas (who was much influenced by Aristotle) did not ask the straightforward causal question, "How do things work?," but rather the teleological question, "What are things for? What end do they serve?" And the answer he gave is that sex exists for the procreation and raising of children. This is why God made us sexual beings, and this therefore is the end towards which we must strive if we are not to violate natural law, that area of the eternal law where we ourselves must make a contribution.

The consequence of Aquinas's position, as he thought, is that all sex outside marriage is wrong because it is a violation of natural law. Thus, quite apart from homosexuality's prohibition on Biblical grounds, for Aquinas it is necessarily barred as being against natural law: as being in conflict with "right reason." Homosexual encounters do not lead to children, therefore they must be wrong. But there is rather more than this. All lust is immoral, but some acts are doubly to be condemned, because "they are in conflict with the natural pattern of sexuality for the benefit of the species." These are termed 'unnatural vices' ("*vitiae contra naturum*"). . . .

MODERN ETHICAL PHILOSOPHIES

Let us turn now to the modern era, the time after the scientific revolution. There are two major, secular moral philosophies, those of the German thinker, Immanuel Kant, and of the (primarily) British utilitarians. Both groups thought their views threw light on the status of homosexual behavior (again, feelings get short shrift). Let us take them in turn.

Kant thought humans are subject to an overriding and necessary moral law, a supreme directive, the "categorical imperative." It is this law which tells us what we ought to do; wherein lies our duty. . . .

As Kant himself recognized, at a quite general level sex and the categorical imperative have a rather uneasy relationship. The starting point to sex is the sheer desire of a person for the body of another. . . . This gets dangerously close to treating the other as a means to the fulfillment of one's own sexual desire—as an object, rather than as an end. And this, according to the categorical imperative, is immoral. To escape from this dilemma, and one surely must if the end of the human race is not to be advocated on moral grounds, one must go on to treat the object of one's sexual advances as an end. One does this by broadening one's feelings, so that the personhood of the object of one's desire is brought within one's attraction, and by giving oneself reciprocally—by yielding oneself, body and soul, one shows respect for the other as an end, and not just as a means.

But what about a sincere commitment between two people of the same sex, the sort of homosexual equivalent of heterosexual marriage? At this point Kant invokes the notion of a *crimina carnis,* an abuse of one's sexuality. There are two kinds. First, there are acts which are contrary to sound reason, *crimina carnis secundum naturam.* These are immoral acts which go against the moral code imposed upon us as humans, and include such

things as adultery. Second, there are acts contrary to our animal nature, *crimina carnis contra naturam.* These include masturbation, sex with animals, and homosexuality. They are the lowest and most disgusting sort of vice, worse in a sense even than suicide, and they are practices that we hesitate to mention. . . .

> A second *crimen carnis contra naturam* is intercourse between *sexus homogenii,* in which the object of sexual impulse is a human being but there is homogeneity instead of heterogeneity of sex, as when a woman satisfies her desire on a woman, or a man on a man. This practice too is contrary to the ends of humanity; for the end of humanity in respect of sexuality is to preserve the species without debasing the person; but in this instance the species is not being preserved (as it can be by a *crimen carnis secundum naturam*), but the person is set aside, the self is degraded below the level of the animals, and humanity is dishonoured.[1]

Contrasting with Kantian ethics is that of the utilitarians, the most prominent of whom were Jeremy Bentham and the two Mills, James (father) and John Stuart (son). For them, the key to ethical theory is happiness: "The creed which accepts as the foundation of morals utility or the greatest happiness principle holds that actions are right in proportion as they tend to promote happiness; wrong as they tend to produce the reverse of happiness.". . . .

Bentham thinks homosexual interactions as acceptable morally as Kant finds them pernicious. Such interactions give pleasure to the people engaged in them, and so by the greatest happiness principle they ought to be valued. "As to any primary mischief, it is evident that [a homosexual interaction] produces no pain in anyone. On the contrary it produces pleasure. . . ." Bentham is not advocating homosexual behavior for everyone, only for those who want to so indulge. Then, there will be no harm. Nor is there any real problem stemming from the possibility that homosexual practices might incline or influence others into similar behavior. People who indulge homosexual appetites seem to enjoy themselves; so at most one is inclining others to enjoyable practices.

What of the claim that homosexual behavior runs one down physically, thus as it were reducing one's long-term pleasure in life? Bentham's conclusion is that there is no evidence to this effect. In any case, being in line with medical opinion of the time, and accepting that masturbation is physically debilitating, Bentham pointed out the injustice of trying to eliminate homosexuality through the law, when one did (and obviously could) do nothing about self-abuse. What of the claim that homosexuality is a threat to the keeping of population numbers up to an acceptable level? (Bentham had no doubts that a sizeable population is a good thing.) Again Bentham saw no danger on this score. Men's sexual appetites and capabilities far exceed those of females, particularly in the sense that a man can fertilize many more times than a fertilized female can give birth. . . .

IS HOMOSEXUAL BEHAVIOR BIOLOGICALLY UNNATURAL?

. . . Plato, who introduced the argument, has had the greatest influence on western thought about the worth of homosexuality. Plato stated categorically that homosexuality (the behavior at least) is wrong because it is unnatural—it is not something done by the animals. . . .

It is biology which is the strongest plank in the barrier against the permissibility of same-gender sex. But should *we* condemn homosexual behavior as immoral because it is unnatural, in the sense of being against biology? Should we say that animals do not behave homosexually; therefore humans should not behave homosexually? Is it true that genitals were "designed" for heterosexual ends and that all other uses are a wicked corruption? We must try to answer these questions for ourselves, and to this end a number of points must be raised.

First, it is simply not true, if by "unnatural" one means "not performed by animals" or even "not commonly performed by animals," that homosexuality is unnatural. We know that in species

after species, right through the animal kingdom, students of animal behavior report unambiguous evidence of homosexual attachments and behavior—in insects, fish, birds, and lower and higher mammals. . . . Whatever the moral implications of homosexuality and naturalness may be, it is false that homosexuality is immoral because it does not exist amongst animals. . . .

Even if it turns out that some kinds of sexual behavior have nothing to do with straight biology, even if it turns out that the homosexual is doing him/herself a biological disservice and perhaps even his/her race or species a similar disservice, this does not as such imply that anything sexual, including homosexual, is immoral. What moral obligation has the individual got to reproduce? What moral obligation has the individual got to help his/her species reproduce? It might be argued that any behavior which is so disruptive of society that society itself fails to reproduce is immoral. . . .

But, in reply, first of all it is obvious that homosexual activity today is not so disruptive of society as to prevent overall reproduction. Second, the moral importance of society's reproduction is not that obvious. We may have an obligation to future generations not so to pollute our planet that life for them becomes depressingly difficult, but do we have an obligation to produce future generations? . . .

My conclusions, therefore, are that once you strike out fallacious arguments about biological naturalness, and bring forward modern realizations of the possibilities for homosexuals of meaningful relationships, the Kantian and utilitarian positions come very much closer together. Certainly, at a minimum, there is moral worth in the close-coupled relationships of the Second Kinsey study, and probably more. . . .

SEXUAL PERVERSION

In theory, this should conclude our discussion at this point. Once you have strained out religious elements, once you have dropped outmoded scientific claims, once you have sorted through the proper relationship between "is" and "ought," once you have discovered a little bit about what homosexuals are really like rather than what you think they might be like, moral conclusions start to fall fairly readily into place. Yet there is something about homosexual activity—and, indeed, the whole overt homosexual life style—that other people find disturbing and threatening; something which drives people to conclude that, for all of the fancy arguments of the philosophers, homosexual activity is a wrong: a moral evil. (The feeling is particularly strong for males, by males—an asymmetry to which I shall return.)

What is it about homosexuality—what is it about male homosexuality in particular—that brings forth such negative judgements? One thing, above all else, comes across. Listen to the eminent theologian Karl Barth (1980):[2] "[Homosexuality] is the physical, psychological and social sickness, the phenomenon of perversion, decadence and decay, which can emerge when man refuses to admit the validity of the divine command in the sense in which we are now considering it" (p. 49). Forget about the sickness part of the complaint. God does not condemn the diabetic. What troubles Barth and his God—what troubles virtually all of those who hate homosexuality—is that they see it as a *perversion*. It is the epitome of wrongdoing, and therefore must be censored in the strongest possible way.

Obviously, from our perspective, we have seen a paradox. Homosexual behavior seems not very morally pernicious; yet, through the notion of perversion, this is precisely how it appears to many people—in our society, at least. How can we resolve it? Fortunately, some help is at hand, for the notion of perversion has been much discussed by analytic philosophers in recent years. Typical in many respects, certainly in that which ties in best with our previous discussion, is an analysis by Sara Ruddick. Trying to capture the concept, she turns to traditional arguments, claiming that what people have been arguing

about down through the ages is less a moral question and more one of perversity. She suggests that the natural end of sex is reproduction: that all and only acts which tend to lead to reproduction are natural, and that all unnatural acts are perverted.

> The ground for classifying sexual acts as either natural or unnatural is that the former type serve or could serve the evolutionary and biological function of sexuality—namely, reproduction. "Natural" sexual desire has as its "object" living persons of the opposite sex, and in particular their postpubertal genitals. The "aim" of natural sexual desire—that is, the act that "naturally" completes it—is genital intercourse. Perverse sex acts are deviations. . . . (p. 91)[3]

. . . Naturalness keeps coming up. Perhaps the time has come to make it work for us, rather than against us. And indeed, this is a reasonable move, for people like Ruddick are surely right in thinking naturalness important. . . . Yet a biological definition will not do. Perhaps the time has come to make a break. We are human beings: that means we live in a cultural realm, unlike animals who are fundamentally trapped down at the level of pure biology. What I argue, therefore, is that naturalness ought to be defined in terms of culture and not simple biology. What is unnatural, and what is consequently in some important sense perverse, is what goes against or breaks with our culture. It is what violates the ends or aims that human beings think are important or worth striving for. This may include reproduction, but extends to all the things we hold dear, the things that make us happy and make life worth living generally. And this is why perversity is indeed a value laden term, because a perversion puts itself against human norms and values. . . .

This is the key to perversions: what I like to call the "Ugh! factor." A perversion involves a breaking not of a moral rule, but more of an aesthetic rule. We find perversions disgusting, revolting. But why is this? I would suggest the following reason. A perversion involves going against one of culture's values or ends or things considered desirable, and other members of society cannot understand why one would want to go against the value. . . .

We have come back to the original Platonic position—but with crucial shifts. Unnaturalness is connected to culture, not biology. (As a Darwinian, though, I would never deny that the former comes from and is moulded by the latter. That is why many perversions do involve biologically unsavory acts—like eating feces.) And the values involved are not so much moral as aesthetic. So what about homosexuality? Are homosexual acts perverse acts, and is the inclination to such acts a perverse inclination? Acknowledging that I am trying to offer a descriptive rather than prescriptive analysis, I do not think there is any straightforward answer to these questions. But I look upon this as a strength of my analysis, not a weakness! I think the question of the perversity of homosexuality is to a great extent an empirical matter. How do people feel about homosexual behavior? Can they in some sense relate to it, whether or not they want to do it themselves and whether or not they have homosexual inclinations? . . . I suggest that for some people in our society homosexuality is not a perversion and for some it is. Some other societies

have seen homosexuality totally as a perversion. Some other societies have not seen it as a perversion at all.

What I am arguing, therefore, is that, faced with divided opinion in our society about the perverted nature of homosexuality (inclination and behavior), neither side is absolutely right and neither side is absolutely wrong. There is a crucial element of subjectivity at work here, as with liking or disliking spinach. Perversion, especially as it applies to homosexuality, is a relative concept. . . . If one agrees that homosexuality is not immoral, then surely one ought to persuade people not to regard homosexuals and their habits with loathing. Certainly, one ought to persuade people not to confuse their disgust at a perversion with moral indignation. . . .

NOTES

1. Immanuel Kant, *Lectures on Ethics,* trans. L. Infield (New York: Harper & Row, 1963), p. 170.
2. Karl Barth, "Church Dogmatics." In E. Batchelor (ed.), *Homosexuality and Ethics* (New York: Pilgrim, 1980), pp. 48–51.
3. Sara Ruddick, "Better Sex." In R. Baker and F. Elliston (eds.), *Philosophy and Sex* (Buffalo: Prometheus, 1975), pp. 83–104.

Discussion Questions

1. Does Ruse adequately respond to the argument that homosexuality is a disease? Does his concept of perversion allow for "healthy" perversions? Support your answers.
2. What stereotypes come to mind when you hear the terms *gay man, lesbian,* and *bisexual*? (These stereotypes do not have to be ones that you accept; this is just a brainstorming exercise.) Are these stereotypes based on fact? Discuss how these stereotypes affect your perception of gay, lesbian, and bisexual people, and how these stereotypes affect how people who are gay, lesbian, or bisexual feel about themselves. Discuss how these stereotypes limit the opportunities of people who are gay, lesbian, or bisexual.
3. Discuss Ruse's statement that if we cannot back up our negative feelings about homosexuality with rational arguments, we have a moral obligation to work on changing those feelings.

4. Discuss how the authors of the Vatican's "Declaration of Sexual Ethics" would most likely respond to Ruse's arguments regarding the morality of homosexuality. Which arguments do you find the most morally persuasive and why?

MARGARET H. MARSHALL AND ROBERT J. CORDY

Goodridge v. Department of Public Health (2003)

Goodridge v. Department of Public Health was a landmark state appellate court case that legalized same-sex marriage in Massachusetts, the first state to do so in the United States. Chief Justice Margaret H. Marshall presents the majority opinion in support of the ruling; Justice Robert J. Cordy presents the dissenting opinion.

Critical Reading Questions

1. According to Marshall, why is denying same-sex couples the right to marriage incompatible with the principles of respect for autonomy and equality under the law?
2. On what grounds does Marshall claim that denying the right to marry between whites and blacks is similar to denying the right to marry between same-sex couples?
3. What does Marshall mean when she says that the laws of civil marriage do not privilege procreative heterosexual intercourse between married people?
4. Why does Marshall reject the argument that same-sex marriage should not be legalized because heterosexual marriage is the optimal setting for raising children?
5. How does Marshall respond to the claim that legalizing same-sex marriage will undermine the institution of marriage?
6. On what grounds does Cordy argue that limiting marriage to one man and one woman does not violate any fundamental rights?
7. According to Cordy, why does the court's decision to legalize same-sex marriage violate the separation-of-powers principle?
8. Why is it important to Cordy that our definition of marriage be deeply rooted in our nation's history and tradition?
9. What is the "rational basis standard" and why, according to Cordy, does a law that permits only marriage between a man and a woman satisfy this standard?
10. According to Cordy, why is traditional marriage the optimal social structure in which to bear and raise children and why would same-sex marriage undermine this important function of marriage?

Goodridge et al. v. Department of Public Health et al. 440 Mass. 309 (2003). Notes have been omitted.

CHIEF JUSTICE MARGARET H. MARSHALL, MAJORITY OPINION

Marriage is a vital social institution. The exclusive commitment of two individuals to each other nurtures love and mutual support, it brings stability to our society. For those who choose to marry, and for their children, marriage provides an abundance of legal, financial, and social benefits. In return it imposes weighty legal, financial, and social obligations. The question before us is whether, consistent with the Massachusetts Constitution, the Commonwealth may deny the protections, benefits, and obligations conferred by civil marriage to two individuals of the same sex who wish to marry. We conclude that it may not. The Massachusetts Constitution affirms the dignity and equality of all individuals. It forbids the creation of second-class citizens. In reaching our conclusion we have given full deference to the arguments made by the Commonwealth. But it has failed to identify any constitutionally adequate reason for denying civil marriage to same-sex couples. . . .

[T]he Court affirmed that the core concept of common human dignity protected by the Fourteenth Amendment to the United States Constitution precludes government intrusion into the deeply personal realms of consensual adult expressions of intimacy and one's choice of an intimate partner. The Court also reaffirmed the central role that decisions whether to marry or have children bear in shaping one's identify. . . .

Barred access to the protections, benefits, and obligations of civil marriage, a person who enters into an intimate, exclusive union with another of the same sex is arbitrarily deprived of membership in one of our community's most rewarding and cherished institutions. That exclusion is incompatible with the constitutional principles of respect for individual autonomy and equality under law. . . .

A

The larger question is whether, as the department claims, government action that bars same-sex couples from civil marriage constitutes a legitimate exercise of the State's authority to regulate conduct. . . .

We begin by considering the nature of civil marriage itself. Simply put, the government creates civil marriage. In Massachusetts, civil marriage is, and since pre-Colonial days has been, precisely what its name implies: a wholly secular institution. . . . No religious ceremony has ever been required to validate a Massachusetts marriage. . . .

Without question, civil marriage enhances the "welfare of the community." It is a "social institution of the highest importance." Civil marriage anchors an ordered society by encouraging stable relationships over transient ones. It is central to the way the Commonwealth identifies individuals, provides for the orderly distribution of property, ensures that children and adults are cared for and supported whenever possible from private rather than public funds, and tracks important epidemiological and demographic data.

Marriage also bestows enormous private and social advantages on those who choose to marry. Civil marriage is at once a deeply personal commitment to another human being and a highly public celebration of the ideals of mutuality, companionship, intimacy, fidelity, and family. . . . Because it fulfils yearnings for security, safe haven, and connection that express our common humanity, civil marriage is an esteemed institution, and the decision whether and whom to marry is among life's momentous acts of self-definition. . . .

The benefits accessible only by way of a marriage license are enormous, touching nearly every aspect of life and death. The department states that "hundreds of statutes" are related to marriage and to marital benefits. . . .

Exclusive marital benefits that are not directly tied to property rights include the presumptions of legitimacy and parentage of children born to a married couple . . . and evidentiary rights, such as the prohibition against spouses testifying against one another about their private conversations, applicable in both civil and criminal cases. . . . Other statutory benefits of a personal nature available only to married individuals include qualification for bereavement or medical leave to care for individuals related by blood or marriage . . . an automatic "family member" preference to make medical decisions for an incompetent or disabled spouse who does not have a contrary health care proxy . . . the application of predictable rules of child custody, visitation, support, and removal out-of-State when married parents divorce. . . .

. . . Notwithstanding the Commonwealth's strong public policy to abolish legal distinctions between marital and nonmarital children in providing for the support and care of minors, . . . the fact remains that marital children reap a measure of family stability and economic security based on their parents' legally privileged status that is largely inaccessible, or not as readily accessible, to nonmarital children.

It is undoubtedly for these concrete reasons, as well as for its intimately personal significance, that civil marriage has long been termed a "civil right." See, e.g., *Loving v. Virginia*. . . . ("Marriage is one of the 'basic civil rights of man,' fundamental to our very existence and survival"), *Skinner v. Oklahoma* . . . (1942). . . . The United States Supreme Court has described the right to marry as "of fundamental importance for all individuals" and as "part of the fundamental 'right of privacy' implicit in the Fourteenth Amendment's Due Process Clause." *Zablocki v. Redhail* . . . (1978). . . .

Without the right to marry—or more properly, the right to choose to marry—one is excluded from the full range of human experience and denied full protection of the laws for one's "avowed commitment to an intimate and lasting human relationship.". . . Because civil marriage is central to the lives of individuals and the welfare of the community, our laws assiduously protect the individual's right to marry against undue governmment incursion. Laws may not "interfere directly and substantially with the right to marry.". . .

B

For decades, indeed centuries, in much of this country (including Massachusetts) no lawful marriage was possible between white and black Americans. That long history availed not when the Supreme Court of California held in 1948 that a legislative prohibition against interracial marriage violated the due process and equality guarantees of the Fourteenth Amendment, *Perez v. Sharp* . . . (1948), or when, nineteen years later, the United States Supreme Court also held that a . . . statutory bar to interracial marriage violated the Fourteenth amendment, *Loving v. Virginia* . . . (1967). As both *Perez* and *Loving* make clear, the right to marry means little if it does not include the right to marry the person of one's choice, subject to appropriate government restrictions in the interests of public health, safety, and welfare. . . .

The individual liberty and equality safeguards of the Massachusetts Constitution protect both "freedom from" unwarranted government instrusion into protected spheres of life and "freedom to" partake in benefits created by the State for the common good. . . . Both freedoms are involved here. Whether and whom to marry, how to express sexual intimacy, and whether and how to establish a family—these are among the most basic of every individual's liberty and due process rights. . . . And central to personal freedom and security is the assurance that the laws will apply equally to persons in similar situations. "Absolute equality before the law is a fundamental principle of our own Constitution.". . .

The department [of Public Health] posits three legislative rationales for prohibiting same-sex couples from marrying: (1) providing a "favorable setting for procreation"; (2) ensuring the optimal setting for child rearing, which the department defines as "a two-parent family with one parent of each sex"; and (3) preserving scarce State and private financial resources. We consider each in turn.

The judge in the Superior Court endorsed the first rationale, holding that "the state's interest in regulating marriage is based on the traditional concept that marriage's primary purpose is procreation." This is incorrect. Our laws of civil marriage do not privilege procreative heterosexual intercourse between married people above every other form of adult intimacy and every other means of creating family. General Laws c. 207 contains no requirement that the applicants for a marriage license attest to their ability or intention to conceive children by coitus. . . . While it is certainly true that many, perhaps most, married couples have children together (assisted or unassisted), it is the exclusive and permanent commitment of the marriage partners to one another, not the begetting of children, that is the sine qua non of civil marriage.

Moreover, the Commonwealth affirmatively facilitates bringing children into a family regardless of whether the parent is married or unmarried, whether the child is adopted or born into a family, whether assistive technology was used to conceive the child, and whether the parent or her partner is heterosexual, homosexual, or bisexual. If procreation were a necessary component of civil marriage, our statutes would draw a tighter circle around the permissible bounds of nonmarital child bearing and the creation of families by noncoital means. . . .

The department's first stated rationale, equating marriage with unassisted heterosexual procreation, shades imperceptibly into its second: that confining marriage to opposite-sex couples ensures that children are raised in the "optimal" setting. Protecting the welfare of children is a paramount State policy. Restricting marriage to opposite-sex couples, however, cannot plausibly further this policy. . . . Massachusetts has responded supportively to "the changing realities of the American family," and has moved vigorously to strengthen the modern family in its many variations. Moreover, we have repudiated the common-law power of the State to provide varying levels of protection to children based on the circumstances of birth. . . . The "best interests of the child" standard does not turn on a parent's sexual orientation or martial status. . . .

The department has offered no evidence that forbidding marriage to people of the same sex will increase the number of couples choosing to enter into opposite-sex marriages in order to have and raise children. There is thus no rational relationship between the marriage statute and the Commonwealth's proffered goal of protecting the "optimal" child rearing unit. Moreover,

the department readily concedes that people in same-sex couples may be "excellent" parents. These couples (including four of the plaintiff couples) have children for the reasons others do—to love them, to care for them, to nurture them. But the task of child rearing for same-sex couples is made infinitely harder by their status as outliers to the marriage laws. While establishing the parentage of children as soon as possible is crucial to the safety and welfare of children, . . . same-sex couples must undergo the sometimes lengthy and intrusive process of second-parent adoption to establish their joint parentage. . . . While the laws of divorce provide clear and reasonably predictable guidelines for child support, child custody, and property division on dissolution of a marriage, same-sex couples who dissolve their relationships find themselves and their children in the highly unpredictable terrain of equity jurisdiction. . . . Excluding same-sex couples from civil marriage will not make children of opposite-sex marriages more secure, but it does prevent children of same-sex couples from enjoying the immeasurable advantages that flow from the assurance of "a stable family structure in which children will be reared, educated, and socialized.". . .

In this case, we are confronted with an entire, sizeable class of parents raising children who have absolutely no access to civil marriage and its protections because they are forbidden from procuring a marriage license. It cannot be rational under our laws, and indeed it is not permitted, to penalize children by depriving them of State benefits because the State disapproves of their parents' sexual orientation. . . .

The department suggests additional rationales for prohibiting same-sex couples from marrying, which are developed by some amici. It argues that broadening civil marriage to include same-sex couples will trivialize or destroy the institution of marriage as it has historically been fashioned. Certainly our decision today marks a significant change in the definition of marriage as it has been inherited from the common law, and understood by many societies for centuries. But it does not disturb the fundamental value of marriage in our society.

Here, the plaintiffs seek only to be married, not to undermine the institution of civil marriage. They do not want marriage abolished. They do not attack the binary nature of marriage, the consanguinity provisions, or any of the other gatekeeping provisions of the marriage licensing law. Recognizing the right of an individual to marry a person of the same sex will not diminish the validity or dignity of opposite-sex marriage, any more than recognizing the right of an individual to marry a person of a different race devalues the marriage of a person who marries someone of her own race. If anything, extending civil marriage to same-sex couples reinforces the importance of marriage to individuals and communities. . . .

. . . Alarms about the imminent erosion of the "natural" order of marriage were sounded over the demise of antimiscegenation laws, the expansion of the rights of married women, and the introduction of "no-fault" divorce. Marriage has survived all of these transformations, and we have no doubt that marriage will continue to be a vibrant and revered institution. . . .

The marriage ban works a deep and scarring hardship on a very real segment of the community for no rational reason. The absence of any reasonable relationship between, on the one hand, an absolute disqualification of same-sex couples who wish to enter into civil marriage and, on the other, protection of public health, safety, or general welfare, suggests that the marriage restriction is rooted in persistent prejudices against persons who are (or who are believed to be) homosexual. "The Constitution cannot control such prejudices but neither can it tolerate them. Private biases may be outside the reach of the law, but the law cannot, directly or indirectly, give them effect." *Palmore v. Sidot* . . . (1984). . . . Limiting the protections, benefits, and obligations of civil marriage to opposite-sex couples violates the basic premises of individual liberty and equality under law protected by the Massachusetts Constitution. . . .

So ordered.

JUSTICE ROBERT J. CORDY, DISSENTING OPINION

The court's opinion concludes that the Department of Public Health has failed to identify any "constitutionally adequate reason" for limiting civil marriage to opposite-sex unions, and that there is no "reasonable relationship" between a disqualification of same-sex couples who wish to enter into a civil marriage and the protection of public health, safety, or general welfare. Consequently, it holds that the marriage statute cannot withstand scrutiny under the Massachusetts Constitution. . . . I find these conclusions to be unsupportable in light of the nature of the rights and regulations at issue. . . .

A

Limiting marriage to the union of one man and one woman does not impair the exercise of a fundamental right. Civil marriage is an institution created by the State. . . . [The marriage statutes] were enacted to secure public interests and not for religious purposes or to promote personal interests or aspirations. As the court notes in its opinion, the institution of marriage is "the legal union of a man and woman as husband and wife," *ante* at, and it has always been so under Massachusetts law, colonial or otherwise.

The plaintiffs contend that because the right to choose to marry is a "fundamental" right, the right to marry the person of one's choice, including a member of the same sex, must also be a "fundamental" right. . . . Hence, it concludes that a marriage license cannot be denied to an individual who wishes to marry someone of the same sex. In reaching this result the court has transmuted the "right" to marry into a right to change the institution of marriage itself. This feat of reasoning succeeds only if one accepts the proposition that the definition of the institution of marriage as a union between a man and a woman is merely "conclusory". . . rather than the basis on which the "right" to partake in it has been deemed to be of fundamental importance. In other words, only by assuming that "marriage" includes the union of two persons of the same sex does the court conclude that restricting marriage to opposite-sex couples infringes on the "right" of same-sex couples to "marry.". . .

Supreme Court cases that have described marriage or the right to marry as "fundamental" have focused primarily on the underlying interest of every individual in procreation, which, historically, could only legally occur within the construct of marriage because sexual intercourse outside of marriage was a criminal act. . . .

Supreme Court cases recognizing a right to privacy in intimate decision-making . . . have also focused primarily on sexual relations and the decision whether or not to procreate, and have refused to recognize an "unlimited right" to privacy. . . .

What the *Griswold* Court found "repulsive to the notions of privacy surrounding the marriage relationship" was the prospect of "allow[ing] the police to search the sacred precincts of marital bedrooms for telltale signs of the use of contraceptives.". . .

Although some of the privacy cases also speak in terms of personal autonomy, no court has ever recognized such an open-ended right. "That many of the rights and liberties protected by the Due Process Clause sound in personal autonomy does not warrant the sweeping conclusion that any and all important, intimate, and personal decisions are so protected. . . ." *Washington v. Glucksberg*. . . (1997). Such decisions are protected not because they are important, intimate, and personal, but because the right or liberty at stake is "so deeply rooted in our history and traditions, or so fundamental to our concept of constitutionally ordered liberty" that it is protected by due process. . . .

While the institution of marriage is deeply rooted in the history and traditions of our country and our State, the right to marry someone of the same sex is not. No matter how personal or intimate a decision to marry someone of the same sex might be, the right to make it is not guaranteed by the right of personal autonomy.

The protected right to freedom of association, in the sense of freedom of choice "to enter into and maintain certain intimate human relationships," is similarly limited and unimpaired by the marriage statute. As recognized by the Supreme Court, that right affords protection only to "certain kinds of highly personal relationships," such as those between husband and wife, parent and child, and among close relatives that "have played a critical role in the culture and traditions of the Nation," and are "deeply rooted in this Nation's history and tradition." *Moore v. East Cleveland* (1977). . . . Unlike opposite-sex marriages . . . same-sex relationships, although becoming more accepted, are certainly not so "deeply rooted in this Nation's history and tradition" as to warrant such enhanced constitutional protection. . . .

Finally, the constitutionally protected interest in child rearing . . . is not implicated or infringed by the marriage statute here. The fact that the plaintiffs cannot marry has no bearing on their independently protected constitutional rights as parents which, as with opposite-sex parents, are limited only by their continued fitness and the best interests of the children. . . .

Because the rights and interests discussed above do not afford the plaintiffs any fundamental right that would be impaired by a statute limiting marriage to members of the opposite sex, they have no fundamental right to be declared "married" by the State.

Insofar as the right to marry someone of the same sex is neither found in the unique historical context of our Constitution nor compelled by the meaning ascribed by this court to the liberty and due process protections contained within it, should the court nevertheless recognize it as a fundamental right? The consequences of deeming a right to be "fundamental" are profound, and this court, as well as the Supreme Court, has been very cautious in recognizing them. Such caution is required by separation of powers principles. If a right is found to be "fundatmental," it is, to a great extent, removed from "the arena of public debate and legislative action". . . .

"[T]o rein in" the otherwise potentially unlimited scope of substantive due process right, both Federal and Massachusetts courts have recognized as "fundamental" only those "rights and liberties which are, objectively, 'deeply rooted in this Nation's *history* and tradition,' [*Moore v. East Cleveland*], . . . and 'implicit in the concept of ordered liberty.'" *Palko v. Connecticut*, . . . (1937). . . . In the area of family-related rights in particular, the Supreme Court has emphasized that the "Constitution protects the sanctity of the family precisely because the institution of the family is deeply rooted." *Moore v. East Cleveland.* . . .

Given this history and the current state of public opinion, as reflected in the actions of the people's elected representative, it cannot be said that "a right to same-sex marriage is so rooted in the traditions and collective conscience of our people that failure to recognize it would violate the fundamental principles of liberty and justice that lie at the base of all our civil and political institutions. Neither . . . [is] a right to same-sex marriage . . . implicit in the concept of ordered liberty, such that neither liberty nor justice would exist if it were sacrificed." . . . In such circumstances, the law with respect to same-sex marriages must be left to develop through legislative processes, subject to the constraints of rationality, lest the court be viewed as using the liberty and due process clauses as vehicles merely to enforce its own views regarding better social policies, a role that . . . our Constitution forbids, and for which the court is particularly ill suited.

B

The marriage statute, in limiting marriage to heterosexual couples, does not constitute discrimination on the basis of sex in violation of the Equal Rights Amendment to the Massachusetts Constitution. . . .

The central purpose of the ERA was to eradicate discrimination against women and in favor of men or vice versa. . . . Consistent with this purpose, we have constructed the ERA to prohibit laws that advantage one sex at the expense of the other, but not laws that treat men and women equally. . . . The Massachusetts marriage statute does not subject men to different treatment from women; each is equally prohibited from precisely the same conduct. . . .

"An equal rights amendment will have no effect upon the allowance or denial of homosexual marriages. The equal rights amendment is not concerned with the relationship of two persons of the same sex; it only addresses those laws or public-related actions which treat persons of opposite sexes differently." . . .

C

The marriage statute satisfies the rational basis standard. . . . "The Legislature is not required to justify its classifications, nor provide a record or finding in support of them.". . .

"[I]t is not the court's function to launch an inquiry to resolve a debate which has already been settled in the legislative forum. '[I]t [is] the judge's duty . . . to give effect to the will of the people as expressed in the statue by their representative body. It is in this way. . . . that the doctrine of separation of powers is given meaning.' *Commonwealth v. Leis* . . . (1969). . . .

"This respect for the legislative process means that it is not the province of the court to sit and weigh conflicting evidence supporting or opposing a legislative enactment." . . .

The "time tested wisdom of the separation of powers" requires courts to avoid "judicial legislation in the guise of new constructions to meet real or supposed new popular viewpoints, preserving always to the legislature alone its proper prerogative of adjusting the statues to changed conditions." . . .

1. Classification

The nature of the classification at issue is readily apparent. Opposite-sex couples can obtain a license and same-sex couples cannot. The granting of this license, and the completion of the required solemnization of the marriage, opens the door to many statutory benefits and imposes numerous responsibilities. The fact that the statute does not permit such licenses to be issued to couples of the same sex thus bars them from civil marriage. The classification is not drawn between men and women or between heterosexuals and homosexuals, any of whom can obtain a licence to marry a member of the opposite sex; rather, it is drawn between same-sex couples and opposite-sex couples.

2. State Purpose

Civil marriage is the institutional mechanism by which societies have sanctioned and recognized particular family structures, and the institution of marriage has existed as one of the fundamental organizing principles of human society. . . . Marriage has not been merely a contractual arrangement for legally defining the private relationship between two individuals (although that is certainly part of any marriage). Rather, on an institutional level, marriage is the "very basis of the whole fabric of civilized society,". . . and it serves many important political, economic, social, educational, procreational, and personal functions.

. . . [A]n orderly society requires some mechanism for coping with the fact that sexual intercourse commonly results in pregnancy and childbirth. The institution of marriage is that mechanism.

The institution of marriage provides the important legal and normative link between heterosexual intercourse and procreation on the one hand and family responsibilities on the other. The partners in a marriage are expected to engage in exclusive sexual relations, with children the probable result and paternity presumed. . . . Whereas the relationship between mother and child is demonstratively and predictably created and recognizable through the biological process of pregnancy and childbirth, there is no corresponding process for creating a relationship between father and child. Similarly, aside from an act of heterosexual intercourse nine months prior to childbirth, there is no process for creating a relationship between a man and a women as the parents of a particular child.

The institution of marriage fills this void by formally binding the husband-father to his wife and child, and imposing on him the responsibilities of fatherhood. . . . The alternative, a society without the institution of marriage, in which heterosexual intercourse, procreation, and child care are largely disconnected processes, would be chaotic.

The marital family is also the foremost setting for the education and socialization of children. Children learn about the world and their place in it primarily from those who raise them, and those children eventually grow up to exert some influence, great or small, positive and negative, on society. The institution of marriage encourages parents to remain committed to each other and to their children as they grow, thereby encouraging a stable venue for the education and socialization of children. . . .

This court, among others, has consistently acknowledged both the institutional importance of marriage as an organizing principle of society, and the State's interest in regulating it. . . .

It is undeniably true that dramatic historical shifts in our cultural, political, and economic landscape have altered some of our traditional notions about marriage, including the interpersonal dynamics within it, the range of responsibilities required of it as an institution, and the legal environment in which it exists. Nevertheless, the institution of marriage remains the principal weave of our social fabric. . . .

It is difficult to imagine a State purpose more important and legitimate than ensuring, promoting, and supporting an optimal social structure within which to bear and raise children. At the very least, the marriage statute continues to serve this important State purpose.

3. Rational Relationship

The question we must turn to next is whether the statute, construed as limiting marriage to couples of the opposite sex, remains a rational way to further that purpose. Stated differently, we ask whether a conceivable rational basis exists on which the Legislature could conclude that continuing to limit the institution of civil marriage to members of the opposite sex furthers the legitimate purpose of ensuring, promoting, and supporting an optimal social structure for the bearing and raising of children.

In considering whether such a rational basis exists, we defer to the decision-making process of the Legislature, and must make deferential assumptions about the information that it might consider and on which it may rely. . . .

We must assume that the Legislature (1) might conclude that the institution of civil marriage has successfully and continually provided this structure over several centuries; (2) might consider and credit studies that document negative consequences that too often follow children either born outside of marriage or raised in households lacking either a father or a mother figure, and scholarly commentary contending that children and families develop best when mothers and fathers are partners in their parenting; and (3) would be familiar with many recent studies that variously support the proposition that children raised in intact families headed by same-sex couples fare as well on many measures as children raised in similar families headed by opposite-sex couples, support the proposition that children of same-sex couples fare worse on some measures, or reveal notable differences between the two groups of children that warrant further study.

Taking all of this available information into account, the Legislature could rationally conclude that a family environment with married opposite-sex parents remains the optimal social structure in which to bear children. . . .

The fact that the Commonwealth currently allows same-sex couples to adopt . . . does not affect the rationality of this conclusion. The eligibility of a child for adoption presupposes that at least one of the child's biological parents is unable or unwilling, for some reason, to participate in raising the child. In that sense, society has "lost" the optimal setting in which to raise that child—it is simply not available. In these circumstances, the principal and overriding consideration is the "best interests of child," considering his or her unique circumstances and the options that are available for that child. . . .

There is no question that many same-sex couples are capable of being good parents, and should be (and are) permitted to be so. The policy question that a legislator must resolve is a different one, and turns on an assessment of whether the marriage structure proposed by the plaintiffs will, over time, if endorsed and supported by the State, prove to be as stable and successful a model as the one that has formed a cornerstone of our society since colonial times, or prove to be less than optimal, and result in consequences, perhaps now unforeseen, adverse to the State's legitimate interest in promoting and supporting the best possible social structure in which children should be born and raised. Given the critical importance of civil marriage as an organizing and stabilizing institution of society, it is eminently rational for the Legislature to postpone making fundamental changes to it until such time as there is unanimous scientific evidence, or popular consensus, or both, that such changes can safely be made. . . .

D. CONCLUSION

While "[t]he Massachusetts Constitution protects matters of personal liberty against government incursion as zealously, and often more so, than does the Federal Constitution," this case is not about government intrusions into matters of personal liberty. It is not about the rights of same-sex couples to choose to live together, or to be intimate with each other, or to adopt and raise children together. It is about whether the State must endorse and support their choices by changing the institution of civil marriage to make its benefits, obligations, and responsibilities applicable to them. While the courageous efforts of many have resulted in increased dignity, rights, and respect for gay and lesbian members of our community, the issue presented here is a profound one, deeply rooted in social policy, that must, for now, be the subject of legislative not judicial action.

Discussion Questions

1. What fundamental rights, according to Chief Justice Marshall, are being violated by denying marriage to same-sex couples? On what ground does Justice Cordy argue that these rights are not fundamental rights? Which person makes the better argument and why? Discuss what criteria should be used in determining whether a right is fundamental and, as Cordy puts it, not up for public debate.
2. Evaluate the analogy with interracial marriage that Marshall uses in support of same-sex marriage. Why does Cordy reject it?
3. The Massachusetts courts rejected civil unions on the grounds that civil unions, like the separate-but-equal laws of the segregation era, create an "unconstitutional, inferior, and discriminatory status for same-sex couples." Discuss the court's argument.
4. Discuss the claim that legalizing same-sex marriage will erode traditional marriage. Support your answer using evidence from countries that have legalized same-sex marriage.

RICHARD WASSERSTROM

Is Adultery Immoral?

Richard Wasserstrom is professor emeritus of philosophy at the University of California at Santa Cruz. Wasserstrom argues that although sexual exclusivity is not a necessary condition of marriage, adultery in general is wrong because it involves deception.

Critical Reading Questions

1. What does Wasserstrom mean when he says that deception is prima facie wrong?
2. How does Wasserstrom define adultery?
3. What are the two arguments against adultery, and what is their basis?
4. In what ways might adultery be harmful to the nonparticipating spouse?
5. What is the distinction between active and passive deception?
6. What is the connection between sexual intimacy and the immorality of adultery?
7. What is Wasserstrom's position on the restriction of sexual intimacy to marriage?
8. What are the two positions put forth by advocates of sexual liberation regarding the relationship between sex and love, and what is Wasserstrom's view of these positions?
9. What is an "open marriage"? Is adultery morally permissible in an open marriage?
10. How does Wasserstrom respond to the claim that "sexual exclusivity is a necessary but not a sufficient condition for the existence of a marriage"?
11. How does Wasserstrom respond to the argument that "a prohibition on extramarital affairs helps maintain the institutions of marriage and the nuclear family"?

This article is reprinted from Richard Wasserstrom, ed., *Today's Moral Problems* (New York: Macmillan Co., 1975), with the permission of the author.

. . . Much, if not all, of the recent philosophical literature on the enforcement of morals appears to take for granted the immorality of the sexual behavior in question. . . . I shall consider just one kind of behavior that is often taken to be a case of sexual immorality—adultery. . . .

Before I turn to the arguments themselves, there are two preliminary points that require some clarification. Throughout the paper I shall refer to the immorality of such things as breaking a promise, deceiving someone, and so on. In a very rough way I mean by this that there is something morally wrong in doing the action in question. I mean that the action is, in a strong sense of "prima facie," prima facie wrong or unjustified. I do not mean that it may never be right or justifiable to do the action—just that the fact that it is an action of this description always counts against the rightness of the action. . . .

The second preliminary point concerns what is meant or implied by the concept of adultery. I mean by "adultery" any case of extramarital sex, and I want to explore the arguments for and against extramarital sex, undertaken in a variety of morally relevant situations.

One argument for the immorality of adultery might go something like this: What makes adultery immoral is that it involves the breaking of a promise, and what makes adultery seriously wrong is that it involves the breaking of an important promise. For, so the argument might continue, one of the things the two parties promise each other when they get married is that they will abstain from sexual relationships with third parties. Because of this promise both spouses quite reasonably entertain the expectation that the other will behave in conformity with it. Hence, when one of them has sexual intercourse with a third party, he or she breaks that promise about sexual relationships that was made when the marriage was entered into and defeats the reasonable expectations of exclusivity entertained by the spouse.

In many cases the immorality involved in breaching the promise relating to extramarital sex may be a good deal more serious than that involved in the breach of other promises. This is so because adherence to this promise may be of much greater importance to them than is adherence to many of the other promises given or received by them in their lifetime. The breaking of this promise may be much more hurtful and painful than is typically the case.

Why is this so? To begin with, it may have been difficult for the nonadulterous spouse to have kept the promise. Hence that spouse may feel the unfairness of having restrained himself or herself in the absence of reciprocal restraint having been exercised by the adulterous spouse. In addition, the spouse may perceive the breaking of the promise as an indication of a kind of indifference on the part of the adulterous spouse. If you really cared about me and my feelings, the spouse might say, you would not have done this to me. And third, and related to the above, the spouse may see the act of sexual intercourse with another as a sign of affection for the other person and as an additional rejection of the nonadulterous spouse as the one who is loved by the adulterous spouse. It is not just that the adulterous spouse does not take the feelings of the nonadulterous spouse sufficiently into account; the adulterous spouse also indicates through the act of adultery affection for someone other than the nonadulterous spouse. I will return to these points later. For the present it is sufficient to note that a set of arguments can be developed in support of the proposition that certain kinds of adultery are wrong just because they involve the breach of a serious promise that, among other things, leads to the intentional infliction of substantial pain on one spouse by the other.

Another argument for the immorality of adultery focuses not on the existence of a promise of sexual exclusivity but on the connection between adultery and deception. According to this argument adultery involves deception. And because deception is wrong, so is adultery.

Although it is certainly not obviously so, I shall simply assume in this essay that deception is always immoral. Thus, the crucial issue for my purposes is the asserted connection between extramarital sex and deception. Is it plausible to maintain, as this argument does, that adultery always involves deception and is, on that basis, to be condemned?

The most obvious person upon whom deceptions might be practiced is the nonparticipating spouse; and the most obvious thing about which the nonparticipating spouse can be deceived is the existence of the adulterous act. One clear case of deception is that of lying. Instead of saying that the afternoon was spent in bed with A, the adulterous spouse asserts that it was spent in the library with B or on the golf course with C.

There can also be deception even when no lies are told. Suppose, for instance, that a person has sexual intercourse with someone other than his or her spouse and just does not tell the spouse about it. Is that deception? It may not be a case of lying if, for example, he or she is never asked by the spouse about the situation. Still, we might say, it is surely deceptive because of the promises that were exchanged at marriage. As we saw earlier, these promises provide a foundation for the reasonable belief that neither spouse will engage in sexual relationships with any other person. Hence the failure to bring the fact of extramarital sex to the attention of the other spouse deceives that spouse about the present state of the marital relationship.

Adultery, in other words, can involve both active and passive deception. An adulterous spouse may just keep silent or, as is often the case, the spouse may engage in an increasingly complex way of life devoted to the concealment of the facts from the nonparticipating spouse. . . . Still, neither active nor passive deception is inevitably a feature of an extramarital relationship.

It is possible, though, that a more subtle but pervasive kind of deceptiveness is a feature of adultery. It comes about because of the connection in our culture between sexual intimacy and certain feelings of love and affection. . . . I may, for instance, be willing to reveal my very private thoughts and emotions to my closest friends or to my wife but to no one else. My sharing of these intimate facts about myself is, from one perspective, a way of making a gift to those who mean the most to me. Revealing these things and sharing them with those who mean the most to me is one means by which I create, maintain, and confirm those interpersonal relationships that are of most importance to me.

In our culture, it might be claimed, sexual intimacy is one of the chief currencies through which gifts of this sort are exchanged. One way to tell someone—particularly someone of the opposite sex—that you have feelings of affection and love for them is by allowing them, or sharing with them, sexual behaviors that one does not share with others. This way of measuring affection was certainly very much a part of the culture in which I matured. It worked something like this: If you were a girl, you showed how much you liked a boy by the degree of sexual intimacy you would allow. If you liked him only a little you never did more than kiss—and even the kiss was not very passionate. If you liked him a lot and if your feeling was reciprocated, necking and, possibly, petting were permissible. If the attachment was still stronger and you thought it might even become a permanent relationship, the sexual activity was correspondingly more intense and intimate, although whether it led to sexual intercourse depended on whether the parties (particularly the girl) accepted fully the prohibition on nonmarital sex. The situation for the boys was related but not exactly the same. The assumption was that males did not naturally link sex with affection in the way in which females did. However, since women did link sex with affection, males had to take that fact into account. That is to say, because a woman would permit sexual intimacies only if she had feelings of affection for the male and only if those feelings were reciprocated, the male had to have and express those feelings too, before sexual intimacies of any sort would occur. . . .

. . . If, for example, sexual intercourse is associated with the kind of affection and commitment to another that is regarded as characteristic of the marriage relationship, then it is natural that sexual intercourse should be thought properly to take place between persons who are married to each other. And if it is thought that this kind of affection and commitment is only to be found within the marriage relationship, then it is not surprising that sexual intercourse should only be thought to be proper within marriage.

Related to what has just been said is the idea that sexual intercourse ought to be restricted to those who are married to each other, as a means by which to confirm the very special feelings that the spouses have for each other. . . . Revealing and confirming verbally that these feelings are present is one thing that helps to sustain the relationship; engaging in sexual intercourse is another. . . .

More to the point, an additional rationale for the prohibition on extramarital sex can now be developed. For given this way of viewing the sexual world, extramarital sex will almost always involve deception of a deeper sort. If the adulterous spouse does not in fact have the appropriate feelings of affection for the extramarital partner, then the adulterous spouse is deceiving that person about the presence of such feelings. If, on the other hand, the adulterous spouse does have the corresponding feelings for the extramarital partner but not toward the nonparticipating spouse, the adulterous spouse is very probably deceiving the nonparticipating spouse about the presence of such feelings toward that spouse. Indeed, it might be argued, whenever there is no longer love between the two persons who are married to each other, there is deception just because being married implies both to the participants and to the world that such a bond exists. . . . And if this is so, then the adulterous spouse always deceives either the partner in adultery or the nonparticipating spouse about the existence of such feelings. Thus extramarital sex involves deception of this sort and is for that reason immoral even if no deception vis-à-vis the occurrence of the act of adultery takes place.

What might be said in response to the foregoing arguments? The first thing that might be said is that the account of the connection between sexual intimacy and feelings of affection is inaccurate . . . in the sense that there is substantially

more divergence of opinion than the account suggests. . . .

Second, the argument leaves unanswered the question of whether it is desirable for sexual intimacy to carry the sorts of messages described above. For those persons for whom sex does have these implications there are special feelings and sensibilities that must be taken into account. But it is another question entirely whether any valuable end—moral or otherwise—is served by investing sexual behavior with such significance. That is something that must be shown and not just assumed. It might, for instance, be the case that substantially more good than harm would come from a kind of demystification of sexual behavior—one that would encourage the enjoyment of sex more for its own sake and one that would reject the centrality both of the association of sex with love and of love with only one other person.

I regard these as two of the more difficult unresolved issues that our culture faces today in respect of thinking sensibly about the attitudes toward sex and love that we should try to develop in ourselves and in our children.

Much of the contemporary literature that advocates sexual liberation of one sort or another embraces one or the other of two different views about the relationship between sex and love. One view holds that sex should be separated from love and affection. To be sure, sex is probably better when the partners genuinely like and enjoy being with each other. But sex is basically an intensive, exciting sensuous activity that can be enjoyed in a variety of suitable settings with a variety of suitable partners. The situation in respect to sexual pleasure is no different from that of the person who knows and appreciates fine food and who can have a satisfying meal in any number of good restaurants with any number of congenial companions. One question that must be settled here is whether sex can be thus demystified; another, more important, question is whether it would be desirable to do so. . . .

The second view of the relationship between sex and love seeks to drive the wedge in a different place. On this view it is not the link between sex and love that needs to be broken, but rather the connection between love and exclusivity. For a number of the reasons already given it is desirable, so this argument goes, that sexual intimacy continue to be reserved to and shared with only those for whom one has very great affection. The mistake lies in thinking that any "normal" adult will have those feelings toward only one other adult during his or her lifetime—or even at any time in his or her life. It is the concept of adult love, not ideas about sex, that needs demystification. What are thought to be both unrealistic and unfortunate are the notions of exclusivity and possessiveness that attach to the dominant conception of love between adults in our culture and others. Parents of four, five, six, or even ten children can certainly claim, and sometimes claim correctly, that they love all of their children, that they love them all equally, and that it is simply untrue to their feelings to insist that the numbers involved diminish either the quantity or the quality of their love. If this is readily understandable in the case of parents and children, there is no necessary reason why it is an impossible or undesirable ideal in the case of adults. . . . Or is there something about sexual love, whatever that may be, that makes these feelings especially fitting? Once again, the issues are conceptual, empirical, and normative all at once: What is love? How could it be different? Would it be a good thing or a bad thing if it were different?

. . . [Let] us imagine that a husband and wife have what is today sometimes characterized as an "open marriage." Suppose, that is, that they have agreed in advance that extramarital sex is—under certain circumstances—acceptable behavior for each to engage in. Suppose that as a result there is no impulse to deceive each other about the occurrence or nature of any such relationships and that no deception in fact occurs. Suppose, too, that there is no deception in respect to the feelings involved between the adulterous spouse and the extramarital partner. And suppose, finally, that one or the other or both of the

spouses then has sexual intercourse in circumstances consistent with these understandings. Under this description, so the argument might conclude, adultery is simply not immoral. At a minimum adultery cannot very plausibly be condemned either on grounds that it involves deception or on grounds that it requires the breaking of a promise.

One way to deal with the case of the "open marriage" is to question whether the two persons involved are still properly to be described as being married to each other. Part of the meaning of what it is for two persons to be married to each other, so this argument would go, is to have committed oneself to have sexual relationships only with one's spouse. Of course, it would be added, we know that that commitment is not always honored. We know that persons who are married to each other often do commit adultery. But there is a difference between being willing to make a commitment to marital fidelity, even though one may fail to honor that commitment, and not making the commitment at all. Whatever the relationship may be between the two individuals in the case just described, the absence of any commitment to sexual exclusivity requires the conclusion that their relationship is not a marital one. For a commitment to sexual exclusivity is a necessary but not a sufficient condition for the existence of a marriage.

Although there may be something to this suggestion, it is too strong as stated to be acceptable. To begin with it is doubtful that there are many, if any, *necessary* conditions for marriage; but even if there are, a commitment to sexual exclusivity is not such a condition.

To see that this is so, consider what might be taken to be some of the essential characteristics of a marriage. We might be tempted to propose that the concept of marriage requires the following: a formal ceremony of some sort in which mutual obligations are undertaken between two persons of the opposite sex; the capacity on the part of the persons involved to have sexual intercourse with each other; the willingness to have sexual intercourse only with each other; and feelings of love and affection between the two persons. The problem is that we can imagine relationships that are clearly marital and yet lack one or more of these features. For example, . . . it is possible for two persons to get married even though one or both lacks the capacity to engage in sexual intercourse. Thus, two very elderly persons who have neither the desire nor the ability to have intercourse can nonetheless get married. . . . And we certainly know of marriages in which love was not present at the time of the marriage, as, for instance, in marriages of state and marriages of convenience.

Counterexamples not satisfying the condition relating to the abstention from extramarital sex are even more easily produced. We certainly know of societies and cultures in which polygamy and polyandry are practiced, and we have no difficulty in recognizing these relationships as cases of marriages. It might be objected, though, that these are not counterexamples because they are plural marriages rather than marriages in which sex is permitted with someone other than one of the persons to whom one is married. But we also know of societies in which it is permissible for married persons to have sexual relationships with persons to whom they are not married, for example, temple prostitutes, concubines, and homosexual lovers. . . .

A commitment to sexual exclusivity is neither a necessary nor a sufficient condition for the existence of a marriage. It does, nonetheless, have this much to do with the nature of marriage—like the other indicia enumerated above, its presence tends to establish the existence of a marriage. Thus, in the absence of a formal ceremony of any sort an explicit commitment to sexual exclusivity would count in favor of regarding the two persons as married. The conceptual role of the commitment to sexual exclusivity can, perhaps, be brought out through the following example. Suppose we found a tribe that had a practice in which all the other indicia of marriage were present but in which the two parties were *prohibited* even from having sexual intercourse with each other. Moreover, suppose that sexual intercourse with others was clearly permitted. In such a case we would, I think, reject the

idea that the two persons were married to each other, and we would describe their relationship in other terms, for example, as some kind of formalized, special friendship relation—a kind of heterosexual "blood-brother" bond.

Compare that case with the following one. Again suppose that the tribe had a practice in which all of the other indicia of marriage were present, but instead of a prohibition on sexual intercourse between the persons in the relationship there was no rule at all. Sexual intercourse was permissible with the person with whom one had this ceremonial relationship, but it was no more or less permissible than with a number of other persons to whom one was not so related (for instance, all consenting adults of the opposite sex). While we might be in doubt as to whether we ought to describe the persons as married to each other, we would probably conclude that they were married and that they simply were members of a tribe whose views about sex were quite different from our own.

What all of this shows is that a *prohibition* on sexual intercourse between the two persons involved in a relationship is conceptually incompatible with the claim that the two of them are married. The *permissibility* of intramarital sex is a necessary part of the idea of marriage. But no such incompatibility follows simply from the added permissibility of extramarital sex.

These arguments do not, of course, exhaust the arguments for the prohibition on extramarital sexual relations. The remaining argument that I wish to consider is . . . a more instrumental one. It seeks to justify the prohibition by virtue of the role that it plays in the development and maintenance of nuclear families. . . .

It is obvious that one of the more powerful human desires is the desire for sexual gratification. The desire is a natural one, like hunger and thirst, in the sense that it need not be learned in order to be present within us and operative on us. But there is in addition much that we do learn about what the act of sexual intercourse is like. Once we experience sexual intercourse ourselves—and, in particular, once we experience orgasm—we discover that it is among the most intensive, short-term pleasures of the body.

Because this is so it is easy to see how the prohibition on extramarital sex helps to hold marriage together.... If one consequence of being married is that one is prohibited from having sexual intercourse with anyone but one's spouse, then the spouses in a marriage are in a position to provide an important source of pleasure for each other that is unavailable to them elsewhere in the society.

... When this prohibition is coupled, for example, with the prohibition on nonmarital sexual intercourse, we are presented with the inducement both to get married and to stay married. For if sexual intercourse is only legitimate within marriage, then persons seeking that gratification that is a feature of sexual intercourse are furnished explicit social directions for its attainment, namely, marriage....

Adultery is wrong, in other words, because a prohibition on extramarital sex is a way to help maintain the institutions of marriage and the nuclear family.

I am frankly not sure what we are to say about an argument such as the preceding one. What I am convinced of is that, like the arguments discussed earlier, this one also reveals something of the difficulty and complexity of the issues that are involved. So what I want now to do in the final portion of this essay is to try to delineate with reasonable precision several of what I take to be the fundamental, unresolved issues.

The first is whether this last argument is an argument for the *immorality* of extramarital sexual intercourse. What does seem clear is that there are differences between this argument and the ones considered earlier. The earlier arguments condemned adulterous behavior because it was behavior that involved breaking a promise, taking unfair advantage of or deceiving another. To the degree to which the prohibition on extramarital sex can be supported by arguments that invoke considerations such as these, there is little question but that violations of the prohibition are properly regarded as immoral. And

such a claim could be defended on one or both of two distinct grounds. The first is that action such as promise-breaking and deception are simply wrong. The second is that adultery involving promise-breaking or deception is wrong because it involves the straightforward infliction of harm on another human being—typically the nonadulterous spouse—who has a strong claim not to have that harm so inflicted.

The argument that connects the prohibition on extramarital sex with the maintenance and preservation of the institution of marriage is an argument for the instrumental value of the prohibition. To some degree this counts, I think, against regarding all violations of the prohibition as obvious cases of immorality....

What this should help us see, I think, is the fact that the argument that connects the prohibition on adultery with the preservation of marriage is at best seriously incomplete. Before we ought to be convinced by it, we ought to have reasons for believing that marriage is a morally desirable and just social institution. And such reasons are not quite as easy to find or as obvious as it may seem. For the concept of marriage is, as we have seen, both a loosely structured and a complicated one. There may be all sorts of intimate, interpersonal relationships that will resemble but not be identical with the typical marriage relationship presupposed by the traditional sexual morality. There may be a number of distinguishable sexual and loving arrangements that can all legitimately claim to be called *marriages*. The prohibitions of the traditional sexual morality may be effective ways to maintain some marriages and ineffective ways to promote and preserve others. The prohibitions of the traditional sexual morality may make good psychological sense if certain psychological theories are true, and they may be purveyors of immense psychological mischief if other psychological theories are true.... Irrespective of whether instrumental arguments of this sort are properly deemed moral arguments, they ought not fully convince anyone until questions such as these are answered.

Discussion Questions

1. Is a commitment to sexual exclusivity a necessary condition for the existence of a marriage? Are agreements on the part of spouses to be open to letting the other have extramarital affairs morally valid? Support your answers.
2. Is there an implicit promise of sexual fidelity in steady dating and cohabitation? Relate your answer to the case of Brooke and Adam at the beginning of this chapter. Should their relationship be considered a common-law marriage? Discuss how Wasserstrom might answer this question.
3. Discuss whether it is morally permissible to have an extramarital affair if one is certain of not being caught and is not emotionally involved with the extramarital partner.
4. Is Internet "sex" adultery? Is it immoral? Why or why not? Discuss how Wasserstrom would most likely answer these questions.

LOIS PINEAU

Date Rape: A Feminist Analysis

Lois Pineau was a professor of philosophy at Kansas State University. According to Pineau, good sex requires communication. To engage in sex without consent is rape.

Critical Reading Questions

1. How does Pineau define date rape?
2. Why is physical injury generally required to show that a sexual encounter was rape?
3. Why do courts, according to Pineau, usually shift the burden of proof onto the woman in cases of alleged rape?
4. What assumptions about male and female sexuality enforce the myth that women want to be raped? According to Pineau, why is this a myth?
5. According to Pineau, why is the contract, which supposedly exists when a woman acts provocatively, not binding?
6. According to Pineau, what is the only way to establish the legitimacy of a sexual encounter?
7. What does Pineau mean by "communicative sexuality"? How does this model differ from the "contract" model? Why does Pineau reject the contractual model in favor of the communicative model?
8. How would the communicative model change the way the judicial system currently approaches sexuality and the question of date rape?

"Date Rape: A Feminist Analysis," *Law and Philosophy* 8 (1989): 217–243. Some notes have been omitted.

Date rape is nonaggravated sexual assault, nonconsensual sex that does not involve physical injury or the explicit threat of physical injury. But because it does not involve physical injury, and because physical injury is often the only criterion that is accepted as evidence that the *actus reas* is nonconsensual, what is really sexual assault is often mistaken for seduction. The replacement of the old rape laws with the new laws on sexual assault have done nothing to resolve this problem. . . .

THE PROBLEM OF THE CRITERION

The reasoning that underlies the present criterion of consent is entangled in a number of mutually supportive mythologies which see sexual assault as masterful seduction, and silent submission as sexual enjoyment. Because the prevailing ideology has so much informed our conceptualization of sexual interaction, it is extraordinarily difficult for us to distinguish between assault and seduction, submission and enjoyment, or so we imagine. . . . I therefore want to begin my argument by providing an example which shows both why it is so difficult to make this distinction, and that it exists. Later, I will identify and attempt to unravel the lines of reasoning that reinforce this difficulty.

> The woman I have in mind agrees to see someone because she feels an initial attraction to him and believes that he feels that same way about her. She goes out with him in the hope that there will be mutual enjoyment and in the course of the day or evening an increase of mutual interest. Unfortunately, these hopes of *mutual* and *reciprocal* interest are not realized. We do not know how much interest she has in him by the end of their time together, but whatever her feelings she comes under pressure to have sex with him, and she does not want to have the kind of sex he wants. She may desire to hold hands and kiss, to engage in more intense caresses or in some form of foreplay, or she may not want to be touched. She may have reasons unrelated to desire for not wanting to engage in the kind of sex he is demanding. She may have religious reservations, concerns about pregnancy or disease, a disinclination to be just another conquest. She may be engaged in a seduction program of her own which sees abstaining from sexual activity as a means of building an important emotional bond. She feels she is desirable to him, and she knows and he knows that he will have sex with her if he can. And while she feels she doesn't owe him anything, and that it is her prerogative to refuse him, this feeling is partly a defensive reaction against a deeply held belief that if he is in need, she should provide. If she buys into the myth of insistent male sexuality she may feel he is suffering from sexual frustration and that she is largely to blame.

> We do not know how much he desires her, but we do know that his desire for erotic satisfaction can hardly be separated from his desire for conquest. He feels no dating obligation, but has a strong commitment to scoring. He uses the myth of "so hard to control" male desire as a rhetorical tactic, telling her how frustrated she will leave him. He becomes overbearing. She resists, voicing her disinclination. He alternates between telling her how desirable she is and taking a hostile stance, charging her with misleading him, accusing her of wanting him and being coy, in short of being deceitful, all the time engaging in rather aggressive body contact. It is late at night, she is tired and a bit queasy from too many drinks, and he is reaffirming her suspicion that perhaps she has misled him. She is having trouble disengaging his body from hers, and wishes he would just go away. She does not adopt a strident angry stance, partly because she thinks he is acting normally and does not deserve it, partly because she feels she is partly to blame, and partly because there is always the danger that her anger will make him angry, possibly violent. It seems that the only thing to do, given his aggression, and her queasy fatigue, is to go along with him and get it over with, but this decision is so entangled with the events in process it is hard to know if it is not simply a recognition of what is actually happening. She finds the whole encounter a thoroughly disagreeable experience, but he does not take any notice, and wouldn't have changed course if he had. He congratulates himself on his sexual prowess and is confirmed in his opinion that aggressive tactics pay off. Later she feels that

she has been raped, but paradoxically tells herself that she let herself be raped.

The paradoxical feelings of the woman in our example indicate her awareness that what she feels about the incident stands in contradiction to the prevailing cultural assessment of it. She knows that she did not want to have sex with her date. She is not so sure, however, about how much her own desires count, and she is uncertain that she has made her desires clear. Her uncertainty is reinforced by the cultural reading of this incident as an ordinary seduction.

As for us, we assume that the woman did not want to have sex, but just like her, we are unsure whether her mere reluctance, in the presence of high-pressure tactics, constitutes nonconsent. We suspect that submission to an overbearing and insensitive lout is no way to go about attaining sexual enjoyment, and we further suspect that he felt no compunction about providing it, so that on the face of it, from the outside looking in, it looks like a pretty unreasonable proposition for her.

Let us look at this reasoning more closely. Assume that she was not attracted to the kind of sex offered by the sort of person offering it. Then it would be *prima facie* unreasonable for her to agree to have sex, unreasonable, that is, unless she were offered some pay-off for her stoic endurance, money perhaps, or tickets to the opera. The reason is that in sexual matters, agreement is closely connected to attraction. Thus, where the presumption is that she was not attracted, we should at the same time presume that she did not consent. Hence, the burden of proof should be on her alleged assailant to show that she had good reasons for consenting to an unattractive proposition.

This is not, however, the way such situations are interpreted. In the unlikely event that the example I have described should come before the courts, there is little doubt that the law would interpret the woman's eventual acquiescence or "going along with" the sexual encounter as consent. But along with this interpretation would go the implicit understanding that she had consented because when all was said and done, when

the "token" resistances to the "masterful advances" had been made she had wanted to after all. Once the courts have constructed this interpretation, they are then forced to conjure up some horror story of feminine revenge in order to explain why she should bring charges against her "seducer."

In the even more unlikely event that the courts agreed that the woman had not consented to the above encounter, there is little chance that her assailant would be convicted of sexual assault. The belief that the man's aggressive tactics are a normal part of seduction means that *mens rea* cannot be established. Her eventual "going along" with his advances constitutes reasonable grounds for his believing in her consent. . . .

The position of the courts is supported by the widespread belief that male aggression and female reluctance are normal parts of seduction. Given their acceptance of this model, the logic of their response must be respected. . . .

RAPE MYTHS

The belief that the natural aggression of men and the natural reluctance of women somehow makes date rape understandable underlies a number of prevalent myths about rape and human sexuality. . . .

The claim that the victim provoked a sexual incident, that "she asked for it," is by far the most common defense given by men who are accused of sexual assault. Feminists, rightly incensed by this response, often treat it as beneath contempt, singling out the defense as an argument against it. . . .

The least sophisticated of the "she asked for it" rationales, and in a sense, the easiest to deal with, appeals to an injunction against sexually provocative behavior on the part of women. If women should not be sexually provocative, then, from this standpoint, a woman who is sexually provocative deserves to suffer the consequences. Now it will not do to respond that women get raped even when they are not sexually provocative, or that it is men who get to interpret (unfairly) what counts as sexually provocative. The question should be: Why shouldn't a woman be sexually provocative? Why should this behavior warrant any kind of aggressive response whatsoever?

Attempts to explain that women have a right to behave in sexually provocative ways without suffering dire consequences still meet with surprisingly tough resistance. Even people who find nothing wrong or sinful with sex itself, in any of its forms, tend to suppose that women must not behave sexually unless they are prepared to carry through on some fuller course of sexual interaction. The logic of this response seems to be that at some point a woman's behavior commits her to following through on the full course of a sexual encounter as it is defined by her assailant. At some point she has made an agreement, or formed a contract, and once that is done, her contractor is entitled to demand that she satisfy the terms of that contract. . . .

The rationale, I believe, comes in the form of a belief in the especially insistent nature of male sexuality. . . . At a certain point in the arousal process, it is thought, a man's rational will gives away to the prerogatives of nature. His sexual need can and does reach a point where it is uncontrollable, and his natural masculine aggression kicks in to assure that this need is met. Women, however, are naturally more contained, and so it is their responsibility not to provoke the irrational in the male. . . . One does not go into the lion's cage and expect not to be eaten. Natural feminine reluctance, it is thought, is no protection against a sexually aroused male.

. . . The assumption that women both want to indulge sexually, and are inclined to sacrifice this desire for higher ends, gives rise to the myth that they want to be raped. After all, doesn't rape give them the sexual enjoyment that they *really* want, at the same time that it relieves them of the responsibility for admitting to and acting upon what they want? And how then can we blame men, who have been socialized to be aggressively seductive precisely for the purpose of overriding female reserve? If we find fault at all, we are inclined to cast our suspicions on the motives of the woman. . . .

But if women really want sexual pleasure, what inclines us to think that they will get it through rape? This conclusion logically requires a theory about the dynamics of sexual pleasure that sees that pleasure as an emergent property of overwhelming male insistence. For the assumption that a raped female experiences sexual pleasure implies that the person who rapes her knows how to cause that pleasure independently of any information she might convey on that point. Since her ongoing protest is inconsistent with requests to be touched in particular ways in particular places, to have more of this and less of that, then we must believe that the person who touches her knows these particular ways and places instinctively, without any directives from her.

Thus we find, underlying and reinforcing this belief in incommunicative male prowess, a conception of sexual pleasure that springs from wordless interchanges, and of sexual success that occurs in a place of meaningful silence. The language of seduction is accepted as a tacit language: eye contact, smiles, blushes, and faintly discernible gestures. It is, accordingly, imprecise and ambiguous. It would be easy for a man to make mistakes about the message conveyed, understandable that he should mistakenly think that a sexual invitation has been made, and a bargain struck. But honest mistakes, we think, must be excused.

In sum, the belief that women should not be sexually provocative is logically linked to several other beliefs, some normative, some empirical. The normative beliefs are that (1) people should keep the agreements they make, (2) that sexually provocative behavior, taken beyond a certain point, generates agreements, (3) that the peculiar nature of male and female sexuality places such agreements in a special category, one in which the possibility of retracting an agreement is ruled out, or at least made highly unlikely, [and] (4) that women are not to be trusted, in sexual matters at least. The empirical belief, which turns out to be false, is that male sexuality is not subject to rational and moral control.

DISPELLING THE MYTHS

The "she asked for it" justification of sexual assault incorporates a conception of a contract that would be difficult to defend in any other context, and the presumptions about human sexuality which function to reinforce sympathies rooted in the contractual notion of just deserts are not supported by empirical research.

The belief that a woman generates some sort of contractual obligation whenever her behavior is interpreted as seductive is the most indefensible part of the mythology of rape. In law, contracts are not legitimate just because a promise has been made. In particular, the use of pressure tactics to extract agreement is frowned upon. Normally, an agreement is upheld only if the contractors were clear on what they were getting into, and had sufficient time to reflect on the wisdom of their doing so. . . .

. . . [E]ven if we assume that a woman has initially agreed to an encounter, her agreement does not automatically make all subsequent sexual activity to which she submits legitimate. If during coitus a woman should experience pain, be suddenly overcome with guilt or fear of pregnancy, or simply lose her initial desire, those are good reasons for her to change her mind. Having changed her mind, neither her partner nor the state has any right to force her to continue. . . .

If the "she asked for it" contractual view of sexual interchange has any validity, it is because there is a point at which there is no stopping a sexual encounter, a point at which that encounter becomes the inexorable outcome of the unfolding of natural events. If a sexual encounter is like a slide on which I cannot stop halfway down, it will be relevant whether I enter the slide of my own free will, or am pushed.

But there is no evidence that the entire sexual act is like a slide. . . . Indeed, the available evidence shows that most of the activity involved in sex has to do with building the requisite level of desire, a task that involves the proper use of foreplay, the possibility of which implies control over the form that foreplay will take. Modern sexual

therapy assumes that such control is universally accessible, and so far there has been no reason to question that assumption. Sexologists are unanimous, moreover, in holding that mutual sexual enjoyment requires an atmosphere of comfort and communication, a minimum of pressure, and an ongoing check-up on one's partner's state. . . .

Where the kind of sex involved is not the sort of sex we would expect a woman to like, the burden of proof should not be on the woman to show that she did not consent, but on the defendant to show that contrary to every reasonable expectation she did consent. The defendant should be required to convince the court that the plaintiff persuaded him to have sex with her even though there are no visible reasons why she should.

In conclusion, there are no grounds for the "she asked for it" defense. Sexually provocative behavior does not generate sexual contracts. . . . Secondly, all the evidence suggests that neither women nor men find sexual enjoyment in rape or in any form of noncommunicative sexuality. Thirdly, male sexual desire is containable, and can be subjected to moral and rational control. Fourthly, since there is no reason why women should not be sexually provocative, they do not "deserve" any sex they do not want. . . .

COMMUNICATIVE SEXUALITY: REINTERPRETING THE KANTIAN IMPERATIVE . . .

In thinking about sex we must keep in mind its sensual ends, and the facts show that aggressive high-pressure sex contradicts those ends. Consensual sex in dating situations is presumed to aim at mutual enjoyment. It may not always do this, and when it does, it might not always succeed. There is no logical incompatibility between wanting to continue a sexual encounter and failing to derive sexual pleasure from it.

But it seems to me that there is a presumption in favor of the connection between sex and sexual enjoyment, and that if a man wants to be sure that he is not forcing himself on a woman, he has an obligation either to ensure that the encounter really is mutually enjoyable, or to know the reasons why she would want to continue the encounter in spite of her lack of enjoyment. . . .

The obligation to promote the sexual ends of one's partner implies the obligation to know what those ends are, and also the obligation to know how those ends are attained. Thus, the problem comes down to a problem of epistemic responsibility, the responsibility to know. The solution, in my view, lies in the practice of a communicative sexuality, one which combines the appropriate knowledge of the other with respect for the dialectics of desire.

So let us, for a moment, conceive of sexual interaction on a communicative rather than a contractual model. . . .

The communicative interaction involved in conversation is concerned with a good deal more than didactic content and argument. Good conversationalists are intuitive, sympathetic, and charitable. Intuition and charity aid the conversationalist in her effort to interpret the words of the other correctly and sympathy enables her to enter into the other's point of view. Her sensitivity alerts her to the tone of the exchange. Has her point been taken good-humoredly or resentfully? Aggressively delivered responses are taken as a sign that *ad hominems* are at work, and that the respondent's self-worth has been called into question. Good conversationalists will know how to suspend further discussion until this sense of self-worth has been reestablished. . . .

Just as communicative conversationalists are concerned with more than didactic content, persons engaged in communicative sexuality will be concerned with more than achieving coitus. They will be sensitive to the responses of their partners. . . . Communicative sexual partners will not overwhelm each other with the barrage of their own desires. They will treat negative, bored, or angry responses as a sign that the erotic ground needs to be either cleared or abandoned. Their concern with fostering the desire of the other must involve an ongoing state of alertness in interpreting her responses.

Just as a conversationalist's prime concern is for the mutuality of the discussion, a person engaged in communicative sexuality will be most concerned with the mutuality of desire. As such, both will put into practice a regard for their respondent that is guaranteed no place in the contractual language of rights, duties, and consent. . . .

CULTURAL PRESUMPTIONS

. . . [N]ow that we know what communicative sexuality is, and that it is morally required, and that it is the only feasible means to mutual sexual enjoyment, why not take this model as the norm of what is reasonable in sexual interaction. The evidence of sexologists strongly indicates that women whose partners are aggressively uncommunicative have little chance of experiencing sexual pleasure. . . .

Thus, where communicative sexuality does not occur, we lack the main ground for believing that the sex involved was consensual. . . . All that is needed then, in order to provide women with legal protection from "date rape" is to make both reckless indifference and willful ignorance a sufficient condition of *mens rea* and to make communicative sexuality the accepted norm of sex to which a reasonable woman would agree. Thus, the appeal to communicative sexuality as a norm for sexual encounters accomplishes two things. It brings the aggressive sex involved in "date rape" well within the realm of sexual assault, and it locates the guilt of date rapists in the failure to approach sexual relations on a communicative basis. . . .

CONCLUSION

In sum, using communicative sexuality as a model of normal sex has several advantages over the "aggressive-acquiescence" model of seduction. The new model ties the presumption that consensual sex takes place in the expectation of mutual desire much more closely to the facts about how that desire actually functions. Where communicative sex does not occur, this establishes a presumption that there was no consent. The importance of this presumption is that we are able, in criminal proceedings, to shift the burden of proof from the plaintiff, who on the contractual model must show that she resisted or was threatened, to the defendant who must then give some reason why she should consent after all. The communicative model of sexuality also enables us to give a different conceptual content to the concept of consent. It sees consent as something more like an ongoing cooperation than the one-shot agreement which we are inclined to see it as on the contractual model. Moreover, it does not matter, on the communicative model, whether a woman was sexually provocative, what her reputation is, what went on before the sex began. All that matters is the quality of communication with regard to the sex itself.

But most importantly, the communicative model of normal sexuality gives us a handle on a solution to the problem of date rape. If noncommunicative sexuality establishes a presumption of nonconsent, then where there are no overriding reasons for thinking that consent occurred, we have a criterion for a category of sexual assault that does not require evidence of physical violence or threat. If we are serious about date rape, then the next step is to take this criterion as objective grounds for establishing that a date rape has occurred. The proper legislation is the shortest route to establishing this criterion.

Discussion Questions

1. Is Pineau's communicative model of sexuality the only desirable one? Are there times when it is reasonable for a man to believe that a woman has given her consent to sex even though she has not verbally communicated it? Support your answers.
2. Catharine MacKinnon maintains that in a society where women are oppressed, communication alone is not sufficient to establish consent to sex. Do you agree? Are there times when a woman might consent out of a feeling of powerlessness, rather than a genuine desire for sexual intimacy? Support your answers, using examples. Discuss how Pineau might respond to MacKinnon.
3. Discuss the implications of Pineau's definition of date rape on how such cases should be handled by the courts. Should policies on date rape be instituted on all campuses? Support your answer.
4. In her book *The Morning After: Sex, Fear, and Feminism on Campus* (1993), Katie Roiphe argues that the fuss over date rape, rather than empowering and liberating women, perpetuates the stereotype of them as vulnerable, naive, and in need of protection. The emphasis on communicative consensus, rather than sexually liberating women, has thrown a damper on relationships and created an atmosphere of suspicion between men and women. Has the current focus on date rape empowered women, or made them more fearful? How has it affected the men on your campus and the heterosexual dating scene? Use examples to illustrate your answer.

CASE STUDIES

SEX EDUCATION AND THE ABSTINENCE-ONLY CURRICULUM

Sex education in schools has been fraught with controversy. The abstinence-only movement began in 1996 when the Welfare Reform Bill created $50 million a year in grant money to be given to schools that agreed to limit their sex education curriculum to abstinence-only. By 2006 the budget for the program had expanded to $206 million, and 35 percent of school districts in the United States were receiving funds from the budget for their abstinence-only curriculums.

Not everyone agrees with this approach. While sex education has been credited with reducing the number of teenage pregnancies and abortions, studies have found that students in abstinence-only programs are just as likely to be sexually active as those who aren't in the programs. One of the contentious aspects of the curriculum is that it contains little or no discussion of contraception. Supporters of the program argue that talking about contraception sends a mixed message to students. Opponents of the abstinence-only curriculum point out that kids are going to have sex anyway and need to learn how to protect themselves from unwanted pregnancies and STDs. Indeed, almost half of all high school students have engaged in sex by the time they turn nineteen.[31]

Some states have rejected federal funding for abstinence-only programs based on the lack of conclusive evidence for their effectiveness. Other states are looking for a more comprehensive approach to abstinence-only education, possibly combining it with accurate and age-appropriate information about contraception—an approach that one study found may be working.

Discussion Questions

1. Should teenagers be discouraged from having sex? Support your answers. Discuss also how Ruddick might answer this question.
2. Do abstinence-only programs blur the line between religion and science? Or can they be justified on moral grounds alone? Support your argument.
3. Working in small groups and referring back to the stages of moral development discussed in Chapter 1, design age-appropriate sex education curriculums for eighth graders and twelfth graders.
4. Discuss whether high schools and/or colleges should give out free condoms to students.

---

2. COLLEGE DORMS AND COHABITATION

Several colleges and universities, including Stanford University, Brown University, University of Pennsylvania, and Oberlin College, now allow students of opposite sex to share a dorm room.

Grace and Jeffrey met in their sophomore year and have been dating steadily for the past year and a half. At the end of their junior year, they got engaged and set their wedding date for August following graduation. During the summer they both took jobs in the same seaside resort and rented a cottage together. When they returned for their senior year, they applied to the housing office to share a double room. However, State University, like most colleges and universities, makes no provision for cohabitation in the undergraduate dorms unless the students are married. Consequently, the school turned down their request. Grace and Jeffrey filed a complaint against State University arguing that the housing office was discriminating against them, pointing out that the university provided housing for married students. They also noted that openly gay and lesbian couples were permitted to share dormitory rooms.

Discussion Questions

1. Opponents of cohabitation on campus argue that sharing sexual intimacy should be reserved for marriage and that cohabitation sets students up for marital failure. Is this a legitimate reason to prohibit cohabitation, or do students have a right to choose their roommate, regardless of gender? If so, what is the basis of that right? Support your answers.
2. Discuss the policy on cohabitation at your college and the justification for the policy.
3. Should the university prohibit, in cases where the couples are open about their sexual orientation and relationship, homosexual couples from sharing a dormitory room? If not, is it fair to deny the same opportunity to heterosexual couples? Support your answers. How would Marshall and Cordy most likely respond to these questions?

3. FACULTY–STUDENT SEXUAL RELATIONSHIPS

Kevin, a junior at Keene State, is having a sexual relationship with his political science professor. As a result, the professor is brought up before the faculty senate disciplinary action committee. Aware that this is not an isolated incident, the Keene State administration is considering a policy that will prohibit faculty–student sexual relationships. Many colleges and universities already have such bans.

Those in favor of a ban maintain that faculty–student sexual relationships are sexual harassment and wrong because of the power that the faculty have over students in terms of grading and advising. Furthermore, they believe that the ban should continue even after the class ends because teachers continue to have a duty to students who might at some time need a letter of recommendation from the professor for a job or graduate school. Opponents of the ban point out that college students are adults and, like other adults, should have the right to make decisions about their own private lives.

Discussion Questions

1. Discuss the pros and cons of a policy prohibiting faculty–student sexual relationships. Discuss how a utilitarian and a natural rights ethicist would most likely respond to such a policy.
2. Does your college have a policy prohibiting faculty–student sexual relationships? If so, get a copy of the policy and discuss its merits and weaknesses.
3. Should sexual relationships between employees and employers in the workplace also be prohibited, or at least discouraged? Why or why not?
4. Radical feminists argue that most sexual relationships between men and women, not just those between faculty and students, are coercive because of the unequal economic and social power of women in our society. Would it make a difference, morally, if it was Kevin rather than the professor who initiated the relationship? Is the gender of the professor morally relevant? Support your answer.

4. POLYGAMY: SHOULD IT BE LEGAL?

Many African nations have a tradition of polygamy, in which a man can have more than one wife. Although polygamy was outlawed by the European colonizers, it is still practiced in parts of Africa. While the great majority of American women oppose polygamy, 60 percent of women in a survey in Nigeria stated that they would be "pleased if their husbands took another wife," and 76 percent of women surveyed in Kenya had a positive view of polygamy.[32] A few years ago, former President Charles Taylor of Liberia proposed making polygamy legal, a proposal that caused quite a stir in the country as well as abroad.[33]

African feminist Awa Thiam opposes legalizing polygamy, arguing that it exploits and commercializes women. First wives who agree to it may feel pressured by their husband, and later wives may accept it because of the lack of other social and economic alternatives for women. Supporters of polygamy counter that men are not the only beneficiaries of polygamy. Polygamy has often been practiced when women greatly outnumbered the men because of war or other reasons. Without polygamy, many women would be without the benefit of a husband and their children would be illegitimate. Also, polygamy, they argue, gives women a greater social support system for raising their own children.

Polygamy was outlawed in the United States in 1878. In 2007 the U.S. Supreme Court turned down a case from a Utah polygamist who wanted polygamy legalized. There are still a few fundamentalist Mormans who practice polygamy, even though it has been forbidden by the Morman Church. It has been suggested that polygamy, such as that practiced in Africa, be legalized in the United States so that women, especially single mothers who are now sharing a "husband" with a married woman, can avail themselves of the social and political benefits of marriage.

Discussion Questions

1. Discuss whether polygamy is compatible with sexual intimacy within a marriage. Discuss how both Ruddick and Wasserstrom might answer this question.
2. Opponents of polygamy argue that it is most often found in patriarchal societies in which women have few options other than marriage. However, is monogamous marriage any less oppressive of women?
3. Discuss the moral relevance of the fact that polygamy was a tradition in Africa prior to colonization. Did the Christian European colonizers have a moral right to impose monogamy, which they regarded as morally superior, on Africans?
4. Segun Gbadegesin points out that monogamy limits a person's choice to only one marital partner, whereas polygamy gives adults a greater choice regarding whom to marry.[34] Discuss the parallels between legalizing same-sex marriages and polygamous marriage between consenting adults, as well as the arguments for and against legalizing polygamy in the United States. Discuss also how Justice Margaret Marshall might respond to a court case regarding the legalization of polygamy.

---

5. SAME-SEX MARRIAGE AND PARENTHOOD

Frank and Peter met while graduate students at MIT and were married in Massachusetts where same-sex marriage is legal. After returning to Michigan, Frank's home state, they became foster parents to two small boys. When they filed a joint petition five years later to adopt the boys, their petition was denied because Michigan law prohibits gay couples from adopting. Frank and Peter now face the unhappy prospect of having their foster sons, whom they have raised since infancy, removed from their home and placed in another foster or adoptive home.

Michigan, which does not recognize same-sex marriage, is one of several states that prohibit same-sex couples from adopting a child. Those who support the prohibition argue that it is in the child's best interests to have a mother and a father because same-sex couples tend to be unstable and the children in these homes can face ridicule and censure at school and in the community. Opponents also see it as a stop toward legalizing same-sex marriage. Those who support allowing same-sex couples to adopt counter that there is no evidence that having same-sex parents harms children. Also, there are so many children in the foster system and this gives them a chance to have a home with two legal parents.

Discussion Questions

1. Discuss the arguments for and against allowing same-sex couples to adopt children. Develop an adoption policy for your state, taking into account the moral issues discussed in this chapter.
2. Discuss whether same-sex couples should even be allowed to become foster parents. Did Frank and Peter harm the boys by taking them in as foster children, knowing that they probably would not be allowed to adopt them? Discuss how a utilitarian might answer this question.
3. Frank and Peter decide to appeal their case. The case goes all the way to the U.S. Supreme Court. Discuss what Justice Robert J. Cordy's opinion might be in this case, if he were on the Supreme Court, given his opposition to same-sex marriage. How would you rule if you were a Supreme Court justice? Support your answer.

6. THE RELUCTANT HUSBAND

Joe and Azra have been married fourteen years and have a nine-year-old daughter and a four-year-old son. For the past three years, following his wife's bout with breast cancer and her mastectomy, Joe, once a loving husband, has been uninterested in sex with her and has begun spending many late nights at work as a way of avoiding intimacy with his wife. However, Joe has never been sexually unfaithful because both he and Azra believe strongly that sexual fidelity is important in a marriage. As a result of her husband's neglect, Azra, who valued their moments of sexual intimacy, has become lonely and somewhat depressed.

One day Azra meets Roberto, an unmarried man, at her writer's group. Roberto and Azra share many common interests. They strike up a friendship that becomes a great source of companionship and happiness to both of them. After several months Azra tells Roberto about her mastectomy and her strained relationship with her husband. Roberto loves Azra despite her physical scars and the relationship soon becomes sexually intimate.

Discussion Questions

1. Was Azra's sexual relationship with Roberto immoral or morally permissible in this case? Support your answer. Discuss how Wasserstrom most likely would answer this question.
2. Discuss whether a promise of sexual exclusivity in a marriage entails a promise of ongoing sexual involvement with each other. What about cases in which one spouse is unable to have a sexual relationship because of illness or injury? What about cases in which one spouse is uninterested in sex but still has perfunctory sexual relations with his or her spouse? Support your answers.
3. What is the extent of Roberto's culpability in this situation? Is it immoral for a single person to have sex with a married person and, if so, on what grounds?
4. Joe finds out about Azra's infidelity. In a fit of rage he strikes her, causing bruising on one arm. Was the violence justified in this situation? Support your answer.
5. Joe and Azra agree to seek the assistance of a marriage counselor who works at their church. You are the marriage counselor. How would you advise them?

---

7. GANG RAPE AND COLLEGE FRATERNITIES

Three UCLA undergraduates were arrested in June 1996 for a rape that allegedly occurred during a Zeta Beta Tau fraternity retreat at a Palm Springs hotel.[35] The woman, a member of a UCLA sorority, claimed that she was gang-raped by the three men after she had gone to the hotel room late the previous night.

Although beer kegs at fraternity-sponsored events are a violation, there had been thirty to fifty kegs available that weekend. According to the alleged victim, she and the three men had been drinking alcohol and smoking marijuana in the room while playing a game called Master. During the game, the three fraternity brothers began to undress her and then sexually assaulted her. She told them to stop, but they ignored her protests. A fourth man watched while they raped her.

Following the rape, the distraught woman returned to her own room, where another student took her to a hospital emergency room. She filed charges with the police early the next morning. The police went to the hotel and arrested the three students. The students claimed in their defense that the sex was consensual. Their fraternity brothers stood by their story.

Discussion Questions

1. Are fraternities breeding grounds for sexism and violence against women? If so, should fraternities be banned? Support your answers. Discuss how Pineau might answer these questions.
2. Brotherhood and loyalty are highly valued in fraternities as part of male bonding. In the great majority of rape cases, members of a fraternity will refuse to "rat on" or testify against their brothers or will even make up stories to protect their brothers. Discuss the morality of this type of loyalty. Does the man who watched

the rape have a moral obligation to come forward and testify against his fraternity brothers? Is he morally culpable for not trying to stop the rape? Support your answers.

3. In fraternity gang rapes, men generally select women who are socially isolated, psychologically vulnerable, and either too intoxicated or too afraid to resist or complain to the authorities.[36] Discuss the extent, if any, to which our culture, including the college culture, socializes women to be victims of rape. Discuss how Pineau might respond.

4. According to one survey, 26 percent of men who acknowledged committing sexual assault on a date say they were intoxicated at the time.[37] Women who are intoxicated are also less likely to successfully resist assault. According to some college policies such as that at Antioch College, people who are intoxicated are unable to give consent to sex. Do you agree with this policy? Does this imply that men who rape while intoxicated are also not responsible for their actions? Discuss your answers in light of the UCLA case.

Feminism, Motherhood, and the Workplace

Eight women, all Princeton graduates, sat around a fireplace discussing books in an Atlanta, Georgia, home. Some of the women also had law degrees from Harvard and Columbia. Most of them were no longer working full-time and had voluntarily left to stay at home with their children. "Women today, if we think about feminism at all," says one of the women, a former publisher, "see it as a battle fought for 'the choice.' For us, the freedom to choose work if we want to work is the feminist strain in our lives." "I've had women tell me," replied a former lawyer, "that it's women like me that are ruining the workplace because it makes employers suspicious. I don't want to take on the mantle of all womanhood and fight for some sister who isn't really my sister because I don't even know her." Have these women failed the feminist movement?

FEMINISM

Many women entering college today think that **feminism** is no longer relevant to their lives—that women are liberated, that the days of discrimination in the workplace, home, and classroom are over. This belief that equality has been achieved is perpetuated by the media and other major institutions. However, in reality, women still earn only a fraction of what men earn. Women in families where both spouses are working are still burdened with the great majority of housework and child care. And sexual harassment in the workplace and classroom is still all too common.

British philosopher Mary Wollstonecraft's 1792 book *A Vindication of the Rights of Woman* was the forerunner of the first wave of feminism in the United States, which ran from the early nineteenth to the early twentieth centuries. She argued that biological differences are not a relevant ground for denying women equal rights. Women and men have the same capacity for reason and are governed by the same moral standards. John Stuart Mill took up the same arguments in his essay "Subjection of Women." The first wave of feminists, which included Elizabeth Cady Stanton, Margaret Sanger, and Susan B. Anthony, focused on civil rights, access to contraception, and universal suffrage (the right to vote).

These **liberal feminists** began with the assumption that there is a common rational human nature that transcends gender differences. The purpose of the state is to
provide a sphere of liberty in which citizens can exercise their rights and freely determine their own lives. Social structures and institutions that limit the rational choices
of women are morally wrong because they limit their autonomy. The solution is to
demand equal access to the opportunities and privileges enjoyed by men.

The second wave of liberal feminism, popularly know as the women's liberation
movement, began in the 1960s following the publication of Betty Friedan's controversial book *The Feminine Mystique*. Friedan wrote that "for women to have full identity and
freedom, they must have economic independence. Equality and human dignity are not
possible for women if they are not able to earn. Only economic independence can free
a woman to marry for love, not for status or financial support, or to leave a loveless,
intolerable, humiliating marriage."[1] The movement, which was composed primarily of
white, middle-class women, focused on equal employment opportunities and abortion
rights. Linda Hirshman, in "Homeward Bound," expresses the liberal feminist point of
view. Judith Jarvis Thomson's 1971 article, "A Defense of Abortion," also emerged from
the liberal feminist movement.

In 1968 the liberal feminist National Organization of Women (NOW) published
its *Bill of Rights*. Many, if not most, of their demands still are not realized. There has
also been a move, which has met with some success, to eliminate sexist language that
conveys women's inferior status, as well as to replace male terms in referring to people
in general with gender-neutral terms such as "humans" and "he or she."

The **radical feminist** movement, which emerged in the late 1960s, rejects the liberal feminist claim that there is a common human nature and claims instead that
gender is a cultural construct used to sustain a patriarchy.[2] Liberty rights are a male
notion, something generated by masculine reason for relationships among men.
Men are socialized to be both protectors and sexual predators; women are socialized
to be weak and to be sexual prey. According to radical feminists such as Catharine
MacKinnon (see her reading "Pornography, Civil Rights, and Speech" at the end of
Chapter 9), one cannot be a woman without being objectified by men as an object of
sexual violence. To use a slogan of radical feminists, the most important difference
between men and women is that "men fuck and women get fucked." Although women
are taught to value connectedness, in reality, they claim, women want individuation
and liberation from the shackles of intimacy. Women who want motherhood and marriage are operating under "false consciousness."

Unlike liberal feminists, radical feminists do not place much stock in political or
legal reform. If government and other social institutions, such as capitalism and religion, are patriarchal, then participation in these systems isn't going to help women.
For example, protecting pornographers' freedom of speech to make and sell pornography harms women. Some radical feminists call for lesbianism, not necessarily in
sexual terms but in terms of women working and living together without men and cel-
ebrating "gynergy"—the woman spirit/strength.

Other schools of feminism include Marxist and socialist feminism. **Marxist feminists** believe that the capitalist class system is the cause of oppression for women.
Simone de Beauvoir is a Marxist feminist, although she is sometimes considered a

---

✍ BILL OF RIGHTS: NATIONAL ORGANIZATION FOR WOMEN (NOW)

We Demand

I. That the United States Congress immediately pass the Equal Rights Amendment to the Constitution to prove that "Equality of rights under the law shall not be denied or abridged by the United States or by any state on account of sex.". . .

II. That equal employment opportunity be guaranteed to all women as well as men, by insisting the Equal Employment Opportunity Commission enforces the prohibitions against sex discrimination in employment. . . .

III. That women be protected by law to ensure their rights to return to their jobs within a reasonable time after childbirth without loss of seniority or other accrued benefits, and be paid maternity leave as a form of social security and/or employee benefit.

IV. Immediate revision of tax laws to permit the deduction of home and child care expenses for working parents.

V. That child care facilities be established by law on the same basis as parks, libraries and public schools, adequate to the needs of children from the preschool years through adolescence, as a community resource to be used by all citizens from all income levels.

VI. That the right of women to be educated to their full potential equally with men be secured by federal and state legislation, eliminating all discrimination and segregation by sex, written and unwritten, at all levels of education. . . .

VII. The right of women in poverty to secure job training, housing, and family allowances on equal terms with men, but without prejudice to a parent's right to remain at home to care for his or her children; revision of welfare legislation and poverty programs when they deny women dignity, privacy and self-respect.

VIII. The right of women to control their own reproductive lives by removing from penal code laws limiting access to contraceptive information and devices and laws governing abortion.

---

radical feminist as well. Socialist feminism grew out of Marxist feminism. While Marxist feminists are concerned primarily with the public realm, socialist feminists look at both the public and private realms. They believe that sexism is rooted in the sexual division of labor between the private home (the woman's realm) and the outside public workplace (man's realm). They maintain that this split is a product of capitalism.

Feminists reject **conservatism,** which regards the roles and capacities of men and women as biologically determined and unchangeable and seeks to retain patriarchy and traditional gender roles. The sexual division in the workplace and home, according to conservatives, is a natural expression of these biological differences. Rather than providing a critical analysis of women's oppression, conservatism provides a justification for it. In his reading at the end of this chapter, "The Logic of Patriarchy," Steven Goldberg argues that male dominance is rooted in biological differences.

Gender essentialists believe that there are essential, innate differences between men and women. However, unlike conservatives, they do not see this as justifying men's dominance of women. Instead women's distinctive nature is to be valued and liberated, primarily through consciousness-raising groups like the one in the scenario at the beginning of this chapter. In 1982 psychologist Carol Gilligan published her landmark book *In A Different Voice,* in which she argues that the liberal emphasis on autonomy and separateness from others is a male value. Gilligan maintains that women are fundamentally connected to life and value connection over individuation. Women's moral reasoning and interaction with the world are based on responsibility, intimacy, and care, not on autonomy, justice, and rights reasoning as used by men. The liberal goal of **androgyny,** the sameness of men and women, is striving not toward true equality but toward the male ideal in dress, behavior, and career ambitions and the rejection of traditional female roles such as motherhood and social service. In the reading "Essentialist Challenges to Liberal Feminism," Ruth Groenhout examines gender-essentialist theories and concludes that liberal feminist theory offers a more powerful tool for securing the rights and freedom of women.

Another type of feminism is **ecofeminism,** which links men's desire to control and dominate women to men's domination and exploitation of the environment. Women, ecofeminists argue, should take the lead in preserving the environment because women are more in tune with nature. For more on ecofeminism see Chapter 12.

In the 1980s feminism began moving away from its roots as a radical political movement. In the current postfeminist period, feminist dialogue and gender analysis occur primarily in the universities.

Support for the feminist movement has declined during the past few decades. In a 1986 Gallup poll, 56 percent of women polled considered themselves feminists. This figure dropped to 33 percent in 1992 and to 25 percent in 2001.[3] The decline may be caused, in part, by modern feminism's primary focus on middle-class working women; the marginalization of African American women, poor women, and stay-at-home mothers; and disillusionment with the lack of progress made for women in the workplace, in politics, and at home.[4] Also, the assertion by academic feminists that one must support abortion-on-demand to be a true feminist has alienated many women (see Serrin Foster's reading, "Refuse to Choose: Women Deserve Better Than Abortion," in Chapter 2).

While the feminist movement in developed countries has focused primarily on equality in the workplace and reproductive rights, the issues of poverty and maternal and infant mortality, including death rates from AIDS, are more pressing in many developing nations. Other feminist issues of concern in developing nations are lack of access to education, lack of property rights for married women, and violence against women—both domestic and by military forces—as well as female genital mutilation (circumcision) in Africa, female infanticide and the sex trade in Southeast Asia, and divorce laws in Islamic countries that allow only men to initiate a divorce.

🖊 TYPES OF FEMINISM

Liberal feminism: Men and women are equal. There is a common human nature that transcends gender differences. The purpose of the state is to provide the liberty for women to exercise their freedom and equal rights.

Radical feminism: Patriarchy and rigid gender roles are the cause of oppression of women. Patriarchy must be rejected and, according to some, men as well.

Marxist feminism: The capitalist class system is the cause of oppression for women. To achieve equality, we need to overthrow capitalism.

Socialist feminism: Sexism is rooted in the division between the public (work/government) and private (home) realms. This split is the result of capitalism and calls for a more integrated, socialist approach.

Gender-essentialist feminism: There are essential differences between men and women that should not be ignored.

Ecofeminism: Patriarchy and male domination are harmful to women as well as the environment.

THE PHILOSOPHERS ON WOMEN

Philosophers bear part of the responsibility for perpetuating **sexism**—the belief that women are inferior to men. Plato taught that man is the true humanity and that woman is a deviation. Woman exists as the result of evil and failure to control one's passions. A man's destiny is to use his rational human faculties. If a man fails to control his emotions, he lives unrighteously and will be reincarnated as a woman.

Aristotle continued the philosophical tradition of misogyny. According to him, heat is the fundamental principle of perfection in animals. Women are colder than men and, therefore, less perfect. Aristotle concluded that a female embryo must be a deviation from nature and results from a deficiency in generative heat. A female is a misbegotten male, a "monstrosity," a "mutilated male." Like Aristotle, Goldberg maintains that **patriarchy**—the dominance of men—has a basis in biology. Although not arguing that women are inferior, Goldberg does maintain that patriarchy is inevitable.

The early Christian philosophers embraced the Platonic doctrine that women are inherently inferior to men. According to Augustine (A.D. 354–430), God created woman to be "in sex subjected to the masculine sex." The second creation story in Genesis, in which Eve was created from the rib of Adam, is used to reinforce the subservient role of women.

The philosophical view that privileges reason and equates male thinking with rationality continues to dominate much of Western philosophy. According to the Enlightenment philosophers, it is through reason that humanity progresses, socially and morally. Immanuel Kant believed that women are deficient in reason. Jean-Jacques

Rousseau maintained that men and women have different duties, based on a natural sexual division of labor. Women can be forced to be free by compelling them to fulfill their duties as mothers and wives. Rousseau writes:

> Woman was made especially to please man. . . . This is the law of nature. If woman is formed to please and to live in subjection, she must render herself agreeable to man instead of provoking his wrath; her strength lies in her charms.[5]

British philosopher and liberal feminist Mary Wollstonecraft (1759–1797) wrote *A Vindication of the Rights of Woman* primarily as a response to Rousseau. In "The Subjection of Women," co-authored by Harriet Taylor, John Stuart Mill also denounced patriarchal power, arguing that women need to be freed from subjection to men. The injustices perpetuated on women by an "almost despotic power of husbands over wives" need to be corrected by giving women the same rights and the same protection under the law as men.[6] Friedrich Engels, in his Marxist analysis of women's oppression, notes:

> The husband is obliged to earn a living and support his family, and that in itself gives him a position of supremacy. . . . Within the family he is the bourgeois, and the wife represents the proletariat. . . . Equality will be achieved only when the special legal privileges of the capitalist class have been abolished. . . . and both [men and women] possess legally complete equality of rights. . . . [T]he first condition for the liberation of the wife is to bring the whole female sex back into public industry, and that this in turn demands that the characteristic of the monogamous family as the economic unit of society be abolished.[7]

Freud was developing his theory of psychoanalysis at about the same time that the first wave of feminists were fighting for equal rights for women. Freud believed that such a project was doomed to failure. Girls feel wronged, he argued, because they don't have a penis like boys and fall victim to penis envy and resentment. As the girl grows up, "the wish for a penis is replaced by one for a baby, in particular a son, from her father." Freud maintained that women have little sense of justice, and a weaker social interest, because of the prominent role that envy plays in their lives.

Modern feminists reject theories claiming that women are inherently inferior to men. In *The Second Sex*, Simone de Beauvoir (1908–1986) accuses the philosophical tradition of propagating the view of women as the "other," as deviant human beings. She argues that gender inequalities are primarily the result of upbringing. Gender stereotypes are also reinforced by the media. (See Case Studies 1 and 6.)

MOTHERHOOD

The experience of motherhood is central to many women's lives. Most modern feminists view motherhood as an oppressive patriarchal institution. Radical feminists believe that motherhood is a social construct, rather than something women naturally want. In her 1949 book *The Second Sex*, Simone de Beauvoir wrote that woman's "misfortune is to have been biologically destined for the repetition of life." Women's connection to others, including pregnancy and motherhood, according to radical feminists, is a source of misery and oppression, not celebration and joy.[8] Like sexual intercourse, pregnancy blurs the line between self and other and, hence, is objectionable and debasing. The solution to this "misfortune" is legalized abortion. Indeed, radical feminists maintain that women who claim to enjoy motherhood are operating from a false consciousness and fail to recognize their own oppression.

Despite this admonition, many professional women are choosing to become mothers. Indeed, "raising a family" was listed by both female (76.9 percent) and male (76.5 percent) students in the 2007 American college freshman survey as being an "essential" or "very important" objective in their lives, more important than any other objective including "being well off financially" or "being an expert in my field."[9] According to the National Centers for Health Statistics, women with a college education are more likely to delay childbearing until their 30s or early 40s. As a result, professional women tend to have more problems with infertility than their less educated counterparts.

Assisted reproductive technologies (ART) have increased options for motherhood. The birth of Louise Brown, the first "test-tube baby," in England in 1978 heralded a new era of reproductive technology. Conception could now take place in a petri dish or test tube in a laboratory without the presence of either parent. **In vitro fertilization** (IVF) soon became a popular means of overcoming the problem of infertility. By January 2009, 3 million babies worldwide had been born as a result of IVF. Some feminists criticize ART and the drive to have children who are biologically related for reducing women to their reproductive organs, especially when adoption is an option. Others praise ART for increasing women's choices. (See Case Study 3.)

Surrogate motherhood, in which one woman agrees to bear a child for another, hit the front pages in 1986 when surrogate mother Mary Beth Whitehead, who was also the baby's biological mother, went to court to get custody of the child she had contracted to have for William Stern, the biological father, and his wife. The Whitehead/Stern case raised a public outcry over treating children, and women's reproductive capacities, as commercial commodities. Many states in the United States and some European nations do not permit commercial surrogacy. Because commercial surrogacy was legalized in India in 2002, more and more Americans are turning to women in India to act as surrogate mothers for their children, a practice that some feminists oppose as exploitation of poor women. (See Case Study 2.)

Adrienne Rich, in her book *Of Woman Born* (1976), was one of the first of the contemporary feminists to write at any length about motherhood as an institution, her experiences as a mother, and the patriarchal notion of motherhood as a "sacred calling." Carol Gilligan in *A Different Voice* (1982) and Sara Ruddick in *Maternal Thinking: Towards a Politics of Peace* (1989) further broke down the barrier between feminist theory and discussion of women as mothers and nurturers. Ruddick regards maternal thinking as "one kind of discipline among many [such as engineering or political science] each with identifying questions, methods and aims." She suggests that "maternal practice is a 'natural resource' for peace politics."[10]

Socialist feminists claim that the capitalist relegation of home and motherhood to the private realm has hurt both mothers and children. Because the home is considered outside the public realm in a capitalist society, the contributions of pregnant women and mothers are not valued or compensated. According to the International Labor Organization, women do two-thirds of the world's work and earn 5 percent of the income.[11] Although men in the United States are doing more of the housework and child care than they did forty years ago, women still do twice as much.[12] This creates a "second shift" for working mothers. Indeed, Hirshman argues that it is not so much the "glass ceiling" at work that has held women back, but the "glass ceiling" at home. It is the failure to transform domestic life that is holding women back.

Liberal feminists such as Hirshman are wary of making motherhood the foundation of womanhood because most of the disadvantage imposed on women in the workplace—and at home—is based on women's ability to become pregnant. Liberal feminists' primary concern with motherhood has been how it interferes with the workplace. One solution proposed by liberal feminists is for men and women to share equally in the care of the children. They also support the establishment of twenty-four-hour day-care centers for working mothers and parental leave that would free mothers, as well as fathers, to compete in the job market.

Societal attitudes toward motherhood also contribute to the glass ceiling. During the 2008 presidential election, John McCain's choice of Sarah Palin as his running made was loudly criticized because she was the mother of five children (three of whom would still be living at home in 2009), despite the fact that her husband was going to be a stay-at-home dad had the Republicans won. No similar criticism was ever directed at Barack Obama, who has two young daughters and a wife who worked full-time, nor at any other male presidential candidates, past or present, who had large families.

WOMEN IN THE WORKPLACE

Studies have found that gender is the "best single predictor of the compensation for that job, surpassing in importance education, experience, or unionization."[13] The lack of fair opportunities in the workplace has been a major concern of feminists for almost two centuries. In the United States, women earn about 76 cents for every dollar men make, a figure that has remained relatively unchanged for the past twenty-five years. In fact, the gap between men and women college graduates has increased slightly over the past decade, despite the fact that more and more women are going to college.[14] According to the National Center for Education Statistics, women earned 59 percent of all postsecondary degrees in 2008 and 49 percent of doctorates. The wage gap increases when women start having children.[15] Despite greater encouragement for women to go into professions such as medicine and law, most women have jobs, not careers. According to the United Nations, the gap between men and women in both the developed and the undeveloped world increased between 1990 and 2000, a phenomenon known as the "feminization of poverty."[16] Worldwide, women earn a little more than 50 percent of what men earn. Globalization of the market economy has contributed to the feminization of poverty.

Unlike college graduates at the height of the feminist movement, who combined full-time careers with motherhood, many women graduating from the elite colleges today say they plan to put their career on hold when they have children.[17] In a 2007 Gallup poll, 45 percent of women stated that they favored staying at home over working outside the home. Twenty-nine percent of the men polled by Gallup also said they would prefer to stay at home rather than go to work—an all-time high. Despite this trend, studies show that men's sense of happiness and fulfillment is much more tied to

---

🖋 THE FAMILY AND MEDICAL LEAVE ACT OF 1993

Section 102 (a1) ENTITLEMENT TO LEAVE.—Subject to section 103, an eligible employee shall be entitled to a total of 12 workweeks of [unpaid] leave during any 12-month period for one or more of the following:

(A) Because of the birth of a son or daughter of the employee and in order to care for such son or daughter.

(B) Because of the placement of a son or daughter with the employee for adoption or foster care.

(C) In order to care for the spouse, or a son, daughter, or parent, of the employee, if such spouse, son, daughter, or parent has a serious health condition.

(D) Because of a serious health condition that makes the employee unable to perform the functions of the position of such employee.

---

their work than is women's. While men who are not employed are much less likely to report that they are very happy, there is little difference between the reported levels of happiness of women who are employed and those who are not.[18]

Socialist feminists argue that the primary cause of women's oppression is capitalist assumptions about the value of women's work and of men's work, and the relegation of work to the public sphere and of home and family to the private sphere. By keeping women's wages low in the workplace, men keep women dependent so that women will continue doing the majority of work in the home. Like the home, the workplace is a gendered institution. It is geared toward the needs of a man who has no or minimal home and family obligations. The traditional, inflexible work schedule is hostile to working mothers, who are often forced to compromise their careers. Despite the fact that most family responsibility still falls on women, among college-educated adults, men (55.5 percent) are more likely to have flex-time options at work than are women (39.7 percent).[19] In addition, working mothers are now burdened with two full-time jobs—a career and caring for the children and home. They maintain that the workplace needs to be restructured so it is more family-friendly and flexible. There is also a need for the government to legislate paid maternity leave and subsidized child care.

Conservatives as well as some gender essentialists argue that women do not do as well in the workplace because they are better suited for the home and parenthood than are men. Liberal feminists believe that it is discrimination and the rigid and demanding work schedules that make the workplace less personally satisfying for women. They point out that most professional women who leave their jobs are ambivalent about doing so and often leave only as a last resort. What is needed, liberal feminists argue, are gender-blind policies and legislation to achieve equality.

Critics of liberal feminism charge that while professing to be gender-neutral, liberal feminists define success by the male standard of power, professional achievement, and money. Liberal feminists encourage women to achieve equality by moving into higher-paying, traditionally male professions. However, studies show that even in the same profession, such as law, there are "steep inequalities of pay, promotion, and opportunities."[20] In universities, female faculty earn only 85 to 90 percent of the income of male faculty at the same rank.[21] This inequity is actually greater because male faculty are more likely to be promoted than female faculty.

While many women are frustrated because of workplace discrimination that prevents them from advancing, other professional women, such as the women mentioned in the opening scenario, no longer find the top so attractive. Professional women are suffering from burnout, stress disorders, and fertility problems. A survey found that 26 percent of women at the most senior levels of management who have a chance to advance don't want promotions.

Probably nowhere has the conflict between the liberal "equal treatment" model and the "special treatment" model been so controversial as in work policies related to pregnancy. Liberal feminists argue that treating pregnancy as special demeans women.[22] Instead, they regard pregnancy as a temporary disability, like any other temporary disability, that takes women away from work for a period of time.

Until the early 1970s employers could fire or refuse to hire a woman because of pregnancy. In 1978 Congress passed the Pregnancy Discrimination Act, which prohibited discrimination and denial of benefits to women because of pregnancy. The Family and Medical Leave Act was passed in 1993. Under the act, a woman's job may be protected for a total of twelve weeks, including time taken off before and after birth. The law does not distinguish between mothers and fathers. The United States is currently one of only five countries in the world—the others being Lesotho, Liberia, Papua New Guinea, and Swaziland—that do not legislate paid maternity leave. (See Case Study 4.)

Sexist attitudes also limit women's opportunities in politics, especially at the upper echelons where women are most underrepresented. Most recently, sexism reared its ugly head in the 2008 presidential election. In a survey of female members of the Junior League of Voters, racism was regarded as worse than sexism. While sexism was perceived as an "acceptable joke," racism was seen as "politically incorrect" and "outrageous."[23] See Gloria Steinem's editorial "Women Are Never Front-Runners" at the end of this chapter.

It has been almost fifty years since Betty Friedan wrote in *The Feminine Mystique* that equality and human dignity are not possible for women if they are not able to earn. Are women better off than they were forty years ago? Or have women been duped by feminism, as some conservatives claim? Is the fast-track superwoman, so glorified by feminists, actually "dehumanized by her career" and "uncertain of her gender identity"?[24] Or is the problem the gendered structure of the workplace that prevents many women from finding equality and dignity in their work?

SEXUAL HARASSMENT

Sexual harassment—unwanted sexual attention—continues to be a problem in the workplace, the military, and schools. About half of working women experience sexual harassment on the job. In 2006, the U.S. Equal Employment Opportunity Commission (EEOC) received almost 13,000 charges of sexual harassment. About one-third of active-duty military women also report experiencing sexual harassment.[25] Young women are most likely to be sexually harassed, with two-thirds of college students reporting that they have been harassed on campus. While most harassment comes from peers, 38 percent of students say they have been sexually harassed by teachers or school employees.[26]

The law has been slow to recognize sexual harassment as a form of discrimination against women. Although an amendment was added in 1972 to the Civil Rights Act specifically prohibiting sexual harassment, women are still reluctant to complain, and in many cases courts have ruled against them.

In June 2001, seven California women who were former Wal-Mart employees filed a suit alleging that female workers received lower wages than male workers, were denied promotions, and were constantly subjected to sexual harassment. *Dukes v. Wal-Mart Stores, Inc.*, which covers 1.6 million women who have worked at Wal-Mart since December 1998, is the largest legal case in history involving workplace bias. In 2004, the court ruled in favor of the plaintiffs. Wal-Mart is currently appealing the decision.

Some people believe that charges of sexual harassment are simply instances of miscommunication between men and women, or cultural differences, rather than a misuse of power.[27] They also believe that sexual harassment is a "woman's problem," or that women use charges to get back at men. While not denying that sexual harassment can be a means of oppressing women, Katie Roiphe, in the reading "Reckless Eyeballing: Sexual Harassment on Campus," questions the current definitions of sexual harassment. She argues that these definitions, like the "rape crisis" definitions of date rape, are so broad that they create distrust and suspicion among men and women by implying that men are sexual predators and that women are their helpless victims. Roiphe argues that in many cases women just have to stand up to their harassers instead of playing the role of victim.

THE MORAL ISSUES

Autonomy and Liberty Rights

Women's autonomy and liberty right to pursue their legitimate interests is compromised by discrimination and limited choices in the workplace. The traditional family structure also restricts women's autonomy. Liberal and radical feminists, in particular, emphasize autonomy and choice when it comes to motherhood.

Human Nature

Feminist theory is grounded in certain assumptions about human nature and the nature of women and men. These assumptions have a profound effect on what solutions feminists propose for overcoming the oppression of women. Conservatives believe that women are, by nature, subservient. Patriarchy is natural and society, including the family and workplace, is structured to reflect this reality. Feminist demands for equality are not only unreasonable but harmful to women. These views are still embedded in gender stereotypes that justify division of labor based on gender.

Liberal feminists disagree, arguing that men and women share the same rational nature. Gender essentialists believe that men and women have different natures, with women being more caring and nurturing. However, unlike conservatives, they do not believe the differences between men and women justify the oppression of women. Radical feminists also claim that women and men are different, with men being objectifiers and women being sexually objectified.

Some critics maintain that radical feminists have gone too far by promoting a false view of men as sexual oppressors of women. Others criticize liberal feminists for adopting what they regard as a male model of human nature.

Justice, Discrimination, and Gender Equality

At home women still perform the majority of housework and child care. At work women suffer from job discrimination and earn significantly less than what men earn. Conservatives claim that this discrepancy is natural and based on a natural division of labor.

Liberal feminists maintain that because men and women share the same nature, justice demands that they be treated the same. Liberals promote gender-neutral policies such as the Family and Medical Leave Act to achieve gender equality in the workplace. Some Marxist and socialist feminists recommend a policy of comparable worth to raise the wages in female-dominated occupations to the level paid to men in occupations of comparable worth. Socialist feminists also believe that much of the injustice in the home as well as the workplace is due to the relegation of the home to the private sphere and work to the public sphere. To correct these inequities, they recommend restructuring the work environment so it has flexible work schedules to accommodate the needs of working mothers and fathers.

Utilitarian Considerations: Harms and Benefits

Although parents are more likely to state that they are happy than people with no children, this association disappears once marital status is taken into consideration, since married people are significantly happier than single people.[28] Indeed, some studies have found that having a child is associated with a drop in the level of happiness and an increase in stress in a marriage. What is the source of the unhappiness (harm)? Are women who are mothers today less happy because our culture does not support motherhood, as socialist feminists claim, or because motherhood is by nature an oppressive institution that stymies women's "right to flourish," as Hirshman and de Beauvoir claim?

While conservatives argue that traditional gender roles benefit both men and women, women clearly are getting the short end of the stick. Discrimination in the workplace not only harms women, but harms society by depriving society of the talents and valuable contributions of women. Women who are mothers are especially vulnerable. Women and children from economically disadvantaged families in particular suffer from the "feminization of poverty" as a result of lower wages paid to women and lack of adequate child-care facilities. The creation of more flexible work schedules, reasonable family leave policies, and twenty-four-hour day-care centers have all been proposed by feminists as means of improving the situation of working mothers. Sexual harassment also harms women by creating a work or school environment that interferes with women's ability to participate fully and equally.

CONCLUSION

Discrimination against women permeates our society. Lower wages for working women and sexual harassment are just examples. Different feminist theories propose different solutions for overcoming the problems of oppression. These solutions, which range

---

☙ SUMMARY OF READINGS ON FEMINISM,
MOTHERHOOD, AND THE WORKPLACE

de Beauvoir, "The Second Sex." Sexuality and motherhood are key aspects of
women's oppression.

Groenhout, "Essentialist Challenges to Liberal Feminism." Liberal feminism provides a more powerful tool than gender essentialism in the fight against sexism.

Hirshman, "Homeward Bound." Traditional patterns of motherhood are
harmful to women, who should get out to work in order to be empowered and
flourish.

Young, "The Return of the Mommy Wars." A critique of Hirshman's argument
that women should get out to work.

Steinem, "Women Are Never Front-Runners." Sexism is a greater barrier than
racism in American life and politics.

Goldberg, "The Logic of Patriarchy." Patriarchy and male dominance are not
simply the product of socialization but are rooted in biology.

Roiphe, "Reckless Eyeballing: Sexual Harassment on Campus." The current
definitions of sexual harassment perpetuate stereotypes of women as helpless
victims rather than empowering women.

---

from rejection of motherhood and male institutions altogether to enforcing gender-
neutral policies in the workplace, are based primarily on differing views of women's
and men's nature as well as economic institutions. While liberal feminists believe that
equality can be achieved within the existing capitalist structure, Marxist and socialist
feminists maintain that in order to achieve equality for women we first need to replace
the patriarchal capitalist economic system.

☙ SIMONE DE BEAUVOIR

The Second Sex

French philosopher and author Simone de Beauvoir (1908–1986) wrote *The Second Sex*
in 1949. It is considered one of the classics of feminist literature. De Beauvoir regards
sexuality and motherhood as key aspects of women's oppression. In this selection she
explores what it means to be a woman and to be a mother.

The Second Sex, trans by H. M. Parshley (New York: Alfred A. Knopf, 1953).

Critical Reading Questions

1. How does de Beauvoir answer the question "What is woman?"
2. What does de Beauvoir mean when she says that woman is defined as the Other?
3. In what ways do religions support the subordinate position of women?
4. On what grounds does de Beauvoir reject motherhood as woman's natural "calling"?
5. What is de Beauvoir's view of pregnancy?
6. How does de Beauvoir respond to the claim that pregnancy is a creative act?
7. How does de Beauvoir respond to the preconception that maternity is the crown of a woman's life?
8. How does de Beauvoir respond to the preconception that "the child is sure of being happy in its mother's arms"?
9. What is de Beauvoir's view of mothers having careers?

INTRODUCTION

[W]hat is a woman? "*Tota mulier in utero*," says one, "woman is a womb." . . .

To state the question is, to me, to suggest, at once, a preliminary answer. The fact that I ask it is in itself significant. A man would never get the notion of writing a book on the peculiar situation of the human male. But if I wish to define myself, I must first of all say: "I am a woman"; on this truth must be based all further discussion. A man never begins by presenting himself as an individual of a certain sex; it goes without saying that he is a man. . . . Man superbly ignores the fact that his anatomy also includes glands, such as the testicles, and that they secrete hormones. He thinks of his body as a direct and normal connection with the world, which he believes he apprehends objectively, whereas he regards the body of woman as a hindrance, a prison, weighed down by everything peculiar to it. "The female is a female by virtue of a certain *lack* of qualities," said Aristotle; "we should regard the female nature as afflicted with a natural defectiveness." And St. Thomas for his part pronounced woman to be an "imperfect man," an "incidental" being. This is symbolized in Genesis where Eve is depicted as made from what Bossuet called "a supernumerary bone" of Adam.

Thus humanity is male and man defines woman not in herself but as relative to him; she is not regarded as an autonomous being. . . . He is the Subject, he is the Absolute—she is the Other. . . .

Why is it that women do not dispute male sovereignty? No subject will readily volunteer to become the object, the inessential; it is not the Other who, in defining himself as the Other, establishes the One. The Other is posed as such by the One in defining himself as the One. But if the Other is not to regain the status of being the One, he must be submissive enough to accept this alien point of view. Whence comes this submission in the case of woman? . . .

Here is to be found the basic trait of woman: she is the Other in a totality of which the two components are necessary to one another. . . .

When man makes of woman the *Other*, he may, then, expect her to manifest deep-seated tendencies toward complicity. Thus, woman may fail to lay claim to the status of subject because she lacks definite resources, because she feels the necessary bond that ties her to man regardless of reciprocity, and because she is often very well pleased with her role as the *Other*. . . .

In the bosom of the family, woman seems in the eyes of childhood and youth to be clothed in the same social dignity as the adult males. Later on, the young man, desiring and loving, experiences the resistance, the independence of the woman desired and loved; in marriage, he respects woman as wife and mother, and in the concrete events of conjugal life she stands there before him as a free being. He can therefore feel that social subordination as between the sexes no longer exists and that on the whole, in spite of differences, woman is an equal. As, however, he observes some points of inferiority—the most important being unfitness for the professions—he attributes these to natural causes. When he is in a co-operative and benevolent relation with woman, his theme is the principle of abstract equality, and he does not base his attitude upon such inequality as may exist. But when he is in conflict with her, the situation is reversed: his theme will be the existing inequality, and he will even take it as justification for denying abstract equality.

So it is that many men will affirm as if in good faith that women *are* the equals of man and that they have nothing to clamor for, while *at the same time* they will say that women can never be the equals of man and that their demands are in vain. . . . If the "woman question" seems trivial, it is because masculine arrogance has made of it a "quarrel"; and when quarreling one no longer reasons well. . . .

Quite evidently this problem would be without significance if we were to believe that woman's destiny is inevitably determined by physiological, psychological, or economic forces. . . .

THE MOTHER

It is in maternity that woman fulfills her physiological destiny; it is her natural "calling," since her whole organic structure is adapted for the perpetuation of the species. But we have seen already that human society is never abandoned wholly to nature. And for about a century the reproductive function in particular has no longer been at the mercy solely of biological chance; it has come under the voluntary control of human beings. . . .

Pregnancy is above all a drama that is acted out within the woman herself. She feels it as at once an enrichment and an injury; the fetus is a part of her body, and it is a parasite that feeds on it; she possesses it, and she is possessed by it; it represents the

future and, carrying it, she feels herself vast as the world; but this very opulence annihilates her, she feels that she herself is no longer anything. A new life is going to manifest itself and justify its own separate existence, she is proud of it; but she also feels herself tossed and driven, the plaything of obscure forces. It is especially noteworthy that the pregnant woman feels the immanence of her body at just the time when it is in transcendence: it turns upon itself in nausea and discomfort; it has ceased to exist for itself and thereupon becomes more sizable than ever before. . . . Ensnared by nature, the pregnant woman is plant and animal, a stock-pile of colloids, an incubator, an egg; she scares children proud of their young, straight bodies and makes young people titter contemptuously because she is a human being, a conscious and free individual, who has become life's passive instrument.

Ordinarily life is but a condition of existence; in gestation it appears as creative; but that is a strange kind of creation which is accomplished in a contingent and passive manner. There are women who enjoy the pleasures of pregnancy and suckling so much that they desire their indefinite repetitions; as soon as a baby is weaned these mothers feel frustrated. Such women are not so much mothers as fertile organisms, like fowls with high egg-production. And they seek eagerly to sacrifice their liberty of action to the functioning of their flesh: it seems to them that their existence is tranquilly justified in the passive fecundity of their bodies. If the flesh is purely passive and inert, it cannot embody transcendence, even in a degraded form; it is sluggish and tiresome; but when the reproductive process begins, the flesh becomes root-stock, source, and blossom, it assumes transcendence, a stirring toward the future, the while it remains a gross and present reality. . . . With her ego surrendered, alienated in her body and in her social dignity, the mother enjoys the comforting illusion of feeling that she is a human being *in herself, a value.*

But this is only an illusion. For she does not really make the baby, it makes itself within her; her flesh engenders flesh only, and she is quite incapable of establishing an existence that will have to establish itself. Creative acts originating in liberty establish the object as value and give it the quality of the essential; whereas the child in the maternal body is not thus justified; it is still only a gratuitous cellular growth, a brute fact of nature as contingent on circumstances as death and corresponding philosophically with it. . . . The dangerous falsity of two currently accepted preconceptions is clearly evident. . . .

The first of these preconceptions is that maternity is enough in all cases to crown a woman's life. It is nothing of the kind. There are a great many mothers who are unhappy, embittered, unsatisfied. . . . It is even more deceptive to dream of gaining through the child a plenitude, a warmth, a value, which one is unable to create for oneself; the child brings joy only to the woman who is capable of disinterestedly desiring the happiness of another, to one who without being wrapped up in self seeks to transcend her own existence. . . .

There is nothing *natural* in such an obligation: nature can never dictate a moral choice; this implies an engagement, a promise to be carried out. To have a child is to undertake a solemn obligation; if the mother shirks this duty subsequently, she commits an offense against an existent, an independent human being; but no one can impose the engagement upon her. The relation between parent and offspring, like that between husband and wife, ought to be freely willed. . . . A social and artificial morality is hidden beneath this pseudo-naturalism. That the child is the supreme aim of woman is a statement having precisely the value of an advertising slogan.

The second false preconception, directly implied by the first, is that the child is sure of being happy in its mother's arms. There is no such thing as an "unnatural mother," to be sure, since there is nothing natural about maternal love; but, precisely for that reason, there are bad mothers. And one of the major truths proclaimed by psychoanalysis is the danger to the child that may lie in parents who are themselves "normal." The complexes, obsessions, and neuroses of adults have their roots in the early family life of those adults. . . .

We have seen that woman's inferiority originated in her being at first limited to repeating life . . .

In a properly organized society, where children would be largely taken in charge by the community and the mother cared for and helped, maternity would not be wholly incompatible with careers for women. On the contrary, the woman who works—farmer, chemist, or writer—is the one who undergoes pregnancy most easily because she is not absorbed in her own person; the woman who enjoys the richest individual life will have the most to give her children and will demand the least from them; she who acquires in effort and struggle a sense of true human values will be best able to bring them up properly. If too often, today, woman can hardly reconcile with the best interests of her children an occupation that keeps her away from home for hours and takes all her strength, it is, on the one hand, because feminine employment is still too often a kind of slavery, and, on the other, because no effort has been made to provide for the care, protection, and education of children outside the home. This is a matter of negligence on the part of society; but it is false to justify it on the pretense that some law of nature, God, or man requires that mother and child belong exclusively to one another; this restriction constitutes in fact only a double and baneful oppression. . . .

Discussion Questions

1. Discuss de Beauvoir's claim that religion as an institution supports the oppression of women. If religion does contribute to the oppression of women, how should feminists respond to religion? Discuss whether or not equal opportunity legislation should be passed, as it was for the workplace, that would require religious institutions to treat women equitably.

2. Discuss de Beauvoir's observation that many men are engaged in doublethink by affirming in good faith that women are their equals while at the same time saying that women cannot be men's equals and that their demands are in vain. If you are a male student, examine ways in which you might unintentionally be doing this. If you are a female student, examine ways in which you might both want the benefits associated with being the Other and at the same time want equality with men.

3. Discuss de Beauvoir's analysis of pregnancy and motherhood. Do you agree with her? Support your answer.

RUTH GROENHOUT

Essentialist Challenges to Liberal Feminism

Ruth Groenhout is a professor of philosophy at Calvin College. Groenhout begins by summarizing the basic assumptions of liberal feminist theory regarding human nature. She then contrasts these assumptions with those of gender essentialists. Groenhout concludes that liberal theory provides a more powerful political tool than gender essentialism in the fight against sexual subordination.

Critical Reading Questions

1. What is the basic assumption of liberal political theory?
2. Why, according to Groenhout, are liberalism and feminism a natural alliance?
3. What is the role of government in liberal theory?
4. What does Groenhout mean when she says that "the notion of individual rights has been a politically powerful tool in the fight against sexual oppression"?
5. Why does Groenhout reject communitarianism?
6. What are the four reasons put forth by Groenhout for why feminism should not give up the liberal tradition?
7. What is gender essentialism and how does it differ from liberal feminism?
8. On what grounds do feminists such as Catherine MacKinnon challenge liberal feminism? How does Groenhout respond to MacKinnon's theory?
9. Why does Groenhout reject sociobiology as a foundation for feminist theory?
10. What are some of the problems, according to Groenhout, with both types of gender essentialism?
11. How does Groenhout respond to the claim by gender essentialists that men are more aggressive than women?

"Essentialist Challenges to Liberal Feminism" *Social Theory and Practice* 28, no. 1 (2002): 51–75. Some notes have been omitted.

12. How does Groenhout respond to the critics of liberalism?
13. On what grounds does Groenhout conclude that feminism should not give up liberalism?

Liberal political theory begins with rights, autonomy, and reason. Humans have rights, and their freedom to exercise those rights is properly limited by others' rights. This view of the basic shape of the political terrain is based on certain assumptions about humans. The most basic is the assumption that humans, whatever their other differences, share some basic qualities that make them properly bearers of rights. . . .

Because liberal political thought bases rights on what would seem to be a gender-neutral concept such as rationality, it has been a traditional resource for feminist thinkers, from early thinkers such as Mary Wollstonecraft and Harriet Taylor Mill, to contemporary thinkers. . . .

This easy and obvious association of liberal political thought with feminist theory has been challenged from two directions. On the one hand, some feminist theorists have challenged the tight connection between liberalism and feminism, because, they have argued, the notion of rationality on which liberal rights are based is not as gender-neutral as it seems. So in her critique of objective rationality, Catharine MacKinnon argues that traditional notions of objectivity that underlie claims about rationality are inherently tied to the objectification of women.[1] If rationality/objectivity is inherently connected to the objectification of women, then the "rationality" of women becomes problematic. On this view, women must either deny their nature as women (become honorary men) and objectify other women in order to be rational, or they must accept their status as objectified (not objectifiers) and so be incapable of rationality. In either case, rationality cannot be exercised by women as women. If this account of rationality is accepted, the standard liberal assumption that men and women equally share in rationality must be given up. . . .

In more recent years the rise of evolutionary ethics, or sociobiological accounts of human nature, have also contributed to a general skepticism about an account of human nature as either rational, or autonomous, or gender-neutral. . . .

The aspect of evolutionary ethics that has proved most effective in distancing liberal thought from feminist thought is the assumption, deeply imbedded in evolutionary ethics, that men and women are genetically coded for different behavior due to their differing roles in the reproductive process and the different reproductive strategies these roles require. What counts as "rational" from the perspective of genes that find themselves in a male body is, we are told, profoundly different from what counts as "rational" for genes that find themselves in a female body. Strategies that lead to success in propagation for men are different from strategies that lead to success in propagation for women. These differences, further, have been selected for over millennia of evolutionary processes, and are now ineradicably a part of what it is to be a man or a woman. It follows from this that even if one wanted to continue the liberal project of grounding rights in (say) rationality, one could no longer assume that male rationality is the same as female rationality, and the easy connection between liberalism and feminism is again severed. . . .

1. LIBERALISM AND FEMINISM: A NATURAL ALLIANCE?

. . . The first thing to note is that the term "liberal political thought" can be used to cover an extremely broad range of thinkers, from Mill to Rousseau, from Wollstonecraft to Hegel. . . . I am assuming that the notion of rationality that undergirds liberal thought is an extensive notion, including the ability to reflect on and choose among conceptions of the good life. This account of rationality is needed to make sense of the moral and political claims of liberal thought.

Liberalism grounds its basic rights in human nature, a nature characterized by rationality and autonomy. There are really two separable aspects to this claim. We might call the first the individualism thesis and the second the rights thesis. Both rely on the notion that there is something morally significant to human capacities for rational deliberation. The first notes that humans are properly thought of first as individuals, not as units in a larger whole. The respect that liberalism accords humans is accorded prior to and independently of membership in any particular community or class. . . .

The rights thesis entails that the respect individuals should be accorded is best articulated in terms of rights, politically protected liberties or entitlements. . . . Which rights need to be protected is, of course, a contested issue in liberal thought. Libertarians defend a rather minimalist notion of protection, limited largely to protection of negative rights such as the right to own property. Rawlsian liberals and others defend a more expansive notion of rights, including rights to education and welfare, because these provide the basic necessities for exercising one's rational capacities. But in either case, the rights being protected are justified on the basis of the individual's capacity to exercise rational judgment and so act freely and be held responsible for his or her choices. This notion of rights naturally leads to a third thesis of liberal thought, that of a necessary, but limited state.

Individual rights cannot be protected without some form of governmental structures that protect them against both other individuals and governmental structures themselves. The liberal political theorist is committed to the notion that one cannot dispense with the state. Liberalism operates with a view of human nature that assumes that some political structures are needed to prevent humans from mistreating each other. This is

not the only role the state can play, but it is a fundamental one. . . .

So the state is necessary, but the state must also be limited. Just as humans, left unrestricted by the state, choose on occasion to mistreat others, so the state, left unchecked, will mistreat its citizens. The power of the state must be limited to protect a sphere of liberty for its citizens and for the non-governmental social structures that they create. . . . The notion of individual rights has been a politically powerful tool in the fight against sexual subordination. The history of the struggle against women's oppression has shown that women need to be able to make decisions for and about their lives as individuals. The right to make decisions that determine the course of one's life, in fact, has been a central right in the fight for women's liberation. There is a deep disagreement between feminism and certain versions of communitarianism, both because women know too well the dangers of being treated as a member of the class or social role of Woman and because traditional values have frequently been the source of women's oppression. The struggle to be recognized as an individual in one's own right and the respect accorded that individuality in law and in society have been too hard won to be given up lightly. Further, the individual is not valued, in liberal thought, because of a specific role that she or he is required to play in society, but instead is valued as an autonomous, that is, self-determining being. . . . These are core feminist values as well; feminism's goal is a world in which women are free to determine the course of their own lives and to play a significant role in political and social decision-making. As long as these remain central feminist values, feminists have reason to place themselves in the liberal tradition.

The second reason feminists should be reluctant to give liberalism up is that rights have been and continue to be important conceptual tropes for understanding the wrongness of gender oppression. There may be other moral frameworks for conceptualizing the moral wrong done to women when they are denied their rights, but few that explain that wrong so clearly, so straightforwardly, or so incontrovertibly. As an example, consider the arguments by Islamic feminists, or similar arguments made by Christians for Biblical Equality. In both cases, there are good reasons given for new interpretations of both religious traditions, arguments that support women's autonomy and independence. But in both cases one faces an uphill battle to convince conservative interpreters of the tradition to change their minds. In contrast, Wollstonecraft's arguments are relatively straightforward. No new interpretation of the notion of a right is needed to recognize that if rational agents deserve the rights intrinsic to autonomy, women must deserve those rights. . . .

A third reason why feminism has good reason to continue to locate itself in the liberal tradition is that the basic analysis of power that is central to feminism finds its historical roots in liberal thought. Power analyses are central to feminist theory, and a basic understanding of how power affects human interactions has been a staple of feminist analyses . . . some of the more perspicuous analyses were offered by Harriet Taylor Mill and John Stuart Mill in the nineteenth century. It is no accident that one finds a careful analysis of how power affects relationships between men and women in these thinkers; their liberal commitments provided a natural location from which to analyze the ways in which power affects individual relationships.

Finally, liberal political thought is based on a respect for the rational capacity of the individual. On this view, humans are more than stimulus response machines. They are capable of making decisions that are the result of critical reflection, and critical self-reflection, and are not purely determined in their actions by the biological and social forces that act on them. Both biological and social determinism truncate moral analysis in ways that make the wrongs done to women by sexism too limited. . . .

The liberal picture of human nature, as more than either biologically or socially determined, is a crucial aspect of the feminist analysis of the wrongness of sexist oppression. Sexual oppression, and social systems that perpetuate sexual oppression, are morally evil because they limit or deny women's capacity to reflect on and determine their own lives. . . .

The basic assumption on which a feminist liberalism is based is the notion of a common human nature. Critics who reject such a conception of human nature offer a critique that is, if correct, devastating to feminist liberalism. I would like to begin by presenting the critique, then argue that, carefully examined, it is not correct, and does not provide grounds for a rejection of feminist liberalism.

2. AGAINST LIBERALISM: THE CHALLENGE FROM FEMINISM

Potentially the most devastating feminist critique of liberal thought arises from a denial of the most basic claim in liberalism: the claim that there is some essential human nature that is the source of moral rights. One feminist challenge to this claim arises from the belief that there is no neutral human nature, but rather there are men's natures and women's natures, and the two are radically different. . . .

One theoretical vantage point from which such an attack on liberalism has been made is that of Catharine MacKinnon's account of rationality, objectivity, and legal structures. I should state at the outset that MacKinnon does not consider herself a gender essentialist, since she believes that "man" and "woman" are socially constructed categories. That said, however, she offers no alternative account of what it would be like to be male or female in any other way than as they are currently constructed in terms of men and women. Since she also believes that an oppressive gender hierarchy is a universal feature of human societies,[2] what she describes seems very close to an essentialist picture of men's and women's natures. Men and women are radically different in nature, they are shaped that way by their culture and cannot simply choose to be otherwise, and the very nature of our perceived reality is determined by these differences. . . .

On MacKinnon's view, women's and men's natures are determined by, respectively, their objectification as objects of sexualized violence or their objectification of others as objects of sexualized violence. What it is to be a woman is to be turned into an object that is an appropriate locus for sex and for sexualized violence; to be a woman is to be sexually vulnerable. What it is to be a man is to be one who can sexually objectify another, either through words or actions, and to be capable of sexual predation. Not all men are sexual predators, of course. Some see themselves as protectors of women rather than predators on women. But both of these roles, protector and predator, assume the same things about women—that women are weak and incapable of self-protection, that women are appropriate objects of sexual violence, and that it is men who control sexual access to women, not the women themselves.

On this view, then, women's nature is essentially one of sexual prey. Women are defined in terms of their sexual accessibility and status. Likewise the essence of being a man is being a sexual predator/objectifier. While neither of these roles is, for MacKinnon, biologically or genetically essential, both are essential to the nature of being a man or a woman—the only way to be otherwise is to cease to be a man or a woman, and become we know not what.

MacKinnon offers one version of a sort of gender essentialism, but other feminists have offered other varieties. Others do not rest, as MacKinnon's does, on a sexualized predator/prey relationship, but instead on a sharp dichotomy between male and female natures in terms of value hierarchies. Females, on this view, are primarily oriented toward life-giving, cooperative, nurturing activities, while males are primarily oriented toward death-dealing, aggressive, controlling activities. Sometimes these different orientations are simply assumed to be the case without explanation, sometimes they are explained as a result of a deep Jungian imaginary, or as a result of women's ability to give birth and men's envy of that ability. . . . For the purposes of this paper, however, I would like to focus on MacKinnon's account, because she is concerned directly with the issue of women's participation in a liberal society, and so she addresses precisely the issues with which I am concerned.

If men and women are fundamentally, essentially, different in the ways MacKinnon argues, then the liberal project of identifying basic human rights is misguided. If gender essentialism is correct, then there is no basic human nature, shared rationality, or fundamental similarity among people. There are two different sorts of beings that are lumped together under the rubric "human," but these two sorts of beings think differently, see the world differently, and have completely opposed value systems.

Liberal rights, from this perspective, are rights that are valued by men, generated by masculine reason, and appropriate (if at all) only for relationships among men. MacKinnon writes:

> The rule of law and the rule of men are one thing, indivisible, at once official and unofficial. . . . State power, embodied in law, exists throughout society as male power at the same time as the power of men over women throughout society is organized as the power of the state.[3]

. . . But MacKinnon's critique does not end with the historical record. In addition to noting that rights have, as a matter of historical fact, been the prerogative of men, she also charges that the very notion of rights is an intrinsically masculine construction. Freedom of speech, for example, has functioned, MacKinnon argues, to protect male "speech" in the form of the violent pornographic portrayal of women. Such speech, as she sees it, makes true freedom of speech for women inaccessible, since anything a woman says in the public sphere is undercut by the definition of women as sexual objects in pornographic portrayals. So the legal notion of freedom of speech functions, she claims, to protect male speech and prohibit female speech. In similar manner, abortion rights, framed as privacy rights, function to protect male sexual access to women. Laws against sexual harassment, likewise, have not served to protect working women adequately because of their reliance on the "reasonable man" standard for judging harassment. . . .

This perspectival bias indicates, according to MacKinnon, that these rights really are "basic" only from a male perspective. From the perspective of lived female experience, she argues, rights are the legal structures that both maintain and hide from view male dominance. This offers a serious challenge to any attempt to maintain a feminist liberalism. If liberalism, viewed accurately, is simply male dominance writ large, feminist liberalism is an oxymoron, which makes those who defend it perhaps just morons.

3. GENDER AND GENES: THE CHALLENGE FROM SOCIOBIOLOGY

A similarly serious challenge to feminist liberalism comes from a very different group of theorists. Like MacKinnon, sociobiologists assert that men and women are essentially different.

Sociobiologists argue that the two sexes are shaped by a long history of evolutionary change. That evolutionary change is driven by success in breeding—those traits that lead to reproductive success are genetically passed on to future generations. Men and women play different roles in the reproductive process. Men's reproductive role is one that can be accomplished relatively quickly and does not involve a great deal of investment. Women's reproductive role, on the other hand, involves an extensive investment in terms of time and energy, first in the nine months of pregnancy, and subsequently in the two to five years of breast-feeding and care-giving. . . .

. . . The assumption in sociobiology is that the differential success of these two different strategies has led to genetically based differences in men and women's behavior. Cultural and social differences, then, between men and women are not so much reflections of differing social roles and expectations as they are reflections of basic genetic differences between men and women.

Men, on this view, are genetically programmed for promiscuity and minimal investment in their children. Some have even argued that men are predisposed to rape as a part of their impulse to procreate. Women are programmed for monogamy and heavy investment in their children. . . . Sociobiologists have argued that male and female tendencies to exhibit traits such as aggression and empathy are likewise tied to reproductive success, and so men are, by nature, more prone to aggression in all areas of life while women are more prone to docility and empathetic nurturing.

As I mentioned above, the picture sociobiologists have drawn is not wildly different from the view of masculine and feminine nature offered by feminists such as MacKinnon. On both views, men are inherently more aggressive, sexually promiscuous, prone to violence, and oriented toward dominating women sexually. Women are inherently more nurturing, more submissive (particularly to men), sexually less promiscuous, and less driven by sexual urges, while more concerned about care for children and infants. . . . In contrast to MacKinnon, whose writing is motivated by political concerns, sociobiologists see their work as having bearing on, but not directly dictating, social policy. They do, generally, imply that the differences between men and women will have social effects. Men's natural aggression and sexual dominance will naturally make men the dominant sex in social settings. Women's natural deference and nurturance will generally prevent them from acquiring social power, but will serve the continuance of the human race quite efficiently. . . . Rather than offering social criticism, then, there is a tendency in this literature to offer explanations for why the status quo is what it is. Underlying this explanatory technique, however, there is sometimes the assumption that since the way things are is dictated by the differing natures of men and women, social policy that attempts to change or modify the existing situation is fighting an uphill battle. This is problematic because of the implicit approval it offers to sexist hierarchies. . . . [T]he more problematic version of sociobiology denies that there are any truths about humans not captured by evolutionary science. Humans, on this view, are nothing more than the sum of their evolutionary heritage, and so all accounts of human nature, human rationality, and human morality must be based in evolutionary studies. . . .

If one accepts this view of rationality, then one is forced to reject the notion that men and women share a common rational nature. . . . There may be a fundamental rational principle ("Propagate effectively!") but at the level of evaluation of actions or of social policy there is no shared conception of rationality. What is rational for men is irrational for women, and vice versa.

On this view, liberal rights are merely a thin veneer of illusion over the biological reality of genetics. . . . [F]urther, there is a deep and abiding conviction that hierarchies, particularly hierarchies of gender, are ineluctably written into the human genetic code. So E.O. Wilson famously comments that "a schedule of sex- and age-dependent ethics can impart higher genetic fitness than a single moral code which is applied uniformly to all sex-age groups."[4] And, more recently, Matt Ridley describes the sexual division of labor as "an economic institution that is a vital part of all human societies."[5] Rights and a concern for justice for individuals are all very nice in philosophical treatises, the implication is, but in the real world it is reproductive success that counts.

4. PROBLEMS WITH GENDER ESSENTIALISMS

If either feminist gender essentialism or sociobiological gender essentialism is correct, then feminist liberalism is incoherent. Feminist liberalism assumes that one can speak of a common human nature, but both sorts of gender essentialists hold that men and women have different natures. . . .

There are problems with both forms of gender essentialism, however, that defuse part of their challenge to liberal thought. The first problem is a matter of over-emphasis on difference. The second problem is an overstatement of determinism, in the one case cultural, in the second case genetic. I would like to deal with each of these in turn.

First, the over-emphasis on difference. Both gender-essentialist feminists and sociobiologists focus so heavily on gender difference that they lose sight of the huge areas of similarity between men and women. Two areas where this is particularly obvious are those of aggression and sexual promiscuity. According to both sorts of gender essentialists, men are more aggressive than women. In both cases theorists move from the statement that men are more aggressive than women to the assumption that aggression is a masculine trait. But the second claim is not entailed by the first. Both men and women are aggressive, though their aggression may show itself in different ways and be elicited by different occasions. . . .

Moreover, sweeping generalizations about the aggressiveness of men frequently ignore the complexity of the notion of aggression itself. It often is used as a synonym for violence, and there are innumerable statistics that show that men engage in more violence against both men and women than do women. But aggression involves more than just "committing murders and making weapons"—the research definition used in one study. Aggression is a complex set of behavioral patterns. . . . If those studying aggression begin with the assumption that aggression is a masculine trait, they will interpret behavior by males as aggressive. Research bias is a well documented problem, and a glance at contemporary discussions of primate research indicates that it is not easily overcome.

But, setting aside for the moment the question of research bias and the difficulty of defining aggression, let us imagine that males can be demonstrated, as a class, to have a tendency to exhibit aggression at a higher level than women. What follows from that with respect to men's and women's natures? It certainly does not follow that women are not aggressive. The fact that men are taller than women does not entail the claim that women don't have height, and the same absurdity occurs when a higher level of aggression in males is equated with a female lack of aggression. Women are aggressive; aggression is a necessary attribute for survival in human life. So from the fact that, as a class, men are more aggressive than women, one surely cannot conclude that women are not aggressive. Nor can one conclude that all men are more aggressive than all women—the statistics would clearly not bear that claim out either. . . .

The second criticism of gender-essentialist thought involves a rejection of the deterministic assumptions such essentialism rests on. One can recognize that sex differences matter in life without moving to the further assumption that they entirely determine every aspect of one's life. . . . We are constrained by the social setting within which we are born and socialized, and we are constrained by our physical nature. . . . But nothing warrants the move from constraint to determinism.

On MacKinnon's account, one cannot be a man without being an objectifier, and one cannot be a woman without being objectified. Further, one cannot choose to opt out of being a man or a woman. Similarly, some sociobiological accounts of human nature assume that being male or female is absolutely determinative of personality. . . . In some cases, in fact, biologically based behavior is more amenable to change than is culturally constructed behavior. Medication can diminish the symptoms of obsessive compulsive disorder, but no medication is likely to change a Westerner's deeply ingrained food taboos against, say, eating grubs. Asserting the "naturalness" of certain sorts of behavior, however, implies the opposite. It implies that biological features of our characters and personalities are fixed and determined in ways that are clearly false when we consider the issue carefully.

MacKinnon's own commitment to making legal changes in the way U.S. law deals with pornography suggests, in fact, that she herself has no trouble seeing herself as an agent rather than a sexualized object. Her legal successes suggest that the judicial system is capable of seeing women as more than sexualized objects. Likewise, the dedication to their research that scientists may display suggests that any account of human rationality as determined by the drive to procreate is seriously defective. . . .

5. LIBERALISM AND CRITICS

While I think that the essentialist case is overstated, I also think that there are valuable lessons to be learned from the critics of liberalism. . . . The first area concerns autonomy. MacKinnon rightly pushes us to recognize that autonomy is not something one either has or does not have. Autonomy occurs along a continuum, and one of the things that makes one more or less autonomous is one's enculturation and socialization into a way of life that may enhance or diminish one's capacity to make and act on choices. MacKinnon is right to point out that women's life choices are diminished when the culture they grow up in defines them as appropriate objects for sexualized violence. She is less concerned with the fact that men's lives, likewise, are diminished when they receive a cultural image of manliness as requiring mindless aggression and the sexual subordination of women. These definitions create a culture that is destructive of human lives and human autonomy. . . .

Likewise, criticisms from sociobiology are healthy for liberal political thought as well. Humans are not disembodied rational intellects. We are embodied, physical beings, whose lives and choices occur always in the context of our physical needs, our evolutionary heritage, and our hormonal present. This does not, in and of itself, negate our freedom and responsibility, but it does situate it in important ways. Careful thinkers have always realized that human freedom and responsibility do not merely occur in an embodied context: they require an embodied context for their exercise. Without a physical existence, it is hard to know what respect for another's needs or rights would even be.

Sociobiologists also help us to avoid the tendency to utopian thinking that can be tempting for moral and political theorists. Humans will always need some form of social safeguards, to prevent them from exploiting others and from being exploited in turn. . . .

Knowing that humans may have natural predispositions to act in certain ways is valuable information for moral reasoning. But it can never substitute for moral reasoning, since from the fact that humans naturally do something we cannot conclude that they ought to do that.

Further, both the feminist and the sociobiological critiques keep liberalism more honest about what it can and cannot do. . . . While both views encourage liberalism to remain humble about its limitations, however, a similar caution is needed in each of their respective cases as well. Sociobiology cannot tell us what the good human life must be, and MacKinnon is quite frank about her own inability to offer a determinate picture of a non–sexually objectified woman. Ultimately, each individual needs to be the one who decides what sort of life she will pursue, but in stating this I find myself back on familiar, liberal, terrain.

6. CONCLUSION

. . . The belief that women, as women, can fight and win legal battles is one worth holding on to. It seems to be one that MacKinnon herself holds. But it is in rather serious tension with the notion that women are defined, as women, in terms of their sexual violability. The two ideas do not sit well together. A liberal notion that women, oppressed though they may be, are still more than the sum of that oppression is, I think, exactly what is needed to make sense of the many ways in which women have exercised their agency to bring about political change. And it is a belief that is situated squarely in liberal theory.

Liberalism does have its weaknesses. Among them are the tendencies to erase differences among people and to overlook how culture and physical circumstances affect the very meaning of terms such as rights and autonomy. But having recognized these tendencies, is liberalism to be rejected? Not until a better alternative comes along, and that is what often seems missing from the critics of liberalism. . . . If we are not willing to give up the protection of basic rights, and if we think that individual autonomy is worth defending, then what is called for is a new and improved liberalism, not the rejection of liberal theory.

NOTES

1. Catharine MacKinnon, *Toward a Feminist Theory of the State* (Cambridge, Mass.: Harvard University Press, 1989), pp. 162–63.
2. MacKinnon, *Toward a Feminist Theory of the State,* p. 94.
3. MacKinnon, *Toward a Feminist Theory of the State,* p. 170.
4. E.O. Wilson, "The Morality of the Gene," excerpts from *Sociobiology: The New Synthesis,* in Paul Thompson (ed.), *Issues in Evolutionary Ethics* (Albany: State University of New York Press, 1995), pp. 153–64; see p. 163.
5. Matt Ridley, *On the Origins of Virtue* (New York: Viking, 1996), p. 92.

Discussion Questions

1. Make a list of the premises and conclusions regarding human nature in the arguments put forth by radical feminism (MacKinnon), sociobiology, and liberal feminism. Analyze each argument. Do the premises support their conclusions? Have any premises been omitted or are any overstated?
2. Does Groenhout present a convincing argument against gender essentialism? Discuss how MacKinnon (see her reading in Chapter 9) might respond to Groenhout's critique of radical feminist gender essentialism. Discuss how a sociobiologist such as E. O. Wilson might respond to Groenhout's argument. Which view of gender do you find most convincing? Support your answer.
3. Does liberal theory, as explicated by Groenhout, provide an adequate analysis of motherhood? Support your answer.
4. Discuss whether Groenhout's claim that liberalism is a more powerful tool for social reform has been demonstrated in reality.

5. Discuss whether liberal feminism is adequate for dealing with issues facing women in developing countries, such as poverty, exploitation in sweat shops, high maternal and infant mortality, lack of access to education, lack of property rights for married women, violence against women—both domestic and by military forces, selective abortion and female infanticide, and the sex trade in Southeast Asia.

LINDA HIRSHMAN

Homeward Bound

Linda Hirshman is an author, attorney, and retired professor of Philosophy and Women's Studies at Brandeis University. Hirshman argues that the traditional patterns of motherhood are harmful to women. By emphasizing choice in whether to work or stay home, feminism has failed women. Instead, women ought to get out to work since it is the workplace and public sphere that provide the most opportunities for women to be empowered and to flourish.

Critical Reading Questions

1. According to Hirshman, where is the real "glass ceiling"?
2. What group of women is most likely to opt out of the workplace and why?
3. What is "choice feminism," and what does Hirshman mean when she says it isn't radical enough?
4. On what grounds does Hirshman argue that the family "allows fewer opportunities for full human flourishing than public spheres"?
5. What is the "right to have a flourishing life," and what are the three rules to achieving it?
6. What advice does Hirshman have for female college students and graduates?
7. What suggestions does Hirshman give for avoiding the situation in which women take on more than their share of household duties?
8. What is Hirshman's advice for women who want to have children?
9. Why are decisions to stay home rather than pursue a career harmful to women in general when it comes to decision making in the public sphere?

"Homeward Bound," *American Prospect*, December 20, 2005.

I. THE TRUTH ABOUT ELITE WOMEN

Half the wealthiest, most-privileged, best-educated females in the country stay home with their babies rather than work in the market economy. When in September *The New York Times* featured an article exploring a piece of this story, "Many Women at Elite Colleges Set Career Path to Motherhood," the blogosphere went ballistic, countering with anecdotes and sarcasm. . . .

. . .[A]mong the educated elite, who are the logical heirs of the agenda of empowering women, feminism has largely failed in its goals. There are few women in the corridors of power, and marriage is essentially unchanged. The number of women at universities exceeds the number of men. But, more than a generation after feminism, the number of women in elite jobs doesn't come close.

Why did this happen? The answer I discovered—an answer neither feminist leaders nor women themselves want to face—is that while the public world has changed, albeit imperfectly, to accommodate women among the elite, private lives have hardly budged. The real glass ceiling is at home.

Looking back, it seems obvious that the un-reconstructed family was destined to re-emerge after the passage of feminism's storm of social change. Following the original impulse to address everything in the lives of women, feminism turned its focus to cracking open the doors of the public power structure. This was no small task. At the beginning, there were male juries and male Ivy League schools, sex-segregated want ads, discriminatory employers, harassing colleagues. As a result of feminist efforts—and larger economic trends—the percentage of women, even of mothers in full- or part-time employment, rose robustly through the 1980s and early '90s.

But then the pace slowed. The census numbers for all working mothers leveled off around 1990 and have fallen modestly since 1998. In interviews, women with enough money to quit work say they are "choosing" to opt out. Their words conceal a crucial reality: the belief that women are responsible for child-rearing and homemaking was largely untouched by decades of workplace feminism. Add to this the good evidence that the upper-class workplace has become more demanding and then mix in the successful conservative cultural campaign to reinforce traditional gender roles and you've got a perfect recipe for feminism's stall. . . .

And there is more. In 2000, Harvard Business School professor Myra Hart surveyed the women of the classes of 1981, 1986, and 1991 and found that only 38 percent of female Harvard MBAs were working full time. A 2004 survey by the Center for Work-Life Policy of 2,443 women with a graduate degree or very prestigious bachelor's degree revealed that 43 percent of those women with children had taken a time out, primarily for family reasons. . . .

. . . The 2000 census showed a decline in the percentage of mothers of infants working full time, part time, or seeking employment. Starting at 31 percent in 1976, the percentage had gone up almost every year to 1992, hit a high of 58.7 percent in 1998, and then began to drop—to 55.2 percent in 2000, to 54.6 percent in 2002, to 53.7 percent in 2003. Statistics just released showed further decline to 52.9 percent in 2004. Even the percentage of working mothers with children who were not infants declined between 2000 and 2003, from 62.8 percent to 59.8 percent.

Although college-educated women work more than others, the 2002 census shows that graduate or professional degrees do not increase workforce participation much more than even one year of college. When their children are infants (under a year), 54 percent of females with graduate or professional degrees are not working full time (18 percent are working part time and 36 percent are not working at all). Even among those who have children who are not infants, 41 percent are not working full time (18 percent are working part time and 23 percent are not working at all).

Economists argue about the meaning of the data, even going so far as to contend that more mothers are working. They explain that the bureau changed the definition of "work" slightly in 2000, the economy went into recession, and the falloff in women without children was similar. However, even if there wasn't a falloff but just a leveling off, this represents not a loss of present value but a loss of hope for the future—a loss of hope that the role of women in society will continue to increase.

The arguments still do not explain the absence of women in elite workplaces. If these women were sticking it out in the business, law, and academic worlds, now, 30 years after feminism started filling the selective schools with women, the elite workplaces should be proportionately female. They are not. Law schools have been graduating classes around 40-percent female for decades—decades during which both schools and firms experienced enormous growth. And, although the legal population will not be 40-percent female until 2010, in 2003, the major law firms had only 16-percent female partners, according to the American Bar Association. It's important to note that elite workplaces like law firms grew in size during the very years that the percentage of female graduates was growing, leading you to expect a higher female employment than the pure graduation rate would indicate. The Harvard Business School has produced classes around 30-percent female. Yet only 10.6 percent of Wall Street's corporate officers are women, and a mere nine are Fortune 500 CEOs. . . .

It is possible that the workplace is discriminatory and hostile to family life. If firms had hired every childless woman lawyer available, that alone would have been enough to raise the percentage of female law partners above 16 percent in 30 years. It is also possible that women are voluntarily taking themselves out of the elite job competition for lower status and lower-paying jobs. Women must take responsibility for the consequences of their decisions. It defies reason to claim that the falloff from 40 percent of the class at law school to 16 percent of the partners at all the big law firms is unrelated to half the mothers with graduate and professional degrees leaving full-time work at childbirth and staying away for several years after that, or possibly bidding down.

This isn't only about day care. Half my *Times* brides quit *before* the first baby came. In interviews, at least half of them expressed a hope never to work again. None had realistic plans to work. More

importantly, when they quit, they were already alienated from their work or at least not committed to a life of work. . . .

II. THE FAILURE OF CHOICE FEMINISM

What is going on? Most women hope to marry and have babies. If they resist the traditional female responsibilities of child-rearing and householding, what Arlie Hochschild called "The Second Shift," they are fixing for a fight. But elite women aren't resisting tradition. None of the stay-at-home brides I interviewed saw the second shift as unjust: they agree that the household is women's work. . . .

Conservatives contend that the dropouts prove that feminism "failed" because it was too radical, because women didn't want what feminism had to offer. In fact, if half or more of feminism's heirs (85 percent of the women in my *Times* sample) are not working seriously, it's because feminism wasn't radical enough: It changed the workplace but it didn't change men, and, more importantly, it didn't fundamentally change how women related to men.

The movement did start out radical. Betty Friedan's original call to arms compared housework to animal life. In *The Feminine Mystique* she wrote, "[V]acuuming the living room floor—with or without makeup—is not work that takes enough thought or energy to challenge any woman's full capacity. . . . Down through the ages man has known that he was set apart from other animals by his mind's power to have an idea, a vision, and shape the future to it. . . . when he discovers and creates and shapes a future different from his past, he is a man, a human being."

Thereafter, however, liberal feminists abandoned the judgmental starting point of the movement in favor of offering women "choices." The choice talk spilled over from people trying to avoid saying "abortion," and it provided an irresistible solution to feminists trying to duck the mommy wars. A woman could work, stay home, have 10 children or one, marry or stay single. It all counted as "feminist" as long as she *chose* it. . . .

Great as liberal feminism was, once it retreated to choice the movement had no language to use on the gendered ideology of the family. Feminists could not say, "Housekeeping and child-rearing in the nuclear family is not interesting and not socially validated. Justice requires that it not be assigned to women on the basis of their gender and at the sacrifice of their access to money, power, and honor."

The 50 percent of census answerers and the 62 percent of Harvard MBAs and the 85 percent of my brides of the *Times* all think they are "choosing" their gendered lives. They don't know that feminism, in collusion with traditional society, just passed the gendered family on to them to choose. Even with all the day care in the world, the personal is still political. Much of the rest is the optout revolution.

III. WHAT IS TO BE DONE?

Here's the feminist moral analysis that choice avoided: The family—with its repetitious, socially invisible, physical tasks—is a necessary part of life, but it allows fewer opportunities for full human flourishing than public spheres like the market or the government. This less-flourishing sphere is not the natural or moral responsibility only of women. Therefore, assigning it to women is unjust. Women assigning it to themselves is equally unjust. To paraphrase, as Mark Twain said, "A man who chooses not to read is just as ignorant as a man who cannot read."

. . . If women's flourishing does matter, feminists must acknowledge that the family is to 2005 what the workplace was to 1964 and the vote to 1920. Like the right to work and the right to vote, the right to have a flourishing life that includes but is not limited to family cannot be addressed with language of choice.

Women who want to have sex and children with men as well as good work in interesting jobs where they may occasionally wield real social power need guidance, and they need it early. Step one is simply to begin talking about flourishing. In so doing,

feminism will be returning to its early, judgmental roots. This may anger some, but it should sound the alarm before the next generation winds up in the same situation. Next, feminists will have to start offering young women not choices and not utopian dreams but *solutions* they can enact on their own. Prying women out of their traditional roles is not going to be easy. It will require rules. . . .

There are three rules: Prepare yourself to qualify for good work, treat work seriously, and don't put yourself in a position of unequal resources when you marry.

The preparation stage begins with college. It is shocking to think that girls cut off their options for a public life of work as early as college. But they do. The first pitfall is the liberal-arts curriculum, which women are good at, graduating in higher numbers than men. Although many really successful people start out studying liberal arts, the purpose of a liberal education is not, with the exception of a miniscule number of academic positions, job preparation.

So the first rule is to use your college education with an eye to career goals. Feminist organizations should produce each year a survey of the most common job opportunities for people with college degrees, along with the average lifetime earnings from each job category and the characteristics such jobs require. The point here is to help women see that yes, you can study art history, but only with the realistic understanding that one day soon you will need to use your arts education to support yourself and your family. . . .

After college comes on-the-job training or further education. Many of my *Times* brides—and grooms—did work when they finished their educations. . . . Every *Times* groom assumed he had to succeed in business, and was really trying. By contrast, a common thread among the women I interviewed was a self-important idealism about the kinds of intellectual, prestigious, socially meaningful, politics-free jobs worth their incalculably valuable presence. So the second rule is that women must treat the first few years after college as an opportunity to lose their capitalism virginity and prepare for good work, which they will then treat seriously.

The best way to treat work seriously is to find the money. Money is the marker of success in a market economy; it usually accompanies power, and it enables the bearer to wield power, including within the family. Almost without exception, the brides who opted out graduated with roughly the same degrees as their husbands. Yet somewhere along the way the women made decisions in the direction of less money. Part of the problem was idealism: idealism on the career trail usually leads to volunteer work, or indentured servitude in social-service jobs, which is nice but doesn't get you to money. . . .

If you are good at work you are in a position to address the third undertaking: the reproductive household. The rule here is to avoid taking on more than a fair share of the second shift. If this seems coldhearted, consider the survey by the Center for Work-Life Policy. Fully 40 percent of highly qualified women with spouses felt that their husbands create more work around the house than they perform. According to Phyllis Moen and Patricia Roehling's *Career Mystique,* "When couples marry, the amount of time that a woman spends doing housework increases by approximately 17 percent, while a man's decreases by 33 percent." . . .

How to avoid this kind of rut? You can either find a spouse with less social power than you or find one with an ideological commitment to gender equality. Taking the easier path first, marry down. Don't think of this as brutally strategic. If you are devoted to your career goals and would like a man who will support that, you're just doing what men throughout the ages have done: placing a safe bet. . . .

If you have carefully positioned yourself either by marrying down or finding someone untainted by gender ideology, you will be in a position to resist bearing an unfair share of the family. Even then you must be vigilant. Bad deals come in two forms: economics and home economics. The economic temptation is to assign the cost of child care to the woman's income. If a woman making $50,000 per year whose husband makes $100,000 decides to have a baby, and the cost of a full-time

nanny is $30,000, the couple reason that, after paying 40 percent in taxes, she makes $30,000, just enough to pay the nanny. So she might as well stay home. This totally ignores that both adults are in the enterprise together and the demonstrable future loss of income, power, and security for the woman who quits. Instead, calculate that all parents make a total of $150,000 and take home $90,000. After paying a full-time nanny, they have $60,000 left to live on.

The home-economics trap involves superior female knowledge and superior female sanitation. The solutions are ignorance and dust. Never figure out where the butter is. "Where's the butter?" Nora Ephron's legendary riff on marriage begins. In it, a man asks the question when looking directly at the butter container in the refrigerator. "Where's the butter?" actually means butter my toast, buy the butter, remember when we're out of butter. Next thing you know you're quitting your job at the law firm because you're so busy managing the butter. If women never start playing the household-manager role, the house will be dirty, but the realities of the physical world will trump the pull of gender ideology. Either the other adult in the family will take a hand or the children will grow up with robust immune systems.

If these prescriptions sound less than family-friendly, here's the last rule: Have a baby. Just don't have two. Mothers' Movement Online's Judith Statdman Tucker reports that women who opt out for child-care reasons act only after the second child arrives. A second kid pressures the mother's organizational skills, doubles the demands for appointments, wildly raises the cost of education and housing, and drives the family to the suburbs. . . .

IV. WHY DO WE CARE?

The privileged brides of the *Times*—and their husbands—seem happy. Why do we care what they do? After all, most people aren't rich and white and heterosexual, and they couldn't quit working if they wanted to.

We care because what they do is bad for them, is certainly bad for society, and is widely imitated, even by people who never get their weddings in the *Times*. This last is called the "regime effect," and it means that even if women don't quit their jobs for their families, they think they should and feel guilty about not doing it. . . .

As for society, elites supply the labor for the decision-making classes—the senators, the newspaper editors, the research scientists, the entrepreneurs, the policy-makers, and the policy wonks. If the ruling class is overwhelmingly male, the rulers will make mistakes that benefit males, whether from ignorance or from indifference. Media surveys reveal that if only one member of a television show's creative staff is female, the percentage of women on-screen goes up from 36 percent to 42 percent. A world of 84-percent male lawyers and 84-percent female assistants is a different place than one with women in positions of social authority. Think of a big American city with an 86-percent white police force. If role models don't matter, why care about Sandra Day O'Connor?. . .

. . . Why should society spend resources educating women with only a 50-percent return rate on their stated goals? The American Conservative Union carried a column in 2004 recommending that employers stay away from such women or risk going out of business. Good psychological data show that the more women are treated with respect, the more ambition they have. And vice versa. The opt-out revolution is really a downward spiral.

Finally, these choices are bad for women individually. A good life for humans includes the classical standard of using one's capacities for speech and reason in a prudent way, the liberal requirement of having enough autonomy to direct one's own life, and the utilitarian test of doing more good than harm in the world. Measured against these time-tested standards, the expensively educated upper-class moms will be leading lesser lives. At feminism's dawning, two theorists compared gender ideology to a caste system. To borrow their insight, these daughters of the upper classes will be bearing most of the burden of the work always associated with the lowest caste: sweeping and cleaning bodily waste. . . .

When she sounded the blast that revived the feminist movement 40 years after women received the vote, Betty Friedan spoke of lives of purpose and meaning, better lives and worse lives, and feminism went a long way toward shattering the glass ceilings that limited their prospects outside the home. Now the glass ceiling begins at home. Although it is harder to shatter a ceiling that is also the roof over your head, there is no other choice.

Discussion Questions

1. Hirshman, like de Beauvoir, maintains that the traditional patterns of motherhood are harming women. Evaluate her argument.

2. Hirshman argues that women *ought* to get out to work. If well-educated women choose to opt out and stay at home, then women will be harmed because important decisions will remain in the hands of men who now hold the great majority of powerful positions. Is a stay-at-home mom a traitor to feminism? Support your answer.

3. Lisa Belkin in her article "The Opt-Out Revolution"[29] writes: "We accept that humans are born with certain traits and we accept that other species have innate differences between the sexes. What we are loath to do is extend that acceptance to humans. . . . Mostly this is because so much of recent history (the civil rights movement, the women's movement) is an attempt to prove that biology is not destiny. To suggest otherwise is to resurrect an argument that can be—and has been—dangerously misused." Does the fact that an argument might be misused

justify ignoring possible genetic differences in the behavior of men and women? Support your answer. Discuss how Hirshman might respond to Belkin.

4. Discuss Hirshman's arguments in light of your own future career and family plans. As a woman, do you think that you have a moral obligation to pursue a career and limit the number of children you have to one? As a man, do you think that you have a moral obligation to do your fair share of household and child-care work? Why or why not? Support your answers.

CATHY YOUNG

The Return of the Mommy Wars

Cathy Young is an author and columnist for the *Boston Globe*. In her article Young responds to Hirshman's "get out to work" feminism, arguing that it is patronizing and that what we need to do instead is to expand choices available to both men and women, rather than narrow options for women.

Critical Reading Questions

1. How do cultural values affect mothers' choices and feelings about whether to go to work or stay at home?
2. What does Young mean when she says that "Freud was right that 'love and work are the cornerstones of our humanness'"?
3. According to Young, in what ways does Hirshman sabotage her own argument?
4. According to Young, what is the "brighter side of the female dilemma"?
5. Why does Young disagree with Hirshman's call for women to put aside their own preferences for the sake of the feminist revolution?

Is a stay-at-home mom a traitor to feminism?

After lying dormant for a while, the Mommy Wars reignited late last year with "Homeward Bound," an article by the feminist legal scholar Linda Hirshman in the December *American Prospect*. Hirshman, who is not known for mincing words . . . [declared] that women who leave work to raise children are choosing "lesser lives" [and] boldly assailed the truism that, when it comes to

full-time mothering vs. careers, it's a good thing for women to have a choice.

Hirshman surveyed 33 women whose wedding announcements had appeared in *The New York Times* during a three-week period in 1996. Of the 30 with children, she found, half were not employed and only five were working full-time. Drawing on that and other studies, Hirshman argued that such choices by elite women are a primary reason for the dearth of women in the corridors of political and economic power. . . .

"The Return of the Mommy Wars," *Reason*, April 2006.

While Hirshman conceded the those "expensively educated upper-class moms" seemed happy at home, she insisted that "what they do is bad for them [and] is certainly bad for society." It's bad for society, she argued, because it reinforces a "gendered ideology" of family roles, perpetuates male dominance in government and business, and deprives ambitious women of role models. It's bad for the women who give up careers, Hirshman suggested, because they fall short of a good life, which includes "using one's capacities for speech and reason in a prudent way," "having enough autonomy to direct one's own life," and "doing more good than harm in the world."

Interestingly, Hirshman blamed this state of affairs less on patriarchy or conservatism than on feminism. Specifically, she damned its alleged failure to challenge male/female relations in the home, its embrace of the language of "choice," and its consequent refusal to be "judgmental" toward women who make "bad" choices. . . .

Unquestionably, a working woman's lot would be much easier in a society where stay-at-home motherhood was as rare as stay-at-home fatherhood is today. No mother would have to field a child's guilt-tripping question, "But Mommy, why do you have to work?" Schoolteachers and other parents would not assume that a mother was available for volunteering at school and sewing Halloween costumes. Working women would not have to deal with the lingering suspicion that, having started families, they will quit work or dramatically reduce their job commitments. Nor would they have to compete with men who have the advantage of a homemaker wife to handle most domestic responsibilities. Conversely, a stay-at-home mother would have a far easier time in a society where full-time motherhood was the norm. She would not have to contend with large numbers of women whose professional status might make her feel inadequate. She would not dread the question, "What do you do?" Single-earner families would face less economic pressure, and employers would probably be able to favor male breadwinners without facing legal or social sanctions.

The talk of choice also tends to downplay the fact that no personal choice is made in a cultural vacuum. The belief that women who stay home are better mothers is definitely in the cultural bloodstream: In polls, at least two-thirds of Americans agree that it's better for the children if the mother stays home, a figure that has risen in recent years.

Surely these beliefs can translate into more or less subtle disapproval toward working mothers, and guilt and self-blame on the part of mothers themselves. For all the talk of respecting choices, only half the stay-at-home moms in a recent *Washington Post* poll agreed that it's all right for the mother of a young child to get a job if she's happier working. Hirshman rightly reminds us, too, of the peril of forgetting or dismissing the feminist critique of full-time domesticity and motherhood. Financial dependency aside, I agree that it's not good for adult human beings to have no identity independent of personal relationships or to become too enmeshed in emotional intimacy. Freud was right that "love and work are the cornerstones of our humanness"; and while parenting involves a lot of work, it still belongs to the "love" half of that balance.

So Hirshman tackles some of the right issues; but she tackles them in so wrong-headed a way as to sabotage her own argument. She absurdly overstates her case, claiming, for instance, that four decades of feminism have not changed relations between women and men in the family. (Women today spend twice as much time on housework as men—but 30 years ago, they did six times as much.)

Hirshman's "get thee to the office" hectoring has an obnoxiously patronizing tone. She takes us back to the French feminist Simone de Beauvoir's assertion, in a 1976 interview with Betty Friedan, that "no woman should be authorized to stay at home to raise her children . . . because if there is such a choice, too many women will make that one." Friedan—whose 1964 classic *The Feminine Mystique* Hirshman invokes as a model of pro-work feminism—was understandably appalled by this diktat. Furthermore, one needn't lapse into hand-that-rocks-the- cradle clichés to be put off by Hirshman's contempt for anything traditionally feminine—even for volunteerism and less-than-lucrative jobs tainted by "idealism" (though it's amusing to see so hearty an endorsement of capitalist values in a left-wing magazine).

Focusing only on the drudgery of home life, Hirshman misses the brighter side of the female dilemma: When it comes to work–life balance, women have far more options than men, including more freedom to choose lower-paying but more flexible and fulfilling jobs. Men, by contrast, are often trapped by more rigid social expectations and economic pressures.

While Hirshman deplores women's alleged slide into 1950s-style domesticity, her vision of careers is itself of '50s vintage, with hardly any allowances for the flexibility of the modern workplace or the growth of self-employment and small businesses. Last November, *Fortune* ran a feature by Jia Lynn Yang on women who step off high rungs of the corporate ladder not to trade briefcases for diapers or to flee sexism but to pursue their ventures in business or in new fields. To these women, Yang noted, "taking control of one's own life can feel as bold as wielding power in a corporation.". . . These greater choices can mean greater conflicts; but if there is an answer, it is to expand the choices available to men, not to narrow the options for women.

Hirshman wants to tell women to set aside their own preferences, including the desire for more than one child, for the sake of the feminist revolution. It is resoundingly obvious this is not going to happen. Do we need a conversation about the downside of "opting out," the work and life expectations of women and men, and the benefits to both sexes of more flexible, less gender-bound roles? I think we do. But if Hirshman was hoping to initiate such a discussion, she started it off on the wrong note.

Discussion Questions

1. Young disagrees with Hirshman's analysis of the rhetoric of "choice" in the feminist movement. Discuss the concept of "choice" as well as which person presents the more compelling analysis of it.
2. Discuss Simone de Beauvoir's statement "No woman should be authorized to stay at home to raise her children . . . because if there is such a choice, too many women will make that one."
3. Young argues that by disparaging parenthood, feminists such as Hirschman discourage men from becoming more involved fathers. Discuss the impact the different views of motherhood and work discussed in this chapter have on fatherhood and the role of men in family life. Use specific examples to illustrate your answer.
4. Young writes that Hirshman shows contempt for "anything traditionally feminine—including volunteerism and less-than lucrative jobs"—while heartily endorsing capitalist values. Evaluate Hirshman's assumption. Is capitalism, and the ethical egoism underlying it, the best system for personal self-fulfillment for both women and men? Support your answer.

GLORIA STEINEM

Women Are Never Front-Runners

Gloria Steinem is co-founder of the Women's Media Center. In her editorial, Steinem examines the effects of sexism in the 2008 Democratic presidential primaries and argues that gender, rather than racism, is probably the most restricting force in American life and politics.

Critical Reading Questions

1. What evidence does Steinem use to support her claim that a woman would be unlikely to be elected president of the United States?
2. Why, according to Steinem, is the sex barrier more restrictive than the race barrier?
3. What examples does Steinem use to illustrate sexism in the 2008 Democratic primaries?
4. According to Steinem, why are older women more likely to support Clinton?

The woman in question became a lawyer after some years as a community organizer, married a corporate lawyer and is the mother of two little girls, ages 9 and 6. Herself the daughter of a white American mother and a black African father—in this race-conscious country, she is considered black—she served as a state legislator for eight years, and became an inspirational voice for national unity.

Be honest: Do you think this is the biography of someone who could be elected to the United States Senate? After less than one term there, do you believe she could be a viable candidate to head the most powerful nation on earth?

If you answered no to either question, you're not alone. Gender is probably the most restricting force in American life, whether the question is who must be in the kitchen or who could be in the White House. This country is way down the list of countries electing women and, according to one

"Women Are Never Front-Runners," *New York Times*, January 8, 2008, http://www.nytimes.com/2008/01/08/opinion/08steinhem.html.

study, it polarizes gender roles more than the average democracy.

That's why the Iowa primary was following our historical pattern of making change. Black men were given the vote a half-century before women of any race were allowed to mark a ballot, and generally have ascended to positions of power, from the military to the boardroom, before any women (with the possible exception of obedient family members in the latter).

If the lawyer described above had been just as charismatic but named, say, Achola Obama instead of Barack Obama, her goose would have been cooked long ago. Indeed, neither she nor Hillary Clinton could have used Mr. Obama's public style—or Bill Clinton's either—without being considered too emotional by Washington pundits.

So why is the sex barrier not taken as seriously as the racial one? The reasons are as pervasive as the air we breathe: because sexism is still confused with nature as racism once was; because anything that affects males is seen as more serious than anything that affects "only" the female half of the human race; because children are still raised mostly by women (to put it mildly) so men especially tend to feel they are regressing to childhood when dealing with a powerful woman; because racism stereotyped black men as more "masculine" for so long that some white men find their presence to be masculinity-affirming (as long as there aren't too many of them); and because there is still no "right" way to be a woman in public power without being considered a you-know-what.

I'm not advocating a competition for who has it toughest. The caste systems of sex and race are interdependent and can only be uprooted together. That's why Senators Clinton and Obama have to be careful not to let a healthy debate turn into the kind of hostility that the news media love. Both will need a coalition of outsiders to win a general election. The abolition and suffrage movements progressed when united and were damaged by division; we should remember that.

I'm supporting Senator Clinton because like Senator Obama she has community organizing experience, but she also has more years in the Senate, an unprecedented eight years of on-the-job training in the White House, no masculinity to prove, the potential to tap a huge reservoir of this country's talent by her example, and now even the courage to break the no-tears rule. I'm not opposing Mr. Obama; if he's the nominee, I'll volunteer. Indeed, if you look at votes during their two-year overlap in the Senate, they were the same more than 90 percent of the time. Besides, to clean up the mess left by President Bush, we may need two terms of President Clinton and two of President Obama.

But what worries me is that he is seen as unifying by his race while she is seen as divisive by her sex.

What worries me is that she is accused of "playing the gender card" when citing the old boys' club, while he is seen as unifying by citing civil rights confrontations.

What worries me is that male Iowa voters were seen as gender-free when supporting their own, while female voters were seen as biased if they did and disloyal if they didn't.

What worries me is that reporters ignore Mr. Obama's dependence on the old—for instance, the frequent campaign comparisons to John F. Kennedy—while not challenging the slander that her progressive policies are part of the Washington status quo.

What worries me is that some women, perhaps especially younger ones, hope to deny or escape the sexual caste system; thus Iowa women over 50 and 60, who disproportionately supported Senator Clinton, proved once again that women are the one group that grows more radical with age.

This country can no longer afford to choose our leaders from a talent pool limited by sex, race, money, powerful fathers and paper degrees. It's time to take equal pride in breaking all the barriers. We have to be able to say: "I'm supporting her because she'll be a great president and because she's a woman."

Discussion Questions

1. Discuss how a liberal feminist, a conservative, and a gender-essential feminist would each most likely respond to Steinem's editorial.
2. Looking back at the 2008 presidential race, discuss whether Steinem was correct in her assessment of sexism in political races. Use specific examples to illustrate your answer.
3. If you were able to vote in the 2008 presidential primaries and elections, discuss to what extent the gender of the candidates (including both Clinton and Palin) influenced your decision.

STEVEN GOLDBERG

The Logic of Patriarchy

Steven Goldberg is retired chair of the department of sociology of City College at the City University of New York and the author of *Why Men Rule (The Inevitability of Patriarchy)*. In this reading, Goldberg argues that male–female differences in behavior, such as dominance and aggression, are rooted primarily in biology.

Critical Reading Questions

1. What does Goldberg mean when he talks about differences between males and females that are universal?
2. Which differences between men and women does Goldberg say are hereditary, and what evidence does he offer to support his claim?
3. What is the relationship between social, environmental, and hereditary male–female differences in observed behavior?
4. How does Goldberg respond to the claim that socialization accounts for male–female differences in behavior?
5. How does Goldberg respond to the argument that his theory is reductionist?
6. How does Goldberg define patriarchy?
7. How does Goldberg respond to arguments that credit social and economic reasons as well as sex hormones and women's roles as mothers with the differences in behavior between men and women?
8. Why, according to Goldberg, have modernization and technology not changed the inevitability of patriarchy?
9. What is Goldberg's position on existing discrimination against women and the Equal Rights Amendment?

Much of my career has been devoted to discovering, and attempting to explain, differences between males and females that are universal—differences that are recognized by every one of the thousands of societies that have ever existed, differences that are incorporated into the system of expectations, values, and institutions of every society.

"Universality" does not imply that there are not, in every society, *individual* exceptions. The

"The Logic of Patriarchy," in *Fads and Fallacies in the Social Sciences* (Amherst, NY: Humanity Books, 2003), chapter 8. Notes have been omitted.

height of men and women is the model to keep in mind. There are many individual "exceptions," many women who are taller than many men, but the mean height of men is always greater, the overwhelming percentage of the tallest people are always male, and the best "basketball teams" are always comprised of only males. Any discussion of sex differences that is not founded on an understanding of the statistical, rather than absolute, nature of sex differences is doomed to incoherence. . . .

The basic statistical differences in male and female tendencies, however, are rooted in hereditary sex difference. These different tendencies are observed by a society's population and this observation sets limits on, and gives direction to, expectations and social reality.

There are three universal institutions that concern us here:

1. (Patriarchy) The upper positions of the hierarchies of every society are overwhelmingly filled by men (patriarchy). A Queen Victoria or a Golda Meir is always an exception in her society and is always surrounded by a government of men. (There are a very few, tiny societies with relatively little hierarchy, but in all such societies an informal male dominance plays a role similar to that of patriarchy.)

2. (Male Status Attainment) The highest-status (*non-maternal*) roles are occupied primarily by males. The high-status roles are high status not primarily *because* they are male (ditch-digging is male), but because they have high status. This high status elicits from males, more strongly than from females, the behavior required to attain the status. Which roles are given high status and which behavior is required to attain these roles is, let's agree for argument's sake, socially determined. But the greater impulse to do whatever is necessary to attain whichever roles are given high status is a function of male physiology.

3. (Male Dominance) Both men and women *feel* that the authority resides in the male and that the woman must "get around" the male to attain power. Even when male dominance is absent from law (as in the United States) or formal custom (as in "chivalrous" societies), the expectation is still one of male dominance. This is attested to in the U.S. by, for example, the feminist's detestation of male dominance and her incorrect attempt to explain it in purely social terms.

My purpose here is not to provide the anthropological evidence of universality, nor the psychophysiological evidence supporting an explanation of universality in terms of the differing neuroendocrinological development of males and females. . . . I will mention merely that I explain the universals as inevitable limits on variation imposed by a hereditary male-female difference that engenders in males a greater tendency to sacrifice others of life's pleasures (safety, family, vacation, relaxation, and the like) when dominance and status are available (just as it does a greater readiness of females to serve the infant in distress). The social environment is a *dependent* variable; it conforms to limits and constraints imposed by the primarily *independent* variable of hereditary psychophysiological male-female difference and a population's observation of the differentiated behavioral tendencies of men and women that it engenders. To be sure, there is great variation in the degree to which the male and female tendencies discussed are manifested, but the directions of these tendencies set by the neuroendocrinological differentiation are always the same and possible variation is limited by that differentiation.

Here my purpose is merely to provide a compendium of the commonly invoked fallacious arguments that attempt to deny the primary importance of the hereditary psychophysiological. . . . [T]hose familiar with current work on the relevance of inherent sex differences to social structure and social system, with its abhorrence of the possibility of the primacy of the hereditary-psychophysiological, will recognize that these fallacies infuse much contemporary social science (especially sociology). While the sociological discussions occasionally give lip-service acknowledgement that physiological differentiation "might play some role," such acknowledgement is meaningless in analyses that implicitly assume the causal primacy of the social.

1. *Socialization explains our expectations of males and females and the male-female differences in behavior (cognition, emotion, and action).* There are two fatal problems with this claim:

(A) Socialization does not explain anything, but merely forces us to ask another question: *why* does socialization of men and women always work in the same direction? Just as the male's greater physical strength is not *caused* primarily by our telling little girls that the men are stronger than women, so too is the male's physiologically-based, more readily elicited dominance behavior not *caused* primarily by the socialization. (In the case of dominance behavior, it is neuroendocrinological differentiation and socialization limited by its behavioral effects, not the difference in physical strength, that is responsible for the universals.) Socialization may often increase sex differences, but it is not the primary cause of them.

. . . The point is made merely to make clear that socialization is always a mediator, whether the primary causes be physiological, economic, or whatever, so that the presence of socialization in no way *conflicts* with the claim of the primary importance of inherent sex differences. In other words, one must ask the question: why has the socialization of every society that has ever existed associated dominance behavior with *males*?

(B) The second problem with the explanation in terms of socialization is its implicit assumption that the social environment of expectations, customs, norms, institutions, and the like is an *independent* variable capable of acting as counterpoise to the physiological constituents that make us male and female.

If the association of sex and behavioral characteristic *were* a variable independent of a population's observation of physiological reality then, at least in principle, socialization could act as counterpoise to hereditary sex differences. For example, society could, by having women lift weights throughout life and men remaining sedentary, balance the male's inherent strength advantage.

But in real life this can't happen because the social environment is a *dependent* variable whose limits are set by our psychophysiological construction. . . . In real life a population's observation of the relative physical strength of men and women precludes the possibility that expectation, socialization, and practice will balance the male's greater inherent strength and will result in institutions rendering women as physically strong as men. Likewise, in real life a population observes the male's dominance tendency and develops expectations and socialization concordant with this. . . .

. . . In the case of the male and female differences we discuss, it is precisely the difference in "motivation"—more rigorously, the male's lower threshhold for the elicitation of dominance behavior—that is a function of the physiological differences. A society's norms and values could not, for example, reflect an equal male and female dominance tendency (or tendency to violence or physical strength or immediacy of sexual arousal); the norms and values must fall within the limits set by the psychophysiological differences between males and females and the population's observations of the differentiated male and female behavior. . . .

Note that it is not so much that men (necessarily) limit women's accession to dominance in hierarchies in any *direct* way. This limitation is primarily a side effect of the male's greater "need" of dominance and the behavior this engenders (just as the absence of women from the best basketball leagues is not primarily the result of discrimination, but the inevitable rise to the top of the best players). In the case of hierarchies, it is not necessarily that males do the job better, but that they do what is necessary to attain the positions. And you can't be a good *or* bad Senator until you become a Senator. To be sure, this reality is inevitably manifested in social values that increase sex differences in attainment. (Some societies preclude women's entering the hierarchies altogether. But, as always, the question remains: why in every society is it males who dominate the hierarchies? Why has there never been a matriarchy or "equiarchy"?

2. *The physiological theory of limits is* "reductionist." The problem with this criticism is that a scientific explanation is *supposed* to be reductionist, if by that we mean "capable of explaining the most empirical reality with the fewest hypotheses." "Reductionism" is impotent as criticism unless the criticized analysis attempts to explain more than its explanatory mechanism is capable of explaining. "Reductionism" would be a legitimate charge if, for example, it were claimed that physiology explains the difference between women's roles in the United States and Saudi Arabia. But my theory of constraints on social possibility is a theory

of limits; it makes no claim of explaining any of the variation within the limits (i.e., any variation found from one actual society to another). A criticism of "reductionism" here is akin to one denying the physiological basis of the human need to eat (and the universality of institutions satisfying this) on the grounds that the explanation does not tell us why the French eat French food and the Chinese eat Chinese food, why societies have different numbers of meals per day, or why some societies associate food with religion far more than do others. The physiological explanation does not *claim* to explain this variation. In short, the criticism of "reductionism" is analogous to an accusation of "sophistry" that fails to specify any logical fallacy. It is mere name-calling.

3. *We define "patriarchy" and/or "dominance" differently from the way you do.* In various anthropological writings, even those predating the ideologically-infused works of the past two decades, one can find at least twenty varying definitions of "patriarchy." The one I use is both that which is most often used and the common denominator of most of the other definitions.

But a far more important point is this: It is the empirical reality—not the word one uses to represent it—that is crucial. As long as one uses consistently the word he has chosen, the specific word chosen is unimportant. . . . Likewise: the empirical reality is that the hierarchies of every society without exception are filled primarily by males. . . .

Similar to this avoidance of the fact that there is an empirical fact—the universalities—that must be explained is the invocation of the "exception" that is not an exception, but a reality having nothing to do with those we address. For example, the "fact" that some societies have a highest god who is female—even if true, which it may well not be—would demonstrate only that religion is of little importance to patriarchy (since such societies all exhibit patriarchy) and that the universality of patriarchy must now be explained without reference to religion.

Most claims of "exceptions" have not been of this type, but have been misrepresentations of

ethnographies the claimant got from third-hand sources. . . .

4. *The explanation fails to understand the "complexity of social life" and "the tremendous variation among societies." AND The explanation fails to understand the complexity of the mechanisms mediating neuroendocrinological differences between males and females, the behavioral differences, and the social differences to which the behavioral differences are relevant.* The "complexity" and "variation" invoked here are irrelevant. No society is "so complex" that it lacks the universal institutions. There is not so much variation that any society manages to escape the constraints of the limits discussed here. . . . The neuroendocrinological explanation of universality is a *sufficient* explanation of the limits within which social variation and complexity take place. The issue of "complexity" is simply another version of the "Chinese food" attempt to obfuscate with irrelevant empirical realities that the theory presented here does not attempt to explain. . . .

5. *We have patriarchy for economic reasons.* This is a confusion of cause and function. The realities I discuss no doubt have important economic functions. But to ascribe patriarchy to economic factors is akin to ascribing the human need to eat to McDonald's need to make a profit. At least with reference to sex differences, economies primarily exploit our natures, not cause them. That is why every economic system—communal, slave, feudal, capitalist, socialist, etc.—works within the limits of *patriarchy.*

6. *Patriarchy is a result of the requirements of a hunting culture, or Christianity, or capitalism, etc.* If it is to be at all persuasive, an explanation of universality must be parsimonious; the explanation must invoke a causal factor common to the varying societies that exhibit the universal institution. Just as the explanation in terms of capitalism fails to explain patriarchy in all of the non-capitalist societies, so do explanations in terms of any single factor other than the physiological fail to explain the host of societies for which that factor does not apply. Non-hunting, non-Christian, non-capitalist, etc. societies are all patriarchal. . . .

7. *Societies are patriarchal because women are tied down with giving birth and raising children and because men are bigger than women.* We can ignore the fact that physiology accounts for the fact that women bear and raise children, because there are many societies in which women work harder and longer outside the home—doing objectively more important economic work—than do men. . . . Whatever the non-maternal roles played by women, these never include primary responsibility for hierarchical position. Similarly, while males are everywhere bigger and stronger, all evidence from both human beings and experimental animals imply that it is the CNS difference relevant to dominance behavior, not physical size, that is primarily responsible. . . .

10. *Attitudes have changed tremendously.* Yes, at least those people are willing to acknowledge, they have. But the very point is that, with reference to the behaviors relevant here, attitudes are not all that much more causally important than they are to the sex difference in height. . . .

11. *Modernization and technology render physiology irrelevant.* There is not a scintilla of evidence that modernization renders likely the demise of the universals. To be sure, no modern society could preclude women's playing any suprafamilial role as some non-modern societies did. But it is also true that no modern society is likely to give women the high status some other non-modern societies gave the woman's maternal roles. In any case, even the Scandinavian societies often claimed to be "non-patriarchal"—called this despite the fact that they feel the need of cabinet departments to deal with the "inequality of women"—are, in fact, overwhelmingly patriarchal. (An interesting fact about the Scandinavian countries is that the political plays a less-important role than does the corporate, relative to other countries. While female membership of parliament is the highest in the world (though still far from equal), male control of the corporate world is absolute; there is no corporate "glass ceiling" issue because hardly any women rise high enough to see the "glass ceiling." Perhaps the Scandinavian nations, which have before augured the future of bureaucratic societies, here also intimate coming realities in an increasingly global world.) . . .

12. *Slavery was universal.* No it wasn't. Many societies never had slavery and only one society lacking slavery is necessary to demonstrate that physiology does not render slavery inevitable. *Had* slavery been universal, this would not demonstrate slavery to be inevitable, but it would certainly make it likely. . . .

14. *Gender identity—our sense of our own maleness or femaleness—is purely determined by familial factors and socialization.* No it's not, but let us assume that it is. Sex-associated *behavior* is not. Whether the hormonally feminized chromosomal male sees him/herself as an "aggressive" female or as an "unaggressive" male is irrelevant; it is the CNS-behavior correlation that is relevant here. For nearly all people, of course, there is a concordance of genetic, chromosomal, hormonal, anatomical, and social development with gender identity. . . .

16. *Boys and girls have equal levels of the male hormone, but boys are more aggressive. This shows that the behavior is a function of socialization.* No it doesn't. The real, but less interesting, explanation is that it is simplistic to speak only of hormone levels; it is the fetal sensitization of the male CNS to the relevant properties of testosterone that is relevant. But, even were this not the case, the implication would be that the socialization of boys and girls anticipates the adult physiological reality (when the male testosterone level is much higher). The reason men can grow moustaches is not that we tell little girls that facial hair is unfeminine. . . .

Similar points can be made about the oft-heard claim that the fact that girls equal boys in mathematical aptitude somehow demonstrates that the pubertal and adult male mathematical superiority must be a result of socialization. It is likely that the arithmetical tests given boys and girls are not sufficiently sensitive to a male advantage that already exists. But even if this is not the case, the pubertal male advantage in all likelihood reflects anticipatory socialization recognizing the hereditary advantage that, like facial hair, manifests itself in puberty. . . .

18. *You claim patriarchy is inevitable. Science never dismisses a possibility.* Of course it does, and should. Every hypothesis should specify things that won't happen. It is only by doing this that we have any way of telling whether the hypothesis is likely to be correct. What science does not ever dismiss is an empirical reality that actually exists. Should a non-patriarchal, hierarchical society be found to have existed, presently exist, or come to exist, I will be the first to jettison the theory I present. But the *hope* that this will happen does not qualify.

A similar criticism claims that I argue that "patriarchy is inevitable *because* it is universal. No. Universality leaves open the *possibility* of inevitability (which an exception would preclude) and forces us to assess the likelihood of inevitability on the basis of the cause of the universality. Moreover, in a world of thousands of societies with unimaginable variation, universality demands that we consider the possibility that the universal is rooted in the biological nature of human beings or in the very nature of society, any society. When universality is complemented by an enormous amount of physiological evidence capable of explaining the universality, the likelihood that the limits are manifestation of the psychophysiological is overwhelming. . . .

In short: given the astounding degree of variation societies have demonstrated, the universality of the institutions we discuss must be explained and, as we have seen, the explanation must be parsimonious. And the only explanation of universality that is parsimonious, logical, concordant with the anthropological and physiological evidence, and plausible is one that understands that the institutions are not inevitable *because* they are universal; they are inevitable for the same reason that they are universal. . . .

22. *The author is a sexist and the effects of his work will be politically bad.* The inadequacy of the *ad hominem* and *ad consequentium* arguments has been known for millennia. Even if these charges were true, they would be irrelevant. If biases infect an analysis, the effects on the analysis can be exposed.

If biases do not infect an analysis, it does not matter how biased the author is. In neither case is any social or political consequence of the analysis relevant to the correctness of the analysis. . . .

However, it is important to acknowledge that the individual exceptions often do encounter harmful discrimination and that society's making the statistical absolute can generate greater sex differences than would heredity alone. But the point relevant here is that, with reference to sex roles, the discrimination is possible precisely because the exception is an exception and the exception is an exception precisely because physiology associates the expected characteristic with the non-exception. It is the very *tall* woman (or very *short* man) who encounters discrimination where the equally tall man (or short woman) does not. . . .

I suspect that much of the impulse energizing such denial [of gender difference] is the unwarranted fear that acceptance of the explanation of universality I offer would commit one to a moral or political view he or she finds abhorrent. This fear is unwarranted. No scientific explanation of how the world works can tell us how we should politically or morally act. Science knows nothing of "should." So, for example, one could agree with all that I have written here and argue that this indicates the crucial importance of an equal rights amendment limiting as much as possible a male advantage in attaining positions, an advantage that often has nothing to do with performance in those positions. On the other hand, one could agree with all that I have written and argue that this indicates the need, in a time when role models are so hard to come by, for our emphasizing differences between male and female tendencies and their ability to form the nuclei of strong roles and role models. "'Is' cannot generate 'ought.'" On the issue of good and bad, right and wrong, science must be silent.

Discussion Questions

1. Evaluate Goldberg's argument. Does he present compelling evidence that patriarchy is inevitable and, if so, what are some of the implications of his position for the feminist movement and public policy? Support your answer.

2. Does capitalism, with its emphasis on competitiveness and domination, disadvantage women? If so, what type of social/economic system would be preferable as far as promoting equality and opportunity for both men and women? Support your answers. Discuss also how both Goldberg and Steinem might answer these questions.

3. Even if men are naturally aggressive and dominating, as Goldberg claims, does this justify patriarchy, or should this "instinct" be rechanneled toward "objects" other than women or even repressed? Discuss whether pornography and/or prostitution are morally acceptable means for rechanneling it. Support your answers.

4. Discuss what Goldberg's position would most likely be on affirmative action for women as well as what sort of college curriculum and admissions program he might propose. Would he be in favor of coed colleges, or would he recommend gender-segregated colleges? Should men and women be funneled into different majors?

5. Discuss how Goldberg would explain the prevalence of date rape and sexual harassment on college campuses. What solution might he offer to these problems? Do you agree with this solution? Support your answers.

KATIE ROIPHE

Reckless Eyeballing: Sexual Harassment on Campus

Katie Roiphe is an author and a journalist. She argues that the current fear of rape and sexual harassment has been fueled by exaggerations of their actual incidence on campuses as well as by the rhetoric of "rape crisis feminists." The current broad definitions of sexual harassment and date rape, rather than empowering women, perpetuate stereotypes of women as both sexless and as powerless victims of male oppression.

"Reckless Eyeballing: Sexual Harassment on Campus," in *The Morning After: Sex, Fear, and Feminism on Campus* (Boston: Little, Brown, 1993), 85–112. Some notes have been omitted.

Critical Reading Questions

1. What is the standard definition of sexual harassment? Why does Roiphe have concerns about this definition?
2. What is MacKinnon's view on sexual harassment, and what are its political implications?
3. What view of men and women, according to Roiphe, is implied by the current rhetoric against sexual harassment? Why does such rhetoric create an atmosphere of suspicion and mistrust and reduce the number of meaningful contacts between students and faculty?
4. How, according to Roiphe, do people from other countries view the concern with sexual harassment in the United States?
5. How does Roiphe explain the high incidence of sexual harassment in the United States?
6. What does Roiphe suggest women do instead of focusing so much on the dangers of sexual harassment?
7. On what grounds does Roiphe argue that people have a right to engage in reckless eyeballing, and what are appropriate moral responses to being leered at?
8. Where does Roiphe draw the line between harmless "harassment" and harassment that is a genuine abuse of power?
9. According to Roiphe, why might telling a woman who did not feel victimized that in fact she *was* a victim of date rape or sexual harassment actually harm rather than empower her?

For generations, women have talked and written and theorized about their problems with men. But theories about patriarchy tumble from abstraction when you wake up next to it in the morning. Denouncing male oppression clashes with wanting him anyhow. From playgrounds to consciousness-raising groups, from suffragette marches to pro-choice marches, women have been talking their way through this contradiction for a long time. . . .

Heterosexual desire inevitably raises conflicts for the passionate feminist, and it's not an issue easily evaded. Sooner or later feminism has to address "the man question." But this is more than just a practical question of procreation, more than the well-worn translation of personal into political. It's also a question for the abstract, the ideological, the furthest reaches of the feminist imagination.

Charlotte Perkins Gilman, a prominent feminist writing at the turn of the century, found a fictional solution to the conflict between sex and feminism in her utopian novel, *Herland.* Her solution is simple: there is no sexual desire. . . .

Many of today's feminists, in their focus on sexual harassment, share Gilman's sexual politics. In their videos, literature, and workshops, these feminists are creating their own utopian visions of human sexuality. They imagine a world where all expressions of sexual appreciation are appreciated. They imagine a totally symmetrical universe, where people aren't silly, rude, awkward, excessive, or confused. And if they are, they are violating the rules and are subject to disciplinary proceedings.

A Princeton pamphlet declares that "sexual harassment is unwanted sexual attention that makes a person feel uncomfortable or causes problems in school or at work, or in social settings."[1] The word "uncomfortable" echoes through all the literature on sexual harassment. The feminists concerned with this issue, then, propose the right to be comfortable as a feminist principle.

The difficulty with these rules is that, although it may infringe on the right to comfort, unwanted sexual attention is part of nature. To find wanted sexual attention, you have to give and receive a certain amount of unwanted sexual attention. Clearly, the truth is that if no one was ever allowed to risk offering unsolicited sexual attention, we would all be solitary creatures.

The category of sexual harassment, according to current campus definitions, is not confined to relationships involving power inequity. Echoing many other common definitions of sexual harassment, Princeton's pamphlet warns that "sexual harassment can occur between two people regardless of whether or not one has power over the other." The weight of this definition of sexual harassment, then, falls on gender instead of status.

In current definitions of sexual harassment, there is an implication that gender is so important that it eclipses all other forms of power. The driving idea behind these rules is that gender itself is a sufficient source of power to constitute sexual harassment. Catharine MacKinnon, an early theorist of sexual harassment, writes that "situations of co-equal power—among co-workers or students or teachers—are difficult to see as examples of sexual harassment unless you have a notion of male power. I think we lie to women when we call it not power when a woman is come on to by a man who is not her employer, not her teacher."[2] With this description, MacKinnon extends the province of male power beyond that of tangible social power. She proposes using the words "sexual harassment" as a way to name what she sees as a fundamental social and political inequity between men and women. Following in this line of thought, Elizabeth Grauerholz, a sociology professor, conducted a study about instances of male students harassing their female professors, a phenomenon she calls "contrapower harassment."[3]

Recently, at the University of Michigan, a female teaching assistant almost brought a male student up on charges of sexual harassment. She was offended by an example he used in a paper about polls—a few sentences about "Dave Stud" entertaining ladies in his apartment when he receives a call from a pollster—and she showed the paper to the professor of the class. He apparently encouraged her to see the offending example as an instance of sexual harassment. She decided not to press charges, although she warned the student that the next time anything else like this happened, in writing or in person, she would not hesitate. The student wisely dropped the course. To understand how this student's paragraph about Dave Stud might sexually harass his teacher, when he has much more to lose than she does, one must recognize the deeply sexist assumptions about male-female relations behind the teaching assistant's charge.

The idea that a male student can sexually harass a female professor, overturning social and institutional hierarchy, solely on the basis of some primal or socially conditioned male power over women is insulting. The mere fact of being a man doesn't give the male student so much power that he can plow through social hierarchies, grabbing what he wants, intimidating all the cowering female faculty in his path. The assumption that female students or faculty must be protected from the sexual harassment of male peers or inferiors promotes the regrettable idea that men are natively more powerful than women.

Even if you argue, as many do, that *in this society* men are simply much more powerful than women, this is still a dangerous train of thought. It carries us someplace we don't want to be. Rules and laws based on the premise that all women need protection from all men, because they are so much weaker, serve only to reinforce the image of women as powerless.

Our female professors and high-ranking executives, our congresswomen and editors, are every bit as strong as their male counterparts. They have earned their position of authority. To declare that their authority is vulnerable to a dirty joke from someone of inferior status just because that person happens to be a man is to undermine their position. Female authority is not (and should not be seen as) so fragile that it shatters at the first sign of male sexuality. Any rules saying otherwise strip women, in the public eye, of their hard-earned authority.

Since common definitions of sexual harassment include harassment between peers, the emphasis is not on external power structures, but on inner landscapes. The boundaries are subjective, the maps subject to mood. According to the Equal Employment Opportunity Commission's definition, any conduct may be deemed sexual harassment if it "has the purpose or effect of unreasonably interfering with an individual's work or academic performance or creating an intimidating, hostile or offensive working or academic environment." The hostility or offensiveness of a working environment is naturally hard to measure by objective standards. Such vague categorization opens the issue up to the individual psyche.

The clarity of the definition of sexual harassment as a "hostile work environment" depends on a universal code of conduct, a shared idea of acceptable behavior that we just don't have. Something that makes one person feel uncomfortable may make another person feel great. At Princeton, counselors reportedly tell students, If you feel sexually harassed then chances are you were. At the university's Terrace Club, the refuge of fashionable, left-leaning, black-clad undergraduates, there is a sign supporting this view: "What constitutes sexual harassment or intimidating, hostile or offensive environment is to be defined by the person harassed and his/her own feelings of being threatened or compromised." This relatively common definition of sexual harassment crosses the line between being supportive and obliterating the idea of external reality.

The categories become especially complicated and slippery when sexual harassment enters the realm of the subconscious. The Princeton guide explains that "sexual harassment may result from a conscious or unconscious action, and can be subtle or blatant." Once we move into the area of the subtle and unconscious, we are no longer talking about a professor systematically exploiting power for sex. We are no longer talking about Hey, baby, sleep with me or I'll fail you. To hold people responsible for their subtle, unconscious action is to legislate thought, an ominous, not to mention difficult, prospect.

The idea of sexual harassment—and clearly when you are talking about the subtle and unconscious, you are talking about an idea—provides a blank canvas on which students can express all of the insecurities, fears and confusions about the relative sexual freedom of the college experience. Sexual harassment is everywhere: it crops up in dinner conversations and advertisements on television, all over women's magazines and editorial pages. . . .

The heightened awareness of the potential for sexual encroachment creates an atmosphere of suspicion and distrust between faculty and students. Many professors follow an unwritten rule: never close the door to your office when you and a female student are inside. One professor told a male teaching assistant I know that closing the door to his office with a student inside is an invitation to charges of sexual harassment. . . .

The irony is that these open doors, and all that they symbolize, threaten to create barriers between faculty and students. In the present hypersensitive environment, caution and better judgment can lead professors to keep female students at a distance. It may be easier not to pursue friendships with female students than to risk charges of sexual harassment and misunderstood intentions. The rhetoric surrounding sexual harassment encourages a return to formal relations between faculty and students.

The university, with its emphasis on intellectual exchange, on the passionate pursuit of knowledge, with its strange hours and unworldly citizens, is theoretically an ideal space for close friendships. The flexible hours combined with the intensity of the academic world would appear to be fertile ground for connections, arguments over coffee. Recently, reading a biography of the poet John Berryman, who was also a professor at Princeton in the forties, I was struck by stories about his students crowding into his house late into the night to talk about poetry. These days, an informal invitation to a professor's house till all hours would be a breach of propriety. . . .

Feminists concerned with sexual harassment must fight for an immutable hierarchy, for interactions so cleansed of personal interest there can be no possibility of borders crossed. Although this approach to education may reduce the number of harmful connections between teachers and students, it may also reduce the number of meaningful connections. The problem with the chasm solution to faculty-student relations is that for graduate students, and even for undergraduates, connections with professors are intellectually as well as professionally important.

In an early survey of sexual harassment, a law student at Berkeley wrote that in response to fears of sexual harassment charges, "the male law school teachers ignore female students . . . this means that we are afforded [fewer] academic opportunities than male students."[4] Many male professors have confirmed that they feel more uncomfortable with female students than with male students, because of all the attention given to sexual harassment. They may not "ignore" their female students, but they keep them at arm's length. They feel freer to forge friendships with male students.

The overstringent attention given to sexual harassment on campuses breeds suspicion; it creates an environment where imaginations run wild, charges can seem to materialize out of thin air, and both faculty and students worry about a friendly lunch. The repercussions for the academic community, let alone the confused freshman, can be many and serious. . . .

The university has become so saturated with the idea of sexual harassment that it has begun to affect minute levels of communication. Like "date rape," the phrase "sexual harassment" is frequently used, and it does not apply only to extremes of human behavior. Suddenly everyday experience is filtered through the strict lens of a new sexual politics. Under fierce political scrutiny, behavior that once seemed neutral or natural enough now takes on ominous meanings. You may not even realize that you are a survivor of sexual harassment.

A student tells me that she first experienced sexual harassment when she came to college. She was at a crowded party, leaning against a wall, and a big jock came up to her, placed his hands at either side of her head, and pretended to lean against her, saying, So, baby, when are we going out? All

right, he didn't touch me, she says, but he invaded my space. He had no right to do that.

She has carried this first instance of sexual harassment around in her head for six years. It is the beginning of a long list. A serious feminist now, an inhabitant of the official feminist house on campus, she recognizes this experience for what it was. . . .

Many foreigners think that concern with sexual harassment is as American as baseball, New England Puritans, and apple pie. Many feminists in other countries look on our preoccupation with sexual harassment as another sign of the self-indulgence and repression in American society. Veronique Neiertz, France's secretary of state for women's rights, has said that in the United States "the slightest wink can be misinterpreted." Her ministry's commonsense advice to women who feel harassed by coworkers is to respond with "a good slap in the face."[5]

Once sexual harassment includes someone glancing down your shirt, the meaning of the phrase has been stretched beyond recognition. The rules about unwanted sexual attention begin to seem more like etiquette than rules. Of course it would be nicer if people didn't brush against other people in a way that makes them uncomfortable. It would also be nicer if bankers didn't bang their briefcases into people on the subway at rush hour. But not nice is a different thing than against the rules, or the law. It is a different thing than oppressing women. Etiquette and politics aren't synonyms.

Susan Teres of SHARE said, at the 1992 Take Back the Night march, that 88 percent of Princeton's female students had experienced some form of sexual harassment on campus. . . . No wonder. Once you cast the net so wide as to include everyone's everyday experience, identifying sexual harassment becomes a way of interpreting the sexual texture of daily life, instead of isolating individual events. Sensitivity to sexual harassment becomes a way of seeing the world, rather than a way of targeting specific contemptible behaviors. . . .

As one peruses guidelines on sexual harassment, it's clear where the average man comes in.

Like most common definitions, Princeton's definition of sexual harassment includes "leering and ogling, whistling, sexual innuendo, and other suggestive or offensive or derogatory comments, humor and jokes about sex." . . . These definitions of sexual harassment sterilize the environment. They propose classrooms that are cleaner than Sesame Street and Mr. Rogers' neighborhood. Like the rhetoric about date rape, this extreme inclusiveness forces women into old roles. What message are we sending if we say We can't work if you tell dirty jokes, it upsets us, it offends us? With this severe a conception of sexual harassment, sex itself gets pushed into a dark, seamy, male domain. If we can't look at his dirty pictures because his dirty pictures upset us, it doesn't mean they vanish. It means he looks at them with a new sense of their power, their underground, forbidden, male-only value.

Instead of learning that men have no right to do these terrible things to us, we should be learning to deal with individuals with strength and confidence. If someone bothers us, we should be able to put him in his place without crying into our pillow or screaming for help or counseling. If someone stares at us, or talks dirty, or charges neutral conversation with sexual innuendo, we should not be pushed to the verge of a nervous breakdown. . . .

I would even go so far as to say that people have the right to leer at whomever they want to leer at. By offering protection to the woman against the leer, the movement against sexual harassment is curtailing her personal power. This protection implies the need to be protected. It paints her as defenseless against even the most trivial of male attentions. This protection assumes that she never ogles, leers, or makes sexual innuendos herself.

Interpreting leers and leer-type behavior as a violation is a choice. My mother tells me about the time she was walking down the street in the sixties, when skirts were short, with my older sister, who was then three. A construction worker made a comment to my mother, and my three-year-old sister leaned out of her carriage and said, "Hey, mister, leave my mother alone." My mother, never the conventional sort of feminist, told my sister

that the construction worker wasn't hurting her, he was giving her a compliment.

Although my mother's reaction may not be everyone's, this is a parable about individual responses. There is spectrum of reactions to something like a leer. Some may be flattered, others distressed; some won't notice, and still others, according to some feminist literature, will be enraged and incapacitated. In its propaganda the movement against sexual harassment places absolute value on the leer. According to its rules, whatever that construction worker said to my mother was violating, harmful, and demeaning. According to its rules, my three-year-old sister was right. By rallying institutional authority behind its point of view, by distributing these pamphlets that say leering always makes women feel violated, this movement propels women backward to a time when sexual attention was universally thought to offend. They are saying, as Catharine MacKinnon neatly summarizes it, that "all women live in sexual objectification the way fish live in water."[6] But I think it depends on where you learned to swim.

History offers an example of another time when looks could be crimes, but today feminists don't talk much about what happened to black men accused of "reckless eyeballing," that is, directing sexual glances at white women. Black men were lynched for a previous incarnation of "sexual harassment." As late as 1955, a black man was lynched for whistling at a white woman. Beneath the Jim Crow law about reckless eyeballing was the assumption that white women were the property of white men, and a look too hard or too long in their direction was a flouting of white power. Reckless eyeballing was a symbolic violation of white women's virtue. That virtue, that division between white women and black men, was important to the southern hierarchy. While of course lynchings and Jim Crow are not the current danger, it's important to remember that protecting women against the stray male gaze has not always served a social good. We should learn the lessons: looks can't kill, and we are nobody's property.

All of this is not to suggest that abuses of power are not wrong. They are. Any professor who trades grades for sex and uses this power as a forceful tool of seduction deserves to face charges. The same would be true if he traded grades for a thousand dollars. I'm not opposed to stamping out corruption; I only think it's important to look before you stamp. Rules about harassment should be less vague, and inclusive. They should sharply target serious offenses and abuses of power rather than environments that are "uncomfortable," rather than a stray professor looking down a shirt. The university's rules should not be based on the idea of female students who are pure and naïve, who don't harbor sexualities of their own, who don't seduce, or who can't defend themselves against the nonconditional sexual interests of male faculty and students. . . .

As feminists interested in the issue themselves argue, "Many have difficulty recognizing their experience as victimization. It is helpful to use the words that fit the experience, validating the depths of the survivor's feelings and allowing her to feel her experience was serious."[7] In other words, these feminists recognize that if you don't tell the victim that she's a victim, she may sail through the experience without fully grasping the gravity of her humiliation. She may get through without all that trauma and counseling. . . . To create awareness is sometimes to create a problem.

Education about sexual harassment is not confined to the space of freshman week. As sexual harassment is absorbed into public discussion, it enters grade schools as easily as colleges. An article in *New York* magazine documents the trickle-down effect: "After her first week at a reputable private school in Manhattan, 8-year-old Alexandra didn't want to go back. A 9-year-old boy had been harassing her: 'He said he wanted to hump me.' She wasn't sure what 'hump' meant."[8]

The article describes what happened when Alexandra discovered the name for her traumatic experience. She was listening to Anita Hill's testimony on the radio when she suddenly exclaimed: "'That's what happened to me! He didn't touch me, but his words upset me!'" . . . As Alexandra grows up, will she be better able to deal with sexual abuse, or will she just see it everywhere she looks? Will she blur the line between childish teasing and sexual abuse for the rest of her life? The prospect of a maturing generation of Alexandras, sensitized from childhood to the issue of sexual harassment, is not necessarily desirable from the feminist point of view. As Joan Didion wrote in the sixties, certain segments of the women's movement can breed "women too sensitive for the difficulties of adult life, women unequipped for reality, and grasping at the movement as a rationale for denying that reality."[9]

Responding to sexual harassment in its most expansive definition purges the environment of the difficult, the uncomfortable, and the even mildly distasteful. . . . Whether or not visions of a universe free from "sexual harassment" are practical, the question becomes whether they're even desirable.

Mary Koss, author of the *Ms.* magazine survey of rape, writes that "experiencing sexual harassment transforms women into victims and changes their lives."[10] Koss sees this transformation into victimhood as something caused by sexual harassment, an external event. In Koss's paradigm, after the student has been harassed, her confidence is perilously shaken, her ability to function and trust men disrupted forever. She sees the "lecherous professor" as the agent of transformation. She does not see that it is her entire conceptual framework—her kind of rhetoric, her kind of interpretation—that transforms perfectly stable women into hysterical, sobbing victims. If there is any transforming to be done, it is to transform everyday experience back into everyday experience.

NOTES

1. "What You Should Know About Sexual Harassment." Princeton, N.J.: SHARE.
2. Catharine MacKinnon, *Feminism Unmodified* (Cambridge: Harvard University Press, 1987), 89.
3. *Chronicle of Higher Education,* 24 April 1991.
4. "Sexual Harassment: A Hidden Issue." Washington, D.C.: Project on the Status and Education of Women, 1978.

5. Alan Riding, "France Rethinks Its Wink at Sex Harassment," *New York Times,* 3 May 1992.

6. MacKinnon, *Toward a Feminist Theory of the State,* (Cambridge: Harvard University Press, 1989), 149.

7. Kathryn Quina, "The Victimization of Women," in Michele Paludi, ed., *Ivory Power: Sexual Harassment on Campus* (Albany: State University of New York Press, 1990), 99.

8. *New York,* 16 November 1992.

9. Joan Didion, *The White Album* (New York: Farrar, Straus and Giroux, 1979), 116.

10. Mary Koss, "Changed Lives: The Psychological Impact of Sexual Harassment," in Paludi, ed., 73.

Discussion Questions

1. What does Roiphe mean when she says that broad definitions of sexual harassment "sterilize the environment"? Do you agree? Support your answers using examples from your campus and/or workplace. Working in groups, come up with a definition of sexual harassment that overcomes some of the problems in the current definitions cited by Roiphe.

2. Do people have a right to leer? Discuss some of the pros and cons of including leering under the definition of sexual harassment. Discuss how a liberal feminist and de Beauvoir might each respond to these questions.

3. Discuss Roiphe's claim that feminists such as Lois Pineau (Chapter 7) who tell victims of date rape that they have been "traumatized" are actually perpetuating the old ethos of female victimhood and contributing to the institutionalization of female weakness. Discuss how Pineau might respond to Roiphe's argument.

4. Discuss whether Roiphe adequately addresses the problem of sexual harassment as sexual discrimination and a violation of the right to equal opportunity. Does sexual harassment, even though it may not directly harm a particular woman, create a hostile working or academic environment that, in turn, limits women's opportunities and freedom? Support your answer.

CASE STUDIES

1. LIFE IMITATING ART: SEX-STEREOTYPES IN THE MEDIA

When it comes to the regulation of media that objectify women and portray them as subordinate, feminists focus primarily on adult pornography. However, their efforts may be coming too late. Research shows that children have already formed their sex-role stereotypes by the age of seven. Television and movies, in particular, exert a strong influence on children's perception of gender roles.[30] In most children's shows females are portrayed in passive roles, such as housewives, waitresses, and secretaries. Males are portrayed in active roles such as doctors, detectives, and commanders. Even television shows for very young children promote sex stereotyping. *Teletubbies* and *Barney & Friends,* for example, while opening up the range of acceptable behavior for boys, reinforce sex stereotypes for girls.[31] The media's belittlement of females does not end with children's shows. The media tend to denigrate motherhood and glamorize the childless, single life in the written media as well as in television shows such as *Nanny 911* and *Law and Order: SVU.*

Discussion Questions

1. Do children's shows that portray females in passive, subordinate roles and males as active problem-solvers represent a type of sex discrimination that harms girls and women? Should these shows be censored or regulated? Discuss how a utilitarian, a liberal feminist, and a conservative such as Goldberg would most likely answer these questions.

2. When women play lead roles in television and movies, they are generally gorgeous, thin, childless, and young. Discuss the effects of this image of successful women on women's sense of self as well as their views on motherhood.

3. Magazine covers often show women who fit our cultural stereotypes. For example, in the 1910s, when feminists were demanding suffrage, magazine covers portrayed women as "bad" and a threat to the social structure. In the politically conservative 1950s, images of Doris Day were popular.[32] What stereotypes of women are portrayed in contemporary magazines? How do these stereotypes shape the way women think of themselves and the way men think of women? Do magazine publishers have a moral obligation to present a fair view of women and to avoid the use of stereotypes? Support your answers.

---

2. COMMERICAL SURROGACY

Twenty-four-year-old Chandra Patel, who is eight months pregnant, settles into her comfortable bedroom at a spacious house that she shares with a dozen other women, all carrying babies for couples, mostly from Europe and North America. In each case the man has donated the sperm while the surrogate mother is the biological mother. A team of cooks, maids, doctors, and other medical staff care for the women. This is the third child Chandra has borne for infertile couples from other countries. The child she had with her husband prior to becoming a surrogate died during infancy.

Commercial surrogacy, in which a woman is paid to carry another person's or couple's child, was legalized in India in 2002. The use of Indian surrogates has become increasingly popular with infertile couples from industrialized countries where commercial surrogacy is illegal or very expensive. Clinics in India charge the intended parents between $10,000 and $30,000 for the entire process. Like the other surrogate mothers, Chandra can make as much as she would in 15 years working in another job. Without the income from her surrogacy, Chandra and her husband, an uneducated farmer, and family, would be living in poverty.

Discussion Questions

1. Commercial surrogacy is illegal in Canada, Britain, and France as well as some states in the United States. Opponents argue that commercial surrogacy reduces women to "wombs for rent." They point out that using women from India exploits poor women in these countries. They also question whether a woman whose alternative to serving as a surrogate is poverty can truly give her autonomous consent. Critically analyze these arguments.

2. Defenders of commercial surrogacy maintain that surrogates provide a meaningful service to infertile couples who want their own child. Surrogates, they note, in

addition to giving their informed consent, are well paid and receive excellent medical care.

3. The couple who have paid Chandra to act as their surrogate decide to get divorced a few weeks before the baby's due date. They inform the clinic in India that they no longer want the baby. Chandra decides she wants to keep the baby. Although she and her husband are no longer living in poverty, thanks to the income from the previous two surrogate pregnancies, they cannot afford to reimburse the clinic for the expenses for this child. However, a gay couple, friends of the intended parents, would like to adopt the baby and are willing to pay all the expenses. What should happen to the child? Support your answer.

3. INFERTILITY TREATMENT: ARE EIGHT BABIES TOO MANY?

In 2009, thirty-three-year-old Nadya Suleman gave birth to eight premature babies ranging in weight from 1 pound 8 ounces to 3 pounds 4 ounces. Suleman, a single mother who already had six young children at home, had six embryos implanted from in vitro fertilization, and two of the embyos resulted in twin births. A team of forty-six doctors as well as other medical staff were involved in the delivery. Some of the eight infants were in the hospital for months. The entire cost ran into the millions of dollars, part of which was paid by taxpayers. In addition, some of the infants may have lifetime medical and developmental problems.

Suleman, who says she was lonely as an only child and has "a deep need to connect," is delighted at the new additions to her family. The octuplets' birth, she says, was a "miraculous experience."

Discussion Questions

1. Does a woman's reproductive freedom extend to a right to have has many babies as she wants? Does it matter who pays—the parent(s) or the taxpayers—for the expenses associated with the birth and any health problems the children may have? Does it matter that Suleman is a single mother with no obvious means of financial support? Support your answers.

2. The physician who implanted the six embryos is under investigation for violating the standard procedures put forth by the American Society for Reproductive Medicine, which recommends limiting the number of embryos to two for women under the age of thirty-five. Discuss the morality of the physician's actions. Should legal restrictions be placed on the number of embryos that a physician can implant? Support your answer.

3. Selective reduction (abortion of some of the fetuses) is generally recommended when a woman is carrying more than three fetuses because of the risk of miscarriage and of health and developmental problems associated with multiple births. Suleman knew she was going to have at least seven babies and decided against selective reduction. Discuss the moral issues involved in her decision, as well as what you would have done and why.

4. LILLIAN GARLAND: PREGNANCY LEAVE AND THE WORKPLACE

Lillian Garland was employed as a receptionist by the California Savings and Loan Co. in Los Angeles. Her difficult pregnancy required that she take several months' leave. When she tried to return to work after four months, she expected her job to have been protected by a California law that granted unpaid pregnancy disability leave. However, there was no job awaiting her. She sued her employer for not giving her maternity leave. Her employer argued that unpaid job-protection maternity laws discriminated against men.

Feminist groups such as NOW and the National Women's Political Caucus filed amicus briefs siding with the employer in the court hearing, arguing for "equal treatment" as opposed to "special treatment" for pregnancy. They contended that pregnancy should be treated just like any other disability. Since men are not given disability leave for pregnancy, neither should pregnant women get disability leave. The federal court ruled with the employer and struck down the California law.

The case was taken to the U.S. Supreme Court where in 1987 in *California Savings and Loan v. Guerra* (1987), the Court overturned the earlier ruling and upheld the California law granting unpaid pregnancy disability leave.

Discussion Questions

1. Liberal feminists maintain that "special treatment" for pregnant women demeans women and violates the principle of equality. Gender-essential feminists, however, reject the gender-neutral approach. Women are not just like men. Pregnancy, they argue, is a natural, normal role performed only by women. This difference should be taken into account in laws affecting the workplace. Do you agree? Support your answer. Discuss the merits of the "equal treatment" and the "special treatment" approaches.
2. The current Family and Medical Leave Act applies equally to fathers and mothers. Is this fair, given that many women need to use part of their twelve-week leave prior to the birth of the child? Support your answer. Discuss also how Goldberg might answer this question.
3. Does the Family and Medical Leave Act discriminate against poor people and single mothers, given that unpaid maternity leave is out of the question for many of them? If so, how should pregnancy and parental leave be structured?
4. The level of support in the United States for pregnancy and child rearing is sharply below world standards. Almost all industrialized nations provide medical coverage and paid leave, sometimes up to twelve months, for maternity and parenting. Discuss the merits of the two approaches.

5. THE MILITARY CULTURE OF SEXUAL HARASSMENT

Only since 1976 have women integrated into the once all-male bastion of the military academy. However, many women drop out of the academies and the military because of sexual harassment. According to a 2008 U.S. Department of Defense Report, 34 percent of active-duty service women as well as 6 percent of men reported they had experienced sexual harassment in 2007; 6.8 percent of women and 1.8 percent of men reported unwanted sexual contact.[33] Other surveys indicate that the rate of sexual harassment and assault may be much higher than reported.

Private Sarah Tolaro and four other enlisted women from the Army base at Fort Meade, Maryland, one of whom had wanted to make the Army her career, all left the Army because of sexual harassment. When Tolaro told someone about the harassment, she was told to drop it and "not to make waves." In fact, one of the other women from Fort Meade, rather than make an issue of sexual harassment, accepted the Army's claim—"inability to cope with military life"—as the official reason for her leaving the Army.[34]

Most female cadets who are sexually harassed or assaulted do not report the incident for fear of reprisal, not being taken seriously, or being blamed for the assault. The military places a high priority on training programs related to sexual misconduct, programs they maintain are working. The military also provides the option of "restricted reported," in which a victim is provided with support services without having to give up her anonymity by pursuing legal charges and participating in an investigative process.

Discussion Questions

1. Discuss the military's "restricted reporting" option. Does this policy encourage sexual misconduct by letting perpetrators off the hook, or does it empower victims by enabling them to seek support services without having to go through the public legal process? Support your answer.
2. Female and male cadets are housed together in the same barracks. One of the changes the Air Force Academy is making to cut down on the incidence of sexual harassment and assault is to move women so their rooms are clustered near the women's bathrooms. Discuss the moral issues raised by this policy. What would a liberal feminist and a radical feminist most likely think about this policy?
3. Discuss what type of policy Roiphe and Goldberg would each most likely recommend for dealing with sexual harassment in the military.
4. Seventeen percent of female college students report being subjected to sexual harassment by an instructor.[35] Does this reinforce women's sense of powerlessness? Discuss the implications of this finding on the quality of women's education and self-confidence.

---

6. ANOREXIA NERVOSA AND BULIMIA: THE TYRANNY OF THINNESS

Philosophical views, rather than being merely abstract ideas, have real-life consequences. Philosophers have traditionally associated women with the body and men with the mind. The myth that the female body and female sexuality are evil contributes to another type of violence against women's bodies: anorexia nervosa and bulimia. These two disorders, which were rare thirty years ago, have reached epidemic proportions today. Tyra Banks, at 5 feet 10 inches, weighed 110 pounds when she began her modeling career at the age of eighteen. While her thinness and beauty made her highly sought after as a supermodel, her weight at the time was well below the healthy range. It also would have made her ineligible to model in Brazil or Spain, where models who fall below a certain weight are barred from modeling in fashion shows. According to the National Eating Disorders Screening Program, more than 5 million Americans had eating disorders, including 15 percent of young women. About one hundred women die each year of anorexia nervosa.[36]

After her semiretirement, Banks put on weight. While happy about her new weight, she has had to endure slurs and headlines referring to her as fat and as "America's Next Top Waddle." Fortunately, Banks—unlike many other women—was able to resist the pressure to lose weight. She told *People* magazine, "If I had lower self-esteem I would probably be starving myself right now.[37]

Discussion Questions

1. Discuss how myths about women contribute to anorexia and bulimia. Are these myths generally accepted on your campus? If so, discuss what steps might be taken to counteract these myths.
2. Discuss Banks's experience. To what extent is your self-esteem tied up with your body image? If you are a woman, have you ever felt pressure to lose weight in order to be better liked or more successful? As a man, have you ever felt pressure to change your body to fit a certain image or cultural ideal? Explain.
3. The greatest fear of many women today is not of a nuclear holocaust or environmental catastrophe, but of getting fat. Discuss how, if at all, sexism in the media contributes to this fear.
4. Do you have a moral obligation to try to help friends who are anorexic or bulimic? If so, what is the basis of this obligation? Imagine a situation in which a friend who is anorexic or bulimic comes to you for help. Discuss what you might say to her.

CHAPTER 9

Freedom of Speech

When Seth Greenberg, coach of the California State University at Long Beach basketball team, walked into the visitors' locker room in the Pan American Center at New Mexico State University, he was confronted by the greaseboard message, "SETH, GET READY FOR AN ASS-KICKING, YOU JEW BASTARD." The outpouring of hate continued during the game, with some of the fans yelling obscenities and racial epithets such as "Take one of the niggers out." After the game, the visibly upset coach Greenberg told television interviewers that the slurs were "a sad commentary on life and . . . a sad commentary on this university." A few days later, New Mexico State University Executive Vice President Michael Conroy sent a letter to the president of Long Beach State, demanding an apology from Greenberg and castigating him for impugning the reputation of the university and the entire state of New Mexico.

Who was in the wrong? Should Greenberg have been more tolerant of the racial slurs? Should college campuses have speech codes that restrict hate speech, or should hate speech be protected under freedom of speech?

WHAT IS "FREEDOM OF SPEECH"?

Freedom of speech is a type of liberty right. We have a right to express our opinions without interference from the government or other people. The primary value of freedom of speech is the promotion of truth and expression. John Stuart Mill, in his essay *On Liberty,* argues that freedom of speech is at the heart of democracy. Expression of ideas cannot be prohibited simply because people find them offensive.

Not all forms of verbal expression are considered speech. Yelling "Fire!" in a crowded theater; "fighting words" intended to inflame someone into committing violent actions; and slanderous, false rumors intended to ruin someone's reputation are not generally protected under freedom of speech. Symbols such as swastikas, armbands, and burning crosses, on the other hand, are protected as freedom of expression if they're used in a public place, like a rally or public schools.

There are many gray areas in the freedom-of-speech debate. Should unsolicited calls from political candidates and spam on the Internet be protected speech? What about pornography, or expressions of anti-American sentiment in times of war, flag burning, or speech that condones terrorism? The community is even more deeply divided over the moral permissibility of hate speech. **Hate speech** is defined as "epithets conventionally understood to be insulting references to characteristics such as race, gender, nationality, ethnicity, religion, and sexual preference."[1]

Libertarians argue that, although discrimination is wrong, hate speech should be protected because we have a right to express our ideas. Stanley Fish, in his reading "There's No Such Thing as Free Speech, and It's a Good Thing, Too," disagrees. He argues that speech and action cannot be separated. Charles R. Lawrence III also rejects this distinction, arguing that racist speech and discriminatory conduct are part of a totality that is incompatible with equality.

LIMITATIONS ON FREEDOM OF SPEECH

Like most liberty rights, freedom of speech is not an absolute right but is limited by the rights of others to pursue their equal and similar interests. Every society places limits on speech in order to prevent violence and civil disorder as well as to protect its citizens against fraud, threats, and harassment. Without some rules of order, discussions would degrade into chaos and frustration. The question of how far these restrictions should extend is widely debated.

Liberals argue that the government does not have a right to protect citizens from offensive speech. **Censorship**—the controlling of silencing of speech—can occur without legal sanctions, as Alan Dershowitz points out in his article on political correctness on campuses. Catharine MacKinnon argues that pornography should be censored because it poses a direct threat to women's equality. Nadine Strossen, president of the American Civil Liberties Union (ACLU), argues the opposite; it is censorship of pornography and hate speech that threatens to undermine equality.

Censorship has traditionally rested on the assumption that people in authority possess the truth and are able to make final judgments about what is right and good. People who expressed doubts about these "truths" were labeled heretics, foolish, dangerous, or insane. The oppression of great thinkers like Galileo illustrates how censorship can hold back progress.

The USA Patriot Act, passed shortly after the terrorist attacks of September 11, 2001, gives government enforcement officials increased powers to eavesdrop on international phone calls and to search people's library and bookstore records. (See Case Study 4.) The USA Patriot Act was expanded in 2006 to allow the Justice Department to "detect and disrupt" the activities of suspected terrorists as well as drug dealers and other criminals. Many people argue that the Patriot Act is a violation of Americans' First Amendment right to freedom of speech. The Universal Declaration of Human Rights was adopted by the United Nations in 1948 following World War II as a "common standard of achievement for all peoples and all nations." Article 19 states: "Everyone has the right to freedom of opinion and expression; this right includes freedom to hold opinions without interference and to seek, receive and impart information and ideas through any media and regardless of frontiers."

> ### 🖊 THE FIRST AMENDMENT TO THE UNITED STATES CONSTITUTION
>
> Congress shall make no law respecting an establishment of religion, or prohibiting the free exercise thereof; or abridging the freedom of speech, or of the press; or the right of the people to peaceably assemble, and to petition the Government for a redress of grievances.

THE FIRST AMENDMENT TO THE U.S. CONSTITUTION

The patriots in the American Revolution were no more willing to recognize freedom of speech than the British were and had no qualms about repressing speech that was not favorable to their cause. Indeed, during the American Revolution many loyalists, Quakers, and other political dissenters fled to Canada in fear of their lives.

Nor is there any indication that the Bill of Rights was intended to prevent censorship and regulation of speech. The original purpose of the First Amendment was to delegate the power to restrict freedom of speech to the states; although the federal government could not restrict speech, the state and municipal governments could.

Freedom of speech was not regarded as an end in itself, but rather as a means of informing the citizenry and promoting democracy. The most valued type of speech was political speech. Alexander Hamilton, one of the defenders of free expression, wrote, "The liberty of the press consists in the right to publish, with impunity, truth, with good motives, and for justifiable ends, whether it respects government, magistracy, or individuals." Utterances that abused this liberty (that is, were not made with concern for the truth, or with good motives) could be censored.

World War I gave rise to new concerns about speech that endangered national security. Supreme Court Justice Oliver Wendell Holmes was one of the great champions of freedom of speech in the early twentieth century. In his dissent in *Abrams v. the United States* (1919), Holmes defended freedom of speech on the grounds that society's ultimate good "is better reached by free trade in ideas—that the best test of truth is the power of the thought to get itself accepted in the competition of the market." Holmes's concept of the free marketplace of ideas, adopted from John Stuart Mill's work, has had a major impact on the Supreme Court's thinking about the role of freedom of speech in a democratic society.

In the early 1950s Senator Joseph McCarthy of Wisconsin reported on his investigation of Communist subversion in the United States. His sensationalist report was followed by a series of public hearings in which the careers of many prominent Americans were ruined on the most flimsy, hearsay evidence. Defenders of **McCarthyism** argued that Communist ideas should be repressed to "protect freedom" and democratic values. According to editor and journalist William F. Buckley Jr., for a free market of ideas to thrive, people out to defraud the public with a defective product (Communism) must be exposed.[2]

In 1954 McCarthy was formally censured by the Senate. The demise of McCarthyism was followed by a rapid expansion of the First Amendment. Speech other than political speech—such as sexual speech and pornography, entertainment, commercial speech, non-verbal expressions such as nude dancing and flag burning, and emotional utterances—came to be included under freedom of speech.

The limits of freedom of speech have been tested in attempts to restrict protesters outside abortion clinics. In the 1997 *Schenck v. Pro-Choice Network* decision, the U.S. Supreme Court ruled that abortion protesters may be kept outside a fifteen-foot "bubble zone" protecting those entering and leaving the clinics. In 2000 the Supreme Court in *Dale v. Boy Scouts of America* (BSA) ruled that the BSA's policy banning homosexuals from the Boy Scouts was protected under the First Amendment, stating that "The forced inclusion of an unwanted person in a group infringes the group's freedom of expressive association if the presence of that person affects in a significant way the group's ability to advocate public or private viewpoints."

One of the most contentious issues regarding First Amendment freedom of speech is religious speech in public places. In 1980 displays of the Ten Commandments were banned from public schools. And in 2000 the U.S. Supreme Court sided with those who wanted prayers removed from public schools and universities on the grounds that public prayer violated the separation of church and state. However, in 2005 the Supreme Court sent a mixed message when it upheld a ruling permitting the display of a civic-donated Ten Commandments monument in a public area, while turning down similar displays near two courthouses. The Supreme Court is currently (2009) hearing a case relating to the erection of a Summum monument next to the Ten Commandments in a Utah public park. The Summum religion practices mummification and received its founding revelation from space aliens in 1975.

FREEDOM OF SPEECH IN CYBERSPACE

Questions regarding freedom of speech have also arisen in the context of the electronic and telemarketing media. The Telecommunications Act of 1996 amended the Communication Act of 1934. One of the purposes of the revisions of the 1934 act was to explicate and strengthen the marketplace of ideas and freedom of speech in the communications industry.

Internet use has almost tripled in the United States since 2000. As of 2009, about 1.6 billion people worldwide were Internet users, including 74.4 percent of North Americans, 48.9 percent of Europeans, and 17.4 percent of Asians, with the most rapid growth in Internet use occurring in Africa and the Middle East.[3] Indeed, the 2007 UCLA American freshman survey found that college freshmen were spending more time surfing the Internet and visiting online social networks than studying.[4]

The rapid development of the Internet over the past few decades has raised the question of whether the rules surrounding freedom of speech that apply to traditional forms of broadcast technology should apply to Internet speech. Internet technology is distinguished from traditional broadcast technology in that anyone who has access to a computer can "broadcast" information to people around the world. Because the Internet is so accessible, it has been hailed as "the great equalizer," "the most participatory form of mass speech yet developed," and "the best advancement in democracy since universal suffrage."[5] On the other hand, as Chinese film director Zhang

Xu points out, there is also a downside to the Internet. Web broadcast TV and radio may homogenize the thinking, interests, and tastes of people around the world.[6] And unlike radio and television, where the hours of broadcast can be regulated, the material on the Internet is available twenty-four hours a day. The Communications Decency Act of 1996 provides immunity to websites.

Reno v. American Civil Liberties Union (1997) was the first U.S. Supreme Court decision according First Amendment protection to the Internet. The decision rejected the government's argument that the Internet should be treated like the broadcast industry, striking down the Communications Decency Act (CDA) restrictions, which required that online communication be reduced to a "safe for kids" level. It stated that in the absence of any effective method for preventing minors from accessing offensive information on the Internet, the restriction of speech on the Internet would impose an undue restriction on adults' access to information. In 2002 the Court struck down the Child Pornography Prevention Act, which would have made it a crime to create and distribute sexually explicit images of children, whether the images are digitally altered photos of adults or computer-generated images.

In his article at the end of this chapter on "The First Amendment in Cyberspace," Cass Sunstein addresses some of the moral issues involved in regulating freedom of speech on the Internet. Because the Internet is global, solutions to problems on the Internet will require international cooperation and regulation.

PORNOGRAPHY

The debate over pornography in the past thirty years has moved from arguments over the morality of nonprocreative sex to arguments based on freedom of speech and concerns that pornography may contribute to gender discrimination, rape, and sexual harassment. This shift is due in part to the proliferation of pornography since the late 1970s. The use of the Internet to distribute pornography allows people to view sexual violence without having to leave the comfort of their homes.

In 2007, there were 4.2 million pornographic websites (12 percent of total sites). Pornography is a 12-billion-dollar industry; the revenue from pornography in the United States alone is almost double the combined revenues of ABC, CBS, and NBC.[7] The largest consumers of Internet pornography are teenagers; 80 percent of fifteen- to seventeen-year-olds have had multiple hard-core pornography exposures. Males are much more likely than females to visit pornography sites.

Despite attempts to define pornography, establishing precise criteria has been difficult. Appeals to "offensiveness" run the risk of using subjective feelings or majority rule rather than rational criteria. In 1986 the U.S. Attorney General's Commission on Pornography defined **pornography** as "the category of material featuring actual or unmistakably simulated or unmistakably threatened violence presented in sexually explicit fashion with a predominant focus on the sexually explicit violence." **Erotica,** in contrast, involves a mutually pleasurable sexual expression; there is no clear conqueror or victim.[8] In addition to written works, art that involves nudity, including Picasso's abstract nudes and Michelangelo's statue of David, has been the target of censorship from government or private action. Music, such as some rap and hip-hop, that uses obscene language deemed degrading to women has also been censored.

Canadians have been relatively consistent in their opposition to pornography. In 1978 the Canadian Standing Committee on Justice and Legal Affairs stated that "the clear and unquestionable danger of this type of material is that it reinforces some unhealthy tendencies in Canadian society [and] male-female stereotypes to the detriment of both sexes."[9] Nadine Strossen opposes the Canadian antipornography law. She argues that historically censorship laws are just as often used to suppress the works of feminists and gays and lesbians whose ideas are unpopular.

In the United States, there have been mixed reactions to legal restrictions on pornography. In *Roth v. United States* (1957), the United States Supreme Court ruled that "obscene" material was not constitutionally protected speech. In 1970, however, the Commission on Obscenity and Pornography concluded that pornography was not harmful and recommended that all legal prohibitions against the sale of pornography between consenting adults be removed. In 1986 former Attorney General Edwin Meese's Commission on Pornography recommended that pornography be censored, arguing that it contributes to sexual violence and antisocial attitudes.

One of the arguments used by opponents of censorship is the Aristotelian view that pornography acts as a catharsis or release for harmful, pent-up sexual urges.[10] There is no scientific evidence, however, that pornography has a cathartic effect. If anything, studies suggest that media violence provokes greater feelings of aggression. (See Case Study 6.) Although the evidence is inconclusive, some studies have found viewing violent pornography to be positively correlated to acts of violence against women.[11]

Catharine MacKinnon argues that pornography is immoral because it poses a substantial threat to women's equality and, therefore, directly harms women. MacKinnon's position is based on radical feminism, which focuses on the oppressive patriarchal hierarchy and its harms to women.[12] Her critics, such as Strossen, question whether there is sufficient evidence to establish the claim that violent pornography presents a "clear and present danger" to women. A ban on violent pornography, they argue, would have a "chilling effect" on freedom of speech. Strossen also argues that censorship of pornography and hate speech undermines the struggle for human rights and equality of women and minorities. (See Case Study 1.)

HATE SPEECH AS PROTECTED SPEECH

Radio and television commentator Dr. Laura Schlessinger believes that homosexuals violate scriptural teachings and that homosexual sex is deviant behavior. Her views have incensed many people who have dubbed Dr. Schlessinger "The Queen of Hate Radio." Rather than an adversary whose ideas are to be debated in the free marketplace of ideas, she is regarded as a hateful person who should be censored and silenced. The San Francisco Board of Supervisors has officially warned Schlessinger about "making inaccurate statements about gays and lesbians that incite violence and hate."[13] However, do her antihomosexual views amount to dangerous hate speech that should be suppressed? Where do we draw the line between hate speech and speech, though offensive and perhaps even inaccurate, that should be tolerated in the name of freedom of speech?

📖 *THE VILLAGE OF SKOKIE V. NATIONAL SOCIALIST PARTY*
OF AMERICA (1978): EXCERPTS FROM THE MAJORITY OPINION

Honorable Joseph M. Wosik, Judge, Supreme Court of Illinois, delivering the opinion of the court:

Plaintiff, the village of Skokie, filed a complaint in the circuit court of Cook County seeking to enjoin defendants, the National Socialist Party of America (the American Nazi Party) and 10 individuals as "officers and members" of the party, from engaging in certain activities while conducting a demonstration within the village. . . .

It is alleged in plaintiff's complaint that the "uniform of the National Socialist Party of America consists of the storm trooper uniform of the German Nazi Party embellished with the Nazi swastika"; that the plaintiff village has a population of about 70,000 persons of which approximately 40,500 persons are of "Jewish religion or Jewish ancestry" and of this latter number 5,000 to 7,000 are survivors of German concentration camps; that the defendant organization is "dedicated to the incitation of racial and religious hatred directed principally against individuals of Jewish faith or ancestry and non-Caucasians"; and that its members "have patterned their conduct, their uniform, their slogan and their tactics along the pattern of the German Nazi Party." . . .

"It is firmly settled that under our Constitution the public expression of ideas may not be prohibited merely because the ideas are themselves offensive to some of their hearers" (*Bachellar v. Maryland* (1970)) . . . and it is entirely clear that the wearing of distinctive clothing can be symbolic expression of a thought or philosophy. The symbolic expression of thought falls within the free speech clause of the first amendment . . . and the plaintiff village has the heavy burden of justifying the imposition of a prior restraint upon defendants' right to freedom of speech. . . .

The village of Skokie seeks to meet this burden by application of the "fighting words" doctrine first enunciated in *Chaplinsky v. New Hampshire* (1942). . . . That doctrine was designed to permit punishment of extremely hostile personal communication likely to cause immediate physical response. . . .

The display of the swastika, as offensive to the principles of a free nation as the memories it recalls may be, is symbolic political speech intended to convey to the public the beliefs of those who display it. It does not, in our opinion, fall within the definition of "fighting words." . . .

Nor can we find that the swastika, while not representing fighting words, is nevertheless so offensive and peace threatening to the public that its display can be enjoined. We do not doubt that the sight of this symbol is abhorrent to the Jewish citizens of Skokie, and that the survivors of the Nazi persecutions, tormented by their recollections, may have strong feelings regarding its display. Yet it is entirely clear that this factor does not justify enjoining defendants' speech.

In summary, as we read the controlling Supreme Court opinions, use of the swastika is a symbolic form of free speech entitled to first amendment

(continued)

(continued from p. 451)

protections. Its display on uniforms or banners by those engaged in peaceful demonstrations cannot be totally precluded solely because that display may provoke a violent reaction by those who view it. . . .

We accordingly, albeit reluctantly, conclude that the display of the swastika cannot be enjoined under the fighting-words exception to free speech, nor can anticipation of a hostile audience justify the prior restraint. . . .

In the 1978 *Skokie* case (see box), the American Civil Liberties Union (ACLU) defended the right of neo-Nazis to march in Skokie, Illinois, a predominantly Jewish neighborhood in Chicago where a number of Holocaust survivors resided. The ACLU argued that the principle of justice required impartiality or neutrality in deciding whether a particular type of expression should be restricted. A particular type of expression should not be outlawed simply because some people find the content offensive.

In 1990 Robert A. Viktora and several other white teenagers fashioned a cross out of broken chair legs. They then held a Klan-type cross burning on the lawn of a black family who had just moved into a mostly white neighborhood in St. Paul, Minnesota. Viktora was convicted under the city's hate speech ordinance, which prohibited "**fighting words**"—speech or expressions that were likely to provoke "anger, alarm or resentment in others on the basis of race, color, creed, religion or gender." The Supreme Court had previously ruled, in the 1942 case *Chaplinsky v. New Hampshire,* that "fighting words" were not protected speech.

In *R.A.V. v. St. Paul* (1992), the first U.S. Supreme Court ruling on hate speech, the Court agreed with Viktora that the St. Paul law violated his freedom of speech. Whereas laws restricting fighting words were constitutional, hate speech laws were not, because they exercised "content-based discrimination"; that is, they were aimed at preventing specific types of speech such as expression of racism. At the time of the *R.A.V. v. St. Paul* ruling, there were laws against hate speech in forty-six states. The Court declared most of these laws unconstitutional on the grounds that the First Amendment prohibits "laws silencing speech on the basis of its content."

Charles Lawrence argues that the social context in which hate speech takes place is morally relevant to whether it should be tolerated. Rather than defending abstract principles such as impartiality, we should be more concerned with defending the real victims. (See Case Study 3.)

SPEECH CODES AND FREE SPEECH ZONES ON COLLEGE CAMPUSES

In 1992, when the Supreme Court ruling overturned the St. Paul hate speech ordinance, more than a hundred colleges and universities in the United States had **speech codes** that placed restrictions on some forms of speech, such as hate speech, fighting words, obscenity, or speech that violates civility codes. The University of Michigan had one of the most restrictive campus speech codes. Its policy forbade all conduct that "stigmatizes or victimizes" students on the basis of "race, ethnicity, religion, sex and sexual orientation."[14] The code was created to cut down on the increasing frequency of racist, sexist, and other forms of hate speech. Although legal scholars generally agree that these campus speech codes are unconstitutional, about one-third of colleges in the United States still have codes that restrict speech.[15] Because courts have sided with students when colleges have tried to punish students for violating campus speech codes, most colleges do not punish violations, but use the codes instead to set standards for fostering an environment of civility and tolerance for diversity.

Campus speech codes evolved primarily out of the civil rights movement of the 1960s and 1970s and in response to the escalation of racist incidents on campuses in the 1980s. Sometimes dubbed the "politically correct" movement, these speech codes were intended to restrict offensive and bigoted forms of expression and encourage tolerance of diversity. (See Case Study 2.) The University of Wisconsin's speech code, for example, prohibited speech intended to "create a hostile learning environment" by demeaning another person's gender, race, sexual orientation, disability, creed, or ethnic background.

The **political correctness** movement was the most successful effort in American history to restrict hate speech. It was also one of the first times that students asked professors and administrators to place restrictions on offensive speech. Charles Lawrence was a leader in the movement to curb hate speech on college campuses. His view was shaped by a 1981 boycott of a Harvard Law School course on "Race, Racism and American Law." A group of students demanded that the course be taught by a person of color. When the administration failed to accede to their demands, the students organized their own course. Lawrence was one of the guest lecturers. His legal expertise provided, in part, the sophisticated arguments needed to convince members of the college community to support speech codes.

Have campus speech codes gone too far? Stockport College in England has banned thirty offensive words and phrases, including "lady," "history," and "slaving over a hot stove."[16] The words "lady" and "gentleman," so the rationale goes, have "class implications," while the word "history" has sexist implications. "Slaving over a hot stove" is considered racist.

Like John Stuart Mill, the ACLU maintains that more speech, not less, is the best response to offensive speech. Restricting the speech of one group—whether Nazis, bigots, antiabortionists, or antiwar protesters—jeopardizes everyone because the laws can be used to silence those who wanted the laws to silence others. For example, under an anti–hate speech code at the University of Michigan, twenty black students were accused by white students of using offensive speech. The University of Michigan speech code was struck down as unconstitutional in 1987. In his reading at the end of this chapter, Stanley Fish defends campus speech codes in situations where freedom of speech threatens the academic community's values of tolerance and freedom of expression.

Another way colleges restrict free speech is by designating "free speech zones" on campus. Greg Lukianoff of the Foundation for Individual Rights in Education (FIRE) calls free speech zones an "Orwellian exercise for turning 99 percent of a university's campus into a censorship zone."[17] The main argument for free speech zones is that noisy protests may disturb classes that are in session. Matthew Poe, a senior at West Virginia University, was stopped by campus police for handing out flyers outside a free speech zone. "I think America is a free speech zone, and the university has no business restricting it," said Poe in his defense. "Rather, the university has a moral responsibility to endorse it." He maintains that free speech zones are simply a thinly veiled excuse "to stop campuses from becoming confrontational, like UC Berkeley."[18] At Florida State University, thirty students were arrested after they refused to move their anti-sweatshop protest to a designated free speech zone. In addition to restricting controversial speech by students, campus speech zones place even more onerous restrictions on groups from off-campus, especially those that hold controversial views. The battle over limiting controversial speech to "free speech zones" is gaining momentum as more complaints and First Amendment rights lawsuits are brought against college administrations. Courts have ruled in favor of the student groups in several of these cases.[19]

Supporters of campus hate speech codes and free speech zones, such as Fish, point out that because people should be able to feel secure in their own homes, there should be greater protection against hate speech harassment on residential campuses than might be necessary in a public setting. Agreeing to attend a particular college entails agreeing to abide by a certain set of rules, such as nondrinking rules, restrictions on visiting hours, nonsmoking in dormitories, and restraints on certain forms of offensive speech. In his article toward the end of this chapter, Alan Dershowitz maintains that the political correctness movement, which spawned these speech codes, has done more harm than good.

THE PHILOSOPHERS ON FREEDOM OF SPEECH

Aristotle acknowledged the importance of liberty and freedom of speech in a democracy. He also believed that expression of violent and hateful thoughts might be cathartic and purge violent urges. Plato disagreed. In his *Republic,* Plato argues that literature, art, verse, and even music that is "impious" and "self-contradictory" should be censored if the republic is to be well ordered. According to Plato, though some of this might appear innocuous in small doses, "lawlessness easily creeps in unobserved . . . in the guise of a pastime, which seems so harmless." The current debate over the morality of pornography and violence in the media depends to a large extent on whether one accepts Aristotle's or Plato's position on the benefits of free expression.

John Locke valued freedom of speech primarily as a political value. He writes, "He who takes away the Freedom [of speech in the legislature], . . . in effect takes away freedom of debate in the legislature, and puts an end to the Government."[20] Like Locke, Ayn Rand argues that the right of free speech is a fundamental right. A person, she writes, "has the right to express his ideas without danger of suppression, interference or punitive action by the government."[21] John Rawls also regards freedom of speech as "one of the basic liberties of citizens."[22]

In his essay *On Liberty,* John Stuart Mill argues that the state does not have the right to interfere with citizens' freedoms except where restriction is necessary to protect the person and property of others. According to him, the harm caused by censorship far outweighs any harm that might result from spreading vicious or false opinions. Truth, he notes, is often found not in the opinion of the status quo nor in the opinion of a dissenter, but in a combination of viewpoints. Therefore, freedom of speech and listening to opposing opinions, no matter how offensive they may be to some people, can allow a fuller truth to emerge.

According to the "marketplace of ideas" metaphor, ideas are like a product on the market. Just as the free market tends to deliver the best consumer goods, if everyone comes to the marketplace of ideas to express her or his opinions, the best opinions will eventually win out. This argument is used by those who support teaching intelligent design in schools. (See Case Study 8.) Mill was not suggesting that truth is like a product whose "goodness" is determined by how well it satisfies customer demand. When it comes to expression of ideas, Mill was well aware of the dangers of the tyranny of the majority. In a democracy "there needs to be protection also against the tyranny of the prevailing opinion and feeling, against the tendency of society to impose, by other means than civil penalties, its own ideas and practices as rules of conduct on those who dissent from them."[23]

Although freedom of expression is a necessary condition for human progress, it is not a sufficient condition. We cannot assume that true opinions will triumph in a free marketplace of ideas. We must actively encourage the expression of minority viewpoints because of the tendency for the majority to coerce the minority into conforming. Thus Mill placed the highest value on the speech of those who have the least power in society.[24] Fish, in contrast, argues that there is no such thing as freedom of speech as an absolute value and that speech may have to be restricted to protect other values that are more important to the community.

The concept of abstract rights that exist independently of a particular context is mostly a Western innovation. Buddhist virtue ethics, in contrast, is concerned with the development of a virtuous disposition, rather than abstract rights or legal prohibitions. Speech is one of the modes in which an unvirtuous disposition can be expressed. We have a moral obligation to avoid slanderous and divisive speech and to cultivate speech that is truthful and that strengthens the bonds of friendship. Confucianism also emphasizes the virtue of sincerity in our speech and actions.

THE MORAL ISSUES

Social Order

One reason given for restrictions on the freedom of speech is to preserve public order. Members of a society must share certain core values if the society is to survive. For democracy to thrive, ideas that are subversive to democracy must be discouraged. Education, by its very nature, reinforces certain ideas over others. In the United States our schools routinely indoctrinate students in the virtues of democracy.

The Canadian argument for the legal regulation of pornography is based in part on the argument that the community has the right to enforce standards of public good. Pornography contributes to unhealthy attitudes and stereotypes and poses a threat to society because it weakens the principle of equality upon which society is founded. On the other hand, this criterion also risks the danger of the "tyranny of the majority." Hence, most ethicists in the United States believe that social good, on its own, is not a sufficient justification for outlawing certain types of speech or behavior.

Campus speech codes and free speech zones maintain social order by keeping college campuses from turning into a pandemonium where the advantage goes to those who can shout the loudest and intimidate the most through their persistent expressions of hatred. On the other hand, speech codes can also intimidate and stifle anyone who has an idea that might be offensive to others.

Restrictions on speech in the name of national social order can become overly restrictive. McCarthyism, for example, was carried out in the name of protecting freedom and democratic values against the "clear and present" danger of Communism. Some people fear that the USA Patriot Act also places unnecessary restriction on freedom of speech in the name of maintaining social order.

Liberty Rights, Freedom of Speech, and Autonomy

Radical feminists, such as MacKinnon, accuse libertarians of placing freedom of speech above women's well-being. They argue that pornography restricts women's freedom and, hence, cannot be defended on the grounds of freedom of speech. Furthermore, pornography has no value in the marketplace of ideas because it presents a distorted view of women and, hence, is based on a lie about women's sexuality. Other feminists, such as Katie Roiphe, disagree. They fear that repression of pornography may impede women's liberation by emphasizing women as victims.

Libertarians such as Strossen argue that we cannot get rid of hate speech or pornography without destroying genuine freedom of speech. Even racial slurs and hate speech provide the target with information about the views of the person making the slur. It is better to let false or harmful ideas compete in the marketplace, where they are likely to fade when exposed to the light of truth, than to let the government or others in authority determine what is true and false and what is beneficial and harmful. Restriction of speech stifles the free exchange of ideas by putting people on guard against making any jokes or statements that might be offensive to others. For example, Alan Dershowitz tapes his lectures on rape statutes, because he fears that someone in the class might interpret what he said as a form of sexual harassment.[25]

Lawrence counters that censoring hate speech is not an infringement on our right to free speech. Hate speech, he maintains, is not really speech or an expression of an idea but an attack. Shouting racial slurs is like a slap in the face. Most hate speech is not an invitation to engage in dialogue but an attempt to silence dialogue through intimidation.

Proponents of restrictions on hate speech also point out that liberty rights exist to protect the autonomy of persons. One of the conditions of autonomy is rationality. For speech to be a moral right, the speaker must be coming from a position of reason and openness to judgment and rational dialogue. One of the current issues regarding autonomy and freedom of speech is whether websites have a right to sell essay to students. (See Case Study 7.)

Civility and Respect for Human Dignity

According to deontologists, we have a duty to respect the dignity of other persons. Pornography violates Kant's categorical imperative by dehumanizing women. Rather than being portrayed as autonomous moral beings, women are viewed as means-only instruments of men.

Hate speech likewise creates a hostile environment and a message of exclusion. Rather than subjecting themselves to assaults on their dignity, members of groups targeted by hate speech are likely to avoid these environments. For example, the rash of racist incidents on campuses in the 1980s was accompanied by a decrease in the college enrollment of black men. Thus, hate speech thwarts the aims of education and diversity. Rather than contributing to an open discussion of ideas, hate speech compromises the ability of those targeted by it to respond and to be equal participants in the debate.

Respect for human dignity requires that we refrain from using hate speech. On the other hand, it is not clear that this justifies legislating civility or placing restrictions on people's speech. There are many ways of treating people as moral inferiors—through ignoring or snubbing them, by interrupting them, or by avoiding them—all acts that few think should be legally banned. Furthermore, people cannot be forced into a subordinate position through hate speech in the way they can through segregation laws or discrimination in hiring. Although hate speech puts down its target as a moral inferior, it does not effect an actual change in the target's moral and legal status.

Harm–Nonmaleficence

Most ethicists agree that speech that directly results in physical harm should be prohibited. For example, it is illegal for a prankster to cry "Fire" in a crowded theater. Fraudulent and libelous speech is also restricted because of the harm it causes.

Does the principle of nonmaleficence also justify restrictions on hate speech and pornography? What about commerial advertising of harmful products such as tobacco and junk food? (See Case Study 5.) Although Mill uses the harm principle as a limit on freedom of speech, he is not clear on what constitutes harm to others. Is psychological distress sufficiently harmful to override freedom of speech? Hate speech harms people by creating unequal opportunity in educational and workplace environments, thus depriving its targets of their freedom of speech by intimidating them into silence.

It is not clear how pornography directly harms women. Furthermore, even though it may be a "lower" pleasure, pornography *is* pleasurable to those who use it. Unlike domestic violence, where the direct harms to the victims clearly outweigh the pleasure of the perpetrators, the harms of pornography are not as clear. In order to justify censorship it must first be shown that the benefits of outlawing pornography would outweigh the harms of suppressing freedom of speech. MacKinnon argues that pornography directly harms women by constructing a social environment that interferes with women's ability to participate fully and equally in social and political life. Others maintain that the possible, and as yet unproven, harms of pornography are not sufficient to justify censorship.

We may agree that pornography and hate speech are wrong because of the harm they impose on their victims, yet also believe that legal restrictions are not the best way to control them. Indeed, laws prohibiting hateful and abusive speech may harm the very groups they are meant to protect. One of the first people convicted under the 1976 British Race Relations Act was a black leader, who was sentenced to twelve months' imprisonment for verbally abusing the white community.[26]

The Slippery Slope

Some ethicists worry that restrictions on pornography, hate speech, political speech, and commercial speech may start us down the proverbial slippery slope toward more and more restrictions on our freedom of speech. Indeed, the ACLU argues that this is already happening to some extent with the passage of the USA Patriot Act. Because it is so difficult to decide what is and what isn't acceptable speech, laws and speech codes prohibiting certain types of speech might be expanded to embrace speech that is offensive to the powers that be, as happened during the McCarthy period.

Pluralism and Tolerance

Pluralism and multiculturalism require tolerance of differences. Lawrence maintains that tolerance of hate speech can conflict with pluralism and the elimination of racism. As a moral ideal, pluralism ensures that the most vulnerable groups have a place in society. Much of the motivation behind the politically correct movement and campus speech codes is to ensure that people who are not from the mainstream culture will be able to express their views without fear of intimidation.

On the other hand, restricting the freedom of speech of groups whose ideas are at odds with our own is to lay a trap for ourselves as well. As Strossen points out, legislating intolerance of certain speech to promote tolerance may backfire.

Impartiality, Equal Justice, and Discrimination

MacKinnon argues that pornography is a form of sex discrimination because it requires the abuse and coercion of women for its manufacture. Pornography is not like hate speech, which does not involve the compliance of its victims for its expression. Pornography does not just convey the idea that women are subordinate; it actually subordinates and silences them by putting them in a position of inferiority. Therefore, legal restrictions on pornography are essential if women are to achieve full equality.

According to Lawrence, tolerance of hate speech conflicts with the elimination of discrimination and racism. He argues that the 1954 United States Supreme Court *Brown v. Board of Education* decision, which outlawed school segregation, was really about freedom of speech. Segregated schools are wrong because they communicate a message of unworthiness to black children. Similarly, prohibiting hate speech is necessary in order to ensure equal protection. Laws against racist speech would reaffirm the conviction that all people are equal. Some feminists also make the same argument: Permitting sexist speech is at odds with the more important goal of egalitarianism.

Those who feel that restrictions on freedom of speech should be content-neutral base their argument on the principle of impartiality. Whereas the principle of impartiality in justice may be appropriate in an egalitarian society, in a society where racism and sexism are embedded in the very structure, it only serves to perpetuate inequalities.

🖋 SUMMARY OF READINGS ON FREEDOM OF SPEECH

Mill, "On Liberty." Freedom of speech is essential in a democracy and should be protected.

MacKinnon, "Pornography, Civil Rights, and Speech." The harms of pornography outweigh the benefits of freedom of speech.

Lawrence, "If He Hollers Let Him Go: Regulating Racist Speech on Campus." Protection of racist speech is incompatible with eliminating racism.

Strossen, "Hate Speech and Pornography: Do We Have to Choose Between Freedom of Speech and Equality?" Censoring hate speech and pornography harms minorities and women and undermines equality.

Fish, "There's No Such Thing as Free Speech, and It's a Good Thing, Too." Freedom of speech needs to be weighed against other values.

Dershowitz, "Political Correctness, Speech Codes, and Diversity." Campus speech codes limit rather than promote diversity of expression.

Sunstein, "The First Amendment in Cyberspace." Regulations on cyberspace speech should aim to foster democratic ends.

CONCLUSION

Does society have a moral obligation to protect people from verbal and written assaults on their dignity? Or should we accept the libertarian position that pornography and hate speech should not be legally restricted? Even if we do, this does not entail the claim that pornography and hate speech are morally acceptable. Some hate speech and pornography are clearly inconsistent with respect for persons. We ought not to engage in them. As moral agents we also have a moral obligation to respond to hate speech. Alexander Hamilton once said that the greatest danger to freedom was not restrictions on freedom of expression but an apathetic citizenry. Part of freedom of speech is a duty to speak out against hatred, sexism, and bigotry.

🖋 JOHN STUART MILL

On Liberty

John Stuart Mill, prominent English utilitarian and defender of liberty rights, wrote *On Liberty* in 1859. In it he argues that utility must be grounded in the freedom of people to pursue their own good, as long as they are not attempting to deprive others of their liberty rights. In particular, freedom of speech is essential in a democracy if we want to avoid the "tyranny of the majority" and intellectual stagnation.

From *On Liberty* (London: Longman, Roberts & Green, 1869).

Critical Reading Questions

1. What does Mill mean by the "struggle between liberty and authority"?
2. What does Mill mean by "tyranny of the majority"?
3. What is the "appropriate region of human liberty"?
4. Why is liberty of thought essential if we are to be free?
5. Why is it an evil, according to Mill, to silence the expression of an opinion?
6. How, according to Mill, do wise men acquire wisdom?
7. What happens when a government believes it has a duty to uphold certain beliefs and oppose others to protect the interests of society?
8. How do we treat dissidents like Socrates today?
9. What is the danger of maintaining "all prevailing opinions outwardly undisturbed"?
10. Why is it so important to be open to challenges even to views that we assume to be true or that are accepted doctrines?
11. What is one of the principal reasons why diversity of opinions should be encouraged?
12. Why is it important, in a democracy, for opposing parties to hold divergent views?
13. Why does Mill oppose restricting freedom of speech even when it is intemperate and presented in a nasty and offensive manner?

INTRODUCTORY

. . . The struggle between Liberty and Authority is the most conspicuous feature in the portions of history with which we are earliest familiar, particularly in that of Greece, Rome, and England. But in old times this contest was between subjects, or some classes of subjects, and the Government. By liberty, was meant protection against the tyranny of the political rulers. . . . In time, however, a democratic republic came to occupy a large portion of the earth's surface, and made itself felt as one of the most powerful members of the community of nations; and elective and responsible government became subject to the observations and criticism which wait upon a great existing fact. It was now perceived that such phrases as "self-government," and "the power of the people over themselves," do not express the true state of the case. The "people" who exercise the power are not always the same people with those over whom it is exercised; and the "self-government" spoken of is not the government of each by himself, but of each by all the rest. The will of the people, moreover, practically means the will of the most numerous or the most active *part* of the people; the majority, or those who succeed in making themselves accepted as the majority; the people, consequently *may* desire to oppress a part of their number; and precautions are as much needed against this as against any other abuse of power. . . . [I]n political speculations "the tyranny of the majority" is now generally included among the evils against which society requires to be on its guard. . . .

Protection, therefore, against the tyranny of the magistrate is not enough: there needs protection also against the tyranny of the prevailing opinion and feeling; against the tendency of society to impose, by other means than civil penalties, its own ideas and practices as rules of conduct on those who dissent from them. . . .

There is a sphere of action in which society, as distinguished from the individual, has, if any, only an indirect interest; comprehending all that portion of a person's life and conduct which affects only himself, or if it also affects others, only with their free, voluntary, and undeceived consent and participation. . . . This, is the appropriate region of human liberty. It compromises, first, the inward domain of consciousness; demanding liberty of conscience in the most comprehensive sense; liberty of thought and feeling; absolute freedom of opinion and sentiment on all subjects, practical or speculative, scientific, moral, or theological. The liberty of expressing and publishing opinions may seem to fall under a different principle, since it belongs to that part of the conduct of an individual which concerns other people; but, being almost of as much importance as the liberty of thought itself, and resting in great part on the same reasons, is practically inseparable from it. Secondly, the principle requires liberty of tastes and pursuits; of framing the plan of our life to suit our own character; of doing as we like, subject to such consequences as may follow: without impediment from our fellow-creatures, so long as what we do does not harm them, even though they should think our conduct foolish, perverse, or wrong. Thirdly, from this liberty of each individual, follows the liberty, within the same limits, of combination among individuals; freedom to unite, for any purpose not involving harm to others: the persons combining being supposed to be of full age, and not forced or deceived.

No society in which these liberties are not, on the whole, respected, is free, whatever may be its form of government; and none is completely free in which they do not exist absolute and unqualified. The only freedom which deserves the name, is that of pursuing our own good in our own way, so long as we do not attempt to deprive others of theirs, or impede their efforts to obtain it. . . .

OF THE LIBERTY OF THOUGHT AND DISCUSSION

. . . If all mankind minus one were of one opinion, and only one person were of the contrary opinion, mankind would be no more justified in silencing that one person, than he, if he had the power, would be justified in silencing mankind. Were an opinion a personal possession of no value except to the owner; if to be obstructed in the enjoyment of it were simply a private injury, it would make some difference whether the injury

was inflicted only on a few persons or on many. But the peculiar evil of silencing the expression of an opinion is, that it is robbing the human race; posterity as well as the existing generation; those who dissent from the opinion, still more than those who hold it. If the opinion is right, they are deprived of the opportunity of exchanging error for truth: if wrong, they lose, what is almost as great a benefit, the clearer perception and livelier impression of truth, produced by its collision with error.

It is necessary to consider separately these two hypotheses, each of which has a distinct branch of the argument corresponding to it. We can never be sure that the opinion we are endeavouring to stifle is a false opinion; and if we were sure, stifling it would be an evil still.

First: the opinion which it is attempted to suppress by authority may possibly be true. Those who desire to suppress it, of course deny its truth; but they are not infallible. They have no authority to decide the question for all mankind, and exclude every other person from the means of judging. To refuse a hearing to an opinion, because they are sure that it is false, is to assume that *their* certainty is the same thing as *absolute* certainty. All silencing of discussion is an assumption of infallibility. Its condemnation may be allowed to rest on this common argument, not the worse for being common. . . . There is no such thing as absolute certainty, but there is assurance sufficient for the purposes of human life. We may, and must, assume our opinion to be true for the guidance of our own conduct: and it is assuming no more when we forbid bad men to pervert society by the propagation of opinions which we regard as false and pernicious. . . . There is the greatest difference between presuming an opinion to be true, because, with every opportunity for contesting it, it has not been refuted, and assuming its truth for the purpose of not permitting its refutation. Complete liberty of contradicting and disproving our opinion is the very condition which justifies us in assuming its truth for purposes of action; and on no other terms can a being with human faculties have any rational assurance of being right.... Wrong opinions and practices gradually yield to fact and argument; but facts and arguments, to produce any effect on the mind, must be brought before it. Very few facts are able to tell their own story, without comments to bring out their meaning. The whole strength and value, then, of human judgment, depending on the one property, that it can be set right when it is wrong, reliance can be placed on it only when the means of setting it right are kept constantly at hand. In the case of any person whose judgment is really deserving of confidence, how has it become so? Because he has kept his mind open to criticism of his opinions and conduct. Because it has been his practice to listen to all that could be said against him.... No wise man ever acquired his wisdom in any mode but this; nor is it in the nature of human intellect to become wise in any other manner. The steady habit of correcting and completing his own opinion by collating it with those of others, so far from causing doubt and hesitation in carrying it into practice, is the only stable foundation for a just reliance on it....

In the present age—which has been described as "destitute of faith, but terrified at scepticism"—in which people feel sure, not so much that their opinions are true, as that they should not know what to do without them—the claims of an opinion to be protected from public attack are rested not so much on its truth, as on its importance to society. There are, it is alleged, certain beliefs so useful, not to say indispensable, to well-being that it is as much the duty of governments to uphold those beliefs, as to protect any other of the interests of society. In a case of such necessity, and so directly in the line of their duty, something less than infallibility may, it is maintained, warrant, and even bind, governments to act on their own opinion, confirmed by the general opinion of mankind. It is also often argued, and still oftener thought, that none but bad men would desire to weaken these salutary beliefs; and there can be nothing wrong, it is thought, in restraining bad men, and prohibiting what only such men would wish to practise....

Mankind can hardly be too often reminded, that there was once a man named Socrates, between whom and the legal authorities and public opinion of his time there took place a memorable collision.... This acknowledged master of all the eminent thinkers who have since lived—whose fame, still growing after more than two thousand years, all but outweighs the whole remainder of the names which make his native city illustrious—was put to death by his countrymen, after a judicial conviction, for impiety and immorality. Impiety, in denying the gods recognised by the State; indeed his accuser asserted (see the "Apologia") that he believed in no gods at all. Immorality, in being, by his doctrines and instructions, a "corruptor of youth." Of these charges the tribunal, there is every ground for believing, honestly found him guilty, and condemned the man who probably of all then born had deserved best of mankind to be put to death as a criminal.... Men did not merely mistake their benefactor; they mistook him for the exact contrary of what he was, and treated him as that prodigy of impiety which they themselves are now held to be for their treatment of him.... These were, to all appearance, not bad men—not worse than men commonly are, but rather the contrary; men who possessed in a full, or somewhat more than a full measure, the religious, moral, and patriotic feelings of their time and people: the very kind of men who, in all times, our own included, have every chance of passing through life blameless and respected....

It will be said, that we do not now put to death the introducers of new opinions: we are not like our fathers who slew the prophets, we even build sepulchres to them. It is true we no longer put heretics to death; and the amount of penal infliction which modern feeling would probably tolerate, even against the most obnoxious opinions, is not sufficient to extirpate them. But let us not flatter ourselves that we are yet free from the stain even of legal persecution. Penalties for opinion, or at least for its expression, still exist by law....

But though we do not now inflict so much evil on those who think differently from us as it was formerly our custom to do, it may be that we do ourselves as much evil as ever by our treatment of them. Socrates was put to death, but Socratic philosophy rose like the sun in heaven, and spread its illumination over the whole intellectual firmament. Christians were . . . cast to the lions, but the Christian church grew up a stately and spreading tree, overtopping the older and less vigorous growths, and stifling them by its shade. Our merely social intolerance kills no one, roots out no opinions, but induces men to disguise them, or to abstain from any active effort for their diffusion. With us, heretical opinions do not perceptibly gain, or even lose, ground in each decade or generation; they never blaze out far and wide, but continue to smoulder in the narrow circles of thinking and studious persons among whom they originate, without ever lighting up the general affairs of mankind with either a true or a deceptive light. And thus is kept up a state of things very satisfactory to some minds, because, without the unpleasant process of fining or imprisoning anybody, it maintains all prevailing opinions outwardly undisturbed. . . . But the price paid for this sort of intellectual pacification is the sacrifice of the entire moral courage of the human mind. A state of things in which a large portion of the most active and inquiring intellects find it advisable to keep the general principles and grounds of their convictions within their own breasts, and attempt, in what they address to the public, to fit as much as they can of their own conclusions to premises which they have internally renounced, cannot send forth the open, fearless characters, and logical, consistent intellects who once adorned the thinking world. . . . Those who avoid this alternative, do so by narrowing their thoughts and interest to things which can be spoken of without venturing within the region of principles, that is, to small practical matters, which would come right of themselves, if but the minds of mankind were strengthened and enlarged, and which will never be made effectually right until then: while that which would strengthen and enlarge men's minds, free and daring speculation on the highest subjects, is abandoned. . . .

Let us now pass to the second division of the argument, and dismissing the supposition that any of the received opinions may be false, let us assume them to be true, and examine into the worth of the manner in which they are likely to be held, when their truth is not freely and openly canvassed. However unwillingly a person who has a strong opinion may admit the possibility that his opinion may be false, he ought to be moved by the consideration that, however true it may be, if it is not fully, frequently, and fearlessly discussed, it will be held as a dead dogma, not a living truth.

There is a class of persons (happily not quite so numerous as formerly) who think it enough if a person assents undoubtingly to what they think true, though he has no knowledge whatever of the grounds of the opinion, and could not make a tenable defence of it against the most superficial objections. Such persons, if they can once get their creed taught from authority, naturally think that no good, and some harm, comes of its being allowed to be questioned. Where their influence prevails, they make it nearly impossible for the received opinion to be rejected wisely and considerately, though it may still be rejected rashly and ignorantly; for to shut out discussion entirely is seldom possible, and when it once gets in, beliefs not grounded on conviction are apt to give way before the slightest semblance of an argument. Waiving, however, this possibility—assuming that the true opinion abides in the mind, but abides as a prejudice, a belief independent of, and proof against, argument—this is not the way in which truth ought to be held by a rational being. This is not knowing the truth. Truth, thus held, is but one superstition the more, accidentally clinging to the words which enunciate a truth. . . .

To abate the force of these considerations, an enemy of free discussion may be supposed to say, that there is no necessity for mankind in general to know and understand all that can be said against or for their opinions by philosophers and theologians. That it is not needful for common men to be able to expose all the misstatements or fallacies of an ingenious opponent. That it is enough if there is always somebody capable of answering them, so that nothing likely to mislead uninstructed persons remains unrefuted. That simple minds, having been taught the obvious grounds of the truths inculcated on them, may trust to authority for the rest, and being aware that they have neither knowledge nor talent to resolve every difficulty which can be raised, may repose in the assurance that all those which have been raised have been or can be answered, by those who are specially trained to the task.

Conceding to this view of the subject the utmost that can be claimed for it by those most easily satisfied with the amount of understanding of truth which ought to accompany the belief of it; even so, the argument for free discussion is no way weakened. For even this doctrine acknowledges that mankind ought to have a rational assurance that all objections have been satisfactorily answered; and how are they to be answered if that which requires to be answered is not spoken? or how can the answer be known to be satisfactory, if the objectors have no opportunity of showing that it is unsatisfactory? . . .

If, however, the mischievous operation of the absence of free discussion, when the received opinions are true, were confined to leaving men ignorant of the grounds of those opinions, it might be thought that this, if an intellectual, is no moral evil, and does not affect the worth of the opinions, regarded in their influence on the character. The fact, however, is, that not only the grounds of the opinion are forgotten in the absence of discussion, but too often the meaning of the opinion itself. The words which convey it cease to suggest ideas, or suggest only a small portion of those they were originally employed to communicate. Instead of a vivid conception and a living belief, there remain only a few phrases retained by rote; or, if any part, the shell and husk only of the meaning is retained, the finer essence being lost. The great chapter in human history which this fact occupies and fills, cannot be too earnestly studied and meditated on.

It is illustrated in the experience of almost all ethical doctrines and religious creeds. They are all full of meaning and vitality to those who originate them, and to the direct disciples of the originators. Their meaning continues to be felt in undiminished strength, and is perhaps brought out into even fuller consciousness, so long as the struggle lasts to give the doctrine or creed an ascendancy over other creeds. At last it either prevails, and becomes the general opinion, or its progress stops; it keeps possession of the ground it has gained, but ceases to spread further. When either of these results has become apparent, controversy on the subject flags, and gradually dies away. The doctrine has taken its place, if not as a received opinion, as one of the admitted sects or divisions of opinion: those who hold it have generally inherited, not adopted it; and conversion from one of these doctrines to another, being now an exceptional fact, occupies little place in the thoughts of their professors. Instead of being, as at first, constantly on the alert either to defend themselves against the world, or to bring the world over to them, they have subsided into acquiescence, and neither listen, when they can help it, to arguments against their creed, nor trouble dissentients (if there be such) with arguments in its favour. From this time may usually be dated the decline in the living power of the doctrine. . . . Then are seen the cases, so frequent in this age of the world as almost to form the majority, in which the creed remains as it were outside the mind, incrusting and petrifying it against all other influences addressed to the higher parts of our nature; manifesting its power by not suffering any fresh and living conviction to get in, but itself doing nothing for the mind or heart, except standing sentinel over them to keep them vacant. . . .

The fatal tendency of mankind to leave off thinking about a thing when it is no longer doubtful, is the cause of half their errors. A contemporary author has well spoken of "the deep slumber of a decided opinion." . . .

It still remains to speak of one of the principal causes which make diversity of opinion advantageous, and will continue to do so until mankind shall have entered a stage of intellectual advancement which at present seems at an incalculable distance. We have hitherto considered only two possibilities: that the received opinion may be false, and some other opinion, consequently, true; or that, the received opinion being true, a conflict with the opposite error is essential to a clear apprehension and deep feeling of its truth. But there is a commoner case than either of these; when the conflicting doctrines, instead of being one true and the other false, share the truth between them; and the nonconforming opinion is needed to supply the remainder of the truth, of which the received doctrine embodies only a part. Popular opinions, on subjects not palpable to sense, are often true, but seldom or never the whole truth. They are a part of the truth; sometimes a greater, sometimes a smaller part, but exaggerated, distorted, and disjointed from the truths by which they ought to be accompanied and limited. Heretical opinions, on the other hand, are generally some of these suppressed and neglected truths, bursting the bonds which kept them down, and either seeking reconciliation with the truth contained in the common opinion, or fronting it as enemies, and setting themselves up, with similar exclusiveness, as the whole truth. The latter case is hitherto the most frequent, as, in the human mind, one-sidedness has always been the rule, and many-sidedness the exception. Hence, even in revolutions of opinion, one part of the truth usually sets while another rises. Even progress, which ought to superadd, for the most part only substitutes, one partial and incomplete truth for another; . . .

In politics, again, it is almost a commonplace, that a party of order or stability, and a party of progress or reform, are both necessary elements of a healthy state of political life; until the one or the other shall have so enlarged its mental grasp as to be a party equally of order and of progress, knowing and distinguishing what is fit to be preserved from what ought to be swept away. Each of these modes of thinking derives its utility from the deficiencies of the other; but it is in a great measure the opposition of the other that keeps each within the limits of reason and sanity. Unless opinions favourable to democracy and to aristocracy, to property and to equality, to cooperation and to competition, to luxury and to abstinence, to sociality and individuality, to liberty and discipline, and all the other standing antagonisms of practical life, are expressed with equal freedom, and enforced and defended with equal talent and energy, there is no chance of both elements obtaining their due. . . .

We have now recognised the necessity to the mental well-being of mankind (on which all their other well-being depends) of freedom of opinion, and freedom of the expression of opinion, on four distinct grounds; which we will now briefly recapitulate.

First, if any opinion is compelled to silence, that opinion may, for aught we can certainly know, be true. To deny this is to assume our own infallibility.

Secondly, though the silenced opinion be an error, it may, and very commonly does, contain a portion of truth; and since the general or prevailing opinion on any subject is rarely or never the whole truth, it is only by the collision of adverse opinions that the remainder of the truth has any chance of being supplied.

Thirdly, even if the received opinion be not only true, but the whole truth, unless it is suffered to be, and actually is, vigorously and earnestly contested, it will, by most of those who receive it, be held in the manner of a prejudice, with little comprehension or feeling of its rational grounds. And not only this, but, fourthly, the meaning of the doctrine itself will be in danger of being lost, or enfeebled, and deprived of its vital effect on the character and conduct: the dogma becoming a mere formal profession, inefficacious for good, but cumbering the ground, and preventing the growth of any real and heartfelt conviction, from reason or personal experience.

Before quitting the subject of freedom of opinion, it is fit to take some notice of those who say that the free expression of all opinions should be permitted, on condition that the manner be temperate, and do not pass the bounds of fair discussion. Much might be said on the impossibility of fixing where these supposed bounds are to be placed; for if the test be offence to those whose opinions are attacked, I think experience testifies that this offence is given whenever the attack is telling and powerful, and that every opponent who pushes them hard, and whom they find it difficult to answer, appears to them, if he shows any strong feeling on the subject, an intemperate opponent. But this, though an important consideration in a practical point of view, merges in a more fundamental objection. Undoubtedly the manner of asserting an opinion, even though it be a true one, may be very objectionable, and may justly incur severe censure. But the principal offences of the kind are such as it is mostly impossible, unless by accidental self-betrayal, to bring home to conviction. The gravest of them is, to argue sophistically, to suppress facts or arguments, to misstate the elements of the case, or misrepresent the opposite opinion. But all this even to the most aggravated degree, is so continually done in perfect good faith, by persons who are not considered, and in many other respects may not deserve to be considered, ignorant or incompetent, that it is rarely possible, on adequate grounds, conscientiously to stamp the misrepresentation as morally culpable; and still less could law presume to interfere with this kind of controversial misconduct. With regard to what is commonly meant by intemperate discussion, namely invective, sarcasm, personality, and the like, the denunciation of these weapons would deserve more sympathy if it were ever proposed to interdict them equally to both sides; but it is only desired to restrain the employment of them against the prevailing opinion: against the unprevailing they may not only be used without general disapproval, but will be likely to obtain for him who uses them the praise of honest zeal and righteous indignation. Yet whatever mischief arises from their use is greatest when they are employed against the comparatively defenceless; and whatever unfair advantage can be derived by any opinion from this mode of asserting it, accrues almost exclusively to received opinions. The worst offence of this kind which can be committed by a polemic is to stigmatise those who hold the contrary opinion as bad and

immoral men. To calumny of this sort, those who hold any unpopular opinion are peculiarly exposed, because they are in general few and uninfluential, and nobody but themselves feels much interested in seeing justice done them; but this weapon is, from the nature of the case, denied to those who attack a prevailing opinion: they can neither use it with safety to themselves, nor, if they could, would it do anything but recoil on their own cause. In general, opinions contrary to those commonly received can only obtain a hearing by studied moderation of language, and the most cautious avoidance of unnecessary offence, from which they hardly ever deviate even in a slight degree without losing ground: while unmeasured vituperation employed on the side of the prevailing opinion really does deter people from professing contrary opinions, and from listening to those who profess them. For the interest, therefore, of truth and justice, it is far more important to restrain this employment of vituperative language than the other; and, for example, if it were necessary to choose, there would be much more need to discourage offensive attacks on infidelity than on religion. It is, however, obvious that law and authority have no business with restraining either, while opinion ought, in every instance, to determine its verdict by the circumstances of the individual case; condemning every one, on whichever side of the argument he places himself, in whose mode of advocacy either want of candour, or malignity, bigotry, or intolerance of feeling manifest themselves; but not inferring these vices from the side which a person takes, though it be the contrary side of the question to our own; and giving merited honour to every one, whatever opinion he may hold, who has calmness to see and honesty to state what his opponents and their opinions really are, exaggerating nothing to their discredit, keeping nothing back which tells, or can be supposed to tell, in their favour. This is the real morality of public discussion: and if often violated, I am happy to think that there are many controversialists who to a great extent observe it, and a still greater number who conscientiously strive towards it.

Discussion Questions

1. To what extent do college campuses and American politics fall prey to the "tyranny of the majority"? Do you agree with Mill's solution to the tyranny of the majority? Illustrate your answers with specific examples.
2. Discuss whether or not democracy is the best form of government. What safeguard(s) does the United States have in place to protect citizens against the "tyranny of the majority" when it comes to freedom of speech? Are these safeguard(s) effective? Support your answers, using specific examples.
3. Discuss what Mill would most likely think of campus speech codes or efforts by colleges to prevent hate speech in order to promote diversity. To what extent should offensive, sexist, and/or bigoted speech be allowed on campuses in order to promote the search for truth and wisdom?
4. Mill maintains that it is important for political parties in a healthy democracy to hold widely divergent views in order for freedom of expression to flourish. Discuss whether this is the case in the United States.
5. What would Mill's response most likely have been to the USA Patriot Act? Discuss what solution(s), Mill would most likely propose for keeping the United States safe from terrorism.

CATHARINE A. MACKINNON

Pornography, Civil Rights, and Speech

Catharine MacKinnon is a professor of law at the University of Michigan. MacKinnon argues that some pornography should be legally restricted. According to her, the harm of pornography outweighs the benefit of freedom of speech. The primary harm of pornography is not that it is offensive, but that it is a type of sexual discrimination. Pornography subordinates women. Rather than being harmless fantasy, pornography is a political practice that institutionalizes the sexuality of male supremacy. The end served by pornography is not pleasure but power. Pornography also contributes indirectly to violence against women and to their social and economic inequality.

Critical Reading Questions

1. What is the feminist "discovery" regarding the basic assumption of equality in our society?
2. According to MacKinnon, why don't very many people, including women, believe the feminist view of the world?

"Pornography, Civil Rights, and Speech," in *Feminism Unmodified: Discourse on Life and Law* (Cambridge, Mass.: Harvard University Press, 1987), 168–179, 193–195. Some notes have been omitted.

3. What is pornography? What view of women does pornography construct?

4. What does MacKinnon mean when she says, "What pornography *does* goes beyond its content"?

5. How does pornography harm women, according to MacKinnon?

6. What does MacKinnon mean when she calls sexuality and gender a "social construct"?

7. According to MacKinnon, why can't we consistently defend both pornography and the equality of the sexes?

8. How does pornography differ from obscenity?

9. What does MacKinnon mean when she says that pornography is a political practice?

10. On what grounds does MacKinnon argue that pornography is a type of sex discrimination that violates the guarantee of equal rights?

11. According to MacKinnon, what is the connection between pornography, rape, and sexual harassment?

12. What was the primary reason some people opposed MacKinnon and Dworkin's antipornography ordinance? How does MacKinnon respond to their concerns?

There is a belief that this is a society in which women and men are basically equals. Room for marginal corrections is conceded, flaws are known to exist, attempts are made to correct what are conceived as occasional lapses from the basic condition of sex equality. Sex discrimination law has concentrated most of its focus on these occasional lapses. It is difficult to overestimate the extent to which this belief in equality is an article of faith for most people, including most women, who wish to live in self-respect in an internal universe, even (perhaps especially) if not in the world. It is also partly an expression of natural law thinking: if we are inalienably equal, we can't "really" be degraded.

This is a world in which it is worth trying. In this world of presumptive equality, people make money based on their training or abilities or diligence or qualifications. They are employed and advanced on the basis of merit. In this world of just deserts, if someone is abused, it is thought to violate the basic rules of the community. If it doesn't, victims are seen to have done something they could have chosen to do differently, by exercise of will or better judgment. Maybe such people have placed themselves in a situation of vulnerability to physical abuse. Maybe they have done something provocative. Or maybe they were just unusually unlucky. In such a world, if such a person has an experience, there are words for it. When they speak and say it, they are listened to. If they write about it, they will be published. If certain experiences are never spoken about, if certain people or issues are seldom heard from, it is supposed that silence has been chosen. The law, including much of the law of sex discrimination and the First Amendment, operates largely within the realm of these beliefs.

Feminism is the discovery that women do not live in this world, that the person occupying this realm is a man, so much more a man if he is white and wealthy. This world of potential credibility, authority, security, and just rewards, recognition of one's identity and capacity, is a world that some people do inhabit as a condition of birth, with variations among them. It is not a basic condition accorded humanity in this society, but a prerogative of status, a privilege, among other things, of gender.

I call this a discovery because it has not been an assumption. Feminism is the first theory, the first practice, the first movement, to take seriously the situation of all women from the point of view of all women, both on our situation and on social life as a whole. The discovery has therefore been made that the implicit social content of humanism, as well as the standpoint from which legal method has been designed and injuries have been defined, has not been women's standpoint. Defining feminism in a way that connects epistemology with power as the politics of women's point of view, this discovery can be summed up by saying that women live in another world: specifically, a world of *not* equality, a world of inequality.

Looking at the world from this point of view, a whole shadow world of previously invisible silent abuse has been discerned. Rape, battery, sexual harassment, forced prostitution, and the sexual abuse of children emerge as common and systematic. We find that rape happens to women in all contexts, from the family, including rape of girls and babies, to students and women in the workplace, on the streets, at home, in their own bedrooms by men they do not know and by men they do know, by men they are married to, men they have had a social conversation with, and, least often, men they have never seen before. Overwhelmingly, rape is something that men do or attempt to do to women (44 percent of American women according to a recent study) at some point in our lives. Sexual harassment of women by men is common in workplaces and educational institutions. Based on reports in one study of the federal workforce, up to 85 percent of women will experience it, many in physical forms. Between a quarter and a third of women are battered in their homes by men. Thirty-eight percent of little girls are sexually molested inside or outside the family. Until women listened to women, this world of sexual abuse was *not spoken* of. It was the unspeakable. What I am saying is, if you *are* the tree falling in the epistemological forest, your demise doesn't make a sound if no one is listening. Women did not "report" these events, and overwhelmingly do not today, because no one is listening, because no one believes us. This silence does not mean nothing happened, and it does not mean consent. It is the silence of women of which Adrienne Rich has written, "Do not confuse it with any kind of absence."[1]

Believing women who say we are sexually violated has been a radical departure, both methodologically

and legally. The extent and nature of rape, marital rape, and sexual harassment itself, were discovered in this way. Domestic battery as a syndrome, almost a habit, was discovered through refusing to believe that when a woman is assaulted by a man to whom she is connected, that it is not an assault. The sexual abuse of children was uncovered, Freud notwithstanding, by believing that children were not making up all this sexual abuse. Now what is striking is that when each discovery is made, and somehow made real in the world, the response has been: it happens to men too. If women are hurt, men are hurt. If women are raped, men are raped. If women are sexually harassed, men are sexually harassed. If women are battered, men are battered. Symmetry must be reasserted. Neutrality must be reclaimed. Equality must be reestablished.

The only areas where the available evidence supports this, where anything like what happens to women also happens to men, involve children— little boys are sexually abused—and prison. The liberty of prisoners is restricted, their freedom restrained, their humanity systematically diminished, their bodies and emotions confined, defined, and regulated. If paid at all, they are paid starvation wages. They can be tortured at will, and it is passed off as discipline or as means to a just end. They become compliant. They can be raped at will, at any moment, and nothing will be done about it. When they scream, nobody hears. To be a prisoner means to be defined as a member of a group for whom the rules of what can be done to you, of what is seen as abuse of you, are reduced as part of the definition of your status. To be a woman is that kind of definition and has that kind of meaning. . . .

What women do is seen as not worth much, or what is not worth much is seen as something for women to do. *Women* are seen as not worth much, is the thing. Now why are these basic realities of the subordination of women to men, for example, that only 7.8 percent of women have never been sexually assaulted, not effectively believed, not perceived as real in the face of all this evidence? Why don't *women* believe our own experiences? In the face of all this evidence, especially of systematic sexual abuse—subjection to violence with impunity is one extreme expression, although not the only expression, of a degraded status—the view that basically the sexes are equal in this society remains unchallenged and unchanged. The day I got this was the day I understood its real message, its real coherence: *This is equality for us.*

I could describe this, but I couldn't explain it until I started studying a lot of pornography. In pornography, there it is, in one place, all of the abuses that women had to struggle so long even to begin to articulate, all the *unspeakable* abuse: the rape, the battery, the sexual harassment, the prostitution, and the sexual abuse of children. Only in the pornography it is called something else: sex, sex, sex, sex, and sex, respectively. Pornography sexualizes rape, battery, sexual harassment, prostitution, and child sexual abuse; it thereby celebrates, promotes, authorizes, and legitimizes them. More generally, it eroticizes the dominance and submission that is the dynamic common to them all. It makes hierarchy sexy and calls that "the truth about sex" or just a mirror of reality. Through this process pornography constructs what a woman is as what men want from sex. This is what the pornography means.

Pornography constructs what a woman is in terms of its view of what men want sexually, such that acts of rape, battery, sexual harassment, prostitution, and sexual abuse of children become acts of sexual equality. Pornography's world of equality is a harmonious and balanced place. Men and women are perfectly complementary and perfectly bipolar. Women's desire to be fucked by men is equal to men's desire to fuck women. All the ways men love to take and violate women, women love to be taken and violated. The women who most love this are most men's equals, the most liberated; the most participatory child is the most grown-up, the most equal to an adult. Their consent merely expresses or ratifies these preexisting facts.

The content of pornography is one thing. There, women substantively desire dispossession and cruelty. We desperately want to be bound, battered, tortured, humiliated, and killed. Or, to be fair to the soft core, merely taken and used. This is

erotic to the male point of view. Subjection itself, with self-determination ecstatically relinquished, is the content of women's sexual desire and desirability. Women are there to be violated and possessed, men to violate and possess us, either on screen or by camera or pen on behalf of the consumer. On a simple descriptive level, the inequality of hierarchy, of which gender is the primary one, seems necessary for sexual arousal to work. Other added inequalities identify various pornographic genres or subthemes, although they are always added through gender: age, disability, homosexuality, animals, objects, race (including antiSemitism), and so on. Gender is never irrelevant.

What pornography *does* goes beyond its content: it eroticizes hierarchy, it sexualizes inequality. It makes dominance and submission into sex. Inequality is its central dynamic; the illusion of freedom coming together with the reality of force is central to its working. Perhaps because this is a bourgeois culture, the victim must look free, appear to be freely acting. Choice is how she got there. Willing is what she is when she is being equal. It seems equally important that then and there she actually be forced and that forcing be communicated on some level, even if only through still photos of her in postures of receptivity and access, available for penetration. Pornography in this view is a form of forced sex, a practice of sexual politics, an institution of gender inequality.

From this perspective, pornography is neither harmless fantasy nor a corrupt and confused misrepresentation of an otherwise natural and healthy sexual situation. It institutionalizes the sexuality of male supremacy, fusing the erotization of dominance and submission with the social construction of male and female. To the extent that gender is sexual, pornography is part of constituting the meaning of that sexuality. Men treat women as who they see women as being. Pornography constructs who that is. Men's power over women means that the way men see women defines who women can be. Pornography is that way. Pornography is not imagery in some relation to a reality elsewhere constructed. It is not a distortion, reflection, projection, expression, fantasy, representation, or symbol either. It is a sexual reality.

In Andrea Dworkin's definitive work, *Pornography: Men Possessing Women,* sexuality itself is a social construct gendered to the ground. Male dominance here is not an artificial overlay upon an underlying inalterable substratum of uncorrupted essential sexual being. Dworkin presents a sexual theory of gender inequality of which pornography is a constitutive practice. The way pornography produces its meaning constructs and defines men and women as such. Gender has no basis in anything other than the social reality its hegemony constructs. Gender is what gender means. The process that gives sexuality its male supremacist meaning is the same process through which gender inequality becomes socially real.

In this approach, the experience of the (overwhelmingly) male audiences who consume pornography is therefore not fantasy or simulation or catharsis but sexual reality, the level of reality on which sex itself largely operates. Understanding this dimension of the problem does not require noticing that pornography models are real women to whom, in most cases, something real is being done; nor does it even require inquiring into the systematic infliction of pornography and its sexuality upon women, although it helps. What matters is the way in which the pornography itself provides what those who consume it want. Pornography *participates* in its audience's eroticism through creating an accessible sexual object, the possession and consumption of which *is* male sexuality, as socially constructed; to be consumed and possessed as which, *is* female sexuality, as socially constructed; pornography is a process that constructs it that way.

The object world is constructed according to how it looks with respect to its possible uses. Pornography defines women by how we look according to how we can be sexually used. Pornography codes how to look at women, so you know what you can do with one when you see one. Gender is an assignment made visually, both originally and in everyday life. A sex object is defined on the basis of its looks, in terms of its usability for sexual pleasure, such that both the looking—the quality of the gaze, including its point of view—and the definition according to use become eroticized as part of the sex itself. This is what the feminist concept "sex object" means. In this sense, sex in life is no less mediated than it is in art. Men have sex with their image of a woman. It is not that life and art imitate each other; in this sexuality, they *are* each other. . . .

To defend pornography as consistent with the equality of the sexes is to defend the subordination of women to men as sexual equality. What in the pornographic view is love and romance looks a great deal like hatred and torture to the feminist. Pleasure and eroticism become violation. Desire appears as lust for dominance and submission. The vulnerability of women's projected sexual availability, that acting we are allowed (that is, asking to be acted upon), is victimization. Play conforms to scripted roles. Fantasy expresses ideology, is not exempt from it. Admiration of natural physical beauty becomes objectification. Harmlessness becomes harm. Pornography is a harm of male supremacy made difficult to see because of its pervasiveness, potency, and, principally, because of its success in making the world a pornographic place. Specifically, its harm cannot be discerned, and will not be addressed, if viewed and approached neutrally, because it *is* so much of "what is." In other words, to the extent pornography succeeds in constructing social reality, it becomes invisible as harm. If we live in a world that pornography creates through the power of men in a male-dominated situation, the issue is not what the harm of pornography is, but how that harm is to become visible.

Obscenity law provides a very different analysis and conception of the problem of pornography. In 1973 the legal definition of obscenity became that which the average person, applying contemporary community standards, would find that, taken as a whole, appeals to the prurient interest; that which depicts or describes in a patently offensive way— you feel like you're a cop reading someone's *Miranda* rights—sexual conduct specifically defined by the applicable state law; and that which, taken as a whole, lacks serious literary, artistic, political or scientific value. Feminism doubts whether the average person gender-neutral exists; has more questions about the content and process of defining what community standards are than it does about deviations from them; wonders why prurience counts but powerlessness does not and why sensibilities are better protected from offense than women are from exploitation; defines sexuality, and thus its violation and expropriation, more broadly than does state law; and questions why a body of law that has not in practice been able to tell rape from intercourse should, without further guidance, be entrusted with telling pornography from anything less. Taking the work "as a whole" ignores that which the victims of pornography have long known: legitimate settings diminish the perception of injury done to those whose trivialization and objectification they contextualize. Besides, and this is a heavy one, if a woman is subjected, why should it matter that the work has other value? Maybe what redeems the work's value is what enhances its injury to women, not to mention that existing standards of literature, art, science, and politics, examined in a feminist light, are remarkably consonant with pornography's mode, meaning, and message. And finally—first and foremost, actually—although the subject of these materials is overwhelmingly women, their contents almost entirely made up of women's bodies, our invisibility has been such, our equation as a sex *with* sex has been such, that the law of obscenity has never even considered pornography a women's issue.

Obscenity, in this light, is a moral idea, an idea about judgments of good and bad. Pornography, by contrast, is a political practice, a practice of power and powerlessness. Obscenity is ideational and abstract; pornography is concrete and substantive. The two concepts represent two entirely different things. Nudity, excess of candor, arousal or excitement, prurient appeal, illegality of the acts depicted, unnaturalness or perversion are all qualities that bother obscenity law when sex is depicted or portrayed. Sex forced on real women so that it can be sold at a profit and forced on other real women; women's bodies trussed and maimed and raped and made into things to be hurt and obtained and accessed, and this presented as the nature of women in a way that is acted on and acted out, over and over; the coercion that is visible and the coercion that has become invisible—this and more bothers feminists about pornography. Obscenity as such probably does little harm. Pornography is integral to attitudes and behaviors of violence and discrimination that define the treatment and status of half the population.

At the request of the city of Minneapolis, Andrea Dworkin and I conceived and designed a local human rights ordinance in accordance with our approach to the pornography issue. We define pornography as a practice of sex discrimination, a violation of women's civil rights, the opposite of sexual equality. Its point is to hold those who profit from and benefit from that injury accountable to those who are injured. It means that women's injury—our damage, our pain, our enforced inferiority—should outweigh their pleasure and their profits, or sex equality is meaningless.

We define pornography as the graphic sexually explicit subordination of women through pictures or words that also includes women dehumanized as sexual objects, things, or commodities; enjoying pain or humiliation or rape; being tied up, cut up, mutilated, bruised, or physically hurt; in postures of sexual submission or servility or display; reduced to body parts, penetrated by objects or animals, or presented in scenarios of degradation, injury, torture; shown as filthy or inferior; bleeding, bruised, or hurt in a context that makes these conditions sexual. Erotica, defined by distinction as not this, might be sexually explicit materials premised on equality. . . .

To define pornography as a practice of sex discrimination combines a mode of portrayal that has a legal history—the sexually explicit—with an active term that is central to the inequality of the sexes—subordination. Among other things, subordination means to be in a position of inferiority or loss of power, or to be demeaned or denigrated. To be someone's subordinate is the opposite of being their equal. The definition does not include all sexually explicit depictions *of* the subordination of women. That is not what it says. It says, this which *does* that: the sexually explicit that subordinates women. To these active terms to capture what the pornography *does,* the definition adds a list of what it must also contain. This list, from our analysis, is an exhaustive description of what must be in the pornography for it to do what it does behaviorally. Each item in the definition is supported by experimental, testimonial, social, and clinical evidence. We made a legislative choice to be exhaustive and specific and concrete rather than conceptual and general, to minimize problems of chilling effect, making it hard to guess wrong, thus making self-censorship less likely, but encouraging (to use a phrase from discrimination law) voluntary compliance, knowing that if something turns up that is not on the list, the law will not be expansively interpreted.

The list in the definition, by itself, would be a content regulation. But together with the first part, the definition is not simply a content regulation. It is a medium-message combination that resembles many other such exceptions to First Amendment guarantees. . . .

This law aspires to guarantee women's rights consistent with the First Amendment by making visible a conflict of rights between the equality guaranteed to all women and what, in some legal sense, is now the freedom of the pornographers to make and sell, and their consumers to have access to, the materials this ordinance defines. Judicial resolution of this conflict, if the judges do for women what they have done for others, is likely to entail a balancing of the rights of women arguing that our lives and opportunities, including our freedom of speech and action, are constrained by—and in many cases flatly precluded by, in, and through—pornography, against those who argue that the pornography is harmless, or harmful only in part but not in the whole of the definition; or that it is more important to preserve the pornography than it is to prevent or remedy whatever harm it does. . . .

The harm of pornography, broadly speaking, is the harm of the civil inequality of the sexes made

invisible as harm because it has become accepted as the sex difference. Consider this analogy with race: if you see Black people as different, there is no harm to segregation; it is merely a recognition of that difference. To neutral principles, separate but equal was equal. The injury of racial separation to Blacks arises "solely because [they] choose to put that construction upon it." Epistemologically translated: how you see it is not the way it is. Similarly, if you see women as just different, even or especially if you don't know that you do, subordination will not look like subordination at all, much less like harm. It will merely look like an appropriate recognition of the sex difference.

Pornography does treat the sexes differently, so the case for sex differentiation can be made here. But men as a group do not tend to be (although some individuals may be) treated the way women are treated in pornography. As a social group, men are not hurt by pornography the way women as a social group are. Their social status is not defined as *less* by it. So the major argument does not turn on mistaken differentiation, particularly since the treatment of women according to pornography's dictates makes it all too often accurate. The salient quality of a distinction between the top and the bottom in a hierarchy is not difference, although top is certainly different. . . .

Free speech only enhances the power of the pornographers while doing nothing substantively to guarantee the free speech of women, for which we need civil equality. The situation in which women presently find ourselves with respect to the pornography is one in which more *pornography* is inconsistent with rectifying or even counterbalancing its damage through speech, because so long as the pornography exists in the way it does there *will not be more speech by women.* Pornography strips and devastates women of credibility, from our accounts of sexual assault to our everyday reality of sexual subordination. We are stripped of authority and reduced and devalidated and silenced. Silenced here means that the purposes of the First Amendment, premised upon conditions presumed and promoted by protecting free speech, do not pertain to women because they are not our conditions. Consider them: individual self-fulfillment—how does pornography promote our individual self-fulfillment? How does sexual inequality even permit it? Even if she can form words, who listens to a woman with a penis in her mouth? Facilitating consensus—to the extent pornography does so, it does so one-sidedly by silencing protest over the injustice of sexual subordination. Participation in civic life—central to Professor Meiklejohn's theory—how does pornography enhance women's participation in civic life? Anyone who cannot walk down the street or even lie down in her own bed without keeping her eyes cast down and her body clenched against assault is unlikely to have much to say about the issues of the day, still less will she become Tolstoy. Facilitating change—*this law* facilitates the change that existing First Amendment theory had been used to throttle. Any system of freedom of expression that does not address a problem where the free speech of men silences the free speech of women, a real conflict between speech interests as well as between people, is not serious about securing freedom of expression in this country.

For those of you who still think pornography is only an idea, consider the possibility that obscenity law got one thing right. Pornography is more actlike than thoughtlike. The fact that pornography, in a feminist view, furthers the idea of the sexual inferiority of women, which is a political idea, doesn't make the pornography itself into a political idea. One can express the idea a practice embodies. That does not make that practice into an idea. Segregation expresses the idea of the inferiority of one group to another on the basis of race. That does not make segregation an idea. A sign that says "Whites Only" is only words. Is it therefore protected by the First Amendment? Is it not an act, a practice, of segregation because what it means is inseparable from what it does? *Law* is only words.

The issue here is whether the fact that words and pictures are the central link in the cycle of abuse will immunize that entire cycle, about which we cannot do anything without doing something about the pornography. As Justice Stewart said in

Ginsburg, "When expression occurs in a setting where the capacity to make a choice is absent, government regulation of that expression may coexist with and *even implement* First Amendment guarantees."[2] I would even go so far as to say that the pattern of evidence we have closely approaches Justice Douglas' requirement that "freedom of expression can be suppressed if, and to the extent that, it is so closely brigaded with illegal action as to be an inseparable part of it."[3] Those of you who have been trying to separate the acts from the speech—that's an act, that's an act, there's a law against that act, regulate that act, don't touch the speech—notice here that the illegality of the acts involved doesn't mean that the speech that is "brigaded with" it *cannot* be regulated. This is when it *can* be.

I take one of two penultimate points from Andrea Dworkin, who has often said that pornography is not speech for women, it is the silence of women. Remember the mouth taped, the woman gagged, "Smile, I can get a lot of money for that." The smile is not her expression, it is her silence. . . .

Classically, opposition to censorship has involved keeping government off the backs of people. Our law is about getting some people off the backs of other people. The risks that it will be misused have to be measured against the risks of the status quo. Women will never have that dignity, security, compensation that is the promise of equality so long as the pornography exists as it does now. The situation of women suggests that the urgent issue of our freedom of speech is not primarily the avoidance of state intervention as such, but getting affirmative access to speech for those to whom it has been denied.

NOTES

1. Adrienne Rich, "Cartographies of Silence," in *The Dream of a Common Language* 16, 17 (1978).
2. *Ginsburg v. New York,* 390 U.S. 629, 649 (1968) (Stewart, J., concurring in result) (emphasis added).
3. *Roth v. United States,* 354 U.S. 476, 514 (Douglas, J., dissenting) (citing *Giboney v. Empire Storage & Ice Co.,* 336 U.S. 490, 498 [1949]); *Labor Board v. Virginia Power Co.,* 314 U.S. 469, 477–78 (1941).

Discussion Questions

1. Discuss MacKinnon's argument that censorship of pornography does not violate our freedom of speech. Has she successfully demonstrated that pornography violates Mill's harm principle? Discuss how Mill might respond to MacKinnon's argument.
2. Discuss MacKinnon's claim that pornography is a type of sex discrimination that directly harms women. Can her argument stand without more definitive evidence?
3. Political analysts George F. Will and Ellen Willis warn that "if feminists define pornography per se as the enemy, the result will be to make a lot of women ashamed of their sexual feelings and afraid to be honest about them."[27] Do you agree? Support your answer. Discuss how MacKinnon might respond to this concern.
4. Sexist attitudes flourish in some religious groups, in advertisements, and in television shows. Indeed, this type of sexist message may be more pervasive and harmful than that of pornography. If so, should sexist religious doctrines, ads, and television shows that demean women be censored? Discuss how MacKinnon might respond to this concern.

CHARLES R. LAWRENCE III

If He Hollers Let Him Go: Regulating Racist Speech on Campus

Charles Lawrence III is a professor of law at the Georgetown University School of Law. In the following article, Lawrence examines the morality of regulating racist hate speech on college campuses. He concludes that the protection of racist speech is incompatible with the elimination of racism. Rather than encouraging the free exchange of ideas, the tolerance of hate speech silences and devalues the ideas of minorities.

Critical Reading Questions

1. What does Lawrence mean by the "double consciousness" shared by minorities?
2. According to Lawrence, who is harmed more by oppressive speech: minorities who are targets of the speech, or those using hate speech?
3. On what grounds does Lawrence claim that many civil libertarians are actually fanning the flames of racism?
4. According to Lawrence, what is the relevance of the United States Supreme Court *Brown v. Board of Education* ruling to the regulation of racist speech?

"If He Hollers Let Him Go: Regulating Racist Speech on Campus," *Duke Law Journal* 431 (1990): 431–480. Notes have been omitted.

5. Why does Lawrence insist that we view individual racist remarks as part of a totality rather than as discrete events?

6. Why does Lawrence reject the distinction drawn by many libertarians between conduct and speech?

7. On what grounds does Lawrence claim that racist speech is the functional equivalent of fighting words?

8. What three types of injury does Lawrence argue are caused by racist speech?

9. Why don't blacks have as much faith in free speech as do whites?

10. According to Lawrence, what are some of the effects of racist speech on the marketplace of ideas?

NEWSREEL*

Racist incidents at the University of Michigan, University of Massachusetts–Amherst, University of Wisconsin, University of New Mexico, Columbia University, Wellesley College, Duke University, and University of California–Los Angeles.

The campus ought to be the last place to legislate tampering with the edges of First Amendment protections.

University of Michigan:
"Greek Rites of Exclusion": Racist leaflets in dorms, white students paint themselves black and place rings in their noses at "jungle parties."

Silencing a few creeps is no victory if the price is an abrogation of free speech. Remember censorship is an ugly word too.

Northwest Missouri State University:
White Supremacists distribute flyers stating, "The Knights of the Ku Klux Klan are Watching You."

---

*The events that appear in this newsreel are gathered from newspaper and magazine reports of racist incidents on campuses. Each of them is followed by a statement, appearing in italics, criticizing proposals to regulate racism on campus. The latter have been garnered from conversations, debates, and panel discussions at which I have been present. Some I managed to record verbatim and are exact quotes; others paraphrase the sentiment expressed. I have heard some version of each of these arguments many times over.

Temple University:
White Student Union formed.

Memphis State University:
Bomb Threats at Jewish Student Union.

The harm that censors allege will result unless speech is forbidden rarely occurs.

Dartmouth College:
Black professor called "a cross between a welfare queen and a bathroom attendant" and the Dartmouth Review purported to quote a black student, "Dese boys be sayin' that we be comin' here to Dartmut an' not takin' the classics. . . ."

Yes, speech is sometimes painful. Sometimes it is abusive. That is one of the prices of a free society.

Purdue University:
Counselor finds "Death Nigger" scratched on her door.

More speech, not less, is the proper cure for offensive speech.

Smith College:
African student finds message slipped under her door that reads, "African Nigger do you want some bananas? Go back to the Jungle."

Speech cannot be banned simply because it is offensive.

University of Michigan:
Campus radio station broadcasts a call from a student who "joked": "Who are the most famous black women in history? Aunt Jemima and Mother Fucker."

Those who don't like what they are hearing or seeing should try to change the atmosphere through education. That is what they will have to do in the real world after they graduate.

University of Michigan:

A student walks into class and sees this written on the blackboard: "A mind is a terrible thing to waste—especially on a nigger." . . .

INTRODUCTION

In recent years, American campuses have seen a resurgence of racial violence and a corresponding rise in the incidence of verbal and symbolic assault and harassment to which blacks and other traditionally subjugated groups are subjected. There is a heated debate in the civil liberties community concerning the proper response to incidents of racist speech on campus. Strong disagreements have arisen between those individuals who believe that racist speech, such as that contained in the Newsreel that opens this Article, should be regulated by the university or some public body and those individuals who believe that racist expression should be protected from all public regulation. At the center of the controversy is a tension between the constitutional values of free speech and equality. . . .

The "double consciousness" of groups outside the ethnic mainstream is particularly apparent in the context of this controversy. Blacks know and value the protection the First Amendment affords those of us who must rely on our voices to petition both government and our neighbors for redress of grievances. Our political tradition has looked to "the word," to the moral power of ideas, to change a system when neither the power of the vote nor that of the gun are available. This part of us has known the experience of belonging and recognizes our common and inseparable interest in preserving the right of free speech for all. But we also know the experience of the outsider. The Framers excluded us from the protection of the First Amendment. The same Constitution that established rights for others endorsed a story that

proclaimed our inferiority. It is a story that remains deeply ingrained in the American psyche.

We see a different world than that which is seen by Americans who do not share this historical experience. We often hear racist speech when our white neighbors are not aware of its presence.

It is not my purpose to belittle or trivialize the importance of defending unpopular speech against the tyranny of the majority. There are very strong reasons for protecting even racist speech. Perhaps the most important reasons are that it reinforces our society's commitment to the value of tolerance, and that, by shielding racist speech from government regulation, we will be forced to combat it as a community. These reasons for protecting racist speech should not be set aside hastily, and I will not argue that we should be less vigilant in protecting the speech and associational rights of speakers with whom most of us would disagree.

But I am deeply concerned about the role that many civil libertarians have played, or the roles we have failed to play, in the continuing, real-life struggle through which we define the community in which we live. I fear that by framing the debate as we have—as one in which the liberty of free speech is in conflict with the elimination of racism—we have advanced the cause of racial oppression and have placed the bigot on the moral high ground, fanning the rising flames of racism. Above all, I am troubled that we have not listened to the real victims, that we have shown so little empathy or understanding for their injury, and that we have abandoned those individuals whose race, gender, or sexual orientation provokes others to regard them as second class citizens. These individuals' civil liberties are most directly at stake in the debate. . . .

BROWN V. BOARD OF EDUCATION: A CASE ABOUT REGULATING RACIST SPEECH

The landmark case of *Brown v. Board of Education* is not a case we normally think of as a case about speech. As read most narrowly, the case is about the rights of black children to equal educational opportunity. But *Brown* can also be read more broadly to articulate a principle central to any substantive understanding of the equal protection clause, the foundation on which all antidiscrimination law rests. This is the principle of equal citizenship. . . .

The key to this understanding of *Brown* is that the practice of segregation, the practice the Court held inherently unconstitutional, was *speech*. *Brown* held that segregation is unconstitutional not simply because the physical separation of black and white children is bad or because resources were distributed unequally among black and white schools. *Brown* held that segregated schools were unconstitutional primarily because of the *message* segregation conveys—the message that black children are an untouchable caste, unfit to be educated with white children. Segregation serves its purpose by conveying an idea. It stamps a badge of inferiority upon blacks, and this badge communicates a message to others in the community, as well as to blacks wearing the badge, that is injurious to blacks. Therefore, *Brown* may be read as regulating the content of racist speech. As a regulation of racist speech, the decision is an exception to the usual rule that regulation of speech content is presumed unconstitutional.

The Conduct/Speech Distinction

Some civil libertarians argue that my analysis of *Brown* conflates speech and conduct. They maintain that the segregation outlawed in *Brown* was discriminatory conduct, not speech, and the defamatory message conveyed by segregation simply was an incidental by-product of that conduct. . . . This objection to my reading of *Brown* misperceives the central point of the argument. . . .

Racism is both 100% speech and 100% conduct. Discriminatory conduct is not racist unless it also conveys the message of white supremacy—unless it is interpreted within the culture to advance the structure and ideology of white supremacy. Likewise, all racist speech constructs the social reality that constrains the liberty of non-whites because

of their race. By limiting the life-opportunities of others, this act of constructing meaning also makes racist speech conduct. . . .

RACIST SPEECH AS THE FUNCTIONAL EQUIVALENT OF FIGHTING WORDS

Much recent debate of the efficacy of regulating racist speech has focused on the efforts by colleges and universities to respond to the burgeoning incidents of racial harassment on their campuses. At Stanford, where I teach, there has been considerable controversy over the questions of whether racist and other discriminatory verbal harassment should be regulated and what form that regulation should take. Proponents of regulation have been sensitive to the danger of inhibiting expression, and the current regulation . . . manifests that sensitivity. It is drafted somewhat more narrowly than I would have preferred, leaving unregulated hate speech that occurs in settings where there is a captive audience, speech that I would regulate. But I largely agree with this regulation's substance and approach. I include it here as one example of a regulation of racist speech that I would argue violates neither First Amendment precedent nor principle. The regulation reads as follows:

> Fundamental Standard Interpretation: Free Expression and Discriminatory Harassment
>
> 1. Stanford is committed to the principles of free inquiry and free expression. Students have the right to hold and vigorously defend and promote their opinions, thus entering them into the life of the University, there to flourish or wither according to their merits. Respect for this right requires that students tolerate even expression of opinions which they find abhorrent. Intimidation of students by other students in their exercise of this right, by violence or threat of violence, is therefore considered to be a violation of the Fundamental Standard.
>
> 2. Stanford is also committed to principles of equal opportunity and non-discrimination. Each student has the right to equal access to a Stanford education, without discrimination on

the basis of sex, race, color, handicap, religion, sexual orientation, or national and ethnic origin. Harassment of students on the basis of any of these characteristics contributes to a hostile environment that makes access to education for those subjected to it less than equal. Such discriminatory harassment is therefore considered to be a violation of the Fundamental Standard.

3. This interpretation of the Fundamental Standard is intended to clarify the point at which protected free expression ends and prohibited discriminatory harassment begins. Prohibited harassment includes discriminatory intimidation by threats of violence, and also includes personal vilification of students on the basis of their sex, race, color, handicap, religion, sexual orientation, or national and ethnic origin.

4. Speech or other expression constitutes harassment by personal vilification if it:

a) is intended to insult or stigmatize an individual or a small number of individuals on the basis of their sex, race, color, handicap, religion, sexual orientation, or national and ethnic origin; and

b) is addressed directly to the individual or individuals whom it insults or stigmatizes; and

c) makes use of insulting or "fighting" words or non-verbal symbols.

In the context of discriminatory harassment by personal vilification, insulting or "fighting" words or non-verbal symbols are those "which by their very utterance inflict injury or tend to incite to an immediate breach of the peace," and which are commonly understood to convey direct and visceral hatred or contempt for human beings on the basis of their sex, race, color, handicap, religion, sexual orientation, or national and ethnic origin.

This regulation and others like it have been characterized in the press as the work of "thought police," but it does nothing more than prohibit intentional face-to-face insults, a form of speech that is unprotected by the First Amendment. When racist speech takes the form of face-to-face insults, catcalls, or other assaultive speech aimed at an individual or small group of persons, then it falls within the "fighting words" exception to First Amendment protection. The Supreme Court has held that words that "by their very utterance inflict injury or tend to incite to an immediate breach of the peace" are not constitutionally protected.

Face-to-face racial insults, like fighting words, are undeserving of First Amendment protection for two reasons. The first reason is the immediacy of the injurious impact of racial insults. The experience of being called "nigger," "spic," "Jap," or "kike" is like receiving a slap in the face. The injury is instantaneous. There is neither an opportunity for intermediary reflection on the idea conveyed nor an opportunity for responsive speech. The harm to be avoided is both clear and present. The second reason that racial insults should not fall under protected speech relates to the purpose underlying the First Amendment. If the purpose of the First Amendment is to foster the greatest amount of speech, then racial insults disserve that purpose. Assaultive racist speech functions as a preemptive strike. The racial invective is experienced as a blow, not a proffered idea, and once the blow is struck, it is unlikely that dialogue will follow. Racial insults are undeserving of First Amendment protection because the perpetrator's intention is not to discover truth or initiate dialogue but to injure the victim.

The fighting words doctrine anticipates that the verbal "slap in the face" of insulting words will provoke a violent response with a resulting breach of the peace. When racial insults are hurled at minorities, the response may be silence or flight rather than fight, but the preemptive effect on further speech is just as complete as with fighting words. Women and minorities often report that they find themselves speechless in the face of discriminatory verbal attacks. This inability to respond is not the result of oversensitivity among these groups, as some individuals who oppose protective regulation have argued. Rather, it is the product of several factors, all of which reveal the non-speech character of the initial preemptive verbal assault. The first factor is that the visceral emotional response to personal attack precludes speech. Attack produces an instinctive, defensive psychological reaction. Fear, rage, shock, and flight all interfere with any reasoned response. Words like "nigger," "kike," and "faggot" produce physical symptoms that temporarily disable the victim, and the perpetrators often use these words with the intention of producing this effect. Many victims do not find words of response until well after the assault when the cowardly assaulter has departed.

A second factor that distinguishes racial insults from protected speech is the preemptive nature of such insults—the words by which to respond to such verbal attacks may never be forthcoming because speech is usually an inadequate response. . . .

The subordinated victim of fighting words also is silenced by her relatively powerless position in society. Because of the significance of power and position, the categorization of racial epithets as "fighting words" provides an inadequate paradigm; instead one must speak of their "functional equivalent." The fighting words doctrine presupposes an encounter between two persons of relatively equal power who have been acculturated to respond to face-to-face insults with violence. The fighting words doctrine is a paradigm based on a white male point of view. In most situations, minorities correctly perceive that a violent response to fighting words will result in a risk to their own life and limb. Since minorities are likely to lose the fight, they are forced to remain silent and submissive. This response is most obvious when women submit to sexually assaultive speech or when the racist name-caller is in a more powerful position—the boss on the job or the mob. . . .

The proposed Stanford regulation, and indeed regulations with considerably broader reach, can be justified as necessary to protect a captive audience from offensive or injurious speech. Courts have held that offensive speech may not be regulated in public forums such as streets and parks where a listener may avoid the speech by moving on or averting his eyes, but the regulation of otherwise protected speech has been permitted when the speech invades the privacy of the unwilling listener's home or when the unwilling listener cannot avoid the speech. Racist posters, flyers, and graffiti in dorms, classrooms, bathrooms, and other common living spaces would fall within the reasoning of these cases. Minority students should not be required to remain in their rooms to avoid racial assault. Minimally, they should find a safe haven in their dorms and other common rooms that are a part of their daily routine. I would argue that the university's responsibility for ensuring these students received an equal educational opportunity provides a compelling justification for regulations that ensure them safe passage in all common areas. . . .

Understanding the Injury Inflicted by Racist Speech

There can be no meaningful discussion about how to reconcile our commitment to equality and our commitment to free speech until we acknowledge that racist speech inflicts real harm and that this harm is far from trivial. I should state that more strongly: To engage in a debate about the First Amendment and racist speech without a full understanding of the nature and extent of the harm of racist speech risks making the First Amendment an instrument of domination rather than a vehicle of liberation. Not everyone has known the experience of being victimized by racist, misogynist, and homophobic speech, and we do not share equally the burden of the societal harm it inflicts. Often we are too quick to say we have heard the victims' cries when we have not; we are too eager to assure ourselves we have experienced the same injury, and therefore we can make the constitutional balance without danger of mismeasurement. For many of us who have fought for the rights of oppressed minorities, it is difficult to accept that—by underestimating the injury from racist speech—we too might be implicated in the vicious words we would never utter. Until we have eradicated racism and sexism and no longer share in the fruits of those forms of domination, we cannot justly strike the balance over the protest of those who are dominated. My plea is simply that we listen to the victims. . . .

Again, *Brown v. Board of Education* is a useful case for our analysis. *Brown* is helpful because it articulates the nature of the injury inflicted by the racist message of segregation. When one considers the injuries identified in the *Brown* decision, it is clear that racist speech causes tangible injury, and it is the kind of injury for which the law commonly provides, and even requires, redress.

Psychic injury is no less an injury than being struck in the face, and is often far more severe. *Brown* speaks directly to the psychic injury inflicted by racist speech in noting that the symbolic message of segregation affected "the hearts and minds" of Negro children "in a way unlikely ever to be undone." Racial epithets and harassment often cause deep emotional scarring, and feelings of anxiety and fear that pervade every aspect of a victim's life. Many victims of hate propaganda have experienced physiological and emotional symptoms ranging from rapid pulse rate and difficulty in breathing, to nightmares, posttraumatic stress disorder, psychosis and suicide.

A second injury identified in *Brown* . . . is reputational injury. "[L]ibelous speech was long regarded as a form of personal assault . . . that government could vindicate . . . without running afoul of the Constitution." . . .

Brown is a case about group defamation. The message of segregation was stigmatizing to black children. To be labeled unfit to attend school with white children injured the reputation of black children, thereby foreclosing employment opportunities and the right to be regarded as respected members of the body politic. . . . *Brown* reflects that racism is a form of subordination that achieves its purpose through group defamation.

The third injury identified in *Brown* is the denial of equal educational opportunity. *Brown* recognized that black children did not have an equal opportunity to learn and participate in the school community if they bore the additional burden of being subjected to the humiliation and psychic assault that accompanies the message of segregation. University students bear an analogous burden when they are forced to live and work in an environment where, at any moment, they may be subjected to denigrating verbal harassment and assault. . . .

All three of these very tangible, continuing, and often irreparable forms of injury—psychic, reputational, and the denial of equal educational opportunity—must be recognized, accounted for, and balanced against the claim that a regulation aimed at the prevention of these injuries may lead to restrictions on important First Amendment liberties.

The Other Side of the Balance: Does the Suppression of Racial Epithets Weigh for or Against Speech?

In striking a balance, we also must think about what we are weighing on the side of speech. Most blacks—unlike many white civil libertarians—do not have faith in free speech as the most important vehicle for liberation. The First Amendment coexisted with slavery, and we still are not sure it will protect us to the same extent that it protects whites. It often is argued that minorities have benefited greatly from First Amendment protection and therefore should guard it jealously. We are aware that the struggle for racial equality has relied heavily on the persuasion of peaceful protest protected by the First Amendment, but experience also teaches us that our petitions often go unanswered until they disrupt business as usual and require the self-interested attention of those persons in power. . . .

Blacks and other people of color are equally skeptical about the absolutist argument that even the most injurious speech must remain unregulated because in an unregulated marketplace of ideas the best ideas will rise to the top and gain acceptance. Our experience tells us the opposite. We have seen too many demagogues elected by appealing to America's racism. We have seen too many good, liberal politicians shy away from the issues that might brand them as too closely allied with us. The American marketplace of ideas was founded with the idea of the racial inferiority of non-whites as one of its chief commodities, and ever since the market opened, racism has remained its most active item in trade.

But it is not just the prevalence and strength of the idea of racism that makes the unregulated marketplace of ideas an untenable paradigm for those individuals who seek full and equal personhood for all. The real problem is that the idea of the racial inferiority of non-whites infects, skews, and disables the operation of the market (like a computer virus, sick cattle, or diseased wheat). Racism is irrational and often unconscious. Our belief in the inferiority of non-whites trumps good ideas that contend with it in the market, often without our even knowing it. In addition, racism makes the words and ideas of blacks and other despised minorities less saleable, regardless of their intrinsic value, in the marketplace of ideas. It also decreases the total amount of speech that enters the market by coercively silencing members of those groups who are its targets.

Racism is an epidemic infecting the marketplace of ideas and rendering it dysfunctional. Racism is ubiquitous. We are all racists. Racism is also irrational. Individuals do not embrace or reject racist beliefs as the result of reasoned deliberation. For the most part, we do not recognize the myriad ways in which the racism pervading our history and culture influences our beliefs. In other words, most of our racism is unconscious. . . .

[John Stuart] Mill's vision of truth emerging through competition in the marketplace of ideas relies on the ability of members of the body politic to recognize "truth" as serving their interest and to act on that recognition. . . .

Prejudice that is unconscious or unacknowledged causes even more distortions in the market. When racism operates at a conscious level, opposing ideas may prevail in open competition for the rational or moral sensibilities of the market participant. But when an individual is unaware of his prejudice, neither reason nor moral persuasion will likely succeed.

Racist speech also distorts the marketplace of ideas by muting or devaluing the speech of blacks and other non-whites. An idea that would be embraced by large numbers of individuals if it were offered by a white individual will be rejected or given less credence because its author belongs to a group demeaned and stigmatized by racist beliefs. . . .

Finally, racist speech decreases the total amount of speech that reaches the market. I noted earlier in this Article the ways in which racist speech is inextricably linked with racist conduct. The primary purpose and effect of the speech/conduct that constitutes white supremacy is the exclusion of non-whites from full participation in the body politic. Sometimes the speech/conduct of racism is direct and obvious. When the Klan burns a cross on the lawn of a black person who joined the NAACP or exercised his right to move to a formerly all-white neighborhood, the effect of this speech does not result from the persuasive power of an idea operating freely in the market. It is a threat, a threat made in the context of a history of lynchings, beatings, and economic reprisals that made good on earlier threats, a threat that silences a potential speaker. The black student who is subjected to racial epithets is likewise threatened and silenced. Certainly she, like the victim of a cross-burning, may be uncommonly brave or foolhardy and ignore the system of violence in which this abusive speech is only a bit player. But it is more likely that we, as a community, will be denied the benefit of many of her thoughts and ideas. . . .

"WHICH SIDE ARE (WE) ON?"

. . . There is much about the way many civil libertarians have participated in the debate over the regulation of racist speech that causes the victims of that speech to wonder which side they are on. Those who raise their voices in protest against public sanctions of racist speech have not organized private protests against the voices of racism. It has been people of color, women, and gays who have held vigils at offending fraternity houses, staged candlelight marches, counter-demonstrations and distributed flyers calling upon their classmates and colleagues to express their outrage at pervasive racism, sexism, and homophobia in their midst and show their solidarity with its victims.

Traditional civil libertarians have been conspicuous largely in their absence from these group expressions of condemnation. Their failure to participate in this marketplace response to speech with more speech is often justified, paradoxically, as concern for the principle of free speech. When racial minorities or other victims of hate speech hold counter-demonstrations or engage in picketing, leafleting, heckling, or booing of racist speakers, civil libertarians often accuse them of private censorship, of seeking to silence opposing points of view. When both public and private responses to racist speech are rejected by First Amendment absolutists as contrary to the principle of free speech, it is no wonder that the victims of racism do not consider them allies. . . .

There is also a propensity among some civil libertarians to minimalize the injury to the victims of racist speech and distance themselves from it by characterizing individual acts of racial harassment as aberrations, as isolated incidents in a community that is otherwise free of racism. When those persons who argue against the regulation of racist speech speak of "silencing a few creeps" or argue that "the harm that censors allege will result unless speech is forbidden rarely occurs," they demonstrate an unwillingness even to acknowledge the injury. Moreover, they disclaim any responsibility for its occurrence.

The recent outbreak of racism on our campuses in its most obvious manifestations provides an opportunity to examine the presence of less overt forms of racism within our educational institutions. But the debate that has followed these incidents has focused on the First Amendment freedoms of the perpetrator rather than the university community's responsibility for creating an environment where such acts occur. The resurgence of flagrant racist acts has not occurred in a vacuum. It is evidence of more widespread resistance to change by those holding positions of dominance and privilege in institutions, which until recently were exclusively white. Those who continue to be marginalized in these institutions—by their token inclusion on faculties and administrations, by the exclusion of their cultures from core curricula, and by commitment to diversity and multi-culturalism that seems to require assimilation more than any real change in the university—cannot help but see their colleagues' attention to free speech as an avoidance of these larger issues of equality.

When the ACLU enters the debate by challenging the University of Michigan's efforts to provide a safe harbor for its black, Hispanic, and Asian students (a climate that a colleague of mine compared unfavorably with Mississippi in the 1960s), we should not be surprised that non-white students feel abandoned. When we respond to Stanford students' pleas for protection by accusing them of seeking to silence all who disagree with them, we paint the harassing bigot as a martyred defender of democracy. When we valorize bigotry we must assume some responsibility for the fact that bigots are encouraged by their newfound status as "defenders of the faith." We must find ways to engage actively in speech and action that resists and counters the racist ideas the First Amendment protects. If we fail in this duty, the victims of hate speech rightly assume we are aligned with their oppressors.

Discussion Questions

1. What welfare rights, according to Lawrence, are violated by hate speech? Are you satisfied with Lawrence's suggestions for resolving the moral dilemma between welfare rights and liberty rights? Support your answers. Create a policy for your campus for resolving this conflict.

2. Lawrence argues that John Stuart Mill's so-called marketplace of ideas does not include hate speech. Do you agree? Given that one of the goals of colleges is to be a marketplace of ideas, discuss which would contribute more toward this goal—the tolerance of hate speech on your campus, or the regulation of hate speech.

3. Lawrence argues that the 1954 United States Supreme Court *Brown v. Board of Education* decision, which outlawed school segregation, was really about freedom of speech. Segregated schools are wrong because they communicate a message of unworthiness to black children. Similarly, prohibiting hate speech is necessary to ensure equal protection. Critically analyze Lawrence's argument.

4. Lawrence claims that "in most situations members of minority groups realize that they are likely to lose if they fight back, and are forced to remain silent and submissive." Does this justify restrictions on hate speech? Or do members of minority groups, as well as others who hear hate speech being used, have a moral duty to stand up to it? Support your answers.

NADINE STROSSEN

Hate Speech and Pornography: Do We Have to Choose Between Freedom of Speech and Equality?

Nadine Strossen is a professor of law at New York Law School and president of the Amercian Civil Liberties Union (ACLU). She argues that censoring hate speech and pornography harms minorities and women. Censorship also undermines, rather than advances, equality.

Critical Reading Questions

1. What are the two important current controversies about free speech?
2. What distinguishes U.S. free speech laws from those of other countries?
3. What is the principle of "viewpoint neutrality" when it comes to freedom of speech?
4. What is the "clear and present danger" requirement for placing restrictions on speech and, according to Strossen, does it justify censoring hate speech and pornography?
5. What are some of the reasons Strossen gives for not suppressing hate speech?
6. What are some of the reasons Strossen gives for not suppressing pornography?
7. What does Strossen mean when she says "censoring hate speech and pornography would undermine, rather than advance, equality goals"?
8. Which group of women in particular would censoring pornography harm, and why?

"Hate Speech and Pornography: Do We Have to Choose Between Freedom of Speech and Equality?" *Case Western Reserve Law Review* 46, no. 2 (Winter 1996). Notes have been omitted.

9. Why is freedom of speech especially important for people, such as minorities and women, who have traditionally suffered from discrimination?
10. In what ways does censorship of hate speech and pornography harm minorities and women?
11. How, according to Strossen, does the censorship of sexual expression harm women and feminists?
12. How does restricting sexual expression undermine human rights in general? What examples does Strossen use to support her argument?

INTRODUCTION

Two important current controversies about free speech have been the focus of academic and public policy debates. Both involve unpopular types of speech that are said to cause harm to particular individuals and societal groups, but have been protected under traditional First Amendment principles. Recently, however, these two types of speech have been the focus of new arguments for suppression and have prompted calls for a re-examination and revision of traditional free speech principles.

The first of these two closely related categories of allegedly harmful speech is commonly called "hate speech." It conveys hatred or prejudice based on race, religion, gender, or some other social grouping. Advocates of suppressing hate speech claim that it promotes discrimination and violence against those it describes.

The second, related type of controversial speech is a category of sexually explicit speech that some prominent feminist scholars [such as Catharine MacKinnon and Andrea Dworkin] call for censoring on the theory that it is, in essence, hate speech against women, promoting discrimination and violence against us. Specifically, they want to suppress sexually explicit expression that is "subordinating" or "degrading" to women. They label this expression "pornography" to distinguish it from the subset of sexual speech that the Supreme Court currently deems constitutionally unprotected, and hence subject to banning under the label "obscenity." . . .

A central feature of U.S. free speech law, which distinguishes it from the law of other countries, is the protection of controversial and unpopular speech, including hate speech and pornography. Probably the best known case that reaffirmed this strong free speech concept was *Village of Skokie v. National Socialist Party of America*. In *Skokie*, the American Civil Liberties Union (ACLU) argued that free speech rights extended even to neo-Nazis seeking to stage a peaceful demonstration in Skokie, Illinois. . . .

More recently, the ACLU has been the prime opponent of a new incarnation of anti-hate speech laws that has become popular: codes adopted by colleges and universities that prohibit hate speech on their campuses. In these cases, too, we have been uniformly successful in challenging the codes on First Amendment grounds.

The concept of suppressible pornography that some feminists advocate—pornography as a type of hate speech—was enacted into two municipal laws. The ACLU participated in lawsuits successfully challenging both of them. . . .

TRADITIONAL U.S. FREE SPEECH PRINCIPLES REGARDING HATE SPEECH AND PORNOGRAPHY

. . . Our law's traditional protection of all types of hate speech, including misogynistic speech, reflects two cardinal principles at the core of our free speech jurisprudence. The first specifies what is not a sufficient justification for restricting speech, and the second prescribes what is a sufficient justification.

A. Viewpoint Neutrality Requirement

The first basic principle requires "viewpoint neutrality." It holds that government may never limit speech just because any listener—or even the majority of the community—disagrees with or is offended by its content or the viewpoint it conveys. The Supreme Court has called this the "bedrock principle" of the proud free speech tradition under American law.

In three recent cases, the Court enforced this basic principle to protect speech with a viewpoint deeply offensive to many, if not most, Americans. The first two involved burning an American flag in political demonstrations against national policies and the third involved burning a cross near the home of an African-American family that had recently moved into a previously all-white neighborhood.

The viewpoint-neutrality principle reflects the philosophy that, in a free society, the appropriate response to speech with which one disagrees is not censorship but counterspeech—more speech, not less. Rejecting this philosophy, the movements to censor hate speech and pornography target speech precisely because of its viewpoint, specifically, its discriminatory viewpoint. For this reason, Seventh Circuit Judge Frank Easterbrook struck down an anti-pornography ordinance that the City of Indianapolis had adopted at the behest of some feminists. Stressing that the law's fatal First Amendment flaw was its viewpoint discrimination, Judge Easterbrook explained that, under the ordinance

> Speech treating women in the approved way—in sexual encounters "premised on equality"—is lawful no matter how sexually explicit. Speech treating women in the disapproved way—as submissive in matters sexual or as enjoying humiliation—is unlawful no matter how significant the literary, artistic, or political qualities of the work taken as a whole. The state may not ordain preferred viewpoints in this way.

B. "Clear and Present Danger" Requirement

Any laws restricting hate speech or pornography would also violate the second core principle of U.S. free speech law: namely, that a restriction on speech can be justified only when necessary to prevent actual or imminent harm, such as violence or injury to others. This is often summarized as the "clear and present danger" requirement. To satisfy this requirement, the restricted speech must pose an "imminent danger." It may not just have a "bad tendency," that is, a more speculative, attenuated connection to potential future harm.

If we banned the expression of all ideas that might lead individuals to actions that may adversely impact even important interests such as national security or public safety, then scarcely any idea would be safe, and surely no idea that challenged the status quo would be. This point was emphasized by Judge Easterbrook when he struck down the Indianapolis anti-pornography ordinance. For the sake of argument, Judge Easterbrook assumed the correctnes of the law's cornerstone assumption that "depictions of [women's] subordination tend to perpetuate subordination." Even so, he concluded, the law was unconstitutional. Judge Easterbrook explained,

> If pornography is what pornography does, so is other speech. . . . Efforts to suppress communist speech in the United States were based on the belief that the public acceptability of such ideas would increase the likelihood of totalitarian government. . . .
>
> Racial bigotry, anti-Semitism, violence on television, reporters' biases—these and many more influence the culture and shape our socialization. . . . Yet all is protected as speech, however insidious. Any other answer leaves the government in control of all of the institutions of culture, the great censor and director of which thoughts are good for us.
>
> Sexual responses often are unthinking responses, and the association of sexual arousal with the subordination of women therefore may have a substantial effect. But almost all cultural stimuli provoke unconscious responses. Religious ceremonies condition their participants. Teachers convey messages by selecting what not to cover; the implicit message about what is off limits or unthinkable may be more powerful than the messages for which they present rational argument. . . . If the fact that speech plays a role

in a process of conditioning were enough to permit governmental regulation, that would be the end of freedom of speech. . . .

CENSORING HATE SPEECH AND PORNOGRAPHY WOULD UNDERMINE, RATHER THAN ADVANCE, EQUALITY GOALS

As previously noted, before the government may restrict expression, it must show not only that the expression threatens imminent serious harm, but also that the restriction is necessary to avert the harm.

Undeniably, the interests that advocates of censoring hate speech and pornography seek to promote—namely, the equality and safety of minority groups and women—are compellingly important. However, advocates of suppressive laws cannot even show that these laws would effectively promote the safety and equality of minority groups and women, let alone that they are the necessary means for doing so. To the contrary, from an equality perspective, these censorship measures would be at best ineffective, and at worst counterproductive. . . .

The reasons why suppressing hate speech does not promote, and may well undermine, racial and other forms of equality include the following. Because the pornography concept advocated by some feminists is a type of hate speech, these points apply to it as well.

- Censoring hate speech increases attention to, and sympathy for, bigots.
- It drives bigoted expression and ideas underground, thus making response more difficult.
- It is inevitably enforced disproportionately against speech by and on behalf of minority group members themselves.
- It reinforces paternalistic stereotypes about minority group members, suggesting that they need special protection from offensive speech.

- It increases resentment towards minority group members, the presumed beneficiaries of the censorship.
- Censoring racist expression undermines a mainstay of the civil rights movement, which has always been especially dependent on a robust concept of constitutionally protected free speech.
- An anti-hate-speech policy curbs the candid intergroup dialogue concerning racism and other forms of bias, which is an essential precondition for reducing discrimination.
- Positive intergroup relations will more likely result from education, free discussion, and the airing of misunderstandings and insensitivity, rather than from legal battles; anti-hate-speech rules will continue to generate litigation and other forms of controversy that increase intergroup tensions.
- Finally, censorship is diversionary; it makes it easier to avoid coming to grips with less convenient and more expensive, but ultimately more meaningful, strategies for combating discrimination. Censoring discriminatory expression diverts us from the essential goals of eradicating discriminatory attitudes and conduct.

The following list outlines the specific reasons why suppressing pornography does not promote, and may well undermine, the critically important goals of reducing discrimination and violence against women. Many of these parallel my analysis of anti-hate-speech laws:

- Censoring pornography would suppress many works that are especially valuable to women and feminists.
- Any pornography censorship scheme would be enforced in a way that discriminates against the least popular, least powerful groups in our society, including feminists and lesbians.
- It would perpetuate demeaning stereotypes about women, including that sex is bad for us.

- It would perpetuate the disempowering notion that women are essentially victims.
- It would distract us from constructive approaches to countering discrimination and violence against women.
- It would harm women who voluntarily work in the sex industry.
- It would harm women's efforts to develop their own sexuality.
- It would strengthen the power of the right wing, whose patriarchal agenda would curtail women's rights.
- By undermining free speech, censorship would deprive feminists of a powerful tool for advancing women's equality.
- Finally, since sexual freedom and freedom for sexually explicit expression are essential aspects of human freedom, censoring such expression would undermine human rights more broadly.

. . . [It is] my conclusion that censoring pornography would do more harm than good to the women who earn their living in the pornography business. As even censorship advocates recognize, any censorship scheme would not prevent the production of all pornography, but rather, would drive that production underground. However, this development would be devastating to the women who would continue to work in the pornography business, as [Seventh Circuit] Judge [Richard] Posner explained, from his law and economics perspective:

> When an economic activity is placed outside the protection of the law—as we know from Prohibition, prostitution, the campaign against drugs and the employment of illegal immigrants—the participants in that activity will resort to threats and violence in lieu of the contractual and other legal remedies denied them. The pimp is an artifact of the illegality of prostitution, and the exploitation of pornographic actresses and models by their employers is parallel to the exploitation of illegal immigrant labor by their employers. These women would be better off if all pornography were legal.

I will now expand upon several of the common reasons why censoring hate speech or pornography would be as dangerous for equality rights as for free speech rights.

A. Free Speech Is Especially Important to People Who Have Traditionally Suffered from Discrimination

First and foremost, all groups who seek equal rights and freedom have an especially important stake in securing free speech. Throughout history, free speech consistently has been the greatest ally of those seeking equal rights for groups that have been subject to discrimination. For example, the Civil Rights Movement during the 1950s and 1960s depended on the vigorous enforcement of free speech rights by the U.S. Supreme Court. . . .

Only strong principles of free speech and association could—and did—protect the drive for desegregation. These principles allowed protestors to carry their messages to audiences that found such messages highly offensive and threatening to their most deeply cherished views of themselves and their way of life. Martin Luther King, Jr. wrote his historic letter from a Birmingham jail. . . .

The most disruptive, militant forms of civil rights protest—such as marches, sit-ins, and kneel-ins— were especially dependent on the Warren Court's generous constructions of the First Amendment. Notably, many of these speech-protective interpretations initially had been formulated in cases brought on behalf of opponents of civil rights. The insulting and often racist language that some militant black activists hurled at police officers and other government officials was also protected under the same principles and precedents.

The foregoing history does not prove conclusively that free speech is an essential precondition for equality, as some respected political philosophers argue. But it does belie the central contention of those who claim an incompatibility between free speech and equality: that equality is an essential precondition for free speech. This history also shows the positive, symbiotic interrelationship between free speech and equality. As stated by Benjamin Hooks, former Executive Director of the NAACP, "The civil rights movement would have been vastly different without the shield and spear of the First Amendment."

Like the Civil Rights Movement, the women's rights movement also has always depended on a vibrant free speech guarantee. This point was made by the lower federal court judge who initially struck down the Indianapolis anti-pornography law. . . . In *American Booksellers Ass'n v. Hudnut* . . . federal district court judge . . . Sara Evans Barker . . . emphasized that advocates of women's rights have far more to lose than to gain from suppressing expression: "It ought to be remembered by . . . all . . . who would support [this anti-pornography law] that, in terms of altering sociological patterns, much as alteration may be necessary and desirable, free speech, rather than being the enemy, is a long-tested and worthy ally."

B. Censorship Has Especially Victimized Members of Politically Powerless Groups, Including Racial Minorities and Women

Just as free speech has always been the strongest weapon to advance equal rights causes, censorship has always been the strongest weapon to thwart them. Ironically, the explanation for this pattern lies in the very analysis of those who want to curb hate speech and pornography. They contend that racial minorities and women are relatively disempowered and marginalized.

I agree with that analysis of the problem and am deeply committed to working toward solving it. However, I strongly disagree that censorship is a solution. To the contrary, precisely because women and minorities are relatively powerless, it makes no sense to hand the power structure yet another tool that it can use to further suppress them, in both senses of the word.

Consistent with the analysis of the censorship advocates themselves, the government will inevitably wield this tool, along with others, to the particular disadvantage of already disempowered groups. This conclusion is confirmed by the enforcement record of all censorship measures, around the world, and throughout history. The pattern of disempowered groups being disproportionately targeted under censorship measures extends even to measures that are allegedly designed for their benefit. This is clearly illustrated by the enforcement record in the many countries that have outlawed hate speech, and the one country that has outlawed pornography as defined by some contemporary feminists.

First, consider the historical enforcement record of anti-hate-speech laws. The first individuals prosecuted under the British Race Relations Act of 1965, which criminalized the intentional incitement of racial hatred, were black power leaders. Rather than curbing speech offensive to minorities, this British law instead has been used regularly to curb the speech of blacks, trade unionists, and anti-nuclear activists. In perhaps the ultimate irony, this statute, which was intended to restrain the neo-Nazi National Front, instead has barred expression by the Anti-Nazi League. The British experience is typical. . . .

The general international pattern of disproportionate enforcement of legal measures curbing hate speech against minority group members also holds true on university and college campuses, where such measures have recently been most vigorously advocated in the United States. . . .

. . . The U.S. campus hate speech code about which we have the most enforcement data is one that was in effect at the University of Michigan from April 1988 until October 1989. Because the ACLU brought a lawsuit to challenge the code, the University was forced to disclose information, which otherwise would have been unavailable to the public, about how the code had been enforced.

During the year and a half that the University of Michigan rule was in effect, there were more than twenty cases of whites charging blacks with racist speech. The only two instances in which the rule was used to punish racist speech, as opposed to other forms of hate speech, involved the punishment of speech by black students. The only student who was subjected to a full-fledged disciplinary hearing under the Michigan rule was an African-American student accused of homophobic and sexist expression. In seeking clemency from the punishment that was imposed on him after this hearing, the student said that he had received such harsh treatment in large part because of his race.

Others who were punished at Michigan included several Jewish students accused of anti-Semitic expression and an Asian-American student accused of making an anti-black comment. The Jewish students wrote graffiti, including a swastika, on a classroom blackboard, saying they intended it as a practical joke. The Asian-American student's allegedly hateful remark was to ask why black people feel discriminated against; he said he raised this question because the black students in his dormitory tended to socialize together, making him feel isolated.

The available information indicates that other campus hate speech codes are subject to the same enforcement patterns. . . .

C. Censorship of Sexual Expression Has Particularly Harmed Women and Women's Rights Advocates

What lesson do we learn from the anti-hate-speech enforcement record that I have outlined? It is this: If you belong to a group that has traditionally suffered discrimination, including women, restrictions on hate speech are especially likely to be wielded against your speech. In fact, all forms of censorship have consistently been used to suppress speech by, about, and for women. Of particular importance for the current pornography debate, laws permitting the suppression of sexually-oriented information have often been used to suppress information essential for women's rights, including reproductive freedom.

In the United States, anti-obscenity laws consistently have been used to suppress information about contraception and abortion. The first federal anti-obscenity statute in this country, the "Comstock Law" enacted in 1873, was repeatedly used to prosecute pioneering feminists and birth control advocates early in this century. Its targets included Margaret Sanger, the founder of Planned Parenthood.

Sanger also had the dubious distinction of being one of the first victims of a new form of censorship that was applied to a then-new medium early in this century. The U.S. Supreme Court had ruled in 1915 that movies were not protected "speech" under the First Amendment. One of the first films banned under that decision was *Birth Control,* a 1917 picture produced by and featuring Margaret Sanger. The banning of films concerning birth control and other sexually-oriented subjects of particular interest to feminists continued in the United States into the second half of this century. . . .

We now have actual experience with a feminist-style anti-pornography law in one country: Canada. In 1992, the Canadian Supreme Court incorporated the pro-censorship feminists' definition of pornography into Canada's obscenity law in *Butler v. The Queen.* The court held that, henceforth, the obscenity law would bar sexual materials that are "degrading" or "dehumanizing" to women.

Alas for women, though, the enforcement record under this law has followed the familiar pattern; it has harmed the very groups that it was supposed to help. The particular victims of Canada's new censorship regime have been the writings and bookstores of women, feminists, lesbians, and gay men. Within the first two and a half years after the Butler decision, approximately two-thirds of all Canadian feminist bookstores had materials confiscated or detained by customs. Butler's supposed rationale is to protect women from works that harm them; it is hard to understand how the feminist writings that have been seized under this decision would harm women.

Ironically, some feminist material has been suppressed under Butler on the ground that it is allegedly degrading and harmful not to women, but to men. In the ultimate irony, two books written by a leading U.S. anti-pornography feminist, the New York writer Andrea Dworkin, were seized at the U.S.-Canada border. According to Canadian customs officials, they illegally "eroticized pain and bondage." . . .

D. Restricting Sexual Expression Undermines Human Rights More Broadly

I will now turn to one final example of the adverse impacts on equality goals that follow from censoring any hate speech, including pornography. Recall that the pro-censorship feminists' conception of suppressible pornography is sexually explicit sexist expression. To highlight the dangers of this concept, I would like to underscore the positive role that sexual expression plays in advancing human freedom.

Sexual expression is an integral aspect of human freedom. Hence, governments that repress human rights in general have always suppressed sexual speech. Correspondingly, laws against sexual speech have always targeted views that challenge the prevailing political, religious, cultural, or social orthodoxy.

Sexually explicit speech has been banned by the most repressive regimes, including Communism in the former Soviet Union, Eastern bloc countries, and China, apartheid in South Africa, and fascist or clerical dictatorships in Chile, Iran, and Iraq. Conversely, recent studies of Russia have correlated improvements in human rights, including women's rights, with the rise of free sexual expression.

In places where real pornography is conspicuously absent, tellingly, political dissent is labeled as such. The Communist government of the former Soviet Union suppressed political dissidents under obscenity laws. In 1987, when the Chinese Communist government dramatically increased its censorship of books and magazines with Western political and literary messages, it condemned them as "obscene," "pornographic," and "bawdy." The white supremacist South African government banned black writing as "pornographically immoral." In Nazi Germany and the former Soviet Union, Jewish writings were reviled as "pornographic," as were any works that criticized the Nazi or Communist party, respectively.

Even in societies that generally respect human rights, including free speech, the terms "obscenity" and "pornography" tend to be used as epithets to stigmatize expression that is politically or socially unpopular. Obscenity laws have been enforced against individuals who have expressed disfavored ideas about political or religious subjects. . . .

The pattern holds today. Obscenity laws in the United States regularly have been used to suppress expression of those who are relatively unpopular or disempowered, whether because of their ideas or because of their membership in particular societal groups. Recent major obscenity prosecutions have targeted expressions by or about members of groups that are powerless and unpopular, including rap music of young African-American men and homoerotic photographs and other works by gay and lesbian artists. Likewise, the National Endowment for the Arts (NEA) has been subjected to many political attacks for its funding of art exploring feminist or homoerotic themes. . . .

. . . During the summer of 1994, the City of Cincinnati brought obscenity charges against a gay and lesbian bookstore, the Pink Pyramid, and its owner, its manager, and its clerk. These individuals, who were arrested and handcuffed, faced sentences of up to six months' imprisonment and fines of up to $1,000. Their "crime"? They had rented out a video of the film *Salo, 120 Days of Sodom,* by Pier Paolo Pasolini, a world-renowned Italian filmmaker, novelist, and poet. The film's sexual-political subject is the dark aspect of sexuality that had served Italian fascism. According to film critic Peter Bondanella, Salo "is a desperate . . . attack against . . . a society dominated by manipulative and sadistic power."

Just as the allegedly obscene video itself had a deeply political message, so too did the charges against those who rented it out. These prosecutions were announced on the opening day of a federal lawsuit brought by the ACLU and Lambda Legal Defense & Education Fund challenging a referendum that had overturned gay and lesbian civil rights legislation. As the National Coalition Against Censorship commented, "At best, the timing suggests indifference to the possibility that these prosecutions would exacerbate already existing prejudices and intolerance." At worst, given the frivolous nature of obscenity charges based on a film of such indisputably serious value, the prosecution was a calculated act of harassment. Accordingly the ACLU filed a brief on behalf of an impressive array of individuals and organizations from the worlds of film, art, and academia, urging the court to dismiss these charges before subjecting the defendants to a pointless and chilling criminal trial. The judge rejected this argument.

The historical and ongoing enforcement record of laws against sexual speech make clear that what is at stake is more than freedom of sexual expression, important as that is. Even beyond that, the freedom to produce or consume anything called "pornography" is an essential aspect of the freedom to defy prevailing political and social mores. . . . [P]ornography in general is the samizdat of those who are oppressed or dissident in any respect. . . .

. . . [F]ree sexual expression is intimately connected with equality—hardly at odds with it, as argued by the anti-pornography feminists. Indeed, free sexual expression is an integral aspect of all human freedom, even beyond freedom from discrimination.

Sexual expression is perhaps the most fundamental manifestation of human individuality. Erotic material is subversive in the sense that it celebrates, and appeals to, the most uniquely personal aspects of an individual's emotional life. Thus, to allow freedom of expression and freedom of thought in this realm is to . . . promote diversity and nonconformist behavior in general. . . .

It is no coincidence that one of the first consequences of democratization and political liberalization in the former Soviet Union, Eastern Europe and China was a small explosion of erotic publications. . . . Suppression of pornography is not just a free-speech issue: Attempts to stifle sexual expression are part of a larger agenda directed at the suppression of human freedom and individuality more generally.

CONCLUSION

. . . With twenty-twenty hindsight, we now see how exaggerated our earlier fears were that Communist authoritarianism would defeat individual liberty. I fervently hope that, in the near future, we will have a similar view about current concerns that racism and sexism could triumph over individual equality. In both cases, free speech plays a vital role in defeating doctrines at odds with human rights. Thus, as Supreme Court Justices such as Brandeis and Black repeatedly reminded us, in the very situations when it seems we have the most to fear in defending free speech—then, above all, do we actually have even more to fear in not defending free speech. As Justice Black wrote,

> Fears of [certain] ideologies have frequently agitated the nation and inspired legislation aimed at suppressing . . . those ideologies. At such times the fog of public excitement obscures the ancient landmarks set up in our Bill of Rights. Yet then, of all times, should [we] adhere most closely to the course they mark.

Discussion Questions

1. Strossen maintains that censoring pornography violates the rights of women who work in the sex industry, including prostitution and the pornography industry. Others argue that women working in the sex industry are not doing so voluntarily but are victims of exploitation and patriarchy, and that prostitution and pornography should be illegal. Critically analyze the two positions.

2. Discuss how Strossen would respond to MacKinnon's argument that pornography is harmful to women because it constructs a social reality in which women are subservient to men. Discuss also how MacKinnon might respond to Strossen's counterargument. Which person makes the better argument? Support your answer.

3. Pornography, whose primary audience is teenagers, is one of the fastest-growing Internet businesses. In addition, there are websites devoted to propagating hate and recruiting racists and terrorists. Discuss what policy, if any, Strossen would most likely adopt regarding the regulation of Internet pornography and hate speech, including that which is deemed a threat to national security.

4. Lawrence maintains that civil libertarians, such as Strossen, are actually "fanning the flames of racism." Strossen argues the opposite—that it is people who want to censor hate speech that are contributing to racism. Discuss the two positions. Which person makes the better argument? Use specific examples to support your answer.

5. Does your campus have a speech code against hate speech? If so, bring in a copy of the speech code for analysis. Discuss what Strossen would most likely think of the code.

STANLEY FISH

There's No Such Thing as Free Speech, and It's a Good Thing, Too

Stanley Fish is dean emeritus at the University of Illinois at Chicago. His article was written as a challenge to libertarians such as Strossen. Fish argues that freedom of speech is not a neutral or absolute principle but is inevitably invoked for political reasons. The value of speech in a particular situation needs to be weighed against other values.

Critical Reading Questions

1. What does Fish mean when he says that "abstract concepts like free speech do not have any 'natural' content"?
2. How does Milton's story in the *Areopagitica* illustrate Fish's claim that speech is never a value in itself, but is produced within a particular concept of the good?
3. According to Fish, why can't the First Amendment be absolute?
4. Why is the concept of "fighting words" problematic as a criterion for censoring speech?
5. What is Fish's position on campus speech codes?
6. On what grounds does Fish reject former Yale University president Benno Schmidt's argument that freedom of expression must be given priority when it collides with harmony in the academic community?

"There's No Such Thing as Free Speech, and It's a Good Thing, Too," *Boston Review* 17, no. 1 (February 1992).

7. How does Fish respond to the liberal argument that colleges should respond to harmful speech, not with regulations, but with more speech?
8. What is Fish's view on the "marketplace of ideas" defense of First Amendment freedom of speech?
9. How does Fish respond to the argument that if we restrict freedom of speech, it will lead us down the slippery slope to restricting more and more speech?

Nowadays the First Amendment is the First Refuge of Scoundrels.

—*S. Johnson and S. Fish*

Lately, many on the liberal and progressive left have been disconcerted to find that words, phrases, and concepts thought to be their property and generative of their politics have been appropriated by the forces of neoconservatism. This is particularly true of the concept of free speech, for in recent years First Amendment rhetoric has been used to justify policies and actions the left finds problematical if not abhorrent: pornography, sexist language, campus hate speech. How has this happened? The answer I shall give in this essay is that abstract concepts like free speech do not have any "natural" content but are filled with whatever content and direction one can manage to put into them. "Free speech" is just the name we give to verbal behavior that serves the substantive agendas we wish to advance; and we give our preferred verbal behaviors *that* name when we can, when we have the power to do so, because in the rhetoric of American life, the label "free speech" is the one you want your favorites to wear. Free speech, in short, is not an independent value but a political prize, and if that prize has been captured by a politics opposed to yours, it can no longer be invoked in ways that further your purposes, for it is now an obstacle to those purposes. This is something that the liberal left has yet to understand, and what follows is an attempt to pry its members loose from a vocabulary that may now be a disservice to them.

Not far from the end of his *Areopagitica,* and after having celebrated the virtues of toleration and unregulated publication in passages that find their way into every discussion of free speech and

the First Amendment, John Milton catches himself up short and says, of course I didn't mean Catholics, them we exterminate:

> I mean not tolerated popery, and open superstition, which as it extirpates all religious and civil supremacies, so itself should be extirpated . . . that also which is impious or evil absolutely against faith or manners no law can possibly permit that intends not to unlaw itself.

Notice that Milton is not simply stipulating a single exception to a rule generally in place; the kinds of utterance that might be regulated and even prohibited on pain of trial and punishment constitute an open set; popery is named only as a particularly perspicuous instance of the advocacy that cannot be tolerated. No doubt there are other forms of speech and action that might be categorized as "open superstitions" or as subversive of piety, faith, and manners, and presumably these too would be candidates for "extirpation." . . .

The list will fill itself out as utterances are put to the test implied by his formulation: Would this form of speech or advocacy, if permitted to flourish, tend to undermine the very purposes for which our society is constituted? It might appear that the result would be *ad hoc* and unprincipled, but for Milton the principle inheres in the core values in whose name individuals of like mind came together in the first place. Those values, which include the search for truth and the promotion of virtue, are capacious enough to accommodate a diversity of views. But at some point—again impossible of advance specification—capaciousness will threaten to become shapelessness, and at that point fidelity to the original values will demand acts of extirpation.

I want to say that all affirmations of freedom of expression are like Milton's, dependent for their force on an exception that literally carves out the space in which expression can then emerge. I do not mean that expression (saying something) is a realm whose integrity is sometimes compromised by certain restrictions but that restriction, in the form of an underlying articulation of the world that necessarily (if silently) negates alternatively possible articulations, is constitutive of expression. . . . The exception to unregulated expression is not a negative restriction but a positive hollowing out of value—we are for *this,* which means we are against *that*—in relation to which meaningful assertion can then occur. It is in reference to that value—constituted as all values are by an act of exclusion—that some forms of speech will be heard as (quite literally) intolerable. Speech, in short, is never a value in and of itself but is always produced within the precincts of some assumed conception of the good to which it must yield in the event of conflict. . . .

Despite the apparent absoluteness of the First Amendment, there are any number of ways of getting around it, ways that are known to every student of the law. In general, the preferred strategy is to manipulate the distinction, essential to First Amendment jurisprudence, between speech and action. The distinction is essential because no one would think to frame a First Amendment that began "Congress shall make no law abridging freedom of action," for that would amount to saying "Congress shall make no law," which would amount to saying "There shall be no law," only actions uninhibited and unregulated. If the First Amendment is to make any sense, have any bite, speech must be declared not to be a species of action, or to be a special form of action lacking the aspects of action that cause it to be the object of regulation. The latter strategy is the favored one and usually involves the separation of speech from consequences. . . . The difficulty of managing this segregation is well known; speech always seems to be crossing the line into action, where it becomes, at least potentially, consequential. In the face of this categorical instability, First Amendment theorists and jurists fashion

a distinction within the speech/action distinction: some forms of speech are not really speech because their purpose is to incite violence or because they are, as the court declares in *Chaplinsky* v. *New Hampshire* (1942), "fighting words," words "likely to provoke the average person to retaliation, and thereby cause a breach of the peace."

The trouble with this definition is that it distinguishes not between fighting words and words that remain safely and merely expressive but between words that are provocative to one group (the group that falls under the rubric "average person") and words that might be provocative to other groups, groups of persons not now considered average. And if you ask what words are likely to be provocative to those nonaverage groups, what are likely to be *their* fighting words, the answer is anything and everything, for as Justice Holmes said long ago (in *Gitlow* v. *New York*), every idea is an incitement to somebody and since ideas come packaged in sentences, in words, every sentence is potentially, in some situation that might occur tomorrow, a fighting word and therefore a candidate for regulation.

This insight cuts two ways. One could conclude from it that the fighting words exception is a bad idea because there is no way to prevent clever and unscrupulous advocates from shoveling so many forms of speech into the excepted category that the zone of constitutionally protected speech shrinks to nothing and is finally without inhabitants. Or, alternatively, one could conclude that there was never anything in the zone in the first place and that the difficulty of limiting the fighting words exception is merely a particular instance of the general difficulty of separating speech from action. And if one opts for this second conclusion, as I do, then a further conclusion, is inescapable insofar as the point of the First Amendment is to identify speech separable from conduct and from the consequences that come in conduct's wake, there is no such speech and therefore nothing for the First Amendment to protect. . . . Despite what they say, courts are never in the business of protecting speech per se, "mere" speech (a nonexistent animal); rather, they are in the business of classifying speech (as protected or regulatable) in relation to a value—the health of the republic, the vigor of the economy, the maintenance of the status quo, the undoing of the status quo—that is the true, if unacknowledged, object of their protection.

But if this is the case, a First Amendment purist might reply, why not drop the charade along with the malleable distinctions that make it possible and declare up front that total freedom of speech is our primary value and trumps anything else, no matter what? The answer is that freedom of expression would only be a primary value if it didn't matter what was said, didn't matter in the sense that no one gave a damn but just liked to hear talk. There are contexts like that, a Hyde Park corner or a call-in talk show where people get to sound off for the sheer fun of it. These, however, are special contexts, artificially bounded spaces designed to assure that talking is not taken seriously. In ordinary contexts, talk is produced with the goal of trying to move the world in one direction rather than another. . . .

Take the case of universities and colleges. Could it be the purpose of such places to encourage free expression? If the answer were "yes," it would be hard to say why there would be any need for classes or examinations, or departments, or disciplines, or libraries, since freedom of expression requires nothing but a soapbox or an open telephone line. The very fact of the university's machinery—of the events, rituals, and procedures that fill its calender—argues for some other, more substantive purpose. In relation to that purpose (which will be realized differently in different kinds of institutions), the flourishing of free expression will in almost all circumstances be an obvious good; but in some circumstances, freedom of expression may pose a threat to that purpose, and at that point it may be necessary to discipline or regulate speech, lest, to paraphrase Milton, the institution sacrifice itself to one of its *accidental* features.

Interestingly enough, the same conclusion is reached (inadvertently) by Congressman Henry Hyde, who is addressing these very issues in a recently offered amendment to Title VI of the Civil Rights Act. The first section of the amendment states its purpose, to protect "the free speech rights of college students" by prohibiting private as well as public educational institutions from "subjecting any student to disciplinary sanctions solely on the basis of conduct that is speech." The second section enumerates the remedies available to students whose speech rights may have been abridged; and the third, which is to my mind the nub of the matter, declares as an exception to the amendment's jurisdiction any "educational institution that is controlled by a religious organization," on the reasoning that the application of the amendment to such institutions "would not be consistent with the religious tenets of such organizations." In effect, what Congressman Hyde is saying is that at the heart of these colleges and universities is a set of beliefs, and it would be wrong to require them to tolerate behavior, including speech behavior, inimical to those beliefs. But insofar as this logic is persuasive, it applies across the board, for all educational institutions rest on some set of beliefs— no institution is "just there" independent of any purpose—and it is hard to see why the rights of an institution to protect and preserve its basic "tenets" should be restricted only to those that are religiously controlled. Read strongly, the third section of the amendment undoes sections one and two. . . . [A]n administrator faced with complaints about offensive speech should ask whether damage to the core would be greater if the speech were tolerated or regulated.

The objection to this line of reasoning is well known and has recently been reformulated by Benno Schmidt, former president of Yale University. According to Schmidt, speech codes on campuses constitute "well-intentioned but misguided efforts to give values of community and harmony a higher place than freedom" (*Wall Street Journal,* May 6, 1991). "When the goals of harmony collide with freedom of expression," he continues, "freedom must be the paramount obligation of an academic community." The flaw in this logic is on display in the phrase "academic community," for the phrase recognizes what Schmidt would deny, that expression only occurs in communities—if not in an academic community, then in a shopping mall community or a dinner party community or an airplane ride community or an office community. In these communities and in any other that could be imagined (with the possible exception of a community of major league baseball fans), limitations on speech in relation to a defining and deeply assumed purpose are inseparable from community membership.

Indeed, "limitations" is the wrong word because it suggests that expression, as an activity and a value, has a pure form that is always in danger of being compromised by the urgings of special interest communities; but independently of a community context informed by interest (that is, purpose), expression would be at once inconceivable and unintelligible. Rather than being a value that is threatened by limitations and constraints, expression, in any form worth worrying about, is a *product* of limitations and constraints, of the already-in-place presuppositions that give assertions their very particular point. Indeed, the very act of thinking of something to say (whether or not it is subsequently regulated) is already constrained . . . by the background context within which the thought takes its shape. . . .

Arguments like Schmidt's only get their purchase by first imagining speech as occurring in no context whatsoever, and then stripping particular speech acts of the properties conferred on them by contexts. The trick is nicely illustrated when Schmidt urges protection for speech "no matter how obnoxious in content." "Obnoxious" at once acknowledges the reality of speech-related harms and trivializes them by suggesting that they are *surface* injuries that any large-minded ("liberated and humane") person should be able to bear. The possibility that speech-related injuries may be grievous and *deeply* wounding is carefully kept out of sight, and because it is kept out of sight, the fiction of a world of weightless verbal exchange can be maintained, at least within the confines of Schmidt's carefully denatured discourse.

To this Schmidt would no doubt reply, as he does in his essay, that harmful speech should be answered not by regulation but by more speech;

but that would make sense only if the effects of speech could be canceled out by additional speech, only if the pain and humiliation caused by racial or religious epithets could be ameliorated by saying something like "So's your old man." What Schmidt fails to realize at every level of his argument is that expression is more than a matter of proffering and receiving propositions, that words do work in the world of a kind that cannot be confined to a purely cognitive realm of "mere" ideas.

It could be said, however, that I myself mistake the nature of the work done by freely tolerated speech because I am too focused on short-run outcomes and fail to understand that the good effects of speech will be realized, not in the present, but in a future whose emergence regulation could only inhibit. . . . My mistake, one could argue, is to equate the something in whose service speech is with some locally espoused value (e.g., the end of racism, the empowerment of disadvantaged minorities), whereas in fact we should think of that something as a now-inchoate shape that will be given firm lines only by time's pencil. That is why the shape now receives such indeterminate characterizations (e.g., true self-fulfillment, a more perfect polity, a more capable citizenry, a less partial truth); we cannot now know it, and therefore we must not prematurely fix it in ways that will bind successive generations to error.

This forward-looking view of what the First Amendment protects has a great appeal, in part because it continues in a secular form the Puritan celebration of millenarian hopes, but it imposes a requirement so severe that one would expect more justification for it than is usually provided. The requirement . . . that we endure whatever pain racist and hate speech inflicts for the sake of a future whose emergence we can only take on faith . . . raises more questions than it answers and could be seen as the second of two strategies designed to delegitimize the complaints of victimized groups. The first strategy, as I have noted, is to define speech in such a way as to render it inconsequential (on the model of "sticks and stones will break my bones, but . . ."); the second strategy is to acknowledge the (often grievous) consequences of speech but declare that we must suffer them in the name of something that cannot be named. The two strategies are denials from slightly different directions of the *present* effects of racist speech; one confines those effects to a closed and safe realm of pure mental activity; the other imagines the effects of speech spilling over into the world but only in an ever-receding future for whose sake we must forever defer taking action.

I find both strategies unpersuasive, but my own skepticism concerning them is less important than the fact that in general they seem to have worked; in the parlance of the marketplace (a parlance First Amendment commentators love), many in the society seemed to have bought them. Why? The answer, I think, is that people cling to First Amendment pieties because they do not wish to face what they correctly take to be the alternative. That alternative is *politics*, the realization (at which I have already hinted) that decisions about what is and is not protected in the realm of expression will rest not on principle or firm doctrine but on the ability of some persons to interpret—recharacterize or rewrite—principle and doctrine in ways that lead to the protection of speech they want heard and the regulation of speech they want silenced. (That is how George Bush can argue *for* flag-burning statutes and *against* campus hate-speech codes.) When the First Amendment is successfully invoked, the result is not a victory for free speech in the face of a challenge from politics but a *political victory* won by the party that has managed to wrap its agenda in the mantle of free speech.

It is from just such a conclusion—a conclusion that would put politics *inside* the First Amendment—that commentators recoil, saying things like "This could render the First Amendment a dead letter" or "This would leave us with no normative guidance in determining when and what speech to protect," or "This effaces the distinction between speech and action," or "This is incompatible with any viable notion of freedom of expression." To these statements (culled more or less at random from recent law review pieces) I would reply that the First Amendment has always been a dead letter if one

understood its "liveness" to depend on the identification and protection of a realm of "mere" expression distinct from the realm of regulatable conduct; the distinction between speech and action has always been effaced in principle, although in practice it can take whatever form the prevailing political conditions mandate; we have never had any normative guidance for marking off protected from unprotected speech; rather, the guidance we have has been fashioned (and refashioned) in the very political struggles over which it then (for a time) presides. In short, the name of the game has always been politics, even when (indeed, especially when) it is played by stigmatizing politics as the area to be avoided.

In saying this, I would not be heard as arguing either for or against regulation and speech codes as a matter of general principle. Instead my argument turns away from general principle to the pragmatic (anti)principle of considering each situation as it emerges. The question of whether or not to regulate will always be a local one, and we cannot rely on abstractions that are either empty of content or filled with the content of some partisan agenda to generate a "principled" answer. Instead we must consider in every case what is at stake and what are the risks and gains of alternative courses of action. In the course of this consideration many things will be of help, but among them will not be phrases like "freedom of speech" or "the right of individual expression," because, as they are used now, these phrases tend to obscure rather than clarify our dilemmas. . . . And when someone warns about the slippery slope and predicts mournfully that if you restrict one form of speech, you never know what will be restricted next, one could reply, "Some form of speech is always being restricted, else there could be no meaningful assertion; we have always and already slid down the slippery slope; someone is always going to be restricted next, and it is your job to make sure that the someone is not you." And when someone observes, as someone surely will, that antiharassment codes chill speech, one could reply that since speech only becomes intelligible against the background of what isn't being said, the background of what has already been silenced, the only question is the political one of which speech is going to be chilled, and, all things considered, it seems a good thing to chill speech like "nigger," "cunt," "kike," and "faggot." And if someone then says, "But what happened to free-speech principles?" one could say what I have now said a dozen times, free-speech principles don't exist except as a component in a bad argument in which such principles are invoked to mask motives that would not withstand closer scrutiny. . . .

Discussion Questions

1. Discuss what Fish means when he says, "There's no such thing as free speech, and it's a good thing, too." Do you agree with him? Support your answer.
2. Fish argues that speech and action cannot be separated. What does he mean by this? Do you agree with him? Use specific examples to support your answer. Discuss how MacKinnon and Lawrence might respond to Fish's claim.
3. Explain and critically evaluate Fish's argument in defense of campus speech codes in certain situations. Discuss how both Mill and Strossen might respond to Fish. Which person makes the strongest argument? Support your answer.
4. Matthew Poe, a fourth-year West Virginia University student, was stopped by campus police for handing out flyers outside a free speech zone (see page 454). Discuss what Fish would most likely think regarding Poe's case and free speech zones on college campuses.
5. Discuss what position—MacKinnon's or Strossen's—Fish would most likely take on the censorship of pornography and why. If neither, explain what position Fish would likely defend. Which person makes the strongest argument?

ALAN M. DERSHOWITZ

Political Correctness, Speech Codes, and Diversity

Alan Dershowitz is a law professor at Harvard University and one of the foremost defense lawyers and civil libertarians in the United States. In this article, Dershowitz examines the motives behind the political correctness movement. He concludes that the speech codes promoted by the political correctness movement, while claiming to promote greater diversity, in fact limit diversity of expression.

"Political Correctness, Speech Codes, and Diversity," *Harvard Law Record,* September 20, 1991.

Critical Reading Questions

1. According to Dershowitz, what are two of the basic tenets of the political correctness movement?
2. What is the primary purpose of campus speech codes? Is this purpose, according to Dershowitz, compatible with diversity of expression?
3. Why does Dershowitz question the real motives of the political correctness movement?
4. According to Dershowitz, what is the real motive behind the demand for more diversity on college campuses?
5. What group of people is pushing hardest for political correctness and speech codes?
6. What is the effect of speech codes on political speech?
7. How does Dershowitz respond to students who defend speech codes on the grounds that certain types of speech contribute to "bigotry, harassment and intolerance, and that it makes it difficult for them to learn"?
8. According to Dershowitz, what has been the effect of political correctness and speech codes on discussions and learning in the classroom?

There is now a debate among the pundits over whether the "political correctness" [P.C.] movement on college and university campuses constitutes a real threat to intellectual freedom or merely provides conservatives with a highly publicized opportunity to bash the left for the kind of intolerance of which the right has often been accused.

My own sense, as a civil libertarian whose views lean to the left, is that the "P.C." movement is dangerous and that it is also being exploited by hypocritical right wingers.

In addition to being intellectually stifling, the P.C. movement is often internally inconsistent. Among its most basic tenets are (1) the demand for "greater diversity" among students and faculty members; and (2) the need for "speech codes," so that racist, sexist and homophobic ideas, attitudes and language do not "offend" sensitive students.

Is it really possible that the bright and well-intentioned students (and faculty) who are pressing the "politically correct" agenda do not realize how inherently self-contradictory these two basic tenets really are? Can they be blind to the obvious reality that true diversity of viewpoints is incompatible with speech codes that limit certain diverse expressions and attitudes?

I wonder if most of those who are pressing for diversity really want it. What many on the extreme left seem to want is simply more of their own: more students and faculty who think like they do, vote like they do and speak like they do. The last thing they want is a truly diverse campus community with views that are broadly reflective of the multiplicity of attitudes in the big, bad world outside of the ivory towers.

How many politically correct students are demanding—in the name of diversity—an increase in the number of Evangelical Christians, National Rifle Association members, and Right to Life advocates? Where is the call for more anti-communist refugees from the Soviet Union, Afro-Americans who oppose race-specific quotas, and women who are antifeminist?

Let's be honest: the demand for diversity is at least in part a cover for a political power grab by the left. Most of those who are recruited to provide politically correct diversity—Afro-Americans, women, gays—are thought to be supporters of the left. And historically, the left—like the right—has not been a bastion of diversity.

Now the left—certainly the extreme left that has been pushing hardest for political correctness—is behind the demands for speech codes. And if they were to get their way, these codes would not be limited to racist, sexist, or homophobic *epithets*. They would apply as well to politically incorrect ideas that are deemed offensive by those who would enforce the codes. Such ideas would include criticism of affirmative action programs, opposition to rape-shield laws, advocacy of the criminalization of homosexuality and defense of pornography.

I have heard students argue that the expression of such ideas—both in and out of class, both by students and professors—contributes to an atmosphere of bigotry, harassment and intolerance, and that it makes it difficult for them to learn.

The same students who insist that they be treated as adults when it comes to their sexuality, drinking and school work, beg to be treated like children when it comes to politics, speech and controversy. They whine to Big Father and Mother—the president or provost of the University—to "protect" them from offensive speech, instead of themselves trying to combat it in the marketplace of ideas.

Does this movement for political correctness—this intolerance of verbal and intellectual diversity—really affect college and university students today? Or is it, as some argue, merely a passing fad, exaggerated by the political right and the media?

It has certainly given the political right—not known for its great tolerance of different ideas—a heyday. Many hypocrites of the right, who would gladly impose their own speech codes if *they* had the power to enforce *their* way, are selectively wrapping themselves in the same First Amendment they willingly trash when it serves their political interest to do so.

But hypocrisy aside—since there is more than enough on both sides—the media are not exaggerating the problem of political correctness. It is a serious issue on college and university campuses. As a teacher, I can feel a palpable reluctance on the part of many students—particularly those with views in neither extreme and those who are anxious for peer acceptance—to experiment with unorthodox ideas, to make playful comments on serious subjects, to challenge politically correct views and to disagree with minority, feminist or gay perspectives.

I feel this problem quite personally, since I happen to agree—as a matter of substance—with most "politically correct" positions. But I am appalled at the intolerance of many who share my substantive views. And I worry about the impact of politically correct intolerance on the generation of leaders we are currently educating.

Discussion Questions

1. List some examples of politically correct ideology. Discuss the criteria you used for deciding whether a particular ideology was politically correct or politically incorrect. Are these criteria based on rational moral principles? Support your answer.
2. Some students confound morality with subscribing to the politically correct ideology. Does the politically correct movement encourage substituting ideology for true moral development? Support your answers using specific examples.
3. What does diversity mean to you? Discuss whether diversity and freedom of speech are most likely to flourish on a college campus with, or without, speech codes.
4. Discuss how both Lawrence and Fish might respond to Dershowitz's objection to campus speech codes. Who makes the strongest argument? Support your answer.

CASS R. SUNSTEIN

The First Amendment in Cyberspace

Cass Sunstein is a professor of jurisprudence in the law school and the department of political science at the University of Chicago. In this selection, Sunstein explores the impact of the different interpretations of First Amendment freedom of speech on the regulation of cyberspace speech. He concludes that constitutionally based regulations on cyberspace speech should aim to foster democratic ends, including public debate, political equality, and even virtue.

Critical Reading Questions

1. What are the two models of the First Amendment free speech tradition?
2. What are the implications of these two models for government regulation of speech?
3. Why does Sunstein prefer the Madisonian model over the marketplace model?
4. What are some of the dangers associated with the new communication technology?
5. According to Sunstein, why is universal access to the information superhighway important in a democracy?
6. According to Sunstein, what criteria should be used in deciding whether it is permissible for government to regulate cyberspace speech?
7. What is Sunstein's view on the regulation of obscene, indecent, and sexually explicit material on the Internet? How have the courts handled this in the past?
8. According to Sunstein, what ends justify regulating speech in cyberspace?

. . . The existence of technological change promises to test the system of free expression in dramatic ways. What should be expected with respect to the First Amendment?

MARKETS AND MADISON

There have been in the United States two models of the First Amendment, corresponding to two free speech traditions. The first emphasizes

well-functioning speech markets. It can be traced to Justice Holmes's great *Abrams* dissent, where the notion of a "market in ideas" received its preeminent exposition. . . .

The second tradition, and the second model, focuses on public deliberation. The second model can be traced from its origins in the work of James Madison, with his attack on the idea of seditious libel, to Justice Louis Brandeis, with his suggestion that "the greatest menace to freedom is an inert people." . . .

Under the marketplace metaphor, the First Amendment requires—at least as a presumption—a system of unrestricted economic markets in speech. Government must respect the forces of supply and demand. At the very least, it may not regulate the content of speech so as to push the speech

"The First Amendment in Cyberspace," from *Free Markets and Social Justice* (New York: Oxford University Press, 1997), 168–169, 172, 183, 187–191, 196–198, 200. Notes have been omitted.

market in its preferred directions. Certainly it must be neutral with respect to viewpoint. A key point for marketplace advocates is that great distrust of government is especially appropriate when speech is at issue. . . .

Those who endorse the marketplace model do not claim that government may not do anything at all. Of course, government may set up the basic rules of property and contract; it is these rules that make markets feasible. . . .

The law of free speech will ultimately have to make some hard choices about the marketplace and democratic models. It is also safe to say that the changing nature of the information market will test the two models in new ways. . . .

SPEECH, EMERGING MEDIA, AND CYBERSPACE

New Possibilities and New Problems: Referenda in Cyberspace and Related Issues

It should be unnecessary to emphasize that the explosion of new technologies opens up extraordinary new possibilities. As the Department of Commerce's predictions suggest, ordinary people are starting to be able to participate in a communications network in which hundreds of millions of people, or more, can communicate with each other and indeed with all sorts of service providers—libraries, doctors, accountants, lawyers, legislators, shopkeepers, pharmacies, grocery stores, museums, Internal Revenue Service employees, restaurants, and more. If you need an answer to a medical question, you may be able to push a few buttons and receive a reliable answer. If you want to order food for delivery, you may be able to do so in a matter of seconds. If you have a question about sports, music, or clothing, or about the eighteenth century, you can get an instant answer. People can now purchase many goods on their credit cards without leaving home. It may now be possible to receive a college education without leaving home. . . .

SOME POLICY DILEMMAS

A large question for both constitutional law and public policy has yet to receive a full democratic or judicial answer: To what extent, if any, do Madisonian ideals have a place in the world of new technologies or in cyberspace? Some people think that the absence of scarcity eliminates the argument for governmental regulation, at least if it is designed to promote attention to public issues, to increase diversity, or to raise the quality of public debate. If outlets are unlimited, why is regulation of any value? In the future, people will be able to listen to whatever they want, perhaps to speak to whomever they choose. Ought this not to be a constitutional ideal?

The question is meant to answer itself, but perhaps enough has been said to show that it hardly does that. Recall first that structural regulation, assigning property rights and making agreements possible, is a precondition for well-functioning markets. Laissez-faire is a hopeless misdescription of free markets. A large government role, with coercive features, is required to maintain markets. Part of the role also requires steps to prevent monopoly and monopolistic practices.

Moreover, Madisonian goals need not be thought anachronistic in a period of infinite outlets. In a system of infinite outlets, the goal of consumer sovereignty may well be adequately promoted. That goal has a distinguished place in both law and public policy, but it should not be identified with the Constitution's free speech guarantee. The Constitution does not require consumer sovereignty; for the most part, the decision whether to qualify or replace that goal with Madisonian aspirations should be made democratically rather than judicially. A democratic citizenry armed with a constitutional guarantee of free speech need not see consumer sovereignty as its fundamental aspiration. Certainly it may choose consumer sovereignty if it likes. But instead it may seek to ensure high-quality fare for children, even if this approach departs from consumer satisfaction. It may seek more generally to promote educational and public-affairs programming. . . .

Analogies

An important issue for the future involves the use of old analogies in novel settings. The new technologies will greatly increase the opportunities for intrusive, fraudulent, harassing, threatening, libelous, or obscene speech. With a few brief touches of a finger, a speaker is now able to communicate to thousands or even millions of people—or to pinpoint a message, perhaps a commercial, harassing, threatening, invasive message, to a particular person. A libelous message, or grotesque invasions of privacy, can be sent almost costlessly. Perhaps reputations and lives will be easily ruined or at least damaged. There are difficult questions about the extent to which an owner of a computer service might be held liable for what appears on that service.

At this stage, it remains unclear whether the conventional legal standards should be altered to meet such problems. For the most part, those standards seem an adequate start and must simply be adapted to new settings. For purposes of assessing cyberspace, there are often apt analogies on which to draw. In fact, the legal culture has no way to think about the new problems except via analogies. The analogies are built into our very language: e-mail, electronic bulletin boards, cyberspace, cyberspaces, and much more. . . .

Access

The government has said that "universal access" is one of its goals for the information superhighway. The question of access has several dimensions. To some extent, it is designed to ensure access to broadcasting options for viewers and listeners. Here a particular concern is that poor people should not be deprived of access to a valuable good. Currently, the expense of Internet connections is prohibitively high for many families. This may entail a form of disenfranchisement. There is an additional problem of ensuring access for certain speakers who want to reach part of the viewing or listening public. In cyberspace, of course, people are both listeners and speakers.

Perhaps the goal of universal viewer or listener access should be viewed with skepticism. The government does not guarantee universal access to cars, housing, food, or even health care. It may seem puzzling to suggest that universal access to information technologies is an important social goal. But the suggestion is less puzzling than it appears. Suppose, for example, that a certain technology becomes a principal means by which people communicate with their elected representatives; suppose that such communications become a principal part of public deliberation and in that way ancillary to the right to vote. . . . Universal access could be seen to be part of the goal of political equality. More generally, universal access might be necessary if the network is to serve its intended function of promoting broad discussion between citizens and representatives. . . .

Protecting Against Obscene, Libelous, Violent, Commercial, or Harassing Broadcasting or Messages

New technologies have greatly expanded the opportunity to communicate obscene, libelous, violent, or harassing messages—perhaps to general groups via stations on (for example) cable television, perhaps to particular people via electronic mail. Invasions of privacy are far more likely. The Internet poses special problems on these counts. As a general rule, any restrictions should be treated like those governing ordinary speech, with ordinary mail providing the best analogy. If restrictions are narrowly tailored and supported by a sufficiently strong record, they should be upheld.

Consider in this regard a highly publicized case involving "cyberporn" at the University of Michigan. A student is alleged to have distributed a fictional story involving a fellow student, explicitly named, who was, in the story, raped, tortured, and finally killed. The first question raised here is whether state or federal law provides a cause of action for conduct of this sort. Perhaps the story amounts to a threat, or a form of libel, or perhaps the most plausible state law claim would be based on intentional infliction of emotional distress. The next question is whether, if a state law claim is available, the award of damages would violate the First Amendment. At first glance, it seems that the question should be resolved in the same way as any case in which a writer uses a real person's name in fiction of this sort. . . .

What of a regulatory regime designed to prevent invasion of privacy, libel, unwanted commercial messages, obscenity, harassment, or infliction of emotional distress? Some such regulatory regime will ultimately make a great deal of sense. The principal obstacles are that the regulations should be both clear and narrow. It is easy to imagine a broad or vague regulation, one that would seize on the sexually explicit or violent nature of communication to justify regulation that is far broader than necessary. Moreover, it is possible to imagine a situation in which liability was extended to any owner or operator who could have no knowledge of the particular materials being sent. The underlying question, having to do with efficient risk allocation, involves the extent to which a carrier might be expected to find and to stop unlawful messages; that question depends on the relevant technology.

Consider, more particularly, possible efforts to control the distribution of sexually explicit materials on the Internet. Insofar as the government seeks to ban materials that are technically obscene and imposes civil or criminal liability on someone with specific intent to distribute such materials, there should be no constitutional problem. . . . On the other hand, many actual and imaginable bills would extend beyond the technically obscene, to include (for example) materials that are "indecent," "lewd," or "filthy." Terms of this sort create a serious risk of unconstitutional vagueness or overbreadth. At least at first glance, they appear unconstitutional for that reason.

The best justification for expansive terms of this kind would be to protect children from harmful materials. It is true that the Internet contains pornography accessible to children, some of it coming from adults explicitly seeking sexual

relations with children. There is in fact material on the Internet containing requests to children for their home addresses. Solicitations to engage in unlawful activity are unprotected by the First Amendment, whether they occur on the Internet or anywhere else. . . .

But when government goes beyond solicitation and bans "indecent" or "filthy" material in general, the question is quite different. Here a central issue is whether the government has chosen the least restrictive means of preventing the relevant harms to children. In a case involving "dial-a-porn," for example, the Court struck down a ban on "indecent" materials on the ground that children could be protected in other ways. . . . Under existing law, it seems clear that in order to support an extension beyond obscenity, Congress would have to show that less restrictive alternatives would be ineffectual. The question then becomes a factual one: What sorts of technological options exist by which parents or others can provide the relevant protection? To answer this question, it would be necessary to explore the possibility of creating "locks" within the Internet, for use by parents, or perhaps for use by those who write certain sorts of materials.

Different questions would be raised by the imposition of civil or criminal liability, not on the distributors having specific intent to distribute, but on carriers who have no knowledge of the specific materials at issue and could not obtain such knowledge without considerable difficulty and expense. It might be thought that the carrier should be treated like a publisher, and a publisher can of course be held liable for obscene or libelous materials, even if the publisher has no specific knowledge of the offending material. But in light of the relatively low costs of search in the world of magazine and book publishing, it is reasonable to think that a publisher should be charged with having control over the content of its publications. Perhaps the same cannot be said for the owner of an electronic mail service. Here the proper analogy might instead be the carriage of mail, in which owners of services are not held criminally or civilly liable for obscene or libelous materials.

The underlying theory is that it would be unreasonable to expect such owners to inspect all the materials they transport, and the imposition of criminal liability, at least, would have an unacceptably harmful effect on a desirable service involving the distribution of a great deal of protected speech. If carriers were held liable for distributing unprotected speech, there would inevitably be an adverse effect on the dissemination of protected speech too. In other words, the problem with carrier liability in this context is that it would interfere with protected as well as unprotected speech. . . .

MADISON IN CYBERSPACE?

Do Madisonian ideals have an enduring role in American thought about freedom of speech? The Supreme Court has not said for certain; its signals are quite mixed; and the existence of new technologies makes the question different and far more complex than it once was. It is conceivable that in a world of newly emerging and countless options, the market will prove literally unstoppable, as novel possibilities outstrip even well-motivated government controls.

If so, this result should not be entirely lamented. A world in which consumers can select from limitless choices has many advantages. . . . If choices are limitless, people interested in politics can see and listen to politics; perhaps they can even participate in politics and in ways that were impossible just a decade ago. But that world would be far from perfect. It may increase social balkanization. It may not promote deliberation, but foster instead a series of referenda in cyberspace that betray constitutional goals.

My central point here has been that the system of free expression is not an aimless abstraction . . . Rooted in a remarkable conception of political sovereignty, the goals of the First Amendment are closely connected with the founding commitment to a particular kind of polity: a deliberative democracy among informed citizens who are political equals. It follows that instead of allowing new technologies to use democratic processes for their own purposes, constitutional law should be concerned with harnessing those technologies for democratic ends—including the founding aspirations to public deliberation, citizenship, political equality, and even a certain kind of virtue. If the new technologies offer risks on these scores, they hold out enormous promise as well. . . .

Discussion Questions

1. Which of the two models of the First Amendment free speech tradition do you prefer and why? Discuss the moral principles and concerns, as well as other assumptions or premises, underlying the models. Discuss which model a rights ethicist, a utilitarian, and a Confucian philosopher would most likely support.
2. Discuss the moral issues raised by the University of Michigan "cyberporn" case. If you had been the president of the University of Michigan, what action, if any, would you have taken? Discuss how Lawrence and Dershowitz would most likely have responded had either of them been president of the University of Michigan.
3. Analyze Sunstein's argument that electronic mail carriers should not be held liable for the distribution of libelous and obscene unprotected speech. Should this same protection apply to Internet service providers? Support your answer.
4. Do you agree with Sunstein that it may be permissible to regulate speech for democratic ends? Relate your answer to the restrictions imposed by the USA Patriot Act. Discuss how Ayn Rand and John Locke might respond to this question.

CASE STUDIES

1. *HUSTLER* PUBLISHER LARRY FLYNT: "FREE-SPEECH HERO"

The hard-core porn magazine *Hustler*, which has a monthy circulation of more than a million, is a popular source of sex education and socialization among teenage boys. One *Hustler* journalist instucts readers that men are "basically rapists, because we're created that way. We're irrational, sexually completely crazy. Our sexuality is more promiscuous, more immediate, and more fleeting, possibly less deep. We're like stud bulls that want to mount everything in sight."[28] *Hustler* also helps readers select vulnerable targets. For example, one issue had an article titled "Good Sex with Retarded Girls." *Hustler* also used to run a regular kiddie corner called "Chester the Molester."

The U.S. Supreme Court in 1988 ruled that *Hustler* magazine publisher Larry Flynt does have a right to publish and sell pornography. In the 1996 film *The People vs. Larry Flynt*, producer Oliver Stone portrays Flynt as a free-speech hero. The controversial film is about Flynt's legal battles against those—especially the "religious right"—who want pornography to be censored. Libertarians have declared him a free-speech hero and defender of civil liberties.

Discussion Questions

1. Do pornography magazines such as *Hustler* harm and subordinate women? To what extent, if at all, do they harm men by socializing them to be sexually violent? Do these harms justify the legal regulation of pornography? Does freedom of speech override the possible harms of pornography? Support your answers. Discuss how MacKinnon and Fish might respond to these questions.
2. In response to the Supreme Court ruling, Jerry Falwell said, "Larry didn't save the First Amendment. The First Amendment saved him." What do you think Falwell meant by this? Do you agree with him? Support your answers. Discuss whether the First Amendment is consistent with "morality" in the *Flynt* ruling.
3. Discuss whether or not Mill would consider Larry Flynt to be a "free-speech hero."
4. Scholar Stanley Fish writes that "nowadays the First Amendment is the First Refuge of Scoundrels."[29] Do you agree? Is Flynt a "scoundrel"? Support your answer.

---

2. BROWN STUDENTS DESTROY OFFENDING NEWSPAPERS

When the *Brown Daily Herald* at Brown University decided to run an ad from David Horowitz entitled "Ten Reasons Why Reparations for Slavery Is a Bad Idea—and Racist Too," a coalition of student groups stole nearly 4,000 copies of the newspaper from campus distribution points. Defendants of the action stated that Horowitz's ad was

> an attempt to inject blatantly revisionist and, yes, racist arguments into a legitimate debate about black reparations. . . . [In] denying the central role of blacks in demanding their own freedom, Horowitz does more than lie. He reveals his true conception of whites as the bestowers of humanity and his contempt for blacks who ask for too much humanity. . . . Outrage is perhaps the only appropriate response [to Horowitz].[30]

They also argued that because Horowitz had the $750 to pay for the full-page ad, the issue was not about freedom of speech but about who can afford to print their views.

The *Herald* released a statement condemning the action of the students who stole the newspapers, stating "We cannot condone the actions our critics have taken against us. The recent theft of thousands of copies of the *Herald* from Brown's campus was an unacceptable attempt to silence our voice." The University administration released a statement supporting the *Herald*.

Discussion Questions

1. Did the coalition of students do the right thing in destroying the newspapers? Discuss how Mill and Fish would each most likely respond to the arguments for and against stealing the newspaper.
2. The purpose of free speech, in the words of Supreme Court Justice Brandeis, is "to free men from the bondage of irrational fears. A speaker who attempts to monopolize the forum and prevent or intimidate others from speaking is not coming from a position of rationality." Discuss in light of the above case.
3. One of the professors who supported the students' actions maintained that we have to take a stand "against those who either actively or passively perpetuate oppression by claiming that all acts of speech are equally entitled to legal protection. We should deny freedom of speech to the oppressor." Discuss.
4. In a separate incident Brown students disrupted a talk by Richard Perle who supported the war in Iraq. Do we have a right based on freedom of expression to interrupt or jeer people whose views we find offensive? Is interrupting speech a legitimate form of protest? Support your answer.

---

3. THE *DARTMOUTH REVIEW*[31]

Dartmouth College is one of America's most prestigious colleges. In 1972 this traditionally white, male, liberal arts college decided to admit women and encourage more diversity in the student population. The curriculum was also changed to reflect the new mission. Not everyone was pleased. The conservative independent school paper, the *Dartmouth Review,* vociferously opposed the affirmative action program and criticized the new nontraditional departments as "political indoctrination centers," making personal attacks on certain members of the college community.

In 1983 the *Dartmouth Review* published an article in which it attacked Professor William Cole's music class, calling it the most "outrageous gut" course on campus. They also made personal attacks on Cole. Cole, one of the few black professors on campus, viewed the attacks as racist and demanded an apology. When this was not forthcoming, he filed a libel suit in U.S. district court. Cole charged that the *Dartmouth Review* was trying to interfere with his right to teach in whatever manner he chose. The *Dartmouth Review,* in turn, accused the college of being hostile to its ideas and of trying to restrict its freedom of speech; it had a right to publish whatever it wanted to publish. The case was eventually settled out of court.

Discussion Questions

1. Did the staff members of the *Dartmouth Review* do anything morally wrong? Support your answer.
2. Supporters of campus speech codes argue that hate speech interferes with the learning environment. Critics of speech codes, on the other hand, argue that such codes stifle professors and students who have ideas they fear may be offensive to others on campus. Discuss these two views in light of the above case.
3. Should classrooms be open forums for the discussion of ideas? Do professors have a right to teach however they see fit, even if it is racist or sexist in the opinion of the students and administration? Discuss how Mill and Strossen would most likely respond to these questions.
4. Discuss what sort of policy Lawrence and Dershowitz might each suggest for dealing with the *Dartmouth Review.* Which policy do you think is better from a moral perspective? Support your answer.

4. THE USA PATRIOT ACT AND ACADEMIC FREEDOM

A senior at the University of Massachusetts, Dartmouth was visited at his parents' home by federal agents after he requested a copy of *The Little Red Book,* Mao Tse-Tung's book on communism. The student, who requested the book through the university library's interlibrary loan, was doing a research paper on communism for a class on fascism and totalitarianism. The two agents who came to the student's home said the book was on a "watch list" and that the student's background, which included "significant time abroad," prompted them to investigate.

His professor told reporters that he suspected that there is a lot more monitoring of student and faculty activities by federal agents than most people realize. The professor also reconsidered a class he was going to teach on "terrorism" because he feared it might put the students at risk. "I shudder to think of all the students I've had monitoring al-Qaeda Web sites, what the government must think of that," he said. "Mao Tse-Tung is completely harmless."[32]

The Department of Homeland Security has the authority to monitor college students' and professors' library borrowing records, Internet records, and e-mails as well as international travel and phone calls. The USA Patriot Act overrides library confidentiality laws. In addition, librarians are bound by a gag order. Once records are requested, librarians are not allowed to tell the person who is under investigation.

Discussion Questions

1. Several libraries have protested the Patriot Act. Librarians in Santa Cruz, California, for example, are shredding patron records daily. Libraries in some other states are posting warning signs or passing out leaflets. The American Library Association passed a resolution calling sections of the Patriot Act a danger to constitutional rights. Does the Patriot Act infringe on people's freedom of speech?
2. The Justice Department defends the Patriot Act on the grounds of national security. They point out that several of the September 11 terrorists used library

computers to communicate by e-mail. Discuss how both Stanley Fish and Cass Sunstein might respond to the argument.

3. Imagine that you are a student working at the circulation desk of your college library. Kashaf, a student from Pakistan, comes up to you to check out a copy of a book on al-Qaeda and terrorism. She says it is for a class. You know Kashaf personally. She is kind and well liked, and you cannot imagine her being involved in any terrorist activities. You worry that if Homeland Security finds out she is borrowing this book, she may get in trouble and may be deported. What should you do?

---

5. THE SMOKING GUN: FREEDOM OF SPEECH AND COMMERCIAL ADVERTISING

Commercial speech is protected because of its value in imparting accurate information to consumers about products. Marketing professor Jerry Kirkpatrick argues that advertising is one of the most effective means of combating ignorance and error. According to him, advertising provides us with important knowledge and guides us toward continuous economic progress. "Nothing, as far as I am concerned," Kirkpatrick writes, "could be more benevolent than advertising, beacon of free society."[33]

Not all advertising has such a benevolent goal, however. Some advertising, such as for cigarettes, does not convey information but uses logical fallacies to make children and other potential consumers associate smoking with things they already desire, such as attractiveness, independence, economic success, and popularity.

In 1995 President Clinton initiated a campaign to prevent children from taking up smoking by severely restricting cigarette advertising on billboards, at sporting events, in magazines, and on promotional items. Clinton's proposal also sought to ban tobacco advertising within 1,000 feet of schools and to require that tobacco companies pay for a $150 million advertising campaign aimed at convincing children and young people to stop smoking. The European Union issued a directive phasing out tobacco ads beginning in July 2001. The tobacco companies, including such giants as Philip Morris and R. J. Reynolds, have protested the U.S. government's restrictions on tobacco advertising as McCarthyism and an assault on their freedom of speech.

Discussion Questions

1. Does commercial speech deserve the same protection as political speech, as Kirkpatrick claims? Support your answer.

2. Does cigarette advertising aimed at children combat ignorance and error? Should restrictions be placed on advertisements that promote harmful products or mislead customers? Or should the "buyer beware"? Support your answers. How would Mill most likely answer these questions?

3. Do paternalism and the protection of children (as well as adults) from potential harm justify restrictions on cigarette advertising? What about the advertising of junk food and sugary cereals on children's television shows? Support your answers.

---

6. THE "MEAN WORLD SYNDROME" AND VIOLENCE IN THE MEDIA

Oscar Wilde once said that life imitates art. Perhaps he was right. Epidemiologist Brandon Centerwall of the University of Washington suggests that violence in the media has made us mean people—a situation he labels the "Mean World Syndrome."

In 1995 fourteen-year-old Sandy Charles of La Ronge, Saskatchewan, watched the movie *Warlock* at least ten times in the days leading up to the kidnapping and murder of seven-year-old Jonathan Thimpsen. The 1991 film depicted a satanic murder in which the victim's skull was crushed with a rock and then strips of flesh were peeled off the victim and boiled in liquid fat—the same method used in the murder of Thimpsen. In 1995, three days after the opening of the movie *Money Train,* in which a New York subway token clerk was doused with a flammable liquid and set on fire, two men who had seen the movie carried out a copycat crime, leaving token booth clerk Harry Kaufman in critical condition with burns over 75 percent of his body. In the next few days, two more token booth clerks were attacked or threatened in a similar manner. Copycat crimes have also been carried out based on Oliver Stone's blood-and-guts movie *Natural Born Killers.* A suit against his movie was recently dismissed by the courts.

Murders have also been inspired by printed matter. In 1993 James Perry murdered Mildred Horn, her eight-year-old son, and the son's nurse. When they went through Perry's belongings, police found a book entitled *Hitman: How to Make a Disposable Silencer* about the techniques of professional murder. There were twenty-two instances in which the book's "recommendations" matched actual details in the Perry murders.

The families of the murder victims brought a wrongful-death suit against the publisher, Paul Lind, who responded that the information his company publishes is protected under freedom of speech and the company is not responsible for how people use that information.[34] His insurance carrier decided to settle the lawsuit rather than go to trial, so the question was never resolved.

Discussion Questions

1. Media violence disproportionately portrays minorities and women as victims, and young, lower-class Latino or foreign males as perpetrators. To what extent do you think these negative images fuel hate speech? If there is a connection, would this justify the regulation of media? Support your answers. Discuss how Mill and Lawrence might each respond to these questions.

2. A 1992 study in the *Journal of the American Medical Association* found that the average child in the United States will have watched 10,000 murders and 200,000 acts of violence by the age of eighteen. Reed Hundt, chairman of the Federal Communications Commission, estimated that without television there would be 10,000 fewer murders, 70,000 fewer rapes, and 700,000 fewer assaults in the United States every year.[35] Many scholars believe that there is a causal connection between viewing violence and acting out hatred and aggression.[36] Are these findings relevant to a decision about whether violence in the media, including the Internet, should be regulated? Support your answer.

3. Does the correlation between media and real-life violence justify limiting the freedom of speech of those who produce these shows? If the programming is harmful to children, would this justify regulating such programming for adults as well? Support your answers.

---

7. INTERNET PLAGIARISM AMONG COLLEGE STUDENTS

Internet plagiarism among college students has increased dramatically in the last ten years. In a recent study, 44 percent of college students admitted to cut-and-paste Internet plagiarism, up from 10 percent in 1999. Of the 50,000 students surveyed, 77 percent said they did not regard this sort of plagiarism as a serious offense.[37]

Mona, a senior honor student who has just been accepted into Harvard Medical School, just realized that she has a three-page paper due the next day for a literature class. She also has an important project due for her microbiology class. Since she doesn't have time to do both, she goes to the Internet, finds an obscure website, and cuts and pastes parts of it into a paper. She e-mails it to her professor, as instructed in the syllabus.

In response to the increase in Internet plagiarism, some colleges have started using antiplagiarism software, such as TurnItIn.com, a website that serves thousands of educational institutions worldwide and receives about 100,000 student papers a day. TurnItIn.com uploads the papers into its database and then searches its database and billions of other pages on the Web for matches. Mona's literature teacher sends Mona's paper to TurnItIn.com and finds out that sections of the paper were plagiarized. She calls Mona into her office, confronts her, and tells Mona that she is failing her for the course and reporting her to the Dean. If Mona fails the course, she will not be able to graduate and go to medical school.

Discussion Questions

1. Websites known as "paper mills" that sell essays and dissertations to students have proliferated since 1999. MasterPapers.com, for example, provides a "custom essay, term paper and dissertation writing service." The site states:

   > Experience your academic career to the fullest—exactly the way you want it! . . . Our company is perfectly aware that a number of tutors do not appreciate when their students resort to essay writing services for help. We strongly believe that professional and legitimate research paper writing services do not hamper students [sic] progress in any way, while the contemporary academic environment often leaves them absolutely no choice but to take advantage of our help.

   Discuss the argument put forth by MasterPapers.com. What moral issues are at stake here? Is the fact that students are not plagiarizing (stealing someone else's work without their permission) morally relevant? Support your answer.

2. In 1997 Boston University sued eight companies that sell term papers on the Internet,[38] claiming that they encourage student plagiarism. In response, the companies argued that the suit, which would close down their businesses, violated their First Amendment right to freedom of speech. Critically evaluate their argument.

3. Do companies have a moral right to publish term papers on the Internet even though they know how students will most likely use them? Or do the students bear moral responsibility for how they use the information from these companies? Do colleges and professors have a moral responsibility to make sure that students are not plagiarizing? Support your answers.

8. FREEDOM OF SPEECH IN SCIENCE CLASS: TEACHING INTELLIGENT DESIGN

The legal conflict between religion and science in the classroom dates back to 1925 when the judge in the Scopes "Monkey Trial" ruled that it was illegal for public schools to teach anything that contradicted the biblical story of creation. The battle has recently resurfaced under the banner of intelligent design (ID) versus evolution. ID is presented by its proponents as an evidence-based scientific theory that challenges the assumption of science that everything in nature must be explained in terms of material causes.

Several states are considering changing their science curriculum to include "alternative theories" such as intelligent design.[39] In a highly publicized trial, the ACLU brought suit against the School Board of Dover, Pennsylvania, for requiring high school biology teachers to teach ID alongside the theory of evolution. The judge ruled against the school board, stating that there was "overwhelming evidence" that intelligent design is not a scientific theory and that "ID cannot uncouple itself from its creationist, and thus religious antecedents."[40] As such, it violates the First Amendment clause regarding separation of church and state.

In some school districts, science teachers are forbidden to teach ID. Teachers who want to include ID in the classroom argue that this violates their freedom of speech.

Discussion Questions

1. The public's belief in evolution has never been more than 50 percent in any of the Gallup polls taken since 1982. The discrepancy between the beliefs of mainstream scientists and the public has fueled a controversy over what should be taught in science classes. Discuss whether restricting teachers' freedom to teach creationism and intelligent design alongside evolution contributes to skepticism or promotes a belief in evolution.

2. Former president George W. Bush endorsed the teaching of ID alongside evolution, stating "Both sides ought to be properly taught so people can understand what the debate is all about." Physicist Robert Ehrlich disagrees. He writes that "to require intelligent design to be taught alongside evolution makes as little sense as requiring flat-Earth theory to be taught in science courses, so that students 'can make up their own minds' whether the Earth is round or flat." Discuss whether or not access to all sides of an argument, even ones that may be mistaken, are important in developing students' critical thinking skills in science. Discuss how Mill would most likely respond.

CHAPTER 10

Racial Discrimination and Global Justice

In January 2009 Barack Obama made history when he became the first African American president of the United States. His election was celebrated as evidence of progress in race relations in the United States. If an African American can become president, then racism must not be as much of a barrier as we previously thought, or so the reasoning goes. However, does Obama's election show that we are now living in a postracial America, as some claim? Mark Potak, director of the Southern Poverty Law Center's Intelligence Project, which monitors hate groups, says "no." Already, racial slurs and hate crimes have been reported in response to Obama's bid for the presidency and his election.[1] Potak worries that this may just be the beginning. "Historically," he says, "a major advance is followed by a backlash."[2]

Sadly, racism is still a harsh reality for many African Americans. Racial segregation in schools is back to levels of the late 1960s. African Americans earn only two-thirds of what European Americans earn, and the unemployment rate is about twice as high. In addition, black men are seven times more likely than white men to end up in jail. In this chapter we'll be looking at some of these issues involving racism, both in the United States and globally.

DEFINING THE KEY TERMS

Race is a loose classification of groups of people based on physical characteristics. Race is more than just a set of physical characteristics, however; it is how people define themselves and others. As such, race is also a social construct. For example, although Jews were singled out as a distinct, inferior race in Nazi Germany, in the United States Jews are generally regarded as white. Hispanics, on the other hand, despite their physical and cultural diversity, are sometimes classified as a race in the United States.   .

Racism is an ideology or worldview that makes race one of the key defining characteristics of a person. Two fundamental premises of racism are (1) humans can be divided into distinct biological groups and (2) some of these groups are morally inferior to others. The Nazi worldview of Aryan superiority was based on an elaborate pseudoscientific description of Jewish biological inferiority. Slavery was also bolstered by scientific theories of biological inferiority. Dr. W. H. Holcombe of Virginia wrote in 1861: "The Negro is not a white man with a black skin, but of a different species, . . . the hopeless physical and mental inferior [of the white, and] organically constituted to be an agricultural laborer in tropical climates—a strong animal machine."[3]

Because racial groups are seen as inherently different, racism leads to an "us/other" mentality, thereby justifying granting privileges to certain groups while denigrating others. The "other" is seen as contaminated and to be avoided. The "one drop" of blood criterion, which designates anyone as black who has even one black ancestor, and the scrutinizing of the pasts of Germans for Jewish ancestry illustrate this fear of racial contamination.

Racism implies prejudice. **Prejudice** is based on negative feelings and stereotypes rather than reason. Racist stereotypes can also be used to justify war and police action, as in the stereotype of the Arab terrorist and the violent young black man. Globally, racism manifests itself in the way affluent nations treat nations whose people are predominantly of non-European descent.

Discrimination occurs when we treat people differently based on their group membership. Unjust discrimination occurs when we base our actions on prejudices rather than relevant differences. Racial discrimination can take many forms, including hate speech, the use of Asian and Latin American mail-order bride services by middle-aged American men who blame their problems with women on feminism, and our lack of response to genocide and the suffering of refugees in the Sudan.

Racism occurs on two levels—the personal and the institutional. **Multiculturalists** believe that racism is based primarily on individual ignorance and that education is the solution. Critical race theorists, such as Charles R. Lawrence III, emphasize the political and social aspects of racism that privilege certain interpretations of history and everyday experience. According to Lawrence, to dismantle racism we need to confront the dominant societal and institutional structures—such as the family and religious, economic, and legal systems—that maintain it.

Institutional racism occurs when the law or a social system is set up to provide advantages to one group of people at the expense of another. Institutional racism exists because of the actions of individuals who either have the power to make and carry out discriminatory policies, or allow them to continue. Slavery and Jim Crow laws are two obvious examples of institutional racism. Schools also act as agents in perpetuating racism.[4] The myth that schools promote upward mobility among immigrant and minority groups is directly contradicted by the finding that the social mobility of second- and third-generation Hispanics is downward.[5]

Institutional racism affects foreign as well as domestic policy. The use of people in Third World nations, as well as nonwhite immigrants in this country, as sources of cheap labor reflects institutional racism. Indeed, the very term **Third World** reflects the Western belief in the inferiority of non-Western countries.

Sometimes institutional racism is indirect. For example, the funding of schools with local, rather than state or federal, taxes means that children from poorer neighborhoods, which may be predominantly black, receive an inferior education. Patterns of environmental use, such as the destruction of American Indian lands by mining companies and the placement of toxic waste sites near minority communities, also reflect institutional racism. (See Case Study 6.)

Institutional racism is perpetuated by the media as well as by legal and religious institutions. The 1915 film *The Birth of a Nation,* based on the best-selling book *The Clansman,* degraded blacks and glorified the Ku Klux Klan. The movie was an instant hit, at least with white people.

Like sexism, racism is embedded in our everyday language. The term *American* is assumed to mean white, usually white male. Other groups of Americans are distinguished from "real" Americans by the use of qualifying terms, as in *African American, Asian American, Arab American,* or *Native American.* In contrast, one rarely hears the term *European American.*

THE PHILOSOPHERS ON RACISM

Although the ancient Greek philosophers did not directly address the issue, the elitist theories of Aristotle and Plato have been used—or, more correctly, misused—to justify racism. In his *Republic,* Plato argued that those with the greatest inherited capacity for moral and intellectual attainment should be educated to become the rulers. According to Aristotle, certain humans are more highly developed or perfect in terms of virtue and reason. Those who are more perfected deserve more of what is good than those who are less perfected. Although Aristotle believed that some humans are "slaves by nature" and exist to serve those who are more perfected, he did not associate slavery with any particular race.

During the seventeenth and eighteenth centuries, racism was incorporated into Western philosophy in part as a response to the need to morally justify European colonialism. John Locke's natural rights ethics, for example, while promoting a doctrine of equal human rights, at the same time assumes the superiority of white Europeans and the inferiority of American Indians. Locke's version of natural rights theory became the basis of colonial rights discourse.

Swedish botanist Carolus Linnaeus (1707–1778) classified humans into varieties, or races, based on physical and psychological characteristics. According to his classification, Europeans are "light, active, ingenious"; Asians are "severe, haughty, miserly"; and Africans are "crafty, lazy, negligent . . . governed by whim." Most Western philosophers accepted Linnaeus's classifications without question.

In the early nineteenth century, the Lamarkian theory of the inheritance of acquired traits was used by scientists, theologians, and philosophers to explain the superiority of the white European race and the inferiority of the dark-skinned Africans. Indians and Asians were only slightly above Africans. Jean-Jacques Rousseau speculated that the people of Africa were only slightly ahead of the great apes in their evolution. "Primitive" people, such as the African Bushmen and the Australian Aborigines, were studied by anthropologists in order to gain insight into the thinking of prehistoric white men.

The Lamarkian theory was also used to support the notion of the perfectibility of humans, which, in turn, justified both colonialization and slavery as a means of assisting "primitive" people in their evolution toward perfection and civilization. This racist worldview was incorporated into the ideals of colonial America. Like Locke, Thomas Jefferson accepted the inequality of hereditary endowment in the different human races. The moral principle of equal respect for all persons was thus drowned out by the racist norms of cultural relativism. It was on the basis of these assumptions that the Europeans continued to exercise their "divine and natural right" to conquer, divide up, and exploit the rest of the world for the next two hundred years.

Modern Marxists link racism to capitalism and class exploitation. The Marxist analysis of racism is problematic in that racism is also found in non-Western, non-capitalist economies such as the Hindu caste system. On the other hand, racism is inconsistent with Buddhism, which stresses the moral equality of all humans and the cultivation of the virtue of compassion or "true friendliness."

THE ROOTS OF AMERICAN RACISM

Jesse Jackson once said, "America has never come to grips with slavery. It is a hole in the American soul." Although racism is found in many, if not most, cultures, this chapter focuses primarily on racism in the United States.

Racism in the United States is rooted in colonialism, slavery, and the systematic attempted extermination of the American Indians. The first record of African slaves arriving in the American colonies was in Jamestown, Virginia, in 1619. The slave trade was both lucrative and brutal. About 10 to 15 percent of the 13 million slaves sent from Africa died en route to the New World.[6] Although the framers of the Declaration of Independence and the U.S. Constitution briefly considered outlawing the African slave trade (although not slavery itself), the idea was soon dropped because several of them were slaveholders, including Jefferson, who owned hundreds of slaves. The number of white abolitionists in the United States was never large. Most people either supported slavery or were indifferent to it.

During the early 1800s, more than a hundred thousand slaves escaped to northern states or found refuge among the Indians. Frustrated at the Native Americans' refusal to return the runaway slaves, southerners sought help from the federal government to pass laws that would make it easier for them to retrieve runaway slaves. The Fugitive Slave Law of 1850 allowed any black person, even people who had been freed, to be returned to slavery. There was little protest in the North over the law, as even freed blacks were not particularly welcomed and were regarded by the whites as "a dangerous and useless element." Frustrated and angry, the northern blacks, with the help of abolitionist groups such as the Quakers, set up the Underground Railroad that smuggled slaves from the United States over the border to Canada.

In 1857 Dred Scott, a slave who had moved with his master to a free territory, sued for his freedom. The U.S. Supreme Court ruled against Scott, arguing that blacks were strictly property and had no rights. The Court also ruled that the Missouri Compromise, which made the territory free, was unconstitutional because it deprived white people of their right to enjoy their human property.

When the Civil War broke out in 1861, the conflict was primarily over economic issues rather than slavery. In his 1861 inaugural address, Abraham Lincoln reassured the southern voters: "I have no purpose, directly or indirectly, to interfere with the institution of slavery in the States where it exists." The 1863 Emancipation Proclamation that freed the slaves, rather than being based on moral repugnance toward slavery, was more of a political move calculated to weaken the Confederate forces and bring an end to the

---

🖋 **EXCERPTS FROM U.S. SUPREME COURT**
BROWN V. BOARD OF EDUCATION OF TOPEKA (1952)

OPINION: MR. CHIEF JUSTICE WARREN delivered the opinion of the Court.

. . . Minors of the Negro race, through their legal representatives, seek the aid of the courts in obtaining admission to the public schools of their community on a nonsegregated basis. In each instance, they had been denied admission to schools attended by white children under laws requiring or permitting segregation according to race. This segregation was alleged to deprive the plaintiffs of the equal protection of the laws under the Fourteenth Amendment. In each of the cases . . . [the] court[s] denied relief to the plaintiffs on the so-called "separate but equal" doctrine announced by this Court in *Plessy v. Ferguson,* 163 U.S. 537. Under that doctrine, equality of treatment is accorded when the races are provided substantially equal facilities, even though these facilities be separate. . . .

The plaintiffs contend that segregated public schools are not "equal" and cannot be made "equal," and that hence they are deprived of the equal protection of the laws. . . .

Today, education is perhaps the most important function of state and local governments. . . . It is the very foundation of good citizenship. Today it is a principal instrument in awakening the child to cultural values, in preparing him for later professional training, and in helping him to adjust normally to his environment. . . . These days, it is doubtful that any child may reasonably be expected to succeed in life if he is denied the opportunity of an education.

---

war. Two years later the Thirteenth Amendment to the Constitution guaranteed that "neither slavery nor involuntary servitude . . . shall exist."

Institutional racism did not end with the Thirteenth Amendment, however. The Ku Klux Klan (KKK) was formed in 1866 by a group of Tennessee Confederate veterans. They were soon joined by some of the South's leading businessmen and professionals. During the thirty years following the Civil War, the southern states passed "Jim Crow laws" that prevented blacks from owning property in certain areas, allowed employers to hunt down and whip troublesome black workers, and enforced segregation in restaurants, theaters, schools, public transportation, hospitals, and even graveyards.

In 1896 the U.S. Supreme Court ruled in *Plessy v. Ferguson* that "separate but equal" segregation was constitutional. According to the Court, the Fourteenth Amendment, while guaranteeing political equality, does not guarantee social equality. The *Plessy v. Ferguson* ruling provided the legal justification for institutional racism for the next sixty years, until 1954, when the Supreme Court overturned the "separate but equal" ruling in *Brown v. Board of Education* (see box).

During the late nineteenth and early twentieth centuries, tens of thousands of blacks were raped, beaten, and brutally murdered. Unofficial "lynch laws" in the South allowed white mobs to torture and lynch blacks who couldn't be humbled and controlled

Such an opportunity, where the state has undertaken to provide it, is a right which must be made available to all on equal terms. . . .

To separate [children] from others of similar age and qualifications solely because of their race generates a feeling of inferiority as to their status in the community that may affect their hearts and minds in a way unlikely ever to be undone. The effect of this separation on their educational opportunities was well stated by a finding in the Kansas case by a court which nevertheless felt compelled to rule against the Negro plaintiffs:

> Segregation of white and colored children in public schools has a detrimental effect upon the colored children. The impact is greater when it has the sanction of the law; for the policy of separating the races is usually interpreted as denoting the inferiority of the negro group. A sense of inferiority affects the motivation of a child to learn. Segregation with the sanction of law, therefore, has a tendency to [retard] the educational and mental development of negro children and to deprive them of some of the benefits they would receive in a racial[ly] integrated school system.

. . . We conclude that in the field of public education the doctrine of "separate but equal" has no place. Separate educational facilities are inherently unequal. Therefore, we hold that the plaintiffs and others similarly situated for whom the actions have been brought are, by reason of the segregation complained of, deprived of the equal protection of the laws guaranteed by the Fourteenth Amendment. . . .

by the other laws. The lynchings were advertised in the newspapers and became festive family outings for many white southerners. Race riots followed the migration of southern blacks to the northern cities during the early twentieth century. With the increase in blacks living in the North, KKK activities spread northward as well.

During the 1920s, the growing "nativist" sentiment made it almost impossible for anyone but people from northern Europe to immigrate to the United States. Racial hatred and Klan activities expanded their targets to include Jews, Puerto Ricans, southern Europeans, Asians, Mexicans, and Native Americans. By 1924 the KKK had 4 million members. Following the Japanese attack on Pearl Harbor during World War II, thousands of Japanese Americans were removed from their homes and placed in federal internment camps, even though not a single case of sabotage involving Japanese Americans was ever discovered.

Racial segregation continued to be the norm in the United States until the 1950s. There were separate professional leagues for black and white athletes. In Hollywood, black actors performed in all-black shows. Although segregated neighborhoods had been ruled unconstitutional by the Supreme Court in 1917, "gentlemen's agreements" among realtors and landlords ensured that neighborhoods—and schools—remained segregated.

In 1954 the U.S. Supreme Court, in *Brown v. Board of Education of Topeka, Kansas,* ruled that school segregation was unconstitutional. The following year Rosa Parks refused to give up her seat on a bus to a white man as required by Alabama law. She was promptly arrested. Her act of nonviolent civil disobedience sparked a citywide bus boycott and the civil rights movement. In 1957 Congress created a Civil Rights Commission, which was followed by the passage of civil rights laws. Martin Luther King Jr. (1929–1968) and Malcolm X (1925–1965) emerged as leaders of the movement. In 1963 Martin Luther King Jr. led the March on Washington.

The "Indian problem" was resolved primarily through genocide. By 1675, only fifty-five years after the Pilgrims landed at Plymouth, the Native Americans of New England, who once numbered in the thousands, were almost exterminated. During the early and mid-1800s, the U.S. government undertook the systematic removal of the Indians from their lands. The Bureau of Indian Affairs was created by Congress in 1824. Instead of being advocates for the Indians, however, the bureau was used to legitimate the takeover of their lands. In 1830 Congress passed the Indian Removal Act. Although the law required the tribes' consent before relocation, many were forced to move without consent. One-fourth of the Cherokee and half of the Creek died of starvation, exposure, and disease during the forced removal from their homes in the South to reservations in the West. In addition to making the land available to wealthy slaveowners, removal of the Indians would make it harder for slaves to escape, since the Indians provided refuge for runaway slaves.

The near extermination of Native American populations by European settlers was justified as the fulfillment of **Manifest Destiny**—a "divine" plan for the expansion of the United States from coast to coast. The massacre of more than two hundred Sioux, at Wounded Knee, South Dakota, in 1890 marked the final step in the conquest of Indians' homelands and their removal to reservations.

The American Indians were not the only group in the West to suffer from the slings and arrows of racism. During the mid-1800s, thousands of Chinese came to the United States to work on the transcontinental railroad. Once the railroad was completed, they were no longer welcome. In 1882 Congress passed the Chinese Exclusion Act, which stopped Chinese immigration and prevented resident Chinese from becoming U.S. citizens. Some of the Chinese returned to China; others sought protection from anti-Chinese violence in segregated areas known as Chinatowns. The Chinese Exclusion Act remained in effect until 1943, when it was repealed by Congress as a gesture of friendship to China during World War II.

Federal initiatives to combat racism and social problems are relatively recent. Under the banner of the Great Society, the Johnson administration in the mid-1960s declared war on poverty. Congress allocated $950 billion for the expansion of existing social services and the establishment of new programs such as Medicare, subsidized housing, and job training to help people break the cycle of poverty.

Following his election in 1980, President Ronald Reagan dismantled much of the Great Society legislation aimed at overcoming the social problems associated with institutional racism. Instead of viewing poverty as a result of institutional racism, the Reagan administration blamed the behavior and values of the poor. The social conditions of people of color began to decline. By the late 1980s, black males were worse off than they were in the late 1960s on almost every socioeconomic measure, including employment rate and life expectancy.[7]

RACISM TODAY

Despite government initiatives to combat racism, 46 percent of blacks interviewed in a 2002 Gallup poll believed that "white hostility towards blacks is fairly widespread."[8] Since the late 1980s, many of the positive gains of the civil rights era have been reversed. Blacks and whites continue to segregate themselves by race in their every-day decisions about housing, church attendance, vacations, and on college campuses. Among college freshmen, only 19 percent think that racial discrimination is no longer a major problem today in the United States; this figure is even lower (12.3 percent) at the traditionally black colleges.[9] According to the U.S. Census Bureau (2008), blacks today earn only 62 percent of what whites earn. In addition, 25 percent of black Americans are living in poverty. Not surprisingly, the life expectancy of blacks in the United States is about five years shorter than that of whites. Much of this disadvantage is due to racism, including low wages, high unemployment rates among blacks, lack of adequate health care, and increasingly segregated schools.

Most schools in the United States are more segregated and unequal today than they were in 1954 at the time of the *Brown v. Board of Education* ruling.[10] In a 2007 Gallup poll, unlike white Americans who had a more optimistic view of racial equality, only half (49%) of blacks thought their children had as good a chance to get a good education as white children in their communities, and even fewer (37%) thought they could get any kind of job they were qualified for.[11]

The percentage of blacks attending college began falling in 1980.[12] Indeed, young black men were more likely to go to prison than to college. This trend began reversing in 1990.[13] More than twice as many minorities are enrolled in colleges as in 1980. Forty-nine percent of black high school graduates and 45 percent of Hispanic high school graduates now attend college.[14]

Arab Americans are also targets of discrimination. In 2006 there were an estimated two thousand cases of anti-Muslim discrimination, including unwarranted arrests under the USA Patriot Act for suspected terrorist activities. Since September 11, 2001, there have also been hundreds of lawsuits filed over the right of Muslim women to wear a veil or *higab* (head scarf) in the workplace and in photo IDs, such as driver's licenses.[15]

Hate Crimes

A **hate crime** is any crime motivated by hostility to the victim as a member of a group based on color, creed, gender, ethnicity, or sexual orientation. Although official reports of hate crimes set the figure at about 7,600 per year, unofficial estimates by the Bureau of Justice Statistics are that about 210,000 hate crimes go unreported every year. According to FBI statistics, about 51 percent of hate crimes are racially motivated. Another 13 percent are based on ethnicity and national origin. The border debate has sparked a rise in hate crimes against Hispanics, and hate crimes against Muslims and Arab Americans increased seventeenfold after the September 11 attacks. Although violent hate crimes against Arab Americans have declined in the past two years, they are still much higher than they were before 2001.

Eleven percent of the hate crimes reported in 2007 took place on college campuses and in schools. For example, a rash of hate mail was sent to more than a dozen historically black colleges warning black students of their impending destruction, stating that in 2000 there would be all-out war against blacks.[16] College faculty in Middle East studies and Muslim students have also been subject to harassment and threats. Following the election of Barack Obama there was an outbreak of racist hate crimes on several college campuses, ranging from racially charged graffiti to effigies of Barack Obama hung from nooses.[17] Obama supports the passage of Hate Crime Prevention legislation that would provide federal assistance to states and local jurisdictions to prosecute hate crimes.

Hate crimes are much more likely to involve violence than other types of crime. While violent crime in general has been decreasing in the United States, hate crimes have not, meaning that an increasing portion of violent crimes in the United States are motivated by hate.

Racial and Ethnic Profiling

During the late 1990s another type of insidious racism known as racial profiling made the headlines. **Racial profiling** is the routine, and often unconscious, practice by police and other law enforcement agents, such as the FBI and airport security personnel, of targeting suspects on the basis of their race or ethnicity.[18]

Despite efforts to counter this practice, racial profiling is still common. A 2006 study found that police are twice as likely to search cars driven by minorities.[19] Some people justify this practice by arguing that blacks, Hispanics, and other minorities commit crimes at a higher rate than whites. In fact, the study found that contraband items, such as illegal drugs and weapons, are more likely to be found in vehicles driven by white motorists. Studies have also found that black college students are subjected to racial profiling, such as being followed around when shopping.[20]

Jorge Garcia, in his reading "The Heart of Racism," notes that individual racism may be more difficult to overcome than institutional racism. When police officers who engage in racial profiling were confronted by their supervisors, the majority of officers had no idea that they were doing it. Some even flatly denied the statistics or that they were racist, arguing instead that "those statistics have to be wrong."[21]

Since the September 11 attacks, Arab Americans and Muslim visitors to the United States have been subject to ethnic profiling both by police and at airports, despite airports' official policy of not using ethnic profiling.[22] Hundreds of Muslims and Americans of Arab descent have also been detained and imprisoned under the USA Patriot Act.

Michael Levin in his article at the end of this chapter argues that practices such as racial profiling of African Americans are morally justified because of biological differences between the races. Bernard Boxill, in contrast, supports the **color-blind principle** arguing that color-conscious policies like this violate the principle of distributive justice. Opponents of racial profiling point out that it not only hurts its direct targets but also leads to an erosion of trust in the government, especially in the justice system and the police, the very branches of government that are entrusted to protect citizens from injustice.

Affirmative Action

The first affirmative action legislation was passed in 1959. It was expanded in the 1960s during the civil rights era. In 1965 President Lyndon B. Johnson delivered a commencement speech at Howard University in which he drew his famous analogy between an American Negro and a shackled runner and called for justice for the American Negro. Excerpts from his speech are found at the end of this chapter.

There are several ways to carry out affirmative action. **Affirmative action** may involve giving preference to a minority person or a woman if that individual is equally qualified with a white male. A more controversial type, known as strong affirmative action, involves giving preference to minorities and women who are less qualified than white male applicants. Other affirmative action programs set goals in terms of percentages of minority and female employees. These goals are usually ideals rather than requirements. Quotas, on the other hand, are fixed percentages or numbers set by a company or college for the hiring or admission of minorities and women.

A basic assumption of affirmative action is that positive steps need to be taken to correct certain injustices. Because racism is institutional, affirmative action benefits minorities by breaking the cycle of discrimination and racism. In addition, affirmative action programs bring together people from diverse racial backgrounds, thus creating a more tolerant and multicultural society.

While Gallup polls show that slightly more than half of blacks support it, affirmative action has never enjoyed popular support among whites in the United States. Opponents of affirmative action point out that the most disadvantaged are not in a position to benefit from it. Affirmative action, some argue, also violates the principle of equality and creates resentment, especially among white males who are harmed by reverse discrimination. In 1978 Allan Bakke, a white man, sued the University of California at Davis Medical School because his application was rejected while minorities with lower test scores were admitted. The Supreme Court agreed with Bakke, ruling that reverse discrimination was unconstitutional.

In 1996, with the passage of Proposition 209, California became the first state to ban affirmative action in the public sector. Washington, Texas, Michigan, and Nebraska have also passed referendums banning affirmative action in college admissions. Despite initial concerns that minorities needed affirmative action programs to make up for past injustices, the enrollment of minorities at the University of California rebounded significantly in 2000.[23] However, the increase was primarily at the satellite campuses.

In June 2003, in *Grutter v. Bollinger,* the U.S. Supreme Court found the admissions policy of the University of Michigan Law School, which awarded points to applicants based on race, to be flawed. However, the Court permitted race to be considered as one among many factors in admissions, stating that the Constitution "does not prohibit the Law School's narrowly tailored use of race in admission decisions to further a compelling interest in obtaining the educational benefits that flow from a diverse student body." This ruling was hailed as a major victory for advocates of affirmative action. (See Case Study 1.) Bernard Boxill defends affirmative action and other policies based on race in his reading on "The Color-Blind Principle" in this chapter.

GLOBALIZATION, IMMIGRATION, AND RACISM

The world has become a smaller place, with the nations of the world linked together in one global economic and technological system. Global ethics addresses issues such as the one-sidedness of global economics, the spread of migration from poorer to more affluent nations, and the increasing racism and xenophobia.

Racist attitudes stem in part from our history of colonialism and slavery. (See Case Study 5.) Under **colonialism,** as Jorge Garcia points out in his reading, the European colonists regarded nonwhites as ignorant and in need of civilizing. Depriving people of color of their freedom and culture was justified as benevolence or the "white man's burden." This attitude continues to some extent in the current **globalization** process, in which wealthy "white" nations justify exploiting people in poorer nations, most of which were former colonies, for their resources and labor as creating economic opportunities for "developing nations." In particular, the World Trade Organization has been accused of being racist by favoring the interests of wealthy nations and corporations and perpetuating disparities between the affluent and the poorest nations.

Under globalization the disparity between the richest and the poorest has widened, both nationally and internationally. The percentage of earned income going to the top 1 percent has nearly doubled—to 19.5 percent—since 1975. While globalization has increased competition and compensation packages for executives at the top, it has driven down the wage of the average American worker as more and more jobs are outsourced to low-paid competitors in countries such as China and India. In his reading "World Poverty and Human Rights," Thomas Pogge argues that since the affluent nations have contributed to—and continue to contribute to—the conditions that lead to severe poverty in the world, we have a duty to work toward alleviating it.

Globalization has also been accompanied by immigration from the poorer to the more affluent nations. The number of illegal immigrants living in the United States has increased from 8.5 million in 2000 to 12 million in 2008. Slightly more than half are from Mexico. While drug trafficking and the threat of terrorists sneaking across the border are serious problems, many illegal immigrants are trying to escape lives of abject poverty and hopelessness and provide a better life for their children. Indeed, according to the Mexican foreign ministry, at least 4,500 Mexicans have died since 1994 trying to cross illegally into the United States.[24] In his article, William Robinson draws a connection between globalization, racism, and the influx of illegal Hispanic immigrants into the United States.

Americans are divided on how to deal with illegal immigrants. Twenty percent of Americans think they should be deported and not allowed to return, or allowed only temporarily as "guest workers." This approach is favored by business interests in the United States who depend on cheap, illegal immigration. Another 42 percent of Americans think illegal immigrants should be allowed to return legally and become citizens if they meet certain requirements. And 36 percent think illegal immigrants should be allowed to remain in the United States and apply for citizenship if they meet certain requirements.[25] (See Case Study 4.) In 2006 the U.S. House of Representatives passed a bill (H.R. 4437) that authorized construction of a 700-mile militarized wall between Mexico and the United States.

THE MORAL ISSUES

Human Dignity and Individual Moral Worth

Jorge Garcia defines racism in terms of ill will and a disregard for the dignity and welfare of certain people based on their assigned race. The victims of Hurricane Katrina (2005), mostly poor and black, were left for days without adequate food and water and in unsanitary conditions before FEMA finally took action to assist them. Failure to take their plight as seriously as that of richer, white victims of natural disasters reflects a history of both institutional and individual racism on the part of the government employees and those in power. (See Case Study 2.)

One of the problems in overcoming institutional racism is how to restore the dignity of groups that have suffered discrimination without violating the equal moral worth of members of groups who have historically benefited from that discrimination. This is particularly an issue in the debate on affirmative action.

Justice and Equality

According to the principle of equality, "it is unjust to treat people differently in ways that deny them significant social benefits unless we can show that there is a difference between them that is relevant to the differential treatment."[26] This principle requires that differential treatment be based only on real and relevant differences.

Michael Levin in "Race, Biology, and Justice" argues that discrimination against blacks is justified based on what he claims are real differences between whites and blacks in terms of intelligence and aggressiveness. Others argue that even if it can be shown that members of one race are, on the average, more intelligent or more aggressive than members of another, this tells us nothing about a particular individual. The principle of equality requires that people be judged on their individual merits, not on their membership in a particular group.[27] Bernard R. Boxill questions whether color-conscious programs, such as affirmative action, are necessarily unjust. He maintains that there are times when race, like talent, is relevant in creating public policy.

On a global level, Pogge maintains that wealthy nations have a duty based on justice to work toward alleviating severe poverty in the world. As it stands now, corporations from wealthy nations can take advantage of workers in poorer nations without regard for the labor and environmental laws that protect workers in richer nations. Currently, the international market exists, for the most part, in a "state of nature"—to use Hobbes's term—in which the powerful are free to exploit the weak.

Utilitarian Considerations

Racism hurts. In the 1954 *Brown v. Board of Education* ruling, the U.S. Supreme Court spoke of the irrevocable damage to the "hearts and minds" of black children who were compelled to attend segregated schools. Delays in responses to disasters that affect mainly people of color, or failure to provide a decent standard of living, can also result in long-term harms and even death, as in the case of Hurricane Katrina.

Affirmative action programs are both defended and opposed on utilitarian grounds. Some people argue that preferential treatment of minorities works against their best interests by fostering social tension and resentment against minorities. It also creates the impression that minorities can't make it on their own merits. In their enthusiasm to diversify, some universities have admitted minority students who are poorly qualified academically, thus setting them up for failure. Furthermore, it is argued, strong affirmative action programs waste the talents of those who are most qualified. Defenders of preferential hiring, in response, maintain that it helps minorities who are less qualified because of racism to develop their talents, thus creating a greater pool of qualified workers.

Reparation and Restitution

Restitution is payment made to a group of people for past harms. Restitution is a type of reparation. Blacks, Native Americans, and Japanese Americans have all sought restitution from the U.S. government. In 1988 Congress passed the Civil Liberties Act authorizing the payment of $20,000 to every living Japanese American who was interned in federal camps during World War II. No similar restitution, however, has been offered to blacks or Native Americans.

What do we owe to blacks and Native Americans, if anything, for a legacy of slavery, genocide, and degradation? Is an apology enough? Should the U.S. government return Indian lands or monetarily compensate Native Americans for the loss of their lands? Should descendants of slaves be compensated monetarily, as were the Japanese Americans for their loss of freedom during World War II? Or do we owe only an indirect debt to contemporary blacks, since it was their ancestors, not they, who were brought to this country against their will? Or is it now time to make peace with the past and just put it behind us?

In his controversial anti-reparations ad, David Horowitz argues that the United States does not owe restitution to blacks. Among his reasons are that blacks who are alive today were not enslaved and that American slavery actually benefited today's African Americans, because they have a much higher standard of living than they would have had if they were living in the African countries from which their ancestors were kidnapped and sold into slavery.[28] His ad has been censored by several college newspapers and student groups (see Chapter 9, Case Study 2). Boxill agrees with Horowitz that the argument for compensation to blacks for harm to their slave ancestors is weak. However, he maintains that blacks living now have a claim for compensation for harms from current injustices.

Care Ethics

The analytical utilitarian approach is often contrasted with a care ethics that emphasizes sentiment and human relationships. Racism prevents the development of caring relationships between people of different races. Care ethics, however, can also be used to justify paternalistic caring and colonialism.

One of the weaknesses of care ethics is that it does not provide a strategy for overcoming racism in a segregated society. When a commitment to caring is absent, it is our commitment to an ideal or principle that must motivate us to do what is right.

CONCLUSION

Because racism is woven into the very fabric of society and reinforced by personal prejudices, it is difficult to eliminate. We need to carefully examine ways in which society today normalizes racism. The racism of the Jim Crow era seemed normal and rational to the majority of white Americans, just as slavery was once regarded as part of the natural order, at least by those who benefited from it.

Some people argue that those affected by racist policies should take responsibility for changing the system. The problem of racism, however, is not a "black problem" or a "Hispanic problem"; the problem is white racism. The people who created and maintain racism bear the main responsibility for eradicating it. Those who have the most power to change institutional racism are the very people who have the power to perpetuate it.

Racism needs to be addressed at all levels. Being "tolerant" or "color-blind" is not enough. The majority of whites state that they strongly believe in the ideal of racial equality; but, even though we may not personally feel racial hatred, our actions can be infected by the hatred of others. It is not enough to simply change our own personal attitudes or substitute a politically correct ideology for action. Unless we actively work toward eliminating racism, we are still part of the problem. Martin Luther King Jr. once said that "the choice is ours, and though we might prefer it otherwise, we *must* choose."

✐ SUMMARY OF READINGS ON RACIAL DISCRIMINATION AND GLOBAL JUSTICE

Johnson, "To Fulfill These Rights." American justice must include respect for the dignity of all people and equal civil rights for African Americans.

Garcia, "The Heart of Racism." Racism is grounded in intention, ill will, and disregard for members of certain groups.

Boxill, "The Color-Blind Principle." Discrimination is not necessarily unjust; difference in color can in some cases be justly considered as a criterion in hiring.

Levin, "Race, Biology, and Justice." The attainment gap between whites and blacks is due not only to racism but to genetic differences between the races.

Robinson, " 'Aquí Estamos y No Nos Vamos!' Global Capital and Immigrant Rights." Globalization and transnational migration have fueled racism and the exploitation of immigrant workers.

Pogge, "World Poverty and Human Rights." Affluent nations have a duty to alleviate poverty in poorer nations.

LYNDON B. JOHNSON

To Fulfill These Rights

Lyndon B. Johnson served as president of the United States from 1963, following the assassination of President John F. Kennedy, to 1969. During his presidency Johnson was a tireless advocate of civil rights for blacks. Legislation passed under Johnson's administration included the 1964 Civil Rights Act. Following are excerpts from his commencement address delivered at Howard University on June 4, 1965.

Critical Reading Questions

1. According to Johnson, in what ways have American Negroes been another nation?
2. Why isn't freedom enough to bring tequal opportunity to the American Negro?
3. What does Johnson mean when he says that "ability is not just the product of birth"?
4. What are some of the causes of inequality?
5. What is the difference between white poverty and Negro poverty?
6. What are the roots of the injustice experienced by the American Negro?
7. What, according to Johnson, is the answer to these problems?
8. What does Johnson mean when he says that "American justice is a very special thing" and what does this mean for the American Negro?

Commencement Address at Howard University, June 4, 1965

. . . In far too many ways American Negroes have been another nation: deprived of freedom, crippled by hatred, the doors of opportunity closed to hope.

In our time change has come to this Nation, too. The American Negro, acting with impressive restraint, has peacefully protested and marched, entered the courtrooms and the seats of government, demanding a justice that has long been denied. The voice of the Negro was the call to action. But it is a tribute to America that, once aroused, the courts and the Congress, the President and most of the people, have been the allies of progress. . . .

That beginning is freedom; and the barriers to that freedom are tumbling down. Freedom is the right to share, share fully and equally, in American

"To Fulfill These Rights," *Public Papers of the Presidents of the United States: Lyndon B. Johnson, 1965*, vol. 2, no. 301 (Washington, D.C.: Government Printing Office, 1966), 635–640.

society—to vote, to hold a job, to enter a public place, to go to school. It is the right to be treated in every part of our national life as a person equal in dignity and promise to all others.

But freedom is not enough. You do not wipe away the scars of centuries by saying: Now you are free to go where you want, and do as you desire, and choose the leaders you please.

You do not take a person who, for years, has been hobbled by chains and liberate him, bring him up to the starting line of a race and then say, "you are free to compete with all the others," and still justly believe that you have been completely fair.

Thus it is not enough just to open the gates of opportunity. All our citizens must have the ability to walk through those gates.

This is the next and the more profound stage of the battle for civil rights. We seek not just freedom but opportunity. We seek not just legal equity but human ability, not just equality as a right and a theory but equality as a fact and equality as a result.

For the task is to give 20 million Negroes the same chance as every other American to learn and grow, to work and share in society, to develop their abilities—physical, mental and spiritual, and to pursue their individual happiness.

To this end equal opportunity is essential, but not enough. Men and women of all races are born with the same range of abilities. But ability is not just the product of birth. Ability is stretched or stunted by the family that you live with, and the neighborhood you live in—by the school you go to and the poverty or the richness of your surroundings. It is the product of a hundred unseen forces playing upon the little infant, the child, and finally the man. . . .

For the great majority of Negro Americans—the poor, the unemployed, the uprooted, and the dispossessed—there is a much grimmer story. They still, as we meet here tonight, are another nation. Despite the court orders and the laws, despite the legislative victories and the speeches, for them the walls are rising and the gulf is widening. . . .

We are not completely sure why this is. We know the causes are complex and subtle. But we do know the two broad basic reasons. And we do know that we have to act.

First, Negroes are trapped—as many whites are trapped—in inherited, gateless poverty. They lack training and skills. They are shut in, in slums, without decent medical care. Private and public poverty combine to cripple their capacities.

We are trying to attack these evils through our poverty program, through our education program, through our medical care and our other health programs, and a dozen more of the Great Society programs that are aimed at the root causes of this poverty.

We will increase, and we will accelerate, and we will broaden this attack in years to come until this most enduring of foes finally yields to our unyielding will.

But there is a second cause—much more difficult to explain, more deeply grounded, more desperate in its force. It is the devastating heritage of long years of slavery; and a century of oppression, hatred, and injustice.

For Negro poverty is not white poverty. Many of its causes and many of its cures are the same. But there are differences—deep, corrosive, obstinate differences—radiating painful roots into the community, and into the family, and the nature of the individual.

These differences are not racial differences. They are solely and simply the consequence of ancient brutality, past injustice, and present prejudice. They are anguishing to observe. For the Negro they are a constant reminder of oppression. For the white they are a constant reminder of guilt. But they must be faced and they must be dealt with and they must be overcome, if we are ever to reach the time when the only difference between Negroes and whites is the color of their skin. . . .

Men are shaped by their world. When it is a world of decay, ringed by an invisible wall, when escape is arduous and uncertain, and the saving pressures of a more hopeful society are unknown, it can cripple the youth and it can desolate the men.

There is also the burden that a dark skin can add to the search for a productive place in our society. Unemployment strikes most swiftly and broadly at the Negro, and this burden erodes hope. Blighted hope breeds despair. Despair brings indifferences to the learning which offers a way out. And despair, coupled with indifferences, is often the source of destructive rebellion against the fabric of society.

There is also the lacerating hurt of early collision with white hatred or prejudice, distaste or condescension. Other groups have felt similar intolerance. But success and achievement could wipe it away. They do not change the color of a man's skin. I have seen this uncomprehending pain in the eyes of the little, young Mexican-American schoolchildren that I taught many years ago. But it can be overcome. But, for many, the wounds are always open.

Perhaps most important—its influence radiating to every part of life—is the breakdown of the Negro family structure. For this, most of all, white America must accept responsibility. It flows from centuries of oppression and persecution of the Negro man. It flows from the long years of degradation and discrimination, which have attacked his dignity and assaulted his ability to produce for his family. . . .

There is no single easy answer to all of these problems.

Jobs are part of the answer. They bring the income which permits a man to provide for his family.

Decent homes in decent surroundings and a chance to learn—an equal chance to learn—are part of the answer.

Welfare and social programs better designed to hold families together are part of the answer.

Care for the sick is part of the answer.

An understanding heart by all Americans is another big part of the answer. . . . American justice is a very special thing. For, from the first, this has been a land of towering expectations. It was to be a nation where each man could be ruled by the common consent of all—enshrined in law, given life by institutions, guided by men themselves subject to its rule. And all—all of every station and origin—would be touched equally in obligation and in liberty.

Beyond the law lay the land. It was a rich land, glowing with more abundant promise than man had ever seen. Here, unlike any place yet known, all were to share the harvest.

And beyond this was the dignity of man. Each could become whatever his qualities of mind and spirit would permit—to strive, to seek, and, if he could, to find his happiness.

This is American justice. We have pursued it faithfully to the edge of our imperfections, and we have failed to find it for the American Negro.

So, it is the glorious opportunity of this generation to end the one huge wrong of the American Nation and, in so doing, to find America for ourselves, with the same immense thrill of discovery which gripped those who first began to realize that here, at last, was a home for freedom. . . .

Discussion Questions

1. Do you agree with Johnson that ability isn't enough to bring equal opportunity to American blacks? If so, what policy do you suggest to ensure equal opportunity for people of all races?
2. Organize a debate between Johnson and Levin (later in this chapter) on the causes and solutions to racism. Discuss the shortcomings and merits of each position.
3. If Johnson were still president, how would he most likely approach the issue of profiling and detention of Muslims and Arab Americans as possible terrorists? Support your answer.
4. Discuss how Johnson would most likely respond to both the *Bakke* and the University of Michigan Law School Supreme Court cases.

JORGE GARCIA

The Heart of Racism

Jorge Garcia is a political commentator and a professor of philosophy at Boston College. Garcia argues that the heart of racism is ill will and disregard for members of certain groups. Garcia argues that his virtue-based definition of racism is more consistent with common usage than other definitions, and is better at accounting for inter-racial hostility.

Critical Reading Questions

1. How does Garcia define racism? What is the essence of racism?
2. How does Garcia respond to the claim that because there are no races, there cannot be racism?
3. What is "higher order discrimination"?
4. Why does Garcia believe that racism is rooted in the heart rather than in action?
5. According to Garcia, why is racism always immoral?
6. What is the relationship between individual racism and institutional racism? Which type does Garcia claim is of greater moral importance and why?
7. According to Garcia, can a person be a racist without ever acting on racist attitudes in a way that harms members of another race?
8. What are some examples of unconscious racism?
9. How does Garcia's concept of racism apply to hate speech? What is the difference between hate speech and "racially offensive speech"?
10. On what grounds does Garcia find the gentle but paternal aristocracy of the antebellum period racist?
11. What is the "Kiplingesque" view? Why is the notion of the "white man's burden" racist?
12. Does Garcia think it is wrong for a white woman to avoid black teenagers on the street? How does his answer differ from that of Judith Lichtenberg?
13. Why does Garcia find it necessary to restrict the definition of institutional racism?
14. Under what circumstance does Garcia find preferential hiring based on race morally justified?
15. According to Garcia, in what ways do individual and institutional racism reinforce each other?

A VOLITIONAL CONCEPTION OF RACISM

Kwame Anthony Appiah rightly complains that, although people frequently voice their abhorrence of racism, "rarely does anyone stop to say what it is, or what is wrong with it" (Appiah, 1990: 3). This way of stating the program of inquiry we need is promising, because, although racism is not essentially "a moral doctrine," *pace* Appiah, it is always a moral evil (Appiah, 1990: 13). No account of what racism is can be adequate unless it at the

same time makes clear what is wrong with it. How should we conceive racism, then, if we follow Appiah's advice "to take our ordinary ways of thinking about race and racism and point up some of their presuppositions"? (Appiah, 1990: 4). My proposal is that we conceive of racism as fundamentally a vicious kind of racially based disregard for the welfare of certain people. In its central and most vicious form, it is a hatred, ill-will, directed against a person or persons on account of their assigned race. In a derivative form, one is a racist when one either does not care at all or does not care enough (i.e., as much as morality requires) or does not care in the right ways about people assigned to a certain racial group, where this disregard is based

"The Heart of Racism," *Journal of Social Philosophy* 27, no. 1 (1996): 5–45. Some notes have been omitted.

on racial classification. Racism, then, is something that essentially involves not our beliefs and their rationality or irrationality, but our wants, intentions, likes, and dislikes and their distance from the moral virtues. Such a view helps explain racism's conceptual ties to various forms of *hatred* and contempt. . . .

It might be objected that there can be no such thing as racism because, as many now affirm, "there are no races." This objection fails. First, that "race" is partially a social construction does not entail that there are no races. . . . Second, as many racial anti-realists concede, even if it were true that race is unreal, what we call racism could still be real (Appiah, 1992: p. 45). What my account of racism requires is not that there be races, but that people make distinctions in their hearts, whether consciously or not, on the basis of their (or others') racial classifications. That implies nothing about the truth of those classifications. . . .

. . . Surely, a person can disapprove of a culture or a family of cultures without being racist. However, cultural criticism can be a mask for a deeper (even unconscious) dislike that is defined by racial classifications. If the person transfers her disapproval of the group's culture to contempt or disregard for those designated as the group's members, then she is already doing something morally vicious. When she assigns all the groups disliked to the same racial classification, then we are entitled to suspect racism, because we have good grounds to suspect that her disavowals of underlying racial classifications are false. If S hates the cultures of various Black groups for having a certain feature, but does not extend that disapproval to other cultures with similar features, then that strongly indicates racism.

Even if she is more consistent, there may still be racism, but of a different sort. Adrian Piper [1990] suggests that, in the phenomenon she calls "higher order discrimination," a person may claim to dislike members of a group because she thinks they have a certain feature, but really disapprove of the feature because she associates it with the despised group. This "higher order discrimination" would, of course, still count as racist in my

account because the subject's distaste for the cultural element derives from and is morally infected by race-based disregard.

We should also consider an additional possibility. A person may falsely attribute an undesirable feature to people she assigns to a racial group because of her disregard for those in the group. This will often take the forms of exaggeration, seeing another in the worst light, and withholding from someone the benefit of the doubt. So, an anti-Semite may interpret a Jew's reasonable frugality as greed; a White racist may see indolence in a Black person's legitimate resistance to unfair expectations of her, and so on.

Thinking of racism as thus rooted in the heart fits common sense and ordinary usage in a number of ways. It is instructive that contemptuous, White racists have sometimes called certain of their enemies "Nigger-lovers." When we seek to uncover the implied contrast-term for this epithet, it surely suggests that enemies of those who "love" Black people, as manifested in their efforts to combat segregation, and so forth, are those who hate Black people or who have little or no human feelings toward us at all. This is surely borne out by the behavior and rhetoric of paradigmatic White racists.

This account makes racism similar to other familiar forms of intergroup animosity. Activists in favor of Israel and of what they perceive as Jewish interests sometimes call anti-Semites "Jew-haters." . . . What is important for us is to note that *hostility* toward Jews is the heart of anti-Semitism.

Racism is always immoral. . . . Its immorality stems from its being opposed to the virtues of benevolence and justice. Racism is a form of morally insufficient (i.e., vicious) concern or respect for some others. It infects actions in which one (a) tries to injure people assigned to a racial group because of their XXXXX, or (b) objectionably fails to take care *not* to injure them (where the agent accepts harm to R1s because she disregards the interests and needs of R1s because they are R1s). We can also allow that an action is racist in a derivative and weaker sense when it is less directly connected to racist disregard, for example, when someone (c) does something that (regardless of its intended, probable, or actual effects) stems in significant part from a belief or apprehension about other people, that one has (in significant part) because of one's disaffection toward them because of (what one thinks to be their) race. Racism, thus, will often offend against justice, not just against benevolence, because one sort of injury to another is withholding from her the respect she is owed and the deference and trust that properly express that respect. Certain forms of paternalism, while benevolent in some of their goals, may be vicious in the means employed. The paternalist may deliberately choose to deprive another of some goods, such as those of (licit) freedom and (limited) self-determination in order to obtain other goods for her. Here, as elsewhere, the good end need not justify the unjust means. Extreme paternalism constitutes an instrumentally malevolent benevolence: one harms A to help her. . . .

My account of racism suggests a new understanding of racist behavior and of its immorality. This view allows for the existence of both individual racism and institutional racism. Moreover, it makes clear the connection between the two, and enables us better to understand racism's nature and limits. . . .

Some say that institutional racism is what is of central importance; individual racism, then, matters only inasmuch as it perpetuates institutional racism. I think that claim reverses the order of moral importance, and I shall maintain that the individual level has more explanatory importance.

At the individual level, it is in desires, wishes, intentions, and the like that racism fundamentally lies, not in actions or beliefs. Actions and beliefs are racist by virtue of their *coming from* racism in the desires, wishes, and intentions of individuals, not by virtue of their *leading* to these or other undesirable effects. . . .

How is institutional racism connected to racism within the individual? Let us contrast two pictures. On the first, institutional racism is of prime moral and explanatory importance. Individual racism, then, matters (and, perhaps, occurs) only insofar as it contributes to the institutional racism which subjugates a racial group. On the second, opposed view, racism within individual persons is of prime moral and explanatory import, and institutional racism occurs and matters because racist attitudes (desires, aims, hopes, fears, plans) infect the reasoning, decision-making, and action of individuals not only in their private behavior, but also when they make and execute the policies of those institutions in which they operate. I take the second view. Institutional racism, in the central sense of the term, occurs when institutional behavior stems from (a) or (b) above or, in an extended sense, when it stems from (c). Obvious examples would be the infamous Jim Crow laws that originated in the former Confederacy after Reconstruction. Personal racism exists when and insofar as a person is racist in her desires, plans, aims, etc., most notably when this racism informs her conduct. In the same way, institutional racism exists when and insofar as an institution is racist in the aims, plans, etc., that people give it, especially when their racism informs its behavior. Institutional racism begins when racism extends from the hearts of individual people to become institutionalized. What matters is that racist attitudes contaminate the operation of the institution. . . .

Not only is individual racism of greater explanatory import, I think it is also more important morally. Those of us who see morality primarily as a matter of suitability responding to other people and to the opportunities they present for us to pursue value will understand racism as an offense against the virtues of benevolence and justice in that it is an undue restriction on the respect and goodwill owed people. (Ourselves as well as others; racism, we must remember, can take the form of self-hate.) Indeed, as follows from what I have elsewhere argued, it is hard to render coherent the view that racist hate is bad mainly for its bad effects. The sense in which an action's effects are bad is that they are undesirable. But that is to say that these effects are evil things to want and thus things the desire for which is evil, vicious. Thus, any claim that racial disadvantage is a bad thing presupposes a more basic claim that race-hatred is vicious. . . .

IMPLICATIONS AND ADVANTAGES

There are some noteworthy implications and advantages of the proposed way of conceiving of racism.

First it suggests that prejudice, in its strict sense of "pre-judgment," is not essential to racism, and that some racial prejudice may not be racist, strictly speaking. . . .

A person may hold prejudices about people assigned to a race without herself being racist and without it being racist of her to hold those prejudices. The beliefs themselves can be called "racist" in an extended sense because they are characteristically racist. However, just as one may make a wise move without acting wisely (as when one makes a sound investment for stupid reasons), so one may hold a racist belief without holding it for racist reasons. One holds such a belief for racist reasons when it is duly connected to racial disregard: when it is held in order to rationalize that disaffection or when contempt inclines one to attribute undesirable features to people assigned to a racial group. One whose racist beliefs have no such connection to any racial disregard in her heart does not hold them in a racist way and if she has no such disregard, she is not herself a racist, irrespective of her prejudices.

Second, when racism is so conceived, the person with racist feelings, desires, hopes, fears, and dispositions is racist even if she never acts on these attitudes in such a way as to harm people designated as members of the hated race. (This is not true when racism is conceived as consisting in a system of social oppression.) It is important to know that racism can exist in (and even pervade) societies in which there is no systematic oppression, if only because the attempts to oppress fail. Even those who think racism important primarily because of its effects should find this possibility of inactive racism worrisome for, so long as this latent racism persists, there is constant threat of oppressive behavior.

Third, on this view, race-based preference (favoritism) need not be racist. *Preferential* treatment in affirmative action, while race-based, is not normally based on any racial disregard. This is a crucial difference between James Meredith's complaint against the University of Mississippi and Allan Bakke's complaint against the University of California at Davis Medical School. . . . Appiah says that what he calls "Extrinsic racism has usually been the basis [1] for treating people worse than we otherwise might, [2] for giving them less than their humanity entitles them to" (Appiah, 1992: 18). What is important to note here is that (1) and (2) are not at all morally equivalent. Giving someone less than her humanity entitles her to is morally wrong. To give someone less than we could give her, and even to give her less than we would if she (or we, or things) were different is to treat her "worse [in the sense of 'less well'] than we otherwise might." However, the latter is not normally morally objectionable. Of course, we may not deny people even gratuitous favors out of hatred or contempt, whether or not race-based, but that does not entail that we may not licitly choose to bestow favors instead on those to whom we feel more warmly. . . .

As racist discrimination need not always be conscious, so it need not always be intended to harm. Some of what is called "environmental racism," especially the location of waste dumps so as disproportionally to burden Black people, is normally not intended to harm anyone at all. Nevertheless, it is racist if, for example, the dumpers regard it as less important if it is "only," say, Black people who suffer. However, it will usually be the case that intentional discrimination based on racist attitudes will be more objectionable morally, and harder to justify, than is unintentional, unconscious racist discrimination. Rac*ial* discrimination is not always rac*ist* discrimination. The latter is always immoral, because racism is inherently vicious and it corrupts any differentiation that it infects. The former—racial discrimination—is not inherently immoral. Its moral status will depend on the usual factors—intent, knowledge, motive, and so on—to which we turn to determine what is vicious.

This understanding of racism also offers a new perspective on the controversy over efforts to restrict racist "hate speech." Unlike racially *offensive* speech, which is defined by its (actual or probable) effects, racist *hate* speech is defined by its origins, i.e., by whether it expresses (and is thus an act of) racially directed hate. So we cannot classify a remark as racist hate speech simply on the basis of *what* was said, we need to look to *why* the speaker said it. Speech laden with racial slurs and epithets is presumptively hateful, of course, but merely voicing an opinion that members of R1 are inferior (in some germane way) will count as racist (in any of the term's chief senses, at least) only if, for example, it expresses an opinion held from the operation of some predisposition to believe bad things about R1s, which predisposition itself stems in part from racial disregard. This understanding of racist hate speech should allay the fears of those who think that racial oversensitivity and the fear of offending the oversensitive will stifle the discussion of delicate and important matters beneath a blanket of what is called "political correctness." Racist hate speech is defined by its motive forces and, given a fair presumption of innocence, it will be difficult to give convincing evidence of ugly motive behind controversial opinions whose statement is free of racial insults.

SOME DIFFICULTIES

It may seem that my view fails to meet the test of accommodating clear cases of racism from history. Consider some members of the southern White aristocracy in the antebellum or Jim Crow periods of American history—people who would never permit racial epithets to escape their lips, and who were solicitous and even protective of those they considered "their Negroes" (especially Black servants and their kin), but who not only acquiesced in, but actively and strongly supported the social system of racial separatism, hierarchy, and oppression. These people strongly opposed Black equality in the social, economic, and political realms, but they appear to have been free of any vehement racial hatred. It appears that we should call such people racist. The question is: Does the account offered here allow them to be so classified?

This presents a nice difficulty, I think, and one it will be illuminating to grapple with. There is, plainly, a kind of hatred that consists in opposition to a person's (or group's) welfare.... [T]he attitude in question [does not have] to be especially negative or passionate. Nor need it be notably ill-mannered or crude in its expression. What is essential is that it consists in either opposition to the well-being of people classified as members of the targeted racial group or in a racially based callousness to the needs and interests of such people.

This, I think, gives us what we need in order to see part of what makes our patricians racists, for all their well-bred dispassion and good manners. They stand against the advancement of Black people (as a group, even if they make an exception for "their Negroes"). They are averse to it as such, not merely doing things that have the *side* effect of setting back the interests of Black people. Rather, they *mean* to retard those interests, to keep Black people "in their place" relative to White people....

It may not be clear how the understanding of racism offered here accommodates the common-sense view that the attitudes, rhetoric, behavior, and representatives of the mindset we might characterize as the "white man's burden" view count as racist. One who holds such a Kiplingesque view (let's call her K) thinks non-Whites ignorant, backward, undisciplined, and generally in need of a tough dose of European "civilizing" in important aspects of their lives. This training in civilization may sometimes be harsh, but it is supposed to be for the good of the "primitive" people....

...An important part of respect is recognizing the other as a human like oneself, including treating her like one. There can be extremes of condescension so inordinate they constitute degradation. In such cases, a subject goes beyond more familiar forms of paternalism to demean the other, treating her as utterly irresponsible. Plainly, those who take it upon themselves to conscript mature, responsible, healthy, socialized (and innocent) adults into a regimen of education designed to strip them of all authority over their own lives and make them into "civilized" folk condescend in just this way. This abusive paternalism borders on contempt and it can violate the rights of the subjugated people by denying them the respect and deference to which their status entitles them. By willfully depriving the oppressed people of the goods of freedom even as part of an ultimately well-meant project of "improving" them, the colonizers act with the kind of instrumentally malevolent benevolence we discussed above. The colonizers stunt and maim in order to help, and therein plainly will certain evils to the victims they think of as beneficiaries. Thus, their conduct counts as a kind of malevolence insofar as we take the term literally to mean willing evils.

Of course, the Kiplinesque agent will not think of herself as depriving responsible, socialized people of their rights over their lives; she does not see them that way and thinks them too immature to have such rights. However, we need to ask why she regards Third World peoples as she does. Here, I suspect, the answer is likely to be that her view of them is influenced, quite possibly without her being conscious of it, by her interest in maintaining the social and economic advantages of having her group wield control over its subjects. If so, her beliefs are relevantly motivated and affected by (instrumental) ill-will, her desire to gain by harming others. When this is so, then her beliefs are racist not just in the weak sense that their content is the sort that characteristically is tied to racial disaffection, but in the stronger and morally more important sense that her own acceptance of these beliefs is partially motivated by racial disaffection. She is *being* racist in thinking as she does. I conclude that the account of racism offered here can allow that, and help explain why, many people who hold the "white man's burden" mentality are racist. . . .

SOME CASES . . .

What should we say of some different cases . . . in which a person who herself harbors no racial disregard or disrespect, nonetheless accedes to others' racism by refusing to hire, promote, or serve those assigned to a targeted racial group? Here the agent's action is infected, poisoned by racial hatred. It has such hate in its motivational structure, and that is the usual hallmark of racist behavior. I think what crucially distinguishes this agent's behavior is that it is not *the agent's own* hatred. I suggest that in addition to the two forms of racial disaffection we have already identified—the core concept of racial malevolence and the derivative concept of a race-based insufficiency of goodwill—we can allow that an action may be called racist in an extended sense of the term when it is poisoned by racism, even where the racial disaffection that corrupts it does not lie in the agent's own heart but in those to whom the agent accedes. Thus, the agent in our example, while not herself a racist, performs an action that is in an important way infected by other people's racism. I doubt we should simply say without qualification that her own action is racist, but it is surely morally objectionable. . . . Consider a person who denies service, or promotion, or admission, or employment to people assigned to group G1 in order to appease people with a racial disaffection directed against them. Now suppose further that she herself cooperates in the latter's malevolence by *trying* to harm those classified as G1s in order to placate their enemies. . . . When the agent goes that far, she has internalized racist malice into her own intentions, and thus corrupted her actions in a more grievous way than has the person who merely goes along with neighboring racists in her external actions. This is so whether or not her *feelings* toward people assigned to G1 are hostile.

What should we say of a case Judith Lichtenberg raises, in which, acting from racial fear, a White person crosses the street to avoid Black pedestrians she perceives as possible dangers? Lichtenberg thinks it acceptable for the fearful (and prejudiced?) White person to cross the street in order to avoid proximity with the Black teenagers who approach her at night ([1992] p. 4). She sensibly suggests that this is not racist if the person would respond in the same way with White teenagers. "She might well do the same if the teenagers were white. In that case her behavior does not constitute racial discrimination." . . .

Lichtenberg maintains that the Black teenagers suffer "a minimal slight—if it's even noticed." She even suggests that the White person might spare their feelings "by a display of ulterior motivation, like [pretending to] inspect the rosebushes on the other side" of the street in order to make it look as if it were her admiration for the flowers, and not her fear of Black people, that motivated her to cross the street. The latter pretense is, in my judgment, insulting and unlikely to succeed. More important, this appears to be a guilty response, as if the person is trying to cover up something she knows is wrong. I think that fact should cause Lichtenberg and her imagined agent to reconsider the claim that the action is unobjectionable. It is also quite wrong-headed to think that the harm of insult is entirely a matter of whether a person has hurt feelings. . . .

According to Lichtenberg, it is acceptable for the White woman to try to avoid the Black teenager on the street, but much harder to justify her racially discriminating when he applies for a job. It will be difficult to maintain this position, however. How is this woman—so terrified of contact with young Black males that she will not walk on the same side of the street with them—simply to turn off this uneasiness when the time comes for her to decide whether to offer a job to the Black male? Suppose that the job is to help out in her family's grocery store, and that this is likely to mean that the woman and the teenager will be alone in the store some evenings? Lichtenberg's advice that the woman indulge her prejudice in her private life but rigorously exclude it from their official conduct, seems unstable. . . . It is the worst of liberal bad faith, however, for this woman to practice her tolerance in official decision-making, but only on the condition that it is other people who will have to bear the burden of adjusting to the pluralistic environment those decisions create and of making that environment work. (Compare the liberal politician who boldly integrates the public schools while taking care to "protect" her own kids in all-White private schools.)

Lichtenberg assumes that private discrimination is less serious morally, but this is doubtful.

The heart is where racism, like all immorality, begins and dwells. . . .

Our view of institutional racism is both narrower and wider than some others that have been offered. To see how it is narrower, that is, less inclusive, let us consider the practice of "word-of-mouth" job-recruitment, in which people assigned to a privileged racial group, who tend to socialize only with one another, distribute special access to employment benefits to social acquaintances similarly assigned. Some deem this institutional racism, because of its adverse impact on those considered members of the disadvantaged group. . . .

Consider . . . the so-called "old boy network." Person F, upon hearing of an opening at his place of employment, tells the people he thinks of (who are all White males like himself) about the job and recommends one of them (Person G) to the boss, who hires him. Ignoring the exaggeration in calling anything so informal an "institution," let us explore whether this "institution" of the "old boy network" is racist. Is F (or F's behavior) racist? Is G (or G's behavior) racist? Some are ready to offer affirmative answers. What should we say? First, G cannot be racist just for receiving the job; that's not sufficiently active. What about G's act of *accepting* the job? That can be racist. I think, however, that it is racist only in the exceptional circumstance where the institutions are so corrupt that G should have nothing to do with them. Second, F may be racist insofar as his mental process skips over some possible candidates simply because the stereotypes he uses (perhaps to mask his racial disaffection from himself and others) keep him from thinking of them as possible job candidates. Third, one needs some further reason not yet given to label racist the practice of the "old boy network." It may work "systematically" to the detriment of Black people. That, however, merely shows that, in our society, with our history of racism, Black people can be disadvantaged by many things other than race-based factors. . . . What is important to note is that it is misleading to call all these things racist, because that terminology fails to differentiate the very different ways in which and reasons for which they disadvantage people.

This classification and broad use of the term, then, fails adequately to inform us and, of more practical importance, it fails to direct our attention (and efforts) to the source of the difficulty. It doesn't identify for us *how* things are going wrong and thus *what* needs to be changed.

Some accounts of institutional racism threaten to be excessively broad in other ways. Some implicitly restrict institutional racism to operations *within* a society—they see it as one group maintaining its social control over the other. This is too narrow, since it would exclude, for example, what seem to be some clear cases of institutional racism, such as discrimination in immigration and in foreign assistance policies. However, if this restriction to intra-group behavior is simply removed from these accounts, then they will have to count as instances of institutional racism some actions which do not properly fall within the class. Suppose, for example, the government of a hostile planet, free of any bigotry toward any Earthling racial group, but unenamored of all Earthlings, launches a missile to destroy the Earth. Suppose it lands in Africa. This institutional (governmental) action has a disproportionly adverse impact on Black people, but it is silly to describe it as racist. . . .

We can also profitably turn our account to an interesting case Skillen offers. He writes:

> Suppose Dr. Smythe-Browne's surgery has been ticking over happily for years until it is realized that few of the many local Asians visit him. It turns out that they travel some distance to Dr. Patel's surgery. Dr. Smythe-Browne and his staff are upset. Then they realize that, stupidly, he has never taken the trouble to make himself understood by or to understand the Asians in his area. His surgery practices have had the effect of excluding or at least discouraging Asians. Newly aware, he sets out to fix the situation. . . .
>
> The example shows the possibility of a certain sort of "racism" that, if we must attribute blame, is a function of a lack of thought (energy, resources, etc.). If that lack of thought is itself to be described as "discriminatory" it would need to be shown Dr. Smythe-Browne showed no such lack of attention when one of the local streets

became gentrified. . . . In such cases, it is not racial sets as such that are the focus of attention, but race as culturally "inscribed." In other words, one is concerned with people in respect of how they identify themselves and are identified by others (for example, intimidating institutions or outright racists). (Skillen [1993], p. 81)

Despite what Skillen implies, that an institution intimidates some racial groups ("sets") does not make it racist. . . . Moreover, that Smythe-Browne was thoughtless about what might be needed to attract Asians in no way shows his conduct was racist, not even if he was more sensitive and interested in how to attract "yuppies" brought close by local gentrification. Insensitivity to certain race-related differences is not racist, even if one is sensitive to class-related differences or to differences associated with other racial differences. Smythe-Browne does not so much "discourage" Asians as fail to encourage them. Psychologically and ontologically, that is a very different matter, and those differences are likely to correlate with moral differences as well. (Failure to encourage is likely merely to be at worst an offense of *non*benevolence rather of *male*volence.) *Perhaps* the Asians were "invisible" to Smythe-Browne in a way that he is culpable for. To show this, however, more would need to be said about why he did not notice them, their absence, and their special interests. Is it that he cares so little about Asians and their well-being? If there is nothing like this involved, then there is no racism in Smythe-Browne's professional behavior, I say. And if there is something like this involved, then Smythe-Browne's conduct is not purely "'consequentially' . . . discriminatory." It is corrupted by its motivation in racial disaffection. . . .

Skillen . . . adds further detail to his case, asking us to suppose that Dr. Smythe-Browne "decides that the only way to cope with the situation is to get an Asian doctor, preferably female, onto the staff. He advertises the job and, finding a good person of the sort he needs, she joins the practice, whereas a number of, in other respects at least, equally good applicants (white, male for the most part) do not. Is this 'racism'?" Skillen thinks not, and I think he argues his point well. . . . "Dr. Smythe-Browne's criteria remain medical. His selection is legitimate insofar as we accept that medicine is a human and communicative 'art' in respect of which socially significant variables are relevant. In that sense it is simply not the case that bypassed candidates with better degree results were necessarily 'better candidates" (Skillen [1993], p. 82).

With this understanding and assessment, I agree wholeheartedly. Dr. Smythe-Browne's hiring preference here seems to me to exemplify the sort of race-based distinction that is in its nature and its morality quite different from racist discrimination. . . .

Skillen is correct to observe that oftentimes institutions shape individual intentions and actions. Institutional racism will often exist in reciprocal relation to individual racism. The racism of some individual (or individuals) first infects the institution, and the institution's resultant racism then reinforces racism in that individual or breeds it in others. Once individual racism exists, institutional racism can be a powerful instrument of its perpetuation. This reciprocity of causal influence, however, should not blind us to the question of origins. Individual racism can come into the world without depending on some prior institutionalization. . . . The converse is not true. Institutional racism can reinforce and perpetuate individual racism. Unless an institution is corrupted (in its ends, means, priorities, or assumptions) by a prior and independent racism in some individual's heart, however, institutional racism can never come to exist. . . .

CONCLUSION

These reflections suggest that an improved understanding of racism and its immorality calls for a comprehensive rethinking of racial discrimination, of the preferential treatment programs sometimes disparaged as "reverse discrimination," and of institutional conduct as well. They also indicate the direction such a rethinking should take, and its dependence on the virtues and other concepts from moral psychology. That may require a significant change in the way social philosophers have recently treated these and related topics.

REFERENCES

Appiah, Anthony. "Racisms." In *Anatomy of Racism,* pp. 3–17. Ed. D. T. Goldberg. Minneapolis: University of Minnesota Press, 1990.

———. *In My Father's House: Africa in the Philosophy of Culture.* Oxford: Oxford University Press, 1992.

Lichtenberg, Judith. "Racism in the Head, Racism in the World." *Philosophy and Public Policy* (Newsletter of the Institute for Philosophy and Public Policy, University of Maryland), Vol. 12 (1992).

Piper, Adrian M. "Higher Order Discrimination." In *Identity, Character, & Morality,* pp. 285–309. Ed. Owen Flanagan and Amelie Rorty. Cambridge: MIT Press, 1990.

Skillen, Anthony. "Racism: Flew's Three Concepts of Racism." *Journal of Applied Philosophy.* vol. 10 (1993): 73–89.

Discussion Questions

1. According to Garcia's definition, are white people who take advantage of better schools in affluent white neighborhoods racist by definition? Are people who oppose state or federal (instead of local) funding for schools racists? Support your answers.

2. Discuss Garcia's claim that people who act in ways that retard the interests of blacks, even though they claim to feel no ill will toward them, are racist.

3. Discuss ways in which your actions may be infected by racism even though you yourself may bear no ill will or racial hatred. Use specific examples to illustrate your answer.

4. Discuss the American government's goal of "nation-building" in Iraq in light of Garcia's discussion of the "white man's burden" and the Kiplingesque worldview.
5. Compare and contrast Lichtenberg's and Garcia's analyses of the white woman crossing the street to avoid the black teenager. Which person do you think provides the better analysis? Support your answer.

BERNARD R. BOXILL

The Color-Blind Principle

Bernard Boxill is a philosophy professor at the University of North Carolina in Chapel Hill. Boxill rejects the assumption that law and morality should always be color-blind. Whereas some color-conscious policies, such as Jim Crow laws, are clearly unjust, there are other times, he argues, when it is morally justified to base public policy on color-conscious principles.

Critical Reading Questions

1. Who was Homer Plessy and why was he arrested in 1892? What was the U.S. Supreme Court ruling in the *Plessy* case?
2. What did Justice Harlan mean when he said, "Our Constitution is color-blind"?
3. What are the main arguments used by advocates of the color-blind principle?
4. What is the difference between the racist's and the black nationalist's views on the importance of color?
5. What is the "responsibility criterion" and why does Boxill claim that this can be a false and confusing criterion for creating egalitarian public policies?
6. Why does racial discrimination subordinate the best interests of minority communities?
7. According to Boxill, why are color-conscious principles no less discriminatory than the principles of meritocracy?
8. On what grounds does Boxill argue that "adopting a color-blind principle entails adopting a talent-blind principle"?
9. How does Boxill respond to the objection that affirmative action leads to reverse discrimination against whites?

"The Color-Blind Principle," in *Blacks and Social Justice* (Totowa, N.J.: Rowman & Allanheld, 1984), 9–18. Some notes have been omitted.

PLESSY

In 1892, Homer Plessy, an octoroon, was arrested in Louisiana for taking a seat in a train car reserved for whites. He was testing a state law which required the "white and colored races" to ride in "equal but separate" accommodations, and his case eventually reached the Supreme Court.

Part of Plessy's defense, though it must be considered mainly a snare for the opposition, was that he was "seven-eighths Caucasian and one-eighth African blood," and that the "mixture of colored blood was not discernible in him." The bulwark of his argument was, however, that he was "entitled to every right, privilege and immunity secured to citizens of the white race," and that the law violated the Fourteenth Amendment's prohibition against unequal protection of the laws. Cannily, the court refused the snare. Perhaps it feared—and with reason—that the ancestry of too many white Louisianans held dark secrets. But it attacked boldly enough Plessy's main argument that the Louisiana law was unconstitutional. That argument, Justice Henry Billings Brown wrote for the majority, was unsound. "Its underlying fallacy," he averred, was its "assumption that the enforced separation of the two races stamps the colored race with a badge of inferiority." "If this be so," Brown concluded, "it is not by reason of anything found in the act, but solely because the colored race chooses to put that construction upon it."

Only one judge dissented from the court majority—Justice John Marshall Harlan. It was the occasion on which he pronounced his famous maxim: "Our Constitution is color-blind." In opposition to Justice Brown, Justice Harlan found that the "separation of citizens on the basis of race [was a] badge of servitude . . . wholly inconsistent [with] equality before the law."

Plessy's is the kind of case which makes the color-blind principle seem indubitably right as a basis for action and policy, and its contemporary opponents appear unprincipled, motivated by expediency, and opportunistic. This impression is only strengthened by a reading of Justice Brown's tortuously preposterous defense of the "equal but separate" doctrine. It should make every advocate of color-conscious policy wary of the power of arguments of expediency to beguile moral sense and subvert logic. Yet I argue that color-conscious policy can still be justified. The belief that it cannot is the result of a mistaken generalization from *Plessy.* There is no warrant for the idea that the color-blind principle should hold in some general and absolute way.

"I DIDN'T NOTICE" LIBERALS

In his book *Second Wind*, Bill Russell recalls how amazed he used to be by the behavior of what he called "I didn't notice" liberals. These were individuals who claimed not to notice people's color. If they mentioned someone Russell could not place, and Russell asked whether she was black or white, they would answer, "I didn't notice." "Sweet and innocent," Russell recalls, "sometimes a little proud." Now, the kind of color-blindness the "I didn't notice" liberals claim to have may be a worthy ideal . . . but it is absolutely different from the color-blind principle which functions as a basis for policy. . . .

COLOR-BLIND AND COLOR-CONSCIOUS POLICIES

The essential thing about a color-conscious policy is that it is designed to treat people differently because of their race. But there are many different kinds of color-conscious policies. Some, for example the Jim Crow policies now in the main abolished, aim to subordinate blacks, while others, such as busing and preferential treatment, aim at elevating blacks.

Some color-conscious policies explicitly state that persons should be treated differently because of their race, for example the segregation laws at issue in *Plessy;* others make no mention of race, but are still designed so that blacks and whites are treated differently, for example the "grandfather clauses" in voting laws that many states adopted at the turn of the century. . . .

Advocates of the belief that the law should be color-blind often argue that this would the best means to an ideal state in which people are color-blind. They appeal to the notion that, only if people notice each other's color can they discriminate on the basis of color and, with considerable plausibility, they argue that color-conscious laws and policies can only heighten people's awareness of each other's color, and exacerbate racial conflict. They maintain that only if the law, with all its weight and influence, sets the example of color-blindness, can there be a realistic hope that people will see through the superficial distinctions of color and become themselves color-blind.

But this argument is not the main thesis of the advocates of legal color-blindness. Generally, they eschew it because of its dependency on the empirical. Their favorite argument, one that is more direct and intuitively appealing, is simply that it is wicked, unfair, and unreasonable to penalize a person for what he cannot help being. Not only does this seem undeniably true, but it can be immediately applied to the issue of race. No one can help being white or being black, and so it seems to follow that it is wicked, unfair, and unreasonable to disqualify a person from any consideration just because he is white or black. This, the advocates of color-blindness declare, is what made Jim Crow laws heinous, and it is what makes affirmative action just as heinous.

The force of this consideration is enhanced because it seems to account for one peculiar harmfulness of racial discrimination—its effect on self-respect and self-esteem. For racial discrimination makes some black people hate their color, and succeeds in doing so because color cannot be changed. Furthermore, a racially conscious society has made color seem an important part of the individual's very essence, and since color is immutable it is easily susceptible to this approach. As a result, the black individual may come, in the end, to hate even himself. . . . The black nationalist agrees with the racists' view that his color is an important and integral part of his self, but affirms, in opposition to the racists, that it has value. This strategy, which is exemplified by the slogans "black is beautiful"

and "black and proud," has the obvious advantage of stimulating pride and self-confidence. Nevertheless, it is no panacea. For one thing, it has to contend with the powerful propaganda stating that black is *not* beautiful. And there is a more subtle problem. Since the black cannot choose *not* to be black, he cannot be altogether confident that he would choose to *be* black, nor, consequently, does he really place a special value in being black. Thus, some people, black and white, have expressed the suspicion that the slogan "black is beautiful" rings hollow, like the words of the man who protests too loudly that he loves the chains he cannot escape. In this respect the black who can pass as white has an advantage over the black who cannot. For, though he cannot choose not to be black, he can choose not to be *known* to be black.

THE RESPONSIBILITY CRITERION

A final argument in favor of legal color-blindness is related to, and further develops, the point that people do not choose to be, and cannot avoid being, black or white. This links the question of color-blindness to the protean idea of individual responsibility. . . . Since this argument requires that people be treated differently in ways which profoundly affect their lives only on the basis of features for which they are responsible, I call it the responsibility criterion.

The responsibility criterion also seems to make the principle of color-blindness follow from principles of equal opportunity. Joel Feinberg takes it to be equivalent to the claim that "properties can be the grounds of just discrimination between persons only if those persons had a fair opportunity to acquire or avoid them."[1] This implies that to discriminate between persons on the basis of a feature for which they can have no responsibility is to violate the principle of fair opportunity. . . .

The responsibility criterion may seem innocuous because, though, strictly interpreted it supports the case for color-blindness, loosely interpreted it leaves open the possibility that color-conscious policies are justifiable. . . . For example, it could support the argument that black and white children should go to the same schools because being white is a reliable sign of being middle-class, and black children, who are often lower-class, learn better when their peers are middle-class. Similarly, it might support the argument that preferential hiring is compensation for the harm of being discriminated against on the basis of color, and that being black is a reliable sign of having been harmed by that discrimination.

But however loosely it is interpreted, the responsibility criterion cannot be adduced in support of all reasons behind color-conscious policies. It cannot, for example, sustain the following argument, sketched by Ronald Dworkin, for preferential admission of blacks to medical school. "If quick hands count as 'merit' in the case of a prospective surgeon this is because quick hands will enable him to serve the public better and for no other reason. If a black skin will, as a matter of regrettable fact, enable another doctor to do a different medical job better, then that black skin is by the same token 'merit' as well."[2] What is proposed here is not that a black skin is a justifiable basis of discrimination because it is a reliable sign of merit or some other factor Q. A closely related argument does make such a proposal, viz., that blacks should be preferentially admitted to medical school because being black is a reliable sign of a desire to serve the black community. But this is not the argument that Dworkin poses. In the example quoted above what he suggests is that being black is in *itself* merit, or, at least, something very like merit.

According to the responsibility criterion, we ought not to give A a job in surgery rather than B, if A is a better surgeon than B only because he was born with quicker hands. For if we do, we treat A and B "differently in ways that profoundly affect their lives because of differences for which they have no responsibility." This is the kind of result which puts egalitarianism in disrepute. It entails the idea that we might be required to let fumblers do surgery and in general give jobs and offices to incompetents, and this is surely intolerable. But, as I plan to show, true egalitarianism has no such consequences. They are the result of applying the responsibility criterion, not egalitarian principles. Indeed, egalitarianism must scout the responsibility criterion as false and confused.

Egalitarians should notice first, that, while it invalidates the merit-based theories of distribution that they oppose, it also invalidates the need-based theories of distribution they favor. For, if people are born with special talents for which they are not responsible, they are also born with special needs for which they are not responsible. . . .

At this point there may be objections. First, that the responsibility criterion was intended to govern only the distribution of income, not jobs and offices—in Feinberg's discussion, for example, this is made explicit. Second, that it does not mean that people should not be treated differently because of differences, good or bad, which they cannot help, but rather that people should not get less just because they are born without the qualities their society prizes or finds useful. . . . Qualified in these ways, the responsibility criterion becomes more plausible. It no longer implies, for example, that fumblers should be allowed to practice surgery, or that the blind be treated just like the sighted. But with these qualifications it also becomes almost irrelevant to the color-blind issue. For that issue is not only about how income should be distributed. It is also about how jobs and offices should be distributed.

Most jobs and offices are distributed to people in order to produce goods and services to a larger public. To that end, the responsibility criterion is irrelevant. For example, the purpose of admitting people to medical schools and law schools is to provide the community with good medical and legal service. It does not matter whether those who provide them are responsible for having the skills by virtue of which they provide the goods, or whether the positions they occupy are "goods" to them. No just society makes a person a surgeon just because he is responsible for his skills or because making him a surgeon will be good for him. It makes him a surgeon because he will do good surgery.

Accordingly, it may be perfectly just to discriminate between persons on the basis of distinctions they are not responsible for having. It depends on whether or not the discrimination serves a worthy end. It may be permissible for the admissions policies of professional schools to give preference to those with higher scores, even if their scores are higher than others only because they have higher native ability (for which they cannot, of course, be considered responsible), if the object is to provide the community with good professional service. And, given the same object, if for some reason a black skin, whether or not it can be defined as merit, helps a black lawyer or doctor to provide good legal or medical service to black people who would otherwise not have access to it, or avail themselves of it, it is difficult to see how there can be a principled objection to admissions policies which prefer people with black skins—though, again, they are not responsible for the quality by virtue of which they are preferred.

JUSTICE AND THE RESPONSIBILITY CRITERION

A further point needs to be made in order to vindicate color-conscious policies. The principles of justice are distributive: Justice is concerned not only with increasing the total amount of a good a society enjoys, but also with how that good should be distributed among individuals. Generally, judicial principles dictate that people who are similar in ways deemed relevant to the issue of justice, such as in needs or rights, should get equal amounts of a good, and people who are dissimilar in these regards should get unequal amounts of the good. In terms of these principles certain laws and rules must be considered unjust which would not otherwise be thought unjust. Consider, for example, a policy for admitting persons to medical school which resulted in better and better medical service for white people, but worse and worse medical service for black people. This policy would be unjust, however great the medical expertise—certainly a good—it produced, unless color is relevant to the receiving of good medical attention.

. . . The point is that if black clients tend to trust and confide more in black lawyers and doctors,

then color—functioning as merit—enables a good to be produced and distributed according to some principle of justice.

If these considerations are sound, then the responsibility criterion thoroughly misconstrues the reasons for which racial discrimination is unjust. Racial discrimination against blacks is unjust because it does not enable goods to be produced and distributed according to principles of justice. It is not unjust because black people do not choose to be black, cannot *not* be black, or are not responsible for being black. This is completely irrelevant. . . . [E]ven if black people could choose to become white, or could all easily pass as white, a law school or medical school that excluded blacks because they were black would still act unjustly. Nothing would have changed.

The arguments in support of color-blindness tend to make the harmfulness of discrimination depend on the difficulty of avoiding it. This is misleading. It diverts attention from the potential harmfulness of discrimination that *can* be avoided and brings the specious responsibility criterion into play. Suppose again, for example, that a person is denied admission to law school because he parts his hair on the right side. Though he, far more easily than the black person, can avoid being unfairly discriminated *against,* he does not thereby more easily avoid being the object, indeed, in a deeper sense, the victim, of unfair discrimination. If he parts his hair on the left side he will presumably be admitted to law school. But then he will have knowingly complied with a foolish and unjust rule and this may well make him expedient and servile. Of course, he will not be harmed to the same extent and in the same way as the victim of racial discrimination. For example, he probably will not hate himself. Unlike color, the cause of his ill-treatment is too easily changed for him to conceive of it as essential to himself. Moreover, if he chooses to keep his hair parted on the right side and thus to forego law school, he *knows* that he is not going to law school because he freely chose to place a greater value on his integrity or on his taste in hairstyles than on a legal education. He knows this because he knows he could have chosen to change his hairstyle. As I noted earlier, this opportunity for self-assertion, and thus for self-knowledge and self-confidence, is denied the black who is discriminated against on the basis of his color.

. . . [R]acial discrimination excludes its victims from opportunities on the basis of a belief that their interests are ipso facto less important than the interests of whites. The man without fingers [who wants to be a surgeon] may regret not being born differently, but he cannot resent how he is treated. Though his ambitions may be thwarted, he himself is still treated as a moral equal. There is no attack on his self-respect. Racial discrimination, however, undermines its victims' self-respect through their awareness that they are considered morally inferior. The fact that racial discrimination, or any color-conscious policy, is difficult to avoid through personal choice merely adds to its basic harmfulness if it is in the first place unjust, but is not the *reason* for its being unjust.

It remains to consider Feinberg's claim that if people are discriminated for or against on the basis of factors for which they are not responsible the equal opportunity principle is contravened. This I concede. In particular, I concede that color-conscious policies giving preference to blacks place an insurmountable obstacle in the path of whites, and since such obstacles reduce opportunities, such policies may make opportunities unequal. But this gives no advantage to the advocates of color-blind policies. For giving preference to the competent has exactly the same implications as giving preference to blacks. It, too, places obstacles in the paths of some people, this time the untalented, and just as surely makes opportunities unequal. Consequently, an advocate of color-blindness cannot consistently oppose color-conscious policies on the grounds that they contravene equal opportunity and at the same time support talent-conscious policies. Nor, finally, does my concession raise any further difficulty with the issue of equal opportunity. As I argue later, equal opportunity is not a fundamental principle of justice, but is derived from its basic principles. Often these basic principles require that opportunities be made more equal. Invariably, however, these same principles require that the process of equalization stop before a condition of perfect equality of opportunity is reached.

To conclude, adopting a color-blind principle entails adopting a talent-blind principle, and since the latter is absurd, so also is the former. Or, in other words, differences in talent, and differences in color, are, from the point of view of justice, on a par. Either, with equal propriety, can be the basis of a just discrimination. Consequently, the color-blind principle is not as simple, straightforward, or self-evident as many of its advocates seem to feel it is. Color-conscious policies can conceivably be just, just as talent-conscious policies can conceivably be—and often are—just. It depends on the circumstances.

NOTES

1. Joel Feinberg, *Social Philosophy* (Englewood Cliffs, N.J.: Prentice-Hall, 1973), 49.
2. Ronald Dworkin, "Why Bakke Has No Case," *New York Review of Books*, 10 Nov. 1977, 14.

Discussion Questions

1. Philosopher Lisa Newton is opposed to affirmative action.[29] She argues that affirmative action violates the moral ideal of equality and, consequently, entails reverse discrimination, which is unjust. Discuss how Boxill might respond to Newton.
2. Discuss what Boxill would most likely think of the current trend to create minority curriculums in colleges.
3. Alan Bloom in *The Closing of the American Mind* (1987) writes: "The black [college] student who wishes to be just a student and to avoid allegiance to the black group has to pay a terrific price, because he is judged negatively by his black peers and because his behavior is atypical in the eyes of whites."[30] Do you agree with Bloom?

Discuss whether color-conscious policies encourage stereotyping as well as the isolation of minority students.

4. Several civil rights and Native American groups have protested the use of Indian mascots and symbols by professional sports teams such as the Washington Redskins and the Atlanta Braves. Is this practice morally justified under the color-blind principle? Support your answer. Discuss how Boxill would most likely respond.

5. Koreans, like other Asian immigrants, are sometimes referred to as "model minorities." Despite the fact that most Koreans living in the United States are relative newcomers, nearly 40 percent of them own businesses. What does it mean to be called a "model minority," and why do some Asians dislike this designation?

MICHAEL LEVIN

Race, Biology, and Justice

Michael Levin is a professor of philosophy at City College of New York. Levin argues that the attainment gap between whites and blacks is due not to racism but to genetic differences between the races. He argues that affirmative action and other compensatory programs are wrong because, rather than advancing blacks, they annul the natural advantage whites have over blacks.

Critical Reading Questions

1. Why aren't possible biological differences between races openly discussed? Why do some people deny that such differences would matter?
2. What are some documented differences between whites and blacks?
3. What is compensatory justice? In what ways is affirmative action compensatory?
4. What is the "bias-fighting rationale" behind affirmative action? What assumption is integral to this argument?
5. On what grounds does Levin reject Boxill's position on affirmative action?
6. How does Levin account for the attainment gap between blacks and whites?
7. According to Levin, how do differences in IQ between whites and blacks undermine the claim that racism is the cause of the attainment gap?
8. According to Levin, what temperamental characteristics of blacks lead to a propensity toward poverty?
9. On what grounds does Levin discount the role that environment plays in IQ?
10. Why, according to Levin, must the burden of proof be shifted onto blacks who claim that racism has brought about their failure?

"Race, Biology, and Justice," *Public Affairs Quarterly* 8, no. 3 (1994): 267–282. Some notes have been omitted.

11. How does Levin answer the charge that distributive justice requires greater racial equality?

12. How does Levin respond to the argument that slavery and segregation have left blacks disadvantaged?

13. How does Levin use Rawls's difference principle, as well as utilitarian considerations, to support his position?

Genetic black/white differences have played almost no role in recent discussions of interracial justice. This paper explores the relevance of these differences to issues of compensation and distribution.

One reason for the neglect of group differences, of course, is the belief that any talk of them is "racist." Obviously, though, the wickedness of mentioning a phenomenon does not diminish its logical bearing on any issue that may present itself.

At the same time, many writers who do admit the possibility of genetic race differences deny that they would matter if found. One of two reasons is usually offered for this conclusion: 1) it might prove possible to suppress genetic differences by manipulating the environment, or 2) moral principles such as a right to equal treatment are independent of the empirical traits of individuals and groups. . . .

RACE DIFFERENCES

The most thoroughly documented race difference is that in intelligence. It is accepted by every competent student of the subject that blacks score about one standard deviation (SD) below whites on all tests of intelligence; under the conventional scaling of IQ, the mean IQ of whites is 100 and that of blacks a bit below 85. A literature survey by the National Academy of Science concluded "The largest difference in group averages [exists] between blacks and whites on all given tests and at all grade levels." . . . The idea that IQ measures immersion in white culture is contradicted by the performance of Japanese and Chinese on IQ tests, which exceeds that of whites and blacks. Finally,

IQ associates with numerous variables unrelated to socialization. . . .

It would be hasty to suppose that blacks and whites differ in intelligence only. Many writers[1] claim that blacks are on average less inclined to defer gratification, a conjecture consistent with psychometric data. Black self-esteem is higher than white,[2] a common assumption to the contrary notwithstanding, and black scores on the Minnesota Multiphasic Personality Inventory are elevated in the direction of greater impulsivity.[3] Because they are more conjectural, however, race differences in temperament play only a minor role in what follows.

COMPENSATORY JUSTICE

When Jones limps into court to demand compensation from Smith for his broken leg, there are a number of defenses Smith should avoid. Denial that anyone can put a price-tag on a sound leg is pettifogging; appeal to the statute of limitations—the claim that Jones was harmed too long ago to deserve anything now—is legalistic; complaints about the cost of compensation are beside the point, the point being Jones' entitlement. Concentrating too heavily on the immediate cause of injury may be misdirection; Smith is still guilty if Jones broke his leg slipping on ice after being stranded by Smith on a frozen lake. Finally, concern that a large settlement may blunt Jones' zeal for rehabilitation sounds disingenuous coming from Smith.

Smith's best defense is to challenge the factual claim that he directly or indirectly broke Jones' leg. If Jones' lameness is not his doing, Smith is off the hook, morally and legally. No one is liable for what he did not do. . . .

The parallel with race is patent. Blacks limp behind whites at virtually all prestigious and remunerative tasks. This deficit is blamed on whites; blacks are said to fail because discrimination and racism have stifled their competitive ability. Given the principle of compensation—a person damaged by a wrong deserves what he lost, and is owed it by the wrong-doer—whites owe blacks the positions blacks would have occupied but for discrimination. In practical terms, redress means preferring blacks over whites when they compete.

Many defenders of preference deny they are demanding compensation. They are often the first to agree that the whites being asked to step aside now never discriminated against anyone, and that blacks receiving preference now never experienced discrimination. Yet the arguments intended to fill the resulting void are often compensatory in character. For instance, many preference advocates insist that innocent contemporary whites still benefit from past wrongs, and that anyone better off because of a wrong must surrender his illicit advantage to those the wrong has left worse off. So this new rationale for preference, like the original one, represents preference as putting blacks and whites where they would have been but for the misdeeds of (other) whites. Whether this new argument is called "compensatory," it too assumes that the black attainment deficit is the fault of (some) whites.

Or consider the argument that affirmative action provides role models for young blacks. The obvious question is, what is wrong with the present number of role models? Why not let role models distribute themselves race neutrally? Because, role-model theorists usually reply, blacks have fewer role models and lower aspirations than they would have had but for oppression. Whites should step aside for blacks so that young blacks may have hopes they should have developed. So understood, the role-model argument is patently compensatory.

Affirmative action is sometimes deemed necessary to counteract present discrimination, as revealed by the continued statistical underrepresentation of blacks in desirable positions. . . . [T]he bias-fighting rationale, while not compensatory, also assumes black ability is roughly equal to that of whites.

Now, just as Smith should not defend himself against Jones with technicalities and subterfuges, critics of affirmative action should not dodge their issue either. . . .

Smith retains the moral high ground only by showing that he did not break Jones' leg. So too, critics of quotas can retain the high ground only by showing that "racism" did not cause the attainment gap. Enter the race difference in intelligence (and, perhaps, motivation), which explains black failure better than "racism."

RACE DIFFERENCES AND THE ATTAINMENT GAP

Quite apart from the plausibility of its rivals, "racism" as a catch-all hypothesis has been eroded by the sheer passage of time. Slavery ended 130 years ago, school segregation 40 years ago; blacks have enjoyed full civil rights protection since 1964 and the ever-expanding privileges of quotas since 1970. Yet blacks are not doing appreciably better now than in 1954, and by some measures, such as marital stability, far worse. To take one of many striking examples, the National Science Foundation has spent over $1.5 billion on programs reserved for blacks since 1972, yet "20 years later, matters have barely improved" with regard to blacks in science.

It is difficult to argue that blacks were too heavily burdened for gains to appear in thirty or forty years. Equally burdened groups, notably Chinese in the US and Jews in many places, have made longer strides in less time. The Germans and Japanese, whose countries lay destroyed in 1945, were again world economic powers by 1970. To explain differential responses to adversity by attributing to some groups a "tradition of hard work" begs the question of black failure to develop that tradition. Post-war Europe did receive Marshall Plan aid, and it has become something of a cliché that American blacks need a domestic Marshall Plan, but in fact the net transfer of resources to blacks under Aid to Families with Dependent Children and other subsidies already amounts to a Marshall Plan every three years.

Given the weakness of "racism" as an explanation, one turns naturally to endogenous black traits, such as lower levels of intelligence and self-restraint, to account for the attainment gap. . . .

Compensation theorists might reply that talk of *the* cause of the attainment gap is an oversimplification. The proper question is *how much* of the gap is explained by race differences, for whatever portion of the gap is left unexplained by race differences might be due to compensable racism. . . .

The reader should think of IQ in the black and white populations as represented by overlapping bell curves, with the mean of the black curve lying one SD to the left of the white mean. . . . Thus, assuming the black SD equals the white SD, about 16% of all blacks have IQs of 100 or more, while about 50% of whites do, so there are about 1/3 as many blacks as whites whose IQs exceed 100. As the normal distribution is nonlinear, this ratio varies with IQ. There is 1 black for every 8 whites whose IQs exceed 115, and 1 black for every 18 whites whose IQs exceed 130. . . .

The recruitment gap is explained by the IQ difference alone, without reference to slavery or segregation. More generally, discrimination apparently explained a minute proportion at most of black vocational failure in 1970, and by 1980 has ceased to be a factor altogether. On the evidence, black representation caught up with ability some time after World War II and before affirmative action, by which point the effects of slavery and discrimination—whatever they may once have been—had been attenuated to non-existence. If so, the present competitive abilities of blacks are what they would have been had slavery and discrimination never happened, and no white enjoys any significant wrongful advantage over his black competitors because of them. Hence, no white is required by compensatory justice to forego any of his competitive advantage.

Black academic failure, usually blamed wholly on whites, is also explicable by the race difference

in IQ. The correlation between IQ and academic performance exceeds .6 in the lower grades, where the population is most diverse and the race difference most pronounced.[4] The correlation, along with the variance, decreases as one ascends the academic hierarchy, but it still suffices to explain the absence of blacks from graduate education. In 1990, 838 blacks earned the Ph.D. Jensen cites an IQ of 130 as predicting the ability to earn a Ph.D.,[5] and, if the mean IQ in a population is 100, 2.3% of its members have IQs $\geq$ 130. As there are about 420,000 blacks in any one-year cohort, proportionality requires that .023 × 420,000 = 9600 blacks earn the Ph.D. annually. In fact, however, only .13% of blacks have IQs $\geq$ 130, leading to a prediction of .013 × 420,000 = 575 blacks annually capable of earning a Ph.D., close to the actual figure. . . .

The high rejection rate for blacks in the NIH competition is actually one instance of a general tendency for whites to outperform blacks when credentials are held constant—whites outearn blacks when occupation and years of schooling are controlled for. This discrepancy strongly suggests bias, but it too can be explained as a statistical artifact. . . . Since wages correlate with IQ within as well as between occupations, the average income of whites exceeds that of blacks in the same jobs and with the same schooling. Proportionately fewer black scientists are outstanding scientists, capable, for instance, of conceiving research projects which win grants in blind competition.

I know of no study like Gottesman's of the relation of black temperament to poverty, but many commentators—including some preference advocates—see a link.[6] Banfield blames most of the problems of the slums on preference for immediate payoffs. Boxill, who supports quotas, acknowledges that black "chronic tardiness" and other "habits or cultural traits which are debilitating and unproductive." Black sociologist William J. Wilson has consistently found that ghetto males look down on jobs which don't produce a lot of money for relatively little effort.[7] Richard J. Hernstein and James Q. Wilson report that a pervasive attitude in black slums is that "straight jobs" are for "suckers." "Every boy interviewed [in a study cited] had been employed at one time, but the turnover was very high. When asked why they left a job, they typically answered that they found it monotonous or low paying. . . . [B]eing able to 'make it' while avoiding the 'work game' is a strong, pervasive, and consistent goal."[8] Such attitudes obviously impede attainment.

AN OBJECTION

There is an objection so likely to be raised at this point that it seems less an objection than a decisive refutation of my entire argument. Virtually everyone with whom I have ever discussed race differences has raised it, and it has probably occurred to the reader. Perhaps the *immediate* cause of low black attainment is lower intelligence (and greater impulsiveness), but if this difference is itself a result of racism, whites are still responsible at one remove for black failure, and the competitive edge enjoyed by whites today remains illicit. (Smith was not exonerated because he merely left Jones on the slippery ice without actually tripping him.) While some writers do not take overt or "institutional" discrimination to be the immediate cause of black failure, more thoughtful compensation theorists recognize that blacks are now objectively less able than whites. In Lyndon Johnson's famous comparison of blacks to a once-shackled runner, no one is restraining the shackled runner. He is slower than his competitors. But he is slower *because* of what has been done to him, and so deserves a head start. Likewise, if blacks are less intelligent than whites because of past discrimination, or denial of proper nutrition, or because racism discourages blacks from stimulating their children, they would still deserve a head start of some sort. It may be superior mental ability that gives whites their advantage over blacks, but the advantage should be annulled if the cause of this advantaging factor was a wrong. . . .

The only environmental factor that does seem capable of explaining the systematic character of black failure are disadvantages imposed on blacks by the majority society. . . .

GENETIC DIFFERENTIATION

The evidence strongly suggests that the race difference in intelligence is due significantly, perhaps primarily, to genetic differences. To begin with, the interindividual heritability of intelligence is quite high, between .5 and .7. Operationally, this means that if everyone were raised in the same environment, the average difference between the IQs of different individuals would be almost as large as it is at present. . . . The difference between Africa and Alaska, great as it may be, does not explain the difference in height between Masai and Eskimos; no one expects a Masai baby raised by Eskimos in Alaska to grow up short and stocky. Mathematically speaking, the higher the heritability of a phenotype, the greater the difference must be between the mean environments of two groups for environment to explain completely a fixed mean group phenotypic difference. . . . I know of no scalable environmental variable on which blacks and whites differ that widely, and the worlds of American blacks and whites—the language they speak, the movies and television shows they see, the school subjects they are exposed to, the technology available to them—appear quite similar. Black slums are admittedly less stimulating than white suburbs, but, as a neighborhood is the work of its inhabitants, the slum/suburb difference must count as an effect, not a cause, of race differences.

There are three sources of direct evidence of genetic influences on the race difference in intelligence. The first is the performance of African blacks on the most culture-free IQ tests, which averages about 70 to 75.[9] The second is transracial adoption. Were blacks genetically identical to whites with respect to intelligence, black adoptees raised from infancy in upper-middle class white families should develop the mean IQ of whites. The Minnesota Transracial Adoption Study[10] found the reverse in a sample of about 100 such adoptees. By late adolescence, their mean IQ was 89. By contrast the mean IQ of whites adopted by the same families was 105, and that of the natural children of these families was 109. In a reanalysis of this study, I estimate that genetic variation explains 60% to 70% of the between-race variance in intelligence. . . .

BURDENS OF PROOF

It cannot be proven beyond a shadow of a doubt that intelligence is a valid construct, or that IQ measures it. A genetic explanation of race differences is inherently more conjectural still than the race differences themselves. . . . Yet these uncertainties weaken my argument less than might be supposed.

Claims of damage must be *sustained*. Jones cannot simply storm into court, accuse Smith of breaking his leg, and expect to collect. He must *show* that Smith broke his leg. As this is a civil action, the standard he must meet is the relatively undemanding one of the preponderance of the evidence; he need only show it is more likely than not that Smith broke his leg. But show it he must—which means that, to defend himself successfully, Smith need not *prove* that he did not break Jones' leg. Smith need only show it is more likely that he did not break Jones' leg than that he did. Just so, white failure to prove the accusations against them false does not by itself leave them liable to compensatory damages. Since those who demand compensation are obliged to show that their accusations are plausible, whites are vindicated by a showing that black failure is *less likely* to be due to racism than to phenotypic race differences due in turn to genetic factors. The hereditarian analysis need not be certain, just more probable than "racism"— as I believe any disinterested examination of the evidence will find it to be.

Lest it seem legalistic in its own right to force the accuser of whites to carry the burden of proof, the reader should reflect that over the last quarter-century a great many whites have watched jobs and resources go to less qualified blacks because of the "racism" theory. It is only fair to ask that this theory be shown to be more likely than its rivals before more sacrifices from whites are demanded in its name.

DISTRIBUTIVE JUSTICE

It might be argued that greater racial equality is a requirement, not of compensatory, but of distributive justice, understood as what is obligatory in the initial distribution of goods. Many contemporary social philosophers seem to treat equality as the inertial distributive state, deviation from which needs justifying. Black and white shares are plainly unequal, hence prima facie wrong.

. . . Rather than repeat that the effects of these [past] inequalities have lingered, it is more pertinent to distribution to remark that past inequalities almost certainly did not leave blacks with smaller shares than they would have had in Africa. Slavery was common in Africa—white slavers bought blacks from tribal chiefs who had captured them—and no indigenous black society developed democracy, which blacks at least witnessed in the antebellum South. It is unlikely that blacks left on their own would shape conditions more conducive to mental growth than the ones they have been exposed to, for no indigenous black society ever developed an educational system remotely comparable in quality to the segregated schools of the Jim Crow era or the de facto segregated public schools of today. . . .

It may be replied that the benchmark of equality is not what would have been available for blacks in Africa, but what is available where they are, the US. This might be true when "what is available" refers to natural resources, but schools, housing and wealth—the goods blacks are commonly said to have too little of—are produced by human effort. The work of human hands should presumably go to the hands that did the work. By that standard, black holdings in the US seem less like inequity than white generosity.

Rawls cites the arbitrariness of the "natural lottery" to divorce an individual's contribution to wealth from his distributive share in it. The exceptional individual is said to have no right to the fruits of his talents because those talents, having been caused by fortuitous circumstances, are undeserved. His talents belong to everyone,[11] and he should keep only as much of what he produces as is needed as an incentive to keep him active. Rawls' argument has not to my knowledge been applied explicitly to race, probably out of reluctance to admit race differences in talent, but the obviousness of the application may help explain the popularity of *A Theory of Justice*.

At one level Rawls' inference from determinism to socialism collapses without a shove from empirical data, for it patently confuses *entitlement* with *entitlement to entitlement*. I may not deserve to spot a gold nugget in a stream, but this hardly implies that I do not deserve the nugget once I do spot it. Perhaps I deserve to be a finder of nuggets only by cultivating habits of alertness, but all I have to do to deserve the *nugget* is find it. I don't have to be entitled to find it.

At a deeper but still logical level, Rawls confuses the contradictory of "The natural lottery is required by justice" with one of its contraries. From the clear truth that "The natural distribution [of ability] is neither just nor unjust" Rawls infers the wrongness of capitalizing on natural abilities. But the fact that a situation is "not just," in the sense of not *required* by justice, does not leave it *forbidden* by justice. Precisely as Rawls says, the natural lottery is neither just *nor unjust*. So, while whites may not *deserve* to have been made cleverer than blacks by the processes of evolution, it hardly follows that there is any *unfairness* in evolution having done this. If there is no positive reason to accept the consequences of evolution, there is also—unless equality is already assumed desirable—no positive reason to resist them. . . .

Second, Rawls' system is far from egalitarian: his difference principle, that the lot of the better off can be improved only when doing so helps the worst off, accords the worst off a veto power denied to other groups. Assuming blacks among the worst off in American society, the difference principle would seem to give priority to helping them. The ghetto has first claim on the next dollar spent on education. . . . Yet given the relevant facts, the difference principle may imply quite another conclusion. Technical innovations, which originate from the high tail of the bell curve, have historically benefited the worst off more than

anyone else. The computer, the latest product of Caucasoid ingenuity, most dramatically boosts the productivity and with it the marketability of workers whose talents confine them to routine clerical tasks. Vacuum cleaners most benefited those women unable to afford domestic help. If giving that next dollar to the—almost entirely white and Asian—gifted would benefit blacks more than giving it to blacks, the difference principle says give it to the gifted.

The findings of the best-known enrichment programs for black children do not settle the issue. The Milwaukee Project produced short-term gains in the IQ of black children at a cost of $23,000 per point. The net benefit of the Perry Preschool Program, as measured by such factors as increased chances of employment, was $250 per IQ point in the first year (and negative thereafter). . . . Yet what the Rawlsian needs to know is whether these programs did more for blacks than would have been done for blacks by investing the same resources in the—mostly non-black—gifted. Utilitarians need similar data, since for them the disposition of that next dollar hinges on a straight bang-for-the-buck comparison of the educability of black and non-black children. The studies needed to apply maximin and utilitarian criteria have not been done, and it is far from clear what their outcome would be.

THE FINAL REMARK

Having returned to reasons for studying race differences, I would repeat the main one.

The right to cite truths in one's own defense is very nearly absolute. This right emphatically includes the marshaling of truths that embarrass one's accuser. A man asked to pay for a wrong he did not commit may repel the accusation even if to do so raises questions his accuser would rather not answer. Jones may wish to avoid thinking about his misshapen leg. He may be ashamed that this deformity runs in his family. He may not want anyone to call attention to it. *But if he accuses Smith of having broken it, Smith is entitled to talk about Jones' leg all day long.* If Jones isn't prepared to have his leg talked about, he shouldn't open the topic by hurling accusations. If racial egalitarians hurl immoderate charges at whites, they open the topic of race differences by forcing whites to defend themselves.

NOTES

1. E.g., E. Banfield, *The Unheavenly City Revisited* (Boston: Little Brown, 1974).

2. A. Tashakkori, "Race, Gender and Pre-adolescent Self-Structure: A Test of Construct-Specificity Hypothesis [sic]." *Personality and Individual Differences,* vol. 14 (1993).

3. W. Dahlstrom, et al., *MMPI Patterns of American Minorities* (Minneapolis: University of Minnesota Press, 1986).

4. A. Jensen, *Bias in Mental Testing* (New York: The Free Press, 1980), p. 343.

5. *Bias in Mental Testing,* p. 112.

6. I. I. Gottesman, "Biogenetics of Race and Class," in M. Deutch, I. Katz, and A. R. Jensen (eds.), *Social Class, Race, and Psychological Development* (New York: Holt, Rinehart, and Winston, 1968).

7. William J. Wilson, *The Truly Disadvantaged: The Inner City, the Underclass and Public Policy* (Chicago: University of Chicago Press, 1987).

8. R. Hernstein, and J. Wilson, *Crime and Human Nature* (New York: Simon and Schuster, 1985), pp. 304, 335.

9. See e.g., K. Owen, "The Suitability of Raven's Standard Progressive Matrices for Various Groups in South Africa," *Personality and Individual Differences,* vol. 13 (1992), pp. 149–59.

10. R. Weinberg, S. Scarr, and I. Waldman, "The Minnesota Transracial Adoption Study: A Follow-up of IQ Test Performance at Adolescence," *Intelligence,* vol. 16 (1992).

11. J. Rawls, *A Theory of Justice* (Cambridge, MA: Harvard University Press, 1971), pp. 101–102.

Discussion Questions

1. Is Levin a racist? Support your answer.

2. Has Levin adequately demonstrated that there is empirical support for genetic differences between the races? If so, do these differences justify differential treatment? Does Levin support a color-blind or a color-conscious approach?

3. Levin disagrees with Boxill's support of affirmative action. Discuss how Boxill might respond to Levin's criticism of his position.

4. In his article "Response to Race Differences in Crime,"[31] Levin argues that because there is a one-in-four chance that a young black male is a felon, a jogger who sees a black male on the path in front of him or her is justified in turning around and running away. He also believes that police are justified in racial profiling. Do you agree with Levin that this differential treatment of black men is morally justified? Discuss how Garcia and Boxill would each answer this question.

5. When Levin tried to find a publisher for his controversial manuscript *Why Race Matters: Race Differences and Their Implications,* dozen of publishers rejected it, including several academic publishers. Other authors, who have attempted to publish "politically incorrect" views on race differences, such as Arthur Jensen, have met similar obstacles in finding publishers.[32] Does freedom of the press give publishers the right to choose not to publish material they find objectionable? Does publishing controversial ideas on alleged differences between the races work to diminish or increase racism? What is the relationship, if any, between freedom of the press, perpetuation of the status quo, and institutional racism? Support your answers.

WILLIAM I. ROBINSON

"Aqui Estamos y No Nos Vamos!" Global Capital and Immigrant Rights

William I. Robinson is professor of sociology, global and international studies, and Latin American and Iberian studies at the University of California, Santa Barbara. Robinson argues that the globalization of capitalism and the transnational migration that it has engendered have fueled racism and the exploitation of immigrant workers.

Critical Reading Questions

1. What does Robinson mean when he says there is a "transnational immigrant workers' uprising" and what are the immigrant workers protesting?
2. What are some of the abuses immigrants have been subjected to in recent years?
3. How has global capitalism contributed to immigration and global racism?
4. What is the role of the state in keeping immigrant labor marginalized?
5. How have government immigration policies exacerbated racial conflict between blacks and Hispanics in the United States?
6. How will the proposed "guest worker" program for Latino immigrants ensure that employers in the United States have a pool of exploitable labor?
7. What does Robinson mean when he refers to white labor as historically enjoying "caste privileges"?
8. How has globalization eroded white labor privileges and contributed to racist, anti-immigrant sentiments?
9. What solutions does Robinson suggest for ensuring that immigrant workers have civil rights?

A spectre is haunting global capitalism—the spectre of a transnational immigrant workers' uprising. An immigrant rights movement is spreading around the world, spearheaded by Latino immigrants in the US, who have launched an all-out fightback against the repression, exploitation and racism they routinely face with a series of unparalleled strikes and demonstrations. The immediate message of immigrants and their allies in the United States is clear, with marchers shouting: "*aqui estamos y no nos vamos!*" (we're here and we're not leaving!). However, beyond immediate demands, the emerging movement challenges the very structural changes bound up with capitalist globalisation that have generated an upsurge in global labour migration, thrown up a new global working class, and placed that working class in increasingly direct confrontation with transnational capital.

The US mobilisations began when over half a million immigrants and their supporters took to the streets in Chicago on 10 March 2006. It was the largest single protest in that city's history. Following the Chicago action, rolling strikes and protests spread to other cities. . . .

Abridged from "'Aqui Estamos y No Nos Vamos!' Global Capital and Immigrant Rights," *Race & Class* 48, no. 2 (2006): 77–91. Notes have been omitted.

Then on the first of May, International Workers' Day, trade unionists and social justice activists joined immigrants in "The Great American Boycott 2006/A Day Without an Immigrant." Millions—perhaps tens of millions—in over 200 cities from across the country skipped work and school, commercial activity and daily routines in order to participate in a national boycott, general strike, rallies and symbolic actions. The May 1 action was a resounding success. Hundreds of local communities in the south, midwest, northwest and elsewhere, far away from the "gateway cities" where Latino populations are concentrated, experienced mass public mobilisations that placed them on the political map. Agribusiness in the California and Florida heartlands—nearly 100 per cent dependent on immigrant labour—came to a standstill, leaving supermarket produce shelves empty for the next several days. In the landscaping industry, nine out of ten workers boycotted work, according to the American Nursery and Landscape Association. The construction industry suffered major disruptions. Latino truckers who move 70 per cent of the goods in Los Angeles ports did not work. Care-giver referral agencies in major cities saw a sharp increase in calls from parents who needed last-minute nannies or baby-sitters. . . .

These protests have no precedent in the history of the US. The immediate trigger was the passage in mid-March by the House of Representatives of HR4437, a bill introduced by Republican representative James Sensenbrenner with broad support from the anti-immigrant lobby. This draconian bill would criminalise undocumented immigrants by making it a felony to be in the US without documentation. . . .

However, the wave of protest goes well beyond HR4437. It represents the unleashing of pent-up anger and repudiation of what has been deepening exploitation and an escalation of anti-immigrant repression and racism. Immigrants have been subject to every imaginable abuse in recent years. Twice in the state of California they have been denied the right to acquire drivers' licences. This means that they must rely on inadequate or non-existent public transportation or risk driving illegally; more

significantly, the drivers' licence is often the only form of legal documentation for such essential transactions as cashing cheques or renting an apartment. The US-Mexico border has been increasingly militarised and thousands of immigrants have died crossing the frontier. Anti-immigrant hate groups are on the rise. The FBI has reported more than 2,500 hate crimes against Latinos in the US since 2000. Blatantly racist public discourse that, only a few years ago, would have been considered extreme has become increasingly mainstreamed and aired in the mass media.

More ominously, the paramilitary organisation Minutemen, a modern day Latino-hating version of the Ku Klux Klan, has spread from its place of origin along the US-Mexican border in Arizona and California to other parts of the country. Minutemen claim they must "secure the border" in the face of inadequate state-sponsored control. . . .

Minutemen clubs have been sponsored by right-wing organisers, wealthy ranchers, businessmen and politicians. But their social base is drawn from those formerly privileged sectors of the white working class that have been "flexibilised" and displaced by economic restructuring, the deregulation of labour and global capital flight. These sectors now scapegoat immigrants—with official encouragement—as the source of their insecurity and downward mobility. . . .

Latino immigration to the US is part of a worldwide upsurge in transnational migration generated by the forces of capitalist globalisation. Immigrant labour worldwide is conservatively estimated at over 200 million, according to UN data. Some 30 million are in the US, with at least 20 million of them from Latin America. Of these 20 million, some 11–12 million are undocumented (south and east Asia are also significant contributors to the undocumented population), although it must be stressed that these figures are low-end estimates. The US is by far the largest immigrant-importing country, but the phenomenon is global. Racist attacks, scapegoating and state-sponsored repressive controls over immigrants are rising in many countries around the world, as is the fightback among immigrant workers wherever they are found. . . .

THE GLOBAL CIRCULATION OF IMMIGRANT LABOUR

The age of globalisation is also an age of unprecedented transnational migration. The corollary to an integrated global economy is the rise of a truly global—although highly segmented—labour market. It is a global labour market because, despite formal nation state restrictions on the free worldwide movement of labour, surplus labour in any part of the world is now recruited and redeployed through numerous mechanisms to where capital is in need of it and because workers themselves undertake worldwide migration, even in the face of the adverse migratory conditions.

Central to capitalism is securing a politically and economically suitable labour supply, and at the core of all class societies is the control over labour and disposal of the products of labour. But the linkage between the securing of labour and territoriality is changing under globalisation. As labour becomes "free" in every corner of the globe, capital has vast new opportunities for mobilising labour power where and when required. National labour pools are merging into a single global labour pool that services global capitalism. . . .

. . . At the structural level, the uprooting of communities by the capitalist break-up of local economies creates surplus populations and is a powerful push factor in outmigration, while labour shortages in more economically advanced areas is a pull factor that attracts displaced peoples. At a behavioural level, migration and wage remittances become a family survival strategy (see below), made *possible* by the demand for labour abroad and made increasingly *viable* by the fluid conditions and integrated infrastructures of globalisation.

. . . Migrant workers are becoming a general category of super-exploitable labour drawn from globally dispersed labour reserves into similarly globally dispersed nodes of accumulation. To the extent that these nodes experience labour short-ages—skilled or unskilled—they become magnets for transnational labour flows, often encouraged or even organised by both sending and receiving countries and regions.

Labour-short Middle Eastern countries, for instance, have programmes for the importation (and careful control) of labour from throughout south and east Asia and north Africa. The Philippine state has become a veritable labour recruitment agency for the global economy, organising the export of its citizens to over a hundred countries in Asia, the Middle East, Europe, North America and elsewhere. . . .

The division of the global working class into "citizen" and "non-citizen" labour is a major new axis of inequality worldwide, further complicating the well-known gendered and racialised hierachies among labour, and facilitating new forms of repressive and authoritarian social control over working classes. In an *apparent* contradiction, capital and goods move freely across national borders in the new global economy but labour cannot and its movement is subject to heightened state controls. The global labour supply is, in the main, no longer coerced . . . due to the ability of the universalised market to exercise strictly economic discipline, but its movement is juridically controlled. This control is a central determinant in the worldwide correlation of forces between global capital and global labour.

The immigrant is a juridical creation inserted into real social relations. States create "immigrant labour" as distinct categories of labour in relation to capital. While the generalisation of the labour market emerging from the consolidation of the global capitalist economy creates the conditions for global migrations as a world-level labour supply system, the maintenance and strengthening of state controls over transnational labour creates the conditions for immigrant labour as a distinct category of labour. The creation of these distinct categories ("immigrant labour") becomes central to the global capitalist economy, replacing earlier direct colonial and racial caste controls over labour worldwide.

. . . State controls are often intended *not to prevent* but to *control* the transnational movement of labour. A *free* flow of labour would exert an equalising influence on wages across borders whereas state controls help reproduce such differentials.

Eliminating the wage differential between regions would cancel the advantages that capital accrues from disposing of labour pools worldwide subject to different wage levels and would strengthen labour worldwide in relation to capital. . . .

The migrant labour phenomenon will continue to expand along with global capitalism. Just as capitalism has no control over its implacable expansion as a system, it cannot do away in its new globalist stage with transnational labour. But if global capital needs the labour power of transnational migrants, this labour power belongs to human beings who must be tightly controlled, given the special oppression and dehumanisation involved in extracting their labour power as non-citizen immigrant labour. . . .

Latino immigrants have massively swelled the lower rungs of the US workforce. They provide almost all farm labour and much of the labour for hotels, restaurants, construction, janitorial and house cleaning, child care, gardening and landscaping, delivery, meat and poultry packing, retail, and so on. Yet dominant groups fear a rising tide of Latino immigrants will lead to a loss of cultural and political control, becoming a source of counter-hegemony and instability, as immigrant labour in Paris showed itself to be in the late 2005 uprising there against racism and marginality.

Employers do not want to do away with Latino immigration. To the contrary, they want to sustain a vast exploitable labour pool that exists under precarious conditions, that does not enjoy the civil, political and labour rights of citizens and that is disposable through deportation. It is the *condition of deportability* that they wish to create or preserve, since that condition assures the ability to super-exploit with impunity and to dispose of this labour without consequences should it become unruly or unnecessary. . . .

The Bush White House proposed a "guest worker" programme that would rule out legalisation for undocumented immigrants, force them to return to their home countries and apply for temporary work visas, and implement tough new border security measures. There is a long history of such "guest worker" schemes going back

to the *bracero* programme, which brought millions of Mexican workers to the US during the labour shortages of the second world war, only to deport them once native workers had become available again. Similar "guest worker" programmes are in effect in several European countries and other labour-importing states around the world. . . .

THE NATURE OF IMMIGRANT STRUGGLES

Labour market transformations driven by capitalist globalisation unleash what McMichael calls "the politics of global labor circulation and fuel, in labour-importing countries, new nativisms, waves of xenophobia and racism against immigrants. Shifting political coalitions scapegoat immigrants by promoting ethnic-based solidarities among middle classes, representatives of distinct fractions of capital and formerly privileged sectors among working classes (such as white ethnic workers in the US and Europe) threatened by job loss, declining income and the other insecurities of economic restructuring. The long-term tendency seems to be towards a generalisation of labour market conditions across borders, characterised by segmented structures under a regime of labour deregulation and racial, ethnic and gender hierarchies.

In this regard, a major challenge confronting the movement in the US is relations between the Latino and the Black communities. Historically, African Americans have swelled the lower rungs in the US caste system. But, as African Americans fought for their civil and human rights in the 1960s and 1970s, they became organised, politicised and radicalised. Black workers led trade union militancy. All this made them undesirable labour for capital—"undisciplined" and "noncompliant."

Starting in the 1980s, employers began to push out Black workers and massively recruit Latino immigrants, a move that coincided with deindustrialisation and restructuring. Blacks moved from super-exploited to marginalised—subject to unemployment, cuts in social services, mass incarceration and heightened state repression—while Latino immigrant labour has become the new super-exploited sector. Employers and political elites in New Orleans, for instance, have apparently decided in the wake of Hurricane Katrina to replace that city's historically black working class with Latino immigrant labour. Whereas fifteen years ago no one saw a single Latino face in places such as Iowa or Tennessee, now Mexican, Central American and other Latino workers are visible everywhere. . . .

White labour that historically enjoyed caste privileges within racially segmented labour markets has experienced downward mobility and heightened insecurity. These sectors of the working class feel the pinch of capitalist globalisation and the transnationalisation of formerly insulated local labour markets. . . .

The loss of caste privileges for white sectors of the working class is problematic for political elites and state managers in the US, since legitimation and domination have historically been constructed through a white racial hegemonic bloc. Can such a bloc be sustained or renewed through a scapegoating of immigrant communities? In attempting to shape public discourse, the anti-immigrant lobby argues that immigrants "are a drain on the US economy." Yet, as the National Immigrant Solidarity Network points out, immigrants contribute $7 billion in social security a year. They earn $240 billion, report $90 billion, and are only reimbursed $5 billion in tax returns. They also contribute $25 billion more to the US economy than they receive in health-care and social services. But this is a limited line of argument, since the larger issue is the incalculable trillions of dollars that immigrant labour generates in profits and revenue for capital, only a tiny proportion of which goes back to them in the form of wages.

Moreover, it has been demonstrated that there is no correlation between the unemployment rate among US citizens and the rate of immigration. . . .

Immigrant workers become the archetype of these new global class relations. They are a naked commodity, no longer embedded in relations of reciprocity rooted in social and political communities that have, historically, been institutionalised in nation states. Immigrant labour pools that can be super-exploited economically, marginalised and disenfranchised politically, driven into the shadows and deported when necessary are the very epitome of capital's naked domination in the age of global capitalism.

The immigrant rights movement in the US is demanding full rights for all immigrants, including amnesty, worker protections, family reunification measures, a path to citizenship or permanent residency rather than a temporary "guest worker" programme, an end to all attacks against immigrants and to the criminalisation of immigrant communities. While some observers have billed the recent events as the birth of a new civil rights movement, clearly much more is at stake. In the larger picture, this goes beyond immediate demands; it challenges the class relations that are at the very core of global capitalism. . . .

Discussion Questions

1. Working in groups, develop a legislative policy for dealing with the issue of illegal immigrants in the United States. Discuss your policy with others in the class and modify it, if necessary, based on the feedback. Discuss what Robinson would most likely think of your legislation and how you might respond to his concerns.

2. Discuss what Ayn Rand would think about global capitalism and the use of immigrants as a source of cheap labor. Discuss also how Robinson might respond to Rand.

3. Ecologist Garrett Hardin uses the metaphor of a lifeboat in which each rich nation amounts to a lifeboat full of comparatively rich people.[33] Each poor nation is represented by a much more crowded lifeboat in which the poor continually fall out and, after swimming around for a while, head toward the rich lifeboats. However,

the rich lifeboats are already filled almost to capacity, and taking in more people runs the risk of swamping the boats. Under such circumstances, Hardin argues that it would be catastrophic to admit the poor of the world into our nations or lifeboats. Instead, we must protect our borders and keep out immigrants as well as refrain from sending aid to poorer nations, which, in the long run, would only lead to increased reproduction and more poverty in these nations. Evaluate Hardin's argument. Discuss also how Robinson might respond to his argument.

4. In 2006 Congress passed amendments to make English the official language of the United States. While most Americans applauded the action, the English-only movement has been criticized as racist and xenophobic and directed mainly against Hispanics. Do you agree? Discuss how Robinson might stand on this issue.

THOMAS POGGE

World Poverty and Human Rights

Thomas Pogge is a professor of political science and philosophy at Columbia University and an adjunct professor in philosophy at the University of Oslo in Norway. Pogge argues that severe poverty is a harm that citizens of affluent nations inflict on poorer nations and that we have a duty to work toward alleviating poverty in these nations.

Critical Reading Questions

1. What is the attitude of the citizens of rich countries toward severe world poverty, and how do we justify this attitude?
2. What does Pogge mean when he says that world poverty is an ongoing harm that we, as citizens of affluent nations, inflict on poorer countries?
3. Why does Pogge disagree with the common assumption that it would be an act of generosity on our part to reduce severe poverty abroad?
4. How has colonialism contributed to world poverty?
5. According to Pogge, why would Locke find the current inequality in the world morally unacceptable?
6. What are the "three notions of harm," and how are they related to justice and the issue of global inequality?
7. What is explanatory nationalism?
8. Why does Pogge reject the argument that it is up to developing nations to design their institutions and policies to reduce severe poverty in their countries?

"World Poverty and Human Rights," *Ethics and International Affairs* 19, no. 1 (2005): 1–7. The statistics and footnotes in this article were updated by Thomas Pogge in March 2007.

9. How do the WTO and protectionist laws, such as those protecting intellectual property rights, contribute to poverty and global inequality?
10. Why do trade agreements and payments we make to developing nations for their resources often do little to help the very poor in those countries?

Despite a high and growing global average income, billions of human beings are still condemned to lifelong severe poverty, with all its attendant evils of low life expectancy, social exclusion, ill health, illiteracy, dependency, and effective enslavement. The annual death toll from poverty-related causes is around 18 million, or one-third of all human deaths, which adds up to approximately 320 million deaths since the end of the Cold War.[1]

This problem is hardly unsolvable, in spite of its magnitude. Though constituting over 40 percent of the world's population, the 2,735 million people the World Bank counts as living below its more generous $2 per day international poverty line consume only 1 percent of the global product, and would need just 0.7 percent more to escape poverty so defined. The high-income countries, with 1,011 million citizens, by contrast, have about 79 percent of the global product.[2] With our average per capita income nearly 180 times greater than that of the poor (at market exchange rates), we could eradicate severe poverty worldwide if we chose to try—in fact, we could have eradicated it decades ago.

Citizens of the rich countries are, however, conditioned to downplay the severity and persistence of world poverty and to think of it as an occasion for minor charitable assistance. Thanks in part to the rationalizations dispensed by our economists, most of us believe that severe poverty and its persistence are due exclusively to local causes. Few realize that severe poverty is an ongoing harm we inflict upon the global poor.

If more of us understood the true magnitude of the problem of poverty and our causal involvement in it, we might do what is necessary to eradicate it.

That world poverty is an ongoing harm *we* inflict seems completely incredible to most citizens of the affluent countries. We call it tragic that the basic human rights of so many remain unfulfilled, and are willing to admit that we should do more to help. But it is unthinkable to us that we are actively responsible for this catastrophe. If we were, then we, civilized and sophisticated denizens of the developed countries, would be guilty of the largest crime against humanity ever committed, the death toll of which exceeds, every week, that of the recent tsunami and, every three years, that of World War II, the concentration camps and gulags included. What could be more preposterous?

But think about the unthinkable for a moment. Are there steps the affluent countries could take to reduce severe poverty abroad? It seems very likely that there are, given the enormous inequalities in income and wealth already mentioned. The common assumption, however, is that reducing severe poverty abroad at the expense of our own affluence would be generous on our part, not something we owe, and that our failure to do this is thus at most a lack of generosity that does not make us morally responsible for the continued deprivation of the poor.

I deny this popular assumption. I deny that the 1,011 million citizens of the affluent countries are morally entitled to their 79 percent of the global product in the face of three times as many people mired in severe poverty. Does not the radical inequality between our wealth and their dire need at least put the burden on us to show why we should be morally entitled to so much while they

---

[1]World Health Organization, *World Health Report 2004* (Geneva: WHO, 2004), 120–25.

[2]World Bank, *World Development Report 2007* (New York: Oxford University Press, 2006), p. 289 (giving data for 2005).

have so little? In *World Poverty and Human Rights*,[3] I dispute the popular assumption by showing that the usual ways of justifying our great advantage fail. My argument poses three mutually independent challenges.

ACTUAL HISTORY

Many believe that the radical inequality we face can be justified by reference to how it evolved, for example through differences in diligence, culture, and social institutions, soil, climate, or fortune. I challenge this sort of justification by invoking the common and very violent history through which the present radical inequality accumulated. Much of it was built up in the colonial era, when today's affluent countries ruled today's poor regions of the world: trading people like cattle, destroying their political institutions and cultures, taking their lands and natural resources, and forcing products and customs upon them. I recount these historical facts specifically for readers who believe that even the most radical inequality is morally justifiable if it evolved in a benign way. . . . But I can bypass these disagreements because the actual historical crimes were so horrendous, diverse, and consequential that no historical entitlement conception could credibly support the view that our common history was sufficiently benign to justify today's huge inequality in starting places.

Challenges such as this are often dismissed with the lazy response that we cannot be held responsible for what others did long ago. This response is true but irrelevant. We indeed cannot inherit responsibility for our forefathers' sins. But how then can we plausibly claim the *fruits* of their sins? How can we have been entitled to the great head start our countries enjoyed going into the postcolonial period, which has allowed us to dominate and shape the world? And how can we be entitled to the huge advantages over the global poor

we consequently enjoy from birth? The historical path from which our exceptional affluence arose greatly weakens our moral claim to it—certainly in the face of those whom the same historical process has delivered into conditions of acute deprivation. They, the global poor, have a much stronger moral claim to that 1 percent of the global product they need to meet their basic needs than we affluent have to take 79 rather than 80 percent for ourselves. Thus, I write, "A morally deeply tarnished history must not be allowed to result in *radical* inequality" (p. 203).

FICTIONAL HISTORIES

Since my first challenge addressed adherents of historical entitlement conceptions of justice, it may leave others unmoved. These others may believe that it is permissible to uphold any economic distribution, no matter how skewed, if merely it *could* have come about on a morally acceptable path. They insist that we are entitled to keep and defend what we possess, even at the cost of millions of deaths each year, unless there is conclusive proof that, without the horrors of the European conquests, severe poverty worldwide would be substantially less today.

Now, *any* distribution, however unequal, *could* be the outcome of a sequence of voluntary bets or gambles. Appeal to such a fictional history would "justify" anything and would thus be wholly implausible. John Locke does much better, holding that a fictional history can justify the status quo only if the changes in holdings and social rules it involves are ones that all participants could have rationally agreed to. He also holds that in a state of nature persons would be entitled to a proportional share of the world's natural resources. Whoever deprives others of "enough and as good"—either through unilateral appropriations or through institutional arrangements, such as a radically inegalitarian property regime—harms them in violation of a *negative* duty. For Locke, the justice of any institutional order thus depends on whether the worst-off under it are at least as well off as people would be

---

[3]Thomas W. Pogge, *World Poverty and Human Rights: Cosmopolitan Responsibilities and Reforms* (Cambridge: Polity Press, 2002). All in-text citation references are to this book.

in a state of nature with a proportional resource share. This baseline is imprecise, to be sure, but it suffices for my second challenge: however one may want to imagine a state of nature among human beings on this planet, one could not realistically conceive it as involving suffering and early deaths on the scale we are witnessing today. Only a thoroughly organized state of civilization can produce such horrendous misery and sustain an enduring poverty death toll of 18 million annually. The existing distribution is then morally unacceptable on Lockean grounds. . . .

The attempt to justify today's coercively upheld radical inequality by appeal to some morally acceptable *fictional* historical process that *might* have led to it thus fails as well. On Locke's permissive account, a small elite may appropriate all of the huge cooperative surplus produced by modern social organization. But this elite must not enlarge its share even further by reducing the poor *below* the state-of-nature baseline to capture *more* than the entire cooperative surplus. The citizens and governments of the affluent states are violating this negative duty when we, in collaboration with the ruling cliques of many poor countries, coercively exclude the global poor from a proportional resource share and any equivalent substitute.

PRESENT GLOBAL INSTITUTIONAL ARRANGEMENTS

A third way of thinking about the justice of a radical inequality involves reflection on the institutional rules that give rise to it. Using this approach, one can justify an economic order and the distribution it produces (irrespective of historical considerations) by comparing them to feasible alternative institutional schemes and the distributional profiles they would produce. Many broadly consequentialist and contractualist conceptions of justice exemplify this approach. . . . Addressed to them, my third challenge is that we are preserving our great economic advantages by imposing a global economic order that is unjust in view of the massive and avoidable deprivations it foreseeably

reproduces: "There is a shared institutional order that is shaped by the better-off and imposed on the worse-off," I contend. "This institutional order is implicated in the reproduction of radical inequality in that there is a feasible institutional alternative under which such severe and extensive poverty would not persist. The radical inequality cannot be traced to extra-social factors (such as genetic handicaps or natural disasters) which, as such, affect different human beings differentially" (p. 199).

THREE NOTIONS OF HARM

These three challenges converge on the conclusion that the global poor have a compelling moral claim to some of our affluence and that we, by denying them what they are morally entitled to and urgently need, are actively contributing to their deprivations. Still, these challenges are addressed to different audiences and thus appeal to diverse and mutually inconsistent moral conceptions.

They also deploy different notions of harm. In most ordinary contexts, the word "harm" is understood in a historical sense, either diachronically or subjunctively: someone is harmed when she is rendered worse off than she was at some earlier time, or than she would have been had some earlier arrangements continued undisturbed. My first two challenges conceive harm in this ordinary way, and then conceive justice, at least partly, in terms of harm: we are behaving unjustly toward the global poor by imposing on them the lasting effects of historical crimes, or by holding them below any credible state-of-nature baseline. But my third challenge does not conceive justice and injustice in terms of an independently specified notion of harm. Rather, it relates the concepts of *harm* and *justice* in the opposite way, conceiving harm in terms of an independently specified conception of social justice: we are *harming* the global poor if and insofar as we collaborate in imposing an *unjust* global institutional order upon them. And this institutional order is definitely unjust if and insofar as it foreseeably perpetuates large-scale human rights deficits that would be reasonably avoidable through feasible institutional modifications.

The third challenge is empirically more demanding than the other two. It requires me to substantiate three claims: Global institutional arrangements are causally implicated in the reproduction of massive severe poverty. Governments of our affluent countries bear primary responsibility for these global institutional arrangements and can foresee their detrimental effects. And many citizens of these affluent countries bear responsibility for the global institutional arrangements their governments have negotiated in their names.

TWO MAIN INNOVATIONS

. . . The usual *moral* debates concern the stringency of our moral duties to help the poor abroad. Most of us believe that these duties are rather feeble, meaning that it isn't very wrong of us to give no help at all. Against this popular view, some have argued that our positive duties are quite stringent and quite demanding; and others have defended an intermediate view according to which our positive duties, insofar as they are quite stringent, are not very demanding. Leaving this whole debate to one side, I focus on what it ignores: our moral duties not to harm. We do, of course, have positive duties to rescue people from life-threatening poverty. But it can be misleading to focus on them when more stringent negative duties are also in play: duties not to expose people to life-threatening poverty and duties to shield them from harms for which we would be actively responsible.

The usual *empirical* debates concern how developing countries should design their economic institutions and policies in order to reduce severe poverty within their borders. The received wisdom (often pointing to Hong Kong and, lately, China) is that they should opt for free and open markets with a minimum in taxes and regulations so as to attract investment and to stimulate growth.

But some influential economists call for extensive government investment in education, health care, and infrastructure (as illustrated by the example of the Indian state of Kerala), or for some protectionist measures to "incubate" fledgling niche industries until they become internationally competitive (as illustrated by the example of South Korea). Leaving these debates to one side, I focus once more on what is typically ignored: the role that the design of the *global* institutional order plays in the persistence of severe poverty.

Thanks to the inattention of our economists, many believe that the existing global institutional order plays no role in the persistence of severe poverty, but rather that national differences are the key factors. Such "explanatory nationalism" appears justified by the dramatic performance differentials among developing countries, with poverty rapidly disappearing in some and increasing in others. Cases of the latter kind usually display plenty of incompetence, corruption, and oppression by ruling elites, which seem to give us all the explanation we need to understand why severe poverty persists there.

But consider this analogy. Suppose there are great performance differentials among the students in a class, with some improving greatly while many others learn little or nothing. And suppose the latter students do not do their readings and skip many classes. This case surely shows that local, student-specific factors play a role in explaining academic success. But it decidedly *fails* to show that global factors (the quality of teaching, textbooks, classroom, and so forth) play no such role. A better teacher might well greatly improve the performance of the class by eliciting stronger student interest in the subject and hence better attendance and preparation.

Once we break free from explanatory nationalism, global factors relevant to the persistence of severe poverty are easy to find. In the WTO negotiations, the affluent countries insisted on continued and asymmetrical protections of their markets through tariffs, quotas, anti-dumping duties, export credits, and huge subsidies to domestic producers. Such protectionism provides a compelling illustration of the hypocrisy of the rich states that insist and command that their own exports be received with open markets. And it greatly impairs export opportunities for the very poorest countries and regions. If the rich countries scrapped their protectionist barriers against imports from poor countries, the populations of the latter would benefit greatly: hundreds of millions would escape unemployment, wage levels would rise substantially, and incoming export revenues would be higher by hundreds of billions of dollars each year.

The same rich states also insist that their intellectual property rights—ever-expanding in scope and duration—must be vigorously enforced in the poor countries. Music and software, production processes, words, seeds, biological species, and drugs—for all these, and more, rents must be paid to the corporations of the rich countries as a condition for (still multiply restricted) access to their markets. Millions would be saved from diseases and death if generic producers could freely manufacture and market life-saving drugs in the poor countries.

While charging billions for their intellectual property, the rich countries pay nothing for the externalities they impose through their vastly disproportional contributions to global pollution and resource depletion. The global poor benefit least, if at all, from polluting activities, and also are least able to protect themselves from the impact such pollution has on their health and on their natural environment (such as flooding due to rising sea levels). It is true, of course, that we pay for the vast quantities of natural resources we import. But such payments cannot make up for the price effects of our inordinate consumption, which restrict the consumption possibilities of the global poor as well as the development possibilities of the poorer countries and regions (in comparison to the opportunities our countries could take advantage of at a comparable stage of economic development).

More important, the payments we make for resource imports go to the rulers of the resource-rich countries, with no concern about whether they are democratically elected or at least minimally attentive to the needs of the people they rule. It is on the basis of effective power alone that we recognize any such ruler as entitled to sell us the resources of "his" country and to borrow, undertake treaty commitments, and buy arms in its name. These international resource, borrowing, treaty, and arms privileges we extend to such rulers are quite advantageous to them, providing them with the money and arms they need to stay in power—often with great brutality and negligible popular support. These privileges are also quite convenient to us, securing our resource imports from poor countries irrespective of who may rule them and how badly. But these privileges have devastating effects on the global poor by enabling corrupt rulers to oppress them, to exclude them from the benefits of their countries' natural resources, and to saddle them with huge debts and onerous treaty obligations. By substantially augmenting the perks of governmental power, these same privileges also greatly strengthen the incentives to attempt to take power by force, thereby fostering coups, civil wars, and interstate wars in the poor countries and regions—especially in Africa, which has many desperately poor but resource-rich countries, where the resource sector constitutes a large part of the gross domestic product.

Reflection on the popular view that severe poverty persists in many poor countries because they govern themselves so poorly shows, then, that it is evidence not for but against explanatory nationalism. The populations of most of the countries in which severe poverty persists or increases do not "govern themselves" poorly, but *are* very poorly governed, and much against their will. They are helplessly exposed to such "government" because the rich states recognize their rulers as entitled to rule on the basis of effective power alone. We pay these rulers for their people's resources, often advancing them large sums against the collateral of future exports, and we eagerly sell them the advanced weaponry on which their continued rule all too often depends. Yes, severe poverty is fueled by local misrule. But such local misrule is fueled, in turn, by global rules that we impose and from which we benefit greatly.

Once this causal nexus between our global institutional order and the persistence of severe poverty is understood, the injustice of that order, and of our imposition of it, becomes visible: "What entitles a small global elite—the citizens of the rich countries *and* the holders of political and economic power in the resource-rich developing countries—to enforce a global property scheme under which we may claim the world's natural resources for ourselves and can distribute these among ourselves on mutually agreeable terms?" . . .

Discussion Questions

1. Discuss how a utilitarian might respond to Pogge's argument that our affluent lifestyles directly harm people in very poor nations as well as what policies and laws a utilitarian might suggest to eradicate severe poverty.
2. What is the relationship between colonialism, racism, and severe poverty in the world today? To what extent is globalization an extension of colonialism? Give specific examples to illustrate your answer.
3. To what extent do government restrictions on immigration from poor nations contribute to severe poverty in the world? Should affluent nations have open borders or less restrictive immigration policies? Discuss how both Pogge and Robinson might answer this question. Discuss also how Pogge might respond to Hardin's lifeboat metaphor in question 3 on page 558.
4. What is your moral responsibility, if any, as a citizen of an affluent nation toward alleviating severe poverty in the world? Discuss your answer in light of your career choice and living style as well as actions you might take.

CASE STUDIES

1. *BARBARA GRUTTER V. THE UNIVERSITY OF MICHIGAN LAW SCHOOL*

In 1996 Barbara Grutter, a white resident of Michigan, applied for admission to the University of Michigan Law School. At that time the law school, in order to achieve its "compelling interest in achieving diversity among its student body,"[34] gave additional points to applicants who were members of groups that had been historically discriminated against, including African Americans, Hispanics, and Native Americans. In the U.S. Supreme Court case the law school conceded that Grutter probably would have been admitted had she been a member of one of these racial minority groups. As plaintiff in the case Grutter maintained that the law school's use of racial preferences, and resulting discrimination against white students, in student admission violated the equal protection clause of the Fourteenth Amendment.

The Supreme Court ruled in favor of Grutter. However, while it rejected the use of points as a means of achieving diversity, it did allow race to be used as a criterion in considering individual applications. In 2006 the people of Michigan voted in favor of a ban on affirmative action in public colleges and universities.

Discussion Questions

1. What is "diversity"? Discuss whether or not racial diversity is a legitimate and desirable educational goal for colleges and universities.
2. In its ruling the Supreme Court stated that while diversity may be a worthwhile goal, the use of racial group preferences, such as quotas or point systems, undermines the notion of equality "where race is irrelevant to personal opportunity and achievement." Do you agree? Support your answer.
3. How should justice as reparation, in terms of making up for past discrimination, be weighed against the principle of equality in the job market and in accepting applicants for college? Discuss your answer in light of Ross's concept of prima facie duties and Rawls's two principles of justice.
4. In 1992 the application of Cheryl Hopwood, a white student from a poor family, to the University of Texas Law School was turned down even though she had better grades and LSAT scores than many of the minority students who were admitted.[35] Is it fair that minorities who come from middle-class families be given preferential treatment over whites from economically disadvantaged families? Discuss how President Johnson and Boxill might each respond to this question.
5. Many colleges extend preferences to athletes. Compare and contrast this policy with affirmative action policies.

---

2. HURRICANE KATRINA AND RACISM

New Orleans is 67 percent African American and one of the poorest cities in the country. On August 29, 2005, Hurricane Katrina slammed into the Gulf Coast of Louisiana. Almost two thousand people—mostly poor African Americans—died in the wake of Hurricane Katrina, and thousands of others were left homeless. While residents who had private vehicles were able to evacuate the city, thousands of the city's poor remained behind to bear the brunt of the storm. The following day the levee system began giving way, flooding 80 percent of the city. About thirty thousand refugees—mostly poor African Americans—sought shelter in the Superdome, where they remained for days in squalid conditions with insufficient food and water, inadequate toilet facilities, and no air conditioning.

Government relief was slow to come, and when it finally arrived, it was sorely inadequate. Some of the refugees still do not have permanent homes and are still waiting for assistance from FEMA. Headlines throughout the world picked up on the connection between the slow response and racism: "Hurricane Katrina has come and gone—leaving behind one strong message—Racism still exists in America" (*Hindustan Times*, India). "Already the finger of racism is being pointed at official Washington for the slowness of federal agencies in responding to the disaster. . . . Such is the legacy of racism that to this day haunts the American psyche" (*Manila Standard Today*, Philippines).[36]

Discussion Questions

1. A newspaper photo of white people leaving a store in a flooded part of New Orleans with a bag of food was captioned "They're looking for food." A similar picture of black people doing the same was captioned "They're looting." Discuss

how racism in the media can distort our view of an event and perpetuate racism, and what might be done about it.

2. More than seventy countries offered to help with the Hurricane Katrina relief effort. Although the government accepted some of the offers, other help was turned down, including Israel's offer to send physicians and drivers for the search-and-rescue mission and Britain's offer to send thousands of emergency meals. Why do you think this happened? Discuss how Garcia might answer this question.

3. Some of the money that had been allocated by the government to upgrade the levees in New Orleans had been diverted into the war in Iraq.[37] Discuss ways in which racism influences a government's spending priorities.

4. Looking at your own town or city, discuss ways in which racism affects government spending on public facilities such as schools, libraries, and roads, as well as government responses to dangers to public health, poverty, and crime. Discuss possible solutions for creating a more equitable society.

---

3. COLIN FERGUSON AND THE "BLACK-RAGE" DEFENSE

Maryanne Philips was one of hundreds of commuters who took the Long Island Railroad to and from work in New York City. On December 7, 1993, she watched in horror as Colin Ferguson came down the aisle of her train car, pulled out a semiautomatic handgun, and shot twenty-five people, killing six. At the time of his arrest, Ferguson, a Jamaican immigrant, had notes in his pockets that expressed hatred of whites, Asians, and "Uncle Tom Negroes." Ferguson, who had a long history of angry encounters with whites, had earlier been involved in an incident in which he shouted at his perceived enemies: "Black rage will get you!"

Ferguson's lawyers decided to use black rage in their client's defense. The term *black rage* stems from a 1968 study by two psychiatrists who argued that racism has made blacks mistrustful and suspicious of outsiders. According to Ferguson's lawyers, "Being exposed to racist treatment over a long period of time drove Ferguson to violence" and "If you treat people as second-class citizens, they're going to snap."[38] Ferguson, in other words, is not responsible for his actions. Like the people he killed, Ferguson is also a victim—a victim of white racism.

A survey of eight hundred people before Ferguson's trial found that 68 percent of blacks and 45 percent of whites believed that a compelling defense could be made on rage stemming from long-term racism. The jury, however, didn't buy the black-rage defense. Ferguson received two hundred years in prison for the murders.

Discussion Questions

1. Should the black-rage defense be taken into consideration in sentencing Ferguson? If so, is long-term imprisonment the appropriate response, or should Ferguson have received counseling?

2. Journalist Jonathan Alter once asked, "Where does acknowledgment of pain stop and excuse-making begin?" Discuss this question in light of the Ferguson case. Is the lack of rage a sign of servility? Compare and contrast the black-rage defense with the battered-woman defense.

3. Attorney Alan Dershowitz argues that the black-rage excuse is an "insult to millions of law-abiding black Americans." The vast majority of African Americans do not use "the mistreatment they have suffered as an excuse to mistreat others."[39] Do you agree? Discuss how people should respond to mistreatment.
4. Dershowitz also suggests that the argument that blacks as a group have more rage than other people, and hence are more prone to violence, instead of helping us overcome racism merely reaffirms the fear of many white Americans that crime is a "black problem." Do you agree? Discuss how Michael Levin and Bernard Boxill might each respond to Dershowitz's concerns.

---

4. GRANTING ILLEGAL IMMIGRANTS IN-STATE COLLEGE TUITION

A 1982 Supreme Court decision entitled undocumented illegal immigrants to a free education from kindergarten through grade 12. About 65,000 undocumented students graduated from American colleges in 2008.[40] Miguel ("Mike") and his parents crossed the border illegally from Mexico when he was only two. The family has been living in California for the past fifteen years where his father works as a laborer and his mother as a chambermaid. Mike graduated valedictorian of his class and also won a prestigious science award. Given his family's financial situation, he can only go to college because California allows undocumented students who have attended high school in their state to pay in-state tuition at their public colleges and universities. However, Mike may not be able to graduate from college. A lawsuit has been brought against the state of California alleging that the current law discriminates against American citizens because out-of-state citizens have to pay a higher tuition than in-state undocumented immigrants.

Several states have already banned undocumented immigrants from their public colleges and universities, arguing that a college education is a scarce resource and tax money should be spent helping citizens get a college education rather than funding the education of undocumented immigrants. Critics also argue that the policy provides an enticement for people to come to the United States illegally. Supporters of in-state tuition argue that it is wrong to punish children for their parents' actions. In addition, the chance for a college education provides an incentive for bright students to reach their potential as productive members of society.

Discussion Questions

1. Discuss the pros and cons of giving in-state tuition to undocumented students. Discuss also how a cultural relativist, a rights ethicist, and a utilitarian would most likely respond to the debate.
2. Do parents such as Mike's who face a life of abject poverty in their country of origin have a moral right, or even a duty, to move to an area of the world where their children can have a brighter future? Support your answer. Discuss how Robinson and Pogge might answer this question.
3. In 2007 the DREAM (Development, Relief and Education for Alien Minors) Act was voted down by Congress. The Act would have provided undocumented

graduates of American high schools who had been residing in the country at least five years prior to graduation the opportunity to obtain permanent residency by graduating from college (including community college) or serving in the military for two years. Discuss the moral issues raised by the DREAM Act.

5. RACISM, COLONIALISM, AND THE CONFLICT IN DARFUR

The conflict in the Darfur region of western Sudan between the Janjaweed—militia recruited from Arab Abbalaha tribes—and the non-Arab people of the region has resulted in hundreds of thousands of deaths since it began in 2003 and the displacement of 2.5 million people, mostly black Africans, from their villages into refugee camps, according to the United Nations. The Sudan Liberation Movement accuses the Sudanese government of supporting the Janjaweed. The scale of the Janjaweed campaign against non-Arab Africans has been compared to the Rwandan genocide.

Makau Mutua, director of the Human Rights Center at the State University of New York at Buffalo, says that racism is at the root of the conflict.[41] The Sudan is a forced merger of Muslim Arabs in the north and black Africans in the south who are Muslim converts. Like most postcolonial nations in Africa, the Sudan is the result of European imperialism and the carving up of Africa into sovereign states without regard for traditional tribal and ethnic divisions.

Although the United States has imposed economic sanctions on Sudan, Western powers have been accused of covertly worsening tensions in order to deter further oil deals between China and the Sudan.

Discussion Questions

1. Some critics argue that the United States has done so little because of racism and our history of slavery and that if the victims of the violence in Darfur had been white, we would have intervened a long time ago. Do you agree that our lack of effective response to the crisis is partially the result of racism? Support your answer.

2. Do the United States and other Western countries—especially those that have benefited from colonialism—have a moral duty to offer assistance to the people of Darfur who are living in severe poverty and fear for their lives as a result of the conflict? If so, what is the basis of this duty? Do we as individuals also have a duty to provide assistance? Support your answers. Discuss how Pogge would most likely answer these questions.

3. Matua argues that only an inclusive democracy will save the Sudan from being partitioned into two states: one black African and one Arab. Is our interest in bringing democracy to non-Western nations, such as the Sudan and Iraq, another form of colonial or "Kiplingesque" paternalism? Or is it based on genuine respect for the dignity of people living in these nations? Discuss how Garcia might answer this question.

6. "NOT IN MY BACKYARD": ENVIRONMENTAL RACISM AND TOXIC WASTE

In 1991 Chemical Waste Management (Chem Waste), the country's largest hazardous-waste company, received approval to build California's first commercial toxic-waste incinerator at its Kettleman Hills dump site in the San Joaquin Valley. A few weeks later Chem Waste, the state, and the county were slapped with a lawsuit claiming discrimination and violation of the residents' civil rights. The suit alleged that the decision to place the toxic-waste incinerator in the almost entirely Hispanic community was part of a national pattern of situating hazardous-waste facilities near minority areas.

With globalization and the increase in consumer waste as well as tighter environmental regulations in developed nations, the dumping of toxic waste has gone global, with the poorest nations serving as our toxic-waste disposal sites. Although there are international treaties making the exporting of waste illegal, it is still widely practiced.

In 2006, a ship carrying tons of highly toxic and caustic sludge, instead of paying a disposal fee in Europe, emptied its load at various sites around the port city of Abidjan in Côte d'Ivoire (Ivory Coast), resulting in at least ten deaths and thousands of sick people. Junked electronics are also dumped in poorer nations. Nigeria, for example, has received hundreds of containers of used electronic equipment under the guise of donations. Most of the equipment is nonfunctional and burned in open fields, releasing toxic chemicals into the groundwater and carcinogenic fumes into the air. Thus, those who did not create the waste in the first place are made to pay the price of the economic progress of the affluent.

Discussion Questions

1. Discuss whether the above cases are illustrations of institutional racism.
2. According to University of California professor Robert Bullard, minority and poor communities are the least likely to fight back against toxic-waste sites. Indeed, some poor communities welcome waste sites because they create much needed jobs and tax revenue. Would the placement of toxic-waste sites in poor areas be justified under utilitarianism? Support your answer.
3. Discuss how Pogge would most likely respond to the practice of affluent nations dumping toxic waste in poor countries. Do we have a moral responsibility to make up for the harms we have caused the people in these countries, or do we merely have a responsibility to stop the harmful practice? Support your answer.
4. Using a utilitarian calculus, decide whose "backyards" companies should use as toxic-waste dumps. Should the people who contribute the most to society also recieve the most protection from toxic waste? Discuss how Levin would answer this question.

CHAPTER   11

War and Terrorism

On the morning of September 11, 2001, the world watched in horror the televised terrorist attacks on the World Trade Center in New York. Approximately 3,000 people died in the attacks on the World Trade Center, 184 in the attack on the Pentagon, and 40 passengers and crew members in the hijacked plane that went down in Shanksville, Pennsylvania. In addition, nineteen hijackers were killed in the four plane crashes. Following the attacks, President George W. Bush declared war on terrorism and launched a military campaign against Afghanistan's Taliban government and the Afghan-based terrorist organization al-Qaeda, which was held responsible for the attacks on the World Trade Center. In 2003 President Bush launched a preemptive strike on Iraq which, he argued, not only possessed weapons of mass destruction but was harboring terrorist groups bent on destroying America.

BACKGROUND

The September 11 attack and our response to it raise several moral issues. Is terrorism ever morally justified? What is the morally proper response to terrorism? Are preemptive wars or wars of aggression ever morally acceptable? What means should a government use to protect its citizens from attack or threats of attack?

War involves the use of armed violence between nations or between competing political factions to achieve a political purpose. Although there are some societies, such as the Eskimos, who have no term for war and have never engaged in warfare, war has been a fact of life in most organized states (including tribal states). Indeed, some philosophers, such as Thomas Hobbes and Elizabeth Anscombe, argue that war is necessary for the survival of a civil society.

The advent of the modern nation-state and the rise of nationalism increased the scale of war. The nineteenth century witnessed efforts to put an end to war through international peace movements and plans to organize nations to ensure peace. After World War I abolitionists sought to control war through the formation of the League of Nations. Despite some initial hope for international peace and cooperation, the wars of the twentieth century dwarfed all previous wars in terms of their destructiveness. In the twentieth century 191 million people were killed either directly or indirectly by war. Half of these people were civilians. The United Nations (UN) was established in 1945 after World War II to promote world peace and justice. However, this objective was not achieved, possibly because of the UN's lack of judicial and enforcement power. Since the end of World War II there have been more than four hundred wars. Worldwide, wars now kill about 1.6 million people a year. In addition, many millions more die of starvation and other war-related causes, or are maimed or forced to relocate.[1]

Motives for war include self-defense against aggression or threat of aggression, the desire to expand one's territory either directly or indirectly through control of markets and resources, and ideological/religious motives. The concept of a holy war emerged in the Christian tradition during the Crusades and is found today among certain radical Islamic groups. Most wars have mixed motives. For example, the current war on terrorism is a response to the threat of aggression and also has ideological/religious undertones in that both sides portray it as a war of good against evil and each side claims to be doing God's will.

The Islamic term *jihad,* often defined as a holy war, is more broadly defined as an "effort." This effort includes first of all the notion of the struggle against one's own internal problems or inner evil, and second, the struggle against injustice in society or the world. Some Muslims understand *jihad* as peaceful and nonviolent, whereas others interpret it as permitting, and perhaps even requiring, war against external enemies. Islamic views on war and peace are discussed in the reading by Sohail H. Hashmi.

Terrorism involves the use of politically motivated violence to target noncombatants and create intimidation. Terrorism is most often used by groups that lack the power to engage in conventional warfare. It is usually indirect and avoids direct confrontation with enemy military forces. Terrorism can be sponsored by non-state groups, as in the September 11 attacks and the 2008 attacks in Mumbai, India, which killed 179 people. The line between war and terrorism is imprecise. Terrorism can be used as a strategy in the context of a war, such as when the United States dropped nuclear bombs on Hiroshima and Nagasaki during World War II. Terrorism can also be domestic, as was the case in the 1995 bombing of the Federal Building in Oklahoma City. (See Chapter 5, Case Study 2, pages 273–274.)

THE PHILOSOPHERS ON WAR AND TERRORISM

Christian natural law theory has had a major impact on thinking about the morality of war. In his *Summa Theologica,* Thomas Aquinas (1225–1274) lists three conditions that must be met for a war to be just: The war must be waged by a legitimate authority, the cause should be just, and the belligerents should have the right intentions. The just-war tradition is discussed in more detail in the following section.

Italian renaissance thinker Niccolò Machiavelli (1469–1527) maintained that a powerful military was essential for political independence. In *The Prince,* Machiavelli counsels rulers to disregard whether their actions will be considered virtuous or vicious and instead do whatever is necessary to achieve success in battle quickly and efficiently. Machiavelli was part of the public debate on war up until World War II, when the rise of tyrants like Hitler and the advent of nuclear weapons made his by-any-means-necessary ideas too dangerous

---

THOMAS AQUINAS, *SUMMA THEOLOGICA*, PART II, QUESTION 40

Of War. . .

First Article

Whether It Is Always Sinful to Wage War?

. . . In order for a war to be just, three things are necessary. First, the authority of the sovereign by whose command the war is to be waged. For it is not the business of a private individual to declare war, because he can seek for redress of his rights from the tribunal of his superior. . . . And as the care of the common weal is committed to those who are in authority, it is their business to watch over the common weal of the city, kingdom or province subject to them. And just as it is lawful for them to have recourse to the sword in defending that common weal against internal disturbances, when they punish evil-doers, according to the words of the Apostle (Rom. xiii, 4): *He heareth not the sword in vain: for he is God's minister, an avenger to execute wrath upon him that doth evil;* so too, it is their business to have recourse to the sword of war in defending the common weal against external enemies. Hence it is said to those who are in authority (Ps. lxxxi. 4): *Rescue the poor: and deliver the needy out of the hand of the sinner;* and for this reason Augustine says (*Contra Faust.* xxii. 75): *The natural order conducive to peace among mortals demands that the power to declare and counsel war should be in the hands of those who hold the supreme authority.*

Secondly, a just cause is required, namely that those who are attacked, should be attacked because they deserve it on account of some fault. Wherefore, Augustine says (*QQ. in Hept.*, qu. x, *super Jos.*): *A just war is wont to be described as one that avenges wrongs, when a nation or state has to be punished, for refusing to make amends for the wrongs inflicted by its subjects, or to restore what it has seized unjustly.*

Thirdly, it is necessary that the belligerents should have a rightful intention, so that they intend the advancement of good, or the avoidance of evil. Hence Augustine says (*De Verb. Dom.*): *True religion looks upon as peaceful those wars that are waged not for motives of aggrandizement, or cruelty, but with the object of securing peace, of punishing evil-doers, and of uplifting the good.* For it may happen that the war is declared by the legitimate authority, and for a just cause, and yet be rendered unlawful through a wicked intention. Hence Augustine says (*Contra Faust.* xxii. 74): *The passion for inflicting harm, the cruel thirst for vengeance, an unpacific and relentless spirit, the fever of revolt, the lust of power, and such like things, all these are rightly condemned in war.*

---

as guidelines for war. In the reading on "Peace and Security," Jonathan Granoff argues that this Machiavellian philosophy of war is still part of our national security policy and poses a threat to global survival.

Like Aquinas, Dutch statesman and philosopher Hugo Grotius (1583–1645) believed that there should be limits on war. War should only be fought to enforce rights, and it should be fought within the limits of law and good faith. Grotius's belief that war should only be fought in the cause of international interests, such as human rights and maintenance of peace, is found in the Charter of the United Nations.

English philosopher Thomas Hobbes (1588–1679) was convinced that fear of death and the need for security are the psychological underpinnings of civilization. Hobbes also believed that humans are naturally selfish. In a state of nature, violence would be the norm and life would be "mean, brutish, and short." The answer to this unpleasant situation is the formation of a civil society. In civil society the authority to use violence is transferred to the sovereign, whose power is absolute. "The Sovereign," writes Hobbes in the *Leviathan,* "[has] the Right of making Warre and Peace with other Nations, and Commonwealths; that is to say, of Judging when it is for the publique good."[2]

Although Hobbes argued for absolute sovereigns as a hedge against war, in fact nations with totalitarian governments seem more susceptible to civil war than democratic governments. Furthermore, even though the formation of governments resolves the problem of constant violence within societies, without an international government the collection of nations still exists in a state of nature. Indeed Hobbes himself believed that nothing short of a world government with a monopoly of power over all nations would be sufficient to ensure peace.

Prominent Arab historian and philosopher Ibn Khaldun (1332–1406) likewise believed that war is a universal and inevitable part of human existence. This view is found in the Qu'ran and the Sunna (the practice of Muhammad), both of which hold a prominent place in Muslim ethical/legal discussions about war. According to the Qu'ran, man's nature is to live in a state of harmony and peace with other living beings. Peace is not just the absence of war, but surrendering to Allah's will and living in accord with his laws. The prophet Muhammad (c. 570–632) taught that the use of force should be avoided except as a last resort. However, given human capacity for choice we are all capable of being tempted by evil and disobeying Allah's will. Consequently the Qu'ran gives Muslims permission to fight against a wrongful aggressor.

In his essay "Perpetual Peace" Immanuel Kant (1724–1804) writes that although "the desire of every nation is to establish an enduring peace [nature] uses two means to prevent people from intermingling and to separate them: differences in languages and differences in religion, which do indeed dispose men to mutual hatred and to pretexts for war." He proposed the creation of a European confederation of states. He also believed that the maintenance of peace requires the establishment of constitutional government, rather than autocracy.

Unlike Kant, Friedrich Nietzsche (1844–1900) glorified war. "A good war hallows every cause," wrote Nietzsche in *Thus Spake Zarathustra.* War, he believed, is a natural activity for the *Übermensch* or "superman." Nietzsche despised Christian morality that makes a virtue out of submissiveness and turning the other cheek. Nietzsche's philosophy was adopted by some Nazi intellectuals to justify Adolf Hitler's war on the Jews.

Utilitarians such as Jeremy Bentham and John Stuart Mill provided much of the philosophical background for the peace movement in the nineteenth century. War is immoral because it causes pain and diminishes happiness. Because of this, another means must be found for resolving international conflicts.

THE JUST-WAR TRADITION

Just-war theory is not a single theory but an evolving framework. Theories of just war are found in both Western and non-Western religious and secular ethics. In their readings in this chapter Coady and Hashmi both examine the just-war tradition, Coady from a Western philosophical tradition and Hashmi from the perspective of Islamic ethics. The **just-war tradition** addresses the questions of *jus ad bellum* (the right to go to war), and *jus in bello* (the just conduct of war).

Jus ad bellum

Jus ad bellum states that the following conditions should be met before going to war:

1. War must be declared and waged by a legitimate authority.
2. There must be a just cause for going to war.
3. War must be the last resort.
4. There must be a reasonable prospect of success.
5. The violence used must be proportional to the wrong being resisted.[3]

While these conditions seem reasonable in theory, it can be difficult to determine if they are being satisfied. For example, what is meant by a legitimate authority? The Hobbesian belief that the only legitimate authority is an absolute sovereignty is no longer accepted. Today most people regard democratically elected governments as more legitimate. The idea of legitimate authority also raises the question of whether governments are the only legitimate authorities. The United Nations recognizes the right of self-determination of groups of people as well as states. Do groups of disenfranchised people, such as the American colonists who waged war against the British, constitute a legitimate authority?

Also, what constitutes a just cause? Former President George W. Bush reserved the right to make a preemptive or "preventive" strike against any nation he perceived as a threat, even though that nation had not taken any aggressive action against us. Is this consistent with the requirements of *jus ad bellum*? If so, would India be justified in a preventive strike against Pakistan (or vice versa), or would Iran be justified attacking Israel?

Furthermore, how do we know that we have tried all other options before going to war? According to pacifists, there are always nonviolent alternatives to war, including nonviolent resistance toward an occupying force. And how does one determine if the prospect for success is reasonable? When the U.S. and British forces invaded Iraq in March 2003, they felt confident that they had an excellent prospect of quick success. Yet six years later the war is still going on. On the other hand, few reasonable people thought the American colonists could win a war against the British Empire.

Finally, how do we determine what is proportional? Was the destruction of thousands of civilian lives in the atomic bombings of Hiroshima and Nagasaki worth the possible loss of American military lives in an invasion of Japan?

🍃 CHARTER OF THE UNITED NATIONS

Chapter I, Purposes and Principles

Article 1

The Purposes of the United Nations are:

1. To maintain international peace and security, and to that end: to take effective collective measures for the prevention and removal of threats to the peace, and for the suppression of acts of aggression or other breaches of the peace, and to bring about by peaceful means, and in conformity with the principles of justice and international law, adjustment or settlement or international disputes or situations which might lead to a breach of the peace;
2. To develop friendly relations among nations based on respect for the principle of equal rights and self-determination of peoples, and to take other appropriate measure to strengthen universal peace;
3. To achieve international co-operation in solving international problems of an economic, social, cultural, or humanitarian character, and in promoting and encouraging respect for human rights and for fundamental freedoms for all. . .

Article 2

The Organization and its Members, in pursuit of the Purposes stated in Article 1, shall act in accordance with the following Principles. . . .

3. All Members shall settle their international disputes by peaceful means in such a manner that international peace and security, and justice, are not endangered.
4. All Members shall refrain in their international relations from the threat or use of force against the territorial integrity or political independence of any state, or in any other manner inconsistent with the Purposes of the United Nations.

Jus in bello

For a war to be conducted justly, the following two conditions should be met:

1. Noncombatants should not be intentionally targeted.
2. The tactics used must be a proportional response to the injury being redressed.

It is possible for a justly waged war to be fought unjustly. For example, even though World War II was a just war from the perspective of the Allies, some people maintain that the scatter bombing of German cities by the Allies (see Case Study 1) and the dropping of nuclear bombs on Japan violated both principles of *jus in bello*. The My Lai massacre in the Vietnam War also violated the principle of noncombatant immunity. In this incident American soldiers entered a Vietnamese village and found only

Chapter VII, Action With Respect to Threats to the Peace,
Breaches of the Peace, and Acts of Aggression

Article 39

The Security Council shall determine the existence of any threat to the peace,
breach of the peace, or act of aggression and shall make recommendations, or
decide what measures shall be taken in accordance with Articles 41 and 42, to
maintain or restore international peace and security.

Article 41

The Security Council may decide what measures not involving the use of armed force
are to be employed to give effect to its decisions, and it may call upon the Members
of the United Nations to apply such measures. These may include complete or partial interruption of economic relations and of rail, sea, air, postal, telegraphic, radio,
and other means of communication, and the severance of diplomatic relations.

Article 42

Should the Security Council consider that measures provided for in Article 41
would be inadequate or have proved to be inadequate, it may take such action by
air, sea, or land forces as may be necessary to maintain or restore international
peace and security. Such action may include demonstrations, blockade, and
other operations by air, sea, or land forces of Members of the United Nations.

Article 51

Nothing in the present Charter shall impair the inherent right of individual or
collective self-defence if an armed attack occurs against a Member of the United
Nations, until the Security Council has taken measures necessary to maintain
international peace and security.

women, children, and old men. Frustrated that the male combatants had managed to
escape, Lieutenant William Calley ordered his soldiers to open fire on the villagers.

Noncombatants include those who are not agents in directing aggression or carrying it out. However, in modern warfare the line between noncombatants and combatants tends to be blurred. Even children can be drawn into war as combatants, as
happened in Vietnam and is happening in the Sudan (see Case Study 5 in Chapter 10).
Also, is it fair to hold individual soldiers responsible in countries where young people
are forcibly conscripted into military service? Indeed, the politicians who launch the
wars rarely serve on the front lines. Furthermore, is it just to kill enemy combatants
who do not pose a direct threat to our lives, as in the case of the bombing of retreating
Iraqi soldiers during the First Gulf War? Should we treat those who work in weapons factories as enemy combatants? Just-war tradition also does not give adequate guidance
on what constitutes acceptable treatment of prisoners of war or enemy combatants, an

issue addressed by David Luban in his reading in this chapter. Is torture morally acceptable as a means of trying to get information from an enemy combatant about a possible future terrorist attack, information that could potentially save hundreds of lives?

In addition, the just-war tradition does not adequately address *jus post bellum,* or justice after war. Is occupation of a defeated nation or territory morally acceptable and, if so, under what circumstances? To what extent is it just for the victor to attempt to change the political system and culture of the occupied country? Do countries have a moral obligation following a war to make restitution to civilians harmed by war?

WEAPONS OF MASS DESTRUCTION

Unlike conventional weapons, **weapons of mass destruction (WMD),** such as nuclear, chemical, and biological weapons, indiscriminately target both combatants and non-combatants. In the years following World War II nuclear weapons were used as a deterrent by the United States and the Soviet Union. The reasoning behind deterrence is that the consequences of retaliation would be so catastrophic that neither side would risk a first strike with nuclear weapons.

With the end of the cold war, instead of disarmament, the threat of global nuclear war between the two superpowers was replaced by the proliferation of nuclear weapons throughout the world and concerns about the use of nuclear weapons by terrorist groups. In 2002 former President Bush rejected the long-standing commitment of the United States not to use nuclear weapons in a first strike or against nonnuclear nations.

Worldwide, there are about 30,000 nuclear weapons, more than 1,500 of which are ready to launch at a moment's notice. The United States alone has about 10,000 nuclear weapons positioned at sites in the United States and Europe. Russia, Britain, France, China, Israel, India, Pakistan, and North Korea also possess nuclear weapons.[4] Arab nations are particularly concerned about Israel's arsenal of nuclear weapons, whereas Israel is concerned about the possibility that Iran and other Arab nations may be producing nuclear weapons and other WMDs.[5] Jonathan Granoff, in "Nuclear Weapons, Ethics, Morals and Law," questions the legitimacy of using nuclear weapons, even for deterrence, and urges that all countries work toward the elimination of nuclear weapons. President Obama has endorsed this as a long-term goal.

Chemical and biological weapons have been around much longer than nuclear weapons. During the French and Indian War the British gave small-pox-infected blankets to the Delaware Indians. Anthrax and mustard gas were both used by the Germans in World War I. The use, though not the production and possession, of chemical and biological weapons was prohibited by the 1925 Geneva Convention. Despite the prohibition, thousands of people died as a result of Soviet chemical and biological weapons that were used in Afghanistan, Laos, and Cambodia. Saddam Hussein also used chemical weapons against the Kurds in Northern Iraq.

Today many countries have biological weapons programs. Unlike the production of nuclear weapons, which requires expensive facilities and highly enriched uranium, biological and chemical weapons are sometimes called "the poor man's atomic bomb" because their construction is much cheaper and their effects can be just as devastating. In addition, recent developments in biotechnology and genetic engineering have made it possible to produce biological agents that have greater resistance to detection and treatment. More than 140 million people fly into the United States from foreign countries every year.[6] It takes up to two weeks for the symptoms of a contagious disease contracted in another country or on a plane to appear, which gives potential terrorists ample time to go into hiding.

PACIFISM AND CONSCRIPTION

There are different types of **pacifism. Absolute pacifists** believe that all violence is wrong, even for self-defense. This position has been criticized for being contradictory because it assumes a right not to be attacked, but not the right of self-defense to defend that right.[7] It is immoral and irresponsible, critics argue, not to allow countries to defend their citizens against aggression. Some pacifists get around these objections by maintaining that while they have a duty not to meet force with force, this is a **supererogatory duty** (morality that goes beyond what is normally required) and not one that is binding on all people. Other pacifists oppose violence except for self-defense and may even participate, though not as combatants, in a war of self-defense.

Pacifists actively seek peaceful alternatives to war. Indian political activist Mohandas "Mahatma" Gandhi (1869–1948) opposed all war and advocated nonviolent resistance (*satyagraha*) as a response to violence and oppression. *Satyagraha* is not passive "nonviolence," but a method of unconditional love (*ahimsa*) in action. Peace is not simply the absence of war but the presence of justice and the practice of *ahimsa*. In her article, Elizabeth Anscombe rejects pacifism as a morally untenable position and argues that the Bible permits and even requires war in some instances.

Conscription, or mandatory military service, raises issues of justice as well as freedom of conscience. The first national draft in the United States was during the Civil War. However, there was a proviso that allowed a person drafted to buy a substitute for $300 (about a year's wages). The draft was reinstated in World War I. Sixteen million young American men were conscripted between 1917 and the end of the Vietnam War in 1973.

The military defines **conscientious objection** (CO) as "opposition to war, in any form, based on a moral, religious, or ethical code." There were an estimated 37,000 conscientious objectors in World War II and 200,000 in the Vietnam War.[8] In addition to proving they are sincere in their opposition to all wars (no easy task), a conscientious objector still must go through boot camp, although not weapons training, and then be assigned to some sort of civilian duty after the training. Only a small percentage of people who apply for CO status receive it. (See Case Study 3.)

Some objectors choose to engage in civil disobedience and go to prison. Henry David Thoreau, in his essay on "Civil Disobedience" (1849), writes that when breaking an unjust law and engaging in **civil disobedience,** one should do so in a manner that is consistent with moral principles; in keeping with this, civil dissidents must:

1. Use only moral and nonviolent means to achieve their goal.
2. First make an effort to bring about change through legal means.
3. Be open and public about their actions.
4. Be willing to accept the consequences of their actions.

Other conscientious objectors choose to leave the country or go into the military but refuse to fire on the enemy. Sometimes people become conscientious objectors after joining the military and experiencing war. (See Case Study 3.) According to a survey conducted by the U.S. military at the end of World War II, up to 75 percent of soldiers in some of the units refused to fire on the enemy or fired their weapons into the air.[9]

Although the Selective Service System still exists and young men are required to register with it within a month of their eighteenth birthday, conscription was abolished in the United States after the Vietnam War. In 2003, the Universal National Service Act was introduced in Congress in response to the strain being placed on the professional military by the war in Iraq. The act was rewritten and reintroduced in 2005 and again in 2006 and 2007. If it ever passes, it would reinstate conscription, making it "the obligation of every citizen [male and female] of the United States, and every other person residing in the United States, who is between the ages of 18 and 42 to perform a period of [two years] of national service." Deferments would be granted to full-time high school students under the age of 20 and exemptions given for extreme hardship or physical or mental disability as well as for those who have "served honorably in the military for at least six months." People who are conscientious objectors would be assigned to either noncombat or national civilian service.

Americans have a long history of ambivalence about military conscription. The primary moral argument against conscription is based on autonomy. Conscription, which puts the draftee at risk for death or permanent disability, is a violation of a person's liberty rights and lowers the quality and motivation of the military. Ron Paul, in his reading toward the end of this chapter, compares conscription to slavery. On the other hand, the voluntary army is made up disproportionately of poorer people. Indeed, one of the complaints of the current voluntary system is that military recruiters tend to target poor youth in urban centers—the so-called "poverty draft."[10] During the economic recession in 2008/09, military recruitment figures went way up and all branches of the military exceeded their recruitment goals as Americans who were laid off sought stable employment.

Arguments for the draft focus on social justice and equality. In "Sharing the Burden," Stephen Joel Trachtenberg supports conscription on the grounds of equality. He also argues that a draft would promote a sense of unity and a common vision. Opponents of the draft note that equality was not promoted when the draft existed. They claim that a universal draft will accomplish only the indoctrination of draftees into nationalistic and militaristic attitudes. On the other hand, research suggests that democracies that have conscripted armies are more cautious about going to war because people are more personally affected.

THE MORAL ISSUES

Respect for Persons

Pacifists argue that war is incompatible with the moral imperative to treat persons as ends-in-themselves. War, by dividing people into us and the enemy, dehumanizes the so-called enemy and creates an us-versus-them/good-versus-evil mentality. In a 2007

Gallup poll, 70 percent of Americans stated that they had an unfavorable view toward Muslim countries; only 7 percent had a favorable view. Despite our claim that civilians in enemy countries are innocent, their deaths as "collateral damages" are not given the moral weight of deaths of American combatants.

Jonathan Granoff argues that war violates the principle of reciprocity or the Golden Rule, which is based on respect for persons. On the other hand, those who support the just-war theory, such as Aquinas, Anscombe, and Coady, point out that for a government to stand by and not defend its citizens against an aggressive attack involves not taking the personhood and security of its citizens seriously.

Rights

In the military, autonomy is restricted for the sake of the greater good. This is particularly evident in conscription, in which the duty of fidelity to one's country is seen as overriding one's liberty rights. War raises the issue of the rights of political communities as well. Hobbes regarded the right to security and freedom from violence as one of the most basic rights and the primary purpose of the social contract. This entails the right of a state to defend itself against attack. The right to a preemptive strike is generally regarded as an extension of the right to self-defense. However, how great and how imminent does the threat need to be to justify a preemptive strike? Was the 2002 invasion of Iraq morally justified on the grounds of self-defense?

The Universal Declaration of Human Rights and subsequent international human rights laws protect the rights of all people. Noncombatants have a right to life and a basic standard of living. In addition, prisoners of war have a right to decent treatment under international law. However, many nations continue to violate these basic human rights.

The United States has refused to adopt international human rights law, arguing that U.S. law provides adequate protection of human rights. The rights of 250 "enemy combatants" being held, as of January 2009, by the United States government at Guantanamo Bay in Cuba raised questions about the adequacy of this policy. The U.S. Supreme Court in 2006 ruled that former President Bush had overstepped his power in ordering war-crimes trials for detainees and that the procedures set up by the president violated both the Uniform Code of Military Justice and the Geneva Conventions. President Obama has issued an executive order to close down the prison at Guantanamo Bay and end torture and harsh interrogation techniques. (See Case Study 6.)

The USA Patriot Act, which was passed soon after September 11, and the targeting of more than 5,000 Arabs and Muslims for detention and questioning also have serious implications for the protection of human rights. (See Case Study 2.) The U.S. government justifies these policies on the grounds of national security, arguing that the positive right of U.S. citizens to security outweighs the liberty rights of potential terrorists. In his reading, Luban argues that the war on terrorism may be seriously eroding international human rights. In addition, justice is an issue in the ban against permitting those who are openly homosexual to serve in the U.S. military. While some argue that lifting the ban would jeopardize national security, others argue that the ban is based solely on discrimination. (See Case Study 5.)

Consequentialism and Nonmaleficence

The restriction on rights and the harms associated with war are generally justified as a means of preserving the greater good of society. However, is war the most utilitarian means to preserve beneficial ends such as our freedom, culture, and standard of living? Was World War II, for example, the best means, from a utilitarian point of view, of defeating Hitler? What about the war in Iraq? While most people agree that Iraq is better off without Saddam Hussein's regime, many disagree that an American invasion of Iraq was the best means of achieving this end. The question of consequences has come up again with Iran and South Korea. What is the best means—war, negotiation, embargos—of reducing these countries' threat to us and other nations?

Utilitarians such as Bentham and Mill, although not pacifists, were opposed to war because of the grievous harms associated with it. According to the World Health Organization, war is one of the leading public health issues of our time.[11] In the four decades following World War II, more than 100 million people were killed during wars, with millions more dying of starvation and disease related to war.[12] Millions of people have lost their homes and sometimes even their homeland as a result of war. More than 6 million people were displaced in Sudan and Sierra Leone alone as a result of civil wars.

Principle of Double Effect

The principle of double effect is found in Catholic just-war theory. According to this principle, if a course of action, such as bombing a town, is likely to have two quite different effects, one legitimate and the other not, the action may still be permissible if the legitimate effect was intended (e.g., the disabling of a military installation or the bringing of a war to an end) and the illicit effect (e.g., the killing of civilians) unintended. The principle of double effect was used to justify the unintended killing of civilians in Hiroshima and Nagasaki.

One of the problems with this principle is that unintentional harms are still harms. Killing civilians unintentionally with another end in mind does not justify knowingly killing them, especially if the unintended harms of the action outweigh the intended benefits. The principle of double effect also reduces people being unintentionally harmed to a means only, and thus violates Kant's categorical imperative.

Justice

The condition of proportionality in the just-war tradition is based on the principle of justice. This principle states that the violence used must be in proportion to the injury being redressed. Justice is also a concern surrounding conscription and in treatment of citizens in an occupied or conquered country.

Trachtenberg maintains that justice requires that we share the burden of military service through conscription. It is not fair that the burden of protecting our country is borne primarily by those who come from less privileged parts of society, as tends to be the case with a voluntary military.

In "Nuclear Weapons, Ethics, Morals and Law," Jonathan Granoff argues that allowing some nations to possess nuclear weapons while forbidding others to do so violates the principle of equality. Justice is also an issue in the treatment of prisoners of war and civilians in occupied countries. For example, local Iraqi police are paid much less by the occupying coalition than are American police in Iraq. Is this just?

Self-Determination

The United Nations recognizes the right of people to "self-determination, freedom and independence." The efforts of a victorious country to impose its form of government, its concept of freedom, and its cultural and economic values on another country have been criticized as a violation of a people's right to self-determination.

John Stuart Mill argued that self-determination and political freedom are not the same. A state has the right to self-determination even if its citizens are struggling for political freedom. Self-help, not occupation and liberation by another country, is the best way for citizens to develop the virtues necessary for self-governance. One of the arguments for withdrawing American troops from Iraq was that Iraqis should be allowed to determine the future course for their country, even if this means civil war.

On the other hand, assisting people in their struggle for freedom does not always violate their right to self-determination. For example, the French assisted the American colonists in the American Revolution. Knowing where to draw the line between interference and assistance in a people's struggle for self-determination has always been difficult.

Duty of Fidelity

In October 2002 U.S. citizen John Walker Lindh was sentenced to twenty years in a federal prison for his association with al-Qaeda. Treason is considered worse than betrayal by a noncitizen because treason violates the duty of fidelity. Living in a country of one's own volition and benefiting from its protection and advantages create a prima facie duty of fidelity or loyalty to that country. However, what does this duty entail? Do we have a duty to fight for our country or at least not to undermine our country's war efforts? Does the prima facie duty of fidelity justify conscription, or does it merely prohibit treason and terrorist acts against one's own government? What about instances in which one's own government is unjust?

Soldiers and others involved in a war effort also have a duty of fidelity to their commanders. However, this duty must be weighed against other moral duties. The argument by Nazi war criminals that they were just obeying the orders of their superiors was found unacceptable in international courts. People need to take personal responsibility for their choices. The duty of fidelity to serve the country can also come into conflict with the duty of fidelity to one's children. This raises the question of whether parent(s) of young children should be made to serve on active duty. (See Case Study 4.)

Personal Responsibility

Soldiers are not merely passive instruments of war. In the My Lai massacre in Vietnam, while most of the soldiers followed orders to "waste" the villagers, others refused to obey. One junior officer even stood between the soldiers and the villagers in an attempt to stop the slaughter.

✍ SUMMARY OF READINGS ON WAR AND TERRORISM

Anscombe, "War and Murder." War, including preemptive strikes, is justified under limited conditions.

Coady, "War and Terrorism." Examines and critiques the just-war theory and its application to the morality of terrorism.

Hashmi, "Interpreting the Islamic Ethics of War and Peace." Discusses the Islamic ethics of war and the concept of *jihad* and applies them to current issues.

Granoff, "Nuclear Weapons, Ethics, Morals and Law." Possession of nuclear weapons is unethical. We should work toward their elimination.

Luban, "The War on Terrorism and the End of Human Rights." The current war on terrorism may seriously erode international human rights.

Trachtenberg, "Sharing the Burden." Military conscription is desirable because it promotes equality and pluralism and a better understanding of the military.

Paul, "Conscription: The Terrible Price of War." We should not have conscription because it is discriminatory and constitutes forced servitude.

Granoff, "Peace and Security." To prevent global war, we should recognize the interconnectedness of all beings and work for ethically responsible public policy.

Conscientious objection in the face of conscription also entails taking personal responsibility for one's decision. During the Vietnam War many conscientious objectors chose to leave the United States and take up residence in another country. Others engaged in civil disobedience and willingly accepted the punishment for their actions as a means of raising public awareness.

The people who design and produce weapons also must accept responsibility for their actions. Because much of the technology used in the production and delivery of weapons of mass destruction can have both peacetime and military applications, researchers need to be aware how the technology they are developing might be used.

CONCLUSION

Internationally, the world exists in a state of nature or anarchy. Weapons of mass destruction, globalization, and the development of new technologies make war and terrorism a greater threat than ever before. What is the solution? If the formation of a state under a social contract is the best means for controlling violence between individuals, is international government the answer for controlling violence between nations? Or is war just a natural part of life and is the solution to develop and enforce ethics for war, such as the just-war tradition? In the end, the responsibility lies with each of us as individuals to critically examine the justifications given for war and to work toward making the world more peaceful, whether that means taking up arms or becoming a conscientious objector.

ELIZABETH ANSCOMBE

War and Murder

British philosopher Elizabeth Anscombe (1919–2001) was a professor of philosophy at Cambridge University in England. In her essay she distinguishes between war and murder. Using both moral and biblical arguments, she concludes that war, including preemptive strikes, is justified under limited conditions.

Critical Reading Questions

1. What are the two attitudes regarding the exercise of violent coercive power by rulers?
2. According to Anscombe, why is the use of coercive power essential?
3. Why have wars been mostly unjust and "mere wickedness on both sides"?
4. What does it mean to be "innocent"?
5. What is the difference between war and murder?
6. What is "pacifism" and on what grounds does Anscombe reject it?
7. What, according to Anscombe, does the Bible say about the permissibility of war?
8. What is the "principle of double effect" and how does Anscombe apply this principle to the killing of innocent people in war?
9. How does Anscombe respond to critics who say that the just-war theory is no longer relevant in the modern world?

THE USE OF VIOLENCE BY RULERS

Since there are always thieves and frauds and men who commit violent attacks on their neighbours and murderers, and since without law backed by adequate force there are usually gangs of bandits; and

since there are in most places laws administered by people who command violence to enforce the laws against law-breakers; the question arises: what is a just attitude to this exercise of violent coercive power on the part of rulers and their subordinate officers?

Two attitudes are possible: one, that the world is an absolute jungle and that the exercise of coercive power by rulers is only a manifestation of this; and the other, that it is both necessary and right that there should be this exercise of power, that

"War and Murder," in *Nuclear Weapons: A Catholic Response*, ed. by Walter Stein (New York: Sheed and Ward, 1961), 45–62.

through it the world is much less of a jungle than it could possibly be without it, so that one should in principle be glad of the existence of such power, and only take exception to its unjust exercise.

It is so clear that the world is less of a jungle because of rulers and laws, and that the exercise of coercive power is essential to these institutions as they are now—all this is so obvious, that probably only Tennysonian conceptions of progress enable people who do not wish to separate themselves from the world to think that nevertheless such violence is objectionable, that some day, in this present dispensation, we shall do without it, and that the pacifist is the man who sees and tries to follow the ideal course, which future civilization must one day pursue. It is an illusion, which would be fantastic if it were not so familiar.

In a peaceful and law abiding country such as England, it may not be immediately obvious that the rulers need to command violence to the point of fighting to the death those that would oppose it; but brief reflection shews that this is so. For those who oppose the force that backs law will not always stop short of fighting to the death and cannot always be put down short of fighting to the death.

Then only if it is in itself evil violently to coerce resistant wills, can the exercise of coercive power by rulers be bad as such. . . .

Society is essential to human good; and society without coercive power is generally impossible.

The same authority which puts down internal dissension, which promulgates laws and restrains those who break them if it can, must equally oppose external enemies. These do not merely comprise those who attack the borders of the people ruled by the authority; but also, for example, pirates and desert bandits, and, generally, those beyond the confines of the country ruled whose activities are viciously harmful to it. . . . Further, there being such a thing as the common good of mankind, and visible criminality against it, how can we doubt the excellence of such a proceeding as that violent suppression of the man-stealing business which the British government took it into its head to engage in under Palmerston? The present-day conception of "aggression," like so many strongly influential

conceptions, is a bad one. Why *must* it be wrong to strike the first blow in a struggle? The only question is, who is in the right.

Here, however, human pride, malice and cruelty are so usual that it is true to say that wars have mostly been mere wickedness on both sides. Just as an individual will constantly think himself in the right, whatever he does, and yet there is still such a thing as being in the right, so nations will constantly wrongly think themselves to be in the right—and yet there is still such a thing as their being in the right. Palmerston doubtless had no doubts in prosecuting the opium war against China, which was diabolical; just as he exulted in putting down the slavers. But there is no question but that he was a monster in the one thing, and a just man in the other.

The probability is that warfare is injustice, that a life of military service is a bad life "militia or rather malitia," as St. Anselm called it. This probability is greater than the probability (which also exists) that membership of a police force will involve malice, because of the character of warfare: the extraordinary occasions it offers for viciously unjust proceedings on the part of military commanders and warring governments, which at the time attract praise and not blame from their people. It is equally the case that the life of a ruler is usually a vicious life: but that does not shew that ruling is as such a vicious activity.

The principal wickedness which is a temptation to those engaged in warfare is the killing of the innocent, which may often be done with impunity and even to the glory of those who do it. In many places and times it has been taken for granted as a natural part of waging war: the commander, and especially the conqueror, massacres people by the thousand, either because this is part of his glory, or as a terrorizing measure, or as part of his tactics.

INNOCENCE AND THE RIGHT TO KILL INTENTIONALLY

It is necessary to dwell on the notion of non-innocence here employed. Innocence is a legal notion; but here, the accused is not pronounced guilty under an existing code of law, under which he has been tried by an impartial judge, and therefore made the target of attack. There is hardly a possibility of this; for the administration of justice is something that takes place under the aegis of a sovereign authority; but in warfare—or the putting down by violence of civil disturbance—the sovereign authority is itself engaged as a party to the dispute and is not subject to a further earthly and temporal authority which can judge the issue and pronounce against the accused. . . . What is required, for the people attacked to be non-innocent in the relevant sense, is that they should themselves be engaged in an objectively unjust proceeding which the attacker has the right to make his concern; or—the commonest case—should be unjustly attacking him. Then he can attack them with a view to stopping them; and also their supply lines and armament factories. But people whose mere existence and activity supporting existence by growing crops, making clothes, etc. constitute an impediment to him—such people are innocent and it is murderous to attack them, or make them a target for an attack which he judges will help him towards victory. For murder is the deliberate killing of the innocent, whether for its own sake or as a means to some further end.

The right to attack with a view to killing is something that belongs only to rulers and those whom they command to do it. I have argued that it does belong to rulers precisely because of that threat of violent coercion exercised by those in authority which is essential to the existence of human societies. . . .

When a private man struggles with an enemy he has no right to aim to kill him, unless in the circumstances of the attack on him he can be considered as endowed with the authority of the law and the struggle comes to that point. By a "private" man, I mean a man in a society; I am not speaking of men on their own, without government, in remote places; for such men are neither public servants nor "private." The plea of self-defence (or the defence of someone else) made by a private man who has killed someone else must in conscience—even if not in law—be a plea that the death of the other was not intended, but was a side effect of the measures taken to ward off the attack. . . . The deliberate choice of inflicting death in a struggle is the right only of ruling authorities and their subordinates.

In saying that a private man may not choose to kill, we are touching on the principle of "double effect." . . . Thus, if I push a man over a cliff when he is menacing my life, his death is considered as intended by me, but the intention to be justifiable for the sake of self-defence. Yet the lawyers would hardly find the laying of poison tolerable as an act of self-defence, but only killing by a violent action in a moment of violence. Christian moral theologians have taught that even here one may not seek the death of the assailant, but may in default of other ways of self-defence use such violence as will in fact result in his death. The distinction is evidently a fine one in some cases: what, it may be asked, can the intention be, if it can be said to be absent in this case, except a mere wish or desire? . . . [T]he principle of double effect has more important applications in warfare, and I shall return to it later.

THE INFLUENCE OF PACIFISM

Pacifism has existed as a considerable movement in English speaking countries ever since the first world war. I take the doctrine of pacifism to be that it is *eo ipso* wrong to fight in wars, not the doctrine that it is wrong to be compelled to, or that any man, or some men, may refuse; and I think it false for the reasons that I have given. But I now want to consider the very remarkable effects it has had: for I believe its influence to have been enormous, far exceeding its influence on its own adherents.

We should note first that pacifism has as its background conscription and enforced military service for all men. Without conscription, pacifism is a private opinion that will keep those who hold it out of armies, which they are in any case not obliged to join. Now universal conscription, except for the most extraordinary reasons, i.e. as a regular habit among most nations, is such a horrid evil that the refusal of it automatically commands a certain amount of respect and sympathy. . . .

A powerful ingredient in this pacifism is the prevailing image of Christianity. This image commands a sentimental respect among people who have no belief in Christianity, that is to say, in Christian dogmas; yet do have a certain belief in an ideal which they conceive to be part of "true Christianity." It is therefore important to understand this image of Christianity and to know how false it is. Such understanding is relevant, not merely to those who wish to believe Christianity, but to all who, without the least wish to believe, are yet profoundly influenced by this image of it.

According to this image, Christianity is an ideal and beautiful religion, impracticable except for a few rare characters. It preaches a God of love whom there is no reason to fear; it marks an escape from the conception presented in the Old Testament, of a vindictive and jealous God who will terribly punish his enemies. The "Christian" God is a *roi fainéant,* whose only triumph is in the Cross; his appeal is to goodness and unselfishness, and to follow him is to act according to the Sermon on the Mount—to turn the other cheek and to offer no resistance to evil. In this account some of the evangelical counsels are chosen as containing the whole of Christian ethics: that is, they are made into precepts. (Only some of them; it is not likely that someone who deduces the *duty* of pacifism from the Sermon on the Mount and the rebuke to Peter, will agree to take "Give to him that asks of you" equally as a universally binding precept.)

The turning of counsels into precepts results in high-sounding principles. Principles that are mistakenly high and strict are a trap; they may easily lead in the end directly or indirectly to the justification of monstrous things. Thus if the evangelical counsel about poverty were turned into a precept forbidding property owning, people would pay lip service to it as the ideal, while in practice they went in for swindling. "Absolute honesty!" it would be said: "I can respect that—but of course that means having no property; and while I respect those who follow that course, I have to compromise with the

sordid world myself." If then one must "compromise with evil" by owning property and engaging in trade, then the amount of swindling one does will depend on convenience. This imaginary case is paralleled by what is so commonly said: absolute pacifism is an ideal; unable to follow that, and committed to "compromise with evil," one must go the whole hog and wage war *à outrance.*

The truth about Christianity is that it is a severe and practicable religion, not a beautifully ideal but impracticable one. Its moral precepts, . . . are those of the Old Testament; and its God is the God of Israel.

It is ignorance of the New Testament that hides this from people. It is characteristic of pacifism to denigrate the Old Testament and exalt the New: something quite contrary to the teaching of the New Testament itself, which always looks back to and leans upon the Old. How typical it is that the words of Christ "You have heard it said, an eye for an eye and a tooth for a tooth, but I say to you . . ." are taken as a repudiation of the ethic of the Old Testament! People seldom look up the occurrence of this phrase in the juridical code of the Old Testament, where it belongs, and is the admirable principle of law for the punishment of certain crimes, such as procuring the wrongful punishment of another by perjury. People often enough *now* cite the phrase to justify private revenge; no doubt this was as often "heard said" when Christ spoke of it. But no justification for this exists in the personal ethic taught by the Old Testament. On the contrary. What do we find? "Seek no revenge" (Leviticus xix, 18), and "If you find your enemy's ox or ass going astray, take it back to him; if you see the ass of someone who hates you lying under his burden, and would forbear to help him; you must help him" (Exodus xxiii, 4–5). And "If your enemy is hungry, give him food, if thirsty, give him drink" (Proverbs xxv, 21).

This is only one example; given space, it would be easy to shew how false is the conception of Christ's teaching as *correcting* the religion of the ancient Israelites, and substituting a higher and more "spiritual" religion for theirs. Now the false picture I have described plays an important part in the pacifist ethic and in the ethic of the many people who are not pacifists but are influenced by pacifism.

To extract a pacifist doctrine—i.e. a condemnation of the use of force by the ruling authorities, and of soldiering as a profession—from the evangelical counsels and the rebuke to Peter, is to disregard what else is in the New Testament. . . . A centurion was the first Gentile to be baptized; there is no suggestion in the New Testament that soldiering was regarded as incompatible with Christianity. The martyrology contains many names of soldiers whose occasion for martyrdom was not any objection to soldiering, but a refusal to perform idolatrous acts.

Now, it is one of the most vehement and repeated teachings of the Judaeo-Christian tradition that the shedding of innocent blood is forbidden by the divine law. No man may be punished except for his own crime, and those "whose feet are swift to shed innocent blood" are always represented as God's enemies.

For a long time the main outlines of this teaching have seemed to be merely obvious morality: . . . And indeed, that it is terrible to kill the innocent is very obvious; the morality that so stringently forbids it must make a great appeal to mankind, especially to the poor threatened victims. Why should it need the thunder of Sinai and the suffering and preaching of the prophets to promulgate such a law? But human pride and malice are everywhere so strong that now, with the fading of Christianity from the mind of the West, this morality once more stands out as a demand which strikes pride- and fear-ridden people as too intransigent. . . .

Now pacifism teaches people to make no distinction between the shedding of innocent blood and the shedding of any human blood. And in this way pacifism has corrupted enormous numbers of people who will not act according to its tenets. They become convinced that a number of things are wicked which are not; hence, seeing no way of avoiding "wickedness," they set no limits to it. How endlessly pacifists argue that all war must be *à outrance!* that those who wage war must go as far as technological advance permits in the destruction of the enemy's people. As if the Napoleonic wars were perforce fuller of massacres than the French war of Henry V of England. It is not true: the reverse took place. Nor is technological advance particularly relevant; it is mere squeamishness that deters people who would consent to area bombing from the enormous massacres *by hand* that used once to be committed.

The policy of obliterating cities was adopted by the Allies in the last war; they need not have taken that step, and it was taken largely out of a villainous hatred, and as corollary to the policy, now universally denigrated, of seeking "unconditional surrender." (That policy itself was visibly wicked, and could be and was judged so at the time; it is not surprising that it led to disastrous consequences, even if no one was clever and detached enough to foresee this at the time.)

Pacifism and the respect for pacifism is not the only thing that has led to a universal forgetfulness of the law against killing the innocent; but it has had a great share in it.

THE PRINCIPLE OF DOUBLE EFFECT

Catholics, however, can hardly avoid paying at least lip-service to that law. So we must ask: how is it that there has been so comparatively little conscience exercised on the subject among them? The answer is: double-think about double effect.

The distinction between the intended, and the merely foreseen, effects of a voluntary action is indeed absolutely essential to Christian ethics. For Christianity forbids a number of things as being bad in themselves. But if I am answerable for the foreseen consequences of an action or refusal, as much as for the action itself, then these prohibitions will break down. If someone innocent will die unless I do a wicked thing, then on this view I am his murderer in refusing: so all that is left to me is to weigh up evils. Here the theologian steps in with the principle of double effect and says: "No, you are no murderer, if the man's death was neither your aim nor your chosen means, and if you had to act in the way that led to it or else do something absolutely forbidden." Without understanding of this principle, anything can be—and is wont to be—justified, and the Christian teaching that in no circumstances may one commit murder, adultery, apostasy (to give a few examples) goes by the board. These absolute prohibitions of Christianity by no means exhaust its ethic; there is a large area where what is just is determined partly by a prudent weighing up of consequences. But the prohibitions are bedrock, and without them the Christian ethic goes to pieces. Hence the necessity of the notion of double effect.

At the same time, the principle has been repeatedly abused from the seventeenth century up till now. The causes lie in the history of philosophy. From the seventeenth century till now what may be called Cartesian psychology has dominated the thought of philosophers and theologians. According to this psychology, an intention was an interior act of the mind which could be produced at will. Now if intention is all important—as it is—in determining the goodness or badness of an action, then, on this theory of what intention is, a marvellous way offered itself of making any action lawful. You only had to "direct your intention" in a suitable way. In practice, this means making a little speech to yourself: "What I mean to be doing is. . . ."

This same doctrine is used to prevent any doubts about the obliteration bombing of a city. The devout Catholic bomber secures by a "direction of intention" that any shedding of innocent blood that occurs is "accidental." I know a Catholic boy who was puzzled at being told by his schoolmaster that it was an *accident* that the people of Hiroshima and Nagasaki were there to be killed; in fact, however absurd it seems, such thoughts are common among priests who know that they are forbidden by the divine law to justify the direct killing of the innocent.

It is nonsense to pretend that you do not intend to do what is the means you take to your chosen end. Otherwise there is absolutely no substance to the Pauline teaching that we may not do evil that good may come.

SOME COMMONLY HEARD ARGUMENTS

There are a number of sophistical arguments, often or sometimes used on these topics, which need answering.

Where do you draw the line? As Dr. Johnson said, the fact of twilight does not mean you cannot tell day from night. There are borderline cases, where it is difficult to distinguish, in what is done, between means and what is incidental to, yet in the circumstances inseparable from, those means. The obliteration bombing of a city is not a borderline case.

The old "conditions for a just war" are irrelevant to the conditions of modern warfare, so that must be condemned out of hand. People who say this always envisage only major wars between the Great Powers, which Powers are indeed now "in blood stepp'd in so far" that it is unimaginable for there to be a war between them which is not a set of enormous massacres of civil populations. But these are not the only wars. Why is Finland so far free? At least partly because of the "posture of military preparedness" which, considering the character of the country, would have made subjugating the Finns a difficult and unrewarding task. The offensive of the Israelis against the Egyptians in 1956 involved no plan of making civil populations the target of military attack.

In a modern war the distinction between combatants and noncombatants is meaningless, so an attack on anyone on the enemy side is justified. This is pure nonsense; even in war, a very large number of the enemy population are just engaged in maintaining the life of the country, or are sick, or aged, or children. . . .

Whether a war is just or not is not for the private man to judge: he must obey his government. Sometimes, this may be, especially as far as concerns causes of war. But the individual who joins in destroying a city, like a Nazi massacring the inhabitants of a village, is too obviously marked out as an enemy of the human race to shelter behind such a plea.

Finally, horrible as it is to have to notice this, we must notice that even the arguments about double effect—which at least show that a man is not willing openly to justify the killing of the innocent—are now beginning to look old-fashioned. Some Catholics are not scrupling to say that *anything* is justified in defence of the continued existence and liberty of the Church in the West. A terrible fear of communism drives people to say this sort of thing. "Our Lord told us to fear those who can destroy body and soul, not to fear the destruction of the body" was blasphemously said to a friend of mine; meaning: "so, we must fear Russian domination more than the destruction of people's bodies by obliteration bombing."

But whom did Our Lord tell us to fear, when he said: "I will tell you whom you shall fear" and "Fear not them that can destroy the body, but fear him who can destroy body and soul in hell"? He told us to fear God the Father, who can and will destroy the unrepentant disobedient, body and soul, in hell.

. . . So we have to fear God and keep his commandments, and calculate what is for the best only within the limits of that obedience, knowing that the future is in God's power and that no one can snatch away those whom the Father has given to Christ.

It is not a vague faith in the triumph of "the spirit" over force (there is little enough warrant for that), but a definite faith in the divine promises, that makes us believe that the Church cannot fail. Those, therefore, who think they must be prepared to wage a war with Russia involving the deliberate massacre of cities, must be prepared to say to God: "We had to break your law, lest your Church fail. We could not obey your commandments, for we did not believe your promises."

Discussion Questions

1. Anscombe supports preemptive strikes under certain conditions. Discuss whether she would support the United States' preemptive strikes against Iraq.
2. Anscombe argues that the Bible supports war, while Christian pacifists claim that war is inconsistent with the teachings of Jesus. Discuss the merits of both positions.
3. Like Anscombe, former President George W. Bush believes that evil exists and that God permits governments to limit the power of evil through the use of violence. However, the Islamic terrorists also believe that God is on their side and that it is the United States that is evil. Referring to just-war theory, discuss the legitimacy of the use of religious ideology to morally justify war.
4. Martyrdom operations are tactics used by Palestinians as well as al-Qaeda and Iraqi insurgents. While some Muslims regard suicide bombing as merely suicide and a violation of God's law, other Muslims regard suicide bombers as martyrs. Discuss the use of suicide bombers in light of the *jus in bello*.

C.A.J. COADY

War and Terrorism

C. A. J. Coady is senior research fellow and deputy director of the Centre for Applied Philosophy and Public Ethics at the University of Melbourne, Australia. Coady applies the principles of the just-war theory to the morality of terrorism.

Critical Reading Questions

1. According to Coady, what are some of the problems with Hobbes's political philosophy?
2. In what way does Hobbes's position on war mirror the division in the just-war theory?
3. What is *jus ad bellum* and what are the five rules of *jus ad bellum*?
4. What is the requirement for proportionality?
5. What are some of the problems with the condition of "reasonable success"?
6. What is the *jus ad bellum* position on the use of war as self-defense?
7. What is a "humanitarian war" and what is Coady's position on the permissibility of humanitarian wars?
8. What are the two primary rules of *jus in bello*?
9. What is "collateral damage" in war and how does this relate to the principle of noncombatant immunity and the principle of double effect?
10. What is "terrorism" and is it ever justified under the just-war theory?

Our discussion can best begin with Thomas Hobbes since for Hobbes civil society primarily exists to solve the problems posed by the endemic role of violence in human life. Hobbes thought that violence created such miseries in pre-civil or non-civil conditions (his "state of nature") that reason required men to alienate, almost entirely, their natural right to self-protection in order to set up a sovereign with the sole right of the sword. His solution to the problem posed by the widespread violence of the state of nature is to monopolize the potentiality for violence in one agency.

The phenomena of war and terrorism, in their different ways, challenge this solution. Hobbes's political philosophy faces certain notorious problems, but even were it to provide a local solution to the problem of violence, it would do so at the cost of establishing a proliferation of (almost) absolute sovereign powers. They would very probably confront each other (as Hobbes realized) in a stance of permanent hostility akin to the war of all against all with which his problematic begins.

"War and Terrorism," in *A Companion to Applied Ethics*, ed. by R. G. Frey and Christopher Heath Wellman (Oxford, UK: Blackwell, 2003), 254–265.

This "anarchy" of the international order thus poses almost intractable difficulties for the peace that Hobbes took to be a primary objective of the laws of nature and for which sovereign power was to provide the guarantee. . . .

For Hobbes, not only is the sovereign power virtually absolute, but it also defines the contours of justice, inasmuch as nothing the sovereign does can be unjust. . . . The sovereign cannot be accused of injustice but may violate the laws of nature and be answerable to God for what Hobbes calls iniquity. Thus the sovereign has certain obligations as a ruler to preserve the peace, and is bound before God to conform to the tenets of natural law. Consequently, many resorts to war would be ruled out on prudential and moral grounds.

Nor are Hobbes's qualifications restricted to the morality of beginning war, for his brief discussions of honor, cruelty, and necessity in war allow some minimal room for moral restrictions on how a war is conducted (Hobbes, 1969: 78). Hobbes's qualifications mirror the twofold division of discussion within the just-war tradition, the first concerned with the morality appropriate to resort to war at all, and the second with the morality that should govern the way a war is fought. The former is often called *jus ad bellum* and the latter *jus in bello*. The Hobbesian mirroring is reductive: the fulsome shape of the *jus ad bellum* appears in the thin form of "providence" (i.e., prudent foresight) and the demanding conditions of the *jus in bello* are reflected as the (largely unspecified) requirements of honor. . . .

THE JUST WAR: *JUS AD BELLUM*

Although it is common to talk of "just-war theory," the mode of thinking thereby indicated is more a broad tradition than a precisely specified intellectual construction. It is less like the theory of the categorical imperative and more like commonsense morality. None the less, certain rules and maxims are invoked and I will begin with a digest of those that are most central to the argument about when it is right to go to war: the *jus ad bellum*.

1. War must be declared and waged by legitimate authority.
2. There must be a just cause for going to war.
3. War must be a last resort.
4. There must be reasonable prospect of success.
5. The violence used must be proportional to the wrong being resisted.

Each of these conditions raises problems. We shall briefly review some of the difficulties with conditions (3)–(5) and then comment more fully on condition (2). Conditions (3) and (5) are specifications of a commonsense understanding of the rational limits to self-defense. Given the ambiguous benefits and definite risks of most uses of violence, and the inherent tendency it has to move beyond control, the idea of "last resort" registers the desirability of a cautious approach to warfare. None the less, the condition cannot require that a nation must resort to war only after it has tried *every* other option. Some of these will be too absurd or counterproductive; others may delay the inevitable to the grave disadvantage of a just cause. Last resort requires the use of imagination and some degree of risk-taking in the search for reasonable

alternatives to war, but it does not counsel peace at any price. Hence it will be a matter of practical judgment whether the relevant alternatives to war have been exhausted. Moreover, it should not be forgotten that some of the alternatives to war may have their own serious moral costs, as is illustrated by growing disenchantment with the human costs of certain sorts of sanctions.

The requirement of proportionality spans the *jus ad bellum* and the *jus in bello* and insists that lethal violence should not be employed without consideration of the balance between the evil it brings and the good to be achieved in resisting evil. There is here an element of calculating consequences, but the appeal to proportionality is not full-bloodedly consequentialist. This is because its focus is narrower. We are not asked to consider whether going to war is the best thing for the universe, all things considered, but whether the foreseeable costs of this resort to violence are out of kilter with the criminal behavior it seeks to redress. . . .

Condition 4 is also a reflection of common sense, but at an even more basic level, since it is merely an application to warfare of an apparently fundamental condition of rational action. Normally one is irrational to engage in a plan with little or no perceived prospect of success. Yet there are desperate circumstances in which one may need to act against the odds. The mountain climber who faces disaster from an avalanche may be rational to attempt the leap across a ravine even where he thinks it unlikely he can make it. In the case of war, a fight against the odds may be justifiable where the stakes are very high, as when a powerful enemy is determined not only to conquer but enslave. This seems plausible, but it does not refute condition 4 so much as require a more subtle interpretation of "reasonable." . . . Some would argue that there are circumstances in which a fight to the death is preferable to mere capitulation. This has most plausibility where the enemy is bent upon enslavement or extermination. But some would extend the circumstances further to encompass the symbolic assertion of national honor, as Michael Walzer seems to do in his discussion of Finland's "futile" war of defense against the Soviet Union in 1939–40. What these arguments show is that the concept of "success" is open to complex interpretations. At first blush, one naturally takes it to mean winning the war, but the counter-examples suggest other purposes. None the less, enough crimes have been committed in the name of national honor to warrant a note of caution about self-immolation for its sake.

Condition 2 concerning just cause also has its origins in commonsense intuitions but again its interpretation raises problems. There are differences between the older tradition and much contemporary theory. The medieval tradition of the just war stems primarily from St Augustine and was generally more permissive, . . . Although the ground of self-defense had always loomed large in legitimating resort to war, Aquinas and others had also allowed various "injuries" of a religious nature. Hence, in some circumstances, a war to return heretical peoples to orthodoxy or, even, to conquer heathens was a candidate for a just war. Both Vitoria and Suarez and later Grotius are anxious to limit further such recourse, so it is plausible to see them as standing at the beginning of a move toward a more restrictive attitude to just cause (Grotius, 1925: 516–17, 553–4; Suarez, 1944; Vitoria, 1991). The current ban on "aggressive war" can be seen, for all its obscurity, as the outcome of such a development.

The strength of this ban is also, of course, connected with the rise of the modern state and the doctrine of sovereignty that has accompanied it. . . .

Admittedly, the contemporary abhorrence of "aggression" has critics; moreover, the exact meaning of "aggression" is elusive and open to exploitation. None the less, the moral power of the idea of defense against aggression comes from the moral significance of self-preservation and particularly self-defense. It is not a uniquely modern concept, as Anscombe (1970), for instance, seems to believe since it may be found virtually at any time or place where questions about the legitimacy of war are raised. . . . Moreover, ancient Chinese discussions of the morality of war are specifically concerned

to reject the legitimacy of aggressive war, and, although the concept of aggression at work is somewhat different from that enshrined in the UN Charter, it is a recognizable relation (Tzu et al., 1964).

The basic moral intuition draws much of its appeal from the legitimacy of personal resort to self-defense. Hobbes, for instance, treats the legitimacy of self-preservation as the fundamental right of nature. There are certainly problems in extrapolating from the case of an individual to that of a nation-state and in elucidating concepts of national rights, but where the state is clearly defending its people rather than its honor or the power of an elite, then the extension has palpable force. Moreover, it is easy to see the point of some other extensions that have had a place in traditional discussions. If a nation is sometimes entitled to the use of violence in its own defense, then surely other nations may come to its aid as long as their objective is to help repel the attack and no more. This parallels what seems allowed with regard to aid in the case of individuals. Of course, in both the domestic and the international cases, what is abstractly morally permissible is not the whole story. There may be powerful prudential reasons for not helping others defend themselves. When the Soviet Union invaded Hungary and later Czechoslovakia the world stood by, principally because of fear of nuclear war, and those fears were realistic enough at least to make a reasonable case for such agonizing inaction.

Another extension is the idea that a nation may defend against aggression before it has begun. The preemptive war is sometimes defended on the ground that when aggression is genuinely imminent it is rational to strike against the enemy before he gets the advantage of the first blow. There seems to be logical space for this, but it remains worrying. As Sidgwick pointed out, the legitimate pre-emption "easily passes over into anticipation of a blow that is merely feared, not really threatened. Indeed this enlarged right of self-protection against mere danger has often been further extended to justify hostile interference to prevent a neighbour growing strong merely through expansion or coalescence with other states" (Sidgwick, 1898: 101). . . .

How then should we understand "aggression"? The UN Charter defines it as follows: "Aggression is the use of armed force by a State against the sovereignty, territorial integrity or political independence of another State or in any other manner inconsistent with the Charter of the United Nations" (United Nations, 1974). . . . There are three broad types of criticism of the defense against aggression model of just cause. . . .

The first complains that the appeal to aggression is too strong. Sometimes aggression is made to seem as if it obliges those attacked, or their sympathizers, to give a military response. . . . But such insistence ignores the rule of proportionality as illustrated and discussed above, and may well conflict with conditions 3 and 4. At most, defense against aggression satisfies the condition of just cause, but it will only license war if the other conditions are fulfilled.

A second complaint is that the aggression appeal is, in another respect, too weak. This questions modern just-war theory's emphasis upon the central, even unique, role of self-defense, and argues that there are other legitimate causes for war. The basic line of criticism here is that restriction of just wars to defense against aggression (even allowing for the extensions discussed above) leaves evils undealt with in the international order. The criticism is put trenchantly by Anscombe: "The present day conception of 'aggression', like so many strongly influential conceptions, is a bad one. Why must it be wrong to strike the first blow in a struggle? The only question is, who is in the right?" (Anscombe, 1970: 43–4). As stated, this criticism would not seem to jettison the concept of aggression as dramatically as she supposes since her argument seems to presume the existence of a struggle in which actual blows have not yet been struck, though they or something like them have been extensively prepared for. So some form of aggression (different from the UN model) may have occurred already, or we may be in the area of legitimate preemption discussed earlier.

But a more interesting construal of "the first blow in the struggle" would refer to the aggressive blow that initiates armed conflict. . . . It would encompass the idea of military intervention in another state's affairs in order to remove an awful government or remedy some great internal evil, such as persecution of a minority group. Following current fashion, let us call these many diverse situations "humanitarian wars." These are not philosophers' fantasies, as wars in Uganda, Cambodia, Somalia, and Kosovo have recently shown.

Support for humanitarian warfare strengthened amongst philosophers and other theorists at the end of the twentieth century, though politicians were generally less enthusiastic. Some humanitarian wars are harder than others for the aggression model to handle, but the tendency to return to a more permissive attitude to the just war needs to be treated with wariness. There is a presumption against the moral validity of resort to war given what we know of the history of warfare, of the vast devastation it commonly causes and the dubious motives that have so often fueled it. For these reasons, the development of just-war theory has been progressively away from altruistic legitimations of war. Our experience of wars of religion, of trade and imperialist wars, and of what tends to happen when one nation conquers another "for its own good" speak against allowing expansive accounts of "just cause."

This provides a powerful objection to humanitarian war, but the fact remains that there can be extreme cases that challenge the objection. Walzer treats the Indian invasion of Bangladesh in 1971 as such a case where the intervention was to prevent the massacre of a population by what was nominally its own government. The Vietnamese invasion of Cambodia may be a similar case or the Tanzanian of Uganda, though the histories of those nations since then has been less than happy. Anscombe's example of the use of violence against "the man-stealing business" is another case that has good claims to exception from the ban, though the example is complex because it sometimes involved armed action against criminal groups disowned by their own governments. . . .

A third, related problem with the aggression model is that it sanctifies existing national-state arrangements. Critics ask: why should these boundaries and *these* states be given such respect? The question is given added force by the ways in which colonization and decolonization have created states with whimsical boundaries. This is not the place to engage in a full-scale discussion of sovereignty, national determination, nationalism, and the justification for state authority, but we can note two things. One is that any idea of sovereignty that requires absolute immunity from outside involvement has never made much sense and makes even less in the contemporary world; the second is that sovereignty, however qualified, is still usually perceived as having profoundly positive significance by those subject to it. Hence, outside intrusions, no matter how well intentioned, will often face deep moral and political problems. The case for humanitarian war needs to be very conscious of these drawbacks. . . .

THE *JUS IN BELLO*

Moral restrictions on how one conducts oneself in war are apt to be met with incredulity. "You do what needs to be done to win" is a common response. There is a certain appeal in this pragmatic outlook, but it flies in the face not only of just-war thinking but of many common human responses to war. The concept of an atrocity, for instance, has a deep place in our thinking. Even that very tough warrior, the US war ace General Chuck Yeager suffered genuine moral revulsion at orders to commit "atrocities" that he was given and complied with in World War II. He was especially "not proud" of his part in the indiscriminate strafing of a 50-square-mile area of Germany.

The idea that there are non-legitimate targets amongst "the enemy" is the basis of one of the two primary rules of the *jus in bello*: the principle of discrimination. The other is the principle of proportionality, the operation of which parallels its work in the *jus ad bellum,* for there are questions to be raised both about whether the resort to war is a proportional response to some injury, and whether some tactic or means is proportionate to its projected effect.

A major part of the discrimination principle concerns the immunity of noncombatants from direct attack. This is a key point at which utilitarian approaches to the justification of war tend to part company with the classical just-war tradition. Either they deny that the principle obtains at all, or, more commonly, they argue that it applies in virtue of its utility. The former move is associated with the idea that war is such "hell" and victory so important that everything must be subordinated to that end, but even in utilitarian terms it is unclear that this form of ruthlessness has the best outcomes, especially when it is shared by the opposing sides. Hence, the more common move is to argue that the immunity of noncombatants is a useful rule for restricting the damage wrought by wars. Non-utilitarians (I shall call them "intrinsicalists" because they believe that there are intrinsic wrongs, other than failing to maximize goods) can agree that there are such extrinsic reasons for the immunity rule, but they will see this fact as a significant additional reason to conform to the principle. Intrinsicalists will argue that the principle's validity springs directly from the reasoning that licenses resort to war in the first place. This resort is allowed by the need to resist perpetrators of aggression (or, on the broader view, to deal with wrongdoers) and hence it licenses violence only against those agents. This is the point behind distinguishing combatants from noncombatants, or, in another terminology, wrongdoers and innocents. In this context, when we classify people as noncombatants or innocents we do not mean that they have no evil in their hearts, or lack enthusiasm for their country's policies, nor do we mean that the combatants have such evil or enthusiasm. The classification is concerned with the role the individual plays in the chain of agency directing the aggression or wrongdoing. . . .

But even when these distinctions are made, there seems room not only for doubt about the application of the distinction to various difficult categories of person, such as slave laborers coerced to work in munitions factories, but also its applicability at all to the highly integrated citizenry of modern states. It is surely anachronistic to think of contemporary war as waged between armies; it is really nation against nation, economy against economy, peoples against peoples. But although modern war has many unusual features, its "total" nature is more an imposed construction than a necessary reflection of a changed reality. Even in World War II not every enemy citizen was a combatant. In any war, there remain millions of people who are not plausibly seen as involved in the enemy's lethal chain of agency. There are, for instance, infants, young children, the elderly and infirm, lots of tradespeople and workers, not to mention dissidents and conscientious objectors. Moreover, the model of total war that underpins this objection is itself outdated. . . .

In fact, there has been a remarkable change on this issue in the strategic doctrine and military outlook of many major powers since the end of the Cold War. It is now common to pay at least lip service to the principle, as evidenced by certain restraint shown during the Gulf War and the bombing of Serbia, and by the widespread condemnation of Russian brutality in Chechnya. The real question is not so much whether it is immoral to target noncombatants (it is), but how "collateral" damage and death to noncombatants can be defended. This was always a problem in just-war theory, often solved by resort to some form of the principle of double effect. This allowed for the harming of noncombatants in some circumstances as a foreseen but unintended side-effect of an otherwise legitimate act of war. The "circumstances" included the proportionality of the side-effect to the intended outcome. Not everyone agrees with the principle (and this is not the place to discuss it in detail) but the conduct of war in contemporary circumstances is morally impossible unless the activities of warriors are allowed to put noncombatants at risk in certain circumstances. Some modification to the immunity principle to allow indirect harming seems to be in line with commonsense morality in other areas of life, and to be necessitated by the circumstances of war. If it is not available, then pacifism, as Holmes (1989: esp. 193–203) has argued, seems the only moral option.

TERRORISM

For a phenomenon that arouses such widespread anxiety, anger, and dismay, terrorism is surprisingly difficult to define. . . . Rather than extensively reviewing the varieties of definition, I propose to concentrate on one key element in common responses to and fears about terrorism, namely the idea that it involves "innocent" victims. This provides a point of connection with the moral apparatus of just-war theory, specifically the principle of discrimination and its requirement of noncombatant immunity. Of course, terrorism does not always take place in the context of all-out international war, but it usually has a war-like dimension. I will define it as follows: "the use of violence to target noncombatants ('innocents' in the *jus in bello* sense) for political purposes."

This definition has several contentious consequences. One is that states can themselves use terrorism, another is that much political violence by non-state agents will not be terrorist. As to the former, there is a tendency, especially amongst the representatives of states, to restrict the possibility of terrorist acts to non-state agents. But if we think of terrorism, in the light of the definition above, as a tactic rather than an ideology, this tendency should be resisted since states can and do use the tactic of attacking the innocent. Some theorists who think terrorism cannot be perpetrated by governments are not so much confused, as operating with a different definition. They define terrorism, somewhat in the spirit of Hobbes, as the use of political violence by non-state agents against the state. Some would restrict it to violence against a democratic state. This is the way many political scientists view terrorism, and, at least in the case of a democratic state, they see it as morally wrong. Call this the political definition to contrast with the tactical definition.

A further consequence of the tactical definition is that it implies a degree of purposiveness that terrorism is thought to lack. Some theorists have claimed that terrorism is essentially "random," others that it is essentially "expressive." In both cases, the claim is that a reference to political purposes is inappropriate. In reply, it can be argued that talk of terrorism as random is generated by the genuine perception that it does not restrict its targets to the obvious military ones, but this does not mean that it is wild and purposeless. Indeed, most terrorists think that the best way to get certain political effects is to aim at "soft" noncombatant targets. Similarly, there can be no doubt that many terrorist attacks are expressive and symbolic, involving the affirmation of the attitude: "We are still here; take notice of us." Yet the expressive need not exclude the purposive, or even the assertive. "That's a rattle-snake" may express horror, be designed to warn an audience, and state a fact. So terrorist acts can be, and are, both expressive and politically purposive. . . .

The tactical definition faces the problems already discussed concerning the meaning of the term "noncombatant," but even more acutely. In guerilla war, insurgents may not be easily identifiable as combatants and will seek to enlist or involve the villagers and local inhabitants in the campaign thereby blurring their status as noncombatants. On the other hand, many state officials who are not directly prosecuting the campaign against the insurgents may be plausibly viewed as implicated in the grievances the revolutionaries are seeking to redress. There are certainly problems here, but they do not seem insurmountable. In the heat and confusion of battle, it may be difficult and dangerous to treat even children as noncombatants, especially where children are coerced or seduced into combatant roles (as is common in many contemporary conflicts). None the less, a premeditated campaign of bombing regional hospitals to induce civilian lack of cooperation with rebels is in palpable violation of the *jus in bello*. So are the murder of infants and the targeting of state officials, such as water authorities or traffic police, whose roles are usually tangentially related to the causes of the conflict. It is true that some ideologies purport to have enemies so comprehensive as to make even small children and helpless adults into "combatants." Western advocates of "total-war" strategic bombing of cities share with the Islamic fanatics, who incorporate American air travellers and sundry citizens of Manhattan into their holy targets, a simplistic and Manichaean vision of the world that is at odds with the just-war tradition's attempt to bring moral sanity to bear upon the use of political violence.

Is terrorism wrong? Given just-war theory and the tactical definition, the answer is clearly yes. And if one takes the principle of noncombatant immunity to invoke an absolute moral prohibition, as just-war thinkers have commonly done, then it is always wrong. Yet many contemporary moral philosophers, sympathetic to just-war thinking, are wary of moral absolutes. They would treat the prohibition as expressing a very strong moral presumption against terrorism and the targeting of noncombatants, but allow for exceptions in extreme circumstances. So, Michael Walzer thinks that in conditions of "supreme emergency" the violation of the normal immunity is permissible in warfare though only with a heavy burden of remorse (extending even to scapegoating). He thinks the Allied terror bombing of German cities in World War II (in the early stages) was legitimated by the enormity of the Nazi threat. John Rawls has recently endorsed this view while condemning the bombings of Hiroshima and Nagasaki (Walzer, 1992; Rawls, 1999). If this concession is allowed to states, it seems mere consistency to allow it to non-state agents on the same terms. The general reluctance to do so suggests that such categories as "supreme emergency" may mask contestable political judgments.

REFERENCES

Anscombe, G. E. M. (1970) War and murder. In R. Wasserstrom (ed.), *War and Morality*. Belmont, CA: Wadsworth.

Grotius, H. (1925) *The Rights of War and Peace (De jure belli ac pacis libri tres)*, vol. 2, ed. Francis W. Kelsey (orig. pub. 1682). Oxford: Clarendon Press.

Hobbes, T. (1969) *The Elements of Law: Natural and Political*, 2nd ed., ed. Ferdinand Tönnies, with new intro. by M. M. Goldsmith. London: Cass.

Holmes, R. (1989) *On War and Morality*. Princeton, NJ: Princeton University Press.

Rawls, J. (1999) Fifty years after Hiroshima. In S. Freeman (ed.), *Collected Papers*, pp. 565–72. Cambridge, MA: Harvard University Press.

Sidgwick, H. (1898/1998) *Practical Ethics*. New York: Oxford University Press.

Suarez, F. (1944) *Selections from Three Works of Francisco Suarez*, vol. 2, ed. J. Scott. Oxford: Clarendon Press.

Tzu, H., Tzu, H. F. and Tzu, M. (1964) *Basic Writings of Mo Tzu, Hsun Tzu, and Han Fei Tzu*, trans. B. Watson. New York: Columbia University Press.

United Nations (1974) *General Assembly Ruling 3314*. New York: United Nations.

de Vitoria, F. (1991) *Political Writings: Francesco de Vitoria*, ed. A. Pagden and J. Lawrance. Cambridge: Cambridge University Press.

Walzer, M. (1992) *Just and Unjust Wars*, 2nd ed. New York: Basic Books.

Discussion Questions

1. Is the just-war theory, as explicated by Coady, still applicable in modern society? Analyze the theory in light of the prima facie moral duties and rights discussed in Chapter 1.

2. Discuss whether the United States' preemptive strike against Iraq, and the attacks by Iraqis on the occupying coalition forces, are justified under the just-war theory.

3. Discuss whether a policy of nuclear deterrence is justified under the just-war theory.

4. Applying the *jus in bello* reasoning, discuss whether the use of chemical and biological weapons in self-defense is justified if a country is invaded by another country that has greatly superior military strength.

5. In the September 11 attacks, the terrorists chose targets that symbolized what they regarded as the heresy of globalization, destruction of traditional ways of living, and exploitation of the poor of the world by the rich. Discuss whether targeting symbols of "evil" by groups that lack the power to directly attack the military of a superior force is ever legitimate. How would Coady and a utilitarian each most likely answer this question?

SOHAIL H. HASHMI

Interpreting the Islamic Ethics of War and Peace

Sohail H. Hashmi is an associate professor in the International Relations Program at Mt. Holyoke College. Hashmi reviews the origins of Islamic ethics of war and peace. He then discusses *jihad* in the context of the just-war tradition. Finally, he applies Islamic ethics of *jihad* to current issues such as the killing of civilians during the Iraq War and the possession and use of weapons of mass destruction.

Critical Reading Questions

1. What is the source of the controversy regarding the concept of *jihad*?
2. What are the primary sources of the ethical discourse in Islam?
3. Who is Ibn Khaldun and what are his views on war and peace?
4. According to the Qur'an, why is humanity prone to war?
5. What is peace (*salam*)?
6. Under what conditions is the use of force sanctioned by Muslim ethics?
7. Is pacifism an acceptable response to oppression in Islamic ethics?
8. What was the prophet Muhammed's view on the use of war and violence?
9. When is nonviolent resistance preferable to armed conflict?
10. What are the four types of war distinguished by Ibn Khaldun? Which wars are legitimate and which ones are illegitimate?
11. What is the Islamic view on the use of war or force to convert nonbelievers?
12. What is the medieval distinction between *dar al-harb* and *dar al-Islam*?
13. What is the modern fundamentalist Islamic view of the role of *jihad* on an international level?
14. What is the basis for *jus in bello* (just conduct of war) and *jus ad bellum* (just waging of a war) in the Qur'an and Islamic ethics?
15. What is the Islamic position on the use of weapons of mass destruction?

Muslim writers of many intellectual persuasions have long argued that Westerners hold an inaccurate, even deliberately distorted, conception of *jihad*. In fact, however, the idea of *jihad* (and the ethics of war and peace generally) has been the subject of an intense and multifaceted debate among Muslims themselves. So diffusely defined and inconsistently applied has the idea become in Islamic discourse that a number of religious opposition groups have felt compelled to differentiate their cause from competing "false" causes by naming themselves, tautologically, "Islamic" *jihad*.

Nevertheless, when the contemporary Islamic discourse on war and peace is studied in the context of recent historical events, including decolonization and the many conflicts in which Muslims have been involved, one can discern an emerging consensus among Muslim intellectuals on the current meaning of *jihad*. This consensus is by no

means universal, and given the diffuse nature of religious authority in the Islamic tradition, debate on the ethics of war and peace is likely to continue. But as I hope to demonstrate, the concept of *jihad* in contemporary Islam is one that is still adapting to the radical changes in international relations that have occurred since the medieval theory was first elaborated. We are witnessing a period of reinterpretation and redefinition, one characterized by controversy and confusion about how the concept should be applied to contemporary events, but also by movement toward wider agreement on the essential points of an Islamic ethics of war and peace. . . .

Much of the controversy surrounding the concept of *jihad* among Muslims today emerges from the tension between its legal and ethical dimensions. This tension arises because it is the juristic, and not the philosophical or ethical, literature that has historically defined Muslim discourse on war and peace. With the rise of the legalistic tradition, ethical inquiry became a narrow and secondary concern of Islamic scholarship. What we find from the medieval period are legal treatises propounding

"Interpreting the Islamic Ethics of War and Peace," from *The Ethics of War and Peace*, ed. by Terry Nardin (Princeton: Princeton University Press, 1996), 146–166. Some notes have been omitted.

the rules of *jihad* and discussing related issues, but few ethical works outlining a framework of principles derived from the Qur'an and sunna upon which these rules could be based. . . .

CONCEPTIONS OF WAR AND PEACE IN THE QUR'AN

Ibn Khaldun observes in the *Muqaddima*, his celebrated introduction to a history of the world composed at the end of the fourteenth century, that "wars and different kinds of fighting have always occurred in the world since God created it." "War is endemic to human existence," he writes, "something natural among human beings. No nation, and no race is free from it."[1] Ibn Khaldun's brief comment summarizes rather well the traditional Islamic understanding of war as a universal and inevitable aspect of human existence. It is a feature of human society sanctioned, if not willed, by God Himself. The issues of war and peace thus fall within the purview of divine legislation for humanity. Islam, Muslims like to say, is a complete code of life; given the centrality of war to human existence, the moral evaluation of war holds a significant place in Muslim ethical/legal discussion. The Islamic ethics of war and peace is therefore derived from the same general sources upon which Islamic law is based.

The first of these sources, of course, is the Qur'an, which is held by Muslims to be God's final and definitive revelation to humanity. The Qur'anic text, like other revealed scriptures, is not a systematic treatise on ethics or law. It is a discursive commentary on the actions and experiences of the prophet Muhammad, his followers, and his opponents over the course of twenty-three years. But as the Qur'an itself argues in several verses, God's message is not limited to the time and place of its revelation; it is, rather, "a message to all the worlds" (81:27) propounding a moral code with universal applicability (39:41). From this commentary emerge broadly defined ethical principles that have been elaborated throughout Islamic history into what may be termed an Islamic conception

of divine creation and man's place in it. In other words, although the Qur'an does not present a systematic ethical argument, it is possible to derive a consistent ethical system from it.

Why is humanity prone to war? The Qur'anic answer unfolds in the course of several verses revealed at various times, the essential points of which may be summarized as follows:

First, man's fundamental nature (*fitra*) is one of moral innocence, that is, freedom from sin. In other words, there is no Islamic equivalent to the notion of "original sin." Moreover, each individual is born with a knowledge of God's commandments, that is, with the essential aspects of righteous behavior. But this moral awareness is eroded as each individual encounters the corrupting influences of human society (30:30).

Second, man's nature is to live on the earth in a state of harmony, and peace with other living things. This is the ultimate import of the responsibility assigned by God to man as His vicegerent (*khalifa*) on this planet (2:30). True peace (*salam*) is therefore not merely an absence of war; it is the elimination of the grounds for strife or conflict, and the resulting waste and corruption (*fasad*) they create. Peace, not war or violence, is God's true purpose for humanity (2:208).

Third, given man's capacity for wrongdoing, there will always be some who *choose* to violate their nature and transgress against God's commandments. Adam becomes fully human only when he chooses to heed Iblis's (Satan's) temptation and disobeys God. As a result of this initial act of disobedience, human beings are expelled from the Garden to dwell on earth as "enemies to each other" (2:36, 7:24). Thus, wars and the evils that stem from them, the Qur'an suggests, are the inevitable consequences of the uniquely human capacity for moral choice.

The Qur'an does not present the fall of man as irrevocable, however, for God quickly returns to Adam to support and guide him (2:37). This, according to Islamic belief, is the beginning of continuous divine revelation to humanity through a series of prophets ending with Muhammad. God's reminders of the laws imprinted upon each human consciousness through His prophets are a manifestation of His endless mercy to His creation, because all human beings are potential victims of Iblis's guile, that is, potential evildoers, and most human beings are actually quite far from God's laws (36:45–46). When people form social units, they become all the more prone to disobey God's laws through the obstinate persistence in wrongdoing caused by custom and social pressures (2:1.3–1:4, 37:69, 43:22). In this way, the individual drive for power, wealth, prestige, and all the other innumerable human goals becomes amplified. Violence is the inevitable result of the human desire for self-aggrandizement.

Fourth, each prophet encounters opposition from those (always a majority) who persist in their rebellion against God, justifying their actions through various self-delusions. One of the principal characteristics of rejection of God (*kufr*) is the inclination toward violence and oppression, encapsulated by the broad concept *zulm*. When individuals choose to reject divine guidance, either by transgressing against specific divine injunctions or by losing faith altogether, they violate (commit zulm against) their own nature (fitra). . . . When an entire society rejects God, oppression and violence become the norm throughout the society and in relation with other societies as well; the moral anarchy that prevails when human beings abandon the higher moral code derived from faith in a supreme and just Creator, the Qur'an suggests, is fraught with potential and actual violence. . . .

Fifth, peace (salam) is attainable only when beings surrender to God's will and live according to God's laws. This is the condition of *islam,* the conscious decision to acknowledge in faith and conduct the presence and power of God. Because human nature is not sufficiently strong to resist the temptation to evil, it is necessary for man to establish a human agency, that is, a state, to mitigate the effects of anarchy and enforce divine law.

Sixth, because it is unlikely that individuals or societies will ever conform fully to the precepts of Islam, Muslims must always be prepared to fight to preserve the Muslim faith and Muslim principles (8:60, 73). The use of force by the Muslim community is, therefore, sanctioned by God as a necessary response to the existence of evil in the world. As the Qur'an elaborates in an early revelation, the believers are those "who, whenever tyranny afflicts them, defend themselves" (42:39). This theme of the just, God-ordained use of force for legitimate purposes is continued in several other verses. In the first verse that explicitly permits the Muslim community to use armed force against its enemies, the Qur'an makes clear that fighting is a burden imposed upon all believers (not only Muslims) as a result of the enmity harbored by the unbelievers.

Permission [to fight] is given to those against whom War is being wrongfully waged . . . those who have been driven from their homelands against all right for no other reason than their saying: "Our Sustainer is God!" . . .

A subsequent verse converts this permission to fight into an injunction: The rationale given for using armed force is quite explicit: "Tumult and oppression (*fitna*) is worse than killing" (2:191). These two verses clearly undermine the possibility of an Islamic pacifism. One verse in particular offers an implicit challenge to an ethical position based on the renunciation of all violence: "Fighting is prescribed for you, even though it be hateful to you; but it may well be that you hate something that is in fact good for you, and that you love a thing that is in fact bad for you: and God knows, whereas you do not" (2:216). There is, thus, no equivalent in the Islamic tradition of the continuing debate within Christianity of the possibility of just war: There is no analogue in Islamic texts to Aquinas's Question 40: "Are some wars permissible?" The Islamic discourse on war and peace begins from the a priori assumption that some types of war are permissible—indeed, required by God—and that all other forms of violence are, therefore, forbidden. In short, the Qur'an's attitude toward war and peace may be described as an idealistic realism. Human existence is characterized neither by incessant warfare nor by real peace, but by a continuous tension between the two. Societies exist forever in a precarious balance between them. The unending human challenge *jihad fi sabit Allah* (struggle in the way of God) [is] to mitigate the possibility of war to strengthen the grounds for peace. . . .

CONCEPTIONS OF WAR AND PEACE IN THE SUNNA

The second source for the Islamic ethics of war and peace is the practice (sunna) of the prophet Muhammad. It is impossible to comprehend the Qur'an without understanding the life of the Prophet and impossible to comprehend the life of the Prophet without understanding the Qur'an. As the Prophet's wife, Aisha bint Abi Bakr, is reported to have said: "His character (*khuluqhu*) was the Qur'an."

Muhammad was born into a milieu characterized by internecine skirmishes (*ghazwa*) among rival tribes. These were seldom more than raids undertaken for petty plunder of a neighboring tribe's flocks. If the conflict had any "higher" purpose, it was usually collective reprisal for an injury or affront suffered by a single member of the tribe: according to the prevailing *lex talionis*. Larger confrontations for higher stakes, such as the actual conquest of territory, were rare, although not unknown. . . . Naturally, tribal loyalty was the cornerstone of this society's ethos, and virtue was often equated with martial valor. It would, however, be incorrect to view pre-Islamic Arab culture as glorifying war. . . . [T]he ghazw'a was often viewed by its participants as a sort of ongoing game, a struggle to outwit the opponent with a minimum of bloodshed. The aim was not to vanquish the foe but to demonstrate the qualities of courage, loyalty, and magnanimity—all components of masculine nobility included in the term *muruwwa*. Implicit in the Arab martial code were "rules of the game" that prohibited, among other things, fighting during certain months, the killing of noncombatants, and unnecessary spoliation. . . .

We can construct an outline of the Prophet's approach to the ethics of war and peace not only by referring to the Qur'an, but also by making use of the large body of literature comprising the Prophet's sayings and actions (*hadith*) and biography (*sira*) compiled between the second and fourth Islamic centuries. It is clear from these records that from an early age, Muhammad was averse to many aspects of the tribal culture in which he was born. In particular, there is no indication that he ever showed any interest in affairs of tribal honor, particularly in the ghazwa. Throughout the Meccan period of his prophetic mission (610–22 C.E.), he showed no inclination toward the use of force in any form, even for self-defense—on the contrary, his policy can only be described as nonviolent resistance. . . . The Prophet insisted throughout this period on the virtues of patience and steadfastness in the face of their opponents' attacks. When the persecution of the most vulnerable Muslims (former slaves and members of Mecca's poorer families) became intense, he directed them to seek refuge in the realm of a Christian king, Abyssinia. The Prophet's rejection of armed struggle during the Meccan period was more than mere prudence based on the Muslims' military weakness. It was, rather, derived from the Qur'an's still unfolding conception that the use of force should be avoided unless it is, in just war parlance, a "last resort." . . .

The requital of evil is an evil similar to it hence, whoever pardons [his enemy] and makes peace, his reward rests with God—for, verily; He does not love evildoers. Yet indeed, as for any who defend themselves after having been wronged—no blame whatever attaches to them: blame attaches but to those who oppress [other] people and behave outrageously on earth, offending against all right: for them is grievous suffering in store! But if one is patient in adversity and forgives, this is indeed the best resolution of affairs (42:40–43).

The main result of these early verses is not to reaffirm the pre-Islamic custom of *lex talionis* but the exact opposite: to establish the moral superiority of forgiveness over revenge. The permission of self-defense is not a call to arms; military force is not mentioned, although neither is it proscribed. Instead, it should be seen as a rejection of quietism, of abnegation of moral responsibility in the face of oppression. Active nonviolent resistance and open defiance of pagan persecution is the proper Muslim response, according to these verses, and was, in fact, the Prophet's own practice during this period. . . .

THE GROUNDS FOR WAR

Ibn Khaldun continues his discussion of war in the *Muqaddima* by distinguishing four types of war: One arises from petty squabbles among rival foes or neighboring tribes, another from the desire for plunder found among "savage peoples." These two types he labels "illegitimate wars." Then, reflecting the prevailing medieval approach, he divides legitimate wars into two types: *jihad* and wars to suppress internal rebellion. This latter division of legitimate wars is the logical outgrowth of the medieval juristic bifurcation of the world into two spheres, *dar al-Islam* (the realm where Islamic law applied), and *dar al-harb* (the realm of war). According to the Sunni legal schools, *jihad* properly speaking was war waged against unbelievers. Because all Muslims were understood to constitute a single community of believers, wars between Muslim parties were usually classed in a separate category, *fitna* (literally, a "trial" or "test"). Like Plato, who has Socrates declare that Greeks do not make war on one another, the Muslim jurists viewed intra-Muslim disputes as internal strife that should be resolved quickly by the ruling authorities. This approach to war among Muslims, important in medieval theory, has assumed greater significance in modern controversies about the definition of *jihad*.

The descriptions of *jihad* in the medieval texts reflect the historical context in which legal theory was elaborated. Because the medieval juristic conception of *jihad* provided legal justification for the rapid expansion of the Islamic empire that occurred in the decades following the Prophet's death, its connotations are offensive rather than defensive. Relatively little consideration was given to *jihad* defined as "defensive struggle," that is, war undertaken strictly to safeguard Muslim lives and property from external aggression. It was considered obvious that Muslims may wage war in self-defense, according to the Qur'anic verses cited earlier. This defensive war was *fard 'ayn*, a moral duty of each able-bodied Muslim, male or female.

More detailed discussion of *jihad* comes in the context of offensive struggles aimed at expansion of Islamic hegemony, an expansion aimed ultimately at the universal propagation of Islam. In the twelfth century, Ibn Rushd (Averroes) wrote a legal treatise that deals at some length with the conditions of *jihad*.[2] . . .

Because the ultimate end of *jihad* is the propagation of the Islamic faith, not material gain or territorial conquest, Ibn Rushd, like other medieval writers, implicitly, if not always explicitly, separates the grounds for *jihad* from the grounds for war (harb or qitai). Because Islam is viewed as a universal mission to all humanity, *jihad* is the perpetual condition that prevails between dar al-Islam and dar al-harb. Participation in the *jihad* to overcome dar al-harb was a *fard kifaya*, a moral obligation only for those capable of assuming it, namely able-bodied and financially secure adult males. Actual war arose only as the final step in a "ladder of escalation." The first step in any contact between the Muslim state and a foreign power was an invitation to allow the peaceful preaching of Islam. This was consonant with the practice of the Prophet, who allegedly had sent letters to the rulers of Byzantium, Iran, and Egypt for precisely this purpose. If a foreign ruler refused this invitation, he was to be offered the incorporation of his people into the Islamic realm as a protected non-Muslim community governed by its own religious laws, but obliged to pay a tax, the *jizya*, in lieu of performing military service. Only if the non-Muslims refused these conditions were there grounds for active hostilities. At this point, the Muslim ruler was not only permitted but required to wage war against them. . . .

As Ibn Rushd's discussion makes apparent, the medieval juristic literature is characterized by fundamental disagreements on the grounds for war. But most of the legal scholars agree that the object of *jihad* is not the forcible conversion of unbelievers to the Islamic faith. This object would contradict several clear Qur'anic statements enjoining free-dom of worship, including "Let there be no com-pulsion in religion; the truth stands out clearly from error" (2:256), and "If your Lord had so willed, all those who are on earth would have believed: you then compel mankind, against their will, to believe?" (10:99). . . . The object of *jihad* is generally held by these writers to be the subjuga-tion of hostile powers who refuse to permit the preaching of Islam, not forcible conversion. Once under Muslim rule, they reason, non-Muslims will be free to consider the merits of Islam. The medieval theory of an on-going *jihad,* and the bifurcation of the world into dar al-Islam and dar al-harb upon which it was predicated, became a fiction soon after it was elaborated by medieval writers. . . . Nevertheless, the idea that "Islam" and the "West" represented monolithic and mutu-ally antagonistic civilizations underlay much Mus-lim and European writing, particularly during the heyday of European imperialism in the eighteenth and nineteenth centuries. Shades of this viewpoint are very much apparent in our own day.

In his discussion of recent Muslim thinking on the grounds for *jihad,* Bassam ubi outlines two contending approaches, the "conformist" and the "fundamentalist." He suggests that the reinter-pretation of the medieval theory of *jihad* by mod-ernists (as the conformists are more commonly known) is half-hearted and that, in the end, it is the fundamentalists' resurrection of the medieval dar al-harb/dar al-Islam distinction that best char-acterizes the current Muslim view of international relations generally and issues of war and peace in particular. . . . Although the Qur'an's division of mankind into believers and unbelievers lends sup-port for such a view, modernist writers argue that the Qur'anic verses cannot be interpreted to sug-gest a perpetual state of war between the two, nor any territoriality to the "house of Islam," when these verses are taken in the full context of the Qur'anic message. In one of the leading modernist expositions of Islam international law, Mohammad Talaat al-Ghunaimi dismisses the dar al-Islam/dar al-harb distinction as an idea introduced by cer-tain medieval legal thinkers in response to their own historical circumstances, but having no basis in Islamic ethics. . . .

With the emergence of postcolonial Muslim states, political legitimacy and the rights of the people in the face of oppressive regimes have emerged as central issues in Islamic discourse. These issues figure prominently, of course, in all fundamentalist literature. Fundamentalists view themselves as a vanguard of the righteous, pre-paring the way for the elimination of jahili values from their societies and the establishment of a just "Islamic" order. . . . What is clear from these works is the view, supported by experience, that the secu-lar, nationalist regimes ruling most Muslim coun-tries today, backed by their Western supporters, will not willingly cede power, even if the major-ity of the population does not support them. They will maintain power by any means, including the violent repression of dissent. In other words, it is argued that these regimes have declared war on Islam within their countries, and that it is incum-bent upon all true believers to respond by what-ever means are necessary, including violence, to overthrow them. The fundamentalist writings are therefore focused on combating the social and international oppression that they believe face the Muslim community (*umma*) everywhere. *Jihad* is for the fundamentalists an instrument for the realization of political and social justice in their own societies, a powerful tool for internal reform and one required by the Qur'an's command that Muslims "enjoin the right and forbid the wrong" (3:104). The thrust of the modern *jihad* is thus very much inward. Warfare on the international level is considered only to the extent that Western gov-ernments are viewed as archenemies who impose corrupt and authoritarian regimes upon Muslims. *Jihad* as an instrument for the imposition of Islamic rule in non-Muslim states today hardly figures in fundamentalist works. That goal has been post-poned indefinitely, given the fundamentalist posi-tion, which they share with many other Muslim writers, that most of the Muslim countries them-selves do not at present have Islamic governments.

One area in which modernists and fundamental-ists are tending to converge is upon the argument that *jihad* is an instrument for enforcing human rights. For example, the Iranian revolutionary leader Ayatollah Murtaza Mutahhari argues that "the most sacred form of *jihad* and war is that which is fought in defense of humanity and of human rights."[3] Similarly, the Indian/Pakistani scholar Maulana Abu al-A'la Mawdudi writes that *jihad* is obligatory for Muslims when hostile forces threaten their human rights, which in his analysis includes forcibly evicting them from their homes, tampering with their social order, and obstructing religious life.[4] To some extent these arguments are a response to Western writings on the international protection of human rights. But it is interesting to note that whereas there is continuing debate in the West on the legality of humanitarian intervention against sovereign states, continuing ambivalence toward the territorial state in Islamic thought lends weight to the argument in favor of such intervention among a broad range of Muslim writers.

THE CONDUCT OF WAR

Because the goal of *jihad* is the call to Islam, not territorial conquest or plunder, the right conduct of Muslim armies has traditionally been an important concern within Islam. The Qur'an provides the basis for *ius in bello* considerations: "And fight in God's cause against those who wage war against you, but do not transgress limits, for God loves not the transgressors" (2:190). The "limits" are enumerated in the practice of the Prophet and the first four caliphs. According to authoritative traditions, whenever the Prophet sent out a military force, he would instruct its commander to adhere to certain restraints. . . .

Do not act treacherously; do not act disloyally; do not act neglectfully. Do not mutilate; do not kill little children or old men, or women; do not cut off the heads of the palm-trees or burn them; do not cut down the fruit trees; do not slaughter a sheep or a cow or a camel, except for food. You will pass by people who devote their lives in cloisters; leave them and their devotions alone. You will come upon people who bring you platters in

which are various sorts of food; if you eat any of it, mention the name of God over it.

Thus, the Qur'an and the actions of the Prophet and his successors established the principles of discrimination and proportionality of means. . . . In addition, the jurists also dealt with the traditional concerns of ius in bello: the definition and protection of noncombatants and restrictions on certain types of weapon. The legal discussions address three issues: Who is subject to damage in war? What types of damage may be inflicted upon persons? What types of damage may be inflicted upon their property? Underlying the differing opinions on these issues once again are the apparent contradictions between the peace verses and the sword verses. . . .

In current Muslim discourse on war and peace, ius in bello issues receive very little attention. This is true despite the vast changes that have occurred in both the international law and the technology of warfare. The discussion that does occur is usually undertaken by modernists seeking to reinterpret the Qur'an and sunna so that Islamic injunctions correspond to current international practice . . . . More contemporary issues, such as the definition of noncombatant immunity and the use of terrorist methods by some Islamic groups have yet to be treated systematically.

Far more relevant and interesting discussion of right conduct in war occurs in the context of specific conflicts. During the "war of the cities" toward the end of the Iran-Iraq War, for example, Mehdi Bazargan and the Liberation Movement of Iran (LMI) repeatedly protested that Khomeini was violating Islamic prohibitions against targeting civilians when he authorized missile strikes against Baghdad in retaliation for Iraq's Scud missile attacks against Teheran. In one "open letter" to Khomeini, the IMI wrote:

According to Islam, it is justifiable retribution only if we, with our own missiles, hit the commanders or senders of the Iraqi missiles rather than hitting civilian areas and killing innocent people and turning their homes and communities into ghost towns and hills of rubble, all in the name of striking military targets.

. . . ius in bello rather than ius ad bellum concerns dominated Muslim debates on the ethics of the conflict. Among the points raised by opponents of the anti-Iraq coalition's policies was that the conflict should be treated as fitna, that is, a dispute among Muslims. The rules concerning fitna developed by medieval jurists do not permit Muslims to ally themselves with non-Muslims, particularly when military decision-making is in non-Muslim hands. The prohibition was based on the belief that unbelievers would not apply the stricter code of conduct incumbent upon Muslims when fighting other Muslims. Critics of the Gulf War have argued that the conduct of the war by the coalition validates the medieval jurists' concerns. The massive air bombardment of Iraq's governmental and industrial facilities, they charge, was disproportionate to the Iraqi provocation and insufficiently discriminated between military and civilian targets. Moreover, the slaughter of Iraqi troops fleeing Kuwait City on the "highway of death" directly contravened one of the central points of Islamic law, namely that the goal of all military campaigns against other Muslims should be to rehabilitate and not to annihilate the transgressing party.

The most glaring area of neglect in contemporary Islamic analyses of ius in bello concerns weapons of mass destruction. So far, no systematic work has been done by Muslim scholars on how nuclear, chemical, and biological weapons relate to the Islamic ethics of war. This is an astonishing fact in light of the development of nuclear technology by several Muslim countries and the repeated use of chemical weapons by Iraq. In discussing the issue with several leading Muslim specialists in international law, I have found a great deal of ambivalence on the subject. Most scholars cite the Qur'anic verse "Hence, make ready against them whatever force and war mounts you are able to muster, so that you might deter thereby the enemies of God" (8:60) as justification for developing nuclear weaponry. Muslims must acquire nuclear weapons, I have been repeatedly told, because their enemies have introduced such weapons into their arsenals. There is unanimous agreement that Muslims should think of nuclear weapons only as a deterrent and that

they should be used only as a second strike weapon. But Islamic discussion of this topic remains at a very superficial level. There is little appreciation of the logistics of nuclear deterrence and of the moral difficulties to which a deterrence strategy gives rise.

CONCLUSION

Is the Islamic *jihad* the same as the Western just war? The answer, of course, depends upon who is defining the concepts. But after this brief survey of the debates that have historically surrounded the Islamic approach to war and peace and the controversies that are continuing to this day, I think it is safe to conclude that even though *jihad* may not be identical to the just war as it has evolved in the West, the similarities between Western and Islamic thinking on war and peace are far more numerous than the differences.

. . . *Jihad,* like just war, is grounded in the belief that intersocietal relations should be peaceful, not marred by constant and destructive warfare. The surest way for human beings to realize this peace is for them to obey the divine law that is imprinted on the human conscience and therefore accessible to everyone, believers and unbelievers. . . . No war was *jihad* unless it was undertaken with right intent and as a last resort, and declared by right authority. Most Muslims today disavow the duty to propagate Islam by force and limit *jihad* to self-defense. And finally, *jihad,* like just war, places strict limitations on legitimate targets during war and demands that belligerents use the least amount of force necessary to achieve the swift cessation of hostilities. Both *jihad* and just war are dynamic concepts, still evolving and adapting to changing international realities. As Muslims continue to interpret the Islamic ethics of war and peace, their debates on *jihad* will, I believe, increasingly parallel the Western debates on just war. And as Muslims and non-Muslims continue their recently begun dialogue on the just international order, they may well find a level of agreement on the ethics of war and peace that will ultimately be reflected in a revised and more universal law of war and peace.

NOTES

1. Ibn Khaldun, *The Muqaddimah: An Introduction to History,* trans. Franz Rosenthal (Princeton: Princeton University Press, 1967), 2:73.

2. Ibn Rushd, *Bidayat al-mujtahid,* in Rudolph Peters, ed. and trans., Jihad, in *Medieval and Modern Islam* (Leiden: E. J. Brill, 1977), 9–25.

3. Ayatollah Murtaza Mutahhari, "Defense: The Essence of Jihad," in Mehdi Abedi and Gary Legenhausen, eds., *Jihad and Shahadat: Struggle and Martyrdom in Islam* (Houston: Institute for Research and Islamic Studies, 1986), 105.

4. Abu al-A'la Mawdudi, *Al-Jihad fi'l-Islam* (Lahore: Idara Tarjuman al-Qur'an, 1988), 55–56.

Discussion Questions

1. Compare and contrast the Islamic ethics of war and peace with the Judeo-Christian just-war tradition. Discuss what a cultural relativist, a natural law ethicist, and/or a deontologist would each make of the similarities and differences.
2. What is the difference between nonviolent resistance and pacifism, and why is the first justified under Islamic ethics, but not the second?
3. In 2001 Islamic terrorists crashed two airplanes into the World Trade Center, killing thousands, including themselves. Many Muslims regard suicide bombers as contrary to God's law and Muhammed's teachings. Others regard suicide bombers as martyrs and suicide bombing as a legitimate form of self-defense.[13] Discuss the moral validity of these two positions in light of the Islamic teachings on war.
4. Discuss what course of action an Islamic ethicist would most likely suggest for the Muslim world to take in response to Hitler's program of exterminating the Jews during World War II. Support your answer.

JONATHAN GRANOFF

Nuclear Weapons, Ethics, Morals and Law

Attorney Jonathan Granoff is a member of the Lawyers Alliance for World Security and president of the Global Security Institute. In this article, Granoff argues that the possession of nuclear weapons by several modern states not only violates the principle of equality, but also shows a lack of respect for human life. Citing international court rulings regarding the legitimacy of nuclear weapons for the purpose of deterrence, he concludes that we should work toward the elimination of nuclear weapons.

"Nuclear Weapons, Ethics, Morals and Law," presented to the *Nuclear Non-Proliferation Prepcom of 1999* and *The Hague Appeal for Peace,* May 1999. Some notes have been omitted.

Critical Reading Questions

1. According to Granoff, what is the foundation of ethical norms?
2. What are some universal moral norms that are relevant to the debate on nuclear weapons?
3. What is the relationship between ethical values and law?
4. How do nuclear weapons run contrary to the rules of humanitarian law?
5. What is the policy of nuclear deterrence and how do proponents justify it?
6. On what moral grounds do Judge Weeramantry and other members of the International Court reject the reasoning behind nuclear deterrence?
7. What solution does Granoff propose for the elimination of nuclear weapons?

ETHICAL AND MORAL FRAMEWORK FOR ADDRESSING THE ISSUE

In his concurrence with the historic opinion of the International Court of Justice (ICJ) issued July 8, 1996, addressing the legal status of the threat or use of nuclear weapons,[1] Judge Ranjeva stated, "On the great issues of mankind the requirements of positive law and of ethics make common cause, and nuclear weapons, because of their destructive effects, are one such issue."[2] Human society has ethical and moral norms based on wisdom, conscience and practicality. Many norms are universal and have withstood the test of human experience over long periods of time. One such principle is that of reciprocity. It is often called the Golden Rule: "Treat others as you wish to be treated." It is an ethical and moral foundation for all the world's major religions.

Several modern states sincerely believe that this principle can be abrogated and security obtained by the threat of massive destruction. The Canberra Commission highlighted the impracticality of this posture: "Nuclear weapons are held by a handful of states which insist that these weapons provide unique security benefits, and yet reserve uniquely to themselves the right to own them. This situation is highly discriminatory and thus unstable; it cannot be sustained. The possession of nuclear weapons by any state is a constant stimulus to other states to acquire them."

The solution can be stated simply: "States should treat others as they wish to be treated in return."

It is inconsistent with moral wisdom and practical common sense for a few states to violate this ancient and universally valid principle of reciprocity. Such moral myopia has a corrosive effect on the law which gains its respect largely through moral coherence. Can global security be obtained while rejecting wisdom universally recognized for thousands of years?

Judge Weeramantry said, "[E]quality of all those who are subject to a legal system is central to its integrity and legitimacy. So it is with the body of principles constituting the corpus of international law. Least of all can there be one law for the powerful and another law for the rest. No domestic system would accept such a principle, nor can any international system which is premised on a concept of equality."[3]

LAW AND VALUES

Law is the articulation of values. Values must be based on moral foundations to have credibility. The recognition of the intrinsic sacredness of life and the duty of states and individuals to protect life is a fundamental characteristic of all human civilized values. Such civilized values are expressed in humanitarian law and custom which has an ancient lineage reaching back thousands of years. "They were worked out in many civilizations—Chinese, Indian, Greek, Roman, Japanese, Islamic, modern European among others." Humanitarian law "is an ever continuous development. . . . (and) grows as the sufferings of war keep escalating. With a nuclear weapon, those sufferings reach a limit situation, beyond which all else is academic."[4] . . .

We must never forget the awesome destructive power of these devices. "Nuclear weapons have the potential to destroy the entire ecosystem of the planet. Those already in the world's arsenals have the potential of destroying life on the planet several times over."[5]

Not only are they destructive in magnitude but in horror as well.

Notwithstanding this knowledge we permit ourselves to continue to live in a "kind of suspended sentence. For half a century now these terrifying weapons of mass destruction have formed part of the human condition. Nuclear weapons have entered into all calculations, all scenarios, all plans. Since Hiroshima, on the morning of 6 August 1945, fear has gradually become man's first nature. His life on earth has taken on the aspect of what the Qur'an calls 'long nocturnal journey', a nightmare whose end he cannot yet foresee."[6]

Attempting to obtain ultimate security through the ultimate weapon, we have failed, for "the proliferation of nuclear weapons has still not been brought under control, despite the existence of the Non-Proliferation Treaty. Fear and folly may still link hands at any moment to perform a final dance of death. Humanity is all the more vulnerable today for being capable of mass producing nuclear missiles."[7] . . .

A five megaton weapon represents greater explosive power than all the bombs used in World War II and a twenty megaton bomb more than all the explosives used in all the wars in history. Several states are currently poised ready to deliver weapons that render those used in Hiroshima and Nagasaki small. One megaton bomb represents the explosive force of approximately seventy Hiroshimas while a fifteen megaton bomb a thousand Hiroshimas. Judge Weeramantry emphasized that "the unprecedented magnitude of its destructive power is only one of the unique features of the bomb. It is unique in its uncontainability in both space and time. It is unique as a source of peril to the human future. It is

unique as a source of continuing danger to human health, even long after its use. Its infringement of humanitarian law goes beyond its being a weapon of mass destruction, to reasons which penetrate far deeper into the core of humanitarian law."[8]

We are challenged as never before: technology continues to slip away from moral guidance and law chases after common sense.

INTERNATIONAL COURT OF JUSTICE

When the International Court of Justice addressed the legal status of threat or use of nuclear weapons members of the nuclear club, which has since grown, asserted a principled reliance on nuclear weapons. The Court held that "the threat or use of nuclear weapons would generally be contrary to the rules of international law applicable to armed conflict, and in particular the principles and rules of humanitarian law" and that states are obligated to bring to a conclusion negotiations on nuclear disarmament in all its aspects. . . .

The Court stated unequivocally that the rules of armed conflict, including humanitarian law, prohibit the use of any weapon that is likely to cause unnecessary suffering to combatants; that is incapable of distinguishing between civilian and military targets; that violates principles protecting neutral states (such as through fallout or nuclear winter); that is not a proportional response to an attack; or that does permanent damage to the environment.

Under no circumstance may states make civilians the object of attack nor can they use weapons that are incapable of distinguishing between civilian and military targets. Regardless of whether the survival of a state acting in self defense is at stake, these limitations continue to hold.

For this reason the President Judge stated in forceful terms that the Court's inability to go beyond its statement "can in no manner be interpreted to mean that it is leaving the door ajar to the recognition of the legality of the threat or use of nuclear weapons."[9] He emphasized his point by stating that nuclear weapons are "the ultimate evil, destabilize humanitarian law which is the law of the lesser evil. Thus the very existence of nuclear weapons is a great challenge to humanitarian law itself." . . .

The Court said, "[M]ethods and means of warfare, which would preclude any distinction between civilian and military targets, or which would result in unnecessary suffering to combatants, are prohibited. In view of the unique characteristics of nuclear weapons . . . the use of such weapons in fact seems scarcely reconcilable with respect to such requirements."

Discordance between the incompatibility of these devices with the requirements of humanitarian law, the assertion that there could be possible instances in which their use could be legal and the reliance on the doctrine of deterrence compelled the Court to seek a resolution: "the long promised complete nuclear disarmament appears to be the most appropriate means of achieving that result." The requirements of moral coherence and ethical conduct and the need for "international law, and with it the stability of international order which it is intended to govern," drive the imperative of nuclear disarmament.

ONGOING PROBLEM

Legal and moral questions continue to loom before us. We are not faced with nuclear policies founded on a strategy of dropping depth charges in mid-ocean or bombs in the desert. What the world faces is nuclear deterrence with its reliance on the horrific destruction of vast numbers of innocent people, destruction of the environment rendering it hostile to generations yet to be blessed with life.

Deterrence proponents claim that nuclear weapons are not so much instruments for the waging of war but political instruments "intended to prevent war by depriving it of any possible rationale."[10] The United States has boldly argued that because deterrence is believed to be essential to its international security that the threat or use of nuclear weapons must therefore be legal. The United States representative stated: "If these weapons could not lawfully be used in individual or collective self defense under any circumstances there would be no credible threat of such use in response to aggression and

deterrent policies would be futile and meaningless. In this sense, it is impossible to separate the policy of deterrence from the legality of the use of the means of deterrence. Accordingly, any affirmation of a general prohibition on the use of nuclear weapons would be directly contrary to one of the fundamental premises of the national security policy of each of these many states."[11]

It is clear that deterrence is designed to threaten massive destruction which would most certainly violate numerous principles of humanitarian law. Additionally, it strikes at generations yet unborn.

Even in the instance of retaliation the moral absurdity challenges us. As Mexico's Ambassador Sergio Gonzalez Galvez told the Court, "Torture is not a permissible response to torture. Nor is mass rape acceptable retaliation to mass rape. Just as unacceptable is retaliatory deterrence—'You burnt my city, I will burn yours.'"[12]

Professor Eric David, on behalf of the Solomon Islands, stated, "If the dispatch of a nuclear weapon causes a million deaths, retaliation with another nuclear weapon which will also cause a million deaths will perhaps protect the sovereignty of the state suffering the first strike, and will perhaps satisfy the victim's desire for revenge, but it will not satisfy humanitarian law, which will have been breached not once but twice; and two wrongs do not make a right."[13]

Judge Weeramantry rigorously analyzed deterrence theory:

1. Intention: "Deterrence needs to carry the conviction to other parties that there is a real intention to use those weapons in the event of an attack by that other party. A game of bluff does not convey that intention, for it is difficult to persuade another of one's intention unless one really has that intention. Deterrence thus consists in a real intention to use such weapons. If deterrence is to operate, it leaves the world of make believe and enters the field of seriously intended military threats."[14]

2. Deterrence and Mere Possession: "Deterrence is more than the mere accumulation

of weapons in a storehouse. It means the possession of weapons in a state of readiness for actual use. This means the linkage of weapons ready for immediate take off, with a command and control system geared for immediate action. It means that weapons are attached to delivery vehicles. It means that personnel are ready night and day to render them operational at a moment's notice. There is clearly a vast difference between weapons stocked in a warehouse and weapons so ready for immediate action. Mere possession and deterrence are thus concepts which are clearly distinguishable from each other."[15]

For deterrence to work one must have the resolve to cause the resulting damage and devastation. . . .

While deterrence continues to place all life on the planet in a precarious position of high risk, one must wonder whether it provides any possible security against accidental or unauthorized launches, computer error, irrational rogue actions, terrorist attack, criminal syndicate utilization of weapons and other irrational and unpredictable, but likely, scenarios.

Did the Court undermine the continued legitimacy of deterrence? The Court stated clearly that "if the use of force itself in a given case is illegal— for whatever reason—the threat to use such force will likewise be illegal."[16]

The moral position of the nuclear weapons states is essentially that the threat to commit an illegal act—massive destruction of innocent people—is legal because it is so horrible to contemplate that it ensures the peace. Thus the argument is that the threat of committing that which is patently illegal is made legal by its own intrinsic illogic. . . .

An unambiguous political commitment by the nuclear weapon states to the elimination of nuclear weapons evidenced by unambiguous immediate pledges never to use them first as well as placing the weapons in a de-alerted posture pending their ultimate elimination will promptly evidence the good faith efforts by the nuclear weapon states to reduce our collective risks. These steps increase our collective security, but are hardly enough to meet the clear decision of the court and the dictates of reason. Only commencement in good faith of multilateral negotiations leading to elimination of these devices will bring law, morals, ethics and reason into coherence. Only then will we be able to tell our children that ultimate violence will not bring ultimate security, a culture of peace based on law, reason and values will. . . .

NOTES

1. Legality of the Threat or Use of Nuclear Weapons, General List No. 95 (Advisory Opinion of the International Court of Justice of July 8, 1996). Unless otherwise noted, references are to this opinion, which was requested by the General Assembly.
2. Opinion of Judge Ranjeva, para. 105(2)E1.
3. Opinion of Judge Weeramantry, V4.
4. Ibid., I 5.
5. Opinion of Judge Weeramantry, II 3(a).
6. Opinion of President Judge Bedjaoui, para. 2.
7. Ibid., para. 5.
8. Opinion of Judge Weeramantry, II para. 3.
9. Opinion of President Judge Badjaoui, para. 20.
10. Marc Perrinde Brichambaut, France, Verbatim record (trans.), 1 November 1995, p. 33.
11. Michael Matheson, US, Verbatim record, 15 November 1995, p. 78.
12. Verbatim record, 3 November 1995, p. 64.
13. Verbatim record (trans.), 14 November 1995, p. 45.
14. Opinion of Judge Weeramantry, VII 2(v).
15. Ibid.
16. Para. 47.

Discussion Questions

1. Discuss whether the possession of nuclear weapons and the strategy of deterrence can be justified under just-war theory as explicated by Aquinas and Coady.
2. India and Pakistan, both nations with nuclear weapons, have more than once been on the brink of war. Discuss how the United Nations and the United States should respond, if at all, to the threat of nuclear war between the two nations.

3. Discuss whether the mere possession (or suspicion) of weapons of mass destruction by a country, such as Iran, that is a potential threat to another country justifies a preemptive strike. Support your answer, using specific examples.

4. Was the dropping of nuclear bombs on Hiroshima and Nagasaki in World War II an example of war or of terrorism? Was the bombing of these two cities justified? Discuss how Granoff and a just-war theorist would each answer this question.

5. President Obama says it's time to rid the world of nuclear weapons. However, he also says he will not commit to the United States' giving up nuclear weapons until other countries do so. Is this position reasonable? Working in small groups, develop a policy for helping Obama rid the world of nuclear weapons.

DAVID LUBAN

The War on Terrorism and the End of Human Rights

David Luban is a professor of law and philosophy at Georgetown University Law Center. In his reading he notes that the United States government, in its war on terrorism, has blurred the line between the law model and the war model approaches by denying terrorist suspects the protections of either model. Luban concludes that because of this the war on terrorism may seriously erode international human rights.

Critical Reading Questions

1. What is the model of war and the model of law? What are the advantages and disadvantages of each model?

2. What is the hybrid war–law approach and why, according to Luban, did Washington adopt it?

3. What is the legal status of terrorist suspects imprisoned at Guantanamo Bay, and what rights do they have under the hybrid war–law model?

4. What is the source of the term "enemy combatant" and how does the hybrid war–law model go beyond the original meaning of the term?

5. What is the argument against the hybrid war–law model?

David Luban, "The War on Terrorism and the End of Human Rights," in *War After September 11*, ed. Verna V. Gehring (Lanham, MD: Rowman & Littlefield Publishers, 2003), 51–62.

6. According to Luban, how does the war on terrorism threaten international human rights?
7. How does the war on terrorism differ from other kinds of wars?
8. According to Luban, how has the war on terrorism been used by governments as a model to justify attacks on insurgents?

In the immediate aftermath of September 11, President Bush stated that the perpetrators of the deed would be brought to justice. Soon afterwards, the President announced that the United States would engage in a war on terrorism. The first of these statements adopts the familiar language of criminal law and criminal justice. It treats the September 11 attacks as horrific crimes—mass murders—and the government's mission as apprehending and punishing the surviving planners and conspirators for their roles in the crimes. The War on Terrorism is a different proposition, however, and a different model of governmental action—not law but war. Most obviously, it dramatically broadens the scope of action, because now terrorists who knew nothing about September 11 have been earmarked as enemies. But that is only the beginning.

THE HYBRID WAR–LAW APPROACH

The model of war offers much freer rein than that of law, and therein lies its appeal in the wake of 9/11. First, in war but not in law it is permissible to use lethal force on enemy troops regardless of their degree of personal involvement with the adversary. The conscripted cook is as legitimate a target as the enemy general. Second, in war but not in law "collateral damage," that is, foreseen but unintended killing of non-combatants, is permissible. (Police cannot blow up an apartment building full of people because a murderer is inside, but an air force can bomb the building if it contains a military target.) Third, the requirements of evidence and proof are drastically weaker in war than in criminal justice. Soldiers do not need proof beyond a reasonable doubt, or even proof

by a preponderance of evidence, that someone is an enemy soldier before firing on him or capturing and imprisoning him. They don't need proof at all, merely plausible intelligence. Thus, the U.S. military remains regretful but unapologetic about its January 2002 attack on the Afghani town of Uruzgan, in which 21 innocent civilians were killed, based on faulty intelligence that they were al Qaeda fighters. Fourth, in war one can attack an enemy without concern over whether he has done anything. Legitimate targets are those who in the course of combat *might* harm us, not those who *have* harmed us. No doubt there are other significant differences as well. But the basic point should be clear: given Washington's mandate to eliminate the danger of future 9/11s, so far as humanly possible, the model of war offers important advantages over the model of law.

There are disadvantages as well. Most obviously, in war but not in law, fighting back is a *legitimate* response of the enemy. Second, when nations fight a war, other nations may opt for neutrality. Third, because fighting back is legitimate, in war the enemy soldier deserves special regard once he is rendered harmless through injury or surrender. It is impermissible to punish him for his role in fighting the war. Nor can he be harshly interrogated after he is captured. The Third Geneva Convention provides: "Prisoners of war who refuse to answer [questions] may not be threatened, insulted, or exposed to unpleasant or disadvantageous treatment of any kind." And, when the war concludes, the enemy soldier must be repatriated.

Here, however, Washington has different ideas, designed to eliminate these tactical disadvantages in the traditional war model. Washington regards international terrorism not only as a military adversary, but also as a criminal activity and criminal conspiracy. In the law model, criminals don't get to shoot back, and their acts of violence subject them to legitimate punishment. That is what we see in Washington's prosecution of the War on Terrorism. Captured terrorists may be tried before military or civilian tribunals, and shooting back at Americans, including American troops, is a federal crime (for a statute under which John Walker Lindh was indicted criminalizes anyone regardless of nationality, who "outside the United States attempts to kill, or engages in a conspiracy to kill, a national of the United States" or "engages in physical violence with intent to cause serious bodily injury to a national of the United States; or with the result that serious bodily injury is caused to a national of the United States"). Furthermore, the U.S. may rightly demand that other countries not be neutral about murder and terrorism. Unlike the war model, a nation may insist that those who are not with us in fighting murder and terror are against us, because by not joining our operations they are providing a safe haven for terrorists or their bank accounts. By selectively combining elements of the war model and elements of the law model, Washington is able to maximize its own ability to mobilize lethal force against terrorists while eliminating most traditional rights of a military adversary, as well as the rights of innocent bystanders caught in the crossfire.

A LIMBO OF RIGHTLESSNESS

The legal status of al Qaeda suspects imprisoned at the Guantanamo Bay Naval Base in Cuba is emblematic of this hybrid war–law approach to the threat of terrorism. In line with the war model, they lack the usual rights of criminal suspects—the presumption of innocence, the right to a hearing to determine guilt, the opportunity to prove that the authorities have grabbed the wrong man. But, in line with the law model, they are considered *unlawful* combatants. Because they are not uniformed forces, they lack the rights of prisoners of war and are liable to criminal punishment. Initially, the American government declared that the Guantanamo Bay prisoners have no rights under

the Geneva Conventions. In the face of international protests, Washington quickly backpedaled and announced that the Guantanamo Bay prisoners would indeed be treated as decently as POWs—but it also made clear that the prisoners have no right to such treatment. Neither criminal suspects nor POWs, neither fish nor fowl, they inhabit a limbo of rightlessness. Secretary of Defense Rumsfeld's assertion that the U.S. may continue to detain them even if they are acquitted by a military tribunal dramatizes the point.

To understand how extraordinary their status is, consider an analogy. Suppose that Washington declares a War on Organized Crime. Troops are dispatched to Sicily, and a number of Mafiosi are seized, brought to Guantanamo Bay, and imprisoned without a hearing for the indefinite future, maybe the rest of their lives. They are accused of no crimes, because their capture is based not on what they have done but on what they might do. After all, to become "made" they took oaths of obedience to the bad guys. Seizing them accords with the war model: they are enemy foot soldiers. But they are foot soldiers out of uniform; they lack a "fixed distinctive emblem," in the words of The Hague Convention. That makes them unlawful combatants, so they lack the rights of POWs. They may object that it is only a unilateral declaration by the American President that has turned them into combatants in the first place—he called it a war, they didn't—and that, since they do not regard themselves as literal foot soldiers it never occurred to them to wear a fixed distinctive emblem. They have a point. It seems too easy for the President to divest anyone in the world of rights and liberty simply by announcing that the U.S. is at war with them and then declaring them unlawful combatants if they resist. But, in the hybrid war–law model, they protest in vain.

Consider another example. In January 2002, U.S. forces in Bosnia seized five Algerians and a Yemeni suspected of al Qaeda connections and took them to Guantanamo Bay. The six had been jailed in Bosnia, but a Bosnian court released them for lack of evidence, and the Bosnian Human Rights Chamber issued an injunction that four of them be allowed to remain in the country pending further legal proceedings. The Human Rights Chamber, ironically, was created under U.S. auspices in the Dayton peace accords, and it was designed specifically to protect against treatment like this. Ruth Wedgwood, a well-known international law scholar at Yale and a member of the Council on Foreign Relations, defended the Bosnian seizure in war-model terms. "I think we would simply argue this was a matter of self-defense. One of the fundamental rules of military law is that you have a right ultimately to act in self-defense. And if these folks were actively plotting to blow up the U.S. embassy, they should be considered combatants and captured as combatants in a war." Notice that Professor Wedgwood argues in terms of what the men seized in Bosnia were *planning to do,* not what they *did;* notice as well that the decision of the Bosnian court that there was insufficient evidence does not matter. These are characteristics of the war model.

More recently, two American citizens alleged to be al Qaeda operatives (Jose Padilla, a.k.a. Abdullah al Muhajir, and Yasser Esam Hamdi) have been held in American military prisons, with no crimes charged, no opportunity to consult counsel, and no hearing. The President described Padilla as "a bad man" who aimed to build a nuclear "dirty" bomb and use it against America; and the Justice Department has classified both men as "enemy combatants" who may be held indefinitely. Yet, as military law expert Gary Solis points out, "Until now, as used by the attorney general, the term 'enemy combatant' appeared nowhere in U.S. criminal law, international law or in the law of war." The phrase comes from the 1942 Supreme Court case *Ex parte Quirin,* but all the Court says there is that "an enemy combatant who without uniform comes secretly through the lines for the purpose of waging war by destruction of life or property" would "not . . . be entitled to the status of prisoner of war, but . . . [they would] be offenders against the law of war subject to trial and punishment by military tribunals." For the Court, in other words, the status of a person as a non-uniformed enemy combatant makes

him a criminal rather than a warrior, and determines *where* he is tried (in a military, rather than a civilian, tribunal) but not *whether* he is tried. Far from authorizing open-ended confinement, *Ex parte Quirin* presupposes that criminals are entitled to hearings: without a hearing how can suspects prove that the government made a mistake? *Quirin* embeds the concept of "enemy combatant" firmly in the law model. In the war model, by contrast, POWs may be detained without a hearing until hostilities are over. But POWs were captured in uniform, and only their undoubted identity as enemy soldiers justifies such open-ended custody. Apparently, Hamdi and Padilla will get the worst of both models—open-ended custody with no trial, like POWs, but no certainty beyond the U.S. government's say-so that they really are "bad men." This is the hybrid war–law model. It combines the *Quirin* category of "enemy combatant without uniform," used in the law model to justify a military trial, with the war model's practice of indefinite confinement with no trial at all.

THE CASE FOR THE HYBRID APPROACH

Is there any justification for the hybrid war–law model, which so drastically diminishes the rights of the enemy? An argument can be offered along the following lines. In ordinary cases of war among states, enemy soldiers may well be morally and politically innocent. Many of them are conscripts, and those who aren't do not necessarily endorse the state policies they are fighting to defend. But enemy soldiers in the War on Terrorism are, by definition, those who have embarked on a path of terrorism. They are neither morally nor politically innocent. Their sworn aim—"Death to America!"—is to create more 9/11s. In this respect, they are much more akin to criminal conspirators than to conscript soldiers. Terrorists will fight as soldiers when they must, and metamorphose into mass murderers when they can.

Furthermore, suicide terrorists pose a special, unique danger. Ordinary criminals do not target innocent bystanders. They may be willing to kill them if necessary, but bystanders enjoy at least some measure of security because they are not primary targets. Not so with terrorists, who aim to kill as many innocent people as possible. Likewise, innocent bystanders are protected from ordinary criminals by whatever deterrent force the threat of punishment and the risk of getting killed in the act of committing a crime offer. For a suicide bomber, neither of these threats is a deterrent at all—after all, for the suicide bomber one of the hallmarks of a *successful* operation is that he winds up dead at day's end. Given the unique and heightened danger that suicide terrorists pose, a stronger response that grants potential terrorists fewer rights may be justified. Add to this the danger that terrorists may come to possess weapons of mass destruction, including nuclear devices in suitcases. Under circumstances of such dire menace, it is appropriate to treat terrorists as though they embody the most dangerous aspects of both warriors and criminals. That is the basis of the hybrid war–law model.

THE CASE AGAINST EXPEDIENCY

The argument against the hybrid war–law model is equally clear. The U.S. has simply chosen the bits of the law model and the bits of the war model that are most convenient for American interests, and ignored the rest. The model abolishes the rights of potential enemies (and their innocent shields) by fiat—not for reasons of moral or legal principle, but solely because the U.S. does not want them to have rights. The more rights they have, the more risk they pose. But Americans' urgent desire to minimize our risks doesn't make other people's rights disappear. Calling our policy a War on Terrorism obscures this point.

The theoretical basis of the objection is that the law model and the war model each comes as a package, with a kind of intellectual integrity. The law model grows out of relationships within states, while the war model arises from relationships between states. The law model imputes a ground-level community of values to those subject to the law—paradigmatically, citizens of a state, but

also visitors and foreigners who choose to engage in conduct that affects a state. Only because law imputes shared basic values to the community can a state condemn the conduct of criminals and inflict punishment on them. Criminals deserve condemnation and punishment because their conduct violates norms that we are entitled to count on their sharing. But, for the same reason—the imputed community of values—those subject to the law ordinarily enjoy a presumption of innocence and an expectation of safety. The government cannot simply grab them and confine them without making sure they have broken the law, nor can it condemn them without due process for ensuring that it has the right person, nor can it knowingly place bystanders in mortal peril in the course of fighting crime. They are our fellows, and the community should protect them just as it protects us. The same imputed community of values that justifies condemnation and punishment creates rights to due care and due process.

War is different. War is the ultimate acknowledgement that human beings do not live in a single community with shared norms. If their norms conflict enough, communities pose a physical danger to each other, and nothing can safeguard a community against its enemies except force of arms. That makes enemy soldiers legitimate targets; but it makes our soldiers legitimate targets as well, and, once the enemy no longer poses a danger, he should be immune from punishment, because if he has fought cleanly he has violated no norms that we are entitled to presume he honors. Our norms are, after all, *our* norms, not his.

Because the law model and war model come as conceptual packages, it is unprincipled to wrench them apart and recombine them simply because it is in America's interest to do so. To declare that Americans can fight enemies with the latitude of warriors, but if the enemies fight back they are not warriors but criminals, amounts to a kind of heads-I-win-tails-you-lose international morality in which whatever it takes to reduce American risk, no matter what the cost to others, turns out to be justified. This, in brief, is the criticism of the hybrid war–law model.

To be sure, the law model could be made to incorporate the war model merely by rewriting a handful of statutes. Congress could enact laws permitting imprisonment or execution of persons who pose a significant threat of terrorism whether or not they have already done anything wrong. The standard of evidence could be set low and the requirement of a hearing eliminated. Finally, Congress could authorize the use of lethal force against terrorists regardless of the danger to innocent bystanders, and it could immunize officials from lawsuits or prosecution by victims of collateral damage. Such statutes would violate the Constitution, but the Constitution could be amended to incorporate anti-terrorist exceptions to the Fourth, Fifth, and Sixth Amendments. In the end, we would have a system of law that includes all the essential features of the war model.

It would, however, be a system that imprisons people for their intentions rather than their actions, and that offers the innocent few protections against mistaken detention or inadvertent death through collateral damage. Gone are the principles that people should never be punished for their thoughts, only for their deeds, and that innocent people must be protected rather than injured by their own government. In that sense, at any rate, repackaging war as law seems merely cosmetic, because it replaces the ideal of law as a protector of rights with the more problematic goal of protecting some innocent people by sacrificing others. The hypothetical legislation incorporates war into law only by making law as partisan and ruthless as war. It no longer resembles law as Americans generally understand it.

THE THREAT TO INTERNATIONAL HUMAN RIGHTS

In the War on Terrorism, what becomes of international human rights? It seems beyond dispute that the war model poses a threat to international human rights, because honoring human rights is neither practically possible nor theoretically required during war. Combatants are legitimate targets; noncombatants maimed by accident or mistake are regarded as collateral damage rather than victims of atrocities;

cases of mistaken identity get killed or confined without a hearing because combat conditions preclude due process. To be sure, the laws of war specify minimum human rights, but these are far less robust than rights in peace-time—and the hybrid war–law model reduces this schedule of rights even further by classifying the enemy as unlawful combatants.

One striking example of the erosion of human rights is tolerance of torture. It should be recalled that a 1995 al Qaeda plot to bomb eleven U.S. airliners was thwarted by information tortured out of a Pakistani suspect by the Philippine police—an eerie real-life version of the familiar philosophical thought-experiment. The *Washington Post* reports that since September 11 the U.S. has engaged in the summary transfer of dozens of terrorism suspects to countries where they will be interrogated under torture. But it isn't just the United States that has proven willing to tolerate torture for security reasons. Last December, the Swedish government snatched a suspected Islamic extremist to whom it had previously granted political asylum, and the same day had him transferred to Egypt, where Amnesty International reports that he has been tortured to the point where he walks only with difficulty. Sweden is not, to say the least, a traditionally hard-line nation on human rights issues. None of this international transportation is lawful—indeed, it violates international treaty obligations under the Convention against Torture that in the U.S. have constitutional status as "supreme Law of the Land"—but that may not matter under the war model, in which even constitutional rights may be abrogated.

It is natural to suggest that this suspension of human rights is an exceptional emergency measure to deal with an unprecedented threat. This raises the question of how long human rights will remain suspended. When will the war be over?

Here, the chief problem is that the War on Terrorism is not like any other kind of war. The enemy, Terrorism, is not a territorial state or nation or government. There is no opposite number to negotiate with. There is no one on the other side to call a truce or declare a ceasefire, no one among the enemy authorized to surrender. In traditional wars among states, the war aim is, as Clausewitz argued, to impose one state's political will on another's. The *aim* of the war is not to kill the enemy—killing the enemy is the *means* used to achieve the real end, which is to force capitulation. In the War on Terrorism, no capitulation is possible. That means that the real aim of the war is, quite simply, to kill or capture all of the terrorists—to keep on killing and killing, capturing and capturing, until they are all gone.

Of course, no one expects that terrorism will ever disappear completely. Everyone understands that new anti-American extremists, new terrorists, will always arise and always be available for recruitment and deployment. Everyone understands that even if al Qaeda is destroyed or decapitated, other groups, with other leaders, will arise in its place. It follows, then, that the War on Terrorism will be a war that can only be abandoned, never concluded. The War has no natural resting point, no moment of victory or finality. It requires a mission of killing and capturing, in territories all over the globe, that will go on in perpetuity. It follows as well that the suspension of human rights implicit in the hybrid war–law model is not temporary but permanent.

Perhaps with this fear in mind, Congressional authorization of President Bush's military campaign limits its scope to those responsible for September 11 and their sponsors. But the War on Terrorism has taken on a life of its own that makes the Congressional authorization little more than a technicality. Because of the threat of nuclear terror, the American leadership actively debates a war on Iraq regardless of whether Iraq was implicated in September 11; and the President's yoking of Iraq, Iran, and North Korea into a single axis of evil because they back terror suggests that the War on Terrorism might eventually encompass all these nations. If the U.S. ever unearths tangible evidence that any of these countries is harboring or abetting terrorists with weapons of mass destruction, there can be little doubt that Congress will support military action. So too, Russia invokes the American War on Terrorism to justify its attacks on Chechen rebels, China uses it to deflect criticisms of its campaign against Uighur separatists, and Israeli Prime Minister Sharon explicitly links military actions against Palestinian insurgents to the American War on Terrorism. No doubt there is political opportunism at work in some or all of these efforts to piggyback onto America's campaign, but the opportunity would not exist if "War on Terrorism" were merely the code-name of a discrete, neatly-boxed American operation. Instead, the War on Terrorism has become a model of politics, a world-view with its own distinctive premises and consequences. As I have argued, it includes a new model of state action, the hybrid war–law model, which depresses human rights from their peace-time standard to the war-time standard, and indeed even further. So long as it continues, the War on Terrorism means the end of human rights, at least for those near enough to be touched by the fire of battle.

Discussion Questions

1. Apply the just-war theory to the war on terrorism. Can the hybrid war–law model be justified under just-law theory?

2. In January 2009 President Obama issued an executive order closing Guantanamo Bay and suspending military trials of several of the inmates while the judicial process is under review. This order is consistent with an earlier U.S. Court of Appeals ruling that overturned the Bush administration's policy that prisoners being held at Guantanamo are "enemy combatants" being held on foreign soil and hence have no rights to a lawyer under U.S. law. Discuss whether terrorist suspects should be entitled to due process under the American legal system in light of Luban's distinction between the war model and the law model.

3. Some of the prisoners who have since been released from Guantanamo Bay describe how they were kept in two-meter-long cages and interrogated up to sixty times a day. Should the captives who were released receive restitution from the United States government for wrongful imprisonment? Support your answer.

4. Discuss what a rights ethicist, such as John Locke or Ayn Rand, would most likely think about the morality of the hybrid war–law model.

5. Following the September 11 attacks, the United States adopted a policy that permits preemptive war as self-defense. "It's a different world," argued Colin Powell in favor of the policy. "It's a new kind of threat." Weapons of mass destruction, new technology, and the ease with which global terrorist groups can network have increased the likelihood of surprise attacks. Discuss whether these developments justify preemptive strikes as self-defense under the just-war tradition. If so, under what conditions would a preemptive strike be morally justified?

STEPHEN JOEL TRACHTENBERG

Sharing the Burden

Stephen Joel Trachtenberg is president of George Washington University and a professor of public administration. Prior to this, he was an attorney with the U.S. Atomic Energy Commission. Trachtenberg favors conscription, or some type of national service program, on the grounds that sharing the burden of defending the nation promotes equality, national unity, and a better understanding of the military.

Critical Reading Questions

1. Why did some colleges oppose ROTC on their campuses during the Vietnam War, and why does Trachtenberg call this reaction to the war a "false equation"?

2. What is the value of pluralism in America, and why does Trachtenberg think we need a counterbalance to pluralism?

3. How would conscription or national service both strengthen pluralism and promote a common vision at the same time?

4. What does Trachtenberg mean when he says that conscription would give us "a better understanding of the military and military activity"?

5. What is the value in having "citizen-soldiers" rather than simply a professional military?

6. What are some of Trachtenberg's suggestions for implementing a national service?

From Stephen Joel Trachtenberg, "Share the Burden or Fob It Off?" *The World & I*, November 2003. WorldandIJournal.com.

It was in 1970, I think, that a university—its name is not important—got very mad at the Government of the United States. It was unhappy because of the war in Vietnam and decided to do something about it. So the faculty convened and voted to invite the Army ROTC [Reserve Officers Training Corps] program off campus. I hasten to point out, for the historical record, that their vote did not bring an end to that unhappy war on the spot. . . .

The vote equated a reserve officers training program at a liberal arts institution with fighting a hated war. It is a false equation—as, in fact, the failure to end the war by withdrawing from ROTC by nearly all elite colleges and universities amply demonstrated. But it is worse than false; it is harmful. It confuses the issues at hand and devalues the idea of national service. Reinstating ROTC programs at colleges and universities should be one step toward remedying the problem I am discussing here.

Let me put this in a contemporary context. The war in Iraq—and before that, in Afghanistan—has focused our national attention more sharply on war than it has been in many years, perhaps since Vietnam. I am not, however, referring to the debate about the right or the wrong of this war, and I am not even addressing the obvious valor and competence of the men and women in our armed forces. I am thinking of New York Congressman Charles Rangel's proposal to restore Selective Service—the draft. . . .

. . . I think the idea of national service can be—indeed will be—transformational. I say this because I think national service, particularly military service, could address some profound issues.

I will offer three for your consideration. They are: We need a good counterbalance to our healthy respect for pluralism; we need a greater understanding across our entire population of what the military is and does; and we need to make sure that we are protected by citizen-soldiers.

About pluralism: Given our heterogeneous backgrounds, it is not surprising that there have always been some powerful centrifugal forces in America. We are aware of being, in the old phrase, "hyphenated Americans," and many of us still retain the hyphen along with a secondary identity.

But generally, in the course of our history, we have been predominantly American, no matter where we, or our parents or grandparents, came from; the word after the hyphen—American—carried the greater meaning. . . .

Now add to this the high value we place on multiculturalism—a comparatively new idea in our society—which encourages the blooming of many flowers. Factor in the desire of many new arrivals to this country never to forget the life and culture of the old country, as some of the earlier arrivals did to their sorrow. Then add in the "identity politics," by which almost any group of more than eight people can acquire not just an identity according to race, ethnicity, or whatever, but a grievance or a perceived and separate set of rights to go with it. And just for good measure, add in all the recent debates about affirmative action, diversity, and representation. Don't shake well, however; this is a very volatile mixture.

When you combine all these ingredients you realize that the package of things we all knew about and shared in common has been ripped open. The shared and cohesive vision of what America is and what it means (more or less, I grant) to be an American is growing blurry.

I do not mean to say that we must undo pluralism, or that pluralism, whatever shape it happens to take, is bad. No, not at all. I believe, however, that pluralism should not trump a common and cohesive vision.

PROMOTING A COMMON VISION

An institution that furthers what the schools are still trying to do to promote such a vision, then, presents something of importance and great value. That institution, as I have already said, would be national service—including a military option. The advantages are obvious. If young men and women are obliged—not invited—to share in a common effort for the good of their country, they acquire a sense of unity outside their own ethnicity or identity group.

They have to, because they are put randomly in with people who may be unlike them in all ways—at least as far as they can tell. But if you talk with people who have served in the military, they will tell you that these differences get buried quickly if the unit is going to survive.

And they can get buried quickly because, for the most part, they are superficial differences of manner, not of matter—differences more of style than substance. Thus, I think that compulsory national service would be as I said, a good balance for a healthy respect for pluralism.

The second benefit I see is a better understanding of the military and military activity. The reporting on the Iraqi war was instructive, if sometimes a bit dismal. The war began with an astounding ground assault—probably the swiftest in the recorded history of warfare.

Yet after a few days, when progress seemed to slow or stop, many reporters and observers began talking about a "quagmire," reminiscent of Vietnam. They were wrong because they did not understand a basic, if overstated, military aphorism: "Amateurs study tactics; professionals study logistics." . . .

. . . [I]t needed and still needs, to be driven home with most Americans who do not understand how armies function—and have since the time of Alexander. Moreover, practically no Members of Congress or their staff members have served in the military and thus were in no better position than the average citizen or reporter to evaluate truly what was going on.

What this means (and this is melancholy) is that most of us are not particularly sympathetic to military needs because we are ignorant of what the military does and how it goes about doing it. . . .

So, it seems to me, military service offers two civic values: the information all citizens should have to understand the military, if only to keep its instincts classically civilian; and the ability to continue the work of public schools in presenting common, cohesive visions.

This is related to my third point, that there is value in having citizen-soldiers. It is probably unfair to compare our contemporary military with Hessian mercenaries working for a professional Prussian officer class—but it is a useful image nevertheless. Most of the young people I observed in

the Navy were there because they could not afford college, were offered training in a marketable skill, and would have a chance to get a large subsidy if they ultimately went to college.

Moreover, by and large, they came from dying small towns, big city ghettos, and barrios. No matter their race or ethnicity, they were not children of the comfortable American middle class. It is good that the Navy offered them options they never would have had in life.

But what does this create? A military staffed by an underclass and doing it for perfectly understandable financial reasons. While it may have a good admixture of races and sexes, it does not have a fair mix of classes and that is a problem.

When politicians and academics and journalists, who tend to come from the more privileged parts of society, have no stake in the military, it becomes lopsided and ill understood.

SHARED BURDENS

. . . "Shared burden" is not the most popular phrase in the English language (or, rather, the American lexicon) these days, but it goes right to the heart of the matter. Do we want to share burdens, or do we want to fob them off on those who have fewer choices? Do we want to lose the possibility of national cohesion, of shared vision along with shared burden as the price for fobbing off military service? I hope not. . . .

I think it would be an enormous benefit to America and to our young people to let them mix their various qualities and see what rubs off on whom. I think we might be surprised and pleased.

A NATIONAL SERVICE DRAFT

. . . The left used to oppose the draft because it saw it as an instrument of war; it still does, missing the point. The right would now probably oppose it as typical left-wing, big-government interference or social engineering, also missing the point. That does not leave, I am aware, a large political base.

However, that does not daunt me altogether. If the military draft will not by itself work, then why not a national service draft—a draft requiring two years of service, with the military as an option? Let me propose that any other option for service would have to require the intense discipline, group work, and training in particular skills that military duty would require.

And let me propose further that they would have the same rewards: training in some useful skill or occupation, exposure to others of different backgrounds as colleagues, and money for higher education afterward. How we make this work is a topic for another day. But I am convinced that what I am proposing is plausible, not a pipe dream. I think it has a lot to offer.

Speaking as a university president, I think many young people would show up for higher education not merely better financed but infinitely better motivated and clearer on their reasons for pursuing college study.

Speaking as a parent, I would like my sons, like everyone else's children, to make a material contribution to our society and to share that burden with people they might never otherwise know. Speaking as a citizen, I think it would foster that national cohesion that the older ones of us remember. And speaking as a senior citizen, I think there might be fascinating opportunities for national service in retirement. Service need not be a monopoly of the young. . . .

Discussion Questions

1. Trachtenberg supports mandatory national service on the grounds that it will help unify the populace. However, is unification desirable? Support your answer.

2. Young people are far more opposed to conscription, with 84 percent of people between the ages of eighteen and thirty-four being opposed to a draft compared to only 59 percent of people over the age of fifty-five.[14] Discuss whether forcing young people who are opposed to conscription constitutes "involuntary servitude" and, as such, violates the Thirteenth Amendment to the Constitution. Discuss also how Trachtenberg might answer this question.

3. The National Service Act of 2007 has been amended to include women. Discuss whether or not women should be conscripted to serve in the military and in combat duty in particular. If so, should exceptions be made for women who are pregnant, as well as for women (and men) who are the primary caretakers of young children? Develop an argument supporting your position.

4. President Ronald Reagan opposed the draft on the grounds that it "rests on the assumption that your kids belong to the state. If we buy that assumption then it is for the state—not the parents, the community, the religious institutions or teachers—to decide who shall have what values and who shall do what work, when, where and how in our society. That assumption isn't a new one. The Nazis thought it was a great idea."[15] Evaluate Reagan's argument and discuss how Trachtenberg might reply.

RON PAUL

Conscription: The Terrible Price of War

A physician by training, Republican Ron Paul of Texas has been a member of the U.S. House of Representatives since 1996. In this reading, Paul argues against conscription on the grounds that most wars cause senseless suffering and that conscription of young people is discriminatory and constitutes forced servitude.

Critical Reading Questions

1. According to Paul, what is the ultimate cost of most wars?
2. What does Paul mean when he says that "when it comes to war, the principle of deception lives on"?
3. According to Paul, why do unpopular wars invite conscription, whereas truly defensive and just wars do not?
4. Why is conscription, by its very nature, discriminatory?
5. On what grounds does Paul draw an analogy between slavery and conscription?

The ultimate cost of war is almost always the loss of liberty. True defensive wars and revolutionary wars against tyrants may preserve or establish a free society, as did our war against the British. But these wars are rare. Most wars are unnecessary, dangerous, and cause senseless suffering with little being gained. The result of most conflicts throughout the ages has been loss of liberty and life on both sides. The current war in which we find ourselves clearly qualifies as one of those unnecessary and dangerous wars. To get the people to support ill-conceived wars, the nation's leaders employ grand schemes of deception.

Woodrow Wilson orchestrated our entry into World War I by first promising during the election of 1916 to keep us out of the European conflict, then a few months later pressuring and maneuvering Congress into declaring war against Germany. Whether it was the Spanish American War before that or all the wars since, U.S. presidents have deceived the people to gain popular

---

"Conscription: The Terrible Price of War." Speech before the U.S. House of Representatives, November 21, 2003.

---

support for ill-conceived military ventures. Wilson wanted the war and immediately demanded conscription to fight it. He didn't have the guts even to name the program a military draft; instead in a speech before Congress calling for war he advised the army should be "chosen upon the principle of universal liability to service." Most Americans at the time of the declaration didn't believe actual combat troops would be sent. What a dramatic change from this early perception, when the people endorsed the war, to the carnage that followed—and the later disillusionment with Wilson and his grand scheme for world government under the League of Nations. The American people rejected this gross new entanglement, a reflection of a somewhat healthier age than the one we find ourselves in today.

But when it comes to war, the principle of deception lives on. The plan for "universal liability to serve" once again is raising its ugly head. The dollar cost of the current war is already staggering, yet plans are being made to drastically expand the human cost by forcing conscription on the young men (and maybe women) who have no ax to grind with the Iraqi people and want no part of this fight.

Hundreds of Americans have already been killed, and thousands more wounded and crippled, while thousands of others will experience new and deadly war related illnesses not yet identified.

We were told we had to support this preemptive war against Iraq because Saddam Hussein had weapons of mass destruction (and to confront al Qaeda). It was said our national security depended on it. But all these dangers were found not to exist in Iraq. It was implied that lack of support for this Iraqi invasion was un-American and unpatriotic.

Since the original reasons for the war never existed, it is now claimed that we're there to make Iraq a western-style democracy and to spread western values. And besides, it's argued, it's nice that Saddam Hussein has been removed from power. But does the mere existence of evil somewhere in the world justify preemptive war at the expense of the American people? Utopian dreams, fulfilled by autocratic means, hardly qualify as being morally justifiable.

These after-the-fact excuses for invasion and occupation of a sovereign nation direct attention away from the charge that the military industrial complex encouraged this war. It was encouraged by war profiteering, a desire to control natural resources (oil), and a Neo-con agenda of American hegemony with the goal of redrawing the borders of the countries of the Middle East.

The inevitable failure of such a seriously flawed foreign policy cannot be contemplated by those who have put so much energy into this occupation. The current quagmire prompts calls from many for escalation, with more troops being sent to Iraq. Many of our reservists and National Guardsmen cannot wait to get out and have no plans to re-enlist. The odds are that our policy of foreign intervention, which has been with us for many decades, is not likely to soon change. The dilemma of how to win an un-winnable war is the issue begging for an answer.

To get more troops, the draft will likely be reinstated. The implicit prohibition of "involuntary servitude" under the 13th Amendment to the Constitution has already been ignored many times so few will challenge the constitutionality of the coming draft.

Unpopular wars invite conscription. Volunteers disappear, as well they should. A truly defensive just war prompts popular support. A conscripted, unhappy soldier is better off on the long run than the slaves of old since the "enslavement" is only temporary. But in the short run the draft may well turn out to be more deadly and degrading, as one is forced to commit life and limb to a less than worthy cause—like teaching democracy to unwilling and angry Arabs. Slaves were safer in that their owners had an economic interest in protecting their lives. Endangering the lives of our soldiers is acceptable policy, and that's why they are needed. Too often, though, our men and women who are exposed to the hostilities of war and welcomed initially are easily forgotten after the fighting ends. Soon afterward, the injured and the sick are ignored and forgotten.

It is said we go about the world waging war to promote peace, and yet the price paid is rarely weighed against the failed efforts to make the world a better place. Justifying conscription to promote the cause of liberty is one of the most bizarre notions ever conceived by man! Forced servitude, with the risk of death and serious injury as a price to live free, makes no sense. What right does anyone have to sacrifice the lives of others for some cause of questionable value? Even if well motivated it can't justify using force on uninterested persons.

It's said that the 18 year old owes it to his country. Hogwash! It just as easily could be argued that a 50 year-old chicken-hawk, who promotes war and places the danger on innocent young people, owes a heck of a lot more to the country than the 18 year-old being denied his liberty for a cause that has no justification.

All drafts are unfair. All 18 and 19 year olds are never drafted. By its very nature a draft must be discriminatory. All drafts hit the most vulnerable young people, as the elites learn quickly how to avoid the risks of combat.

The dollar cost of war and the economic hardship is great in all wars and cannot be minimized.

War is never economically beneficial except for those in position to profit from war expenditures. The great tragedy of war is the careless disregard for civil liberties of our own people. Abuses of German and Japanese Americans in World War I and World War II are well known.

But the real sacrifice comes with conscription—forcing a small number of young vulnerable citizens to fight the wars that older men and women, who seek glory in military victory without themselves being exposed to danger, promote. These are wars with neither purpose nor moral justification, and too often not even declared by the Congress.

Without conscription, unpopular wars are much more difficult to fight. Once the draft was undermined in the 1960s and early 1970s, the Vietnam War came to an end. But most importantly, liberty cannot be preserved by tyranny. A free society must always resort to volunteers. Tyrants think nothing of forcing men to fight and serve in wrong-headed wars; a true fight for survival and defense of America would elicit, I'm sure, the assistance of every able-bodied man and woman. This is not the case for wars of mischief far away from home in which we so often have found ourselves in the past century.

One of the worst votes that an elected official could ever cast would be to institute a military draft to fight an illegal war, if that individual himself maneuvered to avoid military service. But avoiding the draft on principle qualifies oneself to work hard to avoid all unnecessary war and oppose the draft for all others.

A government that is willing to enslave a portion of its people to fight an unjust war can never be trusted to protect the liberties of its own citizens. The ends can never justify the means, no matter what the Neo-cons say.

Discussion Questions

1. Evaluate the arguments by Trachtenberg and Paul regarding reinstating conscription. Which person makes the better argument? Support your answer.
2. The more recent drafts of the National Service Act allow people to perform national service in place of military service. Discuss whether this overcomes some of Paul's objections to the act.
3. Research suggests that democracies that have conscripted armies are more cautious about going to war. If this is the case, discuss whether it justifies bringing back conscription in the United States. Discuss also how Paul would most likely respond to this argument.
4. The 2001 "No Child Left Behind Act" requires high schools to give military recruiters personal information about students and to allow them into the schools to talk directly to students. Some schools refuse to comply, arguing that the law violates students' privacy rights. Parents also say it entices their children, especially children from lower socioeconomic families, away from going to college. Discuss the pros and cons of this approach to recruiting young people for the military.

JONATHAN GRANOFF

Peace and Security

Jonathan Granoff is a Philadelphia lawyer and president of the Global Security Institute. Granoff argues that our collective existence is threatened by the possibility of war and ecological disasters. In order to prevent global nuclear or ecological disaster, we, as concerned global citizens, must recognize the interconnectedness of living systems and work to promote ethically responsible public policy.

Critical Reading Questions

1. According to Granoff, what responsibility do we have to future generations and why?
2. What issues in particular do we need to address as global citizens?
3. Why is a belief in social Darwinism a threat to global security?
4. What does Granoff mean when he says that fear is the twin of ignorance and compassion the twin of wisdom?
5. What is the principle of reciprocity, and how does it apply to nuclear weapons policies?
6. On what grounds does Granoff maintain that nuclear weapons "can never be ethically legitimate"?
7. How does Granoff define "security of the people"?
8. Why is it important that we change the current paradigm in which security is pursued through military violence?

We are the first generation making ethical decisions that will determine whether we will be the last generation. Science, technology and sophisticated social organizational skills have gifted us with unprecedented capacities for enrichment or destruction. I believe that there is an ethical responsibility to future generations to ensure we are not passing on a future of horrific wars or ecological catastrophe. As individuals and organizations that have received the Nobel Peace Prize, we, particularly, have a heightened responsibility to encourage and empower ethically informed policies.

Each of us knows that our individual life is precious and fragile. We are now reminded that our

collective existence is fragile. This compels us to address, among other issues, ensuring bio-diversity and ending the destruction of thousands of species; reversing the depletion of fishing stocks; controlling ocean dumping; preventing ozone depletion; halting global warming; controlling and eliminating nuclear and other weapons of mass destruction; ending terrorism whether by States or non-State actors; fighting pandemic diseases; ending the tragedy of crushing poverty and lack of clean drinking water; and addressing crises arising from States in chaos. No nation or even a small group of nations can succeed in addressing these issues alone.

Some solutions must be universal. Chlorofluorocarbon from a refrigerant in the US or China can harm the ozone in Chile, New Zealand or anywhere. If one country allows oceanic dumping, others will follow. Viruses do not recognize religions,

"Peace and Security." Presented at the *Fourth World Summit to Nobel Peace Laureates,* Rome, November 28, 2003.

races or borders. Our futures are interconnected in unprecedented ways.

Wise people have been instructing us for millennia to recognize our deeper human unity. But, now necessity alerts us: the galvanizing power of moral leadership cannot be ignored in deference to short-term parochial interests. Our collective challenges require principles that are uplifting, inspiring, affirmative of our highest potential and universal. Hope must overcome fear.

Fear is the twin of ignorance, generating a false realism. Nicolo Machiavelli stated it in *The Prince:* "Where the safety of the country depends upon resolutions to be taken, no consideration of justice or injustice, humanity or cruelty, nor of glory or shame, should be allowed to prevail." This policy of "emergency" can hardly make sense as a norm if we are to be ethical beings living in community. Such so called "realists" invariably assert broadly that power in their own hands is necessary to ensure the security of their individual State.

Overlooking the intricate interconnectedness of living systems, they exalt social Darwinism. Strength is good, ultimate strength is better. In the quest for the ultimate weapon, an absurd result is obtained. The means to security and the pursuit of strength undermine the end of security. Such improved means to an unimproved end is most aptly articulated by nuclear weapons whereby the means of pursuing security undermines the end of security. This is not realistic. This is irresponsible.

They also rely on a rigid world view in which the pursuit of the good and the pursuit of the real are divisible. They say that only what can be measured, predicted and controlled is relevant in policy discussion. What gives our lives meaning, what makes us human, what exalts our lives, is thus not considered. They leave little room in the making of policy for conscience, love, or other immeasurable, formless, human treasures. Not the least of these treasures that give our lives meaning is compassion, the twin of wisdom.

Compassion is essential to our ethical nature and has universally guided every successful culture. It is upon the foundation of ethical principles that policies must become based. Without compassion, law cannot attain justice, and without justice, there is never peace. When kindness and compassion guide our policies, our rules become golden.

Buddhism: "Hurt not others in ways that you yourself would find hurtful." *Udana-Varga, 5:18;* "A state that is not pleasing or delightful to me, how could I inflict that upon another?" *Samyutta Nikaya v. 353.*

Christianity: "All things whatsoever you would that men should do to you, do you even so to them." *Matthew 7:12.*

Confucianism: "Do not unto others what you would not have them do unto you." *Analects 15:23;* "Tsi-kung asked, 'Is there one word that can serve as a principle of conduct for life?' Confucius replied, 'It is the word 'shu'—reciprocity. Do not impose on others what you yourself do not desire." Doctrine of the Mean 13.3; "One should not behave towards others in a way which is disagreeable to oneself." Mencius Vii.A.4.

Hinduism: "This is the sum of duty: do not unto others which would cause you pain if done to you." *Mahabharata 5:1517.*

Islam: "No one of you is a believer until he desires for his brother that which he desires for himself." *Hadith.*

Jainism: "A man should journey treating all creatures as he himself would be treated." *Sutrakritanga 1.11.33;* "Therefore, neither does he [a wise person] cause violence to others nor does he make others do so." *Acarangasutra 5.101–2;* "In happiness and suffering, in joy and grief, we should regard all creatures as we regard our own self." *Lord Mahavira, 24th Tirthankara.*

Judaism: ". . . thou shall love thy neighbor as thyself." *Leviticus 19:18;* "What is hateful to you, do not do to your fellow man. That is the law; all the rest is commentary." *Talmud, Shabbat 31a.*

Native American: "Respect for all life is the foundation." *The Great Law of Peace.*

Roman Pagan Religion: "The law imprinted on the hearts of all men is to love the members of society as themselves."

Shinto: "The heart of the person before you is a mirror."

Sikhism: "I am a stranger to no one; and no one is a stranger to me. Indeed, I am a friend to all. *Guru Granth Sahib, p. 1299.* "As thou hast deemed thyself, so deem others.""

Taoism: "Regard your neighbor's gain as your own gain, and your neighbor's loss as your own loss." *Tai Shang Kan Ying Pien, 213–218.*

Yoruba Wisdom (Nigeria): "One going to take a pointed stick to pinch a baby bird should first try it on himself to feel how it hurts."

Zoroastrianism: "That nature only is good when it shall not do unto another whatsoever is not good for its own self." *Dadistan-I-Dinik, 94:5.*

Philosopher's statements:

Plato: "May I do to others as I would that they should do unto me." *Greece, 4th Century BCE.*
Socrates: "Do not do to others that which would anger you if others did it to you." *Greece, 5th Century BCE.*
Seneca: "Treat your inferiors as you would be treated by your superiors." *Epistle 47:11 Rome, 1st Century CE.*

This principle of reciprocity is the ethical and moral foundation of all the world's major religions. Multilateralism is the logical political outgrowth of this principle. An international order based on cooperation, equity and the rule of law is its needed expression.

Where this rule of reciprocity is violated, instability follows. The failure of the nuclear weapons states to abide by their pledge, contained in the Nuclear Nonproliferation Treaty, to negotiate the elimination of nuclear weapons is the single greatest stimulus to the proliferation of nuclear weapons. For some to say nuclear weapons are good for them but not for others is simply not sustainable.

The threat to use nuclear weapons on innocent people can never be ethically legitimate. Thus, there is a moral imperative for their abolition.

I would like to add two new rules:

First, the Rule of Nations: **"Treat other nations as you wish your nation to be treated."**

Second, the Rule of the Powerful: **"As one does so shall others do."**

We are faced with a moment of collective truth: the ethical, spiritually based insights of the wise coincide with material physical imperatives for survival. The value of the love of power must give way to the power of love. In today's world, leadership must be guided by the duty to love one's neighbor as oneself. This includes the duty to protect the weakest neighbor. And, today, the whole world is one neighborhood—a moral location, not just a physical one.

What was once an admonition as a personal necessity for inner growth has now become a principle that we must learn to utilize in forming public policies. The rule is offended by ethnic and religious exclusivity and prejudice, nationalistic expansionism, economic injustice and environmental irresponsibility.

How should we view the security of people? May I suggest that Timothy Wirth, when he was United States Under Secretary of State for Global Affairs, was correct when he stated that a productive focus of multilateral security should begin with people:

Security is now understood in the context of human security. Human security is about the 1 billion individuals who live in abject poverty. It is about the 800 million people who go hungry every day—the 240 million malnourished. The 17 million who die each year from easily preventable diseases fall into this definition of security, as do the 1.3 billion people without access to clean water and the more than 2 billion people who do not benefit from safe sanitation.

Failure to change from the flawed paradigm in which security is pursued primarily through violence reinforces the brutality inflicted upon millions of daily lives destroyed by conventional weapons, including small arms and anti-personnel land mines. And we cannot overlook the exorbitant economic waste and social costs of militarism—more than ten trillion dollars since the end of the Cold War.

If we do not quickly get over the ridiculous excessive attachment to that which divides us, we will fail to establish effective institutions and policies in our time and we will fail to treat future generations as we would be treated. Such failure cannot be accepted by any parent who has looked into the eyes of their children.

We have developed excessively sophisticated technologies for destruction. For our survival, we require appropriate social and human technologies for cooperation, for disarmament—for our very humanity.

An Eskimo elder at the Millennium World Peace Summit at the United Nations said, "Our history goes back 40,000 years and only now are we finding lakes in the Arctic ice cap. You have technology that is melting the ice. When will we develop a technology to melt the human heart?"

Let our deliberations for peace and security also help develop that technology.

Discussion Questions

1. Granoff argues that a resolution to problems that threaten our collective existence requires moral leadership. What does he mean by this? Discuss what steps you are taking, or could take, to resolve problems that threaten global security.
2. What ethical principles, according to Granoff, are found in the world's major ethical teachings, and what is the relevance of these principles to global security?
3. In what ways does a belief in cultural relativism, as opposed to universal morality, threaten our global security? Discuss the extent to which the United States' national security policy is informed by these two ethical systems.
4. Discuss what Granoff's position would most likely be on the just-war theory. In particular, discuss how Granoff might respond to Elizabeth Anscombe's argument that preemptive nuclear strikes may be justified under limited conditions. Which person presents the stronger argument? Support your answer.
5. Compare and contrast Granoff's position on the permissibility of war or arming for war with Sohail Hashmi's Islamic ethics of war and peace.

CASE STUDIES

1. ALLIED FIREBOMBING DURING WORLD WAR II

In 1942 Winston Churchill responded to the question "How are you going to win the war?" by saying, "We will shatter Germany by bombing . . . the severe, ruthless bombing of Germany on an ever-increasing scale will not only cripple her war effort . . . but will create conditions intolerable to the mass of the German population." This statement was followed by a campaign of firebombing German cities. Firebombing consists of dropping large amounts of high explosives on buildings, followed by incendiary devices to ignite them, then more explosives. This creates a self-sustaining firestorm with temperatures peaking at over 1,500 degrees centigrade.

Allied bombers were ordered to attack Berlin, Leipzig, and other German cities in the east to "cause confusion in the evacuation of refugees from the east" and "hamper the movements of troops from the west."[16] The firebombing of German cities continued until 1945, culminating in an attack on the city of Dresden, a cultural center with little war-related industry. The city at the time was crowded with refugees fleeing the Red Army.

The firebombing of Dresden, which has been called "the worst single event massacre of all time,"[17] killed 100,000 people, more than those killed by the atomic bomb dropped several months later on Hiroshima, and destroyed 85 percent of the city. Kurt

Vonnegut Jr., who was a prisoner of war in Dresden when it was firebombed, later wrote of the horrors of the event in his book *Slaughterhouse Five.*

Discussion Questions

1. The bombings of German cities were justified by the British on utilitarian grounds. Discuss whether utilitarians would agree with Churchill's line of reasoning.
2. Were the firebombings justified under the just-war theory? Support your answer.
3. In an August 9, 1945, radio speech, aired shortly after a second atomic bomb destroyed Nagasaki, President Truman stated: "If Japan does not surrender, bombs will have to be dropped on her war industries and, unfortunately, thousands of civilian lives will be lost. I urge Japanese civilians to leave industrial cities immediately, and save themselves from destruction."[18] Does warning civilians to leave cities relieve the military of moral responsibility for their deaths? Should the citizens of Dresden have been warned ahead of time, or would this have put the bombers and the military operation in too much danger?
4. What is a war crime? Should British Air Marshall Arthur Harris, inventor of area firebombing and the officer who ordered the bombing of Dresden, be tried for war crimes? Is the fact that killing civilians was not the intended purpose of the firebombing (principle of double effect) morally relevant? Support your answers.

2. USA PATRIOT ACT AND THE WAR AGAINST TERRORISM

The USA Patriot Act, an acronym for Uniting and Strengthening America by Providing Appropriate Tools Required to Intercept and Obstruct Terrorism, was passed in October 2001 following the September 11 terrorist attacks and reauthorized in 2006. The act permits federal agents to search homes and offices, bank accounts, and medical and library records, wiretap phones, and read people's e-mails without their permission. Shortly after the act was passed, more than one thousand Arab and Muslim men were arrested as terrorist suspects. Many were held without being told the charges against them.

In 2003 the American Civil Liberties Union filed nine legal challenges against the Patriot Act, arguing that the act violates the Fourth Amendment of the Constitution, which permits searches only with a warrant. Supporters of the act point out that it does not make sense to warn possible terrorists that they will be subject to search and seizure. However, it is the potential for abuse that worries civil libertarians. Several colleges have protested the act, arguing that it infringes on academic freedom and privacy rights (see Chapter 9, Case Study 4). More than 150 local governments, including at least three state governments, have passed resolutions condemning the Patriot Act as an infringement on civil rights.

Discussion Questions

1. Discuss whether or not apprehending and deterring terrorists outweighs the temporary loss of rights of innocent people who are suspected of terrorism.
2. Does the Patriot Act pose a threat to our civil liberties, or does it work to protect our civil liberties? When is it appropriate for a country to override the rule of

law, as explicated by Jonathan Granoff in his readings, in the name of national security? Support your answers.

3. Ben Franklin once said that those who would trade liberty for security deserve neither.[19] Do you agree with him? Is his position unrealistic in today's world? Support your answers. Discuss how Thomas Hobbes would most likely respond to Franklin's statement.

4. In response to a question about what would happen if the United States was hit with a weapon of mass destruction that inflicted many casualties, retired General Tommy Franks replied that the Constitution and our liberty and freedoms would likely be discarded for a military form of government.[20] Do you agree?

---

3. EHREN WATADA: THE OFFICER WHO REFUSED TO BE DEPLOYED

When Ehren Watada, a fist lieutenant in the United States Army, received his order in March 2006 to be deployed to Iraq, he refused to go. Watada maintained that the war in Iraq was illegal because it was based on incorrect information, such as the existence of weapons of mass destruction and the link between Saddam Hussein and al-Qaeda, and because the occupation of Iraq violated the Army's own rules of conduct as well as the UN Charter and Geneva Conventions that prohibit wars of aggression. In response, the Army brought charges of "conduct unbecoming an officer and a gentleman" and of "missing movement" for his refusal to be deployed.

Watada faces the possibility of a court-marital and several years in prison. However, he is willing to face the consequences of his decisions. He stated at a press conference:

> It is my duty as a commissioned officer in the United States army to speak out against grave injustices. My moral and legal obligation is to the Constitution, not to those who issue unlawful orders. I stand before you today because it is my job to serve and protect American soldiers and innocent Iraqis who have no voice. It is my conclusion that the war in Iraq is not only morally wrong, but also a breach of American law.[21]

Several groups, including the ACLU and Amnesty International, have come out in support of Watada. Others, including some members of the Japanese American community and Military Families Voice of Victory, who claim he is helping al-Qaeda, oppose his protest. Watada's first court-martial trial ended in a mistrial.

Discussion Questions

1. Using the criteria for civil disobedience listed on page 579, discuss whether Watada's action is an example of civil disobedience.
2. John Rawls writes, "if justified civil disobedience seems to threaten civil concord, the responsibility falls not upon those who protest but upon those whose abuse of authority and power justifies such opposition. For to employ the coercive apparatus of the state in order to maintain manifestly unjust institutions is itself a form of illegitimate force that men in due course have a right to resist."[22] Discuss Rawls's position, relating it to the Watada case.

3. The Army prosecutor in Watada's court-martial trial argued that Watada had "abandoned his soldiers and disgraced himself and the service."[23] Given that Watada voluntarily joined the Army *after* the war in Iraq had begun, does he have a duty of fidelity to carry through on the commitment to the Army and his unit he made when he joined? Discuss whether Watada's refusal to be deployed would have been different from a moral point of view if he had been conscripted into the Army.

4. During the Vietnam War, many of the young men who were drafted refused to participate in the war. While some chose to go to prison, many more left the country. Indeed, some 50,000 draft-age men moved to Canada during the Vietnam era. Discuss what you would do, and why, if the National Service Act is passed and you are drafted to fight in a war that you believe to be unjust.

---

4. WHEN PARENTAL DUTY CONFLICTS WITH MILITARY DUTY

The United States is the only country in the world that sends soldiers who are mothers of young children into harm's way in war. In the early 1970s, with the push for the Equal Rights Amendment and "equal career opportunities" in the military, Congress began to integrate the genders in the military. By 1980 the United States had almost 200,000 women on active military duty, the largest number in the world.[24] More than half of these women are mothers, many of them of young children.

In November 2003, Simone and Vaughn Holcomb took an emergency leave from military duty in Iraq and returned to Fort Carson, Colorado, to face a custody battle over two of their seven children, ranging in age from four to twelve years old. The children had been staying with Mr. Holcomb's mother who was no longer able to care for them. Mr. Holcomb's former wife was suing for custody for two of the children from his former marriage. The court mandated that one of the parents must remain in Colorado to retain custody of the children. Otherwise, the judge would rule abandonment and turn over custody of the two children to Vaughn's former wife.

The Holcombs decided that Vaughn would return to Iraq and Simone would stay behind. "My children always come first," she told a reporter. However, the Army denied her request to be released from active duty, so she remained in Colorado without the army's permission. Simone Holcomb said in justification of her actions, "The Army accepted our applications to be soldiers, they should appreciate our custody problems. I will fight with all my motherly might to protect my children. If both my husband and I are in Iraq together, these children could lose their parents."[25] Holcomb faced dismissal plus possible jail time for her disobedience. In the end, the Army gave Mrs. Holcomb a "compassionate reassignment" to the Colorado National Guard so she could be with her children.

Discussion Questions

1. Did the judge make the morally right ruling in this case? If you had been the judge, how would you have ruled? Explain your reasoning.

2. In her book *Maternal Thinking, Toward a Politics of Peace,* Sara Ruddick maintains that military thinking and maternal thinking—defined as "preservation love"

or keeping the child alive and healthy in an indifferent or hostile world—are set against each other. Ruddick maintains that maternal practice is a natural resource for peace politics because mothers want to prevent harm to their children. Do you agree? If so, how should this insight be incorporated into policies regarding women and mothers in the military? Support your answers.

3. Studies show that newborns and toddlers who lose or are abandoned by their mothers (as happens when a mother is deployed overseas) are much more likely to suffer emotional and mental disorders later in life and to engage in crime and drug use.[26] Given this, discuss how a utilitarian would feel about conscripting mothers of young children or sending mothers into active combat duty.

4. The United Nations Universal Declaration of Human Rights states: "Motherhood and childhood are entitled to special care and protection." Discuss whether sending mothers of young children into combat duty, particularly when they would prefer not to go, is a violation of mothers' rights and the rights of their children. Support your answers.

5. Elaine Donnelly of The Center for Military Readiness is opposed to the current U.S. policy of allowing women to serve near the front lines, arguing that it "violates the long-standing moral imperative that men must protect women from physical harm.[27] Others oppose giving women combat duty on the grounds that women are not physically strong enough for the demands of combat. Also, female combatants who are captured by the enemy are subject to a high risk of rape. Discuss how a liberal feminist would respond to these arguments.

6. If conscription is reinstated, should mothers of dependent children be exempt? Should fathers of young children also be exempt? Support your answers. Discuss how Trachtenberg might answer these questions.

---

5. HOMOSEXUALS IN THE MILITARY: "DON'T ASK, DON'T TELL"

Petty Officer Rhoda Davis was dismissed by the Navy in 2006 because she disclosed her sexual orientation at a rally supporting same-sex marriage. Davis is one of more than eleven thousand military personnel who have been discharged from the United States military since 1993 when Congress passed a law reaffirming the military's long-standing position that "homosexualty is incompatible with military service."[28] Although openly homosexual people are not allowed in the military, a Clinton-era "Don't ask, don't tell" policy prohibits the military from inquiring about a soldier's sexual orientation unless there is evidence of it or the soldier openly admits his or her homosexuality.

In *Meinhold v. U.S. Department of Defense* (1994), an appellate court upheld the U.S. Navy's action in discharging Keith Meinhold after he said on television, "Yes, I am gay." The court ruled that openly declaring one's homosexual orientation demonstrates "a concrete, fixed, or expressed desire to commit homosexual acts despite their being prohibited." Opponents of the decision disagree, arguing that it is irrational to assume that because people are open about their homosexuality they will engage in homosexual activities when in the military.

The Department of Defense defends its policy, stating that homosexuality disrupts the cohesion, discipline, and morale in military units. They also note that barring homosexuals does not violate their rights because there is no constitutional right to serve in the armed forces. Rather, the law defends the right of men and women serving in the military not to be forced to expose themselves to people who might be sexually attracted to them. President Obama has promised to repeal the "Don't ask, don't tell" policy.

Discussion Questions

1. Discrimination is morally justified if it is based on rational criteria. Is this the case with the ban on homosexuality in the military? Support your answer.
2. Some supporters of the current policy, while admitting that they may be mistaken about the negative effects of having homosexuals in the military, nevertheless argue that it is unreasonable to expect the military to engage in a social experiment by allowing homosexuals in the military because the risks are so high if the experiment fails. Discuss this line of reasoning.
3. Opponents of the "Don't ask, don't tell" policy argue that it violates people's freedom to be open about their sexual orientation—a freedom that is essential for ensuring self-respect and a sense of dignity. Do you agree? If so, discuss how this right should be weighed against the right of heterosexual people in the military not to have to expose themselves when undressing to people who might be sexually attracted to them.
4. Several colleges have banned the Reserve Officers' Training Corps (ROTC) from their campuses in protest against the "Don't ask, don't tell" policy. In response, Congress passed the ROTC Campus Access Act, which cut off all Department of Defense funding to campuses that ban ROTC. Critics of the ban argue that it discriminates against poorer students who depend on ROTC to finance their college education. Discuss whether the ban was the best way to protest the "Don't ask, don't tell" policy.

---

6. PRISONERS OF WAR: TRIALS AND TORTURE

The graphic photographs from Abu Graib prison in Iraq, as well as reports from Guantanamo Bay of prisoners being tortured, raise the question of whether it is ever morally justified to torture military prisoners. The Military Commissions Act of 2006, rather than forbidding the use of torture, forbids only "grave breaches" of the Geneva Conventions. In other words, the new law allowed the use of torture—such as stress positions, half-drowning, and grotesque degradation—against "enemy combatants." It also allowed evidence extracted by torture to be used in trials. In addition, the act authorized a new system of military courts in which prisoners of war could be tried without being represented by a lawyer or being informed of the evidence against them, and without even being present at the trial.

Former President Bush defended the law, saying that Congress should not put restrictions on the president, as commander in chief, to do things—such as torturing enemy combatants to get vital information—that are necessary to protect national security and to effectively fight the "war on terror." Opponents of the new law, such as former Secretary of State Colin Powell and Senator John McCain, argued that legitimizing the use of torture damages U.S. policy interests because it can be used by our enemies to justify the torture of American prisoners of war. It also runs counter to our values as a free and democratic nation that is built on respect for the individual. In January 2009 President Obama banned the use of "harsh interrogations techniques," stating that torture is not consistent with "our values and ideals."

Discussion Questions

1. Discuss the arguments for and against the use of torture on prisoners of war. What if it is strongly suspected that a particular prisoner is a terrorist who has information about plans that may lead to the death of thousands of Americans? Discuss how both a utilitarian and a deontologist might answer this question.
2. Apply the just-war theory to the treatment of prisoners of war or enemy combatants. Does the second condition of *jus in bello*—"The tactics used must be a proportional response to the injury being redressed"—permit the use of torture in limited situations, such as the one described in question 1? Support your answer. Discuss how both Anscombe and Coady might answer this question.
3. Discuss the potential impact of the Military Commissions Act on college students and faculty who protest the Iraq war or engage in library or Internet research on terrorism. Referring back to Case Study 4 on page 509, discuss whether the University of Massachusetts student in question could be classified as an "unlawful enemy combatant" under the new definition of the term.

C H A P T E R   1 2

Animal Rights and Environmental Ethics

In the fall of 1995, Lisa Simpson, one of television's most famous cartoon characters, became a vegetarian with a little help from her friends Linda and Paul McCartney. The episode, watched by 10 million Americans, opened with the Simpsons visiting a petting zoo. That evening the family had lamb chops for dinner, and Lisa faced a moral crisis as she made the connection between the lambs she had been petting at the zoo and the meat on her plate. Lisa decided to quit eating meat. She soon discovered, however, that being a vegetarian wasn't all that easy in a society of carnivores. Her brother, Bart, tormented her mercilessly. Lisa faced another crisis when her father, Homer, hosted a pig roast. When Lisa's offer of vegetarian gazpacho as an alternative was rejected, she destroyed the barbecue and fled in disgust at her family's indifference to animal suffering.

Lisa found solace and moral support from her friends the McCartneys, who were visiting Apu, a vegan from India. Lisa confided in Apu that she eats cheese. "You must think I'm a monster," Lisa said. "Indeed I do," Apu responded. "But I learned long ago to tolerate others rather than forcing my beliefs on them." Lisa realized that one cannot convert others through force but only through reason and example.

THE LEGAL AND MORAL STATUS OF NONHUMAN ANIMALS

Most people, when asked, say that they like animals and disapprove of animal cruelty. They draw the line, however, when it comes to animals having rights. When there is a conflict between animal interests and human interests, no matter how trivial, human interests almost always win out. We eat meat, visit zoos, wear leather shoes, use cosmetics and drugs that have been tested on captive animals, and abandon our dogs and cats at animal shelters when they inconvenience us.

Suggestions that animals have rights that we ought to respect are generally met with ridicule. When Mary Wollstonecraft published *A Vindication of the Rights of Woman* in 1792, her ideas were also ridiculed. One critic wrote that if the idea of equality was applied to women, why shouldn't it also hold for "brutes"? Because the idea of granting rights to other animals is absurd, the critic concluded, it is also absurd to grant rights to women. Women have since been granted rights under the law, although it took more than a century.

In the past four decades, dozens of books and hundreds of articles have been written on animal rights. Thousands of animal-rights and vegetarian groups have proliferated; most colleges have at least one animal-rights group on campus. Much of the inspiration for the current animal-rights movement has come from Eastern philosophy. Gandhi's philosophy, in particular, has had an enormous influence on both the American civil rights movement and the animal-rights movement.

In many Asian countries, such as India, vegetarianism has long been the norm. According to Hindu and Buddhist ethics, meat-eating violates the principle of *ahimsa,* or nonviolence. Meat-eating also contributes to a mentality of violence and has negative karmic consequences. Japan has banned research using great apes (chimpanzees, gorillas, bonobos, and orangutans); in other Asian countries apes have never been used in scientific research.

Among Western nations, the Spanish parliament in 2008 approved a resolution that grants great apes "human rights," including the right to life and protection from harmful research practices and commercial exploitation. Other countries, including the Netherlands, Britain, Austria, Switzerland, Sweden, Australia, and New Zealand, have bans on research using great apes. There is pressure in some of these countries to bestow legal "personhood" on great apes. In the United States there is greater resistance to the idea of extending rights to the great apes or other animals.

In most Western countries nonhuman animals have only instrumental value; they are regarded primarily as commodities or property. One meat-company manager, for example, described a breeding sow as "a valuable piece of machinery whose function is to pump out baby pigs like a sausage machine."[1] For at least ten months out of the year, the pregnant and nursing breeding sow or "mother machine" is isolated in a narrow pen in which she is unable to turn around. She is impregnated forcefully either by being tethered to a "rape rack" for easy access or through "the surgical transplant of embryos from 'supersows' to ordinary sows."[2]

The Animal Welfare Act was enacted in the United States in 1970. The act is not concerned, however, with protecting the welfare of rats, mice, birds, reptiles, frogs, or animals raised for food; nor does it include genetically altered animals. In addition, animal welfare laws do not give animals rights. Concern for animal suffering is based primarily on the concept of "necessary suffering." Suffering is wrong ("unnecessary") only when it does not advance human interests.

Ethical positions regarding public policy can be divided into the abolitionist, reformist, and status quo positions. *Abolitionists* argue that we should stop using animals altogether as a source of food and as tools in scientific experiments. They oppose zoos, circuses, and keeping animals as house pets. Their position is supported by animal-rights activists such as Tom Regan. Although few Western philosophers accept this position, it is more generally accepted in Eastern philosophies such as Hinduism, Buddhism, Taoism, and Jainism, which are based on respect for all living beings.

Reformists accept meat-eating and animal experimentation, but think that we need to improve these institutions. Unlike abolitionists, who sometimes work outside the law, reformist organizations such as humane societies work within the system, promoting reform and legislative initiatives on behalf of animals. Animal-welfare laws that require cages of a certain size for animals in laboratories but do not oppose animal experimentation itself are based on the reformist position.

The *status quo* position maintains that no changes are necessary in the way humans treat other animals. The status quo position is supported by traditional Western philosophies, which regard nonhuman animals as lacking moral value. This philosophical tradition has been one of the most deeply rooted obstacles to any serious consideration of the moral rights of both nonhuman animals and the environment.

THE LEGAL AND MORAL STATUS OF THE ENVIRONMENT

Environmental ethics is concerned with the moral basis of environmental responsibility, including the moral value of nonhuman nature, pollution, population control, food production, and preservation of wilderness and species diversity.

The environmental ethics movement is a relative newcomer on the philosophical scene. In 1967 history professor Lynn White published an article in *Science* in which he blamed Christian anthropocentric thinking for creating an ecological crisis. According to Judeo-Christian tradition, the earth was created by God for the benefit of humans. "By destroying pagan animism," White wrote, "Christianity made it possible to exploit nature in a mood of indifference to the feelings of natural objects."[3]

Philosophers entered the fray in the early 1970s. Their attention was initially focused on Aldo Leopold's essay on land ethics, excerpts of which are included in this chapter. Leopold attacks the anthropocentric relationship between humans and the environment that is based on humans as conquerors of the land. He calls on us to replace the old paradigm with a new ecocentric paradigm in which humans are viewed as members, rather than conquerors, of the greater biotic community.

The **deep ecology** movement began in the mid-1970s. Deep ecology is generally regarded as a radical environmental ethic. The central concern of deep ecologists, such as Arne Naess, George Sessions, and Bill Devall, is to cultivate a sense of identification with nature and an awareness of our interconnectedness.

Ecofeminism emerged as a movement in the 1980s. Ecofeminists such as Karen Warren link environmental ethics to feminism and animal rights, arguing that oppression of women, oppression of nonhuman animals, and oppression of nature are all grounded in the same logic of dominance.

As in the animal-rights debate, the *status quo* position is based on an anthropocentric worldview that regards nonhuman nature as a resource for human consumption. The primary purpose for protecting nonhuman nature, according to this view, is to preserve it for ourselves and future generations. The growing awareness of global warming and the detrimental effects of certain human activities has led to greater concern for protection of the environment.

THE PHILOSOPHERS ON THE MORAL VALUE OF NONHUMAN ANIMALS AND THE ENVIRONMENT

Ancient Greek philosophers were divided regarding the moral value of nonhuman nature. The Pythagoreans, who were vegetarians, taught that other animals should be treated with respect. Aristotle, on the other hand, thought that other animals had only instrumental moral value. Contemporary views on the moral value of nonhuman animals have been shaped primarily by Aristotle's anthropocentric philosophy.

The split between humans and nonhuman nature in Western thought began with the acceptance of the ancient Greek dualism, which split reality into nonthinking material substances (body) and nonmaterial thinking substances (mind or soul). Aristotle argued that reason is an activity of the soul. Humans have a soul; nonhuman animals don't. Because moral value depends on the ability to reason, only humans have intrinsic moral value. Other animals are inferior beings whom nature has made "for the sake of man."[4]

Aristotle's worldview was Christianized by Thomas Aquinas. The world was created by God for humans. "Humans," according to Aquinas, "are the highest in the order of material beings, yet the lowest in the order of spiritual beings . . . the progression from the non-living to humans is one of increasing perfection . . . schematically, humans are at the apex of material creation."[5] According to Genesis 1:26, "God said, 'let us make man in our image, after our likeness; and let them have dominion over the fish of the sea, and over the birds of the air, and over the cattle . . . and over all the earth." Nature and other animals exist only to the extent that they benefit humans.

The belief that humans are separate from, and morally superior to, other animals was affirmed by René Descartes, the "father of modern philosophy." Carrying the hierarchical worldview of his predecessors even further, Descartes concluded that nonhuman animals are merely organic machines, much like clocks, without souls, free will, or consciousness. Because of this, it is not immoral to kill and eat them.

John Locke based his natural rights theory on the belief that humans are a special and unique creation of God. To base rights on equal consideration for the interests of all living beings, rather than on the so-called special nature of humans, is to deny the "natural" order of creation. Locke's anthropocentric, theologically based worldview granted humans the inalienable right to exploit nonhuman nature with impunity.

Francis Bacon (1561–1626), founder of the scientific method, unquestionably accepted the prevailing philosophical view on nonhuman animals. Bacon enthusiastically advocated **vivisection**—the dissection of live animals—for the pure joy of learning. Because of the tremendous success of science in generating results and new technologies, few people bothered to question the morality of sacrificing nonhuman animals to achieve some of these successes.

Immanuel Kant taught that we have no direct duties toward animals because they lack rationality and, hence, are nonpersons. We should, however, "practice kindness towards animals, for he who is cruel to animals becomes hard also in his dealings with men." Cruelty toward animals purely for sport cannot be morally justified because it hardens us. While Kant did not regard other animals or nonhuman nature as having intrinsic worth, he emphasized the importance of the aesthetic experience of nature to human well-being. Just as cruelty toward other animals is wrong because it damages our character, destroying a beautiful area of wilderness is wrong because it damages our human sensibilities. On the other hand, because "animals must be regarded as man's instruments," we can use them for scientific experiments and for food just as we can use the natural environment for justifiable human purposes.

The battle for equal rights for all groups of humans fueled a similar demand for respect for the rights of other animals as well. Mohandas Gandhi, Mary Wollstonecraft,

Susan B. Anthony, and Elizabeth Cady Stanton, to name only a few human-rights advo-cates, also spoke out on behalf of other animals. The utilitarians were among the first advocates for nonhuman animals. According to Jeremy Bentham, it is not reason but the capacity to suffer that is morally relevant.[6] The utilitarian's concern for the happiness of all sentient beings—regardless of their race, gender, or species—reflects the moral ideal of equality that was so important during the late eighteenth century. This ideal gave rise to both the American and French Revolutions. The utilitarians, such as Bentham, hoped that this moral ideal would someday be extended to all sentient beings.

Charles Darwin (1809–1882) also rejected anthropocentricism. Darwin attacked the assumption that only humans are capable of reason. Reason, by definition, involves the ability to form general rules from particular experiences. That other animals are capable of reasoning seemed obvious to Darwin. "Only a few persons now dispute that animals possess some power of reasoning," he wrote in *The Descent of Man* (1871). "Animals may constantly be seen to pause, deliberate, and resolve."[7] But Darwin under-estimated the power of tradition. His theory of evolution was reinterpreted not only to justify the oppression of non-Western people, but to justify the exploitation of other animals and nature by placing humans at the apex of evolution, thus scientifically legitimating the religious view that humans are a special creation.

Like Darwin, primatologist Frans de Waal points out how very similar the emo-tional and moral behavior of humans is to that of other animals.[8] Many social animals demonstrate what seems to be a natural moral sense and will respond to the distress of another animal, even one of another species. Not only are many of these animals capa-ble of reason, but they appear to deliberate and interact with one another according to a sense of fairness and reciprocity.

Feminist philosophers are divided on the issue of animal rights. Nel Noddings argues that we do not have moral obligations toward nonhuman animals because they are incapable of being in reciprocal caring relationships with humans. Other femi-nists, such as Karen Warren, argue that the domination of women and the domination of nonhuman animals are part of the same patriarchal paradigm. Women can achieve autonomy only by rejecting the dualistic ideology that allows humans to subordinate other animals.

ANIMAL FARMING, ENVIRONMENTAL DEGRADATION, AND VEGETARIANISM

Our eating habits are our most direct interaction with the earth. Americans are steeped in the Jeffersonian tradition that regards farmers as "the chosen People of God" and our "most valued citizens."[9] Farming, Jefferson claimed, ennobles humans by keeping them in touch with living nature. However, modern agriculture is not a natural process but a cultural institution shaped by cultural beliefs that prescribe our relationships to the environment. Critics of modern agricultural practices maintain that exploitation of the earth and other animals through agriculture does not ennoble us but instead disrupts our sense of connection and blunts our feelings, particularly of empathy.[10] That agricul-ture has become one of the major causes of environmental degradation is not surprising given our degraded view of the environment and other animal species.

Most people are unaware of the extent to which human practices affect other animals. Each year almost 7 billion animals are killed in the United States in laboratories, for their fur, by sports hunters, and in slaughterhouses. Of these animals, 95 percent are killed for food.

The affluence boom that followed World War II was accompanied by an increase in meat-eating, which was regarded as a status symbol. By the early 1970s, rich nations were feeding more grain to their livestock than all the people of China and India (who make up more than two-thirds of the world's population) consumed directly.

Intensive farming of animals also began in the United States shortly after the war. Intensive farming involves raising animals indoors in large, automated "factories." Several thousand chickens or pigs may be housed in one building. Confining animals in buildings requires less land and less labor. The modern factory farm reflects the traditional Western view of nonhuman animals as machines. In line with this, the Food and Drug Administration (FDA) has recently moved toward approving the creation of genetically engineered animals for meat production.

The institution of animal agriculture is one of the greatest sources of suffering for nonhuman animals. Animals in the modern factory farm are raised in large buildings in crowded cages or stalls. Today almost all egg production comes from caged birds in automated factory buildings.[11] Journalist Joy Williams writes:

> Factory farmers are all Cartesians. Animals are no more than machines—
> milk machines, piglet machines, egg machines—production units converting
> themselves into profits. . . . The factory farm today is a crowded, stinking
> bedlam, filled with suffering animals that are quite literally insane, sprayed
> with pesticides and fattened on a diet of growth stimulants, antibiotics, and
> drugs. Two hundred and fifty thousand laying hens are confined within a single
> building. (The high mortality rate caused by overcrowding is economically
> acceptable; nothing is more worthless than an individual chicken.)[12]

We need to eat to stay alive. We do have a choice, however, in what to eat. Humans do not need meat in their diets. Indeed, heavy reliance on meat is one of the leading causes of disease and obesity.[13]

More and more people in countries such as the United States, Canada, England, and Australia are becoming vegetarians. A **vegetarian** is a person who refrains from eating meat, poultry, and seafood. **Vegans** abstain from all animal products, including eggs and milk. In a 2006 Harris poll, 2.3 percent of the people responded that they were vegetarians, about double the number from a 1977 survey.[14] Asian Americans are the most likely, and white males the least likely, to be vegetarians. Women are twice as likely as men to be vegetarians.[15]

Ethical vegetarians maintain that animals have moral value. Although meat-eating might be justified if we needed meat for survival, the human taste for animal flesh does not justify killing and eating animals. Those who defend meat-eating, such as Jan Narveson, deny that animals have either moral status or rights that we must respect.

Environmental ethicists do not have a unified position on agriculture. Aldo Leopold did not reject agriculture but judged it against its impact on the entire biotic community. While many environmental ethicists advocate for more humane treatment of nonhuman animals, a few support a move toward intensive farming of "farm" animals, blaming grazing "livestock" for the destruction of wildlife habitat. This has led to criticism that environmentalists who identify nature with the pristine wilderness have created an artificial divide not only between humans and nonhuman nature but between "domestic" and "wild" animals. The increased use of genetic engineering in agriculture may further exacerbate this divide if genetically engineered plants and animals are viewed as legal property of their human creators.

Some people adopt a vegetarian lifestyle out of concern for the environment. Green political parties in Europe and Great Britain advocate a vegetarian diet for environmental and political reasons. Animal farming is tremendously damaging to the environment. If we gave up animal farming, there would be enough food for everyone in the world. Many of the world's environmental problems would also be reduced by the elimination of animal agriculture. A meat-based diet uses three times as much fossil fuel as a vegetarian diet. One acre of land can produce 40,000 pounds of potatoes or 250 pounds of beef.[16] Much of the water pollution, depletion of topsoil, and deforestation is the result of animal agriculture. In the United States, most of the agricultural land is dedicated to raising beef.

Solid waste disposal also contributes to environmental degradation. While population growth in the Third World has been blamed for many of the environmental problems we are currently facing, in fact, affluent Westerners are responsible for much of this pollution. The average American produces much more household waste and is responsible for more industrial and agricultural pollution than anyone else in the world. Hazardous waste disposal, including the disposal of nuclear waste, is particularly problematic. In his reading on "Peace and Security" at the end of Chapter 11, Jonathan Granoff also discusses the negative effects of war on the environment.

The environmental justice movement emerged in the United States in the 1980s. Its focus has been on the urban environment rather than on the wilderness. As such, this movement has radically redefined the meaning of environment to include the broader framework of economic, racial, and social justice. The movement's primary concerns have been ending environmental racism and promoting tighter government regulation of industrial pollution and waste disposal.

GLOBAL WARMING AND CLIMATE CHANGE

Back in the sixteenth century, when William Shakespeare took in a breath, 280 molecules out of every million entering his lungs were carbon dioxide. Today, each time you breathe in, 380 molecules out of every million are carbon dioxide (CO_2).[17] Most scientists believe that the increase in CO_2 is primarily due to human activities and that emissions of CO_2 and other greenhouse gases are the leading cause of a phenomenon known as **global warming.**

Global warming and climate change are of concern to environmental ethicists because of the impact of our consumer-oriented lifestyles, especially the use of CO_2-emitting fossil fuels, on global warming. Global warming has been accelerating in the past decade at a faster than predicted rate. Eight of the hottest years on record, since 1880 when accurate meteorological records were first kept, have been in the last decade, with the global surface temperature in 2006 being the sixth warmest on record.[18] The year 2006 was the warmest on record in the United States.

As a result of global warming, the polar ice caps and mountain glaciers are melting, storm activity is increasing, precipitation patterns are changing, and oceans are warming, leading to rising sea levels and coastal flooding. It is predicted that disruption of the ecosystem by global warming will lead to massive species extinction, with 15 to 35 percent of species being at risk by 2050, a trend that has already begun with the destruction of rain forests for lumber and agriculture. (See Case Study 7.)

The United States is the single largest emitter of greenhouse gases. The Kyoto Protocol, which took effect in 2005, assigned the 169 signatory nations mandatory targets for reduction in emissions of greenhouse gases. Although the United States signed the treaty, it refuses to ratify it because of the strain it will place on the U.S. economy and also because of the "uncertainty" surrounding global warming. Despite this, there is considerable grassroots support for the Kyoto Protocol in the United States. President Obama, who supports the development of alternative energy sources, has set a goal of reducing U.S. greenhouse gas emissions back to 1990 levels by 2020.

The issue of global warming and our moral responsibility as a nation and member of the international community is addressed in the speech by Al Gore toward the end of this chapter. (See also Case Study 6.)

ANIMAL EXPERIMENTATION

Millions of nonhuman animals are killed every year in scientific experiments in the United States alone. As with animal agriculture, the practice of animal experimentation is based on an anthropocentric paradigm.

The U.S. Food and Drug Administration (FDA) requires that all new chemical products be tested. Most of these tests are performed on nonhuman animals. One of the more common tests is the Draize eye irritancy test. The Draize test involves placing a rabbit's head in a restraining device and then putting in one of its eyes a substance such as bleach, shampoo, nail polish, chemical cleaning substances, or weed killer. These experiments are extremely painful. Some rabbits snap their necks in their frantic attempts to escape. In protest, some abolitionist groups have engaged in illegal actions, freeing lab animals and ransacking laboratories. (See Case Study 1.)

The medical field, the defense industry, and universities also make extensive use of nonhuman animals in their research. The different types of animal experiments are outlined in the box on page 645. The biggest increase has been in biotechnology and genetic engineering. It may not be long before pigs, genetically altered to contain human genes, will be mass produced as drug factories and to provide organ transplants (**xenographs**) for humans. (See Case Study 2.) Those who defend the status quo, such as Carl Cohen, argue that animals have no rights that we are bound to respect. They also point out the benefits that animal experimentation has brought to humans.

On the other hand, the results of experiments on one species do not necessarily carry over to humans. Thalidomide, which was responsible for so many devastating birth defects, was tested on animals and deemed safe before being released on the market. In 2006, six healthy male volunteers in a drug trial developed extreme adverse reactions within hours of taking a new drug that had been developed to treat chronic

---

🌿 EXPERIMENTS USING NONHUMAN ANIMALS[19]

- **Acute toxicity test.** This test involves force-feeding enormous quantities of a substance to a group of animals, either orally or through a tube. The purpose is to determine the lethal dose at which a given percentage of animals die within two weeks. The tests can cause convulsions, vomiting, diarrhea, paralysis, and rupture of internal organs.
- **Chronic toxicity test.** Animals are force-fed smaller quantities of a substance over time to determine if continuous exposure is lethal.
- **Skin and eye irritation tests.** Animals are immobilized in restraining devices and chemicals are applied to raw skin or sprayed in the eyes.
- **Acute inhalation toxicity test.** Animals are subjected to large amounts of spray from aerosol preparations. They are then killed and their tissues examined.
- **Psychology research.** Animals are used in experiments that include electric shock, "punishment," induced fighting and killing, brain damage, mutilation, drug addiction, maternal deprivation, and overcrowding.
- **Weapons tests.** Animals are used to study the effects of atomic blasts, radiation, chemical warfare, and laser weapons on the body.
- **Biotechnology.** Animals are genetically engineered for use in medical experiments, to produce drugs for human use, and for organ transplants.

---

inflammatory conditions and leukemia. This drug also had been tested extensively on nonhuman animals without any adverse reactions.

Millions of dollars are wasted every year on pointless or repetitive experiments. Eliminating these types of experiments would rule out some animal experimentation, but it would not rule out all of it. Both abolitionists and reformists encourage the use of alternatives to animal research. These include observation of patients, clinical tests, tissue and cell cultures, the use of cadavers, mechanical models, and computer-generated models. Some college students also refuse to participate in dissection and the use of animals in experiments in class.[20]

Although some scientists believe that the advent of biotechnology will increase the demand for animal experimentation, others argue that the completion of the Human Genome Project may render much of animal experimentation obsolete. The new field of pharmacogenetics, for example, which studies the effects of genetics on an individual's reactions to drugs, will increase the likelihood that medications will be tailored for each individual based on his or her particular genome rather than on animal models.[21]

THE MORAL ISSUES

The Moral Standing of Nonhuman Animals and Nature

To attribute moral standing to a being is to claim that it is worthy of moral respect and protection. A common approach for determining moral standing is to ask if a being has cognitive qualities similar to those of a rational human adult. The more the being is like a human adult in this respect, the higher its moral standing. Applying this line of reasoning, traditional philosophers and scientists maintain that other animals lack reason and, therefore, have little, if any, moral standing. Narveson and Cohen represent this view. Singer, on the other hand, argues that some adult mammals are sufficiently like humans in their cognitive abilities to warrant moral consideration.

One of the problems with this approach is in knowing the mental life and intentions, if any, of other animals. Furthermore, although lack of certain cognitive abilities may exclude a being from being a moral agent, it does not logically follow that it should be denied moral standing. Regan, for example, argues that nonhuman animals may not be moral agents, but they can still be moral patients; that is, they have interests, and therefore rights, that we ought to respect. For example, a cat companion may not have any moral duties toward us, but we, as moral agents, have a duty to provide her with food and shelter. (See Case Study 3.)

Utilitarians, such as Singer, maintain that sentience, not reason, is the relevant criterion for moral standing. It is wrong to cause suffering no matter what the cognitive level of the being. Singer employs anthropocentric criteria, however, attributing higher moral standing to those animals, such as adult mammals, that are most like adult humans in their cognitive abilities. Buddhist philosophers, on the other hand, cast the net wide enough to include all living beings in the moral community.

The primary divide in the environmental rights movement is between ecocentrism and anthropocentrism. **Ecocentrists** and biocentrists, such as Leopold, maintain that nature has moral standing and that we have a duty to preserve the integrity of the biotic community. Environmental ethicists who subscribe to the anthropocentric model, on the other hand, maintain that while there are good reasons for preserving nonhuman nature, these reasons are based on human interests. (See Case Study 5.) Caring for nature is good, not because nature has intrinsic worth, but because identification with nature expands and humanizes us.

Social Contract Theory

According to social contract theorists, such as Narveson, morality is a type of voluntary contract among people. We have moral obligations only toward those who have entered into this agreement. Because nonhuman animals, plants, and inanimate objects such as mountains cannot enter into a social contract, we have no direct moral obligations toward them. We ought not to kill someone else's pet, not because the pet has rights, but because we have a duty toward the human not to destroy her property. A pet owner, however, may decide to rid herself of her pet.

The Principle of Utility

What matters, according to utilitarians, is whether animals can feel pain, not whether they can reason. Singer and Regan, in their readings, graphically illustrate the pain and torment caused to animals by human practices. The moral duty to minimize pain and maximize pleasure militates against most human use of animals. For example, the pleasure humans may get from the taste of meat does not outweigh the suffering caused to animals by farming.

We also need to weigh the benefits to humans of animal experimentation against the animals' interests in living a pain-free life. If our concern is to benefit humans, then it could be argued that it would be preferable to use brain-damaged humans rather than nonhuman animals, because the results would be more accurate. Indeed, the use of certain "nonproductive" groups of humans, such as elderly people and children who are mentally retarded, has been justified on utilitarian grounds by researchers in the past. Most people find this implication of utilitarian reasoning to be morally repugnant.

One problem with relying on utilitarian criteria is the definition of "necessary suffering." The concepts of necessary and unnecessary suffering, used by Cohen to justify the use of nonhuman animals in experiments, are notoriously vague as well as biased in favor of human interests. People who torture their dogs are seen as despicable cowards; scientists who conduct painful experiments on dogs are seen as promoting human progress. Thus, talk of benefits and necessary suffering often serves to mask a view of other animals as merely property. The tremendous power of scientists and agribusiness also ensures that the interests of humans will always be given greater weight than the interests of other animals. The Buddhist principle of *ahimsa*, in contrast, states that the suffering of nonhuman animals cannot be justified by its benefits to humans.

Many environmental ethicists, including the deep ecologists and ecofeminists, reject the utilitarian model. They believe that utilitarians define the "common good" too narrowly and instead embrace a concept of the common good that includes all of nature, not just sentient beings. To use the words of Leopold, "a thing is right when it tends to preserve the stability, integrity, and beauty of the biotic community." The **stewardship** model, like Singer's utilitarian theory, is hierarchical, placing more value on beings who are the most sentient.

Rights

Animal-rights advocates argue that just as we ought to respect humans' intrinsic worth, regardless of their utility, we should also treat other animals as ends-in-themselves. Animal welfarists, while acknowledging that animals have welfare rights such as health care, proper nutrition, and a clean living space, do not generally recognize other animals' liberty rights or right to life. Animal-rights advocates, on the other hand, claim that nonhuman animals have both welfare and liberty rights.

Traditional Western philosophy supports a model of rights based on self-assertion. This position is defended by Cohen. According to the *self-assertion model,* a right is a claim or potential claim that one being may exercise against another. Rights arise only among beings that can make moral claims against one another. Because nonhuman animals presumably lack the capacity for moral choice, they lack moral rights.

In contrast, the model of rights adopted by animal-rights advocates, such as Regan, is based on *interests.* The existence of interests is based on the capacity for suffering and for enjoyment. All sentient animals, including humans, have an interest in doing that which brings them pleasure, as well as an interest in avoiding harm and suffering. Under this model of rights, benefits to oneself and others are morally acceptable only if no one else's rights have been violated in achieving these benefits.

Justice, Speciesism, and the Principle of Equality

The **principle of equality** states that it is unjust to treat beings differently unless we can show that there is a difference between them that is relevant to the differential treatment. Singer claims that "**speciesism**," which he defines as "a prejudice or attitude of bias in favor of the interests of members of one's own species and against those of members of another species,"[22] violates the principle of equality. His rule of thumb is that "we should give the same respect to the lives of animals as we give to the lives of those humans at a similar mental level." Both Singer and Warren relate discrimination against other animals to discrimination based on racism and sexism.

The moral equality of sentient beings does not entail that human and nonhuman animals have the same rights. Different species have different interests. There are distinctly human rights, such as the right to religious freedom and the right to a formal education, that other animals lack because they have no interest in either organized religion or formal schooling. All sentient animals, however—including humans, mice, and frogs—have an interest in not being tortured or held captive, not because they are capable of rational thought, but because they have the ability to feel pain.

To most people, speciesism doesn't seem as bad as racism or sexism. In fact, many people find the comparison offensive. Whereas gender or skin color is arbitrary and of no moral importance, they argue, the difference in our treatment of humans and other species is based on morally relevant differences. Only humans, as rational autonomous beings, are able to participate in the moral community. As Singer points out, there are humans who are neither rational nor autonomous. Including these people in the moral community while excluding other animals of equal or greater cognitive capacity violates the principle of equality because it bases moral treatment on group membership rather than on individual differences. Also, there would be no point in using nonhuman animals, such as monkeys and rats, in learning experiments if they were incapable of reason. Indeed, the reason why we use other animals in learning and medical experiments is because they are so much like us.

Natural Law

Defenders of meat-eating point out that other animals eat meat. The human practice of meat-eating is simply part of the natural order. This argument is also used in support of hunting. Opponents of meat-eating maintain that humans are not physiologically suited for a meat-based diet. Indeed, many of our modern ailments are due to our meat-eating habits. This argument also commits the naturalist fallacy: Just because humans can and do eat meat does not mean that they ought to.

CONCLUSION

Gandhi once said that "the greatness of a nation can be judged by the way its animals are treated." Even if we don't accept the claim that other animals have inherent moral worth, we ought to stop and consider the ways in which our lifestyles cause suffering to other animals. The case for vegetarianism, especially when almost all the animals we use for food are now raised on factory farms, is strong whichever position we accept

 SUMMARY OF READINGS ON ANIMAL RIGHTS AND ENVIRONMENTAL ETHICS

Regan, "The Moral Basis of Vegetarianism." Animals have moral rights because they are beings who are experiencing subjects of their own life.

Narveson, "Animals Rights Revisited." Animals have no moral rights that we must respect because they are incapable of entering into a social contract.

Singer, "Animal Liberation." Animals are sentient beings that deserve our moral respect. Therefore, meat-eating and most animal experimentation are immoral.

Cohen, "Do Animals Have Rights?" Animals do not have moral rights because they are incapable of asserting them.

Leopold, "The Land Ethic." We need to replace anthropocentrism with an ecocentric view in which humans are seen as part of the natural world.

Devall and Sessions, "Deep Ecology." We need to develop and act from a deeper ecological consciousness of the value of human and nonhuman life.

Gore, "Perspective on Global Warming." Global warming is a crisis that threatens our survival unless we are willing to take action.

Warren, "The Power and the Promise of Ecological Feminism, Revisited." The domination of women and of nature are grounded in the same value-hierarchy thinking.

on the moral status of nonhuman animals. Morality requires that we be able to justify actions that affect others. Human beings have the power to exploit or to live in harmony with other species and the environment. It is up to each of us to decide how we want to use this power.

TOM REGAN

The Moral Basis of Vegetarianism

Tom Regan is professor emeritus of philosophy and religion at North Carolina State University. Regan provides a rights-based argument for vegetarianism. He argues that the current differential treatment of human and nonhuman animals cannot be morally justified. All animals that are experiencing subjects of their own lives have inherent value.

"The Moral Basis of Vegetarianism," in *All That Dwell Therein: Animal Rights and Environmental Ethics* (Berkeley: University of California Press, 1982), 1–36. Notes have been omitted.

Critical Reading Questions

1. How did Gandhi's life and writings influence Regan's thinking on vegetarianism?
2. Why does Regan reject the view that language is necessary for experiencing pain?
3. According to Regan, why is the principle of nonmaleficence morally relevant to our treatment of nonhuman animals?
4. How does Regan respond to the argument that humans have certain natural rights that animals lack?
5. How does Regan respond to the argument that only humans have the ability to reason?
6. How does Regan respond to the argument that animals cannot have rights because they lack the ability to claim them?
7. What is Regan's position on the use of "intensive rearing methods"?
8. How does Regan respond to the argument that meat-eating may be justified if the meat is bought from farms where intensive rearing methods are not used?
9. Why does Regan claim that the burden of justification rests on the shoulders of meat-eaters rather than on vegetarians?
10. Does Regan oppose all taking of the lives of animals? Under what circumstances might it be morally justifiable to take the life of a nonhuman animal?
11. According to Regan, what would be necessary to justify the differential treatment of humans and nonhuman animals?

My initial interest in vegetarianism grew out of my study of the life and writings of Mahatma Gandhi. Gandhi, as is well known, was an advocate of nonviolence (ahimsā), not only in political affairs but in the conduct of one's life generally. The extreme pacifistic position he advocated, from which he derived the obligatoriness of vegetarianism, struck me as inadequate, and I sought a less radical moral basis for vegetarianism, one that those of us in the Western world would find more hospitable. Since the leading theories were (and remain) one or another version of utilitarianism, on the one hand, and, on the other, theories that proclaim basic moral rights, it seemed to me that the moral basis of vegetarianism would have to be found somewhere among these options. That such a basis may be provided by a rights-based theory is what "The Moral Basis of Vegetarianism" attempts to show. Both the moral right not to be caused gratuitous suffering and the right to life, I argue, are possessed by the animals we eat if they are possessed by the humans we do not. To cause animals to suffer cannot be defended merely on the grounds that we like the taste of their flesh, and even if animals were raised so that they led generally pleasant lives and were "humanely" slaughtered, that would not insure that their rights, including their right to life, were not violated. Despite the Western custom of supposing that vegetarians must defend their "eccentric" way of life, the essay attempts to shift the burden of proof onto the shoulders of those who should bear it—the nonvegetarians.

Now, there can be no doubt that animals sometimes appear to be in pain. On this point, even Descartes would agree. In order for us to be rationally entitled to abandon the belief that they actually do experience pain, therefore, especially in view of the close physiological resemblances that often exist between them and us, we are in need of some rationally compelling argument that would demonstrate that this belief is erroneous. Descartes's principal argument in this regard fails to present a compelling case for his view. Essentially, it consists in the claim that, since animals cannot speak or use a language, they do not think, and since they do not think, they have no minds; lacking in these respects, therefore, they have no consciousness either. Thus, since a necessary condition of a creature's being able to experience pain is that it be a conscious being, it follows, given Descartes's reasoning, that animals do not experience pain. . . .

Imagine a person whose vocal cords have been damaged to such an extent that he no longer has the ability to utter words or even make inarticulate sounds, and whose arms have been paralyzed so that he cannot write, but who, when his tooth abscesses, twists and turns on his bed, grimaces and sobs. We do not say, "Ah, if only he could still speak, we could give him something for his pain. As it is, since he cannot speak, there's nothing we need give him. For he feels no pain." We say he is in pain, despite his loss of the ability to say so.

Whether or not a person is experiencing pain, in short, does not depend on his being able to perform one or another linguistic feat. Why, then, should it be any different in the case of animals? It would seem to be the height of human arrogance, rather than of . . . "superstition," to erect a double standard here, requiring that animals meet a standard not set for humans. If humans can experience pain without being logically required to be able to say so, or in any other ways to use a language, then the same standard should apply to animals as well. . . .

Now, an essential part of any enlightened morality is the principle of noninjury. What this principle declares is that we are not to inflict pain on, or otherwise bring about or contribute to the pain in, any being capable of experiencing it. This principle, moreover, is derivable from the more general principle of nonmaleficence, which declares that we are not to do or cause evil, together with the value judgment that pain, considered in itself, is intrinsically evil. . . .

Given the intrinsic evil of pain, and assuming further that pleasure is intrinsically good, it is clear that cases can arise in which the evil (pain) caused to animals is not compensated for by the good (pleasure) caused humans. The classical utilitarians—Bentham, Mill, and Sidgwick—all were aware of this. . . .

It has already been pointed out that the pain an animal feels is just as much pain, and just as much an intrinsic evil, as a comparable pain felt by a human being. So, if there is any rational basis for rendering conflicting judgments about the two practices, it must be looked for in some other direction.

The most likely and, on the face of it, the most plausible direction in which to look is in the direction of rights. "Humans," this line of reasoning goes, "have certain natural rights that animals lack, and that is what makes the two practices differ in a morally significant way. For in the case of the practice involving humans, their equal natural right to be spared undeserved pain is being violated, while in the case of the practice involving animals, since animals can have no rights, *their* rights are not being ignored. That is what makes the two cases differ. And that is what makes the practice involving humans an immoral one, while the practice involving animals is not."

Natural though this line of argument is, I do not think it justifies the differential treatment of the animals and humans in question. For on what grounds might it be claimed that the humans, but not the animals, have an equal natural right to be spared undeserved pain? Well, it cannot be, as it is sometimes alleged, that all and only human beings have this right because all and only humans reason, make free choices, or have a concept of their identity. These grounds will not justify the ascription of rights to all humans because some humans— infants and the severely mentally defective, for example—do not meet these conditions. Moreover, even if these conditions did form the grounds for the possession of rights; and even if it were true that all human beings met them; it still would not follow that *only* human beings have them. For on what grounds, precisely, might it be claimed that no animals can reason, make free choices, or form a concept of themselves? What one would want here are detailed analyses of these operative concepts together with rationally compelling empirical data and other arguments that support the view that all nonhuman animals are deficient in these respects. It would be the height of prejudice merely to assume that man is unique in being able to reason. To the extent that these beliefs are not examined in the light of what we know about animals and animal intelligence, the supposition that *only* human beings have these capacities is just that—a supposition, and one that could hardly bear the moral weight placed upon it by the differential treatment of animals and humans. . . .

Two objections should be addressed before proceeding. Both involve difficulties that are supposed to attend the attribution of rights to animals. The first declares that animals cannot have rights because they lack the capacity to *claim* them. Now, this objection seems to be a variant of the view that animals cannot have rights because they cannot speak, and, like this more general view, this one too will not withstand a moment's serious reflection. For there are many human beings who cannot speak or claim their rights—tiny infants, for example—and yet who would not be denied the right in question, assuming, as we are, that it is supposed to be a right possessed by *all* human beings. Thus, if a human being can possess this (or any other right) without being able to demand it, it cannot be reasonable to require that animals be able to do so, if they are to possess this (or any other) right. The second objection is different. It declares that the attribution of rights to animals leads to absurdity. For if, say, a lamb has the natural right to be spared undeserved pain, then the wolf, who devours it unmercifully, without the benefit of anesthetic, should be said to violate the lamb's right. This, it is alleged, is absurd, and so, then, is the attribution of rights to animals. Well, absurd it may be to say that the wolf violates the lamb's right. But even supposing that it is, nothing said here implies that such deeds on the part of the wolf violate the lamb's rights. For the lamb can have rights only against those beings who are capable of taking the interests of the lamb into account and [are] trying to determine, on the basis of its interests, as well as other relevant considerations, what, morally speaking, ought to be done. In other words, the only kind of being against which another being can have rights is a being that can be held to be morally responsible for its actions. Thus, the lamb can have rights against, say, most adult human beings. But a wolf, I think it would be agreed, is not capable of making decisions from the moral point of view; nor is

a wolf the kind of being that can be held morally responsible; neither, then, can it make sense to say that the lamb has any rights against the wolf. This situation has its counterpart in human affairs. The severely mentally feeble, for example, lack the requisite powers to act morally; thus, *they* cannot be expected to recognize our rights, nor can *they* be said to violate our rights, even if, for example, they should happen to cause us undeserved pain. For as they are not the kind of being that can be held responsible for what they do, neither can they be said to violate anyone's rights by what they do. . . .

Animals who are raised to be eaten by human beings very often are made to suffer. Nor is it simply that they suffer only when they are being shipped to the slaughterhouse or actually being slaughtered. For what is happening is this: The human appetite for meat has become so great that new methods of raising animals have come into being. Called intensive rearing methods, these methods seek to insure that the largest amount of meat can be produced in the shortest amount of time with the least possible expense. In ever increasing numbers, animals are being subjected to the rigors of these methods. Many are being forced to live in incredibly crowded conditions. Moreover, as a result of these methods, the natural desires of many animals often are being frustrated. In short, both in terms of the physical pain these animals must endure, and in terms of the psychological pain that attends the frustration of their natural inclinations, there can be no reasonable doubt that animals who are raised according to intensive rearing methods experience much nontrivial, undeserved pain. Add to this the gruesome realities of "humane" slaughter and we have, I think, an amount and intensity of suffering that can, with propriety, be called "great."

To the extent, therefore, that we eat the flesh of animals that have been raised under such circumstances, we help create the demand for meat that farmers who use intensive rearing methods endeavor to satisfy. Thus, to the extent that it is known that such methods will bring about much undeserved, nontrivial pain on the part of the animals raised according to these methods, anyone who purchases meat that is a product of these methods—and almost everyone who buys meat at a typical supermarket or restaurant does this—is *causally implicated* in a practice that causes pain that is both nontrivial and undeserved for the animals in question. On this point too, I think there can be no doubt. . . .

Now, there are, as I mentioned earlier, two further objections that might be raised, both of which, I think, uncover important limitations in the argument of this section. The first is that a meat eater might be able to escape the thrust of my argument by the simple expedient of buying meat from farms where the animals are not raised according to intensive rearing methods, a difficult but not impossible task at the present time. For despite the widespread use of these methods, it remains true that there are farms where animals are raised in clean, comfortable quarters, and where the pain they experience is the natural result of the exigencies of animal existence rather than, to use an expression of Hume's, of "human art and contrivance." . . .

The [second] objection reads thus: "Granted, the amount of pain animals experience in intensive rearing units is deplorable and ought to be eliminated as far as is possible; still, it does not follow that we ought to give up meat altogether or to go to the trouble of hunting or buying it from other farmers. After all, all we need do is get rid of the pain and our moral worries will be over. So, what we should do is this; we should try to figure out how to *desensitize* animals so that they do not feel any pain, even in the most barbarous surroundings. Then, if this could be worked out, there would not be any grounds for worrying about the 'morality' of eating meat. Remove the animals' capacity for feeling pain and you thereby remove the possibility of their experiencing any pain that is gratuitous."

Now, I think it is obvious that nothing that I have said thus far can form a basis for responding to this objection, and though I think there are alternative ways in which one might try to respond to it, the case I try to make against it evolves out of my response to the first objection; I try to show, in other words, that an adequate response to this objection can be based upon the thesis that *it*

is the killing of animals, and not just their pain, that matters morally.

. . .

Let us begin, then, with the idea that all humans possess an equal natural right to life. And let us notice, once again, that it is an *equal natural* right that we are speaking of, one that we cannot acquire or have granted to us, and one that we all are supposed to have just because we are human beings. On what basis, then, might it be alleged that all and only human beings possess this right to an equal extent? Well, several familiar possibilities come immediately to mind. It might be argued that all and only human beings have an equal right to life because either (*a*) all and only human beings have the capacity to reason, or (*b*) all and only human beings have the capacity to make free choices, or (*c*) all and only human beings have a concept of "self," or (*d*) all and only human beings have all or some combination of the previously mentioned capacities. And it is easy to imagine how someone might argue that, since animals do not have any of these capacities, *they* do not possess a right to life, least of all one that is equal to the one possessed by humans.

I have already touched upon some of the difficulties such views must inevitably encounter. Briefly, it is not clear, first, that no nonhuman animals satisfy any one (or all) of these conditions, and, second, it is reasonably clear that not all human beings satisfy them. The severely mentally feeble, for example, fail to satisfy them. Accordingly, *if* we want to insist that they have a right to life, then we cannot also maintain that they have it because they satisfy one or another of these conditions. Thus, *if* we want to insist that they have an equal right to life, despite their failure to satisfy these conditions, we cannot consistently maintain that animals, because they fail to satisfy these conditions, therefore lack this right.

Another possible ground is that of sentience, by which I understand the capacity to experience pleasure and pain. But this view, too, must encounter a familiar difficulty—namely, that it could not justify restricting the right *only* to human beings. . . .

The onus of justification lies not on the shoulders of those who are vegetarians but on the shoulders of those who are not. If the argument of the present section is sound, it is the nonvegetarian who must show us how he can be justified in eating meat, when he knows that, to do so, an animal has had to be killed. It is the nonvegetarian who must show us how his manner of life does not contribute to practices that systematically ignore the right to life which animals possess, if humans are supposed to possess it on the basis of the most plausible argument considered here. And it is the nonvegetarian who must do all this while being fully cognizant that he cannot defend his way of life merely by summing up the intrinsic goods—the delicious taste of meat, for example—that come into being as a result of the slaughter of animals.

This is not to say that practices that involve taking the lives of animals cannot possibly be justified. . . . For example, perhaps they are satisfied in the case of the Eskimo's killing of animals and in the case of having a restricted hunting season for such animals as deer. But to say that this is (or may be) true of *some* cases is not to say that it is true of all, and it will remain the task of the nonvegetarian to show that what is true in these cases, assuming that it is true, is also true of any practice that involves killing animals which, by his actions, he supports. . . .

Even if it should turn out that there are no natural rights, that would not put an end to many of the problems discussed here. For even if we do not possess natural rights, we would still object to practices that caused nontrivial, undeserved pain for some human beings if their "justification" was that they brought about this or that amount of pleasure or other forms of intrinsic good for this or that number of people; . . . and we would still object to any practice that involved the killing of human beings, even if killed painlessly, if the practice was supposed to be justified in the same way. But this being so, what clearly would be needed, if we cease to invoke the idea of rights, is some explanation of why practices that are not right when they involve the treatment of people can be right (or at least permissible) when they involve the treatment of animals. What clearly would be needed, in short, is what we have found to be needed and wanting all along—namely, the specification of some morally relevant feature of being human which is possessed by *all* human beings and *only* by those beings who are human. Unless or until some such feature can be pointed out, I do not see how the differential treatment of humans and animals can be rationally defended, natural rights or no.

Discussion Questions

1. Do you have a moral obligation to be a vegetarian? Support your argument.
2. Some "vegetarians" eat free-range animals, including fish. Does eating only free-range animals overcome Regan's objection to meat-eating? Support your answer.
3. Discuss how Regan would stand on the morality of keeping animals in zoos. Do their educational value and protection of endangered species justify the existence of zoos? Support your answer.
4. Regan is opposed to animal experimentation no matter how much it benefits humans. Do you agree with Regan's position? Discuss how Kant might respond to Regan's abolitionist position.
5. Would Regan approve or disapprove of the human practice of keeping pets and, if so, under what conditions? Support your answer. Discuss how Regan might stand on the euthanasia of sick and elderly animal companions.

🌿 JAN NARVESON

Animal Rights Revisited

Jan Narveson is professor emeritus of philosophy at the University of Waterloo in Ontario, Canada. Narveson argues that under social contract theory, animals, being nonrational and lacking language, are not capable of entering into a contractual agreement. Therefore, under the social contract, they have no rights that we are morally bound to respect.

Critical Reading Questions

1. What are the three possible options listed by Narveson regarding our moral obligations to nonhuman animals?
2. Why, according to Narveson, do nonhuman animals have less utility than humans?
3. On what grounds does Narveson argue that raising nonhuman animals for food might actually increase the total utility for that species?
4. Why, according to Narveson, can't nonhuman animals be included in a social contract?
5. What is the connection between being included in a social contract and having moral rights?
6. According to Narveson, what abilities are required to be eligible for moral consideration?
7. On what grounds does Narveson claim that our dealings with other animals need only be based on our own self-interest?
8. How does Narveson respond to the "marginal cases" objection?

What do we owe to the animals? What, that is to say, do we owe them *qua* animal, rather than in their various possible roles as pets, watchdogs, potential sources of protein, or potential sources of knowledge on various matters of medical interest? Our usual repertoire of moral ideas does not give us a very clear answer to this question, for those ideas have been framed for dealing with our fellow humans, by and large. When we address ourselves to this nonstandard case, then, we must scrutinize those ideas rather closely. . . .

"Animal Rights Revisited," in *Ethics and Animals,* ed. by Harlan B. Miller and William H. Williams (Clifton, N.J.: Humana Press, 1983), 45–59.

It may be well to begin by trying to assemble the options, though even to do this is assuredly to begin to do moral theory. Here, then, are the main ones as I see it:

(1) The moral status of animals is simply that of things, potentially useful or dangerous in various ways; the proper way to deal with them is simply whatever way is dictated by our interests in such things.

(2) Animals are in the same moral boat as we are: to wit, they have the capacity to suffer or prosper, to be better or worse off, and we ought to attach the same weight to a given degree of well- or ill-being on their part as we do to our own, endeavoring to do the best we can for all concerned.

(3) Animals are in the same moral boat as we are, but it is a different boat: to wit, they have the right to lead their lives as they choose, without interference from us—but also, without *help* from us, if we do not wish to give it.

This list of options is not exhaustive of the logical possibilities, obviously. I have come to suspect, however, that it exhausts all the *interesting* possibilities. And curiously enough, those are the same possibilities that we obtain with respect to our moral dealings with our fellow humans. . . .

What assumptions is it reasonable to make about the utility of animals? It seems very reasonable indeed to suppose that animals can feel pain and pleasure. It seems reasonable to attribute to them some degree of intelligence (but unclear just what we are attributing to them in doing so, nor whether it is a capacity of the same sort we attribute to humans). Does that matter? Mill thought it did. It is tempting to say that he thought that the utility of intelligent beings counts more than the utility of less intelligent ones, but that surely will not do. What we must say instead, and what Mill really does say (I think), is that intelligent beings have a greater capability of utility than less intelligent ones: the satisfaction of a satisfied Socrates (if that is possible) involves a great deal more utility than the satisfaction of a satisfied pig. For that matter, even the satisfactions of a dissatisfied Socrates outweigh those of the pig. One question to worry about is: Is Mill right, or even believable, about that? Another is: What follows if he is? . . .

We do, certainly, make judgments of the form "people would in general be happier if . . ." Although there is a good deal of disagreement about such judgments, it may also be admitted that we are not entirely out in left field in making them. The problem is to make judgments of the form, "people *and animals* would be happier if . . . ," and that is trickier. It is acutely trickier in just the cases we have to worry about in the present paper—all the cases wherein there is a genuine conflict between the interests of us and the animals: namely, if our main interest in animals is realized, then their interest in *whatever* they may be interested in is thwarted, because they end up on our dinner plates. And that is a loss of utility that, in the case of humans, would certainly not be thought to be outweighed by the gourmet's interest in them, however powerful that interest might be. So we would surely be headed for vegetarianism if there were no reason for downrating the animals' utility quite substantially.

Actually, there are two sorts of "downrating." One way is to claim that the utility of animals, although admittedly quite comparable to ours, simply does not count, or that it counts very little: as if, for instance, we were allowed to multiply the animal's utility score by 0.01. The other way is to claim that animals have very little utility, really, at least by comparison with our own. As we have noted, utilitarianism must surely take the latter tack. It is axiomatic, after all, that everyone counts for one and none for more (or less).

What might reasonably (as opposed to just self-interestedly) persuade us that animals *do* have a lesser capacity for utility than we? Many would point to their supposedly lesser intelligence as a justification for treating them as we do. But they may or may not have in mind intelligence as a factor influencing utility. They may instead be thinking of it as an intrinsic good. Can we find a reason for supposing that intellect affects capacity for utility, then?

One thing that has long intrigued me in this connection is the involvement of intelligent beings with their own, or indeed, any futures. We are acutely aware of the future stretching out before us, and of the past in the other direction. We are, indeed, often so involved with time that we might be accused of neglecting our present. And we can at least conjecture that with animals things are different. Perhaps it is still excessively anthropomorphic to think so, but we do seem to think that animal awareness of their own future, indeed of their own identity in general, is rather dim; this despite homing pigeons and whatnot, who certainly seem to have a clear idea where to go next. But we do suppose that they are, as the saying goes, guided by instinct rather than reason. . . .

Still, *why* might this matter? I have suggested that animals might "experience only more or less isolated sensations and uninterpreted feelings. If such beings are killed, all that happens is that a certain series of such feelings which would otherwise have occurred, do not occur.... When beings having a future are killed, they lose that future; when beings lacking it are killed, they do not. So no interest in continued life is lost in their case."[1] Well, setting aside the critical question of whether some such thing is true of animals, there remains the question just why it might make the kind of difference I supposed it did *on utilitarian grounds.* If two beings, one of whom has and one of whom lacks a future, each had a nonutilitarian-type right to its future, then we could agree that if we painlessly killed each of them, we would have violated one creature's rights, but not the other's. Unfortunately, utilitarians are not entitled to nonutilitarian rights. So if this difference is to make a difference, it must be because beings with futures experience more utility than beings without....

What we need to think, therefore, if we are to remain utilitarians *and* we think that normal humans are much greater in their capacity for utility than animals, is that at each typical moment in the sentient life of a human, he or she is chalking up a much higher utility score than a beast at any typical moment for it. And what the basis of this judgment would be is, again, unclear. There is certainly the danger of anthropocentric bias here....

Perhaps this affords some hold on the matter in the following way. If utility is based on preference, then perhaps we could say that if being X is able to have in mind more possible states of affairs over which to exercise preference than Y then X has a greater capacity for utility. As stated, this raises some rather kinky problems about individuating states of affairs so that we can get a fair count; and there is a lingering suspicion that the whole idea is wrong anyway, and utility should not really be thought of as preference at all. But it might offer some explanation of how we manage to account for so great a proportion of the universe's known supply of utility, or at least why we think we do.

If that amount of elitism is accepted, what about vegetarianism? It is axiomatic that some beings may, in principle, be sacrificed for others, on the utilitarian view. But may animals be sacrificed merely in order to enable humans to have a wider variety of gustatory pleasures? In order for it to be so, the marginal increment of such pleasure for humans has to exceed the marginal cost to the animals. Consider, then, the case of Kentucky Fried Chicken. Suppose that one chicken feeds three people for one meal. We might suppose that the cost of this is all the utility that the chicken might have experienced had it been allowed to live to a ripe old age. But wrongly. For that is only the cost to *that* chicken. But it is also reasonable to believe that, under the carnivorous regime we are investigating, this chicken will be replaced by another one which would not have existed at all if its predecessor were not eaten. In fact, the plot is thicker than that, for ... its predecessor would most likely not have existed either, were it not for the prospect of *its* being eaten. Given that we in fact raise animals to be eaten, it is not unreasonable to believe that the total utility of the animal population is enormously higher than it would be if we did not eat them, because so comparatively few would exist at all otherwise. And if we count that way, then the marginal cost to any given animal is the wrong thing to weigh against the marginal benefit to us of eating it. Viewed globally, those costs are very handily outweighed by the total utility increase in question.

That, of course, is to assume that we can apply "total" rather than average or some other sort of utilitarianism here. If we do not, and insist that it is the average utility of animals that should be our sole concern, the prospects for animal rights are much better, perhaps. Or are they? For now we also must reckon the cost of upkeep and care for the animals, which is borne by people. Their cost would certainly not be borne, in fact, if the animals were not beneficial to people in this way. Chickens would be raised only to lay eggs, cows for milk; but most would have little if any use. It might be argued that the loss in utility to people from having to care for useless beasts would exceed the loss to the beasts if they were (painlessly) killed. So even on average principles, it is far from clear that maximization would preclude the eating of animals.

Of course, if we do use total utilitarianism, then we have another small matter to contend with.

Animals are, in fact, quite an inefficient source of food. If humans ate only vegetarian diets, it would be possible for there to be a great many more of *them*. And if, as has been imagined above, each human is so much larger a source of utility than any animal, it might seem that the tables are turned again, since the large animal population is keeping the human population smaller, and yet the human population is so much more efficient a source of utility than the animal one. But that, in turn, is to assume that the marginal utility change associated with the addition of each further human is in fact positive, and it can be argued that *that* is not so. Perhaps a world with two billion humans would have more total utility than one with ten billion. If so, we would have a global justification of carnivorousness from the above arguments.

I am sure that no one will think me excessively conservative if I conclude with the observation that the situation regarding the ethics of our treatment of animals is not entirely clear if we opt for utilitarianism. This is not exactly a surprise, but it is of some importance that it should be so. The vegetarians do not have things all their way on that theory; and it is, I think, the theory that offers the best prospects for animal rights among those I am considering. . . .

On the contract view of morality, morality is a sort of agreement among rational, independent, self-interested persons, persons who have something to gain from entering into such an agreement. It is of the very essence, on such a theory, that the parties to the agreement know who they are and what they want—what they in particular want, and not just what a certain general class of beings of which they are members generally tend to want. Now, Rawls' theory has his parties constrained by agreements that they would have made if they *did not* know who they were. But if we can have that constraint, why should we not go just a little further and specify that one is not only not to know *which* person he or she is, but also whether he or she will be a person *at all*: reason on the assumption that you might turn out to be an owl, say, or a vermin, or a cow. We may imagine that *that* possibility would make quite a difference. . . . (Some proponents of

vegetarianism, I believe, are tempted by it, and do extend the veil of ignorance that far.)

The "agreement" of which morality consists is a voluntary undertaking to limit one's behavior in various respects. In a sense, it consists in a renunciation of action on unconstrained self-interest. It is, however, self-interested overall. The idea is to come out ahead in the long run, by refraining, contingently on others' likewise refraining, from certain actions, the general indulgence in which would be worse for all and therefore for oneself. There are well-known problems generated by this characterization, and I do not claim to have solutions for them. I only claim that this is an important and plausible conception of morality, worth investigating in the present context.

A major feature of this view of morality is that it explains why we have it and who is a party to it. We have it for reasons of long-run self-interest, and parties to it include all and only those who have *both* of the following characteristics: (1) they stand to gain by subscribing to it, at least in the long run, compared with not doing so, and (2) they are *capable* of entering into (and keeping) an agreement. Those not capable of it obviously cannot be parties to it, and among those capable of it, there is no reason for them to enter into it if there is nothing to gain for them from it, no matter how much the others might benefit.

Given these requirements, it will be clear why animals do not have rights. For there are evident shortcomings on both scores. On the one hand, humans have nothing generally to gain by voluntarily refraining from (for instance) killing animals or "treating them as mere means." And on the other, animals cannot generally make agreements with us anyway, even if we wanted to have them do so. Both points are worth expanding on briefly.

(1) In saying that humans have "nothing generally to gain" from adopting principled restraints against behavior harmful to animals, I am in one respect certainly overstating the case, for it is possible that animal food, for instance, is bad for us, or that something else about animals, which requires such restraint from us, would be for our

long-term benefit. Those are issues I mostly leave on one side here. . . .

(2) What about the capability of entering into and keeping such agreements? . . .

There remains a genuine question about the eligibility of animals for morality on the score of their abilities. A very few individuals among some animal species have been enabled, after years of highly specialized work, to communicate in fairly simple ways with people. That does not augur well for animals' entering quite generally into something as apparently sophisticated as an agreement. But of course agreements can be tacit and unwritten, even unspoken. Should we postulate, at some such inexplicit level, an "agreement" among humans, it is largely tacit there. People do not enter into agreements to refrain from killing each other, except in fairly specialized cases; the rule against killing that we (virtually) all acknowledge is one we adopt out of common sense and antecedent inculcation by our mentors. Still, it is reasonable to say that when one person does kill another one, he or she is (among other things) taking *unfair advantage* of the restraint that one's fellows have exercised with regard toward one over many years. But can any such thing be reasonably said of animals? I would think not.

On the whole, therefore, it seems clear that contractarianism leaves animals out of it, so far as rights are concerned. They are, by and large, to be dealt with in terms of our self-interest, unconstrained by the terms of hypothetical agreements with them. Just exactly what our interest in them is may, of course, be matter for debate; but that those are the terms on which we may deal with them is, on this view of morality, overwhelmingly indicated.

There is an evident problem about the treatment of what I have called "marginal cases" on this view, of course: infants, the feeble-minded, and the incapacitated are in varying degrees in the position of the animals in relation to us, are they not? True: but the situation is very different in several ways. For one thing, we generally have very little to gain from treating such people badly, and we often have much to gain from treating them well. For another, marginal humans are invariably members of families, or members of other groupings, which makes them the object of love and interest on the part of other members of those groups. Even if there were an interest in treating a particular marginal person badly, there would be others who have an interest in their being treated well and who are themselves clearly members of the moral community on contractarian premises. Finally, it does have to be pointed out that there is genuine question about the morality of, for instance, euthanasia, and that infanticide has been approved of in various human communities at various times. On the whole, it seems to me not an insurmountable objection to the contractarian account that we grant marginal humans fairly strong rights.

It remains that we may think that suffering is a bad thing, no matter whose. But although we think so, we do not think it is so bad as to require us to become vegetarians. Here by 'we,' of course, I mean most of us. And what most of us think is that, although suffering is too bad and it is unfortunate for animals that they are turned into hamburgers at a tender age, we nevertheless are justified on the whole in eating them. If contractarianism is correct, then these attitudes are not inconsistent. And perhaps it is.

NOTES

1. Jan Narveson, "Animal Rights," *Canadian Journal of Philosophy,* vol. 7 (1977), 161–178.

Discussion Questions

1. Narveson argues that by breeding animals destined for our plates we are increasing their overall utility, as they would not have had any existence otherwise. How might Jeremy Bentham respond to this argument? Could this argument also be used to justify the breeding or cloning of humans for slavery or organ transplants?

2. Narveson admits that the criteria we use for eliminating nonhuman animals from moral consideration also eliminates some humans. How does he overcome this criticism? Are you satisfied with his response? Support your answers.

3. Narveson bases much of his argument against vegetarianism on John Rawls's social contract theory. Rawls said, however, that his was "not a complete contract theory . . . since it would seem to include only our relationship with other persons and to leave out of account how we are to conduct ourselves toward animals and the rest of nature. . . . it does not follow [from social contract theory] that there are no requirements at all in regard to [animals], nor in our relations with the natural order."[23] Discuss how Rawls might respond to Narveson's argument.

PETER SINGER

Animal Liberation

Australian philosopher Peter Singer is a professor of bioethics at the University Center for Human Values, Princeton University, and laureate professor at the Centre for Applied Philosophy and Public Ethics at the University of Melbourne in Australia. Singer argues that utilitarian theory requires that the interests of all sentient beings be given equal weight. To not take the pain and interests of other animals seriously is to engage in what Singer calls "speciesism."

Critical Reading Questions

1. What is the principle of equality?
2. What is "speciesism"? Why is speciesism wrong, according to Singer?
3. According to Singer, what kind of lives have greater moral value than others?
4. Why does Singer claim that most humans are speciesists? What does he mean when he says that speciesism is analogous to racism and sexism?
5. What is the moral significance of sentience, or the ability to feel pain? In what ways do humans inflict suffering on other animals?
6. According to Singer, what is the moral significance of a being's level of cognitive ability? Does his argument make it morally permissible to experiment on humans with low-level cognitive functioning?
7. What do we need to do, according to Singer, to avoid speciesism? Does a rejection of speciesism imply that all lives are of equal worth?
8. Why, according to Singer, has opposition to experimentation on animals made such little headway?

Animal Liberation (New York: Random House, 1990), 5–94. Notes have been omitted.

9. Why do psychological experiments that use animals pose a dilemma for researchers who claim that other animals are not like us cognitively?
10. According to Singer, when, if ever, is animal experimentation morally justified?
11. Why does Singer claim that the controversy over the benefits derived from animal experimentation is essentially irrelevant?

Jeremy Bentham, the founder of the reforming utilitarian school of moral philosophy, incorporated the essential basis of moral equality into his system of ethics by means of the formula: "Each to count for one and none for more than one." In other words, the interests of every being affected by an action are to be taken into account and given the same weight as the like interests of any other being. . . .

It is an implication of this principle of equality that our concern for others and our readiness to consider their interests ought not to depend on what they are like or on what abilities they may possess. Precisely what our concern or consideration requires us to do may vary according to the characteristics of those affected by what we do: concern for the well-being of children growing up in America would require that we teach them to read; concern for the well-being of pigs may require no more than that we leave them with other pigs in a place where there is adequate food and room to run freely. But the basic element—the taking into account of the interests of the being, whatever those interests may be—must, according to the principle of equality, be extended to all beings, black or white, masculine or feminine, human or nonhuman. . . .

It is on this basis that the case against racism and the case against sexism must both ultimately rest; and it is in accordance with this principle that the attitude that we may call "speciesism," by analogy with racism, must also be condemned. Speciesism—the word is not an attractive one, but I can think of no better term—is a prejudice or attitude of bias in favor of the interests of members of one's own species and against those of members of other species. It should be obvious that the fundamental objections to racism and sexism made by Thomas Jefferson and Sojourner Truth apply equally to speciesism. If possessing a higher degree of intelligence does not entitle one human to use another for his or her own ends, how can it entitle humans to exploit nonhumans for the same purpose?

Many philosophers and other writers have proposed the principle of equal consideration of interests, in some form or other, as a basic moral principle; but not many of them have recognized that this principle applies to members of other species as well as to our own. Jeremy Bentham was one of the few who did realize this. In a forward-looking passage written at the time when black slaves had been freed by the French but in the British dominions were still being treated in the way we now treat animals, Bentham wrote:

> The day *may* come when the rest of the animal creation may acquire those rights which never could have been withholden from them but by the hand of tyranny. The French have already discovered that the blackness of the skin is no reason why a human being should be abandoned without redress to the caprice of a tormentor. It may one day come to be recognized that the number of the legs, the villosity of the skin, or the termination of the *os sacrum* are reasons equally insufficient for abandoning a sensitive being to the same fate. What else is it that should trace the insuperable line? Is it the faculty of reason, or perhaps the faculty of discourse? But a full-grown horse or dog is beyond comparison a more rational, as well as a more conversable animal, than an infant of a day or a week or even a month, old. But suppose they were otherwise, what would it avail? The question is not, Can they *reason?* nor Can they *talk?* but, Can they *suffer?*

In this passage Bentham points to the capacity for suffering as the vital characteristic that gives a being the right to equal consideration. The capacity for suffering—or more strictly, for suffering and/or enjoyment or happiness—is not just another characteristic like the capacity for language or higher mathematics. Bentham is not saying that those who try to mark "the insuperable line" that determines whether the interests of a being should be considered happen to have chosen the wrong characteristic. By saying that we must consider the interests of all beings with the capacity for suffering or enjoyment Bentham does not arbitrarily exclude from consideration any interests at all—as those who draw the line with reference to the possession of reason or language do. The capacity for suffering and enjoyment is *a prerequisite for having interests at all,* a condition that must be satisfied before we can speak of interests in a meaningful way. It would be nonsense to say that it was not in the interests of a stone to be kicked along the road by a schoolboy. A stone does not have interests because it cannot suffer. Nothing that we can do to it could possibly make any difference to its welfare. The capacity for suffering and enjoyment is, however, not only necessary, but also sufficient for us to say that a being has interests—at an absolute minimum, an interest in not suffering. A mouse, for example, does have an interest in not being kicked along the road, because it will suffer if it is. . . .

Racists violate the principle of equality by giving greater weight to the interests of members of their own race when there is a clash between their interests and the interests of those of another race. Sexists violate the principle of equality by favoring the interests of their own sex. Similarly, speciesists allow the interests of their own species to override the greater interests of members of other species. The pattern is identical in each case.

Most human beings are speciesists. . . . Ordinary human beings—not a few exceptionally cruel or heartless humans, but the overwhelming majority of humans—take an active part in, acquiesce in, and allow their taxes to pay for practices that require the sacrifice of the most important interests of members of other species in order to promote the most trivial interests of our own species. . . .

Do animals other than humans feel pain? How do we know? Well, how do we know if anyone, human or nonhuman, feels pain? We know that we ourselves can feel pain. We know this from the direct experience of pain that we have when, for instance, somebody presses a lighted cigarette against the back of our hand. But how do we know that anyone else feels pain? We cannot directly experience anyone else's pain, whether that "anyone" is our best friend or a stray dog. Pain is a state of consciousness, a "mental event," and as such it can never be observed. Behavior like writhing, screaming, or drawing one's hand away from the lighted cigarette is not pain itself; nor are the recordings a neurologist might make of activity within the brain observations of pain itself. Pain is something that we feel, and we can only infer that others are feeling it from various external indications.

In theory, we *could* always be mistaken when we assume that other human beings feel pain. It is conceivable that one of our close friends is really a cleverly constructed robot, controlled by a brilliant scientist so as to give all the signs of feeling pain, but really no more sensitive than any other machine. We can never know, with absolute certainty, that this is not the case. But while this might present a puzzle for philosophers, none of us has the slightest real doubt that our close friends feel pain just as we do. This is an inference, but a perfectly reasonable one, based on observations of their behavior in situations in which we would feel pain, and on the fact that we have every reason to assume that our friends are beings like us, with nervous systems like ours that can be assumed to function as ours do and to produce similar feelings in similar circumstances.

If it is justifiable to assume that other human beings feel pain as we do, is there any reason why a similar inference should be unjustifiable in the case of other animals?

Nearly all the external signs that lead us to infer pain in other humans can be seen in other species, especially the species most closely related to us—the species of mammals and birds. The behavioral signs include writhing, facial contortions, moaning, yelping or other forms of calling, attempts to avoid the source of pain, appearance of fear at the prospect of its repetition, and so on. In addition, we know that these animals have nervous systems very like ours, which respond physiologically as ours do when the animal is in circumstances in which we would feel pain: an initial rise of blood pressure, dilated pupils, perspiration, an increased pulse rate, and, if the stimulus continues, a fall in blood pressure. Although human beings have a more developed cerebral cortex than other animals, this part of the brain is concerned with thinking functions rather than with basic impulses, emotions, and feelings. These impulses, emotions, and feelings are located in the diencephalon, which is well developed in many other species of animals, especially mammals and birds.

We also know that the nervous systems of other animals were not artificially constructed—as a robot might be artificially constructed—to mimic the pain behavior of humans. The nervous systems of animals evolved as our own did, and in fact the evolutionary history of human beings and other animals, especially mammals, did not diverge until the central features of our nervous systems were already in existence. A capacity to feel pain obviously enhances a species' prospects of survival, since it causes members of the species to avoid sources of injury. It is surely unreasonable to suppose that nervous systems that are virtually identical physiologically, have a common origin and a common evolutionary function, and result in similar forms of behavior in similar circumstances should actually operate in an entirely different manner on the level of subjective feelings. . . .

Other differences between humans and animals cause other complications. Normal adult human beings have mental capacities that will, in certain circumstances, lead them to suffer more than animals would in the same circumstances. If, for instance, we decided to perform extremely painful or lethal scientific experiments on normal adult humans, kidnapped at random from public parks for this purpose, adults who enjoy strolling in parks would become fearful that they would be kidnapped. The resultant terror would be a form of suffering additional to the pain of the experiment. The same experiments performed on nonhuman animals would cause less suffering since the animals would not have the anticipatory dread of being kidnapped and experimented upon. This does not mean, of course, that it would be *right* to perform the experiment on animals, but only that there is a reason, which is *not* speciesist, for preferring to use animals rather than normal adult human beings, if the experiment is to be done at all. It should be noted, however, that this same argument gives us a reason for preferring to use human infants—orphans perhaps—or severely retarded human beings for experiments, rather than adults, since infants and retarded humans would also have no idea of what was going to happen to them. So far as this argument is concerned nonhuman animals and infants and retarded humans are in the same category; and if we use this argument to justify experiments on nonhuman animals we have to ask ourselves whether we are also prepared to allow experiments on human infants and retarded adults; and if we make a distinction between animals and these humans, on what basis can we do it, other than a bare-faced—and morally indefensible—preference for members of our own species?

There are many matters in which the superior mental powers of normal adult humans make a difference: anticipation, more detailed memory, greater knowledge of what is happening, and so on. Yet these differences do not all point to greater suffering on the part of the normal human being. Sometimes animals may suffer more because of their more limited understanding. If, for instance, we are taking prisoners in wartime we can explain to them that although they must submit to capture, search, and confinement, they will not otherwise be harmed and will be set free at the conclusion of hostilities. If we capture wild animals, however, we cannot explain that we are not threatening their lives. A wild animal cannot distinguish an attempt to overpower and confine from an attempt to kill; the one causes as much terror as the other.

It may be objected that comparisons of the sufferings of different species are impossible to make and that for this reason when the interests of animals and humans clash the principle of equality gives no guidance. It is probably true that comparisons of suffering between members of different species cannot be made precisely, but precision is not essential. Even if we were to prevent the infliction of suffering on animals only when it is quite certain that the interests of humans will not be affected to anything like the extent that animals are affected, we would be forced to make radical changes in our treatment of animals that would involve our diet, the farming methods we use, experimental procedures in many fields of science, our approach to wildlife and to hunting, trapping and the wearing of furs, and areas of entertainment like circuses, rodeos, and zoos. As a result, a vast amount of suffering would be avoided. . . .

Just as most human beings are speciesists in their readiness to cause pain to animals when they would not cause a similar pain to humans for the same reason, so most human beings are speciesists in their readiness to kill other animals when they would not kill human beings. . . .

This does not mean that to avoid speciesism we must hold that it is as wrong to kill a dog as it is to kill a human being in full possession of his or her faculties. The only position that is irredeemably speciesist is the one that tries to make the boundary of the right to life run exactly parallel to the boundary of our own species. Those who hold the sanctity of life view do this, because while distinguishing sharply between human beings and other animals they allow no distinctions to be made within our own species, objecting to the killing of the severely retarded and the hopelessly senile as strongly as they object to the killing of normal adults.

To avoid speciesism we must allow that beings who are similar in all relevant respects have a similar right to life—and mere membership in our own biological species cannot be a morally relevant criterion for this right. Within these limits we could still hold, for instance, that it is worse to kill a normal adult human, with a capacity for self-awareness and the ability to plan for the future and have meaningful relations with others,

than it is to kill a mouse, which presumably does not share all of these characteristics; or we might appeal to the close family and other personal ties that humans have but mice do not have to the same degree; or we might think that it is the consequences for other humans, who will be put in fear for their own lives, that makes the crucial difference; or we might think it is some combination of these factors, or other factors altogether.

Whatever criteria we choose, however, we will have to admit that they do not follow precisely the boundary of our own species. We may legitimately hold that there are some features of certain beings that make their lives more valuable than those of other beings; but there will surely be some nonhuman animals whose lives, by any standards, are more valuable than the lives of some humans. A chimpanzee, dog, or pig, for instance, will have a higher degree of self-awareness and a greater capacity for meaningful relations with others than a severely retarded infant or someone in a state of advanced senility. So if we base the right to life on these characteristics we must grant these animals a right to life as good as, or better than, such retarded or senile humans.

This argument cuts both ways. It could be taken as showing that chimpanzees, dogs, and pigs, along with some other species, have a right to life and we commit a grave moral offense whenever we kill them, even when they are old and suffering and our intention is to put them out of their misery. Alternatively one could take the argument as showing that the severely retarded and hopelessly senile have no right to life and may be killed for quite trivial reasons, as we now kill animals. . . .

What we need is some middle position that would avoid speciesim but would not make the lives of the retarded and senile as cheap as the lives of pigs and dogs now are, or make the lives of pigs and dogs so sacrosanct that we think it wrong to put them out of hopeless misery. What we must do is bring nonhuman animals within our sphere of moral concern and cease to treat their lives as expendable for whatever trivial purposes we may have. At the same time, once we realize that the fact that a being is a member of our own species is not in itself enough to make it always wrong to kill that being, we may come to reconsider our policy of preserving human lives at all costs, even when there is no prospect of a meaningful life or of existence without terrible pain.

I conclude, then, that rejection of speciesism does not imply that all lives are of equal worth. While self-awareness, the capacity to think ahead and have hopes and aspirations for the future, the capacity for meaningful relations with others and so on are not relevant to the question of inflicting pain—since pain is pain, whatever other capacities, beyond the capacity to feel pain, the being may have—these capacities are relevant to the question of taking life. It is not arbitrary to hold that the life of a self-aware being, capable of abstract thought, of planning for the future, of complex acts of communication, and so on, is more valuable than the life of a being without these capacities. . . .

The practice of experimenting on nonhuman animals as it exists today throughout the world reveals the consequences of speciesism. Many experiments inflict severe pain without the remotest prospect of significant benefits for human beings or any other animals. Such experiments are not isolated instances, but part of a major industry. In Britain, where experimenters are required to report the number of "scientific procedures" performed on animals, official government figures show that 3.5 million scientific procedures were performed on animals in 1988. In the United States there are no figures of comparable accuracy. . . .

Among the tens of millions of experiments performed, only a few can possibly be regarded as contributing to important medical research. Huge numbers of animals are used in university departments such as forestry and psychology; many more are used for commercial purposes, to test new cosmetics, shampoos, food coloring agents, and other inessential items. All this can happen only because of our prejudice against taking seriously the suffering of a being who is not a member of our own species. Typically, defenders of experiments on animals do not deny that animals suffer. They cannot deny the animals' suffering, because they need to stress the similarities between humans and other animals in order to claim that their experiments may have some relevance for human purposes. The experimenter who forces rats to choose between starvation and electric shock to see if they develop ulcers (which they do) does so because the rat has a nervous system very similar to a human being's, and presumably feels an electric shock in a similar way.

There has been opposition to experimenting on animals for a long time. This opposition has made little headway because experimenters, backed by commercial firms that profit by supplying laboratory animals and equipment, have been able to convince legislators and the public that opposition comes from uninformed fanatics who consider the interests of animals more important than the interests of human beings. But to be opposed to what is going on now it is not necessary to insist that all animal experiments stop immediately. All we need to say is that experiments serving no direct and urgent purpose should stop immediately, and in the remaining fields of research, we should, whenever possible, seek to replace experiments that involve animals with alternative methods that do not. . . .

This attitude is illustrated by the following autobiographical statement . . . [that] appeared in *New Scientist:*

> When fifteen years ago I applied to do a degree course in psychology, a steely-eyed interviewer, himself a psychologist, questioned me closely on my motives and asked me what I believed psychology to be and what was its principal subject matter? Poor naïve simpleton that I was, I replied that it was the study of the mind and that human beings were its raw material. With a glad cry at being able to deflate me so effectively, the interviewer declared that psychologists were not interested in the mind, that rats were the golden focus of study, not people, and then he advised me strongly to trot around to the philosophy department next door. . . .

Perhaps not many psychologists would now proudly state that their work has nothing to do with the human mind. Nevertheless many of the experiments that are performed on rats can only be explained by assuming that the experimenters really are interested in the behavior of the rat for its own sake, without any thought of learning anything about humans. In that case, though, what possible justification can there be for the infliction of so much suffering? It is certainly not for the benefit of the rat.

So the researcher's central dilemma exists in an especially acute form in psychology: either the animal is not like us, in which case there is no reason for performing the experiment; or else the animal is like us, in which case we ought not to perform on the animal an experiment that would be considered outrageous if performed on one of us. . . .

Once a pattern of animal experimentation becomes the accepted mode of research in a particular field, the process is self-reinforcing and difficult to break out of. Not only publications and promotions but also the awards and grants that finance research become geared to animal experiments. A proposal for a new experiment with animals is something that the administrators of research funds will be ready to support, if they have in the past supported other experiments on animals. New methods that do not make use of animals will seem less familiar and will be less likely to receive support.

All this helps to explain why it is not always easy for people outside the universities to understand the rationale for the research carried out under university auspices. Originally, perhaps, scholars and researchers just set out to solve the most important problems and did not allow themselves to be influenced by other considerations. No doubt some are still motivated by these concerns. Too often, though, academic research gets bogged down in petty and insignificant details because the big questions have been studied already and they have either been solved or proven too difficult. So the researchers turn away from the well-plowed fields in search of new territory where whatever they find will be new, although the connection with a major problem may be remote. It is not uncommon, as we have seen, for experimenters to admit that similar experiments have been done many times before, but without this or that

minor variation; and the most common ending to a scientific publication is "further research is necessary." . . .

When are experiments on animals justifiable? Upon learning of the nature of many of the experiments carried out, some people react by saying that all experiments on animals should be prohibited immediately. But if we make our demands as absolute as this, the experimenters have a ready reply: Would we be prepared to let thousands of humans die if they could be saved by a single experiment on a single animal?

This question is, of course, purely hypothetical. There has never been and never could be a single experiment that saved thousands of lives. The way to reply to this hypothetical question is to pose another: Would the experimenters be prepared to carry out their experiment on a human orphan under six months old if that were the only way to save thousands of lives?

If the experimenters would not be prepared to use a human infant then their readiness to use nonhuman animals reveals an unjustifiable form of discrimination on the basis of species, since adult apes, monkeys, dogs, cats, rats, and other animals are more aware of what is happening to them, more self-directing, and, so far as we can tell, at least as sensitive to pain as a human infant. (I have specified that the human infant be an orphan, to avoid the complications of the feelings of parents. Specifying the case in this way is, if anything, overgenerous to those defending the use of nonhuman animals in experiments, since mammals intended for experimental use are usually separated from their mothers at an early age, when the separation causes distress for both mother and young.)

So far as we know, human infants possess no morally relevant characteristic to a higher degree than adult nonhuman animals, unless we are to count the infants' potential as a characteristic that makes it wrong to experiment on them. Whether this characteristic should count is controversial—if we count it, we shall have to condemn abortion along with experiments on infants, since the potential of the infant and the fetus is the same.

To avoid the complexities of this issue, however, we can alter our original question a little and assume that the infant is one with irreversible brain damage so severe as to rule out any mental development beyond the level of a six-month-old infant. There are, unfortunately, many such human beings, locked away in special wards throughout the country, some of them long since abandoned by their parents and other relatives, and, sadly, sometimes unloved by anyone else. Despite their mental deficiencies, the anatomy and physiology of these infants are in nearly all respects identical with those of normal humans. If, therefore, we were to force-feed them with large quantities of floor polish or drip concentrated solutions of cosmetics into their eyes, we would have a much more reliable indication of the safety of these products for humans than we now get by attempting to extrapolate the results of tests on a variety of other species. The LD50 tests, the Draize eye tests, the radiation experiments, the heatstroke experiments, and many others could have told us more about human reactions to the experimental situation if they had been carried out on severely brain-damaged humans instead of dogs or rabbits.

So whenever experimenters claim that their experiments are important enough to justify the use of animals, we should ask them whether they would be prepared to use a brain-damaged human being at a similar mental level to the animals they are planning to use. I cannot imagine that anyone would seriously propose carrying out the experiments described in this chapter on brain-damaged human beings. Occasionally it has become known that medical experiments have been performed on human beings without their consent; one case did concern institutionalized intellectually disabled children, who were given hepatitis. When such harmful experiments on human beings become known, they usually lead to an outcry against the experimenters, and rightly so. They are, very often, a further example of the arrogance of the research worker who justifies everything on the grounds of increasing knowledge. But if the experimenter claims that the experiment is important enough to justify inflicting suffering on animals, why is it not important enough to justify inflicting suffering on humans at the same mental level? What difference is there between the two? Only that one is a member of our species and the other is not? But to appeal to that difference is to reveal a bias no more defensible than racism or any other form of arbitrary discrimination. . . .

No doubt there are some fields of scientific research that will be hampered by any genuine consideration of the interests of animals used in experimentation. No doubt there have been some advances in knowledge which would not have been attained as easily without using animals. Examples of important discoveries often mentioned by those defending animal experimentation go back as far as Harvey's work on the circulation of blood. They include Banting and Best's discovery of insulin and its role in diabetes; the recognition of poliomyelitis as a virus and the development of a vaccine for it; several discoveries that served to make open heart surgery and coronary artery bypass graft surgery possible; and the understanding of our immune system and ways to overcome rejection of transplanted organs. The claim that animal experimentation was essential in making these discoveries has been denied by some opponents of experimentation. I do not intend to go into the controversy here. We have just seen that any knowledge gained from animal experimentation has made at best a very small contribution to our increased lifespan; its contribution to improving the quality of life is more difficult to estimate. In a more fundamental sense, the controversy over the benefits derived from animal experimentation is essentially unresolvable, because even if valuable discoveries were made using animals, we cannot say how successful medical research would have been if it had been compelled, from the outset, to develop alternative methods of investigation. Some discoveries would probably have been delayed, or perhaps not made at all; but many false leads would also not have been pursued, and it is possible that medicine would have developed in a very different and more efficacious direction, emphasizing healthy living rather than cure.

In any case, the ethical question of the justifiability of animal experimentation cannot be settled by pointing to its benefits for us, no matter how persuasive the evidence in favor of such benefits may be. The ethical principle of equal consideration of interests will rule out some means of obtaining knowledge. There is nothing sacred about the right to pursue knowledge. We already accept many restrictions on scientific enterprise. We do not believe that scientists have a general right to perform painful or lethal experiments on human beings without their consent, although there are many cases in which such experiments would advance knowledge far more rapidly than any other method. Now we need to broaden the scope of this existing restriction on scientific research.

Finally, it is important to realize that the major health problems of the world largely continue to exist, not because we do not know how to prevent disease and keep people healthy, but because no one is putting enough effort and money into doing what we already know how to do. The diseases that ravage Asia, Africa, Latin America, and the pockets of poverty in the industrialized West are diseases that, by and large, we know how to cure. They have been eliminated in communities that have adequate nutrition, sanitation, and health care. . . .

It does not seem likely that any major Western democracy is going to abolish all animal experimentation at a stroke. Governments just do not work like that. Animal experimentation will only be ended when a series of piecemeal reforms have reduced its importance, led to its replacement in many fields, and largely changed the public attitude to animals. The immediate task, then, is to work for these partial goals, which can be seen as milestones on the long march to the elimination of all exploitation of sentient animals. All concerned to end animal suffering can try to make known what is happening at universities and commercial laboratories in their own communities. Consumers can refuse to purchase products that have been tested on animals—especially in cosmetics, alternatives are now available. Students should decline to carry out experiments they consider unethical. Anyone can study the academic journals to find out where painful experiments are being carried out, and then find some way of making the public aware of what is happening. . . .

The exploitation of laboratory animals is part of the larger problem of speciesism and it is unlikely to be eliminated altogether until speciesism itself is eliminated. Surely one day, though, our children's children, reading about what was done in laboratories in the twentieth century, will feel the same sense of horror and incredulity at what otherwise civilized people could do that we now feel when we read about the atrocities of the Roman gladiatorial arenas or the eighteenth-century slave trade.

Discussion Questions

1. Do you agree with Singer that most humans are speciesists? If you are a speciesist, on what grounds do you morally justify it? In what ways does your lifestyle contribute to the suffering of the members of other species?
2. Do you agree with Singer that speciesism is similar to sexism and racism? Support your answer. Discuss how Narveson might respond to Singer's claim.
3. Singer wants to seek a "middle position that would avoid speciesism but would not make the lives of the retarded and senile as cheap as the lives of pigs and dogs now are, or make the lives of pigs and dogs so sacrosanct that we think it wrong to put them out of hopeless misery." However, can he morally justify drawing the line at this point? Or is this middle point arbitrary? Support your answers.
4. Like Singer, R. G. Frey opposes species membership as the criterion of moral standing.[24] Whereas Singer concludes that the principle of equality should preclude experimentation on nonhuman animals whose cognitive capacity is equivalent to

that of human infants or cognitively impaired humans, Frey draws the opposite conclusion. Humans with an impoverished cognitive life can be used in experiments in
the same way we use animals. Discuss Frey's argument as well as how Singer might
respond to him.

5. Is Singer, as a utilitarian, being inconsistent when he argues that the benefits derived
from animal experimentation are morally irrelevant? Do the benefits of experimentation ever justify the use of nonconsenting humans or nonhuman animals in experiments? Support your answers.

CARL COHEN

Do Animals Have Rights?

Carl Cohen is a philosophy professor at the University of Michigan. Cohen defends the
traditional Kantian view of moral agency and rights. According to Cohen, rights are
based on self-assertion rather than on interests. Because only moral agents can assert
moral claims, only moral agents have rights. Therefore, we do not violate the rights of
nonhuman animals by doing research on them.

Critical Reading Questions

1. Why is the question of whether animals have rights of great importance?
2. How does Cohen define the term *right*?
3. Why does Cohen reject Regan's argument that animals have rights?
4. According to Cohen, what is the relationship between rights and obligations?
5. Why can't nonhuman animals be the bearers of rights? How does Cohen use the
   example of the baby zebra and the lioness to illustrate his position?
6. How does Cohen interpret Regan's concept of nonhuman animals as being moral
   patients?
7. According to Cohen, where do human rights come from?
8. How does Cohen respond to the objection that, under his definition, human
   infants and other cognitively impaired humans don't have rights?
9. What fallacy does Cohen accuse Regan of committing in his use of the term *inherent value*? According to Cohen, how does this fallacy invalidate Regan's conclusion
   that animals have rights?
10. What is Cohen's conclusion regarding the use of nonhuman animals in medical
    experiments?

"Do Animals Have Rights?" *Ethics and Behavior* 7, no. 2 (1997): 91–102. Some notes have been omitted.

Whether animals have rights is a question of great importance because if they do, those rights must be respected, even at the cost of great burdens for human beings. A right (unlike an interest) is a valid claim, or potential claim, made by a moral agent, under principles that govern both the claimant and the target of the claim. Rights are precious; they are dispositive; they count.

You have a right to the return of money you lent me; we both understand that. It may be very convenient for me to keep the money, and you may have no need of it whatever; but my convenience and your needs are not to the point. You have a *right* to it, and we have courts of law partly to ensure that such rights will be respected. . . .

A great deal was learned about hypothermia by some Nazi doctors who advanced their learning by soaking Jews in cold water and putting them in refrigerators to learn how hypothermia proceeds. We have no difficulty in seeing that they may not advance medicine in that way; the subjects of those atrocious experiments had rights that demanded respect. For those who ignored their rights we have nothing but moral loathing.

Some persons believe that animals have rights as surely as those Jews had rights, and they therefore look on the uses of animals in medical investigations just as we look at the Nazi use of the Jews, with moral loathing. They are consistent in doing so. If animals have rights they certainly have the right not to be killed, even to advance our important interests.

Some may say, "Well, they have rights, but we have rights too, and our rights override theirs." That may be true in some cases, but it will not solve the problem because, although we may have a weighty *interest* in learning, say, how to vaccinate against polio or other diseases, we do not have a *right* to learn such things. Nor could we honestly claim that we kill research animals in self-defense; they did not attack us. If animals have rights, they certainly have the right not to be killed to advance the interests of others, whatever rights those others may have.

In 1952 there were about 58,000 cases of polio reported in the United States, and 3,000 polio deaths; my parents, parents everywhere, trembled in fear for their children at camp or away from home.

Polio vaccination became routine in 1955, and cases dropped to about a dozen a year; today polio has been eradicated completely from the Western Hemisphere. The vaccine that achieved this, partly developed and tested only blocks from where I live in Ann Arbor, could have been developed *only* with the substantial use of animals. Polio vaccines had been tried many times earlier, but from those earlier vaccines children had contracted the disease; investigators had become, understandably, exceedingly cautious.

The killer disease for which a vaccine now is needed most desperately is malaria, which kills about 2 million people each year, most of them children. Many vaccines have been tried—not on children, thank God—and have failed. But very recently, after decades of effort, we learned how to make a vaccine that does, with complete success, inoculate mice against malaria. A safe vaccine for humans we do not yet have—but soon we will have it, thanks to the use of those mice, many of whom will have died in the process. To test that vaccine first on children would be an outrage. . . . We use mice or monkeys *because there is no other way* . . . to determine the reliability and safety of new vaccines without repeated tests on live organisms. Therefore, because we certainly may not use human children to test them, we will use mice (or as we develop an AIDS vaccine, primates) *or we will never have such vaccines.*

But if those animals we use in such tests have rights as human children do, what we did and are doing to them is as profoundly wrong as what the Nazis did to those Jews not long ago. Defenders of animal rights need not hold that medical scientists are vicious; they simply believe that what medical investigators are doing with animals is morally wrong. Most biomedical investigations involving animal subjects use rodents: mice and rats. The rat is the animal appropriately considered (and used by the critic) as the exemplar whose moral stature is in dispute here. Tom Regan is a leading defender of the view that rats do have such rights, and may not be used in biomedical investigations. He is an honest man. He sees the consequences of his view and accepts them forthrightly. In *The Case for Animal Rights* (Regan, 1983) he wrote,

The harms others might face as a result of the dissolution of [some] practice or institution is no defense of allowing it to continue. . . . No one has a right to be protected against being harmed if the protection in question involves violating the rights of others. . . . No one has a right to be protected by the continuation of an unjust practice, one that violates the rights of others. . . . Justice *must* be done, though the . . . heavens fall. (pp. 346–347)

That last line echoes Kant, who borrowed it from an older tradition. Believing that rats have rights as humans do, Regan (1983) was convinced that killing them in medical research was morally intolerable. He wrote,

On the rights view, [he means, of course, the Regan rights view] we cannot justify harming a single rat *merely* by aggregating "the many human and humane benefits" that flow from doing it. . . . Not even a single rat is to be treated as if that animal's value were reducible to his *possible utility* relative to the interests of others. (p. 384)

If there are some things that we cannot learn because animals have rights, well, as Regan (1983) put it, so be it.

This is the conclusion to which one certainly is driven if one holds that animals have rights. If Regan is correct about the moral standing of rats, we humans can have no right, ever, to kill them—unless perchance a rat attacks a person or a human baby, as rats sometimes do; then our right of self-defense may enter, I suppose. But medical investigations cannot honestly be described as self-defense, and medical investigations commonly require that many mice and rats be killed. Therefore, all medical investigations relying on them, or any other animal subjects—which includes most studies and all the most important studies of certain kinds—will have to stop. . . .

WHY ANIMALS DO NOT HAVE RIGHTS

Many obligations are owed by humans to animals; few will deny that. But it certainly does not follow from this that animals have rights because it

is certainly not true that *every* obligation of ours arises from the rights of another. Not at all. We need to be clear and careful here. Rights entail obligations. If you have a right to the return of the money I borrowed, I have an obligation to repay it. No issue. If we have the right to speak freely on public policy matters, the community has the obligation to respect our right to do so. But the proposition *all rights entail obligations* does not convert simply, as the logicians say. From the true proposition that all trees are plants, it does not follow that all plants are trees. Similarly, not all obligations are entailed by rights. Some obligations, like mine to repay the money I borrowed from you, do arise out of rights. But many obligations are owed to persons or other beings who have no rights whatever in the matter.

Obligations may arise from commitments freely made: As a college professor I accept the obligation to comment at length on the papers my students submit, and I do so; but they have not the right to *demand* that I do so. . . .

Special relations often give rise to obligations: Hosts have the obligation to be cordial to their guests, but the guest has not the right to demand cordiality. Shepherds have obligations to their dogs, and cowboys to their horses, which do not flow from the rights of those dogs or horses. . . . My dog has no right to daily exercise and veterinary care, but I do have the obligation to provide those things for her.

One may be obliged to another for a special act of kindness done; one may be obliged to put an animal out of its misery in view of its condition—but neither the beneficiary of that kindness nor that dying animal may have had a claim of right.

. . . Some of our most important obligations—to members of our family, to the needy, to neighbors, and to sentient creatures of every sort—have no foundation in rights at all. Correlativity appears critical from the perspective of one who holds a right; your right correlates with my obligation to respect it. But the claim that rights and obligations are *reciprocals,* that *every* obligation flows from another's right, is false, plainly inconsistent with our general understanding of the differences between what we think we *ought* to do, and what others can justly *demand* that we do.

I emphasize this because, although animals have no rights, it surely does not follow from this that one is free to treat them with callous disregard. Animals are not stones; they feel. A rat may suffer; surely we have the obligation not to torture it gratuitously, even though it be true that the concept of a right could not possibly apply to it. We humans are obliged to act humanely, that is, being aware of their sentience, to apply to animals the moral principles that govern us regarding the gratuitous imposition of pain and suffering; which is not, of course, to treat animals as the possessors of rights.

Animals cannot be the bearers of rights because the concept of rights is essentially *human;* it is rooted in, and has force within, a human moral world. Humans must deal with rats—all too frequently in some parts of the world—and must be moral in their dealing with them; but a rat can no more be said to have rights than a table can be said to have ambition. To say of a rat that it has rights is to confuse categories, to apply to its world a moral category that has content only in the human moral world.

Try this thought experiment. Imagine, on the Serengeti Plain in East Africa, a lioness hunting for her cubs. A baby zebra, momentarily left unattended by its mother, is the prey; the lioness snatches it, rips open its throat, tears out chunks of its flesh, and departs. The mother zebra is driven nearly out of her wits when she cannot locate her baby; finding its carcass she will not even leave the remains for days. The scene may be thought unpleasant, but it is entirely natural, of course, and extremely common. If the zebra has a right to live, if the prey is just but the predator unjust, we ought to intervene, if we can, on behalf of right. But we do not intervene, of course—as we surely would intervene if we saw the lioness about to attack an unprotected human baby or you. What accounts for the moral difference? We justify different responses to humans and to zebras on the ground (implicit or explicit) that their moral stature is very different. The human has a right not to be eaten alive; it is,

after all, a human being. Do you believe the baby zebra has the *right* not to be slaughtered by that lioness? That the lioness has the *right* to kill that baby zebra for her cubs? If you are inclined to say, confronted by such natural rapacity—duplicated with untold variety millions of times each day on planet earth—that neither is right or wrong, that neither has a *right* against the other, I am on your side. Rights are of the highest moral consequence, yes; but zebras and lions and rats are totally amoral; there is no morality for them; they do no wrong, ever. In their world there are no rights.

A contemporary philosopher who has thought a good deal about animals, referring to them as "moral patients," put it this way:

> A moral patient lacks the ability to formulate, let alone bring to bear, moral principles in deliberating about which one among a number of possible acts it would be right or proper to perform. Moral patients, in a word, cannot do what is right, nor can they do what is wrong. . . . Even when a moral patient causes significant harm to another, the moral patient has not done what is wrong. Only moral agents can do what is wrong. (Regan, 1983, pp. 152–153)

Just so. The concepts of wrong and right are totally foreign to animals, not conceivably within their ken or applicable to them, as the author of that passage clearly understands.

When using animals in our research, therefore, we ought indeed be humane—but we can never violate the rights of those animals because, to be blunt, they have none. Rights do not *apply* to them.

But humans do have rights. Where do our rights come from? Why are we not crudely natural creatures like rats and zebras? . . .

To be a moral agent (on this view) is to be able to grasp the generality of moral restrictions on our will. Humans understand that some things, which may be in our interest, *must not be willed;* we lay down moral laws for ourselves, and thus exhibit, as no other animal can exhibit, moral autonomy. My dog knows that there are certain things she must not do—but she knows this only as the outcome of her learning about her interests, the pains she may suffer if she does what had been taught forbidden. She does not know, cannot know (as Regan agrees) that any conduct is wrong. The proposition *It would be highly advantageous to act in such-and-such a way, but I may not because it would be wrong* is one that no dog or mouse or rabbit, however sweet and endearing, however loyal or attentive to its young, can ever entertain, or intend, or begin to grasp. Right is not in their world. But right and wrong are the very stuff of human moral life, the ever-present awareness of human beings who can do wrong, and who by seeking (often) to avoid wrong conduct prove themselves members of a moral community in which rights may be exercised and must be respected.

Some respond by saying, "This can't be correct, for human infants (and the comatose and senile, etc.) surely have rights, but they make no moral claims or judgments and can make none—and any view entailing that children can have no rights must be absurd." Objections of this kind miss the point badly. It is not individual persons who qualify (or are disqualified) for the possession of rights because of the presence or absence in them of some special capacity, thus resulting in the award of rights to some but not to others. Rights are universally human; they arise in a *human moral world,* in a moral *sphere.* In the human world moral judgments are pervasive; it is the fact that all humans including infants and the senile are members of that moral community—not the fact that as individuals they have or do not have certain special capacities, or merits—that makes humans bearers of rights. Therefore, it is beside the point to insist that animals have remarkable capacities, that they really have a consciousness of self, or of the future, or make plans, and so on. And the tired response that because infants plainly cannot make moral claims they must have no rights at all, or rats must have them too, we ought forever put aside. Responses like these arise out of a misconception of right itself. They mistakenly suppose that rights are tied to some identifiable individual abilities or sensibilities, and they fail to see that rights arise only in a community of moral beings, and that therefore there are spheres in which rights do apply and spheres in which they do not.

Rationality is not at issue; the capacity to communicate is not at issue. My dog can reason, if rather weakly, and she certainly can communicate. . . . Nor is the capacity to suffer here at issue. And, if *autonomy* be understood only as the capacity to choose this course rather than that, autonomy is not to the point either. But *moral autonomy*—that is, *moral self-legislation*—is to the point, because moral autonomy is uniquely human and is for animals out of the question, as we have seen, and as Regan and I agree. In talking about autonomy, therefore, we must be careful and precise. . . .

WHY ANIMALS ARE MISTAKENLY BELIEVED TO HAVE RIGHTS

From the foregoing discussion it follows that, if some philosophers believe that they have proved that animals have rights, they must have erred in the alleged proof. Regan is a leader among those who claim to *argue* in defense of the rights of rats; he contends that the best arguments are on his side. I aim next to show how he and others with like views go astray. . . . Examining *The Case for Animal Rights,* let us see if we can find the faulty switch.

. . . Regan sought to show, patiently and laboriously, that the common belief that we do have obligations to animals, although they have no rights, has not been defended satisfactorily. That belief cannot be justified, he contended, by direct duty views of which he finds two categories: those depending on the obligation to be kind or not to be cruel, and those depending on any kind of utilitarian calculation. . . .

The case is built entirely on the principle that allegedly *carries over* almost everything earlier claimed about human rights to rats and other animals. What principle is that? It is the principle, put in italics but given no name, that equates moral agents with moral patients:

> *The validity of the claim to respectful treatment, and thus the case for the recognition of the right to such treatment, cannot be any stronger or weaker in the case of moral patients than it is in the case of moral agents.* (Regan, p. 279)

But hold on. Why in the world should anyone think this principle to be true? Back where Regan first recounted his view of moral patients, he allowed that some of them are, although capable of experiencing pleasure and pain, lacking in other capacities. But he is interested, he told us there, in those moral patients—those animals—that are like humans in having *inherent value*. This is the key to the argument for animal rights, the possession of inherent value. How that concept functions in the argument becomes absolutely critical. I will say first briefly what will be shown more carefully later: *Inherent value* is an expression used by Regan (and many like him) with two very different senses—in one of which it is reasonable to conclude that those who have inherent value have rights, and in another sense in which that inference is wholly unwarranted. But the phrase *inherent value* has some plausibility in both contexts, and thus by sliding from one sense of inherent value to the other Regan appears to succeed . . . in making the case for animal rights.

. . . Regan went on to argue for the proposition that all moral agents are "equal in inherent value." Holding some such views we are likely to say, with Kant, that all humans are beyond price. Their inherent value gives them moral dignity, a unique role in the moral world, as agents having the capacity to act morally and make moral judgments. This is inherent value in Sense 1.

The expression *inherent value* has another sense, however, also common and also plausible. My dog has inherent value, and so does every wild animal, every lion and zebra, which is why the senseless killing of animals is so repugnant. Each animal is unique, not replaceable in itself by another animal or by any rocks or clay. Animals, like humans, are not just things; they live, and as unique living creatures they have inherent value. This is an important point, and again likely to be thought plausible; but here, in Sense 2, the phrase *inherent value* means something quite distinct from what was meant in its earlier uses.

Inherent value in Sense 1, possessed by all humans but not by all animals, which warrants the claim of human rights, is very different from

inherent value in Sense 2, which warrants no such claim. The uniqueness of animals, their intrinsic worthiness as individual living things, does not ground the possession of rights, has nothing to do with the moral condition in which rights arise. Regan's argument reached its critical objective with almost magical speed because, having argued that beings with inherent value (Sense 1) have rights that must be respected, he quickly asserted (putting it in italics lest the reader be inclined to express doubt) that rats and rabbits also have rights because they, too, have inherent value (Sense 2).

This is an egregious example of the fallacy of equivocation: the informal fallacy in which two or more meanings of the same word or phrase have been confused in the several premises of an argument. Why is this slippage not seen at once? Partly because we know the phrase *inherent value* often is used loosely, so the reader is not prone to quibble about its introduction; partly because the two uses of the phrase relied on are both common, so neither signals danger; partly because inherent value in Sense 2 is indeed shared by those who have it in Sense 1; and partly because the phrase *inherent value* is woven into accounts of what Regan (1983) elsewhere called the *subject-of-a-life criterion*, a phrase of his own devising for which he can stipulate any meaning he pleases, of course, and which also slides back and forth between the sphere of genuine moral agency and the sphere of animal experience. But perhaps the chief reason the equivocation between these two uses of the phrase *inherent value* is obscured (from the author, I believe, as well as from the reader) is the fact that the assertion that animals have rights appears only indirectly, as the outcome of the application of the principle that moral patients are entitled to the same respect as moral agents—a principle introduced at a point in the book long after the important moral differences between moral patients and moral agents have been recognized, with a good deal of tangled philosophical argument having been injected in between. . . .

Animals do not have rights. Right does not apply in their world. We do have many obligations to animals, of course, and I honor Regan's appreciation of their sensitivities. . . . But he is, I submit, profoundly mistaken. I conclude with the observation that, had his mistaken views about the rights of animals long been accepted, most successful medical therapies recently devised—antibiotics, vaccines, prosthetic devices, and other compounds and instruments on which we now rely for saving and improving human lives and for the protection of our children—could not have been developed; and were his views to become general now (an outcome that is unlikely but possible) the consequences for medical science and for human well-being in the years ahead would be nothing less than catastrophic.

Advances in medicine absolutely require experiments, many of which are dangerous. Dangerous experiments absolutely require living organisms as subjects. Those living organisms (we now agree) certainly may not be human beings. Therefore, most advances in medicine will continue to rely on the use of nonhuman animals, or they will stop. Regan is free to say in response, as he does, "so be it." The rest of us must ask if the argument he presents is so compelling as to force us to accept that dreadful result.

REFERENCE

Regan, T. (1983). *The case for animal rights.* Berkeley: University of California Press.

Discussion Questions

1. Is Cohen a speciesist? Discuss how Singer might respond to Cohen's claim that all and only humans have rights, even those who lack reason and moral autonomy.
2. Cohen acknowledges that inhumane treatment of nonhuman animals is wrong when we can achieve the same results using alternative methods. Is his claim that researchers have a moral obligation to treat nonhuman animals humanely inconsistent with his claim that animals have no rights?
3. Cohen admits that nonhuman animals feel pain and that researchers should not subject them to unnecessary suffering. What does he mean by unnecessary suffering? Compare and contrast Cohen's and Singer's positions on the significance of suffering in the moral justification of experiments using nonhuman animals.
4. Does Cohen do an effective job of discrediting Regan's argument that nonhuman animals have rights? Support your answer. Discuss how Regan might respond to Cohen's criticism of his position.
5. Do you agree with Cohen's claim regarding the qualitative gap between humans and other animals? Discuss how Cohen might respond to Singer's argument that scientists who justify using nonhuman animals in psychology and learning experiments on the grounds that they are not like humans find themselves in a moral dilemma, because there would be no point in using them if they were not like us.

ALDO LEOPOLD

The Land Ethic

Aldo Leopold (1887–1948) was a forester and wildlife manager with the U.S. Forest Service and a professor of wildlife management at the University of Wisconsin. In his essay "The Land Ethic," Leopold expresses concern about the detrimental impact of human activities on the environment. He argues that instead of seeing the environment primarily in terms of its value to humans (anthropocentrism), we should see ourselves as part of the natural world (ecocentrism).

Critical Reading Questions

1. What does Leopold mean when he talks of the "extension of ethics"?
2. What is the premise of current ethics?
3. In what ways does a land ethic change the role of humans in the land community?
4. Why does Leopold reject an ethic based on a conservation system?
5. What is the land pyramid? Where are humans in Leopold's land pyramid?
6. What attitudes toward the land are required in order for humans to have an ethical relationship with the land?
7. What are some of the obstacles impeding the evolution of a land ethic?
8. What strategies does Leopold suggest for overcoming these obstacles?
9. According to Leopold, what are the fundamental criteria for determining if something is ethically right?

When god-like Odysseus returned from the wars in Troy, he hanged all on one rope a dozen slave-girls of his household whom he suspected of misbehavior during his absence.

This hanging involved no question of propriety. The girls were property. The disposal of property was then, as now, a matter of expediency, not of right and wrong.

Concepts of right and wrong were not lacking from Odysseus' Greece: . . . The ethical structure of that day covered wives, but had not yet been extended to human chattels. During the three thousand years which have since elapsed, ethical criteria have been extended to many fields

of conduct, with corresponding shrinkages in those judged by expediency only.

THE ETHICAL SEQUENCE

This extension of ethics, so far studied only by philosophers, is actually a process in ecological evolution. Its sequences may be described in ecological as well as in philosophical terms. An ethic, ecologically, is a limitation on freedom of action in the struggle for existence. An ethic, philosophically, is a differentiation of social from anti-social conduct. These are two definitions of one thing. The thing has its origin in the tendency of interdependent individuals or groups to evolve modes of cooperation. The ecologist calls these symbioses. . . .

The first ethics dealt with the relation between individuals; the Mosaic Decalogue is an example. Later accretions dealt with the relation between

Aldo Leopold, "The Land Ethic," from *A Sand County Almanac: And Sketches Here and There*, 201–226 (1949). By permission of Oxford University Press.

the individual and society. The Golden Rule tries to integrate the individual to society; democracy to integrate social organization to the individual.

There is as yet no ethic dealing with man's relation to land and to the animals and plants which grow upon it. Land, like Odysseus' slave-girls, is still property. The land-relation is still strictly economic, entailing privileges but not obligations.

The extension of ethics to this third element in human environment is, if I read the evidence correctly, an evolutionary possibility and an ecological necessity. . . .

THE COMMUNITY CONCEPT

All ethics so far evolved rest upon a single premise: that the individual is a member of a community of interdependent parts. His instincts prompt him to compete for his place in that community, but his ethics prompt him also to co-operate (perhaps in order that there may be a place to compete for).

The land ethic simply enlarges the boundaries of the community to include soils, waters, plants, and animals, or collectively: the land.

This sounds simple: do we not already sing our love for and obligation to the land of the free and the home of the brave? Yes, but just what and whom do we love? Certainly not the soil, which we are sending helter-skelter downriver. Certainly not the waters, which we assume have no function except to turn the turbines, float barges, and carry off sewage. Certainly not the plants, of which we exterminate whole communities without batting an eye. Certainly not the animals, of which we have already extirpated many of the largest and most beautiful species. A land ethic of course cannot prevent the alteration, management, and use of these "resources," but it does affirm their right to continued existence, and, at least in spots, their continued existence in a natural state.

In short, a land ethic changes the role of *Homo sapiens* from conqueror of the land-community to plain member and citizen of it. It implies respect for his fellow-members, and also respect for the community as such. . . .

SUBSTITUTES FOR A LAND ETHIC

When the logic of history hungers for bread and we hand out a stone, we are at pains to explain how much the stone resembles bread. I now describe some of the stones which serve in lieu of a land ethic.

One basic weakness in a conservation system based wholly on economic motives is that most members of the land community have no economic value. Wildflowers and songbirds are examples. . . .

Lack of economic value is sometimes a character not only of species or groups, but of entire biotic communities: marshes, bogs, dunes, and "deserts" are examples. Our formula in such cases is to relegate their conservation to government as refuges, monuments, or parks. . . .

Industrial landowners and users, especially lumbermen and stockmen, are inclined to wail long and loudly about the extension of government ownership and regulation to land, but (with notable exceptions) they show little disposition to develop the only visible alternative: the voluntary practice of conservation on their own lands.

When the private landowner is asked to perform some unprofitable act for the good of the community, he today assents only with outstretched palm. If the act costs him cash this is fair and proper, but when it costs only forethought, open-mindedness, or time, the issue is at least debatable. The overwhelming growth of land-use subsidies in recent years must be ascribed, in large part, to the government's own agencies for conservation education: the land bureaus, the agricultural colleges, and the extension services. As far as I can detect, no ethical obligation toward land is taught in these institutions.

To sum up: a system of conservation based solely on economic self-interest is hopelessly lopsided. It tends to ignore, and thus eventually to eliminate, many elements in the land community that lack commercial value, but that are (as far as we know) essential to its healthy functioning. It assumes, falsely, I think, that the economic parts of the biotic clock will function without the uneconomic parts. It tends to relegate to government many functions eventually too large, too complex, or too widely dispersed to be performed by government.

An ethical obligation on the part of the private owner is the only visible remedy for these situations.

THE LAND PYRAMID

An ethic to supplement and guide the economic relation to land presupposes the existence of some mental image of land as a biotic mechanism. We can be ethical only in relation to something we can see, feel, understand, love, or otherwise have faith in.

The image commonly employed in conservation education is "the balance of nature." For reasons too lengthy to detail here, this figure of speech fails to describe accurately what little we know about the land mechanism. A much truer image is the one employed in ecology: the biotic pyramid. I shall first sketch the pyramid as a symbol of land, and later develop some of its implications in terms of land-use.

Plants absorb energy from the sun. This energy flows through a circuit called the biota, which may be represented by a pyramid consisting of layers. The bottom layer is the soil. A plant layer rests on the soil, an insect layer on the plants, a bird and rodent layer on the insects, and so on up through various animal groups to the apex layer, which consists of the larger carnivores.

The species of a layer are alike not in where they came from, or in what they look like, but rather in what they eat. Each successive layer depends on those below it for food and often for other services, and each in turn furnishes food and services to those above. Proceeding upward, each successive layer decreases in numerical abundance. Thus, for every carnivore there are hundreds of his prey, thousands of their prey, millions of insects, uncountable plants. The pyramidal form of the system reflects this numerical progression from apex to base. Man shares an intermediate layer with the bears, raccoons, and squirrels which eat both meat and vegetables. . . .

Land, then, is not merely soil; it is a fountain of energy flowing through a circuit of soils, plants, and animals. Food chains are the living channels which conduct energy upward; death and decay return it to the soil. The circuit is not closed; some energy is dissipated in decay, some is added by absorption from the air, some is stored in soils, peats, and long-lived forests; but it is a sustained circuit, like a slowly augmented revolving fund of life. . . .

This interdependence between the complex structure of the land and its smooth functioning as an energy unit is one of its basic attributes.

When a change occurs in one part of the circuit, many other parts must adjust themselves to it. Change does not necessarily obstruct or divert the flow of energy; evolution is a long series of self-induced changes, the net result of which has been to elaborate the flow mechanism and to lengthen the circuit. Evolutionary changes, however, are usually slow and local. Man's invention of tools has enabled him to make changes of unprecedented violence, rapidity, and scope. . . .

THE OUTLOOK

It is inconceivable to me that an ethical relation to land can exist without love, respect, and admiration for land, and a high regard for its value. By value, I of course mean something far broader than mere economic value; I mean value in the philosophical sense.

Perhaps the most serious obstacle impeding the evolution of a land ethic is the fact that our educational and economic system is headed away from, rather than toward, an intense consciousness of land. Your true modern is separated from the land by many middlemen, and by innumerable physical gadgets. He has no vital relation to it; to him it is the space between cities on which crops grow. Turn him loose for a day on the land, and if the spot does not happen to be a golf links or a "scenic" area, he is bored stiff. If crops could be raised by hydroponics instead of farming, it would suit him very well. Synthetic substitutes for wood, leather, wool, and other natural land products suit him better than the originals. In short, land is something he has "outgrown."

Almost equally serious as an obstacle to a land ethic is the attitude of the farmer for whom the land is still an adversary, or a taskmaster that keeps him in slavery. Theoretically, the mechanization of farming ought to cut the farmer's chains, but whether it really does is debatable. . . .

The case for a land ethic would appear hopeless but for the minority which is in obvious revolt against these "modern" trends.

The "key-log" which must be moved to release the evolutionary process for an ethic is simply this: quit thinking about decent land-use as solely an economic problem. Examine each question in terms of what is ethically and esthetically right, as well as what is economically expedient. A thing is right when it tends to preserve the integrity, stability, and beauty of the biotic community. It is wrong when it tends otherwise.

It of course goes without saying that economic feasibility limits the tether of what can or cannot be done for land. It always has and it always will. The fallacy the economic determinists have tied around our collective neck, and which we now need to cast off, is the belief that economics determines *all* land-use. This is simply not true. An innumerable host of actions and attitudes, comprising perhaps the bulk of all land relations, is determined by the land-users' tastes and predilections, rather than by his purse. The bulk of all land relations hinges on investments of time, forethought, skill, and faith rather than on investments of cash. As a land-user thinketh, so is he. . . .

The evolution of a land ethic is an intellectual as well as emotional process. Conservation is paved with good intentions which prove to be futile, or even dangerous, because they are devoid of critical understanding either of the land, or of economic land-use. I think it is a truism that as the ethical frontier advances from the individual to the community, its intellectual content increases.

The mechanism of operation is the same for any ethic: social approbation for right actions; social disapproval for wrong actions.

By and large, our present problem is one of attitudes and implements. We are remodeling the Alhambra with a steam-shovel, and we are proud of our yardage. We shall hardly relinquish the shovel, which after all has many good points, but we are in need of gentler and more objective criteria for its successful use.

Discussion Questions

1. Discuss Leopold's assumption about the evolution of ethics toward a land ethic. Discuss whether or not Leopold's land ethic is compatible with the Judeo-Christian view of creation and our place as human beings in the universe.
2. Richard Watson criticizes Leopold's anti-anthropocentric theory on the grounds that it contains a self-contradiction.[25] Rather than viewing human activities as part of nature and the natural process, they are seen as destructive and in need of curbing. Because Leopold's theory sets humans apart from nature, instead of adopting a genuinely holistic view of nature, it has not broken away from anthropocentricism. Is this a legitimate criticism? Discuss how Leopold might respond to this criticism.
3. What does Leopold mean when he says: "A thing is right when it tends to preserve the integrity, stability, and beauty of the biotic community. It is wrong when it tends otherwise"? Discuss the implications of this statement for your own lifestyle and for public policy regarding the environment.
4. In his essay "Thinking Like a Mountain," Leopold describes watching the death of a wolf he just shot. "We reached the old wolf in time to watch a fierce green fire dying in her eyes. I realized then, and have known ever since, that there was something

new to me in those eyes—something known only to her and to the mountain. I was young then, and . . . I thought that because fewer wolves meant more deer, that no wolves would mean a hunter's paradise. But after seeing the green fire die, I sensed that neither the wolf nor the mountain agreed with such a view." Do you agree with Leopold? Discuss Leopold's experience in light of your own experience.

5. Discuss the implications of Leopold's land ethic for our eating habits and the use of nonhuman animals in medical experiments. How would Tom Regan, Peter Singer, Jan Narveson, and Carl Cohen each most likely respond to Leopold's land ethic?

BILL DEVALL AND GEORGE SESSIONS

Deep Ecology

Bill Devall is professor emeritus of sociology at Humboldt State University in Arcata, California. George Sessions is a philosophy professor at Sierra College in Rocklin, California. Their book has been called a manifesto for the deep ecology movement. In this selection, the authors present the eight principles of deep ecology.

Critical Reading Questions

1. What is the difference between "deep" and "shallow" ecology?
2. What are the foundations of deep ecology?
3. How does the deep ecology worldview differ from the dominant worldview?
4. What are the two ultimate norms of deep ecological consciousness?
5. What is the deep ecology sense of self, and how can society help nurture this self?
6. What is "biocentric equality" and how is it related to self-actualization?
7. What are the eight basic principles of deep ecology?
8. According to Devall and Sessions, what are the implications of deep ecology for human population growth and our relationship to nature?

The term *deep ecology* was coined by Arne Naess in his 1973 article, "The Shallow and the Deep, Long-Range Ecology Movements." Naess was attempting to describe the deeper, more spiritual approach to Nature exemplified in the writings of Aldo Leopold and Rachel Carson. He thought that this deeper

approach resulted from a more sensitive openness to ourselves and nonhuman life around us. The essence of deep ecology is to keep asking more searching questions about human life, society, and Nature as in the Western philosophical tradition of Socrates. As examples of this deep questioning, Naess points out "that we ask why and how, where others do not. For instance, ecology as a science does not ask what kind of a society would be the best for maintaining a particular ecosystem—that

"Deep Ecology," from *Deep Ecology: Living As If Nature Mattered* (Salt Lake City: Peregrine Smith Books, 1985), 65–73. Notes have been omitted.

is considered a question for value theory, for politics, for ethics." Thus deep ecology goes beyond the so-called factual scientific level to the level of self and Earth wisdom. . . .

Ecological consciousness and deep ecology are in sharp contrast with the dominant worldview of technocratic-industrial societies which regards humans as isolated and fundamentally separate from the rest of Nature, as superior to, and in charge of, the rest of creation. But the view of humans as separate and superior to the rest of Nature is only part of larger cultural patterns. For thousands of years, Western culture has become increasingly obsessed with the idea of *dominance:* with dominance of humans over nonhuman Nature, masculine over the feminine, wealthy and powerful over the poor, with the dominance of the West over non-Western cultures. Deep ecological consciousness allows us to see through these erroneous and dangerous illusions.

For deep ecology, the study of our place in the Earth household includes the study of ourselves as part of the organic whole. Going beyond a narrowly materialist scientific understanding of reality, the spiritual and the material aspects of reality fuse together. . . .

From this most basic insight or characteristic of deep ecological consciousness, Arne Naess has developed two *ultimate norms* or intuitions which are themselves not derivable from other principles or intuitions. They are arrived at by the deep questioning process and reveal the importance of moving to the philosophical and religious level of wisdom. They cannot be validated, of course, by the methodology of modern science based on its usual mechanistic assumptions and its very narrow definition of data. These ultimate norms are *self-realization* and *biocentric equality*.

I. SELF-REALIZATION

In keeping with the spiritual traditions of many of the world's religions, the deep ecology norm of self-realization goes beyond the modern Western *self* which is defined as an isolated ego striving primarily for hedonistic gratification or for a narrow sense of individual salvation in this life or the next. This socially programmed sense of the narrow self or social self dislocates us, and leaves us prey to whatever fad or fashion is prevalent in our society or social reference group. We are thus robbed of beginning the search for our unique spiritual/biological personhood. Spiritual growth, or unfolding, begins when we cease to understand or see ourselves as isolated and narrow competing egos and begin to identify with other humans from our family and friends to, eventually, our species. But the deep ecology sense of self requires a further maturity and growth, an identification which goes beyond humanity to include the nonhuman world. We must see beyond our narrow contemporary cultural assumptions and values, and the conventional wisdom of our time and place, and this is best achieved by the meditative deep questioning process. Only in this way can we hope to attain full mature personhood and uniqueness.

A nurturing nondominating society can help in the "real work" of becoming a whole person. The "real work" can be summarized symbolically as the realization of "self-in-Self" where "Self" stands for organic wholeness. This process of the full unfolding of the self can also be summarized by the phrase, "No one is saved until we are all saved," where the phrase "one" includes not only me, an individual human, but all humans, whales, grizzly bears, whole rain forest ecosystems, mountains and rivers, the tiniest microbes in the soil, and so on.

II. BIOCENTRIC EQUALITY

The intuition of biocentric equality is that all things in the biosphere have an equal right to live and blossom and to reach their own individual forms of unfolding and self-realization within the larger Self-realization. This basic intuition is that all organisms and entities in the ecosphere, as parts of the interrelated whole, are equal in intrinsic worth. Naess suggests that biocentric equality as an intuition is true in principle, although in the process of living, all species use each other as food, shelter, etc. Mutual predation is a biological fact of life, and many of the world's religions have struggled with the spiritual implications of this. Some animal liberationists who attempt to sidestep this problem by advocating vegetarianism are forced to say that the entire plant kingdom including rain forests have no right to their own existence. This evasion flies in the face of the basic intuition of equality. Aldo Leopold expressed this intuition when he said humans are "plain citizens" of the biotic community, not lord and master over all other species.

Biocentric equality is intimately related to the all-inclusive Self-realization in the sense that if we harm the rest of Nature then we are harming ourselves. There are no boundaries and everything is interrelated. But insofar as we perceive things as individual organisms or entities, the insight draws us to respect all human and nonhuman individuals in their own right as parts of the whole without feeling the need to set up hierarchies of species with humans at the top.

The practical implications of this intuition or norm suggest that we should live with minimum rather than maximum impact on other species and on the Earth in general. Thus we see another aspect of our guiding principle: "simple in means, rich in ends." . . .

Our vital material needs are probably more simple than many realize. In technocratic-industrial societies there is overwhelming propaganda and advertising which encourages false needs and destructive desires designed to foster increased production and consumption of goods. Most of this actually diverts us from facing reality in an objective way and from beginning the "real work" of spiritual growth and maturity.

Many people who do not see themselves as supporters of deep ecology nevertheless recognize an overriding vital human need for a healthy and high-quality natural environment for humans, if not for all life, with minimum intrusion of toxic waste, nuclear radiation from human enterprises, minimum acid rain and smog, and enough free flowing wilderness so humans can get in touch with their sources, the natural rhythms and the flow of time and place. . . .

As a brief summary of our position thus far, Figure 5-1 summarizes the contrast between the dominant worldview and deep ecology.

III. BASIC PRINCIPLES OF DEEP ECOLOGY

In April 1984, during the advent of spring and John Muir's birthday, George Sessions and Arne Naess summarized fifteen years of thinking on the principles of deep ecology while camping in Death Valley, California. . . .

Readers are encouraged to elaborate their own versions of deep ecology, clarify key concepts and think through the consequences of acting from these principles.

Figure 5-1

Dominant Worldview	*Deep Ecology*
Dominance over Nature	Harmony with Nature
Natural environment as resource for humans	All nature has intrinsic worth/biospecies equality
Material/economic growth for growing human population	Elegantly simple material needs (material goals serving the larger goal of self-realization)
Belief in ample resource reserves	Earth "supplies" limited
High technological progress and solutions	Appropriate technology; nondominating science
Consumerism	Doing with enough/recycling
National/centralized community	Minority tradition/bioregion

Basic Principles

1. The well-being and flourishing of human and nonhuman Life on Earth have value in themselves. . . . These values are independent of the usefulness of the nonhuman world for human purposes.

2. Richness and diversity of life forms contribute to the realization of these values and are also values in themselves.

3. Humans have no right to reduce this richness and diversity except to satisfy *vital* needs.

4. The flourishing of human life and cultures is compatible with a substantial decrease of the human population. The flourishing of nonhuman life requires such a decrease.

5. Present human interference with the nonhuman world is excessive, and the situation is rapidly worsening.

6. Policies must therefore be changed. These policies affect basic economic, technological, and ideological structures. The resulting state of affairs will be deeply different from the present.

7. The ideological change is mainly that of appreciating *life quality* (dwelling in situations of inherent value) rather than adhering to an increasingly higher standard of living. . . .

8. Those who subscribe to the foregoing points have an obligation directly or indirectly to try to implement the necessary changes.

Naess and Sessions Provide Comments on the Basic Principles

RE (1). This formulation refers to the biosphere, or more accurately, to the ecosphere as a whole. This includes individuals, species, populations, habitat, as well as human and nonhuman cultures. From our current knowledge of all-pervasive intimate relationships, this implies a fundamental deep concern and respect. . . .

The term "life" is used here in a more comprehensive nontechnical way to refer also to what biologists classify as "nonliving"; rivers (watersheds), landscapes, ecosystems. For supporters of deep ecology, slogans such as "Let the river live" illustrate this broader usage so common in most cultures. . . .

RE (2). More technically, this is a formulation concerning diversity and complexity. From an ecological standpoint, complexity and symbiosis are conditions for maximizing diversity. So-called simple, lower, or primitive species of plants and animals contribute essentially to the richness and diversity of life. They have value in themselves and are not merely steps toward the so-called higher or rational life forms. . . .

Complexity, as referred to here, is different from complication. Urban life may be more complicated than life in a natural setting without being more complex in the sense of multifaceted quality.

RE (3). The term "vital need" is left deliberately vague to allow for considerable latitude in judgment. Differences in climate and related factors, together with differences in the structures of societies as they now exist, need to be considered (for some Eskimos, snowmobiles are necessary today to satisfy vital needs).

People in the materially richest countries cannot be expected to reduce their excessive interference with the nonhuman world to a moderate level overnight. . . . But the longer we wait the more drastic will be the measures needed. Until deep changes are made, substantial decreases in richness and diversity are liable to occur: the rate of extinction of species will be ten to one hundred times greater than any other period of earth history.

RE (4). The United Nations Fund for Population Activities in their State of World Population Report (1984) said that high human population growth rates (over 2.0 percent annum) in many developing countries "were diminishing the quality of life for many millions of people." . . .

The report concludes that if all governments set specific population targets as public policy to help alleviate poverty and advance the quality of life, the current situation could be improved.

As many ecologists have pointed out, it is also absolutely crucial to curb population growth in the so-called developed (i.e., overdeveloped) industrial societies. Given the tremendous rate of consumption and waste production of individuals in these societies, they represent a much greater threat and impact on the biosphere per capita than individuals in Second and Third World countries.

RE (5). . . . The slogan of "noninterference" does not imply that humans should not modify some ecosystems as do other species. Humans have modified the earth and will probably continue to do so. At issue is the nature and extent of such interference.

The fight to preserve and extend areas of wilderness or near-wilderness should continue and should focus on the general ecological functions of these areas (one such function: large wilderness areas are required in the biosphere to allow for continued evolutionary speciation of animals and plants). Most presently designated wilderness areas and game preserves are not large enough to allow for such speciation.

RE (6). Economic growth as conceived and implemented today by the industrial states is incompatible with (1)–(5). There is only a faint resemblance between ideal sustainable forms of economic growth and present policies of the industrial societies. And "sustainable" still means "sustainable in relation to humans." . . .

Whereas "self-determination," "local community," and "think globally, act locally," will remain key terms in the ecology of human societies, nevertheless the implementation of deep changes requires increasingly global action—action across borders. . . .

RE (7). Some economists criticize the term "quality of life" because it is supposed to be vague. But on closer inspection, what they consider to be vague is actually the nonquantitative nature of the term. One cannot quantify adequately what is important for the quality of life as discussed here, and there is no need to do so.

RE (8). There is ample room for different opinions about priorities: What should be done first, what next? What is most urgent? What is clearly necessary as opposed to what is highly desirable but not absolutely pressing?

Discussion Questions

1. Discuss Devall and Sessions's claim that biocentric equality is intuitively true. How would Cohen most likely respond to this claim?
2. Discuss Devall and Sessions's position that self-realization and spiritual growth are enhanced by going beyond the traditional view of humans to the view espoused by deep ecology. Discuss how Kant and Buddha would each most likely respond to the deep ecologist view of human nature and self-realization.
3. Discuss the implications of each of the eight basic principles, both for your lifestyle and for public policy.
4. In his book *Earth in the Balance,* Al Gore argues that modern civilization is dysfunctional because it assumes a radical separation between humans and nature. This dysfunction is manifested in spiritual malaise as well as in our addiction to consuming ever larger quantities of oil, trees, topsoil, and other "substances we rip from the crust of the earth."[26] However, Gore rejects deep ecology, claiming that it incorrectly portrays humans in the "role of pathogens, a kind of virus giving the earth a rash and a fever, threatening the planet's vital life functions."[27] Gore argues instead that we need to seek a balance between our needs and preservation of the global environment. Our proper role is as God's stewards of the earth. Discuss how Devall and Sessions might respond to Gore.

AL GORE

Perspective on Global Warming

Al Gore was a member of the United States Congress from 1977 to 1993 and vice president under President Bill Clinton from 1993 to 2001. An internationally renowned environmental activist, Gore has been a key figure in calling attention to the issue of global warming and climate change. In 2007 Al Gore and the United Nations Intergovernmental Panel on Climate Change were jointly award the Noble Peace Prize.

Critical Reading Questions

1. What does Gore mean when he says we are facing a "planetary emergency"?
2. What evidence does Gore use to support his position that global warming is occurring and that it is worse than we previously thought?
3. What solution does Gore propose to the climate crisis?
4. What does Gore mean when he says that coming up with a solution to global warming is a "moral moment"?
5. How does Gore respond to the charge that solving global warming will be costly?

Madam Chairman, Senator Inhofe, and members of the Committee, I want to thank you for your gracious invitation to be here today, giving me the opportunity to return to the Senate to talk about the climate crisis.

I want to testify today about what I believe is a planetary emergency—a crisis that threatens the survival of our civilization and the habitability of the Earth. Just six weeks ago, the scientific community, in its strongest statement to date, confirmed that the evidence of warming is "unequivocal." Global warming is real and human activity is the main cause. The consequences are mainly negative and headed toward catastrophic, unless we act. However, the good news is that we can meet this challenge. It is not too late, and we have everything we need to get started.

As many know, the Chinese expression for "crisis" consists of two characters side by side. The

"Vice President Al Gore's Perspective on Global Warming," testimony before the United States Senate Environmental and Public Works Committee, March 21, 2007.

first symbol means "danger." The second symbol means "opportunity." I would like to discuss both the danger and the opportunity here today.

First of all, there is no longer any serious debate over the basic points that make up the consensus on global warming. The ten warmest years on record have all been since 1990. Globally, 2005 was the hottest of all. In the United States, 2006 was the warmest year ever. The winter months of December 2006 through February 2007 make up the warmest winter on record. These rising temperatures have been accompanied by many changes. Hurricanes are getting stronger. Sea levels are rising. Droughts are becoming longer and more intense. Mountain glaciers are receding around the world.

New evidence shows that it may be even worse than we thought. For example, a recent study published by the University of Alaska–Fairbanks indicates that methane is leaking from the Siberian permafrost at five times the predicted levels. Methane is 23 times as potent a greenhouse gas as carbon dioxide and there are billions of tons underneath the permafrost.

However, there is a great deal of new momentum for action to solve the climate crisis. Today, I am here to deliver more than a half million messages to Congress asking for real action on global warming. More than 420 mayors have now adopted Kyoto-style commitments in their cities and have urged strong federal action. The evangelical and faith communities have begun to take the lead, calling for measures to protect God's creation. The State of California, under a Republican governor and a Democratic legislature, passed strong, economy-wide legislation mandating cuts in carbon dioxide. Twenty-two states and the District of Columbia have passed renewable energy standards for the electricity sector. Much more needs to be done, but change is in the air.

I do not believe that the climate crisis should be a partisan political issue. I just returned from the United Kingdom, where last week the two major parties put forward their climate change platforms. The Tory and Labour parties are in vigorous competition with one another—competing to put forward the best solution to the climate crisis. I look forward to the day when we return to this way of thinking here in the U.S.

The climate crisis is, by its nature, a global problem—and ultimately the solution must be global as well. The best way—and the only way—to get China and India on board is for the U.S. to demonstrate real leadership. As the world's largest economy and greatest superpower, we are uniquely situated to tackle a problem of this magnitude.

After all, we have taken on problems of this scope before. When England and then America and our allies rose to meet the threat of global Fascism, together we won two wars simultaneously in Europe and the Pacific.

This is a moral moment of similar magnitude. This is not ultimately about any scientific discussion or political dialogue. It is about who we are as human beings and our capacity to transcend our limitations and rise to meet this challenge.

The solutions to this problem are accessible, but politically—at least in the near term—seem quite difficult. In practice, however, they will turn out to be much easier than they appear to us now.

For example, the Montreal Protocol on Substances that Deplete the Ozone Layer, first negotiated in the 1980s, was opposed by industry for fear it would hurt the economy because its provisions were too stringent. However, governments and industry rose to meet the challenge and the treaty was strengthened twice in quick succession to quickly ramp down the chemicals that were causing the hole in the ozone layer.

There are some who will say that acting to solve this crisis will be costly. I don't agree. If we solve it in the right way, we will save money and boost productivity. Moreover, the consequences of inaction would be devastating to both the environment and the economy. Recent reports make that clear.

When I think about the climate crisis today I can imagine a time in the future when our children and grandchildren ask us one of two questions. Either they will ask: What were you thinking, didn't you care about our future? Or they will ask: How did you find the moral courage to cross party lines and solve this crisis? We must hear their questions now. We must answer them with our actions, not merely with our promises. We must choose a future for which our children and grandchildren will thank us.

Discussion Questions

1. Gore maintains that the current global warming crisis presents us with both opportunities and dangers. What does he mean by this? Relate your answer to your own experience.
2. Do our children and future generations have a right to a bright future? If so, what is the basis of this right and what duties does it impose on you, regarding climate change, both as an individual and as a citizen in a democracy?

3. Discuss how Aldo Leopold might respond to Gore's analysis of the problem of global warming as well as his proposed solutions. What policies might Leopold suggest for reducing global warming?

4. Al Gore, in his film *An Inconvenient Truth,* argues that global warming is primarily a moral rather than a political issue. As people who have contributed to the problem of global warming, we have a moral obligation to think about the consequences of our habits and lifestyle choices. In particular he asks, "Are you ready to change the way you live?" In what ways are you a responsible steward of the environment? Discuss modifications you might make in your lifestyle and career plans to lessen the negative effects of climate change and global warming. Be specific.

5. People from affluent nations such as the United States contribute disproportionately to global warming. Despite this, there has been little change in the consumer-oriented lifestyles of Americans. Do we as Americans have a moral obligation to change our lifestyles so we don't continue contributing to global warming? If so, should legislation be passed to enforce lifestyle changes? Support your answers. Discuss how a utilitarian would most likely answer these questions.

KAREN J. WARREN

The Power and the Promise of Ecological Feminism, Revisited

Karen Warren is a philosophy professor at Macalester College in St. Paul, Minnesota. Warren argues that the domination of women and the domination of nature are both grounded in the same logic of domination and value-hierarchy thinking. Therefore, feminism and environmental ethics are conceptually inseparable.

Critical Reading Questions

1. What is "ecofeminism"?
2. What groups constitute "Others" in Western culture?
3. What are the six basic claims of Warren's ecofeminist philosophy?
4. What is an "oppressive conceptual framework"? What are the five common features of oppressive conceptual frameworks?

This essay is an updated version of Karen J. Warren, "The Power and the Promise of Ecofeminism," *Environmental Ethics* 12, no. 3 (Summer 1990): 125–146. From "The Power and the Promise of Ecofeminism, Revisited," in Michael E. Zimmerman et al., eds., *Environmental Philosophy: From Animal Rights to Radical Ecology*, 4th ed. Upper Saddle River, NJ: Pearson Prentice Hall, 2005, pp. 252, 253, 255–258, 272–275, 277–279.

5. What is a "logic of domination"? What are the assumptions supporting it?
6. How is a logic of domination used to justify both oppression of women and oppression of nature?
7. According to Warren, why is the first-person narrative an effective means of raising important issues in environmental ethics?
8. What is the difference between the "loving eye" and the "arrogant eye"?
9. How does loving perception influence how we define the moral community?

INTRODUCTION TO ECOFEMINIST PHILOSOPHY

Ecofeminism is an ecological and feminist position that takes gender as a starting point for providing analyses of and solutions to the unjustified domination of human and nonhuman Others. These "Others" are those who are excluded, marginalized, exploited, devalued, or naturalized—who become "Others"—in systems of unjustified domination-subordination relationships. At least in Western, Euro-American cultures, "Others" includes both "human Others," such as women, people of color, children, and the poor, and "earth Others," such as animals, forests, the land.

One approach to ecofeminism is known as "ecofeminist philosophy." Ecofeminist philosophy assumes that the domination of Others by the dominant group or culture is neither justified nor inevitable. . . . Ecofeminist philosophy involves advancing positions, advocating strategies, and recommending solutions to the domination and exploitation of Others.

ECOFEMINIST PHILOSOPHY: THE VERSION DEFENDED HERE

Six basic claims characterize the version of ecofeminist philosophy I defend: (1) There are important interconnections among the unjustified dominations of women, other human Others, and nonhuman nature: (2) understanding the nature of these interconnections is important to an adequate understanding of and solutions to these unjustified dominations; (3) feminist philosophy should include ecofeminist insights into women–other human Others–nature interconnections; (4) solutions to gender issues should include ecofeminist insights into women–other human Others–nature connections; (5) solutions to environmental problems should include ecofeminist insights into women–other human Other–nature interconnections; and, (6) ecofeminist philosophy and practice must provide proactive, creative, life-affirming solutions and communities, including ecological communities.

This version of ecofeminist philosophy grows out of and is responsive to the intersection of at least three overlapping areas of concern: feminism (and all the issues feminism raises concerning women and other human Others); nature (the natural environment), science (especially scientific ecology), development, and technology; and local or indigenous perspectives. . . .

OPPRESSIVE CONCEPTUAL FRAMEWORKS

Insofar as ecofeminist philosophy is concerned with *conceptual analysis,* a basic place to start to understand ecofeminist philosophy is with its analysis of "oppressive conceptual frameworks." A *conceptual framework* is a set of basic beliefs, values, attitudes, and assumptions which shape and reflect how one views oneself and one's world. A conceptual framework functions as a socially constructed *lens* through which one perceives reality. It is affected and shaped by such factors as sex-gender, race/ethnicity, class, age, affectional orientation, marital status, religion, nationality, colonial influences, and culture.

An *oppressive* conceptual framework is one that functions to explain, maintain, and "justify" relationships of unjustified domination and subordination. When an oppressive conceptual framework is *patriarchal,* it functions to justify the subordination of women by men.

There are five common features of an oppressive conceptual framework. First, an oppressive conceptual framework involves *value-hierarchical thinking,* that is, "Up-Down" thinking, which attributes greater value to that which is higher, or "Up," than to that which is lower, or "Down." It may put men "Up" and women "Down," whites "Up" and people of color "Down," culture "Up" and nature "Down," minds "Up" and bodies "Down." By attributing greater value to that which is higher, the Up-Down organization of reality serves to legitimate inequality. . . .

Second, an oppressive conceptual framework encourages *oppositional value dualisms,* that is, disjunctive pairs in which the disjuncts are seen as exclusive (rather than inclusive) and oppositional (rather than complementary) and that places higher value (status, prestige) on one disjunct than the other. Examples include value dualisms that give higher status to that which has historically been identified as "male," "white," "rational," and "culture" than to that which has historically been identified as "female," "black," "emotional," and "nature" (or "natural"). According to these value dualisms, it is better to be male, white, or rational, than female, black, or emotional.

Third, an oppressive conceptual framework conceptualizes power primarily as *"power-over" power.* Although there are other kinds of power, in oppressive systems power is understood and exercised as justified power of Ups over Downs. . . . When power-over power serves to reinforce the power of Ups in ways that keep Downs unjustifiably subordinated (which not all cases of power-over power do), such conceptions and practices of power-over power are unjustified.

Fourth, an oppressive conceptual framework creates, maintains, or perpetuates a conception and practice of *privilege* as that systematically advantages Ups and not Downs in morally irrelevant or unjustified ways. The privileges of driving a car, taking out a home equity loan, living in high-income housing areas, or attending a college of one's choice should belong to those who qualify according to an appropriate principle of distributive justice. When the privilege of Ups functions to keep intact dominant-subordinate Up-Down relationships of power and privilege—to systematically advantage Ups over Downs on morally irrelevant or unjustified grounds—they are part of an oppressive conceptual framework and the sets of practices sanctioned by appeal to them.

Fifth, an oppressive conceptual framework sanctions a *logic of domination*—a logical structure of argumentation that "justifies" unjustified domination and subordination. A logic of domination provides the alleged moral stamp of approval for unjustified subordination, since, if accepted, it provides a justification for keeping Downs down. Typically this justification takes the form that the Up has some characteristic (e.g., reason or rationality) that the Down lacks and by virtue of which the subordination of the Down by the Up is justified. . . .

The problem with value-hierarchical thinking, value dualisms, and conceptions of power and privilege that systematically advantage Ups over Downs, is the way in which each of these has functioned historically in oppressive conceptual frameworks to establish the inferiority of Downs and to justify the subordination of Downs by Ups. The logic of domination is what provides that alleged justification of subordination.

THE IMPORTANCE OF THE LOGIC OF DOMINATION

Since the logic of domination provides the moral premise that "justifies" the subordination of Downs by Ups in Up-Down relationships of domination and subordination, the logic of domination is explanatorily basic to both oppressive conceptual frameworks and to behaviors and institutions of oppression. This is true for four reasons.

First, since a logic of domination functions *both* to explain *and* to justify domination-subordination relationships, it is more than simply a logical structure; it also involves a substantive value system.

This value system is what is needed to generate an allegedly morally relevant distinction between Ups and Downs (e.g., that Ups are rational and Downs are not), which, in turn, is used to sanction the justified subordination of what is Down. . . .

This construction of inferiority can take many forms, depending on historical and social contexts. It may not be consciously, knowingly, or even intentionally maintained. Its immediate (or, efficient) cause may be habit, custom, or unexamined prejudice. . . .

A second reason that a logic of domination is explanatorily basic is that without it, a description of similarities and differences would be just that—a description of similarities and differences. In order for differences to make a moral difference in how a group is treated or in the opportunities available to it, other moral premises must be accepted. The logic of domination is one such moral premise: it is necessary both to turn diversity (or difference) into domination and to justify that domination.

To illustrate how differences are turned into justified domination by a logic of domination, let us suppose (even if it turns out to be contrary to fact) that what is unique about humans is our conscious capacity to radically reshape our social environments to meet self-determined ends, as Murray Bookchin suggests.[1] Then one could claim that humans are better equipped to radically reshape their environments in consciously self-determined ways than are rocks or plants—a value-hierarchical way of speaking, without thereby sanctioning any domination or exploitation of the nonhuman environment. To justify such domination, one needs a *logic of domination*—a moral premise that specifies that superiority of humans as Ups (here, their superior ability to radically alter their environment in consciously self-determined ways) justifies the domination of nonhuman natural others as Others, as Downs (here, rocks or plants that do not have this ability).

It is helpful to formalize such reasoning, so that we can see clearly how the derivation of the conclusion about the justified domination of nonhuman nature rests on acceptance of two important claims: a claim about the moral superiority of humans over nonhuman entities on the basis of some ability humans have that nonhuman entities

lack (premise 2 below), and the claim that superiority justifies subordination—the "logic of domination" (premise 4 below):

(A) (1) Humans do, and plants and rocks do not, have the capacity to consciously and radically change the communities in which they live in self-determined ways.

(2) Whatever has the capacity to consciously and radically change the community in which it lives in self-determined ways is morally superior to whatever lacks this capacity.

Thus, (3) Humans are morally superior to plants and rocks.

(4) For any X and Y, if X is morally superior to Y, then X is morally justified in subordinating (dominating) Y.

Thus, (5) Humans are morally justified in subordinating (dominating) plants and rocks.

Notice that premise 2 might well be true; that is a topic debated in environmental philosophy. But even if 2 is true, without the logic of domination, 4, all one has are differences (even if morally relevant differences) between humans and some nonhumans. The moral superiority of humans over nonhuman natural beings, if it exists, does not *by itself* justify domination. In fact, one could argue that such moral superiority imposes on humans extraordinary responsibilities toward (rather than unjustified domination over) others less capable.

Third, a logic of domination is explanatorily basic because, at least in Western societies, the oppressive conceptual frameworks that have justified the dominations of women and nonhuman nature historically have been (at the very least) patriarchal. . . . At least in Western societies, women have been identified in art, literature, and philosophy with nature, body, and the realm of the physical, while men have been identified with culture, reason, and the realm of the mental. These contingent, historical associations occur within *both* patriarchal conceptual frameworks *and* patriarchal institutions and practices that then function to justify the subordination of women, nonhuman animals, and "nature." . . .

CLIMBING FROM TRADITIONAL AND FEMINIST ETHICS TO ECOFEMINIST ETHICS

In articulating feminist ethical positions, many feminists, including ecofeminists, have argued for the relevance of narrative as a way of raising philosophically germane issues in ethics. Unlike more traditional approaches to ethics, a narrative approach contextualizes ethical discourse in ways that make relationships and beings-in-relationships central to ethics. The underlying assumption is that the use of narrative can be more than just a helpful literary device for describing ineffable experience or a methodology for documenting personal and social history; it can be an invaluable vehicle for revealing what is ethically significant in human interactions with humans and the nonhuman world.

So it is that I now turn to a personal narrative I wrote in 1980, after my first rock climbing experience, to describe the process by which my own philosophical thinking, especially about ethics, developed along ecofeminist lines. It was through this experience that I realized early-on in my professional career that a different conception of ethics than traditional philosophical ethics provided was badly needed to capture some of the most important features of ethics, ethical theory, and humans as ethical agents.

On my first day of rock climbing I chose a somewhat private spot, away from other climbers and on-lookers. After studying "the chimney," I focused all my energy on making it to the top. I climbed with intense determination, using whatever strength and skills I had to accomplish this challenging feat. By midway I was exhausted and anxious. I couldn't see what to do next—where to put my hands or feet. Growing increasingly more weary as I clung somewhat desperately to the rock, I made a move. It didn't work. I fell. There I was, dangling midair above the rocky ground below, frightened but terribly relieved that the belay rope had held me. I knew I was safe. I took a look up at the climb that remained. I was determined to make it to the top. With renewed confidence and concentration, I finished the climb to the top.

On my second day of climbing, I rappelled down about 200 feet from the top of the Palisades at Lake Superior to just a few feet above the water level. I could see no one—not my belayer not the other climbers, no one. I unhooked slowly from the rappel rope and took a deep cleansing breath. I looked all around me—really looked—and listened. I heard a cacophony of voices—birds, trickles of water on the rock before me, waves lapping against the rocks below. I closed my eyes and began to feel the rock with my hands—the cracks and crannies, the raised lichen and mosses, the almost imperceptible nubs that might provide a resting place for my fingers and toes when I began to climb. At that moment I was bathed in serenity. I began to talk to the rock in an almost inaudible, childlike way, as if the rock were my friend. I felt an overwhelming sense of gratitude for what it offered me—a chance to know myself and the rock differently, to appreciate unforeseen miracles like the tiny flowers growing in the even tinier cracks in the rock's surface. I came to know a sense of myself as *being in relationship* with the natural environment. It felt as if the rock and I were silent conversational partners in a longstanding friendship. I realized then that I had come to *care about* this cliff which was so different from me, so unmovable and invincible, independent and seemingly indifferent to my presence. I wanted to be *with the rock* as I climbed. Gone was the fierce determination to conquer the rock, to forcefully impose my will on it; I wanted simply to work respectfully with the rock as I climbed. And as I climbed, that is what I felt. I felt myself *caring* about this rock and feeling thankful that climbing provided the opportunity for me to know it and myself in this new way.

This narrative reflects only one person's—my—experience. But since it was through this narrative that I personally began to appreciate the significance of narrative to ethics (including ecofeminist ethics), I want to describe now four features of narrative that I came to see as philosophically significant.

First, narrative can give voice to a felt sensitivity, an emotional disposition, or an attitude, too often lacking in traditional analytic ethical discourse—a sensitivity to conceiving of oneself as fundamentally a being in relationship with others, including other animals and the nonhuman natural world. Narrative is a modality that *takes relationships seriously*. It thereby stands in contrast to a strictly reductionist modality that takes relationships seriously only or primarily because of the nature of the *relators* or parties to those relationships (e.g., relators conceived as moral agents, right-holders, interest-carriers, or sentient beings). A climber's relationship with the rock is itself a locus of value, in addition to and independent of whatever moral status the rock may have.

Second, narrative can give expression to a variety of ethical attitudes and behaviours overlooked or underplayed in mainstream Western ethics (e.g., a difference in attitudes and behaviours toward a rock when one is "making it to the top" and when one thinks of oneself as "friends with" or "caring about" the rock one climbs). These different attitudes and behaviours suggest an ethically germane contrast between types of relationships humans may have toward a rock. . . .

The ability to express felt differences between conquering and caring attitudes in relation to nonhuman animals and the natural environment provides a third reason why the use of narrative is important to ecofeminist ethics. Narrative provides a way of conceiving of ethics and ethical meaning as *emerging out of* particular situations moral agents find themselves in, rather than as being *imposed* on those situations as a derivation from some predetermined, abstract rule or principle. This emergent feature of narrative centralizes the importance of *voice*. When a multiplicity of cross-cultural voices are centralized, narrative is able to give expression to a range of attitudes, values, beliefs, and behaviours that may be overlooked or silenced by imposed ethical meaning and theory.

Lastly, the use of narrative has argumentative significance by suggesting *what counts* as an appropriate conclusion to an ethical situation. Jim Cheney calls attention to this feature of narrative when he claims, "To contextualize ethical deliberation is, in some sense, to provide a narrative or a story, from which the solution to the ethical dilemma emerges as the fitting conclusion."[2] Since

I experienced both, my own narrative helped me realize that my conqueror attitude was at odds with my ethical attitude toward mountains and rocks as deserving of respect and care, not domination and conquest.

Marilyn Frye's work helped me appreciate the ethical significance of these two attitudes. In her essay, "In and Out of Harm's Way: Arrogance and Love," Frye contrasts "the arrogant eye" ("arrogant perception") with "the loving eye" ("loving perception") as one way of getting at this distinction in the ethical attitudes of care and conquest:

> The loving eye is a contrary of the arrogant eye.
>
> The loving eye knows the independence of the other. It is the eye of a seer who knows that nature is indifferent. It is the eye of one who knows that to know the seen, one must consult something other than one's own will and interests and fears and imagination. One must look at the thing. One must look and listen and check and question.
>
> The loving eye is one that pays a certain sort of attention. This attention can require a discipline but not a self-denial. The discipline is one of self-knowledge, knowledge of the scope and boundary of the self. . . . In particular, it is a matter of being able to tell one's own interests from those of others and of knowing where one's self leaves off and another begins.[3]

According to Frye, the loving eye "knows the complexity of the other as something that will forever present new things to be known." It is not an invasive, coercive eye that annexes others to itself. . . .

The ecofeminist ethic I defend involves this shift in attitude of humans toward the nonhuman world from arrogant perception to loving perception (or what I sometimes call "caring perception"). Arrogant perception of others presupposes and maintains *sameness* in such a way that it expands the moral community only to those beings who are thought to resemble (be like, similar to, or the same as) "us" in some morally significant way. An ethic based on arrogant perception thereby builds a moral hierarchy of beings and assumes some common denominator of moral considerability by virtue of which like beings deserve similar treatment or moral consideration and unlike beings do not. . . .

In contrast, loving (or caring) perception presupposes and maintains difference—a distinction between the self and other, between human and at least some nonhumans and nature—in such a way that it is an expression of care about the other who/that is recognized at the outset as independent, dissimilar, different. . . .

An attitude of loving perception toward nonhuman animals and the natural world raises issues about what it means for humans to care about the nonhuman world, a world acknowledged as being independent, different, perhaps even indifferent to humans. Humans *are* different from rocks in important ways, even if they are also both members of a shared or common ecological community. A moral community based on loving perception of oneself in relationship with a rock is one that acknowledges and respects difference, in addition to whatever sameness or commonality also exists. The limits of loving perception are determined only by the limits of one's (e.g. a person's, a community's) ability to care—whether it is care about other humans, nonhuman animals, or the nonhuman world. . . .

One of the goals of ecofeminism is the eradication of all unjustified systems of domination and the creation of a diverse, ecologically sustainable, life-affirming world in which difference does not breed domination—say, a world in 4001.

In 4001, an adequate environmental ethic would be an ecofeminist environmental ethic and the prefix "ecofeminist" would be redundant and unnecessary. Similarly, the prefix environmental in "environmental ethics" would be redundant and unnecessary. But this is *not* 4001, and the current historical and conceptual reality, at least in Western cultures, is that the unjustified dominations of women, other human Others, nonhuman animals and nature are intimately interconnected. Failure to notice or make visible these interconnections in the present perpetuates the mistaken and privileged view that environmental ethics is *not* a feminist issue, that nonhuman animals and nature are *not* feminist issues, and that the prefix eco-*feminist* adds nothing significant to environmental ethics and feminism. . . .

NOTES

1. Murray Bookchin, 'Social Ecology versus 'Deep Ecology," in *Green Perspectives: Newsletter of the Green Program Project* (Summer 1987), 9.
2. Jim Cheney, "Eco-Feminism and Deep Ecology," *Environmental Ethics* 9, no. 2 (Summer 1987), 144.
3. Marilyn Frye, "In and Out of Harm's Way: Arrogance and Love," in *Politics of Reality* (Freedom, CA: The Crossing Press, 1983), 75–6.

Discussion Questions

1. Discuss Warren's claim that being a feminist entails being an ecofeminist. How might Leopold and Cohen each respond to this claim?
2. Care ethicist Nel Noddings, in her article at the end of Chapter 1, maintains that we cannot have meaningful caring relationships with nonhuman animals or the environment. How might Warren respond to Noddings? Discuss which person presents the more compelling argument and why.
3. Using the first-person narrative, describe a recent experience you have had in the "outdoors." Does the use of the narrative make you aware, or more aware, of your relationship with the environment? Discuss some of the philosophical and ethical issues raised by your narrative.
4. President Obama wants to double our use of alternative energy and reduce our dependence on fossil fuel. Discuss and evaluate different strategies proposed for achieving this goal. Which strategies represent what Warren calls the patriarchal "arrogant" perspective, and which represent the ecofeminist "loving" perspective? Based on this distinction, discuss which strategies you would support and why.

5. Are legislative proposals in the United States that call on businesses to reduce their emissions of greenhouse gases ineffective in part because they do not take into account the partriarchal nature of big business and government? Discuss how an ecofeminist such as Warren might respond to this question.

CASE STUDIES

1. ANIMAL LIBERATION IN THE SCIENCE LAB

The Animal Liberation Front (ALF) is a loose organization of radical animal-rights activists in thirty-eight countries who target science laboratories, slaughterhouses, and the fur and lumber industries. In 2008 alone the North American branches of ALF engaged in 183 reported direct actions. One of the most publicized actions in the United States took place in May 1984, when five members of the ALF broke into the Experimental Head Injury Lab at the University of Pennsylvania and stole files and videotapes of experiments. The videotapes showed gruesome scenes of terrified baboons in vises with their heads being smashed by pistons while the researchers joked around. The tapes showed operations being performed on primates without regard for their pain or for standard research procedures. After taking the videotapes, the ALF ransacked the lab.

In the controversy that followed the release of the tapes to the public, Dr. Thomas Gennarelli, the director of the lab, defended the research, claiming that the animals had been properly treated. He also accused the ALF of setting back medical research. Both the university and the National Institutes of Health (NIH), which gave the lab a new grant to repair the damage, supported Dr. Gennarelli.

The ALF responded to the accusation by comparing the lab experiments to those conducted by Nazi Dr. Joseph Mengele on Jews in concentration camps. Protesters supported the ALF by staging demonstrations on campuses and at the offices of the NIH. In 1985 the secretary of Health and Human Services stopped federal funding for the head injury program, and the university agreed to pay a fine for violating the Animal Welfare Act. The members of the ALF were not prosecuted for their actions.

Although the ALF defines itself as nonviolent, the FBI regards groups such as the ALF and its sister organization the Earth Liberation Front (ELF) as "violent animal rights extremists and eco-terrorists [who] now pose one of the most serious terrorist threats to the nation."[28] In 2006 the United States Department of Homeland Security designated the AFL a "terrorist threat."

Discussion Questions

1. Were stealing the tapes and ransacking the lab morally justified? Support your answers. Discuss how a utilitarian, such as Peter Singer, might respond to these questions.
2. Discuss how an abolitionist, a reformist, and a status quo person would respond to this case. What solutions would each of them most likely propose?

3. Would the experiments have been morally justified if Dr. Gennarelli had not violated the Animal Welfare Act and if it could be shown that thousands of human lives have been saved as a result of these experiments? Support your answer.

4. Is the AFL a terrorist organization? Support your answer. Discuss how Leopold and Warren might each answer this question.

5. The Animal Rights Direct Action Coalition has targeted McDonald's restaurants. They drive up to a McDonald's in a pickup truck with a dead cow in the back and a sign reading "Here's your lunch." Discuss the moral implications of these tactics.

2. USING ANIMALS FOR XENOTRANSPLANTS

In 2008 more than 100,000 people in the United States were waiting for organ transplants, according to the United Network for Organ Sharing, which oversees organ donations. Most of these people will die before a suitable donor is found. Xenotransplants, the transplanting of organs from one species of animal into another, may offer a solution to this shortage.

The first animal-to-human transplant occurred in 1906, when French physician Mathieu Jaboulay transplanted a kidney from a pig into a woman. Neither the woman nor the pig survived the procedure. Since then several people have received organs from pigs and baboons. Although baboons are genetically closer to humans, many researchers prefer pigs for xenotransplants because pigs are anatomically very similar to humans. They are also healthier, less likely to carry viruses, and easier to breed. At Duke University, scientists are genetically engineering pigs with human genes so that their livers will be more compatible with humans.

In 2001 the Secretary's Advisory Committee on Xenotransplantation (SACX) was formed to advise the U.S. Department of Health and Human Services. Since other animals, such as pigs, carry viruses that are harmless to them but might be lethal to humans, one concern is the risk of inadvertently introducing an infectious disease via a xenotransplant. Another issue of concern is using children in xenotransplant experiments.

Discussion Questions

1. Although many people have ethical qualms about using baboons for xenotransplants because of their similarity to humans, they have fewer objections to using pigs because pigs are already slaughtered for food. Are we being speciesists in making such a distinction? Support your answer.

2. At what point do animals genetically engineered to have human genes become human and, as such, deserving of the moral respect we normally give other humans? Support your answer. Discuss how Cohen might respond to this question.

3. Xenotransplants raise the possibility of outbreaks of new infectious diseases. Retroviruses that may be harmless in other species can be potentially deadly in humans. For example, many researchers believe that AIDS was transmitted to humans from

monkeys. If xenotransplants might endanger healthy human populations, should they be banned or more closely regulated? Support your answers.

4. Weigh the rights, if any, of nonhuman animals such as pigs and baboons against those of humans who need organ transplants. Discuss whether it is morally acceptable to sacrifice the lives of other animals for humans whose organs have been damaged by their destructive lifestyles, such as heavy drinking or smoking. Support your answer. Discuss how Cohen and Singer might respond to this question.

3. THE ABANDONED CAT[29]

David had always wanted a cat. Although pets were forbidden in his dormitory, shortly after he moved to college David went to the local animal shelter and adopted a young cat, which he kept confined in his room. At the end of the year, David moved back home and left the cat to fend for itself.

After several weeks of wandering around campus, the cat was taken in by one of the department secretaries, who took pity on it. By this time the cat was near starvation; it also had a rash that had caused it to lose much of its fur. The secretary knew that one of the professors in the department, Professor Carey, was thinking of getting a cat. Professor Carey agreed to take the cat home.

When the cat's rash did not clear up, Professor Carey took it to the veterinarian. The vet told the professor that the cat had multiple allergies and would have to receive cortisone shots as well as eat a special diet. In addition, the cat had an overactive thyroid that would require an expensive operation or else medication for the rest of its life. The medication would cost approximately $30 a month and would have to be given to the cat three times a day at six-hour intervals. After thinking about it, Professor Carey decided that the expense and inconvenience were not worth it. She asked the veterinarian to euthanize the cat.

Discussion Questions

1. What are the professor's moral obligations, if any, toward the cat? Is it morally acceptable for her to euthanize the cat? Or does the cat's interest in staying alive outweigh the professor's inconvenience? Are there any conditions under which it is morally acceptable to have an animal companion euthanized? Support your answers. Discuss how Narveson, Cohen, and Singer might respond to this question.

2. Discuss whether it was morally acceptable for David to adopt a cat from the animal shelter, knowing that it was against the rules to keep a cat in the dormitory and knowing that he could not take the cat home with him once the school year ended.

3. Some animal-rights activists, such as Regan, argue that owning house pets (animals that are kept inside or allowed outside only on a leash or in an enclosure) is a type of slavery. Do you agree? Can having a pet or animal companion be compatible with respect? Support your answers.

4. A lot of animal shelters do not allow college students to adopt cats and dogs. Is this policy a violation of the autonomy of college students? Support your answer.

4. ZOOS: PRISONS OR HAVENS?

The first modern zoos were established in Europe in the nineteenth century. Britain's famous London Zoo was opened in the nineteenth century to house animals brought back from British colonies around the world. In the early 1990s, the London Zoo became mired in a financial crisis because of the mismanagement of funds and a steady drop in attendance. Like other zoos around the world, it had also come under attack from animal-rights activists.

In 1993 it was announced that the London Zoo would have to close down. A high-profile "Save Our Zoo" campaign, however, raised enough money to keep the zoo going. Supporters of the zoo argued that zoos are often the first contact young people have with "wild" animals. They also noted the important role that the London Zoo plays in educating people about conservation and in saving endangered species.

Opponents respond that watching captive and anguished animals is hardly a good introduction. The use of documentaries of animals in their natural habitat is a more realistic way to educate young people. They also argue that conservation, including the preservation of endangered species, should take place within the animals' natural habitats.

Discussion Questions

1. Are zoos ever morally justified? If so, under what conditions? What about safari parks, such as Six Flags or Disney's Animal Kingdom, where animals roam free, within limits, and the people remain in their cars? Support your answers.
2. While it may be possible to protect some of these species, such as the black rhino, within their natural habitats, in other cases the habitats have been destroyed by human encroachment. The destruction of the rain forests in Central and South America for agricultural land has already resulted in the extinction of hundreds of species of animals. Discuss whether in such cases the continuation of zoos is morally justified as a means of preserving endangered species. Discuss how Leopold, Devall, and Sessions might each respond.
3. Discuss the institution of zoos in light of Warren's ecofeminist analysis. In what ways, if any, do zoos, and the continued justification of zoos, illustrate a dualistic, patriarchal ideology?

---

5. THE "BAMBI BOOM"

The Teneja family were on the way to the College of William and Mary where nineteen-year-old Baninder Teneja was starting a summer research project. As they exited Interstate 95 on a side trip to nearby Lake Anna, a panicked deer struck and careened off a van ahead of them and came crashing through their front window. Baninder, who was riding in the back seat, was fatally injured when she was struck by the decapitated head of the deer before it smashed through their back window.

This was just one of an estimated 1.5 million deer/vehicle collisions that occur in the United States each year, causing more than 150 human fatalities. Vehicle/deer accidents are causing increasing concern as the deer population in the United States continues to grow at an unprecedented rate. In many parts of the United States, the deer population is two to four times what it was in pre-European times. This population explosion is due to a number of factors, including the milder winters of the last decade and a decline in the number of natural predators such as the wolf.

Humans aren't the only ones being negatively impacted by the "Bambi boom." Some scientists predict that the deer population, if left unchecked, could lead to the catastrophic disintegration of certain biotic communities. Overbrowsing by deer not only damages their own habitat but reduces vegetation that butterflies and songbirds use. Their eating habits are also threatening plant species such as orchids and lilies as well as eastern hemlock and white cedar trees.

Discussion Questions

1. Many people believe that the only way to control the deer herds is through culling—hunting deer with the goal of thinning out the herds. However, some animal-rights activists oppose the use of hunting to control deer populations, arguing that hunting is inconsistent with the belief that other animals have inherent worth. Do you agree? Discuss solutions that Singer and Regan might suggest to the Bambi boom.
2. Discuss how a utilitarian and an ecofeminist might approach the problem of the growing deer population.
3. Aldo Leopold supported the "harvesting" of deer herds to control their population. If what is right is defined in terms of preserving the "integrity, stability and beauty of the biotic community," would the land ethic also justify the culling of human populations where overpopulation is threatening the integrity of the biotic environment? Support your answer. Discuss how Leopold, Devall, and Sessions might respond to this question.
4. Working in small groups, develop an ethical public policy for dealing with the Bambi boom.

6. THE CAPE COD WIND FARM

If it gets the official go-ahead, the proposed $770 million wind farm in Nantucket Sound, Cape Cod, will be the largest in the world, providing clean energy for 75 percent of Cape Cod homes. Some residents of Cape Cod, however, oppose the project. They argue that the 130 offshore wind turbines will be unsightly, depressing property values and disrupting the pristine views from the beaches of Cape Cod, one of the most popular tourist destinations in the United States. Preventing global warming, they argue, does "not justify spoiling a view."[30] Opponents, including Senator Edward Kennedy, also maintain that the wind farm will harm the environment and damage the fishing industry.

A 2009 report by the U.S. Minerals Management Service, however, maintains that the project will have only a minimal environmental impact, except for a "moderate" effect on some sea birds. And, supporters point out, clean energy from wind power will help us lessen the impact of global warming. Indeed, when asked if he supported the Cape Cod wind farm, Al Gore replied that, absent some "fatal flaw," he thought it was a good idea. If approved, the wind farm should be in operation in 2011.

Discussion Questions

1. Using the utilitarian calculus, weigh the harms to the residents within view of the wind turbines against the benefits of the wind farm. Discuss whether the benefits justify constructing the wind farm over the objections of residents.
2. Supporters of the project admit that the blades of the turbines could kill more than 350 birds a year. However, they note that global warming and the use of oil-based fuels are responsible for the deaths of even more animals. Discuss how Peter Singer, Aldo Leopold, and Devall and Sessions might each respond to this argument.
3. Discuss whether we have a moral obligation to reduce our overall energy consumption or if it is morally permissible to continue our current level of consumption if we get a significant portion of it from alternative energy. Discuss your answer in terms of the impact of our energy consumption on global well-being.

---

7. EARTH'S DWINDLING FORESTS

People, like other animals, need nature in order to survive. We use trees for lumber to build our homes, the soil for growing crops, the earth as a source of minerals and energy. However, are there limits to how much we ought to use and, if so, what is the justification for these limits?

Most of the world's forests have been cleared by humans, including about 20 percent of the world's rain forests.[31] Tropical rain forests have been bulldozed to create land for cattle grazing, mining operations, hydroelectric dams, and the cultivation of export crops such as coffee. In addition to destruction of species and wildlife habitat, the lifestyles as well as the lives of indigenous peoples have been threatened by the clearing operations and by epidemics such as measles.

The rain forests are not the only forests that are being destroyed at an alarming rate. In the United States, the U.S. Forest Service has long regarded assisting the logging industry as one of its primary roles. There is little wilderness left in our national forests that is not crisscrossed with logging roads. In some cases the logging has threatened bird species with extinction and destroyed recreational areas, creating animosity between environmentalists and the businesses and workers whose livelihood depends on harvesting natural resources. Deforestation also reduces rainfall and contributes to global warming.

Discussion Questions

1. Discuss the prevailing attitude and practices regarding using natural resources in light of the ecofeminists' concept of the logic of dominance. What policies might Warren suggest for the human use of rain forests and our national forests?

2. Americans drink one-third of the world's coffee.[32] Much of this coffee is grown on land that used to be rain forests. This is because coffee plants grown on bare land are much more productive than coffee plants that are shade-grown. Discuss whether we have a moral obligation either to give up coffee drinking or to drink only shade-grown coffee, even though it is more expensive and harder to find in stores.

3. One of the primary reasons for clearing rain forests is to raise beef for the U.S. market. Do we have a moral obligation to modify our lifestyle in order to use fewer natural resources? If so, what is the source of this moral obligation? Discuss how Regan, Narveson, Leopold, and Warren might each answer this question.

Glossary

abortion: The intentional termination of a pregnancy resulting in the death of the fetus.

absolute pacifism: The belief that all violence is wrong including violence that is done in self-defense.

active euthanasia: Taking direct action to bring about a patient's death.

addiction: A behavioral pattern of drug use characterized by the compulsive use of a drug, the securing of its supply, and a high tendency to relapse after withdrawal.

addiction, disease model of: The theory that addicts are ill, and thus are biologically different from nonaddicts.

addiction, moral model of: The view that addiction is a vice in which individuals freely choose to engage, and that overcoming addiction depends on willpower.

adultery: Consensual sexual intercourse between a married person and someone who is not his or her legal spouse.

affirmative action: Programs designed to encourage increased representation of minorities and women in employment and college admissions.

ahimsa: The Buddhist principle of nonhurting.

androgyny: The theory that men and women share the same nature and that the expression of this sameness is a desirable goal.

anthropocentrism: The belief that human beings are the central or most significant entities in the universe.

applied ethics: The application of normative ethics to real-life cases.

autonomy: Self-determination or the freedom to make one's own decisions.

beneficence, duty of: The duty to do good acts and to promote happiness.

binge drinking: The consumption of five or more drinks of alcohol in a short period of time.

blastocyst: The embryonic stage in mammals consisting of two to eight cells.

capital punishment: See *death penalty.*

capitalism, laissez-faire: An economic system based on the pursuit of rational and prudent self-interest, individual freedom, and minimal government interference.

care ethics: The metaethical theory that caring relationships are more important than impartial moral principles such as justice.

categorical imperative: A term introduced by Immanuel Kant to describe moral injunctions that are unconditionally binding on us.

censorship: The controlling or silencing of speech that is deemed offensive, dangerous, or inappropriate by a government or group.

chimera: Embryo created from the genetic material of two different species.

civil disobedience: The refusal, on moral grounds, to obey certain laws, for the purpose of trying to bring about a change in legislation or government policy.

cloning: The process of producing genetically identical individuals through asexual reproduction.

cohabitation: Unmarried people living together as sexual intimates.

colonialism: The subjection of people in one country to the authority of another country.

color-blind principle: The belief that public policy should not be based on racial considerations.

competent: In medical ethics, a patient who is rational and capable of making decisions about his or her own care.

conscientious objection: Opposition to war, in any form, based on moral or religious beliefs.

conscription: Compulsory, state-mandated military service.

conservatism: The position that the traditional state of affairs is the best and that there is no need for change.

cultural relativism: A type of ethical relativism that maintains that morality is created collectively by groups of humans and that it differs from culture to culture.

death penalty: Infliction of death by the state as punishment for a crime.

deep ecology: A movement begun in the mid-1970s that cultivates a sense of identification with nature.

deontology: The metaethical theory that duty is the basis of morality.

deterrence: In the death penalty debate, the argument that the more severe the punishment for a crime, the more other people are going to be discouraged or deterred from committing that crime.

discrimination: The treatment of others based on their group membership. Unjust discrimination is based on prejudice rather than relevant differences.

distributive justice: The duty to distribute the benefits and burdens of society in a fair manner.

divine command theory: The metaethical theory that something is moral merely because God approves of it.

doctrine of the mean: The doctrine, put forth by both Aristotle and Confucius, that moral virtues, in general, entail moderation or seeking the middle path between excess and deficit.

domestic violence: Violence between intimates or people living in the same household.

double effect, principle of: Principle that where a course of action is likely to have different effects, one morally desirable and the other not, it may be permissible to take that course as long as the desirable effect is intended but not the other.

doublethink: Simultaneously holding two contradictory views and believing both to be true.

drug abuse: Taking a drug for purposes other than those for which the drug was intended, and/or the illicit use of a drug that can cause physical and/or mental harm to oneself and/or others.

drugs: Chemicals that enter the bloodstream and predictably alter the way individuals feel.

ecocentrism: The view that humans are members, rather than conquerors, of the biotic community.

ecofeminism: A movement that links environmental ethics to feminism and animal rights, arguing that oppression of women, nonhuman animals, and nature are all grounded in the same logic of dominance.

environmental ethics: An ethic concerned with the moral basis of environmental responsibility, including the moral value of nonhuman nature, pollution, population control, food production, and preservation of wilderness and species diversity.

equality, principle of: The principle that it is unjust to treat beings differently unless we can show that there is a difference between them that is relevant to the differential treatment.

erotica: Literature and art dealing with sexual love.

ethical egoism: The ethical theory that we ought to act in a way that is in our own best self-interest.

ethical relativism: The theory that morality is created by people and that moral systems can be different for different people.

ethical subjectivism: A type of ethical relativism that claims that morality is relative to each individual person.

ethnocentrism: The belief that one's ethnic or cultural group is morally superior.

eugenics: The science of improving the genetic quality of offspring.

euthanasia: The act of painlessly bringing about the death of a person who is suffering from a terminal or incurable disease or condition. See also *active euthanasia, passive euthanasia,* and *physician-assisted suicide.*

extraordinary treatment: Medical treatment that provides no reasonable hope of benefiting a patient.

feminism: A broad movement that is committed to improving women's position in society.

fidelity, duty of: A moral duty that stems from a commitment or promise made in the past.

fighting words: Words that are inherently likely to provoke a violent reaction.

freedom of speech: The individual right to express opinions without interference from the government or other people.

gender essentialism: The belief that men and women have essentially different natures.

genetic engineering: Alteration of genetic material by artificial means.

genetic enhancement: Manipulation of genetic material in order to improve a person's phenotype.

gene therapy: Introduction of normal or desirable genes into cells to override deleterious genes. See also *germ line therapy* and *somatic cell therapy*.

genome: Genetic blueprint or code containing a complete set of chromosomes.

genotype: The genetic blueprint of a particular individual.

germ cells: The ova (eggs) and sperm.

germ line therapy: Genetic therapy that alters the genetic structure of the sperm and ova so that the genotype of future generations is also altered.

global warming: The increasing temperature of the earth over the past century due, at least in part, to the increase in air pollution.

globalization: The worldwide transmission of Western-style democracy and capitalism.

good will: A will that always acts from a sense of duty and reverence for moral law, without regard for consequences or for immediate inclinations.

gratitude, duty of: A duty based on past favors and unearned services.

habituation: A term used by Aristotle to describe the regular practice of virtuous behavior, much as one practices any other skill, until it becomes second nature.

hate crime: Criminal behavior that is motivated by hatred or bigotry against a particular group or community of individuals.

hate speech: Speech that is likely to provoke anger, alarm, or resentment in others on the basis of race, color, creed, religion, or gender.

homosexual: A person whose sexual attraction is exclusively, or almost exclusively, toward members of the same gender.

hospice: A setting for terminally ill patients that provides palliative care and companionship so they can live the last days of their lives as fully and pain-free as possible.

Human Genome Project: A worldwide cooperative effort to map the entire human genetic code.

in vitro fertilization: Fertilization of an ovum by a sperm outside of the woman's body in a laboratory.

incapacitation: A punishment, such as the death penalty or life imprisonment without parole, which ensures that criminals will never repeat their crimes.

institutional racism: Racism stemming from laws and social systems that are set up to provide advantages to one group of people at the expense of another group.

jihad: An Islamic term often taken to mean "holy war," but more broadly defined as an "effort."

just-war tradition: A framework of theories, guidelines, and beliefs regarding the question of what makes a war just.

justice, duty of: The duty to give each person equal consideration.

juvenile: In U.S. law, a person under the age of eighteen.

legitimate interests: In rights ethics, interests that do not prevent others from pursuing similar and equally important interests.

liberal feminism: The belief that men and women share a common nature and, consequently, that women can achieve liberation through equal access to opportunities and privileges enjoyed by men.

libertarian: A person who is opposed to social or political restraints on individual freedom.

liberty right: The right to be left alone to pursue one's legitimate interests without interference from the government or from others.

Manifest Destiny, doctrine of: The nineteenth-century doctrine that the United States had a divine right to expand its borders from coast to coast.

marginalization: The act of relegating beings or groups to the fringes or margins of the moral community.

Marxist feminism: The belief that the capitalist system is the cause of oppression of women.

McCarthyism: An atmosphere of distrust produced by Senator Joseph McCarthy when he used the free speech of individuals as evidence of their Communist allegiances. His followers believed that Communist ideas should be repressed in order to protect democratic values.

mercy, principle of: The principle based on the duty of non-maleficence that we have an obligation not to cause further pain and suffering and also to relieve pain and suffering.

metaethics: See *theoretical ethics*.

moral community: The community of all beings who have moral worth in themselves and, as such, deserve the protection and respect of the community.

moral development, stage theory of: Theory that humans move through distinct stages of moral development from egoist to acceptance of universal moral values.

moral dilemma: A situation in which there is a conflict between moral values such that no matter what solution is chosen, it will involve doing something that is wrong in order to do what is right.

morning-after pill: A high dose of birth control pills taken over the three days following intercourse to prevent ovulation, prevent fertilization, or prevent the blastocyst from implanting in the uterine wall.

multiculturalists: Individuals who believe that racism is based primarily on individual ignorance and that education can eliminate racism.

natural law ethics: The metaethical theory that morality is grounded in rational human nature.

natural rights ethics: The ethical theory that people's entitlements as members of society are the basis of ethics.

naturalist fallacy: A type of faulty reasoning in which it is argued that something is moral because it is natural.

noncombatant: An individual who does not serve as an agent of aggression in war.

nonmaleficence, duty of: The duty to do no harm and to prevent harm.

normative ethics: The study of the values and guidelines by which we live.

objectivist theory: The metaethical theory that morality is discovered by humans and that universal moral truths exist that are true for all humans.

opinion: A statement that is based on feeling rather than on fact.

pacifism: An opposition to war or violence based on principle.

palliative care: Pain relief, comfort, and compassion.

"partial-birth" abortion: Late-term form of abortion that involves partial delivery of a live fetus baby.

passive euthanasia: Withholding or withdrawing medical treatment, resulting in a patient's death.

paternalism: Relationship in which an authority, such as the government or a physician, overrides a person's own decision and decides what is best for that person in order to protect him or her.

patriarchy: Social organization in which men hold the positions of authority.

persons: Beings who are worthy of respect as valuable in themselves rather than because of their usefulness or value to others; members of the moral community.

physician-assisted suicide: A type of active euthanasia in which a physician assists a patient in bringing about his or her death.

political correctness: In academia, subscribing to particular views based on their popularity, rather than their truth, and the suppression of opposing views.

pornography: Material featuring actual or unmistakably simulated or unmistakably threatened violence presented in a sexually explicit fashion with a predominant focus on the sexually explicit violence.

prejudice: Personal judgment that is based on negative feelings and stereotypes rather than reason.

prima facie duty: A duty that is morally binding unless it conflicts with a more pressing moral duty.

pro-choice: In the abortion debate, the position that a woman should have the right to make her own choice about whether or not to have an abortion at any time during the pregnancy.

pro-life: In the abortion debate, the position that abortion is immoral except when it is used to save the life of the mother.

proportionality: A principle of retributive justice in which the severity of the punishment must be proportionate to the crime.

psychological egoism: The theory that humans by nature are selfish and out for themselves.

race: A loose classification of groups of people based on physical characteristics; a social construct that forms an important component of personal identity.

racial profiling: The routine, and often unconscious, practice by police or other law enforcement agents of targeting suspects on the basis of their race or ethnicity.

racism: An ideology or worldview based on the belief that people can be classified according to race and that some races are morally inferior to others.

radical feminism: The theory that men are socialized to be both protectors and sexual predators, and that women are objectified by men as objects of sexual violence.

rape: Nonconsensual sex.

reciprocity, principle of: The moral principle in Confucian ethics that states that we have a moral duty to treat others as we would wish to be treated ourselves.

reductionism: The belief in science and medicine that the human body can be reduced to or described as an elaborate machine.

reparation, duty of: A duty that stems from past harms to others.

restitution: Reparation made by giving a person or group compensation for past harms.

retributive justice: The principle that punishment for wrongdoing should be in proportion to the crime.

retributive justice: In the death penalty debate, the idea that those who violate other people's right to life by murdering them in turn forfeit their own right to life.

same-sex marriage: Marriage between two people of the same gender.

satyagraha: In the philosophy of Mohandas "Mahatma" Gandhi, *satyagraha* is the skill of nonviolent resistance.

selective abortion: Abortion performed because a particular fetus, rather than the pregnancy itself, is unwanted, usually because the fetus has a genetic defect or is the "wrong gender."

self-improvement, duty of: The duty to improve our knowledge and virtue.

sentient being: A being with the capacity to experience pain and pleasure.

sexism: The worldview or belief that women are morally inferior to men.

sexual harassment: Unwanted sexual attention that makes a person feel uncomfortable at work, at school, or in social situations.

social contract: Agreement among individuals to freely give up some of their liberties in exchange for living in a well-ordered and just society.

sociobiology: The branch of biology that applies evolutionary theory to the social sciences.

sociological relativism: The observation that there is disagreement among cultures regarding moral values. Unlike cultural relativism, sociological relativism is neither an argument nor a moral theory. It is merely a descriptive statement about societies.

sociopath: A person without a conscience.

somatic cell therapy: Genetic therapy in which a normal or desirable gene is introduced into cells to override the effects of deleterious genes. The genetic structure of the germ cells remains unchanged.

speciesism: A term coined by utilitarian Peter Singer to describe a prejudice or bias in favor of the interests of members of one's own species and against those of members of another species.

speech codes: Codes that place restrictions on some forms of speech, such as hate speech, fighting words, or speech that violates civility codes.

state of nature: In Hobbes's philosophy, the hypothetical condition in which people lived before the formation of civil states.

stem cell: A cell that gives rise to a particular type of tissue. Embryonic stem cells have the potential to turn into any of the types of tissue that make up the human body.

stewardship: Religious doctrine that God has given humans dominion or stewardship over the lives of other animals and the planet.

supererogatory duty: A duty that exceeds the normal expectations of moral behavior.

surrogate motherhood: Arrangement whereby a woman agrees to gestate a child for another woman.

terrorism: The use of politically motivated violence that targets noncombatants and creates intimidation.

theoretical ethics: The subdivision of ethics concerned with appraising the logical foundations and internal consistencies of ethics systems.

theory: A conceptual framework for explaining a set of facts or concepts.

Third World: A term referring to nonindustrial or developing nations.

transgenic: Animals and plants with genes introduced from another species.

universalist theories: Metaethical theories that claim there are objective, universal moral principles and values that are true for all human beings.

utilitarianism: The metaethical theory that actions producing the most pleasure are good and those that produce pain are bad.

utility, principle of: Also known as the greatest happiness principle, it states that we have a duty to maximize pleasure or happiness and to minimize pain or unhappiness for the greatest number.

vegan: A person who abstains from all animal products, including eggs and milk.

vegetarian: A person who refrains from eating meat, poultry, and seafood.

veil of ignorance: A conceptual device used by John Rawls to establish a social contract that is unbiased and based on impartiality.

viability: In the abortion debate, the capacity of the fetus to survive disconnection from the placenta.

virtue: An admirable character trait or disposition to habitually act in a manner that benefits oneself and others.

virtue ethics: The metaethical theory concerned primarily with character and the type of people we should be rather than with our actions.

vivisection: Cutting or operating on a live animal for the sake of scientific research.

voluntary euthanasia: Intentionally bringing about the death of a competent patient at his or her request.

war: The use of armed violence between nations or between competing political factions within a nation to achieve a political purpose.

Way, the: In Eastern philosophy, the path of equilibrium and harmony.

weapons of mass destruction (WMD): Nuclear, chemical, and biological weapons that, unlike conventional weapons, indiscriminately target both combatants and noncombatants.

welfare rights: The right to receive primary social goods such as adequate nutrition, housing, education, and police and fire protection.

xenograph: Cross-species tissue transplantation.

Endnotes

CHAPTER 1

1. *Obedience* is available on video.

2. Stanley Milgram, *Obedience to Authority* (New York: Harper & Row, 1969), 6.

3. Elliot Turiel, Carolyn Hildebrandt, and Cecilia Wainryb, "Judging Social Issues: Difficulties, Inconsistencies, and Consistencies," *Monographs of the Society for Research in Child Development* 56, no. 2, 1991.

4. Lawrence Kohlberg, *The Philosophy of Moral Development* (New York: Harper & Row, 1981).

5. This is not to say that religious people are necessarily cultural relativists; many people who are religious believe that morality exists independently of religion; religious teachings confirm, rather than create, morality.

6. Gontran de Poncins, *Kabloona* (New York: Reynal & Hitchcock, 1941).

7. Nancy L. Jacobs, Alison Landes, and Mark A. Siegel (eds.), *Capital Punishment—Cruel and Unusual* (Wylie, Tex.: Information Plus, 1996), 85.

8. Turiel et al., "Judging Social Issues."

9. Stephen A. Satris, "Student Relativism," *Teaching Philosophy* 9, no. 3 (1986): 193–200.

10. Carol Gilligan, *In a Different Voice* (Cambridge, Mass.: Harvard University Press, 1982).

11. From Norma Haan, *On Moral Grounds: The Search for Practical Morality* (New York: New York University Press, 1985).

12. Adapted from Lawrence Kohlberg, *The Philosophy of Moral Development* (San Francisco: Harper & Row, 1984), 510–511.

13. Paul M. Valliant, "Personality, Peer Influence, and Use of Alcohol and Drugs by First-Year University Students," *Psychological Reports* 77, no. 2 (1995): 401–402.

14. Eva Skoe and Rhett Diessner, "Ethic of Care, Justice, Identity, and Gender: An Extension and Replication," *Merrill-Palmer Quarterly* 40, no. 2 (1994): 272–289.

15. Carol Gilligan and Jane Attanucci, "Two Moral Orientations: Gender Differences and Similarities," *Merrill-Palmer Quarterly* 34, no. 3 (1988): 223–227; R. Blotner and D. J. Bearison, "Developmental Consistencies in Socio-Moral Knowledge: Justice Reasoning and Altruistic Behavior," *Merrill-Palmer Quarterly* 30, no. 4 (1984): 349–357; Nancy Stiller and Linda Forrest, "An Extension of Gilligan and Lyon's Investigation of Morality: Gender Differences in College Students," *Journal of College Student Development* 31, no. 1 (1990): 54–63.

16. For more on moral development in college students, see Alexander Astin and Gregory Blimling, "Developing Character in College Students," *NASPA Journal* 27, no. 4 (1990): 268; and Dwight Boyd, "The Condition of Sophomoritis and Its Educational Cure," *Journal of Moral Education* 1 (1980): 24–39.

17. Children by the age of four, regardless of their culture, recognize the duty of justice, even though they mostly apply it egocentrically, protesting only when they are unjustly treated. William Damon, *The Moral Child* (New York: Free Press, 1993), 36.

18. The film *Obedience* on the Milgram study is an excellent example of this occurring.

19. James Rest, "Research on Moral Development: Implications for Training the Counseling Psychologist," *The Counseling Psychologist* 12, no. 2 (1984): 26.

20. Study by William Damon of Stanford University.

21. Although Confucianism and Buddhism are sometimes included under the rubric of religion, they are philosophies.

22. David Domke, "Divine Dictates?" *Baltimore Sun*, February 6, 2005.

23. See Kwame Gyekye, *An Essay on African Philosophical Thought: The Akan Conceptual Scheme* (New York: Cambridge University Press, 1964), 184–185.

24. An exception here is fundamentalist religion, such as fundamentalist Christianity or Islam, in which the Bible and the Qur'an are interpreted literally and are regarded as the final word on certain moral issues such as drinking and homosexuality.

25. Thomas Hobbes, *Leviathan* (New York: Macmillan, 1962), 100.

26. Ruut Veenhoven, *Conditions of Happiness* (Dordrecht, Netherlands: D. Reidel, 1984).

27. John Stuart Mill, "Utilitarianism," in *Utilitarianism*, ed. Mary Warnock (New York: Meridian Books, 1962), 257.

28. John Rawls, *A Theory of Justice* (Cambridge, Mass.: Belknap Press, 1971), 30.

29. Chang Wing-tsit, *A Source Book in Chinese Philosophy* (Princeton, N.J.: Princeton University Press, 1963), bk. 3:1.

30. Immanuel Kant, "Duties to Oneself," in *Lectures on Ethics* (Indianapolis: Hackett, 1775–1780/1963), 123.

31. Jeane Kirkpatrick, "Establishing a Viable Human Rights Policy," *World Affairs* (Winter 1980/81): 323–334.

32. Confucius, *The Analects*, bk. 2:1.

33. Adapted from Aristotle's *Nicomachean Ethics*, bk. 2.

34. Virginia Held, "The Meshing of Care and Justice," *Hypatia* 10, no. 2 (1995): 128–132.

CHAPTER 2

1. Centers for Disease Control, "Abortion Surveillance—United States 2007," *Surveillance Summaries*, November 23, 2007/55(SS9), p. 1.

2. Centers for Disease Control, "Abortion Surveillance—United States 2003," pp. 1–2.

3. Lawrence Finer et al., "Reasons U.S. Women Have Abortion: Quantitative and Qualitative Perspectives," *Perspectives on Sexual and Reproductive Health* 37, no. 3 (September 2005): 110–118.

4. "Abortion Statistics," www.abortiontv.com/Misc/AbortionStatistics.htm.

5. http://www.johnstonarchives.net/policy/abortion/wrip338sd.html.

6. Gilda Sedgh, "Legal Abortion Worldwide: Incidence and Recent Trends," *Perspectives on Sexual & Reproductive Health* 39, no. 4 (Dec. 2007): 216–225.

7. Brief of 281 American Historians as *Amici Curiae* Supporting the Appellees in *Webster v. Reproductive Services*, 1988.

8. James C. Mohr, *Doctors and the Law: Medical Jurisprudence in Nineteenth-Century America* (New York: Oxford University Press, 1993): 42–43.

9. Reva Siefel, "Reasoning from the Body: A Historical Perspective on Abortion Regulation and Questions of Sexual Protection," *Stanford Law Review* 44 (1992): 286.

10. Elizabeth Cady Stanton, "Child Murder," *The Revolution* 1, no. 10 (1868): 146–147.

11. Susan B. Anthony, "Marriage and Maternity," *The Revolution* 1, no. 1 (1869): 4.

12. Elizabeth Cady Stanton, "Infanticide," *The Revolution* 1, no. 4 (1868): 57–58.

13. Judith Blake, "Abortion and Public Opinion: The 1960–1970 Decade," *Science* 171 (1971): 540–548.

14. Clifford Grobstein, *Science and the Unborn* (New York: Basic Books, 1988), 109.

15. Alex M. Gallup and Frank Newport, eds., *The Gallup Poll: Public Opinion 2007* (Lanham, Md.: Rowman & Littlefield, 2008), 212.

16. Linda Sax et al., *The American Freshman National Norms for Fall 2007* (Higher Education Research Institute, University of California, Los Angeles, December 2007).

17. S. K. Henshaw, "Abortion Incidence and Services in the United States, 2000," *Family Planning Perspectives* 35 (January/February 2003).

18. For more on the Islamic Perspective, see "Abortion: Religious Traditions," Warren T. Reich, *Encyclopedia of Bioethics*, vol. 1 (New York: Simon & Schuster, 1995), 38–42.

19. "Data on 'Partial Birth' Abortion in the United States." November 28, 2006, www.johnstonarchive.net.

20. Robert J. White, "Partial-Birth Abortion: A Neurosurgeon Speaks," Testimony by U.S. House Committee on the Judiciary, June 19, 1996.

21. For a defense of this definition of personhood, see Baruch Brody, "The Morality of Abortion," in *Abortion and the Sanctity of Human Life: A Philosophical View* (Cambridge, Mass.: MIT Press, 1975).

22. Therese Hesketh and Zhu Wei Xing, "Abnormal Sex Ratios in Human Populations: Causes and Consequences," *Proceedings of the National Academy of Sciences* 3, no. 36 (September 5, 2006): 13271–13275.

23. Dorothy Wertz and John Fletcher, "Ethics and Medical Genetics in the United States,"

American Journal of Medical Genetics 29 (April 1988): 815–827.

24. See http://news.bbc.co.uk/1/hi/sci/tech/325979 .stm for more on genetic research on a "gay gene."

25. Marc Miringoff, *The Index of Social Health, 1989: Measuring the Social Well-Being of Children* (New York: Fordham Institute for Innovations in Social Policy, Fordham University, 1989), 7–8.

26. Martha Goldsmith, "Researchers Amass Abortion Data," *JAMA* 26 (September 15, 1989): 1431–1432.

27. Marc L. Miringoff, "2003 Index of Social Health: Monitoring the Social Well-Being of the Nation," Fordham Institute for Innovation in Social Policy.

28. Mary Benedict, Roger White, and Donald Cornely, "Maternal Perinatal Risk Factors and Child Abuse," *Child Abuse and Neglect* 9 (1985): 222.

29. Philip Ney, "Infant Abortion and Child Abuse: Cause and Effect," in *The Psychological Aspects of Abortion,* ed. David Mall and Walter Walls (Washington D.C., University Publications of America, 1979), 26. See also Judith Boss, "Pro-Child, Pro-Choice: An Exercise in Doublethink?" *Public Affairs Quarterly* 7 (1993): 85–91.

30. "The Right Ear," *Human Events* 53, no. 45 (1997): 24.

31. Deroy Murdock, "United Nations' Social Welfare Produces Scant Results," *Headway* 9, no. 10 (1997): 20.

32. James M. Humber, "Maternity, Paternity, and Equality," in *Reproduction, Technology, and Rights,* ed. James M. Humber and Robert F. Almeder (Totowa, N.J.: Humana Press, 1996), 27–41.

33. Steven D. Hales, "More on Fathers' Rights," in *Reproduction, Technology, and Rights,* ed. James M. Humber and Robert F. Almeder (Totowa, N.J.: Humana Press, 1996), 43–49.

34. "Ultrasound Effects," *Economist* 336, no. 7926 (1996): 34.

35. Paul A. Logli, "Drugs in the Womb: The Newest Battlefield in the War on Drugs," *Criminal Justice Ethics* (Winter/Spring 1990): 25.

36. www.pcrm.org/issues/Ethics_in_Human _Research/ethics_human-birthdefects.html (September 10, 2003).

37. "Supreme Court: Debates Pregnancy Drug Testing Policy," *American Health Line* 29 (February 2000).

38. Quoted in "A Proposal to Control Fetal Alcohol Hell," *Report,* February 17, 2003, p. 19.

39. J. M. Lawrence, "Police Say Arsonist Set N.H. Abortion Clinic Fire," *Boston Herald,* May 30, 2000, p. 2.

40. "National Task Force on Violence Against Health Care Providers," U.S. Department of Justice, 2008, http://www.usdoj.gov.crt/crim/faceweb.php.

41. "Abortion-Related Crime Increased in 1997," *Providence Journal* 18 (January 1998): F5.

42. "New Study Reports on Attacks Against U.S. Abortion Clinics." *Medical News Today,* October 1, 2006, www.medicalnewstoday.com.

43. "For what reasons are partial-birth abortions usually performed?" www.nric.org/abortion/pba/ pbafact10.html.

CHAPTER 3

1. Plato, *Republic,* bk. 3:410; bk. 4:456–461.

2. For updated information on the Human Genome Project, go to http://www.ornl.gov.sci/ techresources/Human_Genome.shtml.

3. Sheryl Bay Stolberg, "A Small Leap to Designer Babies," *New York Times,* January 1, 2000, p. E7.

4. Ibid.

5. David Stipp, "Speed-Reading Your Genes," *Fortune* 148, no. 4 (September 1, 2003): 150–152.

6. Mitochondria are slender microscopic filaments that provide energy to the cell.

7. *The Opinion of the Advisers to the President of the European Commission on the Ethical Implications of Biotechnology,* May 28, 1997.

8. See www.pollingreport.com/science.htm for the latest polling results.

9. "Moral Acceptability of New Stem Cell Research," *The Gallup Poll: Public Opinion 2007* (Lanham, Md.: Rowman & Littlefield, 2008), 262–263.

10. "Vatican Condemns Birth Technologies," *Facts on File World News Digest,* March 13, 1987, p. 158-F1.

11. For information on issues related to the Human Genome Project, visit their website at www.ornl .gov/TechResources/Human_Genome.

12. Quoted in Bob Harris, "Second Thoughts about Cloning Humans," *The Humanist* (May/June 1997): 43.

13. "The Right to Be Beautiful," *Economist* 367, no. 8325 (May 24, 2003): 9.

14. John Travis, "Cloning Extends Life of Cells—and Cows?" *Science News* 157, no. 18 (April 29, 2000): 279.

15. David Stipp, "Speed-Reading Your Genes," *Fortune* 148, no. 4 (September 1, 2003): 150.

16. Judith B. Hall, "Mendel Might Get Dizzy," *Canadian Medical Association Journal* 157, no. 12 (1997): 1669–1670.

17. "Clonaid Claims Birth of First 5 Cloned Babies," www.globalchange.com/clonaid.htm.

18. "Company Gets Funds to Clone Baby," *Science,* September 29, 2000.

19. "The Moo Two: Any Way You Splice It," *Newsweek,* February 2, 1998, p. 65.

20. Roger Dobson, "Cloning of Pigs Bring Xenotransplants Closer," *British Medical Journal* 320 (March 2000): 826.

21. "Transgenic Animals: The Latest in Anti-Terror Technology," *The Pew Initiative on Food and Biotechnology,* August 26, 2003, http://pewagbiotech .org/newsroom/summaries.

22. This is a fictional case study set in the future.

23. Glenn Zorpette, "Off With Its Head!" *Scientific American,* January 1998, p. 41.

24. Andrew Blattman, "Patently Animals—Where Does Singapore Sit?" *Managing Intellectual Property,* no. 130 (June 2003): 56–57.

25. This case study is based on correspondence to British geneticist and author Dr. Patrick Dixon, November 1997.

CHAPTER 4

1. Quoted in Sogyal Rinpoche, *The Tibetan Book of Living and Dying* (San Francisco: HarperCollins, 1992), 375.

2. One exception was David Hume who, in his 1783 essay "On Suicide," argued that suicide may sometimes be part of our duty to society.

3. Robert Jay Lifton, *The Nazi Doctors: Medical Killing and the Psychology of Genocide* (New York: Basic Books, 1986), 63.

4. *The Gallup Poll: Public Opinion 2007* (Lanham, Md.: Rowman & Littlefield, 2008).

5. "Euthanasia Debate Revives in China," *New York Times,* December 22, 2006.

6. Qur'an 17:33 and 3:145.

7. Studies cited in Barbara Dority, "The Ultimate Liberty," *Humanist* 57, no. 4 (1997): 16–20.

8. Wim Weber, "Dutch Proposal for Children's Right to Euthanasia Withdrawn," *Lancet* 356, no. 9226 (July 22, 2000): 322.

9. "Number of Euthanasia Cases Rise, Dutch News On," April 29, 2008. www.dutchnews.nl/ news/archives/2008/04/number_of_euthanasia_ cases_ris.php

10. Hilary White, "Dutch Oversight Authorities Find Euthanasia on the Rise," May 2, 2006, LifeSiteNews .com.

11. Layne Cameron, "Death Becomes Him," *American Legion Magazine,* October 1997, pp. 33, 64.

12. Cicely Saunders, "A Commitment to Care," *Raft, The Journal of Buddhist Hospice Trust* 2 (Winter 1989/90): 10.

13. Martha L. Twaddle, "Hospice Care," in *Dignity and Dying,* ed. John F. Kilner, Arlene F. Miller, and Edmund D. Pellegrino (Grand Rapids, Mich.: William B. Eerdmans, 1996), 183.

14. Willamette University College of Medicine, "Recent Developments in Physician-Assisted Suicide," March 2003, www.willamette.edu/wucl/pas/pasup datemarch2003.html.

15. Stuart N. Davidson, "Pain and Opiophobia," *Healthcare Forum Journal* (May/June 1997): 64–67.

16. Raymond S. Duff and A. G. M. Campbell, "Moral and Ethical Dilemmas in the Special-Care Nursery," *New England Journal of Medicine* 289 (1973): 890–894.

17. "Dutch, U.S. Doctors' Views on Assisted Suicide Vary," *Star Tribune* (Minneapolis), January 23, 2000, p. 5E.

18. www.efmoody.com/longterm/dying.html.

19. Harry A. Cole and Martha M. Jablow, *One in a Million* (Boston: Little, Brown, 1993).

20. Quoted in Steve Hallock, "Physician-Assisted Suicide: 'Slippery Slope' or Civil Right?" *Humanist* 56, no. 4 (1996): 7–14.

21. Tom Koch, "Living Versus Dying 'With Dignity': A New Perspective on the Euthanasia Debate," *Cambridge Quarterly Healthcare Ethics* 5, no. 1 (1996): 50–61.

22. Richard Selzer, "A Question of Mercy," *New York Times Magazine,* September 22, 1991, pp. 32–38.

23. Case study adapted from Judith A. Boss, *Perspectives on Ethics* (Mountain View, Calif.: Mayfield, 1997), 312.

24. "Kevorkian Charged in Assisting 3 Suicides," *Patriot Ledger* (Quincy, Mass.), November 1, 1996, p. 11.

25. Doreen Iudica Vigue, "The Top 10 Local News Stories of 1996," *Boston Globe,* January 1, 1997, p. B1.

26. Derek Humphry, "Prisoner of Conscience, Dr. Jack Kevorkian, Prisoner #284797," January 29, 2000, www.finalexit.org/drkframe.html.

27. John Stuart Mill, "Utilitarianism," in *Utilitarianism,* ed. by Mary Warnock (New York: Meridian Books, 1962), 308.

28. Kim Murphy, "Graphic How-to Program on Suicide to Air on TV in Oregon, Sparking Debate," *Los Angeles Times,* February 1, 2000, p. A13.

29. Ibid.

30. Sharon Doyle Driedger, "Should Latimer Go Free?" *Maclean's,* November 17, 1997.

CHAPTER 5

1. Amnesty International, "Facts and Figures on the Death Penalty," December 2008, http://amnesty.org.

2. Robert F. Drinan, "Catholics and the Death Penalty," *America* 170 (June 1994): 13–15.

3. George Pettinico, "Crime and Punishment: America Changes Its Mind," *Public Perspective* (September/October 1994): 29–32.

4. Bureau of Justice Statistics, "Capital Punishment," December 1999, NCJ-179012.

5. Bureau of Justice Statistics, "Capital Punishment Statistics," August 24, 2003, www.ojp.usdoj.gov/bjs.

6. Solomon Moore, "Executions and Death Sentences in United States Dropped in 2008, Report Finds," *New York Times,* December 11, 2008, p. A42.

7. Jimmy Moore, "Ashcroft Calls for Expanding Death Penalty to Terrorists," *Talon News,* June 6, 2003.

8. Hoover Institute, "Facts on Policy: Incarceration Rates," March 4, 2008, http://www.org/research.factsonpolicy/facts/16084042.html.

9. For the latest statistics, go to the Department of Justice website at http://www.ojp.usdoj.gov/bjs/cp.htm.

10. Solomon Moore, "Executions and Death Sentences in United States Dropped in 2008, Report Finds," *New York Times,* December 11, 2008, p. A42.

11. Linda Sax et al., *The American Freshman National Norms for Fall 2007* (Higher Education Research Institute, University of California, Los Angeles, December 2008), p. 37.

12. *The Gallup Poll: Public Opinion 1991* (Wilmington, Del.: 1992), pp. 130–131.

13. George Gallup Jr., *The Gallup Poll: Public Opinion 2002* (Wilmington, Del.: Scholarly Resources Inc., 2003), 147.

14. Ernest van den Haag, "The Ultimate Punishment: A Defense," *Harvard Law Review* 99 (1986): 1662–1669.

15. Helen Prejean, *Dead Man Walking* (New York: Random House, 1993), 47.

16. Margaret Talbot, "The Executioner's I.Q. Test," *New York Times Magazine,* June 29, 2003.

17. Amnesty International, "Methods of Execution in the U.S.," 2008. www.amnestyusa.org/death-penalty/death-penalty/methods-of-execution/

18. Leah Brumer, "Lethal Objection," *New Physician* (January/February 1997): 52.

19. Emma Marris, "DNA Tests Put Death Penalty Under Fire," *Nature* 439 (January 12, 2006): 126–127.

20. Death Penalty Information Center. http://www.deathpenaltyinfo.org/news/past/15/2009

21. John Locke, *The Second Treatise of Government* (Indianapolis: Bobbs-Merrill, 1952), ch. 2.

22. Jeremy Bentham, *An Introduction to the Principles of Morals and Legislation,* in *Utilitarianism,* ed. Mary Warnock (Cleveland: Meridian, 1962).

23. John Stuart Mill, "Parliamentary Debate on Capital Punishment Within Prisons Bill," in *Hansard's Parliamentary Debates,* 3rd ser. (London: Hansard, 1868).

24. Immanuel Kant, *The Philosophy of Law,* pt. 2, trans. W. Hastie (Edinburgh: T. T. Clark, 1887), 194–198.

25. Prejean, *Dead Man Walking,* 110.

26. *The Death Penalty* (London: Amnesty International Publications, 1987), 18.

27. Brian Gilmore, "Spotlight on the Death Penalty," *Progressive* 67, no. 8 (August 2003): 38.

28. Joe Soss, Laura Langbein, and Alan Metelko, "Why Do White Americans Support the Death Penalty?" *Journal of Politics* 397 (2003): 397–421.

29. *Times Union,* September 22, 2003, www.deathpenaltyinfo.org/article.php?did=108&scid=7.

30. Solomon Moore, "Executions and Death Sentences in United States Dropped in 2008, Report Finds," *New York Times,* December 11, 2008, p. A42.

31. Stewart Alexander, "Capital Punishment: Cruelty and Cost," December 24, 2006, www.indybay.org/newsitems/2006/12/24/18340433.php.

32. "Study Reveals Flaws in U.S. Death Sentences," *Facts On File* 60, no. 3106 (June 15, 2000): 404.

33. Lawrence Kohlberg, P. Scharf, and J. Hickey, "The Justice Structure of the Prison: A Theory and Intervention," *Prison Journal* 51 (1972): 3–14.

34. Clarence Darrow, *Crime and Criminals* (Charles H. Kerr & Co., 1902).

35. Dan Malone, "Views from Death Row," *Providence Sunday Journal,* May 25, 1997, p. D1.

36. Andrew O. Selskey, "9/11 Suspects Ask to Make Confessions," December 9, 2008, http://news.aol.com/article/911-suspects-ask-to-make-confessions/271343.

37. Albert Camus, *Reflections sur la Peine Capital* (Paris: Calmann-Levy, 1957), 199.

38. Martha Stout, *The Sociopath Next Door* (New York: Broadway Books, 2005), 82.

39. John Larrabee, "At 21, RI Serial Killer Soon Will Go Free," *USA Today,* June 6, 1994, p. A8.

40. Malone, "Views from Death Row," p. D5.

CHAPTER 6

1. *Global Health Research, Drugs and Beyond* (Alberta, Canada: Global Health, 1995), 7.

2. Jerome Jaffe's definition, quoted in Francis F. Seeburger, *Addiction and Responsibility* (New York: Crossroad, 1996), 48.

3. Listed are the effects of small or moderate amounts of these drugs. Excessive amounts may be accompanied by other, sometimes harmful, effects.

4. For an excellent history of drug and alcohol use in the United States, see David R. Musto, *The American Disease* (New Haven: Yale University Press, 1973), and his article "Legal Control of Harmful Substances," in the *Encyclopedia of Bioethics,* vol. 5 (New York: Simon & Schuster, 1995), 2439–2443.

5. World Health Organization, *Report on the Global Tobacco Epidemic,* 2008.

6. Michael Bloomberg, "The Way to Save Millions of Lives Is to Prevent Smoking," *Newsweek,* September 29, 2008.

7. "It's Time to Open the Doors of Our Prisons," *Newsweek* 133, no. 16 (April 19, 1999): 10.

8. "Drug Statistics," 2008, http://www.drug-statistics .com/marijuana.htm.

9. Alec M. Gallup and Frank Newport, *The Gallup Poll: Public Opinion 2007* (Lanham, Md.: Rowman & Littlefield Publishers, Inc., 2008), 456–457.

10. Ross Atkins, "Homefront: Keeping Kids 'Clean,'" *Christian Science Monitor* 95, no. 7 (December 4, 2002): 11.

11. Barry Stimmel, *Drug Abuse and Social Policy in America* (New York: Haworth, 1996), 3.

12. Atkins, "Homefront: Keeping Kids 'Clean,'" 11.

13. "Drug Statistics," 2008, http://www.drug-statistics. com/marijuana.htm.

14. Ibid.

15. J. B. Treaster, "Drugs Not Just an Urban Problem, Study Finds," *New York Times,* October 1, 1991, p. B1.

16. John Iwasaki, "Forum Tackles Race and Drug Use," *Seattle Post,* December 6, 2002, http://seattlepi .nwsource.com/local/98767_drug06.shtml.

17. American Lung Association, "Trends in Tobacco Use," January 2006.

18. Centers for Disease Control, "Decline in Adult Smoking Rates Stall," October 26, 2006, http://cdc .gov.od/oc/media.pressrel/r061026a.htm.

19. Office of Applied Statistics, U.S. Department of Health and Human Services, http://www .drugabusestatistics.samhsa.gov/2k6/college/ collegeUnderage.cfm.

20. Centers for Disease Control, "General Information on Alcohol Use and Health," June 2006.

21. Adam Cohen, "Battle of the Binge," *Time,* September 8, 1997, p. 55.

22. Ibid.

23. Office of Applied Statistics, U.S. Department of Health and Human Services, http://www .drugabusestatistics.samhsa.gov/2k6/college/ collegeUnderage.cfm.

24. "Clean up Campuses," *Maclean's,* September 1996, p. 14.

25. Mary E. Larimer, Daniel L. Irvine, Jason R. Kilmer, and G. Alan Mariatt, "College Drinking and the Greek System: Examining the Role of Perceived Norms for High-Risk Behavior," *Journal of College Student Development* 38, no. 6 (1997): 587–598.

26. Jürgen Rehm et al., "The Relationship of Average Volume of Alcohol Consumption and Patterns of Drinking to Burden of Disease: An Overview," *Addiction* 98 (2003): 1220–1221.

27. Henry Wechsler et al., *Secondary Effects of Binge Drinking on College Campuses* (Newton, Mass.: Higher Education Center for Alcohol and Other Drug Prevention, 1996).

28. Antonia Abbey et al., "Alcohol and Dating Risk Factors for Sexual Assault Among College Women," *Journal of Women Quarterly* 20, no. 1 (1996): 147–169.

29. U.S. Bureau of Justice Statistics, "Drug Use," www.ojp.usdoj.gov/bjs/dcf/du.htm.

30. John H. Pryor, Sylvia Hurtado, Jessica Sharkness, and William Korn, *The American Freshman National Norms for Fall 2007* (Higher Education Research Institute, University of California, Los Angeles, December 2007), 37.

31. Kennet Jost, "Are Stronger Anti-Doping Policies Needed?" *Congressional Quarterly Researcher,* July 23, 2004.

32. "Steroid Cloud Mars Baseball," *Milwaukee Journal Sentinel,* October 15, 2000, p. 1C.

33. Nweze Nnakwe, "Anabolic Steroids and Cardiovascular Risk in Athletes," *Nutrition Today* 31, no. 5 (1996): 206–208.

34. ACSM, "Position Statement: Senate Hearing on the Abuse of Anabolic Steroids," July 2004.

35. See E. M. Jellinek, *The Disease Concept of Alcoholism* (Highland Park, N.J.: Hillhouse Press, 1960).

36. Alison M. Goate, "Molecular Biology," *Alcohol Health and Research World* 19, no. 3 (1995): 217–220.

37. Aristotle, *Nicomachean Ethics*, bk. 3, ch. 5.

38. *Encyclopedia of Religion*, vol. 12, ed. Mircea Eliade (New York: Macmillan, 1987), 129.

39. John Stuart Mill, *On Liberty* (Indianapolis: Hackett, 1859/1978), 9.

40. H. Thomas Milhorn, *Drug and Alcohol Abuse* (New York: Plenum, 1994), 3.

41. E. Webb, C. H. Ashton, P. Kelly, and F. Kamali, "Alcohol and Drug Use in UK University Students," *Lancet* 348, no. 9032 (1996): 922–925.

42. Jean Kinney and Gwen Leaton, *Understanding Alcohol* (St. Louis: Mosby Year Book, 1992), 20.

43. Cohen, "Binge," 54–56.

44. "Alcohol Illness Cited as Big Cost," *New York Times*, September 12, 1993, p. A22.

45. Mark S. Gold, *"Addiction and Dependence,"* in *Encyclopedia of Bioethics*, vol. 5, ed. Warren T. Reich (New York: Simon & Schuster, 1995), 2145.

46. "Drug Offenders in the Corrections System—Prison, Jails and Probation," DrugWarFacts.org.

47. "Drug Statistics," 2008, http://www.drug-statistics.com/marijuana.htm.

48. "Legislators Aim to Snuff Out Penalties for Pot Use," July 20, 2008, CNNPolitics.com.

49. For a description of who is eligible to possess marijuana for medical purposes, see the Health Canada website: www.hc-sc.gc.ca/english.protection/marijuana.html.

50. Gold, "Addiction and Dependence," 2416.

51. Cohen, "Binge," 54–56.

52. "Discussing Drinking," *NIH News in Health*, September 2006.

53. H. Wesley Perkins and Henry Wechsler, "Variation in Perceived College Drinking Norms and Its Impact on Alcohol Abuse: A Nationwide Study," *Journal of Drug Issues* 26, no. 4 (1996): 961–974.

54. Clayton L. Thomas, ed., *Taber's Cyclopedic Medical Dictionary*, 16th ed. (Philadelphia: F. A. Davis, 1989), 1045.

55. Alvin H. Moss and Mark Siegler, "Should Alcoholics Compete Equally for Liver Transplants?" *Journal of the American Medical Association* 265, no. 10 (1991): 1295–1297.

56. "Liver Transplant: Treating End-Stage Liver Disease," December 15, 2006, MayoClinic.com.

57. John Taylor, "Live and Let Die: In Praise of Mickey, Jerry, and the Reckless Life," *Esquire*, December 1995, p. 120.

58. This case study is based on questions used in a 1995 poll of U.S. Olympians or aspiring Olympians as reported in Michael Bamberger and Don Yaeger, "Over the Edge," *Sports Illustrated*, April 1997, pp. 60–67.

59. Stimmel, *Drug Abuse*, 41.

60. Case study adapted from Judith A. Boss, *Perspectives on Ethics* (Mountain View, Calif.: Mayfield, 1998), 222–223.

61. Peter D. Kramer, *Listening to Prozac* (New York: Viking, 1993), 294.

62. Ibid., 291.

63. Ibid., 258.

64. Ibid.

65. This case study is adapted from "AA Made Me Confess," in Alan Dershowitz, *The Abuse Excuse* (Boston: Little, Brown, 1994), 69–71.

66. This is a fictional case.

CHAPTER 7

1. Elizabeth Llorente, "Homosexuals Seek U.S. Political Asylum," *The Report*, August 11, 1996, p A1.

2. Alan Goldman, "Plain Sex," *Philosophy and Public Affairs* 5 (Spring 1977): 267–287.

3. Elizabeth Anscombe, "Contraception and Chastity," orthodoxytoday.org/articles/AnscomebeChastity.shtml.

4. Neil Gross, "The Detraditionalization of Intimacy Reconsidered," *Sociological Theory* 23, no. 3 (September 2005): 301–302.

5. Barbara Dafoe Whitehead and David Popenoe, "The Station of Our Unions: The Social Health of Marriage in America 2001," The National Marriage Project, Rutgers University, 2001.

6. Arif Khan, "Marriage between Muslims and Non-Muslims," www.jannah.org/sisters/intermarriage.html.

7. Ralph Wedgewood, "The Fundamental Argument for Same-Sex Marriage," *Journal of Political Philosophy* 7, no. 3 (September 1999): 233.

8. Carolyn A. Kapinus and Michael P. Johnson, "Personal, Moral and Structural Commitment to Marriage: Gender and the Effects of Family Life

Cycle Stage," *Sociological Focus* 35, no. 2 (May 2002): 189–205.

9. Matthew 19:4–6.

10. These include Denmark, Norway, Sweden, France, Hungary, Portugal, and Croatia.

11. David Crary, "Study Claims 95 Percent of Americans Have Had Premarital Sex," Associated Press, December 20, 2006.

12. Diana West, "Opening the Door: College Romance in the New Century," *Jewish World Review,* August 3, 2001.

13. http://personalwebs.myriad.net/Roland/cohab1.html.

14. Department of Health and Human Services, *Vital and Health Statistics: Cohabitation, Marriage, Divorce and Remarriage in the United States,* Series 23, no. 22, July 2002, p. 19.

15. George Gallup Jr., *The Gallup Poll: Public Opinion 2002* (Wilmington, Del.: Scholarly Resources Inc., 2003), 240.

16. http://health.discovery.com/centers/loverelationships/articles/marriage_myths.html.

17. Immanuel Kant, "Of Duties to the Body in Regard to the Sexual Impulse," in *Lectures on Ethics,* trans. Louis Infield (New York: Cambridge University Press, 1930), 159.

18. Ibid., 161.

19. *G.W.F. Hegel Philosophy of Right,* trans. T. M. Knox (New York: Oxford University Press, 1942).

20. Alec M. Gallup and Frank Newport, *The Gallup Poll: Public Opinion 2007* (Lanham, Md.: Rowman & Littlefield Publishers, Inc., 2008), 241.

21. Amanda Orr, "Unfaithfully Yours," *People* 59, no. 19 (September 19, 2003): 159.

22. "New Law Offers Stronger Weapons Against Domestic Violence," *Providence Journal,* October 29, 2000, p. A4.

23. www.kstatecollegian.com/issues/v101/sp/n133/city-dviolence-dsfritchen.html.

24. Susan Brownmiller, *Against Our Will: Men, Women and Rape* (New York: Simon & Schuster, 1975), 13.

25. See Patricia Yancey Martin and Robert A. Hummer, "Fraternities and Rape on Campus," *Gender and Society* 3, no. 4 (1989).

26. Ibid.

27. National Institute of Justice, *Extent, Nature and Consequences of Intimate Partner Violence* (Washington, D.C.: U.S. Department of Justice, 2000).

28. Kimberly Klinger, "Prostitution, Humanism, and a Woman's Choice," *Humanist* 63, no. 1 (January/February 2003): 16–19.

29. Catharine MacKinnon, *Toward a Feminist Theory of the State* (Cambridge, Mass: Harvard University Press, 1989), 245.

30. George Gallup Jr., *The Gallup Poll: Public Opinion 2002* (Wilmington, Del.: Scholarly Resources Inc., 2002), 83.

31. Del Stover, "Politics and Policy," *National School Board Journal,* November 2006, p. 37.

32. Sherif Abdel Azim, "Women in Islam Versus Women in the Judaeo-Christian Tradition: The Myth and the Reality," http://islamicity.com./mosque/w_islam/poly.htm.

33. Some claim it was already legal by an 1892 law. See Siahyonkron Nyanseor and James Mamoo Coleman, "Evaluation of Polygyny (Polygamy) and Female Circumcision," *Perspective,* September 7, 2006.

34. Segun Gbadegesin, "The Ethics of Polygyny," *Quest* 7, no. 2 (December 1993): 2–27.

35. Marie Blanchard, "Students Arrested in Alleged Rape Case," *Daily Bruin Online,* June 6, 1996.

36. Naomi B. McCormick, "Fraternity Gang Rape: Sex, Brotherhood, and Privilege on Campus," *Archives of Sexual Behavior* 24, no. 3 (1994): 355–358.

37. Jill Rhynard, Marlene Krebs, and Julie Glover, "Sexual Assault in Dating Relationships," *Journal of School Health* 67, no. 3 (1997): 89–93.

CHAPTER 8

1. Betty Friedan, *The Feminine Mystique* (New York: Dell Books, 1963), 370–371.

2. See Catharine MacKinnon, *Toward a Feminist Theory of State* (Cambridge, Mass: Harvard University Press, 1989).

3. Jennifer Robison, "Feminism—What's in a Name?" www.gallup.com/poll/6715/Feminism_Whats_Name.aspx

4. For more on this topic, see Barbara Dafoe Whitehead and David Popenoe, *The State of Our Unions: The Social Health of Marriage in America 2006,* The National Marriage Project, Rutgers University, 2006.

5. Jean-Jacques Rousseau, *Emile* (London: Dent, 1974).

6. John Stuart Mill, *On Liberty* (Indianapolis: Hackett, 1978/1859), 104.

7. Friedrich Engels, *The Origin of the Family, Private Property, and the State* (New York: International Publishers, 1942), 144–145.

8. See Jeffner Allen, "Motherhood: The Annihilation of Women," in Joyce Trebilcot, *Mothering: Essays in*

Feminist Theory (Towota, N.J.: Rowman & Allanheld, 1984), 315–330.

9. John H. Pryor, Sylvia Hurtado, Jessica Sharkness, and William S. Korn, *The American Freshman National Norms for Fall 2007* (Higher Education Research Institute, University of California, Los Angeles, December 2007), pp. 58, 80.

10. Sara Ruddick, *Maternal Thinking: Toward a Politics of Peace* (Boston: Beacon Press, 1989), 24.

11. Lena Graber and John Miller, "Economy in Numbers: Wages for Housework: The Movement and the Numbers," *Dollars and Sense,* no. 243 (September/October, 2002): 45.

12. Sarah Glazer, "Future of Feminism," *Congressional Quarterly Researcher* 16, no. 14 (April 14, 2006).

13. H. Remick, ed., *Comparable Worth and Wage Discrimination* (Philadelphia, Pa.: Temple University, 1984), ix.

14. "College Educated Women Trail Men on Pay Scale," *Providence Journal,* December 24, 2006, p. A4.

15. Sarah Glazer, "Future of Feminism."

16. "The Feminization of Poverty," www.un.org/women watch/daw/followup/session/presskit/fs1.htm.

17. Louise Story, "Many Women at Elite Colleges Set Career Path to Motherhood," *New York Times,* September 20, 2005.

18. Pew Research Center, "At First Blush, Parents Are More Likely to Be Happy," http:/pewresearch .org/social/chart.php?ChartID=20.

19. American Association of University Women, "Women at Work (2003)," http//www.aauw.org/ research/womenatwork.cfm.

20. N. Bernstein, "Study Finds Equality Eludes Most Women in Law Firms," *New York Times,* January 6, 1996, p. A9.

21. Margaret Gibelman, "So How Far Have We Come? Pestilent and Persistent Gender Gap in Pay," *Social Work* 48, no. 1 (January 2003): 23.

22. Lisa Vogel, "Debating Difference: Feminism, Pregnancy and the Workplace," *Feminist Studies* 16, no. 1 (Spring 1990): 9.

23. Randi Kaye, "Some Voters Say Sexism Less Offensive Than Racism," http://www.cnn.com/2008/ POLITICS/02/15/Kaye.ohioracegender/index.html.

24. See N. Holla, "Blame It on Feminism," *Mother Jones* 16, no. 5 (September 1991): 24–29.

25. U.S. Department of Defense, "Report on Sexual Assault in the Military," 2007. http://www.sapr.mil.

26. AAUW, "Nearly Two-Thirds of College Students Say They Have Been Sexually Harassed," 2006, www. aauw.org.

27. Vaughana Macy Feary, "Sexual Harassment: Why the Corporate World Still Doesn't 'Get It,'" *Journal of Business Ethics* 13 (1994): 648–662.

28. Pew Research Center, "At First Blush, Parents Are More Likely to Be Happy."

29. Lisa Belkin, "The Opt-Out Revolution," *New York Times,* October 26, 2003.

30. F. E. Barcus, *Images of Life on Children's Television: Sex-roles, Minorities, and Families* (New York: Praeger, 1983), 20–22.

31. Kimberly A. Powell and Lori Abels, "Sex-Role Stereotypes in TV Programs Aimed at the Preschool Audience: An Analysis of *Teletubbies* and *Barney and Friends*," *Women and Language* 25, no. 1 (2002): 14–22.

32. Jennifer Scanlon, "Not Just a Pretty Face," *Women's Review of Books* 19, no. 6 (2002): 18–20.

33. http://www.defenselink.mil/releases/release. aspx?released=11757.

34. Linda Bird Francke, "The Military Culture of Harassment," in *Sexual Harassment: Issues and Answers,* ed. Linda LeMoncheck and James P. Sterba (New York: Oxford University Press, 2001), 95–102.

35. Hilary M. Lips, "Female Powerlessness: A Case of 'Cultural Preparedness'?" in *Power/Gender: Social Relations in Theory and Practice,* ed. H. Lorraine Radtke and Henderikus J. Stam (London: Sage, 1994), 99.

36. American Anorexia Bulemia Association, www.aabainc.org/general.

37. "Tyra Talks Back," *People,* cover story, January 25, 2007.

CHAPTER 9

1. Larry Alexander, "Banning Hate Speech and the Sticks and Stones Defense," *Constitutional Commentary* 13, no. 1 (1996): 71.

2. William F. Buckley Jr., and L. Brent Bozell, *McCarthy and His Enemies* (Chicago: Henry Regnery, 1954).

3. "Internet Usage Statistics," March 2009. http://www.internetworldstats.com/stats.htm

4. John H. Pryor, Sylvia Hurtado, Jessica Sharkness, and William S. Korn, *The American Freshman National Norms for Fall 2007* (Higher Education Research Institute, University of California, Los Angeles, Dec. 2007), p. 8.

5. Reid Goldsborough, "Free Speech in Cyberspace—Both a Privilege and a Burden," *Community College Week* 12, no. 1 (August 23, 1999): 27.

6. Kevin Platt, "With a Click, Chinese Vault Cultural Walls," *Christian Science Monitor* 92, no. 133 (June 1, 2000): 1.

7. Jerry Ropelato, "Internet Pornography Statistics," *Internet Filter Review,* 2007, http://internet-filter-review.toptenreviews.com/internet-pornography-statistics.html.

8. See Gloria Steinem, "Erotica and Pornography: A Clear and Present Difference," *Ms.* magazine, November 1978, for a more in-depth discussion of the difference between erotica and pornography.

9. House of Commons, Standing Committee on Justice and Legal Affairs, *Report on Pornography* 22, no. 18 (March 1978): 4.

10. Ronald J. Berger, Patricia Searles, and Charles E. Cottle, *Feminism and Pornography* (New York: Praeger, 1991), 4.

11. Cynthia A. Stark, "The War Against Pornography," *Social Theory and Practice* 23, no. 2 (1997): 279. For a critique of some of these studies, see Ann Garry, "Pornography and Respect for Women," *Social Theory and Practice* 4 (Spring 1978): 395–421.

12. For more on radical feminism and liberal feminism, see Chapter 8.

13. John Leo, "Watch What You Say," *U.S. News & World Report* 128, no. 11 (March 20, 2000): 18.

14. *Doe v University of Michigan,* 721 F. Supp. 852 (E.D.Mich. 1989).

15. Sara Lipka, "Campus Speech Codes Said to Violate Rights," *Chronicle of Higher Education* 53, no. 18, (January 5, 2007): A32.

16. Martin Bentham, "College Guide Bans 'Lady' and 'History' as Offensive Words," *Sunday Telegraph* (London), June 11, 2000, p. 3.

17. Marla Fisher, "Free Speech v. Censorship," *Community College Week,*" May 19, 2008, p. 7.

18. Christian Mignot, "Lawsuits, Debate Intensify over University 'Free Speech Zones,'" *Daily Bruin* (UCLA), October 1, 2002.

19. "Campus Speech Rules Scrutinized by Courts, Students, Advocates: Opponents Say Policies Violate First Amendment Right to Protest and Distribute Material," *College Censorship* 21, no. 1 (Winter 2002–2003): 6.

20. John Locke, *The Second Treatise of Government* (New York: Cambridge University Press, 1960), 457.

21. Ayn Rand, "Man's Rights," in *The Virtue of Selfishness* (New York: Penguin, 1964), 114.

22. John Rawls, *A Theory of Justice* (Cambridge, Mass.: Harvard University Press, 1971).

23. John Stuart Mill, "On Liberty," in *Collected Works of John Stuart Mill* (Toronto: University of Toronto Press, 1977), 220.

24. For more on this interpretation of Mill's theory of free speech, see Jill Gordon, "John Stuart Mill and the 'Marketplace of Ideas,'" *Social Theory and Practice* 23, no. 2 (1997).

25. "Forbidden Thoughts: A Roundtable on Taboo Research," *The American Enterprise,* January/February 1995, p. 69.

26. D. F. B. Tucker, *Law, Liberalism and Free Speech* (Totowa, N.J.: Rowman & Allanheld, 1985), 141.

27. Keith Burgess-Jackson, "Justice and the Distribution of Fear," *Southern Journal of Philosophy* 32 (1994): 367–388.

28. Quoted by Sarah J. McCarthy, "Pornography, Rape, and the Cult of Macho," *Humanist,* September/October 1980, p. 15.

29. This is a paraphrase of Samuel Johnson's famous statement, "Patriotism is the first refuge of scoundrels."

30. "The Real Meaning Behind Horowitz Advertisement," Op-Ed, *Brown Daily Herald* 139, no. 93, 2001, www.browndailyherald.com/stories .sep?dbversion+2&storyID+4243.

31. For a more complete description of this case study, see Christopher McMahon, "Preserving the Bastion: The Case of the *Dartmouth Review,*" in *Hate Speech on Campus,* ed. Milton Heumann and Thomas W. Church (Boston: Northeastern University Press, 1997), 192–212.

32. Aaron Nicodemus, "Agents' Visit Chills UMass Dartmouth Senior," *Standard Times,* December 17, 2005.

33. Jerry Kirkpatrick, *In Defense of Advertising: Arguments from Reason, Ethical Egoism, and Laissez-Faire Capitalism* (Westport, Conn.: Quorum, 1994), 154.

34. See Calvin Reid, "Appeals Court Reviewing 'Hitman' Ruling," *Publishers Weekly,* May 19, 1997, p. 14.

35. Brandon S. Centerwall, "Exposure to Television as a Cause of Violence," in *Public Communication and Behavior,* vol. 2, ed. G. Comstock (Orlando: Academic Press, 1989), 1–58.

36. Richard B. Felson, "Mass Media Effects on Violent Behavior," *Annual Review of Sociology* 22 (1996): 103–128.

37. http://academicintegrity.org/cal%5fresearch.asp

38. See Sharon Machlis, "University Sues Over Internet Term-Paper Site," *Computerworld,* October 1997, p. 3; and Julianne Basinger and Kelly McCollum, "Boston U. Sues Companies for Selling Term

Papers Over the Internet," *Chronicle of Higher Education,* October 31, 1997, pp. A34–A35.

39. Charles C. Haynes, "The Harm of Teaching 'Both Sides' in Evolution Debate," *Providence Sunday Journal,* August 21, 2005, p. E5.

40. *Kitzmiller v. Dover Area School District,* United States District Court for the Middle District of Pennsylvania, 12/20/05, Case No. 04cv2688, www.pamd.uscourts.gov/kitzmiller/kitzmiller_342.pdf.

CHAPTER 10

1. Cyril Josh Barker, "Obama Blacklash Already?" *New York Amsterdam News,* November 13, 2008.

2. Diane Cole, "Spread Tolerance," *U.S. News and World Report* 145, no. 14 (December 29, 2008): 68.

3. William H. Holcombe, "Characteristics and Capabilities of the Negro Race," *Southern Literary Messenger* 33 (1986): 401–410.

4. See Jonathan Kozol, *Savage Inequalities: Chidren in America's Schools* (New York: Crown, 1991).

5. Barbara Kantrowitz and L. Rosado, "Falling Further Behind: A Generation of Hispanics Isn't Making the Grade," *Newsweek,* August 19, 1991, p. 60.

6. Jonathan Alter, "The Long Shadow of Slavery," *Newsweek,* December 8, 1997, p. 62.

7. Ronald L. Taylor, "Black Males and Social Policy: Breaking the Cycle of Disadvantage," in *The American Black Male: His Present Status and His Future,* ed. Richard G. Majors and Jacob U. Gordon (Chicago: Nelson-Hall, 1994), 148–166.

8. George Gallup Jr., *The Gallup Poll: Public Opinion 2002* (Wilmington, Del.: Scholarly Resources Inc., 2003), 179.

9. John H. Pryor, Sylvia Hurtado, Jessica Sharkness, and William S. Korn, *The American Freshman National Norms for Fall 2007* (Higher Education Research Institute, University of California, Los Angeles, December 2007), 37.

10. Kozol, *Savage Inequalities.*

11. Alec M. Gallup and Frank Newport, *The Gallup Poll: Public Opinion 2007* (Lanham, MD: Rowman & Littlefield Publishers, Inc., 2008), 286–287.

12. Carroll P. Horton and Jessie Carney, eds., *Statistics Record of Black America* (Detroit: Gale Research, 1990).

13. Lydia Lum, "A Welcome Increase," *Black Issues in Higher Education* 20, no. 18 (October 2003): 36–37.

14. U.S. Census Bureau, "School Enrollment in the United States: 2006." http://www.census.gov/prod/2008pubs/p20-559.pdf

15. Matthew Philips, "School Veil," *Newsweek,* November 13, 2006, p. 14.

16. "Time to Tell Hate, 'Not on Our Campus'," *Black Issues in Higher Education* 16, no. 27 (March 2, 2000): 48.

17. Susan Snyder, "Hate Crimes Up on Campuses, Group Says," *Philadelphia Inquirer,* November 15, 2008.

18. "Race, Crime and Justice," *Christian Century* 117, no. 11 (April 5, 2000): 379.

19. Bruce Landis, "Traffic Stops Still Show Disparities," *Providence Sunday Journal,* June 4, 2006, p. A1.

20. Shaun Gabbidon, Ronald Craig, Nonso Okafo, Lakiesha Marzette, and Steven Peterson, "The Consumer Racial Profiling Experiences of Black Students at Historically Black Colleges and Universities: An Exploratory Study," *Journal of Criminal Justice* 36, no. 4 (August 2008): 354–361.

21. Landis, "Traffic Stops Still Show Disparities."

22. See Robert H. Bork, "Civil Liberties After 9/11," *Commentary* 116, no. 1 (July/August 2003): 29–35; and Sarfraz Mansoor, "I'm a Muslim but I Can Still Fly," *New Statesman* 131, no. 4614 (November 18, 2002): 32–33.

23. Herbert I. London, "Minority Enrollment Rebounds at California Schools," *Human Events* 56, no. 24 (June 30, 2000): 24.

24. "FACTBOX: Some Facts about U.S. Mexico Ties," January 11, 2009, http://www.reuters.com/article/politicsNews/idUSTRE50A1QG20090111.

25. Gallup and Newport, *The Gallup Poll: Public Opinion 2007,* 177–178.

26. Barbara MacKinnon, *Ethics: Theory and Contemporary Issues* (Belmont, Calif.: Wadsworth, 1995), 238.

27. See Ayn Rand, "Racism," in *The Virtue of Selfishness* (New York: Penguin, 1964), 147–161.

28. See David Horowitz, "Ten Reasons Why Reparations for Blacks Is a Bad Idea for Blacks—and Racist, Too!" www.adversity.net/reparations/anti_reparations_ad.htm.

29. Lisa Newton, "Reverse Discrimination Is Unjustified," *Ethics* 83, no. 4 (July 1973): 308–312.

30. Alan Bloom, *The Closing of the American Mind* (New York: Simon & Schuster, 1987), 95.

31. Michael Levin, "Response to Race Differences in Crime," *Journal of Social Philosophy* 23, no. 1 (1992): 5–29.

32. Kevin Lamb, "IQ and PC," *National Review,* January 27, 1997, pp. 39–42.

33. Garrett Hardin, "Living on a Lifeboat," *BioScience* 24, no. 10 (October 1974): 561–568.

34. *Barbara Grutter v. Lee Bollinger et al.*, U.S. Supreme Court, 2003, p. 4.

35. See *Cheryl Hopwood v. The State of Texas*, 78 F.3d 932 (5th Cir. 1996).

36. For other headlines, see "Katrina and Racism: The World View" at www.tolerance.org/news/article_print.jsp?id=1291.

37. Article in *New Orleans City Business*, February 16, 2004. See also Lee Sustar, "Hurricane Katrina Exposes Racism and Inequality," *Socialist Worker*, September 1, 2005.

38. Quoted in Sophfronia Scott Gregory, "Black Rage: In Defense of a Mass Murderer," *Time*, June 6, 1994, p. 31.

39. Alan Dershowitz, *The Abuse Excuse* (Boston: Little, Brown, 1994).

40. Eddy Ramirez, "Should Colleges Enroll Illegal Immigrants?" *U.S. News & World Report*, 3 August 2008. www.usnews.com/articles/education/2008/08/07/should-colleges-enroll-illegal-immigrants.html

41. Makau Mutua, "Racism at Root of Sudan's Darfur Crisis," *Christian Science Monitor*, July 14, 2004, p. 9.

CHAPTER 11

1. Paul W. Williams, "The Twentieth Century and Beyond," *Vital Speeches of the Day* 55, no. 20 (1989): 624.

2. Thomas Hobbes, *Leviathan* (New York: Cambridge University Press, 1996), 126.

3. C. A. J. Coady, "War and Terrorism," in *A Companion to Applied Ethics*, ed. R. G. Frey and Christopher Heath Wellman (Oxford, UK: Blackwell, 2003), 256.

4. Greenpeace International, "The Vital Statistics," http://www.greenpeace.org/internationalcampaigns/peace/abolish-nuclear-weapons/the-vital-statistics.

5. "Israel's Nuclear Programme," *BBC News*, December 22, 2003.

6. "U.S. Unprepared for Disease Outbreak," *USA Today Magazine* 131, no. 2697 (June 2003): 16.

7. See Jan Narveson, "Pacifism: A Philosophical Analysis," *Ethics* 75, no. 4 (July 1965).

8. Gabriel Packard, "Hundreds of U.S. Soldiers Emerge as Conscientious Objectors," April 15, 2003, InterPress Service, www.commondreams.org/headlines03/0415-11.htm.

9. John Keegan, "Men in Battle," *Human Nature* 1, no. 6 (June 1978): 36.

10. Packard, "Hundreds of U.S. Soldiers Emerge as Conscientious Objectors."

11. World Health Organization, *World Report on Violence and Health*, 2002, www.who.int/violence_injury_prevention/violence/world_report/wrvh1/en.

12. Williams, "The Twentieth Century and Beyond," 624.

13. For more on these two positions, see John Kelsey, "Suicide Bombers," *Christian Century* 119, no. 17, p. 23.

14. Survey USA News Poll #6000, June 27, 2005.

15. Ronald Reagan, "A Coercive 'National Service,'" *Human Events*, April 28, 1979, p. 19.

16. http://en.wikipedia.org/wiki/Bombing_of_Dresden_in_World_War_II.

17. www.rense.com/general19/flame.htm.

18. *Public Papers of the Presidents of the United States: Harry S. Truman, Containing the Public Messages, Speeches and Statements of the President April 12 to December 31, 1945* (Washington, D.C.: U.S. Government Printing Office, 1961), 212.

19. Randall Hamud, "We're Fighting Terror, But Killing Freedom," *Newsweek*, September 1, 2003, p. 11.

20. "Perspectives," *Newsweek*, December 1, 2003, p. 21.

21. "First Officer Announces Refusal to Deploy to Iraq," June 7, 2006, Truthout.org.

22. John Rawls, "Definition and Justification of Civil Disobedience," from *Civil Disobedience in Focus*, ed. Hugo Bedau (London: Routledge, 1991), 121.

23. "Mistrial Ends Watada's Court-Martial: War Objector May Have to Be Tried Again," *Seattle Post-Intelligencer*, February 7, 2007.

24. Allan Carlson, "Mothers at War: The American Way?" *World Net Daily*, April 11, 2003.

25. Joanne Laurier, "Colorado Woman Faces Charges by Military: Interview with U.S. Soldier Who Refused to Abandon Children and Return to Iraq," *World Socialist Website*, November 7, 2003, www.ccmep.org/2003_articles/Iraq.

26. Carlson, "Mothers at War: The American Way?"

27. Joseph A. D'Agostino, "Center for Military Readiness," *Human Events* 59, no. 18 (May 26, 2003): 20.

28. Peter J. Smith, "Homosexuals Howl at Military Policy Banning Them from Service," August 16, 2006, LifeSiteNews.com.

CHAPTER 12

1. David Coats, *Old MacDonald's Factory Farm* (New York: Continuum, 1989), 32.

2. Coats, *Factory Farm*, 34.

3. Lynn White, "The Historical Roots of Our Ecological Crisis," *Science* 155, March 10, 1967, p. 1205.

4. Aristotle, "Politics," bk. 1, ch. 8, in *The Oxford Translation of Aristotle,* trans. Benjamin Jowett (Oxford: Oxford University Press).

5. Thomas Aquinas, *Summa Contra Gentiles,* bk. III, pt. II, ch. CXII, trans. by the English Dominican Father (Chicago: Benziger Brothers, 1928).

6. Jeremy Bentham, *Principles of Morals and Legislation* (London: Clarendon Press, 1907), 1.

7. Charles Darwin, *The Descent of Man,* excerpt from Tom Regan and Peter Singer, eds., *Animal Rights and Human Obligations* (Englewood Cliffs, N.J.: Prentice-Hall, 1989), 30.

8. See Frans de Waal, *Primates and Philosophers: How Morality Evolved* (Princeton, N.J.: Princeton University Press, 2006).

9. Thomas Jefferson, *Writings* (New York: Literary Classics of the United States, 1984), 290, 818.

10. See Judith Boss, "Treading on Harrowed Ground: The Violence of Agriculture," in *Institutional Violence,* ed. Deane Curtin and Robert Litke (Amsterdam: Rodopi, 1999), 263–277.

11. Jim Mason and Peter Singer, *Animal Factories* (New York: Crown, 1990), 3.

12. Joy Williams, "The Inhumanity of the Animal People," *Harper's,* August 1997, 61.

13. See John Robbins, *Diet for a New America* (Walpole, N.H.: Stillpoint, 1987).

14. Charles Stahler, "How Many Adults Are Vegetarians?" *Vegetarian Journal,* no. 4 (2006).

15. John Fetto, "It Ain't Easy Eating Greens," *American Demographics* 22, no. 5 (May 2000): 13.

16. *Discussing Vegetarianism with a Meat-Eater: A Hindu View* (Kapaa, Hawaii: Himalayan Academy Publications).

17. Robert H. Socolow, "Can We Bury Global Warming?" *Scientific American* 293, no. 1 (July 2005).

18. United Nations World Meteorological Organization.

19. Adapted from *PETA Factsheet on Animal Experiments,* no. 1.

20. See Rutgers Animals Rights Law Center, *1996 Supplement to Vivisection and Dissection in the Classroom.*

21. "The President of Europeans for Medical Advancement Responds to the Prediction That the Mapping of the Human Genome Will Increase Animal Experimentation," *The Independent* (London), June 28, 2000, p. 2.

22. Peter Singer, *Animal Liberation* (New York: Random House, 1990), 6.

23. John Rawls, *A Theory of Justice* (Cambridge, Mass.: Harvard University Press, 1971), 17, 512.

24. R. G. Frey, "Moral Community and Animal Research in Medicine," *Ethics and Behavior* 7, no. 2 (1997): 123–136.

25. Richard Watson, "A Critique of Anti-Anthropocentric Ethics," *Environmental Ethics* 5, no. 3 (Fall 1983): 245–256.

26. Al Gore, *Earth in the Balance: Ecology and the Human Spirit* (Boston: Houghton Mifflin, 1992), 221.

27. Ibid., 216.

28. Terry Frieden, "FBI, ATF Address Domestic Terrorism," May 19, 2005, CNN.com.

29. This is based on a true story. However, the professor in question—the author—did not have the cat euthanized.

30. Anna Badkhen, "Residents Upset over Cape Cod Wind-Farm Plan," *San Francisco Chronicle,* November 2004, p. A-2.

31. Michael Astor, "Researchers: Warming May Change Amazon," Associated Press, 2006, www.physorg.com/printnews.php?newsid=86677664.

32. Steve La Rue, "More Retailers Warming to Rainforest-Friendly Coffee," *San Diego Union-Tribune,* November 5, 2000, p. B-1.

Credits

Index

abortion, 73–130
  abortion clinics, 77, 78, 82, 127–128, 448
  attitudes toward, 74–75, 77, 78–79, 114, 115
  consequentialist arguments, 84–85
  father's rights and, 83, 117–125
  fetus, moral status of, 75, 76–77, 78–79, 80–82
  Foster, Serrin M., 74, 82, 113–116
  Hales, Steven D., 34, 82, 83, 117–125
  historical overview, 72–78
  Marquis, Don, 82, 108–112
  maternal drug/alcohol use, 82, 126–127
  methods of, 79–80
  Noonan, John, 80, 97–101
  partial-birth, 78, 80, 81, 129
  pro-choice movement, 75, 84, 312
  pro-life movement, 75, 84
  rape and, 82, 88, 92–93, 96, 128
  religion and, 78–79, 98
  rights and, 34, 75, 76, 78, 81, 82–83, 88–93, 103, 105–107, 118–124
  Roe v. Wade (1973), 75–78
  selective, 78, 83–84, 125–126, 141
  therapeutic, 73, 75
  Thomson, Judith, 81, 82, 86–97, 121
  viability, 75, 76–77, 78, 81, 98–99
  Warren, Mary Anne, 11, 80, 82, 102–108
"Abortion and Fathers' Rights" (Hales), 83, 117–125
Abraham and Isaac, 17
Abrams v. the United States (1919), 447
abstinence-only curriculum, 383–384
Abu Graib prison, 635
"Active and Passive Euthanasia" (Rachels), 190–194
acute toxicity test, 645
addiction. *See also* drug and alcohol use
  definition, 278, 285, 292, 296
  disease (medical model of), 285–286
  "Ethics of Addiction, The" (Szasz), 291–298
  moral model of, 286

"Address to the Prisoners in the Chicago County Jail" (Darrow), 244
Adkins, Janet, 184, 217
adoption, 8, 168, 364, 387–388, 559
adultery. *See* marriage, adultery
advertising/commercial speech, 448, 457, 505, 510
affirmative action, 35, 525, 532, 534, 539, 543–545, 565–566. *See also* color-conscious policies
Afghanistan, 571, 578, 614, 621
Africa, 331, 386, 448, 516, 551, 564, 599, 672
African Americans. *See also* affirmative action; racism; slavery
  abortion, 74, 79
  black-rage, 567–568
  capital punishment, 231, 237, 241–242
  civil rights, 453, 488–489, 520, 523, 557
  college, 521
  marriage/family, 333, 529–530
  racial profiling, 522
  reckless eyeballing, 437
  reparation, 35, 507–508, 526
Agabi, Kanu, 277
Against Our Will: Men, Women and Rape (Brownmiller), 337
"Against the Legalization of Drugs" (Wilson), 299–306
aggression, 19, 410, 411, 412, 450. *See also* war and terrorism, wars of aggression
agriculture. *See also* animals, nonhuman, animal farming
  environmental degradation, 641–642, 644, 699–700
  factory/intensive farming, 642, 646–647, 652–653
  genetic engineering, 142, 642
  Jeffersonian tradition, 641
  Leopold, Aldo, 642–643
  migrant labor, 555–557
ahimsa, 28, 186, 235, 579, 647
AIDS/HIV, 90, 175–176, 203, 329, 333, 338, 696

Aid to Families with Dependent Children (AFDC), 549
Akan (Ghana), 17
Alabama, 520
Alaska, 75
alcohol. *See* drug and alcohol use, alcohol
Alcoholics Anonymous (AA), 286, 328
alcohol-related end-stage liver disease (ARESLD), 325–326
Alexander the Great, 43
Alien 3, 275
Alito, Samuel, 78
Allen, Floyd, 228
Allied firebombing. *See* war and terrorism, obliteration bombing
"Almost Absolute Value in History, An" (Noonan), 97–101
al Muhajir, Abdullah, 616
al-Qaeda, 16, 274, 583, 591, 614, 615, 619, 632
Alter, Jonathan, 567
altruism, 20, 48–49
American Booksellers Ass'n v. Hudnut, 489
American Civil Liberties Union (ACLU), 304, 446, 452, 453, 458, 483, 485, 489, 491–492, 631, 632
American Indians. *See* Native Americans
American Library Association, 509
American Medical Association (AMA), 74, 75, 177–178, 191, 193, 233, 280, 286, 325, 333
American Revolution, 447, 575, 583, 641
American Society of Reproductive Medicine (ASRM), 156
Amnesty International, 232, 237, 618, 632
Analects (Confucius), 68–70
anarchy. *See* state of nature
androgeny, 393
Anglin, Douglas, 304
Animal Liberation (Singer), 660–668
Animal Liberation Front (ALF), 694–695
"Animal Rights Revisited" (Narveson), 655–659

animals, nonhuman
  animal experimentation, 638, 640,
    644–645, 647, 663–668, 694–695
  animal farming, 638, 641–643,
    652–654, 657, 664, 679
  "Bambi boom," 697–698
  biotechnology/genetic engineering,
    131, 133, 134–135, 138, 140,
    142–143, 171–172, 173–174, 638,
    642, 644, 645, 695–696
  Cohen, Carl, 646, 647, 669–675
  deer/vehicle collisions, 698
  hunting, 648, 653–654, 698
  moral standing, 34, 35, 71–72,
    637–639, 645–646, 647, 655,
    671–675
  Narveson, Jan, 646, 655–659
  natural law and 648
  pets, 646, 696
  reason, 641, 661–662
  Regan, Tom, 638, 646, 647, 649–654,
    670–675
  rights, 638, 647, 650–654, 657–658,
    670–675
  Singer, Peter, 646, 647, 648, 660–668
  social contract theory, 646, 658–659
  speciesism, 648, 660–665, 668
  suffering/pain, 638, 640, 647,
    651–653, 661–667, 672
  utilitarianism and, 23, 646–647
  xenotransplantation, 695–696
  zoos, 664, 697
Animal Welfare Act, 638, 694
anorexia nervosa, 443–444
Anscombe, Elizabeth, 571, 579,
  585–591, 594, 595
Anthony, Susan B., 7, 74, 113, 114, 115,
  390, 641
anthrax, 578
anthropocentrism, 3, 132, 639–640,
  641, 644, 646, 656–657, 679, 690
antidepressants, 285
Anti-Drug Abuse Act (1986), 308
Antinori, Severino, 151, 152
Antioch College, 337, 389
Anti-Saloon League, 279
Appiah, Kwame Anthony, 531
applied ethics, 2
"Aqui Estamos y No Nos Vamos!"
  (Robinson), 554–558
Aquinas, Thomas
  ensoulment, 79
  just war theory, 572–573, 581, 594, 602
  marriage/sexuality, 335, 356
  natural law theory, 16–17
  nonhuman animals, 639–640
  suicide, 179
  Summa Theologica, 573
  women, 403
Arab Americans, 521, 522, 581, 631
Areopagitica (Milton), 494
Aristotle
  background, 42
  distributive justice, 30

doctrine of the mean, 38, 45–47
drug use, on, 286–287
eudaimonia/happiness, 44, 321
euthanasia, 179
freedom of speech, 454
justice, 38
Nichomachean Ethics, 43–47, 321
nonhuman animals, 640
reason, 38, 43, 640
sexuality and marriage, 335
slavery, 516
virtue ethics, 37–38, 44–47
women, 394, 403
Armstrong, Lance, 285
Arthur, Joyce, 127
Ashcroft, John, 182, 231
Ashcroft v. Oregon (2002), 182
Asian Americans, 519, 520,
  522, 546, 547, 642. See also
  Japanese Americans
assisted reproductive technologies
  (ART), 152, 153, 154, 396, 441
Atkins v. Virginia (2003), 232
Atlanta Braves, 546
Augustine, 335, 394, 594
Australia, 228, 282, 516, 638, 642
Austria, 282, 638
autonomy, 35, 82, 84, 106, 140–141,
  185–186, 198–200, 289, 297, 322,
  352, 366, 400, 672

Baby Doe, 188, 226
Bachellar v. Maryland (1970), 451
Bacon, Francis, 640
Bakke, Allan, 523, 534
"Bambi boom," 697–698
Banfield, E., 549
Bangladesh, 595
Banks, Tyra, 443–444
Bantu, 139
Barbara Grutter v. The University of
  Michigan Law School (2003), 565
Barney & Friends, 439
Barth, Karl, 359
Bassam ubi, 605
Battin, Margaret Pabst, 28, 186, 188,
  203, 195–202
Bazargan, Mehdi, 606
Bedau, Hugo Adam, 29, 235, 236, 242,
  251–261, 264
Belgium, 182, 282, 334
Belkin, Lisa, 420
beneficence, duty of, 28, 55, 69, 70, 147,
  220, 221, 246, 250
benevolence. See beneficence, duty of
Bennett, William, 311, 312
Bentham, Jeremy
  biographical sketch, 22, 50
  death penalty, 234, 236, 244, 255
  equality of pleasures, 23, 51
  happiness, 51, 357

homosexuality, 357–358
"Introduction to the Principles of
  Morals and Legislations, An," 50–51
nonhuman animals, 641, 661–662
pleasure and pain/suffering, 22,
  50–51, 641, 661
principle of utility, 50–51
rights, 244
utilitarianism, 22, 50–51
war and peace, 574, 581
Berlin, Germany, 630
Berryman, John, 435
"Better Sex" (Ruddick), 346–352
Bible
  Corinthians 6:9–10, 356
  Exodus 23:4–5, 588
  Genesis 1:26, 640
  Leviticus 18:22–23, 356
  Leviticus 19:18, 588, 628
  Leviticus 20:30, 356
  Luke 10:30–35, 94
  Matthew 7:12, 628
  Matthew 25, 269
  Proverbs 25:21, 558
  Romans 1:2–27, 356
  Romans 12:19, 356
  I Timothy 1:9–10, 356
bin Laden, Osama, 274
biocentrism, 646, 681–682
biological weapons, 578–579
biotic communities, 677–679
Birth of a Nation, The, 516
black-rage defense, 567–568
blastocyst (embryo) splitting, 133, 134,
  135, 138
Bloom, Alan, 4, 545
Bloomberg, Michael, 238
Boas, Franz, 5
Boisselier, Brigitte, 170
Bondanella, Peter, 491
Bookchin, Murray, 690
bootlegging, 280
Bosnia, 615–616
Boston University, 512
Bouvier, Elizabeth, 200
Boxill, Bernard, 35, 522, 523, 525, 526,
  540–545
Boyle, Robert, 137
Brandeis, Louis D., 502, 508
Brazil, 443
Brennan, William J., 244
Brinkerhoff, Mattie, 116
Britain. See England
British Medical Society, 177
British Race Relations Act, 458, 489
Brothers Karamazov, The (Dostoyevsky), 18
Brown, Henry Billings, 541
Brown, Louise, 396
Brown Daily Herald, 507–508
Brownmiller, Susan, 337
Brown University, 384, 507–508
Brown v. Board of Education (1954), 458,
  477–478, 481, 484, 518–519, 525
Buckley, William F., Jr., 447

Buck v. Bell (1927), 131
Buddhism
  animal rights, 36, 71, 638
  compassion, 37, 239, 517, 628
  death penalty, 29, 179, 236
  drug/alcohol use, 287
  ecological consciousness, 681
  euthanasia, 177
  mindfulness trainings, 71–72
  nonviolence (ahimsa), 28, 29
  speech, 72, 455
  virtue ethics, 39, 455
bulimia, 443–444
Bullard, Robert, 570
Bush, George H. W., 282, 289
Bush, George W.,
  Guantanamo Bay, 581, 635
  intelligent design theory, 513
  nuclear weapons, 578
  stem call research, 136, 137, 167–169
  war/terrorism, 16, 231, 571, 578, 581, 591, 614
Butler v. The Queen (Canada, 1992), 490

California, 75, 181, 217, 233, 238, 442, 523, 555, 568, 570, 686
California Natural Death Act (1976), 181
California Savings and Loan Co., 442
California State University, 445
Cambodia, 578, 595
campus. *See* college
Camus, Albert, 238, 259, 274
Canada
  commercial surrogacy, 440
  death penalty, 228, 235
  drug/alcohol use, 282, 283, 306, 329
  freedom of speech/pornography, 447, 450, 455, 490
  genetic engineering, 173
  prostitution, 338
  same-sex marriage, 334
  slavery, 517
  Vietnam War era, 633
Canadian Marijuana Medical Access Regulations (2001), 306
Canberra Commission, 609
Cape Cod Wind farm, 698–699
capitalism, 20, 33, 48–49, 391, 396, 429, 503, 556–557. *See also* globalization
capital punishment. *See* death penalty
"Capital Punishment" (Bedau), 251–261
Capone, Al, 280
Career Mystique (Moen/Roehling), 419
care ethics, 39–41
  death penalty, 239
  ecofeminism, 692–693
  euthanasia, 220–221
  feminism, 31, 40–41, 67, 393, 400
  Gilligan, Carol, 12–13, 39–40, 393
  Hume, David, 40, 66
  Noddings, Nel, 40, 65–67
  Prejean, Helen, 40, 239
  racism and, 526

Caring: A Feminine Approach to Ethics and Moral Education (Noddings), 65–67
Carson, Rachel, 680
Case for Animal Rights, The (Regan), 671–674
"Case for Euthanasia, The" (Battin), 28, 195–202
categorical imperative, 26–27, 56–58, 234, 331
Catholic Church, 79, 229, 271, 332, 342–345
censorship. *See* freedom of speech, censorship
Center for Military Readiness, 634
Centerwall, Brandon, 511
Chaplinsky v. New Hampshire (1942), 451, 452, 495
character, 55
Charles, Sandy, 511
Charter of the United Nations. *See* United Nations, Charter of
Chechnya, 597, 619
Chemical Waste Management, 570
chemical weapons, 578
Chi K'ang Tzu, 70
Child Pornography Prevention Act, 449
children. *See also* schools
  abortion and, 84–85, 98, 384
  abuse, 72, 85, 126, 147, 469
  cigarette advertising, 510
  commodification of, 153, 161, 163–164, 396
  crime, 273, 275
  drug/alcohol use, 282, 283, 288, 295–296, 300, 303, 313–316
  euthanasia, 182, 188, 226
  experimental subjects, 666–667, 673
  genetically engineered, 133, 137, 138, 146–150, 153, 159–165
  infanticide, 74, 103, 104–105, 197
  military/war and, 583, 598
  moral development, 12, 147
  pornography, 449, 505
  punishment, 232, 277
  rights of, 34, 140, 363
  same-sex parents, 363–364, 368–369, 369, 386–387
  sex selection, 78, 83–84
  sexual abuse, 72, 338
  social view of, 153–154
  television, 439, 511
Chile, 491
chimeras, 133, 173–174
China. *See also* Confucianism
  abortion/sex selection, 74, 78, 83–84
  death penalty, 229, 237
  drinking age, 316
  freedom of speech, 419
  gene patents, 138
  global capitalism, 563, 569
  global warming, 686
  immigration, 281, 520
  nuclear weapons, 578

opium wars, 586
period of the hundred philosophers, 68
Uighur separatists, 619
Chinese Exclusion Act, 520
Christianity. *See also* Bible
  death penalty, 229, 271
  ecological consciousness, 681
  freedom of speech, 463
  homosexuality, 344, 354, 356–357
  Nietzsche, 39
  pacifism, 586, 587–589
  patriarchy, 429
  war and peace, 573, 586–591
  women's inferiority, 394
Chung-kung, 69
Churchill, Winston, 630, 727
civil disobedience, 520, 579, 584, 632
"Civil Disobedience" (Thoreau), 579
Civil Liberties Act (1988), 526
Civil Rights Movement, 453, 488–489, 520, 523
civil society, 33, 39, 60–62, 64, 571, 574, 592
Clansman, The, 516
climate change, 643–644, 685–686
Clinton, Bill, 334, 424, 510
Clinton, Hillary, 424, 425
Clonaid, 135, 151, 152, 169–170
cloning, 133–135, 150–165
  animals, nonhuman, 142–143
  extinct species, 135, 174
  fertility treatment, 134, 142
  human, 137, 139, 140, 141–142, 150–165
  interference with nature, 139–140
  Johnson, Judith, 139, 150–157
  Jurassic Park (Crichton), 174
  Kass, Leon, 158–165
  public opinion, 135
  reproductive, 134, 140, 142, 151, 152–154, 157, 161
  repugnance toward, 160–165
  right to be unique, 139
  therapeutic, 151, 154–157
  Williams, Erin, 139, 150–157
Cloning Prohibition Act (1997), 135
Closing of the American Mind, The (Bloom), 545
Coady, C. A. J., 575, 581, 591–599
cocaine, 280–281, 283, 302, 306
cohabitation, 334–335, 384–385
Cohen, Carl, 644, 646, 647, 669–675
Cold War, 597
Cole, Jackie, 189
Cole, William, 508
college
  affirmative action, 523, 543–544
  cohabitation, 334, 384–385
  dorms, 325, 384–385
  drug/alcohol use, 278, 283–284, 285, 288, 289, 314–316, 324–325
  faculty-student sexual relationships, 385

college (*continued*)
  fraternities, 278, 284, 324–325, 337, 388
  free speech zones, 452, 453–454, 456
  hate speech/crimes, 445, 476–483, 494, 496–498, 522
  illegal immigrant tuition, 568–569
  Internet, 448, 456, 512
  moral development, 12, 15–16
  plagiarism, 512
  political correctness, 446, 499–501
  pregnancy/motherhood and, 114, 115, 416, 418
  racism, 453, 457, 476–483, 521–522
  Reserve Officers Training Corps (ROTC), 635
  sexual harassment, 399, 433–436, 469
  speech codes, 445, 452–454, 456, 485, 489–490, 498, 500–501
  USA Patriot Act, 509–510, 631
  violence/rape, 335, 337, 388
Collins, Kevin, 275
colonialism, 139, 524, 526, 536, 561, 569, 596, 605
color-blind principle, 522, 540–545
"Color-blind Principle, The" (Boxill), 540–545
color-conscious policies, 525, 541–545. *See also* affirmative action
Columbine High School, 232
Commonwealth v. Leis (1969), 367
Communications Decency Act (1996), 449
communism, 447, 456, 486, 491, 492, 591
communitarianism, 408
compassion, 37, 186, 272, 628–629
Comstock Law (1873), 490
Confucianism
  Analects, 68–70, 628
  compassion, 628
  deontology, 27
  doctrine of the mean, 38, 628
  freedom of speech, 455
  virtue ethics, 38–39
Confucius, 27, 37, 38–39, 68–71, 235, 287, 628
Congressional Research Service's Report for Congress on Human Cloning, 135
Connecticut, 74, 279, 334
Connelly, Harold, 320
Connelly, Patricia, 320
Conroy, Michael, 445
conscientious objection (CO). *See* war and terrorism, conscientious objection (CO)
conscription, military. *See* war and terrorism, conscription
"Conscription: The Terrible Price of War" (Paul), 624–626
consequentialism. *See* utilitarianism
conservation. *See* environmental ethics, conservation model

consumerism, 682, 684
contraception, 73, 83, 111, 331, 366, 384, 390, 490
contractarian theory, 246–250, 648–659, 660. *See also* social contract
Cordy, Robert J., 361, 365–369
Côte d'Ivoire, 570
Cowart, Donald, 225–228
Cox, Donald, 328
crack. *See* cocaine
Crichton, Michael, 174
Crick, Francis, 131
criminal justice system, 238–239, 270, 308, 522. *See also* death penalty
critical race theory, 515
Cruzan, Nancy, 181, 183, 222–223
Cruzan v. Director, Missouri Department of Health (1990), 181, 183–184, 222–223
Cuba, 615
cultural relativism, 5–8, 9, 39
Curlander v. Bio-Science Laboratories (1980), 140–142
Curren, Franklin, 223
Curren, Judith, 188, 223
cyberspace, 448–449, 502–506. *See also* Internet
Czechoslovakia, 594

Dalai Lama, 179
Dale v. Boy Scouts of America (2000), 448
Dar al-harb, 604–605
Dar al-Islam, 604–605
Darfur, 569
Darrow, Clarence, 244–245
Dartmouth College, 476, 508
Dartmouth Review, 476, 508–509
Darwin, Charles, 131, 641
date rape, 324, 377–383
"Date Rape: A Feminist Analysis" (Pineau), 377–383
David, Eric, 611
Davis, Rhoda, 634
Dean-Mooney, Laura, 284, 314–315
death penalty, 228–277
  abolition of, 228–229, 235, 237, 241, 242, 255, 260–261
  adultery and, 276–277
  Bedau, Hugo Adam, 29, 235, 236, 242, 251–261
  Christianity, 268, 271
  cruel and unusual punishment, 230, 232, 238, 250
  death row, 229, 231, 237, 238, 259, 268–270, 273, 276
  deterrence, 234, 235, 237, 242–243, 258–259, 262, 265, 267
  dignity of persons, 236, 244, 252, 254–257, 271
  discrimination and, 237, 241–242, 260, 269–270
  distributive justice, 237, 246–247
  DNA testing, 229, 233, 238

electric chair, 259, 270, 271
finality/risk of errors, 238–239
forfeiture theory, 247–248, 250, 253–254
Gregg v. Georgia (1976), 228, 229, 230–231
historical overview, 228
incapacitation, 235–236, 257
innocence and, 233, 239
justice, 236, 237, 246, 247, 248, 249, 250, 254–255, 256, 259–260
juveniles, 232
Kant, Immanuel, 29, 234–235, 244, 254–255, 264
lethal injection, 232–233, 259, 267, 271, 273, 276
Locke, John, 233, 252, 253–254, 255
medicalization of executions, 232–234
mental retardation and, 232
moral standing, 237, 245, 247–250
Morris, Christopher, 245–250
poverty, 249–250, 260, 269, 270
Prejean, Helen, 267–272
principle of equality, 237, 241–242, 260
public support, 229, 231–232, 237
racism, 231, 237, 260, 269–270
Reiman, Jeffrey, 261–267
retributive justice, 236, 237, 259–260, 263–266
sanctity of life, 236–237, 244, 252, 256
stoning, 276–277
terrorism, 273–274
van den Haag, Ernest, 234, 235, 237, 239, 240–244
death with dignity, 184, 186
de Beauvoir, Simone, 391–392, 395–396, 402–405, 422, 423
Decalogue, 17
deception, 322, 336, 371–374, 376, 624
Declaration of Independence, 33, 297
"Declaration on Sexual Ethics" (Vatican), 341–345
decriminalizing marijuana, 310–313, 329
deep ecology, 639, 647, 680–684
"Deep Ecology" (Devall/Sessions), 680–684
deer/vehicle collisions, 697–698
"Defense of Abortion, A" (Thomson), 28, 86–96, 121, 391
Defense of Marriage Act (1996), 332, 334
deforestation, 699–700
democracy, 30, 47, 447, 455, 460, 502–503, 506, 575, 580
deontology, 26–32
  Confucius, 27, 68–70
  duties, 27–30, 57–58
  Kant, Immanuel, 26–27, 55–58
  Rawls, John, 30, 59–62
  rights and, 33–34, 35
  Ross, W. D., 27–29, 30–31

de Poncins, Gontran, 9
Dershowitz, Alan M., 446, 454, 456, 499–501, 568
Descartes, René, 640, 650–651
Descent of Man, The (Darwin), 641
Devall, Bill, 639, 680–684
de Vitoria, F., 594
de Waal, Frans, 641
Diamond v. Chakrabarty (1980), 173, 174
Diaz, Angel Nieves, 238
Didache, 79
Didion, Joan, 438
dignity, human
 cloning, 137, 140, 154
 consensual sex, 339
 death penalty, 244, 252, 254–257, 260, 271
 drug abuse, 287–288
 duty to respect, 36
 euthanasia, 186, 205, 206, 210
 racism, 525
 stem-cell research, 168–169
dilation and curettage (D&C), 80
discrimination. *See also* racism; sexism
 cultural relativism, 7, 10
 genetic, 148
 homosexuals, 340, 367
 pornography and, 468
 selective abortion, 83–84
 speciesism, 648
disease, 133, 139, 147, 166–167, 168, 171, 285–286, 288
distributive justice. *See* justice, distributive
District of Columbia, 686
divine command theory, 16
divorce. *See* marriage, divorce
DNA testing, 233, 238
"Do Animals Have Rights?" (Cohen), 669–675
doctrine of the mean, 38, 45–47, 287
Dolly, 131, 135, 171
domestic violence. *See* sexual intimacy, violence
domination, 427–429, 470–473, 682, 688–691, 693
Donnelly, Elaine, 634
"don't ask, don't tell" policy, 634–635
Donum Vitae, 152
dopamine, 306
Dostoyevsky, Fyodor, 18
double effect, principle of, 180, 187, 582, 587, 589–590, 597, 631
doublethink, 8, 406, 589
Douglas, Justice, 474
Down's syndrome, 188, 191–192, 226
Draize eye irritancy test, 644, 667
DREAM Act (2007), 568–569
Dred Scott v. Sanford (1857), 10
Dresden, Germany, 630–631
drug and alcohol use, 278–329. *See also specific types of drugs*
 addiction, 285–286, 288, 292, 293–294, 305, 306

alcohol, 72, 278, 279–280, 281, 283–284, 286, 293–294, 295–296, 305–306, 309, 312, 314–317, 324, 325, 328
cocaine, 280–281, 283, 302, 303, 305, 306
crime and, 272, 273, 289, 303–304, 309, 328, 388
definitions, 278, 309
disease model of addiction, 280, 285–286, 288, 290
drug classifications, 279
drug education, 289–290, 304, 313
drug screening/testing, 284, 285, 307
good life, 287, 290
harms, 72, 288–290, 293, 311–312, 315–316, 320–323
heroin, 279, 280, 281, 293, 294, 295, 296, 300–303, 305, 309, 318
historical overview, 279–281
human dignity, 287–288
Husak, Douglas N., 287, 289–290, 307–313
legalization of drugs, 282, 293, 299–306, 310–311, 329
LSD, 279, 280, 293
marijuana, 279, 280, 281, 282, 284, 295, 296–297, 303, 306, 308, 319, 320
maternal drug use, 126–127
medicinal use, 280, 282, 301, 329
methadone, 279, 295, 297, 301
moral model of addiction, 280, 286
morphine, 279–280, 281, 287, 292, 295
Murray, Thomas H., 285, 288, 317–323
opiates, 280, 281, 293–294, 301
paternalism, 288–289, 311
performance enhancing/steroids, 50, 279, 284–285, 288, 317–323, 326
pregnancy and, 126–127, 289
principle of noninterference, 288
prohibition, 279–280, 281, 289, 292–293, 310–312, 316
race and, 280, 283, 310
self-medication, right of, 295–296, 297
sports, 150, 284–285, 288, 317–323, 326–327
stimulants, 279, 306, 319–320
Szasz, Thomas, 286, 291–298
tobacco, 281, 283, 289, 290, 293, 296, 304, 309, 312, 509
Wilson, James Q., 289, 299–306
dualism, 640, 689
Dukes v. Walmart Stores, Inc., 400
Durkheim, Emile, 5
duty, 6, 26–30, 57–58. *See also specific duties*
duty to die, 188–189, 207–213
duty to punish, 264
Dworkin, Andrea, 471, 472, 474, 485, 490
Dworkin, Ronald, 543

Earth in the Balance (Gore), 684
Earth Liberation Front (ELF), 694
Easterbrook, Frank, 486
eating disorders, 443–444
ecocentrism, 639, 646, 676
ecofeminism, 393, 394, 639, 647, 687–693
ecoterrorism, 694–695
egg procurement, 156
egoistic moral reasoning, 12, 14
Egypt, 590, 618
Ehrlich, Robert, 513
Emancipation Proclamation, 517
embryonic stem cell research. *See* stem cell research
Emerson, Ralph Waldo, 64
endangered/extinct species, 134, 135, 174, 697
enemy combatants. *See* war and terrorism, prisoners of war
energy consumption, 644, 686, 699
Engels, Friedrich, 395
England
 alcohol/drug use, 279, 282, 303
 animal experimentation, 638, 665
 climate crisis, 686
 commercial surrogacy, 440
 nuclear weapons, 578
 vegetarianism, 642
 war, 586
environmental ethics
 biocentrism, 646, 677–679, 681–682
 climate change/crisis, 643–644, 685–687
 conservation model, 679
 deep ecology, 639, 647, 680–684
 deforestation, 699–700
 Devall, Bill, 639, 680–684
 ecocentrism, 639, 646, 676
 ecofeminism, 393, 394, 639, 647, 687–693
 environmental racism, 515, 534, 570
 global warming, 564, 643–644, 685–687, 698–699
 Leopold, Aldo, 23, 639, 647, 676–679, 680, 682, 698
 moral standing of nature, 639, 644
 pollution, 564
 Sessions, George, 639, 680–684
 stewardship model, 647
 Warren, Karen, 40, 639, 641, 687–693
environmental racism, 515, 534, 570
Epicurus, 22, 246
Equal Employment Opportunity Commission (EEOC), 399, 435
equality, principle of
 affirmative action and, 523
 animals, nonhuman, 648, 661–664
 death penalty and, 234, 236, 237, 264
 euthanasia and, 188
 fathers and abortion, 83, 119–121, 124
 justice as fairness, 60, 62
 pornography and, 455, 487–488
 racism and, 525

equality, principle of (*continued*)
  rights and, 36
  same-sex marriage, 340, 367
  women and, 78, 399, 404
erotica, 449
Eskimos, 8, 9, 571, 630, 654
"Essentialist Challenges to Liberal
  Feminism" (Groenhout), 393,
  406–414
ethical egoism, 19–22, 47–49
ethical relativism, 3, 4–8, 12
ethical subjectivism, 4–5, 8, 12, 19, 81
ethics education, 14–15
"Ethics of Addiction, The" (Szasz),
  291–298
ethnocentrism, 10
eudaimonia, 321
eugenics, 131, 153
Europeans, 516
European Union, 135, 173, 229, 510
euthanasia, 177–227
  active, 177, 178, 185, 187, 191–192,
    200, 215
  advanced directives, 181, 221
  American Medical Association
    (AMA), 178–179, 191, 193, 216
  argument against self-interest,
    205–206
  argument from nature, 205
  argument from practical effects, 206
  autonomy, 185–186, 198–200
  Baby Doe, 188, 226
  Battin, Margaret, 186, 188, 203,
    195–202
  depression and, 182, 188, 199, 217
  duty to die, 188–189, 202–213
  equality, principle of, 188
  feminist view, 214–221
  "Final Exit" (Humphrey), 224
  Gay-Williams, J., 186, 203–206
  gender and, 180, 188, 214–221
  Hardwig, John, 29, 179, 187, 188,
    207–213
  involuntary, 177, 178, 182
  justice, 188, 189, 200–201, 202,
    210–211
  Kevorkian, Jack, 17, 35, 182, 184, 187,
    203, 207, 217, 219, 223, 225
  Latimer, Robert, 227
  legislation, 181–182
  mercy, principle of, 186, 196–198, 202
  pain and suffering, 186–187, 196–198
  passive euthanasia, 177, 178, 180, 187,
    191–194, 200, 204
  patient competence, 182, 185, 187,
    188, 212
  persistent vegetative state/coma,
    177–178, 180, 183, 186, 187, 189,
    199, 202, 222
  physician-assisted suicide, 182, 184,
    187–188, 202, 208, 214–221, 223
  public opinion, 180–181
  quality of life, 186–187
  Rachels, James, 178, 186, 190–194

religion, 178, 179–180, 185
sanctity of life, 185
self-determination, 185–186
slippery slope argument, 24, 189,
  201–202, 206
voluntary euthanasia, 177, 178, 185, 206
Wolf, Susan M., 185–186, 188,
  214–221
Evangelium Vitae, 229
evolution, 24, 513, 641, 676, 678, 684
Ex parte Quirin, 616
experimentation, scientific
  animal, 152, 638, 640, 645, 647,
    663–668, 675, 694, 695
  human, 172, 647, 663, 666–667, 694
explanatory nationalism, 563–564
extinction of species, 683, 699
extraordinary vs. ordinary treatment,
  180, 187

Falwell, Jerry, 507
Family and Medical Leave Act (1993),
  398, 399, 401, 442
Fan Ch'ih, 70
farming. *See* agriculture
fascism, 491
Fatal Attraction, 337
fatherhood, 34, 83, 114, 117–125, 130,
  140, 401, 633
Feinberg, Joel, 542, 543, 545
FEMA, 566
Feminine Mystique, The (Friedan), 391,
  399, 417, 422
feminism. *See also* women
  abortion and, 74, 113–114, 391, 393
  autonomy/liberty rights, 391, 400
  care ethics, 31, 40–41, 67
  choice feminism, 418
  conservatives, 392, 393, 398, 399,
    400, 401, 417
  de Beauvoir, Simone, 395, 402–405
  ecofeminism, 393, 394, 639, 647,
    687–693
  euthanasia and, 214–221
  gender equality, 391, 398
  gender essentialism, 393–394,
    406–414
  Goldberg, Steven, 426–431
  Groenhout, Ruth, 406–414
  Hirshman, Linda, 415–420
  historical overview, 390–393
  liberal feminism, 391, 394, 398–399,
    400, 401, 402, 406–414, 417–418
  MacKinnon, Catharine, 468–469,
    472, 474
  Marxist feminist, 391, 394, 401, 402
  patriarchy, 426–431
  pornography, 450, 456, 467–474
  radical feminist, 391, 394, 395,
    400–401, 450, 456
  Roiphe, Katie, 432–439
  socialist feminism, 392, 394, 396,
    398, 401, 402
  Steinem, Gloria, 424–425

women in workplace, 397–399
  Young, Cathy, 421–425
"Feminist Critique of Physician-Assisted
  Suicide, A" (Wolf), 214–221
Feminists for Life, 114, 115
Ferguson, Colin, 567
fertility treatment, 140–141, 142, 156,
  168, 441
fetal alcohol syndrome, 82, 126–127,
  289, 302
fidelity, duty of, 28, 29, 34, 69, 337, 352,
  374, 583
fighting words. *See* freedom of speech,
  fighting words
"Final Exit" (Humphrey), 224
Finkbine, Sherri, 73, 75
Finland, 590, 594
"First Amendment in Cyberspace, The"
  (Sunstein), 502–506
Fish, Stanley, 446, 453, 443–449
"Five Mindfulness Trainings, The"
  (Thich Nhat Hanh), 71–72
Florida, 555
Florida State University, 313–314, 454
Flynt, Larry, 507
Foot, Philippa, 197–198
Ford, Gerald, 151, 154, 157
forgiveness, 21, 39, 262, 264
Fort Carson, Colorado, 633
Fort Meade, 443
Foster, Serrin M., 74, 82, 113–116
Foundation for Individual Rights in
  Education (FIRE), 453
Fountainhead (Rand), 47–49
Fox, Michael J., 136
France, 180, 285, 300, 440, 578, 583
Franklin, Ben, 632
Franks, Tommy, 632
fraternities. *See* college, fraternities
Freedom of Access to Clinic Entrances
  Act (1994), 127
freedom of expression. *See* freedom
  of speech
freedom of speech, 445–513
  abortion clinic buffer zones and, 78,
    448
  advertising and, 510
  campus speech codes/zones, 452–454
  censorship, 446, 453, 454–455, 456,
    457, 473, 474, 487–488, 489–491
  clear and present danger require-
    ment, 486–487
  conduct/speech distinction, 478,
    495–496, 498
  cyberspace. *See* Internet
  Dershowitz, Alan, 499–501
  fighting words, 445, 451–452,
    478–480, 495
  First Amendment, 446, 447–448, 449,
    451, 452, 454, 477–479,
    481, 485, 486, 488, 490, 494,
    495–496, 497–498, 501, 502,
    505, 506, 512, 513
  Fish, Stanley, 455, 493–499

Hustler, 507
Internet, 448–449, 503–506
Lawrence, Charles, 475–483
liberty rights, 456, 459–466
MacKinnon, Catherine, 446, 467–474
"marketplace of ideas," 447, 448, 450, 455, 466, 482, 483, 501
Mill, John Stuart, 459–466
offensive speech, 446, 449–450, 453, 458
political correctness, 446, 458, 499–501
racist speech, 452–453, 475–483
slander/libel, 445, 457
Strossen, Nancy, 456, 458, 484–492
Sunstein, Cass, 502–506
viewpoint neutrality, 486
Freud, Sigmund, 333, 395, 422, 469
Frey, R. G., 668
Friedan, Betty, 391, 399, 417, 420, 422
Friedman, Milton, 300
friendship, 69, 336, 455
Frye, Marilyn, 692–693
Fugitive Slave Law (1850), 517
Fundamental Principles of the Metaphysics of Ethics (Kant), 54–58
Furman v. Georgia (1972), 228, 229, 230

Galton, Francis, 131
Galvez, Sergio Gonzalez, 611
Gandhi, Mohandas "Mahatma," 579, 638, 640, 648
Garcia, Jerry, 326
Garcia, Jorge, 522, 524, 525, 530–539
Garland, Lillian, 442
Gay-Williams, J., 178, 186, 189, 203–206
gender. *See also* feminism; men; women
   death penalty, 272–273
   differences, 407, 411–413, 426–431, 473
   inequality/discrimination, 390, 401, 468–471, 473–474, 523
   moral reasoning, 12–13, 39–40
   physician-assisted suicide, 214–221
   roles/stereotypes, 392–393, 399, 401, 403–405, 424, 431, 439–440, 450, 487
   vegetarianism, 642
genetically modified (GM) crops, 133
genetic engineering, 131–176
   aging and, 170–171
   animals, nonhuman, 131, 133, 134–135, 140, 142–143, 171–172, 695–696
   autonomy, 140
   consequentialist arguments, 141–142
   gene therapy, 132–133, 134, 138, 141, 146, 148, 171
   genetic discrimination, 148–149
   genetic enhancement, 132, 133, 141, 144–150
   genetic (DNA) testing, 141, 146, 275–276

historical overview, 131–132
Human Genome Project, 132, 138
reproductive rights, 140–141
Genetic Information Nondiscrimination Act (2008), 141
"Genetic Interventions and the Ethics of Enhancement of Human Beings" (Salvulescu), 144–150
Geneva Conventions, 578, 581, 614, 615, 632, 635
Gennarelli, Thomas, 694
genocide, 16, 81, 520
Germany, 10, 131, 180, 491, 598, 630–631
germ line therapy, 132, 133, 138
Gilligan, Carol, 12–13, 31, 39–40, 65, 216, 217, 220, 393, 396
Gilman, Charlotte Perkins, 433
Ginsberg, Morris, 15
Gitlow v. New York (1925), 495
Glass, Shirley, 336
Glesinger, Jesse, 141
global capitalism, 554–558. *See also* globalization
globalization, 397, 524, 554–557, 559–565, 570
global justice, 524, 526, 554–565
global warming, 643–644, 685–686, 698–699
Goldberg, Steven, 393, 394, 426–431
Golden Rule, 17, 27, 263, 264, 609, 628, 677
Goldman, Alan H., 248
Gonzales v. Oregon (2006), 182
good life, 35, 38, 147, 408
Goodridge v. Department of Health (2003), 340, 361–369
good will, 26, 40, 55
Gore, Al, 34, 644, 684, 685–686, 687, 699
Gottesman, I. I., 549
Graczyk, Michael, 276
Granoff, Jonathan, 573, 578, 581, 582, 608–612, 627–630
gratitude, duty of, 28, 29
Grauerholz, Elizabeth, 434
"Great American Boycott 2006/A Day Without an Immigrant," 555
Great Britain. *See* England
greatest happiness principle, 23, 52
Greenberg, Seth, 445
Gregg, Tony, 228
Gregg v. Georgia (1976), 228, 229, 230–231
Griswold v. Connecticut (1969), 75, 331, 366
Groenhout, Ruth, 393, 406–414
Grotius, Hugo, 573–574, 594
Grutter, Barbara, 565
Grutter v. Bollinger (2003), 523
Guantanamo Bay, 35, 273–274, 581, 615, 619, 635
Gulf War, 578, 597, 607
Gyge's ring, 19

habituation, 37, 38, 44–45
Hales, Steven D., 34, 82, 83, 117–125
hallucinogens, 279, 280
Hamdi, Yasser Esam, 616
Hamilton, Alexander, 447, 459
happiness, 21, 22–23, 39, 53, 72, 397–398, 401, 641. *See also* pleasure
Hardin, Garrett, 558–559
Hardwig, John, 29, 179, 187, 188, 207–213
Harlan, John Marshall, 541
Harris, Arthur, 631
Harris, Eric, 232
Harrison Narcotic Act, 297
Hart, Myra, 416
Harvard University, 136, 453
Hashmi, Sohail H., 572, 599–608
hate speech/crimes, 445, 450–454, 457, 478–480, 483, 484–492, 497–498, 521–522, 534–535. *See also* freedom of speech; racism
"Hate Speech and Pornography: Do We Have to Choose Between Freedom of Speech and Equality?" (Strossen), 484–492
Hawaii, 75
headhunting, 6, 10
"Heart of Racism, The" (Garcia), 530–539
Heaton, Joan, 274
Heaton, Patricia, 114
hedonistic paradox, 21
Hegel, Georg F. W., 244, 263, 264, 335
Held, Virginia, 40
Hemlock Society, 224
Herland (Gilman), 433
Hernstein, Richard J., 549
heroin, 279, 280, 281, 293, 294, 295, 296, 300–303, 305, 309, 318
Hill, Paul, 128
Hill v. Colorado (2000), 78
Hinduism, 78, 179, 333, 628, 638
Hippocratic Oath, 179, 196, 233
Hiroshima, Japan, 572, 575, 582, 590, 598, 610, 630
Hirshman, Linda, 391, 397, 401, 415–420, 421, 422–423
Hispanics/Latinos
   cocaine use, 283
   environmental racism, 570
   hate crimes, 521
   immigrants, 524, 554–558, 568
   marginalization of, 10
   racism, 514, 515, 522
Hitler, Adolf, 1, 201, 572, 574
Hitman: How to Make a Disposable Silencer, 511
Hobbes, Thomas, 19, 246, 248, 249, 571, 574, 581, 592–593, 594, 597
Holcomb, Simone and Vaughn, 633
Holcombe, W. H., 515
Holmes, Oliver Wendell, 295, 447, 502
"Homeward Bound" (Hirshman), 391, 415–420, 421

homosexuality
    attitudes toward, 340, 367
    biologically unnatural, 355–356, 358,
        359–360
    Goodridge v. Department of Public Health
        (2003), 340, 361–369
    Judeo/Christian tradition, 344, 354,
        356–357
    military and, 581, 634–635
    parenthood, 363–364, 368–369, 369,
        386–387
    Ruse, Michal, 353–360
    same-sex marriage, 333–334,
        356–360
    sexual perversion, 333–334, 358–360
    Sodom and Gomorrah, 356
Hong Kong, 563
Hopwood, Cheryl, 566
Horn, Mildred, 511
Horowitz, David, 507–508
hospice, 40, 184–185, 186
Howard University, 523, 528
HR4437, 524, 555
"Human Cloning" (Johnson/Williams),
    24, 150–157
Human Cloning and Human Dignity, 151
human dignity. *See* dignity, human
Human Genome Diversity Project
    (HGDP), 138–139
Human Genome Project (HGP), 132,
    138, 645
Human Life Amendment, 77
Humber, James, 125
Hume, David, 22, 37, 40, 66, 246, 248
Humphry, Derek, 224
Hundt, Reed, 511
Hungary, 594
hunting, 648, 653–654, 698
Hurlbut, William, 154
Hurricane Katrina, 525, 558, 566–567
Husak, Douglas N., 287, 289–290,
    307–313
Hussaini, Safiya Yakubu, 276–277
Hussein, Saddam, 578, 582, 625, 632
Hustler, 507
Hyde, Henry, 496
hypothetical imperative, 57, 58
hysterectomy, 80
hysterotomy, 80

Ibn Khaldun, 574, 604
Ibn Rushd, 604
identity. *See* self-identity
"If He Hollers Let Him Go: Regulating
    Racist Speech on Campus"
    (Lawrence), 475–483
Illinois, 451–452
immigrants. *See also specific countries
    and groups*
    globalization and, 524, 554, 556–558
    guest worker programs, 524, 557, 558
    illegal/undocumented immigrants,
        524, 555, 557, 568
    immigrant rights movement, 554, 558

migrant workers, 554–558
    racism/hate crimes, 281, 519, 555,
        557, 558
imperialism. *See* colonialism;
    globalization
In a Different Voice (Gilligan), 216,
    393, 396
"In and Out of Harm's Way: Arrogance
    and Love" (Frye), 692
Inconvenient Truth, An (Gore), 687
India
    abortion/sex selection, 28,
        83–84, 125
    commercial surrogacy, 396, 440
    global warming, 686
    marijuana laws, 282
    Mumbai terrorist attack, 572
    nuclear weapons, 578, 612
    tobacco-related deaths, 281
Indianapolis anti-pornography law,
    486, 489
Indian Removal Act, 520
Indians. *See* Native Americans
individualism, 20–21, 39, 209, 295,
    298, 408
Indonesia, 281
Industrial Revolution, 22, 50
"Inevitability of Patriarchy, The"
    (Goldberg), 426–431
infanticide. *See* children, infanticide
intelligent design (ID), 455, 513
International Court of Justice, 609–611
international government. *See* world
    government
International Workers' Day, 555
Internet, 336, 445, 448–449, 502–506,
    512–513
"Interpreting the Islamic Ethics of War
    and Peace" (Hashmi), 599–608
"Introduction to the Principles of
    Morals and Legislation, An"
    (Bentham), 50–51
in vitro fertilization (IVF), 152, 154,
    156, 166, 168, 396, 441. *See also*
    assisted reproductive technologies
    (ART)
Iowa, 334
Iowa v. Marzel Jones (2003), 288
Iran, 232, 491, 578, 582, 606, 619
Iraq, 491, 540, 577, 578, 580, 583,
    591, 606–607, 619, 621, 622, 625,
    632–633
"Is Adultery Immoral?" (Wasserstrom),
    336, 339, 370–376
"Is Homosexuality Bad Sexuality?"
    (Ruse), 353–360
Islam. *See also* Arab Americans
    abortion, 78
    adultery, 277, 331
    compassion, 628
    death penalty, 229
    drug/alcohol use, 287
    euthanasia, 179, 181, 185
    homosexuality, 333

jihad, 572, 600–601, 604,
    605–606, 607
    marriage, 330, 332, 333, 393
    Qur'an, 17, 601–606, 610
    terrorism, 16
    war and peace, 16, 572, 574, 599–608
    women/feminism, 409
Israel, 575, 578, 590
"Is There a Duty to Die?" (Hardwig),
    179, 207–213
Ivory Coast. *See* Côte d'Ivoire

Jaboulay, Mathieu, 695
Jackson, Jesse, 517
Jainism, 628, 638
Jamaica, 280, 282
Japan
    abortion, 74
    animal research, 638
    atomic bombing of, 572, 575, 576,
        582, 590, 610, 631
    gene patents, 138
Japanese Americans, 519, 526,
    626, 632
Jefferson, Thomas, 33, 62, 516, 517,
    641, 661
Jellinek, Elvine M., 286
Jensen, Arthur, 549, 553
Jesus of Nazareth, 37, 39, 53, 239, 268,
    269, 343–344
jihad. See Islam, *jihad*
Jim Crow Laws, 437, 515, 518, 527, 533,
    535, 541–542, 551
John Paul II, Pope, 186, 271
Johnson, Dr., 590
Johnson, Jennifer, 126–127
Johnson, Judith A., 24, 139, 142,
    150–157
Johnson, Lyndon B., 520, 523,
    528–530, 550
Johnson, S., 494
Judaism. *See also* Bible
    abortion, 78–79
    anti-Semitism, 451–452, 532.
        See also Nazis
    compassion, 628
    death penalty, 229
    euthanasia, 179, 181, 185
    marriage, 332, 354, 356
Jurassic Park (Crichton), 174
justice, 29–31
    compensatory, 547–548, 549, 550,
        551. *See also* restitution
    by convention, 246–247
    death penalty, 236, 237, 246, 249, 254,
        259–260
    distributive, 29–30, 35, 61,
        200–201, 237, 246–247, 544–545,
        551–552, 561
    euthanasia, 188, 189, 200–201, 202
    fairness, 30, 59–62, 141, 210–211
    feminism and, 401
    perspective, 13, 31–32, 239
    racism and, 535

retributive, 29, 229, 234, 236, 237, 239, 242, 243, 246, 248, 253, 254–255, 256, 259–260, 263, 264, 265, 611, 606
Theory of Justice, A (Rawls), 59–62
war and terrorism, 582–583
just-war tradition, 575–578, 592–598
    Aquinas, Thomas, 572–573, 601
    double-effect, principle of, 582, 589–590
    Islam, 602, 606–607
    Jus ad bellum, 575, 593–596, 607
    Jus in bello, 575–578, 596–597, 598, 606–607
    modern warfare and, 590–591
    noncombatant immunity, 577, 590, 596, 597, 598, 606–607
    proportionality, principle of, 582, 593, 595, 596, 597, 606–607
juveniles. *See* children

Kabloona, 9
Kansas State University, 336
Kant, Immanuel
    animal rights, 59, 640, 671
    categorical imperative, 26–27, 56–58, 287–288, 357, 582
    death penalty, 29, 234–235, 236, 244, 254–255, 264
    deontology/duty, 26–27, 31–32, 55–58, 66
    Fundamental Principles of the Metaphysics of Ethics, 54–58
    humans, 137, 210, 213, 254, 255
    "Perpetual Peace," 574
    sexuality, 335, 357
    suicide/euthanasia, 35, 58, 180
    women, 394–395, 457
Kass, Leon, 137, 139, 140, 141–142, 154–155, 158–165
Kaufman, Harry, 511
Kennedy, Edward, 699
Kennedy, John F., 425
Kenya, 386
Kevorkian, Jack, 17, 35, 182, 184, 187, 203, 207, 217, 219, 223, 225
Khaldun, Ibn, 601, 604
Khalid Sheik Mohammed, 273
Khomeini, 606
King, Martin Luther, Jr., 7, 17, 488, 520, 527
King, Stephen, 175
Kirkpatrick, Jeane, 36
Kirkpatrick, Jerry, 510
Klebold, Dylan, 232
Kluckhohn, Clyde, 9
Kohlberg, Lawrence, 3–4, 11–13, 216, 220, 239
Koop, C. Everett, 115, 182
Koran, 229
Koss, Mary, 438
Kramer, Peter, 327–328
Krueger, Scott, 278
Ku Klux Klan (KKK), 518–519

Kurami, Amina Lawal, 277
Kuwait, 607
Kyoto Protocol, 644, 686

laissez-faire capitalism. *See* capitalism
Lamarkian theory, 516
Lamm, Richard, 208
"Land Ethic, The" (Leopold), 23, 639, 676–679
land pyramid, 678
Langevin, James R., 136, 142, 166–167
Laos, 578
Latimer, Laura, 227
Latimer, Robert, 227
Latimer, Tracy, 227
Latinos. *See* Hispanics
Lawrence, Charles R., III, 32, 33, 446, 448, 452, 453, 456, 458, 475–483, 515
Lawrence v. Texas (2003), 334
League of Nations, 571, 624
Lee, Barbara Coombs, 224
leer, right to, 437
legal moralism, 311
legitimate interests, 34–35, 400
Leipold, Alexander, 284
Leopold, Aldo, 23, 639, 647, 676–679, 680, 682, 698
Lesotho, 399
Leviathan (Hobbes), 21, 574
Levin, Michael, 522, 525, 546–553
Lewis, David, 203
lex talionis, 229, 243, 259–260, 263, 264, 265–267, 603. *See also* justice, retributive
Liberation Movement of Iran (LMI), 606
Liberia, 386, 399
libertarians, 35, 36, 287, 408, 456, 459
liberty rights, 33, 34–35, 61, 408, 456, 460–461, 465. *See also specific liberty rights*
Lichtenberg, Judith, 536–537
Lincoln, Abraham, 517
Lind, Paul, 511
Lindh, John Walker, 583, 615
Linnaeus, Carolus, 516
Listening to Prozac (Kramer), 327, 328
Little Red Book, The (Mao Tse-Tung), 509
liver transplants, 326–327
living wills, 181. *See also* euthanasia, advanced directives
Locke, John
    death penalty, 233, 236, 237, 252, 253–254, 255
    freedom of speech, 454
    native Americans, 516
    natural rights ethics, 33, 35, 62–64, 253, 516, 640
    retributive justice, 272
    self-killing/suicide, 179–180
    state of nature, 561–562
    Two Treatises of Civil Government, 62–64

"Logic of Patriarchy, The" (Goldberg), 426–431
London Zoo, 697
Long Island Railroad, 567
Los Angeles, 555
Louisiana, 267–268, 541, 566
Louisiana State University, 324
love, 57, 331–332, 355, 629
Loving v. Virginia (1967), 363
Luban, David, 578, 581, 613–619
Lukianoff, Greg, 453–454
Luxembourg, 182
lying, 56
lynch laws, 518–519

Machiavelli, Niccolò, 572, 628
MacKinnon, Catharine
    liberal feminism, 407, 409–411, 413–414
    pornography, 410, 413, 446, 450, 456, 457, 458, 467–474, 485
    "Pornography, Civil Rights, and Speech," 391, 410, 467–474
    sexual harassment, 434, 437
    women as prey, 410, 413
    women's rights, 34, 383, 390
Madison, James, 502
Maine, 334
Malcolm X, 520
mammoth, 135, 174
Manifest Destiny, 520
Mantle, Mickey, 325–326
Mao Tse-Tung, 509
marijuana, 279, 280, 281, 282, 284, 295, 296–297, 303, 306, 308, 320, 329
marketplace of ideas. *See* freedom of speech
Marquis, Don, 82, 108–112
marriage, 332–336. *See also* sexual intimacy
    adultery, 276–277, 336, 338, 340, 346, 387–388
    attitudes toward, 330–331, 366–367
    contractual model, 333
    divorce, 277, 333, 335, 339, 340, 364–365, 393
    domestic violence, 218, 335
    feminist perspectives, 333, 339
    Goodridge v. Department of Public Health (2003), 340, 361–369
    happiness and, 401
    interracial, 363
    love, 331–332, 343–344, 351, 372–374
    marrying down, 419
    open marriage, 374
    polygamy, 331, 375, 386
    premarital agreements, 333
    premarital education, 383–384
    priests and, 332, 345
    procreation and, 159, 160–165, 330, 332, 343–344, 356, 363–364
    purpose of, 332–333, 335–336, 343–344, 363–364, 365, 368
    right to marry, 363, 365–366

ntinued)
.., 333–334, 339–340,
  570, 386–387
  ies, 335–336, 339
  ious attitudes, 330, 333, 342–345
  hall, Margaret H., 340, 361–365
  x, Karl, 234, 235
  irxism, 391–392, 401
  iassachusetts, 334, 361–369, 698
Massachusetts Institute of Technology
  (MIT), 278
masturbation. *See* sexual intimacy,
  masturbation
materialism, scientific, 681
maternal drug use, 126–127
*Maternal Thinking: Towards a Politics of
  Peace* (Ruddick), 396, 633
Mawdudi, Abual-A'la, 606
Mbuti, 139
McCain, John, 397, 635
McCardell, John, 284, 314, 315–316
McCarthy, Joseph, 447–448
McCarthyism, 447, 456
McCartney, Linda and Paul, 637
McDonald's (restaurant), 695
McVeigh, Timothy, 273–274
mean world syndrome, 511
meat-eating, 642, 648, 652. *See also*
  vegetarianism
media. *See also* advertising/commercial
  speech; Internet
  sex stereotypes, 439–440
  racism, 516, 566–567
  violence, 454, 511
Medicare, 289, 520
Meese, Edwin, 450
Meilkejohn, A., 474
Meinhold v. U.S. Department of Defense
  (1994), 634
Memphis State University, 476
men. *See also* fatherhood; patriarchy
  aggression, 379–380, 410–412
  dominant nature, 393, 394, 427–431,
    470–473
  drug/alcohol, 294
  housework and, 392, 396–397
  moral development, 12–13
  pornography, 449, 507
  reverse discrimination, 523
  socialization, 391, 427–428,
    430, 507
  status attainment/power, 427, 434
  workplace and, 335–336, 390, 392,
    397–398
Mengele, Josef, 694
mercy, principle of, 186, 196–198,
  202. *See also* nonmaleficence,
  duty of
mercy killing. *See* euthanasia
Meredith, James, 534
metaethics, 2
Mexico
  drug use/trafficking, 280, 300, 524
  immigration to U.S., 519, 524, 557

Michigan, 387, 523. *See also* University
  of Michigan
Midgley, Mary, 173
Mifepristone, 79
Milgram, Stanley, 1
Milgram experiment, 1, 15
military. *See also* war and terrorism,
  conscription
  homosexuals, 634–635
  rape/sexual harassment, 399,
    442–443, 634
  women, 393, 399, 442–443, 623,
    633–634
Military Commission Act (2006), 635
Military Families Voice of Victory, 632
Mill, Harriet Taylor. *See* Taylor, Harriet
Mill, James, 52, 357
Mill, John Stuart
  animal rights, 53–53, 651, 656
  death penalty, 234, 255
  deontology, critique of, 31
  freedom of speech, 453, 454, 455,
    457, 459–466
  greatest happiness principle, 357
  harm principle, 311, 457
  marriage, 336, 395
  "On Liberty," 7, 298, 445, 454,
    459–466
  pleasure, 23
  power and gender, 409
  self-determination, 583
  "Subjection of Women," 390, 395
  tyranny of the majority, 7, 455–456
  Utilitarianism, 52–54
  war and peace, 574, 582
Millennium World Peace Summit, 630
Miller, Sherry, 217
Milton, John, 494–495
Milwaukee Project, 552
mindfulness, 71–72
Minnesota, 452
Minnesota Transracial
  Adoption Study, 550–551
Minutemen, 555
Missouri Compromise, 517
Moen, Phyllis, 419
Mohammed, Khalid Sheik, 273
Money Train, 511
Montreal Protocol, 686
Moore, Bob, 228
Moore v. East Cleveland (1977), 366–367
"Moral Basis of Vegetarianism, The"
  (Regan), 649–654
moral community, 9–10, 648, 693
moral development, 12–15, 216
  Americans, 3–4
  children, 12, 147
  college students, 13–14
  gender and, 12–13
  Gilligan, Carol, on, 12–14
  Kohlberg, Lawrence, on, 12–13, 14
  prison and, 239
  stages of, 12–13, 14
moral disagreement, 8–9

"Moral Right to Use Drugs, A" (Husak),
  307–313
"Moral Significance of Birth, The"
  (Warren), 102–108
moral theory, 1–72. *See also specific
  moral theories and philosophers*
  Buddhist ethics, 39, 71–72
  care ethics, 39–41, 65–68
  Confucian virtue ethics, 38–39,
    68–69
  cultural relativism, 5–8, 9
  deontology, 26–32, 54–62
  divine command theory, 16
  ethical egoism, 19–22, 47–49
  ethical relativism, 3, 4–8, 12
  ethical subjectivism, 4–5
  moral disagreement, 8–9
  natural law theory, 16–17
  natural rights ethics, 35–38, 62–64
  psychological egoism, 19–20
  rights-based ethics, 32–37
  universal moral theory, 18–41
  utilitarianism, 22–26, 50–54
  virtue ethics, 37–41, 42–47
Mormon Church, 386
morning-after pill, 79
*Morning After: Sex, Fear, and Feminism on
  Campus, The* (Roiphe), 383
morphine, 280, 281, 295
Morris, Christopher W., 237, 245–250
Mosaic Decalogue, 676
motherhood, 395–397. *See also* abortion
  attitudes toward, 397
  autonomy and, 391, 393, 400
  de Beauvoir, Simone, 403–405
  false consciousness and, 391, 386
  feminist perspectives, 391, 395–396,
    403–405, 415–423
  gender roles and, 392–393, 396–397,
    416, 418, 419, 422–423
  happiness, 401, 405
  maternal drug/alcohol use, 82,
    126–127, 289, 302
  maternity leave, 392, 398–399, 442
  military, 623, 633–634
  "mommy wars," 417, 421–423
  patriarchal institution, 395
  pregnancy, 404–405, 411
  stay-at-home, 416–417, 421–422
  surrogate, 396, 440–441
  workplace and, 397, 398–399, 401,
    416–420
  Young, Cathy, 421–425
Mothers Against Drunk Driving
  (MADD), 314–315
Muqaddima (Ibn Khaldun), 601, 604
Muhammad (the Prophet), 574, 601,
  603–604, 606
Muir, John, 682
Murray, Thomas H., 285, 288, 317–323
Muslims. *See* Islam
Mutahhari, Murtaza, 606
Mutua, Makau, 569
My Lai Massacre, 576–577, 583

Nadelmann, Ethan, 304–305
Naess, Arne, 639, 680, 681, 682, 683
Nagasaki, 572, 575, 582, 590, 598, 631
Nagel, Thomas, 349
Nanny 911, 439
Nantucket Sound, 698
Narveson, Jan, 646, 655–659
National Association for the
    Advancement of Colored People
    (NAACP), 482, 489
National Bioethics Advisory
    Commission (NBAC), 151, 152
National Institutes of Health,
    (NIH), 694
nationalism, 571
National Minimum Legal Drinking Age
    Act, 315
National Organization of Women, 391,
    392, 442
National Service Act, 580, 622–623.
    See also war and terrorism,
    conscription
Native Americans, 282–283, 515, 516,
    517, 519, 520, 526, 546, 578, 628
Natural Born Killers, 511
naturalistic fallacy, 6–7, 140, 648
Natural law theory, 16–17, 18, 179,
    342–345, 648
natural lottery, 30, 149
natural rights ethics, 33–34, 35, 62–64,
    408
Nazis, 131, 180, 201, 251, 451–452, 485,
    489, 491, 514, 574, 584, 590, 670
Neanderthal, 135, 174
Nebraska, 78, 523
Neiertz, Veronique, 436
Netherlands
    animal rights, 638
    euthanasia, 178, 180, 182, 188, 189
    marijuana, 282
    same-sex marriage, 334
Nevada, 338
New Guinea, 6, 139, 399
New Hampshire, 334
New Mexico State University, 445
Newton, Lisa, 545
New York State, 73
New Zealand, 638
Nichomachean Ethics (Aristotle), 42–47, 321
Nietzsche, Friedrich, 39, 66, 574
Nigeria, 276–277, 386, 570, 629
1984 (Orwell), 11
Nitschke, Dr., 225
Noblitt, Cindy, 224–225
No Child Left Behind Act (2001), 626
Noddings, Nel, 31, 40, 65–67, 641
noninterference, principle of, 288
nonmaleficence, duty of, 28, 29, 186,
    289–290, 457, 582, 651
Noonan, John, 80, 97–101
normative ethics, 2
North Korea, 578, 619
Northwest Missouri State
    University, 476

Norton, Sarah, 113
nuclear deterrence, 611–612
Nuclear Non-Proliferation Treaty,
    610, 629
nuclear weapons, 572, 575, 576, 578,
    582, 590, 607, 608–613, 627, 629
"Nuclear Weapons, Ethics, Morals and
    Law" (Granoff), 582, 608–612
nuclei transfer using adult cells, 135
nuclei transfer using embryonic or
    fetal cells, 134–135
Nye, Phillip, 85

Oates, Captain, 208
Obama, Barack
    "don't ask, don't tell" policy, 635
    global warming/alternative energy,
        644, 694
    Guantanamo Bay, 237, 581, 619, 636
    nuclear weapons, 578
    presidential campaign, 397, 424, 425
    racism, 514, 522
    stem cell research, 136
    taxes, 50
    torture, 636
obedience, 1, 15, 17
Oberlin College, 384
objectivist moral theories, 3
obscenity laws, 471, 472, 473, 474, 485,
    490, 491, 505
Odyssey (Homer), 336, 676
Of Woman Born (Rich), 396
Oklahoma City bomber, 273, 572
Olympics, 284, 319–320, 322, 326
oncomouse, 138
On Liberty (Mill), 8, 298, 445, 459–466
opiates, 279, 280
opiophobia, 187
"Opt-Out Revolution, The" (Belkin), 420
Oregon, 181–182, 219
Oregon Death with Dignity Act,
    181–182
organ donation, 172, 695
Orwell, George, 8, 11
outsourcing, 524. *See also* globalization

pacifism, 257, 579, 586, 587–589, 597, 602
Padilla, Jose, 616
pain and suffering, 22, 23, 25,
    71–72, 82, 139, 154, 155, 166, 184,
    186–187, 196–198, 206, 219, 243,
    661–667
Pakistan, 232, 575, 578, 612
Palestine, 591
Palin, Sarah, 397
Palko v. Connecticut (1937), 367
palliative care, 184, 186–187, 221
Palmerston, Lord, 586
Palmore v. Sidot (1984), 365
parenthood, 140, 146, 153, 161, 164,
    363–364, 386–387, 583. *See also*
    fatherhood; motherhood
Paris, 557
Parks, Rosa, 519–520

partial-birth abortion, 78, 80, 81, 129
Partial-Birth Abortion Act of 2003, 78
Pasolini, Paolo, 491
Pasteur, Louis, 173
patents, gene, 138–139, 173–174
paternalism, 199, 200, 288–289, 526,
    533, 535–536
patriarchy, 338, 395, 400, 402, 427,
    429–431, 433, 689, 691
Patriot Act. *See* USA Patriot Act
Paul, Ron, 580, 624–626
"Peace and Security" (Granoff), 627–630
peace (anti-war) movements, 571
pedophilia, 337
Pennsylvania, 116, 513, 571
Pentagon, 571
People vs. Larry Flynt, The, 507
performance-enhancing drugs, 279,
    284–285
Perle, Richard, 508
"Perpetual Peace" (Kant), 574
Perry, James, 511
personhood
    definition, 10
    embryonic stem cell research,
        136, 137
    fetal, 80–81, 87–88, 95, 98–101, 102,
        107, 110–112
    great apes and, 638
"Perspective on Global Warming"
    (Gore), 685–686
perversity. *See* sexual perversion
Pet Sematary (King), 175
peyote, 280, 282
pharmacogenetics, 645
Philip Morris, 510
Philippines, 556
Philips, Maryanne, 567
physicians
    abortion, 74–75, 84, 126
    death penalty, 233, 276
    domestic violence, 336
    drug use, 136, 280, 286, 292, 297, 301
    euthanasia, 181, 182, 187–188, 202,
        206, 212, 214–221, 292
    Nazi, 670
    physician-assisted suicide, 182, 184,
        187–188, 202, 208, 214–221, 223
Pineau, Lois, 331, 337, 377–383
Pinker, Steven, 108
Pink Pyramid (bookstore), 491
Piper, Adrian, 532
Pius XII, Pope, 190
plagiarism, 512
Planned Parenthood, 75, 77
*Planned Parenthood of Central Missouri
    v. Danford (1976)*, 83
Planned Parenthood v. Casey (1992), 77
Plato, 19, 43, 131, 178, 275, 354–356,
    358, 394, 454, 516, 604, 629
pleasure, 22–23, 25, 52–54, 288, 347,
    350, 352. *See also* utilitarianism
Plessy, Homer, 541
Plessy v. Ferguson (1896), 518, 541

8

..w, 454, 499
.omas, 21, 524, 559–565
.correctness, 453–454, 458,
    ,–501, 527, 535, 553
.cal Correctness, Speech Codes,
    .nd Diversity" (Dershowitz),
    499–501
.lygamy, 331, 340, 386
.ornography, 336, 410, 446, 449–450,
    455–456, 457, 467–474, 484–492,
    504–505
"Pornography, Civil Rights, and
    Speech" (MacKinnon), 391,
    467–474
Pornography: Men Possessing Women
    (Dworkin), 471
Portugal, 316
Posner, Richard, 488
Potak, Mark, 83
poverty, 21, 74, 520, 524, 559–565, 529,
    549, 629, 683
Powell, Colin, 620, 635
"Power and the Promise of Ecological
    Feminism, Revisited, The"
    (Warren), 687–603
PPL Therapeutics, 171
preemptive war. *See* war and terrorism,
    preemptive war
preferential treatment. *See* affirmative
    action
Pregnancy Discrimination Act,
    (1978), 399
pregnancy leave, 116, 440
Prejean, Helen, 17, 29, 40, 235, 236,
    237, 238, 239, 267–272
prejudice, 22, 237, 286, 463,
    465–466, 515, 527, 534, 537. *See also*
    discrimination; racism, individual
premarital education programs,
    383–384
prenatal diagnosis/screening, 83, 84,
    125–126, 132, 141
President's Council on Bioethics, 151,
    152, 154, 155, 156, 157
Price, Craig, 5, 274–275
prima facie duties, 27–29
Prince, The (Machiavelli), 572, 628
Princeton University, 433–434, 435,
    436–437
principles, moral. *See specific principles*
privacy rights, 34, 75, 76, 127, 363, 366,
    504–505, 635
property rights, 33, 35, 36, 61, 63–64,
    71, 517, 564
proportionality, principle of, 236, 582,
    593, 595, 596, 597
Proposition 209 (California), 523
prostaglandins, 80
prostitution, 331, 338, 488, 492
Prozac, 327–328
psychological egoism, 19–20
punishment, 228, 232, 234, 236, 237,
    239, 241, 243, 246–250, 252,

253–254, 255–256, 257, 262,
    263–264, 265–266, 588, 617. *See also*
    capital punishment
"Punishment and Loss of Moral
    Standing" (Morris), 245–250
Purdue University, 476
Pure Food and Drug Act (1906), 281
Pythagoreans, 179, 639

Quakers, 17
quality of life, 145, 186–187
Quinlan, Karen Ann, 177, 204
Qur'an, 17, 181, 330, 574, 601–606

"Race, Biology, and Justice" (Levin),
    525, 546–553
Rachels, James, 178, 186, 187,
    190–194
racial differences, 516, 525, 529,
    546–553
racism, 514–570. *See also* African
    Americans; Arab Americans; His-
    panics/Latinos; Native Americans
black-rage defense, 567–568
Boxill, Bernard, 35, 522, 523, 525,
    526, 540–545
colonialism, 139, 524, 526, 561
color-blind principle, 522, 527,
    540–545
critical race theory, 515
death penalty, 231, 237, 260,
    269–270
definitions, 514, 525, 531–532
distributive justice, 551–552
environmental racism, 534, 570
Garcia, Jorge, 525, 530–539
globalization, 524, 559–565
hate speech/crimes, 445, 450–454,
    457, 478–480, 483, 484–492,
    497–498, 508, 514, 521–522,
    534–535
historical overview, 516–520
immigrants and, 524, 554–558
individual, 522, 525, 527, 533, 539
institutional, 515–516, 518, 520,
    522, 523, 525, 527, 533, 537–538,
    539, 550
Jim Crow Laws, 437, 515, 518, 527,
    533, 535, 541–542, 551
Johnson, Lyndon, 520, 523,
    528–530, 550
Levin, Michael, 522, 525, 546–553
lynch laws, 518–517
Pogge, Thomas, 559–565
racial profiling, 522
reparations/compensation, 526,
    547–551
Robinson, William, 524, 554–565
segregation, 457, 474, 518–520, 551
stereotypes, 424–425, 515, 516
rain forests, 644, 697, 699–700
Rand, Ayn, 20–21, 33–35, 47–49, 454
Rangel, Charles, 621
Ranjeva, Judge, 609

rape, 82, 88, 92–93, 96, 128, 337, 339,
    351, 377–383, 388–389, 437, 438,
    469, 470
Rastafarians, 280, 282, 329
Ratzinger, Joseph, 137
R.A.V. v. St. Paul (1992), 452
Rawls, John
    civil disobedience, 632
    contractarian theory, 648–659, 660
    justice, 30, 59–62, 246–247,
        551–552
    natural lottery, 551–552
    rights, 408, 454
    Theory of Justice, A, 59–62, 552
    utilitarianism, 24, 25
    veil of ignorance, 30, 59, 60, 658
    war, 598
Reagan, Nancy, 136, 151, 154, 157
Reagan, Ronald, 520, 623
reason, 40, 38, 407–408, 641
reciprocity, principle of, 27, 67, 237,
    581, 609, 629
"Reckless Eyeballing: Sexual
    Harassment on Campus"
    (Roiphe), 400, 432–439
reductionism, 137, 428–429, 692
Reeve, Christopher, 136
"Refuse to Choose: Women Deserve
    Better Than Abortion" (Foster), 74,
    113–116
Regan, Tom, 34, 36, 638, 646, 647,
    649–654, 671–675
Reiman, Jeffrey, 234, 236, 261–267
religion. *See also specific religions*
    abortion, 78–79
    animals/environment, 24
    compassion, 628–629
    death penalty, 229, 267–269, 271
    divine command theory, 16
    ethics and, 15–18
    euthanasia, 179–180
    homosexuality, 356–357
    intelligent design theory, 513
    natural law theory, 16–17, 18
    religious freedom, 277, 329
    reparation, duty of, 28, 526
    reproductive rights, 33, 140–141,
        164–165, 175, 441, 490
    sexuality and marriage, 330–331
Republic (Plato), 19, 131, 275, 454, 516
Reserve Officers' Training Corps
    (ROTC), 635
"Response to Race Differences in
    Crime" (Levin), 553
responsibility criterion, 542–544
restitution, 236, 238, 526. *See also*
    racism, reparations/compensation;
    religion, reparation, duty of
retaliation, 234, 611
retributive justice. *See* justice,
    retributive
"Return of the Mommy Wars, The"
    (Young), 421–425
revenge, 236, 268, 588, 611

reverse discrimination. *See* affirmative action
Revolution, The, 113
Rhode Island, 275, 338
Rich, Adrienne, 396, 469
right of refusal, 119–124
right to be unique, 139, 161, 164
right to life
    abortion, 88–93, 103, 105
    animals, nonhuman, 638, 650, 653–654, 664
    death penalty, 233, 237, 244, 249, 252, 253–254
    stem cell research, 169
right to marry, 363, 365–366, 367
right to punish, 234, 256, 262
right to reproduce. *See* genetic engineering, reproductive rights; religion, reproductive rights
rights, forfeiture of, 247–248, 250
rights ethics, 32–37. *See also specific rights*
R. J. Reynolds, 510
Roberts, John, 78
Robinson, William I., Jr., 524, 554–558
Roehling, Patricia, 419
Roe v. Wade (1973), 73, 75–78
Roiphe, Katie, 337, 383, 400, 432–439, 456
romantic love, 331, 332
Roper v. Simmons (2005), 232
Rosenberg, Ethel and Julius, 242
Roslin Institute (Scotland), 131
Ross, W. D., 27–28, 30–31, 67, 253
ROTC Campus Access Act, 635
Roth v. United States (1957), 450
Rousseau, Jean-Jacques, 4, 246, 335, 394–395, 516
RU 486. *See* Mifepristone
Ruddick, Sara, 331, 346–353, 359, 396, 633–634
Rumsfeld, Donald, 615
Ruse, Michael, 330, 340, 353–360
Russell, Bill, 541
Russia, 74, 491, 578, 591, 597, 619. *See also* Soviet Union
Rutgers University, 325
Rwanda, 569

Sacco, Nicola, 242
"Salo, 120 Days of Sodom" (Pasolini), 491
Salvulescu, Julian, 144–150
same-sex marriage. *See* marriage, same-sex
sanctity of life, 136, 179, 181, 185, 206, 236–237, 244, 252, 256. *See also* right to life
Sand County Almanac, A (Leopold), 676
Sandel, Michael, 145
Sanger, Margaret, 390, 490
Sartre, Jean-Paul, 352
Satris, Stephen, 11
Saudi Arabia, 232

Saunders, Cicely, 184–185
Scandinavia, 430
Schenck v. Pro-Choice Network (1997), 448
Schiavo, Terri, 177, 180, 186
Schlessinger, Laura, 450
Schmidt, Benno C., 496–497
schools. *See also* college
    drugs and alcohol use, 288, 296, 304, 510
    evolution/intelligent design, 513
    military recruiters, 626
    "No Child Left Behind Act" (2001), 626
    prayer, 448
    racism, 458, 478, 481, 514, 515, 518–519, 521, 525
    segregation, 458, 478, 514, 518–519, 521, 525, 543, 551
    sex education, 383–384
    violence/harassment, 232, 399, 522
Schuster, Stephen, 174
science experimentation. *See* experimentation, scientific
scientific view of body, 137
SCNT. *See* somatic cell nuclei transfer (SCNT)
Scopes "Monkey Trial," 513
Scott, Dred, 517
Second Sex, The (de Beauvoir), 395, 402–405
Second Treatise of Government (Locke), 62–64, 233–234
Second Wind (Russell), 541
segregation. *See* racism; schools, segregation
Selective Service System, 580, 621. *See also* war and terrorism, conscription
self-actualization. *See* self-realization
self-awareness criterion, 103, 104–105
self-defense, right to, 257, 579, 581, 592, 594, 603–604. *See also* war and terrorism, defensive wars
self-determination, right of, 185, 188, 200, 219, 225, 575, 583, 690
self-hate, 533
self-identity, 137, 139, 153, 162, 164
self-improvement, duty of, 29, 285
self-interest, 20–21, 48–49, 55, 149, 205–206
self-love, 57
self-preservation, right to. *See* self-defense, right to
self-realization, 21, 327, 681–682
self-sacrifice, 13, 39, 48, 186, 188, 215, 216, 217, 218
Seneca, 629
Sensenbrenner, James, 555
sentience, 22, 53, 103–106, 646, 653
September 11, 2001, 16, 273, 274, 446, 522, 571, 581, 599, 608, 618, 619, 631
Serbia, 597
Sermon on the Mount, 588

Sessions, George, 639, 680–684
Sex and the City, 439
sex education, 383–384
sexism, 10, 215–216, 394, 424–425, 458, 468–474, 492, 648, 689
sex trade. *See* prostitution
sexual harassment
    college, 385, 399–400, 432–439, 456, 469–470
    definition, 399, 434–435
    laws against, 410
    military, 442–443
    workplace, 399–400, 401, 410, 469–470
sexual intimacy, 330–389. *See also* marriage
    adultery/infidelity, 71, 336, 340, 356, 357, 370–376, 387–388
    Buddhism and, 71–72
    chastity, 343, 345
    cohabitation, 330, 335, 339, 340
    communicative model, 381–383
    complete sex acts, 347–353
    consent, 331, 339, 378–379, 381–383
    contractual model, 381, 383
    dating, 331, 339
    desire, 348–349, 350, 351, 352, 355, 357
    dignity, 338–339, 342–344
    homosexuality, 333–334, 353–360
    infidelity, 336, 352, 370–376, 387–388
    love, 331–332, 355, 374
    masturbation, 292, 335, 344–345, 352, 357, 358
    natural/unnatural sex, 340, 347, 349, 350, 355–356, 358, 359–360
    pedophilia, 337
    Pineau, Lois, 377–383
    pleasure, 347, 349–350, 351–352, 353, 373, 376, 380, 382
    premarital sex, 334–335, 343–344
    rape, 337, 377–383, 388
    religious/cultural attitudes, 330–331, 342–345
    Ruddick, Sara, 346–352
    Ruse, Michael, 353–360
    seduction, 378–379, 381
    sex education, 334, 383–384
    stalking, 337
    Vatican's position, 341–345
    violence, 218, 335, 336–337, 340
    Wasserstrom, Richard, 370–376
sexual perversion, 349, 350–351, 358–360
"Shallow and the Deep, Long-Range Ecology Movements, The" (Naess), 680
Sharia courts, 277
"Sharing the Burden" (Trachtenberg), 30, 620–623
Sharon, Ariel, 619
Shaw, Anthony, 191
Shintoism, 181, 628
Siberia, 685

...iia, 142
...iry, 594, 651
..., 628
...9
..., Fred, 228
..., *The,* 637
...ore, 282
..., Peter, 646, 647, 648, 660–668
...en, Anthony, 538–539
...nner v. Oklahoma (1942), 363
...okie trial, 451–452, 485
Slaughterhouse Five (Vonnegut), 631
slavery, 6, 481, 514–515, 516, 517–518, 520, 526, 529, 551, 661
Slay, Brandon, 284
slippery slope argument, 24, 87, 155, 164, 188, 201–202, 206, 458
Smith College, 476
smoking. *See* tobacco
social contract, 14, 30, 60, 61, 234, 238, 246–250, 646, 660
social Darwinism, 628
socialism, 37, 391–392, 394
sociobiology, 20, 407, 411–412, 413, 414
sociological relativism, 6, 9
sociopaths, 5, 13, 148, 274–275
Socrates, 19, 53, 251, 455, 462–467, 604, 629
Solis, Gary, 616
somatic cell nuclei transfer (SCNT), 133, 134–135, 138, 144, 151, 154
somatic cell therapy, 133, 134–135, 175–176
Sonnier, Patrick, 268, 269, 270–271, 272
South Africa, 334, 491
South Carolina, 126
South Korea, 563, 583
Soviet Union, 491, 492, 594
Spain, 334, 443, 638
Spanish American War, 624
species integrity, 140
speciesism, 648, 660–665, 668
speech. *See* freedom of speech
sports, 150, 284–285, 288, 317–323, 326–327, 519
stalking, 337
Stanford University, 478–479, 480, 483
St. Anselm, 586
Stanton, Elizabeth Cady, 74, 113, 390, 641
State Children's Health Insurance Program (SCHIP), 116
"Statement in Support of H.R. 810, the Stem Cell Research Enhancement Act" (Langevin), 166–167
state of nature, 19, 33, 60, 63–64, 234, 525, 561–562, 574, 584, 592
Steinem, Gloria, 399, 424–425
stem cell research, 136, 138, 142, 166–169, 172–173
Stem Cell Research Enhancement Act of 2005, 136, 166–167
"Stem Cell Research Policy" (Bush), 167–169

Stenberg v. Carhart (2000), 78
Stephen, Sir James Fitzjames, 242–243
sterilization, mandatory, 131
Stern, William, 396
steroids. *See* drug and alcohol use, performance enhancing/steroids
stewardship model, 647
Stewart, Justice, 474
Stock, Gregory, 133
Stockport College (England), 453
Stoics, 178–179
Stone, Oliver, 507, 511
Strossen, Nadine, 446, 450, 456, 458, 484–492
Suarez, F., 594
"Subjection of Women" (Mill), 390, 395
substance abuse. *See* drug and alcohol use
Sudan, 569, 577, 582
suffering. *See* pain and suffering
suicide, 27, 35, 58, 179, 182, 188, 202, 217, 219–220, 221, 225, 284, 289, 293. *See also* euthanasia; physicians, physician-assisted suicide
suicide bombing, 591, 616, 617
Suleman, Nadya, 441
Summa Theologica (Aquinas), 572, 573
Summum Monument (Utah), 448
Sumner, William Graham, 5
Sunna. *See* Muhammad (the Prophet)
Sunstein, Cass, 449, 502–506
supererogatory duty, 579
Support 21 Coalition, 315
surgical abortion, 80
surrogate motherhood. *See* motherhood, surrogate
sympathy, 22, 40
Swaziland, 399
Sweden, 73, 618
Switzerland, 182
Szasz, Thomas, 286, 291–298, 300

Talaat al-Ghunaimi, Mohammad, 605
Taoism, 629, 638
Taylor, Charles, 386
Taylor, Harriet, 335, 395, 407, 409
Taylor, John, 326
Telecommunications Act (1996), 448
Teletubbies, 439
television, 224, 429. *See also* media
temperance movement, 279–280
Temple University, 476
Teneja, Baninder, 697–698
"Ten Reasons Why Reparations for Slavery Is a Bad Idea—and Racist Too" (Horowitz), 507–508
Teres, Susan, 436
terrorism, 231, 249, 273–274, 446, 571, 572, 591, 597–598, 694–695. *See also* war and terrorism; war on terrorism
Texas, 75, 276, 523
Thailand, 182
Thalidomide, 73, 75, 644–645

theoretical ethics, 2–3, 41
Theory of Justice, A (Rawls), 30, 59–61, 552
"There's No Such Thing as Free Speech, and It's a Good Thing, Too" (Fish), 493–499
Thiam, Awa, 386
Thich Nhat Hanh, 28, 71–72
Thimpsen, Jonathan, 511
"Thinking Like a Mountain" (Leopold), 679
Third World, 515, 684
Thomson, Judith Jarvis, 28, 82, 86–97, 121, 391
Thoreau, David, 579
Thus Spoke Zarathustra (Nietzsche), 574
Tibet, 237
tobacco, 281, 283, 289, 293, 304, 309, 312, 510
"To Fulfill These Rights" (Johnson), 528–530
Tolaro, Sarah, 443
tolerance, 4, 21, 86, 477, 527
Tooley, Michael, 110
torture, 238, 578, 581, 618, 635–636
toxic waste, 570
Trachtenberg, Stephen Joel, 30, 580, 582, 620–623
trade, principle of, 20
transgenic animals and plants, 133, 134, 143, 171–172
Trans Ova Genetics, 171
transplantation, organ, 134, 171, 172–173
treason, 583
Truman, Harry, 631
Truth, Sojourner, 661
Tucker, Judith Stadtman, 419
Tucker, Karla Faye, 238, 272–273
Turkey, 300
Twain, Mark, 418
twins, 137, 139, 140, 153
"Two Takes on the 21 Drinking Age" (Dean-Mooney and McCardell), 314–316
Two Treatises of Civil Government (Locke), 62–64
tyranny of the majority, 7, 455–456, 460, 477

übermensch, 39
Uganda, 595
Ultimate Punishment: A Defense of Capital Punishment, The (van den Haag), 240–244
Underground Railroad, 517
United Nations, 135, 229, 237, 251, 571–572, 575, 576–577, 583, 634, 683
United Nations, Charter of, 574, 576–577, 594, 595, 632
United Nations Universal Declaration of Human Rights, 33, 271, 446, 581, 634
United Network for Organ Sharing, 695

United States
abortion, 73–78, 84
animals, nonhuman, 638, 641–643, 665, 698
Civil War, 517–518, 579
crime, 231, 232, 235, 241, 274
death penalty, 10, 228–232, 235, 237, 241, 261–267
drug/alcohol use, 279–283, 288, 289, 294, 301, 308–313, 329
environment, 643–644, 698–699
euthanasia, 177–178, 180–184, 188, 215
feminist movement, 390–393
freedom of speech, 446–448, 450–454, 485, 489, 502–504
genetic engineering/cloning, 135, 138, 173
homosexuality, 331, 333–334, 361–369
immigration policy, 555
peace (anti-war) movements, 571–572
polygamy, 386
prostitution, 338
racism, 476–483, 517–521
war, policy on, 578, 580, 581, 611, 632, 633, 635–636
United States Conference of Catholic Bishops (USCCB), 151, 152, 155, 157
United States Constitution
First Amendment, 446, 447–448, 449, 451, 452, 454, 468, 473–474, 477–479, 481, 485, 486, 488–489, 490, 494, 495–496, 497–498, 501, 502, 505, 506, 512, 513
Fourth Amendment, 618, 631
Fifth Amendment, 618
Sixth Amendment, 618
Eighth Amendment, 230, 231, 232
Thirteenth Amendment, 173, 518, 623, 625
Fourteenth Amendment, 10, 75, 76, 230, 231, 362, 363, 518, 519, 541, 565
Eighteenth Amendment, 279, 281
Twenty-First Amendment, 280
United States Food and Drug Administration (FDA), 644
United States Supreme Court. See specific cases
universalist moral theories, 3–4, 18–19. See also specific theories
universalization, 26, 27, 56
Universal National Service Act. See National Service Act
University of California, 389, 454, 523, 534
University of Massachusetts, 509
University of Michigan, 434, 452–453, 476–477, 483, 489–490, 504, 523, 565
University of Mississippi, 534

University of Pennsylvania, 141, 384, 694
University of Texas, 566
University of Wisconsin, 453
USA Patriot Act, 446, 456, 458, 509, 522, 581, 631
USSR. See Soviet Union
Utah, 386
utilitarianism, 22–26
abortion, 84–85
animal rights/interests, 23, 53, 646–647, 656–657
Bentham, 22, 23, 50–51, 236, 244, 255
death penalty, 236, 237–238, 255, 263
Mill, 23, 52–54
principle of utility, 23
racial/gender discrimination, 401, 525–526
social reform, 23–24
strengths/limitations, 24–25
utilitarian calculus, 23, 211
war and peace, 596
Utilitarianism (Mill), 52–54
utility, principle of, 23, 51, 52

vaccination, polio, 670
vacuum aspiration (D&E), 80
Valium, 327
value-hierarchical thinking, 689
van den Haag, Ernest, 29, 234, 235, 237, 239, 240–244
Vanzetti, Bartolomeo, 242
Vatican, "Declaration on Sexual Ethics," 330
vegetarianism, 638, 642–643, 648, 649–654, 656–659, 682
veil of ignorance, 30, 59, 60, 658
Venter, Craig, 132
Vermont, 334
Vietnam War, 576–577, 579, 580, 583–584, 621, 626, 633
Viktora, Robert A., 452
Village of Skokie v. National Socialist Party of America, The (1978), 451–452, 485
Vindication of the Rights of Women, A (Wollstonecraft), 113, 335, 390, 395, 637
Violence against Women Act (1994), 336
Virginia, 279, 517
virtue, definition of, 37
virtue ethics, 37–41
Aristotle, 37–38
Buddhist, 39
care ethics, 39–41
Confucian, 37, 38–39
doctrine of the mean, 38, 45–47, 287
Nietzsche, Friedrich, 39
strengths/limitations, 41
vivisection, 640
Volstead Act, 296
Vonnegut, Kurt, Jr., 630–631
voting, 61

Walker, Adele, 328
Wal-Mart, 400
Walters, John, 329
Walzer, Michael, 593–594, 595, 598
Wantz, Marjorie, 217, 219
"War and Murder" (Anscombe), 585–591
war and terrorism, 571–636. See also just-war tradition; specific wars
Allied firebombing, 630–631. See also war and terrorism, obliteration bombing
Anscombe, Elizabeth, 571, 579, 585–591, 594, 595
biological weapons, 578–579
chemical weapons, 578
Coady, C. A. J., 591–599
collateral damages, 581, 597, 614, 618
conscientious objection (CO), 579–580, 584, 623, 632–633
conscription, 577, 579–580, 582, 583, 584, 587–588, 620–626
defensive wars, 572, 581, 587, 595, 604, 624, 625
definitions, 571–572
"don't ask, don't tell" policy, 634–635
enemy combatants. See war and terrorism, prisoners of war
environmental damage and, 610, 611, 627
Granoff, Jonathan, 573, 578, 581, 582, 608–612, 627–630
Guantanamo Bay, 581, 619, 635
guerilla war, 598
Hashmi, Sohail, 572, 599–608
Hobbes, Thomas, 574
holy war, 572
humanitarian war, 595–596
hybrid war-law approach, 614–615, 619
illegitimate wars, 604
Luban, David, 578, 581, 613–619
national service draft, 623
obliteration bombing, 589–590, 591, 598, 630–631
pacifism, 579–580, 586, 587–589
Paul, Ron, 624–626
pre-emptive wars, 575, 594, 625
principle of double effect, 582, 589–590, 631
prisoners of war, 577, 581, 582–583, 614–616, 619, 635–636
September 11, 2001 terrorist attacks, 16, 571, 599
terrorism, 571, 572, 591–599, 614–619
Trachtenberg, Stephen Joel, 30, 580, 582, 620–623
wars of aggression, 571, 586, 587, 594–595
weapons of mass destruction (WMD), 571, 578–579, 610, 617, 625, 627. See also nuclear weapons
women and, 399, 442–443, 623, 633–634
"War and Terrorism" (Coady), 591–599